STATION TO STATION

STATION TO STATION

STEVEN PARISSIEN

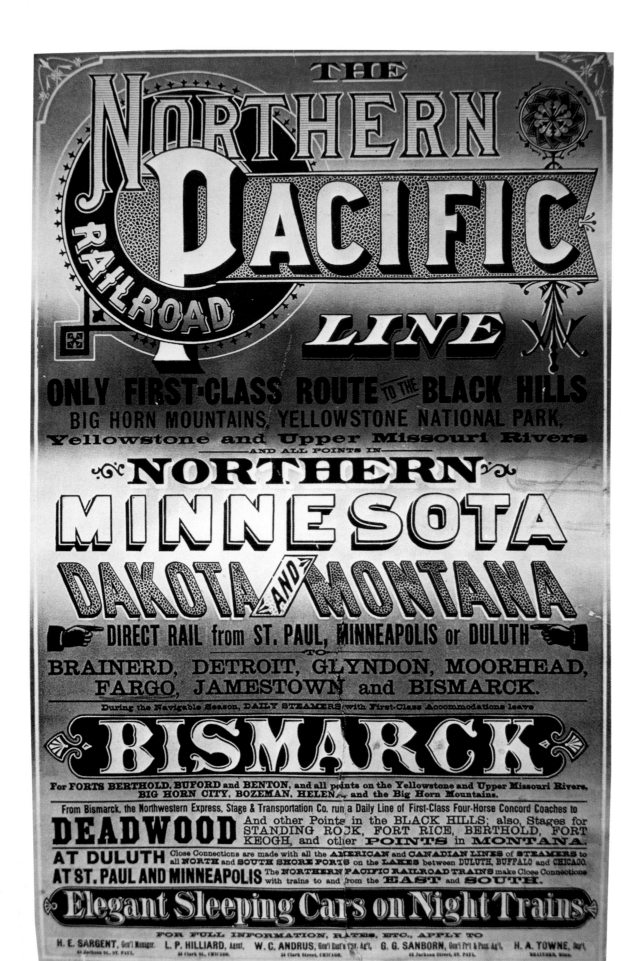

INTRODUCTION
THE LIFE AND TIMES OF THE RAILWAY STATION

Railroad architecture has, or would have,
a dignity of its own if it were only left to its work.[1]
JOHN RUSKIN, 1849

Since the world's first railway station, Darlington, opened in 1826, stations have always maintained a special place in the public's affection. The lure of the great railway terminus has always been especially strong: the breathtaking grandeur, swagger and opulence of the architecture inextricably fused with the dizzying prospects of adventure, romance, escape or challenge offered by far-flung destinations.

Many have seen stations as the churches of the Industrial Revolution. To Théophile Gautier large stations were 'cathedrals of the new humanity' and 'the centre where all converges', which constituted 'the meeting points of nations'.[2] G K Chesterton also saw them as modern-day cathedrals, declaring in 1909 that the great terminus 'has many of the characteristics of a great ecclesiastical building … vast arches, void spaces, coloured lights', a 'recurrence of ritual' and the opportunity for 'quietude and consolation'.[3] Over thirty years earlier the American *Building News* celebrated the great railway terminus as being 'to the nineteenth century what monasteries and cathedrals were to the thirteenth'.[4] Metropolitan termini were, it concluded, the 'only real representative buildings' the Victorian era possessed; moreover, they were also 'the leaders of art spirit of our time'. Writing in 1913, during the heyday of the giant railway stations, James Scott saw in great termini 'the sense of immensity and importance'. To Kasimir Malevich they were 'volcanoes of life'; to Cendrars they were 'the most beautiful churches in the world' and 'palaces of modern industry where the religion of the century is displayed';[5] to Marcel Proust 'tragic places, for in them the miracle is accomplished whereby scenes which hitherto have no existence save in our minds are about to become the scenes among which we shall be living'.[6] To Erich Mendelsohn they constituted 'frozen music'.[7]

The advent of rail travel enjoyed a mixed public reception. The fête-like atmosphere of the opening of the Stockton to Darlington Railway on 27 August 1825 is captured in the contemporary print, opposite; and the handbill below boasts of a 3½ hour journey on the London to Nottingham route in 1856. Early pitfalls were, however, depicted in satirical prints, such as 'The Perils of Steam Transport', below left, and the etching, 'The Pleasures of the Rail Road – showing the Inconvenience of a Blow-Up' by Henry Hughes, 1831, boiler explosions being rather frequent occurrences.

To Thomas Wolfe in 1934, the great railway terminus encapsulated all of the spiritual resonance and transcendent, ethereal timelessness of a medieval church:

Few buildings are vast enough to hold the sound of time, and now it seemed … that there was a superb fitness in the fact that the one which held it better than all others should be a railroad station. For here, as nowhere on earth, men were brought together for a moment at the beginning or end of their innumerable journeys, here one saw their greetings and farewells, here, in a single instant, one got the entire picture of the human destiny.[8]

Others looked to great stations as catalysts of urban renewal. As early as 1850 the British economist Dr Dionysus Lardner was stating of the newly built rail termini in his *Railway Economy* that: 'It is impossible to regard the vast buildings and their dependencies … without feelings of inexpressible astonishment at the magnitude of the capital and boldness of the enterprise.' During the American Civil War, General William T Sherman, the nemesis of the Deep South, ominously identified the railroad terminus as 'the heart of the modern artery of business … second only in the importance to the buildings of the confederate government itself as a subject for elimination.'[9] In 1912, the American architect W S Richardson observed that 'a terminal is considered not as the end of a line, but as the distributing-point in any city of the first magnitude'. As such, stations should, he suggested, always be provided with one of the most pivotal sites in the urban mesh, 'attractively placed, facing large squares and surrounded by important streets and boulevards'.[10] As a more recent study has noted, even in the smaller centres of population 'an impressive terminal was felt to be a requisite sign of civic wellbeing and better things to come'.[11]

More recently, great stations have been regarded both as international melting pots or, conversely, as the epitome of national character. Jean Dethier saw the principal rail terminus as 'a modern-day Tower of Babel' as well as 'a place of theatricality and mobility'. However, great stations were rarely deliberately intended to form expressions of international amity; on the whole the inspiration behind their construction was based firmly on the foundations of civic pride, national pretension or corporate ambition.

Not everyone has always acclaimed the railway station as the architectural and social wonder of the age. While Émile Zola was asserting in a poem of 1878 the principle that a station could be attractive as well as impressive, ('You, modern poet, you detest modern life/You go against your gods, you don't really accept your age./Why do you find a railway station ugly? A

The Liverpool and Manchester Railway. Above, 'Liverpool and Manchester Railway – Taking Water at Parkside', 1831, by D&R. Harell, shows the impact of rail travel on the landscape; and on people's lives: the commemorative medal, below, was produced in 1830 to mark the opening of the line.

A Train of the First Class of Carriages, with the Mail.

A Train of the Second Class for outside Passengers.

A Train of Waggons, with Goods, etc., etc.

A Train of Carriages with Cattle.

PLATE XX.
TRAVELLING ON THE LIVERPOOL AND MANCHESTER RAILWAY.

station is beautiful.'),[12] across the Channel two years later the most influential art critic of the nineteenth century was identifying 'evil tendencies' and 'impertinent folly' in the design of railway stations. Here, declared John Ruskin, 'people are deprived of that portion of temper and discretion which is necessary to the contemplation of beauty'. It would be better, he concluded, for railway companies to 'bury gold in the embankments' than to 'put it in ornaments over the stations'.[13]

Stations not only heralded a new age of travel. They also provided urban and rural populations with a social centre, acting as the focal point for the community as well as a transportation hub. In the catalogue to his ground-breaking exhibition *Les Temps des Gares* of 1978, Jean Dethier noted that great stations presented 'a veritable microcosm of industrial society, a public

'Travelling on the Liverpool and Manchester Railway', above, shows the hierarchies of travel: from first class and mail carriages, to the open-air for second class, and wagons for goods and livestock. Left, an early Director's ticket.

place where all social classes rub shoulders'. Given the understandable tendency in station planning to institutionalize class distinctions, railway stations often revealed rather more of the social presumptions of their critics than was intended. In 1876 *Murray's Handbook for Holland and Belgium* lamented that there was no separation of the different classes in Belgian stations – pining perhaps for the early days of the Great Western Railway, when passengers travelling in each class were penned into separate areas until the train arrived. The 1904 edition of E B Ivatts's *Railway Management at Stations* observed that 'the British Biped likes to meander up and down a railway platform', while the French preferred to wait for their services indoors. In 1923 G L Boag noted with horror that Spanish railway passengers were even more reluctant than the British or French to use waiting rooms, and smoked, talked and – God forbid – actually ate while strolling up and down the platforms.

Termini are the places where things happen, where real-life dramas occur and around which fictional dramas pivot. Little can match for pathos and irony the death of William Huskisson MP at Lancashire's Parkside Station, on the occasion of the opening of the Liverpool to Manchester Railway in 1830. President of the Board of Trade, Huskisson had been tipped as a future Tory leader; yet he died pathetically at the feet of his Prime Minister, the Duke of Wellington. Huskisson had stepped down on to the railway line to talk to the Duke but, unused to the speed of the locomotive (George Stephenson's *Rocket*, no less), had hesitated when the train approached, and did not jump clear in time.

Rather more well-remembered than Huskisson's unfortunate demise was the fictional station-platform suicide of Anna Karenina, in Leo Tolstoy's eponymous novel of 1878:

In a flash she remembered the man who had been run down by the train the day she first met Vronsky, and knew what she had to do. Quickly and lightly she descended the steps that led from the watertank to the rails, and stopped close to the passing train … And exactly at the moment when the space between the wheels drew level with her … dropped on her hands under the truck, and with a light movement, as though she would rise again at once, sank onto her knees. At the same instant she became horror-struck at what she was doing. 'Where am I? What am I doing? Why?' She tried to get up, to throw herself back, but something huge and relentless struck her on the head and dragged her down on her back. 'God forgive me everything!' she murmured, feeling the impossibility of struggling.[14]

Anna's was not the first fictional station suicide. Two years before the publication of Tolstoy's novel, Anthony Trollope's *The Prime Minister* featured the melodramatic suicide of Ferdinand Lopez at Tenway Junction. Lopez, having had a breakfast of 'a mutton

A scene from the Clarence Brown film of *Anna Karenina* of 1935, with the two leads, Greta Garbo as Anna and Frederic March as Vronsky. Tolstoy chose a station platform as the fitting setting for the Anna's dramatic suicide, under the wheels of an oncoming train.

Services for passengers became increasingly sophisticated. A mobile ticket office for British Railways excursions at Marylebone Station, London is shown above; and right, Cinema Trains were introduced for the rail traveller's entertainment. Here a cinema attendant of 1935 dispenses tickets on the LNER King's Cross to Peterborough route.

chop and some tea' at Euston, travelled 'some six or seven miles' to Tenway. (Tenway can be therefore identified with Willesden Junction, in northwest London. Trollope mischievously described the station's layout as 'a marvellous plan, quite unintelligible to the uninitiated'.)[15] Lopez threw himself under the Euston–Inverness express: 'With quick, but still with gentle and apparently unhurried steps, he walked down before the flying engine – and in a moment had been knocked into bloody atoms.'

Stations have long been the stage for real-life departures and arrivals. The bodies of Queen Victoria (for whom a separate royal entrance had been added to Windsor and Eton Riverside Station), King Edward VII and King George V all passed through Brunel's Paddington, while in 1945 Franklin D Roosevelt's body was brought with almost equal pomp into Washington Union from Warm Springs, Georgia. Lenin's arrival on a train from Stockholm at St Petersburg's Finlandski terminus on the night of 16 April 1917 can be said to have initiated the momentous events of the Russian Revolution, and ranks as perhaps

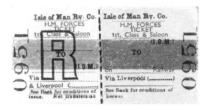

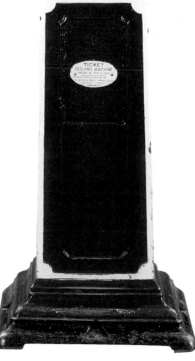

Tickets and their dispensers came in various forms. These tickets, far left, top to bottom, depict a range of service and destinations, from Britain, Germany and the Welsh town with the unpronouncable name. The red and white ticket machine, shown left, dispensed penny platform tickets for both the Great Western and the Great Central Railway.

the most auspicious of all station arrivals. Even at the time, the significance of the train's approach was not lost on the revolutionary crowds: the station was specially lit by military searchlights and military bands played the Marseillaise, while on alighting Lenin was instantly taken to the Tsar's special waiting room.

Countless politicians have always been eager to employ the station, with its massive spaces, its sense of theatricality and its inherent egalitarianism, as a backdrop for their polemic. Throughout the nineteenth and early twentieth centuries numerous American politicians campaigned at railroad stations, speaking from platforms, from specially constructed stages or, more usually, from the back of trains. President Woodrow Wilson announced the crucial legislation introducing the eight-hour working day at Washington Union Station, choosing to sign the Adamson Act while sitting in a private railroad car. Wilson's fellow Democrat, Harry Truman, addressed his first great audience following his surprise election victory of 1948 not at a large hotel or in a public square but in the echoing, vaulted hall of New York's Grand Central Station. Ten years later, on 19 May 1958, General Charles de Gaulle picked the Salle des Fêtes at Paris's voluptuous Orsay terminal as the ideal venue from which to offer his services to France, a declaration which was to hasten the collapse of the Fourth Republic. A further ten years on, De Gaulle's own retirement was precipitated by the anti-government crowds of May 1968 using the Gare de Lyon as their rallying point.

Great stations have often been designed, or at least perceived, as trenchant symbols of national pride and national achievement: Helsinki's great terminal of 1904 was the first real expression of the Finnish independence movement; Milan Central was devised

Rail travel in the Third Reich. Hitler says a fond farewell to Mussolini. While few stations of advanced design were built in Hitler's Germany, Mussolini, as well as allegedly making trains run on time, also encouraged the adoption of a surprisingly advanced modernism for Italy's principal termini. The German Railways, Deutsch Reichsbahn (logo shown below), transported the Nazi party's leading figures.

Stations were the settings for triumphant arrivals. In a scene from a painting by M Solokov, above, Lenin steps out to applause at St Petersburg's Finlandski Terminus, in April 1917 – surely one of the most celebrated and resonant station arrivals of the Railway Age. His colleague Trotsky, right, architect of the Red forces' victory in the post-revolutionary Civil War, harangues troops of his Red Army from the steps of his carriage in 1917. Trotsky famously exploited the wartime possibilities of the railways to great effect, using his personal command train to link the widely-flung theatres.

as a monument to Mussolini's Fascist hegemony; Bombay Victoria was intended to demonstrate how the British Raj had successfully fused native architectural traditions with British technological expertise; while the rebuilding of Metz Station in 1905 was a propaganda exercise by the German conquerors of Alsace-Lorraine, who attempted to show that French and Germans could, after all, work in harmony under the Prussian yoke.

Inevitably, overt political associations tended to attract protest or derision as circumstances changed. The fabric of the new station at Metz was fortunate to survive the Allied victories of 1918 and 1945. The station at Villepinte was not so lucky: having been identified by the Corsican Independence Movement as a symbol of French colonialism, it was blown up in 1977.

Large stations have always been central to the prosecution of war. Unique among public buildings of the industrial age, the railway terminus served a dual function in wartime: as the distribution centre for

troops and war material, and as the gathering point for those who had come to collect, or see off, their relatives or loved ones. Paris Gare de l'Est, for example, was the principal centre for troop dispersal in the wars against Germany of 1870, 1914–18 and 1939–40, as Berlin Stettiner was for soldiers being sent west to fight the French. During the First World War, Paddington was enlarged (a fourth span being added in 1915 to the east of Isambard Kingdom Brunel and Sir Matthew Digby Wyatt's train shed) to cope with the vast numbers of troops arriving by Great Western from Wales and the West, bound for the Western Front. Paris Est was similarly extended after 1918. During the Second World War, it was at the Gare Montparnasse, that De Gaulle's Free French authorities staged the formal surrender of the German forces, on 25 August 1944.

The station concourse was where wives kissed their husbands goodbye, or where mothers came to support wounded servicemen. Thomas Hardy encapsulated the emotions of a station goodbye in his poem *In a Waiting Room*:

A soldier and his wife, with haggard look
Subdued to stone by strong endeavour;
And then I heard
From a casual word
They were parting as they believed for ever.

Vera Brittain's last goodbye to her lover Roland Leighton in 1915 was similarly poignant:

To my amazement, taut and tearless as I was, I saw him hastily mop his eyes with his handkerchief, and in that moment … I realized how much more he cared for me than I had supposed or he had ever shown … And then, all at once, the whistle sounded again, and the train started … he sprang on to the footboard, clung to my hand, and, drawing my face down to his, kissed my lips with a sudden vehemence of despair. And I kissed his, and just managed to whisper 'Good-bye!' The next moment he was walking rapidly down the platform, with his head bent and his face very pale. Although I had said that I would not, I stood by the door as the train left the station and watched him moving through the crowd. But he never turned again.[16]

Leighton was killed in France later that year.

The station was the setting for equally poignant scenes during the next war. In 1985 the *Life* magazine

photographer Alfred Eisenstaedt still vividly recalled his Second World War assignments in Pennsylvania Station, a key assembly point for troops destined for Europe, the Pacific or merely for US training camps:

The light was beautiful – so subdued. The atmosphere in the station was sad and exciting, and many people were crying. The men were very shy – it was difficult for some of them to embrace in public. Their mothers couldn't go beyond the train gates, and they stood there, looking down at the tracks, crying. It was very difficult to focus and be unobtrusive.[17]

On film, it was from Paris's Gare de Lyon that Humphrey Bogart left to escape the encroaching Germans – but without Ingrid Bergman – in the legendary *Casablanca* of 1942. In reality, the scenes at the Parisian termini serving the southwest in June 1940 were even more confused and chaotic. (On 10 June the government itself boarded trains at Paris Austerlitz for the Loire, leaving in its wake an administrative vacuum and a capital ripe for capture.) It was from the great London termini that the children of Britain were evacuated during the Second World War; in 1939 617,000 travelled from London's principal stations on 1,577 special trains, with another half million following in 1940. Across the channel, however, the great stations of Europe were soon being pressed into grimmer service. By 1942 railway termini all over the Nazi-occupied continent were functioning as the departure point from which Jews and other political, sexual and racial 'undesirables' were deported in cattle trucks for the concentration camps of Germany and Eastern Europe.

Stations were also obvious wartime targets. The First World War offered a foretaste of what the railways could expect in the next war. On 17 February 1918 five bombs were dropped on London St Pancras by a Zeppelin, damaging the hotel; in October 1940, it was hit far more comprehensively, and duly closed to traffic, while nearby Euston's famous Great Hall was gutted. Between 1942 and 1945 numerous stations in

The train was a vehicle for transporting statesmen in both the heat of campaign battles and in death. Above, left, F D Roosevelt supported by his son, Franklin Junior, on the campaign trail to Bismarck, North Dakota in 1936. It was only shortly before his death that many Americans became aware that the president was seriously crippled and could not stand unaided. Below, the Presidential funeral train for Abraham Lincoln, 1865.

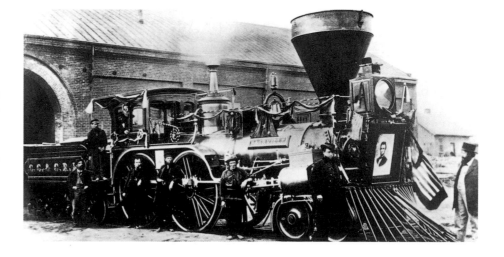

Germany and occupied Europe fell victim to the long-range bomber, taking thousands of passengers to more ultimate destinations than they had originally planned.

Given the station's central importance during wartime, it inevitably metamorphosed into a war memorial. James Robb Scott's immense Victory Arch at London Waterloo of 1922 transformed the station into an echo of Edwin Lutyens's famous Whitehall Cenotaph. Scott included representations of the goddesses of War and Peace, a winged Victory and, to emphasize the station's symbolic nationalism, a 'central group of Britannia, seated and triumphant holding aloft the sacred torch of Liberty to her own greatness and glory, and for the guidance of her children and the benefit of mankind in general'. That this vast piece of triumphalist architectural sculpture should be added to a station whose name commemorated one of Britain's most famous victories made it doubly effective.

During the Second World War the optimistic jingoism of the Great War was toned down in favour of more direct and ostensibly democratic remembrances of the fighting man and woman. Typical of the time were the wartime additions at New York's Pennsylvania Station. In 1942 a star-studded banner was suspended across the Great Waiting Room, gold stars representing those railroad company employees killed in action and blue stars those serving with the forces. Three years later Raymond Loewy installed a 60-foot florescent Stars and Stripes over the entrance and six 40-foot photomurals on the west wall, each showing one of the professions in which the company's employees were helping the war effort.

Given the dramas that unfold daily within their walls, and the exuberance of their architecture, it is unsurprising that great railway stations have featured prominently in film throughout the twentieth century. The images of stations that the moving pictures have left us with have been strikingly memorable: Vivien Leigh picking up returning soldiers at Waterloo (or at least Hollywood's idea of Waterloo) in *Waterloo Bridge* of 1931; Judy Garland agreeing to meet Robert Walker by the clock at Penn Station in *The Clock* of 1945; and, perhaps most memorable of all, Trevor Howard and Celia Johnson gazing into each other's eyes in the refreshment room (actually at Carnforth Station) in the immortal *Brief Encounter* of 1945. Sometimes the stations themselves became the star – either intentionally, as in John Schlesinger's evocative study of Waterloo, *Terminus*, of 1961, or unintentionally, as in Vittorio de Sica's *Indiscretion of an American Wife* of 1953, in which the International Modernism of Rome's Termini station threatens to eclipse the rather conventional dramatic action.

Trains and railway stations have long provided the film industry with dramatic settings for human dramas. Above, Michael Redgrave and Margaret Lockwood encounter spy Dame May Whitty in Alfred Hitchcock's *The Lady Vanishes*, 1938; and the unforgettable farewell scene between Celia Johnson and Trevor Howard in the iconic *Brief Encounter*, 1945, directed by David Lean, right. While the sentiment of *Brief Encounter* survives, widely celebrated as a paradigm of British emotional understatement, the evocative, shadow-strewn setting does not. The train shed at Carnforth was ruthlessly demolished in the 1960s.

Facilities at stations for travellers developed through time. Left, an early poster advertises travel services, whilst the sixpence-in-the-slot luggage locker, below right, brought with it a new level of convenience, shown here at Euston Station, London in 1949. The press-button timetable, with its information window, was introduced as early as 1936, shown here, above right, at King's Cross Station, London.

Great railway stations have often been the subject of great paintings. Stations particularly appealed to the French Impressionists of the late nineteenth century and their British followers, and during the 1870s leading artists experimented with *plein-air* views of stations, buildings which fulfilled their criteria of utilitarian function combined with striking and even heroic architecture. Most renowned were Monet's and Manet's canvases of Paris's St Lazare terminus; at the same time, however, Camille Pissarro was painting intimate portrayals of more mundane, suburban subjects such as Norwood's Lordship Lane Station. Inspired by these acclaimed paintings, over the next twenty years many British, Irish and American 'realist' Impressionists such as Walter Osborne and William Kennedy seized upon the station as an ideal model for their depictions of the modern cityscape and of the daily life of unposed subjects from both the working and middle classes.

The importance of terminal stations is not merely a social one. As perhaps the most characteristic building type of the late nineteenth and early twentieth centuries, they remain of immense architectural significance. Their well-earned (but often overlooked) place in the architectural canon derives from two principal factors. Firstly, the railway terminus often served as the focus for the planning or replanning of the town or city centre; as such, the station quickly became the most prominent, well-known and influential building in the city centre. Secondly, city centre railway stations were without direct

architectural precedent. Their lack of uniform style – even railway companies which favoured standard plans and elevations for their smaller stations were forced to adapt these to suit local conditions and preferences – gave them a marvellous flexibility which often eluded other, more pedestrian public buildings in the city centre. Their diversity was both tempered and fuelled by the very precise requirements of their design: a great station that failed to deal with the sudden arrival and departure of great crowds of people, and thus signally failed to realize the business targets expected by the railway, was not long for this world.

Often the station took the form of a city gate. This could either be literal – as in the case of Philip Hardwick's Euston Arch of 1838, Auguste Payen's Neoclassical gateway to his Brussels Midi of 1869, or Julius Rochlitz's vast imperial arch of 1881 at Budapest East – or metaphorical. In 1912 the project architect of New York's recently completed Pennsylvania Station, W S Richardson, claimed that his firm's design sought

INTERNATIONALE DES WAGONS
ORIENT - EXPRESS
PARIS - STRASBOURG - STUTTGART
NÜRNBERG - PRAHA - BOHUMIN - WARSZAWA
TARE 56t5

Rail travel as glamorous and
thrilling. The luxurious Orient-
Express traversed Europe in
style. Left: at Strasbourg-Ville
on its way to Warsaw; and above:
a railside vendor makes a sale at
Milan Central in 1951. The train
was the intriguing setting for the
film of Agatha Christie's *Murder
on the Orient Express* (1974), with
Albert Finney and Richard
Widmark below left, and Sir
John Gielgud and Jean-Pierre
Cassel, below.

The bustle and industry of the late-nineteenth-century station was a source of fascination for contemporary artists. Above: social interaction of the upper middle classes in *The Railway Station*, 1862, by William Powell Frith (1819–1909); and *Gare St-Lazare*, 1870s, by Claude Monet (1840–1926), one of his several depictions of the Paris station. Overleaf: George Earl (1824–1908) was famous for his dog portraits, and ensured that dogs were prominently featured in his *Coming South: Perth Station* of 1895. This splendid depiction of a bustling Late Victorian railway terminus was designed to be a companion piece to his celebrated *Going North* of 1893. While the latter showed London's King's Cross, this painting centred on the gaslit train shed of 1848 (by Sir William Tite) at Perth Station in Scotland. Earl took care to include himself in both pictures; here he is the old moustachioed gentleman on the right, admiring the two well-heeled women.

to introduce passengers to Manhattan 'in the same way as the Brandenburg Gate in Berlin, through which a great part of the traffic enters that city'.[18] At the same time, the erection of a great station in a run-down city-centre neighbourhood often acted as a spur for urban revitalization. At the opening of Penn Station the critic Montgomery Schuyler wrote not only that the terminus 'could not be a more impressive demonstration of the power which the great corporations of transportation have attained', but also that it had given 'value to a quarter which has sunk into neglect and decay'.[19]

By 1910, indeed, most industrialized cities were keen to attract termini that were close to the centre. As early as 1838 the City of York had been prepared to scythe through the world-famous medieval city walls to admit the Great Northern's station into the heart of the city and the environs of the Minster. Ultimately, York Station was only permitted to stare across at the venerable masonry of the city walls from the outside. However, by the turn of the century the regenerative role of the station had become a factor that no city government could afford to ignore.

Although it is one of the most instantly recognizable of all public buildings, the railway terminus was, at least until 1945, couched in a surprisingly varied array of architectural styles. Given the architectural climate of the 1840s, the first great decade of station building, it was inevitable that the public face of the earliest stations was articulated in a Gothic or Classical (and usually Italianate) revivalist style. This does not mean,

however, that railway stations, auguries of a new age of urban development as well as of mass transportation, were backward-looking in their design. The architect E M Barry was at pains to point out that 'so-called revivals are often difficult to distinguish from practical innovations'. In the case of great stations, it was the stylistic freedom to chose from a variety of architectural idioms that enabled both architects and engineers to fuse the latest technological advances with the railway companies' desired goals of convenience, comfort and nobility. In the opinion of architectural historian Carroll Meeks, the 'creative eclecticism' employed by the best station designers helped to create a situation in which 'architects could claim freedom and rebel against dogma'.[20] Historicism could, railway architects discovered, liberate, rather than hinder, good modern design.

By 1850, these revivalist styles were wholly familiar to the travelling public – and to the railway directors. The principal goal of the station architect was not always, as Richards and Mackenzie have suggested, 'to comfort and reassure those concerned about the new-ness of it all';[21] however, it clearly helped if the clients and passengers were at least greeted by something with which they could identify. In the late 1970s the French critic Jean Dethier asserted that traditional building styles were used by station architects in a deliberate attempt to 'disguise the upheavals of the introduction of the railway into the town'; moreover, he alleged, architects and patrons sought to employ 'pastiche and historical fetishism' so as to fend off 'the coming of a modernity which … worried more than it reassured'.[22] Yet there seems little evidence to support this view, which perhaps says more about the architectural politics of the 1970s than about the design ethics of the 1840s. The most successful of the world's great stations, whether of 1850 or of 1950, successfully synthesized technological innovations and stylistic scholarship in a manner which was unique to architecture and always decidedly contemporary.

Such syntheses did, it is true, produce a stunning array of architectural treatments. However, the existence of a diversity of styles should not imply that one was intrinsically inferior to another. All stations served a very specific and extremely exacting function, whether they were the early giants of London King's Cross or Paris Gare de l'Est or the hollowed-out oak tree that was being used as a ticket office at Moreton-

on-Lugg (on the Shrewsbury and Hereford Railway) as late as the 1860s. Some railway companies preferred particular styles; others preferred to give their architects free rein. In Britain, for example, while the London, Brighton and South Coast and the London and Southampton Railways favoured a resolutely Italianate treatment for their station buildings, the Great Western Railway espoused a home-grown 'Tudorbethan'.

Early termini often exhibited an academic purity of style rarely seen in their larger and more complex successors. Sir William Tite's Southampton Station of 1839 featured a rusticated, arched ground floor which distinctly recalled the austerely Neo-Palladian terraces of Inigo Jones's Covent Garden Piazza in London, built two centuries before. (Tite was, incidentally, one of the few first-rank architects to

The railway brought about new possibilities for people to venture further afield on day trips. A postcard, right, of *c*1908 shows the excursion's wide appeal; and, below, an upper middle class family have a compartment to themselves, in Thomas Crane's drawing in *Anne and Jack in London, c*1885. Opposite, a porter shows off the Lost Property truck, piled high with gloves, umbrellas and even a child's toy.

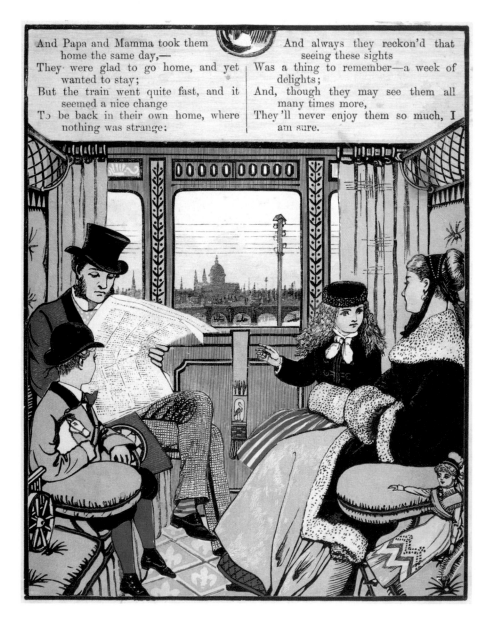

And Papa and Mamma took them home the same day,—
They were glad to go home, and yet wanted to stay;
But the train went quite fast, and it seemed a nice change
To be back in their own home, where nothing was strange:

And always they reckon'd that seeing these sights
Was a thing to remember—a week of delights;
And, though they may see them all many times more,
They'll never enjoy them so much, I am sure.

be employed by British railway companies, which by 1870 tended to prefer in-house professionals. The problems encountered and expense incurred by the Midland Railway in employing George Gilbert Scott at St Pancras after 1868 merely confirmed this prejudice.) At Leicester's Campbell Street Station of 1840, William Parsons designed for the Midland Railway a Palladian villa, complete with Tuscan portico, which incorporated no symbols denoting its railway function. At Lowell, Massachusetts, a small Doric temple was erected as the station in 1835, again, with no obvious architectural indication of its purpose. And the South Eastern Railway's station of 1852 at Battle in Sussex, designed by Tite's pupil William Tress, was even less like a railway station, incorporating Early English lancet windows and thirteenth-century tracery.

It is easy to generalize about the development of railway-station architecture. Designs varied from country to country, from region to region, from company to company, even from station to station. It is, for example, not entirely true to state, as Carroll Meeks did in 1957, that by the 1860s the symmetrical, Italianate station had largely disappeared in favour of the picturesque, asymmetrical Gothic that Tress used at Battle and which Tite was to employ at Windsor and Eton. Designs inspired by the palaces of Renaissance Italy and the villas of Ancient Rome continued to be built in Europe and the Americas during the 1860s and 70s, the resulting stations becoming increasingly ambitious and overblown as the territorial ambitions of the railway companies and the civic ambitions of the towns they served became more pronounced. The end product of this Neoclassical pomp was the grandiose

'Beaux-Arts' style, derived from the classically grounded teaching of the highly influential École des Beaux-Arts in Paris. Beaux-Arts theory had a profound effect on the design of railway termini from 1870 through to the beginning of the First World War, and beyond into the 1920s and 30s. If any one style can be said to have epitomized the aspirations and achievements of the climactic years of the Railway Age, it is Beaux-Arts classicism.

Jean Dethier's sweeping declaration that it was only after 1918 that architects began to employ forms which reflected the 'machine cult' of the station is also rarely borne out by the evidence. If anything, the station buildings of the Modernist era reflected the transport ethic and railway functions less than their supposedly 'historicist' predecessors. Even the most oversized and pompous Beaux-Arts temple, such as Daniel

Burnham's Washington Union of 1903–7, or the most exotic Art Deco confection, such as Victor Laloux's Tours Station of 1895–8, mirrored the functional spanning arches of their train shed in the facades of their head buildings, in a manner which instantly communicated the building's nature to the travelling public. In contrast, the bland, repetitive International Modernism of most postwar stations, from Rome Termini of 1951 to Manchester Piccadilly of 1960 and London Euston of 1968, does little to identify the buildings' real purpose.

While the history of station style is necessarily complex and eclectic, the history of station planning is inevitably more logical. The first stations were constructed with the administrative building on one side of the track or tracks, a form which easily metamorphosed into the two-sided station. In the case

"The **CORONATION**
THE FIRST STREAMLINE TRAIN
KING'S CROSS FOR SCOTLAND

DOMINION OF CANADA

LONDON & NORTH EASTERN RAILWAY

London King's Cross was the point of departure and arrival for trains to Scotland via the east coast of Britain. It became the London 'home' of such famous trains as 'The Flying Scotsman' and 'The Coronation', seen, above, at the station's approach. Left, a promotional brochure boasts of the fast new service on the LNER, created by the Grouping of 1923.

of termini, two-sided stations were often disposed so that arriving and departing trains, together with their passengers, would be kept entirely separate. It was only with the opening of Paris Gare de l'Est in 1852 that the concept of containing all of the booking facilities and waiting rooms in the head building, placed between the stub-end tracks and the street, was introduced into terminus architecture.

Certain architectural motifs and forms are common to many of the world's larger stations. The most obvious, and most fundamental, is the arched train shed. The task of spanning the area over the tracks and platforms was often left to the engineer, while the architect was left to deal with the surrounding fabric. However, the train shed was frequently the element which defined the architecture, dimensions and tone of the rest of the site. During the second half of the nineteenth century, the curved, glazed train-shed roof was the feature which did most to determine the station's function and its status. When François Duquesney's Paris Est opened, the facade's vast, central lunette window, while couched in a familiar, Renaissance idiom, directly expressed the nature and form of Sérinet's arched, glazed train shed behind. 'Perfectly appropriate to the purpose' declared the critic James Fergusson of the composition in 1862;[23] 'the most striking example of railway architecture'

wrote Perdonnet in 1865.[24] (The eastern replication of Duquesney's station, topped by a sculptural representation of Verdun, dates from the end of the First World War.) In a similar manner, the twin-span train shed at Lewis Cubitt's King's Cross, which also opened in 1852, was reflected in the double span of the brick elevation. The central, Italianate clock tower was the only element which relieved the stark, functional symbolism of the facade. As Cubitt himself wrote: 'The building will depend for its effect on the largeness of some of the features, its fitness for its purpose and its characteristic expression of that purpose.'[25]

Each of the train shed's spans, at 105 feet wide, were broader than those of the Crystal Palace. However, unlike Paxton's great work, the roof ribs were not of iron but of laminated wood, each rib comprising sixteen one-and-a-half inch boards bolted together and bound with an iron band. (It was only in 1866 that their replacement with iron ribs was begun.) Nevertheless, the basic principle of light, wide-spanning ribs, glazed and unencumbered by obvious supports was eagerly taken up by subsequent station designers and engineers. Increasing spans in other contemporary structures, such as that of Ferdinand Dutert and Victor Contamin's Palais des Machines at the Paris Exposition of 1889, inspired the railway-station engineers to even greater flights of fancy and function.

DE CHANGE
EXCHANGE
THOS COOK
ENTRANCE TO
HAMPSTEAD & HIGH
THOS. COOK & SO
TWO
EVEN
AFTE
VICTORY
SOMME
GREAT PUSH
SOMME

The first arched iron roof was introduced into a station at Liverpool Lime Street, in 1849. By 1890 massive iron spans had been built at stations such as St Pancras, where William Barlow and R M Ordish's 240-feet train shed incorporated girders pierced with quatrefoils, circles and stars; Franz Schwechten's Berlin Anhalter of 1872–80; and Frankfurt-am-Main, where the massive, three-span shed was unveiled in 1888. Frankfurt's multi-arched train shed was the direction of the future; in 1895 the new St Louis Union featured a five-span shed, while 1914 saw the opening of the biggest train shed of all, Wilhelm Lossow and Max Hans Kühne's Leipzig Hauptbahnhof, which included no less than six parallel sheds. After the First World War, however, the trend was to economy, in spatial if not always in financial terms, a trend which signalled the beginning of the end for the great arched train shed. Even behemoths such as Pennsylvania Station (whose project architect, W S Richardson, was ironically one of the first to identify the arched train shed as a defining element of any station design) were by 1910 not equipped with multi-span sheds; here, as elsewhere in the United States, the need to economize on space led to the train shed being sited underneath, rather than adjacent to, the station services.

Equally redolent of the great railway terminus, and an important part of its architectural vocabulary, was a feature not connected with train operation, but one borrowed from large-scale urban design: the entrance archway. Given that the railway terminus was more often than not intended as the new gateway to the city, the Railway Age's counterpart to the medieval city gate, it was not surprising that many of the largest stations were adorned with massive arches, either situated in their forecourts or incorporated into the main building. These features not only fulfilled a practical function, denoting the station's main point of entry, but also served to reflect the train shed behind (thus providing a simple but potent and easily recognizable symbol of the building's function), to advertise the importance of the station in the city, and to underline the station's ancestry from the triumphal entrance gateways of the Classical world via the gate in the city wall.

While early examples of the great entrance arch were kept entirely separate from the main business of the station, by 1880 the triumphal gateway was being included as part of the facade of the head building itself. This was not only more economic but it also helped to circumvent the problems caused by increased traffic flow through arch entrances designed to take far fewer vehicles. One of the earliest of these incorporated arches can be found at Jacques-Ignace

Hittorf's Paris Gare du Nord of 1861–4; by the early twentieth century it had become the defining motif of a large number of termini, wholly dominating the composition of stations such as Eliel Saarinen's Helsinki Station of 1910–14 and Alfred Fellheimer and Stewart Wagner's Cincinnati Union of 1928–33. The entrance arch was even more flexible than the arched train shed it mirrored: an architectural symbol that successfully distinguished the railway terminus from other principal historic buildings, its simplicity and ability to divest itself of historicist veneer enabled the great arch to become just as relevant to the Futurist and Art Deco designs of the 1930s and the Modernist stations of the 1960s as it had been to Hardwick and Hittorf.

A modification of the arch motif was to transform

the single span into a tripartite element, which frequently reflected the corresponding growth of the arched shed at the rear. This was first popularized by the great German stations of the immediate post-imperial eras, most notably at Johan Jacobstahl's Strasbourg of the early 1870s, Theodore Stein's Berlin Stettiner of 1876, Hubert Stiers's Hanover of 1876–9 and, most famously, at Georg P Eggert's Frankfurt-am-Main of 1883–8 and Ernst Giese and Paul Weidner's Dresden of 1892–8. After 1900 this motif was used not only by the Germans (appearing at Wiesbaden of 1904–6, Basel of 1903–7 and the Wilhelm Lossow and Max Hans Kühne's monumental Leipzig Hauptbahnhof of 1907–15) but became especially prevalent in the giant American Beaux-Arts termini of the early twentieth century – stations such as Daniel Burnham's Washington Union of 1903–7 and Jarvis Hunt's Kansas City Union of 1914. Alternatively,

Liverpool's Lime Street Station, seen opposite, saw the first arched iron roof, constructed in 1849. Above, motorbuses wait patiently in the courtyard outside Paris's first major railway terminal, Duquesney's Gare de l'Est, in 1905. For such an early design, the station shows astonishing assurance and sophistication.

the three-arched entrance could be brought forward from the main facade to form a fully fledged porte-cochère, a tradition which began with John Dobson and Thomas Prosser's Newcastle Central of 1846–55 and effectively ended with Ulisse Stacchini's giant Milan Central, completed in 1931.

By the close of the nineteenth century another key element was being widely introduced to help distinguish the railway terminus from its urban neighbours. The addition of a tall clock tower to the composition helped the railway to signal the building's location, much in the manner of the towers of a cathedral or the minaret of a mosque. It also helped to break up the monotonous, yet increasingly common, horizontality of the station's principal facade, adding a welcome vertical emphasis while providing a refreshing contrast to the well-signed symmetry of the main elevation and the logical functionalism of the whole site's operation. Meeks traced the origin of the motif to the early Gothic Revival in Britain:

Pugin seems to have introduced it at Scarisbrick Hall, Lancashire, in 1837. Some years later he built a much larger version that was destined to become a symbol of the whole Victorian era: Big Ben in Westminster. That striking silhouette, with its overhanging upper stage surmounted by a steep pyramidal roof interrupted by a lantern or belfry, is familiar to millions.[26]

George Gilbert Scott transferred the clock tower from the country house to the station when he introduced it into his design for St Pancras of 1868; from there it passed into the repertoire of countless architects in Northern Europe and North America, where it retained the bold, Gothic asymmetricality of A W N Pugin and Scott.

Not all architects used the clock tower as an asymmetrical device. Cubitt's 112-foot clock tower at King's Cross – the earliest use of a clock in such a prominent position and a feature which did much to relieve the stark utilitarianism of the rest of the facade – was placed squarely between the two arches of the principal elevation. (Until the grouping of 1923, when Britain's railway companies were formed into four systems, the time on the tower's Dent clock rarely agreed with that at the top of the clock tower of neighbouring St Pancras.) At Berlin's Stettiner Station of 1876, the twin clock towers gave the station the appearance of a medieval German cathedral. However, it was the asymmetrical clock tower which found most favour with turn-of-the-century designers.

The prevalence of station clock towers in the Northern Hemisphere was not, according to Dethier, entirely coincidental. 'In Europe', he argues, 'station

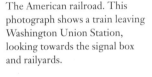
The American railroad. This photograph shows a train leaving Washington Union Station, looking towards the signal box and railyards.

towers are most rare in the Latin countries, where the notion of time is less strict, whereas they abound in countries renowned for their social discipline.' Undoubtedly, clock towers did abound in the larger stations of turn-of-the-century America. Massive campaniles, with little direct function except to display the time, almost overwhelmed the design of Worcester Union, Massachusetts (William Ware and Henry van Brunt, 1875–7) and St Louis Union (Theodore C Link and Edward D Cameron, 1891–4), while fantasy Gothic clock towers were an unmistakable feature of the great American termini of the 1880s, among them C L W Eidlitz's Detroit Michigan (1882–3) and Chicago Dearborn (1883–5), Isaac Taylor's Detroit Union (1889), Thomas Rodd's Indianapolis Union (1886–9), Spencer Beaman's Chicago Central (1888–90) and Charles Frost's Milwaukee of 1889. By 1920 the lofty, off-centre clock tower was a common feature of station design in Northern Europe and the United States, from McKim, Mead and White's Waterbury, Connecticut of 1909 and Saarinen's Helsinki of 1910–14 to Gonthier's Limoges Bénédictins of 1925–9, Henri Pacon's Le Havre Ville of 1930–3 and Donald and John Parkinsons' Los Angeles Union of 1934–9.

The architecture of stations has never been very comprehensively covered in print. In the past, railway enthusiasts have often tended to overlook the station buildings themselves in favour of the rolling stock, track layout and company operation. Even the works of such celebrated railway writers as O S Nock and John Day include only passing references to the stations through which they must have passed, and even to the great termini where they must have embarked. Similarly, many travel writers – and even the authors of international architectural guides – have dismissed the station as little more than a functional transportation issue, to be mentioned only in the 'How to Get There' section. (Samuel Sheppard's classic guide to Bombay of 1912, for example, fails to mention what is now regarded as one of the world's most outstanding buildings from the industrial era: Victoria Terminal. It merely informs the reader that the Great Indian and Peninsula Railway 'now has the greatest length of electrified miles in the British Empire'.)

In-depth analyses of the station as a building, or as a social phenomenon, have until recently been few and far between. John A Droege's *Passenger Terminals and Trains* of 1916 was the first study to properly examine the design, disposition and workings of the principal station. Droege, however, wrote from the point of view of a New York railroad official, and there is an understandably strong American bias in his book. Yet

there was a forty-year gap before an architectural historian, Carroll L V Meeks, seriously addressed the subject; *The Railway Station, An Architectural History* dramatically changed the way in which the architecture of major stations was appraised. Meeks attempted to assign common characteristics and consistent parameters to the history of station architecture, dividing the chronology into a period of functional pioneering (from c1830 to c1850) followed by 'Standardization' (the 1850s), 'Sophistication' (1860–90), 'Megalomania' (1890–1914) and 'Post-First World War'. These subdivisions have effectively been used by most historians since 1957, and serve as the bases, and inspiration, for the following chapters.

Yet it was not until the 1970s that Meeks's pioneering study was redefined at an international level. (David Lloyd and Donald Insall's thought-provoking 1967 polemic, *Railway Station Architecture*, undoubtedly represented an important contribution to station conservation, but dealt only with Britain.) Jean Dethier's exhibition *Les Temps des Gares*, held at the Georges Pompidou Centre in Paris in 1978, was the first attempt to reconcile (admittedly with varying success) the architectural development of the station with accepted Modernist ideology. The exhibition's catalogue remains a key text in the historiography of station architecture, and was one of the significant publications of the late 1970s which helped to provide the catalyst for a great surge of interest in this most attractive, yet neglected, of disciplines.

As the 1970s saw a significant increase in the number of published studies on station architecture, so this

Pride in hard work. This photograph of the 1890s shows the crew of a Stroudley locomotive on the London to Brighton line, England.

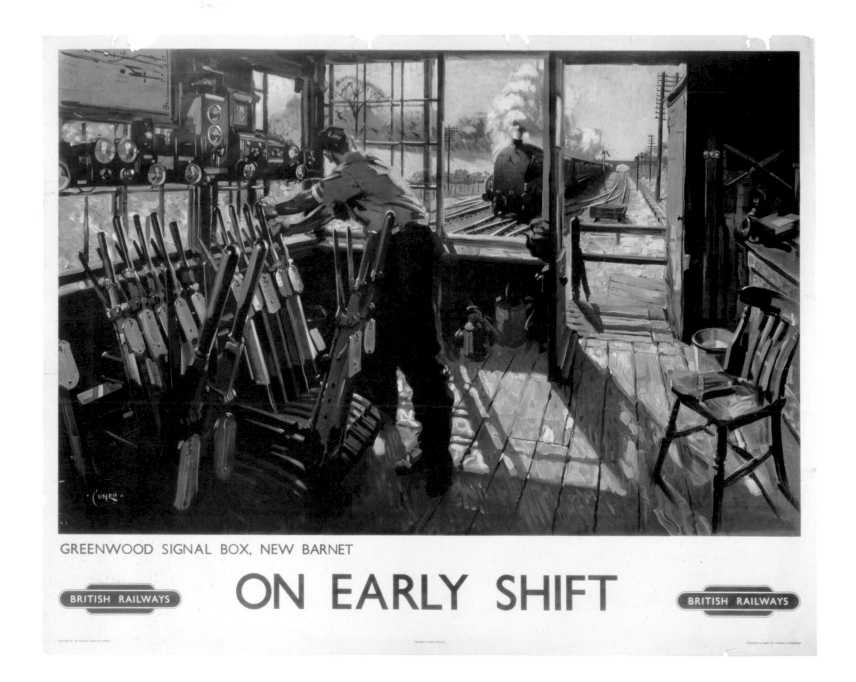

GREENWOOD SIGNAL BOX, NEW BARNET

ON EARLY SHIFT

BRITISH RAILWAYS   BRITISH RAILWAYS

Signal box operations, the subject of posters and photographs. Above: a British Railways poster by Terence Cuneo. Opposite, above: an early 1900s photograph and, below, a picture from a 1930s storybook.

decade also witnessed the emergence of interest in trying to protect those great stations which survived. The 1960s had been characterized by the closure and demolition of countless stations in America, Britain, France and elsewhere. Some of the most prominent and loved landmarks of the world's greatest cities fell to corporate greed and stylistic fashion, among them London's Euston terminus and New York's outstanding and much-hymned Pennsylvania Station. In Britain, the orgy of destruction that followed the short-sighted Beeching report of 1963 (whose author was Chairman of the British Transport Commission) made British Rail, in the expert opinion of Marcus Binney and David Pearce, 'the biggest corporate

vandal and iconoclast Britain has seen since the Tudor dissolution of the monasteries'. In the United States during the same period over 20,000 stations were shut.

The architectural and economic scars left by the sudden withdrawal of rail services and the demolition of local stations prompted a sense of dislocation rarely seen since the dawn of the Industrial Age. One beneficial by-product of the demise of so many first-rate station buildings, however, was the impetus that this destruction gave to the emerging conservation movement during the 1970s.

Key events helped to galvanize public opinion during this decade. In Britain, the Victorian Society's campaign to save St Pancras and sixty other important railway stations in England was in 1977 augmented by SAVE Britain's Heritage's influential 'Off the Rails' exhibition at the RIBA's Heinz Gallery in London. This hard-hitting study detailed the irrecoverable loss of excellent station architecture since the Beeching Report (3,539 stations, they claimed, had been closed in Britain alone between 1963 and 1977) and alerted professionals and public to the long-term damage being done to the country's historic environment. In France, Jean Dethier's wide-ranging Pompidou Centre exhibition of 1978, *Les Temps des Gares*, did the same on an international basis. In America, the determined campaign by the Municipal Arts Society of New York, assisted by a glittering array of celebrities, politicians and architects, prevented the demolition of Grand Central Station, proving to the rest of the country that the great stations of the past did not have to be consigned to the wrecker's ball. As this victory was being won, the United States Government launched a new programme to promote the reuse of historic railroad stations.

These campaigns, studies and exhibitions helped to redefine the case for preserving historic stations, encouraging the public, and the railways themselves, to begin to resist the pressure for outright demolition and instead to take a fresh look at the options of refurbishment and complete or partial conversion. Compared to the dismal record of the 1960s, the 1970s boasts a number of landmark restorations and conversions. As early as 1973 Paris's celebrated Orsay terminal had been saved from demolition, and had been earmarked for conversion to an art gallery; Strasbourg's fine but empty Imperial Terminus had not, as was originally planned, been razed, but had become a public market; Zürich Hauptbahnhof was reprieved from the bulldozer, and was being restored as a working terminal; and work had begun on converting much of Washington Union Station into the capital's Visitor Centre. Later in the decade St Louis Union became a cultural centre; Brunswick and Lincoln, Nebraska, became banks; Chattanooga (already a celebrity thanks to Glenn Miller), a restaurant and office complex; and Bath's Neoclassical Green Park Station became a supermarket.

Inevitably, not every conservation battle was won, and not every triumph could be sustained. Glasgow's fine Victorian St Enoch's train shed was destroyed during European Architectural Heritage Year in 1978. Birmingham's Snow Hill terminus was reopened in 1987, thanks to an imaginative rethink of the West Midland's transit needs, but the impressive station of 1852 had already been razed in 1972. Windsor and Eton Central's much-publicized 'Royalty and Empire'

concourse display, run by Madame Tussaud's, closed in 1993; across the Atlantic, Washington Union's ambitious Visitor's Centre had by 1980 become a leaking liability. At the time of writing both stations rely on banal shopping complexes for their survival.

Some great stations survive only as fragments of their former selves. Others (Den Hague Central or Hull Paragon come immediately to mind) survive only by cowering behind insensitive and uncompromising modern office slabs. Countless others are reduced by the unthinking addition of poorly sited and incompetently designed services, concession stands and signage. In this manner even termini of international significance, such as London's King's Cross, Amsterdam Central and Tokyo Central, have been mutilated to the extent that their carefully planned architecture begins to make little sense. As Peter Davey wrote in the *Architectural Review* in September 1993: 'even journeys that start at wonderful places like Grand Central or King's Cross are made revolting by absurd modern alterations to these splendid buildings'.

Today, however, the future looks brighter for the great railway station than at any time since 1945. Recent, sympathetic restorations of outstanding international termini, among them Kuala Lumpur and Paris Nord, have shown that the economics of modern transportation systems are not incompatible with the retention, or indeed the celebration, of the railway's historic fabric. At the same time, the past ten years have witnessed the construction of the most exciting and well-designed termini since the age of the great Beaux-Arts leviathans of the early twentieth century. Even if some railway companies, and indeed some nations, appear slow to acknowledge the perennial appeal of stations, the public is well aware of the continuing allure of this most evocative of building types. In 1990 Gordon Biddle noted that: 'The attractions of living in a former station are so high that the [British Rail] Property Board cannot satisfy the demand.'[27] And as corporations, authorities and governments begin to acknowledge once more that rail systems represent an extremely efficient, green, cost-effective and pleasant means of transporting large numbers of people for long or short distances, the prospects for railways and for railway stations in the next century begins to look increasingly encouraging. If this book helps to heighten the awareness of the irreplaceable value of the world's built railway heritage, it will have served a useful purpose.

Overleaf: as the *Coronation* negotiates the signals on the LNER line, the trains provide a source of fascination for two young bystanders.

2 NEW CATHEDRALS OF TRANSPORT
NINETEENTH-CENTURY GOTHIC

We may regret the plainness of the Great Northern station, but it is better it should remain as it is, rather than that it should be disfigured with incongruous medievalism like the station of the Midland Railway.[1]
JAMES FERGUSSON on St Pancras Station, 1873.

Early railway stations incorporated head or side buildings couched in a variety of architectural idioms. However, it was the Gothic style, with all its variants, that by 1870 was perceived as being peculiarly suited to station building. Like the railway companies and civic authorities whose aspirations it represented, Gothic was ambitious, soaring and yet endearingly familiar. Tudor Gothic in particular, with its rectangular forms, repetitive decoration and large areas of glazing, was especially suited to the requirements of iron-framed construction and mass-produced decoration, as well as allowing the designer to provide the interior – whether booking hall or train shed – with far more illumination than was often possible with Italianate or Greek forms.

The first designer to give serious consideration to the architecture of the train shed alone was Isambard Kingdom Brunel (1806–59). Brunel was one of the greatest entrepreneurs as well as one of the most gifted engineers of the age. The son of a French engineer who fled to the United States in 1789 and then on to Britain in 1795, he was barely thirty when Parliament passed an act assenting to the construction of his projected Great Western Railway, linking London with Bristol and the West Country. In June 1838 Brunel completed the London–Maidenhead section of the railway, and began work at the Bristol end. In 1840 the two ends met at Wootton Bassett in Wiltshire, and construction began on the railway's principal western terminal: Bristol's Temple Gate (later Temple Meads) station, sited three-quarters of a mile from the medieval city centre. Hardly had the last rail been laid at Temple Gate when the first train steamed in, carrying the GWR directors, on 30 June 1841.

Brunel's Temple Gate train shed was one of the first examples of Victorian Gothic used for a large commercial building. Its novel and impressive

The view towards Scott's exuberant Gothic Midland Grand Hotel and St Pancras Station offices of 1868–73, looking up the staircase from Cubitt's King's Cross, photographed shortly after restoration and safeguarding work had been completed in 1995. St Pancras's elevated site gave it an immediate advantage over its lowly neighbour. *First Class*, 1855, by William Solomon, left.

mock-hammerbeam roof supported on a 'Tudor' colonnade (itself 15 feet above ground level) was inspired by the medieval architecture of Bristol, and in particular by the city's fine late Gothic churches. Even the plan was ecclesiastically derived: the train shed's 'nave' spanned the five tracks, while the 'aisles', each side of the iron columns, covered the two side platforms. The shed's overall span of 72 feet was wider than that of London's fourteenth-century Westminster Hall, on whose impressive hammerbeams Brunel's non-structural roof supports were modelled.

The architecture of Temple Gate Station was, like its designer, daring, irreverent and iconoclastic. Not all, however, were impressed by his engineering *tour-de-force*. A W N Pugin, the self-appointed arbiter of academic Gothicism, predictably dubbed the terminal a 'mere caricature', whose mock hammerbeams and 'mock-castellated' Tudorbethan street elevation contributed to 'a design at once costly and offensive and full of pretension'.[2]

Unusually for such an early example of a great railway terminus, Brunel's train shed still stands today. This survival is due to the fact that later additions were

Wyatt's new Tudorbethan
Temple Meads Station, Bristol,
1865–78, built on the site of
Brunel's old Bristol and Exeter
Railway terminus, has long been
criticized for its lack of grandeur
and its lighthearted detailing.
The tower's pyramidal roof,
shown here in 1905, opposite
above, was removed by the
Great Western Railway in 1933,
as seen, right, in a contemporary
view. The original iron-framed
shed, by Brunel of 1839–40,
opposite below, with its Tudor
detailing and mock hammerbeams purporting to support the
roof, now functions, most
appropriately, as the setting for a
museum of the British Empire.

Rain, Steam and Speed –
The Great Western Railway, 1844,
by Joseph Mallord William
Turner (1775–1851) evocatively
captures the early age of steam
travel.

made not on the site of Brunel's station, but to the
southeast, enabling a through line to be added to
Brunel's stub-end terminus. In 1845 the Bristol and
Exeter Railway (also engineered by Brunel) arrived at
Bristol and built its own through station at right angles
to Brunel's GWR terminus. (The new station's neo-
Jacobean facade, by S C Fripp of 1852, was even more
repugnant to Puginian Goths than Brunel's
lighthearted Tudor.) With the arrival of the Midland
Railway in Bristol in 1854, though, the double-station
site became overcrowded; accordingly, the Bristol and
Exeter station was demolished to make way for a
grander design by Sir Matthew Digby Wyatt
(1820–77), built between 1865 and 1878.

Wyatt's principal elevation (the construction of
which necessitated the demolition of the southern
wing of Brunel's original facade) was couched in what

can best be described as 'Toytown Tudorbethan': its
ungainly and rather ludicrous central tower, crowned
not only with pinnacles but also with a pyramidal roof,
which was removed in 1933. Wyatt's new, curved train
shed, engineered by Francis Cox, paid obeisance to
Brunel's design by including a pointed Gothic roof,
suggestions of hammerbeam supports, and vaguely
Tudor detailing for its brickwork. In 1932–5 this shed
was extended yet further to the south, in a consciously
moderne style.

Few have admired Wyatt's new station. However, its
construction has allowed Brunel's shed to survive to the
present day as one of the outstanding relics of the early
Railway Age. In 1902 the GWR suggested levelling the
site and building a terminus closer to the city's centre,
but were dissuaded by the City Council from this
dramatic move. (The following year the GWR's

two-hour express between London and Bristol became one of the fastest trains in the world.) Brunel's pioneering train shed lasted another sixty years; it was only in the aftermath of the Beeching cuts, in 1965, that it finally ceased to be used for railway traffic. Initially the building was ignominiously converted into a car park. In a rare act of far-sighted civic planning, however, Bristol City Council refused to grant British Railways permission to raze the shed, which immediately joined the Victorian Society's new, sixty-strong list of railway stations to be targeted for listing.[3]

At the London end of Brunel's great railway lay Paddington Station. This great building of the 1850s was immortalized in William Powell Frith's celebrated canvas of 1860, *The Railway Station*. The painting, a follow-up to his enormously successful *Derby Day* of 1856–8, depicted a rather extraordinary day in the life of a great railway terminus. Frith included himself and his family, together with two of the most famous detectives of the day, Haydon and Brett, who became the station's policemen. The foreigner arguing with a taxi driver was, Frith admitted, 'a mysterious individual who taught my daughters Italian', while the man talking to the engine driver was the art-dealer Louis Flatow, who was subsequently to organize the exhibition of the painting, to which over 80,000 visitors came in six months. As an evocation of the bustle and drama of a great station, it is unrivalled.

As at Bristol, however, the virtuosity of Paddington's Gothic train shed of 1850–4, so graphically evoked by Frith, was not matched by the architecture of the rest of the station – in this instance, by the hotel of 1852–4, which separated the main concourse from Praed Street. A surprisingly pedestrian composition by the

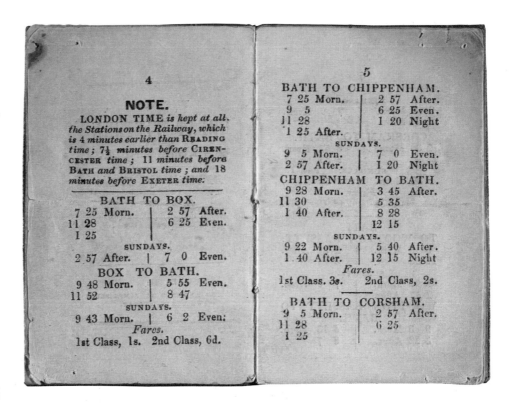

One of the earliest GWR timetables, from the early 1840s, above. The train shed at Paddington Station, London 1850–4 was designed by M D Wyatt and the engineer I K Brunel, seen left. An episode from Paddington's busy and varied life, below: the last train to use Brunel's original broad gauge leaving Brunel and Wyatt's glazed train shed in 1892.

Scenes at Paddington Station during the General Strike of 1926: workers take a break, below; and a view of the twin aisles of Brunel's ingenious train shed platforms 7 and 8, near right. The inspiration for the ridge-and-furrow glazing was taken from Paxton's gigantic Great Exhibition conservatory – the 'Crystal Palace' – of 1851; indeed the contractors for the Crystal Palace, Fox, Henderson and Company, were also employed by Brunel at Paddington. The GWR coat of arms, centre. Opposite, a 1933 view of Wyatt's curious Moorish iron detailing at the end of the shed. These applied additions, which were not designed to fulfill any structural function, were devised with the aid of the revolutionary designer Owen Jones.

younger Philip Hardwick, the hotel does not bear comparison with George Gilbert Scott's later Midland Grand further east, nor even with Lewis Cubitt's contemporary Great Northern. (What remained of Hardwick's interiors was removed in the 1930s.) Its position at the head of the concourse forced passengers to enter the station through the booking hall on the western side of the site until the station was extended to the east in 1915.

At Paddington Brunel was responsible for the design of the train shed alone. What he produced was an impressive exercise in iron and glass, in the vein of Joseph Paxton's celebrated Crystal Palace of 1851. (Brunel had been a member of the Great Exhibition Building Committee which had engaged Paxton, while the contractors at Paddington, Fox, Henderson and Company, had also erected the Crystal Palace.) The resulting train shed – 'one of the wonders of British architecture and the nineteenth century', in the words of the historian David Lloyd[4] – was, after John Dobson's Newcastle Central, the first station building to use arched braces to support a large span. It also incorporated two transepts, half-way along the shed's length. As at Temple Gate, Brunel was keen to invoke medieval ecclesiastical precedents for his cathedral of

Queen Victoria, depicted right, was an enthusiastic supporter of the railways and her frequent rail journeys did much to convince many of her more doubtful subjects of the advantages of travelling in this fashion. The rich decoration of her private car, below, demonstrates the vast differences, however, between the monarch's carriage and those of her subjects. Even the ceiling of the Royal Saloon is lined with buttoned fabric. Above, Queen Victoria's funeral cortège is seen here arriving at Paddington in 1901, from where the coffin was carried in state to Windsor in a train pulled by the Royal Sovereign Engine, opposite.

The bold, theatrical outline of Wyatville's Windsor Castle dominates this view of the approaches to William Tite's Windsor and Eton Riverside Station, Berkshire, of 1851, right. The tablet, left, commemorates both the comprehensive rebuilding of Windsor and Eton Central Station, Berkshire, 1897, and its enduring royal connections. During 1997 Central Station was refurbished by the L & R Group to accommodate forty upmarket shops and restaurants, a development which involved restoring and reopening Queen Victoria's long-shut Royal Waiting Room, below.

the Railway Age. However, like Temple Gate's hammerbeams, this innovation was ignored by later designers; indeed, today Paddington's own transepts remain a rather forlorn and forgotten part of the plan.

In his design, Brunel made provision for almost every conceivable eventuality. The iron columns which supported the ridge-and-furrow roof also carried hidden rainwater downpipes, which drained underneath the concourse floor. (Sadly, Brunel's original cast-iron supports are now replaced by steel columns, while only a small, restored section of his ridge-and-furrow glazing remains.) Even the pierced-iron roof beams had another function. The stars and planets with which they were perforated, to provide a vision of an industrial heaven for the tired travellers below, were deliberately sized so as to admit scaffolding poles when workmen were required to repair the roof.

The architectural trimmings and adjacent offices to Brunel's shed were added by Wyatt, over a decade before he was employed to enlarge Temple Meads. Given that Wyatt was advised by Owen Jones, it is not surprising to find that much of the bolted-on iron detailing is more Moorish than Gothic. Even the huge fanlight illuminating the concourse from the south end of the shed was provided with curious, sinuous Arab forms, which today make the composition resemble an Art Deco creation of the 1930s. When Wyatt worked solely on his own, however – such as at the oriel window projecting from the first floor – the result was a wholly orthodox exercise in Perpendicular Gothic.

Given that the GWR served Windsor, it is unsurprising that Paddington was, and indeed still is, much used by royalty. Queen Victoria, an early and enthusiastic railway traveller, arrived at Paddington on her first railway journey on 13 June 1842. (The Queen had actually come from Slough, since Windsor's GWR

terminus had not been built, and alighted at the first, temporary Paddington terminus. Brunel and Wyatt's building was not officially opened until 16 January 1854.) To provide easier access for the monarch and her retinue, a private royal entrance was provided to the departure platform at Paddington, incorporating a royal waiting room hung with pink and silver silk. It was from here that the funeral trains of the Queen (on 2 February 1901), Edward VII (20 May 1910), George V (28 January 1936) and George VI (15 February 1952) departed on their way to Windsor. Today the platform (now platform number 1) is still used by Windsor-bound royalty; the waiting room now houses the new-born Great Western's First Class Lounge.

At Windsor itself, rival companies vied for royal patronage. The GWR's Central station, originally a Brunel-designed timber train shed, was impressively rebuilt in the Queen's Diamond Jubilee year, 1897. (It was at this station in 1882 that the Queen narrowly survived an assassination attempt by the crazed Roderick McLean.) The new terminal, whose author is unknown, was equipped with one of Britain's last iron sheds and with a porte-cochère at right angles to the entrance drive, which passed under a glazed elliptical arch to terminate directly opposite the royal castle. At the rear of the new station was a separate royal entrance, stone-faced where the rest of the building was brick-faced. Above its entrance, leading into a vestibule lit by a glass dome, was Victoria's royal cipher, joined in 1901 by that of her son.

While the GWR's Windsor terminal was certainly impressive enough to constitute the Queen's principal gateway to London, for trips to the south the monarch used the London and South-Western's nearby Windsor and Eton Riverside terminus, whose architecture was one notch above that of the later Central station. The LSWR station was built to the designs of the architect Sir William Tite (1798–1873), one of the few leading architects who enthusiastically involved himself in station design. Tite, who made his name as the architect of London's Royal Exchange of 1842–4, was subsequently made President of the RIBA (in 1861–3 and again in 1867–9), and still found time to represent the City of Bath as its MP from 1855 to 1870. By the 1840s much of his practice (at least until his virtual retirement from architecture in 1851) was taken up with station design, particularly for the London and Southampton Railway and its successor, the LSWR. Tite's design for Windsor was, like Brunel's Temple Gate, phrased in Tudorbethan Gothic. The main building was characterized by large, flat-arched Tudor windows, the largest of which illuminated the booking hall. The asymmetrical, gabled front elevation was

Country Gothic. Left, Wateringbury, Kent, built to William Cubitt's domestically-scaled design in 1844. Centre, the splendid Renaissance arcading and Dutch gable-ends of Maldon East, built in 1846. This highly unusual branch-line terminus, closed following the Beeching cuts, survives in private hands. Below, Carshalton and Wallington, a delightfully simple building of 1850, demolished in 1900.

complemented by a long wall along Datchet Road, with twelve-arched openings each fitted with double doors large enough to accommodate the Queen's mounted Life Guard. To advertise the royal association still further, the diaper patterns in the brickwork featured a series of relevant monograms, beginning with 'VR' and 'PA' for the Queen and her Consort, and continuing with 'WC' (indicating not the location of facilities, but the LSWR's chairman, William Chaplin), 'WT' (for Tite) and LSWR. To cap it all, the wall culminated in a feature explicitly designed both to help speed the royal journey and to put the GWR's corporate nose thoroughly out of joint: an arched entrance, flanked by the royal monograms and topped with a tall turret, from which LSWR staff could catch a glimpse of the monarch's carriage as it approached. Inside the royal pavilion (which now serves as an office) plaster vaulting imitated the ceiling of Henry VII's Chapel in Westminster Abbey, where most of England's medieval monarchs are buried.

Advance notice of a monarch's arrival was vital, since royal train journeys were such complex processes:

WOOLFERTON RAILWAY-STATION

The Queen's own saloon was always kept in special care at an equable temperature. The electricians were apprised so that all electrical appliances could be in perfect order. The Locomotive Department and the District Superintendant were advised, in order to ensure the clear road required not only for the train but for the pilot engine running fifteen minutes in advance. The Engineering Department received notice, so that the whole length of the line could be watched and patrolled, because of constant fears of a Fenian outrage.[5]

Queen Victoria passed through the LSWR's Riverside station on numerous occasions. To get to London, however, she preferred the more direct, GWR route; and, as we have seen, the GWR also secured the royal funeral trade. The arrival of Edward VII's funeral party at the GWR's Central Station in 1910 was an especially grand affair. The station was closed, and every available surface draped in royal purple; following the arrival of the special trains carrying the royal family, government ministers and foreign heads of state, the funeral train drew in, and, under the eyes of a guard of honour from HMS *Excellent*, the coffin, on which was precariously balanced the royal standard, the crown and the coronation regalia, was carried into the royal waiting room. From here it was solemnly borne to St George's Chapel in the castle grounds.

Windsor was not the only place to have a royal station or two. The Great Eastern Railway's station at Wolferton in Norfolk, a Gothic confection of the early 1860s, had a series of royal waiting rooms added in 1876, to serve those who were visiting the local Sandringham Estate, which the Prince of Wales had bought in 1862. The Prince's eldest son, the mentally unstable Duke of Clarence, was later to be indirectly responsible for the station's vandalism when, on his twenty-first birthday, an elephant from Sanger's Circus, engaged to provide the entertainment, escaped and demolished the station entrance. On another, possibly apocryphal, occasion Rasputin was said to have arrived at Wolferton, but to have been turned away at the gate by the stationmaster. Both George V and his second son, George VI, died at Sandringham, and their funeral trains started from Wolferton. The station was nevertheless closed as part of the Conservative government's Beeching Report cuts in the mid-1960s, and British Rail proposed demolishing the building and erecting homes on the site. A former railwayman rescued the station, restored and reopened it as a railway museum.

In 1860 it was station architect Sir William Tite who headed the deputation to Prime Minister Palmerston to protest at George Gilbert Scott's daringly Gothic design for the Foreign Office. In helping to frustrate Scott's Gothic Foreign Office scheme, however, Tite may have inadvertently laid the foundations for one of the world's most outstanding railway stations: St Pancras, a building which (together perhaps with Bombay's Victoria Terminal) can be said to epitomize the style and sentiments of the High Victorian Goths and of the Late Victorian Empire more than any other secular building.

The Midland Railway was, until 1867, based in Derby. From February 1858 it ran trains into London; by arrangement with the Great Northern Railway, these terminated at the GNR's King's Cross station. In 1862, with crowds flocking to London for the International Exhibition, pressure on the two platforms at King's Cross was enormous, and understandably, the GNR gave precedence to their own traffic. This in turn prompted the Midland directors to establish their own route into London, which, they were determined, would eclipse the neighbouring stations at Euston and King's Cross.

By 1865 the Midland line had reached the Euston Road, and work on the train shed began the following year. The man primarily responsible for the design was the Midland's own Chief Engineer, William Henry Barlow(1812–1902). Chief Engineer of the Midland Railway since 1844, he was the co-designer of the new Tay and Forth railway bridges. At St Pancras Barlow was advised by Sir John Alleyne, General Manager of the Butterley Iron Company of Derbyshire, and assisted by R M Ordish, an expert on iron construction who had worked at the Crystal Palace and at Birmingham New Street.

Barlow and Ordish's concept was audacious: a single span of a size never built before. The twenty-five principal iron ribs of the shed, each just over 29 feet apart, spanned an astonishing 243 feet, which remained the widest span in the world for years. Indeed the shed as a whole was the largest iron structure in the world for over two decades, until Dutert built his Palais des Machines for the Paris Exhibition of 1889. The iron ribs, like everything at St Pancras, were supplied by companies which lay within the Midland's network in this case, by the Butterley Iron Company. The manner in which they were anchored to the ground provides yet another surprise. What appears to be ground level – the floor of the concourse and platforms – actually constitutes a massive tie for the roof ribs, suspended above the real floor. Barlow himself had realized that 'the floor girders across the station formed a ready-made tie sufficient for an arched roof crossing the station in one span'.[6] Originally he intended to fill the space below with rubble excavated from the Metropolitan and St John's Wood Railway's extension to Swiss Cottage of 1868. Ultimately, however, he resolved to utilize this space in a far more productive fashion. Between the 720 cast-iron columns and brick piers which carried the concourse floor were stored barrels of Bass beer, brought straight from the Bass brewery in Burton-on-Trent, Staffordshire, by the Midland's own trains. On arrival at St Pancras, barrels were unloaded at the far end of the platform and brought below the floor level by hydraulic lift; the distance between each brick-and-iron concourse support being sized to accommodate one barrel.[7]

Barlow and Ordish's spectacular iron roof comprised two acres of glazing. (Originally the supporting ironwork was painted brown, but from 1876 it was repainted sky blue, at the behest of the Midland's General Manager.) The span itself was not phrased as a simple semicircle, but came to a visible point. This feature, said Barlow, was to give protection against the wind, though he admitted that it did also improve 'the architectural effect'. Architect George Gilbert Scott was delighted by Barlow's design, later declaring that its Gothic profile was 'as if in anticipation' of his design for the adjacent office and hotel block.

Initial reaction to Barlow and Ordish's shed was mixed. The *Engineer* of 1867 decided that: 'There is no possible utility in constructing a roof of dimensions similar to those of … St Pancras station', a roof which it subsequently termed (with some geometric inexactitude) as a 'gigantic rotundity'. By the 1930s, however, it had become well-loved – far more so, in fact, than Scott's adjoining hotel. In 1939 the Beaux-Arts champion Sir Albert Richardson even suggested demolishing Scott's towering block so as to improve the view of the train shed. By 1952 Nikolaus Pevsner was prepared to declare the shed to be 'one of the outstanding surviving examples of Victorian functionalism and daring'.[8]

George Gilbert Scott (1811–78) was originally approached for the St Pancras commission by one of the Midland Railway's directors. He was, he recalled in his 1879 memoirs, 'persuaded (after more than once declining) by my excellent friend Mr Joseph Lewis … to enter into a limited competition for the new terminus'.[9] Scott's competition design was worked up while he was staying with his family on Hayling Island

E W Elmslie was principally known as a designer of Gothic churches, as is demonstrated by the exquisite Gothic detailing of the fine Great Malvern Station, Worcestershire, 1860–1 – most notably seen in the superb cast-iron capitals, above. After a serious fire in 1986 the station building was painstakingly restored by the local authority and the Railway Heritage Trust, and the unused portion let to tenants. Elmslie went on to design Great Malvern's Imperial Hotel (1861–2), Britain's first Gothic hotel.

in the autumn of 1865. Its Gothic style was reminiscent of his recently rejected Gothic scheme for the Foreign Office, but, as the architect later wrote, 'divested of the Italian element'. The myth that Scott's station was simply the Foreign Office scheme resubmitted has no foundation in fact, and the two designs are quite dissimilar.[10] Following the fierce battle over the Whitehall offices, Scott was simply 'glad to be able to erect one building in that [Gothic] style in London'. It was certainly a building of which he was inordinately proud; remarking that: 'It is often spoken to me as the finest building in London', he added that it was in his own opinion 'possibly *too good* for its purpose'.[11]

The competition for the station hotel and offices, advertised on 3 May 1865, attracted not only Scott, then widely acknowledged as Britain's premier architect, but also leading designers such as E M Barry and F P Cockerell. Early in 1866 it was announced that Scott had won, even though his scheme was over £50,000 more than the next most expensive, and £180,000 more than the cheapest submission. In the event, Scott's scheme as executed omitted two floors of offices and one floor of the hotel, to trim the costs. The result was not the first Gothic hotel in Britain, but the largest secular Gothic building in Britain, a leviathan which demonstrated that Gothic was not to be reserved just for educational purposes.

Work on the hotel and offices began in March 1868, and was not far advanced when the first trains ran into St Pancras on 1 October 1868. Nearly all of the building materials stipulated by Scott came from the Midlands, and had been transported to London by the Midland Railway: Gripper patent bricks; Ketton stone and terracotta; graduated Leicestershire slates; Derbyshire fossil marble; Mansfield sandstone; Ancaster limestone; and iron and brass fittings from Coventry. Not all the materials, though, were from the Midlands. Grey and red Peterhead granite was used for columns and piers inside the hotel, as was Connemara limestone. Scottish and Cornish granites were employed for the staircase and for the marble shafts both inside and out, while the preferred wood for the floorboards was Baltic pine – Danzig red or Swedish or Russian yellow. Yet as far as possible the physical links between the Midland's London terminus and the Midland's network were made as explicit as the budget would allow.

From the outside, Scott's Gothic facade was undeniably eclectic, 'composed of Lombardic Venetian, Street's, Spanish and North Italian, Milanese terra-cotta, fragments from Salisbury, Lincoln, Westminster and King's Gothic Study Book, sprinkled with Ruskin's aphoristic sauce', as Richardson wrote.

The main block's innately Gothic verticality was greatly enhanced by the bewildering array of Gothic turrets and pinnacles, and by the 270-foot high clock tower. Britannia, placed high on the clock tower, was the only sculpted figure permitted on the main elevation by the Midland Construction Committee.

Inside, Scott's attention to detail was immediately apparent, from the linen-fold panelling on the walls of the oak-lined booking hall to the Minton ceramic tiles on the floor of the dramatically curved main corridor. The booking hall was provided with an open-trussed roof, with carved hammerbeams complementing the Tudor linen folds; in its blind arcade were placed four sculptures of typical railwaymen. Inside the hotel itself, the walls of the ground-floor corridor were studded with columns of Derbyshire fossil marble on Ancaster pedestals and decorated in a colour scheme featuring red and brown Tudorbethan motifs on a stone-coloured ground. (By 1885 this paintwork had become discoloured by gas from the light fittings, and when electric lighting was fitted in 1886–9 the opportunity was taken to replace this scheme with a more lurid combination of greens, reds and browns.)

The centrepiece of Scott's building was the grand staircase, a breathtaking example of structural function made to serve an aesthetic purpose. The girders of Scott's cantilevered staircase were not hidden under plaster or masonry but, moulded and pierced, were made to work as decorative elements. Six granites were used to frame the staircase – pink Shap, grey Shap, grey Aberdeen, pink Devon and two Cornish varieties – and the stone-coloured walls were overpainted with a vaguely Tudor, strapwork-style scheme of red and brown (replaced after 1885 with the scarlet finish, studded with gold fleurs-de-lys, which still remains). However, it was the virtuoso ironwork which dominated the composition. Even the stair carriages were pierced; and where the ironwork might seem too plain, it was provided with additional enrichment in the form of applied ornaments in timber, plaster or carton pierre, a type of papier-mâché.

On the first-floor landing was fixed a delightfully bucolic, canvas-backed mural, *The Garden of Deduit – Romance à la Rose*, painted by T W Hay. (Hay was also the author of the murals in the coffee lounge, inexplicably eradicated after 1935.) At the top of the stair was a series of vibrant, striking figures, painted in the vaulting spandrels by the historical and landscape painter Benjamin Donaldson. Unlike Hay's mural, these paintings were executed directly on to plaster (and were consequently in need of considerable restoration by 1993). The figures represented the nine Virtues; some, such as Industry and Charity, were

The ecclesiastically derived Gothic of George Gilbert Scott's bold Euston Road elevation of St Pancras Station, London, 1868–73, opposite, has long inspired controversy. The cost for the hotel-and-office block was itself a source of dispute; Scott's original estimate of £316,000 (which made his design the most expensive of all the competition entries) ultimately proved to be rather conservative: the finished building cost over £500,000. Nevertheless, the Midland Railway was determined to outshine the neighbouring King's Cross. Scott's elevation relied principally on the products of two fine Midland firms: the salmon-coloured bricks of Edward Gripper of Nottingham and the virtuoso ironwork of FA Skidmore of Coventry. The *See Britain by Train* poster, above, of 1951 is by Abram Games.

Barlow and Ordish's revolutionary train shed at St Pancras Station, London, 1865–8, under construction in 1865, above. The old churchyard at St Pancras before it was razed to enable the Midland Railway to reach Euston Road, centre. George Gilbert Scott's competition-winning design for the hotel and office block, 1865–73, below.

NEW CATHEDRALS OF TRANSPORT

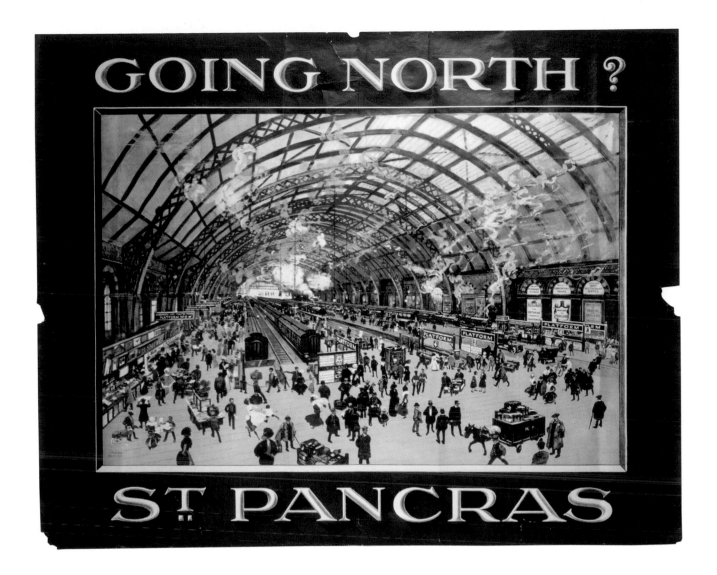

GOING NORTH ?

ST PANCRAS

posed in classical dress, much in the manner of Albert Moore or Lawrence Alma-Tadema; others, such as Temperance (depicted with his sword in his hand and his finger pressed to his lips) were fitted with medieval dress or armour. All are eminently Victorian, both in terms of subject and treatment.

By the time that Donaldson was starting on the spandrel paintings, in December 1876, Scott had lost control of the building's decoration. Three years previously, decisions on the disposition of the interiors passed from Scott to the Midland's Construction Committee. Already in 1872 a tender from the renowned cabinet-makers and interior decoration specialist Gillows of Lancaster had been accepted for carpets and furnishings. (Their representative was none other than Benjamin Donaldson.) And in January 1873 Frederick Sang began work on a decorative

concept for the hotel rooms. Sang, trained as an architect but also an accomplished watercolourist, was appointed at Scott's recommendation, but by August 1873 it was obvious that he, too, was running well over budget. Scott's failure to have the well-known firm of Clayton and Bell hired to assist Sang (who was himself sacked in January 1874) was his last involvement with the project. In December 1873 the Construction Committee members wrote to their architect to say that they had decided 'to appoint their own decorator who shall act under their own instructions', and left Gillows in charge of the interiors.

The basic planning of the first floor, however, remained Scott's. His was the curved dining hall, the arcaded ladies' room, and the sumptuous coffee lounge. Scott's concept drawing for the latter survives in the RIBA Drawings Collection; even with the

Destinations in the Midlands and North are advertised in this early poster for services from St Pancras.

mutilations necessitated by the horrific suspended ceiling of the 1960s, and the grey paint which has obliterated both Hay's murals and the marble columns, it is still possible to use this drawing to envisage what the room was like in the late nineteenth century.[12] Sang was responsible for the decoration of the ladies' room, (which in 1890 became the world's first ladies' smoking room) where each of the three arcade soffits was carved in the latest Arts and Crafts manner, including one with a distinctly Morrisian pomegranate motif. The colours of this room were originally Pompeiian red with buff decoration; in the 1880s this was replaced with a scheme of green, buff and gold. (By 1900 the ladies' smoking room was, as historians Michael Hunter and Robert Thorne have noted, 'equipped with an electrophone which linked guests by telephone line to the Queen's Hall and other London halls and churches'.)[13]

The Construction Committee members were not the only ones to question the value of Scott and Sang's work. In 1872 a poisonous article by J T Emmett in the *Quarterly Review* bitterly attacked the decoration of the hotel's interiors, alleging that those responsible had produced 'a complete travesty of noble associations' and had taken 'not the slightest care to save these from sordid contact'. Emmett clearly found Scott's Gothic hard to stomach: 'An elaboration that might be suitable for a chapter-house of a Cathedral choir, is used as an advertising medium for bagmen's bedrooms and the costly discomforts of a terminus hotel',[14] while Scott's architecture and Sang's decoration were 'catering for the low enjoyments of the great travelling crowd'. In April 1874 the *Architectural Review*'s correspondent visited the site (which had actually opened on 5 May 1873, though barely half-finished) and sniffily found

Whereas the GNR had opted to tunnel under the Regent's Canal to reach King's Cross, the Midland chose to bridge over it. The practical result of this was that, despite a downward gradient leading into the terminus, St Pancras Station was still built significantly above ground level. Thus the 'splendid Gothic pile' of St Pancras dominated the contemporary city skyline, as seen in *From Pentonville Road Looking West: Evening*, 1884, by John O'Connor.

the coffee room's decoration 'too loud' and the remarkably hygienic toilet facilities 'overdone'.[15]

Given this criticism, and the less public nature of the higher rooms, Gillows's decorative solutions for the hotel's second floor were more restrained than those advocated by Sang for the floors below. The corridor walls were provided with stencilled decoration and trellis-patterned wallpaper; above were pierced iron beams, stained-glass fanlights and aggressive heraldic beasts in the stone tympana. Inside the rooms, decoration was more subdued, relying on wallpaper and tiled or papered dados.

The whole complex was finally completed in 1877. With its handsomely equipped bathrooms, its pneumatic postal system, its billiard room, smoking rooms, reading rooms, gas chandeliers, electric bells and revolutionary Armstrong hydraulic lifts (based on Elisha Otis's United States patent design of 1857) as well as innovatory rubbish chutes, the 400-bed hotel was by far the most luxurious in London. It was certainly the most expensive: its dinner and breakfast rate of 1879 for its premier room, 14 shillings, was the highest in London. The hotel prided itself on its luxury, and on its attention to its guests' needs.

Given the strength and unashamed Gothicism of the architecture and the boldness of the decoration, the initial response to St Pancras Station was fairly predictable. The influential critic James Fergusson set the trend for a century of unfavourable comparisons with its Great Northern neighbour in 1873. While King's Cross remained for him 'an unaffected piece of engineering skill', and Barlow's shed was at least judged to be 'an engineering *tour de force*' – even if in the final analysis Fergusson declared the shed to be too big ('the carriages and engines look like toy trains') – Scott's building was derided for its 'curious clumsiness'.[16]

Fergusson's, however, was not the last word, and over the next century familiarity bred favour. In 1878 no less an authority than *The Times* declared St Pancras 'the most beautiful terminus in London, remarkable alike for its convenience and its inspiring effect';[17] almost twenty years later the *Queen's London* of 1897 thought it a 'splendid Gothic pile' whose rich red brickwork was 'well calculated to defy the begriming aspects of the London atmosphere',[18] while another contemporary critic remarked that: 'It Stands without rival … [with] touches of Milan and other Italian terra-cotta buildings, interlaced with good reproductions of details from Winchester and Salisbury Cathedrals and … ornaments of Amiens, Caen and other French edifices'.[19]

St Pancras spawned few direct imitators: I C Buckhout's train shed of 1871 for New York's Grand Central Station was closely based on Barlow's, as was that of Jersey City Station of 1888, which was only ten feet wider. After the First World War, however, the station's architecture grew increasingly less fashionable, and the hotel less profitable. Following the grouping of 1923, the station's new owners, the London Midland and Scottish Railway (LMS), expressed dissatisfaction with both the station's design and the hotel's performance. The Midland Grand – which in 1934 made a profit of only £2,781, compared with Euston's £7,039 and the Manchester Midland's £50,579 – was the first to go. In 1935 the LMS closed the hotel and clumsily converted its rooms into utilitarian offices.

For the next sixty years the hotel's story was one of unrelieved vandalism and neglect: the entrance lobby's splendid wooden screen and revolving doors were ripped out; walls were overpainted in bland, dull colours; shoddy partitions were installed, scything through the cornices; and suspended ceilings, their supports ruthlessly punched through the plasterwork, made nonsense of the rooms' proportions. In one of the few areas that still remained in public use, Scott's Tudor booking hall, the damage of the Second World War was poorly repaired, the original vaulted ceiling being replaced by a characterless flat covering.

Scott's block was not the only element of the site to be threatened with destruction: Barlow's train shed was also at risk. In the 1930s the LMS's notorious president, Lord Stamp, had complained that it was impossible to alter the building 'without meeting with the same obstacles that would be encountered in modifying the Rock of Gibraltar'. Yet in 1966 the BTC announced plans to amalgamate King's Cross and St Pancras into a 'single modern terminal',[20] a scheme which would involve the complete demolition of the latter, if not the former. The following year, British Rail unveiled a plan to build a sports centre or exhibition hall on the site of St Pancras Station, a plan that clearly took its cue from the Madison Square Garden complex at Penn Station.

In the event, St Pancras did not go the way of Penn Station, nor of Euston. By the early 1960s opinions had already begun to change on the merits of Scott's and Barlow's designs. In 1952 Nikolaus Pevsner was still faintly embarrassed by Scott's uncompromising Gothic, preferring to single out for special mention only that 'the carriage ramp up to the drive-in should

… delight the eye of the modern designer'.[21] In 1957, however, Carroll Meeks, though a Modernist at heart, commended the harmony between the shed and the head building-cum-hotel, applauding Scott's 'unrivalled, uninhibited display of towers'. And the years which followed the founding of the Victorian Society in 1958 saw a new appreciation of the great architectural achievements of the Railway Age. In 1964 David Piper eulogized the romantic qualities of Scott's 'great Gothic phantasmagoria': 'Its value to the London skyline is inestimable … high as a cliff crowned with a pinnacled castle in a Grimm's fairy-story, drawing up with complete confidence into a sky-assaulting rage of turrets.'[22] Three years later architect Donald Insall was equally rhapsodic: he especially delighted in St Pancras's 'delicate Gothic bridges which leap its entrances', which were, he averred, 'more delicious than any bridge of sighs'.[23]

By 1967 the Victorian Society was marshalling its forces to face the new threat of demolition. Pevsner (now Chairman of the Society) was now giving the station his full support, and wrote in the *Guardian* that St Pancras was not an ugly and unfashionable white elephant but 'a masterpiece of modern architecture'. In November 1967 the Labour government accepted this view, and gave the train shed and hotel block a Grade I listing. St Pancras thus became one of the first major buildings to enjoy the protection of the new, tougher historic buildings legislation which the Wilson administration had recently introduced.

The hotel, alas, was not so lucky. In 1980 the offices were abandoned and the building's decay accelerated. During the ensuing decade schemes to convert the hotel came to nothing. Instead, companies began to chose the evocative, decaying interiors for film shoots or as the setting for PR events. Some principal scenes of Tim Burton's *Batman* of 1991 were filmed in the potent Gothic atmosphere of the ladies' smoking room, while shortly before Christmas 1994 theatrical entrepreneur Cameron Mackintosh celebrated the first night of his *Oliver* revival with a spectacular party centred on the hotel's breathtaking grand stair.

In 1993 some work was done on the badly damaged interior and exterior. Sadly, though, all this valuable work came to a premature end in 1995. The stabilising of Scott's great building had aroused great public interest, with thousands attending the hotel's open days in 1994 and 1995. Yet the fate of the station, and particularly of Scott's hotel, now depends on the site's post-privatization owners.

The potential for political symbolism in Romanesque Revival was certainly used to great effect at Metz Station, in what is now the eastern French province of Lorraine. The province had for centuries been a bone of contention between France and Germany, with the city of Metz regularly passing between the two countries since the Middle Ages, yet at the outbreak of the Franco-Prussian War of 1870 the city's population was largely Francophone. Fed by Paris's Est terminus at the western end of the line, Metz was one of the centres of Napoleon III's doomed war effort. The city station, however, rapidly became an ominous metaphor for the whole French campaign: platforms were often blocked, trains arrived days late, and others had to unload their precious cargoes of material far from the terminus. Shortly after the French collapse at Sedan, when Napoleon III himself was captured by the Prussians, Metz fell into the hands of the invaders. As a result of the ignominious peace terms subsequently dictated by Berlin, the provinces of Alsace and Lorraine were ceded to the newly declared German Empire, where they remained until 1918.

To underline the altered status quo, and to prepare for the expected rematch against France, the German government began crisscrossing the region with military railways, and studding the system with German-built stations. As part of this policy the French station in Metz (erected in 1875–80, and the second building on the site) was demolished in 1905. In its place the Germans built a wholly different

terminus, to the designs of the German architect Jürgen Kröger. The new station's powerful, squat Romanesque lines were in sharp contrast to the playful Beaux-Arts idiom of contemporary French termini such as Paris Orsay and Tours. Metz Station's solemn, brooding, humourless presence, and its evocation of a Rhenish town hall rather than a French railway station, was a constant reminder to the local population of the German occupation. Some effort was made to lighten the heavy symbolism: sculptural groups on the facade optimistically represented French and Germans working together in harmony, and even (on one capital) embracing each other. However, elsewhere on the elevation Teutonic knights stood guard. The message was unmistakable: accept the new order or face the consequences.

Metz is rare in France not only in being couched in a decidedly Teutonic fashion, but in being in any Gothic style at all. Outside Britain, the British colonies and the United States, wholeheartedly Gothic stations were uncommon; it appears that other nations were reluctant to follow the Anglo-Saxons' championing of a style which many still regarded as exclusively ecclesiastical or academic. Few great American Gothic termini of the nineteenth century survive today, most having succumbed either to a neoclassical replacement or, more usually, to outright demolition during the 1960s or 70s. Of those Gothic stations that were built

Jürgen Kröger's muscular and distinctly Teutonic Romanesque architecture, while initially repugnant to the German-ruled French inhabitants of Metz, has helped Metz Station, France, 1905–8, to shrug off the modern incursions which can ruin a historic building. It has even been able to withstand postwar accretions such as the insensitive entrance block, below, and the inevitable proliferation of internal signage, opposite.

by the British at the height of the Victorian era, though, one that happily does survive is Bombay's Victoria Terminus. In Bombay Victoria, India possesses not only one of the world's greatest railway terminals, but also one of the most impressive secular Gothic buildings.

Indian stations have always exerted a strong attraction to visitors. They were of especial importance in the administration and pacification of British India; at the same time, they represented microcosms of the nation. And they still do, as Paul Theroux has observed: 'Much of Indian life is lived within sight of the tracks or the station, and often next to the tracks, or inside the station.'[24] V S Naipaul described a typical Indian railway terminal in 1964:

… the shouts of stunted, sweating porters, over-eager in red turbans and tunics, the cries of tea-vendors with their urns and clay cups (the cups to be broken after use), the cries of *pan*-vendors and the vendors of fried or curried messes (the leaf-plates, pinned together by thin dried twigs, to be thrown afterwards on to the platform or on the tracks, where the pariah dogs, fierce only with their fellows, will fight over them …), the whole scene – yet animated only in the foreground, for these stations are havens as well as social centres, and the smooth, cool concrete platforms are places where the futile can sleep – the whole scene ceilinged by low fans which spin in empty frenzy.[25]

The first Indian railway was the Bombay–Thana line, officially opened at Bombay in 1853. The inaugural ceremony was not auspicious: the Governor (Lord Falkland), the army Commander-in-Chief (Lord Frederick FitzClarence) and the Bishop of Bombay (The Right Reverend John Hardinge) all 'left for the hills the previous evening in disregard of the memorable character of the occasion', as the *Bombay Times* sourly observed.[26] Yet the local officials saved the day: a public holiday was declared, and the first train left Bombay to a twenty-one-gun salute.

During the next forty years the Indian railway network spread eastwards, and became studded with great stations, executed in a distinctly European Gothic or classical idiom and, though staffed by locals, invariably run by a British stationmaster. Most spectacular of the great stations of the interior was Lahore, built in 1864 to the design of William

The bizarre, fortress-like silhouette of Lahore Station, India, 1861–4, as originally conceived by William Brunton, above. Opposite, a poster advertising the Calcutta–Bombay service on the Bengal–Nagpur Railway, 1935.

Brunton, Chief Engineer of the Amritsar and Multan Railway. (Few Indian stations were designed by established or well-known architects. Calcutta Sealdah of 1862, designed by Brunel in a hybrid Oriental-Italianate manner, is a rare exception.) The form of Lahore Station strongly recalled a medieval European castle, with its crenellated towers, giant iron doors and loopholes. The parallel was not accidental. Memories of the Indian Mutiny of 1857–8 were still vivid; together with the constant threat from the northwestern tribes, this made security a prime consideration in the design of a major railway station. The loopholes were not, as in Victorian England, intended to be purely decorative, but were designed to accommodate the nineteenth century's answer to the medieval bow: the musket. And the towers were built not to withstand ancient cannonades, but the explosive effects of the latest bombs or shells, while also

providing contemporary defenders with a commanding view. Only later were Lahore's substantial towers provided with clocks, in the manner of a regular railway terminus.

It was from Lahore, 'the fort-like railway station', that Rudyard Kipling's Kim set out on a pilgrimage to the holy city of Benares, and adventure, accompanied by a holy lama:

'This is the work of devils!' said the lama, recoiling from the hollow echoing darkness, the glimmer of rails between the masonry, and the maze of girders above. He stood in a gigantic stone hall paved, it seemed, with the sheeted dead – third-class passengers who had taken their tickets overnight and were sleeping in the waiting-rooms … The lama, not so well used to trains as he had pretended, started as the 3.25am south bound roared in. The sleepers sprung to life, and the station filled with clamour and shoutings, cries of water and sweetmeat vendors, shouts of native policemen, and shrill yells of women gathering up their baskets, their families, and their husbands.[27]

The true home of India's railways, however, remained Bombay. From here the Great Indian Peninsular Railway (GIPR) ran east to Allahabad, where it connected with the East India Railway (EIR), which ran to Lahore and the northwest. In 1873 Jules Verne chose to set much of his *Around the World in Eighty Days* in the city's stations; it was, for example, at the old GIPR terminus that Inspector Fix attempted to detain Phileas Fogg: 'Fix had followed Fogg to the station, and was there on the platform. He now perceived that the rogue was leaving Bombay, and at once made up his mind to accompany him as far as Calcutta, or farther, if necessary.'

Bombay was the commercial capital of the Raj, and this was reflected in the astonishing contrasts and juxtapositions of its vibrant railway termini – places 'of refugees and fortune hunters, smelling of dirt and money', as Paul Theroux has put it.[28] Teeming, exciting, and at times frightening, Bombay's great buildings were correspondingly grand, often laughably pretentious and sometimes theatrically sham. In the 1930s the travel writer Robert Byron termed the city 'an architectural Sodom' studded with 'daemonic buildings'.[29]

To mirror the growing importance of the city, and of the railway company's operations, the GIPR had by the 1870s decided to rebuild their principal terminus in a more heroic mould. The result was one of the world's most stupendous buildings. Victoria Terminal has been labelled 'an oriental St Pancras' or 'St Pancras Station splendidly crossed with a Moghul Mausoleum'. However, it was far more than just an imitation of Scott's London terminus; it was a powerful piece of socio-political theatre. Its political symbolism was scarcely less evident than at Metz, as it sought to fuse Indian national imagery with an unmistakably

European architectural heritage in the grandest manner available. It was reputedly the largest building in the whole of Asia when completed, and its significance was not lost on British India: the British were in India to stay. As Jean Dethier has written: 'Its mass dominated the town and glorifies the virtues of the Victorian age and the spirit of eternity of a foreign power.'[30] Between them, Bombay Victoria and Lahore epitomized the goals of British India: the use of military prowess, technological superiority and, above all, ceremonial bombast in order to achieve a degree of commercial gain.

Victoria Terminal was built on the site of a former Portuguese church (later the setting for a Portuguese gallows) and was next door to a former Hindu temple to the mouthless goddess Mumba Devi, the Mother Goddess who gave her name to the city. ('Mumbai' is still the vernacular name for Bombay.) Its architect was not a figure of the international renown of Brunel or Scott, but was an engineer named F W Stevens (1847–1900) who was born in Bath, and had trained there in the office of Charles E Davis. In 1867 he travelled to Bombay to take up a post as an assistant engineer in the new Public Works Department under Lt Col James Fuller, subsequently the architect of the

Early English-style Bombay Law Courts of 1871–9. Stevens resigned from government service in 1884, before Victoria Terminal was completed, but continued to practise in the city. The Municipal Buildings opposite Victoria Terminal were also built to his design, in 1888–93. (Their Gothic-Saracenic synthesis has been acclaimed by Philip Davies as Stevens's masterpiece: 'For sheer ebullience it is unsurpassed in British India, and more than any other building, it exudes the twin qualities of Imperial and Civic pride.') Stevens also designed Bombay's

Churchgate terminus of 1894–6 in a vaguely Byzantine style for the Bombay, Baroda and Central India Railway. Unfortunately, the BBCIR completely rebuilt this station in a mundane, workaday style in 1928.

Even for an experienced and celebrated architect, Victoria Terminal – begun in 1878 and finished in time for Queen Victoria's Golden Jubilee in 1887 – would have been an astonishing achievement. Yet what has been justly termed 'the most famous Victorian building in India' was the product of a little-known corporation engineer.[31] The exterior of the building was a breathtaking fusion of English Gothic, Venetian Gothic, Romanesque and Moghul, its two huge wings stretching out in the manner of a French Renaissance palace or an Elizabethan country house to embrace the visitor. No expense was spared on the materials; nor did Stevens stint on the political and cultural symbolism. Marbles from the Mediterranean and granite from Aberdeen were imported for the interior. Thomas Earp was commissioned to design stone medallions for the front elevation, the Imperial lion and Indian tiger for the two giant gate piers and the 14-foot high statue of Progress atop the central dome (the first true dome to be applied to a Gothic building). Much of the sculptural decoration on the facade, however, originated closer to home. The sculptured panels of Engineering, Agriculture, Commerce, Science and Trade in the gables, the cameo busts of the GIPR directors, the monkey-gargoyles, the medallions of elephants, the reliefs of locomotives and the carved capitals were all executed by students at the local Bombay School of Art.

Inside the station were Aberdeen granite columns, stained-glass windows, and more evidence of the sculptural talent to be found at the School of Art. On the floor were ceramic tiles by Maw and Company from the cradle of the Industrial Revolution: Ironbridge in Shropshire. (Maw's was later to supply floor tiles to a number of major railway stations, among them the Gothic extravaganzas of St Louis Union and Montreal Windsor.) The wooden, groin-vaulted ceilings were painted blue, and decorated with gold stars, in the same vein as Sang's interiors for the Midland Grand Hotel. In the entrance corridor decorated rib vaulting sprang not from standard corbels but from the backs of grotesquely carved animals, while the central bosses, from which the gas lanterns were originally hung, were fashioned in the shape of lion and tiger heads.

It was entirely appropriate to the symbolic nature of the station that Victoria Terminal opened on the Jubilee Day of the Empress of India herself. The reaction of the spectators to the building was generally supportive, although the Vicereine, Lady Dufferin, sniffily opined that the architecture was 'much too magnificent for a bustling crowd of railway passengers'.[32] Over the next sixty years Victoria Terminal was indissolubly linked with the image and administration of the British Raj. It was from Victoria Terminal that all British civilians and army officers departed for the interior, after the arrival of the P&O's steamships after the thirteen-day voyage from Britain. Every Friday the GIPR's first class and mail-only express left Victoria Terminal for Calcutta Howrah, travelling the sixty-six-hour journey at what was in 1900 an astonishing average speed of 35 mph, and equipped with sumptuous dining facilities:

For *chota-hazri* (little breakfast), which we took just after daybreak, we would have a cup of tea and some toast or bread-and-butter. Breakfast proper followed this at 9 or 10 o'clock, then tiffin at 1, and dinner about 6 in the evening. All the meals were exceptionally good. For dinner there would be, besides soup and fish, beef, mutton, snipe, duck, partridge, quail, pastry, four or five different kinds of fruits, and the universal curry and rice. The tables were laid more in the style of a first-class club than a railway refreshment room; and there was a native servant to every two passengers who partook of meals. The guard or some other official of the train came to our carriage and asked what wine or beer we wished to have, and he would then send a wire for it to be put on ice.[33]

From the 1920s this service was supplemented by the weekly expresses to Madras and Delhi, designed principally for the Raj's British administrators. The Delhi express was for a time the country's fastest train, taking twenty-seven hours to run the 957 miles, with only eighteen stops. By the late 1930s, however, the Deccan Queen was able to cover the short 119-mile journey from Bombay to Poona even more rapidly, carrying potential spectators for the Poona horse races at an average speed of 52 mph. In contrast to the squalid conditions of most carriages departing from Victoria Terminal, first class trains enjoyed spacious compartments with berths, lavatories and showers, and even a small bath. Over the carriage windows were placed mats, moistened by tanks on the roof, which helped to keep the compartment interiors cool.

Typical of the flights of fancy which British architects felt free to indulge in once in India, here the Romanesque fenestration of Central Station, Madras, India, 1868, competes with French-Gothic towers. Curiously, such architectural bravado, while characteristic of the great Indian railway stations, was rarely repeated in the termini of other British Dominions or colonies.

Railways of the Indian Empire.
— 1860 —

Original Design of one of the first Third-class Carriages run on the Bombay Baroda and Central India Railway. Built in the old workshops at Amroli in 1860.

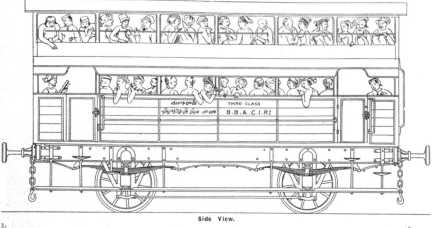

Side View.

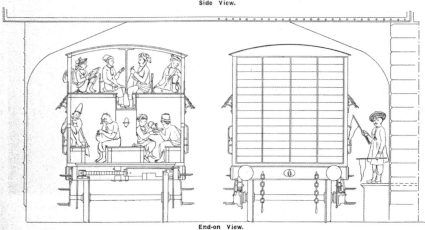

End-on View.

By 1921, the year in which Victoria Terminal was enlarged (a new administration block and five new platforms were added), large stations such as Victoria were generally provided with an adjacent compound, which enclosed special quarters for senior British railway officers, an Anglican church or chapel, a railway club (for the senior staff) and a railway institute (for all employees). With independence in 1947, however, this cosy colonial arrangement came to an end. On 24 August 1947, only nine days after the nation's independence had been declared, the frontier mail arrived at Victoria Terminal having been held up by a gang of Muslim bandits, its contents looted and many of its passengers murdered. Worse was to come, as trains of Hindus and Muslims all over the Indian subcontinent were ambushed, and their passengers massacred. Meanwhile, Victoria Terminal was being overwhelmed by refugee Hindus, who had fled to the city, and by Muslims awaiting transport to Pakistan.

Railways of the Raj. This early drawing, above, shows the railway carriages of the trains of the Bengal–Nagpur Railway. Jamanagar Station, above, is a handsome, low-slung design. The building in the background of this 1910 view, below, could easily be in Surrey or the Swiss Alps; in fact, it lies on the Calcutta to Darjeeling Railway.

Today these horrors are a fading memory. Victoria Terminal, though, remains the heart of a fizzing metropolis, a city which has firmly established itself as the commercial capital of India. The terminus now handles two million passengers and 900 trains daily, and its Calcutta express now takes only thirty-six hours. Sadly, Indian Railways did nothing to celebrate Victoria Terminal's 100th anniversary in 1987. This was left up to the Post Office, who released a special commemorative stamp, and the *Times of India*, which published a long, celebratory article extolling the station as 'an unprecedented gallery of life' where 'you can see friezes of faces from all parts of the country'.[34] More than any other great railway terminus in the world, Bombay Victoria is a mirror of its evolving nation. At the time of writing it is even proposed to rename the station Chatrapati Shivaji (after the heroic Maratha king) in an attempt to eradicate associations of British rule. Given the building's unmistakable visual evocation of the Raj, however, it will, surely, always be known as the Victoria Terminal.

Grandiose High Gothic sentiment was not to everyone's taste – or purse. By the end of the nineteenth century some of the less ostentatious railway companies were, in designing their major stations, turning away from Gothic braggadocio and neoclassical grandiloquence in favour of a more light-hearted (and cheaper) approach, which revived the forms of the Gothic-Classical hybrid architectural styles of Western Europe in the sixteenth and seventeenth centuries.

In Britain, this Renaissance–Gothic fusion proved popular for stations in the smaller towns and the new suburbs. An early example is Slough, the GWR's junction for Windsor. The station of 1879–82 made no attempt to echo the Regency Gothic of Sir Jeffry Wyatville's Windsor Castle, the Perpendicular-Tudorbethan Gothic of Tite's Windsor and Eton Riverside (for the rival LSWR), nor even the genuine sixteenth-century Gothic of nearby Eton College. Instead, the architect-engineer J E Danks opted for a surprisingly sophisticated French château style, with high, curved roofs and large *œil-de-bœuf* windows for both the main block and the two sizable end pavilions. The result was a small piece of sixteenth-century France in the midst of what has never been a particularly attractive industrial town. Everyone remembers John Betjeman's notorious plea of 1937: 'Come, friendly bombs, and fall on Slough,/It isn't fit for humans now…' Today, when what remained of the Victorian town centre of Betjeman's day has been swept away as part of a series of ruthless civic developments, this good-humoured, decidedly

Francophile station is easily the town's most impressive building, and still survives in remarkably good condition.

It was in Continental Europe, rather than in Britain or the United States, that the architectural manner based loosely on the hybrid Gothic forms of the late Renaissance was most often adapted for large railway stations. The most famous is Amsterdam Central, which was built in 1881–9 by P J H Cuypers (1827–1921), also the architect of the city's famous Rijksmuseum of 1885. The station building was entirely grouped on one side of the tracks, facing south towards the city centre. This long frontage was executed in local brickwork, and in a domestically derived, seventeenth-century manner which revealed nothing of the building's true purpose. Yet Cuypers' building (or at least its facade) was one of the most spectacular in the city, its appearance being further enhanced by a large forecourt – the Stationsplein. Cuypers was a follower of Eugène Viollet-le-Duc, and was keen to employ the medium of Renaissance Gothic to celebrate Holland's illustrious past. Ironically, though, Cuypers was a Catholic, while the period the architecture of the station evokes – the late sixteenth and early seventeenth centuries – was exactly the time of The Netherlands' bitter and protracted revolt against the Catholic yoke of Spain.

Cuypers' station was built on an artificial island in the harbour; hence the room available for the Stationsplein. Its construction actually cut off the view of the harbour from that part of the city; however, such was the popularity of Cuypers' design that this loss was quickly forgotten. As Charles Ford's guide to Amsterdam enthuses, 'the style is a Northern

Union Station, Springfield, Massachusetts by Shepley, Rutan and Coolidge, built in 1889 (though now demolished), is a squat, asymmetrical, rubble walled station much in the manner of the Romanesque pioneer H H Richardson. This photograph was taken in 1905.

NEW CATHEDRALS OF TRANSPORT

Renaissance pot-pourri reminiscent of the great town halls of the Flemish cities to the South'.[35] The long facade of the station is covered in decorative motifs recalling Amsterdam's maritime past, and specifically her domination of seaborne trade in the seventeenth century. The materials used – principally plain red brick, with stone dressings – also suggest the buildings of the era of Admirals de Tromp and de Ruyter, and of the nation's finest hour.

After the showy evocation of Dutch glories on the main facade, the brick-lined entrance hall is surprisingly plain and utilitarian. The entrance to the platforms is even more starkly functional: two dark, plainly tiled tunnels run under the tracks, from which stairs ascend to island platforms covered by a pair of simple, unornamented train sheds of 1922. It is these bare, even ominous features, rather than Cuypers' theatrical facade, which help to remind the traveller of the station's wartime role: the railhead from which Holland's Jews were transported to incarceration and death in Nazi Germany's concentration camps. It was from these severe platforms, on 11 September 1944, that Anne Frank and the seven other occupants of her secret annexe embarked on cattle trucks for Westerbork transit camp. From Westerbork they left on the last train to leave for Auschwitz-Birkenau. As is well known, Anne died at Bergen-Belsen on 12 April 1945, only weeks before the camp was liberated by the British. Today Amsterdam Central's bleak, dark tunnels bear silent witness to the helpless passengers of fifty years ago, mocking the cheerful, almost naïve exuberance of the historicist facade.

Where Cuypers' led, few followed. Even at the height of the station-building era at the turn of the twentieth century, nearly all of the new European termini were deliberately phrased in a more robust, masculine Classicism, which more properly reflected the city's, and the nation's, strength of purpose. Of the great European stations of this era, only one principal terminus – Lisbon's Rossio station – was built in a recognizably Gothic style. Like Amsterdam Central, its Gothicism was used to evoke the architecture, and the glories, of the country's illustrious past; and like Amsterdam, its peculiarly home-grown historicism (see Chapter 4) failed to appeal to the muscle-flexing Great Powers of Central Europe. In 1900 most of the great railway stations that had been recently erected on the Continent – among them Brussels Midi, Frankfurt-am-Main, Dresden, Zürich, Budapest East – had been designed in a pompous Classical idiom far removed from the light-hearted quotations of Amsterdam and Lisbon. Only in America was the Gothic terminus celebrated and developed.

The stunning, Renaissance-derived principal elevation of P J H Cuypers' Central Station, Amsterdam, 1881–9, phrased in an idiom which few other architects were prepared to adapt for large city termini. The brick-built facade still survives, virtually intact today; however, the luscious interiors depicted in a local magazine at the time of the station's opening, above, have largely been excised. Cuypers' shed has gone, replaced by two functional but anonymous structures in 1922.

THE MONUMENTAL AGE OF RAIL
IMPERIAL NEOCLASSICISM

'The day will certainly come when railway stations will be considered as significant as other great buildings, when architecture will be expected to deploy all its resources in their construction, and when their design will be on a monumental scale. Railway stations may then have the same importance as those vast and splendid monuments erected for their Public Baths by the Romans.'[1]
CÉSAR DALY, 1846.

As well as being used to recapture and amplify the drama of the great medieval cathedrals, railway termini were used to give expression to the imperial ambitions of the nation, using the austere, imposing and suitably severe medium of gigantically-proportioned Neoclassicism. Bombay Victoria was very much a stylistic exception to the hegemony which the Classical style enjoyed in railway systems elsewhere within the British Empire. From Junagadh in India to Vancouver at Canada's western edge haughty Classical edifices were built to mark the progress of Britain's railways and Britain's Imperial civilization.

One of the most celebrated of these was London's Euston terminus. Even shortly before its untimely demolition it was still much appreciated. In 1950 Christian Barman declared of Euston: 'Never again was railway architecture to rise to such a sense of high occasion. It was the railway builders' monument to their conquest of the greatest city in the world.'[2] Two years later even Nikolaus Pevsner enthused that 'Here was something as grandiose of its kind as anything the Greeks ever had accomplished.'[3] The demolition of Euston a decade later – and in particular, that of the celebrated Euston Arch – was a wholly avoidable tragedy. More than any other single event in the 1960s, it helped to define the emerging conservation movement and, indirectly, to persuade the incoming Labour administration to tighten the legislation protecting the nation's built heritage.

The London to Birmingham Railway was formed in 1831, only one year after the pioneering Liverpool and Manchester company. Four years later Parliament granted the extension of the L&B line to London. Negotiations to share a terminus with the GWR, however, had foundered: the L&B's directors loftily declared in November 1834 that Brunel's Great

Philip Hardwick's unforgettable railway monument, the Doric Arch at Euston, 1837–8, here seen under construction, left, and in use in 1890, opposite. The unjustified demolition of this masterpiece still rankles today; in 1996, twenty-five years after it was razed, a society was founded in London dedicated to campaigning for its resurrection.

Western was not 'in a condition to make a legal agreement'. Accordingly, the line was ended just to the north of the Euston Road at what was then London's first main-line terminus, planned by Robert Stephenson. The first, temporary station opened on 20 July 1837, only one month after Queen Victoria's accession to the throne. The timber-framed, double-span train shed was designed by Charles Fox (1810–74), an enthusiastic engineer later knighted for his work on the Great Exhibition of 1851, who also drove locomotives on the Liverpool and Manchester Railway (once arriving at Liverpool with a level-crossing gate on his buffers).

For the permanent station, however, the L&B turned to one of the leading architects of the day. In July 1836, while the wooden terminal was still being constructed, the directors asked Philip Hardwick to prepare elevations for the principal building. Hardwick (1792–1870) was the son of the architect Thomas Hardwick, who in turn had been a pupil of Sir William Chambers, one of the most influential

architects of the second half of the eighteenth century. Philip thus came from a strong Classical tradition; James Wyatt's opinion of his father – 'a regular bred, classical architect' – was equally appropriate to the son. Philip went into partnership with his father in 1819 and, following appointments at the notorious Bridewell Prison and the equally infamous Bethlehem ('Bedlam') Hospital, was appointed architect to the Goldsmiths' Company in 1828, for whom he built his most famous surviving building, the austerely Greek Goldsmiths' Hall of 1835. A founder member of the new Institute of British Architects in 1834, he became the organization's vice-president in 1839 and 1841. In 1843, however, his health deteriorated at the relatively young age of fifty-one, and he was forced to turn much of his practice over to his son, Philip Charles (1822–92), who had already learned his trade as his father's principal assistant at Euston Station.

The centrepiece of Hardwick's new Euston was the Neoclassical great hall, which formally opened on 27 May 1849. It represented something wholly new in

It was not only the imposing Classical space of the Great Hall (1846–9) at Euston Station that helped make it such a memorable interior; the standard of decoration – the dramatic double stairs and sinuous, scrolled lamp standards, opposite; the statuary and bas-reliefs by John Thomas, centre and right – was also unusually high. This naturally served to escalate the cost, which soon soared above £150,000. Hardwick was forced to make economies, among them abandoning the frescoes for the walls (which were instead rendered and painted grey) and substituting painted plaster columns for the planned marble. Meanwhile, critics were increasingly pointing out the disparity between the grand but cramped Neoclassicism of the Great Hall and the inexpensive functionalism of the workman-like train shed behind.

Top, GWR Booking Office at Euston, *c*1910; LNER timetable from 1930, above, listing services from King's Cross, Liverpool Street and Marylebone stations; LMS/Cunard Poster advertising the route taken by those travelling abroad; the suffragette, Emmeline Pankhurst en route to the USA boarding the boat train at Euston, opposite.

British and indeed in world railway architecture: the use of direct references to the great buildings of the antique world (and, more specifically, of the Roman Empire) to create a building that was sufficiently imposing to impress visitors, yet at the same time functioned as a highly efficient welcoming and dispersal area. It was also a structure whose magnificent Classical rhetoric properly befitted this newest and most heroic of building types, and whose brazen showmanship communicated the depth of the railway's commercial aspirations. At 139-feet long by 62-feet wide, and lined with a 20-foot high colonnade of Ionic columns painted to resemble red granite shafts with white marble capitals, the scale of the interior recalled the basilicas and baths of ancient Rome, while its double-cube proportions were reminiscent of Inigo Jones's royal Whitehall Banqueting House of 1622–9. Unfortunately, though, the standards of construction were not always as high as those of Vitruvius or Jones: during building work the columns collapsed, killing three workmen. Luckily for Hardwick, the main contractor William Cubitt, supported by Hardwick's professional colleagues William Tite and Edward Blore, testified that the brick cores for the columns were perfectly sound; they were, however, subsequently rebuilt using internal iron supports.

The hall's plaster ceiling, its design taken directly from the fourth-century church of St Paul's-outside-the-walls in Rome, was said in 1849 to have the largest span of any ceiling in the world. Its only visible support was from the massive wall brackets, themselves balanced on giant lion heads. Thus the cast-iron

technology of the Industrial Revolution was allied to the forms of the ancient world, in a manner which anticipated the great Beaux-Arts stations of the early twentieth century. Some of the Roman ceiling panels were even perforated to allow the hot-water pipes behind to help heat and ventilate the hall.

The decoration was as impressive as the technological feats. Punctuating the walls were eight plaster bas-reliefs depicting the principal destinations of the railway: London, Liverpool, Manchester, Birmingham, Carlisle, Chester, Lancaster and, oddly, Northampton. (In 1846 the L&B had merged with the Liverpool and Manchester, the Manchester and Birmingham, and the Grand Junction railways to form the famous London and North Western Railway – the LNWR.) The sculptor chosen for this commission was, like Hardwick, one of the most highly regarded and fashionable designers of the day. John Thomas was both prolific and remarkably successful. Frequently employed both as sculptor and as architect by the Prince Consort (for whom he had in 1849 just completed the figures of 'Peace' and 'War' for Buckingham Palace), he had recently carved almost all

of the sculptural decoration on the exterior of the Houses of Parliament for Charles Barry. In addition to the bas-reliefs at Euston, he was responsible for the stone group over the hall door to the general meeting room, comprising a figure of Britannia resting on the head of a lion and supported by the Arts and Sciences and Mercury (then just beginning to be employed as an allegorical emblem of rail transport). Below Britannia was the great double staircase of Craigleith granite, in front of which was Thomas's statue of George Stephenson. (A bronze of Stephenson's brother Robert was commissioned from Carlo Marochetti twenty years later, but when completed in 1870 was inexplicably relegated to the forecourt of the station.) Originally Hardwick planned to have the hall's walls also executed in granite; this, however, ultimately proved too expensive, and they were instead constructed in plaster painted to resemble granite.

Hardwick's great hall was the first enclosed courtyard to be used for a railway purpose, and the first truly Neoclassical interior to grace a terminus complex. The effect of the Euston hall's finished interior was dramatic. A visitor of 1911 was still able to marvel at its scale and facilities:

> … it is spacious, well lit and of imposing height. A gallery with ornamental railings is carried around the hall thus forming a pleasing break in the massiveness of the walls. In the centre of the hall … the floor is occupied by rows of seats for waiting passengers, train indicators, models of the steamers running from Holyhead to Ireland, afternoon tearooms, weighing and chocolate machines and all the usual equipment of a station waiting hall.[4]

The other celebrated structure at Euston was the great sandstone arch in the station's forecourt, a 72-foot high propylaeum completed in May 1838. Five years after it was built, A W N Pugin used his *An Apology for the Revival of Christian Architecture in England* (1843) to deride the arch as a perfect symbol of the excessive, pagan Neoclassicism he so detested: 'a piece of Brobdingnagian absurdity which must have cost the company a sum which would have built a first-rate station'. However, to a more sympathetic observer such as John Britton, writing in 1839, it was 'a most successful adaptation of the pure Grecian Doric; admirably suited, by its massiveness and boldness of its design and execution, for an approach … connecting the British Metropolis with the most important towns of the kingdom'.[5] A century later the arch was being widely acclaimed, by Pevsner and others, as 'the greatest monument to the passing Railway Age'.

Sadly, with the exceptions of the great hall and the arch, Euston Station was not designed to an

William Tite's 1848 Waterloo Station was demolished at the end of the nineteenth century; in its place was built a far larger terminus by J R Scott and J W Jacomb Hood, 1900–22, whose construction necessitated the razing of the old Necropolis Station and two brothels. Scenes from Waterloo; the timetable boards, right, and the milk bar, below. Opposite, *LMS – Best Way* poster, 1925 by A M Cassandre.

exceptionally high standard. The other elements in the complex were built by Philip Charles Hardwick, using the same contractors his father had used: William Cubitt and Company. Yet while the hall alone had cost £150,000, and the arch £35,000, the rest of the station cost a mere £122,562 to build, a discrepancy which explains the mean, uninspiring banality of the design. Samuel Sidney's criticisms of Euston of 1851 – that the 'vast hall with magnificent roof and scagliola [sic] pillars appears to have swallowed up all the money, and all the light of the establishment' – appear to have been well founded. Lewis Cubitt, the younger brother of the Hardwicks' contractor and the designer of King's Cross Station, agreed, telling the Great Northern directors that 'a good station could be built at King's Cross for less than the cost of the ornamental archway at Euston'. While Cubitt was undoubtedly exaggerating, the cost of the L&B's grand gesture was undeniable. Nevertheless, for their money the railway's directors had bought a superb piece of urban theatre, one which could have lasted for centuries.

Euston, as the capital's oldest and in many ways grandest railway terminal, and as the gateway to the Empire's powerhouses – Birmingham, Manchester, Liverpool and Glasgow – was always central to the life of the nation. On 29 May 1856 the whole station was illuminated to celebrate the end of the Crimean War. Four years later, when the fear of invasion from Napoleon III's France was at its height, the St Pancras Volunteers were allowed to drill in the station crypt, provided they did not alarm the passengers. During the Great War, the station played a crucial role in receiving troops from Scotland, Wales and the Midlands as they passed on their way to the Western Front.

Outside the great hall, however, the service areas and circulating spaces gradually became increasingly cramped as the traffic to and from the terminus expanded. As early as 1898 the LNWR was proposing to build an entirely new station; however, the second Boer War intervened, and the Hardwicks' complex remained. A new booking concourse was added to the south of the great hall, in the old cab yard, in 1913–14. The great hall itself was somewhat disfigured by a 1927 refurbishment by Edwin Lutyens, when it was repainted and the old gas globes were finally replaced with electric fittings. The magnificent interior suffered a further indignity in 1933, when a new ticket office was erected, couched in what John Betjeman dryly termed 'a restrained jazz-modern style'.[6]

The momentous year of 1933 also saw Sir Josiah Stamp, Chairman of the London, Midland and Scottish Railway (into which the LNWR had been absorbed as part of the 1923 grouping), use the

opportunity of the RIBA's annual dinner to float the proposal for the demolition of both Euston and St Pancras. Sir Josiah was a trained economist, raised to the peerage in 1938 by his friend Neville Chamberlain, who designated Stamp Chancellor of the Exchequer shortly before his government's ignominious fall in 1940. To Stamp the expensive leviathans of the Euston Road were merely 'useless' and 'obsolete'. It was thus no surprise when in 1935 he announced that no less an architectural authority than the RIBA's President, Percy Thomas, would direct the design and erection of a single, new station to replace both Euston and St Pancras. Thomas promptly devised a scheme which included a hotel (although Stamp had in fact just closed the Midland Grand) and, in a bizarrely futuristic

gesture, a rooftop helicopter pad. On 12 July 1938 Stamp threw a switch in Hardwick's 400-seat Shareholders' Meeting Room to begin the quarrying of limestone for the new station.

After the Second World War prospects for Euston looked good; in 1951–3, for example, the great hall was restored to something approaching its appearance in Hardwick's day. Yet there was still a widespread feeling, especially within the higher echelons of the newly nationalized British Railway, that Euston was too old, too cramped, and wholly unsuited to the brave, new postwar Britain. Even the addition at the end of the 1950s of two new main-line and suburban booking offices either side of the main hall, introducing London's first mechanized ticket machines into the

WATERLOO STATIC
1848 A CENTENARY OF UNINTERRUPTED SERVICE DURING PEAC
SOUTHERN RAILWAY

ND WAR 1948

capital's oldest terminus, did not quell the dissenting voices. In 1959 British Railways asked the London County Council (LCC) for statutory permission to demolish both the principal listed buildings on the site: the arch and the great hall. The LCC acceded, adding the lame proviso that the arch be re-erected on an appropriate site. Following some very creative accounting, British Rail or rather, BR's parent, the British Transport Commission (BTC), announced that, while demolition would cost only £12,000, re-erection would cost a massive £190,000, and that BR were not prepared 'to bear this financial burden'. Nor would the government: in July 1961, Ernest Marples, Harold Macmillan's Minister of Transport, declared that the arch, too, was to be swept away.

The public response was furious, as the pusillanimity and philistinism of the government and the BTC served to unite all sections of the architectural world. While John Betjeman and the Earl of Rosse led the conservationists' campaign to save the great hall and the arch, the voice of contemporary architecture, the *Architect's Journal*, argued passionately for the retention of the station and especially the arch:

[The Euston Arch] is the last great classical building in the English sequence with an architectural merit which would make it welcome in almost any setting. Second, it is an important common-place in Victorian London… Third, it is a splendid reminder of our country's leadership in the early Railway Age. WE CANNOT POSSIBLY LET IT BE DESTROYED.[7]

The pioneering Modernist architect Alison Smithson, in a famous published celebration of Hardwick's station, was subsequently to extend this argument to apply to all valuable old buildings. 'Preservation', she argued, 'is a positive way… to bring about good new buildings by retaining a standard for comparison.'[8]

The main booking hall at Waterloo, as illustrated in this 1948 poster printed to mark the centenary of the station, left, was completed in 1911; Scott's Victory Arch, above, was not opened until 1922. The latter was conceived as the London and South-Western Railway's war memorial; vast stones bore the names of the principal campaigns – Belgium, Dardanelles, Mesopotamia, the North Sea. Detail of the clock beneath the Victory Arch, below. Actor Jack Hawkins and his wife are greeted as they arrive at Waterloo.

Handbill, 1904, for the Hull and
Barnsley Railway, right.
The fine timber detailing and
tiled walls of Bell's new booking
hall at Hull Station, East
Yorkshire, of 1904, below, neatly
complemented the bold Classical
lines of Andrews' imposing
station.
John Dobson saw great railway
stations as 'a new class of
structures'. His masterpiece was
Newcastle Central, 1847–50,
opposite, one of the most
imposing of all early Victorian
stations. As at York, Newcastle
train shed curved dramatically.
Cast iron columns supported
iron ribs which themselves
carried what was originally a
timber-and-glass roof, later
replaced by a wholly iron-
framed span. In the middle
of the picture can be seen wall
plaques commemorating the
opening of the station by
Victoria and Albert in 1850.

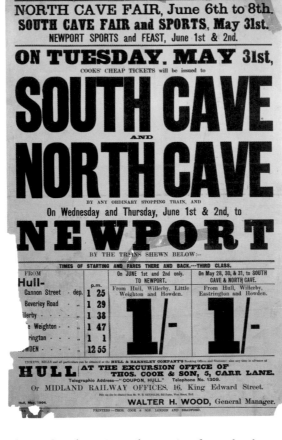

On 24 October 1961 a deputation from the three
leading national amenity societies (the Society for the
Protection of Ancient Buildings, the Georgian Group
and the Victorian Society), the London Society and the
Royal Academy met the Prime Minister. Harold
Macmillan, however, remained adamant that the
BTC's estimated £190,000 was too much to pay for one
of the nation's most cherished and important
monuments. Meanwhile, the Victorian Society
actually found a firm of Canadian contractors who
would move the arch on rollers to a new site for less
than half the BTC's spurious quote. But still the
government remained obdurate, while the slippery and
over-accommodating Chair of the LCC's Planning
Committee, Reginald Stamp, persistently refused to
object to the proposals.

Demolition of the arch began on 6 November 1961.
Little is now left to remember old Euston by. Stansby's
entrance lodge and the bronze of Robert Stephenson
stand guard over the bus station, while Thomas's
Britannia sits unhappily inside the new terminal. In
place of Hardwick's great hall is a long, low box, not
designed by any of the leading practitioners of the
1960s, Hardwick's modern-day equivalents, but by the
BTC's London Midland Region architect R L
Moorcroft. With predictable crassness the 200-foot

long concourse, clad in black granite and white mosaic
facings, was named the 'great hall'. Opened on 14
October 1968, the new Euston has over the years been
repeatedly condemned by conservationists and
architects alike. It is perhaps fitting that Euston Station
is today more famous for its drunks and teenage
runaways than for its architecture.[9]

Even countries that were not officially part of the
Empire, but were economically tied to Britain, were
soon studded with British-built stations in the
Neoclassical idiom, dignified testimonies of the long
arm of the Empire's commercial strength. Buenos
Aires' Retiro Station, for example, was devised as a
Classically phrased statement both of Argentina's
Latin American ambitions and Britain's trading
influence, and was sited, appropriately enough, on the
Plaza Britannica. (In 1982, at the time of the Falklands
War, this was for obvious reasons renamed the Plaza de
la Fuerta Aerea – 'Air Force Plaza'.) At the time of its
opening in 1915, all twelve of Argentina's railway
companies were British-owned. Retiro's design
reflected this economic obeisance: its massive booking
hall, 200 feet by 60 feet, and great hall, 480 feet by 82
feet, were decorated in Royal Doulton faience, straight
from Staffordshire. *The Times*, aware of the British
origin of its design and most of its materials, termed
Retiro the finest railway terminus south of the equator,
and asserted that, 'in point of convenience and
completeness, [it] challenges comparison with any in
the world'.

Euston was not the only great Neoclassical terminus
to perish in Britain after the Second World War. Sir
William Tite's impressive station at Gosport,
Hampshire, of 1841 incorporated a novel, fourteen-
bay Tuscan colonnade of Portland stone, set between
two stuccoed pavilions to the south side of the tracks.
In the 1960s the historian David Lloyd termed Tite's
grand gesture 'one of the finest pieces of exterior
station architecture surviving from the beginning of
the railway age'. However, the station was inexplicably
closed in 1954, leaving Gosport as one of the nation's
largest towns without a railway service. Mysteriously
damaged by fire a year later, the station lost its goods
service in 1966, and by the 1980s the building was a
forlorn wreck. Only emergency work funded by
English Heritage has prevented the remains of this
once-proud structure from disappearing. The bitter
irony is that, at the time of writing, local government is
reconsidering re-establishing a rail link to the town. It
may be too late for what is left of Tite's station.

Other fine stations of the 1840s, specifically
designed to reflect Britain's increasingly imperial self-
confidence and growing wealth, happily survive. By a

The Canadian Pacific Railway. The entrepreneurial energy of William Van Horne forced the Canadian Pacific Railway west, creating small towns on the way to a grand Neoclassical terminus at Vancouver. The railway under construction, above right; the first transcontinental train (named, somewhat ahead of time, *Victoria's Golden Jubilee*) arriving at Vancouver on 24 May 1881, below; and a CPR sleeping car of the 1890s, opposite below. The coast-to-coast service began in June 1903, opposite far right.

strange coincidence, all of them in are the Northeast. Huddersfield, built in 1847 by J P Pritchett (1789–1868) for the Lancashire & Yorkshire and Huddersfield & Manchester railways, is an imposing two-storey block behind a giant, hexastyle Corinthian portico, linked by colonnades to wing pavilions. The station represents Pritchett's finest hour; Gordon Biddle and O S Nock have termed it 'the foremost classical station frontage … in the country after Euston'.[10] Pritchett's original plan was to use the station as the centrepiece for a new, planned piazza, St George's Square; yet his projected Town Hall, designed to complement the architecture of the station, was never built (the disappointing Town Hall of today was built in 1878–81 on a different site), and

the plan never came to fruition. Nevertheless, Huddersfield Station still dominates the town centre, providing an impressive termination to the vista up Northumberland Street. The fabric has lasted well, having been partly tenanted by the local council following a threat by BR to demolish in 1960. The train shed of 1886 also survives in good condition.

The Paragon Station at Hull was opened in 1848. Built for the Hull and Selby Railway, the station, and its adjacent hotel of 1851, were designed by G T Andrews (1805–55), also the author of York's first station. It was Andrews who provided the station with its grand, Doric-arched porte-cochere; the hotel's wings, however, were added by William Bell (1843–1919) in 1904–5 in a more Italianate, Renaissance style. At the same time as Bell's wings were added, the train shed was also rebuilt, incorporating the last large arched roof to be used in a British station. Bell's Art Nouveau kiosks – containing a hairdressing salon, refreshment room (complete with a glass dome), 'temperance room', tearoom and lavatories – largely survive today, as does the marvellous oak-panelled booking hall with its polychrome tiled walls. The booking hall was restored in 1979–80, and now forms the rear of the W H Smith shop which faces onto the concourse. Hull was also the site of the first station milk bar in Britain, added in 1938. Sadly, this does not survive.

The largest of all the great Northeastern Neoclassical stations of the 1840s is Newcastle Central, built in 1845–50 for the York, Newcastle and

Berwick Railway to the designs of John Dobson (1787–1865). Born and bred on the Tyne (he also died in Newcastle), Dobson had begun his career as a talented watercolourist. By the 1820s, however, he was being employed by the speculative builder Richard Grainger to help realize the latter's plans for transforming the city of Newcastle into a showcase for Neoclassical design. Newcastle Central was a key element in this plan. Like Huddersfield, it was intended to be the focus of a new, rationally planned urban scheme; and as at Huddersfield, while the station was indeed constructed, the grand town plan was only partly executed. Nor did the station ever quite achieve the Classical purity envisaged by Dobson. His majestic Corinthian portico was never built; instead, the railway opted for a cheaper, and smaller, Doric porte-cochere, added by Thomas Prosser in 1863.

Nevertheless, what was built remains very impressive. The 600-foot, arcaded entrance front recalls the elemental wings at Sir John Vanbrugh's country house Seaton Delaval, a powerful Baroque pile of the early eighteenth century that lay only a few miles north of Newcastle. And while this imposing principal facade was built in a straight line along the street, there is a surprise inside, where the three-span shed (the central span of which is slightly higher than that of its neighbours) is dramatically curved to fit the swooping tracks. Newcastle was the first large station to be built on such a pronounced curve, and its shed quickly became one of the sights of the city. Its glazed timber roof was supported on iron ribs, each carried by cast

Chemin de Fer du Nord, Vitesse
Luxe Confort poster of 1929 by
A M Cassandre.

iron columns 22 feet high; every third rib rested on cross-girders, and each rib had an open spandrel. Such was the building's fame that railway enthusiast Queen Victoria was prevailed upon to open the station, on 29 August 1850. Stone plaques of Victoria and Albert inserted into the concourse wall are a lasting reminder of the station's importance in the Victorian era.

Dobson's station was of the highest architectural quality. Exactly a century after it opened, architectural historian Christian Barman lauded it as 'the crowning achievement of British railway architecture'.[11] In Dobson's own day, the critic James Fergusson inevitably found some fault with the design. In 1862, Fergusson acknowledged that the station possessed 'some excellent points of design', but he also suggested that the building was 'neither quite truthful nor quite appropriate'[12] although he neglected to mention what he thought *was* appropriate for a modern railway terminus. 'The ornamentation', he continued, 'has too much the character of being put there for ornament's sake alone.' Dobson had an answer to Fergusson's carping comments: his station scheme had already won the Medal of Honour at the Paris Exhibition of 1855.

Newcastle Central was originally devised as two separate stations, one for the Newcastle and Berwick and one for the Newcastle and Carlisle Railways. In 1862, shortly before Prosser's cut-price porch was built, the two were merged into the North Eastern Railway (NER), the headquarters of which were further south at York. In spite of York's administrative dominance, however, Newcastle remained the busier station – so much so that in 1890 the NER's William Bell had to add a series of new platforms. By 1924 the station boasted 730 staff – as many as most of the London rail termini, and more than such major stations as Dresden Hauptbahnhof and Milan Central.

In the frosty light of the Beeching era, however, neither Newcastle's bustling traffic nor its outstanding Classical architecture were considered of sufficient importance to merit the retention of the station's historic fabric and unique plan. In 1970 British Railways announced plans to develop the whole site, involving the demolition of all of the station except for Prosser's porte-cochere (which of course had not been part of Dobson's original scheme). In 1972 BR went further, and proposed razing the Victorian building. Thankfully, pressure from both the City Council and the Victorian Society averted this dismal fate. Today Newcastle Central's architecture is as highly regarded as that of its contemporaries further south.

To the north of the American continent was an even more glaring expression of British economic colonialism expressed as a railway terminus. On

23 May 1887 the first transcontinental train arrived at a wooden depot west of Granville Street in Vancouver, British Columbia, to the strains of the local fire brigade band. The way to Vancouver had been fraught with difficulties, both natural and political. The province of British Columbia had only joined Canada in 1871, upon which agents of the United States' Northern Pacific Railroad had tried to arrange a secret deal with the Canadian authorities which would favour their own American route to Canada's western shore. The public revelation of this arrangement, however, prompted the fall of Conservative Prime Minister Sir John Macdonald's government in 1872; six years later Alexander Mackenzie's Liberal administration took matters in hand and resolved that the western terminus of the trans-Canada route, promoted by the Canadian Pacific Railway (CPR), would be at the mouth of the Fraser River.

The architect of the new railway and the inspiration behind its westernmost terminus was the Canadian adventurer-industrialist William van Horne, the General Manager of the CPR, dubbed 'the ablest railroad general in the world' by one American railway entrepreneur. Van Horne was not only interested in

In Paris the imposing centrepiece of Hittorf's Gare du Nord facade fused the giant arched window – a representation of the train shed behind, and an architectural symbol which clearly denoted the station's function – with the giant order (in this case, of Ionic pilasters) and the sculptural figures of a triumphal gateway that even Meeks acknowledged made 'a powerful and often admired spectacle'.

Jacques-Ignace Hittorf's Gare du Nord terminus, 1857–66, opposite, above, was disposed as a cathedral, with one broad nave and two side aisles. While the supports for the roof, right, were cast iron, the roof trusses themselves were originally of wood (oak and pine) and glass. Today the station also functions as the Paris terminus for the Eurostar services which run through the Channel Tunnel to London.

railways: he had one of the world's finest collections of Japanese porcelain, as well as a fine array of French Impressionist paintings. Today he is principally remembered as the driving force behind the CPR, and the effective creator of the bustling city of Vancouver. He even renamed the settlement, after the British sea captain who had claimed the area for Britain in 1792, but who had actually stayed only one day: George Vancouver. Even the Chinese labourers Van Horne imported to build the CPR were persuaded to stay in the new, railway-inspired city; today their descendants still form the basis of Vancouver's thriving Chinese community.

The original modest, wooden terminus at Vancouver was (like Bombay Victoria on the other side of the world) opened in the year of Victoria's Golden Jubilee, 1887. This precarious structure was not replaced until 1912, when work began on a more substantial terminus which more properly fulfilled the role of the western gateway to the British Empire. The heavy, Ionic colonnade of the main, Cordova Street elevation, designed by Barott, Blackader and Webster, gave the station and the city an impressive Neoclassical portal. Inside, the booking hall was decorated with painted landscapes of the territory which Van Horne's CPR had encompassed to the east.

The new station was a fitting testimony not only to the westward march of Britain's world Empire but also to the imperial ambitions of the CPR. The Canadian Pacific did much to forge the shape, location and character of the new cities of the Canadian West, fostering over 800 new towns and cities in the westward drive to the Pacific. Its Vancouver terminal was as much a tribute to its own achievement in creating a new nation as a Pacific gateway to Britain's dominions. While the provincial seat of government was sited further west, at Victoria on Vancouver Island, Vancouver remained at heart a CPR town.

Today, alas, what remains of the CPR's passenger services has been absorbed into the national rail network, while CPR's solemn Vancouver terminus itself is empty of trains and passengers. Rail services to the 1912 building ended in the early 1970s, following which the main station building was in 1976–8 converted to mixed office and retail use, in a reasonably sympathetic manner, by Hawthorn Mansfield Towers. The pathetically few trains which do still manage to terminate at the former Empire's Pacific gate (only one passenger train a day now arrives at Vancouver) pull into the former Canadian Northern station, sited some way to the east of downtown Vancouver. This terminal – also couched in a rather dramatic, if in this case somewhat clumsy, Neoclassical style – was built to the design of Pratt and Ross in 1917–19. It was intended to be the Canadian Northern's rejoinder to the mighty CPR; yet shortly after it was completed, the British-financed Grand Trunk railway system of which it was part collapsed, and the network was incorporated into the new, nationalized Canadian National system. Today even this terminus, like the railway that serves it, is merely a shadow of its former self. Part-converted to a bus station in 1993, and currently sited in an undeveloped wasteland of demolition and decay, Vancouver's last railway terminal bears evocative witness to the fall of the Empire, and to the seemingly inexorable decline of North America's once-proud railroad systems.

In Europe, another of the world's most important Classical stations also managed to survive until its architectural qualities were better appreciated. In 1958 the celebrated Gare du Nord, formerly the Chemins de Fer du Nord's Paris flagship, was in an advanced state of decay, and was earmarked for demolition. Yet while Paris's fine Montparnasse terminal did indeed succumb to the bulldozers (demolished in 1965 to make way for a characterless, curtain-walled slab of 1969), the Gare du Nord stayed, its only concession to the mediocre Modernism of the ever-hungry developers being the addition of a hideous multi-storey car park to the eastern end of the principal elevation.

The first Nord station was built by the architect and engineer F C Reynaud in 1847. By the 1860s, though, Reynaud's terminus was patently unable to cope with the 7.1 million passengers who used the station each year. The architect chosen to rebuild the station was a great Classical architect coming to the end of an

illustrious career: Jacques-Ignace Hittorf (1792–1867) was born in Cologne, but moved to Paris in 1810 (a move facilitated by the Napoleonic hegemony over Western Europe). In Paris he became a pupil of the highly influential architect and interior designer Charles Percier, after which he joined the office of François-Joseph Bélanger, with whom he worked on the revolutionary, iron-framed Halle aux Blés. During the uninspiring rule of the obese Bourbon Louis XVIII, Hittorf was appointed 'architect of the King's entertainments' – a post not as frivolous as the title might suggest – and during the 1820s he visited Italy, Britain (where he became a close friend of the young Charles Barry) and Berlin, where he met Karl Friedrich Schinkel, an architect who would have been ideally suited to the Railway Age had he not died in 1842. Hittorf's subsequent Sicilian travels resulted in two important studies of the island's rich Graeco-Roman and Renaissance heritage, and kindled a passionate, lifelong devotion to the Greek Revival.

After the July Revolution of 1830 Hittorf, the consummate survivor, was commissioned by Louis Philippe to plan what became the Place de la Concorde and the Champs Elysées. Having served the First Empire, the restored Bourbons and the House of Orléans, during the 1850s he became close to the self-proclaimed Napoleon III. However, while he cultivated the friendship of the Emperor, he managed to alienate the ambitious and influential Paris Prefect Baron Haussmann, causing what had been an extremely lucrative practice to atrophy.

Hittorf's new station was designed not just to improve the operation of the railway, but also to rejuvenate the area by creating a dramatic Neoclassical portal as its focus. In 1854 the local populace had sent a petition to the Prefect of the Seine, detailing the appalling state of the station's environs and demanding the quarter's reconstruction:

Posters celebrate the railways in emphatic style. Above, in a cartoon of 1860, a buffered character announces the way forward (in German) – to the railway station. Below, a poster of 1935 by Jupp Wiertz marks a centenary of rail travel exhibition in Nuremberg, showing the advancements made through time.

100 JAHRE
DEUTSCHE EISENBAHNEN
AUSSTELLUNG NÜRNBERG 1935
14. JULI · ANFANG SEPTEMBER

The surroundings of the Nord terminus represent an eyesore: they leave much to be desired in the matter of easy traffic … There is no direct wide street opening from the front of the station. The side road, parallel to the Lariboisière hospital, is a frightful dead-end, a permanent tip for unspeakable refuse, well-deserving of police attention … Even the station waiting-rooms are stifling black holes for travellers.[13]

'The works of reconstruction', the petition concluded, 'can no longer be put off.' Embarrassed by the public outcry, and encouraged by Napoleon III, the Prefecture authorised the rebuilding of a far larger station in 1857. That Hittorf himself was not approached to design the building until January 1861, shortly before work began on the site, indicates that the railway had already devised the scope, if not the details, of the project. Nevertheless, the overture to one of the country's leading architects was a public affirmation of the scheme's importance to the city's development. It may indeed have influenced the Midland Railway's decision to approach George Gilbert Scott, an architect of similar stature to Hittorf, a few years later.

The Nord railway was well aware of the commercial and promotional benefits to be gained by building an imposing Neoclassical gateway into the city, one that at the same time overshadowed the nearby Est terminus. In 1860 the railway's Council resolved that the 'imposing effect [of] an isolated building will be preferable', although they were concerned that a monumental facade might alienate 'a large section of the public which believes that convenience and economy are the two major factors in any architecture'. In the event, to ensure that the principal elevations remained simple in composition and relatively uncluttered by ancillary buildings, the railway's administrators were housed in new offices on the other side of the station's forecourt. Today this building is home to the regional headquarters of SNCF.

Hittorf's responsibilities were defined in a manner which the Midland would have done well to emulate at St Pancras. Although he was the principal architect of both the head building and its shed, the railway retained control over the day-to-day running of the construction site and, most importantly, over the project's budget. Hittorf – increasingly helped by his son Charles – was initially required only to design the front and side facades; it was only when they were completed that the Hittorfs were allowed to turn their attention to the form and decoration of the train shed.

Hittorf's principal facade was an impressive and powerful gateway, whose simple geometry instantly communicated the building's nature while advertising the wealth and success of Napoleon III's imperial capital. The centrepiece comprised a central, 100-foot high arch flanked by two, lower arches. Arcaded wings

led to two pedimented pavilions, each dominated by a giant lunette window which immediately recalled the great structures of Imperial Rome. Unlike that of St Pancras, begun two years after this station was completed, the Gare du Nord's facade was liberally sprinkled with prominent sculptures. Over the central arch was placed a statue representing Paris, by Pierre-Jean Cavelier; to the right and left were allegorical female representations of twenty-two cities and towns reached by the Nord network, executed by thirteen of the country's leading sculptors. Some of the destinations (Arras, Amiens, Rouen) were familiar and close; others (London, Berlin and Amsterdam) were more far-flung. Hittorf even managed to include his birthplace, Cologne, in this litany of travel.

Above the destinations, placed high up on the

Anhalter Bahnhof, Berlin, by Franz Schwechten, 1872–80. Anhalter's simple composition, above, with three-arched entrances to both the porte-cochere on the street elevation (for passengers) and the rear of the train shed (for trains) and the same pattern of round-arched lights in the fanlights at either end of the shed, was eminently logical and comprehensible. Boarding a train at Anhalter in 1937, left, supervised by the inevitable uniformed official.

In contrast to many of the great German stations of the early twentieth century, where provision was made for future passage of large bodies of troops, the concourse of Schwechten's Berlin Anhalter, left, did not leave much room for manœuvre. Anhalter after 1945, above, when Allied bombing had left it as a gaunt shell. Demolition of the shell in 1961, right; as the Berlin Wall was going up, one of Imperial Germany's finest stations was coming down.

The wide station platforms
beneath the soaring arches of the
roof at Frankfurt am Main's
Hauptbahnhof, pictured below
in 1959, allowed for easy access
for both travellers and their
luggage – seen piled high on the
concourse, on a British inter-war
travel brochure, above right, and
on the station platform, right.

entablatures which flanked the central lunettes, were statues of the ancient gods – an appropriate adornment to a station which deliberately recalled the glories of ancient Rome in order to suggest a parallel with Napoleon III's ever-ambitious Second Empire. More down to earth were the statues, sited at the western (departure) side of the building, of the fathers of steam traction: Papin for France and James Watt for Britain. Watt's statue was to adorn the facades of many great international termini, from Budapest to Buenos Aires. Ironically, however, none of the great British stations ever so honoured the British inventor.

Half-way through construction, Hittorf's arch-enemy, Baron Haussmann, intervened in the project in an astonishingly high-handed manner, insisting that the whole complex be moved back to create a larger open space in front. Thankfully, this proposal – which would have involved (as it was probably meant to) the demolition of most of Hittorf's new station – was successfully resisted by the railway, who opened the station to services in 1864. Final work was finished in 1866. A year later Hittorf was dead; he was thus saved the potentially career-ending embarrassment of conquering troops from Berlin, and his home town of Cologne, parading in triumph past this soi-disant symbol of French imperial might in 1870.

On the station's completion, the *Magasin Pittoresque* was moved to acclaim the Gare du Nord as 'a veritable temple to steam'.[14] Not all contemporary critics, however, were so generous. The *Encyclopédie d'Architecture* of 1863 completely missed the point of a bombastic terminus such as the Nord station:

What strikes us immediately about this building is the lack of any relationship between its exterior and interior… If we examine the interior, we see clearly that the purpose was to satisfy bare necessities … As for the design of the facade, it would seem to have had an entirely different rationale; necessity has had little influence on it; neither the nature of the materials nor their function have governed the thickness of the walls; it is not the discipline of necessity which dictated the forms … [but] wild imaginativeness.[15]

The *Encyclopédie*'s was not the only commentary to damn the design. In 1897 the great Renaissance historian Jacob Burckhardt, in an outburst of surprising vehemence, labelled the station 'one of the most frightful architectural infamies of our century'.[16] By 1924, however, Georges Gromort was prepared to praise it as a 'powerful, bold work':

… the Gare du Nord is not only the least outmoded of all the great buildings of its kind, but it is also the one which in its structure, its mass, its general appearance is most nearly related, in spite of its Graeco-Roman aspects, to what would be tomorrow's architecture.[17]

As recently as 1986 the architectural writer Thomas van Joest found Hittorf's design to be without fault, the 'logical rigour' of the main facade 'perfectly expressing the plan of the building'.[18] Today the Gare du Nord remains a powerful statement of civic pride, and a lasting reminder of the soaring ambitions and precipitous fall of the Second Empire.

Having crushed Napoleon III's France with astonishing ease in 1870, the new German Empire set about not only linking the disparate elements of the new nation with new rail links, but also creating vast new termini that would properly reflect the pride and strength of Europe's great military colossus. The only possible style for these behemoths was a giant-order Neoclassicism. And in their scale, itself a statement of Germany's political ambitions, the new German stations were explicitly designed to eclipse the great termini of France and Britain.

Large railway stations both demonstrated

The three, massive glazed sheds at Frankfurt-am-Main's Hauptbahnhof of 1879–88, pictured here in 1905, were intended not simply to cover the eighteen incoming tracks but to symbolize the three regional identities of the railway companies brought together in this capacious new terminus. The vast concourse and head-building by Georg P Eggert in turn represented the new German Empire that had brought them all together.

Germany's new-found unity and the country's position at the forefront of the industrial world. They were also cogent symbols of the power and efficiency of the Empire's military machine, which increasingly depended on the operation of the railways and, in particular, on the great stations, which were devised to act as embarkation points for troops and materials. The logical result of this railway-led military expansion were the events of 1 August 1914, when a horrified Kaiser Wilhelm II was told by General von Moltke that the precise timetabling of the military railway network meant that Germany's mobilization could not be halted: 'Those [railway] arrangements took a whole year of intricate labour to complete ... and once settled, cannot be altered.'

The first, and perhaps the greatest, of these new imperial monuments was Berlin's Anhalter terminus. Begun in 1872 – only two years after the empire was declared by Chancellor Bismarck – it was built to the designs of Franz Schwechten (1841–1924). Its sumptuous, sophisticated Neoclassicism recalled Schinkel's dramatic Neoclassical legacy in Berlin, continuing to stress, as Schinkel had done in pre-Imperial Prussia, the country's affinity with the great empires of the ancient world. It was also a thoroughly rational station, with no inessential decoration and no doubling of facilities. The result was, in Carroll Meeks's opinion, 'the finest head station since the Gare de l'Est'.[19]

Anhalter's main facade featured the standard, centrally-placed glazed arch; what was different about Schwechten's design was that this vast arch was

punctuated with tall, vertical openings. Inside, the booking hall's glazed roof led directly to the glazed, single-span train shed, whose rear was provided with a three-arched train exit which directly quoted the three-arch porte-cochère on the front elevation. All was logical and symmetrical in a tidy and inescapably Teutonic way.

Berlin Anhalter was gutted by bombing in 1944–5. The walls, though, remained standing throughout the 1950s, at the end of which a proposal was floated to convert the site into that most appropriate of uses, a museum of transport. Given the attitudes of the time, it is not surprising that this inventive proposal was turned down, and the ruins of one of Europe's most important stations were demolished in 1961–2.

Almost contemporary with Anhalter was the even larger terminus at Frankfurt-am-Main, built by Georg P Eggert (1844–1914) between 1879 and 1888. Frankfurt's basic form epitomized the success of the new German Empire in fusing distinctive national and regional identities. Its triple shed, covering eighteen tracks, corresponded to the three regions the lines served; as the regions had in 1870 been brought together in one new state, so the separate lines were now gathered into one great terminal. The train shed needed to accommodate all this traffic was inevitably vast: an astounding 610 feet long and 549 feet wide in total, it was divided into three equal spans, each 183 feet wide and 93 feet high, and almost entirely glazed.

Outside, the main facade was dignified by a vast lunette window flanked by two turrets, a composition which immediately signalled the building's function. Visitors entered through a massive domed booking hall, which fed into the concourse or into the waiting rooms and restaurants. The concourse was built on a heroic scale, in order to allow for easy passage of crowds and large numbers of troops. Direct access from the platforms to the street also facilitated troop movement as well as the exit of incoming passengers.

Frankfurt escaped total destruction in the Second World War, and was restored in 1958. Not all the great imperial stations of Germany, however, were as lucky. The Romanesque station Georg Frentzen (1854–99) built at Cologne in 1892–4 was so severely damaged by bombing that it was completely rebuilt in a vapid Modernist style in the 1950s. (Frentzen had lost the competition at Frankfurt to Eggert, who was nevertheless instructed to incorporate elements of Frentzen's design; Frentzen, meanwhile, went on to build the massive Beaux-Arts terminus at Bucharest of 1893–7.) Ernst Giese and Paul Weidner's domed pile at Dresden of 1892–8 succumbed to the terrible bombing and subsequent firestorm of 13–14 February 1945,

while the immense complex by Heinrich Reinhardt and Georg Sössengarth of 1903–6 at Hamburg was wrecked, along with much of the rest of the city, and rebuilt after the war in an appropriately modern style.

One German railway terminus which does still survive provides a curious epilogue to the story of the country's imperial ambitions. The new empire sought not only to consolidate its German territory, but to obtain some colonies to emulate, and if possible surpass, its European rivals. Before the scramble for Africa was finished, Germany had, by Bismarck's swift action in 1884, carved itself a large, if somewhat useless, slice of territory on Africa's West Coast. A railway line was planned from the colony's capital, Windhoek, to the British coastal enclave of Walvis Bay, via the German port of Swakopmund. The impetus for

the line, originally devised to serve only 2,000 German colonists, was the need to crush an uprising of the Herero tribe. However, by the time work was started on the railway in 1897, the outbreak of a bovine flu epidemic ('rinderpest') had brought the Herero nation to its knees. Thomas Pakenham has vividly described the tribe's plight:

Their herds withered like grass. Once the cattle had numbered 250,000 head of stock. Now the Herero villages were almost empty. In desperation, individual Herero began to sell their land to German settlers to pay for vaccination, to buy new cattle, or simply to buy food and save their families from starvation. When the first census was taken a few years later, a few hundred German settlers owned 40,000 head of cattle, about the same number as belonged to the whole Herero people.[20]

The line to Windhoek provided German Southwest Africa with essential transport links into the interior with many small stations along the way. The principal reason for its construction was not commercial but military: troops were regularly ferried to and from the astonishing Rhenish-Classical hybrid station at Swakopmund, 1904, above, and indeed ran the system, below. The Cape-Cairo Route in a poster of 1930, opposite.

The German railway was still needed, though, since rinderpest had wiped out the region's usual form of overland transport, the ox wagon. It was largely due to the construction of the railway that the number of Europeans in Southwest Africa grew from 2,000 in 1896 to 4,700 in 1903. In 1904 the line was completed, and a fine new Neoclassical terminal, its facade suitably severe and forbidding, was built at Windhoek. Both terminus and railway soon proved their military worth: they were vital in crushing a renewed Herero revolt. General Lothar von Trotha found the line invaluable, using it to transport his army of 10,000 from Swakopmund to the Herero land that lay between him and the capital during the summer of 1904. The importance of the railway, and of the railway station, to imperial conquest had been decisively demonstrated. The Herero, of course, paid the human price for this German success.[21]

The ease of Trotha's victory, however, was illusory. Shortly after the outbreak of hostilities in 1914, Walvis Bay was briefly occupied by the Germans. Yet the latter were in turn ejected both from the British enclave and from their new colony, complete with its brand-new railway and shiny new terminal, by General Botha's South Africans.

Germany was not the only central European power

keen to display its imperial might by means of ever-grander railway stations. Following their dismal performance and ignominious defeat in the Austro-Prussian War of 1866 (resulting in the loss of Austria's last toehold in northern Italy and her expulsion from the German Confederation), the Austrians turned in frustration towards the east. In 1867, by the terms of the new 'Dual Monarchy', the Austrian Emperor, in his capacity as King of Hungary, raised the neighbouring Hungarians to be the Viennese court's imperial partner in its self-appointed mission to tame the Balkans. While the Empire's Czech, Polish and Croat subjects were outraged, Hungary was naturally delighted, and set about transforming its ancient capital, Budapest.

As part of this reconstruction, both of the main railway termini in Budapest were rebuilt to reflect Hungary's new status. Budapest West (Nyugati) was built by Alfons de Serres, from Gustav Eiffel's French practice, in 1873–7. On its principal facade, an eccentric, glazed pediment connected two massive and ungainly turreted pavilions – not a composition that Hardwick, Hittorf or Schwechten would have dared use. The exuberance of its main elevation, however, belied an oddly plain concourse and train shed, and distinctly dull railway offices. (Carroll Meeks dryly commented of the station: 'We may presume from the richness of the building with which [De Serres] surrounded the simple shed that he was following the law of contrast.')[22] All was paper-thin imperial bombast, wrapped up in a rather exotic and ill-assembled departure from Classical orthodoxy. In many ways, the image of the imperial rhetoric of Nyugati's facade, masking what was in reality an empty shell, was an unwitting metaphor for the Austro-Hungarian Empire itself, as proved by its dismal performance after 1914. By 1918 the Dual Monarchy had collapsed, and the empire with it; all it left as its memorial were bizarre monuments such as Budapest West.

Budapest West's epilogue was provided thirty-six years later, when De Serres' bizarre confection became a symbol of a very different kind. Hundreds of refugees filled the station in 1956, attempting to flee the country for Austria as the Russians advanced into the city. Fittingly for such a theatrical gateway, the station found itself at the epicentre of great real-life drama. As in 1918, however, the ending was far from happy.

Even more bombastic and florid than its pompous neighbour was Budapest's Eastern (Keleti) station, built to the design of Julius Rochlitz (1827–86) in 1881–84. (The station was not actually in the east of the city; its designation derives from the fact that it served the eastern part of the country.) At the East

THE CAPE·TO·CAIRO ROUTE.
Special Supplement to The Illustrated London News.
(This Supplement has been compiled by LEO WEINTHAL, C.B.E., F.R.G.S., Chief Editor of "The African World.")

SOUTH AFRICAN RAILWAYS

In co-operation with the principal Shipping Companies, Tourist Agencies, etc., the South African Government Railways undertake all travel

Station the composition of the facade was more coherent than De Serres', and, in contrast to the latter's French fancies, was more obviously Teutonic in inspiration. The main elevation was dominated by a massive triumphal arch, of the type already closely identified with the vast new termini of Bismarck's Germany, placed between long, low wings. Rochlitz's design was in fact directly borrowed from a German precedent, Lapierre's Berlin Lehrter terminal of 1869–71, which itself was derived from Jean-Marie Viel's entrance to the Paris Exhibition of 1855. However, Rochlitz's detailing was far more luxuriant than had been the case with Viel's or Lapierre's solemn buildings. The passenger entered not simply under the central, elliptical glazed arch, but passed through a

Right, Alfons de Serres's bizarre solution to the problem of equating the relationship between head building and train shed at Budapest Nyugati of 1873–7: a glazed shed sandwiched between two pompous pavilions. Volgograd Station, Russia by Khourovskin and Briskin in 1953, below, is an eccentric wedding-cake of a building, whose monolithic centrepiece seems strangely out-of-scale with the rest of the station.

terminus had become thoroughly debased. Classical forms were employed as a lazy shorthand for status and success, and deployed in a vague and clumsy manner which would have appalled architects such as Hardwick or Hittorf, trained in the heyday of the Greek revival and deeply inculcated with the seriousness and sacredness of their purpose. Volgograd represents the twilight of the style, a building in which formerly evocative elements are reduced to an almost comic assembly of tired motifs and empty symbolism. Designed by Khourovskin and Briskin, the station's fatuous, gestural architecture encapsulates the overtly imperial, yet fundamentally backward-looking, Soviet Russia of Stalin's last years. A stripped-Classical triumphal arch (in the midst of which was placed the inevitable sculptural representation of the nation's triumph) was surmounted in turn by a square lantern, a pedestal, a spire and the Soviet star. The result was a ludicrously inflated composition, not improved by the dull, Classical banality of the long, low flanking wings. Inside, however, the architects were permitted greater licence; the result was a stunning, almost Beaux-Arts series of high rooms with marble floors, massive, arched doorways, theatrically exaggerated cornices, elaborate Neoclassical plasterwork and splendid painted ceilings. It is difficult to believe, though, that this Hollywood-style set dates from the mid-1950s.

Imperial Neoclassicism had clearly reached the end of the road. Stalin's death, just as work was beginning on Volgograd Station, ensured that no further attempts were made to revive this most evocative, if most misused, of railway styles. When, seven years later after Volgograd was begun, the Soviet authorities finally decided to rebuild the celebrated but severely war-damaged Finlandski terminus in Leningrad, they chose not the bombastic Neoclassicism of Stalinist Russia but an anonymous, bland International Modernism more in keeping with the times.

hexastyle portico – a juxtaposition of Neoclassical imagery which made for a very overcrowded elevation. Unfortunately, the entrance facade was simply tacked directly on to the arched gable of the train shed, which could be easily seen through the glazing at the front. Once again, subtlety and depth had been sacrificed for outward show.

Fifty years after the completion of Budapest East, the solemn bombast of Schwechten, Eggert and even Julius Rochlitz was becoming increasingly out of date in most countries of the world. The imperial resonance of oversized Classical motifs and heavy-handed antique symbolism was still welcomed, however, by the more retrogressive totalitarian regimes of Europe and South America. By the time that Volgograd (formerly Stalingrad) Station was built in 1953, the concept of imperial Neoclassicism as applied to the railway

The imposing Neoclassical gateway to Brussels' premier terminus, Midi, was devised by Auguste Payen, the first architect to be engaged by Belgian Railways in 1841, opposite below and right. This Classical confection of 1869 was wholly demolished to make way for the grim, functional terminus necessitated by the disastrous interwar plan to link the Midi and Nord stations, a goal which was achieved only by clearing a path through the historic city centre.

THE ECLECTICISM OF STATION STYLE
NEW CENTURY EXOTIC

'These were the high-class European courtesans among stations, glittering, sensual, elegant, veritable Mata Haris and Lola Monteses among terminals, the architectural equivalents of Zola's Nana, Manet's Olympe, and Dumas fils's Camille, complete with fans, pendants, and feather boas rendered in stone. They were also regularly penetrated day and night by a variety of trains of different lengths and sizes.'[1]
JEFFREY RICHARDS AND JOHN M MACKENZIE, 1986.

By 1900 the accepted architectural vocabulary of the typical railway terminus was increasingly adapted to fit the architect's more personal vision or to reflect the railway company's self-confidence. This tendency to singularity and originality in the design of even the largest stations reached its zenith in the heady, over-confident years immediately before the Great War. The Edwardian era saw the erection of not only the first Beaux-Arts leviathans (detailed in Chapter 5) but also of some of the most unusual, individual and bizarre railway termini. The fundamental currency of station architecture – in particular the great glazed arch signalling the station's main entrance and mirroring the train shed behind – was still widely employed. Yet this basic language was now being interpreted in a more offhand manner, unfettered by traditional Gothic or Classical doctrines and increasingly remote from the more sedate and orthodox approaches of the mid-nineteenth century. By the beginning of the twentieth century the railways were widely recognized as constituting the lifeblood of industrialized society; the networks were growing, trains were getting faster, a second Railway Age seemed about to dawn. In eschewing the straitjacket of accepted architectural style, the great railway stations of this productive era helped to emphasize the railway companies' quest for modernity, energy and individualism.

Many of the excesses of the Edwardian period were anticipated in the 1890s. St Louis Union of 1891–4, by Theodore C Link (1850–1923) and Edward D Cameron, was Gothic gone mad: a fantasy village complete with 200-foot high Alpine clock tower – equipped with an asymmetrical bartizan, a pyramidal roof and battlements – and a grossly inflated pastiche of the Abbot's Kitchen at Glastonbury Abbey. Link, a local man, had won the 1890 competition for the new

At St Louis Union's Great Hall, Theodore C Link achieved a sumptuous, rich decorative effect rarely to be seen in great American stations of the early twentieth century. Note how the motif of the torch-bearing goddess, opposite, prominent in the frescoes above, is also employed for the gallery's lamp standards. *The Route to California*, Truckee River, Sierra Nevada, 1871 (lithograph), left, depicts the Central Pacific railway coming west through the mountains to the California Coast.

COAST TO COAST IN 48 HOURS

(Daily Through service effective from New York July 7—from Port Columbus July 8, 1929)

The schedule and meal arrangements for the through route between New York, N. Y. and Los Angeles, Cal., and San Francisco, Cal., are given below. Passengers will be ticketed from Pittsburgh, Cleveland or any station on the Pennsylvania Railroad on convenient connecting train service to and from Columbus. Tickets will be also sold from all stations for any combination of rail and air service included in the through route.

WESTBOUND

Pennsylvania Railroad
THE AIRWAY LIMITED
Eastern Time
Lv. New York (Penna. Sta.),
 N. Y. *............ 6.05 PM
Lv. North Philadelphia, Pa. 7.50 PM
Lv. Washington, D. C.... 6.30 PM
Lv. Baltimore, Md...... 7.30 PM
Ar. Port Columbus, O.†... 7.55 AM

Transcont'l Air Transp. Inc.
Lv. Port Columbus, O.... 8.15 AM
 Central Time
Ar. Indianapolis, Ind..... 9.13 AM
Lv. Indianapolis, Ind..... 9.28 AM
Ar. St. Louis, Mo....... 12.03 PM
Lv. St. Louis, Mo. ‡.... 12.18 PM
Ar. Kansas City, Mo..... 2.47 PM
Lv. Kansas City, Mo..... 3.02 PM
Ar. Wichita, Kansas.... 4.56 PM
Lv. Wichita, Kansas..... 5.11 PM
Ar. Airport, Okla. (Landing
 Field)§............ 6.24 PM
Transfer to Waynoka by Aero Car

Atch., Topeka & Santa Fe Ry.
*Sleeping car ready for occupancy
at 8.00 P.M*
 Central Time
Lv. Waynoka, Okla....... 11.00 PM
Ar. Clovis, N. M. ‖....... 8.20 AM
Transfer to Portair by Aero Car

Transcont'l Air Transp. Inc.
 Mountain Time
Lv. Portair, N. M. Landing
 Field............. 8.10 AM
Ar. Albuquerque, N. M.... 10.17 AM
Lv. Albuquerque, N. M.... 10.32 AM
Ar. Winslow, Ariz........ 1.12 PM
Lv. Winslow, Ariz. ‡..... 1.27 PM
 Pacific Time
Ar. Kingman, Ariz....... 2.31 PM
Lv. Kingman, Ariz....... 2.46 PM
Ar. Los Angeles, Cal..... 5.52 PM
*(Grand Central Air Terminal, Glendale,
Cal. Passengers will be transferred by
Aero Car to and from the central section
of Los Angeles.)*

EASTBOUND

Transcont'l Air Transp. Inc.
 Pacific Time
Lv. Los Angeles, Cal ..... 8.45 AM
 (Grand Central Air Terminal,
 Glendale)
Ar. Kingman, Ariz....... 11.18 AM
Lv. Kingman, Ariz.‡..... 11.33 AM
 Mountain Time
Ar. Winslow, Ariz........ 2.14 PM
Lv. Winslow, Ariz........ 2.29 PM
Ar. Albuquerque, N. M.**. 4.40 PM
Lv. Albuquerque, N. M.... 5.10 PM
Ar. Portair, N. M. Landing
 Field.............. 6.54 PM
Transfer to Clovis by Aero Car

Atch., Topeka & Santa Fe Ry.
*Sleeping car ready for occupancy
at 9.00 P.M*
 Central Time
Lv. Clovis, N. M......... 11.35 PM
Ar. Waynoka, Okla. ◎.... 8.10 AM
Transfer to Airport by Aero Car

Transcont'l Air Transp. Inc.
 Central Time
Lv. Airport, Okla. Landing
 Field............... 8.55 AM
Ar. Wichita, Kansas..... 9.55 AM
Lv. Wichita, Kansas..... 10.10 AM
Ar. Kansas City, Mo...... 11.43 AM
Lv. Kansas City, Mo.‡.... 11.58 AM
Ar. St. Louis, Mo........ 2.00 PM
Lv. St. Louis, Mo........ 2.15 PM
Ar. Indianapolis, Ind...... 4.22 PM
Lv. Indianapolis, Ind...... 4.37 PM
 Eastern Time
Ar. Port Columbus, O..... 7.13 PM

Pennsylvania Railroad
THE AMERICAN
Lv. Port Columbus, O.*... 7.46 PM
Ar. North Philadelphia, Pa. 8.05 AM
Ar. New York (Penna. Sta.),
 N. Y............... 9.50 AM

Ar. Baltimore, Md....... 9.05 AM
Ar. Washington, D. C..... 10.05 AM

San Francisco passengers upon arrival at Los Angeles will be given the option of using overnight trains either from Los Angeles or Glendale, or they may remain overnight in Los Angeles and proceed by Maddux Airline plane morning service from Glendale Airport to San Francisco. Transfers will be provided by aero car between Glendale and the central section of Los Angeles. Tickets for whichever plan is selected by passenger will be furnished by the Transcontinental Air Transport, Inc.

From San Francisco passengers will be given the option of using overnight trains from San Francisco, arriving Glendale next morning, making direct connection with eastbound airplane, or they may leave San Francisco via Maddux Airline afternoon plane, arriving Grand Central Air Terminal, Glendale and will be transported by Aero car to the central section of Los Angeles. The next morning they will be transported by Aero car to the airport at Glendale.

*Dinner and breakfast on Pennsylvania Railroad Dining Car. †A new station stop (Port Columbus) seven (7) miles east of Columbus, O. ‡Luncheon on plane— Fred Harvey Service. §Transfer to Harvey House, Waynoka, Okla., where dinner will be served. ‖Breakfast at Harvey House, Santa Fe Station—**Dinner at Albuquerque, Airport—Fred Harvey Service. ◎Breakfast at Harvey House

Apply to any Pennsylvania Railroad agent for full information as to fares, checking baggage, other schedules, etc.

PENNSYLVANIA RAILROAD

Market Street station site, and proceeded to build what was in 1894 the largest station in the world. The vast, barrel-vaulted concourse (which Meeks described as 'cavelike') was phrased in the virile Romanesque idiom made popular by fellow-American H H Richardson, and was lightened by large panels of stained glass and ornamental plasterwork in a deliberate homage to the hall at Adler and Sullivan's recent Auditorium Hotel in Chicago. The other public areas were equally splendid, the waiting room ('Grand Hall') being decked out in yellow, green and gold frescoes, and the dining room being lined with Gothic-styled oak panelling. Behind the concourse was George H Pegram's gigantic, five-span train shed, which all contemporary commentators noted was an astonishing 606 feet long. Everything about the building was exaggerated; its very footprint covered an area of over thirteen acres. However, only ten years after it opened, the new Union station had to be enlarged to cope with the extra traffic generated by St Louis' World's Fair of 1904; further remodelling (by local architect H B Deal) was also necessary in 1942–4, to accommodate the vast wartime increase in both passengers and freight.

The excess and extravagance of St Louis Union was mirrored across the Atlantic in the station at Tours –

The glittering frescoes of the Grand Hall of St Louis Union, above left. While the station no longer has rail services, it survives as a giant shopping mall, food court and hotel. The soaring Gothic tower, complete with bartizans and machicolations as well as clock faces, dominates Link's almost Disneyesque conception, photographed in the 1950s, above. George H Pegram's vast if starkly utilitarian trainshed, photographed in 1907, left. Opposite, a Pennsylvania Railroad timetable poster for the coast-to-coast service, 1929.

begun in 1895, a year after St Louis was completed, and opened in 1898. This overblown Art Nouveau confection, with its massive sculptural figures atop the giant columns which separated the two great entrance arches, was designed by French architect Victor Laloux (1850–1937), and was less a rehearsal for his more conventionally Beaux-Arts composition of Paris Orsay of 1898–1900 (see Chapter 5) than an exuberant expression of the importance of the railways, phrased in a deliberately over-the-top parody of seventeenth-century château architecture. Laloux dispensed with the convention of a tall clock tower, so prominently used at St Louis, by placing Tours' external station clock in the centre of the facade; he did, however, include in his facade two massive, arched reflections of the train shed behind, a feature which American stations of the period generally omitted. In the event Laloux's station did, in a sense, come to St Louis: six years after its completion the design was shamelessly plagiarized by E L Masqueray for his Transportation Building at the St Louis Exhibition of 1904.

At the turn of the century railway-station architects were making even more assiduous use of non-conformist styles. In Belgium, Cloquet's Ghent St Pieters of 1900–12 was a riot of Mediterranean influences, motifs that in truth looked a little out of place in temperate Flanders. Ghent's oddly bulbous

clock tower, complex roof line and Moorish detailing were something wholly new in station design; ironically, this almost Middle Eastern confection was constructed at exactly the same time as the Islamic city of Constantinople was being provided with a distinctly Northern European railway terminal at Hyderpasha. Inside, Ghent's entrance hall was lit by clerestories, roofed by a flat, painted ceiling and decorated with murals of Belgian cities. Alas, today this highly individual composition is disfigured by poor signage and by a lack of repair unusual for Belgian Railways.

Down the line from Ghent is Brussels Schaerbeek, the Clapham Junction of the Belgian capital. As St Pieters was being opened, work was progressing on a wholly new guise for this important railway centre. The form it took was not Moorish, as at Ghent, but an equally eccentric, vaguely neo-Renaissance manner. Begun in 1887 to the design of Belgian State Railways' principal architect, Franz Seulen, its polychrome brick walls supported a bizarre roof line incorporating a high-pitched central block with pinnacled roof *à l'imperiale* and two false gables, each provided with a small clock tower. A conventional large glazed arch was included to light the booking hall; unusually, it was placed at right angles to the platforms and the shed, and not on the main elevation.

Schaerbeek's comic-opera facade conceals a darker

history. The new station was only completed in 1913, just in time to be captured by the Germans in 1914 and put to use as one of the foremost supply centres for the nearby Western Front. Having been used to transport troops and other instruments of death in the First World War, during the Second World War Schaerbeek was used by the occupying Nazis as the departure point for trains carrying Jews and so-called 'undesirables' to the concentration camps further east. Few of those who left from Schaerbeek's platforms on these grim journeys ever returned.

Further north lies an even more original product of Edwardian railway architecture: Copenhagen Central. The result of a competition of 1900 won by H E Wenck (1851–1936), it was begun in 1906 and completed in 1911. The tracks and platforms were sited below the station forecourt and main building; the latter, though relatively small for the principal railway terminus of a capital city, was couched in a romantic, castle-like manner of great individuality and humour, which makes it appear bigger than it really is.

Forty years after Copenhagen opened, station architecture's first true historian – writing in the context of the no-nonsense Modern Movement – was unsure what to make of Wenck's unashamed levity. Regretting the loss of J D Herholdt's old Copenhagen Station of 1863–4, Carroll Meeks suggested that the 'old red brick building with its big arches had a dignified monumentality which is lacking in the new one'. Meeks was prepared to acknowledge that Wenck's witches' castle silhouette 'clothes one of the best organised stations of the period, with six possible platforms, seven separate luggage platforms and clear separation of incoming and outgoing passengers'.[2] However, even though Copenhagen incorporated some of the most advanced planning of its time Meeks preferred to spend more time eulogizing progressive termini of a more orthodox nature such as Karlsruhe, where the enterprising use of concrete and rejection of stereotypical railway-station motifs appealed far more to the Modernist 1950s than the pinnacles and turrets of Copenhagen Central.

Some great Edwardian termini were considered so outrageous in terms of their design that they were not even mentioned in Meeks's otherwise admirable history. Perhaps the best known of these is Prague Central by Josef Fanta (1856–1954), a bizarre, Art Nouveau-influenced composition. Built between 1900 and 1909, its central, semicircular glazed arch is surmounted by a stepped gable that looks more Dutch than Czech. The two, immensely tall side towers which flank this feature are today adorned with two glazed bubbles, products of the station modernization of

1980. The unwieldy influence of party dogma can be seen in these unsympathetic additions of the last years of the Communist regime; they try hard to look bravely modern and forward-looking, but today simply look as outdated as the system that built them. Following the Czechs' Velvet Revolution of 1989, however, the building has been allowed to express itself once more, and the railway has been encouraged to celebrate, rather than to excuse or hide, the concourse's glazed dome and effusive sculpture.

Even more eccentric than Prague Station are two of the principal Moscow termini, stations often admired by travellers but, again, unsurprisingly omitted from Meeks's history. Moscow Yaroslavl is the terminus for trains to Archangel and the Arctic north as well as, most famously, for the Trans-Siberian Railway. As if to compensate for the grim conditions in these fabled destinations, its architecture is warm and bright, and far more redolent of Western European Art Nouveau than of native Russian styles. Originally built in 1902–4 by F O Schechtel, its theatrical asymmetry, its Gothic towers and steeply pitched roof are today the only reminder of its Edwardian glory, the interior having been starkly modernized in the 1960s. More complete is Moscow's other great railway terminus of this

The theatrical swagger of the Beaux-Arts school is entirely missing from Franz Seulen's bizarre confection of Brussels' Schaerbeek Station, below. The use of polychromatic brick and prominent gable ends suggests more the architecture of sixteenth-century Flanders than 1887. Seulen also designed similar stations at Turnhout and Vilvorde.

At Yaroslavl Station, Moscow, F O Schechtel fused together a seemingly unrelated assortment of styles and scales. A low, domestically-scaled Renaissance range of eight bays is sandwiched between a dramatically pitched, Second Empire roof and a Neoclassical entrance topped by a Gothic spire. The admirably restrained detailing of the corner quadrant appears to belong to an entirely different design. Below, *Lenin on the train to Petrograd, 1917* by A M Lopukhov, 1957.

period, Kazan. It was begun in 1912 by Alexei Shchusev and was not completed until well after the First World War and the Revolution, in 1926. However, the crudely nationalist historicism of its exterior – and indeed the magnificent, overblown Rococo decoration of its astonishing dining room – were well suited to the cultural conservatism of the new Stalinist era. In essence a neo-medieval composition, the facade incorporated a high tower and spire based on the Syuyumbekin Tower of the Kremlin at Kazan, at the other end of the line. Even Stalin could not argue with such an unambiguously patriotic quotation from the nation's past.

Nationalist expression was not limited to the stations of Russia's capital. At the other end of Europe, Portugal's architects turned to evocations of the great periods of their country's history. At Porto São Bento, of 1913–16, an affectionate pastiche of eighteenth-century style was used, and inside the walls decorated with tiles showing scenes from Portuguese history, rural life and industrial progress – a progress which, naturally, featured the construction of the railway at its centre. Lisbon's Central Station – more generally known as Rossio Station – went even further back for

inspiration, to the Manueline architecture of the Portuguese Renaissance. The two, horseshoe-shaped entrances recalled a time of Portuguese greatness, of the wealth and opulence of the Portuguese Empire before the ignominious Spanish annexation of 1580. Its architect, José Luis Monteiro, deliberately sought to evoke the great days of his nation's past in its impressive facade. Unfortunately, the theatrical historicism of the principal elevation is not matched by equivalent grandeur elsewhere. In contrast with the imperialist echoes of the entrance, the side walls are rather more prosaic – its medallions advertising Portuguese regional produce – while the interior is a great disappointment.

During the first years of the new century in the United States, the overt nationalist sentiment of these European termini was rejected in favour of a robust and inventive individuality. At Worcester Union, Massachusetts, Ware and Van Brunt's long, low terminus of 1875–7, with conventional three-arch windows, a three-window clerestory and a soaring, Gothic clock tower was extended by Watson and Huckel in 1909–11 in an even more bizarre guise, complete with a pair of white marble towers. Also

At Alexei Shchusev's Kazan terminus in Moscow of 1912–26, the asymmetrical confusion of the neo-Renaissance elevation sits uneasily with the adjacent pastiche of the Syuyumbekin Tower. The unsophisticated, wedding cake gradation of the latter was to become one of the most familiar architectural motifs of the Stalinist era.

begun in 1909 was McKim, Mead and White's Waterbury, Connecticut, with its staggeringly high campanile erupting from one end of a low, squat entrance block executed in the standard Beaux-Arts mould. The result is a dramatic but rather unbalanced composition; small wonder, Meeks observed, that this tower (said to have been imposed on the architects by the Pennsylvania Railroad President after a trip to the cathedrals of Europe) was 'the last to appear on an important American station for a quarter of a century'.

In the Deep South, P Thornton Marye built two highly individual Edwardian termini for the Southern Railroad. Birmingham, Alabama, of 1905–9 was a cross between a Moorish palace and an Italian church, with a central, domed entrance flanked by two higher towers, each 130 feet tall and crowned with Baroque cupolas. To the east a long, low, wing housed the baggage facilities; to the west, the 'Coloured Waiting Room'. ('The whites-only equivalent was, naturally, at the centre of the station complex, 300 yards away.) As Birmingham was begun, Marye was also at work further to the east, completing Atlanta Terminal for the Southern and the Atlanta and West Point railroads. Where Birmingham was dizzily eclectic, Atlanta resembled nothing more than a large villa of the later Italian Renaissance, with its ground-floor loggias, two projecting wings and a centrepiece flanked by tall, distinctly Italianate towers. Marye's bold and far-sighted concept of surrounding the building with a shopping plaza was, sadly, not executed.

Both the Birmingham and Atlanta terminals were proud and powerful symbols of the New South which had emerged from the wreckage of the Civil War. Atlanta's old Union Station – made famous for the cinema-goers of the twentieth century by its prominent role in the 1939 epic *Gone with the Wind* – had been deliberately razed by Sherman's artillery, while the city of Birmingham was largely a product of the postbellum Reconstruction of the 1870s. However, the Southern Railroad never seemed to grasp either their symbolic or their architectural significance. Atlanta's train shed was demolished in 1925, the station's two towers clumsily truncated in 1940, and the whole site cleared in 1971. By this time Birmingham, too, had been demolished.

Out West the rugged individualism of the new population was, as the twentieth century dawned, invariably extended to the architecture of the region's great railway stations. Charles Reed (d 1911) and Allen Stem's (1856–1931) Tacoma Union, Washington, built in 1910 for the Northern Pacific Railroad, was like a Neoclassical utopia by Étienne-Louis Boullée, its vast central-domed waiting room lit by an immense glazed

The interior of Kazan train shed seen in this contemporary view, opposite. Warning posters for the Russian railway, above.

While the arches and pediments of the principal facade of José Luis Monteiro's Rossio Station in Lisbon, right, suggest a sixteenth-century urban palace, they do little to advertise the real function of the building. The small clock tower is the only concession to traditional station design. Once in the plain train shed, below, however, the identity of the building is all too obvious.

arched window and flanked by two-storey wings. Shawnee, Oklahoma, was a complete contrast. Built in 1902–3 by an unknown designer for the famous Aitchison, Topeka and Santa Fe Railroad, its style is reminiscent of the heavy Romanesque revival of H H Richardson and Frank Furness. It is in the form of a Disneyesque castle, with stepped gables and a massive, tapering crenellated tower of local red sandstone. The building still survives, although it has lost its passenger service; as does another eccentric Santa Fe station of the Edwardian era: Barstow, California, of 1912. Like many California stations of the time, Barstow abandoned the more customary railway-station motifs borrowed from Northern Europe and instead took up the forms and features of the Iberian Peninsula and its Central American colonies. However, Barstow was more than just another Spanish Mission-style station; it so strongly resembled a Mediterranean villa that it was known locally as the 'Casa del Desierto'.

While Mediterranean-style stations were being built on America's Pacific Coast, on the eastern shores of the Mediterranean the forms of Northern Europe were

appearing. At the turn of the century the ambitious German Reich had turned to an alliance with the ailing Ottoman Empire – spurned by Britain and France and threatened by Russia. Attracted by the historically rich markets in the Middle East, Germany, as one of the world's leading industrialized powers, also discovered that the eastern borders of the Ottoman Empire were rich in oil. In 1901 a German technical commission reported that Mesopotamia was a 'lake of petroleum', and in 1904 the Deutsche Bank surveyed the oilfields of the Tigris and Euphrates valleys. The best way to exploit these resources, the Germans believed, was to open up the area to railways; accordingly, the Deutsche Bank promoted the idea of a German-built, German-financed Berlin to Bagdad Railway. Not only could this allow Germany to grab much of the precious oil reserves; in addition, the Vienna *Zeit* predicted in 1901, once the Berlin-Bagdad line was built, 'Anatolia, northern Syria, Mesopotamia and Iraq will export at least as much grain as all of Russia.'[3] To the Turks it was a chance to recapture lost wealth and to turn back the clock. As E M Earle wrote at the time of Turkey's postwar rebirth under Kemal Atatürk, the Ottoman government hoped that the railway 'would bring back

Ware and Van Brunt's jaunty Gothic clock tower and low-lying concourse of the 1870s (top, to right of picture) were deemed too modest and insufficiently imperial by the Edwardian directors of the Boston and Albany Railroad. The result was Frank Rushmore Watson and Samuel Huckel's pompous, twin-towered Beaux-Arts extravaganza, seen here, top (centre of picture) and above, shortly after opening in 1911. The second terminal still survives today, albeit in a shockingly dilapidated condition.

Overleaf, the NYC *Twentieth Century Limited* pauses in Buffalo in 1934. The Central Terminal's Tower can be seen behind.

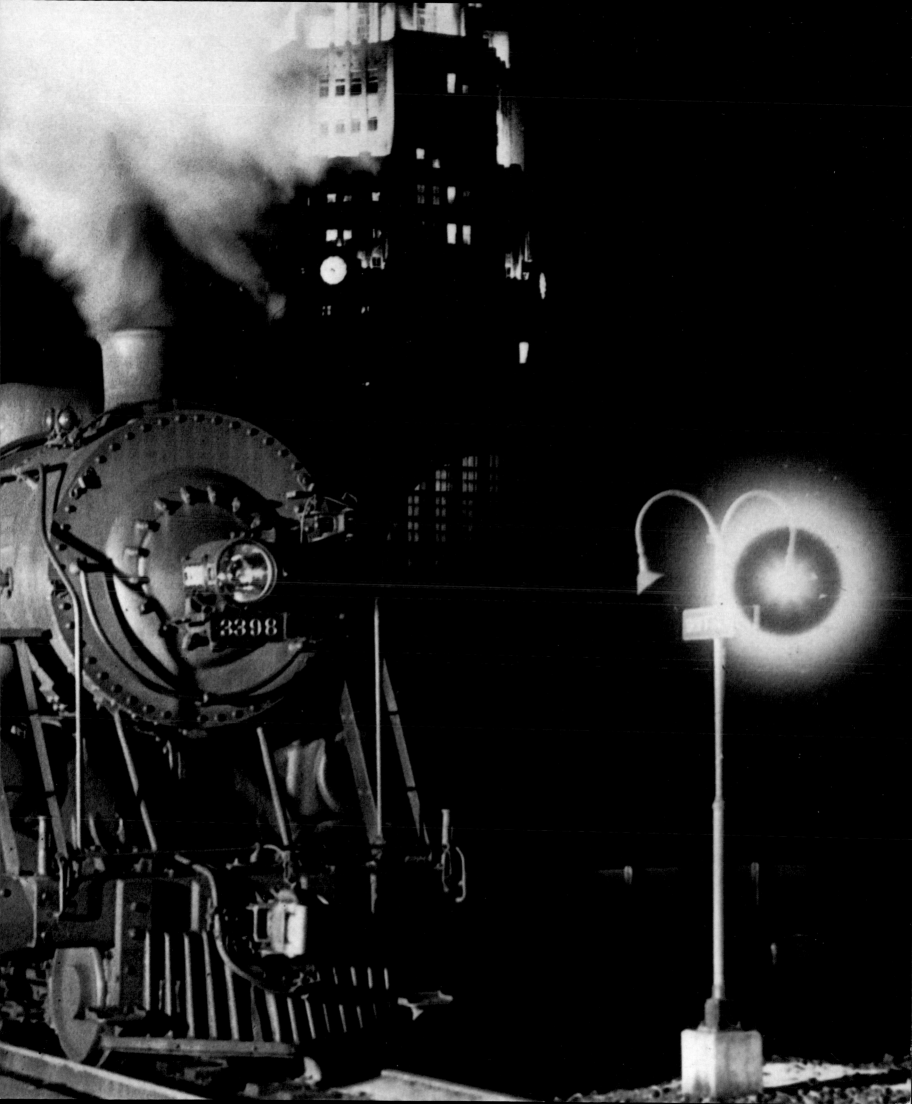

The temple-like qualities of P Thornton Marye's distinctive Birmingham Station, Alabama, building can clearly be seen in this view of the late 1960s, right. Shortly after this photograph was taken, the station was demolished – in the face of, as Marjorie White has noted, 'only mild civic opposition'. As has happened in so many towns and cities in the USA, the faceless, low-profile design of its dismal replacement has led many to forget the railroad entirely. The result is that Birmingham is now only served by one main-line passenger train each way a day. *Across the Continent*, 'Westward the Course of the Empire takes its Way', 1868, by J M Ives, below.

Elements of the facade of Richard Montfort's 1900 Nashville Union Station, Tennessee, below, suggest the neo-Renaissance styles of Belgium or Holland. However, the porte-cochere and the booking hall betray the unmistakable influence of the muscular Romanesque Revival of H H Richardson. In 1991–2 the station's interiors were converted into a hotel and two restaurants, a most appropriate re-use of a fine building.

to Anatolia, Syria and Mesopotamia some of the prosperity and prestige they had enjoyed before the explorations of the Portuguese and the Spaniards had opened the new sea routes to the Indies'.

Initial work on the Berlin-Bagdad railway had started as early as 1888, under the direction of the Ottoman government's German railway expert, Wilhelm von Pressel. With Britain preoccupied with the Second Boer War after 1899, the turn of the century seemed an excellent time to press on with construction. Like Cecil Rhodes' dream of a Cape to Cairo route, however, the idea of a Berlin–Bagdad line ultimately came to nothing. The railway never reached Bagdad, and German expresses from Berlin stopped on the European side of the Bosporus. Aleppo and Nisibin were reached in October 1918, but on 30 October Turkey signed an armistice with the Allies, ending all German hopes of eastward expansion. At the Versailles Conference all German rights to the Berlin–Bagdad line were rescinded, and responsibility for the project passed to an Ottoman–American syndicate. The subsequent break-up of the old Ottoman Empire effectively prevented any nation or company from taking advantage of what was already built; by 1923 the scheme was quite dead.

The Germans did, nevertheless, leave some Teutonic memorials of the Berlin–Bagdad project behind them. Undeniably the most impressive of these is Istanbul's Hyderpasha Station, whose towering outline can easily be seen across the Bosporus. Hyderpasha marked the beginning of the Asian half of the Berlin–Bagdad line; its design, however, had little to do with its role as the Gateway to Asia, and much to do with Germany's imperial ambitions. Built in 1909, no attempt was made to incorporate native architectural traditions or Ottoman forms. Instead, it is in the form of a massive Hanseatic town hall – something you would expect to see in Hamburg rather than Istanbul. Hyderpasha Station announced Germany's new-found military and economic influence to the world in an unmistakable fashion.

Much of the station was destroyed in a mysterious explosion which rocked the harbour in September 1917. It was comprehensively rebuilt after the First World War, when its conspicuously Germanic facade looked somewhat out of place in Atatürk's new Turkey. Today Hyderpasha remains as evocative a symbol of Europe's expansionist ambitions as Bombay Victoria or Windhoek. In the early 1970s Paul Theroux still detected a lingering Teutonic quality in the station: 'The steam locomotives, used by Turkish railways for short runs, were being stoked at the platform; they poured soot over the boarding passengers and

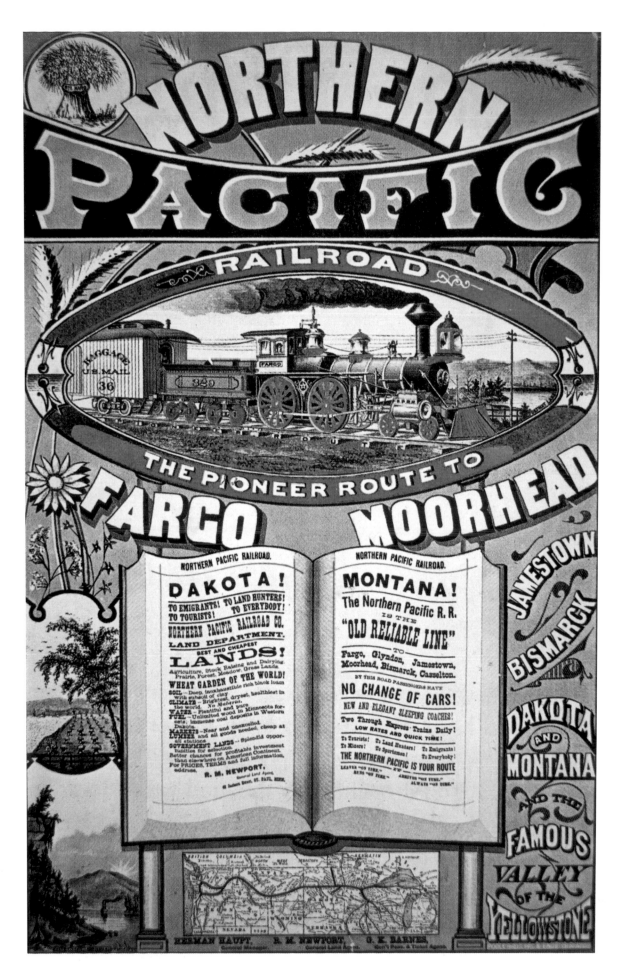

The swansong of the clock tower, above: McKim, Mead and White's distinctly European and undeniably phallic addition of 1909 to Waterbury Station, Connecticut, seen in 1912. While the station is today still served by trains connecting with the east coast main line, most of the building's interiors have been converted for use as offices. Left, Northern Pacific line poster, *c*1875, advertising services to the west.

darkened the sky with smoke, giving the German station a German atmosphere.'[4]

The Berlin–Bagdad scheme bequeathed another European-influenced railway terminus to the Middle East. In 1900 Sultan Abdul Hamid II (the ruler subsequently deposed by the 'Young Turks' in 1909) announced that a new line would be built linking the holy cities of Mecca and Medina with Damascus and, ultimately, with the Berlin–Bagdad route. This new Hejaz line would, he claimed, make the 'Haj' (the pilgrimage to Mecca), incomparably easier for the thousands of Muslims who travelled there each year. Unlike the main Berlin–Bagdad route, the construction of this explicitly Islamic line was not to be financed by Christian Europeans, but by Islamic sources. For example, the city of Lucknow contributed 29,000 rupees, while the Shah of Persia donated over one million francs. With these and other funds the Ottoman government was able to hire German, Austrian and French (but not British) engineers to build the new line, which was, in contrast to the stop-start progress of the main Berlin–Bagdad project, finished promptly in 1908. However, the Young Turks' uprising of that year, and the partial dismantling of the old regime, did put a brake on construction of the principal stations. It was not until 1912 (by which time the Young Turks had shown themselves to be

The Berlin–Bagdad Railway, Turkey. Above right, the first spike being driven into the ground for the Konia section of the ambitious Berlin–Bagdad project in 1903. British suspicions of Germany's real intentions in promoting and constructing the railway are neatly revealed in this cartoon of 1913, above. Below right, the European detailing of the internal features such as the ground-floor windows and iron railings blend well with the more ostentatiously Islamic motifs of Fernando de Aranda's skilful design of Hejaz Station, Damascus, 1913–17, photographed in 1995.

remarkably similar to the Old Turks they had replaced) that a competition was announced for the design of the Hejaz terminus, to be sited in the Kadem quarter of the Syrian capital of Damascus. The competition was won by Fernando de Aranda (1890–1969), a Spaniard. Aranda's father had been music master to the Sultan and Director of the Imperial Band, and had been made a pasha by a grateful Abdul Hamid. Following Abdul Hamid's deposition, the Aranda family returned to Barcelona; except, that is, for Fernando, who stayed in Damascus until his death at the age of ninety-one, and who, in good Muslim fashion, married two wives. Aranda was not a trained architect; but in the years following the creation of the new Turkey, he won the commission for a large number of the capital's government buildings, including the Parliament building and the Ministry of Defence.

It was Aranda's Hejaz Station which made his name. The building's European influences were far more blatant than in his later works, and the finished product reflected the peculiar mix of national identities within the architect's soul. The disposition of the main facade was reminiscent of a French château of the seventeenth century, with large, pointed windows which were a cross between traditional Islamic forms and French

Gothic openings. Inside, the detailing of the booking hall was more eclectic, with black-painted fretwork, stepped brackets and long wooden galleries in the Islamic manner above European-style panelling. The ceiling's elaborate brass chandelier epitomized the fusion of Western European and Middle Eastern styles.

Damascus Hejaz was completed in 1917, only months before T E Lawrence's Arab army blew up the Hejaz line some thirty miles further south, using the intermediate station of Deraa as a base for their raids. The newly opened railway was rapidly put out of action, but survived the fall of Damascus on 1 October 1918 and the city's subsequent plundering by the occupying British and Arab armies – even though it had been one of the Arabs's principal objectives in the city. Lawrence wrote of his first impression of the site on that glorious day: 'The uproar of the night had shrunk to a stiff tall column of smoke, which rose in sullen blackness from the store-yard by Kadem, terminus of the Hejaz line.'[5]

Today the building still stands, although the service is very limited and the booking hall virtually deserted. Trains run to Deraa and to Amman in Jordan via the strangely Alpinesque stations of the Hejaz, supplemented in the summer by a steam service to Zabandani. In 1968 the ninety-year-old Aranda actually proposed demolishing his own station and replacing it with a major road system. Thankfully, this scheme – a rare case of an architect seeking to obliterate his own work – was dropped upon Aranda's death the following year, thus saving an important part of Damascus's historic environment.

The European–Eastern melange found at Hejaz Station was also the basis for the design of one of the most odd and imposing of Britain's colonial railway termini. Calcutta Howrah was built in 1906 for the East India Railway to the designs of the British architect Halsey Ricardo (1854–1928), better known as a key figure in the Arts and Crafts movement and a builder of eccentric English homes. Howrah was a vast red-brick complex, with no less than eight towers and numerous domes and spires – a 'huge … conglomerate

of mixed Tibetan monastic and English penal suggestion.'[6] Its windows were, like those at Damascus Hejaz, a curious fusion of Gothic and Moorish. Yet it is wholly symmetrical, with not one but two porte-cocheres flanking the forbidding main entrance. Unfortunately, it was also erected on the wrong side of the river: to save expenditure on a bridge, the station was sited on the west bank of the Hooghly, and passengers bound for the city were forced to cross by ferry and pontoon.

Perhaps more than any other Indian station, Calcutta Howrah is an embodiment of all the nation's virtues and ills, of its history and culture. The bizarre and startling juxtaposition of Ricardo's elephantine, strangely ponderous architecture (an awfully long way from his Kensington villas) and the poverty of many of the station's users has always astonished observers. In 1928 R B Porter was fascinated by the station, naïvely confusing potential passengers with what were actually almost permanent inhabitants of the station's platforms:

An amazing sight is witnessed here … the natives make certain of not missing their trains by arriving sometimes as much as twelve hours before they are due to leave and camp out in batches all over the space between the platform barriers and the station offices. The day the writer travelled was Easter Sunday and he had to step over several sleeping families on his way from the booking hall to the train.[7]

Fifty-five years later Jan Morris's Howrah sounded much the same:

Inside all is thrust and movement. It is true that huddled here and there across the concourses are silent heaps of humanity, lapped about with bundles, mattresses, baskets and cardboard boxes, apparently permanently inert. But all round these lifeless deposits there is motion. There is a whirring of great fans, an incessant flashing of lights from automatic vending-machines, a drifting and spouting of steam from the platforms beyond, a shuddering of diesels, a rattle of trolleys, an unimaginable rush of people here and there … night and day, dark and light, have little meaning in this vast caravanserai, which looks much the same at any time, snorting, seething and flashing indifferently.[8]

Howrah Station, Calcutta, below, was a big departure for an architect best known for his English suburban housing. Halsey Ricardo's executed design of 1906 was certainly imposingly imperial in scale, but lacked any central definition – its somewhat chaotic elevation unintentionally reflecting the character of the vast city it faced.
Left, the railway station at Hyderabad, in south central India, was a fusion of Indian and Imperial influences.

A few years before that indefatigable railway traveller Paul Theroux was rather less impressed with the spectacle:

… at every pillar squatters huddled amid the rubbish they had created: broken glass, bits of wood and paper, straw, and tin cans… Families sought refuge beside the pillars, under counters and luggage carts: the hugeness of the station intimidated them with space and drove them to the walls.[9]

Howrah, Asia's largest station, epitomized the grandiose, pompous and rather indigestible nature of the British Empire. Its fortress-like walls were in sharp contrast to one of the Empire's other great Far Eastern termini, Kuala Lumpur. In the late 1840s Chinese traders had been attracted to this remote area of Selangor province, on the Klang river, by the discovery of tin, and by 1857 there was a small community of riverside huts here. During the next fifty years the British gradually increased their hold on the Malay peninsula – to the advantage of Kuala Lumpur, which was handily situated in the middle of the country. In 1880 the British Resident of Selangor, the swaggering, audacious diplomat-adventurer Frank Swettenham, ended the Selangor Civil War and established Kuala Lumpur as the province's capital. The city's population increased tenfold between 1880 and 1900, and on the creation of the Federated Malay States in 1896 the city was designated the new nation's capital. By this time it had become one of the Far East's most important trading centres, and was notorious for quick profits and unscrupulous dealing; not for nothing did Jean Cocteau term the city 'Kuala l'impure'.[10] By 1903 the railway linking Kuala Lumpur with Singapore and

Singora in the north was completed, and by 1919 the entire peninsula was firmly under British control.

The Malayan capital's new station of 1911 was not in the same authoritarian vein as Ricardo's Howrah. It remains, however, one of the most recognizable and best-loved stations in Asia. Its author was British: AB Hubbock, a little-known architect who had previously designed one building in a hybrid, semi-Islamic style: Kuala Lumpur's Jame Mosque of 1909. Hubbock's railway station was a Moorish–European synthesis, which took more notice of Eastern architecture and Islamic tradition than Damascus Hejaz, Bombay Victoria or Calcutta Howrah, even if Hubbock did tend to ignore genuine Malay buildings for the Indian structures he knew better. The building's borrowings from the Moghul mosques of Northern India were evident in the seven minarets and hundred-foot high onion domes. Paul Theroux was entranced by this combination, which gave it 'the general appearance of Brighton Pavilion, but twenty times larger'.[11]

Both the station and the similarly styled Malayan Railway Administration Building, across the Jin Damasara, survived the Japanese invasion of 1941–2 and subsequent occupation. Both buildings also managed to survive the Emergency of the 1950s unscathed, and since 1957 have been treated in exemplary fashion by the Malaysian government. While during the 1960s many of the city's old buildings were forced to make way for some exceptionally mediocre modern blocks, making Kuala Lumpur one of the less architecturally distinguished cities of

Unlike many European stations of the time, where a magnificent head building backed on to a disappointingly plain shed, the booking hall, concourse and train shed at Kuala Lumpur, Malaysia, were all conceived as one unified design. A B Hubbock took the idea of a hybrid 'Moorish' style from the nearby Abdul Samad Building of 1894–7, which now houses Malaysia's High and Supreme Courts. Hubbock's Indo-Malaysian external detailing, above and opposite, while never pretending to academic authenticity, was remarkably successful.

A bustling scene in *Adelaide Railway Yards* by the Australian landscape painter Sir Hans Heysen (1877–1968). Below, an Australian commemorative stamp of 1954, marking the centenary of the railway.

Southeast Asia, the restoration of both the station and the Railway Administration offices (originally converted for use as the Majestic Hotel, now housing the National Art Gallery) provide a lesson of which other Western countries would be wise to take note.

Further east still, Britain's Australasian colonies were rarely equipped with stations of the quality and individuality of those in India and Malaya. However, at Melbourne Flinders Street, J W Fawcett and H P C Ashworth created a bizarre terminus wholly unlike other great stations of the area, and which could stand comparison with the other eccentric termini of the Edwardian period. Having won the competition for the station site of 1899, Fawcett and Ashworth designed a station, built between 1905 and 1910, which was an imperial monument almost on the scale of Howrah, Victoria Terminus or its exact American contemporary, Washington Union. Cupolas flanked an enormous central dome, below which was a giant pediment, brusquely pierced by the station's external clock, and a gaping, arched entrance. The whole scale of the building is immense: the facade disappearing into the haze down Flinders Street. In 1971 the

terminus was acclaimed as 'one of the world's busiest stations', and its concourse clocks had become one of the city's most famous meeting places. Proposals to demolish Flinders Street in the mid-1970s came to nothing, and the station is well placed to remain one of the city's principal landmarks into the next century.

Britain was, of course, not the only country to build out-of-the-ordinary testaments to Empire during the first years of the twentieth century. The great German termini of the period – Hamburg Hauptbahnhof of 1903–6, Nuremberg of 1900–6, Wiesbaden of 1904–6 and Leipzig Hauptbahnhof, begun in 1907 – were overt symbols of Kaiser Wilhem II's overweening imperial ambition. Across the northwestern border, however, a rather more debonair evocation of imperial confidence was being constructed. At Antwerp Central, the local Bruges architect Louis de la Censerie (1835–1909) created a fitting allegory of the fervent and transparent national aspirations of this chaotic period. Built at the height of Belgium's ultimately disastrous imperial experiment, its walls were being raised as King Leopold II was personally intervening in the affairs of Central Africa.

Leopold had been granted the Congo in 1885, and proceeded to run this territory almost as a personal fiefdom. In 1890 he financed an expedition by H M Stanley to explore the interior; when Stanley returned to Brussels's Gare du Midi on 19 April he was, as Thomas Pakenham relates, 'welcomed by a guard of honour, and then whisked off into the King's carriage, driving through streets lined with crowds shouting "Viva", straight to the royal palace. There he was given the scarlet and gilt "imperial" apartments, normally reserved for kings and emperors.'[12] After this, however, things started to go wrong. Between 1890 and 1892 Leopold sent four expeditions into the interior, all of which were decimated by disease. By October 1892 the Belgians were at war with the Arab traders, 'with both armies eagerly supported by cannibals'. By 1895, when work began on Antwerp Central, even the normally unruffled Leopold was becoming disillusioned with his Congo venture, and almost transferred the sovereignty of the colony to the Belgian State; yet an improvement in the rubber trade instead led him to commission yet another expedition, aimed at the Nile. This foray was to end in disaster two years later, when the Belgian officers were massacred by their mutinous troops. However, for the moment the King was full of his usual confidence and optimism.

Antwerp Central was an embodiment of Leopold's colonial enterprise in stone, iron and glass. Completed in 1905, ten years after Leopold's crisis of confidence in the Congo, the station was explicitly devised as a tribute to Leopold's imperial excesses and to the newly elevated place in the world which the annexation of the Congo afforded the country. It was in essence a monument to Leopold, with the king's cipher prominently placed over the entrance doorways.

The architecture of the head building was almost a parody of the great Classical stations of the preceding decades. Antwerp included many of the standard elements that were to be found in many other Western European termini of the late nineteenth century. The

vast, single-span train shed by the engineer Van Bogaerde was mirrored in the giant lunette window high on the wall separating the concourse from the main booking hall, and again by the four lunettes which lit the main hall's domed clerestory. However, the station was finished in an overblown, ostentatious manner that would have shocked the relatively restrained railway-station architects of the mid-Victorian period. An exuberant, elaborately decorated central dome (not dissimilar to one at the Paris Exposition of 1889) was, in its ostentatious pomp, a splendid metaphor for Leopold's buccaneering colonialism. Jostling with the dome for attention were two lantern-crowned octagonal towers and ten smaller turrets, each with innumerable finials and pendentives. Inside were more elaborately framed clocks than any traveller could possibly want, and the almost entirely glazed train shed with its span of 212 feet. Almost any element could be used as an excuse for an imperial statement, from the grandiose flights of stairs up to the the concourse, to the reassuringly expensive decoration of the dome's interior. As Richards and Mackenzie have recently written, the station 'is like one of those Edwardian showgirls who married into the aristocracy. The curving shapes are there but she is in her Sunday best, positively dripping in spires, swags, pilasters, finials, and coats of arms, the better to proclaim her respectability and superiority.'[13]

The station's desperate need to convince travellers of its swaggering importance is an appropriate analogue for the country's rapidly assembled imperial status, and of the tragi-comic nature of Belgium's African Empire. While the involvement in the Congo ended in catastrophe and horror in the early 1960s, however, the station itself has lasted rather better. In the 1950s even Meeks, though not a fan of the station's posturing style, was prepared to admit that 'the iron, in spite of forty years service, was in sound condition'.[14] Today, while Belgium prefers to forget Leopold II and the Congo colony, Antwerp Central has been splendidly restored to its original magnificence.

Half-way round the world from Antwerp is another example of Western intervention in an alien culture. At Tokyo Station, however, the intervention was purely architectural. Belgian and Dutch stations, particularly Amsterdam Central, are often said to have been the primary influence on Tokyo. And certainly the general appearance of the original Tokyo Station, and the widespread use of red brick for the walling, resembles that of a building of the northwestern corner of Europe rather than of Central Japan. However, in its massing and in its detailing the resemblance between Tokyo and Amsterdam is only passing; if anything, Tokyo,

In the years before the First World War even the designs of some of the great German behemoths began to turn away from the rigid formulae and sedate imperial neoclassicism that had characterised their predecessors. Two of the best examples of this short-lived tendency were the theatrically-oversized entrance at Nuremberg Station of 1900–6, below, and Jürgen Klingholz's boldly asymmetrical Wiesbaden of 1904–6, below left, photographed in 1954.

with its principal brick buildings connected by long, low wings to terminating pavilions, most resembles the French Renaissance composition of Danks's Slough Station (see Chapter 2) or Düsseldorf Hauptbahnhof of 1890 (demolished in 1930). Whatever the direct inspiration for the Japanese capital's principal railway terminus, though, Tokyo Station remains one of the most surprising and interesting buildings in Japan, and one of the most striking termini of the remarkably prolific and eclectic period of station-building just before the outbreak of the First World War.

Japan's railways, like Tokyo's great station, were heavily influenced by the West. By the end of the 1860s British engineers were busily constructing the country's first railway lines: in 1872, when the Mikado opened the first segment of the new network, from Yedo to Yokohama, 94 out of the 104 engineers were British. Not until 1879 were trains entrusted to Japanese crews, and then only during the day. (It was widely believed by Westerners that the Japanese could not see properly at night, a myth that persisted until Pearl Harbour and the invasion of Malaya in 1941.)

Services to Tokyo originally terminated at Shimbashi, south of Ginza. It was not until 1908 that all the capital's principal lines were brought into a new, central station, which replaced all the existing city termini except for Ueno and Shinjuku. By 1914 the new station building was complete, its Western-styled design foreshadowing Japan's eagerness to follow its European allies into the forthcoming Great War.

The author of the new terminal was not European but Japanese, and one of the country's leading architects, Tatsuno Kingo, who was assisted by a Briton, William Burton, and was the pupil of another: Josiah Conder, a former assistant to William Burges, who had been invited to preside over Tokyo's new Imperial College of Engineering in 1878. Conder had already been responsible for a number of European-style buildings in the Marunouchi quarter, in downtown Tokyo. His brick-clad Mitsubishi Hall No 1 of 1894 looked like something one would expect in Chelsea or Marylebone, and was the first component of what became known, for obvious stylistic reasons, as the 'London Block' ('Itcho Rondon'). Kingo had also designed the Bank of Japan in Honkokucho in a Western idiom before he tackled the station; this, though, was a dull Neoclassical structure which bore little resemblance to Kingo's later work.

For the Tokyo Station commission, the Director of Japanese Railways urged Kingo to produce something startling that would announce Japan's membership of the exclusive club of industrialized powers to the world. What Kingo produced was just that, an exercise

The dramatic view from the concourse of Central Station, Antwerp. In 1978 the French critic Jean Dethier sniffily dismissed this rumbustuous design as 'eclectic architecture run wild'. The combination of Louis de la Censerie's Neoclassical detailing of 1895–9, with its vast openings and huge scale, cannot fail to uplift even the most jaded traveller.

Tokyo Central by Tatsuno Kingo and William Burton, 1914, was rebuilt after the earthquake of 1923. This is the principal western entrance, above, which faces the Imperial Palace. Below, the symbol of Japan's postwar rebirth and, more particularly, its recognition of the importance of fast, reliable railway links: a 'Shinkansen' bullet train from Tokyo Central, bound for Fukuoka at an average of 160 miles per hour.

in the seventeenth-century Renaissance style of Western Europe which looks even more astonishing today, surrounded by vast, blank modern towers, than it did in 1914.

Kingo's first scheme was even more flamboyant than the executed building: in addition to the octagonal domes over the two end pavilions of the final version, the connecting wings (which in 1914 were punctuated by two-bay turrets, today only by a projecting canted bay) were interrupted by two large blocks with curved roofs and Wren-style cupolas. In addition, Kingo originally envisaged a projecting portico and lantern for the central block, again more Wrenaissance than Henri IV. The execution was more French in appearance, and less dramatically scaled than Kingo's first scheme; nonetheless, it was still most impressive. The wing pavilions were a *tour de force*, each provided with not only a giant single arch flanked by two bartizans but also with a massive octagonal dome studded with large *œil-de-bœuf* windows. In 1914 these pavilions represented the principal public entrances; the central block was reserved for the imperial family, whose palace the station faced. Today such distinctions have disappeared (although the Imperial Palace grounds are still across the road from the main facade); yet the pavilions are, with the ravages of time, only a shadow of their former selves.

Not only is it surprising that Tokyo Central was built in such a recognizably Western idiom; what is even more remarkable is that, while virtually all of the capital's European-style buildings (and indeed almost all of Tokyo's built heritage) have been destroyed over the years, this particular symbol of Western influence has been allowed to remain, becoming in the process an unlikely symbol of the nation's postwar rebirth and subsequent commercial success.

The first disaster to befall the station was the great earthquake of 1923, a natural catastrophe that was immediately followed by a giant tidal wave. The station was grievously damaged, while the headquarters of Japanese Railways was destroyed. However, the building was not only comprehensively rebuilt, but rebuilt in the same European style.

The earthquake was not the only drama to affect the station during the interwar years. In 1921 and 1931 respectively two prime ministers, Hara Takashi and Hamaguchi Osachi, were assassinated on the station's concourse, both shot by militarist fanatics angered by Japan's participation in international naval treaties. (Takashi, in particular, was widely despised by the right wing as the first non-Samurai premier, and the irony of these anti-Western gestures being staged in a Western-style building was presumably not lost on the assassins.) By the late 1930s Japanese politics had swung firmly to the right, and the conservative, military-dominated government was using the Central Station as a ceremonial centre for welcoming fraternal delegates from their new allies, Nazi Germany and Fascist Italy.

America's saturation bombing of the Japanese capital during 1944–5 completely gutted the station. However, the new government – quietly encouraged by Douglas MacArthur's occupation administration – resolved to restore the building to something approaching its prewar appearance. The station's imperial pomp was gone: the pavilions lost their domes (replaced by simple octagonal roofs) and much of their articulation, while the whole frontage was rebuilt one-storey lower than before. Today Tokyo Central and the Banker's Club, both in the Marunouchi district, are the only historic buildings in downtown Tokyo to survive the Second World War and the demolition mania of the ensuing decades.

The Tokyo Central that MacArthur saw in 1945 was a scene of utter devastation. However, the capital's principal terminus was soon transformed into a potent symbol of national regeneration. In the 1950s the rear, eastern side of the complex was completely opened up. (An eastern entrance had been built in 1929, but was intended only for the poorer commuters. Long-distance travellers still had to buy tickets from the main, eastern entrance, adjacent to the Imperial Palace.) This new, 'Yaesuguchi' entrance was able to serve a far bigger population than the old, Palace-oriented portal, and the eastern side of the station soon spawned into a vast, underground shopping centre – one of the world's first giant, purpose-built malls – and by 1960 was the largest retailing area in the Far East.

While shops and services were burrowing beneath

the tracks, exciting new train services were being initiated above ground. In 1959 the government gave its approval for the construction of a new high-speed, electrified line between Tokyo Central and Osaka, a line which ran with almost no perceptible curves and which used multiple-unit trains which, unlike the locomotive-hauled services of the rest of the world's main lines, did not need to be substituted or turned around at the terminus. In March 1963 the prototype test train ran at a staggering 150 mph; when the line formally opened in October 1964 the 'Hikari' class train managed an average speed of 100 mph, making it by far the fastest train in the world.

The psychological boost which the establishment of Japan's high-speed, 'Shinkansen' lines from Tokyo gave the population cannot be underestimated. The nation had shown not only that it had recovered from the devastation of the war, but that it was now an industrial and technological power to be reckoned with, and no longer merely the source of cheap plastic goods and copycat electronics. It was also a society which had clearly appreciated the value of efficient mass transportation: at a time when Europe and the United States were closing their stations and levelling their great termini, Japan was extending her railway network into entirely new areas of the country and was breathing new life into her historic termini.

During the 1970s Japanese Railways were able to build on the evident success of the first Shinkansen service, extending the high-speed network throughout the country.

The station, too, has profited by this success. Many visitors have been attracted to the Yaesuguchi Shopping Centre, despite its uninspired design and confusing layout.[15] And as the eastern side and the underbelly of the station were developed, Kingo's main entrance blocks found themselves increasingly used for non-railway purposes. Having survived a brief threat of demolition in the mid-1980s, the principal elevation's central block now houses an art gallery, in addition to restaurants and bars. In sharp contrast, the ground-floor interiors of the two wing pavilions currently look very shabby; yet at least their future appears secure.

The synthesis of custom and technology is nowhere more apparent in modern Japan than Tokyo Central. The high-speed network continues to be the envy of those nations which are still relatively serious about railway operation: fast, clean, extremely efficient and enduringly popular, its internationally famous trains demonstrate the key role that well-run railways and well-maintained stations can play in an increasingly gridlocked world.

A print of the 1870s showing the opening ceremony of the first railway terminus, Shimbashi, in Tokyo. Note the presence of what appears to be a Western train crew. After the Central station was built, Shimbashi was relegated to the status of a freight office, and was finally demolished in 1923.

THE APOGEE OF THE RAILWAY AGE
BEAUX-ARTS STYLE

'As time passes the indubitable merits of picturesque eclectic
buildings will receive wider recognition and the ruthless
destruction of them can be halted.'[1]
CARROLL MEEKS, 1956.

The Beaux-Arts movement originated in France in the
last decades of the nineteenth century, taking its name
from the school which was to exert such a profound
influence over so many station architects, the
celebrated École des Beaux-Arts in Paris. From here
architects of all nationalities went forth to spread the
Beaux-Arts gospel, allying technological advances with
the Classical architecture of the ancient world and the
Renaissance. In practice the lofty ideals of the Beaux-
Arts practitioners often fell to earth with a dull thud;
what was intended to be a pure and honest doctrine was
often expressed as an oversized parody, less a Roman
temple, an Italian palazzo or a French château than a
rather repetitive exercise in corporate Neoclassicism.
However, it was a style whose connotations of imperial
grandeur, monumental wealth and unlimited power
proved enduringly appealing.

By the 1890s, the Beaux-Arts approach was
beginning to be applied to the buildings which most
epitomized this fertile period: the great railway
stations. The style's pre-eminence at the Chicago
World's Fair of 1893 set the tone for the rest of the
decade, the whole exhibition – which also witnessed
the auspicious unveiling of America's first petrol-
powered car, built by Karl Benz – being housed in a
complex of Beaux-Arts buildings known as the 'White
City'. However, outside France and the Americas the
appeal of Beaux-Arts classicism was largely limited to
government buildings. In Britain and Germany it was
regarded as too ostentatious and theatrical, while in
many other countries railway companies were
dissuaded by the vast expense which Beaux-Arts
monuments often entailed. Only in France and North
America was it widely used for station design.

The most influential of these Beaux-Arts stations
was Victor Laloux's Orsay terminal in Paris, begun in

Mercury, the personification of
travel and speed (as well as, in
Whitney Warren's words, 'the
glory of Commerce'), at the
summit of the triumphal arch
of New York's Grand Central
Station's main elevation. The
scale, movement and articulation
of this giant sculptural group,
carved by none other than the
École des Beaux-Arts' Professor
of Sculpture, Jules Alexis
Coutan, ensured that it was
closely integrated with Warren's
facade, opposite. Left, a New
York, New Haven & Hartford
stock certificate of 1906.

The Seine facade, rather than the main passenger entrance on the western side, was always intended to be the Gare d'Orsay's principal architectural attraction. As at all of the great Beaux-Arts stations of the early twentieth century, the imposing blocks of masonry were in reality suspended from the building's steel frame.

1898 and finished only two years later, in time for the Paris Exposition of 1900. Orsay's importance in the history of the railway station and of transport in general should not be underestimated. Meeks called Orsay 'a model station, destined to influence many others', and pointed out that the terminus itself was one of the principal attractions to the 1900 Fair. More recently, the construction and electrification of the station has been called 'the most decisive event in the pioneer history of electric traction'.[2]

On 12 September 1896 the French Ministry of Works set up an enquiry into whether it would be feasible to extend the Orléans Railway from its current Austerlitz terminal, in southeast Paris, to a city-centre railhead at the Quai d'Orsay, across the Seine from the Louvre Palace. The railway company believed this scheme was their only hope to attract suburban traffic; writing in 1902, the critic Alfred Dumas noted that 'the distance between the terminal station and the city centre has no doubt been one of the main reasons why, until now, Parisians have almost completely avoided moving to the suburban areas along the Orléans railway line'.[3] The new station was to be for commuters only; goods, military trains and postal services were to

remain at Austerlitz, which was to be linked with the Quai d'Orsay by a two-track railway running twenty feet underground along the left bank of the Seine. The new terminal was to be on the site of the old Cour des Comptes and Barracks of the former Orsay Palace, ruined in the revolutionary Communard terror of 24 May 1871.

The Orsay project was formally approved on 29 November 1897. Not everyone exhibited the same enthusiasm as the Orléans Railway: the City of Paris was worried that the scheme would encourage other railways into the heart of the historic cityscape, while *La Construction Moderne* warned that the development might involve the demolition of the famous Hôtel de Salm, which had been so admired by Thomas Jefferson soon after its construction in 1782.[4] (It did not, and, anyway, the Hôtel had already been rebuilt from ruins in 1878.) L C Boileau was concerned that visitors to the Louvre Museum across the river would be 'disturbed by the shrill whistling of the locomotives, the steam and smoke, and the hubbub of the coaches'. How long before 'a veritable transport factory is erected on the opposite bank of the Seine?' *l'Illustration* simply bemoaned the onward march of industrial society:

The utilitarian architecture of Orsay station will follow on from the military architecture of the Quai d'Orsay barracks. An appealing area will entirely vanish as if through a trap-door. Electric coaches, laden with parcels, will cross the Tuileries! … there are times when the march of progress seems too brutal, and inevitable amputations somewhat too painful.[5]

The design – and particularly the electrification – of the station was to calm these fears. For this the railway originally approached the Paris Exposition's chief architect, Hénard, but he declared he was too busy with the exhibition. The railway then launched a competition between three nominated architects: Lucien Magne, Emile Bénard and Victor Laloux. Each was asked to draw up three variants: a station without a hotel, with a medium-sized hotel and with a luxury hotel. In April 1898 it was announced that the winner of the competition was Victor Laloux.

Laloux (1850–1937) was then aged forty-eight, a former student at the École des Beaux-Arts and winner of the Grand Prix de Rome. In 1898 he was basking in the acclaim for his recently completed station at Tours, with its breathtakingly monumental façade, and was thus well acquainted with the discipline of station design. He immediately told the press that, in order to balance 'the requirements of a modern station with those of the architectural setting', he would face his iron-framed building with stone to create 'a fitting balance for the Tuileries'. However, this did not mean he intended merely to resort to a pastiche of Louis XIV's palace on the opposite bank of the Seine. 'To copy the Louvre in order to create a railway station', he declared, 'would have been a downright monstrosity.'[6] Laloux, requested by the railway to incorporate a medium-sized hotel of 230 beds, also resolved that the hotel would obscure neither the station's main entrance nor its Seine elevation, the element which most passers-by would see.

Work began immediately and was completed remarkably quickly: the foundations were completed in May 1899, and the station and the hotel were both finished in record time, ready to open on the first Bastille day of the new century, 14 July 1900.

Laloux's finished complex comprised a head building, a hotel on the south side and a long frontage to the river, behind which were sited the platforms. No arched iron shed was needed, as there were no steam locomotives to accommodate. The brave decision had been taken to electrify the line from Austerlitz, an option which was partly dictated by the subterranean nature of the line, but which had never before been adopted for a major station. Electrification solved a number of problems at a stroke: the danger of accidents due to smoke obscuring the tunnels, the possibility of passenger suffocation, and the likelihood that the sooty emissions from steam trains would cause damage to the dense urban environment – including a large number of government buildings and national monuments – adjacent to the line and the terminus.

The 172-foot long Seine elevation was suitably impressive, as befitted a major addition to the Paris cityscape. At each end was a giant pavilion, provided with an illuminated clock 16 feet in diameter. Between these was the main arcade of seven arches, decorated with cartouches featuring the railway's cipher ('PO' – Paris Orléans) and names of the network's principal destinations in west and southwest France. Above the cornice were three giant statues representing, as those atop Hittorf's Gare du Nord had done, the principal destinations of the railway: Bordeaux (by Jean-Baptiste Hugues), Toulouse (by Laurent Marqueste) and Nantes (by Antoine Injalbert), which was provided with the face of Mme Laloux. Behind these statues was a slate mansard roof studded with rooflights, a stone obelisk and zinc finials.

The Seine façade was considered as much a part of the city's river front as Notre Dame or the Pont Neuf. The American architect W S Richardson found it 'not only singularly appropriate and expressive of its use' but also a structure which 'gives an impression of real beauty';[7] he did warn, however, that its unrestrained Beaux-Arts exuberance 'may possibly be somewhat over-ornate for average Anglo-Saxon taste'. The other facades were deliberately couched in a quieter language. The station's main entrance, on the Rue de Bellechasse, featured a giant glazed fanlight – the ubiquitous symbol of the late nineteenth-century terminus – behind a restrained, nine-bay centrepiece with a simple glazed porch, set between two modest pavilions. The hotel's 530-foot long, six-storey Rue de Lille elevation was even more utilitarian, harmonizing well with the adjacent streets in a quiet, unassuming

Detail of one of the ten foot-wide pavilion clocks of the Gare d'Orsay, above. Below, passengers arriving at the Gare d'Orsay's main entrance on the Rue de Bellechasse, in 1900.

Representations of the Orléans Railway's principal destinations – Bordeaux, Toulouse and Nantes – atop the superbly detailed attic of the Seine front of Laloux's Gare d'Orsay, Paris, below. At the summit of the slate mansard roof behind is one of the giant stone-and-zinc finials.
Near right: cross-section of the glazed steel train shed of 1898, showing the hotel rooms to the right. Today the suburban RER line runs directly underneath this shed, using a tunnel begun in 1939.

way that was entirely different in execution and object from the river front on the other side of the station.

Inside the terminus, there were three main spaces: the barrel-vaulted entrance arcade, top-lit with a rooflight; the booking hall, also top-lit, and with painted landscapes by Cormon; and the glazed train shed, its nine arches corresponding to the divisions of the Seine front. At the eastern, exit end of the shed was another glazed fanlight, surmounted by the head of Mercury, the god of travel; inside, on the west wall, was a fabulous clock set in an ornately gilded plaster frame, perhaps the most lavish of all the many station clocks of this splendid era. Between lay the platforms, each with special luggage-handling gangways expressly designed to keep the baggage separate from the passengers. The gangways led to conveyor belts and a goods lift, from where luggage was taken to the baggage room to be reunited with its owners; incoming luggage descended by spiral ramps on to the platforms.

At the western end of the complex lay the most impressive of the station's interiors. On the first floor was the *salle des fêtes*, profusely decorated with gilded plasterwork and with ceiling panels painted by Pierre Fritel, and the sumptuous *salon mauresque*, with

overdoors by Adrien Moreau-Néret. The decoration of the hotel's dining room was similarly lavish, with Louis XV walls and a vast ceiling painting – an 'Allegory on Time', reminding the diners that their trains would not wait for dessert – by Gabriel Ferrier.

On its opening the station met with widespread approval, and indeed with relief. W S Richardson (subsequently the project architect for New York's Penn Station) wrote that it was 'in some respects the best railway entrance to any city yet achieved', while the French critic Henry Haguet noted:

The Orsay station, with the great architectural beauty and majestic external aesthetics with which we are already familiar, displays some very unexpected arrangements internally … which make it one of Europe's most attractive and best ordered railway stations. Here everything works automatically and speedily, electricity makes everything move.[7]

Alfred Dumas declared that Laloux had masked 'the great metallic vessel most opportunely'; if the steelwork had been left exposed, as was the custom at other great termini, it would, he suggested, 'have had a less than happy effect when set opposite the Tuileries and the Louvre Palace'.[8]

By the 1960s, however, Orsay was, along with many of its great contemporaries, rather less well-loved by the critics, who despised its good-humoured, if inflated, historicism and who, reversing Dumas's judgement of sixty years before, now condemned Laloux for submerging the station's metal frame beneath a masonry coat. Jean Autin derided the station as 'a dreadful blot on the face of the Seine', and even critic Michel Ragon ridiculed its 'chocolate-box form'.[9] By 1979 J G Garcias and J J Trentel felt they were being even-handed with their faint praise, while damning the building (and effectively the whole ethos of the Beaux-Arts school) for daring to combine historical reference with the latest technology. Orsay was, they declared with confidence, 'typical of the overblown *style pompier* architecture of the *arrière-garde*. It combines showpieces of modernity – conveyor belts, passenger and goods lifts of every kind – with such outdated symbols as statuary, mosaics, frescoes, coffered ceiling and the like.'[10] Whereas at the beginning of the century such comments could be interpreted as positive recognition of what the architect was trying to achieve, after the Second World War the goals of the Beaux-Arts swiftly became as up-to-date as the top hat. Exactly the same criticisms had been made of America's great Beaux Arts stations; whereas many of these masterpieces were demolished or mutilated, Orsay, however, managed to survive long enough to be rediscovered at a time when Modernist dogma was tempered by historical perspective.

Even before the Second World War, Orsay appeared to be ripe for disposal; indeed, at the time of the fall of France in 1940 the station was quite empty. During the 1920s it became increasingly obvious that the station was difficult to reach by car and that the platforms could not accommodate the new, longer trains. In 1929 the Orléans Railway first floated the idea of terminating all services at Austerlitz once more, and merely running a shuttle to Orsay. Six years later Paris City Council suggested replacing the complex with a Festival and Sports Palace – a proposal that was uncannily similar to the scheme then being proposed for London's St Pancras, and to that carried out on the site of McKim, Mead and White's New York Pennsylvania Station in the early 1960s. Raymond Lopez's Sports Palace scheme for the Orsay site was undeniably futuristic: with its large, funnel-like tower rising up at the site's western end and its striking Modern Movement lines it was a slap in the face for Laloux's considered Beaux-Arts compromise. And for a while it seemed as if the fate of the old terminal was sealed. On 23 November 1939 all main line services were terminated at Austerlitz, and a shuttle begun to an underground platform underneath Laloux's station. Only the German invasion of May 1940 prevented the building from being razed and Lopez's bright new Palace from being erected on its grave. Even then, the fleeing government of the Third Republic left for the

Platforms, left, and the main concourse with various services, pictured in 1902–3 above, at the Gare d'Orsay, Paris, show the attention to detail and combination of historical reference with up-to-date technology.

Loire the following month from Austerlitz, not Orsay.

After 1940 Orsay passed into a twilight existence, its echoing train shed only rarely being put to practical use. In 1945 the station was used as a reception centre for returning prisoners of war and deportees, but after 1947 lapsed again into silence. The hotel survived for a few years – as we have seen, it was here that De Gaulle made his historic appeal to the nation, presaging the end of the Fourth Republic, on 19 May 1958 – but finally succumbed to closure in January 1973.

In 1961 came the inevitable: SNCF announced a competition for a design that would replace the old station with a new hotel. One of the entrants was none other than Le Corbusier himself, who rapidly attracted the backing of much of the architectural and political establishment. Le Corbusier was enthused by the possibilities of the site – but then, given the long Seine frontage, the downtown location and the proximity of the Louvre, who would not be? Terming it a 'privileged location', he declared with Olympian certainty that, 'The gigantic station (of which nothing will be seen) is to become a belvedere where theatre will be created from every window and on every level.' Orsay, he announced, 'unleashes the future massing of Paris'.[11] Unfortunately, even some of his own supporters admitted that the vapid, dreary slab which the incomparable Corb unveiled as his scheme for the site, featuring two immense blind walls, made little of the 'privileged location'. André Chastel, no friend of historicism, dared to write in *Le Monde* of the design's 'sterility' and 'off-hand nature', suggesting that to erect this block would be 'like bringing the United Nations skyscraper and putting it on the banks of the Seine, but without the clouds, the sea breeze and the formidable tension of the Hudson'.[12]

Faced with such comments, SNCF decided to start again with a new competition in 1963. This round was won by Condon and Gillet, who proposed a long, low slab of stultifying banality. Nevertheless, in 1969 this dismal scheme received government approval. Across the Channel the indefatigable campaigner against architectural mediocrity, Ian Nairn, commented that 'it now seems certain that [Orsay] will be replaced by some wall-eyed exposition of *l'urbanisme*'.[14] Sure enough, on Christmas Eve 1970 the Paris Préfecture issued their consent to demolish.

The 1970s, however, offered renewed hope to Orsay, as this decade did to so many other of the world's great railway stations. And unlike most other countries, in the case of Orsay it was the national government who intervened to save the station – a sharp contrast to the British government's complicity in Euston's demolition and to New York City's

Edwardian views of the interior of the Orsay train shed, right, showing the vast glazed fanlight at the west end and the huge clock, fifteen feet across, with its exuberant plaster surround. In Laloux's hands, established Beaux-Arts features such as the coffering and arched supports of the roof always remained light and graceful.
In 1986, Orsay Station was reborn as the Musée d'Orsay. Top, a commemorative stamp from 1987, and, above, a detail of Gae Aulenti's treatment of the interior, with some of the museum's excellent collection of pre-First World War French sculpture.

connivance in the destruction of Pennsylvania Station. On 25 February 1971, before demolition work had begun on the site, the Minister of Cultural Affairs, Jacques Duhamel, formally objected to the scale and context of the new development planned for the Quai d'Orsay: '… whatever its intrinsic value, its massing and height are badly integrated with an area encompassing the Place de la Concorde, the Tuileries gardens, the Louvre Palace and the banks of the Seine as far as Notre-Dame'. This official view was repeated until 1975, when the government ruled that the hotel's construction 'would obviously detract from the interest of the surrounding area'.[13] Meanwhile, the Republic's president, Georges Pompidou, had begun to take a personal interest in the site. It was Pompidou who helped to give the station statutory protection in March 1973; the following month he announced that the station was not, after all, to be demolished, but was to be converted into a museum for nineteenth-century French art. With Pompidou's support, suddenly anything was possible. The team already used to plan Richard Rogers and Renzo Piano's Pompidou Centre of 1972, Patrick O'Byrne and Claude Pequet, worked out an architectural brief in July 1974. In July 1976 the project received the enthusiastic blessing of the new president, Valéry Giscard d'Estaing, who announced that the new museum would contain French art from the period 1848–1914. A competition to convert the building was held in 1978; in 1979 Giscard declared the winner to be Pierre Colboc of ACT Architecture, while at the same time appointing Gae Aulenti to handle the project's interior design.

The station, meanwhile, had not been entirely abandoned. In 1962 Orson Welles filmed his version of Kafka's *The Trial* in the desolate train shed, paying Anthony Perkins and the rest of the cast out of his own pocket. The shed subsequently became home to a rifle range, a car park, a theatre, and, from January 1974, to an auction house.

ACT's scheme was a long way from the all-or-nothing approach of Le Corbusier or Condon and Gillet. The firm's fundamental brief was to respect the fabric of Laloux's station as far as was practically possible. Thus the roof and walls were largely undisturbed, the museum's central avenue followed exactly the line of the former tracks, while the hotel's magnificent dining room became the museum's first-floor restaurant. The new exhibition spaces were simply inserted into the shell of Laloux's shed. Even the muted colours of the cream-coloured partitions, the bare Burgundian stone walls and the brown or green ironwork were designed to complement the greys, greens and browns of the limestone and iron structure.

Despite major changes of government, successive French administrations continued to back the new scheme. Giscard's successor of 1981, François Mitterrand, devoted much of his time to the project during the early 1980s, and helped to increase its budget to more practical levels. Fittingly, it was Mitterrand who formally opened the glittering new Musée d'Orsay to the public in 1986.

Where Paris led in 1900, New York soon followed. The Beaux-Arts approach used so successfully at Orsay was, ten years later, used as the basis for the design of two of the world's most magnificent stations: New York's Pennsylvania and Grand Central termini.

New York Pennsylvania's strengths lay not merely in its architecture, which fused the pretension and bombast of Beaux-Arts Neoclassicism with the latest steel-frame technology, but also in the radical nature in which it was planned. During its brief but illustrious history, Penn Station was variously described as not only the greatest (and, at the time of its opening in 1910, the largest) station in the world, but also as one of the greatest building projects of the early twentieth century. In 1911 the *Architectural Review*, having complimented the 'quiet dignity of the architecture' and the 'lack of ostentatious display', confidently claimed the station as 'one of the greatest modern architectural achievements'.[14] Seventy years later Professor Carl Condit counted Penn amongst 'the four greatest achievements of American building art'.[15]

Prior to Penn's construction, Pennsylvania Railroad (PRR) passengers arriving in New York from the west had to catch a ferry across the Hudson River from the railway's terminus in Jersey City, which the PRR had reached in 1871. A similar situation existed in the east, where the Long Island Railroad (bought by the PRR in 1900) ended on the eastern shore of the East River, necessitating a ferry journey across to Manhattan. Pressure for a road or railway crossing of the Hudson and the East River during the 1880s and 90s had met with little success; in the event, the implementation of the tunnel links and the building of Penn Station were largely the work of one man: Alexander Cassatt of the PRR. It was Cassatt who, in April 1902, commissioned Charles McKim of architects McKim, Mead and White to draw up a plan for tunnels, linking central Manhattan with the eastern and western shores, which would terminate in a large, new station and hotel. Work on the tunnels began in June 1903.

Taking his cue from Orsay, Cassatt used the novel concept of electrification to solve the problems presented by the approach tunnels. On 8 January 1902 locomotive smoke had caused a major accident on the New York Central line in which fifteen people were

1962: a derelict Orsay is the setting for Orson Welles's film of Kafka's *The Trial*. Anthony Perkins is Joseph K.

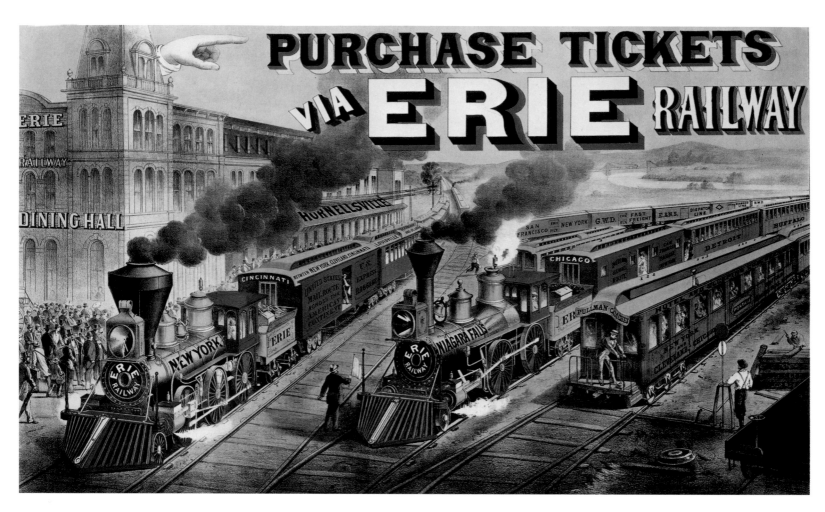

PURCHASE TICKETS VIA ERIE RAILWAY

Above, an 1874 poster for the Erie line depicting Hornellsville, Erie Railway, a trunk line running between New York City and the Western States and Territories. Below, a cartoon from 1883, depicting 'A Deadhead Passenger' – an intelligent animal stealing a free ride on the railroad.

A DEADHEAD PASSENGER.
HOW AN INTELLIGENT ANIMAL REFUSED TO BE BUFFED OFF THE TRACK BY THE COWCATCHER, AND STOLE A FREE RIDE ON THE RAILROAD.

killed when two trains collided, an incident which prompted the city to announce a ban on the use of steam locomotives in Manhattan from July 1908. Cassatt instantly sent an observer to see how work on the new, electrified terminus and approach tracks at Orsay was progressing, and attended the Paris station's opening ceremony in person. The following year he also appointed a PRR Board of Engineers specifically to assess the feasibility of the Orléans Railway's innovations. The Baltimore and Ohio Railroad had already shown that electric train operation in America was safe and reliable; their experience, together with the example of Orsay, prompted Cassatt to build the first, smoke-free electric railway terminus outside Paris, at a time when Italy, Germany and even Britain were still experimenting with main-line electrification.

Pennsylvania Station was always intended by Cassatt and the PRR to be the most impressive gateway into New York City, grander than the port and more magnificent than the New York Central's Grand Central terminus. As *Scientific American* observed on the occasion of Penn's opening in 1910, McKim, Mead and White's design 'endeavoured to give to the building the character of a monumental entrance to the commercial metropolis of the country, which would at

the same time conform to the traditional aspects of a great railway terminus'.[16]

The firm appointed by Cassatt as the architects for Penn Station was America's most renowned champion of the Beaux-Arts movement. McKim, Mead and White's three principal partners were nevertheless remarkably disparate in character. Charles Follen McKim (1847–1909), the partner designated to head the Penn Station project, was the anchor of the practice – a withdrawn, scholarly son of Quaker and radical abolitionist parents. William Rutherford Mead (1846–1928) was a quiet, thoughtful administrator from Vermont who outlived both his colleagues, dying in 1928. In contrast, Stanford White (1853–1906) was far more celebrated. White represented to many observers the creative whirlwind of the firm; he was a man whose talents, the *American Architect* claimed, 'verged on genius', yet whom J P Morgan alleged was 'always crazy'. At the time of Penn Station's opening White was more renowned for his lurid private life than for his architectural achievements. On 25 June 1906 White, a renowned womanizer and bon viveur, was shot and killed in the theatre restaurant at the top of Madison Square Tower – a building he had himself designed – by deranged millionaire playboy Harry

K Thaw, who had discovered that his 'virginal' young bride had formerly been White's mistress. Thaw – ironically, a major shareholder of the PRR – was declared insane and sent to Matteawan Asylum in 1908, though not before alleging that White had seduced 378 girls in his Madison Square apartment.

McKim was the partner who perhaps most enshrined the practice's commitment to Beaux-Arts ideals in the twenty years after 1887. Having studied engineering – not architecture – at Harvard, and spent one summer in the office of the noted Goth, Russell Sturgis, in 1867 McKim began three years' study under Daumet at the École des Beaux-Arts. Returning to the United States and to the office of H H Richardson in 1870, he set up on his own in a practice devoted to the Neoclassical ideals and straightforward precepts of the Beaux-Arts. Most importantly for the immediate future of American architecture, he was an enthusiastic backer of and participant in the great World's Columbian Exposition in Chicago of 1893.

By 1902 McKim had become responsible for winning the majority of the practice's larger contracts, including Pennsylvania Station, to which the firm was directly appointed by Cassatt. Cassatt and McKim did not always see eye to eye. Cassatt wanted to add a large hotel to the site; McKim – who, with his Classical training, was vehemently opposed to high-rise, 'anti-urban' buildings – did not. In the event McKim won the argument, and retained the contract. It is a bitter irony that the addition of Cassatt's revenue-earning tower block to the station might have helped to stave off the demolition of the 1960s.

McKim's and project-architect W S Richardson's goal in planning Pennsylvania Station was to allow freedom and rapidity of movement into, out of and within the station complex. Although the station site filled four large blocks, lateral space was at a premium, allowing very little room for grandiose train sheds over the platforms. Accordingly, McKim placed the tracks *below* the station's facilities, an arrangement which had the added advantage of shortening the distance which the passengers had to travel to reach their trains. The tracks and their platforms were installed 45 feet below street level, and were themselves undercut by smaller tunnels needed for baggage handling and for water and electrical services. (It was a major priority of McKim's plan to prevent passengers from carrying their baggage too far, or from being run over by the baggage trucks.) From the track bed, 650 steel columns rose up to support the massive structures above: the concourse, 18 feet above, the exit concourse (a low-ceilinged, intermediate area, allowing incoming passengers access to the street without having to force their way

through the crowds on the main working floor), and the great waiting room and its attendant areas. Even the waiting rooms were still 14 feet below street level, and reached the street level by ascending stairs or, preferably, by ramps.

In terms of architectural language, McKim divided the station into two distinct areas: the exposed steel-framed train concourse, with platforms below, and the Classically inspired, stone-clad service area, which revolved around the cavernous great waiting room. The distinction made by McKim between these two vocabularies was deliberately stark, and was designed to reflect the different functions of the two zones: dramatically but ruthlessly functional below, in those spaces intended primarily for train use, and theatrically Classical above, in those areas reserved for passengers. The railway tracks themselves were so far underground that McKim resolved that any expression of a traditional train shed at this level would be impossible.

For the main floor, in particular the great waiting room, McKim sought to combine the structural freedom afforded by the latest steel-frame technology with the Classical language of ancient Rome. The constant reference to antique models was not devised, though, purely for aesthetic reasons. As Richardson noted in 1912, Rome's monumental buildings provided 'the greatest examples in architectural history of large roofed-in areas adapted to assemblages of people'.[17] They were also, he suggested, the product of a culture that was remarkably analogous to that of early twentieth-century America; everyday life in the turn-of-the-century United States was, he alleged, 'more nearly akin to the life of the Roman Empire than that of any other known civilisation'. While in Rome on behalf of the McMillan Commission in 1901, McKim had inspected the ruined Baths of Caracalla. He even had photographs made of the site, hiring locals to give a sense of human scale and to replicate the flow of large crowds within its spaces. In the central 'tepidarium' (or at least in its conjectural restorations), McKim found the inspiration for the interior of the great waiting room. The Roman tepidarium was simply enlarged by 20 per cent: the Roman dimensions of 80 feet by 175 feet by 100 feet high were expanded to 102 by 278 by 147 feet high. And the coffered barrel vaults and clerestory windows were reproduced almost exactly – although, unlike the load-bearing vault of the ancient baths, the decorative, coffered plaster ceiling at Penn Station was merely suspended from the steel frame.

The entrance into the great waiting room itself, down a 40-foot wide stair, was breathtakingly Baroque. As Richardson delighted in pointing out, the dimensions of this cavernous hall were similar to those

Fred Wright, a porter who had served the New Haven Railroad for over 55 years, receives his long-service medal in 1947.

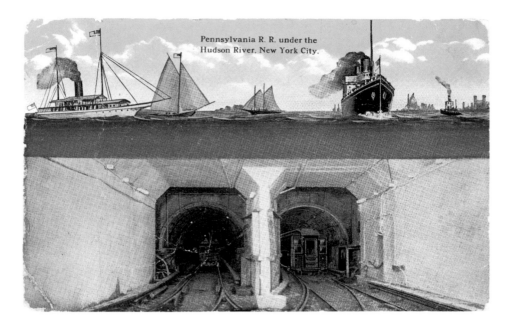

Pennsylvania R. R. under the Hudson River, New York City.

NEW YORK—PHILADELPHIA TRAINS

Schedule in effect 12.01 A. M., December 11, 1917.
Subject to change without notice.

PENNSYLVANIA
RAILROAD
The Standard Railroad of the World

EXPRESS TRAINS
BETWEEN
NEW YORK
AND
PHILADELPHIA

R. L. O'DONNEL   JAS. F. ANDERSON
Assistant General Manager   Passenger Traffic Manager
    DAVID N. BELL   OLIVER T. BOYD
General Passenger Agent   General Passenger Agent

Early postcard depicting the tunnels under the Hudson, above right. Pennsylvania Railroad timetable, above. Below right, postwar view of the principal, Seventh Avenue entrance of Pennsylvania Station, New York. The severe, sober hybrid-Doric order devised by McKim and his project architect W S Richardson for the main elevations provided New York with a suitably evocative imperial gateway.

of the nave of St Peter's, and constituted 'the largest and most monumental single room in the world today'. Along the walls was a giant order of eight Corinthian columns, each 59.5 feet high; above were huge, coffered groin vaults, 150 feet high at their apex. A smaller order of Ionic pilasters, 31 feet high, rose to half the height of the wall at either end, while massive clerestory lunettes, each 68 feet in diameter, provided the direct light for the monumental interior.

The steel latticework of the concourse was a complete contrast. Montgomery Schuyler was not the last to point out the contradiction between the ruthlessly utilitarian design of this area, its glazed umbrella-roof and branching supports lacking any decorative embellishments, and the Beaux-Arts pomposity of the Great Waiting Room, 'incrusted with a quite meaningless coffering' and 'columns which supported nothing'.[18] Forty years later Lewis Mumford contrasted the 'shopworn tags of McKim's classical design' with the 'reassuring' stability of the concourse area.[19] The shape of the concourse's exposed steel vaults was dictated by the engineers, rather than the architects, but their basic form derived from McKim's masterplan, which had envisaged an appropriately transitional vocabulary to link the 'purely architectural' character of the great waiting room and its attendant spaces with the 'purely utilitarian and structural treatment' of the tracks and platforms below. The immense steel arches and glazed roofs were the nearest Penn Station came to the great iron-and-glass train sheds of Europe; indeed, in 1912 Richardson declared that the steel columns had been introduced 'to give as distinctive a railway expression as was possible'.[20]

At the time of its opening, Pennsylvania Station incorporated not only the latest technology but also unrivalled passenger facilities. There were 158 drinking fountains, all supplied from the famously reliable New York City mains. In the public rooms these were supplemented by vending machines which, William Couper boasted, would 'dispense paraffined-paper cups at one cent each'. There were hot-water radiators, and fans to expel noxious fumes and admit fresh air. The ladies' waiting room had a matron on duty (although, unlike at the Grand Midland Hotel at London's St Pancras Station, women were not provided with their own smoking room), while in the gentlemen's changing room were toilet facilities complete with towels and silver-handled whisks. 'A boon to the commuter are the luxurious pay toilets' trilled Couper in 1912; fifty years later Ken Macrorie, eyeing the thirty white marble urinals, could not but agree, declaring that 'One feels important going to the toilet here'. The Travelers' Aid Society maintained an office in the station for the 'bewildered', while, for the 'distressed', the Corinthian room dispensed tea from silver pots. There was also a 'thoroughly equipped emergency hospital with attendant physician'.[21]

The design of the station even provided facilities for

the bereaved. Private rooms were designated for the sole use of funeral parties, who were thus able to await trains away from the bustle of the waiting rooms. To aid the speedy departure of the departed, technology was once again enlisted in order that the coffin could be transported as quickly and as silently as possible – six electric funeral trucks being provided by the PRR specifically for this purpose. Upstairs, much of the fourth floor of the building was given over to facilities for the railroad employees. All of the 8th Avenue frontage at attic level was fitted up for the PRR's very own YMCA, and equipped with assembly hall, lecture rooms, library, billiard room, bowling alley and gym. Few institutions, let alone railway stations, could boast such an impressive array of employee comforts.

Penn Station opened on 8 September 1910 to a rapturous welcome. Couper's official history proudly announced Penn to be 'the largest building in the world constructed at one time' – the giant scale of the interiors allowing for 'no audible evidence of the hastening throngs seen all around us'. *Scientific American* suggested that the station was 'so spacious, that it could contain, bodily, the New York City Hall';[22] the *New York Architect* called it 'a lasting monument worthy of a great city of which it was to form the western gateway';[23] while the *American Architect* enthusiastically noted both that it was 'a wide departure from the conventional railway station' (lacking 'turrets and towers and … the lofty arched train shed') as well as being 'unique among all the railway stations of the world in the number and convenience of its entrances and exits'.[24]

McKim's first biographer, Alfred Granger, was more rhapsodic about what was in 1913 still the largest

An early photograph of Penn Station, below, showing the point of entry from the western carriageway. Foot passengers from 31st Street walked over the bridge.

railway station in the world. Constituting 'a perpetual gateway to a great modern city', the station's timeless qualities of 'calmness, order, beauty' were, he declared, characteristics that 'the civilization of tomorrow demands'. The great waiting room, with its 'supreme beauty of line and function', was just as important as the concourse, which Granger likened to 'the lean, lithe frame of a young athlete stripped of every ounce of superfluous flesh'. On entering the station, he noted, 'instinctively one lowers one's voice as one takes in slowly the intense beauty'.[25]

Twenty years later Thomas Wolfe enlarged on this observation in *You Can't Go Home Again*. Wolfe's hero George Webber was captivated by what he beheld once inside the Great Waiting Room:

Great, slant beams of moted light fell ponderously athwart the station's floor, and the calm voice of time hovered along the walls and ceiling of that mighty room, distilled out of the voices and movements of the people who swarmed beneath. It had the murmur of a distant sea… It was elemental, detached, indifferent to the lives of men.[26]

The interior which Wolfe beheld, however, was not quite as empty as he implied. In 1929 a most unlikely addition had been made to the great waiting room: a Ford Trimotor aeroplane, which Amelia Earhart had christened the *City of New York*. The Trimotor was designed to publicize the air–rail service that Transcontinental Air Transport had recently inaugurated between New York and California, in which the PRR had invested. Unlikely as it may seem, the railroad was crucial to the operation of this new service. Passengers travelling from New York to Los Angeles actually took the train from Penn Station to Columbus, Ohio, where they finally boarded a plane. (The Trimotor could not fly over mountain ranges, and yet another rail journey was necessary before the second plane touched down in California.) In 1930

TAT was sold to Western Air Express – later to metamorphose into TWA – and the PRR's shares were sold. However, the Trimotor lingered on in the waiting room. In the late 1930s William Faulkner saw it there, 'motionless, squatting, with a still, beetling look like a huge bug preserved in alcohol'.[27]

During the 1930s Penn Station was being used by over 170 million passengers a year, with nearly 3,000 PRR employees to serve them, including 76 ticket clerks and 355 redcaps to carry baggage. From Penn ran some of the most celebrated and glamorous trains in the world: the *Crescent* to New Orleans, the *Havana Special* to Miami and the *Florida Keys*, and, most famous of all, the *Broadway Limited*, which carried the illustrious and the hopeful to Chicago, Los Angeles – and Hollywood. The *Broadway Limited* competed fiercely for distinguished trade with the New York Central's *Twentieth Century Limited*, which ran from Grand Central.

'The largest and most monumental single room in the world today' – the cavernous General Waiting Room of Pennsylvania Station, opened in 1910, above. McKim's debt to the great public buildings of Imperial Rome is unmistakable. Opposite, looking out from the stone-clad public waiting areas into the steel-and-glass concourse, shown below and overleaf. The concourse's unadorned steel arches appear to spring almost organically from the upright, trunk-like supports. Not only the structure but also the contents of the great British glasshouses of the 1840s and 50s are immediately recalled.

THE APOGEE OF THE RAILWAY AGE

During the Second World War Penn worked to full capacity. In the harsh light of peacetime, however, the terminus became increasingly viewed by its owners as a missed chance for increased revenue. In 1956 a brand-new oval ticketing counter was inserted into the middle of the great waiting room. Designed by architect Lester C Tichy in the guise of an airline facility the steel and aluminium canopy was suspended from McKim's wall colonnade, while the addition necessitated the demolition of the gentlemen's and ladies' waiting rooms.

The new ticketing counter was the beginning of the end for Penn Station. In May 1960 the railroad told its stockholders that the station operated at a $1.5 million annual loss, and that it was thus financially imperative to develop the site's air rights. And on 21 July 1961 the PRR published its new plans in the *New York Times*, unveiling its scheme for a resited Madison Square Garden sports and entertainment centre – 25 per cent of which would be owned by the railroad – while glossing over the demolition of the Beaux-Arts station.

The following year, leading modern architects formed the Action Group for Better Architecture for New York (AGBANY), specifically to save Penn Station. A station rally of 2 August 1962 persuaded New York City Mayor Robert F Wagner to meet the movement's leaders, who pleaded with him to persuade his new Landmarks Preservation Commission to save the station. However, financial muscle ultimately prevailed. Even as AGBANY representatives were talking to Mayor Wagner, the Madison Square Garden Corporation was beginning to rent office space in the proposed new development, lamely suggesting that eighteen of McKim's granite columns from the facade be resited in run-down Battery Park or in Central Park. To no-one's surprise, Wagner dismissed the objections and gave the go-ahead for the station's destruction.

On 29 October 1963 Adolph Weinmann's 5,700-pound stone eagles were lowered from the 7th Avenue entablature of Penn Station, and by July 1966 little trace remained above ground of the original building; the only physical reminders were two stone eagles, now placed incongruously in front of the dismally uninspired Madison Square Garden complex which rose above the equally mediocre subterranean station.

Thankfully, New York City still possesses one world-class railway terminus from the Beaux-Arts era: Grand Central. As early as 1911 it was already being hailed as 'the greatest railway station in the world'; more recently, it has been declared to have 'shaped the destiny of Manhattan' and to have constituted 'the foundation of a positive and optimistic urban

philosophy which is one of New York's greatest contributions to twentieth-century life'.[28]

Certainly few stations have been the subject of, or the backdrop to, so many films, articles and books. Grand Central's numerous movie credits run from *The Grand Central Murder* of 1942 (in which Van Heflin investigates an actress's murder at the terminus) to the celebrated concourse waltzing scene in Lawrence Kasdan's *The Fisher King* of 1986. It has also always been central to the life of the city. By 1946 the station's biographer David Marshall was calling the complex 'the unofficial Community Hall of New York';[29] even today the concourse clock remains New York City's most renowned meeting place.

The first station on the site was built in 1871 by John B Snook for the great railway magnate Cornelius Vanderbilt, who had bought the New York Central Railroad (NYC) four years previously. The station's enlargement in 1898–1900, when a new facade and three new storeys were added, only served to postpone large-scale redevelopment. Between 1890 and 1910 passenger volumes on the NYC doubled.

The station's rebuilding was hastened by the City's decision to electrify both the existing NYC line, and the PRR's planned east–west crossing of Manhattan, announced in May 1903. The idea of electrification

Penn Station's spartan arrivals concourse was designed explicitly to keep incoming passengers separate from those buying tickets and boarding trains, by providing the former with exits directly on to street level. Opposite, Raymond Loewy's photomural of 1945, featuring Pennsylvania Railroad staff who were helping the war effort, either directly or indirectly. The fluorescent flag over the entrance to the concourse was 60 feet long and weighed 200 pounds. PRR posters of June 1944 supporting the war effort, right, and 'One Hundred Years of Transportation Progress', in 1946, above.

was seized on eagerly by the father of the new terminus, William J Wilgus. Wilgus had begun as a NYC draughtsman, and was now the system's Chief Engineer. He envisaged a station that, in the absence of steam locomotives, could exist on more than one level, passengers passing up and down as well as across the site. He planned a terminal that would cover 76 acres, rather than the present 23, and that rose 105 feet above ground level while burrowing 45 feet into the Manhattan bedrock. This was, moreover, not to be a stub-end terminus in the traditional sense. The tracks would continue past the arrival platforms in an underground loop which finished back at the departure tracks. (In the finished building, three out of the four tracks were used for incoming services in the morning rush hour; in the evening, this arrangement was reversed.) To the north of the station, Wilgus aimed to exploit the line's air rights. The streets were carried across the tracks by steel bridges as far as 97th Street; above ground Wilgus sold the recovered land in an effort to make a profit out of the whole enterprise, something that had not been achieved by the PRR's ambitious project.

In January 1903 the NYC announced that an architectural competition would be held for the design of the new electrified terminal. Four firms were shortlisted: McKim, Mead and White of New York; D H Burnham and Co of Chicago; Samuel Huckel Jr of Philadelphia; and Reed and Stem of St Paul. McKim, Mead and White's position at the head of the American

Beaux-Arts movement was well known, and McKim had already been asked to submit proposals for nearby Penn Station. The firm's scheme for Grand Central involved a fourteen-storey terminal and a sixty-storey tower which, if executed, would have been the tallest building in the world. Burnham was also widely tipped for success, being the author of the station for the 1893 Chicago World's Fair – a design, based on the Baths of Caracalla, which was to heavily influence the Beaux-Arts termini of the early twentieth century – and the architect currently responsible for the erection of the vast new station of Washington Union. (Burnham's Grand Central design has been lost, so it is impossible to determine its resemblance to Washington.) And while Reed and Stem were already employed on small commissions by the NYC, Samuel Huckel was the architect who had remodelled the interior of the old Grand Central in 1900.

In the event it was Charles Reed and Allen Stem who were judged the winners, a victory which perhaps owed as much to the fact that Reed was Wilgus's brother-in-law as to their scheme's superiority. The competition-winning design featured a massive hotel block and, most unusually, an elevated roadway (which they called a 'circumferential plaza') built around the site, to unlock the 42nd Street bottleneck. To the north was a grand 'court of honor' in the manner of the 1893 Chicago World's Fair, with Beaux-Arts blocks grouped on both sides of a vastly widened Park Avenue, very much in the manner of Imperial Rome.

Reed and Stem's euphoria was short-lived. Hardly had the ink dried on the contract than, in February 1904, the firm were told that they would have to work with a practice that was not even on the competition shortlist: Warren and Wetmore. Once again, family connections were to blame. The ebullient Whitney Warren was a cousin of William K Vanderbilt, and the Vanderbilts still controlled the NYC – whatever Wilgus might say. While Charles Wetmore was the firm's backroom lawyer, Warren was its driving force. Having studied and taught at the École des Beaux-Arts

Opposite, the view from Park Avenue today of Grand Central Station, New York, by Warren and Wetmore, Reed and Stem, 1911–13. While Warren's splendid Beaux-Arts façade appears crushed by the weight of the MetLife (formerly Pan-Am) Building above, it is fortunate to have survived at all. Top, a postcard view of the projected station of 1905, showing Reed and Stem's concept of an elevated roadway grafted on to Warren and Wetmore's design for the terminal itself. The view to the north was blocked off firstly by Warren and Wetmore's own New York Central Building (now the Helmsley Building) of 1928–30, and after 1959 by the monolithic Pan-Am Building. Detail of clock and Jules Alexis Coutan's Mercury above the triumphal arch, above.

Concourse, Grand Central I, 1996, by Bill Jacklin, right. The celebrated, four-faced brass clock in the centre of Grand Central's main concourse, below. Opposite, beams of sunlight from the clerestory lunettes illuminate the main concourse of Grand Central in the late 1940s. Twenty years later this magnificent interior narrowly escaped destruction at the hands of the railroad's developers.

for almost ten years after 1884, he had come to the notice of New York with his adventurous design for the New York Yacht Club of 1899. A devotee of the Beaux-Arts manner, he was in 1895 one of the founders of America's counterpart to his beloved École, the Society of Beaux-Arts Architects (more prosaically renamed the Beaux-Arts Institute of Design in 1911), and in 1913 he instituted the annual Beaux-Arts Ball, devised to raise funds for scholarships to the Paris École. It was Warren's arrogance which led him to use his family connections to muscle in on the Grand Central competition; as he was well known as an amateur boxer as well as an excellent swimmer, few would argue.

Warren and Wetmore's alternative scheme, the final version of which centred on a twenty-two-storey building, was entirely different from Reed and Stem's competition winner. Nevertheless, it became the basis for the executed station, with only the elevated driveway being retained from Reed and Stem's concept. Unsurprisingly, relations between the two firms were very tense. And things deteriorated even further when, only four days after the death of Charles Reed on 12 November 1911, Whitney Warren persuaded the NYC to issue a new contract giving his firm sole control over the project. When Grand Central opened two years later, it was presented to the public and even to fellow-professionals merely as a Warren and Wetmore design. Belatedly, in July 1916, Allen Stem sued Warren and Wetmore – not for the besmirching of his firm's good name, but for the loss of fees. As a result of the action, Whitney Warren was expelled from the American Institute of Architects in 1920, and despite two appeals was, in 1922, ordered to pay Stem $400,000 in compensation.

Work had begun on extending the site as early as 1903. However, the completed station was not opened until ten years later. Work was delayed not only by the architects' disputes over responsibility; unlike at the brand-new Pennsylvania terminal, the network's existing train services also had to be accommodated during the works. As at Penn Station, however, the redevelopment of the site involved the demolition of numerous buildings, including over two hundred 'time-worn and smoke-stained churches, hospitals and stores', as Wilgus happily announced in 1907.[30]

Astonishingly, the unhappy fusion of two entirely different schemes from two different practices still managed to produce a stunning building. The exterior was pure Beaux-Arts, and pure Warren. On the north

THE APOGEE OF THE RAILWAY AGE

facade was a Roman triumphal arch, symbolizing the station's role as the gateway to the city; to the south, paired Corinthian columns in Connecticut granite framed three vast arched windows. Above the entablature of the latter was a large, 1,500-ton and 60-foot-wide sculptural group in Bedford limestone by Jules-Alexis Coutan, above a vast clock (behind each of whose numbers was a small window, to allow for easy maintenance).

Inside the station, the ancient world was harnessed to modern science in typical Beaux-Arts fashion. Whereas the Roman Empire had made use of ramps to elevate chariots, at Grand Central they were employed, in place of stairs, to move vast crowds. Where the stone-lined tunnels at Rome's Colosseum were designed to act as the conduits for spectators eager for entertainment, at Grand Central the throngs came to worship at an entirely different shrine, one which would get them to the office, or home, in the shortest possible time. In a suitably practical update of Roman practice, the concourse – 120 feet by 375 feet, and 125 feet high ('higher than the cathedral of St John the Divine' as the publicists boasted) – was sheathed, not in travertine, but below the dado in Tennessee marble and, above, washable reconstituted 'Caen stone', applied in inch-thick wide boards. Like the great baths of ancient Rome, the room was lit at both ends by vast lunette windows. In contrast to Penn, however, no glimpse of the building's steel frame was allowed to be seen, so as to preserve the outward impression of a great Roman monument or an eighteenth-century Neoclassical fantasy.

In general, the planning of the interior at Grand Central was easier to comprehend than that of Penn. Slap in the middle of the concourse was the four-faced golden clock – one of seventy-five clocks in the whole complex – under which, entirely logically and instantly visible, was the information booth. All the ticket windows and baggage facilities were concentrated around the concourse perimeter, leaving the adjoining main waiting room a much quieter area. At one end of the concourse was a grand double stair (recalling Charles Garnier's equally dramatic sweep at the Paris Opera), leading to offices and smaller waiting rooms via the 'kissing gallery' where people waited to meet incoming travellers. Above all of this hung the suspended plaster ceiling, painted by the French portrait painter Paul Helleu. This was a representation of the night sky, in which the major stars were lit by light bulbs and 2,500 others were picked out in gold leaf. Helleu had, appropriately, sprung to fame

through his depiction of one of the most famous members of the family which owned the NYC: Consuelo Vanderbilt, society beauty and ninth Duchess of Marlborough. At Grand Central, however, he appears to have been rather overcome by the enormity of the commission, and painted the winter night sky of his native France (and not that of New York), and that back to front.

Down below, underneath the low exit concourse, crouched the oyster bar. Its shallow vaults were lined in the revolutionary manner of the Catalan designer Raphael Guastavino, cream-coloured tiles lining an ultra-thin, steel-supported plaster shell. This oasis was subsequently made famous throughout the city by the enthusiasm of its flamboyant first manager, Slovakian-born Viktor Yesensky, who ran the restaurant from 1913 until his retirement in 1946. Today the bar is as

Grand Central's famous Oyster Bar, above. The flat, arched vaults are still lined with the same Guastavino tiles in place when the restaurant opened in 1913. By the year 2000 this mecca for seafood-lovers, currently isolated in the gloomy, under-used lower concourse, will be surrounded by a wide variety of other shops and restaurants. Opposite, escalators from the Met Life Building arrive at the main concourse. The gallery above is to reopen in 1998, with its stunning, egg-shaped light fittings of nickel and brass beautifully restored by Beyer Blinder Belle.

popular and lively as ever, a key element in the life of thousands of New Yorkers.

Outside the oyster bar little of the station's original interior decoration survives. Most of the wall decoration was thoughtlessly overpainted in the 1950s; the only Edward Trumbull mural to survive, of 1931, can be found in the exit passageway to Lexington Avenue, and features appropriate transport imagery. What does remain, however, are the constant reminders of the Vanderbilt family. Carvings of the three acorns and oak leaves from the family arms (inevitably embellished with the familiar motto, 'Great oaks from little acorns grow') can be found above the entrances to the lower level tracks and the stairs to the upper floor offices. In case these references were too subtle, in 1929 the bronze statue of Commodore Vanderbilt (originally cast in 1869, and formerly adorning the St John's Park freight station) was moved to the centre of the south facade.

The Vanderbilts' new terminus was opened with little formality on 12 February 1913. (The first large-scale party to be held under its echoing vaults was, unfortunately for posterity, a party for Kaiser Wilhelm II.) On the day of the opening the NYC took out a full-page advertisement in *Harper's Weekly* declaring Grand Central to be 'the greatest civic development ever undertaken', while the *New York Times* applauded the terminus as 'a thing of convenience as well as of size and beauty' and Edward Hungerford declared in the *Outlook* that the reliance on ramps rather than stairs 'is going to be a boon to invalids, a paradise to a tired man with arms filled with packages or baggage'.

Not everything worked perfectly. Within ten years fungi had grown on the poorly ventilated ceiling; in 1944 this was finally opened up, lined with asbestos and replastered and painted. Above ground, however, everything went as Wilgus had planned. The Biltmore Hotel (named after the Vanderbilts' vast North Carolina mansion) was erected over the arrivals area, and the Commodore Hotel over the loop tracks to the southeast. By the mid-1920s all of the available air rights had been sold over the tracks between 42nd and 52nd Streets, making Park Avenue the most prestigious residential area in Central Manhattan. Grand Central had become, in the words of one academic, 'the generator of a vast concentration of new urban development'.[31]

In 1929 the concourse's 'kissing gallery', the east balcony, became the setting for a display of the first plane to fly the Atlantic westwards, the German machine *Bremen*. (After 1945 this was replaced by a replica of the NYC's first locomotive, the *DeWitt Clinton*.) More importantly, Grand Central had

The New York Central Railroad. As Lorraine Diehl has noted 'The [NYC's] *Broadway Limited* was an all-Pullman train with no inexpensive coaches, consisting of sleeping and parlor cars staffed by a barber and a stenographer in addition to a piano player in the observation lounge. It was the train of presidents and kings and of movie stars …'

Trains such as the *Twentieth Century Limited*, which took a mere 16 hours to reach Chicago, lent sophistication to the NYC and its New York terminal. The *Limited*, pictured at the La Salle Street Depot, above left, and on a matchbook cover, above. Opposite, above, a poster from 1941 depicts a couple embarking on a romantic trip on the train; and an earlier version from the 1920s shows off glamorous passengers. A chef of the 1920s is seen at work in his galley of a Baltimore and Ohio train, opposite, above left.

become the social focus of Midtown Manhattan. Fund-raising events were held here; politicians addressed large crowds here; and, after December 1941, war rallies were conducted here. The station even had its own, thirty-three-man orchestra of redcaps, who played both in the concourse and waiting room and at engagements throughout the city. The Second World War brought some material alterations: the large windows were painted over for the blackout (in case the Germans were able to bomb Grand Central). Yet sufficient illumination still streamed in from the vast clerestory windows.

After the war, Grand Central was targeted along with Penn Station by those who wished to see these station sites used 'more profitably'. In 1954 two proposals surfaced, both involving the introduction of a tower of over eighty storeys immediately to the north of the concourse. These were submitted by William Zenckendorf (his project architect the young I M Pei) and by Alfred Fellheimer and Stewart Wagner – ironically, the successor to Reed and Stem. (After Stem's 1922 victory over Whitney Warren, he had entered into partnership with Alfred Fellheimer.) As was to be the case at Penn, though, an impressive array of modern architectural talent, including Serge

Chermayeff and Philip Johnson, joined in protest against this proposed mutilation. In an open letter to the NYC in *Architectural Forum*, this group of architects argued that the Grand Central concourse was not only 'probably the finest big room in New York' but also exerted an appeal which 'recognises the top limit of sophistication, no bottom limit … [from] the most exacting architectural critic [to] the newsboy at the door'.[32]

The official response was predictable. The architect L L Rado (not quite such a household name as Chermayeff or Saarinen) replied with the Modernist mantra that: 'You cannot stop progress for sentimental reasons.'[33] ('Grand Central', he declared with the confidence of a less-than-experienced practitioner, 'is not a cultural or historic treasure.') Alfred Fellheimer condescendingly argued that the forty-year-old station had 'become an obstacle to the attainment of important public objectives',[34] namely easing traffic flow and increasing office accommodation. Yale professor Carroll Meeks, on the other hand, snorted that Fellheimer's argument was complete nonsense, and that 'a more utilitarian transfer point can never achieve its uniquely successful blend of efficiency and civic dignity'.[35]

Thanks to the efforts of its many supporters, and the lacklustre schemes of the NYC, Grand Central was saved – but at a cost. In 1958 Ervin Wolfson unveiled a new variation on the Zenckendorf/Fellheimer tower-block concept, which Emery Roth had worked up with the help of Pietro Belluschi and no less an authority than Walter Gropius. Faced with such a glittering array of big names, and the perceived need to gain some additional revenue from the site, the railroad and the city capitulated. The result was that a fifty-nine-storey tower, subsequently known as the Pan-Am Building after its first owner, scythed through the north side of the complex, preventing easy movement to 45th Street and crushing the handsome, Beaux-Arts facade beneath a featureless monolith. In 1907 Wilgus had claimed that a barrel pushed from any of Grand Central's ramped street entrances would roll easily and directly down to the main concourse. The Pan-Am Building ended all that, since some of the northern exits were now permanently closed.

To the developers the Pan-Am Building was merely a foot in the door. By 1968 Marcel Breuer had been commissioned by British developer Morris Saady to design a vast, Mies-like tower, higher than Wolfson's block, that would have obliterated the station's southern facade and whose foundations were designed either to separate the main concourse from the main waiting room or to be carried on pilotis over the demolished southern entrance. At best, the concourse interior would remain; at worst, the whole site would

be levelled. The vociferous journalist Ada Louise Huxtable was unambiguous about her response to this scheme: it would, she wrote in her *New York Times* column, result in 'a huge sandwich board' comprising the 'waffle-faced slab of the Breuer building and the existing Pan-Am tower, with Grand Central trampled underfoot'. This would, she declared, be 'like a slap in the eye' to the city.[36]

Breuer's scheme was not immediately executed, but this did not mean that Grand Central would not go the way of Penn Station. Redevelopment seemed imminent after 1972, when Penn Central – the result of the 1968 merger of the NYC and the PRR – went bankrupt. New York City declared the terminal a landmark; yet Penn Central repeatedly appealed against this designation, arguing that the decision was unconstitutional and was deliberately preventing an economically viable scheme from being built. In 1975 the State Supreme Court Justice, Irving L Saypol, sensationally resolved in favour of Penn Central, overturning Grand Central's landmark status and allowing the planned mutilation to proceed.

The renewed threat to the terminus swiftly mobilised New York's 'Great and Good'. Jackie Kennedy Onassis and Senator Daniel Moynihan publicly joined the growing campaign to save the station, inaugurated by the Municipal Arts Society of New York. And with their help, the battle went all the way to the top. In 1978, ten years after Breuer's scheme was first suggested, the US Supreme Court ruled that the city's landmark designation was, after all, wholly constitutional, and that the station did enjoy legal protection. Since then, the station has never looked back. In Ada Huxtable's words, Grand Central continues to be 'part of the city's essential image and remaining elegance' while representing 'one of the most stunning achievements in the history of urban design'. In February 1988 Metro-North (who in 1983 had taken over the former Penn Central lines, operated since 1976 by the Consolidated Rail Corporation) celebrated Grand Central's Diamond Jubilee, issuing a special commemorative brochure for the occasion. Today, although the station is served by a fraction of the train service of fifty years ago, the historic terminal is thriving. The concourse is always busy; New Yorkers still meet by the central clock; and the oyster bar is always full and animated. You lose some, you win some.

The third station in the triumvirate of the great American Beaux-Arts stations of the early twentieth century was Washington Union. It, too, has survived – though only just. Built in 1903–7 by D H Burnham and Co, and jointly owned by the PRR and the Baltimore and Ohio, it was built on a greenfield site chosen by a

The Beaux-Arts sprawl of D-H Burnham's vast, hunched Washington Union station, 1903–7, above, nearly helped to contribute to its demise in the 1960s. However, the possibilities afforded by its echoing, dignified Neoclassical interiors were exploited in two wholly different rejuvenation schemes of the 1970s and 80s. Today the magnificent concourse, below and opposite, houses a vast shopping mall.

The Columbus fountain by
Lorado Z Taft stands in front of
Union Station, *c*1920. Below,
Washington Union's General
Waiting Room, with its
appropriately antique coffering
and Tuscan screen, in the 1920s.

D H Burnham's death in 1912, at
an early stage of the scheme for
Chicago Union may have been
the reason why this vast, bulky
building of 1916–25 lacked the
accustomed brio of the Beaux-
Arts pioneer's 'Burnham
Baroque' style. While the
exterior is rather ungainly and
uninspired, however, the
concourse, below, is, along with
New York's Grand Central, one
of the most frequently-filmed of
all American public interiors. Its
recent screen credits include
movies, TV soaps and
documentaries, from *The
Untouchables* to *ER*.

committee which included Charles McKim and Daniel
Burnham (1846–1912). Externally, its 120-foot long,
three-arched entrance block, with its long, low wings
(making the whole main facade 650 feet long) was
couched in a typical, if rather unexciting, Beaux-Arts
manner. Sculptural groups were added by Louis St
Gaudens and Lorado Taft to make the whole
composition suitably majestic for the nation's capital.
Their statues depicted appropriately industrial or
American subjects: Fire, Electricity, Freedom,
Imagination, Agriculture and Mechanics; inside, to
reinforce the Beaux-Arts imagery, Roman legionnaires
were placed over the main entrance to the concourse.

The main doorway led, via a vestibule, to the general
waiting room. Measuring 220 feet by 130 feet, with a
coffered barrel vault in the manner of the Baths of
Diocletian, the room was, like that at Penn, lit at either
end by a giant lunette window. To the east of the
general waiting room was a large dining room, able to
seat 1,000 diners, plus a lunch room, women's room
and offices. There was even a separate suite for the
president, which could also be used by senior
government officials and visiting dignitaries and which

had its own exit to the train concourse. To the west were the ticket lobby, smoking room, luggage room and the carriage porch. As at Penn, there was also a waiting room for funeral parties. The concourse, a vast area of 130 feet by 760 feet with a plain, simply-vaulted ceiling, was said by Richardson in 1912 to be 'the largest room devoted to any purpose in the world'. Burnham himself boasted that the station was 'superior to any structure ever created for [a] railway purpose'.[37]

By the 1960s Washington Union, like so many American railway terminals, was threatened with demolition – despite being declared a National Landmark as early as 1964, in the wake of Penn

Station's controversial destruction. As Madison Square Garden was opened in 1968, salvation came for Burnham's Washington Union, in the form of a congressional resolution that the station was to be converted into a National Visitors' Centre.

Work on this grand project finally began in 1973, just as the Watergate scandal was breaking, and was completed in time for the Bicentennial celebrations of July 1976. Yet the conversion had ruthlessly expunged much of Burnham's fine interior. As David Morton wrote in *Progressive Architecture* in November 1977, 'we can be grateful that Union Station has been saved'; nevertheless, what had seemed such a good idea in the late 1960s had plainly 'turned sour in the 1970s'. Shortly before Morton's article appeared, Amtrak abandoned what was left of the station; three years later the whole complex, its roof leaking badly, was shut.

This could easily have been the end of the station. In 1981, however, the Reagan administration promised funding for restoration, on condition that the bulk of the site be used for retail purposes. Washington Union was thus transformed into the quintessential 80s building type: the shopping mall. The $150-million conversion, planned and executed by Harry Weese and Associates and by Benjamin Thompson and Associates, was completed in 1988.

Today the station houses 210,000 square feet of retail space on three levels, with over one hundred shop units. There is, incidentally, also a small Amtrak station within the complex (with trains serving Philadelphia, New York and the Northeast Corridor and, less frequently, New Orleans and the Deep South), and an even newer Metro station. Washington Union is not what it was; but it is more than just a fading memory or a sepia photograph. It is still the setting for great events: most recently, the station's Presidential Suite held Margaret Thatcher's $1,000-a-plate seventieth-birthday banquet. How appropriate that one of the principal begetters of the consumer culture of the 1980s should dine in the midst of one of the world's biggest shopping malls.

The Beaux-Arts architecture of Penn, Grand Central and Washington was a great influence on the development of the railway terminal in North America. In 1914, for example, work began on a new Union Station for Toronto, jointly owned by the Canadian Pacific and the Grand Trunk (Canadian National Railways after 1919). Three firms of architects collaborated on what became a Beaux-Arts behemoth: Ross and MacDonald, Hugh G Jones, and John M Lyle. The end product of their efforts was a vast, highly repetitious limestone facade (its planned sculptures were never executed) masking a set of

A dispute between the two major railroads and the city meant that Toronto Union by Ross and MacDonald, Hugh G Jones, and John M Lyle, of 1914–19, opposite above, did not open until 1927, long after its American Beaux-Arts cousins. Here the Telegraph office is shown soon after the visit of King George VI of May 1939, opposite below. A 1947 poster for the Chicago and Northwestern Railway, right.

JUNE 29, 1947

CHICAGO AND NORTH WESTERN SYSTEM

SF-1

400

Serves the

WEST, NORTHWEST PACIFIC COAST NORTH WESTERN UNION PACIFIC

The Overland Route

The disastrous Dieppe raid of 1942 had already been a reminder to those seeing off their loved ones from Toronto Union that many would not be coming back.

In 1968 – that *annus horribilis* for the great railway station – the CPR and CNR jointly announced that they intended to completely redevelop the site. In 1969 they unveiled the details of their proposed scheme: the station was to be replaced with, unsurprisingly, a high-rise tower block, designed by Hugh Taylor. Reassuringly, though, the scheme encountered unexpected resistance and was dropped. Toronto Union thus survives as one of the few Beaux-Arts monuments in modern Canada. Like Washington Union, it now houses a shopping mall, although there is still a reduced railway service. Yet there remains enough of the old station's atmosphere to remind visitors of a time of optimism and power, when North America truly believed in the importance of the railways, and when the great Beaux-Arts stations were widely regarded as the building type best suited to embodying the lofty aspirations of the new century.

interiors which owed much to the great United States termini of the preceding decade. Its Beaux-Arts pedigree was unmistakable. The 757-foot long main front was provided with a monotonous, pseudo-Doric colonnade taken from the ancient Temple of Apollo at Delos, and was surmounted by a tripartite attic, as at Penn. The great hall – 250 feet by 84 feet, its ceiling vaulted with vitrified Guastavino tiles and its walls lined with artificial 'Zumbro stone' from Missouri – was closely based on academic recreations of the central hall at the Roman Baths of Caracalla. (The same coffered ceiling vault and giant lunette windows had already been used by Ross and MacDonald for the waiting room at their Ottawa Union of 1908 and 1912.)

Toronto Union was completed in 1919, but due to a protracted dispute over whether the railways or the city should pay for the new viaduct carrying the lines into the new station, it did not actually open until eight years later. Even then, the occasion was less than auspicious. On 6 August 1927 the Prince of Wales, watched in some embarrassment by the prime ministers of both Britain and Canada, took exactly eleven minutes to tour the station before he abruptly left, clearly having better things to attend to.

Despite this ignominious beginning, Toronto Union was heavily used, and during the 1930s became one of the principal entry points for immigrants to Canada. (The flow of these crowds was eased by the provision of a separate basement concourse for incoming passengers, along the lines of those at Penn and Grand Central.) As late as 1961 *The Times* observed that throngs of European refugees and immigrants still used the station: 'Laden with bulging suitcases and holding small fretful children, they wait bewildered and apprehensive as a large crowd of friends and relatives … scan the faces of the new arrivals'.[38]

Toronto was also a major centre of activity in the Second World War. Cleric Dr Peter Bryce observed the comings and goings there during October 1943:

TOWARDS A NEW CENTURY OF TRAVEL
EXPRESSIONISM

'A microcity that embraces a great multiplicity of elements divided
between those introduced for comfort and convenience of passengers on
one hand and those essential to the movement of trains and servicing of
cars on the other'.[1]
CARL CONDIT on the great railway terminus, 1977.

As the twentieth century progressed, some railway
companies began to commission designs that were not
looking backwards to the revivalism and eclecticism of
the past century, nor to the lessons of the ancient
world, but which looked forward to a new era, to a new
Railway Age. The architecture of many of the great
stations of the new century, while inevitably
incorporating some of the more characteristic and
familiar aspects of station design, and while never
entirely free of historical associations, sought to
associate itself more with the new technology of the
day rather than with outmoded concepts of style and
form. Some also sought to use the terminus's central
place in the city's consciousness to make a political
statement relevant to a world that had, by 1918, seen
its borders, institutions and presumptions
comprehensively altered.

Nowhere was railway station design used to express
a political movement and a national awakening more
clearly than in turn-of-the-century Finland. Here the
principal railway terminal of the country's capital was
devised not only to be an unmistakable symbol of the
new century, but to represent in stone and iron the
Finns' desire for independence from the Russian
imperialist yoke. The fact that both the design of the
station and the quest for independence had, by the end
of the First World War, proved highly successful was
not lost on contemporary observers.

While Finland's cultural links were traditionally
with the neighbouring Swedes – during the nineteenth
century most educated Finns still spoke Swedish as
their first language – since 1809 the country had been
placed under Russian rule. For the next ninety years it
was administered as an autonomous grand duchy; after
the succession of the ill-fated Tsar Nicholas II in 1894,
however, things rapidly deteriorated. In 1898 the Tsar,

Eliel Saarinen's distinctly Nordic
lantern-bearers at Helsinki
Station appeared to grow out of
the stone itself – a device
subsequently used by Stacchini
at Milan Central. These figures
constituted the only sculptural
decoration on the executed
station; the rather quaint frogs
and bears that adorned his
designs of 1904 and 1906 were
soon swept away.

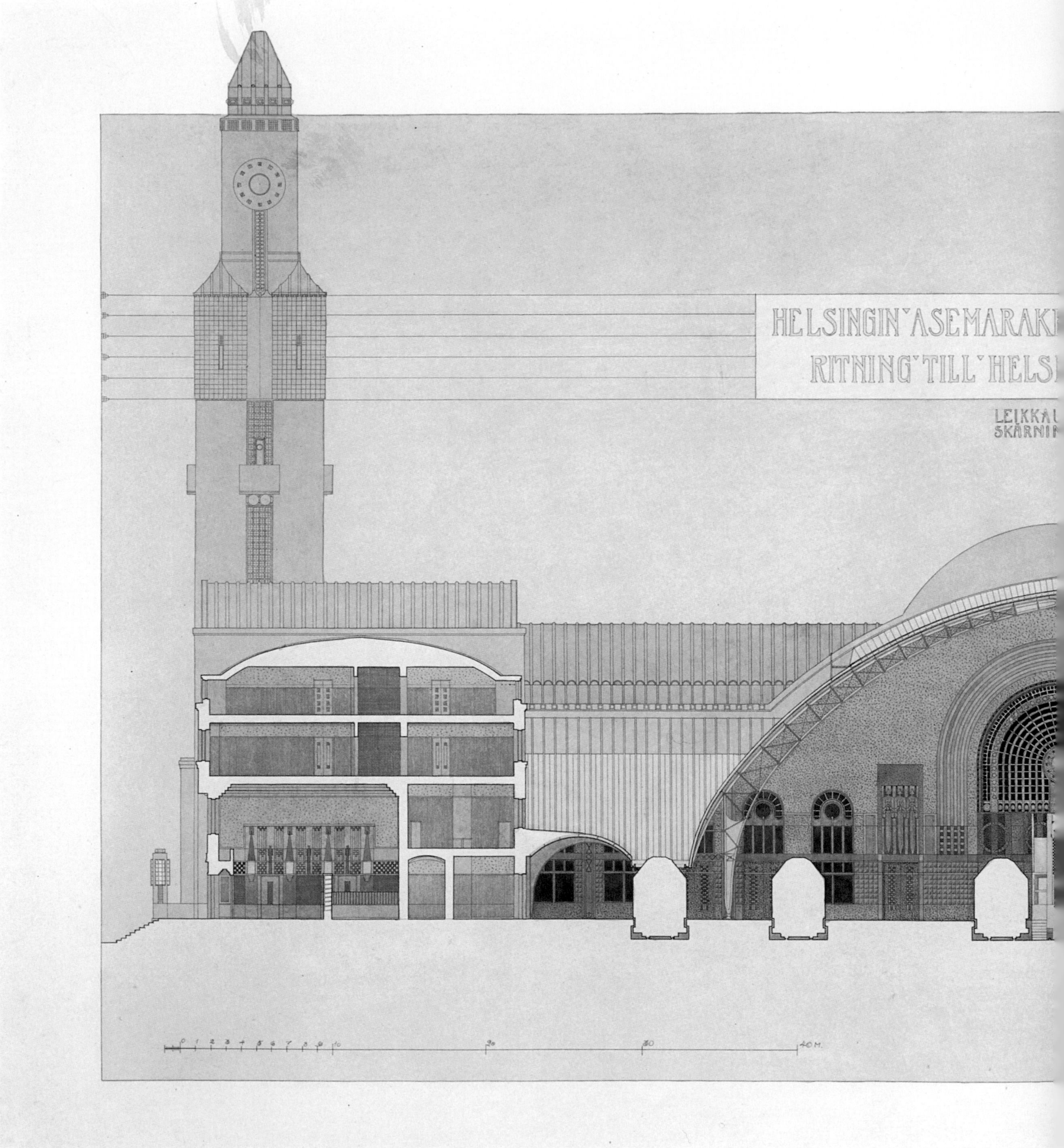
HELSINGIN ASEMARAKE
RITNING TILL HELS
LEIKKAU
SKÄRNIN
0 1 2 3 4 5 6 7 8 9 10
20
30
40 M.

KSEN' PIIRUSTUS

RS' BANGÄRD

Gesellius, Saarinen and Lindgren's competition design of 1904, opposite, was a natural precursor of Saarinen's bold, forward-looking station of 1910–14. However, the clean lines and ribbed arches of the executed building owe much to Gesellius' personal input.

Saarinen incorporated two of the most familiar symbols of station architecture in his design: the entrance archway and the clock tower. However, both motifs were reinterpreted in strikingly new ways. The arched window was given the plainest of reeded frames and underscored by a massive, slab-like canopy, while the tight massing of the tower and the ribbed supports of the dining room, below, looked forward to the Art Deco forms of the 1920s and 30s.

with the lack of foresight and insight that was to characterize his career, ordered his brusque Governor-General, Nikolai Bobrikov, to Russify the grand duchy. The Finnish army was absorbed into the Russian armed forces, and by 1901 had ceased to exist, while by Nicholas II's decree of 15 February 1899 all autonomy for the country was quashed. Peaceful Finnish demonstrators turned in frustration to violence, and on 16 June 1904 Bobrikov was assassinated by a young official of the embryonic nationalist movement. Russia's disastrous performance in the Russo–Japanese War of 1904–5 led to a damaging general strike, which had soon spread to Finland, and to a rehearsal of the Revolution, all of which forced the Tsar to make concessions both in Russia and in Finland. Yet Nicholas still refused to learn; five years later his

solemn guarantee of Finnish autonomy was swiftly revoked, and Bobrikov's former chief of staff was appointed governor-general. The Finns' initial reply was to resort to symbolic protests; after all, they had no official standing army. The victory of many Finnish athletes in the Stockholm Olympics of 1912, for example, was exploited as a rallying point for nationalist feeling. More blatant, however, was the deliberate nationalist symbolism of Helsinki's new railway station of 1910–14.

The architect of this dramatic new building was himself a Finn. Born in East Finland, Eliel Saarinen (1873–1950) was well qualified to be the author of the country's architectural response to the imposition of Russian cultural values. Although he was sent to school in Central Finland, Saarinen was raised in Ingermanland, the area of the country which had always been ruled directly from St Petersburg.

In 1902 the Finnish Architects' Club's response to the worsening political situation was to announce a competition to revitalize one of the capital's most neglected central areas, adjacent to the old station. This initiative resulted in two potent symbols of Finnish self-assertion: the National Museum of 1902–11 and Helsinki Station of 1910–14. The firm that won both these commissions, Saarinen, Gesellius and Lindgren, had become a partnership as recently as 1896, and had made its name with the Finnish Pavilion at the Paris Exposition of 1900. While the National Museum was a team effort, however, the design of the station was largely left to Saarinen. He based his initial, competition-winning scheme on the far more radical, and far smaller, station at Viipuri that he and Herman Gesellius built in 1904. However, in contrast to the stark functionalism and Art Nouveau decoration of Viipuri (which succumbed to Russian bombing in the desperate Winter War of 1939–40), Saarinen's original proposal for Helsinki was far more consciously historicist. While Viipuri relied on simple shapes for its effect – the vast entrance arch, the stubby columns, the sinuously curving ribbed roof and, in particular, the progressive concrete vaulting by Talman Castrén – in his original design for the capital Saarinen took refuge in neomedievalism. A tall, square-sectioned granite campanile with tiny window openings and a spire (very similar to the tower at Saarinen's National Museum) rose above a central, arched entrance, flanked by two octagonal towers and preceded by a simplified Classical porte-cochere.

Saarinen's initial scheme was designed to encapsulate the new romantic nationalism then sweeping the country, to effectively provide an architectural counterpart to the new music of the nationalist Finnish composer Jean Sibelius. However, to some of the critics Saarinen's initial scheme was not muscular or bold enough for these revolutionary times.

Saarinen's Helsinki was evidently strongly influenced by his work with Herman Gesellius on the smaller but equally radical station at Viipuri, 1904–13. The ribbed roof, emphasised verticals, single entrance arch, and flanking twin pedestals topped with sculptural figures (in this case, Finnish bears) all presage the design of the capital's new terminus.

TOWARDS A NEW CENTURY OF TRAVEL

Compared with the brave lines of Viipuri, Helsinki Station's architecture seemed retrogressive and unassertive, its romanticism too unfocused and apolitical. The scheme's failings were ruthlessly advertised as part of a savage pamphlet attack by the architects Gustav Strengell and Sigurd Frosterus on the woolly historicism of national romanticism. To the authors, anything that did not reflect the machine technology of the Industrial Age in its outward form was unacceptable; designs that were truly functional, structurally authentic and that were designed 'from the inside out' were, they declared, the only way forward. Saarinen's station project, with its medieval towers and its half-comic sculptures of frogs and bears, was singled out for especial criticism – hardly surprising, given that Frosterus was a disappointed competition entrant.

Saarinen took this criticism to heart, and during the next five years substantially revised his design on the basis of first-hand experience of the latest German and British stations. The result was the station begun in 1910. Gone were the sculptures and the medievalism; in their place was a more futuristic terminus, asymmetrically-planned and clean-lined. Its well-emphasized vertical piers comprised no capitals or footings; its only concession to representative art was the inclusion of two immense lantern-bearers, holding vast globe lights, flanking the vast single entrance arch. (Saarinen had a liking for such semi-abstract human figures merging into the masonry; this in turn was an obvious influence on Stacchini's Milan Central of twenty years later.) The station still retained a tall tower, but one that was recognizably modern, rising in vertical shafts around an octagon to a multi-faceted dome and a massive, American-style clock.

Helsinki Station as executed clearly had nothing to do with Russian architecture, nor much to do with the nineteenth century. The design looked instead to Germany (a potential ally against the Russians) and to democratic America for inspiration in its transparent architectural protest against the stifling repression of the Romanovs. Its resemblance to the work of Peter Behrens and other contemporary Germans did not go unnoticed; in 1914 one of the first architectural historians to deal with the railway station type, Karl Osthaus, placed Helsinki Station 'firmly in the German sphere of interest'. As such, Saarinen's terminus was one of the first expressions of Finno-German friendship, which was to find direct expression in the 40,000 troops the German Empire sent to help the Finns in 1917. Only four years after the station was completed, Finland won its independence from Russia, the victorious Finnish General Mannerheim riding into Helsinki on 16 May 1918. Five years later

Saarinen left for the United States; looking at the clean American lines of his now-famous TWA terminus, this move should not have been hard to predict.

Disappointingly, owing to the cost constraints imposed by the outbreak of the European war in 1914 (and the fact that the Russian army immediately converted most of the station into a military hospital), the excellence of Saarinen's magnificent facade was never matched by its interior; the impressive vaulted spaces and the curved steel and glass train shed roof that he and Viipuri's engineer Castrén had planned were never executed. The great shed was instead replaced by what Meeks termed 'miserable wooden sheds over the platforms'. Yet Saarinen's station remains an evocative symbol of Finland's hard-won independence, and of the fervour for democratic self-determination that was sweeping the world in the early twentieth century.

Equally progressive stations were being built further south at the same time as Helsinki. August

Both interior, above, and exterior, top, of the mammoth Leipzig Hauptbahnhof, Germany, were couched in a severe neoclassical idiom. The bold, clean-limbed train shed at Stürzenacker's daring Karlsruhe station in Germany, 1908–13, below. 'The Comfortable Railroad journey' by Friede, 1935, opposite.

Paul Bonatz and F F Scholer took the stripped Classicism of Leipzig and Helsinki to its logical conclusion, arriving, in Stuttgart Hauptbahnhof of 1911–28, at a starkly functional head building which merely suggested, rather than included, Classical columns. Surrounds and other mouldings were eradicated wherever possible, as was any sculptural decoration, while the principal elevation was faced with unforgiving rubble-walling, below. The result was a brooding, rather sinister composition, opposite.

Stürzenacker's Karlsruhe Station of 1908–13 was remarkably different from the vast Neoclassical buildings which were the rule for most German railway companies. As at Saarinen and Gesellius's Viipuri, at Karlsruhe Stürzenacker made much use of reinforced concrete to construct his glazed, simply coffered concourse – a bare, echoing place that harked back to the utopian Neoclassical projects of the late eighteenth century. On the facade were none of the customary arches alluding to the train shed behind; instead, the elevation comprised a pointed gable end with two flanking square pavilions, the whole composition decorated not with figurative sculpture but with abstract patterns. The glazing in the centrepiece and the entrances was very simple; each opening was square-headed, not semicircular, and was given no emphasis or elaboration. 'Few stations of the period have shown more distinction', judged Meeks in 1957.[2]

In a similar vein was Karl Moser's Basle Station, begun in 1910 – the same year as Helsinki – and provided with a tall, blunt clock tower reminiscent of

Saarinen's executed design. Slightly different in conception, but equally forward-looking, was Paul Bonatz and F F Scholer's Stuttgart, begun in 1911 but not finished, due to the war and its chaotic aftermath, until 1928. Like that at nearby Karlsruhe, Stuttgart's facade eschewed round-headed arches, except for the single-arched window over the markedly plain entrance canopy; in contrast to Stürzenacker's almost Arts and Crafts composition, though, Bonatz and Scholer preferred unadorned, cube-like forms. The result lacked the grace and elegance of Karlsruhe, the architects appearing to have been overawed by the site's sheer size. With its plain elevations, its rubble walling and its complete lack of sculptural or incised decoration, it seemed almost painfully utilitarian. It was a building whose puritanical lines certainly appealed to the emerging Nazi party.

Stark functionalism characterized the other great German station begun before the First World War. Leipzig Hauptbahnhof, begun in 1909, was the largest station in Europe when it was finished in the dark days

Overleaf, at the Krupp Works at Essen, during the postwar years, locomotives were repaired and produced in the former munitions factories.
One of Berlin's many railway stations, Friedrichstrasse, 1920–26, by C T Brodführer, has strong Expressionist influences, in its detailing and the structure of its train shed.

of 1915. If it had been built in America, it would have been designated a Union station: six different railway companies ran services into the terminus (in which the states of Saxony and Prussia still retained separate ticket offices), which was partly paid for by the city of Leipzig and partly by the German state. The design, by Dresden architects Wilhelm Lossow (1852–1914) and Max Hans Kühne (b 1874), was produced for a competition of 1906. Its vast, blank facade, with suggestions of vestigial Classicism, fronted a train shed of reinforced concrete comprising six parallel spans, each 147 feet wide and divided by giant concrete arches. Yet this expression of the cult of the colossal was, like Stuttgart, not necessarily handsome. Even Meeks was disappointed that engineers Karig and Eisler's enormous concrete sheds were 'walled in, as if they were something to be ashamed of, behind a forbidding fortress'.

France failed to follow Germany's lead in pioneering the use of reinforced concrete in station architecture. Even after the First World War French railway companies generally preferred to use designs that were more retrospective and less brutal than those of the German giants, and whose light-hearted historicism recalled the great days of the French past. For the one major French railway terminus of the 1920s, reinforced concrete was used, but to create not a machine for transportation, nor an expression of national virility, but a gigantic, megalomaniacal

Baroque parody. Roger Gonthier's Limoges Bénédictins was originally planned in the years after 1908, but the war prevented its execution until 1925–9. It was a bizarre domed confection – half-cathedral, half-mosque – which outdid any American or German station of the period in terms of demonstrative ostentation. The concourse, vaulted by massive, flat arches, was lit by stained glass by the local artist Francis Chigot. And in contrast to the more obviously progressive termini of the period (and streamlined, futuristic French buildings of the time such as Auguste Perret's Notre-Dame du Raincy of 1923), the exterior was covered with profuse decoration and sculptural figures. Either side of the entrance were allegorical figures representing the local porcelain industry by Henri Varenne; at each corner of the concourse were figurative symbols of the Orléans company's four principal destinations. The model was more Orsay, the railway's Paris terminal, than Helsinki.

Rouen station of 1913–28 by Adolphe Dervaux (b 1871) was one exception to this rule. Like Limoges, it made structural use of reinforced concrete. But unlike Limoges, its design looked forward – albeit in a typically French manner, which was far less brutal than the sheer walls of Stuttgart or Leipzig. Its recognizably Classical forms were greatly simplified, as at Helsinki, and glazed arched entrance metamorphosed into a giant, five-bay feature covered by a ribbed concrete roof, as at Viipuri. And much in the manner of its illustrious American contemporaries, New York

Pennsylvania, New York Grand Central and Kansas City Union, the tracks and platforms were placed below the concourse, which was bridged over the tracks by means of reinforced-concrete supports. In the mid-1930s Rouen was still being acclaimed as the first truly modern railway station in France.

The trend towards fashioning new compositions which borrowed familiar elements from the old, and in particular for using new forms to symbolize a robust, aggressive nationalist spirit, was nowhere better expressed than in one of the world's most celebrated and individual stations, Milan Central. By 1906 the old main station of 1864 was considered too small and insufficiently grand; accordingly, a competition was held for a replacement, ultimately won by Arrigo Cantoni. The city authorities, however, subsequently changed their mind, and declared in 1912 that Cantoni's conventional, Neoclassical design was too timid and too retrospective for the city, and that a new competition should be held for a new head building – the shed being left to the engineers. In his desperation Cantoni called on the services of the gifted young futurist Antonio Sant'Elia (1888–1916), who transformed Cantoni's original essay in Second Empire style into an elaborate, domed, shed-like structure, bound by semicircular iron trusses, supported by massive, tapering pylons, and covered in stylized Art Nouveau motifs. Many of the elements of Sant'Elia's 1912 design were strongly redolent of Saarinen's Helsinki. Over the main entrance a vast lunette was

France's exact counterpart to Stuttgart was a terminus which was phrased in a more accessible and lighthearted idiom. Roger Gonthier's Limoges Bénédictins of 1908 and 1925–9, was expressively retrospective – while at the same time using steel and reinforced concrete to achieve its inflated Beaux-Arts effects, bottom. Limoges's exuberant excesses were slightly tamed at the Gare de l'Ouest, Rouen, 1913–28, below. Here Adolphe Dervaux's concrete-and-steel construction could be glimpsed behind the Art Nouveau finials and the Expressionist sculpture.

flanked by robust piers, at the summit of which hunched human figures (probably designed by Sant'Elia's friend Possamai) held out globe lights; all of these were, of course, elements to be found in Saarinen's great Finnish terminus. In the event, though, Cantoni found Sant'Elia's designs too radical to stomach, submitting a variant of the 1907 scheme. This fared no better the second time round; the new competition was won by Ulisse Stacchini, while Cantoni's own scheme came a dismal seventh.

Stacchini (1871–1947) had already beaten Sant'Elia in the competition for the cemetery in Monza the previous year. His victorious competition design lacked the brio of Sant'Elia's, being an eclectic mix of Beaux-Arts, Renaissance Revival and Venetian Gothic, with a standard arched porte-cochere as the main front entrance. During 1913–14, however, Sant'Elia himself persisted with wholly new designs for Milan. These relied not on historicist references or on accepted forms, but on the architect's astonishing Futurist vision. The result was a giant terminus, the like of which had never been seen before. Gone were the familiar lunette window and the central dome. In their place rose a colossal, ziggurat-like building, its entrances – a series of broad but incredibly flat arches – marked by two soaring, unmoulded towers. Sant'Elia's biographer Esther da Costa Meyer has graphically described the sheer power and emotion which this astonishing scheme still generates:

Powerful oblique buttresses shoulder the immense mass, which slopes down dramatically only to rise again in the form of two mighty pylons. Low dark vaults conjoin and brace the pylons in the center, while on either side of the main entrance they flare out unsupported, forming a marquee.[3]

Two years after producing this breathtaking project, however, Sant'Elia was dead. The young architect, aged only twenty-eight, was killed on 10 October 1916 while fighting the Austrians on the Trieste front. Nevertheless, his ideas did not wholly die with him. In the years after the First World War, Stacchini gradually incorporated more and more elements of Sant'Elia's last scheme. In 1918 two severely rectilinear clock towers, directly cribbed from Sant'Elia's 1913–14 project, were added to the existing design. These boldly Futurist towers were in the event never executed.

Yet the finished building owed far more to Antonio Sant'Elia – and to Eliel Saarinen – than to its Italian predecessors. Sant'Elia's vertical massing and even his compact, cubic figures were all assimilated into the station, which as completed in 1931 bore little resemblance to Stacchini's competition winner of 1912. The familiar, two-arched entrance porch still

survived, yet the dimensions and planning of the booking hall behind were unusual: 200 feet long and impressively vaulted, the hall emptied out on to the side streets as well as to the Piazza Andrea Doria at the front. While the booking hall's decorative panels showing the network's principal destinations, the two large lunette windows at either end, and the use of travertine marble and pink Baveno granite were all elements borrowed from the Beaux-Arts tradition, the proportions, the massing and the decoration of the rest of the building were undeniably derived from Sant'Elia. The walls of the 700-foot long concourse, reached by monumental stairs or vast escalators, were covered with stylized sculptures of mythical beasts and mighty men, carved on a superhuman scale by Giannino Castigliani. The immense, threatening

faces, directly recalling the figurative additions to Sant'Elia's competition designs as well as Saarinen's executed facade at Helsinki, were partly embedded in the walls, and threatened to erupt into the station concourse at any moment.

The overall design was an astonishing feat of imagination, quite unlike any other railway terminal – and quite unlike anything that Stacchini had previously devised. And, given the building's incorporation of vast supermen and its use of massive, overpowering forms, it did not take long for observers to decipher heavy-handed allusions to the muscular Fascism of Benito Mussolini, dictator of Italy during most of the station's construction. If the masonry did not communicate the message sufficiently clearly, there was always the giant inscription carved over the entrance arch: a dedication both to King Victor Emmanuel III and to Benito

Giannino Castigliani's Imperial imagery – from the Assyrian winged horses and the bronze lions heads to Mussolini's faces – vies for attention on Ulisse Stacchini's deeply articulated facade with the bizarre, grotesque faces which appear to be surfacing from deep within the masonry, top. The effect is to make the elevation, which from a distance appears immutably solid, to be on closer inspection surprisingly fluid and organic. Above, the dimensions of the laterally sited entrance hall were deliberately intended to rival those of the great American Beaux-Arts termini. Opposite, Sant'Elia's astonishing scheme of 1912 for an airport railway station.

Mussolini, dated '1931 dell'Era dei Christi' and 'IX dell'Era dei Fasci'.

It was surely no coincidence that by 1931 the man who had clearly inspired the new station had himself been raised to the status of a Fascist hero. In 1921 Sant'Elia was proudly reburied, and the circumstances of his death swiftly transformed into a fictional tale. Conveniently ignoring Sant'Elia's socialist past, Fascist mythology had him declaiming shortly before he expired: 'Men, tonight we shall sleep either in Trieste or in paradise with the heroes.' (Trieste was to the Fascists a powerful symbol of Italy's so-called 'unredeemed territories', which Mussolini hoped to annex after 1940.) By 1931 the Fascists' appropriation of Sant'Elia was complete. As Da Costa Meyer has observed: 'He had been endowed with heroism, vitality, and a sacrificial death, crucial prerequisites of the new role models of the regime'. In 1933 even Mussolini's son Vittorio was declaring to the population that 'In matters of modernity we young people must follow the words of the patriot, soldier and futurist Antonio Sant'Elia, who died on the battlefield.'[4] By boldly reworking his designs for Milan Central, Ulisse Stacchini – with an understandable eye on future government patronage – fashioned a building which represented both a tribute to the exceptional vision of a Fascist idol and a testimony to the vaunted strength, virility and progressiveness of Mussolini's Fascist state.

Milan Central's political symbolism has since 1945 tended to obscure its architectural worth. While in 1958 the British railway authority Ernest Carter magnanimously termed the station 'a truly magnificent building' and, 'although of somewhat doubtful architectural style … undoubtedly one of the best-designed stations in the world', Carroll Meeks expressed his disgust at a scheme which 'began as a fresh Art Nouveau conception … [and] in execution sank to the depths of bombastic retrogressive

monumentality'.[5] What particularly outraged Meeks was the fact that Milan's five massive sheds, ascending in height to the central span and each lit by elliptical lunettes placed just above springing level, were totally obscured from view by Stacchini's monument to a resurgent, aggressive Italian nation. ('A bank of five sheds, among the most beautiful ever built, is entirely concealed from the piazza by a grotesque brontosaurus of a fore-building'.) Twenty years later Jean Dethier was prepared to be a bit more forgiving and objective in his assessment of the station. Milan Central, he wrote in the catalogue to his splendid station exhibition of 1978:

conveys a disturbing spirit of enormity and imperialist visions, expressed with a megalomaniac delirium of Assyrian-Babylonian inspiration: the architecture serves to support a triumphal and menacing iconography, with a mixture of fascist emblems, references to the grandeur of the Roman empire and glorifications of physical strength and combat.[6]

Although the station's political allusions now appear dated and devalued, the building itself has in fact continued to perform very well. As a functional interchange it works just as smoothly, if not better, than many of the starkly functional termini of the postwar era. Some of the original facilities have disappeared –

The simple geometry of the five-span train shed at Milan, opposite, left and overleaf, has long won praise, even when the Fascist monumentalism of the head building was considered highly embarrassing. Today, however, Stacchini's fusion of Neoclassical pretension and Futurist aspiration, as seen in his majestic, 210-foot long concourse, above right, is once more in vogue.

the waiting room for invalids, for example, and the umbrella-hire service (both, interestingly, services originated in Mussolini's Italy) – but today the mid-concourse bank of shops and restaurants, reassuringly close to the tracks, is still thriving, and vast crowds of people are still able to pass freely through the terminal even at the busiest times.

After 1945 the Italians were understandably embarrassed by the Fascist overtones of the station. While Rome's principal terminus was refashioned in Modernist garb (see Chapter 7), at Milan a project of 1952 by Minoletti and Gentili envisioned inserting a thin but immensely tall, piloti-supported slab directly in front of the station entrance. This immense intrusion – similar to the contemporary plans for a block on the north side of New York's Grand Central – would have completely hidden Stacchini's facade from the Piazza dei Cinquecento. This, of course, was its

main objective, the daring brutality of which was ultimately too much even for the abashed, style-conscious Milanese of the 1950s. Today Stacchini's colossal testimony to the genius of Sant'Elia, to the power of the railways, and to the rise and fall of the man who made them run on time now enjoys a relatively safe haven in a more architecturally tolerant age.

As Milan Central was being opened, work was progressing on another of the great stations of the era, one that was more conventional in its recognizably railway-orientated composition and Art Deco detailing, but one which was, like Milan, redolent of the aesthetic and political currents of a bold new age. As early as 1904 it was proposed to rebuild Cincinnati's undistinguished Union terminal of 1882–3; however, owing to rivalries between the railroad companies and problems in finding a suitable new site, the final decision was not taken until 1923. The new station was

to be as near to the city centre as was practically feasible. (Carl Condit observed in his history of the city's transportation systems that 'genuine union stations centrally located and designed for the use of all lines serving the city were by long odds the exception rather than the rule in the English-speaking lands.')[7] Accordingly, the tracks of the seven companies due to use the new terminal – the Baltimore and Ohio, the Chesapeake and Ohio, the NYC, the PRR, the Southern, the Louisville and Nashville, and the Norfolk and Western – were extended and rerouted.

In 1928 the New York firm of Alfred Fellheimer and Stewart Wagner (the heirs, as already noted, of Grand Central's Reed and Stem) were awarded the commission for the new Cincinnati Union. Five years earlier Fellheimer had used *Railway Age* to advertise his criteria for the design of railway termini, an article which clearly did him no harm in alerting potential clients to his familiarity with the requirements of a modern station. (His strictures were not particularly novel; perhaps the most helpful was the recommendation that ticket offices and other service facilities were best placed along the lines of movement from street to train.) Fellheimer, however, entrusted the detailed design of the project to one of his office architects: the unfortunately named Roland A Wank (1898–1970). Wank was born in Budapest, and after training at the Paris École des Beaux-Arts emigrated to the United States in 1924. Cincinnati Union was his greatest building, and won him the American Institute of Architects (AIA) Gold Medal. In later years he became the chief architect for Roosevelt's Tennessee Valley Authority, and in 1945 founded his own firm of Wank, Adams and Slavin.

Wank's design combined strong Art Deco motifs with the vocabulary of the Beaux-Arts and the rational simplicity of the Modern Movement. The limestone facade was dominated by a massive single arch, 200 feet in diameter – 'the unchallenged giant of station portals', as Meeks put it in 1956.[8] To the side, two quadrant wings embraced the forecourt in the manner of St Peter's in Rome; behind, concrete trusses supported a plaster concourse vault that was 106 feet high at its apex.

At the rear of Cincinnati's main concourse, a long, narrow train concourse ran out for 450 feet directly over the tracks, first passing under a low tower which housed the railroad offices. There was no single train shed; each platform merely possessed its own canopy – which, like the rest of the station, was steel-framed. Baggage and mail were dealt with underneath the platforms, in the manner of the Beaux-Arts stations of the East Coast.

For the principal elevation of Union Station, Cincinnati, Roland Wank borrowed the familiar concept of the single arch, below, from the great German termini of the late nineteenth century and, more recently, from Saarinen's Helsinki. However, he clothed it in the Art Deco forms that had become internationally popular in the late 1920s. The result was a very cosmopolitan as well as assured design. Ironically, though, the great arch does not reflect the disposition of the train sheds behind.

TOWARDS A NEW CENTURY OF TRAVEL

The result was a stunning, glowing interior, far more welcoming than anything the Modern Movement was to devise over the next forty years. Sadly, though, the fashion for such rich stations seems to have been a brief one. The trend was already on the way out after the Modernist lessons of Chicago's 'Century of Progress' exhibition of 1933–4; by 1945 it was quite dead.

Cincinnati opened in March 1933, having cost $41 million. Yet there had already been a big fall in the area's railroad traffic since 1929; indeed the number of trains serving the city had, largely due to the Depression, almost halved over the preceding five years. It was thus not a good time to be opening a vast new Union station. The only time that the terminus was used to its full capacity was during the Second World War; by the time that Amtrak was created, in 1971, Cincinnati was served by only one passenger train a day each way.

Thankfully, Cincinnati did not go the way of so many other great American termini. In 1972, as the station was being declared a National Historic Landmark, the railroads introduced a scheme to level the site which was roundly attacked by the local media. The *Cincinnati Post and Times-Star* declared it 'would be a sad day' if this 'true gateway toward a futuristic environmental design' was demolished.' Backed by regional newspapers and TV stations, the University of Cincinnati resolved to lead the fight against the building's destruction.

Initially the prospects looked bleak: the Southern Railroad bought the concourse, intending to demolish it to provide space for modernized freight operations. Having diverted services to a poky underground terminal on River Road, in late 1972 the Southern actually began demolition of the rear train concourse and platforms. Almost the last straw appeared to be the transfer of the Reiss murals to the city airport, an act of crushing symbolism. A last-minute reprieve came in 1973, when the City stepped in. The demolition of the

Although the station's external colour scheme was, like those of its Beaux-Arts predecessors, rather muted – the walls being executed in limestone or buff brick, with terracotta dressings for the arch (which were, sadly, replaced by aluminium cladding in 1945) – the interiors were a riot of bold, warm hues. The decorative scheme for Cincinnati Union was largely the work of the Philadelphia architect Paul P Cret, invited in 1930 by Fellheimer and Wagner to assist Wank with the interiors. Cret's rich, autumnal palette of reds, browns and yellows worked brilliantly. The lower walls of the concourse were covered with mosaic murals, designed by the German-born Winold Reiss and executed by the Ravenna Mosaic Company; the mosaic scenes depicted aspects of leading Cincinnati industries, and the far wall a world map, augmented by clocks telling the time all over the world. The concourse vaulting was finished in red Verona, Tennessee fleuri and black Virginia marbles; the floor was of red and tan terrazzo; the men's lounge was finished in zebrawood, walnut and holly veneer, arranged to form transport-derived motifs; and the restaurant walls were lined with zebrawood, birch, and red and black marbles. The station was even equipped with a theatre, which was provided with walls of black and white marble and a rich mulberry carpet.

The postwar optimism of Winold Reiss's mosaic murals on the walls of the circular concourse, above and above left, nicely complemented the bold lines of Wank's architecture, opposite. By the mid-1930s their industrial subjects also served to encapsulate the job-creation programmes of Roosevelt's 'New Deal'.

In most of the subsidiary public areas of Cincinnati Union, such as the men's lounge, Paul Cret's warm autumnal tones proved a welcome relief to the austerity of the American Beaux-Arts stations. The circular concourse, below, was a bold departure from accepted tradition; today its stripped Classicism and uncompromising Art Deco signage are as effective as when the building opened in 1933.

An early 50s postcard showing the *Super Chief* of the Santa Fe Railroad travelling through the orange groves of California. In a sharp reaction to the vast scale of the Beaux-Arts termini of twenty years before, the head building at Union Station, Los Angeles, by Donald and John Parkinson, above and opposite, was phrased in a more contemporary idiom that used local building traditions and took care to employ a more human scale. The result was a station which, while not as evocative of the railway age as its predecessors, asserted its function in an economical and assured fashion.

main concourse was halted and the City authorities commissioned Hardy Holzman Pfeiffer Associates to devise a scheme by which the central concourse and its attendant areas would be converted to museum use. Today the head building houses no less than four fine civic museums, while retaining much of Wank and Cret's Art Deco detailing. Though the building stands in a wasteland of urban uncertainty, its vast entrance arch and its engaging, instantly recognizable profile have ensured it a position as one of the city's principal attractions and best-loved landmarks.

While the design of Cincinnati Union had looked to the future, for the railways the future actually offered very little comfort. Cincinnati was not, as its designers believed, the first of a new kind of railway terminus, but instead one of the last of the great American stations.

The accolade of being the very last in a great tradition probably belongs to Los Angeles Union, built in 1934–9 by father-and-son Donald (1895–1946) and John Parkinson (1861–1935). The Parkinsons's design fused the ubiquitous Californian 'Spanish Mission' manner with Art Deco styling and a perceptible Modernist ethos. To ensure its structural stability in an area notorious for its earthquakes and tremors, the station was originally devised as thirty separate but interconnected units, with sufficient space between each module to allow for the building's survival in the event of a natural disaster. The station's 860-foot long frontage along Alameda Road, complete with cantilevered concrete porch, was phrased in a simplified, quasi-Modernist style, though with a varying, irregular roof line and a 125- foot high clock tower (surmounted by what was described at the time as a 'Moorish finial'). As at Cincinnati, colour played an important part in the composition. The facade's off-white walls contrasted pleasingly with the blue paint of the steel windows and the red of the tiled sills and

the roof tiles. Its church-like arched entrance, with five bronze-framed glazed doors, was bordered with grey, green, blue and Siena mosaic tiles. Inside, the floors were of Vermont, Tennessee or Montana marble, or of red quarry tiles, and the dado of black Belgian marble, with American black walnut used for the woodwork. The restaurant's design harked back to the Mission Style, being themed in an avowedly 'Eighteenth Century Provincial' manner. But the centrepiece of the station was the waiting room, decorated by local artist Robert E McKee. The walls were covered with mosaics in blue, olive and brown, above a black Belgian marble base; the floor was in two-tone red quarry tiles, with a marble border; while the blue-painted windows were provided with evocative amber glass.

For the next fifty years no station as thrilling or as exciting as Cincinnati or Los Angeles was built. Certainly never again were railway stations to be so sumptuously decorated or brilliantly coloured. In 1940 the Union Pacific claimed that Los Angeles Union was not only 'one of the most workable' stations in the United States, but also 'the nation's most outstandingly attractive railroad station'.[10] For once the railroad's PR was right. Los Angeles achieved a synthesis of pleasing decoration and human scale which eluded most station architects of the subsequent decades. Yet the colourful new Railway Age it hoped to herald did not materialize. Already by 1950 it was widely known as a centre of crime. (In that year, Rudolph Maté's *Union Station* was filmed here, with William Holden – 'I'm a cop twenty-four hours a day. All I care about is my railroad station' – as its star.) Los Angeles Union survives, but the station is a sad testimony to the fate of the American railroad, given that few inhabitants of the city or its sprawling hinterland are even aware of its location.

In contrast to the Mission Style and Art Deco references prominent on the exterior of the head-building, the arcaded entrance, opposite, and the waiting room interior, below, of Los Angeles Union – the last of the great American railroad stations of the twentieth century – betrayed their debts to the Beaux-Arts tradition. The red quarry tiles of the waiting room floor and the blue-and-olive colouring of the walls, however, provides a more homely touch. In Los Angeles, Hollywood's impact is never far away: Buster Keaton in a scene from *Go West*, 1925, above.

THE MODERN MOVEMENT AND BEYOND
THE RENAISSANCE OF RAIL

'In the second half of this century, airports have assumed the monumental character once unique to the great railroad stations. In turn, the new stations created by the rail revival of the 1980s and 90s have an expressive quality which has nothing to do with hiding the train away; they act as a necessary celebration of the survival and revival of rail travel.'[1]
KENNETH POWELL, 1996.

The first traces of Modernist design and theory being used for the structure of larger railway stations can be detected in the 1930s, some time after this doctrine had been applied to other commercial and industrial buildings in the Western World. Three large stations of this era stand out: Henri Pacon's Le Havre Ville of 1930–3, Giovanni Michelucci's Santa Maria Novella in Florence of 1932–3 and I I J Schelling's Amsterdam Amstel, begun in 1939. All three buildings rejected even the most subtle and perfunctory of historicisms – and with it much of the accepted vocabulary and symbolism of the station facade – in favour of a soberly Modernist approach. Inevitably, these new stations were rapidly heralded as the buildings of the future.

At the Le Havre terminus (built to replace the old station so lovingly analysed in Zola's 1890 *La Bête Humaine*), Pacon grouped low, cubic shapes to form a hunched and entirely rational head building. It was Pacon's belief that the station should concentrate on just three principal elements: vestibule, barrier and platforms. In practice, though, he was forced to accede to demands to include some more familiar aspects of station design. Yet even the subsequent addition of a tall, excessively plain clock tower, complete with an odd, Futurist spire, did not detract from the station's remarkable and, in the context of the history of French station architecture, singularly brave design. In Carroll Meeks's view, the inclusion of the tower demonstrated that the SNCF had lost its nerve and 'did not care to follow Le Corbusier's architectural lead' by rejecting all the familiar elements of the traditional station.[2] In 1939, however, the English architect and critic Sir Albert Richardson (better known as a champion of the Beaux-Arts style) went out of his way to praise Pacon for Le Havre's 'graceful engineering'.

Equally adventurous, and highly influential on the

To mark the opening of the Channel Tunnel on 6 May 1994 Queen Elizabeth II travelled by Royal Eurostar, from London to Paris, left. Opposite, Santiago Calatrava's magnificent Lyon Satolas Station was built to accommodate France's related TGV services.

stations of the postwar era, was Amsterdam Amstel. It bore none of the hallmarks of traditional terminus architecture. Instead, it comprised a large, glazed box housing the main concourse, which was supplemented by long, low, unobtrusive wings for the railway offices. There were a few references to past practices: the glazed box was given a slightly pitched roof (Schelling wisely making provision for heavy rainfall) and, although most of the building was constructed of functional red brick above a granite plinth, the east elevation was faced with French limestone, as a concession to outward display. In general, however, the building attempted to eliminate the compromises of the past. All passenger facilities were grouped into the main box, which was simply proportioned and glazed in the manner of Charles Holden's London Transport underground stations of the 1930s, while the platforms were covered by equally simplistic glass cages.

Perhaps the most astonishing great station of the decade was, however, Florence's Santa Maria Novella terminus. A showcase for Mussolini's Fascist state, Florence SMN's uncompromisingly rigid, box-like design was light years away from the pompous and empty theatrical Classicism of Stalinist Russia or Nazi Germany, where such unambiguous expressions of Modernism were considered decadent. Its designer, Giovanni Michelucci, won the competition of 1931 and enlistd the help of the 'Tuscan Group' of architects to introduce full-blooded Modernism to the railway station. The station was long, low, and flat-roofed, its lateral concourse strung out along the entrance drive to allow as much space to unload vehicles as possible; it was thus the first purpose-built terminus of the car age. Aside from the marble-clad royal entrance, almost all traditional station references were expunged; only the porte-cochere survived, in the form of an ambiguous, block-like glazed projection. Most notably, the main facade was entirely blank, with no openings, sculpture, incised patterns, or selection of materials. Glass only appears on the elevation over the main entrance.

Michelucci's horizontal mass was shockingly new, particularly since Stacchini's bombastic Milan Central was still fresh in everyone's mind. Richard Etlin has alleged that Santa Maria Novella's lateral emphasis was deliberately 'reminiscent of the Florentine walls';[3] however, this is about all it has in common with the historic city. Richardson declared that 'the new station at Florence is typical of the volte-face which has taken place' against the 'pompous columnar treatment' of other Italian termini.[4] And after the war Meeks rejoiced in its uncompromising vocabulary: 'The Rockefellers poring over plans for Williamsburg could hardly have been more shocked by the sight of a

modern design than the Florentines were at their first sight of this sensational station.'[5] As Meeks hints, however, not all Florentines were so ecstatic.

By 1940, with termini such as Amsterdam Amstel and Florence SMN, Modernism had finally arrived at the great railway station. Commentators of the 1950s and 60s invariably found these designs exhilarating; in 1956 Carroll Meeks admitted that he was delighted that 'no echo is heard of Burnham Baroque or other antique vocabularies of ornament' in such schemes; stations such as Amstel, he declared, 'are raised to the level of the best contemporary architecture, a level more familiar to us in our schools and churches'. Whether, of course, this brave Modernism actually made this type of station any more efficient or pleasant to use than those of the 1840s or early twentieth century is another matter.

Opposite, Peter Alma's mural at H G Schelling's Amsterdam Amstel, begun in 1939. The exterior of Amstel Station, Amsterdam, 1940, above: a large glazed block with low office wings. Top, commemorative Dutch railway stamps.

LA STAZIONE PARLANTE

A volte basta un nulla per l'artista:
qualcosa che colpisca la sua vista!
come, ad esempio, un grosso valigione...
fa germogliar l'idea della Stazione!

It is instructive to remember that the striking Santa Maria Novella Station, Florence – which Meeks declared 'followed the spirit rather than the forms of Renaissance Florence' – was the product not of the brave new postwar Europe but of Mussolini's Italy. Like its exact contemporary, Los Angeles Union, Florence SMN was one of the first great stations to ensure not only that motor car access was well provided for, but that the needs of the car were second only to those of the passengers. While the glazed attic, top, recalls the Beaux-Arts termini of the United States, the alignment of the principal facade and the booking hall so that both lead directly to the access driveway, opposite, was wholly new. A cartoon in *Il Brivido* depicted the building as two large packing crates, inside which was the real station.

At Termini Station, Rome, Eugenio Montuori and his partners took the rather earthbound contours of Florence SMN and pulled them skywards. The result was the stunning, S-shaped steel and glass canopy which not only covered the booking hall but which also invited the passenger in, above and right. After a *tour-de-force* of such stunning simplicity, the mean barrel vaults over the concourse and platforms, come as something of a surprise.

After the Second World War the Italians, Germans and Dutch led the way in the design of Modern Movement stations. It was in Italy, however, that the best-known terminus of the immediate postwar era was built. The decision to replace Rome's principal terminus of the 1870s was personally taken by Mussolini. The subsequent competition was won in 1931 by the architect Angiolo Mazzoni, to many as surprising a choice as the uncompromisingly Modernist style of Florence SMN. Mazzoni was a government architect in Mussolini's Ministry of Communications, yet he was a confirmed rationalist. At Rome he was obliged to include a degree of Neoclassical magniloquence; however, even his early designs for the station combined a heavy Classical colonnade on the principal (eastern) facade with plain Modernist treatments of the long side elevations. In 1995 Eric Hobsbawm suggested that 'compared to the cultural achievements and international influence of post-1945 Italy, the Fascist era does not look impressive. One has only to compare the Fascist plan for Rome's railway station … with what was actually constructed after 1947.'[6] However, Mazzoni's development of the Termini design belies this claim.

His revised scheme of 1936–7 was startlingly advanced for its time: the side elevation facing the ancient Servian wall was little more than a horizontal block, supported on doubled pilotis and pierced by a continuous band of glazing; the result was a 'modern crystalline wafer'.[7] That such a courageously modern building was constructed in the heart of Mussolini's capital says much for the breadth of his architectural vision – a cultural tolerance which his fellow dictators in Germany and Russia clearly did not possess.

Work finally began on the new station's wings in 1938. By the time Italy entered the war in 1940, however, little genuine progress had been made on the project – work had not even begun on the principal facade and its massive colonnade – and by the time of the country's capitulation to the Allies in 1943 construction had stopped altogether.

Predictably, Mazzoni's identification with Il Duce's Fascist regime called for an entirely new approach after the war's conclusion. Accordingly, in 1947 a new competition was held for the site. This was won by Eugenio Montuori, assisted by Castellazzi, Fadigati, Pinotello and Vitellozzi, and the engineer Leo Calini. Avoiding the ancient walls of the Agger Serviano to the northeast, the design of the new station was far removed from the Neoclassical pomp of Mazzoni's terminus or the totalitarian eccentricity of Stacchini's Milan. Instead Montuori introduced a dispassionate exercise in International Modernism. The main facade merely comprised a glass wall, which in turn supported a cantilevered canopy which curved sinuously over the laterally oriented booking hall – a device borrowed from Stacchini at Milan. Over the restaurant block which separated the booking hall and the tracks were four floors of offices; to the east the concourse was roofed with low, flat arches pierced with glass bricks, which abutted the unexceptional, flat-roofed platform awnings that substituted for an overall train shed. Like

A scene from Vittorio de Sica's *Indiscretion of an American Wife*, 1953, with Montogomery Clift and Jennifer Jones shot in Montuori's Rome Termini.

The dramatic curved span of Nicholas Grimshaw's train shed, above right and overleaf, brought romance and theatre as well as first-class design back to the British railway terminus. At the same time, the shed roof was ingeniously fanned so as to admit the inclusion of as many standard-sized powder-coated aluminium panels as possible, overleaf, and provided with extensive glazing in the manner of the great Victorian train sheds. The map, above, details the routes of the early Eurostar services. Opposite: the sweeping arrivals concourse, with its Zumtobel lighting and Jean-Luc Vilmouth's marvellous fish sculptures.

so many buildings of the time, the interiors were largely devoid of colour, the monochrome of the steel and glass walls being relieved only by the pale pink granite floor and the red granite benches.

Equally impressed was the film director Vittorio de Sica, who shot most of his *Indiscretion of an American Wife* in and around the station's stark, gleaming new interiors. The film was originally devised as a deliberate homage to Montuori's design, being initially named *Terminal Station*, but it was subsequently retitled – and savagely cut – by producer David O Selznick. Nevertheless, at least some of the vignettes of station life survived:

De Sica sketches in the life of the station, skilfully establishing the texture of existence going on around the lovers: a gaggle of priests buying their tickets, a school party being kept in order, singing sports fans. There is much activity by *carabinieri* and top-hatted officials connected with a red carpet for the arrival of the President, who comes and goes during the film. Unlike *Brief Encounter*, where it is the homely formality of the surroundings that points up the grand tragedy in their midst, here it is the spacious, glittering echoing modernity of the new station, angular, cold, and unfriendly, heightening the sense of alienation…[8]

Sadly, for many Termini Station is today more renowned as the haunt of ubiquitous pimps and thieves than for its pioneering architecture.

In contrast to the high standard of design exhibited at Rome Termini, most of the major new stations built during the 1950s and 60s were decidedly mediocre. There were, of course, a few exceptions. Two were British: Banbury and Manchester Oxford Road. British Rail Western Region's Banbury of 1959 incorporated a glazed main building with a slightly pitched roof with a

reinforced-concrete frame, concrete platform coverings, concrete wall slabs (faced with Derbyshire spar chips or the ghastly 'Tyrolean rendering' that was to become so common on houses over the next twenty years). Few of these features had previously graced a large British station.

Even more innovatory than Banbury was Manchester Oxford Road of 1961, perhaps the most architecturally significant British station of the whole postwar period, by the London Midland Region's regional architect W R Headley. Its 'ship's prow' entrance and series of three shell roofs, each rising towards the entrance front, both provided an echo of the grand, framed station archways of the nineteenth century and, more directly, of Jørn Utzon's celebrated Sydney Opera House, begun in 1957. Headley's shell roofs were not quite as glamorous as Utzon's, but they were undoubtedly more structurally reliable, and, incomparably, less controversial. Supported on brick arches, the shells were made of laminated wood (three layers of hemlock) to keep their weight down; concrete, the accepted building material for structures of this type in the early 60s, would have been far too heavy for the delicate roof profile. Underneath the main shell was the concourse, lit by a lunette window much in the manner of Eero Saarinen's TWA Terminal at Idlewild (now JFK) Airport, built the following year. The concourse's detailing was also in wood, the provision of which emphasized the building's visual coherence while also keeping the cost down. Headley's design was not only radical and cheap; his use of traditional materials also guaranteed structural

stability, in marked contrast to the poor performance of many of the postwar concrete structures. In November 1995 its evident success was rewarded with statutory protection.

While many of the great stations of the Railway Age were demolished in the mid-1960s, few buildings of any real quality were erected in their place. Tilburg in The Netherlands, built in 1965 to the design of Koem van der Gaast, was one of the few exceptions. Its revolutionary zig-zag roof was something completely new in station design, and anticipated the High-Tech rooflines of twenty years later. The roof of John P Parkin's unsubtle and top-heavy Ottawa Station of 1967 also deserves a brief mention: the vast, graceless box of steel trusses was ingeniously supported over the featureless one-floor concourse by delicate pin connections balanced on tapered concrete columns. Ottawa is thus the ancestor of the great High-Tech termini of the early 1990s. Whatever the merits of Parkin's roof, however, it must be remembered that not only was the new station built on the ruins of the fine Beaux-Arts Union terminal of 1910, but, like most of the examples of its time, it deliberately eschewed the accepted forms of railway architecture in favour of an approach to design more usually associated with airports and shopping malls.

It was not really until the railway revival of the mid-1980s that serious attention was once more given to the great railway terminus as a significant and discrete building type, one that actually dared to exploit the spatial and dramatic qualities of that almost-forgotten element, the arched train shed. Over the past decade, rail termini have, for the first time in years, been designed to look both distinctive and exciting.

The first of the great new termini of the late twentieth century was Nicholas Grimshaw and Partners' justly fêted International Terminal at London Waterloo. Commissioned in 1988, the new station was completed long before the Channel Tunnel was opened to passenger traffic on 14 November 1994. Grimshaw's new building is not a new freestanding structure, but was added onto the north end of the old Waterloo terminal. As such, it was forced to reproduce the curving alignment of the adjacent platforms. Grimshaw worked closely with David Kirkland of structural engineers YRM Anthony Hunt Associates to find an exciting and inexpensive solution. The 1,300-foot long shed was the product of this collaboration: supported by blue-painted, bowstring-shaped steel trusses, its span narrows 53 feet from the booking hall end to the track exits. The bowstring profile was chosen in order to maximize internal space while allowing sufficient clearance for trains at the north end

of the site. It is worth noting that a bowstring truss was also used as the defining element in Harry Reijnders's impressive Rotterdam Blaak Station of 1989–93. In this instance the huge, single truss used (which supports a vast, glazed canopy, opening upwards like a scallop shell) is, most appropriately, banana coloured.

To augment the blue trusses at Waterloo, structural glass, and not steel or concrete, was used to create a more delicate and coherent effect. Glass fins were employed as beams, running alongside the blue trusses to give additional support to the standard-sized, overlapping glass sheets which formed the basis of the train shed's cladding. Altogether 245 tons of structural glazing was used to supplement the 12,000 square yards of stainless steel in the roof. The result is a structure of extraordinary brilliance, which admits

direct light during the day and serves as an illuminated sculpture at night. Yet, despite its apparent fragility, the shed is also able to endure considerable weight and vibration. Not only are the trains unusually heavy and long; they also run on tracks placed over two levels of passenger facilities and an underground car park.

The floors below the train shed were designed to cope with 15 million passengers a year. Their design was intended as a deliberate contrast to the brilliant elegance of the train shed: while the latter is dominated by the blue trusses, the arrival and departure areas are muted and monochrome; the ubiquitous steel and concrete is relieved only occasionally, for example by the black granite used for the toilet walls and the ticket-desk surface, and the red upholstery of the Charles Eames chairs used for the standard-class waiting area on the departures floor.

To admit as much natural light as possible, Peter Rice's almost weightless roof, top and opposite, was poised as gently as possible on top of Duthilleul's economically-designed concourse and platforms at Lille Europe. The result was an effortlessly impressive station which demonstrated that station architecture no longer need be physically subservient to its immediate surroundings. It also showed that the train, rather than the car, could be used as the regenerative hub of even the largest of urban developments. Above, a Lille-bound Eurostar train emerges from the Channel Tunnel.

THE MODERN MOVEMENT AND BEYOND

Placing the terminal's services below the tracks allows a clear, uninterrupted view of the shed and the train carriages while also providing easy access to and from the ground-floor arrivals concourse and the first-floor departures area. Grimshaw had little choice but to establish a vertical arrangement of services. The new platforms clearly had to be at the same level as the existing ones; yet passengers at Waterloo have always had to ascend either the stairs under the 1922 Victory Arch or the taxi ramp to the south in order the reach the concourse. Grimshaw dealt with this requirement as rationally as possible in his International Terminal. Departing passengers arrive at the ground-floor booking hall, rather awkwardly sandwiched between the eastern end of the new shed and the main concourse. Having passed through the control area, they then use escalators or glass lifts to reach the first-floor departures concourse and the second-floor platforms.

From Waterloo International trains leave for the Channel Tunnel and the impressive French high-speed line, on which trains can currently reach a top speed of 190 mph. The principal station on this new line, currently served by tunnel trains from London to Brussels as well as by TGV services, is another brand-new structure: Lille Europe, designed by SNCF's chief architect Jean-Marie Duthilleul (assisted by Etienne Tricaud and Pierre Saboya) and the engineer Peter Rice, and built in 1990–4.

Immediately the decision was taken in January 1986 to build the Channel Tunnel, the cities of northeast France (in sharp contrast to the apathy and suspicion of the towns of southeast England) vied with each other to attract the new high-speed line. By 1988 Lille had beaten its closest rival Amiens to the prize. In addition, aided by £114 million of civic funds, the powerful mayor of Lille and former socialist prime minister, Pierre Mauroy, persuaded SNCF to divert the course of the line via the city centre rather than the airport, through which it was originally designated to run.

As a result of Mauroy's victory, Lille's new Europe station is close both to the old city and to the existing railway terminus, Lille Flandres (which continues to serve TGVs from Paris and the south). The new terminal is also the focus of a vast new office and retail complex, 'Euralille'. The fact that this new development could be so near to the city centre, and not marooned on an out-of-town greenfield site, was due to the proximity of a redundant former barracks area on the fringes of the city centre. Pierre Mauroy declared that he wanted Euralille to constitute 'a strong architectural signal',[9] and that is exactly what he got. Dutch architect Rem Koolhaas (who had achieved

Roissy Station's situation at the heart of Paris' principal international airport, Charles de Gaulle, above, inevitably dictated that the station's profile was lower than its SNCF contemporaries. However, Peter Rice's 'croissant beams' and nautical roof trusses rose to the occasion, creating a seamless web apparently open to the sky.

The glazed rotunda which acts as the new entrance to the revamped Atocha terminus for the AVE trains, Spain's equivalent of the French TGVs, right, provides a welcoming uplift for incoming passengers. Sadly, this is not equalled by the grid-like train shed, above. At Atocha, Rafael Moneo chose to ignore the original 1892 train shed altogether, and to site his new structure at its mouth. The resulting interface of walkways and glazed span is not always successful.

notoriety in the 1970s for his plan to relocate New York's Central Park atop a forest of skyscrapers) was in 1990 appointed as the masterplanner for the site, working in conjunction with the regional Office of Metropolitan Architecture.

Koolhaas's intention is that the Euralille park should be closely integrated with the new station, with easy access and related architectural styling. Thus, Duthilleul's low station roof was actually straddled by one of the most interesting of the site's new blocks, designed by Christian de Portzamparc – a strikingly-profiled building which was immediately likened by the locals to a ski boot.

On entering the station, the most noticable aspect of Duthilleul's comparatively reticent design is the wave-like roof. Largely the work of the late British engineer Peter Rice, it was based directly on the latter's Pavilion of the Future at Seville's Expo '92, and more indirectly on Montuori's S-shaped roof at Rome Termini of forty years before. Since it does not have to fulfil any

loadbearing function, the roof is as light as possible; although clad principally in steel, the metal is so thin that, on a bright day, light is able to permeate into the station concourse. Half-way along, the gentle curve is interrupted by François Deslaugier's elegant, understated road bridge.

The building below is in turn set above the tracks, which had to be sited below ground in order to reach so far into the city centre. Koolhaas was keen to ensure that, even though the platforms were below street level, as much of the station as possible should be visible, making the station the central element of the plan. To achieve this, he sloped the ground down towards the station site, making possible Duthilleul's transparent walls of float glass. Incoming passengers arrive at what is actually the highest of three floors, then travel by escalator or lift to the main concourse in a reversal of the arrangement at Waterloo.

The concourse is dominated by Duthilleul's slender arches, which seem to be effortlessly supporting the whole of Peter Rice's sinuous roof but which actually constitute only one component of the supporting structure. The roof itself actually rests on cross-braces emanating from a horizontal beam, which is in turn carried by a series of small vertical supports. Above them, Rice's graceful steel arches are reinforced by unobtrusive steel ties. These, too, appear at first glance to be unequal to their structural job. However, the ties are actually more reliable than conventional columns. Below the level of the concourse the underground tracks are supported at their sides by V-shaped steel trusses and, directly below the concourse itself, by concrete columns.

The completed station is undeniably impressive. Its graceful roof recalls the great train sheds of the past, its vertically-oriented planning the achievements of the great New York termini. However, in contrast with the great stations of the past, Lille's concourse is strangely empty of shops or services. In the case of this building, and many other new SNCF stations, it seems that the

Stirling-Wilford's Bilbao Abando Station, Spain, represents another catalyst for urban renewal; the model, above, shows the passenger interchange.

The crisp lines and forms of
Antonio Cruz and Antonio
Ortiz's Santa Justa station,
Seville, Spain, made a striking
impact on visitors to Expo 92.

station planners have been almost too reverential towards the architecture.

Built at exactly the same time as Lille Europe, from 1989 to 1994, were two new termini constructed by SNCF to serve large airports: Lyon Satolas and Roissy-Charles de Gaulle. Both these buildings were designed to accommodate the latest TGV trains, and were devised as part of France's increasing commitment to a fully integrated transport system. Both also serve as a sharp rejoinder to other Western governments' lack of interest in this crucial aspect of urban planning.

Roissy Station opened in November 1994. Built to receive TGV services into Paris's Charles de Gaulle Airport, it is perhaps the more conventional of the two. Replacing Paul Andreu's mundane, Brutalist concrete railway terminus of 1976, it was inserted between the sites of the airport's existing Terminal 2 and the planned Terminal 3. The station's six tracks – four for the TGVs and two for the Paris-bound RER trains – were placed below ground, as at Lille Europe and Lyon Satolas (see below). Like Lille, the design was masterminded by SNCF's Jean-Marie Duthilleul and the Paris-based British engineer Peter Rice. The station was more earthbound than some of its French contemporaries; its steel-tube and glass roof rises only gradually, breaking at the centre to make way for the insertion of a new, ship-like hotel of six storeys. Rice's roof was nevertheless a spectacular achievement. Marcus Binney has eloquently described it as 'the rigging of a great sailing ship', which 'only needs the ship's company to scale the masts, run out along the booms and salute the admiral as he reviews the fleet'.[10] Rice's trusses were not conventionally arched, as was the case at Lille, but were actually constructed as upside-down U's. Not for nothing did Rice call them 'croissant beams'. Aside from the trusses and the pylons which supported them, almost the whole roof was glazed. As Rice's project leader explained: 'in the quest for transparency, the structural capacity [of glass] had been exploited so as to dispense with aluminium glazing bars'. The end product is a delicate, subtle structure of white-painted steel and diamond-like glass, brilliant by day and a magic lantern by night.

The form of Lyon Satolas was even more exciting than those of Duthilleul's two stations. The man principally responsible was the remarkable Spanish architect-engineer Santiago Calatrava, who at Lyon combined resonant images of flight – the main concourse was shaped like a butterfly, while the outstretched wings made an obvious reference to Eero Saarinen's bird-like TWA Terminal – with those architectural symbols which for a century and a half have been indissolubly linked with the great railway terminus: the single glazed arch and the vaulted concourse. The result can only be called one of the world's greatest stations, a monument which is a fitting symbol of the revival in railways' fortunes and a highly public testimony to the late twentieth century's rediscovery of the splendour that can be achieved in a great railway station.

As at Roissy, the TGV tracks at Satolas were sited below ground in order to penetrate to the heart of a busy international airport. (Lyon Airport, itself a glum Brutalist complex of 1974, was swiftly overpowered by Calatrava's virtuoso addition.) Over the tracks was the long, low train shed, 1,650 feet long and supported on giant, flat arches. And in the centre of the train shed was placed the main concourse building: a dramatic, bird-like structure, popularly called 'l'Oiseau', which perches atop the gently curving train shed roof like some splendid peacock, in the manner of one of Sant'Elia's most outrageous concepts. The whole of the concourse is supported by fantastic steel ribs – none of which is exactly vertical, just as none of the roof elements is precisely horizontal. Structural glass is once more used to create sharp, elegant supports, wall cladding, and internal partitioning. To prevent the prevalence of glazing from turning the concourse into a greenhouse, the partitions can be automatically lowered to admit air from outside.

Below the concourse are the six tracks, supported on concrete beams rising from triangular concrete supports. Since two of these tracks carry non-stopping services through the station at enormous speeds, they are enclosed in a concrete box. Vaulted walkways connect the platforms with the concourse, and the concourse to the nearby air terminal, only 590 feet away. The overriding image, and indeed the very atmosphere, is of a medieval cathedral – or perhaps one of the great, echoing American Beaux-Arts termini – rendered aerobatically transparent by modern technology. As at Lille and Roissy, and indeed as at Penn Station and Grand Central, the use of strong colour is not much in evidence, either inside or outside. All is monochrome, with only SNCF's standard dark blue signage to relieve the steel greys, concrete beiges and glass whites. Lighting is also kept simple and unobtrusive. Calatrava prefers to rely on the effects of natural light on glass to provide visual interest; it is only at night that the subdued lighting comes into its own, providing the airport and its environs with a stunning illuminated sculpture.

Calatrava's breathtaking *tour de force* has inevitably not been to everyone's taste. Before it even opened, one prominent British architectural critic had already labelled Calatrava's architecture as 'perilously close to

The graceful canopy of Richard Brosi and Robert Obrist's Chur Station, Switzerland, above, distinctly recalls the great glazed train sheds of the late nineteenth century.

kitsch' and far too light-hearted for the serious world of modern design. After the station's unveiling, one sympathetic observer predicted that 'Some undoubtedly will see l'Oiseau as sheer self-indulgence, out of tune with today's revival of modernist simplicity'.[11] Moreover, it did not go unnoticed that, while the whole station project cost $64 million, the station's concourse actually offered few services for the travelling public – only two shops and a restaurant.

The proof of the enduring quality of Calatrava's design, however, lies in its evident popular appeal. The exhibition of the designs for the station and other recent Calatrava projects, held at the RIBA in London in 1992, proved to be the most successful exhibition ever held at the Institute. When the station opened to the public in July 1994, prior to the official inauguration of rail services, over 30,000 visitors

crowded in to get a glimpse of the new building.

Not since the era of St Pancras, Bombay Victoria and Pennsylvania Station has station design been so eagerly awaited, or so architecturally exciting. At termini such as Grimshaw's Waterloo International (1990–3), Richard Brosi and Robert Obrist's Chur, Switzerland (1992–3), Harry Reijnders's Leiden Central (1992–5) and Stirling Wilford's Bilbao Abando (1990–5), the Victorian concept of the great arched train shed has been revived and, by employing the very latest in constructional technology, even improved. At Chur the shed, engineered once again by the talented Peter Rice, not only protects the tracks from driving snow but provides a stunningly simple but enormously appealing and gracefully curved canopy which instantly defines the structure as a great railway terminus. At Leiden the shed runs laterally across

rather than along the line of the tracks, touching down on the platforms with incredible grace and elegance. And at Bilbao Abando, (planned just before James Stirling's death in 1993), Stirling Wilford's bold, sweeping station roof is the centrepiece for a vast new scheme of urban regeneration, funded by central government to appease the local Basque nationalist MPs. The firm's first project for this site, of 1986–7, simply comprised two train sheds flanking a public plaza. By 1990, however, the parameters for the scheme had widened; what the architects ultimately produced was a development that not only provides a dramatic foil for the high-speed trains which serve it, and an impressively theatrical gateway to Spain, but also constitutes a vital link between Bilbao's historic medieval quarter and the nineteenth-century city to the west. At the same time, the station site has been ingeniously adapted to fit neatly into the existing street pattern: another example of a major railway station serving to bind, rather than to fracture, the extant urban grain. As at Duthilleul and Calatrava's contemporary SNCF stations, Abando's six tracks are buried underground, and covered by a low, glazed span, engineered by Ove Arup and Partners. At one side of the shed, over the principal entrance, is the drum-like form of the World Trade Centre, at the other the cube-like tourist centre, 'inclined towards the rail tracks as if to invite exploration'.[13]

Other major termini are also currently in the process of construction. Prominent among them are Terry Farrell's ambitious station at Kowloon, Hong Kong – which will be ready just in time for the British departure from the colony – and Calatrava's vast complex in Lisbon, being built to serve Expo '98. The scale and vision of these projects demonstrates not only that theatre and grandiloquence are once more back in vogue, but, more importantly, that the great railway station is a key architectural icon once more. Freed from the dogmatic shackles of the early twentieth century, the railway terminus is now fully able to express itself in a language which combines references to the architectural imagery of the station, with elements derived directly from the requirements of everyday use and from contemporary design. The result is some of the most impressively confident public buildings of the last twenty years, buildings which are both symbols of a new-found public confidence in modern architecture and testimonies to the role that a revitalized railway system can play in urban regeneration. Looking at the soaring train sheds of Waterloo International, Bilbao Abando and Lyon Satolas, one can truly believe in the birth of a new Railway Age.

The glazed, arched dihedral fans of Santiago Calatrava's giant butterfly, above and overleaf, alight on the long, low shed of Lyon Satolas, creating surely the most glamorous and instantly recognisable profile of any modern railway station. The view overleaf shows Calatrava's 'Oiseau' turning, almost threateningly, to face Guillaume Gillet's humdrum airport. Opposite, the tapering concrete beams gently encase both the platforms and the 190-mph TGVs. In 1993 Catherine Slessor wrote that standing by the tracks was 'like being inside the bleached ribcage of some prehistoric behemoth'. Top, a commemorative stamp portrays a prototype for the TGV.

PORTE RHÔN

NOTES

1 INTRODUCTION

1 John Ruskin, *The Seven Lamps of Architecture*, London (1849), p 222.

2 Quoted in Jean Dethier, *All Stations* (1981), p 6.

3 G K Chesterton, *Tremendous Trifles* (1909), p 219.

4 *Building News*, 1875, quoted in Carroll L V Meeks, *The Railroad Station, An Architectural History*, (1956), Preface.

5 Quoted in Jean Dethier, *Les Temps des Gares*, Paris (1978).

6 Marcel Proust, *Remembrance of Things Past* (1983), p 694.

7 Quoted in Jean Dethier, *Les Temps des Gares, op cit.*

8 Thomas Wolfe, *You Can't Go Home Again*, New York (1934).

9 Quoted in *Bulletin of the Railroad Station Historical Society*, vol 4 (1971).

10 From William Couper (ed), *The History of the Engineering, Construction and Equipment of the Pennsylvania Railroad Company's New York Terminal and Approaches*, New York (1912).

11 Quoted in Jeffrey Richards and John M Mackenzie, *The Railway Station, A Social History*, Oxford (1986).

12 M Baroli, *Le Train dans la littérature française* (1963), quoted in Richards and MacKenzie, *op cit*, p 346.

13 From Ruskin's *The Seven Lamps of Architecture* of 1880. Ruskin's opinion was clearly inherited from his father, who in 1848 had declared that 'A grand railway station is disgusting and a profit only to builders and carpenters': Mary Lutyens, *The Ruskins and the Grays* (1972), p 111.

14 Leo Tolstoy, *Anna Karenina*, Harmondsworth (1954), pp 801–2. Richards and Mackenzie, *op cit*, point out that Tolstoy himself died at a station, Astapovo, in 1910.

15 Anthony Trollope, *The Prime Minister*, London (1876).

16 Quoted in Richards and MacKenzie, *op cit*, p 262.

17 Quoted in Lorraine B Diehl, *The Late, Great Pennsylvania Station* (1985), p 132.

18 From William Couper (ed), *op cit.*

19 Montgomery Schuyler, 'The New Pennsylvania Railroad Station' in The International Studio, vol 41, October 1910.

20 Carroll L V Meeks, *op cit.*

21 Richards and Mackenzie, *op cit.*

22 Jean Dethier, *op cit.*

23 James Fergusson, *A History of the Modern Styles of Architecture*, London (1862).

24 Quoted in Jean Dethier, *op cit.*

25 *The Builder*, vol ix (1851).

26 Carroll LV Meeks, *op cit*, p 95.

27 Gordon Biddle, *The Railway Surveyors*, London (1990), p 242.

2 NEW CATHEDRALS OF TRANSPORT

1 Quoted in Jack Simmons, *St Pancras Station*, London (1968).

2 Quoted in Gordon Biddle, *Great Railway Stations of Britain*, Newton Abbot (1986).

3 In the mid-1980s the former terminus, by now listed Grade I, was converted for use as a national centre for engineering design, a scheme backed by both the city and British Rail. Predictably, though, this excellent training initiative was soon sacrificed to commercial interests. At the time of writing the centre is being reconverted into the Empire and Commonwealth Museum – admittedly a fitting use for the creation of one of the Empire's most resourceful and colourful figures.

4 David Lloyd and Donald Insall, *Railway Station Architecture*, Newton Abbot (1976).

5 Richards and MacKenzie, *op cit*, p 163.

6 Quoted in Jack Simmons, *op cit.*

7 The Burton beer traffic continued until the 1960s; the space which once housed Bass's famous products is now merely a car park.

8 Nikolaus Pevsner, *The Buildings of England: London 2*, Harmondsworth (1952), p 369.

9 George Gilbert Scott, *Personal and Professional Recollections*, London (1879).

10 This story was propagated by Kenneth Clark's *Gothic Revival* of 1928 and repeated in 1939 by Albert Richardson, who ridiculed St Pancras's 'mountain-top scenery and pinnacled summits'. A E Richardson, 'Railway Stations' in *RIBA Journal*, vol 46, 8 May 1939.

11 George Gilbert Scott, *op cit*.

12 An American visitor of 1882 noted that the drab-and-gold wallpaper in the room was complemented by 'a sort of sarcophagus chimney piece surmounted by an antique mirror of bevelled glass.'

13 Michael Hunter and Robert Thorne in Scott, *op cit*. p 82.

14 J J Emmett in *Quarterly Review*, vol 132 (1872).

15 Quoted in Hunter and Thorne, *op cit*, p 80.

16 James Fergusson, *A History of the Modern Styles of Architecture*, second edition, London (1873).

17 Quoted in Jack Simmons, *op cit*.

18 *Ibid*.

19 *Ibid*.

20 *Ibid*.

21 Nikolaus Pevsner, *op cit*.

22 David Piper, *A Companion Guide to London*, London (1964).

23 Lloyd and Insall, *op cit*, p 47.

24 Paul Theroux, 'By Rail Across the Indian Subcontinent' in *National Geographic*, vol 165, June 1984.

25 V S Naipaul, *An Area of Darkness* (1964).

26 Quoted in Richards and MacKenzie, p 69.

27 Rudyard Kipling, *Kim* (1901), p 37–8.

28 Paul Theroux, *The Great Railway Bazaar* (1975), p 140.

29 Quoted in Gillian Tindall, *City of Gold*, London (1982).

30 Jean Dethier, *All Stations* (1981), iv.

31 Gavin Stamp, 'British Architecture in India 1857–1947', *Journal of the Royal Society of Arts*, May 1981.

32 Quoted in Michael Satow and Rory Desmond, *Railways of the Raj*, London (1980).

33 Sir William Acworth, *Railways of England* (1900), quoted in Richards and MacKenzie, p 295.

34 Quoted in Bill Aitken, *Exploring Indian Railways*, Delhi (1994).

35 Charles Ford, *The Blue Guide: Amsterdam*, London (1993), p 64.

3 THE MONUMENTAL AGE OF RAIL

1 César Daly in 'Des Gares de Chemin de Fer' in *Revue Generale d'Architecture* (1845–6), trans Kate Wedd.

2 Christian Barman, *An Introduction to Railway Architecture*, London (1950).

3 Nikolaus Pevsner, op cit, p 366.

4 Quoted in K J Ellaway, *Euston* (1994), p 7.

5 John Britton and A C Pugin, *The Public Buildings of London*, 1839.

6 John Betjeman, 'Dictating to the Railways' in *Architectural Review*, vol 74, September 1933.

7 Alison and Peter Smithson, *The Euston Arch*, London (1968).

8 *Ibid*.

9 Deakin and Willis, *Johnny Go Home* (1976), quoted in Richards and MacKenzie, *op cit*, p 105.

10 Gordon Biddle and O S Nock, *The Railway Heritage of Britain*, London (1983).

11 Christian Barman, *op cit*, p 32.

12 James Fergusson, *op cit*, 1862 ed.

13 Quoted in Thomas van Joest, 'Hittorf et la Nouvelle Gare du Nord' in *Hittorf*, Paris (1986), p 269, trans Kate Wedd.

14 *Ibid*, p 267.

15 *Ibid*, p 275.

16 Quoted in Marcus Binney, Manfred Hamm and Axel Foehl, *Great Railway Stations of Europe*, London (1984).

17 Quoted in Thomas van Joest, *op cit*, p 273.

18 *Ibid*, p 275.

19 Carroll L V Meeks, *op cit*, p 98.

20 Thomas A Pakenham, *The Scramble for Africa*, London (1991), p 606.

21 *Ibid*, p 615.

22 Carroll L V Meeks, *op cit*, p 99.

4 THE ECLECTICISM OF STATION STYLE

1 Richards and Mackenzie, *op cit*.

2 Carroll LV Meeks, *op cit*, p 113.

3 Quoted in E M Earle, *Turkey, the Great Powers and the Bagdad Railway*, London (1923).

4 Paul Theroux, *The Great Railway Bazaar*, Harmondsworth (1975), p 59.

5 T E Lawrence, *Seven Pillars of Wisdom*, Harmondsworth (1962), p 665. It is ironic that Lawrence was to lose the original manuscript of this work at another major railway station, Reading General.

6 Jan Morris, *The Stones of Empire* (1986), p 128.

7 R B Porter, in *Railway Magazine*, vol 63, December 1928.

8 Jan Morris, *op cit*.

9 Paul Theroux, *op cit*, p 198.

10 *Ibid*, p 258.

11 *Ibid*, p 257.

12 Thomas A Pakenham, *op cit*, p 393.

13 Richards and Mackenzie, *op cit*, p 30.

14 Carroll L V Meeks, *op cit*, p 119.

15 Peter Davey, in *Architectural Review*, vol 193, September 1993.

5 THE APOGEE OF THE RAILWAY AGE

1 Carroll L V Meeks, *op cit*, p 165.

2 Quoted in Jean Jenger, *Orsay the metamorphosis of a monument*, London (1987), p 27.

3 *Ibid*.

4 *Ibid*, p 30.

5 *Ibid*, p 38.

6 W S Richardson, 'The Terminal – The Gate of the City' in *Scribner's Magazine*, vol 52, October 1912, p 416.

7 Jean Jenger, *op cit*, p 48.

8 *Ibid*.

9 *Ibid*.

10 J C Garcias and J J Trentell, 'Où en eut le Musée d'Orsay?', in *Techniques et Architecture*, September 1979.

11 Jean Jenger, *op cit*, p 55.

12 *Ibid*, p 56.

13 Ian Nairn, *Nairn's Paris*, Harmondsworth, 1968.

14 *Ibid*, p 57.

15 *Architectural Review*, vol 30, August 1911.

16 Carl W Condit, The Port of New York, Chicago (1980).

17 *Scientific American*, vol 103, 10 September 1910.

18 W S Richardson, 'The Architectural Motif of the Pennsylvania Station' in William Couper (ed), *op cit*.

19 Montgomery Schuyler, *op cit*.

20 Lewis Mumford, 'The Skyline – The Disappearance of Pennsylvania Station' in *New Yorker*, 7 June 1958.

21 Richardson in William Couper (ed), *op cit*.

22 Ken Macrorie, 'Arriving and Departing' in *The Reporter*, 13 September 1962, p 52–55.

23 *Scientific American*, vol 102, 14 May 1910.

24 *New York Architect*, vol 4, September 1910.

25 *The American Architect and Building News*, vol 89, 30 June 1906.

26 Alfred Hoyt Granger, *Charles Follen McKim*, Boston (1913).

27 Thomas Wolfe, *op cit*.

28 William Faulkner, 'Pennsylvania Station' in *Collected Stories*, New York (1950).

29 *Architectural Review*, July 1911, p 72, quoted by Kenneth Powell in *Grand Central Terminal*, London (1996), p 4.

30 David Marshall, *Grand Central*, New York (1946).

31 James M Fitch, *Grand Central Terminal and the Rockefeller Centre*, New York (1974).

32 Carl W Condit, *op cit*.

33 *Architectural Forum*, vol 101, November 1954.

34 *Ibid*.

35 *Ibid*.

36 *Ibid*.

37 Quoted in Ada Huxtable, *Goodbye History, Hello Hamburger*, Washington (1986).

38 Richardson in William Couper (ed), *op cit*.

39 Quoted by Richard Débout, *The Open Gate – Toronto Union Station*, Toronto (1972).

40 *Ibid*.

6 TOWARDS A NEW CENTURY OF TRAVEL

1 Carl W Condit, *The Railroad and the City*, Columbus (1977).

2 Carroll L V Meeks, *op cit*, p 139.

3 Esther da Costa Meyer, *The Work of Antonio Sant'Elia*, New Haven (1995), p 93.

4 Esther da Costa Meyer, *op cit*, pp 197–8.

5 Carroll L V Meeks, *op cit*, p 141.

6 Jean Dethier, *op cit*.

7 Carl W Condit, *The Railroad and the City*, *op cit*.

8 Carroll L V Meeks, *op cit*, p 158.

9 Quoted in *Art Journal*, vol 32, Spring 1973.

10 Union Pacific Railroad press release, 1940 (New York Public Library).

7 THE MODERN MOVEMENT AND BEYOND

1 Kenneth Powell, *Grand Central Terminal*, London (1996).

2 Carroll L V Meeks, *op cit*, p 149.

3 Richard A Etlin, *Modernism in Italian Architecture*, Cambridge MA (1991).

4 A E Richardson, 'Railway Stations' in *RIBA Journal*, vol 46, 8 May 1939.

5 Carroll LV Meeks, *op cit*, p 151.

6 Eric Hobsbawm, *Art and Power: Europe under the Dictators*, London (1995), Foreword.

7 Richard A Etlin, *op cit*.

8 Richards and MacKenzie, *op cit*, p366.

9 Quoted in *Architectural Review*, vol 193, September 1993.

10 Marcus Binney, *Architecture of Rail*, London (1995), p 21.

11 *Ibid*, p37.

12 David Jenkins in *RIBA Journal*, September 1993, p52.

BIBLIOGRAPHY

INTRODUCTION

For those seeking a brief introduction to the history of the railway station, I can do no better than recommend Carroll Meeks's highly authoritative *The Railroad Station* of 1956, which, although now forty years old, is still the best – indeed the only – comprehensive architectural history of the great station. It is now once more widely available, having recently (1995) been reprinted by the inestimable Dover Publications of New York. And for a broader view of the station in its social, political and cultural context, Jeffrey Richards and John M MacKenzie's excellent and highly readable *The Railway Station, A Social History* of 1986 cannot be bettered.

The 1980s saw a sudden increase in the publication of detailed and perceptive studies of station architecture. In Britain the primary influences have been the railway historian Gordon Biddle and architectural historian Marcus Binney, who is best known as one of the founders of the successful architectural pressure group SAVE Britain's Heritage. Gordon Biddle's in-depth studies of surviving stations have provided an essential bedrock for any study of this area, while Binney's thought-provoking books, the definitive *Railway Architecture* of 1983 (written with David Pearce, another SAVE stalwart), *Great Railway Stations*

of Europe of 1985 (which specifically aimed 'to champion the cause of railway architecture' in the face of widespread threats of demolition or unacceptable redevelopment), together with his recent survey of contemporary station design in Europe, *Architecture of Rail* of 1995, have established the railway station as a wholly legitimate branch of architectural history and helped to re-establish discussion of new station architecture at the top of the professional agenda. In Germany, Mihaly Kubinsky's scholarly *Bahnhöfe Europas* of 1969 and Ulrich Krings's *Bahnhofsarchitektur* of 1985 did the same for the German-speaking world, concentrating especially on an area on which little has been written: the stations of Central and Eastern Europe. And in France, Jean Dethier followed up his ground-breaking stations exhibition of 1978 (whose catalogue was translated into English and published as *All Stations* in 1981) with a more detailed study: *Gares d'Europe*, of 1988.

The 1980s also saw an increase in the number of critics and historians who were prepared to look at individual stations as exceptional buildings rather than just as another of the same building type, or a necessary outlet of mass transportation. Jack Simmons's splendidly enthusiastic analysis of St

Pancras of 1968 had been the first biography of a station since René Clozier's thorough but dry *Gare du Nord* of 1940. However, following the lead of Carl Condit's masterly 1977 examination of Cincinnati Union as a building and a product of urban planning and corporate rationalization, during the 1980s a number of monographs were produced on key stations such as Milan Central (1981), Berlin Anhalter (1984) and New York Pennsylvania (1985). This trend has continued into the 1990s, with studies such as K J Ellaway's *Euston* of 1994. American stations have been particularly well served by photographic collections; Edwin P Alexander, Julian Cavalier and H Roger Grant and Charles Bohi's volumes (see below) are particularly useful in this respect. A comprehensive history of US stations, however, still has to be written. Even the most impressive of American railroad stations have been little regarded outside the specialist architectural and railway magazines. The exceptions are the two great New York termini, Penn Station and Grand Central, both of which have been the subject of a number of detailed studies, from John A Droege's *Passenger Terminals and Trains* of 1916 to the author's *Pennsylvania Station* and Kenneth Powell's *Grand Central Station*, eighty years later.

WORLD

Christian Barman, *An Introduction to Railway Architecture* (London: Art and Technics, 1950)

Bund Deutscher Architekten (ed), *Renaissance of Railway Stations*, (Braunschweig: Freiedrich Vieweg & Sohn, 1996).

Anthony Burton, *The Railway Empire* (London: John Murray, 1994)

E F Carter, *Famous Railway Stations of the World* (London: Frederick Muller, 1958)

Jean Dethier, *Le Temps des Gares* (Paris: Centre Georges Pompidou, 1978)

Nicholas Faith, *The World the Railways Made* (London: Bodley Head, 1990) and *Locomotion* (London: BBC, 1993)

Michael Frayn, et al, *Great Railway Journeys of the World* (London: BBC, 1981)

Henry–Russell Hitchcock, *Architecture: The Nineteenth and Twentieth Centuries* (Harmondsworth: Penguin, 4th edn, 1977)

Carroll Meeks, *The Railroad Station – An Architectural History* (New Haven: Yale, 1956)

Present and Past Views of Railroad Station Architecture (Monticello, IL: Bibliographical Research Library, 1984)

C H Reilly, 'Railway Stations' in *Architectural Review*, vol 78, October 1935

Jeffrey Richards and John M MacKenzie, *The Railway Station, A Social History* (Oxford: OUP, 1986)

Rob Shortland-Ball (ed), *Common Roots – Separate Branches* (London: Science Museum, 1994)

BRITAIN

John Betjeman, *London's Historic Railway Stations* (London: John Murray, 1972)

Gordon Biddle, *Victorian Stations* (Newton Abbot: David & Charles, 1973); *Great Railway Stations of Britain* (Newton Abbot: David & Charles, 1977); and Jeoffry Spence, *The British Railway Station* (Newton Abbot: David & Charles, 1977); and O S Nock, *The Railway Heritage of Britain* (London: Michael Joseph, 1983); and *The Railway Surveyors* (London: Ian Allan, 1990)

Marcus Binney and David Pearce, *Railway Architecture* (London: Bloomsbury, 1979)

Geoffery Body, *Railway Stations of Britain* (Wellingborough: Patrick Stephens, 1990)

Michael Bowers, *Railway Styles in Building* (London: Almark, 1975)

Gordon A Buck, *A Pictorial Survey of Railway Stations* (Oxford: Oxford Publishing Co, 1992)

H M Colvin, *A Biographical Dictionary of British Architects* (London: Yale, 1995)

Edwin Course, *London's Railways Then and Now* (London: Batsford, 1987)

J Horsley Denton: *British Railway Stations* (London: Ian Allan, 1965)

James Fergusson, *A History of the Modern Styles of Architecture* (London: John Murray, 1862)

Michael Hanson, 'British Fail' in *Architect*, vol 123, March 1977

John R Kellett, *Railways and Victorian Cities* (London: RKP, 1979)

David Lloyd and Donald Insall, *Railway Station Architecture* (Newton Abbot: David & Charles, 1976)

David Lloyd, 'All Change' in *Architectural Review*, vol 139, February 1966

Bill Pertwee, *The Station Now Standing* (London: Hodder & Stoughton, 1991)

A E Richardson, 'Railway Stations' in *RIBA Journal*, vol 46, 8 May 1939

John Ruskin, *The Seven Lamps of Architecture* (London: George Allen, 1880)

James Scott, *Railway Romance and Other Essays* (London: Hodder & Stoughton, 1913)

Jack Simmons, *The Railway in Town and Country 1830–1914* (Newton Abbot: David & Charles, 1986)

LONDON WATERLOO INTERNATIONAL

Architect's Journal, vol 198, 18 August 1993

Architectural Review, vol 193, September 1993

Marcus Binney, *Architecture of Rail* (London: Academy Editions, 1995)

Building, vol 257, 8 May 1992

LONDON ST PANCRAS

J T Emmett in *Quarterly Review*, vol 132, 1872

James Fergusson, *A History of the Modern Styles of Architecture* (London: 2nd edn, John Murray, 1873)

Michael Hunter and Robert Thorne (eds), *Change at King's Cross* (London: Historical Publications, 1990)

Alan A Jackson, *London's Termini* (Newton Abbot: David & Charles, 1969)

Chris Miele, *Spandrel Painting in the Grand Staircase, The Midland Grand Hotel* (London: English Heritage report, 1993)

Steven Pilcher, 'St Pancras', *Railway World*, December 1994

George Gilbert Scott, *Personal and Professional Recollections* (London: Sampson Low, Marston, Searle & Rivington, 1879)

Jack Simmons, *St Pancras Station* (London: George Allen & Unwin, 1968)

Gavin Stamp and Colin Amery, *Victorian Buildings of London 1837–87* (London: Architectural Press, 1980)

LONDON PADDINGTON

John Betjeman, *London's Historic Railway Stations* (London: John Murray, 1972)

Frank Booker, *The Great Western Railway* (Newton Abbot: David & Charles, 1977)

Elain Harwood and Andrew Saint, *London* (London: HMSO, 1993)

Alan A Jackson, *London's Termini* (Newton Abbot: David & Charles, 1969)

LONDON EUSTON

'The Euston Murder', *Architectural Review*, vol 115, April 1962

John Betjeman, 'Dictating to the Railways', *Architectural Review*, vol 74, September 1933

K J Ellaway, *Euston* (Oldham: Irwell Press, 1994)

Hermione Hobhouse, *Lost London* (London: Macmillan, 1971)

Nikolaus Pevsner, *The Buildings of England: London Except the Cities of London and Westminster* (Harmondsworth: Penguin, 1952)

S M Phillips in *Railway Magazine*, vol 6, 1900

G Royde Smith, *Old Euston* (London: Country Life, 1938)

Alison and Peter Smithson, *The Euston Arch* (London: Thames & Hudson, 1968)

BRISTOL TEMPLE MEADS

R A Buchanan and M Williams, *Brunel's Bristol* (Bristol: Radcliffe Press, 1982)

Clare Crick, *Victorian Buildings in Bristol* (Bristol: Bristol & West Building Society, 1975)

Andor Gomme, Michael Jenner and Bryan Little, *Bristol* (London: Lund Humphries, 1979)

L T C Rolt, *Isambard Kingdom Brunel* (London: Longman, 1957)

MANCHESTER OXFORD ROAD

Architect, vol 219, 22 February 1961

NEWCASTLE–UPON–TYNE CENTRAL

John Dobson, 'The Central Railway Station, Newcastle-upon-Tyne' in *Civil Engineer's and Architect's Journal*, vol 11, 1848

K Hoole, *Railway Stations of the North East* (Newton Abbot: David & Charles, 1985)

EUROPE

'The Architecture of Railroads', *Architectural Record*, vol 104, October 1948

Marcus Binney, Manfred Hamm and Axel Foehl, *Great Railway Stations of Europe* (London: Thames & Hudson, 1984)

Jean Dethier, *Gares d'Europe* (Paris: Denoël, 1988)

Ulrich Krings, *Bahnhofsarchitektur* (Munich: Prestel, 1985)

Mihaly Kubinszky, *Bahnhöfe Europas* (Stuttgart: Franckh'sche Verlagshandlung, 1969)

Michel Ragon, *L'architecture des gares* (Paris: Denoël, 1984)

George Wade, 'Famous Continental Railway Stations', *Railway Magazine*, vols 16 and 17, 1905

FRANCE

Marcus Binney, *Architecture of Rail* (London: Academy Editions, 1995)

Michel Chlastacz, 'Les Belles Gares des Provinces Francaises', *La Vie du Rail*, no 2505, 19–25 July 1995

Jacques Reda and Marc Ribaud, *Gares et trains* (Paris: ACE, 1983)

PARIS NORD

Réné Clozier, *La Gare du Nord* (Paris: J-B Baillière et Fils, 1940)

César Daly, 'Des Gares de Chemin de Fer', *Revue Générale d'Architecture*, 1845–6

Thomas von Joest, 'Hittorf et la Nouvelle Gare du Nord', *Hittorf* (Paris: Musée Carnavalet, 1986)

PARIS ORSAY

Carl W Condit, *The Port of New York* (Chicago: University of Chicago Press, 1980)

J G Garcias and J J Treuttel in *Revue des Monuments Historiques*, vol 6, 1971

Jean Jenger, *Orsay, the metamorphosis of a monument* (Paris: Electa, 1986)

Michel Laclotte, *The Musée d'Orsay* (London: Thames & Hudson, 1987)

LILLE EUROPE

Architectural Review, vol 193, September 1993

LYON SATOLAS

RIBA Journal, vol 101, August 1994

BELGIUM

Thierry Demey, *Les Gares Bruxelloises* (Brussels: Region de Bruxelles-Capitale Service des Monuments et Sites, 1994)

HOLLAND

'The Architecture of Railroads', *Architectural Record*, vol 104, October 1948

Marcus Binney, *Architecture of Rail* (London: Academy Editions, 1995)

GERMANY

BERLIN ANHALTER

Alfred Gottwald, 'The railway buildings of Berlin' in Rob Shortland-Ball (ed), *Common Roots – Separate Branches* (London: Science Museum, 1994)

Helmut Maier, *Berlin Anhalter Bahnhof* (Berlin: Asthetik & Kommunikation, 1984)

FRANKFURT-AM-MAIN

Ulrich Krings, *Bahnhofsarchitektur* (Munich: Prestel, 1985)

ITALY

MILAN CENTRAL

Ernest F Carter, *Famous Railway Stations of the World* (London: Frederick Muller, 1958)

Esther da Costa Meyer, *The Work of Antonio Sant'Elia* (New Haven: Yale, 1995)

P M K Bishop, *Italian Railways* (Newton Abbot: David & Charles, 1973) and *La Stazione Centrale di Milano* (Milan: Ferrovia della Stato/Di Baio Editore, 1981)

FLORENCE SANTA MARIA NOVELLA

Richard A Etlin, *Modernism in Italian Architecture 1890–1940* (Cambridge, MA: MIT, 1991)

ROME TERMINI

'Rome Termini', *Architectural Review*, vol 109, April 1951

SPAIN

ABANDO

David Jenkins in *RIBA Journal*, vol , September 1993

FINLAND

HELSINKI

Albert Christ–Janer, *Eliel Saarinen* (Chicago: University of Chicago Press, 1948)

Marika Hausen, et al, *Saarinen Projects* (Helsinki: Otava, 1990)

Eino Jutikkala, *A History of Finland* (London: Weilin & Goos/Heinemann, 1979)

Markku Komonen (ed), *Saarinen in Finland* (Helsinki: Museum of Finnish Architecture exhibition catalogue, 1984)

Kirmö Mikkola, *Architecture in Finland in the 20th Century* (Huhmari: Finnish-American Cultural Institute, 1981)

USA

Edwin P Alexander, *Down at the Depot* (New York: Clarkson N Potter, 1970)

Julian Cavalier, *Classic American Railroad Stations* (San Diego: A S Barnes, 1980)

John A Droege, *Passenger Terminals and Trains* (New York: McGraw-Hill, 1916)

Samuel A Dun, 'The Problem of the Modern Terminal', *Scribner's Magazine*, vol 52, October 1912

Alfred Fellheimer, 'Modern Railway Passenger Terminals', *The Architectural Forum*, vol 53, December 1930

H Roger Grant and Charles Bohi, *The Country Railroad Station in America* (Boulder, CO: Pruett Publishing Co, 1978)

Laurence Grow, *Waiting for the 5.05: Terminal, Station and Depot in America* (New York: Universe, 1977)

Douglas Haskel, 'Railroad Stations – A Neglected Opportunity', *Architectural Record*, vol 94, December 1943

Herbert H Harwood, 'The Train Stopped Here', *Historic Preservation*, vol 30, April–June 1978

Stewart H Holbrook, *The Story of American Railroads* (New York: Crown, 1947)

Office of Archaeology and Historic Preservation, *National Register of Historic Places: Historic Railroad Stations* (US Department of the Interior, July 1974)

Janet Greestein Potter, *Great American Railway Stations,* (New York: John Wiley, 1996)

Railroad and Bus Terminal and Station Layout (American Locker Co Inc, nd [1945])

Railroad Station Historical Society Bulletin, vols 1–24, 1968–91

John F Stover, *Life and Decline of the American Railroad* (New York: OUP, 1970)

Margo B Webber and Paul J McGinley [Anderson Notter Finegold], *Reuse of Historically and Architecturally Significant Railroad Stations* (Washington, DC: US Department of Transportation, 1978)

Margo B Webber [Anderson Notter Finegold], *Recycling Historic Railroad Stations: A Citizen's Manual* (Washington, DC: US Department of Transportation, 1978)

NEW YORK PENNSYLVANIA

Alfred Granger, *The Architecture of McKim, Mead and White* (1915; reprint, New York: Dover, 1990)

Carl W Condit, *The Port of New York* (Chicago: University of Chicago Press, 1980)

Patricia B Davis, *End of the Line* (New York: Neale Watson, 1978)

Lorraine B Diehl, *The Late, Great Pennsylvania Station* (Lexington, MA: The Stephen Greene Press, 1985)

John A Droege, *Passenger Terminals and Trains* (New York: McGraw-Hill, 1916)

Ada L Huxtable, *Goodbye History, Hello Hamburger* (Washington, DC: Preservation Press, 1986)

Charles Moore, *The Life and Times of Charles Follen McKim* (Boston: Houghton Mifflin, 1929)

Lewis Mumford, *From The Ground Up* (New York: Harcourt Brace, 1956)

Steven Parissien, *Pennsylvania Station, New York, 1905–10* (London: Phaidon, 1996)

Pennsylvania Railroad Company (ed William Couper), *The History of the Engineering, Construction and Equipment of the Pennsylvania Railroad Company's New York Terminal and Approaches* (Philadelphia: PRR, 1912)

C H Reilly, *McKim, Mead and White* (London: Ernest Benn, 1924)

Leland M Roth, *McKim, Mead and White, Architects* (London: Thames and Hudson, 1983)

Robert Sobel, *The Fallen Colossus* (New York: Weybright and Talley, 1977)

NEW YORK GRAND CENTRAL

Architectural Forum, vol 101, November 1954 and vol 128, January/February 1968

James M Fitch, *Grand Central Terminal and the Rockefeller Centre* (New York: New York State Parks and Recreation, 1974)

Grand Central Terminal – 75th Anniversary (New York: Metro-North Commuter Railroad, 1988)

H Roger Grant, *Living in the Depot* (Iowa City: University of Iowa Press, 1993)

David Marshal, *Grand Central* (New York: McGraw-Hill, 1946)

William D Middleton, *Grand Central* (San Marino, CA: Golden West, 1977)

Deborah Nevins (ed), *Grand Central Terminal: City Within the City* (NY: Municipal Arts Society of New York, 1982)

Kenneth Powell, *Grand Central Terminal* (London: Phaidon, 1996)

Donald Martin Reynolds, *The Architecture of New York City* (New York: John Wiley, 1994)

CINCINNATI UNION

Art Journal, vol 32, Spring 1973

Carl W Condit, *The Railroad and the City* (Columbus, OH: Ohio State University Press, 1977)

Alfred Fellheimer, 'The Principles of Terminal Stations', *Railway Age*, 21 July 1923

WASHINGTON UNION

Architectural Review, vol 30, August 1911

Thomas Finnegan, *Saving Union Station* (Albany, NY: Washington Park Press, 1989)

David Morton, 'A Terminal Case?', *Progressive Architecture*, vol 58, November 1977

Thornton H Waite, 'Union Station, Washington, DC', *Railroad Station Historical Society Bulletin*, vol 22, March/April 1989

CANADA

Pierre Berton, *The Great Railway* (Toronto: McClelland & Stewart, 1972)

Julian Cavalier, *North American Railroad Stations* (Cranbury, NJ: A S Barnes, 1979)

TORONTO UNION

Richard Bébout, *The Open Gate – Toronto Union Station* (Toronto: Peter Martin, 1972)

Robert F Legget, *Railways of Canada* (Newton Abbot: David & Charles, 1973)

OTTAWA

'Ottawa Station', *Progressive Architecture*, August 1967

VANCOUVER CPR

Nicholas Faith, *The World the Railways Made* (London: Bodley Head, 1990)

Raymond Hull, *Vancouver's Past* (Seattle: University of Washington Press, 1974)

ASIA

O S Nock, *Railways of Asia and the Far East* (London: A & C Black, 1978)

Paul Theroux, *The Great Railway Bazaar* (London: Hamish Hamilton, 1975)

ISTANBUL HYDERPASHA

E M Earle, *Turkey, the Great Powers and the Bagdad Railway* (London: Macmillan, 1923)

DAMASCUS HEJAZ

Brigid Keenan in *Interiors*, vol 15, March 1995

BOMBAY VICTORIA

Bill Aitken, *Exploring Indian Railways* (Delhi: OUP, 1994)

Philip Davies, *Splendours of the Raj* (London: John Murray, 1985)

Jan Morris, *Stones of Empire* (Oxford: OUP, 1986)

Michael Satow and Ray Desmond, *Railways of the Raj* (London: Scolar Press, 1980)

Gavin Stamp, 'British Architecture in India 1857–1947', *Journal of the Royal Society of Arts*, vol CXXIX, May 1981

Gillian Tindall, *City of Gold* (London: Temple Smith, 1982)

J N Westwood, *Railways of India* (Newton Abbot: David & Charles, 1974)

CALCUTTA HOWRAH

Jan Morris, *Stones of Empire* (Oxford: OUP, 1986)

Railway Magazine, vol 63, December 1928

KUALA LUMPUR

B W and L Andaya, *History of Malaysia* (London: Macmillan, 1982)

Peter Chay, *Kuala Lumpur* (Kuala Lumpur: Foto Technik, 1989)

TOKYO

Kami Ryosuke, *Tokyo Sights and Insights* (Tokyo: Tuttle, 1992)

Edward Seidensticker, *Low City, High City* (New York: Alfred A Knopf, 1983) and *Tokyo Rising* (New York: Alfred A Knopf, 1990)

Paul Walen, *Tokyo Now and Then* (Tokyo: Weatherhill, 1984) and *Tokyo, City of Stories* (Tokyo: Weatherhill, 1991)

Richard Wurman, *Tokyo Access* (Tokyo: Kodanska, 1984)

AUSTRALASIA

David B Leitch, *Railways of New Zealand* (Newton Abbot: David & Charles, 1972)

O S Nock, *Railways of Australia* (London: A & C Black, 1971)

Railways of New South Wales 1855–1955 (Sydney: New South Wales Department of Railways, 1955)

L C Staffan, 'Railway Station Buildings – An Historical Survey', *Journal of the New Zealand Institute of Architects*, vol 32, March 1965

AFRICA

E D Brant, *Railways of North Africa* (Newton Abbot: David & Charles, 1971)

John R Day, *Railways of Southern Africa* (London: Arthur Baker, 1963)

Nicholas Faith, *The World the Railways Made* (London: Bodley Head, 1990)

Thomas Pakenham, *The Scramble for Africa* (London: Weidenfeld and Nicolson, 1991)

INDEX

PICTURE CREDITS

TO JULIA

ACKNOWLEDGEMENTS

I would like to thank everyone who has helped in the research for and production of this book. Those who helped me to travel abroad: in particular Paula Folkard, Mark Johnson and British Airways, Guy and April Nobes, Amy Ostenso, Malcolm Parsons and European Passenger Services, and Daria and Jeanne-Marie Teutonico. Also those who have generously shared their expertise or have provided me with invaluable information, among whom I must mention Ian Clift, Margaret Davies, James Edgar, David Fraley, Kent Hannah and the RSHS, Julian Holder, Chris Miele, Timothy Mowl, Graeme Overall, Steve Pilcher, Glenn Scoggins, Carolyn Stoddard, The Victorian Society and Albert Zimmer. Especial thanks go to Andrew Holt, for his invaluable help in France, Belgium and the Netherlands; Kate Wedd, for her French translations; and my wife, for her advice, guidance and peerless proofreading.

AUTHOR'S NOTE

This book was not intended as an exhaustive history of station architecture. (Carroll Meeks's *The Railroad Station* is still unsurpassed in this respect.) It is rather an analysis of the phenomenon of the great railway station and its development over 150 years of railway history, through the medium of a very personal selection of the world's greatest railway terminals. The focus is very much on the architecture of the station and on how its principal components – the waiting rooms, the services, the concourse, the train shed, the platforms – have been reinterpreted and adapted.

The subjects dealt with do not include station hotels, unless (as in the case of London's St Pancras) those hotel buildings incorporate services connected with the operation of the station. Station hotels, fascinating as they are, constitute a wholly separate subject, one that has already been enthusiastically tackled elsewhere.

Some station and place names have been anglicized for clarity and Imperial measurements have been used throughout.

Phaidon Press Ltd
Regent's Wharf

All Saints Street
London N1 9PA

First published 1997

© 1997 Phaidon Press Limited

ISBN 0 7148 3467 X

A CIP catalogue record for this
book is available from the
British Library.

Printed in Hong Kong.

Introduction to
BUSINESS
2nd Edition

Jeff Madura
Florida Atlantic University

SOUTH-WESTERN
★
TM
THOMSON LEARNING

Australia · Canada · Mexico · Singapore · Spain · United Kingdom · United States

Introduction to Business, 2e, by Jeff Madura

Publisher: Dave Shaut
Acquisitions Editor: Dave Shaut
Developmental Editor: Leslie Kauffman, Litten Editing and Production, Inc.
Executive Marketing Manager: Steve Scoble
Marketing Coordinator: Erin Powers
Production Editor: Barbara Fuller Jacobsen
Media Developmental Editor: Sally Nieman
Media Production Editor: Robin K. Browning
Manufacturing Coordinator: Sandee Milewski
Internal Design: Liz Harasymczuk
Cover Design: Joe Devine
Cover Photographer: ©TSM/Jose Fuste Raga, 2000
Production House: Litten Editing and Production, Inc.
Compositor: GGS Information Services, Inc.
Printer: Quebecor World

Printed in the United States of America
1 2 3 4 5 03 02 01 00

For more information contact South-Western College Publishing, 5101 Madison Road, Cincinnati, Ohio 45227 or find us on the Internet at http://www.swcollege.com

For permission to use material from this text or product, contact us by

- Telephone: 1-800-730-2214
- Fax: 1-800-730-2215
- Web: http://www.thomsonrights.com

0-324-06474-8 (core book, Business Plan book, Business Plan CD-ROM, and InfoTrac)
0-324-00675-6 (core book only)
0-324-06475-6 (Business Plan book)
0-324-00680-2 (Business Plan CD-ROM)
0-324-10159-7 (looseleaf book, Business Plan book, Business Plan CD-ROM, and InfoTrac)
0-324-00676-4 (looseleaf book only)

Library of Congress Cataloging-in-Publication Data

Madura, Jeff.
  Introduction to business / Jeff Madura.
    p. cm.
  ISBN 0-324-00675-6 (alk. paper)
1. Industrial management. 2. Business. I. Title.

HD31 .M2815 2001
658—dc21   00-033858

To Mary

Brief Contents

Contents

29   Chapter 2
Selecting a Form of Business Ownership

55   Chapter 3
Business Ethics and Social Responsibility

PART II

89 Business Environment

91 Chapter 4
Economic Environment

119 Chapter 5
Industry Environment

231 Chapter 9
Production Management

259 Chapter 10
Improving Production Quality and Efficiency

385 Chapter 14
Distribution Strategies

409 Chapter 15
Promotion Strategies

493 **Chapter 18**
Business Investment

581 Chapter 21
Synthesis of Business Functions

607 Appendix A
How to Invest in Stocks

Preface

Whether college students select business or some other area as their major, they typically pursue a career that is in a business setting. For example, students who major in science commonly work for biotechnology firms, and can benefit from an understanding of business. Students who select journalism as a major commonly work for media and publishing firms, and therefore benefit from an understanding of business. Even students who plan to work for the government benefit from an understanding of business, since the government has become more focused on recognizing its revenue and its expenses as if it were a business.

A course in Introduction to Business can be one of the most important courses for shaping a student's career. It provides the foundation of business knowledge that can enable students to utilize their talent in the business world. It also provides a survey of the different business topics, allowing students who plan to major in business to determine the field of business (management, marketing, etc.) they would like to pursue.

Focused Around a Business Plan

The underlying approach of the text revolves around the development of a business plan. The chapters follow the structure of a business plan and are organized into seven parts. Part I of the text explains how to establish a business, how to choose a type of business organization, and how to establish ethics guidelines for the business. Part II describes how the business environment (economic, industry, and global conditions) can affect a business. Parts III and IV focus on the management of a business, while Part V focuses on the marketing, and Part VI explains the financial management of the business. Part VII discusses other business topics.

Focused on Key Business Concepts

This textbook is designed to prepare students for the business world by focusing on business concepts, without dwelling only on definitions. It uses a unique approach to place students in positions as decision-makers so that they can truly understand the dilemmas faced by businesses. Here are some examples of key business concepts that are discussed in this text:

▶ What are the objectives of managers, and what potential conflicts of interest can occur?
▶ How can a firm use the Internet to enhance its performance?
▶ How does the level of competition within an industry affect a firm's performance?
▶ How can firms benefit by expanding overseas? How can they be adversely affected by expanding overseas?
▶ Why do firms restructure their operations?
▶ How can firms motivate their employees?
▶ How should firms promote their products?
▶ How does the Federal Reserve System (the Fed) affect a firm's performance?
▶ How are the roles of different business departments intergrated?

The concepts in this text are intended to make students think, rather than just rely on memory. This enables students to understand business strategy, so that they can not only survive but also be successful in the business world.

Focused on Learning Methods Endorsed by the AACSB

This text enables students to learn concepts through learning methods (such as decision making, teamwork, and communication) that are endorsed by the American Association of Collegiate Schools of Business (AACSB). For example, students are challenged to be creative by forming their own business idea. The cases and other end-of-chapter exercises frequently put students in positions in which they must make business decisions. There are teamwork exercises so that students become experienced in working with others to resolve business dilemmas. There are communication exercises that enable students to improve their writing and speaking skills, and thus learn how to communicate their ideas, as they learn business concepts.

Special Features That Distinguish This Text From Others

This text is loaded with features that help students learn business concepts. In particular, six special features differentiate this text from other texts:

- ▶ Emphasis on Technology
- ▶ Practical, Real-World Applications and Team Building Projects
- ▶ The Coca-Cola Annual Report Project
- ▶ Small Business Applications
- ▶ Value Creation First, Definitions Second
- ▶ Cost-Saving Features
- ▶ Reinforcement of Key Concepts

Emphasis on Technology

Business Online

New!

The Internet is now being used in some manner by most businesses. Each chapter has two or more sections called **Business Online**, which illustrate how the Internet is used by businesses to apply a particular business concept discussed in that chapter. Featured websites include **Adobe** (Chapter 2, p. 34), **Blockbuster** (Chapter 6, p. 146), and **Monster.com** (Chapter 12, p. 317).

Spotlight on Technology

The role technology plays in business continues to grow. **Spotlight on Technology** explores the integration of technology in business, both now and in the future, and develops the relationship between technology resources and each functional area of business. Examples include *Online Resources for Starting a Business* on p. 18 in Chapter 1, *Online Recruiting and Recruitment Software* on p. 329 in Chapter 12, and *Distribution through the Internet* on p. 401 in Chapter 14.

Dell Computer's Formula for Success

New!

Dell Computer is one of the most successful firms in the last decade. Each chapter has a section called **Dell Computer's Formula for Success** (an example follows at top of next page) that explains how Dell applied the key concepts in that chapter to achieve high performance.

Applications for Dell Computer

At the end of each part, students are asked how specific business concepts covered in that part can be applied to Dell Computer's business. An emphasis is placed on the use of the application of the Internet and technology to Dell Computer's business. This ensures that students understand how Dell Computer has been able to achieve success by applying technology and other business concepts.

Internet Applications

Internet Applications at the end of each chapter send students out to real-company websites to research and answer questions related to the chapter concepts.

Practical, Real-World Applications and Team-Building Projects

Global Business

Global Business boxes in each chapter show how global realities impact every area of business and emphasize how international opportunities and dilemmas affect the value-creation ability of the firm. For example, see *Global Quality Standards* on p. 267 in Chapter 10 and *Promoting Products Across Countries* on p. 422 in Chapter 15.

Self-Scoring Exercises

Self-Scoring Exercises scattered throughout the text prepare students for the business world by helping them understand their strengths and weaknesses and how those characteristics can successfully fit into a business setting. Questions posed include *Assessing the Ethical Standards of the Firm Where You Work* (Chapter 3, p. 71), *Are You an Empowered Employee?* (Chapter 11, p. 303), and *How Much Risk Can You Take?* (Appendix A, p. 615).

Cross-Functional Teamwork

Cross-Functional Teamwork boxes emphasize the need for managers of different functional areas to work as a team in order to maximize profits, focusing on planning errors that occur when individual units are NOT working together toward the same goal.

Investing in the Stock of a Business

Students acquire the annual report of a company in which they want to invest, then track that company's stock price throughout the semester. Students also investigate how their company manages its business operations, analyze how it markets products, and generally learn how it conducts business.

Stock Market Game

This new feature, appearing at the end of each part, allows students to simulate the management of a stock portfolio. It keeps track of the portfolio as the student trades over time, and determines the market value of the portfolio on a daily basis. The last part includes a project that allows the student to determine the performance of their investments.

Integration of Business Concepts

The text integrates business concepts throughout. There is a **Part Introduction** at the beginning of each part that introduces the chapters in that part and explains how those chapters are related. At the end of the part, a **Part Summary** summarizes how various concepts covered within the part are integrated.

As previously mentioned, the "Cross-Functional Teamwork" feature in each chapter explains how various business strategies discussed within the chapter require teamwork and interaction among employees of different departments. The final chapter of the text (Chapter 21) summarizes the entire text and integrates many of the key business functions that were described throughout the text.

The Coca-Cola Co. Annual Report Project

Introduction to Business includes exercises after each chapter that specifically reference The Coca-Cola Company's annual report and show practical applications of chapter topics. This stimulating hands-on look at The Coca-Cola Company gives students first-hand, real-life exposure to how all functional areas of a company work together to propel one of the world's most recognizable products into the 21st Century. Updated questions for the most recent Coca-Cola Company annual report are found on the text's web site at **http://madura_intro_bus.swcollege.com**.

THE *Coca-Cola* COMPANY ANNUAL REPORT PROJECT

Questions for the current year's annual report are available on the text web site at **http://madura_intro_bus.swcollege.com**.

The following questions apply concepts learned in this chapter to The Coca-Cola Company. Go to The Coca-Cola Company web site (**http://www.cocacola.com**) and find the index for the 1999 annual report.

QUESTIONS

1 Look at the information on the "Impact of Inflation and Changing Prices." How could inflation affect The Coca-Cola Company's future profitability? What does The Coca-Cola Company generally

do to counteract inflationary effects?

2 Look at the information on "Euro Conversion." Does the management of The Coca-Cola Company perceive any problems to be associated with the introduction of the euro, the new European currency?

3 Look at "Middle & Far East Group." Given that it is impossible to predict future economic conditions, what might be a general strategy of a large firm such as The Coca-Cola Company to insulate against shifts in the economic environment of any particular country?

Small Business Applications

Examples from Fortune 500 companies are beneficial, but it's also important to recognize issues facing smaller businesses. This text gives you many flexible options to do just that.

College Health Club: Business Dilemma

This on-going simulation tracks the dilemmas of Sue Kramer's new business, College Health Club, from start-up through the growth phase. The **Business Dilemma** is tied closely to specific issues in individual chapters as students encounter the problems and opportunities faced by Sue and her business.

Small Business Survey

Who are the board members of small firms? Do employees want more influence in business decisions? How do CEOs allocate their time when managing employees? Answers to these and similar questions are discussed in **Small Business Survey**, providing your students with a reality-based picture of how small business managers conduct day-to-day business.

Running Your Own Business

The **Running Your Own Business** project at the end of each part of the text takes students step-by-step through issues and decisions they would face in running their own business. Students choose their own business and develop a business plan as they go through the chapters of the text. Questions guide them through the issues they would face. At the end of the project, students can convert their accumulated answers into a formal business plan. An accompanying business plan booklet and CD-ROM provide templates where students can document their business plan.

Managing Campus.com

In the **Managing Campus.Com** project, students are given an idea for a small business that would sell information about college campuses to prospective students over the Internet. They are asked to make decisions about how to apply business concepts covered within each part of the text. By the end of the semester, they will have completed a business plan for this small business. An accompanying business plan booklet and CD-ROM provide templates where students can document their business plan. This project also offers the opportunity for students to work in teams and to develop their communication skills by sharing their ideas with their team or with the class.

Value Creation First, Definitions Second

Introduction to Business provides complete and thorough definitions to the hundreds of terms this course requires. **Key terms** are highlighted in four different ways:

▶ Boldfaced within the text
▶ Placed in the margin with full definitions
▶ Listed at the end of the chapter where they first appear
▶ Assembled in a glossary at the end of the text and page-referenced to where the definition appears.

But this isn't a dictionary of business terms. It emphasizes business concepts and strategy, which are much more important to your students' success in understanding business than memorizing a list of terms.

Introduction to Business reaches students through a variety of vignettes, exercises, and projects. In addition, end-of-chapter material reinforces this practical application through four distinct elements for each chapter:

▶ **Review Questions** that emphasize the review of basic chapter concepts
▶ **Discussion Questions** that ask students to apply chapter concepts to business situations
▶ **Cases** that present real-world scenarios for students to analyze and make decisions about the direction of a business
▶ **Video Cases** that allow you to bring a real business into the classroom, where students can discuss the situation faced by the business and the results of the action the business decided to take.

Cost-Saving Features

In-Text Study Guide

Found at the end of each chapter, the **In-Text Study Guide** questions essentially serve as a study guide without the additional cost. Segments focus on test preparation, with 10 true/false and 25 multiple-choice questions per chapter. Answers to these questions, along with page references for where the answers can be found, are provided in Appendix C of the text. In-Text Study Guide questions are repeated in a separate section of the test bank for instructors who want to provide an incentive for students to work through the questions.

Loose-Leaf Version of *Introduction to Business*

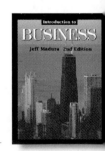

If you're concerned about keeping costs down for your students, or if you prefer to teach the topics in a different order, you should look into the loose-leaf version of *Introduction to Business*. (ISBN 0-324-10159-7)

Reinforcement of Key Concepts

Many of the features just described reinforce the key concepts in each chapter. This leads to better understanding on the part of the student. In turn, instructors have more flexibility to focus on current events and class discussion exercises. To illustrate how this text can ensure a clear understanding through reinforcement, consider the concept of making a decision on how to promote a product, which is discussed in Chapter 15. The Spotlight on Technology discusses electronic shopping offered by firms. The Small Business Survey section in that chapter discusses the opinions of small businesses about the skills that are necessary to be successful in sales. The Global Business section in that chapter explains why promotion strategies need to be adjusted to appeal to customers in foreign countries. The Business Dilemma section in that chapter explains the dilemma of a health club that is considering various strategies to promote its services. The Investing in the Stock of a Business exercise in that chapter asks students to determine how the firm that they decided to invest in at the beginning of the term promotes its products. The Case in that chapter illustrates the decisions involved in promoting a product on a website. The Video Case illustrates promotion strategies for Red Roof Inn. The Internet Application in that chapter observes the promotion strategies of Amazon.com. The Coca-Cola Company Annual Report Project in that chapter enables students to determine the ways in which The Coca-Cola Company promotes its products. Finally, the In-Text Study Guide in that chapter allows students to test their understanding of promotion strategies. Students are consistently empowered to make decisions as if they were managers of a firm.

Every key concept in the text can be reinforced with one or more of the text features just described. While instructors may vary in their emphasis of features in this text to reinforce each concept, they have a variety of features available to them.

The Supplement Package

We know how vital the supplement package is to the success of your Introduction to Business course, so we're pleased to provide an extensive package to accompany *Introduction to Business*.

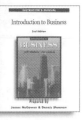

Instructor's Manual

The **Instructor's Manual**, prepared by James McGowen and Dennis Shannon of Belleville Area College, includes chapter outlines, discussion questions for boxed material in the text, suggestions for research topics, suggestions for guest speakers, and solutions to end-of-chapter materials.

Test Bank

The **Test Bank**, prepared by James McGowen and Dennis Shannon of Belleville Area College, includes over 2,000 true/false, multiple-choice, and essay questions. Each question notes the text page reference and difficulty level. Questions from the in-text study guide are included in a separate section.

ExamView Testing Software

ExamView Testing Software contains all of the questions in the printed test bank. This program is an easy-to-use test creation software compatible with Microsoft Windows. Instructors can add or edit questions, instructions, and answers; and select questions by previewing them on the screen, selecting them randomly, or selecting them by number. Instructors can also create and administer quizzes online, whether over the Internet, a local area network (LAN), or a wide area network (WAN).

PowerPoint Presentation Slides

PowerPoint Presentation Slides, prepared by Stephen M. Peters of Walla Walla Community College and President of Cool Pictures & MultiMedia Presentations, are available to qualified adopters. The slides that accompany *Introduction to Business* include custom presentations that contain chapter outlines and key exhibits from the text.

Video Case Segments

Each chapter concludes with a video case that puts chapter concepts into action within the context of a real business. This edition includes all new video cases describing the specific challenges of the featured companies and the choices they must make to solve them. Featured companies include Yahoo!, Ben & Jerry's, World Gym, and Burton Snowboards. In all cases, students hear the story in the words of those who know it best.

Business Plan Booklet

A **Business Plan Booklet** and **Electronic Templates** are tied to both the *Campus.com* and *Running Your Own Business* end-of-part projects. These templates provide predesigned documents for students to fill in so that they can complete their business plans for these projects.

CD-ROM

A **CD-ROM**, packaged with each text, provides the electronic templates for the *Campus.com* and *Running Your Own Business* business plans, as well as the PowerPoint slides. The slides can be printed three to a page with space for student note-taking.

Acetate Transparencies

Full-color **Acetate Transparencies** of key text exhibits and PowerPoint slides are provided for qualified adopters.

Web Site

A text support **Web Site** at **http://madura_intro_bus.swcollege.com** offers many resources for both instructors and students. Instructors can access downloadable supplement materials and additional video cases. Students can access interactive quizzes, key-term flashcards, chapter links, career-related links, and updated questions for *The Coca-Cola Company Annual Report Project* related to its most recent annual report.

For more information about supplement availability and qualifications, contact your local South-Western College Publishing representative.

Acknowledgments

Several reviewers completed surveys and analyzed drafts of chapters for the second edition, and helped improve the final product. They are acknowledged here in alphabetical order.

Ronald J. Cereola	James Madison University
Swee Chia	Baruch College-CUNY
Steven Christian	Jackson Community College
Robert Costi	Concordia University
Sam Crowley	DeVry Institute
H. Leroy Drew	Central Maine Technical College

Ken Fairweather	LeTourneau University
Dennis Foster	Northern Arizona University
Abhay Burjor Ghiara	DeVry Institute
Debbie Gilliard	Metropolitan State College of Denver
Robert A. Hall	Adult Vocational Training Center-DOC Lakes Region Facility
Bruce J. Hanson	Pepperdine University
Annette Johnson	Johnson County Community College
David B. Klenosky	Purdue University
Mary Beth Klinger	Charles County Community College
Barbara Luck	Jackson Community College
Richard J. Magjuka	Indiana University
Rosalie Martin	El Paso Community College
Jim Miles	Anoka Ramsey Community College
Pete Moutsatson	Montcalm Community College
Susan Ockert	Charles County Community College
Kathy Parkison	Indiana University Kokomo
Camille Reale	Sacred Heart University
Bernard Schmit	FMU-Fort Lauderdale College Campus
Pat Setlik	William Rainey Harper College
Laurie Shapero	Miami-Dade Community College
Peter Mark Shaw	Tidewater Community College
Carolou Skeans	Miami University-Middletown
Manny Stein	Queensborough Community College of The City University of New York
Charlene Terninko	Associate Dean, Keiser College
Linda Tucker	Brooks College
Michael Vijuk	Harper College
Jeffrey Walls	Indiana Institute of Technology
Joel Wisner	University of Nevada-Las Vegas
Mary E. Zimmerer	Mesa State College

In addition, many others offered insight and suggestions on particular business concepts, including Carol Annunziato, John Bernardin, Ed Diarias, Bob Duever, Dick Fenton, Dan Hartnett, Joan Hedges, Victor Kalafa, Dave Lynde, Randy Rudecki, Mike Suerth, Tom Vogl, Rachel Zera, and Peter Zutty. In addition, Jarrod Johnston contributed to the parts of the text that were focused on technology and management information systems. And Oliver Schnusenberg provided the Business Online and Dell Computer features, as well as contributed to new end-of-chapter materials.

Special thanks go to Dave Shaut, Vice President/Team Director and acting Acquisitions Editor for his creative ideas; to Leslie Kauffman, Developmental Editor–Litten Editing and Production, for managing the project and pulling all its pieces together; to Barb Fuller-Jacobsen, Production Editor, and Malvine Litten, Project Manager–Litten Editing and Production, for keeping the project on schedule and ensuring a quality final product; to Erin Powers, Marketing Coordinator, for her promotional and marketing efforts; to Joe Devine, Senior Designer, and Rick Moore, Design Coordinator, for their design and creative efforts. Finally, I wish to thank my wife Mary and my parents for their moral support.

Jeff Madura

About the Author

Jeff Madura is the SunTrust Professor of Finance at Florida Atlantic University. He has written several other textbooks as well, including *International Financial Management* and *Financial Market and Institutions*. He has had articles on business published in numerous journals, including *Journal of Financial and Quantitative Analysis*, *Journal of Banking and Finance*, *Journal of Business Research*, *Financial Review*, *Journal of Financial Research*, *Columbia Journal of World Business*, *Journal of International Money and Finance*, and *Journal of Business Strategies*. He has received awards for teaching and research and has served as a consultant for many businesses. He has served as Director for the Southern Finance Association and the Eastern Finance Association and has also served as President of the Southern Finance Association.

Organization of a Business

A business is created to provide products or services to customers. The first step in understanding how businesses operate is to recognize their most important functions and how a business is initially organized. Part I, which contains Chapters 1 through 3, provides this background. Chapter 1 describes key business functions and explains how to develop a plan for a new business. Chapter 2 describes the possible forms of business ownership that the creators of a new business can select. It also explains how business owners are exposed to risk when they establish a business. Chapter 3 describes the ethical and social responsibilities of owners who establish a business and of employees who are hired to manage the business. This chapter is included in Part I because a business should recognize ethical and social responsibilities as soon as it is established. Overall, Part I explains the main decisions that owners must make when they create a new business. These decisions serve as a foundation for other decisions that are made by employees as the business develops. Consequently, these initial decisions affect the performance of the firm and ultimately its value.

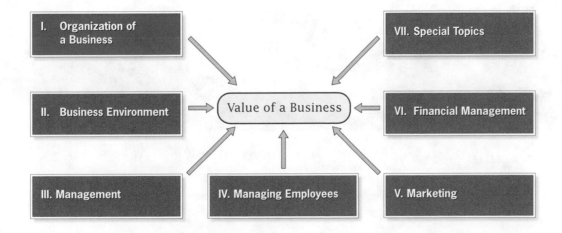

I. Organization of a Business

VII. Special Topics

II. Business Environment → Value of a Business ← VI. Financial Management

III. Management — IV. Managing Employees — V. Marketing

The Learning	1	Identify the key stakeholders that are involved in a business.
Goals of this	2	Describe the key functions of a business.
chapter are to:	3	Explain how to develop a business plan.

Planning a Business

A business (or firm) is an enterprise that provides products or services that customers desire. According to the U.S. Labor Department, more than eight hundred thousand businesses are created in the United States every year. Many businesses, such as Dell Computer, Kodak, and Ford Motor Company, develop products for customers. Others, such as American Airlines and Hilton Hotels, provide services rather than products. Common types of service organizations include travel agencies and health care, law, and accounting firms. Managing a business that provides services can be as challenging and rewarding as managing a business that provides products.

Key Stakeholders in a Business

① Identify the key stakeholders that are involved in a business.

Every business conducts transactions with people. Those people are affected by the business and therefore have a stake in it. They are referred to as **stakeholders,** or people who have an interest (or stake) in the business. Five types of stakeholders are involved in a business:

stakeholders people who have an interest in a business; the business's owners, creditors, employees, suppliers, and customers

▶ Owners
▶ Creditors
▶ Employees
▶ Suppliers
▶ Customers

Each type of stakeholder plays a critical role for firms, as explained next.

Owners

entrepreneurs people who organize, manage, and assume the risk of starting a business

Every business begins as a result of ideas about a product or service by one or more people, called **entrepreneurs,** who organize, manage, and assume the risk of starting a business. More than 8 million people in the United States are entrepreneurs. Entrepreneurs are critical to the development of new business because they create new products (or improve existing products) desired by consumers.

An entrepreneur who creates a business initially serves as the sole owner. However, as a business grows, it may need more funding than the entrepreneur can provide. Consequently, the entrepreneur may allow other people to invest in the firm and become co-owners.

When the ownership of the firm is shared, the proportion of the firm owned by existing owners is reduced. Consider a bakery that two people created with a $100,000 investment each. Each person owns one-half of the firm. They can obtain more funds by allowing a third person to invest in the firm. If the third person invests $100,000, each of the three people will own one-third of the firm. Any profits (or earnings) of the firm that are distributed to owners will be shared among three owners. However, when the firm accepts investment from more owners, it may be able to expand its business so that the original owners may benefit despite their decreased share of ownership.

stock certificates of ownership of a business

stockholders (shareholders) investors who wish to become partial owners of firms

Many large firms periodically sell **stock** (certificates of ownership of a business) to investors who wish to become partial owners (called **stockholders** or **shareholders**) of those firms. Large firms such as ExxonMobil, IBM, and General Motors have millions of stockholders. Their stock can be sold to other investors who wish to invest in these firms. When a firm's performance improves, its value may increase as well, as reflected in a higher stock price for those who own the stock. As an extreme example, stockholders of Dell Computer have doubled their investment in some years because Dell has performed so well. At the other extreme, stockholders of many firms have lost their entire investment because the firms failed.

Creditors

Firms typically require financial support beyond that provided by their owners. When a firm is initially created, it incurs expenses before it sells a single product or service. Therefore, it cannot rely on cash from sales to cover its expenses. Even firms that have existed for a long time, such as Little Caesars Pizza, Disney, and Nike, need financial support as they attempt to expand. A fast-growing business such as Little Caesars Pizza would not generate sufficient earnings to cover new investment in equipment or buildings.

creditors financial institutions or individuals who provide loans

Many firms that need funds borrow from financial institutions or individuals called **creditors,** who provide loans. Bank of America, SunTrust Bank, and thousands of other commercial banks commonly serve as creditors for firms. Firms that borrow from creditors pay interest on their loans. The amount borrowed represents the debt of the firm, which must be paid back to the creditors along with interest payments over time. Large firms such as General Motors and DuPont have billions of dollars in debt.

Creditors will lend funds to a firm only if they believe the firm will perform well enough to pay the interest on the loans and the principal (amount borrowed) in the future. The firm must convince the creditors that it will be sufficiently profitable to make the interest and principal payments.

Employees

Employees of a firm are hired to conduct the business operations. Some firms have only a few employees; others, such as General Motors and IBM, have more than two hundred thousand. Those employees who are responsible for managing job assignments of other employees and making key business decisions are called **managers.** The performance of a firm is highly dependent on the decisions of its managers. Although managers' good decisions can help a firm succeed, their bad decisions may cause a firm to fail.

managers employees who are responsible for managing job assignments of other employees and making key business decisions

Goals of Managers The goal of a firm's managers is to maximize the firm's value. Maximizing firm value is an obvious goal for many small businesses since the owner and manager are often the same. When a firm has publicly traded stock, most of its stockholders do not work for the firm. They rely on the firm's managers to maximize the value of the stock held by stockholders. The following statements from recent annual reports illustrate the emphasis firms place on maximizing shareholder value:

" *Our mission is to build value for our shareowners.* "

—Ameritech

Steve Rees is owner of School Wise Press Internet Company. His managerial decisions affect the firm's value and therefore affect his wealth.

❝ *We are not promising miracles, just hard work with a total focus on why we're in business: to enhance stockholder value.* ❞

Zenith Electronics

❝ *We believe that a fundamental measure of our success will be the shareholder value we create over the long term.* ❞

—Amazon.com

❝ *Everything we do is designed to build shareholder value over the long haul.* ❞

—Wal-Mart

❝ *We create value for our share owners, and that remains our true bottom line.* ❞

—The Coca-Cola Company

Maximizing the firm's value encourages prospective investors to become shareholders of the firm.

To illustrate how managers can enhance a firm's value, consider the case of Compaq Computer, a computer firm. Compaq's managers created a competitive advantage with an efficient system for producing computers. This resulted in low costs and allowed Compaq to provide high-quality computers at low prices. In this way, Compaq's sales increased substantially over time, as did its profits. The ability of Compaq's managers to control costs and sell computers at low prices satisfied not only the customers but also the owners (shareholders).

Suppliers

Firms commonly use materials to produce their products. For example, automobile manufacturers use steel to make automobiles, while home builders need cement, wood siding, and many other materials. Firms cannot complete the production process if they cannot obtain the materials. Therefore, their performance is partially dependent on the ability of their suppliers to deliver the materials on schedule.

Customers

Firms cannot survive without customers. To attract customers, a firm must provide a desired product or service at a reasonable price. It must also ensure that the products or services produced are of adequate quality so that customers are satisfied. If a firm cannot provide a product or service at the quality and price that customers desire, customers will switch to the firm's competitors. Motorola and Saturn (a division of General Motors) attribute some of their recent success to recognizing the types of products that consumers want. These firms also are committed to quality and price their products in a manner that is acceptable to customers.

BUSINESS ONLINE

Customer Satisfaction Information

http://www.saturnfans.com

LIKE ALL SUCCESSFUL COMPANIES, SATURN REALIZES THAT IT CANNOT survive without customers. Consequently, Saturn uses the Internet to gather information on customers' reactions to its products. On the website shown here, it is even possible to enter a Saturn group discussion, where customers meet to discuss and compare the quality of their product.

DELL® COMPUTER'S FORMULA FOR SUCCESS

One of the five factors Dell considers responsible for its success in the computer industry is closeness to its customers or customer contact. To achieve a high level of customer contact, Dell segments the computer marketplace into well-defined customer groups, each of which has unique computing needs. For example, large corporations have a high need for global service capabilities, while medium-sized businesses place a high value on product repair and help-desk support. By segmenting the marketplace in this manner, Dell is able to address varying customer needs with greater precision and speed, thereby satisfying its customers.

Summary of Key Stakeholders

Firms rely on entrepreneurs (owners) to create business ideas and possibly to provide some financial support. They rely on other owners and creditors to provide additional financial support. They rely on employees (including managers) to produce and sell their products or services. They rely on suppliers to provide the materials needed for production. They rely on customers to purchase the products or services they produce. The president of Goodyear Tire and Rubber Company summarized the relationship between a firm and its stakeholders in a recent annual report: "Last year I reaffirmed our values—protecting our good name, focusing on customers, respecting and developing our people [employees], and rewarding investors."

Interaction among Stakeholders The interaction among a firm's owners, employees, customers, suppliers, and creditors is illustrated in Exhibit 1.1. Managers decide how the funds obtained from owners, creditors, or sales to customers should be utilized. They use funds to pay for the resources (including employees, supplies, and machinery) needed to produce and promote their products. They also use funds to repay creditors. The money left over is profit. Some of the profit (or earnings) is retained and reinvested by the firm. Any remaining profit is distributed as **dividends,** or income that the firm provides to its owners.

dividends income that the firm provides to its owners

Creating a Business Idea

People will be willing to create a business only if they expect to be rewarded for their efforts. The rewards of owning a business come in various forms. Some people are motivated by the chance to earn a large income. Others desire to be their own boss rather than work for someone else. Many people enjoy the challenge or the prestige associated with owning a business. Most business owners would agree that all of these characteristics motivated them to start their own business.

A recent survey by the Center for Entrepreneurial Leadership found that 69 percent of high school students were interested in starting their own business. Yet, about 86 percent of the students rated their business knowledge as very poor to fair. People need to learn how a business operates before they consider creating a business.

To be successful, a business needs to achieve a **competitive advantage,** or unique traits that make its products more desirable than those of competitors. Some businesses create a competitive advantage by offering products similar to their competitors' prod-

competitive advantage unique traits that make a business's products more desirable than those of its competitors

Exhibit 1.1

Interaction among Owners, Employees, Customers, Suppliers, and Creditors

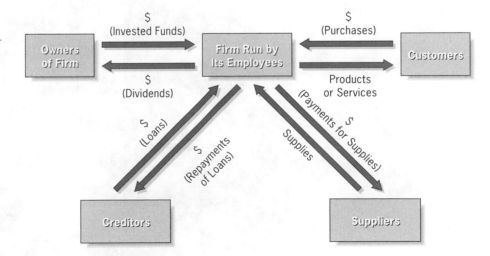

ucts but at a lower price. Other businesses attempt to provide a product that is of higher quality than those produced by competitors. Some other businesses offer more convenient services.

Examples of Successful Business Ideas

Many of today's successful businesses require a high degree of technology, a large amount of funds, or both. Yet, numerous business ideas can be implemented without relying on technology or much funding, as the following success stories illustrate:

1 Domino's Pizza (of Ann Arbor, Michigan) is a classic example of a business that started with little funding. It was established when Tom Monaghan (a college dropout) and his brother bought a bankrupt pizza parlor in 1960. Tom had to borrow the $500 that he needed to invest in the firm. Later, he bought his brother's interest in the business. Domino's Pizza now generates sales of about $1 billion per year.

2 Jeremy's Micro Batch Ice Cream (of Philadelphia, Pennsylvania) has applied the microbrewery concept to ice cream: it makes ice cream in small quantities and sells it in limited editions. The owner, Jerry Kraus, created the business idea for a class project when he was a student at the University of Pennsylvania.

3 Glow Dog, Inc. (of Concord, Massachusetts) sells light-reflective clothing for pets. The owner, Beth Marcus, thought of this business idea when she was walking her dog at night and realized that the dog was not visible to passing motorists. After just two years in business, her firm generates annual sales of more than $1 million.

Impact of Technology on the Creation of Businesses

technology knowledge or tools used to produce products and services

information technology technology that enables information to be used to produce products and services

Technology has contributed to the creation of many successful businesses in recent years. **Technology** can be defined as knowledge or tools used to produce products and services. An important subset of technology, **information technology,** involves the use of information to produce products and services. It includes the use of computers to transfer information among departments within a firm and the use of the Internet to transfer information about a firm's production process.

Rollerblades went from being a summer training product for ice skaters to becoming one of the most popular recreational products in the country in just a few years.

Information technology accounts for only about 8 percent of the total output produced in the United States, but it represents more than one-third of the growth in the U.S. output produced. A recent study by the U.S. Commerce Department estimates that about half of all U.S. workers will soon be employed in industries that produce information technology. It also found that information technology has reduced the cost of producing products and resulted in lower prices of products. Furthermore, workers in the technology industries earn about $53,000 per year on average versus $30,000 for workers in other industries.

VARIOUS COMPANIES FROM DIFFERENT INDUSTRIES USE THE INTERNET TO provide customers with information on upcoming events. On the site shown below, IBM lists upcoming technical conferences, which both companies and individuals can attend. Thus, companies can use the Internet both to fulfill their customers' needs and as a marketing tool.

BUSINESS ONLINE

Customer Needs Fulfillment

http://www-3.ibm.com/
services/learning/conf/

electronic business (e-business) or electronic commerce (e-commerce) use of electronic communications, such as the Internet, to produce or sell products and services

A related type of technology is **electronic business (e-business),** also referred to as **electronic commerce (e-commerce),** which is the use of electronic communications to produce or sell products and services. E-business includes both business transactions, such as the sales of products over the Internet, and the interactions between a firm and its suppliers over the Internet. In fact, many people use the terms *information technology* and *e-commerce* interchangeably. A recent study by the University of Texas estimates that e-business generated about $301 billion in revenue during 1998 and created 1.2 million jobs.

An example of a successful e-business idea is Amazon.com, which enables customers to purchase books and other products online (over the Internet). Amazon.com's creativity is not the product (books) but an alternative method of reaching customers. Its customers use the Internet to have their book orders delivered to them rather than having to go to a retail bookstore. Several other firms have applied the same idea to their own businesses. Computer firms now sell computers over the Internet, toy manufacturers sell toys over the Internet, and automobile manufacturers sell automobiles over the Internet. Hotels, airlines, and cruiselines now allow customers to make reservations over the Internet.

Exhibit 1.2 describes some of the successful firms that have been created to capitalize on e-business. Notice from the descriptions that these businesses started out

Exhibit 1.2 Successful Internet Businesses

Business Name	Business Description	How the Business Was Created
1. Amazon.com Value = $18 billion	This online bookseller is frequently cited as an Internet success story. Customers can purchase books and music and participate in auctions at its website. Amazon's innovative bookselling idea allows the company to offer popular titles at deeply discounted prices due to low overhead costs.	Jeff Bezos, 35, founded the company in 1994. Bezos quit his job as vice-president of a Wall Street firm, moved to Seattle, and started the business in his garage. When Amazon.com opened for business in July 1995, Bezos himself frequently dropped off the packages at the post office. Bezos's estimated net worth (value of his house and other assets after paying off any debts) is now $10 billion.
2. Yahoo! Value = $29.5 billion	This Internet search engine is the most visited site on the Web. It has evolved to offer a wide variety of other products to attract users. Free e-mail, Web page hosting, and custom-designed start-up pages are just a few of the options available. Revenues are generated through advertising sales.	David Filo, 32, and Jerry Yang, 29, were Ph.D. students at Stanford who had put together an electronic directory of their favorite websites. It was essentially a list of their bookmarks that they titled Yahoo! (which stands for Yet Another Hierarchical Officious Oracle). The site was generating so much traffic that the students dropped out of school and launched their company in 1995. Each of the founders now has a net worth of nearly $4 billion.
3. America Online Value = $121 billion	This company is the largest Internet service provider and purchased Netscape in 1998. It generates revenues by selling advertising and charging subscription fees to its users. In 2000, America Online acquired Time Warner, becoming AOL Time Warner. The value of the company is far above the value of huge companies such as Disney and General Motors.	The company, founded by James Kimsey in 1985, was originally a bulletin board service for Commodore users. Steve Case was the 24th employee hired by Kimsey. Kimsey, 60, now has an estimated net worth of $130 million, and Case, 41, has an estimated net worth of $540 million.
4. Netscape	Netscape grew rapidly as a popular browser used to navigate the Web. The company had 65 million users within 18 months after its introduction. The company was acquired by AOL for $4.2 billion in December 1998.	Marc Andreessen, 28, worked at the National Center for Supercomputing Applications (NCSA) for $6 an hour while an undergraduate at the University of Illinois. At the NCSA, he assisted in the creation of Mosaic, an early browser. Jim Clark, founder of Silicon Graphics, approached Andreessen about a variety of business ventures. Andreessen decided to create an improved Mosaic and build a business around it. Netscape Navigator was launched in December 1994. Andreessen's net worth exceeds $60 million, and Clark's net worth is about $400 million.
5. RealNetworks Value = $4.4 billion	This company promotes audo-video through the Internet. The general idea is that everything from video advertisements through music videos will become commonplace on the Internet and that RealNetworks software will be the foundation for those creations.	Rob Glaser, 36, left Microsoft in 1993 to start RealNetworks. He had spent 10 years at Microsoft and had become a vice-president. His estimated net worth exceeds $400 million.
6. Ameritrade Value = $4.2 billion	This company is one of the most popular online brokerage services. It offers users the ability to buy and sell stock for $8 per trade. The size and power of online brokerages continue to grow as more investors transfer accounts. Online accounts are expected to number nearly 14 million by the year 2001.	Joe Ricketts, 57, founded the company with $12,500. Ricketts began his career as a stockbroker for Dean Witter after spending nine years working on his bachelor's degree in economics. His estimated net worth is $4.7 billion.

continued

Exhibit 1.2   concluded

Business Name	Business Description	How the Business Was Created
7. Broadcast.com Value = $4 billion	The Internet's leading broadcast company, Broadcast.com, is located in a converted warehouse in Dallas. From there it plays radio shows from all over the country. Users are able to listen to their favorite radio station, listen to sports events, or watch local television news.	Two University of Indiana alumni began the company in 1995 because they were unable to hear Hoosier basketball games deep in the heart of Texas. Mark Cuban, 41, and Todd Wagner, 39, began the company in Cuban's spare bedroom with a Packard Bell 486 computer. The company was running out of money in late 1995 and began selling $30,000 increments to friends around Dallas. In 1996, they attracted investment through private placements, and the company began to grow rapidly. Cuban has an estimated net worth exceeding $250 million, and Wagner's net worth exceeds $150 million.
8. @Home Value = $13.2 billion	This company plans to become the most popular Internet service provider through the use of cable modems. They offer connection speeds that are 100 times faster than traditional dial-up modems. The fiber-optic system is able to deliver videos, music, sports talk, concerts, and multiplayer gaming.	The company was founded by Will Hearst, a publishing heir, and was supported by TCI and the venture capital firms of Kleiner, Perkins, Caufield, and Byers. The company lured Tom Jermoluk away from Silicon Graphics to become CEO. Jermoluk, 42, has an estimated net worth exceeding $160 million.
9. eBay Value = $18.3 billion	eBay is an online auction service that enables users to sell goods to each other. The person-to-person services attract a wide variety of goods, most of them used. Sellers develop a reputation, which creates some level of trust and excuses eBay from any repsonsibility. The company profits by charging fees based on the sale price.	The company evolved out of a method that Pierre Omidyar, 32, devised to help his girlfriend collect Pez candy dispensers. By 1996, the volume of goods traded forced Omidyar to quit his job at General Magic and devote all his time to the company. The company has been profitable since 1996. Omidyar's net worth is estimated at $7.8 billion, similar to the value of Sears, Roebuck and Company.

very small and were created to offer a product or service that was not being provided by other firms. Thus, these new businesses were created to accommodate the needs or preferences of customers. The success of firms in e-business triggered the creation of many other e-businesses. Exhibit 1.3 identifies various types of e-business that exist today.

Although businesses' use of the Internet to serve consumers has attracted considerable attention, the Internet is also having an important impact on the way businesses serve other businesses (referred to as "business-to-business e-commerce" or "B2B e-commerce"). Business-to-business e-commerce might be used, for example, when a firm needs construction work to repair its facilities, wants an outside firm to conduct seminars to improve relationships among employees, or requires specific supplies for its production process. The firm can request bids online from several prospective businesses that may serve its needs and then select the firm that provides the best bid. This process is much easier and faster than calling various firms and waiting for return phone calls. Furthermore, having to send a message online forces the bidders to specify their bids in writing.

Business-to-business e-commerce has already reduced the expenses associated with transactions between firms and is expected to reduce them even further once all firms take full advantage of the technology. In particular, firms that rely on other businesses for supplies, transportation services, or delivery services can reduce their expenses substantially by using business-to-business e-commerce.

Exhibit 1.3

Types of e-Business

Firm	Description
Amazon.com	Books, music
AOLTimeWarner	Internet content
Autobytel	Guide to new and used cars
Beyond.com	Consumer software
eBay	Auctions
Emusic.com	Music recordings
eToys	Children's products
E-Trade	Brokerage
iTurf	Women's apparel
Net.Bank	Banking
Preview Travel	Travel reservations
Ticketmaster	Guides, tickets
Yahoo!	Web guide

Key Functions of a Business

2 Describe the key functions of a business.

The five key functions involved in operating a business are management, marketing, finance, accounting, and information systems. These five functions are the focus of this text because they must be conducted properly if a business is to be successful. Each of the functions is briefly introduced here and will be thoroughly discussed in other chapters.

management means by which employees and other resources (such as machinery) are used by the firm

marketing means by which products (or services) are developed, priced, distributed, and promoted to customers

finance means by which firms obtain and use funds for their business operations

accounting summary and analysis of the firm's financial condition

information systems include information technology, people, and procedures that work together to provide appropriate information to the firm's employees so they can make business decisions

Management is the means by which employees and other resources (such as machinery) are used by the firm. **Marketing** is the means by which products (or services) are developed, priced, distributed, and promoted to customers. **Finance** is the means by which firms obtain and use funds for their business operations. **Accounting** is the summary and analysis of the firm's financial condition and is used to make various business decisions. **Information systems** include information technology, people, and procedures that work together to provide appropriate information to the firm's employees so they can make business decisions.

Interaction among Business Functions

Most business decisions can be classified as management, marketing, or finance decisions. Examples of these types of decisions are provided in Exhibit 1.4. Notice from this exhibit that management decisions focus on the use of resources, marketing decisions focus on the products, and finance decisions focus on obtaining or using funds.

A firm's earnings (or profits) are equal to its revenue minus its expenses. The effect that each type of business decision has on a firm's earnings is illustrated in Exhibit 1.5. Since management decisions focus on the utilization of employees and other resources, they affect the amount of production expenses incurred. Since marketing decisions focus on strategies that will make the product appealing to customers, they affect the firm's revenue. Marketing decisions also influence the amount of expenses incurred in distributing and promoting products. Since finance decisions focus on how funds are obtained (borrowing money versus issuing stock), they influence the amount of interest expense incurred. As the management, marketing, and finance decisions affect either a firm's revenue or expenses, they affect the earnings and value of the firm.

Much interaction takes place between management, marketing, and finance in making decisions. For example, production managers at Compaq Computer receive

Exhibit 1.4   Common Business Decisions

Management Decisions
1. What equipment is needed to produce the product?
2. How many employees should be hired to produce the product?
3. How can employees be motivated to perform well?

Marketing Decisions
1. What price should be charged for the product?
2. Should the product be changed to be more appealing to customers?
3. Should the firm use advertising or some other strategy to promote its product?

Finance Decisions
1. Should financial support come from the sale of stock or from borrowing money? Or a combination of both?
2. Should the firm attempt to obtain borrowed funds for a short-term period (such as one year) or a long-term period?
3. Should the firm invest funds in a new business project that has recently been proposed (such as expansion of its existing business or development of a new product), or should it use these funds to repay debt?

sales projections from the marketing managers to determine how much of a product to produce. The finance managers must receive the planned production volume from production managers to determine how much funding is needed.

How Some Business Functions Enhance Decision Making

Proper business decisions rely on accounting and information systems.

Accounting Managers of firms use accounting to monitor their operations and to report their financial condition to their owners or employees. They can also assess the performance of previous production, marketing, and finance decisions. They may even rely on accounting to detect inefficient uses of business resources that can be eliminated. Consequently, a firm's accounting function can be used to eliminate waste, thereby generating higher earnings.

Information Systems Firms use information systems to continually update and analyze information about their operations. This information can be used by the firm's managers to make business decisions. In addition, the information can be used by any employee within the firm who has access to a personal computer. For example, FedEx uses information on its computer system to track deliveries and determine when packages will arrive at their destination.

Exhibit 1.5

How Business Decisions Affect
a Firm's Earnings

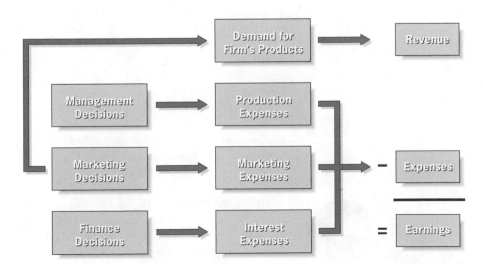

Developing the Business Plan

business plan a detailed description of the proposed business, including a description of the business, the types of customers it would attract, the competition, and the facilities needed for production

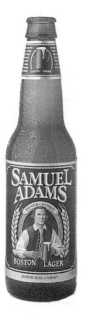

The Boston Beer Company, producer of Samuel Adams beer, implemented a business plan to achieve a reputation for quality.

Once entrepreneurs create a business idea, they consider how to apply the business functions just described to make the business successful. They create a **business plan,** which is a detailed description of the proposed business, including a description of the business, the types of customers it would attract, the competition, and the facilities needed for production.

The business plan is not only for the entrepreneur but also for any investors or creditors who may provide financial support. Entrepreneurs commonly provide their plan to those investors who may be willing to serve as partial owners. They also provide their plan to creditors (such as commercial banks) that may be willing to provide business loans. Thus, the business plan should be clear and must convince others that the business will be profitable. If investors do not believe in the business plan, they will be unwilling to invest funds in the business. If creditors do not believe in the plan, they will not provide any loans. In this case, entrepreneurs would have to rely completely on their own funds, which may not be sufficient to support the business.

In 1985, Jim Koch developed a business plan for Boston Beer Company to produce Samuel Adams beer. He invested $100,000 of his own money and raised $140,000 in additional funds to begin his business. He focused on the specialty beer market and emphasized selling the beer within four months after it was bottled, because beer can become stale over time. This was the first application of freshness dating to beer. Samuel Adams beer developed a reputation for its quality. The success of this business is partially attributed to its excellent business plan.

The business plan is typically about eight to twelve pages long. It describes how the business functions identified earlier can be applied to a business idea so that the idea can be implemented successfully. The business plan is developed with a focus on stakeholders. Specifically, the plan describes how the business idea will utilize employees, suppliers, and creditors, and how it will satisfy customers and the owners of the business. Thus, the business idea involves managing the resources to be used, marketing the idea, and financing the idea. A complete business plan normally includes an assessment of the business environment, a management plan, a marketing plan, and a financial plan, as explained in detail next.

Assessment of the Business Environment

The business environment surrounding the business includes the economic environment, the industry environment, and the global environment.

Economic Environment The economic environment is assessed to determine how demand for the product may change in response to future economic conditions. The demand for a product can be highly sensitive to the strength of the economy. Therefore, the feasibility of a new business may be influenced by the economic environment.

Industry Environment The industry environment is assessed to determine the degree of competition. If a market for a specific product is served by only one or a few firms, a new firm may be able to capture a significant portion of the market.

One must also ask whether a similar product could be produced and sold at a lower price, while still providing reasonable earnings. A related question is whether the new business would be able to produce a higher-quality product than the competitors. A new business idea is more likely to be successful if it has either a price or a quality advantage over its competitors.

Global Environment The global environment is assessed to determine how the demand for the product may change in response to future global conditions. The global demand for a product can be highly sensitive to changes in foreign economies, the number of foreign competitors, exchange rates, and international trade regulations.

Management Plan

A management plan, which includes an operations plan, focuses on the proposed organizational structure, production, and human resources of the firm.

Organizational Structure An organizational structure identifies the roles and responsibilities of the employees hired by the firm. The organizational structure of a new factory is more complicated than that of a pizza delivery shop. If the owner plans to manage most of the operations, the organizational structure is simple. Some businesses begin with the owner assuming most responsibilities, but growth requires the hiring of managers. Even if owners initially run the business, they should develop plans for the future organizational structure. The job descriptions of each employee should be identified, along with the estimated salary to be paid to each employee.

Production Various decisions must be made about the production process, such as the site (location) of the production facilities and the design and layout of the facilities. The location decision can have a major effect on a firm's performance because it influences both the cost of renting space in a building and the revenue generated by the business.

The proposed design and layout of the facilities should maximize the efficiency of the space available. This proposal should contain cost estimates on any machinery or equipment purchased. The cost estimates for factories are normally more complicated than those for retail stores.

Human Resources Human resources (employees) are critical to the success of a firm. A business must set up a work environment that will motivate the employees to help the business succeed. It must also develop a plan for monitoring and evaluating employees and for compensating them. By monitoring and compensating employees properly, the business can ensure that the employees are striving to maximize its performance.

Marketing Plan

A marketing plan focuses on the target market, as well as product characteristics, pricing, distribution, and promotion.

customer profile characteristics of the typical customer (based on gender, age, hobbies, and so on)

target market market of customers that fit the customer profile

Target Market The **customer profile,** or characteristics of the typical customer (based on gender, age, hobbies, and so on), should be identified. This helps to determine the **target market,** which consists of customers that fit the customer profile. A paperback book of fiction for adults has a much larger target market than one for young children.

Product Characteristics The characteristics of the product should be described, with an emphasis on what makes the product more desirable than similar products offered by competitors. A product may be desirable because it is easier to use, is more effective, or lasts longer. Any competitive advantage of this product over similar products should be identified.

Pricing The proposed price of the product should be stated. Prices of similar products sold by competitors should also be mentioned. The price will influence the demand for the product.

Distribution The means by which the product will be distributed to the customers should be described. Some products are sold to customers directly, while others are distributed through retail outlets.

Promotion The means by which the product will be promoted should be described. The promotion strategy should be consistent with the customer profile. For example, products that appeal to college students may be advertised in student newspapers.

Financial Plan

The financial plan should demonstrate why the business is feasible and should propose how the business will be financed. That is, how much of the funds will come from owners and how much from creditors?

Feasibility The benefits and costs of the business must be estimated to determine whether it is feasible (whether the benefits exceed the costs). The business must be judged feasible by the owner and by any creditors who will provide financial support.

The details of the business plan can be used to create forecasts of expected revenue and expenses of the business over time. Forecasts of the sales volume and product price could be used to forecast periodic revenue. The proposed organizational structure, location, design, and layout can be used to estimate the expenses involved in the proposed business.

The estimated revenue and expenses (including payments to creditors) can be used to forecast periodic earnings. These earnings can be evaluated to determine whether they provide an acceptable profit to the owners. In addition, the risk of the business should be assessed by measuring the uncertainty of future earnings. If the risk is high, owners should be willing to implement the project only if the potential profits adequately compensate for the risk involved.

Financing the Business The business must be financially supported. Most businesses require a large initial outlay to cover purchases of machinery, equipment, and possibly a building. While the owners normally use some of their own funds to support the business, they may need additional financing. If they decide to request financing from a financial institution (such as a commercial bank), they will need to present a detailed business plan. Then the lending institution can determine whether the proposed business deserves a loan. If the lending institution believes that the projected revenue is overestimated or the projected expenses are underestimated, it may decide not to provide financing.

An alternative source of funds is to issue stock to the public. However, most firms rely heavily on funding from the entrepreneurs who established them and from loans when they were initially created. They may consider issuing stock only after demonstrating adequate performance for several years. Recently, firms such as Prodigy and MarketWatch.com have issued stock in order to obtain funds.

Summary of a Business Plan

The key parts of a business plan are summarized in Exhibit 1.6. Notice that the business plan is based on key business functions: management, marketing, and finance.

Assessing a Business Plan

Many business ideas that seem reasonable at first may not be undertaken because the entrepreneur has various concerns after developing the business plan. Some concerns may relate to the potential revenue to be generated by the business. Perhaps the potential demand for the product or service is highly uncertain. Other concerns may relate to the expense of producing the product or service. For example, the entrepreneur may believe that the costs of production may be too high. Any concerns about the revenue or the expenses raise questions about the potential profitability. If the business

Exhibit 1.6   Contents of a Typical Business Plan

1. DESCRIPTION OF PROPOSED BUSINESS
▶ Describe the product (or service) provided by the proposed business.

2. ASSESSMENT OF THE BUSINESS ENVIRONMENT
▶ Economic Environment: Describe the prevailing economic conditions, and the exposure of the firm to those conditions.
▶ Industry Environment: Describe the competition in the industry and the general demand for the product in the industry.
▶ Global Environment: Describe the prevailing global conditions that relate to the business, such as foreign markets where the business may sell products in the future or obtain supplies.

3. MANAGEMENT PLAN
▶ Organizational Structure: Describe the organizational structure and show the relationships among the employee positions. This structure should also identify the responsibilities of each position in overseeing other positions and describe the specific tasks and salaries of managers and other employees.
▶ Production Process: Describe the production process, including the site, design, and layout of the facilities needed to create a product. Also, describe the planned amount of production per month or year.
▶ Managing Employees: Describe the work environment used to motivate employees and the plans for training, evaluating, and compensating employees.

4. MARKETING PLAN
▶ Target Market: Describe the profile (such as the typical age and income level) of the customers that would purchase the product and therefore make up the target market. (Who will buy the product?)
▶ Product Characteristics: Explain desirable features of the product. (Why will customers buy the product?)
▶ Pricing: Describe how the product will be priced relative to competitors' products. (How much will customers pay for the product?)
▶ Distribution: Describe how the product will be distributed to customers. (How will customers have access to the product?)
▶ Promotion: Describe how the product will be promoted to potential customers. (How will customers be informed about the product?)

5. FINANCIAL PLAN
▶ Feasibility: Estimate the revenue, expenses, and earnings of the proposed business over the next five years. Consider how the estimates of revenue, expenses, and earnings of the proposed business may change under various possible economic or industry conditions.
▶ Funds Needed: Estimate the amount of funds needed to establish the business and to support operations over a five-year period.

BUSINESS ONLINE

Business
Planning Tools

http://www.palo-alto.com/index
.cfm

SOFTWARE IS NOW AVAILABLE TO AID ENTREPRENEURS IN DEVELOPING A business plan. Many software companies, such as PaloAlto, use the Internet to advertise their products. Thus, the Internet provides entrepreneurs with a variety of information they can use in developing their business plan. Also note that companies such as this provide a variety of other products related to the development of a business.

idea does not have much potential for profit, the entrepreneur may decide to search for alternative business ideas.

If the estimated costs of the business are too high, this does not necessarily mean that the business idea should be completely discarded. Perhaps one or more aspects of the proposed business need to be changed to make the idea feasible. For example, the establishment of a video store may not be feasible in a business district because of the high costs of renting space in that location. An alternative location may significantly reduce the cost of renting a facility. Yet, the firm's revenue may also be affected

SPOTLIGHT ON TECHNOLOGY

Online Resources for Starting a Business

 Starting a small business can be a difficult process. Business publications and the Small Business Administration (SBA) have been the usual sources for advice. Financing has primarily been available through local financial institutions and has been relatively difficult to obtain.

The Internet has made this process much easier. A variety of sites provide advice about beginning a business. Information on government grants, advice about specific industries, business plan templates, and discussions of legal issues are readily available.

Yahoo's Small Business site (**http://smallbusiness .yahoo.com**) is a good place to find links to more specific information. American Express (**http://americanexpress .com/smallbusiness**) provides information about building a business. The SBA (**http://www.sbaonline.sba.gov**) offers information about government programs and other relevant information for small businesses.

Obtaining financing is crucial to beginning any business, and there are sites to facilitate this process, too. Quicken Small Business (**http://www.quicken.com/small_ business**) matches entrepreneurs with lenders. Once a questionnaire has been completed, the site offers advice on the most appropriate financing. It also provides a list of interested banks and the appropriate applications. Garage.com (**http://www.garage.com**) targets start-up companies in the high-tech sector and matches the companies with venture capitalists. The Elevator (**http://www.thelevator.com**) also matches entrepreneurs with investors and does not restrict itself to high-tech firms. The Internet is always changing, so the sites listed here may become obsolete. Nevertheless, a simple search for small business resources will find numerous sites with much information.

Business planning software is another tool that entrepreneurs can use to ease the start-up process. A good business plan is a complex document that is demanded by lenders and potential investors and can provide a valuable guide for the business. It details the nature of the company, the competition, and a forecasted financial analysis. In the past, putting a business plan together was both time-

consuming and expensive. Today, business plan software can make the process much easier.

Most of the software packages contain a collection of options, which can be used to create a thorough business plan. The best packages incorporate many of the following capabilities:

▶ *Business Plan Outlines* Packages normally offer one or more outlines of business plans that can be altered to fit most businesses. Some packages take entrepreneurs through a series of questions in order to create a tailor-made plan.

▶ *Text Generation* Much of the information that goes into a business plan is standardized. Business plan software can insert such text directly into the plan, making the appropriate substitutions for company names and products. Once in place, the text can be edited as needed.

▶ *Forecasting* Any business plan software packages should include the ability to create consistent projections. The software package should be able to predict sales and costs in various ways (for example, using percentage growth models, market share models, or values that are individually specified by the planner) and should ensure that interrelated data are consistent. For example, when the planner changes values in a table of projected market shares, forecasted sales in other parts of the document should automatically be updated.

▶ *Graphics* Business plan software offers the ability to create charts of several different types (bar charts, pie charts, line charts) and should also allow users to draw other common charts, such as organizational charts.

▶ *Supplementary Documents* A number of business plan packages offer supplementary documents, such as disclosure agreements, which are often used in conjunction with business plans, although not necessarily as part of the document.

A few hours on the computer are all that is now needed to gather information and apply for financing. Prior to the advances in technology described here, this process might have taken weeks. The result has been a rise in the number of small businesses and a more competitive environment as the barriers to entry have decreased.

by a different location. An entirely new cost-benefit analysis should be conducted after revising the proposed location or any other part of the business plan for a specific business.

BUSINESS DILEMMA | **College Health Club**

Developing a
New Health
Club Business

IN EVERY CHAPTER OF THIS TEXT, SOME OF THE KEY CONCEPTS ARE ILLUStrated with an application to a small health club business. The "Business Dilemma" section in each chapter allows students to recognize the dilemmas and business decisions that they may face in the future. For this chapter, the application is on the development of a business plan for the health club.

Background Sue Kramer is a business major in her senior year. Although she has limited funding, she has always wanted to own a business. Throughout her college years, she has belonged to a health club that is a thirty-minute drive from campus. This club has all types of weight and exercise machines but does not offer any aerobics classes. Sue's informal discussions with several other students who also use the club have revealed that they would prefer a health club that not only has weight and exercise machines but also offers aerobics classes. The students would also prefer a health club that is inexpensive and more convenient to the college campus.

Sue begins to seriously consider establishing her own business, a health club that would serve the needs of other students at the college. She hands out a brief questionnaire to two hundred students on campus to determine whether they might be interested in joining a new health club and what types of club facilities they desire. She then checks a local yellow pages directory and other sources to identify any other health clubs that would be considered competitors within the local area.

Next Sue inquires about the price of renting space at a small shopping mall across the street from the college campus. She also starts pricing weight and exercise machines that she would need to purchase or rent to start this business. To reduce the initial outlay necessary for the business, she plans to rent the machines rather than purchase them.

Dilemma

Sue cannot establish the health club until she determines that the idea is feasible and obtains financial support. How can Sue prove to a bank that she has a well-developed plan that will make her business successful?

Solution

Sue develops a business plan for a local bank and determines that she would need a $40,000 loan. Her plan is summarized in Exhibit 1.7, although an actual business plan would contain more details. Review this business plan before continuing.

The business plan summarized in Exhibit 1.7 can help Sue (the owner) estimate the revenue and expenses resulting from the business. Although these estimates are normally completed for a five-year period, they are provided for only the first year in Exhibit 1.8.

Estimation of Revenue The estimated number of memberships per period can be multiplied by the price to derive an estimate of revenue. In our example, the estimated demand in the first year is 300 memberships, and the price per membership is $250. Thus, the estimated revenue is $75,000 (300 × $250 per membership) as shown in row (3) of Exhibit 1.8.

Exhibit 1.7	Summary of Business Plan for College Health Club (CHC)

Description of Proposed Business

The proposed business is a health club called College Health Club (CHC) that would be located at the corner of 1st Street and Bell Avenue. Space for the health club would be obtained by leasing (renting) four connected units within the shopping mall. The health club would offer weight machines, exercise machines, and aerobics classes.

Assessment of the Business Environment

▶ Economic Environment: The economic conditions are expected to be stable. Inflation and interest rates have been stable. The business is not highly exposed to economic conditions.

▶ Industry Environment: The demand for health club services is increasing in the local area. This business would compete against other health clubs in the area but would focus on students at the local college.

▶ Global Environment: The business may consider purchasing equipment from Canada in the future. In general, it is not highly exposed to global conditions.

Management Plan

▶ Production Process: This business would produce health club services. The facilities needed to provide the health club services are (1) four connected units in the shopping mall across from the campus, (2) numerous weight machines and exercise machines, (3) a small locker room with showers, and (4) miscellaneous items. The units can be leased for a total of $40,000 per year. The weight and exercise machines would be rented for a total of $10,000 per year. The insurance and utility expenses are included within the rent expense.

   The facilities should be able to handle five hundred memberships. If the memberships increase beyond that amount, the facilities would be expanded.

▶ Organizational Structure: Sue Kramer would be the sole owner and president of CHC and would oversee all policies established by CHC. Sue would earn a salary of $20,000. Her salary is intended to cover only her general living expenses. Most earnings will be reinvested in the firm to support any growth in the business. Initially, Sue will be the only full-time employee. She will spend much of her time on marketing tasks in order to boost memberships.

   Lisa Lane (friend of Sue's and a senior at the college) would work at the firm on a part-time basis. She would be an aerobics instructor for some of the classes. She will probably be paid about $10,000 in the first year, but will receive a higher salary as the club's memberships increase.

   Lisa reports to Sue. As the business grows, the organizational structure and the human resource plans will need to be developed.

Marketing Plan

▶ Target Market: CHC would target students and employees of the college.

▶ Product (or Service) Characteristics: This health club would offer benefits over existing competitors. It would offer weight machines, exercise machines, aerobics classes, convenience, and affordability. Two competing health clubs are in the area. One is thirty minutes away by car; it does not offer aerobics classes at the present time. The other is ten minutes away by car; it offers a wide variety of exercise and weight machines and aerobics. However, the membership fee is much higher than that of the first club.

▶ Pricing: CHC would charge an annual membership fee of $250 to customers. This price is much lower than the fee charged by the competitor club that is ten minutes away by car.

▶ Distribution: CHC would distribute its health club services on its own facilities.

▶ Promotion: CHC would advertise regularly in the college's newspaper. Its promotion efforts would focus on college students and employees. It would attempt to develop a close relationship with the college and would create promotions for college students. The total promotion expense would be about $10,000 per year.

Financial Plan

▶ Feasibility: The earnings of the health club are forecasted as the estimated revenue minus estimated expenses. The source of revenue is annual memberships, and the key factor affecting revenue is the number of people who will sign up for membership each year. The membership level is expected to grow each year. The main expenses are the cost of leasing the space, the cost of renting the weight and exercise machines, and salaries paid to the two employees.

   The revenue is expected to be $21,000 less than the business expenses in the first year (negative earnings). In the second year, the revenue is expected to equal business expenses (zero earnings). Earnings are expected to be $40,000 in Year 3, $80,000 in Year 4, and $90,000 in Year 5.

▶ Funds Needed: Various expenses must be paid before any revenue is generated by CHC. Sue Kramer desires to have $50,000 to start the business. Part of this amount would be used to pay the lease expense over the first few months. Also, the equipment and miscellaneous items need to be purchased immediately. Sue has $10,000 that she has saved over the years. She plans to invest that amount and would like to borrow the remaining $40,000 from the commercial bank. She believes she would be able to pay off the loan in three years, based on her expectations of revenue and expenses. If she decides to expand the business in the future, she may need to borrow additional funds to support the expansion.

Exhibit 1.8

Estimates of Revenue and Expenses of CHC in First Year

(1) Estimated Demand for the Service	300
(2) Price of the Service (Membership Fee)	$250
(3) Revenue = (1) × (2)	**$75,000**
(4) Salary Expense (Sue and Lisa's Salaries)	$30,000
(5) Rent Expense (Leasing Space)	40,000
(6) Machine Rental Expense	10,000
(7) Marketing Expense	10,000
(8) Interest Expense	6,000
(9) Total Expenses = (4) + (5) + (6) + (7) + (8)	**$96,000**
(10) Earnings = (3) − (9)	**−$21,000**

Estimation of Expenses The total expenses can be estimated by deriving an estimate of each type of expense, as shown in rows (4) through (9) of Exhibit 1.8. The estimated salary expense of $30,000 is the combination of Sue and Lisa's salaries specified in the business plan. The rent, machine rental expenses, and marketing expenses are stated in the business plan. The interest expense is based on the $40,000 Sue wishes to borrow at an annual interest rate of 15 percent (15% × $40,000 = $6,000).

Estimation of Earnings The business earnings are estimated as the difference between the estimated revenue and estimated expenses. To simplify the example, taxes are not considered here. Although the earnings are expected to be negative in the first year, the firm's performance should improve if memberships increase over time. It is not unusual for a firm to incur a loss in its first year.

Given that the salary, lease, and machine rental expenses are somewhat predictable, much of the uncertainty about this firm's earnings involves the firm's revenue; that is, the demand for CHC's services is uncertain. If the revenue is overestimated, the earnings will likely be overestimated as well. Even if the health club has zero memberships (resulting in zero revenue), it will still incur the expenses just described.

While Sue recognizes this uncertainty, she is confident that the health club will generate her predicted earnings. She decides to submit her business plan to her local commercial bank.

Additional Issues for Discussion

1 Why would Sue attempt to obtain the $40,000 from a creditor rather than from a second owner?

2 Assume that the enrollment at the college is expected to grow by 10 percent each year. How will this affect the estimated earnings for CHC?

3 Sue needs four connected units in the shopping mall to create CHC. Assume that there are two more connected units that Sue could lease as well. What would be an advantage of leasing more space? What is the main disadvantage of leasing more space?

SUMMARY

The key stakeholders in a business are owners, creditors, employees, suppliers, and customers. The owners invest in the firm, while creditors lend money to the firm. Employees are hired to conduct the firm's business operations efficiently in order to satisfy the owners. Suppliers provide the materials that the firm needs to produce its product. The firm's revenue is generated by selling products or services to customers.

 The key functions in operating a business are management, marketing, finance, accounting, and information systems. Management decisions determine how the firm's resources are allocated. Marketing decisions determine the product to be sold, along with the pricing, distribution, and promotion of that product. Finance decisions determine how the firm obtains and invests funds.

Business decisions are improved as a result of accounting and information systems. Accounting is used to monitor performance and detect inefficient uses of resources in order to improve business decisions. Information systems provide the firm's employees with information that enables them to improve business decisions.

③ A business plan forces an owner of a proposed business to specify all the key plans for the business. The business plan normally consists of (1) an assessment of the business environment, (2) a management plan that explains how the firm's resources are to be used, (3) a marketing plan that explains the product pricing, distribution, and promotion plans, and (4) a financial plan that demonstrates the feasibility of the business and explains how the business will be financed.

KEY TERMS

accounting *12*
business plan *14*
competitive advantage *7*
creditors *4*
customer profile *15*
dividends *7*
electronic business (e-business) *9*

electronic commerce (e-commerce) *9*
entrepreneurs *3*
finance *12*
information systems *12*
information technology *8*
management *12*

managers *4*
marketing *12*
stakeholders *3*
stock *4*
stockholders (shareholders) *4*
target market *15*
technology *8*

REVIEW QUESTIONS

1 Identify the five key stakeholders in a business and explain their roles.

2 Why has information technology received so much attention in business recently?

3 If you were to start your own business, discuss the key functions needed to operate the business. Discuss some decisions made by each function.

4 Discuss the environmental factors that may impact the success of a business.

5 Why should a business plan be clear and precise? Explain what is included in a business plan.

6 What are the three major decisions within a business plan?

7 Explain why business plans are closely reviewed by creditors or investors.

8 What is included in a marketing plan? Give a brief explanation of the elements.

9 Give a brief description of a typical financial plan in starting a new business.

10 Explain the concerns an entrepreneur would have in starting a new business.

DISCUSSION QUESTIONS

1 Assume you are in a rock band that performs at the college you attend. Is a product or a service being provided? Is the management function more important or less important than the marketing function for your band?

2 You are planning to open your own record store in a local mall. Discuss this statement: "The customer is king."

3 Assume you are about to launch a business. You believe employees do not work as hard as owners do; therefore, you do not need them. In addition, you do not believe in keeping financial records and will not need an accountant for your business. Discuss your assumptions.

4 What characteristics of a potential firm enable it to use the In-

ternet to plan its business? What characteristics of a firm enable it to use the Internet to promote its business once it is established?

5 Wal-Mart is planning to open a new store in your local area. Since Wal-Mart is nationally known, is it necessary for this store to have a marketing plan designed for this particular location?

INVESTING IN THE STOCK OF A BUSINESS

The following exercise allows you to apply the key concepts covered in each chapter to a firm in which you are interested.

If you had funds available right now to purchase the stock of a firm, which stock would you purchase? Record the stock price of that firm by reviewing today's stock quotations in your local paper or in *The Wall Street Journal*. Your instructor may explain how to find these quotes. If the stock was issued by a large U.S. firm, it is probably listed on the New York Stock Exchange (NYSE). Otherwise it may be on the American Stock Exchange (AMEX) or on the Over-the-Counter Exchange, which includes Nasdaq.

Record the following information:

▶ Name of the Stock_____
▶ Today's Date _____
▶ Present Stock Price per Share_____
▶ Annual Dividend per Share _____
▶ Standard & Poor's (S&P) 500 Index _____

The price and dividend information is provided for each stock within the stock quotations.

The S&P 500 index is based on the stock prices of five hundred large firms. It indicates the general level of stock prices and is quoted in the section of the newspaper that provides stock price quotations. It also serves as a benchmark with which you can compare your stock's performance at the end of the term.

At the end of each part, the section "Investing in the Stock of a Business" will allow you to determine how the key concepts apply to that firm. You will need the firm's annual report, which can often be found on the firm's website or can be ordered by calling or writing to the firm's shareholder relations department. Addresses of many firms are available at your local library. For your information, Appendix A (near the end of this text) provides a background on investing in stocks.

You should also monitor how the price of your stock moves over time in response to specific conditions. This will help you recognize the factors that can affect the firm's stock price (and therefore its value). At the end of the school term, the "Investing in the Stock of a Business" project at the end of the last chapter will help you determine the performance of your investment.

The Stock Market Game

Many firms are owned by individuals such as yourself who buy stock. When individuals buy stock, they become partial owners of the firm, yet rely on the firm's managers to manage the firm. Investors attempt to invest in firms that have much potential to perform well in the future. If a firm's performance improves, its value increases, and its stock price should increase as well. Here is an opportunity for you to test your skills at selecting stocks.

A great website (Fantasy Stock Market) enables you to participate in the Stock Market Game exercise, which allows you to invest in stocks, change the composition of your stock portfolio over time, and monitor how the market value of your portfolio changes on a daily basis. This exercise not only illustrates how stock prices change, but it enables you to recognize how business concepts discussed throughout the text can influence the stock price of the firm.

Go to **http://www.fantasystockmarket.com.** To get started, register your name, e-mail address, and password as requested. Once you register, your "log-in" name in the future is your e-mail address. Make sure you remember your password.

INSTRUCTIONS
You are allocated $100,000 cash in fantasy money to create your stock portfolio. You should create your stock portfolio at the beginning of the school term. You can purchase any stocks that are sold on the major U.S. stock exchanges.

You can make a stock transaction by clicking on "Fantasy Transactions." If you do not know the ticker symbol of a stock you wish to purchase or want to know the current price (quote) of a specific stock, click on "Quotes & Lookup."

Your balance is updated daily so that you can monitor how the market value of your portfolio changes over time. You can sell some of your stocks at any time and use the proceeds to buy other stocks. For every stock transaction, you are charged a commission of $19.95.

INFORMATION PROVIDED TO YOU
As you change your stock portfolio, your balance will automatically be adjusted. The balance shows the following for each stock that you own:
▶ Ticker symbol.
▶ Number of shares you own.
▶ Current price of the stock.
▶ Stock total (market value), which is the number of shares multiplied by the current price.

The balance also shows additional information that you can obtain about each of the stocks that you own:
▶ Click on "Headline News" to obtain news about the stock.
▶ Click on "Charts" to see the price movements of the stock over the last five years.
▶ Click on "Report" to obtain financial information about the stock.

MONITORING YOUR PERFORMANCE
Your goal is to manage your portfolio so that you earn a high return on your investment. At the end of each part in

the text, you will be asked to check the value of your portfolio (which is continuously provided by the Fantasy website for you). You may also be asked to compare the performance of your portfolio to the performance of other students' portfolios and to determine why your portfolio performed better or worse than theirs.

You will also be asked to determine whether the prices of any of your stocks changed because of concepts covered in that part of the text. By doing this, you will see how many of the concepts affect the value of a business, and therefore its stock price.

A stock's price can be influenced by changes in the business environment (discussed in Part II), management decisions (discussed in Parts III and IV), marketing decisions (discussed in Part V), and financial decisions (discussed in Part VI). To determine whether the recent stock price movements of one of your stocks are attributed to any firm-specific conditions, you can click on News where your Fantasy balance is shown. Review the recent news and assess whether the stock price movements were influenced by that news. This exercise will help you understand how the decisions that managers make can affect the value (stock price) of their business.

CASE PLANNING A NEW BUSINESS

Mike Cieplak has just created an idea for a business. He wants to provide lessons to people on how to use the Internet and e-mail. He believes that this idea will work because many people (especially older people) do not know how to use the Internet. He will provide hands-on experience and will also show people how to do searches for information, how to buy products online, and how to use other services that are available online. He also will teach people how to create a website.

Mike knows that many people need this service, which is why he thinks this business will be successful. He also knows that he needs a business plan so that he can make this business run efficiently. In particular, he wants to make people aware of his business. He must also decide where he will provide the lessons and what price he will charge for his services.

Mike is currently finishing his degree at a university and will not start on this business full-time until he completes his degree in about three months. Mike does not believe he will need much money to run this business, but the amount of money he will need is partially dependent on his other business decisions within his business plan.

QUESTIONS

1 What are the key decisions that Mike must make when developing his management plan? Relate these decisions to his business.

2 What are the key decisions that Mike must make when developing his marketing plan? Relate these decisions to his business.

3 What are the key decisions that Mike must make when developing his financial plan? Relate these decisions to his business.

4 What do you think will determine whether Mike's business is successful?

VIDEO CASE BUSINESS PLANNING BY YAHOO!

Yahoo!'s original owners were students who created informational websites as a hobby. They realized how valuable this service was to people and turned their hobby into a business. Yahoo has become a very successful business over a short period of time. It has expanded the information it provides on its website to include stock quotations, sports, weather, yellow pages, and business news. Its popularity has generated revenue from firms that pay Yahoo! to advertise their products on its website. Yahoo! is continually changing its website to provide additional information. It attempts to provide whatever information customers want so that it will become even more popular and attract even more advertising revenue. It relies on customer feedback to determine what customers like about its website. It receives a substantial amount of immediate feedback every day in the form of e-mail from its customers.

QUESTIONS

1 What do you think Yahoo!'s business plan is regarding its production of a service and how it generates revenue?

2 Given that Yahoo!'s business plan seems to be working, why is it still necessary for Yahoo! to focus on continual improvement through feedback from its customers?

3 Why might Yahoo!'s business plan change over time?

INTERNET APPLICATIONS

http://www-3.ibm.com/services/learning/conf/

What are some of the upcoming technical conferences IBM is hosting in the future? How do you think these conferences benefit IBM? How do you think these conferences benefit IBM's customers and employees? Do you think establishing an Internet site such as this one is useful for a company that is just starting its operations? Why or why not?

THE *Coca-Cola* COMPANY ANNUAL REPORT PROJECT

Questions for the current year's annual report are available on the text website at **http://madura_intro_bus.swcollege.com.**

You are probably familiar with the product Coke. The producer of that product is The Coca-Cola Company. Throughout this book there are questions related to The Coca-Cola Company's annual report. *Fortune* magazine recently conducted a survey of leading executives and named The Coca-Cola Company as America's most admired corporation. This exercise will provide you with some insights about the operations of one of the world's most successful business organizations.

The following questions apply concepts learned in this chapter to The Coca-Cola Company.

Go to The Coca-Cola Company website (**http://www.cocacola.com/** and find the message to the share owners in the company's 1999 annual report.

QUESTIONS

1 Why do you think The Coca-Cola Company's main goal is to satisfy stockholders?

2 In the message to the share owners, how does the Chairman of the Board view the business of The Coca-Cola Company?

3 What is The Coca-Cola Company's objective in the future? How does the Chairman think this objective should be achieved?

4 How is The Coca-Cola Company fundamentally a local business? In terms of conducting business in foreign countries, what does being a "local business" mean?

5 Go to **http://hoovers.com** and locate the NEWS SEARCH. Type in The Coca-Cola Company in the space provided, and review the recent news stories about the firm. Summarize any (at least one) recent news story about The Coca-Cola Company that applies one or more of the key concepts in this chapter of the text.

IN-TEXT STUDY GUIDE

Answers are in an appendix at the back of the book.

TRUE OR FALSE

1 Creditors organize, manage, and assume the risks of the business.

2 A firm's earnings (or profits) are equal to its revenue plus its expenses.

3 Managers use accounting to monitor and assess the performance of a business.

4 A business plan is intended to provide information for potential investors or creditors of a proposed business.

5 Dividend payments are made to repay loans from creditors.

6 A marketing plan focuses on various decisions that must be made about the production process, such as site location and design and layout of the facilities.

7 Firms use information systems primarily to determine how to finance their businesses.

8 The goal of a firm's management is to maximize the firm's value, which is in the best interests of the firm's owners.

9 Assessing the business environment includes information from industry, economic, and global environments.

10 A firm must satisfy its customers by providing the products or services that customers desire at a reasonable price.

MULTIPLE CHOICE

11 An enterprise that provides products or services that customers desire is a(n):
a) institution.
b) philanthropy.
c) market.
d) agency.
e) business.

12 The five types of stakeholders involved in a business include all of the following except:
a) owners.
b) creditors.
c) couriers.
d) employees.
e) customers.

13 The function of business responsible for the efficient use of employees and other resources (such as machinery) is:
a) finance.
b) accounting.
c) management.
d) information systems.
e) marketing.

14 When an entrepreneur allows other investors to invest in the business, they become:
a) creditors.
b) brokers.
c) employees.
d) sponsors.
e) co-owners.

15 A certificate of ownership of a business is a:
a) bond.
b) stock.
c) mutual fund.
d) co-article.
e) contract.

16 Many firms that need funds borrow from financial institutions or individuals called:
a) debtors.
b) creditors.
c) collateral.
d) joint ventures.
e) investors.

17 The function of business that gathers information about a firm and then provides that information to management for use in decision making is known as:
a) management.
b) information systems.
c) economics.
d) finance.
e) marketing.

18 All of the following describe the products or services provided by successful firms except:
a) obsolete.
b) properly designed.
c) adequate quality.
d) desired by customers.
e) customer satisfying.

19 The purpose of an industry environmental assessment is to determine the:
a) degree of competition.
b) inflation rate.
c) unemployment rate.
d) population growth.
e) economic growth.

20 The business environment assesses the industry of concern to determine the degree of:
a) competition.
b) ownership.
c) debt.
d) inventory.
e) collateral.

21 Management, marketing, and finance are key parts of a(n):
a) accounting plan.
b) production strategy.
c) inventory plan.
d) business plan.
e) information systems plan.

22 A business plan is a detailed description of the proposed business that includes all of the following except:
a) description of the business.
b) types of customers it would attract.
c) competition.
d) facilities needed for production.
e) monetary and fiscal policy.

23 Employees responsible for making key business decisions are:
a) stockholders.
b) owners.
c) managers.
d) business agents.
e) creditors.

24 The business function that focuses on strategies to make the product more appealing to customers and improve the firm's revenue is:
a) production.
b) marketing.
c) manufacturing.
d) personnel.
e) finance.

25 Most business owners would agree that the following characteristics motivated them to start their own business except:
a) earning large incomes.
b) being their own boss.
c) independence of ownership from management activities.
d) prestige associated with owning a business.
e) risk.

26 Firms anticipate how the consumer demand for products changes by:
a) production control.
b) accounting.
c) empowering management.
d) incorporating.
e) monitoring consumer behavior.

27 The function of business that summarizes the firm's financial condition and is used to make various business decisions is:
a) accounting.
b) information systems.
c) production.
d) marketing.
e) management.

28 The management plan that identifies the roles and responsibilities of the employees hired by the firm is the:
a) unity of command.
b) division of work.
c) degree of specialization.
d) organizational structure.
e) standardization concept.

29 A marketing plan focuses on all the following except:
a) financing the business.
b) a profile of typical customers.
c) product characteristics.
d) pricing of the product.
e) distribution of the product.

30 The _____ identifies the characteristics of the typical customer.
a) stockholders' report
b) customer profile
c) Dun & Bradstreet report
d) credit report
e) production schedule

31 A plan that demonstrates why the business is feasible and proposes how the business should be financed is the:
a) production report.
b) marketing plan.
c) financial plan.
d) human resource plan.
e) bottom-up plan.

32 _____ is the business function that is responsible for obtaining the necessary funds to be used by the firm.
a) Finance
b) Marketing
c) Accounting
d) Information systems
e) Management

33 The key stakeholders of a firm include all of the following except:
a) owners.
b) creditors.
c) employees.
d) suppliers.
e) government officials.

34 Managers rely on _____ to detect the inefficient use of resources.
a) owners
b) creditors
c) marketing research
d) marketing mix studies
e) accounting data

35 The function of business by which products are created, priced, distributed, and promoted to customers is:
a) finance.
b) information systems.
c) accounting.
d) management.
e) marketing.

The Learning	1	Explain how business owners select a form of business ownership.
Goals of this	2	Describe methods of owning existing businesses.
chapter are to:	3	Explain how business owners can measure their business performance.

CHAPTER 2

Selecting a Form of Business Ownership

When entrepreneurs establish a business, they must decide on the form of business ownership. The choice of a specific form of business ownership can affect various business characteristics that influence the firm's value.

Consider the case of Outback Steakhouse, which has more than 235 restaurants spread from California to New Jersey. Outback's sales have recently grown substantially. What is the ideal form of business ownership for Outback? What factors did Outback consider when it selected a form of business ownership? What are the risks of Outback from the perspective of its owners? This chapter provides a background on business ownership, which can be used to address these questions.

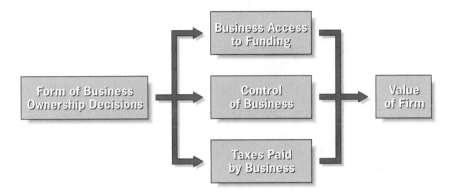

Possible Forms of Business Ownership

Entrepreneurs choose one of three possible forms of business ownership:

► Sole proprietorship
► Partnership
► Corporation

① Explain how business owners select a form of business ownership.

Sole Proprietorship

sole proprietorship a business owned by a single owner

sole proprietor the owner of a sole proprietorship

A business owned by a single owner is referred to as a **sole proprietorship**. The owner of a sole proprietorship is called a **sole proprietor**. A sole proprietor may obtain loans from creditors to help finance the firm's operations, but these loans do not represent ownership. The sole proprietor is obligated to cover any payments resulting from the loans but does not need to share the business profits with creditors.

Typical examples of sole proprietorships include a local restaurant, a local construction firm, a barber shop, a laundry service, and a local clothing store. About 70 percent of all firms in the United States are sole proprietorships. But because these firms are relatively small, they generate less than 10 percent of all business revenue. The earnings generated by a sole proprietorship are considered to be personal income received by the proprietor and are subject to personal income taxes imposed by the Internal Revenue Service (IRS).

Characteristics of Successful Sole Proprietors Sole proprietors must be willing to accept full responsibility for the firm's performance. The pressure of this responsibility can be much greater than any employee's responsibility. Sole proprietors must also be willing to work flexible hours. They are on call at all times and may even have to substitute for a sick employee. Their responsibility for the success of the business encourages them to continually monitor business operations. They must exhibit strong leadership skills, be well organized, and communicate well with employees.

Many successful sole proprietors had previous work experience in the market in which they are competing, perhaps as an employee in a competitor's firm. For example, restaurant managers commonly establish their own restaurants. Experience is critical to understanding the competition and the behavior of customers in a particular market.

Advantages of a Sole Proprietorship The sole proprietor form of ownership has the following advantages over other forms of business ownership:

1 *All Earnings Go to the Sole Proprietor* The sole proprietor (owner) does not have to share the firm's earnings with other owners. Thus, the rewards of establishing a successful firm come back to the owner.

2 *Easy Organization* Establishing a sole proprietorship is relatively easy. The legal requirements are minimal. A sole proprietorship need not establish a separate legal entity. The owner must register the firm with the state, which can normally be done by mail. The owner may also need to apply for an occupational license to conduct a particular type of business. The specific license requirements vary with the state and even the city where the business is located.

3 *Complete Control* Having only one owner with complete control of the firm eliminates the chance of conflicts during the decision-making process. For example, an owner of a restaurant can decide on the menu, the prices, and the salaries paid to employees.

4 *Lower Taxes* Because the earnings in a proprietorship are considered to be personal income, they may be subject to lower taxes than some other forms of business ownership, as will be explained later in this chapter.

Disadvantages of a Sole Proprietorship Along with its advantages, the sole proprietorship has the following disadvantages:

1 *The Sole Proprietor Incurs All Losses* Just as sole proprietors do not have to share the profits, they are unable to share any losses that the firm incurs. For example, assume you invested $10,000 of your funds in a lawn service and borrowed an additional $8,000 that was invested in the business. Unfortunately, the revenue was barely sufficient to pay salaries to your employees, and you terminated the firm. You not only lost all of your $10,000 investment in the firm but also are liable for the $8,000 that you borrowed. Since you are the sole proprietor, no other owners are available to help cover the losses.

unlimited liability no limit on the debts for which the owner is liable

2 *Unlimited Liability* A sole proprietor is subject to **unlimited liability**, which means there is no limit on the debts for which the owner is liable. If a sole proprietorship is sued, the sole proprietor is personally liable for any judgment against that firm.

3 *Limited Funds* A sole proprietor may have limited funds available to invest in the firm. Thus, sole proprietors have difficulty engaging in airplane manufacturing, shipbuilding, computer manufacturing, and other businesses that require substantial funds. Sole proprietors have limited funds to support the firm's expansion or to absorb temporary losses. A poorly performing firm may improve if given sufficient time. But if this firm cannot obtain additional funds to make up for its losses, it may not be able to continue in business long enough to recover.

4 *Limited Skills* A sole proprietor has limited skills and may be unable to control all parts of the business. For example, a sole proprietor may have difficulty running a large medical practice because different types of expertise may be needed.

Partnership

partnership a business that is co-owned by two or more people

partners co-owners of a business

general partnership a partnership in which all partners have unlimited liability

limited partnership a firm that has some limited partners

limited partners partners whose liability is limited to the cash or property they contributed to the partnership

general partners partners who manage the business, receive a salary, share the profits or losses of the business, and have unlimited liability

A business that is co-owned by two or more people is referred to as a **partnership**. The co-owners of a business are called **partners**. The co-owners must register the partnership with the state and may need to apply for an occupational license. About 10 percent of all firms are partnerships.

In a **general partnership**, all partners have unlimited liability. That is, these partners are personally liable for all obligations of the firm. Conversely, a **limited partnership** is a firm that has some **limited partners**, or partners whose liability is limited to the cash or property they contributed to the partnership. Limited partners are only investors in the partnership and do not participate in its management. Yet, because they invested in the business, they share the profits or losses of the business. A limited partnership has one or more **general partners**, or partners who manage the business, receive a salary, share the profits or losses of the business, and have unlimited liability. The earnings distributed to each partner represent personal income and are subject to personal income taxes imposed by the IRS.

Advantages of a Partnership
The partnership form of ownership has three main advantages:

1 *Additional Funding* An obvious advantage of a partnership over sole proprietorships is the additional funding that one or more partners can provide. Therefore, more money may be available to finance the business operations.

2 *Losses Are Shared* Any business losses that the partnership incurs do not have to be absorbed by a single person. Each owner will absorb only a portion of the loss.

3 *More Specialization* A partnership can allow partners to focus on their respective specializations and serve a wide variety of customers. For example, an accounting firm may have one accountant who specializes in personal taxes for individuals and another who specializes in business taxes for firms. A medical practice partnership may have doctors with various types of expertise.

Disadvantages of a Partnership
Along with its advantages, the partnership has the following disadvantages:

1 *Control Is Shared* The decision making in a partnership must be shared. Partners may disagree about how a business should be run, which may destroy business and personal relationships. Some owners of firms do not have the skills to manage a business.

2 *Unlimited Liability* General partners in a partnership are subject to unlimited liability, just like sole proprietors.

3 *Profits Are Shared* Any profits that the partnership generates must be shared among all partners.

S-corporation A firm that has seventy-five or fewer owners and satisfies other criteria. The earnings are distributed to the owners and taxed at the respective personal income tax rate of each owner.

S-Corporations
A firm that has seventy-five or fewer owners and satisfies other criteria may choose to be a so-called **S-corporation.** The earnings of an S-corporation are distributed to the owners and taxed at the respective personal income tax rate of each owner. Thus, the owners are subject to limited liability (like owners of corporations), but they are taxed as if the firm were a partnership. Some state governments impose a corporate tax on S-corporations. Many accounting firms and small businesses select the S-corporation as a form of ownership.

limited liability company (LLC) a firm that has all the favorable features of a typical general partnership but also offers limited liability for the partners

Limited Liability Company (LLC) A type of general partnership called a **limited liability company (LLC)** has become popular in recent years. An LLC is a firm that has all the favorable features of a typical general partnership but also offers limited liability for the partners. It typically protects a partner's personal assets from the negligence of other partners in the firm. This type of protection is highly desirable for partners, given the high frequency of liability lawsuits. The assets of the company (such as the property or machinery owned by the company) are not protected. Although S-corporations may also provide liability protection, various rules may restrict some partners of S-corporations from limited liability. The LLC does not impose such stringent rules.

The LLC must be created according to the laws of the state where the business is located. The precise rules on liability protection vary among the states. Numerous general partnerships (including many accounting firms) have converted to LLCs to capitalize on the advantages of a partnership, while limiting liability for their owners.

Comparison of a Proprietorship with a Partnership A general comparison of a proprietorship with a partnership can be illustrated by considering how your earnings and losses would be affected by the form of business you choose. Exhibit 2.1 shows the earnings of your business over four years if you were the sole proprietor, versus the earnings if you were a co-owner (partner) in a partnership. In the first two years when the business incurred losses, your loss would be larger if you were the sole owner of the business rather than a co-owner. In the next two years, however, when the business generated positive earnings, your gain would be larger if you were the sole owner of the business. The comparison illustrates the relative advantage of being the sole owner when the business performs well and the relative disadvantage when the business incurs losses.

Exhibit 2.1

Your Portion of Earnings (or Losses) on a Proprietorship versus a Partnership

Year	Total Business Earnings (or Loss)	Earnings to a Sole Owner	Earnings to One Partner
1	−$40,000	−$40,000	−$20,000
2	−$20,000	−$20,000	−$10,000
3	+$40,000	+$40,000	+$20,000
4	+$80,000	+$80,000	+$40,000

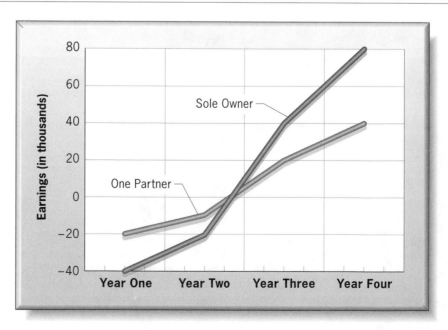

Corporation

corporation a state-chartered entity that pays taxes and is legally distinct from its owners

A third form of business is a **corporation,** which is a state-chartered entity that pays taxes and is legally distinct from its owners. About 20 percent of all firms are corporations. Yet, corporations generate almost 90 percent of all business revenue. Exhibit 2.2 compares the relative contributions to business revenue made by sole proprietorships, partnerships, and corporations.

charter a document used to incorporate a business. The charter describes important aspects of the corporation.

To form a corporation, an individual or group must adopt a corporate **charter,** or a document used to incorporate a business, and file it with the state government. The charter describes important aspects of the corporation, such as the name of the firm, information about the stock issued, and a description of the firm's operations. The people who organize the corporation must also establish **bylaws,** which are general guidelines for managing the firm.

bylaws general guidelines for managing a firm

Since the shareholders of the corporation are legally separated from the entity, they have limited liability, meaning they are not held personally responsible for the firm's actions. The most that the stockholders of a corporation can lose is the amount of money they invested.

The stockholders of a corporation elect the members of the board of directors, who are responsible for establishing the general policies of the firm. One of the board's responsibilities is to elect the president and other key officers (such as vice-presidents), who are then given the responsibility of running the business on a day-to-day basis.

If the board of directors becomes displeased with the performance of the key officers, the board has the power to replace them. Similarly, if the stockholders become displeased with the performance of members of the board, the stockholders can replace the directors in the next scheduled election. In some corporations, one or a few individuals may serve as a stockholder, as a member of the board of directors, and as a key officer of the firm. For example, Louis Gerstner is the chief executive officer of IBM, is the chairman of the board, and holds more than eighty thousand shares of IBM stock.

How Stockholders Earn a Return on Their Investment Stockholders can earn a return on their investment in a firm in two different ways. First, they may receive dividends from the firm, which are a portion of the firms recent earnings over the last three months that are distributed to stockholders. Second, the stock they hold may increase in value. When the firm becomes more profitable, the value of its stock tends to rise, meaning the value of stock held by owners has increased. Thus, they can benefit by selling that stock for a much higher price than they paid for it. In recent years, stock prices of many well-known firms such as IBM and Motorola have more than doubled.

Exhibit 2.2

Relative Contributions to Business Revenue of Sole Proprietorships, Partnerships, and Corporations

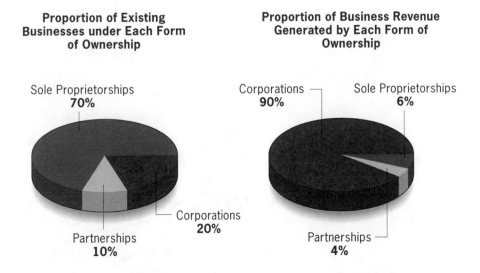

Proportion of Existing Businesses under Each Form of Ownership

Sole Proprietorships 70%

Partnerships 10%

Corporations 20%

Proportion of Business Revenue Generated by Each Form of Ownership

Corporations 90%

Sole Proprietorships 6%

Partnerships 4%

Large corporations have an annual shareholder meeting in which key officers of the firm summarize the firm's performance and future prospects. In this photo, John Welch, chief executive officer of General Electric, addresses a group of shareholders at the annual meeting.

Corporate Information

http://www.adobe.com/aboutadobe/main.html

MANY CORPORATIONS, SUCH AS ADOBE, USE THE INTERNET TO PROVIDE information about their corporations. Companies use the Internet both to market their product and to provide detailed information about their company to investors and customers. For example, by clicking on "About Adobe," financial information and recent press releases can be accessed.

privately held ownership is restricted to a small group of investors

Privately Held versus Publicly Held Corporations People become owners of a corporation by purchasing shares of stock. Many small corporations are **privately held**, meaning that ownership is restricted to a small group of investors. Some well-known privately held firms include L. L. Bean, Enterprise Rent-A-Car, and Rand

Yahoo! went public so that it could obtain more funds to support its business expansion. Its stock is listed in the Nasdaq market, while its stock options are traded on the Chicago Board of Trade (CBoe).

publicly held shares can be easily purchased or sold by investors

McNally and Company. Most large corporations are **publicly held**, meaning that shares can be easily purchased or sold by investors.

Stockholders of publicly held corporations can sell their shares of stock when they need money, are disappointed with the performance of the corporation, or simply expect that the stock price will not rise in the future. Their stock can be sold (with the help of a stockbroker) to some other investor who wants to invest in that corporation.

going public the act of initially issuing stock to the public

Although virtually all firms (even Ford Motor Company) were privately held when they were created, some of these firms became publicly held when they needed funds to support large expansion. The act of initially issuing stock to the public is called **going public.** Recently, well-known firms such as Barnesandnoble.com, United Parcel service (UPS), and Prodigy have gone public to raise funds.

Publicly held corporations can obtain additional funds by issuing new common stock. This means that either their existing stockholders can purchase more stock, or other investors can become stockholders by purchasing the corporation's stock. By issuing new stock, corporations may obtain whatever funds are needed to support any business expansion. Corporations that wish to issue new stock must be able to convince investors that the funds will be utilized properly, resulting in a reasonable return for the investors.

Advantages of a Corporation   The corporate form of ownership offers the following advantages:

1 *Limited Liability* Owners of a corporation have limited liability (as explained earlier), whereas sole proprietors and general partners typically have unlimited liability.

2 *Access to Funds* A corporation can easily obtain funds by issuing new stock (as explained earlier). This allows corporations the flexibility to grow and to engage in new business ventures. Sole proprietorships and partnerships have less access to funding when they wish to finance expansion. To obtain more funds, they may have to rely on their existing owners or on loans from creditors.

3 *Transfer of Ownership* Investors in large, publicly traded companies can normally sell their stock in minutes by calling their stockbrokers or by selling it online over the Internet. Conversely, owners of sole proprietorships or partnerships may have some difficulty in selling their share of ownership in the business.

Disadvantages of a Corporation Along with its advantages, the corporate form of ownership has the following disadvantages:

1 *High Organizational Expense* The expense of organizing a business normally is greater for the corporate form of business than for the other forms. The higher expense results from the necessity of creating a corporate charter and filing it with the state. Some expense also may be incurred in establishing bylaws.

2 *Financial Disclosure* When the stock of a corporation is traded publicly, the investing public has the right to inspect the company's financial data, within certain limits. As a result, firms may be obligated to publicly disclose more about their business operations and employee salaries than they would like. Privately held firms are not forced to disclose financial information to the public.

3 *Agency Problems* Publicly held corporations are normally run by managers who are responsible for making decisions for the business that will serve the interests of the owners. Managers may not always act in the best interests of stockholders, however. For example, managers may attempt to take expensive business trips that are not necessary to manage the business. Such actions may increase the expenses of running a business, reduce business profits, and therefore reduce the returns to stockholders. When managers do not act as responsible agents for the shareholders who own the business, a so-called **agency problem** results. Such a problem normally does not occur with proprietorships, because the sole owner may also serve as the sole manager and make most or all business decisions.

4 *High Taxes* Since the corporation is a separate entity, it is taxed separately. The annual taxes paid by a corporation are determined by applying the corporate tax rate to the annual earnings. The corporate tax rate is different from the personal tax rate. Consider a corporation that earns $10 million this year. Assume that the corporate tax rate applied to earnings of corporations is 30 percent this year (the corporate tax rates can be changed by law over time). Thus, the taxes and after-tax earnings of the corporation are as follows:

$$
\begin{aligned}
\text{Earnings before Tax} &= \$10,000,000 \\
\text{Corporate Tax} &= \underline{3,000,000} \ (\text{computed as 30\% of \$10,000,000}) \\
\text{Earnings after Tax} &= \underline{\$\ 7,000,000}
\end{aligned}
$$

agency problem when managers do not act as responsible agents for the shareholders who own the business

Corporations, just like individuals, have to pay taxes. Apple Computers pays hundreds of millions of dollars in taxes each year.

If any of the after-tax earnings are paid to owners as dividends, the dividends represent personal income to stockholders. Thus, the stockholders will pay personal income taxes on the dividends. Continuing with our example, assume that all of the $7 million in after-tax earnings is distributed to the stockholders as dividends. Assume that the personal tax rate is 20 percent for all owners who will receive dividends (personal tax rates depend on the person's income level and can be changed by law over time). The actual dividend income received by stockholders after paying income taxes is as follows:

$$
\begin{aligned}
\text{Dividends Received} &= \$7,000,000 \\
\text{Taxes Paid on Dividends} &= \underline{\quad1,400,000\quad} \text{ (computed as 20\% of \$7,000,000)} \\
\text{Income after Tax} &= \underline{\underline{\$5,600,000}}
\end{aligned}
$$

Since the corporate tax was $3,000,000 and the personal tax was $1,400,000, the total tax paid as a result of the corporation's profits was $4,400,000, which represents 44 percent of the $10,000,000 profit that the corporation earned.

This example shows how owners of corporations are subject to double taxation, because the corporation's entire profits from their investment are first subject to corporate taxes. Then, any profits distributed as dividends to individual owners are subject to personal income taxes. Exhibit 2.3 shows the flow of funds between owners and the corporation to illustrate how owners are subject to double taxation.

To recognize the disadvantage of double taxation, consider what the taxes would have been for this business if it were a sole proprietorship or partnership rather than a corporation. The $10,000,000 profit would have been personal income to a sole proprietor or to partners and would have been subject to personal taxes. Assuming a personal tax rate of 20 percent, the total tax amount would be $2,000,000 (computed as 20 percent of $10,000,000). This tax amount is less than half of what would be paid out by a corporation that earned the same profit. Even if the personal income tax rate of a sole proprietor or a partner was higher than 20 percent, the taxes paid by a corporation would probably still be higher. A comparison of the tax effects between corporations and sole proprietorships is provided in Exhibit 2.4.

Exhibit 2.3

Illustration of Double Taxation

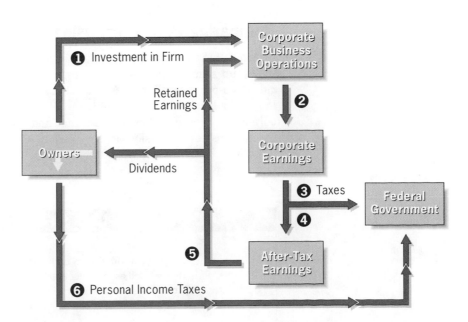

Exhibit 2.4

Comparison of Tax Effects between Corporations and Sole Proprietorships

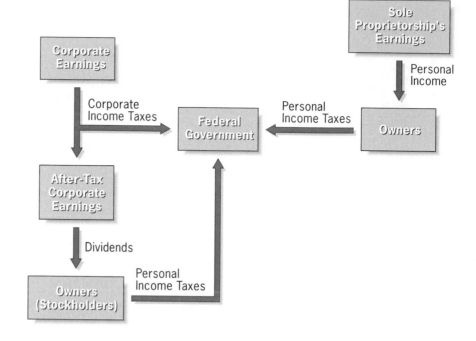

One way that the corporation may reduce the taxes paid by owners is to reinvest its earnings (called "retained earnings") rather than pay the earnings out as dividends. If owners do not receive dividends from a corporation, they will not be subject to personal taxes on the profits earned by the corporation. This strategy makes sense only if the corporation can put the retained earnings to good use.

capital gain the price received from the sale of stock minus the price paid for the stock

When stockholders of a corporation sell their stocks for more than they paid for them, they earn a **capital gain**, which is equal to the price received from the sale of stock minus the price they paid for the stock. The stockholders must pay a so-called capital gains tax on the capital gain. Whether stockholders receive income from selling the stock at a gain or from receiving dividend payments, they are subject to taxes.

Comparing Forms of Business Ownership

No single form of business ownership is ideal for all business owners. An individual setting up a small business may choose a sole proprietorship. Some people who decide to co-own a small business may choose a partnership. However, if they prefer to limit their liability, they may decide to establish a privately held corporation. If this corporation grows substantially over time and needs millions of dollars to support additional business expansion, it may convert to a publicly held corporation so that it can obtain funds from stockholders.

DELL® COMPUTER'S FORMULA FOR SUCCESS

Dell Computer uses the corporate form of ownership. Its board of directors includes nine directors, with Michael Dell as the chief executive officer (CEO). Furthermore, Dell's corporate structure includes seventeen executive officers. Dell Computer has approximately 36,500 employees in thirty-four countries.

Methods of Owning Existing Businesses

(2) Describe methods of owning existing businesses.

Many people become sole owners of businesses by starting their own business. Some people, however, become the sole owners without starting the business. The following are common methods by which people become owners of existing businesses:

- ▶ Assuming ownership of a family business
- ▶ Purchasing an existing business
- ▶ Franchising

Assuming Ownership of a Family Business

Many people work in a family business and after a period of time assume the ownership of it. This can be an ideal way to own a business because its performance may be somewhat predictable as long as the key employees continue to work there. Major decisions regarding the production process and other operations of the firm have been predetermined. If the business has historically been successful, a new owner's main function may be to ensure that the existing operations continue to run efficiently. Alternatively, if the business is experiencing poor performance, the new owner may have to revise management, marketing, and financing policies.

Purchasing an Existing Business

Businesses are for sale on any given day in any city. They are often advertised in the classified ads section of local newspapers. Businesses are sold for various reasons, including financial difficulties and the death or retirement of an owner.

People considering the purchase of an existing business must determine whether they have the expertise to run the business or at least properly monitor the managers. Then they must compare the expected benefits of the business with the initial outlay required to purchase it. Historical sales volume may be provided by the seller of the business and can be used to estimate the future sales volume. However, the prospective buyer must be cautious when using these figures. In some businesses such as dentistry and hair styling, personal relationships between the owner and customers are critical. Many customers may switch to competitors if the ownership changes. For these

This photo shows the first McDonald's restaurant, in Des Plaines, Illinois. McDonald's restaurants use a franchise arrangement, which allows investors to purchase a franchise and manage it. This franchise arrangement is probably the most successful in the world, as evidenced by McDonald's more than 25,000 restaurants in 120 countries.

types of businesses, the historical sales volume may substantially overestimate future sales. For some other, less personalized businesses such as grocery stores, a change of ownership is not likely to have a significant effect on customer preferences (and therefore on sales volume).

Franchising

franchise arrangement whereby a business owner allows others to use its trademark, trade name, or copyright, under specific conditions

franchisor firm that allows others to use its trade name or copyright, under specified conditions

franchisee firm that is allowed to use the trade name or copyright of a franchise

A **franchise** is an arrangement whereby a business owner (called a **franchisor**) allows another (the **franchisee**) to use its trademark, trade name, or copyright, under specified conditions. Each individual franchise operates as an independent business and is typically owned by a sole proprietor.

Franchises in the United States number over five hundred thousand, and they generate more than $800 billion in annual revenue. Some well-known franchises include McDonald's, Thrifty Rent-a-Car System, Mail Boxes Etc., Dairy Queen, Super 8 Motels Inc., TGI Fridays, Pearle Vision Inc., and Baskin-Robbins. The costs of purchasing a franchise can vary significantly, depending on the specific trademarks, technology, and services provided to the franchisees.

BUSINESS ONLINE

Forms of Ownership Information

http://www.dairyqueen.com/ idq/dq/lease/home.htm

DAIRY QUEEN, ONE OF THE MOST POPULAR FRANCHISORS IN THE WORLD, uses the Internet to provide information to existing and potential franchisees. For example, Dairy Queen provides information on its website regarding its new training program for its franchisees and the information on how to apply for franchises in the United States and abroad.

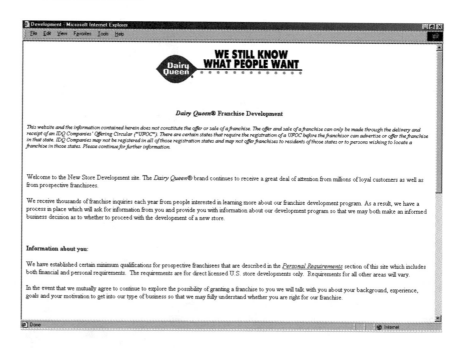

distributorship a type of franchise in which a dealer is allowed to sell a product produced by a manufacturer

chain-style business a type of franchise in which a firm is allowed to use the trade name of a company and follows guidelines related to the pricing and sale of the product

manufacturing arrangement a type of franchise in which a firm is allowed to manufacture a product using the formula provided by another company

Types of Franchises   Most franchises can be classified as a distributorship, a chain-style business, or a manufacturing arrangement.

In a **distributorship**, a dealer is allowed to sell a product produced by a manufacturer. For example, Chrysler and Ford dealers are distributorships.

In a **chain-style business**, a firm is allowed to use the trade name of a company and follows guidelines related to the pricing and sale of the product. Some examples are McDonald's, CD Warehouse, Holiday Inn, Subway, and Pizza Hut.

In a **manufacturing arrangement**, a firm is allowed to manufacture a product using the formula provided by another company. For example, Microsoft might allow a foreign company to produce its software, as long as the software is sold only in that country. Microsoft would receive a portion of the revenue generated by that firm.

Advantages of a Franchise The typical advantages of a franchise are as follows:

1 *Proven Management Style* Franchisees look to the franchisors for guidance in production and management. McDonald's provides extensive training to its franchisees. The management style of a franchise is already a proven success. A franchise's main goal is to duplicate a proven business in a particular location. Thus, the franchise is a less risky venture than a new type of business, as verified by a much higher failure rate for new businesses.

2 *Name Recognition* Many franchises are nationally known because of advertising by the franchisor. This provides the franchisee with name recognition, which can significantly increase the demand for the product. Therefore, owners of Holiday Inn, Pizza Hut, and other franchises may not need to spend money on advertising because the franchises are already popular with consumers

3 *Financial Support* Some franchisees receive some financial support from the franchisor, which can ensure sufficient start-up funds for the franchisee. For example, some McDonald's franchisees can receive funding from McDonald's. Alternatively, franchisees can purchase materials and supplies from the franchisor on credit, which represents a form of short-term financing.

Disadvantages of a Franchise Two common disadvantages of franchising are as follows:

1 *Sharing Profits* In return for services provided by the franchisor, the franchisee must share profits with the franchisor. Annual fees paid by the franchisee may be 8 percent or more of the annual revenue generated by the franchise.

2 *Less Control* The franchisee must abide by guidelines regarding product production and pricing, and possibly other guidelines as well. Consequently, the franchisee's performance is dependent on these guidelines. Owners are not allowed to revise some of the guidelines.

Though decision making is limited, owners of a franchise still make some critical decisions. They must decide whether a particular franchise can be successful in a particular location. In addition, even though the production and marketing policies are somewhat predetermined, the owners are responsible for managing their employees. They must provide leadership and motivation to maximize production efficiency. Thus, a franchise's performance is partially dependent on its owners and managers.

How Owners Measure Business Performance

3 Explain how business owners can measure their business performance.

Owners who invest in a firm focus on two key criteria to measure a firm's performance: (1) return on their investment and (2) risk of their investment. These two criteria are discussed now, because the business strategies that managers implement should be intended to satisfy the business owners. Managers must determine how various business strategies will affect the firm's return on investment and risk.

Return on Investment

The return on investment in a firm is derived from the firm's profits (also called "earnings" or "income"). As a firm produces income, a portion of these earnings is paid to the Internal Revenue Service as income taxes. The remaining (after-tax) earnings represent the return (in dollars) to the business owners. However, dollar value of a firm's after-tax earnings is not necessarily a useful measure of the firm's performance unless

SPOTLIGHT ON TECHNOLOGY

Organizing Your Business by Using the Internet

The decision on the form of business ownership can have long-term implications for taxes, liability, and control of the business. For these reasons, it should not be made lightly and will usually require a lawyer. Unfortunately, good legal advice does not come cheap. Therefore, entrepreneurs should familiarize themselves with the issues involved in organizing their businesses prior to retaining legal counsel. In recent years, the Internet has become an excellent place for finding out about such issues.

Perhaps the best starting point for learning more about business organization is the Small Business Administration (SBA). The SBA's home page (**http://www.sbaonline.sba.gov/**), pictured in Exhibit 2.5, represents an excellent starting point for further research. Among the resources offered are the following:

▶ Information on local SBA offices.
▶ Access to the Service Corps of Retired Executives (SCORE), consisting of over ten thousand retired businesspeople who have volunteered to help small businesses for free.
▶ SBA publications. As illustrated (Exhibit 2.6), the range of topics covered by the publications is enormous, and each can be copied directly to the entrepreneur's computer at no charge.

All of these services are also available through local SBA offices, but the entrepreneur can reach them far more quickly over the Internet.

Exhibit 2.5 The Small Business Administration's Home Page

Exhibit 2.6 List of SBA Publications on the Internet

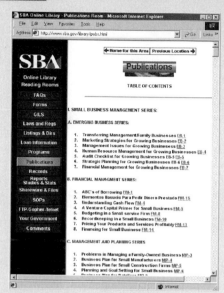

In addition to government agencies, such as the SBA, many private organizations provide information and services to small businesses just setting up. Many of these organizations, such as The Company Corporation (Exhibit 2.7), allow corporations and other forms of businesses to be set up entirely over the Internet. A particularly attractive feature of these services is their low cost—often hundreds or thousands of dollars less than using a lawyer. The entrepreneur is cautioned, however, that "undoing" the wrong form of ownership can often be expensive. Therefore, unless the entrepreneur has extensive knowledge of various forms of ownership, establishing a long-term relationship with a local attorney is generally prudent.

Exhibit 2.7 The Company Corporation Home Page

equity the total investment by the firm's stockholders

return on equity (ROE) earnings as a proportion of the equity

it is adjusted for the amount of the firm's **equity**, which is the total investment by the firm's stockholders. For this reason, business owners prefer to measure the firm's profitability by computing its **return on equity (ROE)**, which is the earnings as a proportion of the equity:

$$\text{Return on Equity} = \frac{\text{Earnings after Tax}}{\text{Equity}}$$

For example, if a firm was provided with $1,000,000 by stockholders, and if its after-tax earnings last year were $150,000, its return on equity last year was:

$$\text{ROE} = \frac{\$150,000}{\$1,000,000}$$

$$= .15, \text{ or } 15\%.$$

Thus, the firm generated a return equal to 15 percent of the owners' investment in the firm.

To recognize why a "return" measurement such as ROE is more useful than the dollar value of profits, consider the following situation for Firms A and B in a particular industry:

	Firm A	Firm B
Earnings after taxes last year	$15 million	$15 million
Stockholders' equity	$100 million	$300 million
Return on equity	15%	5%

Notice that the firms had the same dollar value of earnings after taxes. However, it took three times the investment in Firm B to achieve the same level of annual profit. Therefore, the return on equity (measured as earnings after taxes divided by stockholders' equity) is much higher for Firm A than for Firm B. Thus, Firm A is apparently making better use of the funds invested by stockholders.

As a realistic application, the return on equity for IBM for 1999 is derived in Exhibit 2.8. Notice that IBM generated earnings before taxes of about $12 billion. Of this amount, $4 billion (30 percent) was used to pay corporate taxes. The remaining $8 billion represents after-tax earnings. Given the total investment (equity) in IBM of about $19 billion, the after-tax earnings represent a return of about 32 percent (computed as $8 billion divided by $20 billion).

Risk

risk the degree of uncertainty about a firm's future earnings

The **risk** of a firm represents the degree of uncertainty about the firm's future earnings, which reflects an uncertain return to the owners. A firm's future earnings are dependent on its future revenue and its expenses. Firms can experience losses if the revenue is less than expected or if the expenses are more than expected. Some firms that experience severe losses ultimately fail. In these cases, the owners may lose most or all of the funds they invested in the firms. Also, creditors may not be repaid for the loans that they provided to the firms.

To illustrate the risk of a business, consider the uncertainty of the future revenue and expenses of a lawn service firm. Revenue generated by the firm could be less than expected if unusually cold weather prevents grass and shrubs from growing. In addition, other lawn service firms may be created and compete for any available business. Given a limited number of lawns in a community, any lawn jobs done by new lawn service firms take away business that was previously provided by this firm. The ex-

Exhibit 2.8

Return on Equity for IBM

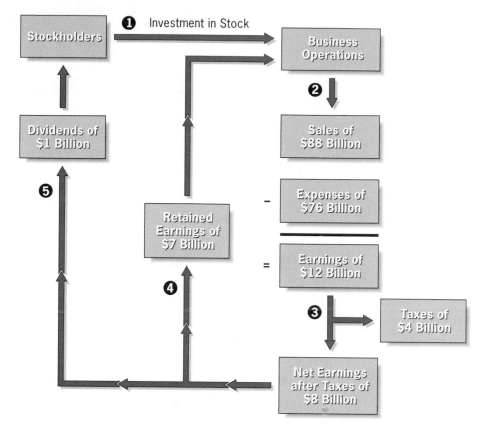

Return on Equity (ROE)

Given that IBM equity was about $20 billion, its ROE was:

$$\text{ROE} = \frac{\text{Earnings after Taxes}}{\text{Equity}}$$

$$= \frac{\$8 \text{ billion}}{\$20 \text{ billion}}$$

$$= 32\%$$

penses of a lawn service may be higher than expected if lawn mowers break down or if the cost of hiring employees rises. Exhibit 2.9 illustrates how business risk applies to the lawn service. This exhibit shows that the owner of the lawn service anticipated that the firm's earnings would be $30,000 in one year. However, since actual revenue was $40,000 less than expected and expenses were $4,000 more than expected, the firm incurred a loss of $14,000. Large firms such as KMart and Smith Corona (typewriters) have experienced losses following a decline in the demand for their products.

Firms cannot control some factors that may affect their revenue or expenses. Nevertheless, firms should recognize how possible adverse conditions can affect demand, so that they can develop a realistic forecast of revenue. In addition, to create a more realistic expectation of the total expenses, they should anticipate that some repairs on their machinery may be needed.

Exhibit 2.9

Example of Business Risk

	Expected	Actual
Revenue	$90,000	$50,000
Expenses	60,000	64,000
Earnings	$30,000	−$14,000

To prepare for potential problems, the risks of each business should be recognized. Although many new businesses become success stories, many failures occur as well. Some new businesses fail simply because the entrepreneur did not recognize the risks. The Self-Scoring Exercise offers a self-test for assessing your own skills for success in business. However, recognize that some people may be successful as managers but not as entrepreneurs because they do not recognize the risks involved in establishing a new business.

SELF-SCORING EXERCISE

Do You Have the Skills Necessary to Succeed in Business?

According to the U.S. Department of Labor, achieving success in the workplace, now and in the future, will require that a person possess three enabling skills as a foundation for the five functional skills required in the business environment. Answer each of these three basic questions:

1. Do you believe you possess the basic reading, speaking, listening, and mathematics skills required for future learning?
2. Do you believe you possess the intellectual skills for effective decision making and problem solving?
3. Do you believe you possess the affective skills required for you to cooperate with others and achieve effective sociability?

If you answered yes to each question, you have the basic skills needed to enable you to master five functional skills in the business environment. How do you rate yourself in each of these five functional skill areas? In the blank before each skill, place the number from 1 (very good) to 5 (needs improvement) that reflects your self-rating.

_____ 1. Resource management skills, such as human resource management, time management, and financial resources management.
_____ 2. Information management skills, such as identifying and interpreting information.
_____ 3. Personal interaction skills, such as teamwork, negotiation, and working with customers.
_____ 4. Systems behavior and performance skills, such as anticipating consequences of behavior and cause-and-effect relationships.
_____ 5. Technology utilization skills, such as selecting, using, maintaining, and/or troubleshooting technology.

If you rated yourself a 4 or 5 on any of the five functional skills, you may want to talk with your instructor or the university's career and counseling office about specific opportunities that will enable you to strengthen those skills.

Relationship between Risk and Return Some firms have a much higher degree of risk than others because the demand for their products is highly uncertain. Potential owners will support these high-risk firms only if they are expected to provide a higher return. For example, people may be willing to become owners of an exotic jewelry store only if they expect the store to generate high profits. The people could have used their money to invest in a less risky business, such as a retail bookstore or a grocery store, but investing in the exotic jewelry store offers the possibility of earning a higher return on their investment.

Like business investors, creditors will provide funds to a risky firm only if they have the potential to earn a relatively high return on the funds provided. The return to creditors is the interest rate charged on the loans they provide. To compensate for the higher risk, creditors charge a higher rate of interest when lending funds to a risky business.

CROSS-FUNCTIONAL TEAMWORK

Sources of Risk Across Business Functions

A firm relies on the management of resources (including human resources and other resources such as machinery), marketing, and finance functions to perform well. Poor performance can normally be attributed to poor management of resources, poor marketing, or poor financing, as explained next.

If resources are not properly managed, the firm will incur excessive expenses. The following are typical mistakes that can cause excessive production expenses:

1 Hiring more employees than necessary, which results in high operating expenses.

2 Hiring fewer employees than necessary, which prevents the firm from achieving the desired volume or quality of products.

3 Hiring employees who lack proper skills or training.

4 Investing in more equipment or machinery than necessary, which results in high operating expenses.

5 Investing in less equipment or machinery than necessary, which prevents the firm from achieving the desired volume or quality of products.

The following are typical marketing mistakes that can cause poor performance:

1 Excessive spending on marketing programs.

2 Ineffective marketing programs, which do not enhance the firm's revenue.

The following are typical finance mistakes that can cause poor performance:

1 Borrowing too much money, which results in a high level of interest expenses incurred per year.

2 Not borrowing enough money, which prevents a firm from investing the necessary amount of funds to be successful.

Since business decisions are related, a poor decision in one department can affect other departments. For example, Compaq Computer's production volume is based on the forecasted demand for computers by the marketing department. When the marketing department underestimates the demand, Compaq experiences shortages.

Risk of Small Businesses Small businesses tend to be riskier than larger businesses because small businesses have neither the managerial expertise nor the funds to diversify into other businesses. Thus, if their single line of business experiences problems, they are highly susceptible to failure. Any event that affects the single industry they have entered (such as a workers' strike in a supplier firm or reduced demand for the type of products they produce) can result in failure. In addition, the death or retirement of a key manager can have a greater impact on a small business. Larger businesses typically have several employees in high-level positions who can make key decisions, so no one person is irreplaceable.

Investors recognize the higher risk of small businesses and will invest in them only if the potential for high profitability outweighs the risk involved. Creditors will lend to small businesses only if they will receive a higher return (higher interest rate) that properly reflects the risk. Consequently, the cost of financing for a small business is generally higher than for a large corporation.

BUSINESS ONLINE

Small Business Information

THE SMALL BUSINESS ADMINISTRATION (SBA) OF THE U.S. GOVERNMENT USES the Internet to provide information and list the requirements for qualifying as a small business. Sites such as this are highly useful for individuals considering the establishment of a new business, as they provide information about legal liability and taxes. Contact information and online brochures containing information about starting and financing small businesses are also available.

http://www.sbaonline.sba.gov

Ownership of Foreign Businesses

OPPORTUNITIES IN FOREIGN COUNTRIES HAVE ENCOURAGED MANY ENTRE-preneurs in the United States to establish foreign businesses in recent years. A common method for an entrepreneur to establish a foreign business is to purchase a franchise created by a U.S. firm in a foreign country. For example, McDonald's, Pizza Hut, and KFC have franchises in numerous foreign countries. The potential return on these franchises may be higher than in the United States if there is less competition.

Another popular method for U.S. entrepreneurs to own a foreign business is to purchase a business that is being sold by the foreign government. During the 1990s, many governments in Eastern Europe and Latin America sold a large number of businesses that they had owned. They also encouraged more competition among firms in each industry. Entrepreneurs recognized that many businesses previously owned by the government were not efficiently managed. Consequently, many businesses were perceived as having relatively low values, thus enabling some entrepreneurs to purchase the businesses at low prices. However, these businesses were subject to a high degree of risk because the foreign environment was unstable. Since most of the businesses in these countries had been managed by their respective governments, the rules for privately owned businesses were not completely established. The tax rates that would be imposed on private businesses were uncertain. The degree of competition was also uncertain, as firms were now free to enter most industries.

Given the uncertainties faced by new businesses in these foreign countries, some entrepreneurs made agreements with existing foreign firms rather than establishing their own business. For example, suppose that an entrepreneur recognizes that various household products will be popular in some Latin American countries but prefers not to establish a firm there because of uncertainty about tax rates and other government policies. The entrepreneur may make an agreement with an existing firm that distributes related products to retail stores throughout Latin America. This firm will earn a fee for selling the household products produced by the entrepreneur. This example is just one of many possible arrangements that allow U.S. entrepreneurs to capitalize on opportunities in a foreign country without owning a business there.

| BUSINESS DILEMMA | College Health Club |

Ownership Decision at College Health Club

SUE KRAMER HAS COMPLETED HER BUSINESS PLAN FOR COLLEGE HEALTH Club (CHC), as explained in Chapter 1, in which she would be a sole proprietor. She believes that she is well prepared to run her own health club. She submits the plan to her local bank along with a request for a business loan. Shortly after submitting her plan, she learns that a national health club chain is planning to establish a health club franchise near a huge corporate office complex at the other end of town. Sue does not perceive this franchise as a competitor to CHC because it is far away from the campus and is targeted at employees who work in the office complex. Nevertheless, the franchise is of interest to her because it is searching for someone to purchase it. Sue decides to consider purchasing the franchise. The franchisee will be trained by the national chain on how to run the health club and will receive a percentage of the revenue earned by the franchise. Although similar types of health clubs are in the area, the national chain believes that there is room for at least one more competitor.

Dilemma

Sue has to decide whether to purchase the franchise or establish CHC. For this reason, she needs to consider the advantages of purchasing the franchise health club versus establishing CHC. What are the advantages of each alternative? Which alternative should Sue select?

Solution

One advantage of the franchise health club is that it would offer training. Second, it has a well-established plan for managing health clubs. Third, the club has a national name that potential customers recognize.

Owning CHC, however, also offers advantages. One advantage is that CHC would be less expensive than the franchise health club. Second, CHC would allow Sue to capitalize on her specific idea of targeting college students. Third, Sue would be able to manage CHC without any interference, whereas the franchise would have to be managed in a manner dictated by the national chain. Fourth, Sue would not have to pay a percentage of her revenue to the national chain if she establishes her own health club.

Given the balanced advantages of each alternative business opportunity, the choice is dependent on personal preferences and abilities. Since Sue feels that she has the skills to run her own health club, she decides to do it on her own rather than purchase a franchise.

Additional Issues for Discussion

1 Sue could also have considered purchasing one of the existing health clubs that are for sale in the area. What is an advantage of purchasing an existing health club? What is a disadvantage?

2 One advantage of a partnership is that it allows partners to focus on their respective specializations. Should this advantage cause Sue to search for a partner for her health club business?

3 How will CHC be taxed given that Sue plans to be the sole owner?

SUMMARY

When starting a new business, entrepreneurs must select from among three forms of ownership:

▶ A sole proprietorship, owned by a single person who often manages the firm as well.

▶ A partnership, composed of two or more co-owners who may manage the firm as well. A partnership can allow for more financial support by owners than a sole proprietorship, but it also requires that control and profits of the firm be shared among owners.

▶ A corporation, which is an entity that is viewed as separate from its owners. Owners of a corporation have limited liability, while owners of sole proprietorships and partnerships have unlimited liability.

The common methods by which people become owners of existing businesses are as follows:

▶ Assuming ownership of a family business

▶ Purchasing an existing business

▶ Franchising

Assuming the ownership of a family business is desirable because a person can normally learn much about that business before assuming ownership. Yet, many people are not in a position to assume the family business. To purchase an existing business, one must estimate future sales and expenses to determine whether making the investment is feasible. Franchising may be desirable for people who will need some guidance in running the firm. However, the franchisee must pay annual fees to the franchisor.

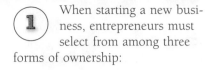

A firm's performance is measured by its owners using two criteria: return on the owner's investment (equity) and risk. Owners of a business commonly assess the return on their investment by measuring the firm's return on equity (ROE), which represents a firm's after-tax earnings as a percentage of the total investment by owners.

The risk of a business represents the uncertainty about its future earnings. Firms that have more uncertain revenue or expenses will have more uncertain earnings, and therefore higher risk. The owners and creditors require a higher return when providing funds to firms whose future earnings are more uncertain.

KEY TERMS

agency problem   36
bylaws   33
capital gain   38
chain-style business   40
charter   33
corporation   33
distributorship   40
equity   43
franchise   40
franchisee   40

franchisor   40
general partners   31
general partnership   31
going public   35
limited liability company (LLC)   32
limited partners   31
limited partnership   31
manufacturing arrangement   40
partners   31

partnership   31
privately held   34
publicly held   35
return on equity (ROE)   43
risk   43
S-corporation   31
sole proprietor   29
sole proprietorship   29
unlimited liability   30

REVIEW QUESTIONS

1 What are the differences between a sole proprietorship, a partnership, and a corporation?

2 Discuss the advantages and disadvantages of a sole proprietorship.

3 Distinguish between a general partnership and a limited partnership.

4 Identify the advantages of an S-corporation.

5 Identify and explain the differences between an S-corporation and a limited liability company.

6 How can stockholders earn a return on their investment?

7 Identify and explain the differences between privately held and publicly held corporations.

8 Explain why stockholders have a concern that managers do not always act in their best interests.

9 Explain the difference between the corporate tax rate and the personal tax rate.

10 Identify and explain the advantages and disadvantages of a franchise.

DISCUSSION QUESTIONS

1 Assume you are a management consultant. For the following situations, recommend an appropriate form of business ownership:
   a. Four physicians wish to start a practice together, and each wants to have limited liability.
   b. A friend wants to start her own convenience store.
   c. An entrepreneur wants to acquire a large U.S. steel business.
   d. Five friends want to build an apartment complex and are not concerned about limited liability.

2 Discuss the basic steps that should be undertaken to organize a corporation in your state.

3 Discuss and give examples of what you believe is the most common form of business ownership in your hometown.

4 Assume you are starting your own business. What decisions do you have to make concerning the type of ownership and control of your business?

5 Discuss the advantages and disadvantages of starting your own business compared to buying a franchise.

INVESTING IN THE STOCK OF A BUSINESS

Using the annual report of the firm in which you would like to invest, complete the following:

1 Each annual report contains an income statement, which discloses the firm's earnings before taxes, its taxes, and its earnings after taxes over the most recent year. Search for the table called "Income Statement" and determine your firm's earnings before taxes, taxes paid, and earnings after taxes last year. What proportion of your firm's earnings were eventually paid as taxes?

2 Is your firm involved in franchising? If so, describe the details on its franchises. Check its website to obtain franchise information.

3 Describe any conditions mentioned in the annual report that expose the firm to risk.

4 Explain how the business uses technology to provide information about its form of business ownership. For example, does it use the Internet to disclose the form of business ownership it uses?

5 Go to **http://hoovers.com** and locate the NEWS SEARCH. Type in the name of the firm in the space provided, and review the recent news stories about the firm. Summarize *one* recent news story about the firm that applies to one or more of the key concepts within this chapter.

CASE DECIDING THE TYPE OF BUSINESS OWNERSHIP

Paul Bazzano and Mary Ann Boone are lifelong friends and have decided to go into business. They are not sure of the form of business ownership and control. Paul has stated he would like to invest his savings of $25,000, but he does not want to take an active role in managing the day-to-day operations of the business. Mary Ann, on the other hand, is a self-starter, enjoys cooking and baking, and has a vast number of pizza recipes. An existing pizza business is for sale for $50,000. Paul and Mary Ann both like the idea of getting into a business investment. Mary Ann has $5,000 she would like to contribute and believes that buying an existing business has certain advantages. She likes the idea that Paul will not be an active owner and that she will have full control of the pizza operation.

The existing business has sales of $150,000 and generates earnings after taxes of $32,500. Mary Ann believes the business can be expanded and foresees future growth to expand into different locations throughout the Boston area. She projects two more stores in the next five years.

QUESTIONS

1 What form of business ownership would you recommend for this business?

2 Would Mary Ann's form of ownership be any different from Paul's?

3 How could Paul and Mary Ann determine the return on their investment after their first year of business?

4 Describe the risk of this business.

VIDEO CASE BUSINESS ORGANIZATION AT SECOND CHANCE BODY ARMOR

Richard Davis was shot while he was working at a pizza restaurant. When he recovered, he thought of a way to create a bulletproof vest that would be so flexible that it could be worn all day. He decided to turn this idea into a business (called Second Chance Body Armor) that would produce vests that would enhance the safety of police officers around the country. He began the firm as a sole proprietorship and started with just $70. Any revenue that he received was used to pay for marketing the concealable body armor that he created. Once law enforcement agencies learned of his product, they began to order it. Consequently, Second Chance Body Armor became a success. In time, the firm hired many employees and converted into a corporation.

QUESTIONS

1. Why do you think Richard Davis initially began his firm as a sole proprietorship?
2. When Richard Davis started his firm, how could he have benefited from creating a partnership with a few other owners? What would be a disadvantage of using this form of business ownership instead of a sole proprietorship?
3. Why do you think Richard Davis decided to convert his sole proprietorship into a corporation?

INTERNET APPLICATIONS

http://www.ibm.com

What were IBM's most recent quarterly earnings (total and per share)? Compute IBM's return on equity (ROE) for the last quarter. How does a corporate website such as this allow investors to evaluate the performance of a company such as IBM? What other information do you think a website such as this could provide to evaluate corporate performance?

THE Coca-Cola COMPANY ANNUAL REPORT PROJECT

 Questions for the current year's annual report are available on the text website at **http://madura_ intro_bus.swcollege.com.**

The following questions apply concepts learned in this chapter to The Coca-Cola Company.

Go to The Coca-Cola Company website (**http://www .cocacola.com**) and find the index for the 1999 annual report.

1. Why do you think The Coca-Cola Company is organized as a corporation rather than a sole proprietorship or a partnership?
2. According to its 1999 annual report, The Coca-Cola Company has increased its dividend thirty-eight years in a row. Why might this be an advantage to shareholders?

3. Look at the "Total Return to Share Owners." If you had invested in The Coca-Cola Company ten years ago, what would your average annual compound return have been?
4. Do you think a global company such as The Coca-Cola Company would experience more or fewer agency conflicts than a corporation operating solely within the United States?
5. Go to **http://hoovers.com** and locate the NEWS SEARCH. Type in The Coca-Cola Company in the space provided, and review the recent news stories about the firm. Summarize any (at least one) recent news story about The Coca-Cola Company that applies one or more of the key concepts within this chapter of the text.

IN-TEXT STUDY GUIDE

Answers are in an appendix at the back of the book.

TRUE OR FALSE

1. One advantage of sole proprietorships is that this form of ownership provides easy access to additional funds.
2. The legal requirements for establishing a sole proprietorship are very difficult.
3. When a corporation distributes some of its recent earnings to stockholders, the payments are referred to as capital gains.

4 If the board of directors becomes displeased with the performance of the key officers, the board has the power to replace them.

5 Publicly held corporations can obtain additional funds by issuing new common stock.

6 Publicly held corporations are required to disclose financial information to the investing public.

7 To incorporate a business, one must adopt a corporate charter and file it with the state government where the business is to be located.

8 The limited liability feature is an advantage in owning a sole proprietorship.

9 Distributorships, chain-style businesses, and manufacturing arrangements are all common types of franchises.

10 Limited partners are investors in the partnership and participate in the management of the business.

MULTIPLE CHOICE

11 People become owners of a corporation by purchasing:
a) shares of stock.
b) corporate bonds.
c) retained earnings.
d) inventory.
e) accounts receivable.

12 The following are possible forms of business ownership except for a:
a) sole proprietorship.
b) partnership.
c) bureaucracy
d) corporation.

13 The return on investment in a firm is derived from the firm's ability to earn:
a) assets.
b) liabilities.
c) profits.
d) expenses.

14 Joe wants to form his own business. He wants to get started as quickly and inexpensively as possible and has a strong desire to control the business himself. He is confident he will be successful and wants to keep all the profits himself. Joe's goals indicate he would probably choose to operate his business as a(n):
a) limited partnership.
b) limited liability company.
c) S-corporation.
d) franchise.
e) sole proprietorship.

15 A firm that has seventy-five owners or less and also meets other criteria may choose to be a so-called:
a) cooperative.
b) proprietorship.
c) joint venture.
d) S-corporation.
e) bureaucracy.

16 A disadvantage of a sole proprietorship is that:
a) sole proprietors have very little control over the operations of the business.
b) sole proprietors have unlimited liability.
c) it is more difficult and expensive to establish than other forms of business.
d) its earnings are subject to higher tax rates than other forms of business.
e) sole proprietors are required to share the firm's profits with employees.

17 Sharing profits and less control of the business ownership are two common disadvantages of:
a) sole proprietorships.
b) downsizing.
c) divestiture.
d) franchising.

18 Partners have unlimited liability in a:
a) general partnership.
b) corporation.
c) limited partnership.
d) cooperative.

19 An arrangement whereby business owners allow others to use their trademark, trade name, or copyright under specified conditions is a:
a) franchise.
b) labor union.
c) bureau.
d) joint venture.
e) cartel.

20 The degree of uncertainty about future earnings, which reflects an uncertain return to the owners, is known as:
a) certainty.
b) profits.
c) risk.
d) equity.
e) dividends.

21 The members of the board of directors of a corporation are chosen by the corporation's:
a) president and chief executive officer.
b) creditors.
c) general partners.
d) stockholders.
e) charter members.

22 When stockholders of a corporation sell shares of stock for more than they paid for them, they receive a(n):
a) dividend.
b) premium.
c) capital gain.
d) discount.
e) stock option.

23 A business that is allowed to use the trade name of a company and follows guidelines related to the pricing and sales of the products is a:
a) joint venture.
b) monopoly.
c) chain-style business.
d) sole proprietorship.

24 A corporate charter contains general guidelines for managing the company called:
a) rules of order.
b) bylaws.
c) indenture agreements.
d) control procedures.
e) disclosure clauses.

25 A general partnership that protects a partner's personal assets from the negligence of other partners is called a:
a) limited liability company.
b) cooperative.

c) private corporation.

d) master limited partnership.

e) protected partnership.

26 A corporation is:

a) easier to form than other types of businesses.

b) a state-chartered entity that is legally distinct from its owners.

c) a business that is owned and operated by a government agency.

d) a form of business that is legally exempt from paying taxes on earnings.

e) simply another term for a large sole proprietorship.

27 When ownership of a small corporation is restricted to a small group of investors, it is:

a) publicly held.   d) privately held.

b) government owned.   e) perfectly competitive.

c) bureaucratic.

28 All of the following are common types of franchise arrangements except:

a) business agencies.

b) chain-style businesses.

c) manufacturing arrangements.

d) distributorships.

29 The total amount invested in a company by its owners is called:

a) the corporate margin.

b) equity.

c) working capital.

d) the stock premium.

e) treasury stock.

30 A business owned by a single owner is referred to as a:

a) partnership.

b) sole proprietorship.

c) limited partnership.

d) corporation.

e) subchapter S-corporation.

31 In a limited partnership:

a) all partners have limited liability.

b) the partnership exists only for a limited time period, or until a specific task is accomplished.

c) the limited partners do not participate in management of the company.

d) the partners agree to operate in a limited geographic area.

e) no more than seventy-five partners may invest in the company at any one time.

32 When a corporation's shares can be easily purchased or sold by investors, it is:

a) publicly held.   d) monopolized.

b) privately held.   e) franchised.

c) institutionalized.

33 Important aspects of the corporation, such as the name of the firm, information about the stock issued, and a description of the firm's operations, are contained in a:

a) mission.   d) plan.

b) policy.   e) venture.

c) charter.

34 When two or more people, having complementary skills, agree to co-own a business, this agreement is referred to as a:

a) partnership.   d) corporation.

b) sole proprietorship.   e) joint venture.

c) cooperative.

35 When entrepreneurs establish a business, they must first decide on the form of:

a) divestiture.   c) joint venture.

b) global expansion.   d) ownership.

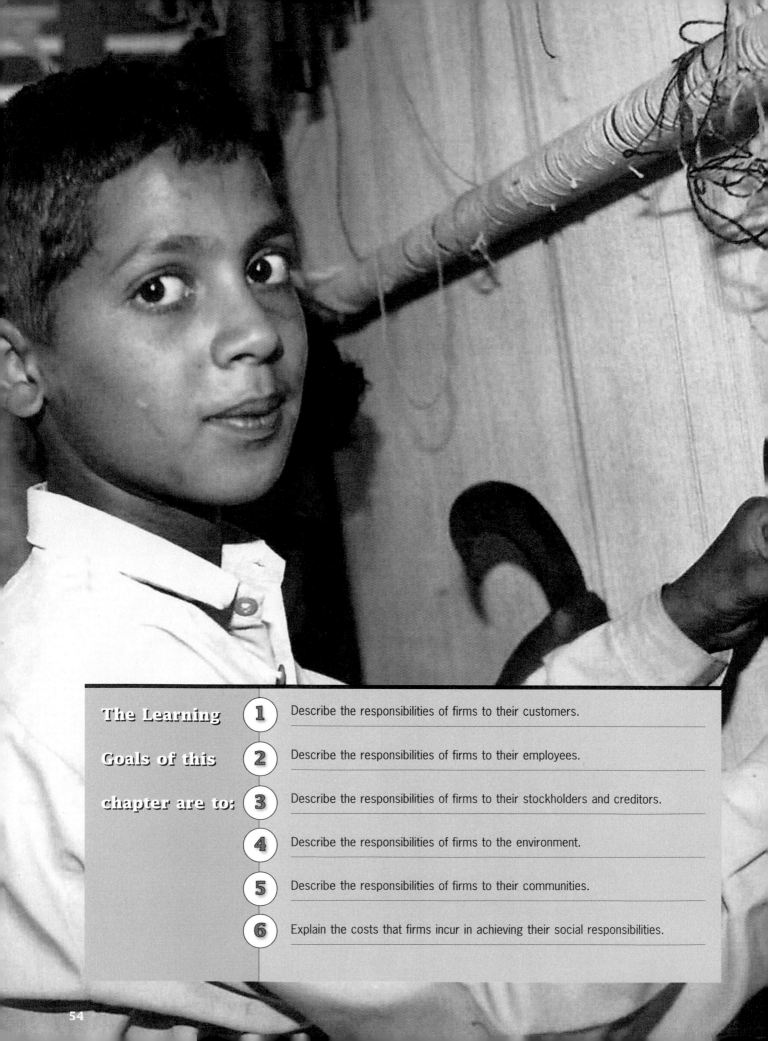

The Learning Goals of this chapter are to:

1 Describe the responsibilities of firms to their customers.

2 Describe the responsibilities of firms to their employees.

3 Describe the responsibilities of firms to their stockholders and creditors.

4 Describe the responsibilities of firms to the environment.

5 Describe the responsibilities of firms to their communities.

6 Explain the costs that firms incur in achieving their social responsibilities.

Business Ethics and Social Responsibility

A firm's employees should practice business ethics, which is a set of principles that should be followed when conducting business. Each firm has a social responsibility, which is the firm's recognition of how its business decisions can affect society. The term *social responsibility* is sometimes used to describe the firm's responsibility to its community and to the environment. However, it may also be used more broadly to include the firm's responsibility to its customers, employees, and creditors. Although the business decisions a firm makes are intended to increase its value, the decisions must not violate its ethics and social responsibilities.

To illustrate how business ethics can affect the value of a business, consider the case of Homestake Mining Company, which focuses on gold mining in the United States, Canada, and other countries. What responsibilities does Homestake have toward its employees who are involved in min-

ing? What responsibilities does Homestake have toward the environment in which it conducts mining operations? What responsibilities does Homestake have toward the stockholders who have invested their funds in the firm? Can Homestake satisfy all of these responsibilities simultaneously? This chapter provides a background on a firm's social responsibilities that can be used to address these questions.

Impact of Unethical Decisions

Employees continually make business decisions that may be influenced by business ethics. The following are examples of common unethical business decisions:

1 An employee of a car dealership wants to sell a car at the sticker price to any customers who are not aware that the usual selling price is at least $2,000 less than the sticker price. The employee is paid on commission and will receive a higher income if the customer pays a higher price.

Result: Benefit to car salesperson, adverse effect on customer

2 An employee of a computer company who is paid on commission attempts to sell a much more expensive computer to a customer than the customer needs.

Result: Benefit to employee, adverse effect on customer

3 A manager hires a friend, even though the friend is not the most qualified applicant for the job.

Result: Benefit to manager, adverse effect on other applicant who deserved the job

4 An employee who is the buyer of supplies at a manufacturing plant buys most supplies from a supplier who sends him tickets to the Super Bowl each year. This supplier charges 20 percent more than another supplier. Since the cost of supplies is so high, the firm's earnings are lower.

Result: Benefit to employee who is assigned to buy supplies, adverse effect on other supplier and on the firm's shareholders

5 A manager of a firm attempts to avoid paying some employees for some hours worked so that she can reduce her expenses and possibly earn a higher bonus for keeping expenses low.

Result: Benefit to manager, adverse effect on other employees

6 The president of a firm uses most of this year's earnings to purchase a private jet for the firm. The jet supposedly was obtained for business purposes, but the president uses it to fly to golf outings and other forms of entertainment for himself. Consequently, a smaller amount of dividends is distibuted to the shareholders who own the firm.

Result: Benefit to president, adverse effect on the firm's shareholders

7 To keep expenses low, an employee of a factory throws several pollutants into the garbage rather than disposing of them properly.

Result: Benefit to employee, adverse effect on the environment

8 The manager of a factory decides to close it and build a new factory in his hometown, where he wants to live. The expenses of the new factory will be higher, but the manager will be able to move back to his hometown.

Result: Benefit to manager, adverse effect on the first community and on the firm's shareholders

Notice that each of these decisions was directly beneficial to the person who made the decision, at the expense of one or more stakeholders of the firm or the environment. Unethical decisions usually occur when the decision maker makes a decision that is intended to benefit himself or herself, rather than the firm's stakeholders.

Assess each of the eight unethical decisions, and consider how such decisions can be prevented. In each case, some form of monitoring may be needed to ensure that decision makers of firms maintain their responsibilities to their stakeholders and to the environment. This chapter describes these responsibilities and discusses how firms can ensure that the decision makers will uphold them.

Impact of Unethical Practices on Firm Value

Unethical business practices can adversely affect a firm's value. As an illustration, consider the case of Columbia Hospital, which was accused of overbilling for its hospital services in 1998. It experienced numerous employee resignations, and its value (as measured by its stock price) declined substantially, as shown in Exhibit 3.1.

As a related example, Sunbeam used unusual accounting practices that appeared to overstate its earnings. In June 1998, it was alleged that Sunbeam's earnings were overstated to enhance the compensation of its high-level managers (their pay was tied to performance). Once the allegations were publicized, many investors who held Sunbeam's stock sold the stock. This caused the stock price to decline substantially, as shown in Exhibit 3.2.

Responsibility to Customers

1 Describe the responsibilities of firms to their customers.

A firm's responsibility to customers goes beyond the provision of products or services. Firms have a **social responsibility** when producing and selling their products, as discussed next.

Exhibit 3.1

Columbia's Stock Price after Overbilling

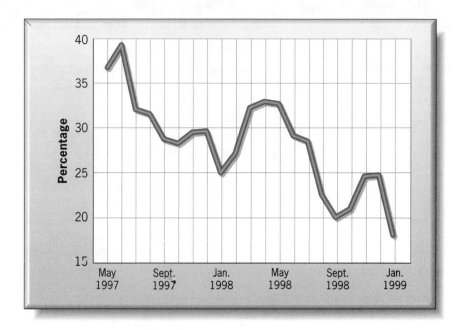

social responsibility a firm's recognition of how its business decisions can affect society

Responsible Production Practices

Products should be produced to ensure customer safety. Proper warning labels should be attached to products to prevent accidents that could result from misuse. For some products, proper information on possible side effects should be provided. For example, Tylenol gelcaps, Nyquil cough syrup, and Coors beer all have warning labels about possible adverse effects.

Responsible Sales Practices

Firms need guidelines that discourage employees from using overly aggressive sales strategies or deceptive advertising. They may also use customer satisfaction surveys to ensure that customers were treated properly by salespeople. The surveys should be conducted after customers make a purchase to determine whether the product worked as the salesperson said that it would.

Exhibit 3.2

Sunbeam's Stock Price after It Was Accused of Overstating Its Earnings

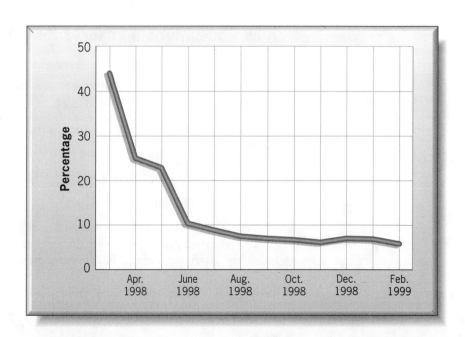

How Firms Ensure Responsibility toward Customers

A firm can ensure responsibility toward its customers by following these steps:

business ethics a set of principles that should be followed when conducting business

1 *Establish a Code of Ethics* Firms can establish a code of **business ethics** that sets guidelines for product quality, as well as guidelines for how employees, customers, and owners should be treated. The pledge (from an annual report) by Bristol-Myers Squibb Company in Exhibit 3.3 is an example of a code of ethics. Many firms have a booklet on ethics that is distributed to all employees.

2 *Monitor Complaints* Firms should make sure that customers have a phone number that they can call if they have any complaints about the quality of the product or about how they were treated by employees. The firm can attempt to determine the source of the complaint and ensure that the problem does not occur again. Many firms have a department that receives complaints and attempts to resolve them. This step may involve assessing different parts of the production process to ensure that the product is produced properly. Or it may require an assessment of particular employees who may be violating the firm's code of responsibility to its customers.

3 *Customer Feedback* Firms can ask customers for feedback on the products or services they recently purchased, even if the customers did not call in to complain. This process may detect some other problems with the product's quality or with the way customers were treated. For example, automobile dealers such as Saturn send a questionnaire to customers to determine how they were treated by salespeople. Customers may also be asked whether they have any complaints about the automobile they recently purchased. Once the firm is informed of problems with either production defects or customer treatment, it should take action to correct these problems.

DELL® COMPUTER'S FORMULA FOR SUCCESS

Dell uses custom configuration to ensure a high level of product quality and thereby fulfill its responsibility to customers. Specifically, Dell custom configures hardware and software as it builds computer systems, one order at a time. This single-step integration is efficient for Dell and its customers and produces higher-quality products because it reduces the number of times systems are handled. Partly as a result of this practice, Dell has consistently received high service and reliability ratings in a *PC World* magazine survey.

How Consumerism Ensures Responsibility toward Customers

consumerism the collective demand by consumers that businesses satisfy their needs

The responsibility of firms toward customers may be enforced not only by the firms but also by specific groups of consumers. **Consumerism** represents the collective demand by consumers that businesses satisfy their needs. Consumer groups became popular in the 1960s and have become increasingly effective as a result of their growth.

How the Government Ensures Responsibility toward Customers

In addition to the codes of responsibility by firms and the wave of consumerism, the government attempts to ensure responsibility to customers with various laws on product safety, advertising, and industry competition.

Government Regulation of Product Safety   The government protects consumers by regulating the quality of some products produced by firms. For example,

Exhibit 3.3

Excerpts from a Pledge of
Ethics and Responsibility by
Bristol-Myers Squibb Company

THE BRISTOL-MYERS SQUIBB PLEDGE

TO THOSE WHO USE OUR PRODUCTS . . .
We affirm Bristol-Myers Squibb's commitment to the highest standards of excellence, safety and reliability in everything we make. We pledge to offer products of the highest quality and to work diligently to keep improving them.

TO OUR EMPLOYEES AND THOSE WHO MAY JOIN US . . .
We pledge personal respect, fair competition and equal treatment. We acknowledge our obligation to provide able and humane leadership throughout the organization, within a clean and safe working environment. To all who qualify for advancement, we will make every effort to provide opportunity.

TO OUR SUPPLIERS AND CUSTOMERS . . .
We pledge an open door, courteous, efficient and ethical dealing, and appreciation of their right to a fair profit.

TO OUR SHAREHOLDERS . . .
We pledge a companywide dedication to continued profitable growth, sustained by strong finances, a high level of research and development, and facilities second to none.

TO THE COMMUNITIES WHERE WE HAVE PLANTS AND OFFICES . . .
We pledge conscientious citizenship, a helping hand for worthwhile causes, and constructive action in support of civic and environmental progress.

TO THE COUNTRIES WHERE WE DO BUSINESS . . .
We pledge ourselves to be a good citizen and to show full consideration for the rights of others while reserving the right to stand up for our own.

ABOVE ALL, TO THE WORLD WE LIVE IN . . .
We pledge Bristol-Myers Squibb to policies and practices which fully embody the responsibility, integrity and decency required of free enterprise if it is to merit and maintain the confidence of our society.

---

the Food and Drug Administration (FDA) is responsible for testing food products to determine whether they meet specific requirements. The FDA also examines new drugs that firms have recently developed. Because potential side effects may not be known immediately, the FDA tests some drugs continually over several years.

Government Regulation of Advertising The federal government also has established laws against deceptive advertising. Yet, it may not be able to prevent all unethical business practices. Numerous examples of advertising could be called deceptive. It is difficult to know if a product is "new and improved." In addition, a term such as "lowest price" may have different meanings or interpretations.

Government Regulation of Industry Competition Another way in which the government ensures that consumers are treated properly is to promote competition in most industries. Competition between firms is beneficial to consumers, because firms that charge excessive prices or produce goods of unacceptable quality will not survive in a competitive environment. Because of competition, consumers can avoid a firm that is using deceptive sales tactics.

monopoly a firm that is the sole provider of goods or services

A firm has a **monopoly** if it is the sole provider of goods or services. It can set prices without concern about competition. However, the government regulates firms that have a monopoly. For example, it regulates utility firms that have monopolies in specific locations and can control the pricing policies of these firms.

In some industries, firms created various agreements to set prices and avoid competing with each other. The federal government has attempted to prevent such activity by enforcing antitrust laws. Some of the more well-known antitrust acts are summarized in Exhibit 3.4. All of these acts share the objective of promoting competition. Yet, each act focuses on particular aspects that can influence the degree of competition within an industry.

The trucking, railroad, airlines, and telecommunications industries have been deregulated, allowing more firms to enter each industry. In addition, banks and other financial institutions have been deregulated since 1980 and now have more flexibility on the types of deposits and interest rates they can offer. They also have more freedom to expand across state lines. In general, deregulation results in lower prices for consumers.

Responsiblity to Employees

2 Describe the responsibilities of firms to their employees.

Firms also have a responsibility to their employees to ensure safety, proper treatment by other employees, and equal opportunity.

Employee Safety

Firms ensure that the workplace is safe for employees by closely monitoring the production process. Some obvious safety precautions are to check machinery and equipment for proper working conditions, require safety glasses or any other equipment that can prevent injury, and emphasize any special safety precautions in training seminars.

Firms that create a safe working environment prevent injuries and improve the morale of their employees. Many firms now identify workplace safety as one of their main goals. Levi Strauss and Company imposes safety guidelines not only on its U.S. facilities but also on Asian factories where some of its clothes are made. Starbucks Coffee Company has developed a code of conduct in an attempt to improve the quality of life in coffee-producing countries.

Proper Treatment by Other Employees

Firms are responsible for ensuring that employees are treated properly by other employees. Two key issues concerning the treatment of employees are diversity and the prevention of sexual harassment, which are discussed next.

Exhibit 3.4	Key Antitrust Laws

Sherman Antitrust Act (1890)	Encouraged competition and prevented monopolies.
Clayton Act (1914)	Reinforced the rules of the Sherman Antitrust Act and specifically prohibited the following activities because they reduced competition:
	Tying agreements Forced firms to purchase additional products as a condition of purchasing the desired products.
	Binding contracts Prevented firms from purchasing products from a supplier's competitors.
	Interlocking directorates The situation in which the same person serves on the board of directors of two competing firms.
Federal Trade Commission Act (1914)	Prohibited unfair methods of competition; also called for the establishment of the Federal Trade Commission (FTC) to enforce anti-trust laws.
Robinson-Patman Act (1936)	Prohibited price policies or promotional allowances that reduce competition within an industry.
Celler-Kefauver Act (1950)	Prohibited mergers between firms that reduce competition within an industry.

Diversity In recent years, the workforce has become much more diverse. More women have entered the job market, and more minorities now have the necessary skills and education to qualify for high-level jobs. Exhibit 3.5 shows the proportions of various job categories held by women, African-Americans, and Hispanics.

Many firms have responded to the increased diversity among employees by offering diversity seminars, which inform employees about cultural diversity. Such information can help employees recognize that certain statements or behavior may be offensive to other employees.

The following statement from a recent annual report of General Motors reflects the efforts that have been made by many firms to encourage diversity:

" Internally, we are working to create an environment where diversity thrives. We are trying to remove barriers that separate people and find new ways to engage teams to maximize productivity and profitability. This is being done through communication, teamwork, mutual support, and pulling together to achieve common objectives. Our challenge is to seek a diverse population in leadership roles with a wide range of backgrounds, views, and experiences to ensure we capture diverse perspectives to meet and exceed customer expectations. "

Johnson and Johnson, MCIWorldCom, The Coca-Cola Company, IBM, Merrill Lynch, Sara Lee Corporation, and many other firms have made major efforts to promote diversity. Rockwell International has a diversity task team that developed guidelines for workforce diversity planning in each of its businesses. Xerox has improved its workplace diversity in recent years.

sexual harassment
unwelcome comments or actions of a sexual nature

Prevention of Sexual Harassment Another workplace issue is **sexual harassment,** which involves unwelcome comments or actions of a sexual nature. For example, one employee might make unwelcome sexual advances toward another and use personal power within the firm to threaten the other employee's job status. Firms attempt to prevent sexual harassment by offering seminars on the subject. Like diversity seminars, these seminars can help employees recognize how some statements or behavior may be offensive to other employees. These seminars are not only an act of responsibility to employees but also can improve a firm's productivity by helping employees get along.

Exhibit 3.5

Proportion of Women and Minorities in Various Occupations

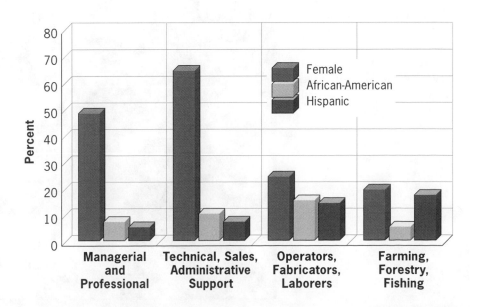

Equal Opportunity

Employees who apply for a position at a firm should not be subjected to discrimination because of their national origin, race, gender, or religion. The Civil Rights Act of 1964 prohibits such forms of discrimination. The act is enforced by a federal agency known as the Equal Employment Opportunity Commission (EEOC). Beyond the federal guidelines, many firms attempt to ensure equal treatment among applicants for a position by assigning someone to monitor the hiring process. The concept of equal treatment applies not only to the initial hiring of an employee but also to annual raises and promotions within the firm.

affirmative action a set of activities intended to increase opportunities for minorities and women

Many firms and government agencies implement **affirmative action** programs. Some people expect affirmative action programs to ensure equal treatment among prospective and existing employees. Other people expect these programs to establish quotas, which would designate specific positions for minorities or women. Most people would agree that affirmative action programs have good intentions, but quotas may be viewed as a form of reverse discrimination.

Denny's (a restaurant business) was charged with racial discrimination in 1993. That same year, it began implementing a program to promote diversity. In recent years, Denny's has increased both its minority management and the number of franchises owned by African Americans.

How Firms Ensure Responsibility toward Employees

To ensure that employees receive proper treatment, many firms establish a grievance procedure for employees who believe they are not being given equal opportunity. A specific person or department is normally assigned to address such complaints. This method of addressing employee complaints is similar to that of addressing customer complaints. By recognizing the complaints, the firm attempts both to resolve them and to revise its procedures to prevent further complaints.

Starbuck's has been proactive in monitoring working conditions in coffee-producing countries. A portion of their statement of beliefs reads, "We respect human rights and dignity. We believe that people should work because they want or need to, but not because they are forced to do so. We believe that people have the right to freely associate with whichever organizations or individuals they choose. We believe that children should not be unlawfully employed as laborers."

A good example of a firm's effort to resolve employee complaints is Marriott, which implemented three strategies. First, it created a mediation process, in which a neutral person outside the firm (called a mediator) assesses the employee complaint and suggests a solution. The mediator does not have the power to enforce a final judgment but may help the employee and the firm resolve the conflict.

Second, Marriott offers a toll-free number for employees to call if they believe they were subjected to discrimination, harassment, or improper firing. Marriott begins to investigate the complaint within three days of the call.

Third, Marriott allows the employee to voice complaints in front of a panel of other employees who determine whether the employee's complaints are valid, based on Marriott's existing guidelines.

Marriott's procedure for resolving employee complaints has shown positive results. EEOC complaints against Marriott by its employees declined by 50 percent in the year after the procedure was implemented and by 83 percent in the next year. Since more employee complaints are resolved within the firm, employees are more satisfied with their jobs and focus on satisfying customers.

The cost of attempting to listen to every employee complaint can be substantial for a firm. Furthermore, some of the complaints may not be valid. Firms must attempt to distinguish between complaints that are valid and those that are not and then focus on resolving the valid complaints.

Conflict with Employee Layoffs

Some business decisions are controversial because although they improve the firm's performance, they may adversely affect employees in the local community. Consider the following example, which reflects a common dilemma that many firms face. As your firm's business grew, you hired more employees. Unfortunately, demand for your product has declined recently, and you no longer need twenty of the employees that you hired over the last two years. If you lay off twenty employees, you will reduce your expenses substantially and satisfy your stockholders. However, you may be criticized for not serving employees' interests. This situation is unpleasant because the layoffs may be necessary (to cut expenses) for your firm to survive. If your firm fails, all your other employees will be out of work as well.

This dilemma has no perfect solution. Many firms may do what's best for the business, while attempting to reduce the adverse effects on their employees. For example, they may help laid-off employees find employment elsewhere or may even attempt to retrain them for other jobs within the firm.

GLOBAL BUSINESS

Global Ethics

U.S. FIRMS TYPICALLY HAVE A CODE OF ETHICS THAT PROVIDES GUIDELINES to the employees. However, these guidelines may be much more restrictive than those generally used in some foreign countries. Consider a U.S. firm that sells supplies to manufacturers. The employees of this firm may be subject to rules that prevent them from providing payoffs ("kickbacks") to any employees of the manufacturing companies that order the firm's supplies. Yet, other competitors may provide payoffs to employees of the manufacturing companies ordering supplies from their company. In some countries, this type of behavior is acceptable. Thus, the U.S. supplier is at a disadvantage because its employees are required to follow a stricter code of ethics. This is a common ethical dilemma that U.S. firms face in a global environment. The employees of U.S. firms must either ignore their ethical guidelines or be at a disadvantage in certain foreign countries.

Another ethical dilemma that U.S. firms face in some foreign countries is their relationship with foreign governments. Firms that conduct business in foreign countries are subject to numerous rules enforced by the local government. Officials of some foreign governments commonly accept bribes from firms that need approval for various business activities. For example, a firm may need to have its products approved for safety purposes, or its local manufacturing plant may need to be approved for environmental purposes. The process of approving even minor activities could take months and prevent the firm from conducting business. Those firms that pay off government officials may receive prompt attention from the local governments. Employees of Lockheed were charged with bribing Egyptian government officials to win a contract to build new aircraft. Executives of IBM's Argentina subsidiary were charged with bribing Argentine government officials to generate business from the government.

A recent assessment of foreign countries by the U.S. Commerce Department and intelligence agencies detected numerous deals in which foreign firms used bribes to win business contracts over U.S. competitors. Many of these foreign firms are located in France, Germany, and Japan, as well as in some less-developed countries.

Many U.S. firms attempt to follow a worldwide code of ethics that is consistent across countries. This type of policy reduces the confusion that could result from using different ethical standards in different countries. Although a worldwide code of ethics may place a U.S. firm at a disadvantage in some countries, it may also enhance the firm's credibility.

Responsibility to Stockholders

 Describe the responsibilities of firms to their stockholders and creditors.

Firms are responsible for satisfying their owners (or stockholders). Employees may be tempted to make decisions that satisfy their own interests rather than those of the owners. For example, some employees may use the firm's money to purchase computers for their personal use rather than for the firm.

How Firms Ensure Responsibility

Managers of a firm monitor employee decisions to ensure that they are made in the best interests of the owners. Employee salaries may be directly tied to the firm's performance. In this way, employees stay focused on maximizing the firm's value.

Owners of a firm recognize that the firm will incur costs in meeting responsibilities such as employee safety and prevention of pollution. The firm's efforts to provide a safe and pollution-free environment represent a necessary cost of doing business.

BUSINESS ONLINE

Stockholder Information

http://www.goodyear.com/investor/index.html

COMPANIES SUCH AS GOODYEAR USE THE INTERNET TO PROVIDE THEIR INvestors with detailed information about the firm's financial performance. For example, Goodyear summarizes the most significant information, such as the level of its stock price and recent dividends, right in the body of its website. Other information, such as the most recent annual report, can be obtained by clicking the links on the left. Sites such as these provide investors with the resources they need to monitor closely the management of the companies they own.

How Stockholders Ensure Responsibility

shareholder activism the
active efforts of stockholders to
influence a firm's management
policies

institutional investors financial
institutions that purchase large
amounts of stock

In recent years, there has been much **shareholder activism,** which refers to the active efforts of stockholders to influence a firm's management policies. Stockholders have been especially active when they are dissatisfied with the firm's executive salaries or other policies.

The stockholders who have been most active are **institutional investors,** or financial institutions that purchase large amounts of stock. For example, insurance companies invest a large portion of the insurance premiums that they receive in stocks. If institutional investors invest a large amount of money in a particular stock, the return on their investment is highly dependent on how that firm performs. Since many institutional investors commonly invest $10 million or more in a single firm's stock, they pay close attention to the performance of any firm in which they invest.

If an institutional investor believes the firm is poorly managed, it may attempt to meet with the firm's executives and express its dissatisfaction. It may even attempt to team up with other institutional investors who also own a large proportion of the firm's stock. This gives them more negotiating power because the firm's executives are more likely to listen to institutional investors who collectively hold a large proportion of the firm's stock. The institutional investors do not attempt to dictate how the firm should be managed. Instead, they attempt to ensure that the firm's managers make decisions that are in the best interests of all stockholders.

Conflict with Excessive Executive Compensation

A firm's managers can attempt to satisfy its stockholders by ensuring that funds invested by the stockholders are put to good use. If these funds are used to cover unnecessary expenses, the firm's profits are reduced, which reduces the return that stockholders receive on their investment. A major concern of stockholders is the salaries provided to the firm's chief executive officer (CEO) and other executives. The following example illustrates the potential effect that excessive executive salaries can have on a firm's performance (and therefore on the returns to stockholders).

Consider two firms called Firm C and Firm D, which are in the same industry and have similar revenue and expenses, as shown in Exhibit 3.6. Assume that the only difference is that Firm C pays its top five executives a total of $30 million in annual salary,

Ben and Jerry, shown here, have been recognized nationally for their focus on employees, the community in which they operate, and society as a whole. No employee of Ben & Jerry's can receive more than eight times the salary of the lowest paid employee. In 2000, Ben & Jerry's was acquired by Unilever. Yet, Ben & Jerry's still operates as a separate business and maintains its focus on social responsibility.

Exhibit 3.6

Impact of Executive Salaries on a Firm's Performance

	Firm C	Firm D
Revenue	$200,000,000	$200,000,000
− Expenses (except executive salaries)	−150,000,000	−150,000,000
− Executive salaries expense	− 30,000,000	− 5,000,000
= Profits	=$20,000,000	=$45,000,000

while Firm D pays its top five executives a total of $5 million. As shown in Exhibit 3.6, the annual profits of Firm D are $25 million above those of Firm C. This difference is attributed to Firm C's higher executive salary expenses. Thus, the return to the stockholders of Firm C is smaller than the return to stockholders of Firm D.

Although it may be possible to justify very high compensation for CEOs who have been successful, it is difficult to justify such compensation for CEOs whose companies have performed poorly. The firms listed in Exhibit 3.7 paid very high compensation to their CEOs over the last five years but did not provide much return to stockholders. As a basis of comparison, many firms generated a return of more than 20 percent per year on average over this period. The firms listed in Exhibit 3.7 not only experienced poor results, but they paid their CEOs very well. Thus, it appears that these CEOs were not rewarded according to the firm's performance.

A different issue arises when firms pay high salaries but also provide high returns to stockholders. Some customers and stockholders may argue that firms paying executives such high salaries are not meeting their social responsibilities. These firms may be serving the interests of the executives and not the stockholders who own the firm. However, the counterargument is that these executives deserve high salaries because their contribution to the value of the firm exceeds the amount of their compensation.

BUSINESS ONLINE

CEO Compensation Information

http://www.wabio.com/ind/csba_survey.htm

SOME ORGANIZATIONS, SUCH AS THE COUNCIL OF STATE BIOTECHNOLOGY Associations (CSBA), use the Internet to publish surveys on CEO compensation in their industry. The CSBA contracted the Washington Biotechnology and Biomedical Association to conduct the survey and publish it on its website. Both average salaries and bonuses earned by CEOs are published. Sites like these allow shareholders to ensure that the funds they invest are put to good use and are not used to pay excessive salaries to the CEO of the company.

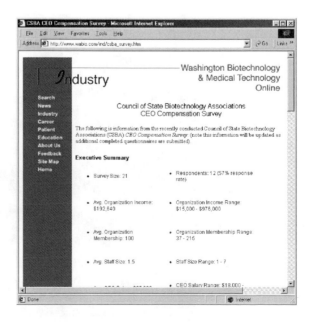

Exhibit 3.7
High Compensation to
CEOs but Low Returns to
Stockholders

Firm	Approximate Compensation Paid to CEO over the Last 5 Years (in millions)	Annual Return to Stockholders over the Last 5 Years
Integrated Health Services	$ 43.5	−36%
Cendant	135	7%
Occidental Petroleum	125	8%
HealthSouth	148	10%
Advanced Micro	38	−10%

Responsibility to Creditors

Firms are responsible for meeting their financial obligations to their creditors. If firms are experiencing financial problems and are unable to meet their obligations, they should inform creditors. Sometimes creditors are willing to extend payment deadlines and may even offer advice to firms on how to improve their financial condition. A firm has a strong incentive to satisfy its responsibility to creditors. If the firm does not pay what it owes to creditors, it may be forced into bankruptcy.

Responsibility to the Environment

4 Describe the responsibilities of firms to the environment.

The production processes that firms use, as well as the products they produce, can be harmful to the environment. The most common abuses to the environment are discussed next, along with recent actions that firms have taken to improve the environment.

Air Pollution

Some production processes cause air pollution, which is harmful to society because it inhibits breathing. For example, the production of fuel and steel, as well as automobile use, increases the amount of carbon dioxide in the air.

How Firms Prevent Air Pollution Automobile and steel firms have reduced air pollution by revising their production processes so that less carbon dioxide escapes into the air. For example, firms such as Allied Signal and Inland Steel spend substantial funds to prevent pollution. Ford Motor Company has developed an environmental pledge, which states that it is dedicated to providing environmental solutions, and intends to preserve the environment in the future.

How the Government Prevents Air Pollution The federal government has also become involved by enforcing specific guidelines for firms to limit the amount of carbon dioxide caused by the production process. In 1970, the Environmental Protection Agency (EPA) was created to develop and enforce pollution standards. In recent years, pollution control laws have become more stringent.

Land Pollution

Land has been polluted by toxic waste resulting from some production processes. A related form of land pollution is solid waste, which does not deteriorate over time. As a result of waste, land not only looks less attractive but also may no longer be useful for other purposes, such as farming.

How Firms Prevent Land Pollution Firms have revised their production and packaging processes to reduce the amount of waste. They now store toxic waste and deliver it to specified toxic waste storage sites. They also recycle plastic and limit their use of materials that would ultimately become solid waste.

Many firms have environmental programs that are designed to reduce damage to the environment. For example, Homestake Mining Company recognizes that its mining operations disturb the land, and it spends money to minimize any effect on the environment. PPG Industries restructured its production processes to generate about six thousand fewer tons of waste in a single year. Kodak recycles more than a half-billion pounds of material a year and also supports a World Wildlife Fund environmental education program. IBM typically spends more than $30 million a year for environmental assessments and clean-up. Chevron and DuPont spend hundreds of millions of dollars every year to comply with environmental regulations. Rockwell International has reduced its hazardous waste by more than 50 percent in recent years.

As an example of how a lack of responsibility can adversely affect a firm's value, consider the case of Monsanto. In 1998, Monsanto received bad publicity regarding its effects on the environment, which caused many of its investors to sell their holdings of Monsanto stock. Consequently, Monsanto's value (as measured by its stock price) declined as shown in Exhibit 3.8.

Conflict with Environmental Responsibility

Although most firms agree that a clean environment is desirable, they may disagree on how much responsibility they have for improving the environment. Consider two firms called Firm A and Firm B, which have similar revenue and expenses. Firm A, however, makes a much greater effort to clean up the environment; it spends $10 million, while Firm B spends $2 million. The profit of each firm is shown in Exhibit 3.9. Firm A has an annual profit of zero, while Firm B has an annual profit of $8 million. If you could invest in the stock of either Firm A or Firm B, where would you invest your money? Most investors desire to earn a high return on their money. Although they recognize that a firm may have some environmental cleanup expenses, they do not want those expenses to be excessive. Therefore, most investors would prefer to invest in Firm B rather than Firm A.

Exhibit 3.8

Monsanto's Stock Price after Receiving Bad Publicity about Its Effects on the Environment

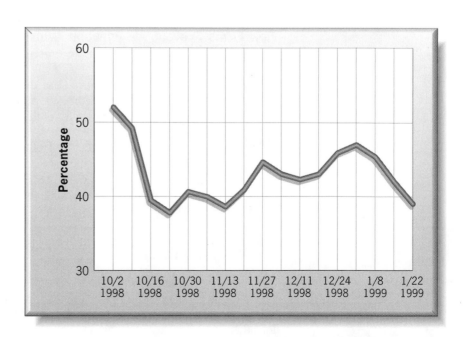

Exhibit 3.9

Effect of Environmental
Expenses on Business
Performance

	Firm A	Firm B
Revenue	$90,000,000	$90,000,000
Total operating expenses	−80,000,000	−80,000,000
Environmental cleanup expenses	−10,000,000	− 2,000,000
Profit	0	$8,000,000

Firm A could attempt to recapture its high environmental cleanup expenses by charging a higher price for its product. In this way, it may be able to spend heavily on the environment, while still generating a reasonable return to its stockholders. This strategy makes the customers pay for its extra environmental cleanup. However, if Firm A charges a higher price than Firm B, many customers would switch to Firm B in order to pay the lower price.

This example illustrates that there is a limit to how much firms can spend on improving the environment. Firms have a responsibility to avoid damaging the environment. However, if they spend excessively on environmental improvement, they will not satisfy most of their customers or owners.

Although firms have increased their efforts to clean up the environment, they do not necessarily agree with the guidelines enforced by the government. Oil refineries that are losing money remain open to avoid the cleanup that the EPA would require if they closed down. Some refineries would pay about $1 billion for cleanup costs because of the EPA's strict guidelines. Firms have questioned many other environmental guidelines imposed by the EPA.

Responsibility to the Community

5 Describe the responsibilities of firms to their communities.

When firms establish a base in a community, they become part of that community and rely on it for customers and employees. Firms demonstrate their concern for the community by sponsoring local events or donating to local charities. For example, Sun-Trust Bank, IBM, and many other firms have donated funds to universities. Bank of America has provided loans to low-income neighborhoods and minority communities.

Conflict with Maximizing Social Responsibility

The decisions of a firm's managers that maximize social responsibility could conflict with maximizing firm value. The costs involved in achieving such a goal will have to be passed on to consumers. Thus, the attempt to maximize responsibility to the community may reduce the firm's ability to provide products at a reasonable price to consumers.

Many companies support charitable organizations that promote nutrition, education, performing and visual arts, and amateur athletics. Even though this social support requires a considerable financial commitment, the firm can gain from an enhanced image in the eye of the consumer to whom it sells its products. In a sense, the charitable support not only can help society but also can be a valuable marketing tool to create a desired image for the firm. Consequently, society and stockholders can benefit from the charitable support. If a company properly identifies a charitable cause that is related to its business, it may be able to simultaneously contribute to society and maximize the firm's value. For example, a running shoe manufacturer may sponsor a race, or a tennis racket manufacturer may sponsor a tennis tournament.

Computer firms commonly donate computers to schools. This not only demonstrates support for the communities, it also promotes the computer's name to potential future customers.

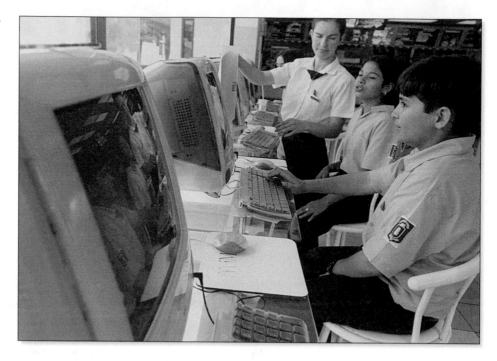

Apple and IBM invest substantial funds in local education programs. This investment not only is helpful to the communities but also results in computer sales to schools. Home Depot donates to community programs that use much of the money for housing projects. Many Checkers restaurants have been located in inner-city areas. They not only provide jobs to many minorities but also have been profitable.

One of the best examples of a firm that has demonstrated its social responsibility in a manner that can also enhance its performance is The Coca-Cola Company. It initiated a ten-year, $60 million sponsorship of Boys & Girls Clubs of America—the largest amount of funds donated by a firm to a specific cause. The sponsorship involves several events, such as basketball and golf tournaments, and after-school read-

SPOTLIGHT ON TECHNOLOGY

Ethical Misconduct

Information technology has greatly increased the potential for ethical misconduct in a variety of areas. Recent studies indicate that many employees believe that playing computer games, pirating company software for personal use, and sending personal e-mail are not unethical.

The integration of company systems allows more employees to have access to confidential books and records. A well-publicized breach of ethics was disclosed when the Internal Revenue Service revealed that celebrity returns had been accessed unnecessarily by a number of employees. In another incident, an employee of Texas Instruments provided information to an investor chat line on the Internet. The employee did not realize that the information was pri-

vate company information and that disclosing it may have violated regulations of the Securities and Exchange Commission.

Another area of concern is the protection of company information. According to a recent survey by the American Society for Industrial Security, U.S. companies lose about $250 billion annually due to theft of intellectual property. In the past, companies were primarily concerned about protecting product formulas. Now, marketing strategies and business strategies must also be protected.

A number of methods have been developed to combat ethics violations. Some are as simple as establishing a written policy regarding the appropriate use of e-mail, copying software, and accessing data. More complex methods must be used to guard against the theft of intellectual property. Computer security procedures must be developed and continually examined to protect against theft of information.

Nike's Stock Price after It Improved Its Social Responsibilities

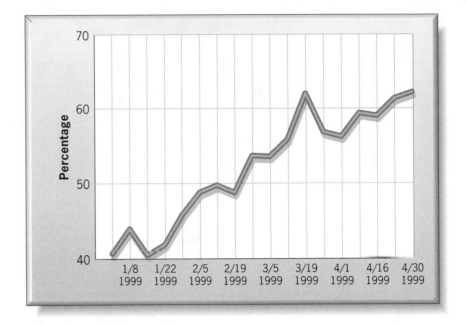

ing sessions Coca-Cola's name will be promoted at the events, which can help attract new young customers to its products.

As an illustration of how a firm may benefit from its efforts to improve social responsibilities, consider the case of Nike. During 1998, Nike was criticized for poor working conditions in its manufacturing plants in Asia. In 1999, Nike hired a former executive of Microsoft to help increase its attention to its social responsibilities. This created a more favorable public perception of Nike, and its value (as measured by its stock price) increased significantly, as shown in Exhibit 3.10.

Summary of Business Responsibilities

Firms have many responsibilities to customers, employees, the environment, the community, stockholders, and creditors that must be recognized when doing business. The general concern of firms about ethics and social responsibility can be illustrated with the following quotations from recent annual reports.

" *A comprehensive annual ethics training program heightens the awareness of our employees and provides guidelines to resolve issues responsibly.* "

—Rockwell International

" *Boise Cascade is committed to protecting the health and safety of our employees, being a responsible corporate citizen in the communities in which we operate, and providing active stewardship of the timberlands under our management.* "

—Boise Cascade

" *We . . . believe that to create long term value for shareholders, we must also create value in our relationships with customers, employees, suppliers and the communities in which we operate.* "

—Briggs & Stratton

Assessing the Ethical Standards of the Firm Where You Work

Think about the organization you currently work for or one you know something about and complete the following Ethical Climate Questionnaire.

Please use the scale below and write the number that best represents your answer in the space next to each item.

To what extent are the following statements true about your company?

Completely false 0	Mostly false 1	Somewhat false 2	Somewhat true 3	Mostly true 4	Completely true 5

_____ 1. In this company, people are expected to follow their own personal and moral beliefs.

_____ 2. People are expected to do anything to further the company's interests.

_____ 3. In this company, people look out for each other's good.

_____ 4. It is very important here to follow strictly the company's rules and procedures.

_____ 5. In this company, people protect their own interests above other considerations.

_____ 6. The first consideration is whether a decision violates any law.

_____ 7. Everyone is expected to stick by company rules and procedures.

_____ 8. The most efficient way is always the right way in this company.

_____ 9. Our major consideration is what is best for everyone in the company.

_____ 10. In this company, the law or ethical code of the profession is the major consideration.

_____ 11. It is expected at this company that employees will always do what is right for the consumer and the public.

To score the questionnaire, first add up your responses to questions 1, 3, 6, 9, 10, and 11. This is subtotal number 1. Next, reverse the scores on questions 2, 4, 5, 7, and 8 (5 = 0, 4 = 1, 3 = 2, 2 = 3, 1 = 4, 0 = 5). Add the reverse scores to form subtotal number 2. Add subtotal number 1 to subtotal number 2 for an overall score.

Subtotal 1 _____ + Subtotal 2 _____ = Overall Score _____ .

Overall scores can range from 0 to 55. The higher the score, the more the organization's culture encourages ethical behavior.

Assessing Whether Specific Situations Are Ethical

The purpose of this exercise is to explore your opinions about ethical issues faced in organizations. The class should be divided into twelve groups. Each group will randomly be assigned one of the following issues:

1. Is it ethical to take office supplies from work for home use? Make personal long-distance calls from the office? Use company time for personal business? Or do these behaviors constitute stealing?

2. If you exaggerate your credentials in an interview, is it lying? Is lying to protect a co-worker acceptable?

3. If you pretend to be more successful than you are to impress your boss, are you being deceitful?

4. How do you differentiate between a bribe and a gift?
5. If there are slight defects in a product you are selling, are you obligated to tell the buyer? If an advertised "sale" price is really the everyday price, should you divulge the information to the customer?
6. Suppose you have a friend who works at the ticket office for the convention center where Shania Twain will be appearing. Is it cheating if you ask the friend to get you tickets so that you won't have to fight the crowd to get them? Is buying merchandise for your family at your company's cost cheating?
7. Is it immoral to do less than your best in work performance? Is it immoral to accept worker's compensation when you are fully capable of working?
8. What behaviors constitute emotional abuse at work? What would you consider an abuse of one's position of power?
9. Are high-stress jobs a breach of ethics? What about transfers that break up families?
10. Are all rule violations equally important? Do employees have an ethical obligation to follow company rules?
11. To what extent are you responsible for the ethical behavior of your co-workers? If you witness unethical behavior and don't report it, are you an accessory?
12. Is it ethical to help one work group at the expense of another group? For instance, suppose one group has excellent performance and you want to reward its members with an afternoon off. The other work group will have to pick up the slack and work harder if you do this. Is this ethical?

Once your group has been assigned its issue, you have two tasks:

1. First, formulate your group's answer to the ethical dilemmas.
2. After you have formulated your group's position, discuss the individual differences that may have contributed to your position. You will want to discuss the individual differences presented in this chapter as well as any others that you believe affected your position on the ethical dilemma.

Your instructor will lead the class in a discussion of how individual differences may have influenced your positions on these ethical dilemmas.

CROSS-FUNCTIONAL TEAMWORK

Ethical Responsibilities across Business Functions

 The perception of a firm's ethical standards is dependent on its team of managers. The ethical responsibilities of a firm's managers vary with their specific job assignments. Production managers are responsible for producing a product that is safe. They should also ensure that the production process satisfies environmental standards.

Marketing managers are responsible for marketing a product in a manner that neither misrepresents the product's characteristics nor misleads consumers or investors. Marketing managers must communicate with production managers to ensure that product marketing is consistent with the production. Any product promotion by marketing managers that makes statements about quality should be assessed by production managers to ensure accuracy.

Financial managers are responsible for providing accurate financial reports to creditors or investors who may provide financial support to the firm. They rely on information from production and marketing managers when preparing their financial reports.

A firm earns a reputation for being ethical by ensuring that ethical standards are maintained in all business functions. If some members of its team of managers are unethical, the entire firm will be viewed as unethical.

Most firms have procedures in place to ensure that social responsibilities are satisfied. They also enforce codes that specify their responsibilities. Prudential Securities has created a position called "Corporate Values Officer" to ensure that its social responsibilities are satisfied.

Some firms may make more of an effort to follow ethical standards than others. The first Self-Scoring Exercise (page 72) allows you to assess the ethical standards of the firm where you work. Employees may vary in their perception of what behavior is ethical. The second Self-Scoring Exercise (page 72) provides a variety of situations that would probably be perceived as unethical by some people but as acceptable by others.

SEVERAL COMPANIES, INCLUDING PROCTER & GAMBLE, DISCUSS THEIR PRODUCTION and product development practices on their websites, as shown here. Sites such as these facilitate investment decisions by existing and potential investors in these companies. The sites also allow the companies' customers to assess the degree of social responsibility practiced by these companies.

Business Responsibilities in an International Environment

When firms compete in an international environment, they must be aware of cultural differences. Firms from some countries do not necessarily view certain business practices such as payoffs to large customers or to suppliers as unethical. This makes it difficult for other firms to compete for international business. Nevertheless, firms typically attempt to apply their ethical guidelines and corporate responsibilities in an international setting. By doing so, they establish a global reputation for running their business in an ethical manner.

The Cost of Ensuring Social Responsibilities

6 Explain the costs that firms incur in achieving their social responsibilities.

A summary of possible expenses incurred as a result of social responsibilities is provided in Exhibit 3.11. Some firms incur large expenses in all areas of social responsibility. For example, automobile manufacturers such as Ford Motor Company and General Motors must ensure that their production of automobiles does not harm the

Exhibit 3.11	Possible Expenses Incurred as a Result of Social Responsibilities

Responsibility to:	Expenses Incurred as a Result of:
Customers	Establishing program to receive and resolve complaints Conducting surveys to assess customer satisfaction Lawsuits by customers (product liability)
Employees	Establishing program to receive and resolve complaints Conducting surveys to assess employee satisfaction Lawsuits by employees based on allegations of discrimination
Stockholders	Disclosing financial information periodically Lawsuits by stockholders based on allegations that the firm's managers are not fulfilling their obligations to stockholders
Environment	Complying with governmental regulations on environment Complying with self-imposed environmental guidelines
Community	Sponsoring community activities

environment. Second, they must ensure that all employees in their massive workforces are treated properly. Third, they must ensure that they deliver a safe and reliable product to their customers.

In recent years, many new government regulations have been imposed to create a cleaner environment and ensure other social responsibilities. Normally, all the firms in an industry will raise their prices to cover the expenses associated with following new government regulations. For example, restrictions on cutting down trees resulted in higher expenses for paper companies. These companies raised their prices to cover these higher expenses. Maintaining social responsibilities is necessary but costly, and customers indirectly pay the expenses incurred.

Cost of Lawsuits

When assessing the expense involved in dealing with customer or employee complaints, firms normally consider the cost of hiring people to resolve the complaints. However, they must also consider the cost of defending against possible lawsuits by customers and employees. Customers suing firms for product defects or deceptive advertising and employees suing their firms for discrimination are common practices today.

A number of expenses can be associated with a lawsuit. First, the court may fine a firm that is found guilty. Some court-imposed fines have amounted to several million dollars. Second, some lawsuits are settled out-of-court, but the settlement may require the firm to make some payment to customers or employees. Third, a firm may incur substantial expenses when hiring an attorney. Many lawsuits continue for several years, and the expenses of the attorney (or a law firm) for a single case may exceed $1 million. Fourth, an indirect cost of a lawsuit is the decline in demand for a firm's product because of bad publicity associated with the lawsuit. This results in less revenue to the firm.

Even when firms establish and enforce a comprehensive code of social responsibility, they do not necessarily avoid lawsuits. They must recognize this when estimating the expenses involved in social responsibility. Consider the situation in June 1993, when the media announced that some customers had found syringes in their Pepsi cans. After this announcement, other customers reported similar findings. This not only caused potential product liability lawsuits but also caused some consumers to switch to other soft drinks. Within two weeks of the first claim, several people were arrested for false tampering charges. One person was even caught on videotape placing a syringe in a Pepsi can. It became clear that the product was not defective but that people were claiming a defect to win large cash settlements through lawsuits. Although the conclusion in this case was favorable, PepsiCo spent millions of dollars attempting to determine whether the claims were valid and then convincing the public that the claims were false.

Firms must recognize that they will incur some expenses arising out of customer or employee claims (whether the claims are valid or not). They may also incur expenses from purchasing product liability insurance to cover potential lawsuits. In some businesses (such as specific medical fields), a major expense to the firm is liability insurance. The threat of liability lawsuits may even discourage entrepreneurs from establishing some types of businesses.

BUSINESS DILEMMA | **College Health Club**

Social Responsibility at College Health Club

AS A COLLEGE STUDENT, SUE KRAMER ALWAYS HAD AN INTEREST IN THE SOcial responsibility of businesses. Now that she is establishing the College Health Club (CHC), she can apply her beliefs about social responsibility to her own business.

Dilemma

Sue recognizes that being socially responsible may either reduce her firm's earnings or result in higher prices to her customers because attending to many social responsibilities can increase expenses. Sue's goal is to develop strategies for satisfying CHC's social responsibilities in a manner that can still maximize the value of CHC. What responsibilities should Sue have toward her customers? Employees? Environment? Community?

Solution

Sue identifies the following specific responsibilities of CHC to her customers, employees, environment, and community:

▶ *Responsibility to Customers* Sue plans to spend some of her time talking with customers at the health club to determine whether the customers (members) are satisfied with the facilities that CHC offers. She also plans to send out a survey to all the members to obtain more feedback. Furthermore, she offers a money-back guarantee if the customers are not satisfied after a two-week trial period.

Sue's efforts are intended not only to fulfill a moral responsibility but also to increase the firm's memberships over time. In the health club business, the firm's reputation for satisfying the customer is important. Many customers choose a health club because of referrals by other customers. Therefore, Sue hopes that her efforts will identify ways in which she can make CHC more appealing to potential members. She also wants to show her interest in satisfying the existing members.

▶ *Responsibility to Employees* Sue started the business with herself as the only full-time employee. However, she has one part-time employee (Lisa Lane) and expects to hire more employees over time as the number of memberships increases. Sue plans to pay employee wages that are consistent with those of other health clubs in the area. She also plans to have employees who are diverse in gender and race. Her goal is not just to demonstrate her willingness to seek diversity but also to attract diversity among customers as well. For example, she wants her health club to have a somewhat even mix of males and females and believes that an even mix of employees over time might attract an even mix of customers.

▶ *Responsibility to the Environment* Since the health club is a service, no production process is involved that could damage the environment. However, Sue will establish recycling containers for cans of soft drinks consumed at CHC.

▶ *Responsibility to the Community* Sue feels a special allegiance to the local college she has attended over the last four years. She volunteers to offer a free seminar on health issues for the college students. She believes that this service will not only fulfill her moral responsibility but also allow her to promote her new health club located next to the college campus. Therefore, her community service could ultimately enhance the value of CHC.

▶ *Summary of CHC's Social Responsibilities* In general, Sue develops strategies that will not only satisfy social responsibilities but also retain existing customers and attract new customers.

Additional Issues for Discussion

1 Sue was recently asked if she wanted to sell aerobics clothing in her health club. A clothing firm has the clothing produced in Asia and would sell it to Sue at low prices. Sue could then sell it to her customers at reasonable prices and still earn a profit. This would be beneficial to the customers and to CHC. Sue has heard that the clothing in some Asian countries is sometimes produced by young children under poor working conditions. Should Sue purchase the clothing?

2 Based on the information in the previous question, what is Sue's social responsibility (if any) toward preventing improper treatment of employees in other countries?

3 Recently, several college students have asked Sue for jobs at CHC. Although Sue would like to help the students out, she does not need any more employees at this time. Should she hire them anyway?

SUMMARY

1 The behavior of firms is molded by business ethics, which represent a set of moral values. Firms have a responsibility to produce safe products and to sell their products without misleading the customers. They ensure social responsibility toward customers by establishing a code of ethics, monitoring customer complaints, and asking customers for feedback on products that they recently purchased.

2 Firms have a responsibility to safety, proper treatment, and equal opportunity for employees. They can ensure responsibility toward employees by enforcing safety guidelines, by offering seminars on diversity, and by establishing a grievance procedure that allows employees to state any complaints.

3 Firms have a responsibility to satisfy the owners (or stockholders) who provided funds. They attempt to ensure that managers make decisions that are in the best interests of stockholders.

4 Firms have a responsibility to maintain a clean environment when operating their businesses. However, they incur expenses when attempting to fulfill their environmental responsibility.

5 Firms have a social responsibility to the local communities in which they attract customers and employees. They provide donations and other benefits to local communities.

6 When firms ensure their social responsibilities, they may incur substantial expenses. These expenses are ultimately incurred by the customers, since the prices of products charged by firms are influenced by the expenses incurred.

KEY TERMS

affirmative action *62*
business ethics *58*
consumerism *58*
institutional investors *65*
monopoly *59*
sexual harassment *61*
shareholder activism *65*
social responsibility *57*

REVIEW QUESTIONS

1 Define business ethics and describe an ethical situation in which you had to decide right from wrong.

2 Identify and explain the major areas of social responsibility with which a business should be concerned.

3 Identify the steps a firm develops to ensure social responsibility to its customers.

4 How can a business ensure social responsibility to its customers and still earn a profit?

5 Explain how the government becomes socially responsible to consumers.

6 Describe a firm's social responsibility to its community and the environment.

7 Describe the most common abuses to the environment and how businesses can prevent them.

8 How does a business's environmental responsibility affect product prices?

9 Identify and explain the conflicting objectives that often challenge a manager's responsibility.

10 Identify expenses that a firm may incur when assuming social responsibility for customers and employees.

DISCUSSION QUESTIONS

1 Assume that you are a manager. How would your firm's business ethics and social responsibility affect your decision making, and what effect would these issues have on the organization's bottom line (earnings)?

2 Assume that you are a manager. What are your ethical responsibilities to the following: (a) employees, (b) stockholders, (c) customers, and (d) suppliers?

3 How could a firm use the Internet to promote the business ethics and social responsibility it practices?

4 You are an advertising manager. You have just left a meeting, having been made aware of truth in labeling laws. Would you be obligated to disclose the ingredients in your product, especially if that product has a potential side effect?

5 Discuss the pros and cons of affirmative action programs and how they affect businesses' recruiting and selection efforts. Do they constrain or aid business?

INVESTING IN THE STOCK OF A BUSINESS

Using the annual report of the firm in which you would like to invest, complete the following:

1 Many firms disclose their policies on ethics and social responsibilities within their annual reports. Does your firm mention any specific policies that encourage employees' ethical behavior? Does the firm give any specific examples of how it accomplishes these goals?

2 Describe your firm's policies on its social responsibility toward its community and the environment. Does the firm give any specific examples of how it accomplishes these goals?

3 Explain how the business uses technology to enhance its business ethics and social responsibility. For example, does it use the Internet to provide information regarding its business practices? Does it provide a place for customer complaints on the Internet?

4 Go to **http://hoovers.com** and locate the NEWS SEARCH. Type in the name of the firm in the space provided, and review the recent news stories about the firm. Summarize any (at least one) recent news story about the firm that applies to one or more of the key concepts within this chapter.

CASE RESPONSIBILITIES TO EMPLOYEES

David Thomas, a supervisor in the bearings department at the ABC Corporation, a rollerblade manufacturer, manages a nonunion plant where the work atmosphere appears to be a "good ol' boy" system. He desires to give preference to males by giving them the better jobs and newer equipment, and favoritism is often extended to them. Currently, there are no females in management positions throughout the plant. Females tend to occupy to-

ken positions, often starting out as clerk-typists or file clerks, and few female employees advance into higher positions. Presently, twenty people work in Mr. Thomas's department; only two are female. All perform the same job; skills, responsibility, and authority are the same. Males are paid $10.50 per hour; females with the same seniority earn $7.50 per hour. Working conditions throughout the department are often unsanitary, and neglect on the supervisor's part has made the department unsafe. Recently, many complaints have been made from Mr. Thomas's employees concerning the poor working conditions. Mr. Thomas is a profit maximizer with a bottom-line orientation and often ignores any safety policy directive that comes from top management.

In his office, Mr. Thomas has pinups on every wall. On his desk are sexually explicit slogans that some females have found offensive. His language tends to be off-color and is often upsetting to many people throughout the plant.

Mr. Thomas has just received a memo. He has been asked by the company president to attend a meeting on the firm's responsibilities. The memo reads, "The company is going in a new direction. We would like your input on responsibility issues that this company should adopt." Mr. Thomas's immediate reaction is, "This com-

pany has always been a profit-maximizing firm and should not concern itself with any social issues because they constrain and impact the bottom line of the company's operations." Thus, he refuses to attend the meeting.

QUESTIONS

1. Is Mr. Thomas ignoring any responsibility issues in his department operations?
2. Is Mr. Thomas correct in saying that the ABC Corporation should be a profit-maximizing firm at all costs?
3. Is Mr. Thomas discriminating against females and, if so, in what areas?
4. What are the potential costs to the firm as a result of Mr. Thomas's actions?

VIDEO CASE SOCIAL RESPONSIBILITY AT BEN & JERRY'S ICE CREAM

Ben & Jerry's Ice Cream began as a small business and has grown into an international corporation. Its mission statement includes provisions about (1) producing a good product for its customers, (2) providing an economic reward (profits) to its shareholders, and (3) fulfilling its social responsibility. These three goals have no particular order. Ben & Jerry's believes that it should not focus on any one goal but should achieve all three goals.

Ben & Jerry's directs 7.5 percent of its pretax profits to a foundation, which donates money to specific charitable organizations. In another effort to fulfill its social responsibility, Ben & Jerry's works with small businesses, as its owners remember that it was once a small business. It relies on small businesses for some of the materials used in its production process.

Ben & Jerry's has proved that it can achieve its economic mission while fulfilling its social mission. Its social commitment has enhanced Ben & Jerry's reputation, increased its name recognition, and stimulated demand for its ice cream. Thus, the company's social mission has enhanced its profits and therefore is aligned with its economic mission.

QUESTIONS

1. Why do you think Ben & Jerry's has a social mission?
2. Does the firm's social mission conflict with its economic mission?
3. Do you think the shareholders disapprove of Ben & Jerry's social mission?

INTERNET APPLICATIONS

http://www.pg.com/about/about.htm

Based on Procter & Gamble's Environmental Progress Updates, what has the company done in the last couple of years to fulfill its responsibilities to the environment? In a few words, describe the type of information provided

in P&G's most recent Sustainability Report. Has P&G won any environmental awards? What are some of the initiatives and programs P&G conducts regarding the environment? Overall, do you think P&G is an environmentally responsible company? Why or why not?

THE *Coca-Cola* COMPANY ANNUAL REPORT PROJECT

Questions for the current year's annual report are available on the text website at **http://madura_intro_bus.swcollege.com**.

The following questions apply concepts learned in this chapter to The Coca-Cola Company. Go to The Coca-Cola Company website (**http://www.cocacola.com**) and find the index for the 1999 annual report.

1. Look at the "Our Business" section. Do you think The Coca-Cola Company has an advantage over other large companies with respect to its impact on the environment?
2. Study the "Citizenship" section. How does The Coca-Cola Company contribute to society in countries such as Mexico and Venezuela while at the

same time accomplishing its mission of creating long-term value for its shareholders?

3 Do you think The Coca-Cola Company's acts of "corporate responsibility," such as investing in countries with poor economic performance, conflict with the goal of satisfying shareholders?

4 Look at "Investments." Why does The Coca-Cola Company invest in "anchor bottlers"? Why does the company acquire a controlling interest in some bottling operations?

5 Go to **http://hoovers.com** and locate the NEWS SEARCH. Type in The Coca-Cola Company in the space provided, and review the recent news stories about the firm. Summarize any (at least one) recent news story about The Coca-Cola Company that applies one or more of the key concepts within this chapter of the text.

IN-TEXT STUDY GUIDE

Answers are in an appendix at the back of the book.

TRUE OR FALSE

1 The responsibility of firms toward customers can be enforced by specific groups of consumers.

2 The government protects consumers by regulating the quality of some products that firms produce.

3 Deregulation results in lower prices for consumers.

4 Marketing managers are primarily responsible for providing accurate financial information to creditors and investors.

5 In recent years, pollution laws have become less stringent.

6 Employees commonly sue firms for product defects or deceptive advertising.

7 In recent years, stockholders have been active in trying to influence a firm's management practices.

8 An attempt by a firm to maximize social responsibility to the community may reduce the firm's ability to provide products at a reasonable price to consumers.

9 U.S. firms that conduct business in foreign countries are not subject to the rules enforced by the local government.

10 The Clayton Act is intended to restrict competition.

MULTIPLE CHOICE

11 The act that prohibits unfair methods of competition is the:
a) Humphrey Act.
b) Civil Rights Act of 1964.
c) Federal Trade Commission Act.
d) Garn Act.
e) Reagan Antitrust Act.

12 An active role by stockholders in influencing a firm's management policies is called:
a) empowerment.   d) quality circles.
b) reengineering.   e) shareholder activism.
c) self-managed teams.

13 Tying agreements, binding contracts, and interlocking directorates are prohibited by the:

a) Clayton Act.
b) Sherman Antitrust Act.
c) Robinson-Patman Act.
d) Celler-Kefauver Act.
e) Federal Trade Commission Act.

14 Many U.S. firms provide guidelines of behavior to employees through a code of:
a) reciprocity.
b) cartel arrangements.
c) kickback arrangements.
d) technical production manuals.
e) ethics.

15 Compensation that is based on the volume of an employee's sales of the firm's products is called:
a) share of stock.   d) promotion.
b) stock certificate.   e) commission or bonus.
c) corporate bond.

16 One example of a firm's attempt to ensure the proper and equal treatment of all employees is the establishment of a:
a) labor contract.   d) walkout.
b) strike.   e) lockout.
c) grievance procedure.

17 Unwelcome comments or actions of a sexual nature are examples of:
a) business as usual.
b) sexual harassment.
c) equal employment opportunities.
d) workplace diversity.
e) deregulation.

18 The act that prohibits mergers between firms that reduce competition within an industry is the:
a) Robinson-Patman Act.
b) Celler-Kefauver Act.
c) Federal Trade Commission Act.
d) Clayton Act.
e) Sherman Antitrust Act.

19 Which of the following terms describes a set of activities intended to increase opportunities for minorities and women?

a) affirmative action
b) Americans with Disabilities Act
c) minimum wage law
d) antitrust action
e) consumerism

20 The recognition of how a firm's business decisions can affect society is its:
a) moral code.
b) social responsibility.
c) conservation policies.
d) recycling program.
e) consumer bill of rights.

21 A firm's decision to maximize its social responsibilities may conflict with its responsibility to:
a) monopolize the marketplace.
b) provide safe products for customers.
c) maximize the opportunities for women and minorities.
d) maximize the firm's value for stockholders.
e) follow government regulations.

22 Which of the following represents legislation passed to prevent firms from entering into agreements to set prices and avoid competition?
a) affirmative action laws
b) deregulation codes
c) antitrust laws
d) consumerism laws
e) Food and Drug Administration Act

23 If a firm is the sole provider of a good or service, it is a(n):
a) unsuccessful organization.
b) sole proprietorship.
c) deregulated firm.
d) institutional investor.
e) monopoly.

24 If a firm fails to meet its responsibilities to _____, it may be forced into bankruptcy.
a) its employees   d) its creditors
b) the environment   e) its owners
c) the government

25 Shareholder activism is most commonly practiced by:
a) customers.
b) chief executive officers.
c) institutional investors.
d) managers.
e) the government.

26 _____ represents the collective consumer demand that businesses satisfy their needs.
a) Conservationism   d) Business ethics
b) Consumerism   e) Recycling
c) Social responsibility

27 Assuming everything else is the same, a firm that pays higher executive salaries will experience a _____ rate of return on the stockholders' investment than a firm that pays lower executive salaries.

a) more stable   d) steadier
b) lower   e) more erratic
c) higher

28 Most firms have procedures in place as well as codes to ensure individual employee accountability. This is a part of their:
a) program network.   d) social responsibility.
b) division of work.   e) recycling program.
c) local area network.

29 Firms are responsible to their creditors by meeting their:
a) dividend payments.
b) financial obligations.
c) retained earnings.
d) stockholders' equity.
e) treasury stock.

30 Guidelines for proper treatment of employees, customers, and owners can be found in:
a) business policies.   d) business ethics.
b) procedures.   e) work standards.
c) rules.

31 The act that prohibits discrimination due to national origin, race, gender, or religion is the:
a) Clayton Act.
b) Sherman Antitrust Act.
c) Federal Trade Commission Act.
d) Civil Rights Act of 1964.
e) Robinson-Patman Act.

32 The following industries have been deregulated, allowing more firms to enter the industry, except for:
a) trucking.   d) boating.
b) railroads.   e) telecommunications.
c) airlines.

33 The firm's management is responsible for satisfying its:
a) union demands.
b) owners or stockholders.
c) business agents.
d) competition.
e) friends.

34 The act that prohibits price differences on promotional allowances that reduce competition within an industry is the:
a) Celler-Kefauver Act.
b) Robinson-Patman Act.
c) Clayton Act.
d) Sherman Antitrust Act.
e) Federal Trade Commission Act.

35 The act that encourages competition and prevents monopolies is the:
a) Deregulation Act.
b) Federal Trade Commission Act.
c) Robinson-Patman Act.
d) Celler-Kefauver Act.
e) Sherman Antitrust Act.

Summary of Part I

The success of a business may depend on the initial decisions that are made by its owners when it is established. The first set of decisions is made within the business plan (Chapter 1), which requires management, marketing, and financial plans. The management plan consists of decisions about production, organizational structure, and employee job descriptions. Management policies are discussed in more detail in Parts II and III. The marketing plan consists of pricing, distribution, and promotion decisions and is discussed in more detail in Part IV. The financial plan consists of financing decisions and business investment decisions, which are discussed in detail in Part V.

In addition to the business plan, owners who establish a new business must select the proper form of ownership (Chapter 2). The possible forms of ownership are sole proprietorships, partnerships, and corporations. This decision is based on various characteristics of the business, such as the potential liability of the business and the amount of funds needed to support the business.

Owners of a new business also need to establish ethical and social responsibilities (Chapter 3), which provide guidelines for proper treatment of its customers, employees, stockholders, and creditors. Overall, the business plan, form of business ownership, and ethical guidelines establish a foundation that can be used by the firm's managers to make future decisions.

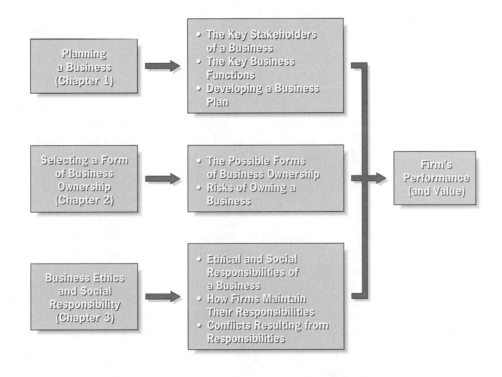

Developing a Business Plan for Campus.com

Following is a business idea called Campus.com that has been created for you. It is your job to develop a business plan for the business during the school term, applying many of the key concepts discussed in each chapter. At the end of each part, questions will guide your development of a portion of the plan that relates to that part. By the end of the school term, you will have developed a complete business plan for Campus.com. This exercise not only enhances your understanding of business concepts but also demonstrates the integration of concepts and can enhance your teamwork and communication skills.

Your instructor will tell you whether you will be developing the business plan by yourself or as part of a team. There is no single perfect method for developing the business, so your (or your team's) business plan may vary from the plans created by other students (or student teams). However, the manner in which you develop the business plan should be based on logical business concepts discussed in the chapters.

As you (or your team) answer the questions at the end of each part, you can insert your answers in the Business Plan booklet or on the Business Plan CD-ROM that are supplied with the text. Once you (or your team) complete the questions at the end of each part, you will have completed the business plan for Campus.com and will be ready to implement your plan.

Business Idea (related to Chapter 1)

Campus.com will provide an information service for high school students who are assessing different colleges to which they may apply. It will provide information on the lifestyles of any college that they select. High school students might find this service useful for several reasons. First, many books compare academic requirements at colleges but provide very limited information on student lifestyles. Second, some high school students do not rely on the lifestyle information in these books because they question whether the authors really understand students. Third, students do not necessarily want to purchase an entire volume on all colleges across the country just to obtain information on the few colleges to which they may apply. Fourth, students recognize that the material in these books can become outdated.

For these reasons, the business of Campus.com can satisfy high school students. The business does not require any physical facilities initially. It requires a website that provides information to high school students who wish to purchase the information. The website will show an index of all colleges. Customers will click on those colleges for which they want information. They must submit a credit card number and will be charged $1 for each college that they select. They will receive immediate information on their computer about the campus lifestyles of each college selected.

The main expenses for Campus.com are the creation of the website and gathering information about every college campus from reliable sources. Initially, this information will be gathered by ordering back issues of campus newspapers for the last year and then summarizing the campus activities for each college. In addition, the plan is to send a brief survey to about thirty students at each school (offering $20 to each respondent who fills out the survey), asking them to answer general questions about their opinions of the activities and to rate the campus in terms of its sports activities, entertainment on campus, and nightlife. You hope to receive responses from at least twenty students before you summarize the information for each college. The information will be updated every three months by paying some of the same students who filled out the first survey to fill out an updated survey. Thus, the information that you provide to customers is frequently updated, which is an advantage over any books they could buy in stores.

Ownership (related to Chapter 2)

Decide the optimal form of business ownership for this firm, and indicate that form in your business plan for Campus.com. To answer this question, consider whether you would prefer to be the sole owner of Campus.com or to invite other individuals into the firm to form a partnership. If you are working with a team of students, you already have a partnership. In your business plan, explain your reasons for the optimal form of ownership for Campus.com. What are the advantages of forming a partnership for this firm? What are the disadvantages of forming a partnership?

Main Sources of Revenue and Expenses

The success of this business is highly dependent on your revenue and expenses. What will be the main source of your revenue? What will be the main source of your expenses? Should you pay yourself a salary, or will you reinvest any earnings in the firm? Summarize your comments in your business plan for Campus.com.

Responsibility to Customers, Employees, and Owners (related to Chapter 3)

Describe the mission of the business as part of your business plan for Campus.com. Include statements on how the business will fulfill its responsibilities to its customers, its employees, and its owners.

Communication and Teamwork

Your instructor may ask you (or your team) to hand in and/or present the sections of your business plan that relate to this part of the text. As you build the plan at the end of each part of the text, you can continue to use the Business Plan booklet or disk.

PART I

Applications for Dell Computer

Refer to "Dell Computer's Formula for Success" where necessary.

1 Dell's customer contact
   a. How does Dell achieve a high level of customer contact?
   b. How does Dell achieve a high level of customer contact with its individual customers?
   c. Why do you think Dell Computer considers customer contact important to its success?

2 Dell's ownership structure
   a. What advantages does Dell gain by using the corporate form of ownership?
   b. What disadvantages does Dell face by using the corporate form of ownership?
   c. Why do you think Dell is organized as a corporation rather than as a sole proprietorship or a partnership?

3 Dell's social responsibility
   a. How could Dell Computer use the Internet to fulfill its responsibility to customers?
   b. How could Dell Computer use the Internet to fulfill its responsibility to its stockholders?
   c. How could Dell Computer use the Internet to fulfill its responsibility to its employees?

PART I

The Stock Market Game

Go to **http://www.fantasystockmarket.com**. Enter your name (e-mail address) and password as requested and check your portfolio balance, which is updated continuously by the Fantasy website.

Check Your Stock Portfolio Performance

1 What is the value of your stock portfolio today?

2 What is your return on your investment? (This return is shown on your balance.)

3 How did your return compare to those of other students? (This comparison tells you whether your stock portfolio's performance is relatively high or low.)

Changing Your Stock Portfolio   At the end of each of the following parts, you will be prompted to assess the performance of your portfolio since you created it at the beginning of the school term. At this point, you should decide whether you want to change your portfolio. You can change it at any time throughout the semester. You should consider changing the portfolio if you no longer wish to hold one or more of the stocks in which you invested. If you do not want to change your portfolio, however, you can leave it as is.

PART I

Running Your Own Business

The following exercise allows you to apply the key concepts covered in each chapter to a business that you would like to create for yourself. Applying these concepts to a business in which you are interested enables you to recognize how these concepts are used in the business world. Since this part focused on the organization of a business, you will be asked specific questions about the organization of a business of your choice. Chapter 1 focused on the creation of a business idea, so the first questions will ask you to create your own business idea. Give this some serious thought, because you will be developing specific details about your business idea at the end of each part. In Chapter 1, you learned how a college student developed a health club business. One could develop numerous types of small businesses without necessarily being a business expert. If you do not have any ideas initially, consider the types of businesses that are in a shopping mall. Or consider the firms that produce and sell products to those businesses. You might look through the yellow pages to find other types of small businesses.

The "Running Your Own Business" exercise at the end of each part will apply the key concepts in the chapters in that part to the business that you create. You can record good business ideas in the Business Plan booklet or on the Business Plan disk that are supplied with the text. By developing a business idea, you may actually implement it someday. Alternatively, you may realize from developing your idea why such a business could fail, which may lead you to alternative business ideas.

When developing your business idea, try to create a business that will require you to hire at least a few employees in the future. By doing this, you will find it easier to apply the concepts related to managing employees in later chapters.

1 Describe in general terms the type of business that you would like to create.

2 Explain in general terms how your business would offer some advantage over competing firms.

3 Explain whether your business will be a sole proprietorship, a partnership, or a corporation. Why did you make this decision?

4 Describe the risk of your business. That is, explain what conditions could result in lower revenue or higher expenses than you expect.

5 Describe the ethical dilemmas (if any) that you might face in your business. How do you plan to handle these situations?

6 What types of social responsibilities would your business have toward your employees, customers, or community? What, if any, special policies would you set to take better care of your employees, customers, or community?

7 Explain how your business would use the Internet to provide relevant information to its customers, employees, and shareholders. Would it use the Internet to fulfill some of its social responsibilities? How?

Business Environment

The success of a firm is partially dependent on its environment. Although managers of a firm cannot control the business environment, they can attempt to make business decisions that benefit from that environment or that offer protection against adverse conditions. To do this, they need to understand how the business environment affects their firm.

A firm is exposed to three different parts of the business environment: (1) economic conditions, (2) industry conditions, and (3) global conditions. Chapter 4 describes how economic conditions affect a firm's performance. It also explains how government policies affect firms indirectly by influencing economic conditions. Chapter 5 explains how a firm's performance is affected by industry conditions, and Chapter 6 explains how it is affected by global conditions.

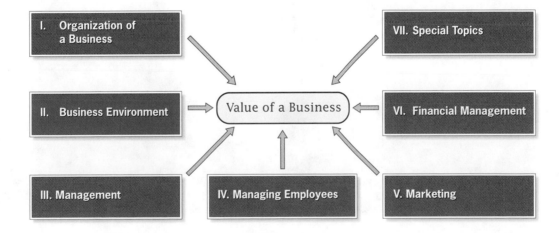

The Learning	**①**	Identify the macroeconomic factors that affect business performance.
Goals of this	**②**	Explain how market prices are determined.
chapter are to:	**③**	Explain how the government influences economic conditions.

Economic Environment

Economic conditions reflect the level of production and consumption for a particular country, area, or industry. **Macroeconomic conditions** reflect the overall U.S. economy; **microeconomic conditions** are more focused on the business or industry of concern. This chapter focuses on the macroeconomic factors, and the following chapter focuses on microeconomic (industry) factors.

Economic conditions can affect the revenue or expenses of a business and therefore can affect the value of that business.

To illustrate how economic conditions can affect the performance and value of a business, consider the case of Inland Steel Industries, whose steel is purchased by Harley-Davidson, Ford Motor Company, and numerous other manufacturers. A change in the demand for motorcycles, automobiles, and other products produced with steel affects the demand for Inland's steel. How

would weak economic conditions affect the demand for Inland's steel? How would inflation affect Inland's expenses? How would rising interest rates affect the demand for Inland's steel? How do the federal government's policies influence Inland's performance? This chapter provides a background on the economic environment that can be used to answer these questions.

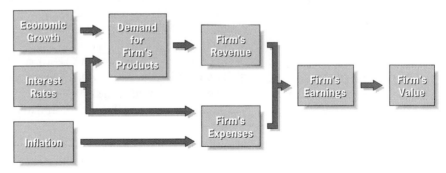

Macroeconomic Factors that Affect Business Performance

1 Identify the macroeconomic factors that affect business performance.

The performance of most firms is highly dependent on three macroeconomic factors:

▶ Economic growth
▶ Inflation
▶ Interest rates

Economic Growth

economic growth the change in the general level of economic activity

A critical macroeconomic factor that affects business performance is **economic growth,** or the change in the general level of economic activity. When U.S. economic growth is higher than normal, the total income level of all U.S. workers is relatively high, so there is a higher volume of spending on products and services. Since the demand for products and services is high, firms that sell products and services should receive higher revenue. When economic growth is negative for two consecutive quarters, the period is referred to as a **recession.**

recession two consecutive quarters of negative economic growth

Although high economic growth enhances a firm's revenue, slow economic growth results in low demand for products and services, which can reduce a firm's revenue. The potential impact of slower economic growth is reflected in the following statements:

❝ *Our caution stems largely from the macroeconomic environment, in which some forecasts are for slower growth.* ❞

—Hewlett-Packard

❝ *[The company] expects to experience significant fluctuations in future [performance] due to . . . general economic conditions.* ❞

—Amazon.com

General Motors and Ford Motor Company commonly shut down some factories in response to low economic growth.

aggregate expenditures the total amount of expenditures in the economy

Indicators of Economic Growth Two common measures of economic growth are the level of total production of products and services in the economy and the total amount of expenditures (also called **aggregate expenditures**). The total production level and total aggregate expenditures in the United States are closely related, because a high level of consumer spending reflects a large demand for products and services. The total production level is dependent on the total demand for products and services.

gross domestic product (GDP) the total market value of all final products and services produced in the United States

Businesses can monitor the U.S. total production level by keeping track of the **gross domestic product (GDP),** which is the total market value of all final products and services produced in the United States. The GDP is reported quarterly in the United States. The trend of GDP is shown in Exhibit 4.1. Notice that GDP was stagnant dur-

Exhibit 4.1

Trend of Gross Domestic Product (GDP)

ing the early 1990s but has grown substantially since then. Economic growth is commonly interpreted as the percentage of change in the GDP from one period (such as a quarter) to another. Businesses tend to monitor changes in economic growth, which may signal a change in the demand for their products or services.

An alternative indicator of economic growth is the unemployment level. Various unemployment indicators may be monitored because they can indicate whether economic conditions are improving. The four different types of unemployment are as follows:

frictional unemployment
people who are between jobs

▶ **Frictional unemployment** (also referred to as natural unemployment) represents people who are between jobs. That is, their unemployment status is temporary, as they are likely to find employment soon. For example, a person with marketable job skills might quit her job before finding a new one because she believes she will find a new job before long.

seasonal unemployment
people whose services are not needed during some seasons

▶ **Seasonal unemployment** represents people whose services are not needed during some seasons. For example, ski instructors may be unemployed in the summer.

cyclical unemployment
people who are unemployed because of poor economic conditions

▶ **Cyclical unemployment** represents people who are unemployed because of poor economic conditions. When the level of economic activity declines, the demand for products and services declines, which reduces the need for workers. For example, a firm may lay off factory workers if the demand for its product declines.

structural unemployment
people who are unemployed because they do not have adequate skills

▶ **Structural unemployment** represents people who are unemployed because they do not have adequate skills. For example, people who have limited education may be structurally unemployed.

Of the four types of unemployment, the cyclical unemployment level is probably the best indicator of economic conditions. When economic growth improves, businesses hire more people and the unemployment rate declines. Unfortunately, determining how much of the unemployment level is cyclical can be difficult. Some people assume that when the unemployment rate changes, the change is primarily attributed to economic cycles. A lower unemployment rate may be interpreted as an indicator of increased economic growth. Conversely, a higher unemployment rate is commonly interpreted as a sign of reduced economic growth. The trend of U.S. unemployment is shown in Exhibit 4.2. Notice that the U.S. unemployment level was at its peak in 1992, when U.S. economic conditions were weak, but it declined in the middle and late 1990s when economic growth was strong.

Many other indicators of economic growth, such as the industrial production index, new housing starts, and the personal income level, are compiled by divisions of the federal government and reported in business magazines and newspapers.

Exhibit 4.2

Trend of U.S. Unemployment

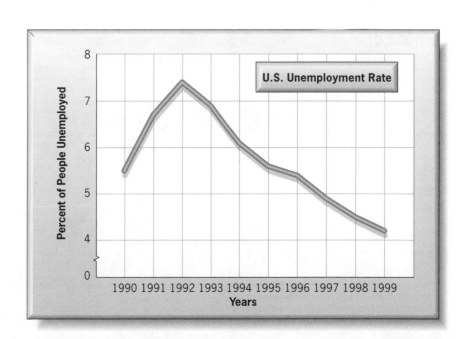

Sensitivity of a Firm to Economic Growth Some firms are more sensitive than others to economic conditions because the demand for their product is more sensitive to such conditions. For example, the demand for the product (food) provided by McDonald's is not very sensitive to economic conditions because people still purchase McDonald's food even when the economy is weak. However, the demand for new automobiles is more sensitive to economic conditions. When the economy is weak, the demand for new automobiles declines. Ford Motor Company experienced negative profits during the 1991–1992 period, when the United States experienced an economic recession, but earned high profits in the late 1990s during strong economic conditions.

Inflation

inflation the increase in the general level of prices of products and services over a specified period of time

Inflation is the increase in the general level of prices of products and services over a specified period of time. The inflation rate can be estimated by measuring the percentage change in the consumer price index, which indicates the prices on a wide variety of consumer products such as grocery products, housing, gasoline, medical services, and electricity. The annual U.S. inflation rate is shown in Exhibit 4.3. Notice that the inflation rate was generally higher in the 1970s than in the 1980s and 1990s.

Inflation can affect a firm's operating expenses from producing products by increasing the cost of supplies and materials. Wages can also be affected by inflation. A higher level of inflation will cause a larger increase in a firm's operating expenses. A firm's revenue may also be high during periods of high inflation because many firms charge higher prices to compensate for their higher expenses.

cost-push inflation the situation when higher prices charged by firms are caused by higher costs

Types of Inflation Inflation may result from a particular event that increases the costs of production. For example, when oil prices rise, gasoline prices increase and the costs of transporting products increase. Firms that incur higher costs from transporting their products increase their prices to cover the higher costs. This situation, when firms charge higher prices due to higher costs, is referred to as **cost-push inflation.** For example, beverage producers such as PepsiCo and Anheuser-Busch raised prices when the cost of aluminum (used to make cans) increased. Procter & Gamble raised prices on paper towels following an increase in pulp (used in the production process). Advances in information technology reduced some production costs, so cost-push inflation was not a problem during the late 1990s.

Inflation can also be caused by strong consumer demand. Consider a situation in which consumers increase their demand for most products and services. Some firms

Exhibit 4.3

U.S. Inflation Rates over Time

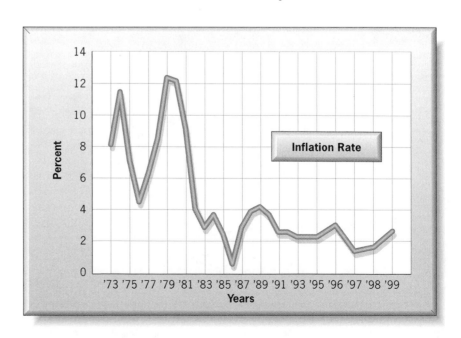

demand-pull inflation the situation when prices of products and services are pulled up because of strong consumer demand

may respond by increasing their prices. This situation, when prices of products and services are pulled up because of strong consumer demand, is referred to as **demand-pull inflation.** In periods of strong economic growth, strong consumer demand can cause shortages in the production of some products. Firms that anticipate shortages may raise prices because they are confident they can sell the products anyway.

Strong economic growth may place pressure on wages as well as prices. Strong economic growth may mean fewer unemployed people, so workers may negotiate for higher wages. Firms may be more willing to provide higher wages to retain their workers when no other qualified workers are available. As firms pay higher wages, production costs rise, and firms may attempt to increase their prices to recover the higher expenses.

Interest Rates

Interest rates represent the cost of borrowing money. Businesses closely monitor interest rates because they determine the amount of expense a business will incur if it borrows money. If a business borrows $100,000 for one year at an interest rate of 8 percent, the interest expense is $8,000 (computed as .08 × $100,000). At an interest rate of 15 percent, however, the interest expense would be $15,000 (computed as .15 × $100,000). Imagine how the interest rate level can affect firms such as General Motors, which has borrowed more than $1 billion at any time. An interest rate increase of just 1 percent on $1 billion of borrowed funds results in an extra annual interest expense of $10 million.

Changes in market interest rates can influence a firm's interest expense, since the loan rates that commercial banks and other creditors charge on loans to firms are based on market interest rates. Even when a firm obtains a loan from a commercial bank over several years, the loan rate is typically adjusted periodically (every six months or year) based on the prevailing market interest rate at that time.

Exhibit 4.4 illustrates the annual interest expense for a reputable U.S. firm that borrows $1 million from a bank each year and earns $100,000 in annual profits before paying its interest expense. The interest expenses are adjusted each year according to the interest rate that existed in the United States that year. As this exhibit shows, interest rates can significantly influence a firm's profit.

Notice that the firm incurred much higher interest expenses in the early 1980s than in the 1990s. Because the interest rate in 1982 was almost twice as high as in 1999, the interest expense in 1982 was almost twice the expense incurred in 1999 for the same amount of funds borrowed.

Since interest rates affect the cost of financing, some possible projects considered by the firm that would be feasible during periods of low interest rates may not be feasible during periods of high interest rates. That is, the project may not generate an adequate return to cover financing costs. Consequently, firms tend to reduce their degree of expansion when interest rates are high.

Interest rates affect a firm's revenue as well as its interest expenses. For example, when interest rates rise, the cost of financing the purchase of new homes increases. Therefore, the demand for new homes typically declines, and firms that build homes experience a decline in business. In addition, firms such as Caterpillar and Weyerhaeuser that produce equipment and construction products experience a decline in business. This explains why firms involved in the construction industry are highly influenced by interest rate movements.

Impact of Interest Rates on a Firm's Value To illustrate how interest rates can affect a firm's value, consider the case of Home Depot. In the 1997–1999 period, low interest rates in the United States encouraged consumers to purchase homes (using borrowed funds with low interest expenses). As a result, demand for home-building products sold by firms such as Home Depot was strong. Home Depot's performance and value (as measured by its stock price) increased substantially over the 1998–1999 period, as shown in Exhibit 4.5.

Exhibit 4.4

Effect of Interest Rates on Interest Expenses and Profits

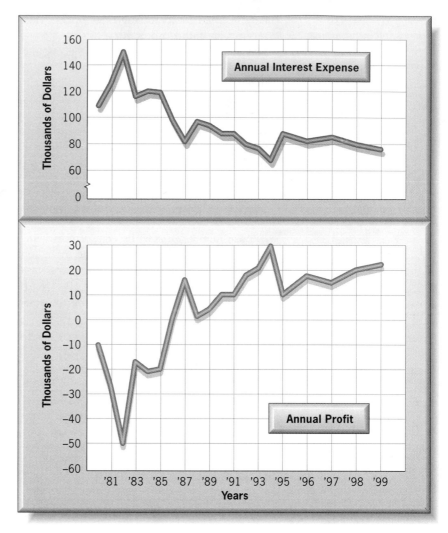

Note: Assume that the firm's revenue equals $400,000 and its operating expenses equal $300,000.

Exhibit 4.5

Value of Home Depot during the 1997–1999 Period of Low Interest Rates

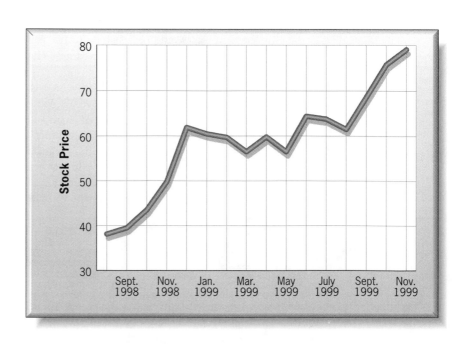

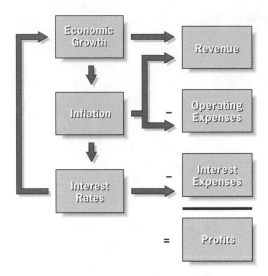

Summary of Macroeconomic Factors That Affect a Firm's Performance

A summary of how the three macroeconomic factors affect a firm's performance is provided in Exhibit 4.6. The firm's revenue is affected by economic growth, which influences the demand for the firm's products. Its revenue and operating expenses are affected by inflation. Its interest expenses are affected by interest rate movements.

MANY ORGANIZATIONS, SUCH AS THE FEDERAL RESERVE BOARD OF GOVERnors and the Federal Reserve district banks, publish macroeconomic data on the Internet. For example, the Federal Reserve uses the Internet to make available a variety of interest rates, such as those on commercial paper and certificates of deposit (CDs). Since interest rates represent the cost of borrowing money and changes in interest rates can affect a firm's financial performance, sites such as these are highly useful to both individuals and corporations.

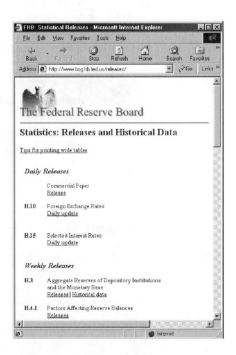

THE DEMAND FOR A FIRM'S PRODUCTS IS DEPENDENT ON THE ECONOMIC growth where the products are sold. Given the mature economy of the United States, the potential for economic growth is limited. Less-developed countries, however, have much greater potential for economic growth because they have not yet taken full advantage of existing technology. Furthermore, the governments of many less-developed countries have encouraged more business development by entrepreneurs, which accelerates economic growth. Many of these governments have also allowed U.S. firms to enter their markets. U.S. firms have attempted to capitalize on changes in economic and political conditions in less-developed countries by selling their products in those countries.

The Coca-Cola Company is among many U.S. firms that have targeted countries with high potential for economic growth. Its sales have increased substantially in Brazil, Chile, East Central Europe, Northern Africa, and China. The Coca-Cola Company's increased sales in these countries can be attributed in part to economic growth, which increases the amount of consumer spending. It can also be attributed to reductions in government restrictions imposed on U.S. firms that desire to conduct business in these countries.

Other U.S. firms are planning major expansion in less-developed countries to capitalize on the changes in economic and political conditions. General Motors plans to expand in various Asian markets, including China, India, and Indonesia, where the potential for economic growth is strong.

U.S. firms that attempt to capitalize on economic growth in foreign countries can be adversely affected if these countries experience a recession. However, if a U.S. firm diversifies its business among several different countries, a recession in any single foreign country should not have a major effect on the firm's worldwide sales.

How Market Prices Are Determined

2 Explain how market prices are determined.

The performance of firms is affected by changes in the prices they charge for products (which influence their revenue) and the prices they pay for supplies and materials (which influence their operating expenses). The prices of products and supplies are influenced by demand and supply conditions.

The following framework uses demand and supply conditions to explain how prices of products change over time. The market price of a product is influenced by the total demand for that product by all customers. It is also affected by the supply of that product produced by firms. The interaction between demand and supply determines the price, as explained in detail next.

DELL® COMPUTER'S FORMULA FOR SUCCESS

The website for Dell Computer, Inc. is **www.dell.com**. Customers visiting this website can configure, price, and order computer systems twenty-four hours a day, seven days a week. Thus, Dell uses the Internet to let its customers partly determine the market price they are willing to pay.

Demand Schedule for a Product

demand schedule a schedule that indicates the quantity of a product that would be demanded at each possible price

The demand for a product can be shown with a **demand schedule,** or a schedule that indicates the quantity of the product that would be demanded at each possible price. Consider personal computers as an example. Assume that the demand schedule for a particular type of personal computer is as shown in the first and second columns in Exhibit 4.7 for a given point in time. If the price is relatively high, the quantity demanded by consumers is relatively low. For example, if the price is $3,000, only 8,000

Exhibit 4.7

How the Equilibrium Price Is Determined by Demand and Supply

If the Price of a Particular Computer Is:	The Amount of These Computers Demanded by Consumers Will Be:	The Amount of These Computers Supplied (Produced) by Firms Will Be:
$3,000	8,000	30,000
2,500	14,000	24,000
2,000	18,000	18,000
1,500	22,000	16,000
1,000	25,000	10,000

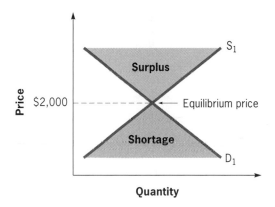

of these computers will be demanded (purchased) by consumers. At the other extreme, if the price is $1,000, a total of 25,000 of these computers will be demanded by customers. The quantity of personal computers demanded is higher when the price is lower.

The graph in Exhibit 4.7, which is based on the table, shows the relationship between the price of a computer and the quantity of computers demanded by consumers. The demand curve (labeled D_1) shows that as price decreases, the quantity demanded increases.

Supply Schedule for a Product

supply schedule a schedule that indicates the quantity of a product that would be supplied (produced) by firms at each possible price

The supply of a product can be shown with a **supply schedule,** or a schedule that indicates the quantity of the product that would be supplied (produced) by firms at each possible price. Assume that the supply schedule for the type of personal computer already discussed is as shown in the first and third columns of Exhibit 4.7 for a given point in time. When the price at which the personal computer can be sold is relatively high, firms will produce a large supply of this computer. For example, if the price is $3,000, 30,000 of these computers will be produced. Firms are willing to produce the computers at this price because they will earn a high profit if they can sell the computers at such a high price.

At the other extreme, if the price of computers is only $1,000, only 10,000 of these computers will be produced. The quantity supplied is much smaller at a low price because some firms will be unwilling to produce the computers if they can sell them for only $1,000. If some firms' actual cost of producing the computers is above this price of $1,000, these firms will be unwilling to produce the computers.

The graph accompanying Exhibit 4.7, which is based on the table, shows the relationship between the price of a computer and the quantity of computers supplied (produced) by firms. The supply curve (labeled S₁) shows that as price increases, the quantity of computers supplied increases.

Interaction of Demand and Supply

The interaction of the demand schedule and supply schedule determines the price. Notice from Exhibit 4.7 that at relatively high prices of computers (such as $3,000), the quantity supplied by firms exceeds the quantity demanded by customers, resulting in a so-called **surplus** of computers. For example, at the price of $3,000 the quantity supplied is 30,000 units and the quantity demanded is 8,000 units, resulting in a surplus of 22,000 units. This surplus occurs because consumers are unwilling to purchase computers when the price is excessive.

When the price of a computer is relatively low, the quantity supplied by firms will be less than the quantity demanded by customers, resulting in a so-called **shortage** of computers. For example, at a price of $1,000, the quantity demanded by customers is 25,000 units, while the quantity supplied by firms is only 10,000 units, causing a shortage of 15,000 units.

Notice from Exhibit 4.7 that at a price of $2,000, the quantity of computers supplied by firms is 18,000 units, and the quantity demanded by customers is also 18,000 units. At this price, there is no surplus and no shortage. The price at which the quantity of a product supplied by firms equals the quantity of the product demanded by customers is called the **equilibrium price.** This is the price at which firms normally attempt to sell their products.

At any price above the equilibrium price, the firms will be unable to sell all the computers they produce, resulting in a surplus. Therefore, they would need to reduce their prices to eliminate the surplus. At any price below the equilibrium price, the firms will not produce a sufficient quantity of computers to satisfy all the customers willing to pay that price (resulting in a shortage). The firms could raise their price to correct the shortage.

The demand and supply concepts just applied to a particular type of computer can also be applied to every product or service that firms produce. Each product or service has its own demand schedule and supply schedule, which will determine its own equilibrium price.

surplus the situation when the quantity supplied by firms exceeds the quantity demanded by customers

shortage the situation when the quantity supplied by firms is less than the quantity demanded by customers

equilibrium price the price at which the quantity of a product supplied by firms equals the quantity of the product demanded by customers

---

BUSINESS ONLINE

Supply and Demand Conditions

http://www.norfolkco-op.com/ mcm/soyfuture.html

SUPPLY AND DEMAND CONDITIONS FOR A VARIETY OF PRODUCTS ARE AVAILable on the Internet, as shown here for U.S. soybeans. For both supply and demand, three different scenarios are projected. Since supply and demand conditions interact to determine the equilibrium market price, individuals and corporations can use this information to budget their expenses and set their prices.

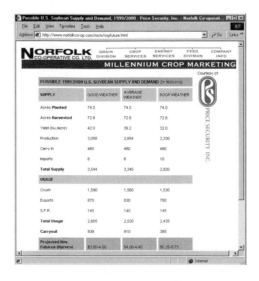

The supply of 7'1" basketball players of the caliber of Shaquille O'Neal is very small. At the same time, every NBA team would love to have a player like him. This combination of low supply and high demand results in very high salaries for these players.

Effect of a Change in the Demand Schedule

As time passes, changing conditions can cause a demand schedule or a supply schedule for a specific product to change. Consequently, the equilibrium price of that product will also change. Reconsider the previous example and assume that computers become more desirable to potential consumers. Assume that the demand schedule for the computer changes as shown at the top of Exhibit 4.8. At any given price, the quantity demanded is now 10,000 units higher than it was before the computer became more popular. The graph accompanying Exhibit 4.8 shows how the demand curve shifts outward from D_1 to D_2.

Now consider the effect of this change in the demand schedule on the equilibrium price of computers. Assuming that the supply schedule remains unchanged, the effect of the change in the demand schedule on the equilibrium price is shown in Exhibit 4.8. At the original equilibrium price of $2,000, the quantity of computers demanded is now 28,000, while the quantity of computers supplied is still 18,000. A shortage of computers occurs at that price. However, at a price of $2,500, the quantity of computers supplied by firms equals the quantity of computers demanded by customers. Therefore, the new equilibrium price is $2,500. The graph at the bottom of Exhibit 4.8 confirms that the shift in the demand schedule from D_1 to D_2 causes the new equilibrium price of computers to be $2,500.

The graph illustrating the effect of a shift in the demand schedule on the equilibrium price of a product can be supplemented with simple logic. When a product becomes more popular, consumers' demand for that product increases, resulting in a shortage. Under these conditions, firms recognize that they can sell whatever amount they produce at a higher price. Once the price is raised to the level at which the quantity supplied is equal to the quantity demanded, the shortage is corrected.

Effect of a Change in the Supply Schedule

Just as the demand for a product may change, so might the supply. A change in the supply can also affect the equilibrium price of the product. To illustrate this effect, re-

Exhibit 4.8

How the Equilibrium Price Is Affected by a Change in Demand

If the Price of a Particular Computer Is:	The Quantity of the Computers Demanded by Consumers Was:	But the Quantity of These Computers Demanded by Consumers Will Now Be:
$3,000	8,000	18,000
2,500	14,000	24,000
2,000	18,000	28,000
1,500	22,000	32,000
1,000	25,000	35,000

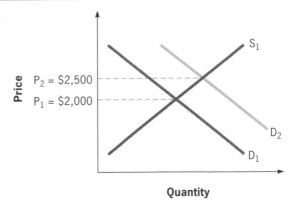

Michael Dell, CEO of Dell Computer. Dell Computer helped increase the supply of IBM compatible personal computers and was thus instrumental in sharp declines in computer prices over the last five years.

consider the original example in which the equilibrium price of computers was $2,000. Now assume that improved technology allows firms to produce the computer at a lower cost. In this case, firms will be willing to produce a larger supply of computers at any given price, which reflects a change in the supply schedule.

Assume that as a result of the improved technology (lower production costs), the supply schedule changes as shown in Exhibit 4.9. At any given price, the quantity

Exhibit 4.9

How the Equilibrium Price Is Affected by a Change in Supply

If the Price of a Particular Computer Is:	The Quantity of These Computers Supplied by Firms Was:	The Quantity of These Computers Supplied by Firms Will Now Be:
$3,000	30,000	36,000
2,500	24,000	30,000
2,000	18,000	24,000
1,500	16,000	22,000
1,000	10,000	16,000

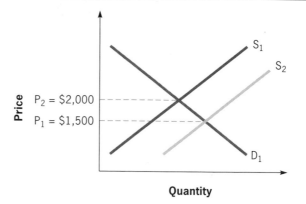

supplied is now 6,000 units higher than it was before the improved technology. The graph accompanying Exhibit 4.9 shows how the supply schedule shifts outward from S_1 to S_2.

Now consider the effect of this change in the supply schedule on the equilibrium price of computers. Assuming that the demand schedule remains unchanged, the effect of the change in the supply schedule on the equilibrium price is shown in Exhibit 4.9. At the original equilibrium price of $2,000, the quantity of computers demanded is 18,000, while the quantity of computers supplied (produced) is now 24,000. A surplus of computers occurs at that price. However, at a price of $1,500, the quantity of computers supplied by firms equals the quantity of computers demanded by consumers. Therefore, the new equilibrium price is $1,500. The graph at the bottom of Exhibit 4.9 confirms that the shift in the supply schedule from S_1 to S_2 causes the new equilibrium price of computers to be $1,500.

The graph illustrating the effect of a shift in the supply schedule on the equilibrium price of a product can be supplemented with simple logic. When improved technology allows firms to produce a product at a lower cost, more firms will be willing to produce the product. This results in a larger supply produced, which causes a surplus. Firms recognize that the only way they will be able to sell all that is supplied (produced) is to lower the price of the product. Once the price is lowered to the level at which the quantity supplied is once again equal to the quantity demanded, the surplus is eliminated.

Effect of Demand and Supply on the General Price Level

The discussion so far on demand and supply has focused on one product to show how the equilibrium price of that product might change. Now consider how the general price level for all products might change. The general price level is an average of prices of all existing products and services. If the total (aggregate) demand by consumers for all or most products suddenly increases (perhaps because of an increase in the income level of most consumers), the general level of prices could rise. The general price level may also be affected by shifts in the supply schedules for all goods and services. If the supply schedule of all or most products suddenly decreases (perhaps because of increasing expenses when producing the products), the general level of prices should rise.

Factors That Influence Market Prices

Thus far, examples have illustrated how the demand by customers or the supply produced by firms can change, causing a new market price. Shifts in the demand schedule or the supply schedule can be caused by several factors, some of which are identified next.

Consumer Income

Consumer income determines the amount of products and services that individuals can purchase. A high level of economic growth results in more income for consumers. When consumers' income rises, they may demand a larger quantity of specific products and services. That is, the demand schedules for various products and services may shift out in response to higher income, which could result in higher prices.

Conversely, when consumers' income level declines, they may demand a smaller quantity of specific products. For example, in the early 1990s, the average income level in the United States declined substantially in specific areas where firms relied on government contracts (such as for building missiles and so on). The federal government's cutbacks for such expenditures resulted in less work for firms in specific regions of the country. As income declined, the demand for new homes in these areas declined, causing a surplus of new homes. The firms that were building new homes were forced to lower their prices because of the surplus.

Consumer Preferences

As consumer preferences (or tastes) for a particular product change, the quantity of that product demanded by consumers may change. There are numerous examples of products whose prices rose in response to increased demand. For example, in early March 1995, a scalped ticket for a Chicago Bulls basketball game in Chicago sold for less than $50. In late March, Michael Jordan came back from retirement, and some scalped tickets for his first game in Chicago sold for $500.

When a product becomes less popular, the demand for the product declines. The resulting surplus may force firms to lower their prices to sell what they produce. For example, when specific clothes become unpopular, clothing manufacturers sell these clothes at discounted prices just to eliminate the surplus.

Production Expenses

Another factor that can affect equilibrium prices is a change in production expenses. When firms experience lower expenses, they are willing to supply (produce) more at any given price (as explained earlier). This results in a surplus of the product, forcing firms to lower their price to sell all that they have produced. For example, the prices of musical compact discs have declined every year since they were first introduced.

When expenses of firms increase, the opposite result occurs. For example, insurance companies that had insured south Florida homes in the early 1990s incurred high expenses in the aftermath of Hurricane Andrew. Some of these companies decided that they would no longer supply this insurance service in south Florida. Those companies that were still willing to provide insurance were able to raise their prices.

Government Influence on Economic Conditions

The federal government can influence business by imposing regulations or by enacting policies that affect economic conditions. Since the regulations tend to vary by industry, they are discussed in the chapter on the industry environment. To influence economic conditions, the federal government implements monetary and fiscal policies, which are discussed next.

> ③ Explain how the government influences economic conditions.

Monetary Policy

money supply demand deposits (checking accounts), currency held by the public, and traveler's checks

In the United States, the term **money supply** normally refers to demand deposits (checking accounts), currency held by the public, and traveler's checks. This is a narrow definition, as there are broader measures of money supply that count other types of deposits as well. Regardless of the precise definition, any measure of money represents funds that financial institutions can lend to borrowers.

Federal Reserve System the central bank of the United States

monetary policy decisions on the money supply level in the United States

The U.S. money supply is controlled by the **Federal Reserve System** ("the Fed"), which is the central bank of the United States. The Fed sets the **monetary policy,** which represents decisions on the money supply level in the United States. The Fed can easily adjust the U.S. money supply by billions of dollars in a single day. Because the Fed's monetary policy affects the money supply level, it affects interest rates.

How the Fed Can Reduce Interest Rates The Fed maintains some funds outside the banking system, which are not loanable funds. These funds are not available

Members of the finance community pay close attention to the comments of Fed Chairman Alan Greenspan.

to firms or individuals who need to borrow. The Fed can use these funds to purchase Treasury securities held by individuals and firms. These purchases provide individuals and firms with new funds, which they deposit in their commercial banks. Consequently, the money supply increases because the commercial banks and other financial institutions can loan out these funds. In other words, the Fed's action increases the supply of loanable funds. Assuming that the demand for loanable funds remains unchanged, the increase in the supply of loanable funds should cause interest rates to decrease. The impact of the supply of loanable funds on interest rates is discussed in more detail in the Chapter 17 appendix.

How the Fed Can Increase Interest Rates   When the Fed reduces the U.S. money supply, it pulls funds out of commercial banks and other financial institutions. This reduces the supply of funds that these financial institutions can lend to borrowers. Assuming that the demand for loanable funds remains unchanged, the decline in the supply of loanable funds should cause interest rates to rise.

When the Fed affects interest rates with its monetary policy, it directly affects a firm's interest expenses. Second, it can affect the demand for the firm's products if those products are commonly purchased with borrowed funds. The amount of expansion by firms is highly influenced by the interest rate they must pay on funds borrowed to support the expansion.

Fiscal Policy

fiscal policy decisions on how the federal government should set tax rates and spend money

Fiscal policy represents decisions on how the federal government should set tax rates and spend money. These decisions are relevant to businesses because they affect economic growth and therefore can affect the demand for a firm's products or services.

Revision of Personal Income Tax Rates   Consider a fiscal policy that reduces personal income taxes. This policy would give people a higher after-tax income, which may encourage them to spend more money. Such behavior reflects an increase in the aggregate demand for products and services produced by businesses, which can improve the performance of businesses.

Revision of Corporate Taxes

Fiscal policy can also affect a firm's after-tax earnings directly. For example, assume the corporate tax rate is reduced from 30 percent to 25 percent for corporations. If a specific corporation's before-tax earnings are $10 million, its corporate taxes would have been $3 million (computed as 30% × $10,000,000) at the old tax rate. However, at a corporate tax rate of 25 percent, its corporate taxes are now $2.5 million (computed as 25% × $10,000,000). Therefore, the corporation's after-tax earnings are now $500,000 higher, simply because the corporate taxes are now $500,000 lower.

excise taxes taxes imposed by the federal government on particular products

Revision in Excise Taxes

Excise taxes are taxes imposed by the federal government on particular products. These taxes raise the cost of producing these goods. Consequently, manufacturers tend to incorporate the tax into the price they charge for the products. Thus, consumers indirectly incur the tax. The tax may also discourage consumption of these goods by indirectly affecting the price. Excise taxes are imposed on various products, including alcohol and tobacco.

Revision in the Budget Deficit

The fiscal policy set by the federal government dictates the amount of tax revenue generated by the federal government and the amount of federal spending. If federal government spending exceeds the amount of federal taxes, a **federal budget deficit** results.

federal budget deficit the situation when the amount of federal government spending exceeds the amount of federal taxes and other revenue received by the federal government

When the federal government receives less revenue than it spends, it must borrow the difference. For example, if the federal government plans to spend $900 billion but receives only $700 billion in taxes (or other revenue), it has $200 billion less than it desires to spend. It must borrow $200 billion to have sufficient funds for making its expenditures (as shown in Exhibit 4.10). If the federal government needs to

---

SPOTLIGHT ON TECHNOLOGY

Monitoring the Economic Environment

In a world tied together by information technology, it has become increasingly important for companies to be aware of the economic environment. Mortgage brokers, for example, typically serve the financing needs of home buyers and homeowners in their local region. They cannot, however, afford to be local in their outlook. The potential lenders that they rely on for channeling funds to homeowners are located across the United States. Their business is also dramatically affected by economic factors such as recession and interest rate fluctuations. For example, during periods of falling interest rates, much of a mortgage broker's business comes from refinancing existing mortgages for homeowners. During periods of rising rates, however, that business virtually disappears. As a consequence, year-to-year swings in loan volume of 50 to 60 percent are common.

Some of the most progressive mortgage brokers have recognized their dependence on information and are employing information technology to acquire it. Austin Kazinetz, president of the American Financial Network, Inc.,

in Boca Raton, Florida, describes the systems he put in place as follows:

"Right now, we are hooked into every valuable source of data that we've been able to identify. The ISC system gives us online access to county tax rolls, providing data on comparable sales, tax deeds, and foreclosures. The Ready system hooks us into the local Board of Realtors, providing us with information on what's on the market and how it is being priced, based upon multiple listing service (MLS) listings. We can link directly to the tax collector's rolls. The Data Trace system allows us to perform online title searches. The Mortgage Banker's Association of America provides us with bulletin board system (BBS) access to various data, such as being able to identify FHA/VA case numbers and appraiser assignments. That BBS also allows us to exchange information with many lenders. We are tied into a number of providers of online credit information, so we can perform credit searches in-house. We have even installed a satellite dish, which allows us up-to-the-minute access to financial market news. . . . As a result, nobody has as much data as American Financial Network."

He believes these systems were instrumental in his company's ability to prepare for changes in the economic environment.

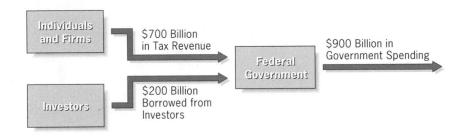

borrow additional funds, it creates a high demand for loanable funds, which may result in higher interest rates (for reasons explained earlier).

In 1998 and 1999, the federal government spent less funds than it received, which resulted in a small surplus. Under these conditions, the government's budget policy does not place upward pressure on interest rates.

Summary of Government Influence on Economic Factors

Exhibit 4.11 provides a summary of how the federal government can affect the performance of firms. Fiscal policy can affect personal tax rates and therefore influence consumer spending behavior. It can also affect corporate tax rates, which influence the earnings of firms. Monetary policy can affect interest rates, which may influence the demand for a firm's product (if the purchases are sometimes paid for with borrowed funds). By influencing interest rates, monetary policy also affects the interest expenses that firms incur.

BUSINESS ONLINE

The Government and Economic Conditions

http://www.fms.treas.gov/
citizensreport/index.html

THE U.S. GOVERNMENT USES THE INTERNET TO PROVIDE THE PUBLIC WITH economic data and with information about its financial performance. As shown here, the Financial Management Service (FMS), a bureau of the Department of the Treasury, provides information about both the annual budget surplus or deficit and economic data. For example, by clicking on the most recent fiscal year under economic data, interested parties can obtain information on unemployment, GDP growth, and inflation rates. Since government policies have a large effect on economic conditions, information on its own performance is very useful to individuals and corporations.

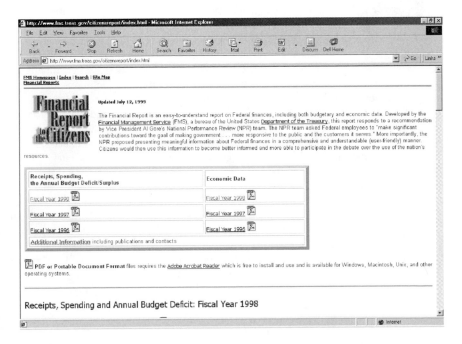

Exhibit 4.11

How Government Policies Affect Business Performance

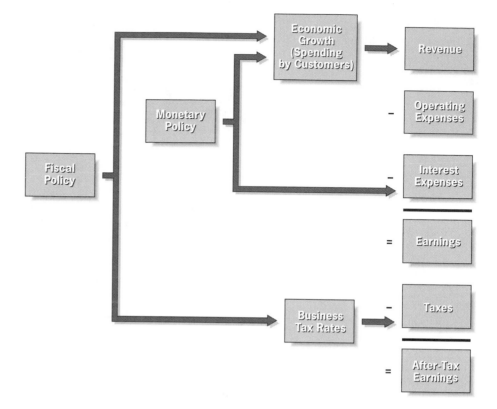

CROSS-FUNCTIONAL TEAMWORK

Economic Effects across Business Functions

Since managers of a firm have different responsibilities, they assess different aspects of the economic environment. Managers who focus on production monitor the changes in economic conditions that could affect the firm's production costs. They tend to monitor inflationary trends, or changes in the price levels of specific supplies or equipment that they purchase.

Marketing managers attempt to forecast sales of their products and assess economic conditions that affect the demand for the products, such as economic growth. They may also monitor interest rates if the products are commonly purchased with borrowed funds, since the demand for the products might increase in response to a reduction in interest rates. Since the firm's production volume is dependent on the forecasted demand for the product, it is influenced by economic conditions.

Marketing managers assess economic conditions because their marketing decisions can be affected by the strength of the economy. Some of a firm's products (such

as necessities and relatively inexpensive products) may be marketed more heavily when economic conditions are weak because these products may be more popular at that time. Conversely, the firm may market its expensive products more heavily when economic conditions are more favorable.

The firm's financial managers monitor the economic conditions that affect the cost of financing. They tend to focus on interest rates because the firm's financing expenses are directly affected by changes in interest rates.

When different types of managers forecast economic conditions so they can make business decisions, they should work as a team. Otherwise, a forecast of some economic conditions may vary across managers, which may cause their business decisions to be different. For example, if the marketing managers of an automobile manufacturer expect low interest rates, they will expect a high sales volume, which will require a large production of automobiles. However, if the production managers expect high interest rates, they will expect a lower level of sales and will be concerned that a large production volume could cause excessive inventories.

Some firms assign one person or department to develop the forecasts of all economic conditions, which the managers use in all business functions. In this way, all managers make decisions according to the same forecasts of economic conditions.

Dilemma of the Federal Government

The federal government faces a dilemma when attempting to influence economic growth. If it can maintain a low rate of economic growth, it can prevent inflationary pressure caused by an excessive demand for products. A restrictive monetary or fiscal policy may be used for this purpose. A restrictive monetary policy leads to low growth in the money supply over time, which tends to place upward pressure on interest rates. This discourages borrowing and therefore can reduce total spending in the economy. A restrictive fiscal policy results in high taxes and low government spending.

Although restrictive monetary and fiscal policies may keep inflation low, a critical trade-off is involved. The unemployment rate may be higher when the economy is stagnant. The federal government can use a more stimulative policy (such as low tax rates or a monetary policy designed to reduce interest rates) to boost economic growth. Although these policies increase economic growth, they may also cause higher inflation.

Rarely is a consensus reached on whether the government should use a stimulative or restrictive policy at a given point in time. During the late 1990s, the federal government used stimulative monetary policies because inflation was very low and was not expected to be a serious problem. This monetary policy helped to increase economic growth during that period.

Managers of firms commonly attempt to forecast how future fiscal and monetary policies will affect economic conditions. This information is then used to predict the demand for the firm's product, its labor and material costs, and its interest expenses. To illustrate, assume an automobile manufacturer forecasts that next year's interest rate on consumer loans will decrease by 2 percent. This forecast of interest rates will be used to forecast the demand for the firm's automobiles. Lower interest rates will probably create higher demand, because more consumers will be willing to finance their purchases of new automobiles. Assume that the firm believes that for every 1 percent decrease in interest rates, demand for its automobiles will increase by 3 percent. Thus, it anticipates a 6 percent increase in sales volume in one year.

BUSINESS DILEMMA | **College Health Club**

Economic Effects on College Health Club

SUE KRAMER, OWNER OF COLLEGE HEALTH CLUB (CHC), IS TRYING TO EStimate the performance of CHC over the next three years. The annual memberships of $250 are paid to CHC with cash. Many of the members are college students who work part-time.

CHC incurs interest expenses on its $40,000 loan. The loan has a variable rate that is based on the prevailing market interest rate. The annual interest paid is $6,000, based on a prevailing interest rate of 15 percent (15% × $40,000 = $6,000).

Sue reviews several business publications to find a consensus forecast of economic conditions:

1 The consensus forecast for the economy (including the local area) is strong economic growth over the next three years. Since many students at the local university rely on jobs to pay their tuition, the university's enrollment is expected to increase due to the economic growth. Sue expects that this will result in about ten more annual memberships in each of the next three years.

2 The inflation rate will be about 3 percent in each of the next three years.

3 The Federal Reserve will raise interest rates by 2 percent over the next year, but interest rates are expected to remain steady for the following two years. This means that the interest rate that Sue pays on her business loan will rise to 17 percent next year and will remain at that level the following two years.

Dilemma

Sue is concerned about how economic conditions could affect CHC. She wants to forecast how CHC will be affected based on the forecasts of economic conditions. How will the change in economic conditions affect revenue? Expenses? Earnings (before taxes)?

Solution

A summary of Sue's analysis is provided next.

Economic Growth   The economic growth will result in more part-time work for the college students and should cause an increase in the demand for annual memberships at CHC. Sue increases her forecast of annual memberships by ten over each of the next three years. At a membership fee of $250 per person, the extra ten memberships will generate an extra $2,500 per year.

Inflation   The increase in inflation could result in higher prices for equipment. However, since CHC has a leasing agreement, the expense of leasing the equipment will not be affected. Wages may also rise nationwide as a result of inflation, but the effect will be minor at CHC, which has only one employee besides Sue.

Interest Rates   The increase in interest rates will result in higher financing costs. CHC has a $40,000 loan with an interest rate that rises in response to higher market interest rates. The interest rate on CHC's loan will be 2 percentage points higher than it was, which results in extra annual interest payments of $800 (computed as 2% × $40,000).

The effects of changing economic conditions on CHC are as follows:

	Year		
	1	**2**	**3**
Change in revenue	$2,500	$2,500	$2,500
− Change in operating expenses	0	0	0
− Change in financing expenses	800	800	800
= Change in earnings	1,700	1,700	1,700

The extra revenue resulting from economic growth exceeds the extra financing expenses resulting from higher interest rates. Overall, CHC should benefit from the forecasted economic conditions.

Additional Issues for Discussion

1   Should Sue more closely monitor economic growth in the United States as a whole or economic growth in her local area? Why?

2   Assume that the federal government is expected to raise income taxes for all people, regardless of income level. How could this change possibly affect CHC?

3   Should Sue more closely monitor inflation in the United States as a whole or inflation in her local area? How could Sue be affected by land and rental prices in the local area?

SUMMARY

1 A firm's performance is highly dependent on three macroeconomic factors: (1) economic growth, (2) inflation, and (3) interest rates. A high level of economic growth tends to increase the overall demand for a firm's products and services. Inflation affects the costs of supplies and wages, which represent the firm's operating expenses. Higher inflation tends to cause higher operating expenses. Interest rates affect the firm's interest expenses. An increase in interest rates will typically result in higher interest expenses for the firms.

2 Market prices are determined by demand and supply conditions. The demand for a product is influenced by consumer income and preferences. Higher consumer income generally results in a higher demand for products. The amount of a product produced is influenced by production expenses. Firms will supply products to the market only if the market price is sufficiently high to more than cover expenses.

3 The federal government influences macroeconomic conditions by enacting monetary or fiscal policies. Its monetary policy affects the amount of funds available at commercial banks and other financial institutions and therefore affects interest rates. Its fiscal policy affects the taxes imposed on consumers, which can influence the amount of spending by consumers and therefore affect the performance of firms. Fiscal policy is also used to tax the earnings of firms.

KEY TERMS

aggregate expenditures   *92*
cost-push inflation   *94*
cyclical unemployment   *93*
demand schedule   *98*
demand-pull inflation   *95*
economic growth   *92*
equilibrium price   *100*
excise taxes   *106*

federal budget deficit   *106*
Federal Reserve System   *104*
fiscal policy   *105*
frictional unemployment   *93*
gross domestic product (GDP)   *92*
inflation   *94*
macroeconomic conditions   *91*
microeconomic conditions   *91*

monetary policy   *104*
money supply   *104*
recession   *92*
seasonal unemployment   *93*
shortage   *100*
structural unemployment   *93*
supply schedule   *99*
surplus   *100*

REVIEW QUESTIONS

1 Discuss macroeconomic factors that affect business performance.

2 Describe the four different types of unemployment and explain which type a college graduate would face upon entering the job market.

3 Why should firms be concerned with the changes in interest rates?

4 How are market prices determined?

5 Define and explain price equilibrium for businesses and consumers. What is the effect when there is a surplus or shortage?

6 Discuss the factors that will influence a shift in the demand curve for products or services.

7 Explain why a supply curve would shift due to improved technology for a firm. What effect would this have on price?

8 Define monetary policy. Who is responsible for regulating the monetary growth in the United States?

9 Distinguish macroeconomics from microeconomics. Which of the two economic theories would apply when the government establishes a fiscal policy?

10 Discuss the two primary responsibilities of the federal government in establishing economic policies. What does it mean to have a budget deficit?

DISCUSSION QUESTIONS

1 In your community, do businesses and housing show signs of economic growth or evidence of decay? What effect do these conditions have on inflation and interest rates?

2 How could a firm use the Internet to assess the current level of some macroeconomic factors that may affect business performance, such as economic growth and inflation? How could a firm use the Internet to determine the demand for its products?

3 Assume that you are a manager in a plant that produces rollerblades. What factors would you consider in determining price for this product?

4 When college students are given federal grants (such as Pell Grants) that cover some education expenses, does this reflect a form of fiscal policy or monetary policy? Explain your answer.

5 Discuss the effect when the federal government spends more tax dollars than it takes in. Is this practice unhealthy for our economy?

INVESTING IN THE STOCK OF A BUSINESS

Using the annual report of the firm in which you would like to invest, complete the following:

1 Was your firm's performance affected by economic growth last year? If so, how? Are these trends expected to continue? What does your firm plan to do about the economic conditions it faces?

2 Was your firm's performance affected by inflation or interest rates last year? If so, how?

3 Explain how the firm uses technology to assess its economic environment. For example, does it use the Internet to assess the economic environment?

4 Go to **http://hoovers.com** and locate the NEWS SEARCH. Type in the name of the firm in the space provided, and review the recent news stories about the firm. Summarize any (at least one) recent news story about the firm that applies to one or more of the key concepts within this chapter.

CASE IMPACT OF ECONOMIC CONDITIONS

Gold Autoparts, Inc., produces automobile parts which are purchased by various automobile manufacturers that are building new cars. Gold has had some success in selling its parts to automobile manufacturers because they do not have to produce those parts if they can rely on Gold to do so.

Gold has recently created a website that lists all of its parts and the prices charged for them. The automobile manufacturers can order parts online, and Gold tries to fill these orders quickly.

Gold attempts to anticipate when orders will increase so that it can produce enough parts to fill orders. It realizes that the demand for its auto parts is dependent on economic conditions that affect the demand for new cars. When demand for new cars increases, more new cars are produced, and there is greater demand for Gold's parts.

Tom Gold, president of Gold Autoparts, expects that economic growth will increase this year. He expects that interest rates will be relatively low over the next year. He also expects that foreign car manufacturers will introduce many new types of cars into the U.S. market. At this time, Gold Autoparts focuses its business on U.S. automobile manufacturers.

QUESTIONS

1 How will Gold Autoparts, Inc., be affected if economic growth increases as expected?

2 How will Gold Autoparts be affected if interest rates decline as expected?

3 How might the introduction of many new cars by foreign car manufacturers affect Gold's business?

4 Overall, do you think conditions will cause an increase or decrease in the demand for Gold's auto parts?

VIDEO CASE EXPOSURE TO WEAK ECONOMIC CONDITIONS

Linda Russell's CollectionCenter found itself in a can't-squeeze-blood-out-of-a-turnip situation. Major job sources in Wyoming—oil, gas, coal, uranium, and timber—were in trouble, a trouble especially deep in the area around

Rawlins, location of Russell's collection and credit-reporting agency. Rawlins was experiencing a very weak economy, which reduced the ability of customers to pay their bills.

Russell takes a gentle approach to debt collection, with a philosophy of helping people figure out ways to pay what they owe, rather than browbeat them. The approach had been working well.

However, CollectionCenter had strengths: a team of skilled, dedicated people and a reputation for outstanding service. The team included Russell's husband, Jerry, a lawyer with an outside practice who served as CollectionCenter's executive vice president.

The Russells huddled with some of the team, the office, collection, and credit-reporting managers. It was agreed that CollectionCenter would shrink and die if its territory didn't expand. Input was solicited from everyone else on the team, and the company moved into Wyoming's two largest cities, Casper and Cheyenne, buying existing agencies there.

"We were off and running," says Linda Russell, "but we found we were in real need of more expertise in the rapidly changing world of computers with which we had to deal."

Since then, the company has expanded farther, to Ft. Collins and Grand Junction in Colorado and Salt Lake City, Utah. Its team has increased from 12 to 69.

QUESTIONS

1 Explain why the revenue generated by Linda Russell's CollectionCenter may decline when the local economy is weak, while the expenses of the CollectionCenter do not decline.

2 Explain how expansion of the CollectionCenter business into other locations can reduce the firm's exposure to the economic conditions of Rawlins, Wyoming. Would expansion into new locations where the economic conditions were similar to Rawlins, Wyoming, be a useful strategy for the CollectionCenter? Explain.

3 Assume that the one executive of the CollectionCenter suggested that the entire firm be moved to Salt Lake City, where the economic conditions are presently more favorable than all other regions. Is this an appropriate strategy to prevent any adverse effects of economic conditions over the next several years?

INTERNET APPLICATIONS

http://www.bog.frb.fed.us/policy.htm

Briefly describe the Federal Open Market Committee. When is the next scheduled meeting of the committee?

What type of information is provided in the Humphrey-Hawkins report? How is this type of information useful for decision making by a business?

THE *Coca-Cola* COMPANY ANNUAL REPORT PROJECT

Questions for the current year's annual report are available on the text website at **http://madura_intro_bus.swcollege.com**.

The following questions apply concepts learned in this chapter to The Coca-Cola Company. Go to The Coca-Cola Company website (**http://www.cocacola.com**) and find the index for the 1999 annual report.

QUESTIONS

1 Look at the information on "Impact of Inflation and Changing Prices." How could inflation affect The Coca-Cola Company's future profitability? What does The Coca-Cola Company generally do to counteract inflationary effects?

2 Look at the information on "Euro Conversion." Does the management of The Coca-Cola Company perceive any problems to be associated with the introduction of the euro, the new European currency?

3 Look at "Selected Market Results." Given that it is impossible to predict future economic conditions, what might be a general strategy of a large firm such as The Coca-Cola Company to insulate against shifts in the economic environment of any particular country?

4 Look at "A Message from Doug Daft." According to the chairman, what did The Coca-Cola Company have to do to fuel further investment and to reshape the company in light of increased technological changes?

5 Go to **http://hoovers.com** and locate the NEWS SEARCH. Type in The Coca-Cola Company in the space provided, and review the recent news stories about the firm. Summarize any (at least one) recent news story about The Coca-Cola Company that applies one or more of the key concepts within this chapter of the text.

IN-TEXT STUDY GUIDE

Answers are in an appendix at the back of the book.

TRUE OR FALSE

1 A higher level of inflation will cause a larger decrease in a firm's operating expenses.

2 The total amount of expenditures in the economy is known as aggregate expenditures.

3 An increase in aggregate demand will cause the general price level to fall.

4 The Federal Reserve System sets the monetary policy that determines the money supply in the United States.

5 Macroeconomics is focused on a specific business or industry of concern.

6 Structural unemployment refers to workers who lose their jobs due to a decline in economic conditions.

7 The demand for a product can be shown with a demand schedule, which indicates the quantity of the product that would be demanded at each possible price.

8 Inflation is usually measured as the percentage change in gross domestic product.

9 When the U.S. economic growth is lower than normal, the total income level of all U.S. workers is relatively high.

10 Economic growth represents the change in the general level of economic activity.

MULTIPLE CHOICE

11 The total market value of all final goods and services produced in the United States is known as:
a) gross domestic product.
b) aggregate expenditures.
c) fiscal output.
d) the production quota.
e) aggregate supply.

12 The type of unemployment that represents people who are unemployed because of poor economic conditions is:
a) functional unemployment.
b) cyclical unemployment.
c) seasonal unemployment.
d) structural unemployment.
e) general unemployment.

13 Over the next several years, economic growth in less-developed nations is:
a) unlikely to occur due to lack of natural resources in most of these countries.
b) likely to occur, but at a much slower rate than growth in the United States.
c) likely to be greater than the growth in the United States, thus providing U.S. firms with important market opportunities.

d) unlikely to occur because of the anti-growth attitudes of their governments.
e) likely to be quite rapid, but U.S. firms are unlikely to benefit since they view the opportunities in less-developed countries as being too risky.

14 _____ represent the cost of borrowing money.
a) Discount factors   d) Dividends
b) Depreciation rates   e) Interest rates
c) Inflation premiums

15 Taxes that the federal government imposes on particular products are called:
a) excise taxes.   d) quotas.
b) import taxes.   e) embargoes.
c) export taxes.

16 _____ conditions reflect the overall performance of the nation's economy.
a) Microeconomic   d) Proto-economic
b) Multi-economic   e) Supraeconomic
c) Macroeconomic

17 The type of inflation that requires firms to increase their prices to cover increased costs is referred to as:
a) demand-pull inflation.
b) stagflation.
c) cost-push inflation.
d) disequilibrium.
e) unemployment.

18 Jan is currently between jobs, but she has marketable job skills and is confident she will find work in the near future. Jan's current situation would be an example of _____ unemployment.
a) seasonal   d) frictional
b) structural   e) cyclical
c) functional

19 The prices firms pay for supplies or materials directly influence their:
a) operating expenses.   d) stockholders' equity.
b) operating revenue.   e) economic assets.
c) dividends.

20 A typical demand schedule shows that:
a) as price decreases, quantity demanded will also decrease.
b) as price decreases, quantity demanded will increase.
c) quantity supplied can never be less than quantity demanded.
d) the total quantity of goods consumers want to buy will fall during periods of inflation.
e) a firm can always increase its revenue by increasing the prices it charges for its products.

21 At the equilibrium price for a good, the:
a) firms in the market are maximizing their total revenue.

b) consumers in the market have spent all of their income.

c) firms in the market are maximizing their total output.

d) firms in the market are just breaking even.

e) quantity demanded by consumers equals the quantity supplied by firms.

22 If the market price of a good is above the equilibrium price:

a) a surplus will exist, which will put downward pressure on prices.

b) the supply curve will shift to the right as firms rush to take advantage of the high price.

c) the demand curve will shift to the left as consumers decrease the quantity they buy.

d) the government will intervene to force the price downward.

e) a shortage will exist, which will force the price even higher.

23 Which of the following is the best example of the federal government's use of fiscal policy?

a) The Federal Reserve places new regulations on the nation's banks that require them to make more loans to minorities and women.

b) The U.S. Treasury announces that it has redesigned the nation's paper money to make the bills more difficult to counterfeit.

c) Congress enacts, and the president signs, a bill to cut income taxes during an economic downturn.

d) The president appoints a new commission to look into concerns about how pollution is damaging the environment.

e) The Federal Reserve gives banks more funds in order to allow them to make more loans.

24 If the market price is below the equilibrium price:

a) quantity demanded will exceed quantity supplied, resulting in a shortage.

b) quantity demanded will exceed quantity supplied, resulting in a surplus.

c) quantity supplied will exceed quantity demanded, resulting in a shortage.

d) quantity supplied will exceed quantity demanded, resulting in a surplus.

e) the supply curve will shift to the left and the demand curve will shift to the right.

25 The _____ of the United States is defined as the total amount of demand deposits, currency held by the public, and traveler's checks.

a) financial wealth

b) financial reserves

c) money supply

d) total banking assets

e) gross domestic product

26 If consumer incomes increase, the effect on consumer decisions about how much they want to buy can be shown by:

a) shifting the demand curve outward (to the right).

b) shifting the supply curve outward.

c) shifting the demand curve inward (to the left).

d) moving downward to the right along the demand curve.

e) shifting the supply curve inward.

27 The central bank of the United States, where the money supply is controlled and regulated, is the:

a) Federal Reserve System.

b) Senate.

c) Department of Congress.

d) Council of Economic Advisors.

e) Board of Directors.

28 A supply schedule shows:

a) the relationship between quantity supplied and quantity demanded.

b) how the quantity firms supply in the market affects their total profits.

c) the quantity firms are willing to supply at each possible price.

d) the average cost of supplying various quantities of a good.

e) the relationship between the amount of labor and other inputs the firm employs and the quantity of output the firm can produce.

29 A major effect of the Federal Reserve's monetary policies is to bring about changes in the:

a) stock of gold held by the government to back the money supply.

b) income tax rates paid by households and businesses.

c) size of the federal budget deficit.

d) amount the government spends to finance social programs.

e) interest rates banks charge when they make loans.

30 An increase in the demand for a product is likely to cause:

a) a matching decrease in supply.

b) an increase in the equilibrium price.

c) the supply curve to shift to the right.

d) a decrease in equilibrium price.

e) the government to attempt to increase production quotas.

31 When the amount of federal government spending exceeds the amount of federal taxes, the result is a so-called:

a) trade deficit.

b) federal budget deficit.

c) balance of payments.

d) price equilibrium.

e) opportunity cost.

32 All of the following would be examples of macro-economic concerns except:
a) a drop in the nation's gross domestic product.
b) an increase in the rate of inflation.
c) a strike by workers at a local bakery.
d) an increase in the amount of cyclical unemployment.
e) an increase in the rate of interest charged on bank loans.

33 An increase in the general level of prices of products and services over a specified period of time is called:
a) inflation.
b) stagflation.
c) unemployment.
d) disinflation.
e) equilibrium.

34 Restrictive monetary and fiscal policies may keep inflation low, but the critical trade-off is that they may also cause:
a) disinflation.
b) environment problems
c) massive crime.
d) unemployment.
e) higher inflation.

35 The government can prevent inflationary pressure caused by an excessive demand for products by maintaining a low rate of:
a) fiscal policies.
b) economic growth.
c) monetary policies.
d) unemployment.
e) savings.

The Learning	1	Identify the industry characteristics that influence business performance.
Goals of this	2	Explain why some firms are more exposed to industry conditions.
chapter are to:	3	Explain how a firm can compete within its industry.

Industry Environment

Just as a firm is affected by macroeconomic conditions, it is also affected by microeconomic conditions related to the firm and its respective industry.

online access? By increased competition from Yahoo! and other large Internet providers? By free Internet access offered by some companies? This chapter provides a background on the industry environment that can be used to answer these questions.

To illustrate how the industry environment can affect the value of a business, consider the case of AOL/Time Warner, which provides Internet and other various media services. How will AOL/Time Warner earnings and value be affected by increasing demand for

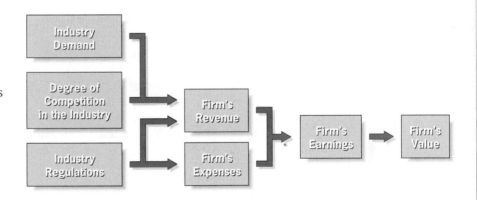

Industry Characteristics That Influence Business Performance

① Identify the industry characteristics that influence business performance.

The performance of the firm can be highly dependent on the following industry characteristics:

▶ Industry demand
▶ Industry competition
▶ Labor environment
▶ Regulatory environment

Industry Demand

industry demand total demand for the products in an industry

Over a given time period, a specific industry can perform much better than others because the total demand for the products in the industry (called **industry demand**) is high. The industry demand for baby clothes is highly dependent on the number of children that are born. The industry demand for hotels in Florida during the winter is partially dependent on the weather in the northern states. Therefore, it would be a

Industry demand for family-oriented vacation spots has increased the popularity of such towns as Branson, Missouri. Branson has grown into a highly visited destination, as evidenced here by the traffic on its "strip"—a busy 10-mile stretch lined with hotels, restaurants, and theaters.

mistake for a firm to conclude that it will perform well over the next year just because of favorable economic conditions in the United States.

As industry demand changes, so does the performance of firms in the industry. For example, the performance levels of DaimlerChrysler and General Motors are related over time because they are similarly affected by industry conditions. Both firms experienced relatively poor performance in the early 1990s when the economy was weak and the demand for new automobiles was low. These firms performed much better in the mid- and late-1990s when the demand for new automobiles increased.

Industry demand can change abruptly and therefore is monitored closely by a firm's managers. It can be affected by changes in consumer income levels or preferences. For example, consumer preferences have substantially increased the demand for minivans in recent years, which has favorably affected DaimlerChrysler and other manufacturers of minivans. Consumer preferences have also recently increased the demand for athletic footwear, which has favorably affected Nike, Reebok International, and other athletic shoe manufacturers.

Just as an increase in industry demand is beneficial to firms in that industry, a decline in industry demand has adverse effects. For example, as the demand for missiles and other products in the defense industry has declined, TRW and other firms that produce these products have been adversely affected. Chevron's performance was adversely affected by a decline in the industry demand for petroleum.

The following examples illustrate how industry competition can change in response to a change in industry demand. Compaq benefited from the increased industry demand for computers in the mid-1990s. However, as new computer firms recognized the large industry demand and entered the industry, Compaq faced more intense competition.

As a second example, consider the case of Bell Sports Corporation, which was once the largest producer of motorcycle helmets. In the early 1990s it experienced a decline in business because the demand for these helmets leveled off. In response to the increased demand for bicycles, Bell switched its production process to make bicycle helmets instead. However, other firms also recognized the popularity of bicycles and began to compete in this market. In response to the intense competition in the bicycle helmet industry, Bell began to produce other bicycle accessories, such as child seats, safety lights, and car racks. In this way, it diversified its product line so that it was not completely reliant on its bicycle helmet business.

As a third example, consider the case of Pizza Hut, which initially benefited from the increased demand for pizza delivery. However, competition from Little Caesars and

Domino's caused a decline in Pizza Hut's earnings. Pizza Hut responded by offering a more diversified menu, including sandwiches and pasta, at some of its restaurants. By diversifying in this way, Pizza Hut attempted to reduce its reliance on pizza delivery.

Industry Competition

market share a firm's sales as a proportion of the total market

Each industry is composed of various firms that compete against each other for the customers who want their products. The level of competition varies across industries. When a firm is subject to less competition in an industry, it will typically be more profitable for the following reasons. A firm's sales as a proportion of the total market (called **market share**) are normally higher when it faces little competition. In addition, a firm can charge a higher price without losing its customers if it faces little competition. Total revenue is dependent on the quantity (Q) of units sold and the price (P) per unit:

$$\text{Revenue} = Q \times P$$

A firm that faces little competition can sell a high quantity at a high price and therefore generate a high level of revenue. A high degree of competition has the opposite effect. First, it can reduce each firm's market share, thereby reducing the quantity of units sold by each firm in the industry. Second, a high degree of competition may force each firm in the industry to lower its price to prevent competitors from taking away its business.

As an illustration of how a firm's performance can be affected by competition, consider the case of Robert Half, an employee search firm. The demand for Robert Half's services declined substantially when online employee search firms (such as Hot Jobs) appeared on the Internet. Consequently, Robert Half's performance and value (as measured by its stock price) declined, as shown in Exhibit 5.1.

DELL® COMPUTER'S FORMULA FOR SUCCESS

Dell Computer sells a variety of desktop computers. Recently, sales of the OptiPlex and Dell Dimension desktop computers grew at four times the industry rate, and the products garnered an unprecedented 174 awards for performance, reliability, and service. Furthermore, sales growth for Dell's notebook computers was three times the overall industry rate in a recent year. Thus, Dell Computer uses its ability to custom configure computers to maintain its position in the computer industry.

Exhibit 5.1   Impact of Increased Competition on Robert Half's Stock Price

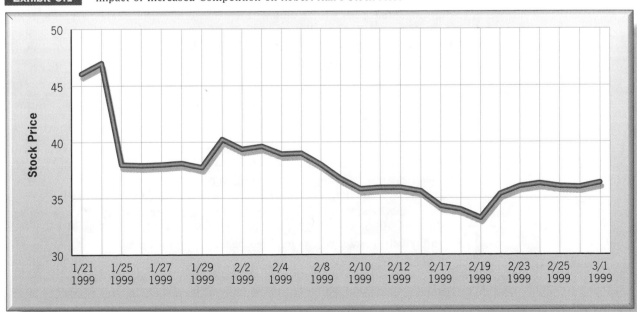

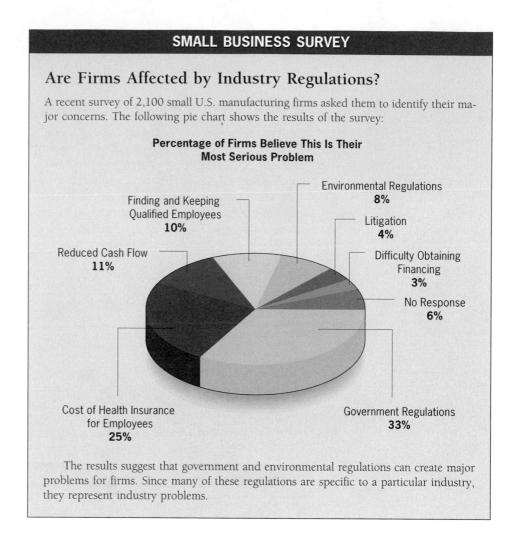

SMALL BUSINESS SURVEY

Are Firms Affected by Industry Regulations?

A recent survey of 2,100 small U.S. manufacturing firms asked them to identify their major concerns. The following pie chart shows the results of the survey:

Percentage of Firms Believe This Is Their Most Serious Problem

- Environmental Regulations 8%
- Litigation 4%
- Difficulty Obtaining Financing 3%
- No Response 6%
- Government Regulations 33%
- Cost of Health Insurance for Employees 25%
- Reduced Cash Flow 11%
- Finding and Keeping Qualified Employees 10%

The results suggest that government and environmental regulations can create major problems for firms. Since many of these regulations are specific to a particular industry, they represent industry problems.

Labor Environment

Some industries have peculiar labor characteristics. The cost of labor is much higher in specific industries (such as health care) that require specialized skills. Unions may also affect the cost of labor. Some manufacturing industries, particularly those in the northern states, have labor unions, and labor costs in these industries are relatively high. Industries that have labor unions may also experience labor strikes. Understanding the labor environment within an industry can help a firm's managers estimate the labor expenses to be incurred from its business.

Regulatory Environment

The federal government may enforce environmental rules or may prevent a firm from operating in particular locations or from engaging in particular types of business. All industries are subject to some form of government regulation.

In 1995, an effort was made to reduce federal regulations. Congress eliminated sixteen thousand pages of regulations. Nevertheless, complying with existing regulations can still be very expensive. Often businesses involved in federal contracts must comply with more than one hundred pages of specifications.

Regulation is much more restrictive in some industries than others. Automobile and oil firms have been subject to increased environmental regulations. Firms in the banking, insurance, and utility industries have been subject to regulations on the types of services they can provide. An entrepreneur who wishes to enter any industry must recognize all the regulations that are imposed on that industry.

The Justice Department of the U.S. federal government attempts to prevent price-fixing, in which two or more firms in the same industry set prices. In the early 1990s, U.S. airlines were forced to provide millions of dollars in discounts to passengers to settle a price-fixing lawsuit.

Firms that have already been operating within an industry must also monitor industry regulations because they may change over time. For example, recent reductions of regulations in the banking industry have allowed banks more freedom to engage in other types of business. Some banks have attempted to capitalize on the change in regulations by offering new services.

Summary of Industry Characteristics

All of the industry characteristics just identified must be considered to determine their impact on a firm's performance. The means by which these characteristics affect a firm's profits are shown in Exhibit 5.2. Changes in industry demand and competition affect the demand for a firm's products and therefore affect its revenue. Since these industry characteristics influence the quantity of products that the firm produces, they also affect operating costs, such as manufacturing and administrative expenses. Any changes in the labor and regulatory environments typically affect a firm's expenses. The overall effect on profits is dependent on the impact each individual characteristic has on either the firm's revenue or expenses. The potential impact of industry demand and competition on a firm's performance can be confirmed by consulting any business periodical that discusses how a particular industry performed recently.

BUSINESS ONLINE

Detailed Industry Information

http://www.activemedia-guide .com/industry_profile_cp.htm

INTERNET PUBLICATIONS SUCH AS U.S. BUSINESS REPORTER PUBLISH A VARiety of industry information. For example, for each industry listed, trends, issues, characteristics, and the industry environment can be assessed. This information is highly useful to investors trying to make investment decisions, to customers considering purchase decisions, and to firms competing in a given industry.

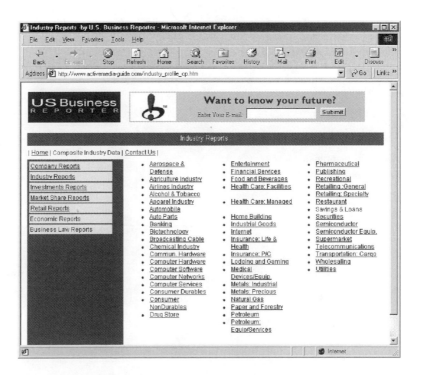

Exhibit 5.2

Industry Effects on a Firm's Performance

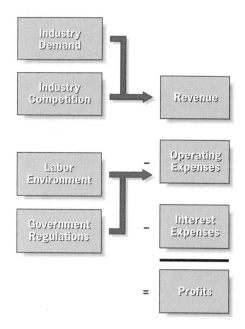

Industry Sources

Although a firm can attempt to monitor its industry's characteristics, it may also rely on other sources for industry information. The following sources provide useful information about the characteristics of each industry:

1 *Value Line* The Value Line Investment Survey provides valuable information about numerous publicly traded companies, including financial characteristics, forecasts of earnings, and general information about the respective industries.

2 *Standard and Poor's* The Standard and Poor's Industry Outlook provides industry data and assessments for several different industries. A firm can use this source to forecast the industry demand, competition, labor environment, and regulatory environment.

MANY COMPANIES SUCH AS INVESTORLINKS USE THE INTERNET TO PUBLISH industry analyses they perform. By clicking on a link, recent trends in a particular in-

BUSINESS ONLINE

Industry
Analysis

http://www.investorlinks.com/
industry/index-indus.html

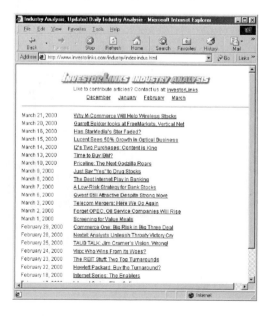

dustry and a discussion of their effect on the financial performance of companies in the industry are displayed. Examples of specific companies in each industry and how they are affected by these trends are also provided. Sites such as these are highly useful to investors, because industry characteristics, such as industry demand and competition, can significantly affect a firm's performance.

Exposure to Industry Conditions

② Explain why some firms are more exposed to industry conditions.

The exposure of a firm to a given industry's conditions is dependent on its particular characteristics. Some firms are more exposed to industry conditions, which means that their performance is affected more by those conditions. Two of the key characteristics that affect a firm's exposure to industry conditions are the firm's market share and the firm's focus on its main industry.

Firm's Market Share

The degree to which a firm is affected by a change in industry conditions is dependent on its market share, or its share of total sales in the industry (or market). A firm that controls a larger share of the market will normally benefit more from an increase in industry demand. For example, Hewlett-Packard benefits more than small firms from an increase in the demand for fax machines.

Firms that have the most market share, however, are also hurt more than smaller firms as a result of a decrease in industry demand. Exhibit 5.3 illustrates how firms with a larger market share are affected more by changes in industry demand. It assumes that an industry has just two firms: Firm X with 80 percent market share and Firm Y with 20 percent market share. In Year 1, total industry sales were equal to 10,000,000 units. In Year 2, however, total industry sales declined to 5,000,000 units. Assuming that each firm's market share remained unchanged, Firm X's sales declined by about 4,000,000 units whereas Firm Y's sales declined by about 1,000,000 units.

A firm does not have much control over the industry demand. Nevertheless, it may attempt to forecast industry demand, which may allow it to forecast the demand for its own product. For example, assume that a firm expects industry demand to equal 5,000,000 units over the next year. If its market share is 20 percent, its forecast of the demand for its product is as follows:

Exhibit 5.3

Influence of Market Share on Exposure to Industry Conditions

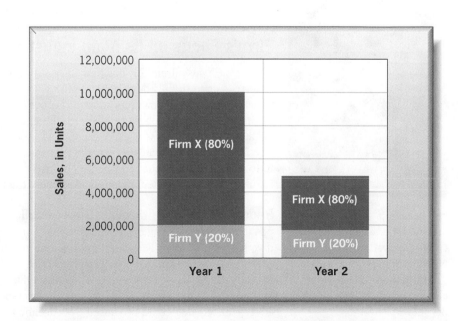

$$\begin{aligned}
\text{Demand for Firm's Product} &= \text{Firm's Market} \times \text{Industry} \\
&\qquad\quad \text{Share} \qquad\quad \text{Demand} \\
&= \quad 20\% \quad \times \ 5{,}000{,}000 \text{ units} \\
&= 1{,}000{,}000 \text{ units}
\end{aligned}$$

If changing conditions cause industry demand to decline, the forecasted demand for the firm's product should be revised. For example, if the forecasted industry demand from the previous example is revised to 4,000,000 units, the demand for the firm's product would be only 800,000 units (computed as 20% × 4,000,000 units).

BUSINESS ONLINE

Market Share Information

http://www.cctc.ca/ ncth/stats/industry/ ind-global-mktshr.html

INFORMATION ON COMPANIES' MARKET SHARES IN THEIR INDUSTRY IS AVAILable on the Internet, as illustrated here. Because a firm's exposure to industry conditions is contingent on the firm's market share in that industry, this information is highly useful to potential investors and customers.

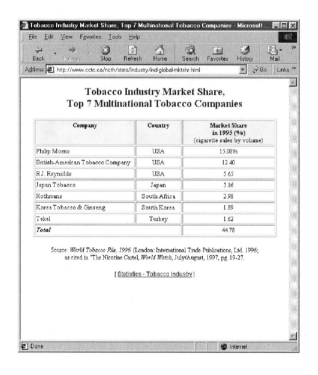

Tobacco Industry Market Share, Top 7 Multinational Tobacco Companies

Company	Country	Market Share in 1995 (%) (cigarette sales by volume)
Philip Morris	USA	15.08%
British-American Tobacco Company	USA	12.40
R.J. Reynolds	USA	5.65
Japan Tobacco	Japan	5.16
Rothmans	South Africa	2.98
Korea Tobacco & Ginseng	South Korea	1.89
Tekel	Turkey	1.62
Total		44.78

Source: *World Tobacco File, 1996* (London: International Trade Publications, Ltd. 1996; as cited in "The Nicotine Cartel, *World Watch*, July/August, 1997, pg. 19-27.

[Statistics - Tobacco Industry]

The Coca-Cola Company has been a world leader in diversifying into overseas markets. It is the leading seller of soft drinks in many countries including Prague, Czech Republic, shown above.

Firm's Focus on Its Main Industry

Firms that focus all of their business in one industry are generally more exposed to the industry's conditions. For example, Smith Corona Corporation, which focused its business on producing typewriters and word processors, was highly exposed to any changes in the total demand for these office machines. When the demand for these machines declined due to increased use of computers, Smith Corona filed for bankruptcy.

Exhibit 5.4 illustrates how changes in performance can vary substantially among industries. The aluminum and airlines industries weakened over the period, while other industries such as biotechnology and semiconductors strengthened.

Reducing Exposure through Diversification A firm may desire to reduce its exposure to the possibility of poor conditions in its respective industry. One solution is to diversify its businesses across several different industries. Consider a firm that does business in electronics and real estate development. If this firm anticipates a large decline in the demand for its real estate development services, it may adjust its operations to focus more on electronics and less on real estate development. In this way, it can reduce any adverse effects that could be caused by a decline in any particular industry. Ford Motor

Exhibit 5.4

Comparison of Performance across Industries

Note: Numbers reflect the mean percentage change in values of firms for each industry shown during January 2000.

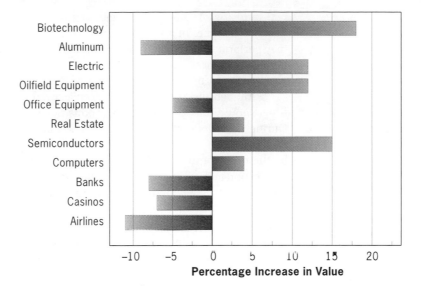

Exhibit 5.4

Comparison of Performance across Industries

Note: Numbers reflect the mean percentage change in values of firms for each industry shown during January 2000.

Company has diversified by producing a variety of trucks along with its cars. When demand for its cars is stagnant, it may still benefit from an increase in demand for trucks.

Seagrams Company traditionally focused on sales of alcoholic beverages, but its performance was adversely affected by the decline in demand for alcoholic drinks. It has responded by producing nonalcoholic beverages to reduce its risk of poor performance because of exposure to a single industry.

The following comments from a recent annual report by Textron (a large diversified firm) confirm the potential benefits of diversification:

> *Textron's presence in diverse industries helps achieve balance and stability in a variety of economic environments by providing insulation from business and industry cycles. More specifically, we were able to maintain consistent growth . . . because the growth of our Aircraft, Automotive, Industrial and Finance businesses more than offset the downturns in the Systems and Components segment.*

Exhibit 5.5 shows the average return on equity for two related industries and for a combination of those two industries. Notice how a diversified combination of the

Exhibit 5.5

How Diversification Can Influence the Return on Equity

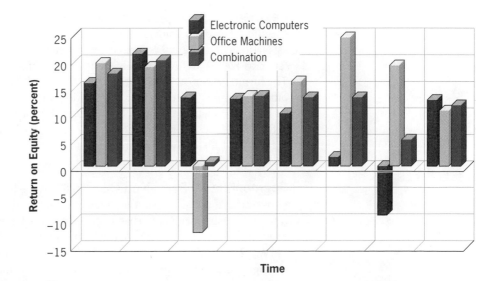

two industries creates a more stable return on investment than either individual industry over time. In a period when one industry performs poorly, the other industry may perform well. Exxon (now ExxonMobil) benefited from diversifying into the petrochemical businesses because the performance of its oil business was highly exposed to changes in the market price of crude oil.

Although diversification can effectively reduce a firm's exposure to one industry, firms should only diversify across industries in which they have sufficient expertise. During the 1980s, many firms diversified across industries completely unrelated to their expertise. Many of these unrelated businesses performed poorly and were sold by the firms during the 1990s. For example, Chrysler (now DaimlerChrysler) entered the corporate aircraft business, military defense business, and car rental business. It lost its focus by attempting to engage in too many different businesses and incurred higher expenses than expected. W. R. Grace (producer of chemicals) engaged in health care, coal mining, and numerous other businesses. It recently sold many of these businesses so that it could focus on its chemicals business.

Competing within an Industry

3 Explain how a firm can compete within its industry.

Intense competition can separate the performance of the well-managed firms from that of the poorly managed firms in an industry. When the airlines industry became more competitive, some of the poorly managed airlines failed. The well-managed airlines captured some of the market share lost by those that failed. Similarly, when the banking industry became more competitive and many commercial banks failed, the well-run commercial banks were able to capture some of the market share lost by those that failed.

Given the influence of industry competition on a firm's performance, a firm should perform two tasks:

▶ Assess the competitors.
▶ Develop a competitive advantage.

Assess the Competitors

segments subsets of a market that reflect a specific type of business and the perceived quality

Every firm should be able to identify its competitors and measure the degree of competition. Each industry has **segments,** or subsets that reflect a specific type of business and the perceived quality. Thus, an industry can be narrowly defined by segmenting the industry according to type of business and quality. Segmenting the industry in this way helps identify the main competitors so that they can be assessed.

Segmenting by Type of Business Within an industry, some firms may focus on specific types of customers. For example, in the car rental industry, some firms (such as National Car Rental Systems) focus heavily on business customers, while others (such as Hertz) are more evenly split between businesses and individuals on vacation. The furniture industry has segments such as outdoor furniture, bedroom furniture, and office furniture. The degree of competition within each segment may vary. There may be heavy competition in bedroom furniture but little competition in outdoor furniture. A firm that focuses only on the production of outdoor furniture is not concerned with the demand for office furniture. Therefore, it is helpful for a firm to narrowly define its industry before assessing the degree of competition.

Segmenting by Perceived Quality Once the firm defines its industry by the type of business, it should assess the different quality segments that exist. Exhibit 5.6 shows different quality segments (based on customer perceptions) in the market for small cars. Each type of car in this market is represented by a point. Some cars, such as the BMW 325 and the Corvette, are perceived to have high quality (measured according to engine size and other features that customers desire) and a relatively high price.

Exhibit 5.6

Identifying Industry Segments

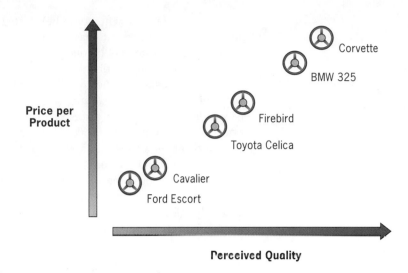

Other small cars have a moderate quality level and a lower price, such as the Toyota Celica and the Firebird. The Ford Escort and the Cavalier represent cars in a lower quality and price segment. Because each consumer focuses only on one particular market segment, the key competitors are within that same segment. For example, the Escort and Cavalier are competitors within the low-priced segment. The Escort is not viewed as a competitor to the higher-priced cars.

Many firms create products that are designed for different population segments. Firms commonly expand by producing different types of the same product, which are offered to various segments. General Motors produces the Cavalier for the low-priced, small-car segment, the Firebird for the moderate-priced segment, and the Corvette for the high-priced segment. A firm may produce a high-quality product for consumers who can afford to pay a high price and a low-quality product for consumers who are less concerned about quality and more concerned about price. Tire companies such as Goodyear and Michelin produce tires that fit the high-priced and low-priced segments. Beer producers such as Anheuser-Busch and Miller Brewing produce different types of beer to satisfy high-priced and low-priced segments. Most airlines provide first-class (high-priced) and coach (low-priced) seats to satisfy different segments.

Anticipating Changes in Competition The competitors within an industry segment change over time. New firms may enter the market; others that were in the market but were unsuccessful may exit. Many competing firms in the same market attempt to expand. It is not unusual for every firm competing within a specific industry segment to share the same goal of increasing market share. Yet, all competitors within an industry segment cannot increase their market share at the same time. When some competitors gain market share, other competitors lose.

As an illustration of how a firm assesses its competition, consider the following statements made by Amazon.com in a recent annual report:

“ The retail book market is extremely competitive. The Company's current or potential competitors include various online booksellers . . ., a number of indirect competitors that specialize in online commerce, . . . and publishers, distributors and retail vendors of books, music, and videotapes, including Barnes & Noble Inc. . . . The Company believes that the principal competitive factors in its market are . . . convenience, price, accessibility, customer service, quality . . . reliability, and speed of fulfillment. . . . The company believes that competition in the online commerce market will intensify in the future. ”

To understand how firms can be affected by changes in competition, consider the airline industry. In recent years, many new airlines began servicing specific routes. They attracted customers by offering low airfares. In response, some existing airlines reduced their airfares to discourage customers from switching to the new airlines. In general, the existing airlines were adversely affected by the new competition in two ways. First, their sales of airline tickets declined, as some customers switched to the new airlines. Second, the prices of many airline tickets were reduced to match the prices of new competitors. Both effects resulted in a decline in the revenue of the existing airlines, as well as a decline in their earnings. Recent annual reports by airlines, such as Delta Air Lines, confirm the adverse effects of increased competition.

Firms in various other industries have also acknowledged that they have been adversely affected by more intense competition. Kellogg Company has said that it was adversely affected by increased competition in the cereal industry. Federal Express claimed that its earnings were hurt by fierce competition in the express mail industry.

Develop a Competitive Advantage

Once a firm has identified and assessed its key competitors, it must search for ways to increase or at least maintain its market share. A firm must assess its specific industry segment to determine whether it has a competitive advantage. The following characteristics could create a competitive advantage for a firm:

▶ Low-cost production
▶ Better quality
▶ Product differentiation

Low-Cost Production If a firm can produce a product of similar quality at a lower cost, it could price the product lower than its competitors. This should enable that firm to attain a larger market share. For example, assume that a firm can produce high-quality outdoor furniture at a lower price than the other firms in the high-priced segment. This may allow the firm to charge a lower price so that it can capture a larger share of the high-priced outdoor furniture market. The low production cost may result from efficient management of its employees (human resources) and its production process.

The Gap has established a competitive advantage by delivering style, service, and value to customers of all ages.

Some firms attempt to achieve a price advantage even when they do not have a cost advantage. For example, an entrepreneur may notice that the only gas station in a populated area has set high prices on its gasoline. The entrepreneur may consider establishing a new gas station in the area, with lower prices as its competitive advantage. However, the existing gas station may lower its gas prices in response to the new competitor. In this example, the entrepreneur's competitive advantage may be eliminated unless it has a cost advantage.

Airlines commonly attempt to achieve a price advantage over their competitors by advertising special fares on various routes over a particular period. The objective is to attract a higher demand by pulling customers away from other airlines. In many cases, other airlines respond by lowering their airfares by the same amount. If some of the airlines are less efficient, however, they may not be able to continue the low fares for a long period of time (because their costs may exceed the fares charged). Thus, the more efficient firms may drive the inefficient competitors out of the industry.

Better Quality If a firm can produce a product of better quality without incurring excessive costs, it has a competitive advantage over other competitors in the same price range. For example, in the low-priced outdoor furniture market, one firm may be perceived to produce higher quality furniture than other firms. If its furniture is priced about the same as others in its segment, its superior quality creates a competitive advantage within the low-priced outdoor furniture segment.

Various characteristics may cause a product to be of better quality. It may be easier to use, may last longer, or may have better service. The specific characteristics that determine perceived quality vary among products. For soft drinks, quality may be measured by taste. For outdoor furniture, quality may be measured by durability. For computers, quality may be measured by ease of use, the service provided, and processing speed. By achieving higher quality, a firm can satisfy customers to a greater degree.

Product Differentiation Firms commonly attempt to identify particular needs of some customers so that they can differentiate their product (or service) to satisfy those needs. For example, some contact lenses are made for permanent wear. Other lenses

Competitive Advantage

Advances in information technology are changing many industries, including the retail grocery industry. A few firms in that industry are building competitive advantages through state-of-the-art technology.

Grocery stores have typically been labor-intensive. In the past, cashiers entered every item and inventory was taken manually. Most stores have converted to scanners, which reduce the time required to check out a customer and allow the store to keep the inventory electronically. The firms that committed to this technology early have prospered while others have lagged behind. Many other advances are occurring as the grocery industry goes through a transition.

Kroger Company is one of the firms that have adopted advanced self-scanning technology. Kroger introduced the system in mid-1998 and has been gradually expanding its

use. A major reason for the adoption of self-scanners has been a shortage of cashiers. With self-scanners, a store can open additional checkouts even when it is not adequately staffed. Customers come in waves to grocery stores, creating long lines at peak periods and overstaffing problems during nonpeak times. Self-scanning can help remedy this problem and lower costs.

Grocers and other retailers have also been using other advances in technology to create effective frequent-shopper programs. Customers of Schultz Sav-O are able to log on to a web page and access targeted discounts by entering their frequent-shopper account numbers. Sav-O customizes the discounts based on customer purchase histories. The system creates strong customer loyalty and enables the store to effectively evaluate its incentive program.

These are just a few examples of how information technology is changing the retail grocery industry. More recent developments include online shopping and delivery.

must be cleaned daily because some customers cannot wear lenses permanently. A third type of lens is disposable for those customers who are unable to keep the lenses clean and frequently need new lenses. Rarely can a particular product serve all customers, because customers desire different features in a given product.

Computer firms tend to differentiate their computers in ways that attract customers with specific preferences. Computers vary in power, size (some are portable), warranty, and service. They are also made to allow for replaceable components so that the product can precisely fit customers' needs.

Customer preferences for each particular type of service also vary, allowing firms in each service industry to differentiate their service. Some travel agencies specialize in cruise vacations. Others focus on international travel packages. The choice of a travel agent may be dependent on specific customer needs.

As time passes, customer preferences for a particular product's features can change. Firms must attempt to recognize these changes in the industry so that they can revise the products they offer. Failure to adapt can result in a reduction in the firm's market share. For several years, IBM conducted business without paying close attention to changes in industry conditions (such as a preference by many business customers for personal rather than mainframe computers). During that time, its annual report stated that "IBM failed to keep pace with a significant change in the industry." General Motors was also slow to react to changes in customer preferences in the automobile industry. These firms improved their performance once they recognized the importance of responding to changes in customer preferences.

Firms commonly use *SWOT analysis* to develop a competitive advantage. The acronym SWOT stands for strengths, weaknesses, opportunities, and threats. Thus, in SWOT analysis, the firm assesses its own strengths and weaknesses, as well as external opportunities and threats. For example, Amazon.com may consider its strengths to include the creativity of its employees and its ability to apply technology. Its weakness may be its lack of traditional retail outlets to sell books (although that is also a strength because Amazon.com can avoid intermediaries). Its opportunities may be the potential market for other related products (in addition to books) online and the potential growth in the demand for online services in foreign countries. Its threats may include

Industry Effects across Business Functions

Managers of a firm have different responsibilities and therefore assess different aspects of the industry environment. Production managers monitor changes in labor costs in a particular industry when anticipating how their production costs may change. They monitor changes in the industry's technology, because their production costs will be influenced by the level of technology. They also monitor regulatory changes in the industry that could require revisions to the production process. Such revisions may also affect the cost of production. They may also monitor the level of industry demand so that they can determine the proper volume of products that their firm should produce.

Marketing managers monitor new competitors in the industry to become aware of the features of competing products. The managers consider this industry information when they search for strategies to make their product superior to those sold by competitors. Marketing managers must obtain production cost information from production managers when deciding how to make their product superior.

Financial managers monitor the industry environment to determine how much money they can afford to borrow. If the competition in the industry is intense, the firm may lose its market share to other competitors. Therefore, a firm should limit its debt so that it is capable of covering future interest payments on that debt. Financial managers should obtain information from the marketing managers about the intensity of competition in the industry so that they can determine the amount of funds that will be available (from sales) to cover future interest payments.

In general, the industry environment can affect a firm's production, marketing, and finance functions in different ways. The overall assessment of potential industry effects requires input from each function.

specific competitors that are creating similar online book businesses that provide the same type of services for consumers. SWOT analysis can help direct a firm's future business by using the firm's strengths to capitalize on opportunities, while reducing its exposure to threats. For example, if Amazon.com believes that one of its strengths is its technology, it may attempt to improve that technology to make its direct sales of books to customers even more convenient. Thus, even if competitors attempt to copy its existing business, Amazon.com will have advanced technology that allows it to offer better service than the competitors.

GLOBAL BUSINESS

Assessing the Industry Environment from a Global Perspective

WHEN U.S. FIRMS ENGAGE IN INTERNATIONAL BUSINESS, THEY MUST CONsider the segments within the foreign countries of concern. A specific product that is classified in a specific segment in the United States may be classified in a different segment in other countries. A product that is perceived as an inexpensive necessity in the United States may be perceived as an expensive luxury product in less-developed countries. U.S. firms may revise the quality and price of their products to satisfy a particular market segment. For example, Procter & Gamble produces a wide variety of household products that U.S. consumers may view as basic necessities. Yet, those products are not affordable to consumers in some less-developed countries. Rather than ignore those countries, Procter & Gamble has revised its product and pricing strategies to fit the country of concern. As stated in a recent annual report: "In some countries where incomes are low, striking this balance between quality and price requires us to market a diaper that offers more basic features, at a substantially lower price, than the premium diaper we sell in many countries." This example illustrates how a firm's assessment of market segment can vary across countries and therefore how its product and pricing strategies may be revised in accordance with each foreign country's characteristics.

BUSINESS DILEMMA | **College Health Club**

Industry Effects on College Health Club

SUE KRAMER, OWNER OF COLLEGE HEALTH CLUB (CHC), IS ASSESSING THE expected earnings of CHC. She expects that the two main industry characteristics that will affect CHC's future earnings are industry demand and industry competition, so she summarizes her view of these two characteristics.

Industry Demand
The industry demand for health club services will continue to rise as people continue to focus on health and fitness. Sue is concerned about industry demand only within the local area, since the only potential customers live or work within thirty miles of CHC.

Industry Competition
Currently, CHC has two competitors. One competitor is about thirty miles away. It has prices similar to those of CHC but offers only weight room facilities (no aerobics classes). The other competitor is a few miles from CHC but has not focused on college students. It has more facilities, but its annual membership fees are much higher than those of CHC.

Sue carefully assessed these two competitors when she opened her health club across from the local college campus. The fact that no club was accommodating the college students motivated her to establish CHC. In the few months since its opening, CHC has been successful in attracting students. Sue still expects to achieve her initial goal of three hundred memberships in the first year, at an annual membership fee of $250.

Dilemma

Sue's main concern is that new competitors will be established and will pull away some of her customers. She expects that if a new competitor is established near the college campus, CHC may bring in only about two hundred annual memberships over the first year (assuming she does not lower CHC's membership fee). CHC's expenses (such as the lease expense and the equipment) would not be affected by the number of memberships. Sue wants to forecast how CHC's performance (specifically earnings) would be affected if a new competitor enters the industry. She also wants to forecast CHC's performance if she lowers the annual membership fee (to existing and potential members) to $200 as a way of competing against any new competitors. At such a low fee, Sue believes that CHC would attract 240 memberships even if a new competitor did enter the industry.

Estimate the first year's revenue, total expenses, and earnings of CHC under Situation 1 (no new competition), Situation 2 (new competition and no change in CHC's membership fee), and Situation 3 (new competition and a reduction in CHC's membership fee).

Solution

Since CHC's expenses are generally fixed regardless of the quantity of memberships, Sue focuses on how CHC's revenue would be affected by competition. Yet, to show how the profits would be affected, the forecasted operating expenses (of $90,000) and interest expenses (of $6,000) are also shown in Exhibit 5.7 (these estimates were initially developed in Chapter 1).

Based on the information provided, the expected impact on CHC's performance over its first year is shown in Exhibit 5.7. Situation 1 reflects the existing situation, in which no new competitors enter the industry. Situation 2 reflects the entrance of a new competitor, resulting in only two hundred memberships for CHC. This results in revenue of $50,000, which is $25,000 less than Sue originally anticipated. Situation 3 reflects a lower membership price for CHC as a means of battling the new competition. This strategy can reduce the adverse effect of new competition on CHC memberships. However, it also means that CHC will receive less revenue from each member. Given Sue's expectations of 240 annual memberships at a membership price of $200, CHC's revenue would be $48,000.

Based on her assessment, Sue decides that she will not lower the membership price even if a new competitor does enter the industry. However, she recognizes that she may need to differentiate CHC's services in various ways to compete with any new competitors. CHC may incur some additional expenses when differentiating its services.

Exhibit 5.7 Assessment of Profits of CHC under Three Different Situations

	Situation 1: No New Competition	Situation 2: New Competition and No Change in Membership Fee	Situation 3: New Competition and a Reduced Membership Fee
Price of membership	$250	$250	$200
× Quantity of memberships	× 300	× 200	× 240
= Revenue	= $75,000	= $50,000	= $48,000
− Operating expenses	− $90,000	− $90,000	− $90,000
− Interest expenses	− $ 6,000	− $ 6,000	− $ 6,000
= Earnings	= − $21,000	= − $46,000	= − $48,000

Additional Issues for Discussion

1 Explain how the increased popularity of exercise videos and portable weight machines could affect CHC's earnings.

2 How could Sue Kramer differentiate her services to maintain her customers (mostly college students) even if a new competitor enters the market?

3 Like other industries, the health club industry has segments that reflect a specific type of business and quality. Describe the characteristics of CHC that appeal to college students.

SUMMARY

 The main industry characteristics that influence business performance are:

▶ industry demand,
▶ industry competition,
▶ labor environment, and
▶ regulatory environment.

Industry demand and the degree of industry competition affect the demand for a firm's products or services and therefore affect the firm's revenue. The labor and regulatory environments typically affect the firm's expenses. Since a firm's prof-

its equal its revenue minus its expenses, its profits are influenced by these industry factors.

 A firm is more exposed to an industry's conditions when it has a large market share and focuses most of its business within that industry. As the industry's conditions change, most of the firm's business will be affected. Firms can reduce their exposure to industry conditions by diversifying their business across industries.

3 A firm can battle the competition by assessing its main competitors and then attempting to develop a competitive advantage. To identify its main competitors, it must recognize the segment of the industry that it serves. It can develop a competitive advantage within that industry segment through efficient production (which allows it to charge a lower price), better quality, or product differentiation.

KEY TERMS

industry demand   *119*

market share   *121*

segments   *128*

REVIEW QUESTIONS

1 Identify and explain the main characteristics of the automobile industry that influence business performance.

2 Explain why the cost of labor is so much higher in some industries (such as the health-care industry).

3 What outside resources are available that would enable a firm to monitor the industry in which it operates?

4 Discuss what happens to a firm that has a large market share in an industry in which demand suddenly increases.

5 When a firm is subject to less competition in an industry, why is it typically more profitable?

6 Identify the tasks a firm should complete before deciding to compete in a specific industry.

7 Give some examples of how

firms can be affected by changes in competition.

8 List some characteristics that could create a competitive advantage for a firm.

9 Explain the production manager's responsibility in assessing the industry environment.

10 Distinguish between the responsibilities of a marketing manager and a financial manager in monitoring a particular industry.

DISCUSSION QUESTIONS

1 Do you believe business enterprise should be regulated by the federal government or should the marketplace determine price? Discuss.

2 A group is discussing how competitive forces must be preserved at all costs within the marketplace of a free enterprise system. What are your views?

3 How could a firm use the Internet to determine how its competitors are performing and how they are affected by industry conditions?

4 Assume that you are a production manager in the automobile industry. Should your operation be labor intensive or capital (machinery) intensive? Discuss.

5 Consider a car that was typically classified in the low-price segment. Yet, it has been unable to compete there because it is priced higher than the other cars in that segment. What alternative strategies are possible for the car as it is redesigned for the next year?

INVESTING IN THE STOCK OF A BUSINESS

Using the annual report of the firm in which you would like to invest, complete the following:

1 Describe the competition within your firm's industry. If the annual report does not contain information, try to find a magazine or newspaper article that discusses the competitive environment within your firm's industry. How successful is your firm compared with its competitors?

2 Was your firm's performance affected by industry conditions last year? If so, how?

3 Explain how the business uses technology to assess its industry environment. For example, does it use the Internet to assess the industry environment? Does it use the Internet to assess the performance of its competitors?

4 Go to **http://hoovers.com** and locate the NEWS SEARCH. Type in the name of the firm in the space provided, and review the recent news stories about the firm. Summarize any (at least one) recent news story about the firm that applies to one or more of the key concepts within this chapter.

CASE IMPACT OF INDUSTRY CONDITIONS

Phoenix Shoes has recently established a shoe store that sells high-quality, high-priced shoes to customers of all ages. Its main source of revenue, however, is from the sale of children's shoes. Its store is located in a large shopping mall. The store has been very successful in the year that it has been open. However, Stephanie Scheck, the owner of Phoenix Shoes, is worried about the following industry conditions.

First, she is concerned that the general demand for high-quality shoes could decline because parents may not be so willing to purchase high-quality shoes for children who quickly grow out of them. She is also concerned because published surveys suggest a preference by parents toward casual footwear for their children. Phoenix has focused on formal footwear.

Second, Stephanie is concerned about a new competitor shoe business at the other end of the mall that sells relatively low-quality shoes at low prices.

Third, Stephanie is concerned about another new competitor shoe business that sells high-quality shoes online through its website. The quality of these shoes is similar to that of Phoenix's shoes, but they are priced at 10 percent less.

Stephanie recognizes that the store's future performance is influenced by industry conditions that affect the general demand for its products, as well as its market share within its industry. She wants to assess how Phoenix might be affected by the recent industry conditions and how it can protect its market share.

QUESTIONS

1 How can Stephanie Scheck attempt to protect Phoenix's market share, given the recent preference for more casual footwear?

2 Will the demand for shoes at Phoenix be affected by the new shoe business at the other end of the shopping mall? If so, how can it protect its market share?

3 Will the demand for shoes at Phoenix be affected by the new online shoe business? If so, how can Phoenix protect its market share?

4 Is there any way that Phoenix could expand its product line to increase its revenue?

VIDEO CASE   WORLD GYM'S POSITION IN THE FITNESS INDUSTRY

World Gym Showplace Square in San Francisco was created to serve customers that prefer to be in between the high-end (luxury fitness centers) and the low-end fitness centers. Its facilities were established in a busy area where many people work. There was a strong demand for fitness facilities in the area, but little competition. The World Gym set a price that was lower than their competitors. In this way, it encouraged customers to try its services. The membership increased from 500 to 2,500 in the first year, and now is about 8,000. As new competitors (such as Gold's Gym) entered the market, World Gym responded by improving its facilities and lowering

prices. Thus, it encouraged its customers to continue their membership rather than switching to other fitness facilities.

QUESTIONS

1. Explain how the World Gym is focused on a specific market segment.
2. Explain how the World Gym used pricing to attract demand.
3. Why do you think the World Gym responded with lower prices and improved facilities when new competitors entered the area?

INTERNET APPLICATIONS

http://www.activemedia-guide.com/industry_profile_cp.htm

Click on an industry of your choice, such as "Entertainment." What is the industry environment of this industry? What are some of the issues firms operating in this industry face, and what are some of the industry trends?

Describe any international aspects of the industry. What type of firm do you think would be highly exposed to industry conditions? Why? What type of firm do you think would be able to compete successfully within this industry? Why?

THE Coca-Cola COMPANY ANNUAL REPORT PROJECT

Questions for the current year's annual report are available on the text website at **http://madura_intro_bus.swcollege.com.**

The following questions apply concepts learned in this chapter to The Coca-Cola Company. Go to The Coca-Cola Company website (**http://www.cocacola.com**) and find the index for the 1999 annual report.

QUESTIONS

1. Look at "Selected Market Results." How does The Coca-Cola Company's average annual five-year growth rate in U.S. unit case volume compare with the rest of the industry?
2. Study the "Worldwide Unit Case Volume" section. Do you think The Coca-Cola Company's competition varies by specific products (Coca-Cola, Sprite, Minute Maid, etc.) that it sells? Do you think The Coca-Cola Company views tap water as a major competitor? Why?

3. Look at "Selected Market Results."
   a. What is The Coca-Cola Company's current market share of sales for nonalcoholic ready-to-drink beverages on a worldwide basis?
   b. What is its market share of the nonalcoholic ready-to-drink beverages in Mexico? In China? In Germany?
4. Look at "Selected Market Results." By how much did the increase in The Coca-Cola Company's Great Britain unit case volume exceed the growth of the Great Britain soft drink industry?
5. Go to **http://hoovers.com** and locate the NEWS SEARCH. Type in The Coca-Cola Company in the space provided, and review the recent news stories about the firm. Summarize any (at least one) recent news story about The Coca-Cola Company that applies one or more of the key concepts within this chapter of the text.

IN-TEXT STUDY GUIDE

Answers are in an appendix at the back of the book.

TRUE OR FALSE

1. Total revenue is dependent on the quantity of units sold and the expenses of producing those units.

2. A firm that faces a high degree of competition can sell a low-quality product at a high price and therefore generate a high level of profit.
3. The cost of labor is high in industries that require specialized skills.

4 Firms that focus all of their business in one industry are generally less exposed to the industry's conditions.

5 All industries are subject to some form of government regulation.

6 Typically, a firm will have less control over its market share than over the total industry's demand.

7 Diversification can reduce a firm's exposure to poor performance in a particular industry.

8 Market share refers to an individual firm's sales expressed as a proportion of the total industry sales.

9 Improved product quality could create a competitive advantage for a firm.

10 A firm can safely conclude that it will perform well over the next year if there are favorable economic conditions in the United States.

MULTIPLE CHOICE

11 Managers will monitor changes in labor costs in order to control:
a) marketing costs.
d) social responsibility.
b) macroeconomics.
e) industry demand.
c) production costs.

12 The performance of a firm can be highly dependent on the following industry characteristics except for:
a) regulatory environment.
b) labor environment.
c) industry competition.
d) industry demand.
e) gross domestic product.

13 During the 1980s, many firms diversified across industries completely unrelated to their:
a) business ethics.
b) expertise.
c) management styles.
d) social responsibility.
e) goal of high performance.

14 Intense competition within an industry will likely _____ the performance of well-managed firms while the performance of poorly managed firms will likely _____.
a) stabilize; improve
d) decrease; improve
b) improve; suffer
e) harm; suffer
c) improve; improve

15 Total revenue is the result of multiplying the selling price of the product times the:
a) quantity of units sold.
b) quantity of units produced.
c) quantity of labor hours used.
d) quality demanded by consumers.
e) quantity of government regulations.

16 Over a given time period, a specific industry with strong total demand can perform better than industries experiencing relatively weak demand. This performance difference is due to differences in:
a) industry supply.
d) industry demand.
b) market share.
e) industry condition.
c) equilibrium price.

17 Labor costs are often higher in industries that have:
a) labor unions.
d) demand schedules.
b) unemployment.
e) interest expense.
c) savings.

18 Industry demand is commonly affected by changes in consumer preferences and:
a) consumer ethics.
b) consumer income levels.
c) labor supply schedules.
d) activity level of labor unions.
e) production technology advancements.

19 According to the text, industry regulations have recently been reduced in the:
a) automobile industry.
d) banking industry.
b) chemical industry.
e) steel industry.
c) oil industry.

20 Monitoring changes in market tastes and preferences can enable a firm to stay in touch with changes in consumer demands. This strategy will enable a firm to maintain or improve its:
a) technology schedule.
b) social responsibility.
c) business ethics.
d) market share.
e) equilibrium salary schedule.

21 When monitoring changes in industry characteristics, managers will focus on all of the following except:
a) industry demand.
b) gross domestic product.
c) technology.
d) labor costs.
e) regulatory changes.

22 A firm's share of total sales in the industry is measured by its:
a) industry demand.
b) regulatory environment.
c) market share.
d) competition.
e) employee turnover.

23 The demand for a firm's product equals the firm's market share times:
a) industry demand.
b) gross national product.
c) gross domestic product.
d) inflation rate.
e) unemployment rate.

24 Even if a firm does not have a cost advantage, it may still create a(n):
a) inflation advantage.
b) condition advantage.

c) monopoly advantage. e) ethics advantage.
d) price advantage.

25 Once a firm has identified and assessed its key competitors, it must search for ways to increase or at least maintain its:
a) labor environment.
b) regulatory environment.
c) market share.
d) competition.
e) social costs.

26 After a firm identifies a specific industry, it can segment that industry by:
a) level of employees.   d) conservationism.
b) scrap reworked.   e) quality segments.
c) labor environment.

27 An industry characteristic that influences business performance is:
a) social responsibility.
b) competition.
c) machinery.
d) inflation throughout the United States.
e) gross domestic product.

28 As industry demand changes, so does the _____ of firms in the industry.
a) performance
b) business ethics
c) consumerism
d) conservationism
e) regulatory environment

29 Another name for subsets in an industry that reflect a specific type of business and the perceived quality is:
a) demographics.   d) segments.
b) marketing.   e) economics.
c) sales.

30 A firm must assess its specific industry segment to determine whether it has a(n):
a) forecast.
b) competitive advantage.
c) industry condition.
d) cost differential.
e) shift in supply.

31 A firm can charge a higher price without losing its customers if it does not have much:
a) production.   d) advertising.
b) competition.   e) industry demand.
c) marketing.

32 To reduce its exposure to the possibility of poor conditions in its respective industry, a firm needs to:
a) diversify.   d) commercialize.
b) socialize.   e) increase its size.
c) privatize.

33 Changes in industry demand and competition affect both the demand for a firm's products and the firm's:
a) location.   d) recycling.
b) customer service.   e) segmentation.
c) revenue.

34 Two of the key characteristics that affect a firm's exposure to industry conditions are the firm's market share and the firm's focus on its:
a) recycling.   d) fringe market.
b) downsizing.   e) labor union.
c) main industry.

35 A firm may attempt to conduct an industry forecast; however, it does not have much control over:
a) revenue.
b) production costs.
c) production schedules.
d) industry demand.
e) employee hiring.

The Learning	**1**	Explain why U.S. firms engage in international business.
Goals of this	**2**	Describe how firms conduct international business.
chapter are to:	**3**	Explain how foreign characteristics can influence a firm's international business.
	4	Explain how exchange rate movements can affect a firm's performance.

Global Environment

Many U.S. firms have capitalized on opportunities in foreign countries by engaging in international business. The amount of international business has grown in response to the removal of various international barriers. Even small U.S. firms are now engaging in international business by purchasing foreign supplies or by selling their products in foreign countries.

International economic conditions affect a firm's revenue and expenses and therefore affect its value.

To illustrate how international economic conditions can affect the value of a business, consider the case of The Coca-Cola Company, which generates more than two-thirds of its revenue in foreign countries. In what ways can The Coca-Cola Company attempt to expand its business in China? What characteristics of China could influence the company's decision to expand there? How will The Coca-Cola Company's performance in China be affected by changes in the value of Chinese currency (the renminbi)? This chapter provides a background on the international environment that can be used to address these questions.

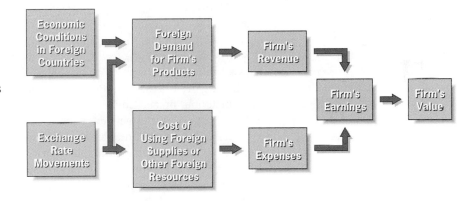

Why Firms Engage in International Business

1 Explain why U.S. firms engage in international business.

A firm may have several possible motives for engaging in international business. The following are some of the more common motives:

▶ Attract foreign demand
▶ Capitalize on technology
▶ Use inexpensive resources
▶ Diversify internationally

Attract Foreign Demand

Some firms are unable to increase their market share in the United States because of intense competition within their industry. Alternatively, the U.S. demand for the

A boy rides his bike past a Pizza Hut van in Moscow. Russian streets are cluttered with English billboards, store shelves are glutted with foreign products, but a backlash seems to be welling up—the Russian equivalent of the English-only movement in the United States and the Francophone movements in France and Canada.

firm's product may decrease because of changes in consumer tastes. Under either of these conditions, a firm might consider foreign markets where potential demand may exist. Many firms, including DuPont, IBM, and PepsiCo, have successfully entered new foreign markets to attract new sources of demand. Wal-Mart Stores recently opened stores in numerous countries, including Mexico and Hong Kong. Boeing (a U.S. producer of aircraft) recently received orders for jets from China Xinjiang Airlines and Kenya Airways.

During the 1990s, Avon Products opened branches in twenty-six different countries, including Brazil, China, and Poland. McDonald's is now in more than eighty different countries and generates more than half of its total revenue from foreign countries. Blockbuster Entertainment has more than two hundred stores in Asia and plans to have about one thousand by the early 2000s. Hertz has set a goal to increase sales by expanding its agencies in Europe and in other foreign markets. Amazon.com plans to expand its business by offering its services in many foreign countries.

Exhibit 6.1 shows how The Coca-Cola Company's business has expanded globally over time. Now the company has a significant presence in almost every country. It expanded throughout Latin America, Western Europe, Australia, and most of Africa before 1984. Since then, it has expanded into Eastern Europe and most of Asia.

Capitalize on Technology

Many U.S. firms have established new businesses in the so-called less-developed countries (such as those in Latin America), which have relatively low technology. AT&T and other firms have established new telecommunications systems in less-developed countries. Other U.S. firms that create power generation, road systems, and other forms of infrastructure have extensive business in these countries. Ford Motor Company and General Motors have attempted to capitalize on their technological advantages by establishing plants in less-developed countries throughout Asia, Latin America, and Eastern Europe. IBM is doing business with the Chinese government to capitalize on its

Exhibit 6.1   The Coca-Cola Company's Global Expansion

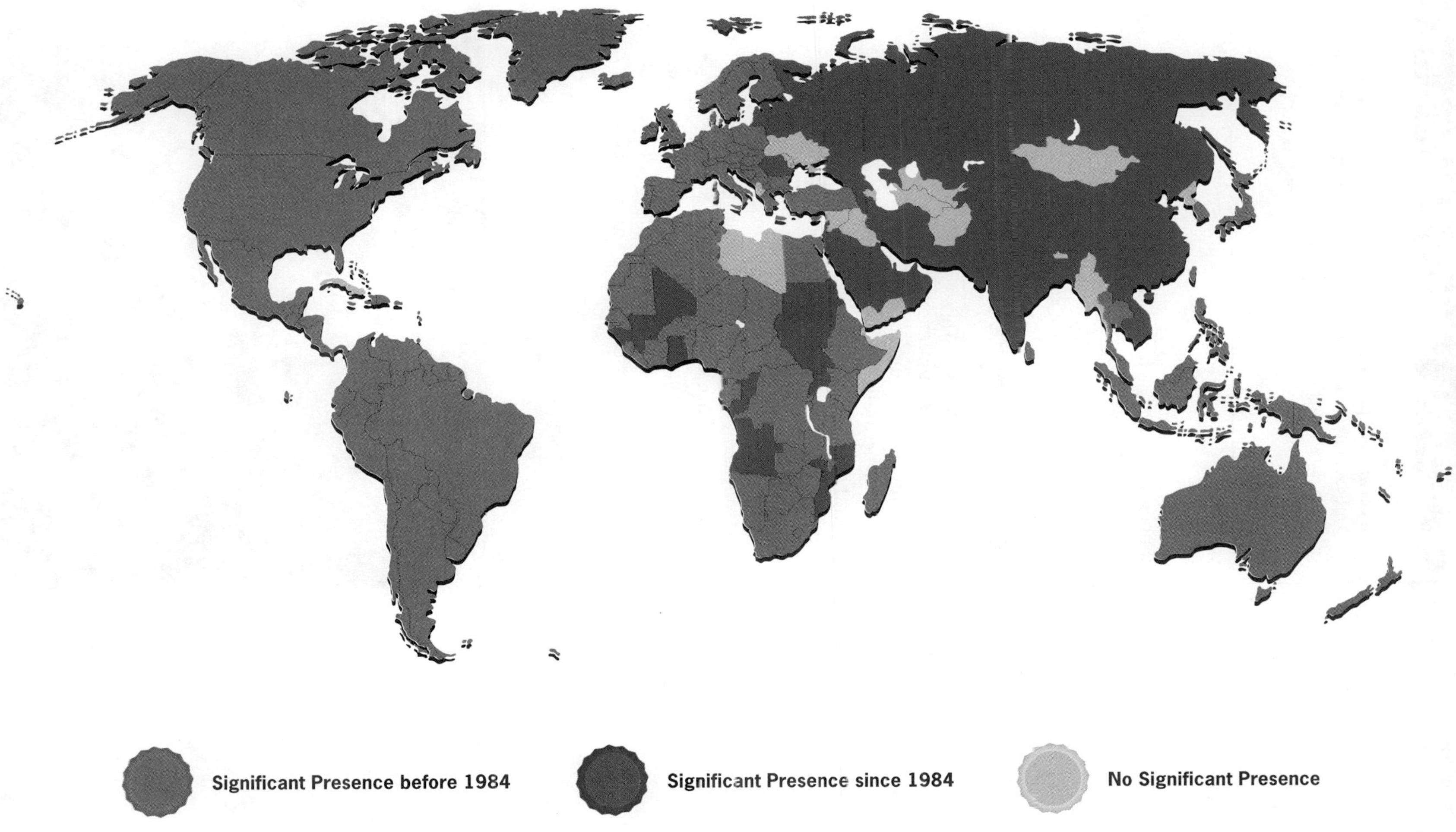

Significant Presence before 1984

Significant Presence since 1984

No Significant Presence

DELL® COMPUTER'S FORMULA FOR SUCCESS

Dell Computer's physical expansion is not limited to the United States. For example, Dell recently acquired a manufacturing plant in Ireland. Furthermore, Dell will soon open an integrated customer center and production facility in China. Doing business around the world allows Dell to give customers consistent product quality and services wherever they are needed.

---

technology. Amazon.com can capitalize on its technology advantage by expanding in foreign countries where technology is not as advanced.

Use Inexpensive Resources

Labor and land costs can vary significantly among countries. Firms often attempt to set up production at a location where land and labor are inexpensive. Exhibit 6.2 illustrates how hourly compensation (labor) costs can vary among countries. The costs are much higher in the developed countries (such as the United States and Germany) than in other countries (such as Mexico or Taiwan). Numerous U.S. firms have established subsidiaries in countries where labor costs are low. For example, Converse has shoes manufactured in Mexico. Dell Computer has disk drives and monitors produced in Asia. General Electric, Motorola, Texas Instruments, Dow Chemical, and Corning have established production plants in Singapore and Taiwan to take advantage of lower labor costs. Many firms from the United States and Western Europe have also developed plants in Hungary, Poland, and other parts of Eastern Europe, where labor costs are lower. General Motors pays its assembly-line workers in Mexico about $10 per day (including benefits) versus about $220 per day for its assembly-line workers in the United States.

Many U.S. firms, such as Reebok, have established subsidiaries in Asia to capitalize on low-cost labor for producing their products.

Exhibit 6.2   Approximate Hourly Compensation Costs for Manufacturing across Countries

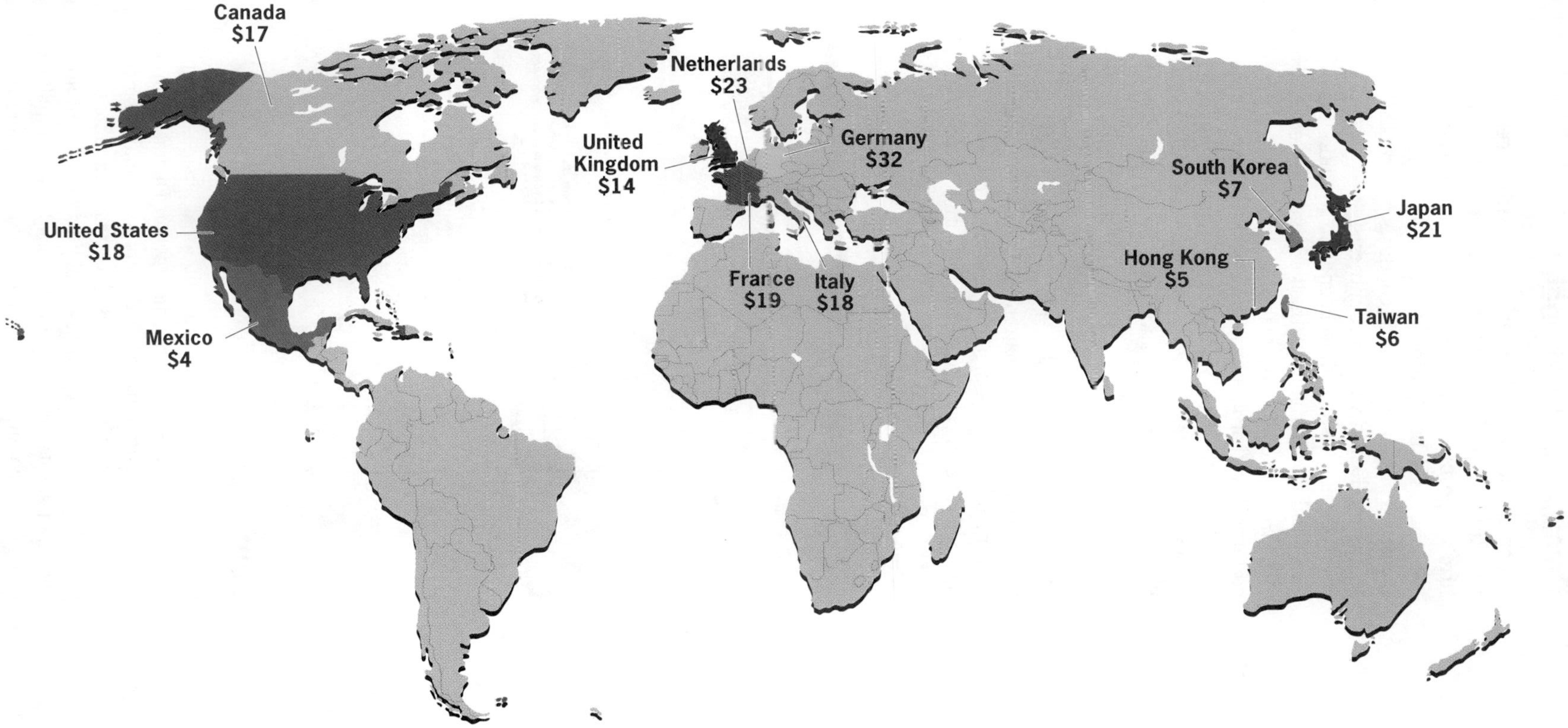

Japan
$21

Taiwan
$6

South Korea
$7

Hong Kong
$5

Germany
$32

Italy $18

Netherlands
$23

France
$19

United
Kingdom
$14

Canada
$17

United States
$18

Mexico
$4

Diversify Internationally

When all the assets of a firm are designed to generate sales of a specific product in one country, the profits of the firm are normally unstable. This instability is due to the firm's exposure to changes within its industry or within the economy. The firm's performance is dependent on the demand for this one product and on the conditions of the one economy in which it conducts business. The firm can reduce such risk by selling its product in various countries.

Exhibit 6.3 shows how economic conditions can vary among countries. U.S. firms that conduct international business are affected less by U.S. economic conditions. A U.S. firm's overall performance may be more stable if its product is sold in various countries, so that its business is not solely influenced by the economic conditions in a single country. For example, the demand for PepsiCo's products in Mexico might decline if the Mexican economy is weak, but at the same time economic growth in Brazil, the Netherlands, and Spain might result in a higher overall demand for PepsiCo's products.

BUSINESS ONLINE

International Corporate Information

http://www.blockbuster.com/ co/index.jhtml

MANY COMPANIES, SUCH AS BLOCKBUSTER ENTERTAINMENT, USE THE INternet to provide information on their recent international expansions. The information includes the reasons for the expansion, such as increasing market share or international diversification. Such information is useful to investors, who try to assess the level of market share, and to customers, who are looking for quality service domestically and internationally.

Combination of Motives

Many U.S. firms engage in international business because of a combination of the motives just described. For example, when Digital Equipment Corporation (subsidiary of Compaq Corporation) engaged in international business, it attracted new demand from customers in foreign countries. Second, it was able to capitalize on its technology, since local firms in these countries did not have its technology. Third, it was able to use low-cost land and labor in some countries in Asia. Finally, it was able to diversify its business among countries. It also reduced its exposure to U.S. economic conditions by increasing its international business over time.

General Electric has also expanded internationally in recent years. As Exhibit 6.4 shows, General Electric has substantial business in Europe. Its sales have also increased

Exhibit 6.3   Ratings of Economic Conditions among Countries

Note: The highest rating is 10.

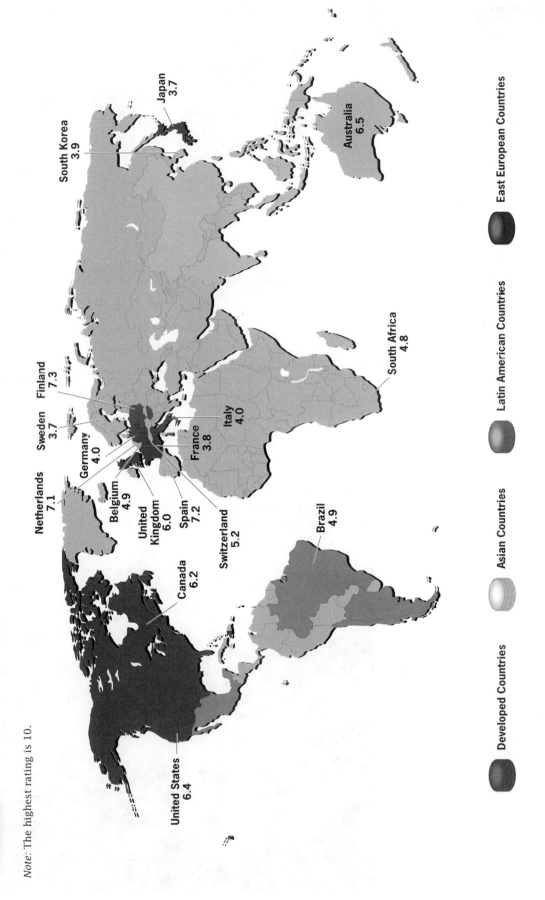

Exhibit 6.4

General Electric's International
Expansion

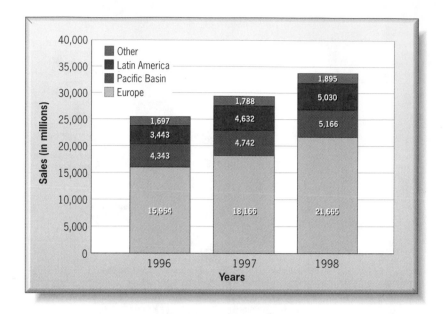

in Latin America and the Pacific Basin. Wal-Mart is another example of a firm that has been motivated by the reasons just described to expand into foreign countries. Its foreign expansion has resulted in a substantial improvement in its sales and its value (as measured by its stock price), as shown in Exhibit 6.5.

Foreign Expansion in the United States

Just as U.S. firms have expanded into foreign countries, foreign firms have expanded into the United States. Some foreign firms have established new subsidiaries (or branches) in the United States, such as Toyota (expanded its Kentucky plant), Mitsubishi Materials (built a silicon plant in Oregon), and Honda (expanded its Ohio

Wal-Mart has expanded in foreign markets to attract foreign demand and to diversify its business among countries.

Exhibit 6.5

Impact of International Expansion on Wal-Mart's Stock Price

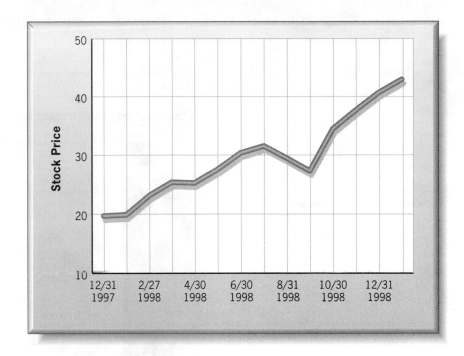

plant). Other foreign firms such as Sony have acquired firms in the United States. Many foreign firms have spent hundreds of millions of dollars to develop or expand their U.S. businesses. Since foreign firms have expanded into the United States, even those U.S. firms that only sell their products domestically are subject to foreign competition.

Foreign Competition

Most industries in the United States are susceptible to foreign competition. Some foreign firms control a significant share of the U.S. market for the following reasons. Some countries, such as China, Mexico, and Thailand, have extremely low labor costs. The production costs of foreign firms in these countries can be especially low for labor-intensive industries, such as clothing. Competing in these industries is difficult for U.S. firms because the production expenses are higher in the United States.

A second reason why foreign firms are successful in the United States is that some foreign-made products may be perceived as having higher quality than U.S.-made products. For example, many U.S. consumers considered Japanese automobiles to be of higher quality than U.S. automobiles. Although this general perception of the automobile industry has changed, some foreign products (such as furniture, watches, and wine) are still considered more desirable because of a quality perception.

In some industries, such as the automobile, camera, and clothing industries, many foreign firms offer their products in the United States. The U.S. firms in these industries must compete against the foreign firms for the U.S. market share. In industries that do not have much foreign competition, the U.S. firms compete only among themselves. For example, service industries such as accounting and hairstyling normally are not exposed to much foreign competition because foreign firms cannot easily offer these services.

BUSINESS ONLINE

Foreign Competition in the United States

http://www.daimlerchrysler.com /homepage/homepage_e.htm

SOME FOREIGN COMPANIES, SUCH AS DAIMLER, PENETRATE THE U.S. MARket via direct foreign investment. For Daimler, this direct investment took the form of a merger with Chrysler. Such companies then use the Internet to provide useful information about corporate operations and events in both countries to customers and investors in both countries.

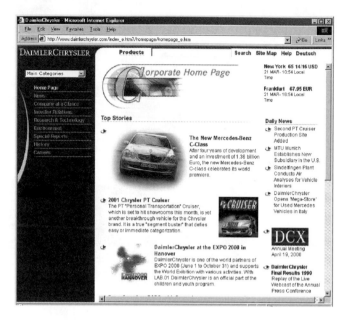

How Firms Conduct International Business

2 Describe how firms conduct international business.

Firms engage in various types of international business. Some of the more popular types are:

▶ Importing
▶ Exporting
▶ Direct foreign investment (DFI)
▶ Strategic alliances

Importing

importing the purchase of foreign products or services

Importing involves the purchase of foreign products or services. For example, some U.S. consumers purchase foreign automobiles, clothing, cameras, and other products from firms in foreign countries. Many U.S. firms import materials or supplies that are used to produce products. Even if these firms sell the products locally, they can benefit from international business. They import foreign supplies that are less expensive or of a higher quality than alternative U.S. supplies.

tariff a tax on imported products

Factors That Influence the Degree of Importing The degree to which a firm imports supplies is influenced by government trade barriers. Governments can impose a **tariff** (or tax) on imported products. The tax is normally paid directly by the importer, who typically passes the tax on to consumers by charging a higher price for the product. Thus, the product may be overpriced compared with products produced by firms based in that country. When foreign governments impose tariffs, the ability of foreign firms to compete in those countries is restricted.

quota a limit on the amounts of specific products that can be imported

Governments can also impose a **quota** on imported products, which limits the amounts of specific products that can be imported. This type of trade barrier may be even more restrictive than a tariff because it places an explicit limit on the amount of a specific product that can be imported.

Many large products are exported out of the United States by ship. Shown here is a port in Seattle.

In general, trade barriers tend to both discourage trade and protect specific industries from foreign competition. In recent years, however, many trade barriers have been removed. In 1993, the North American Free Trade Agreement (NAFTA) was passed, which removed many restrictions on trade between Canada, Mexico, and the United States. Consequently, U.S. firms are more capable of expanding their businesses in Canada and Mexico. At the same time, however, they are also more exposed to competition from foreign firms within the United States. Since NAFTA, other trade agreements have also occurred among the European countries and among countries in Southeast Asia.

Exporting

exporting the sale of products or services (called exports) to purchasers residing in other countries

Exporting is the sale of products or services (called exports) to purchasers residing in other countries. Many firms, such as DuPont, Kodak, Intel, and Zenith, use exporting as a means of selling products in foreign markets. Many smaller firms in the United States also export to foreign countries.

Trend of U.S. Exports and Imports The trend of U.S. exports and imports is shown in Exhibit 6.6. Notice that the amount of U.S. exports and imports more than tripled between 1980 and the mid-1990s, reflecting the increased importance of international trade.

balance of trade the level of exports minus the level of imports

trade deficit the amount by which imports exceed exports

The U.S. **balance of trade,** which is also shown in Exhibit 6.6, is equal to the level of U.S. exports minus the level of U.S. imports. A negative balance of trade is referred to as a **trade deficit** and means that the United States is importing (purchasing) more products and services from foreign countries than it is selling to foreign countries. The U.S. trade deficit has been consistently negative since 1980 and has grown in recent years.

Direct Foreign Investment (DFI)

direct foreign investment (DFI) a means of acquiring or building subsidiaries in one or more foreign countries

Many firms engage in **direct foreign investment (DFI),** which is a means of acquiring or building subsidiaries in one or more foreign countries. For example, Ford Motor

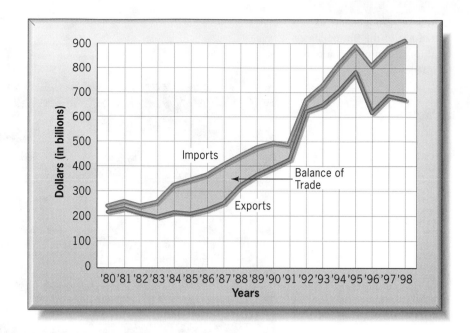

Company has facilities in various countries that produce automobiles and sell them in those locations. Blockbuster Video has stores in various countries that rent videos to customers in those countries. A U.S. firm may either build a subsidiary in a foreign country or acquire an existing foreign firm and convert that into its subsidiary. Many U.S. firms acquire foreign firms to expand internationally. They most commonly acquire firms in Canada and the United Kingdom but have recently increased their acquisitions in countries such as Brazil, the Czech Republic, and Hungary. Direct foreign investment is feasible under a variety of situations, including the following:

1 A firm that has successfully exported to a foreign country desires to reduce its transportation costs. It establishes a subsidiary in the foreign country that manufactures the product and sells it in that country. Kellogg Company uses this strategy and has production plants in nineteen different countries, including China and India.

2 A firm that has been exporting products is informed that the foreign government will impose trade barriers. Therefore, it establishes a subsidiary that can manufacture and sell products in that country. In this way, it avoids the trade barrier.

3 A foreign country is desperately in need of advanced technology and offers a U.S. firm incentives, such as free use of land, to establish a subsidiary in its country. The foreign country also expects that the firm will employ some local workers.

4 A U.S. firm believes that it could substantially reduce its labor costs by shifting its production facilities to a developing country where the labor and land are less expensive.

Although direct foreign investment can often be feasible, firms should conduct a thorough analysis of its costs and benefits before implementing the idea. Once the funds are spent on direct foreign investment, the decision cannot be easily reversed because the foreign facilities would have to be sold at a loss in most cases.

Strategic Alliances

strategic alliance a business agreement between firms whereby resources are shared to pursue mutual interests

U.S. and foreign firms commonly engage in **strategic alliances,** which are business agreements that are in the best interests of the firms involved. Various types of inter-

joint venture an agreement between two firms about a specific project

national alliances between U.S. firms and foreign firms can be made. One type is a **joint venture,** which involves an agreement between two firms about a specific project. Joint ventures between U.S. and non-U.S. firms are common. The U.S. firm may produce a product and send it to a non-U.S. firm, which sells the product in that country. The non-U.S. firm is involved because it knows the culture of that country and is more capable of selling the product there.

An alternative type of joint venture involves the participation of two firms in the production of a product. This type of joint venture is common in the automobile industry. The automakers in the United States are involved in a variety of ventures with foreign manufacturers. General Motors dealerships and Ford Motor Company dealerships sell cars manufactured by firms in France, Japan, and South Korea. RJR Nabisco has engaged in joint ventures with some food producers in some of the former Soviet republics. This gives Nabisco access to local production facilities and skilled workers. These joint ventures reflect the improved commercial relations with the former Soviet republics that have led to a major change in attitude by U.S. companies about doing business in those areas.

international licensing agreement a type of alliance in which a firm allows a foreign company (called the "licensee") to produce its products according to specific instructions

Another type of alliance is an **international licensing agreement,** in which a firm allows a foreign company (called the "licensee") to produce its products according to specific instructions. Many U.S. beer producers engage in licensing agreements with foreign firms. The foreign firm is given the technology to produce the products. As the foreign firm sells the products, it channels a portion of revenue to the *licensing firm.* The advantage of licensing is that the firm is able to sell its product in foreign markets without the costs involved in exporting or direct foreign investment. One disadvantage, however, is that the foreign firm shares the profits from products sold in the foreign country.

GLOBAL BUSINESS

Nonverbal Communications in Different Cultures

NONVERBAL BEHAVIOR CAN ONLY BE INTERPRETED WITHIN A SPECIFIC CULtural context. Here are five common nonverbal behaviors and how they are interpreted in different countries or geographic areas. Caution is always the better part of valor in using nonverbal behaviors outside your native land.

Withholding eye contact:
▶ In the United States, it indicates shyness or deception.
▶ In Libya, it is a compliment to a woman.
▶ In Japan, it is done in deference to authority.

Crossed legs when seated:
▶ In the United States, it is done for comfort.
▶ In Arab countries, it is an insult to show the soles of the feet.

Displaying the palm of the hand:
▶ In the United States, it is a form of greeting, such as a wave or handshake.
▶ In Greece, it is an insult.

Joining the index finger and thumb to make an O:
▶ In the United States, it means "okay."
▶ In Mediterranean countries, it means "zero" or "the pits."
▶ In Japan, it means money.
▶ In Tunisia, it means "I'll kill you."
▶ In Latin America, it is an obscene gesture.

Standing close to a person while talking:
▶ In the United States, it is an intrusion, and the speaker is viewed as pushy.
▶ In Latin America and southern Europe, it is the normal spatial distance for conversations.

How Foreign Characteristics Influence International Business

③ Explain how foreign characteristics can influence a firm's international business.

When a firm engages in international business, it must consider the following characteristics of foreign countries:

▶ Culture
▶ Economic system
▶ Economic conditions
▶ Exchange rates
▶ Political risk

Culture

Because cultures vary, a firm must learn a foreign country's culture before it engages in international business. Poor decisions can result from an improper assessment of a country's tastes, habits, and customs. For example, a U.S. firm may decide to allocate millions of dollars toward promoting a program to export a product to a particular country. The business could fail if the people in that country do not desire that type of product. Many U.S. firms know that cultures vary and adjust their products to fit the culture. For example, McDonald's sells vegetable burgers instead of beef hamburgers in India. PepsiCo (owner of Frito Lay snack foods) sells Cheetos without cheese in China because Chinese consumers dislike cheese, and it has developed a shrimp-chip to satisfy consumers in Korea. Beer producers sell nonalcoholic beer in Saudi Arabia, where alcohol is not allowed.

Economic System

A firm must recognize the type of economic system used in any country where it considers doing business. A country's economic system reflects the degree of government ownership of businesses and intervention in business. A U.S. firm will normally prefer countries that do not have excessive government intervention.

Although each country's government has its own unique policy on the ownership of businesses, most policies can be classified as capitalism, communism, or socialism.

capitalism an economic system that allows for private ownership of businesses

Capitalism **Capitalism** allows for private ownership of businesses. Entrepreneurs have the freedom to create businesses that they believe will serve the people's needs. The United States is perceived as a capitalist society because entrepreneurs are allowed to create businesses and compete against each other. In a capitalist society, entrepreneurs' desire to earn profits motivates them to produce products and services that satisfy customers. Competition allows efficient firms to increase their share of the market and forces inefficient firms out of the market.

U.S. firms can normally enter capitalist countries without any excessive restrictions by the governments. Typically, though, the level of competition in those countries is high.

communism an economic system that involves public ownership of businesses

Communism **Communism** is an economic system that involves public ownership of businesses. In a purely communist system, entrepreneurs are restricted from capitalizing on the perceived needs of the people. The government decides what products to produce and in what quantity. It may even assign jobs to people, regardless of their interests, and sets the wages to be paid to each worker. Wages may be somewhat similar, regardless of individual abilities or effort. Thus, workers do not have much incentive to excel because they will not be rewarded for abnormally high performance.

In a communist society, the government serves as a central planner. It may decide to produce more of some type of agricultural product if it recognizes a shortage. Since the government is not concerned about earning profits, it does not focus on satisfying consumers (determining what they want to purchase). Consequently, people are unable to obtain many types of products even if they can afford to buy them. In addition, most people do not have much money to spend because the government pays low wages.

Countries in Eastern Europe, such as Bulgaria, Poland, and Romania, were viewed as communist before 1990. During the 1990s, however, government intervention in these countries declined. Prior to the 1990s, communist countries restricted most U.S. firms from entering, but as they began to allow more private ownership of firms, they also allowed foreign firms to enter.

socialism an economic system that contains some features of both capitalism and communism

Socialism **Socialism** is an economic system that contains some features of both capitalism and communism. For example, governments in some so-called socialist countries allow people to own businesses and property and to select their own jobs. However, these governments are highly involved in the provision of various services. Health-care services are run by many governments and are provided at a low cost. Also, the governments of socialist countries tend to offer high levels of benefits to unemployed people. Such services are indirectly paid for by the businesses and the workers who earn income. Socialist governments impose high tax rates on income so that they have sufficient funds to provide all their services.

Many businesses and workers in socialist countries would argue that the tax rates are excessive. Entrepreneurs have less incentive to establish businesses if the government taxes most of the income to be earned by the business. Entrepreneurs could establish businesses in other countries where taxes are lower.

Socialist countries face a trade-off when setting their tax policies. If the government wants to provide many services to the poor or unemployed, it must charge higher tax rates, which discourages entrepreneurs from starting new businesses. But if the government uses a low tax rate, it may not generate enough tax revenue to provide the services.

A socialist society may discourage not only the establishment of new businesses but also the desire to work. If the compensation provided by a socialist government to unemployed workers is almost as high as the wages earned by employed workers, unemployed people have little incentive to look for work. Employed people are typically subject to high tax rates in socialist countries, which also discourages people from looking for work.

Comparison of Socialism with Capitalism In socialist countries, the government has more influence because it imposes higher taxes and can spend that tax revenue as it chooses. In capitalist countries, the government has less influence because it imposes fewer taxes and therefore has less funds to spend on the people. Businesses and highly skilled workers generally prefer capitalist countries because there is less government interference.

Even if a capitalist county is preferred, people may disagree on the degree of government influence in that country. For example, some people in the United States believe that the government should provide fewer services to the unemployed and the poor, which would allow for lower taxes. Other people believe that taxes should be increased so that the government can allocate more services to the poor.

Many countries exhibit some degree of capitalism and socialism. For example, the governments of many developed countries in Europe (such as Sweden and Switzerland) allow firms to be privately owned but control various services (such as health care) for the people. Germany's government provides child-care allowances, health care, and retirement pensions. The French government commonly intervenes when firms experience financial problems.

European countries have recently attempted to reduce their budget deficits as part of a treaty supporting closer European relations. This may result in less government control because the governments will not be able to spend as much money.

privatization the sale of government-owned businesses to private investors

Privatization Historically, the governments of many countries in Eastern Europe, Latin America, and the Soviet Bloc owned most businesses, but in recent years they have allowed for private business ownership. Many government-owned businesses have been sold to private investors. As a result of this so-called **privatization,** the governments are reducing their influence in numerous countries and allowing firms to compete in each industry. This allows firms to focus on providing the products and services that people desire and forces the firms to be more efficient to ensure survival. About one thousand businesses in the Soviet Bloc were privatized each month during 1994. Some U.S. firms have acquired businesses sold by the governments of the former Soviet republics and other countries. Privatization has provided an easy way for U.S. firms to own businesses in many foreign countries.

Privatization in many countries, such as in Brazil, Hungary, and the former Soviet Bloc, is an abrupt shift from tradition. Most people in these countries were not experienced in owning and managing a business. Even those people who had managed government-owned businesses were not used to competition because the government had typically controlled each industry. Therefore, many people who wanted to own their own businesses were given some training by business professors and professionals from capitalist countries such as the United States. In particular, the MBA Enterprise Corps, headquartered at the University of North Carolina—Chapel Hill, has sent thousands of business students to less-developed countries.

Even the industrialized countries have initiated privatization programs for some businesses that were previously owned by the government. The telephone company in Germany has been privatized, as have numerous large government-owned businesses in France.

Economic Conditions

To predict demand for its product, a firm must attempt to forecast the foreign country's economic conditions. The firm's performance in a foreign country is dependent on that country's economic growth and inflation, as explained next.

Economic Growth When a foreign country experiences a high degree of economic growth, foreign demand for a U.S. firm's products may be high. Conversely, when the foreign country experiences weak economic conditions, foreign demand for the U.S. firm's products may be low. Many U.S. firms experienced lower revenue from their European business in 1993 when Europe's economy was weak. During the 1994–1995 period, however, U.S. firms such as Alcoa, Dow Chemical, DuPont, Gillette, and Procter & Gamble experienced higher revenue in Europe because the European economy improved. PepsiCo also experienced strong performance in this period as a result of the increased demand for its products in China, India, and Latin America. Hewlett-Packard experienced higher earnings as a result of the strong global demand for its computer products in 1995.

Many U.S. firms have recently expanded into smaller foreign markets because they expect that economic growth in these countries will be strong, resulting in a strong demand for their products. For example, Heinz has expanded its business throughout Asia. General Motors, Procter & Gamble, AT&T, Ford Motor Company, and Anheuser-Busch plan new direct foreign investment in Brazil. The Coca-Cola Company has expanded in China, India, and Eastern Europe.

The primary factor influencing the decision by many firms to expand in a particular foreign country is the country's expected economic growth, which affects the potential demand for their products. If firms overestimate the country's economic growth, they will normally overestimate the demand for their products in that country. Consequently, their revenue may not be sufficient to cover the expenses associated with the expansion.

Firms must recognize that foreign countries may experience weak economies in some periods. For example, during the Asian crisis of 1997–1998, Asian economies were weak, and U.S. firms with business in Asia, such as Nike and Hewlett-Packard, experienced a decline in the demand for their products.

Inflation For U.S. firms with production facilities in foreign countries, production expenses will be affected by inflation. For example, inflation in some Latin American countries has exceeded 100 percent annually, meaning that prices and wages more than doubled in a single year. Some U.S. firms established facilities in Latin American countries to produce products at a low cost; however, the production expenses turned out to be much higher than the U.S. firms anticipated.

A U.S. firm's exposure to a foreign country's economy is dependent on the firm's proportion of business conducted in that country. To illustrate, compare the influence of Canada's economy on two U.S. firms (Firm X and Firm Y), as shown in Exhibit 6.7. Assume that Firm X typically generates 20 percent of its total revenue from selling its products in Canada and 80 percent of its total revenue from the United States. Firm Y typically generates 60 percent of its total revenue from Canada and 40 percent of its total revenue from the United States. A weak economy in Canada will likely have a more negative effect on Firm Y because it relies more on its Canadian business.

Some U.S. firms, such as The Coca-Cola Company, Dow Chemical, and Exxon-Mobil, generate more than half of their total revenue from foreign countries. Nevertheless, they are not heavily influenced by any single foreign country's economy because their international business is scattered across many countries. The Coca-Cola Company, for example, conducts business in more than two hundred foreign countries. The demand for The Coca-Cola Company's soft drink products may decline in some countries where the weather is cooler than normal, but this unfavorable effect can be offset by a higher demand for Coca-Cola's products in other countries where the weather is warmer than normal.

Exchange Rates

Each country has its own currency. The U.S. uses dollars ($), the United Kingdom uses British pounds (£), Canada uses Canadian dollars (C$), and Japan uses Japanese yen (¥). Eleven European countries have recently adopted the euro (€) as their currency. Exchange rates between the U.S. dollar and any currency fluctuate over time. Consequently, the number of dollars a U.S. firm needs to purchase foreign supplies may change even if the actual price of supplies charged by the foreign producer does not. When the dollar weakens, foreign currencies strengthen; thus, U.S. firms need more dollars to purchase a given amount of foreign supplies. Exchange rate fluctuations can also affect the foreign demand for a U.S. firm's product because they affect the actual price paid by the foreign customers (even if the price in dollars remains unchanged).

Political Risk

political risk the risk that a country's political actions can adversely affect a business

Political risk represents the risk that a country's political actions may adversely affect a business. Political crises have occurred in many countries throughout Eastern Eu-

Exhibit 6.7 Comparing the Influence of the Canadian Economy on Two U.S. Firms

U.S. Firm	Total Annual Revenue	Proportion of Canadian Business	Proportion of U.S. Business	Annual Revenue from Canadian Business	Annual Revenue from U.S. Business
Firm X	$100,000,000	20%	80%	$20,000,000	$80,000,000
Firm Y	10,000,000	60%	40%	6,000,000	4,000,000

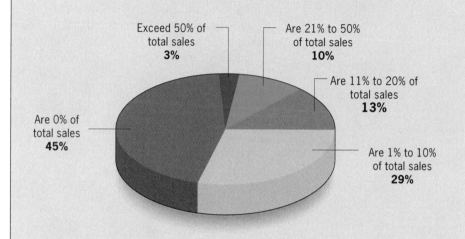

SMALL BUSINESS SURVEY

Do Small Firms Conduct International Business?

A recent survey asked 384 Entrepreneur of the Year award winners whether they conducted international business. About one-third of the firms had annual sales of less than $15 million. Results of the survey are disclosed in the following pie chart:

Firms Whose International Sales:

Exceed 50% of total sales
3%

Are 21% to 50% of total sales
10%

Are 11% to 20% of total sales
13%

Are 0% of total sales
45%

Are 1% to 10% of total sales
29%

The results suggest that many successful small firms rely on international sales for a significant portion of their business.

---

rope, Latin America, and the Middle East. U.S. firms are subject to policies imposed by the governments of the foreign countries where they do business. As an extreme form of political risk, a foreign government may take over a U.S. firm's foreign subsidiary without compensating the U.S. firm in any way. A more common form of political risk is that the foreign government imposes higher corporate tax rates on foreign subsidiaries.

Firms must understand how government characteristics could affect their businesses in foreign countries. For example, some governments impose a tax on funds sent by a subsidiary to the parent firm (headquarters) in the home country. They may even restrict the funds from being sent for a certain period of time. Government-imposed taxes on business earnings and environmental laws vary among countries. These laws can affect the feasibility of establishing a subsidiary in a foreign country.

There were numerous examples of political risk affecting U.S. firms in the 1990s. A McDonald's restaurant in China was given an eviction notice from Beijing's city government, which ignored the firm's twenty-year agreement to use the land. Some U.S. firms operating in Russia were surprised to learn that they had to pay a wage tax on all salaries over the minimum salary and a large social security tax. Governments of various foreign countries have failed to honor agreements with U.S. automobile manufacturers.

CROSS-FUNCTIONAL TEAMWORK

Managing International Business across Business Functions

When a firm plans to conduct business in a foreign country, it should request input from its managers across various departments. The production managers may assess a country according to the expenses associated with production, and therefore may focus on the following questions.

1 What is the cost of hiring the necessary labor?
2 What is the cost of developing a new facility?
3 What is the cost of purchasing an existing facility?
4 Does the country have access to the necessary materials and technology?

The answers to these questions are dependent on the specific part of the country where the firm considers producing a product.

The marketing managers may assess a country according to the potential revenue to be earned from selling a product in that country and therefore may focus on the following questions:

1 What is the foreign demand for the firm's product?

2 What changes need to be made in the product to satisfy local consumers?
3 What types of marketing strategies would be effective in that country?
4 What is the cost of marketing the product in that country?

The financial managers may assess a country according to the costs of financing any business conducted in that country and therefore may focus on the following questions:

1 Is it possible to obtain a local loan in that country?
2 What is the interest rate charged on local loans?
3 Should the firm use some of its retained earnings from its domestic business to support any foreign business?
4 How would the firm's earnings increase as a result of doing business in the foreign country?

Because of these cross-functional relationships, the decision to establish a business in a foreign country must consider input across departments. The production department cannot properly estimate the production costs in a specific country until the marketing department determines whether the product must be revised to satisfy the local consumers. Also, the financial managers cannot estimate the earnings from this business until they receive estimates of revenue (from the marketing department), production expenses (from the production department), and marketing expenses (from the marketing department).

How Exchange Rate Movements Can Affect Performance

 4 Explain how exchange rate movements can affect a firm's performance.

International trade transactions typically require the exchange of one currency for another. For example, if a U.S. firm periodically purchases supplies from a British supplier, it will need to exchange U.S. dollars for the British currency (pounds) to make the purchase. This process is shown in Exhibit 6.8.

Exhibit 6.8

Example of Importing by a U.S. Firm

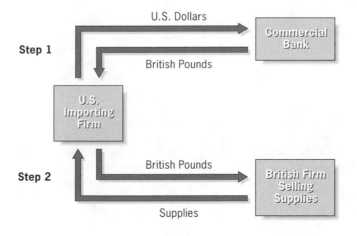

Generally, the exchange rates between each currency and the U.S. dollar fluctuate daily. When the exchange rate changes, U.S. firms involved in international trade are affected. The impact of exchange rate movements on a U.S. firm can be favorable or unfavorable, depending on the characteristics of the firm, as illustrated by the following examples.

Impact of a Weak Dollar on U.S. Importers

Assume that the value of the pound (£) at a given point in time is $2.00. That is, each dollar is worth one-half of a British pound. If a U.S. firm needs £1,000,000 to purchase supplies from a British supplier, it will need $2,000,000 to obtain those pounds, as shown:

$$\text{Amount of \$ Needed} = (\text{Amount of £ Needed}) \times (\text{Value of £})$$
$$= £1,000,000 \times \$2.00$$
$$= \$2,000,000$$

appreciates strengthens in value

Now assume that the pound **appreciates** (or strengthens in value) against the dollar. This also means that the dollar weakens (is worth less) against the pound. For example, assume the pound is now equal to $2.02 instead of $2.00. The amount of dollars needed is $20,000 more than the amount needed before the pound appreciated.

Thus, the cost of the supplies has increased for the U.S. firm as a result of the appreciation in the British pound (a weaker dollar). This illustrates why a weak dollar adversely affects U.S. firms that frequently import supplies.

Impact of a Strong Dollar on U.S. Importers

depreciates weakens in value

Now consider a situation in which the pound **depreciates,** or weakens in value against the dollar. This also means that the dollar strengthens against the pound. For exam-

---

SPOTLIGHT ON TECHNOLOGY

Moving Technology across Borders

Technologies that are highly effective in one country may have to be modified substantially before they are suitable for another country. A good example of the challenges of moving technology across borders can be found in the case of AucNet, the satellite used car auctioning system.

AucNet was developed in the mid-1980s in Japan as a substitute for traditional used car auctions. It used laser disk and later satellite technology to permit dealers from around the country to view the used cars that were going to be sold. Dealers could also view the results of inspections conducted by AucNet's team of on-site inspectors. After they had been given the opportunity to study the cars, dealers were then able to participate in online auctions. Participating in such auctions offered dealers two major advantages: they did not have to go to the auction sites, and they did not have to take their vehicles to the auction sites. As a result of its innova-

tive approach, the company became a major force in the Japanese used car business, participating in the sale of over a million cars during its first ten years of operation.

In 1995, AucNet entered the U.S. market, first in the Atlanta area and then expanding to California. However, because the used cars were typically much older, a simple inspection of a vehicle could not guarantee its actual condition. Also, used car dealers in the United States were less specialized than those in Japan and therefore were interested in a broader range of cars.

In attempting to address these problems, AucNet U.S.A., Inc. took two key steps: (1) it chose to focus on the high-priced market segment of cars, and (2) it increased the scope of its inspection program. Specifically, whereas the Japanese inspections had been almost entirely cosmetic, for the U.S. operations inspectors checked 120 specific items, both cosmetic and mechanical, and took each vehicle on a test drive. The final rating of each vehicle was then determined using custom-designed inspection software. In addition, a digital camera was used to take three photos of each car, which could then be downloaded by potential bidders. These changes were deemed necessary to make AucNet's approach attractive to the U.S. market.

ple, assume the pound's value was $2.00, but has changed to $1.90 over the last month. If the U.S. firm needs to obtain £1,000,000, it will be able to purchase them for $100,000 less than was needed before the pound depreciated. That is, the U.S. firm can obtain the pounds for $100,000 less than before. Its payment has declined by 5 percent because the pound's value has declined by 5 percent.

This example shows how the depreciation of a foreign currency against the dollar (a stronger dollar) reduces the expenses of a U.S. firm that is purchasing foreign supplies. This explains why a strong dollar favorably affects U.S. firms that frequently import supplies.

Actual Effects of Exchange Rate Movements on U.S. Importers

To illustrate how exchange rate movements can affect firms engaged in international business, actual exchange rate movements of the British pound (£) are shown at the top of Exhibit 6.9. The amount of dollars paid by a U.S. importer that owes £1,000,000 every quarter to a British supplier is shown at the bottom of Exhibit 6.9. Notice that the pound depreciated substantially in some periods, such as 1981–1984 and 1991–1993. In other periods, such as 1985–1987, the pound appreciated. When the pound appreciated, the amount of dollars needed to buy British imports increased. Conversely, when the pound depreciated, the amount of dollars needed to buy British imports declined. Exhibit 6.9 illustrates how the expenses of a U.S. importing firm are highly sensitive to changes in the value of the pound.

The exchange rates of currencies in less-developed countries fluctuate more than those in developed countries. For example, the Mexican peso depreciated by 45 per-

Exhibit 6.9

How Exchange Rate Movements
Can Affect the Price of Imports

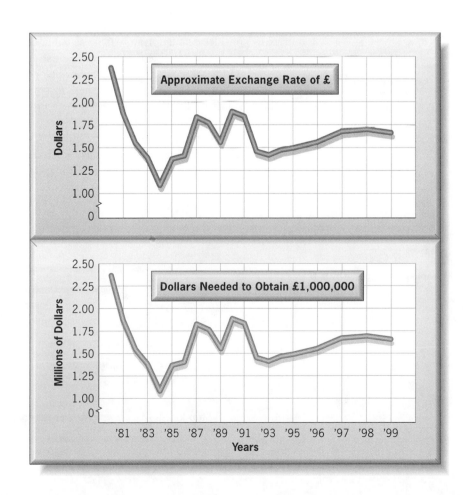

cent during the month of December 1994. U.S. firms that do business in less-developed countries are exposed to wide swings in exchange rates.

Impact of a Weak Dollar on U.S. Exporters

Just as exchange rate movements can affect U.S. importing firms, they can also affect U.S. firms that export products to other countries. The effect of a weak dollar will be examined first, followed by the effect of a strong dollar.

Consider how a U.S. firm that exports equipment to a British firm is affected by a weak dollar. The exporting process is shown in Exhibit 6.10. If the U.S. exporter wants to receive U.S. dollars for its equipment, the British firm must first exchange its currency (pounds) into dollars at a commercial bank (Step 1 in Exhibit 6.10). Then the British firm uses these dollars to purchase the equipment of the U.S. exporting firm (Step 2).

If the dollar weakens, the British firm can obtain the dollars it needs with fewer pounds. Therefore, it may be willing to purchase more equipment from the U.S. exporting firm. The U.S. firm's revenue will rise in response to a higher demand for the equipment it produces. Therefore, its profits should increase as well.

This example shows how a weak dollar can result in higher revenue and profits for U.S. firms that frequently export their products. U.S. exporting firms tend to benefit from a weak dollar because their prices are perceived as inexpensive by foreign customers who must convert their currencies into dollars. A weak dollar favorably affects U.S. firms that export heavily because foreign demand for the products they export increases substantially when the dollar is weak.

Impact of a Strong Dollar on U.S. Exporters

Now consider a situation in which the value of the pound depreciates against the dollar. As the pound's value declines, the British firm must exchange more British pounds to obtain the same amount of dollars as before. That is, it needs more pounds to purchase equipment from the U.S. firm. Consequently, it may reduce its purchases from the U.S. firm and perhaps will search for a British producer of the equipment to avoid obtaining dollars.

This example shows how a strong dollar can result in lower revenue for U.S. firms that frequently export their products. A strong dollar adversely affects U.S. exporting firms because the prices of their exports appear expensive to foreign customers who must convert their currencies into dollars. When the dollar strengthens, U.S. export-

Exhibit 6.10

Example of Exporting by a U.S. Firm

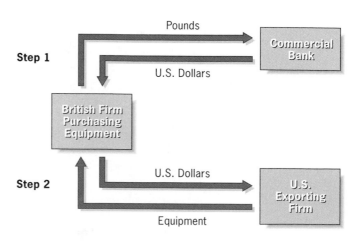

ing firms such as Procter & Gamble, Boeing, and Eastman Kodak are adversely affected.

Hedging against Exchange Rate Movements

hedge action taken to protect a firm against exchange rate movements

U.S. firms commonly attempt to **hedge,** or protect against exchange rate movements. They can hedge most effectively when they know how much of a specific foreign currency they will need or will receive on a specific date in the future.

Hedging Future Payments in Foreign Currencies Consider a firm that plans to purchase British supplies and will need £1,000,000 in ninety days to pay for those supplies. It can call a large commercial bank that exchanges foreign currencies and request a so-called **forward contract,** which states an exchange of currencies that will occur for a specified exchange rate at a future point in time. In this case, the forward contract will specify an exchange of dollars for £1,000,000 in ninety days. In other words, the firm wants to purchase pounds ninety days forward.

forward contract states an exchange of currencies that will occur at a specified exchange rate at a future point in time

forward rate the exchange rate that a bank will be willing to offer at a future point of time

The bank will quote the so-called **forward rate,** or the exchange rate that the bank would be willing to offer at a future point in time. The forward rate is normally close to the **spot exchange rate,** which is the exchange rate quoted for immediate transactions. Assume that the bank quotes a ninety-day forward rate of $1.80 for the British pound. If the firm agrees to this quote, it has agreed to a forward contract. It will lock in the purchase of £1,000,000 in ninety days for $1.80 per pound, or $1,800,000 for the £1,000,000. Once the firm hedges its position, it has locked in the rate at which it will exchange currencies on that future date, regardless of the actual spot exchange rate that occurs on that date. In this way, the U.S. firm hedges against the possibility that the pound will appreciate over that period.

spot exchange rate the exchange rate quoted for immediate transactions

Hedging Future Receivables in Foreign Currencies U.S. firms can also hedge when they expect to receive a foreign currency in the future. For example, consider a U.S. firm that knows it will receive £1,000,000 in ninety days. It can call a commercial bank and negotiate a forward contract in which it will provide the £1,000,000 to the bank in exchange for dollars. Assuming that the ninety-day forward rate is $1.80 (as in the previous example), the firm will receive $1,800,000 in ninety days (computed as $1.80 × £1,000,000). By using a forward contract, this firm locks in the rate at which it can exchange its pounds for dollars, regardless of the spot exchange rate that occurs on that date. In this way, the U.S. firm hedges against the possibility that the pound will depreciate over the period of concern.

Limitations of Hedging A major limitation of hedging is that the hedge offsets not only unfavorable exchange rate movements but also favorable rate movements. For example, reconsider the initial example in which the firm locks in the purchase of pounds ninety days ahead at a forward rate of $1.80. If the actual spot exchange rate in ninety days is $1.70, the firm would have been better off without the hedge. Nevertheless, it is obligated to fulfill its forward contract by exchanging dollars for pounds at the forward exchange rate of $1.80. This example illustrates why many U.S. firms hedge only when they expect that their future international business transactions will be adversely affected by exchange rate movements.

How Exchange Rates Affect Foreign Competition

Many U.S. firms compete with foreign firms in the U.S. market. Exhibit 6.11 shows a common situation in the United States. RCA is a U.S. firm that sells televisions in the U.S. market. It competes with many foreign competitors that export televisions to the United States. Retail stores purchase televisions from RCA as well as other firms.

Exhibit 6.11

How Exchange Rates Affect the
Degree of Foreign Competition

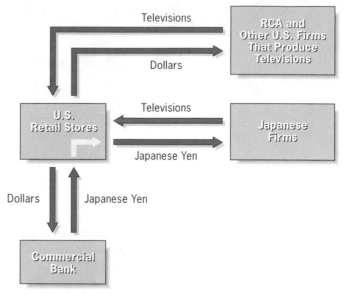

Scenario	Result
1. Japanese yen depreciates against the dollar.	U.S. retail stores can purchase Japanese televisions with fewer dollars, so the demand for Japanese televisions increases (and therefore the demand for U.S. televisions decreases).
2. Japanese yen appreciates against the dollar.	U.S. retail stores must pay more dollars to purchase Japanese televisions, so the demand for Japanese televisions decreases (and therefore the demand for U.S. televisions increases).

Assume that the stores mark up the price of each television by 20 percent. When these stores purchase Japanese televisions, they convert dollars to Japanese yen (the Japanese currency). If the value of the yen depreciates against the dollar, the store needs fewer dollars to purchase the Japanese televisions. If it applies the same markup, it can reduce its price on the Japanese televisions. Therefore, increased foreign competition (due to depreciation of one or more foreign currencies) may cause RCA to lose some U.S. business.

If the foreign currency appreciates against the dollar, the foreign competitors may be unable to compete in the United States because the prices of imported products will rise. Using our example, if the Japanese yen appreciates, the retail store will need more dollars to purchase the Japanese televisions. When applying its markup, it will need to increase its price on the Japanese televisions. Therefore, U.S. firms such as RCA may gain more U.S. business.

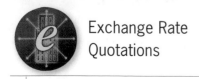

BUSINESS ONLINE

Exchange Rate
Quotations

FOREIGN EXCHANGE RATES ARE AVAILABLE ON THE INTERNET FOR THE USE of companies conducting international trade or operating in foreign countries. The website shown here allows the user to convert a specific amount from any one currency to any other currency. Historical exchange rates are also available. This information is useful for companies attempting to hedge against exchange rate movements.

http://www.oanda.com/ converter/classic

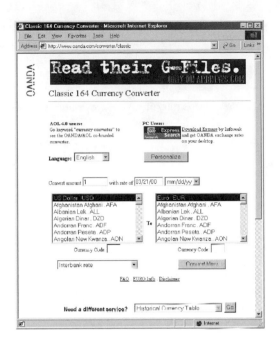

| BUSINESS DILEMMA | College Health Club |

Exchange Rate Effects at College Health Club

WHEN SUE KRAMER OPENED COLLEGE HEALTH CLUB (CHC), SHE LEASED THE exercise equipment. Now, however, she is considering purchasing exercise equipment from a Canadian manufacturer. The price of the equipment is C$20,000. If Sue purchases the equipment, she will have to pay the bill in ninety days. Sue recognizes that the value of the Canadian dollar changes each day. She learns that a business newspaper recently predicted that the Canadian dollar will be valued at $.84 in ninety days. However, a business expert predicts that the Canadian dollar will be valued at $.88 in ninety days.

Dilemma

Sue decides that she will purchase the equipment only if her cost is less than $16,000. Estimate the price of the equipment in U.S. dollars. Should Sue purchase the Canadian equipment?

Solution

Sue does not know what the exchange rate of the Canadian dollar will be in ninety days, but she can use the two different predictions that were provided. She can estimate the purchase price by multiplying the C$20,000 times the expected exchange rate at the time the payment is due. Her analysis is as follows:

1 If the exchange rate in ninety days is C$ = $.84:

$$\text{Expected Amount of \$ Needed} = \text{C\$20,000} \times \text{Exchange Rate}$$
$$= \text{C\$20,000} \times \$.84$$
$$= \$16,800$$

2 If the exchange rate in ninety days is C$ = $.88:

$$\text{Expected Amount of \$ Needed} = \text{C\$20,000} \times \text{Exchange Rate}$$
$$= \text{C\$20,000} \times \$.88$$
$$= \$17,600$$

Based on these estimates, the expected expense to CHC will be either $16,800 or $17,600, depending on which exchange rate exists in ninety days. Since the expected expense exceeds $16,000, Sue decides not to purchase the equipment. She will continue leasing equipment but will reconsider purchasing the Canadian equipment if the value of the Canadian dollar depreciates to a rate of C$ = .80 or less. At an exchange rate of C$ = .80, Sue will need only $16,000 to obtain C$20,000.

Additional Issues for Discussion

1 Assume that CHC becomes highly successful over time, and Sue Kramer considers establishing some health clubs in a foreign country. What characteristics would she assess in that country before deciding whether to establish health clubs there?

2 Assume that a large foreign country has no health clubs. Does this mean Sue would benefit by establishing a health club there? (Assume no political barriers exist.)

3 Do you think CHC is more exposed or less exposed to foreign competition than U.S. manufacturing firms? Why?

SUMMARY

 The main reasons why U.S. firms engage in international business are to:

▶ attract foreign demand,
▶ capitalize on technology,
▶ use inexpensive resources, or
▶ diversify internationally.

The first two reasons reflect higher revenue, while the third reason reflects lower expenses. The fourth reason reflects less risk by reducing exposure to a single economy.

 The primary ways in which firms conduct international business are:

▶ importing,
▶ exporting,
▶ direct foreign investment, and
▶ strategic alliances.

Many U.S. firms have used all of these strategies.

3 When firms sell their products in international markets, they assess the cultures, economic systems and conditions, exchange rate risk, and political risk in those markets. A country's economic conditions affect the demand by its citizens for the firm's product. The larger the proportion of the firm's total sales generated in a specific foreign country,

the more sensitive is the firm's revenue to that country's economic conditions.

4 Exchange rate movements can affect U.S. firms in various ways, depending on their characteristics. U.S. importers benefit from a strong dollar. U.S. exporters benefit from a weak dollar but are adversely affected by a strong dollar. U.S. firms competing with foreign firms that export to the U.S. market are adversely affected by a strong dollar, because the products exported by foreign firms appear inexpensive to U.S. consumers when the dollar is strong.

KEY TERMS

appreciates 160
balance of trade 151
capitalism 154
communism 154
depreciates 160
direct foreign investment (DFI)
  151
exporting 151

forward contract 163
forward rate 163
hedge 163
importing 150
international licensing agreement
  153
joint venture 153
political risk 157

privatization 156
quota 150
socialism 155
spot exchange rate 163
strategic alliance 152
tariff 150
trade deficit 151

REVIEW QUESTIONS

1 Explain why a business may want to sell its product or service in a foreign country.

2 Discuss why the U.S. market is so susceptible to foreign competition.

3 Explain how tariffs or quotas affect the price of imports.

4 Distinguish exporting from importing. Can a business such as McDonald's be involved in both exporting and importing?

5 Identify and explain the various types of international alliances between U.S. firms and foreign firms.

6 Explain the difference between a direct foreign investment and a strategic alliance undertaken by an international business.

7 Identify and explain the foreign characteristics that will influence international business investment.

8 Explain the differences between capitalism, communism, and socialism.

9 Identify the economic factors that must be assessed before a firm can internationalize its operation in a foreign market.

10 Explain why many U.S. firms may increase their foreign acquisitions due to exchange rates.

DISCUSSION QUESTIONS

1 Discuss the advantages and disadvantages of foreign ownership in the United States. Are there any types of businesses that should *not* be for sale to a foreign investor?

2 Assume you are a business entrepreneur. Do you support free trade among nations, or do you believe that there should be tariffs and quotas on imported goods? How would each position affect the economy?

3 How could a firm use the Internet to attract foreign demand? How could a firm use the Internet to access the current level of exchange rates?

4 Should Americans buy U.S.-produced goods and services or buy foreign goods and services? Does either practice affect the U.S. balance of trade? Comment.

5 Discuss the implications of a stronger dollar in relation to other foreign currencies for an exporter, as well as for someone who is planning to travel to a foreign country. Are there differences between the two parties?

INVESTING IN THE STOCK OF A BUSINESS

Using the annual report of the firm in which you would like to invest, complete the following:

1 Describe the means (if any) by which the firm engages in global business. Does it export? Does it import? Does the firm have foreign subsidiaries overseas? Joint alliances or ventures?

2 In what foreign countries does the firm do business? Is the firm seeking to expand into new foreign markets? How does its overseas sales growth compare with its domestic sales growth?

3 Does the firm's annual report specifically mention foreign firms as a source of competition?

4 Was the firm's performance affected by exchange rate movements last year? If so, how?

5 Explain how the business uses technology to assess the global environment in which it operates. For example, does it use certain websites to determine its exchange rate risk? Does it use the Internet to determine its global competition?

6 Go to **http://hoovers.com** and locate the NEWS SEARCH. Type in the name of the firm in the space provided, and review the recent news stories about the firm. Summarize any (at least one) recent news story about the firm that applies to one or more of the key concepts within this chapter.

CASE GLOBAL EXPANSION BY LINTON RECORDS

Linton Records is a U.S. producer of soul music, which is sold in the United States and exported to Europe. A year ago, the company entered into a joint venture with a distributor in London to retail its records. It is planning to import British rock into the United States, as it has just entered into a strategic alliance with this distributorship. Sales are expected to increase 20 percent a year over first-year sales of £12.5 million. Linton receives payment for its exports in British pounds. The dollar has been weakening against the British pound.

Linton Records has learned that its product line will be subject to a tariff on goods imported into Europe. The tariff is related to the common market alliance that exists throughout Europe. The company has expressed concern because it believes that political intervention disrupts the free flow of trade as it exists in the United States.

Management is developing a strategic alliance with a French manufacturer to produce compact discs for the entire operation. The company is expected to cut production costs by 25 percent because of the French firm's advanced technology. In this strategic alliance, the French manufacturer will buy all its raw materials from a company in Bonn, Germany. In addition to the distributorship in London, Linton Records plans to open new markets in six different countries throughout Western Europe in the future.

QUESTIONS

1 Discuss the primary reasons why Linton Records may benefit from its international business.

2 How will Linton Records be affected if the dollar weakens further?

3 Should music imported by U.S. firms from England be subjected to a tariff?

VIDEO CASE   GLOBAL BUSINESS BY ETEC

Enforcement Technology (ETEC) uses technology to manufacture the AutoCite system for parking enforcement. It sells its technology to parking enforcement agencies in the United States so that they can monitor parking meters. In recent years, it has received orders from parking enforcement agencies in foreign countries. When ETEC creates an AutoCite system for a foreign agency, it must adjust the technology to fit the system used in that country. For example, Australian agencies require much more information on parking tickets than U.S. agencies do, so the AutoCite system had to be adjusted to allow for this information.

QUESTIONS

1 Why is it so important for ETEC to adjust its product to satisfy various types of customers (parking enforcement agencies) in different countries?

2 Do you think that ETEC's performance is highly exposed to U.S. economic conditions? Explain.

3 Do you think ETEC's performance is highly exposed to exchange rate fluctuations?

INTERNET APPLICATIONS

http://asiarisk.com/library5.html

The brief article displayed here describes some of the aspects of political risk in foreign countries. Briefly describe what they are. According to the article, which country has the highest degree of political risk? In which country is it most difficult to do business? Are the rankings of political risk and difficulty of doing business identical? Why or why not? Briefly discuss how this information is useful to firms competing in a global environment.

THE *Coca-Cola* COMPANY ANNUAL REPORT PROJECT

Questions for the current year's annual report are available on the text website at **http://madura _intro_bus.swcollege.com.**

The following questions apply concepts learned in this chapter to The Coca-Cola Company. Go to The Coca-Cola Company website (**http://www.cocacola.com**) and find the index for the 1999 annual report.

QUESTIONS

1 Study the "Worldwide Unit Case Volume" section. Do you think The Coca-Cola Company's products have achieved a global presence?

2 Look at "Selected Market Results."
   a. In terms of per capita consumption, what are The Coca-Cola Company's major successes?
   b. Where are its major opportunities for increasing per capita consumption?

3 Look at "Financial Risk Management." In some situations, The Coca-Cola Company may receive cash inflows from foreign countries that can be affected by exchange rate changes.
   a. How does it measure these currency fluctuations?
   b. How does it hedge against these currency fluctuations?

4 Look at "Selected Market Results." How many of The Coca-Cola Company's products does the average resident of Central Europe consume in a year?

5 Go to **http://hoovers.com** and locate the NEWS SEARCH. Type in The Coca-Cola Company in the space provided, and review the recent news stories about the firm. Summarize any (at least one) recent news story about The Coca-Cola Company that applies one or more of the key concepts within this chapter of the text.

IN-TEXT STUDY GUIDE

Answers are in an appendix at the back of the book.

TRUE OR FALSE

1 An important reason U.S. firms establish new businesses in less-developed countries is to capitalize on technological advantages.

2 The best way for a firm to stabilize its profits over time is to focus its efforts on producing and selling one specific product in one specific country.

3 U.S. firms that provide services are more likely to face strong foreign competition than firms that produce manufactured goods.

4 A firm's performance in a foreign country is dependent on that country's economic growth and inflation.

5 A tax placed on imported goods is called a tariff.

6 Competition among firms is usually more intense in communist economies than it is in capitalist economies.

7 A key advantage of socialist economies is the emphasis on keeping tax rates as low as possible.

8 Land and labor costs can vary significantly among countries.

9 The values of most currencies are not allowed to change relative to the dollar.

10 If firms overestimate the economic growth in a particular country, they will normally overestimate the demand for their products in that country.

MULTIPLE CHOICE

11 All of the following are important reasons why U.S. firms engage in international business except to:
a) attract foreign demand.
b) capitalize on technology.
c) take advantage of lower taxes in socialist economies.
d) use inexpensive labor and natural resources available in less-developed countries.
e) diversify internationally.

12 With the implementation of NAFTA in 1993:
a) most trade restrictions between the United States, Canada, and Mexico were removed.
b) European nations began using a common currency.
c) U.S. firms were encouraged to invest in the less-developed nations of Asia, Central America, and Africa.
d) the World Bank was given the authority to set interest rates on international business loans.
e) countries were no longer allowed to have trade deficits continue for more than three years.

13 Eleven European nations recently agreed to share a common currency known as the:
a) gifspen.   d) euro.
b) francmarc.   e) NAFTA.
c) European pound.

14 The main reason U.S. firms want to achieve international diversification is that it:
a) exposes them to cultural diversity.
b) enables them to take big tax write-offs.
c) helps them stabilize profits, thus reducing their risk.
d) allows them to acquire more advanced technology.
e) allows them to offer stock to foreign investors, thus increasing their financial base.

15 An exchange rate that is quoted for immediate transactions is the:
a) spot rate.
b) forward rate.
c) world bank rate.
d) prime rate.
e) international monetary fund.

16 When businesses take action to lock in a specific exchange rate for a future international transaction in order to reduce risk, their strategy is referred to as:
a) rate fixing.   d) hedging.
b) trading on reserve.   e) trading on margin.
c) selling short.

17 The acquisition of a foreign business by a U.S. firm is an example of:
a) direct foreign investment.
b) exporting.
c) importing.
d) international licensing.
e) a joint venture.

18 When governments limit the amount of specific products that can be imported, they are imposing a/an:

a) tariff.   d) cartel.
b) embargo.   e) bribe.
c) quota.

19 A negative balance of trade is referred to as a:
a) trade deficit.
b) trade surplus.
c) favorable balance of payments.
d) direct investment.
e) hedge.

20 The purchase of foreign supplies by IBM is an example of:
a) direct foreign investment.
b) exporting.
c) importing.
d) international licensing.
e) a joint venture.

21 If you plan to convert dollars to obtain Japanese yen today, you would pay the:
a) spot rate.   d) hedge rate.
b) open market rate.   e) forward rate.
c) discount rate.

22 The sale of film produced by Kodak in the United States to Chinese firms is an example of:
a) direct foreign investment.
b) exporting.
c) importing.
d) international licensing.
e) a joint venture.

23 A _____ states an exchange of currencies that will occur at a specified exchange rate at some future point in time.
a) reserve clause
b) forward contract
c) limit order
d) market order
e) fixed time exchange contract

24 The dollar weakens against the British pound if the value of the pound:
a) depreciates.   d) appreciates.
b) sells off.   e) declines.
c) softens.

25 The purchase of foreign products or services is called:
a) importing.   d) financial exchange.
b) exporting.   e) economic growth.
c) hedging.

26 _____ is an economic system that allows some private ownership of businesses and property but also has an active government sector and high tax rates to support the government's programs.
a) Socialism   d) Mercantilism
b) Capitalism   e) Dualism
c) Feudalism

27 In recent years, governments of many nations have sold government-owned and -operated businesses to private investors. This process is known as:
a) public disinvestment.
b) privatization.
c) repatriation.
d) democratization.
e) public capitalization.

28 Under _____ the government owns most businesses and decides what products to produce and in what quantity.
a) socialism   d) dualism
b) capitalism   e) pluralism
c) communism

29 The U.S. government just imposed a numerical limit on the amount of widgets that may be imported, which is called a:
a) quota.   d) exchange factor.
b) tariff.   e) limit order.
c) call rate.

30 When a firm in one country acquires or builds a subsidiary in another country, it is engaging in:
a) arbitrage.
b) a joint venture.
c) foreign aid.
d) a forward contract.
e) direct foreign investment.

31 The sale of products or services to purchasers residing in other countries is called:
a) importing.   d) smuggling.
b) hedging.   e) financial exchange.
c) exporting.

32 A(n) _____ is a strategic alliance in which a firm allows a foreign company to produce its products according to specific instructions.
a) international cartel
b) international licensing agreement
c) joint venture
d) international limited partnership
e) limited liability contract

33 If the dollar depreciates relative to the Japanese yen:
a) Japanese goods will seem cheaper to American importers.
b) gold will flow from the United States to Japan.
c) American goods will seem less expensive to Japanese consumers.
d) the dollar must appreciate relative to some other Asian currency.
e) the U.S. government will have to intervene to increase the value of the dollar.

34 In a _____ economy, businesses are privately owned and profit-seeking entrepreneurs are free to start businesses they believe will serve the people's needs.

a) capitalist
b) communist
c) feudalist
d) mercantilist
e) pluralist

35 One disadvantage of hedging is that it:
a) is illegal in many foreign countries.
b) requires businesses to pay additional taxes on their earnings.
c) is considered unethical behavior by some investors.
d) offsets not only unfavorable, but also favorable changes in exchange rates.
e) greatly increases the risk of doing business in foreign countries.

Summary of Part II

A firm is exposed to economic conditions (Chapter 4), industry conditions (Chapter 5), and global conditions (Chapter 6). The economic conditions that affect a firm's performance are economic growth, inflation, and interest rates. Economic growth influences the demand for products and services produced by firms. Inflation influences the production expenses of materials, machinery, or employees. Interest rates influence the demand for products that are typically purchased with borrowed funds.

They also influence the cost of financing. In general, a firm's performance is improved as a result of strong economic growth, low inflation, and low interest rates.

The industry conditions that affect a firm's performance are the demand for a specific type of product (industry demand), the industry competition, the labor environment, and the regulatory environment. A firm's performance is typically improved when industry demand is high, industry competitors are weak,

the supply of available labor is high, and regulations do not impose excessive restrictions.

The global conditions that affect a firm's performance are economic conditions in foreign countries and exchange rates. A U.S. firm's performance may be improved when the foreign countries where it sells some of its products experience a high rate of economic growth. A U.S. firm may also benefit from a weak dollar if it exports products or from a strong dollar if it imports products.

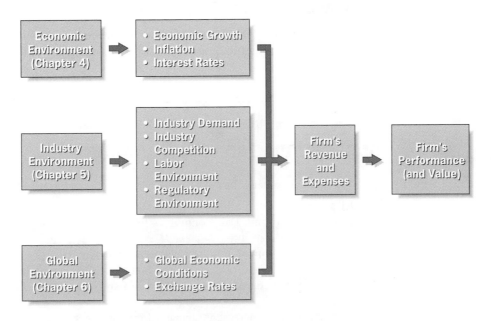

173

PART II	

Assessing the Business Environment within the Business Plan for Campus.com

Exposure to Economic Conditions (related to Chapter 4)

In your business plan for Campus.com, explain whether and how the firm's performance may be affected if economic conditions change. For example, would the demand for Campus.com's services be affected if economic conditions deteriorate? Why?

Industry Segments (related to Chapter 5)

In your business plan, identify the various segments of the industry that Campus.com could target. The business was initially created to serve high school students who are about to graduate. Could the business offer different levels of service to its main market (high school students) and charge higher prices for some types of services?

Competition (related to Chapter 5)

In your business plan for Campus.com, describe any existing competition for its product, including services that provide general information about colleges throughout the United States.

Global Conditions (related to Chapter 6)

Describe in the business plan how Campus.com could expand outside the United States. In this part of the plan, identify the logical choice of a foreign country that Campus.com could target.

Communication and Teamwork

You (or your team) may be asked by your instructor to hand in and/or present the section of your business plan that relates to this part of the text.

PART II	**Applications for Dell Computer**

Refer to "Dell Computer's Formula for Success" where necessary.

1 Dell's economic environment
   a. How do you think Dell Computer's financial performance would be affected by an increase in interest rates?
   b. How do you think Dell's financial performance would be affected by an increase in the prices of desktop and notebook computers, assuming that prices for the components necessary to manufacture these products stay the same?
   c. How would an increase in demand for computers affect the price of computers sold by Dell?

2 Dell's industry environment
   a. Do you think Dell Computer is highly exposed to conditions in the computer industry? Why or why not?

   b. How would you describe Dell's competitive advantage over its competitors?

   c. How does Dell use the Internet to operate within its industry environment?

3 Dell's global environment

   a. How could Dell Computer use the Internet to attract foreign demand?

   b. Do you think Dell should diversify internationally?

   c. Do you think Dell should be concerned with exchange rate risk? If yes, how could Dell hedge against this risk?

PART II

The Stock Market Game

Go to **http://www.fantasystockmarket.com**. Enter your name (e-mail address) and password as requested and check your portfolio balance, which is updated continuously by the Fantasy website.

Check Your Stock Portfolio Performance

1 What is the value of your stock portfolio today?

2 What is your return on your investment? (This return is shown on your balance.)

3 How did your return compare to those of other students? (This comparison tells you whether your stock portfolio's performance is relatively high or low.)

Keep in mind that you can change your portfolio at any time during the school term.

Explaining Your Stock Performance
Stock prices are frequently influenced by the economic environment, including economic, industry, and global conditions. Review the latest news about some of your stocks on the Fantasy website by clicking on News and typing the ticker symbol of your stock.

1 Identify one of your stocks whose price was affected (since you purchased it) as a result of the business environment (the main topic in this part of the text).

2 Identify the specific changes in the business environment (interest rate movements, industry competition, etc.) that caused the stock price to change.

3 Did your stock's price increase or decrease in response to changes in the business environment?

PART II

Running Your Own Business

1 How would the performance of your business be affected by economic conditions in the local area? How would it be affected by economic conditions across the United States? How would your company be affected by global economic events?

2 How would the performance of your business be affected by an increase in interest rates?

3 Describe the main competitors that would be competing against your business. Would it be easy for additional competitors to enter your market? Could you effectively expand your business?

4 How would the performance of your business be affected by industry conditions? Explain.

5 What competitive advantage can your business be affected by industry conditions? Explain.

6 Explain whether your business would benefit from importing any supplies from foreign countries.

7 Will your business attempt to export any products to foreign countries? Identify which countries could be targeted. Will your business compete against foreign competitors?

8 Explain how the performance of your business would be affected in any way by exchange rate movements.

9 How could your business use the Internet to assess its competition, its industry environment, and its global environment?

Management

Management is the use of human and other resources in a manner that best achieves the firm's objectives. Four key components of management are (1) understanding the characteristics necessary for managers to be effective, (2) assigning job responsibilities, (3) managing the process by which products are produced, and (4) monitoring and improving the quality of the products produced. Chapter 7 provides a background on the characteristics necessary for managers to be effective, and Chapter 8 explains how job responsibilities are assigned. Chapter 9 describes how the resources used in the production process can be allocated efficiently, and Chapter 10 explains how the quality of products produced can be monitored and improved.

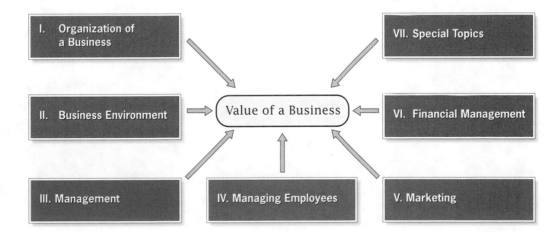

The Learning	**1**	Identify the levels of management.
Goals of this	**2**	Identify the key functions of managers.
chapter are to:	**3**	Describe the skills that managers need.
	4	Describe methods that managers can use to utilize their time effectively.

Fundamentals of Effective Management

Management represents the utilization of human resources (employees) and other resources (such as machinery) in a manner that best achieves the firm's plans and objectives. According to a recent survey by Shareholder Surveys, shareholders ranked good management and long-term vision as the two most important characteristics of a firm. Effective management can improve the firm's performance and therefore increase the firm's value for shareholders.

Consider the case of Intel Corporation, which produces computer chips, boards, and software for computer firms. What types of planning should Intel do over the next one to five years? How can Intel ensure that its various business tasks are being conducted properly? What types of management skills are needed to ensure Intel's continued success? This chapter discusses the fundamentals of management, which can be used to answer these questions.

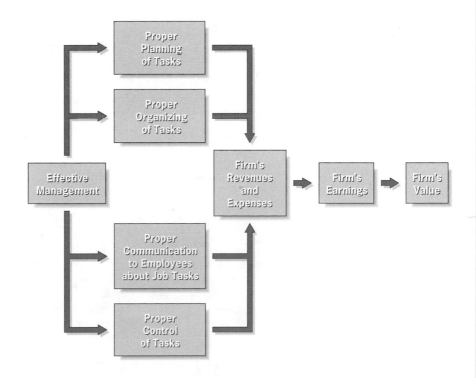

Levels of Management

① Identify the levels of management.

Employees who are responsible for managing other employees or other resources serve as managers, even if their official title is different. The functions of managers vary with their respective levels within the firm. **Top (high-level) management** includes positions such as president, chief executive officer (who commonly also serves as president), chief financial officer, and vice-president. These managers make decisions regarding the firm's long-run objectives (such as three to five years ahead).

Middle management is often responsible for the firm's short-term decisions, as these managers are closer to the production process. Middle managers resolve problems and devise new methods to improve performance. Middle management includes positions such as regional manager and plant manager.

Supervisory (first-line) management is usually highly involved with the employees who engage in the day-to-day production process. Supervisors deal with problems such as worker absenteeism and customer complaints. Supervisory management includes positions such as account manager and office manager. The types of functions that each level of management conducts are summarized in Exhibit 7.1.

The relationships among top, middle, and supervisory managers can be more fully understood by considering a simple example. Exhibit 7.2 shows the responsibilities of all managers in light of new plans by a firm to expand production and increase sales. The middle and top managers must make production, marketing, and finance decisions that will achieve the new plans. The supervisory managers provide specific instructions to the new employees who are hired to achieve the higher production level.

top (high-level) management
managers in positions such as president, chief executive officer, chief financial officer, and vice-president who make decisions regarding the firm's long-run objectives

middle management
managers who are often responsible for the firm's short-term decisions

supervisory (first-line) management managers who are usually highly involved with the employees who engage in the day-to-day production process

Exhibit 7.1

Comparison of Different Levels of Management

Title	Types of Decisions
Top Management	
President	1) Should we create new products? 2) Should we expand? 3) How can we expand? Through acquisitions?
Chief Financial Officer	1) Should more funds be borrowed? 2) Should we invest available funds in proposed projects?
Vice-President of Marketing	1) Should an existing product be revised? 2) Should our pricing policies be changed? 3) Should our advertising strategies be changed?
Middle Management	
Regional Sales Manager	1) How can we boost sales in a particular city? 2) How can complaints from one of our largest customers be resolved? 3) Should an additional salesperson be hired?
Plant Manager	1) Should the structure of the assembly line be revised? 2) Should new equipment be installed throughout the plant?
Supervisory Management	
Account Manager	1) How can workers who process payments from various accounts be motivated? 2) How can conflicts between two workers be resolved?
Supervisor	1) How can the quality of work by assembly-line workers be assessed? 2) How can assembly-line tasks be assigned across workers? 3) How can customer complaints be handled?

Exhibit 7.2

Comparison of Responsibilities among Managers

Top Management

1. Set new plan to expand production and increase sales.
2. Communicate those plans to all managers.

Middle and Top Managers

1. Determine how many new employees to hire.
2. Determine how to charge lower prices to increase sales.
3. Determine how to increase advertising to increase sales.
4. Determine how to obtain funds to finance the expansion.

Supervisory Managers

1. Provide job assignments to the new employees who are hired.
2. Set time schedules for new employees who are hired.

Functions of Managers

2 Identify the key functions of managers.

Most managerial functions can be classified into one of the following categories:

▶ Planning
▶ Organizing
▶ Leading
▶ Controlling

Planning

planning the preparation of a firm for future business conditions

mission statement a description of a firm's primary goal

The **planning** function represents the preparation of a firm for future business conditions. As the first step in the planning process, the firm establishes its **mission statement,** which describes its primary goal. For example, here is the mission statement of Bristol-Myers Squibb:

❝ *The mission of Bristol-Myers Squibb is to extend and enhance human life by providing the highest quality health and personal care products.* ❞

Most mission statements are general, like that of Bristol-Myers. The mission of General Motors is to be the world's leader in transportation products, and the mission of Ford Motor Company is to be the world's leading consumer company providing automotive products and services. The mission of the former Amoco Corporation (now part of BP Amoco) was to provide quality petroleum and chemical products to

Managers are more effective when they communicate directly with employees, as shown in this photo.

customers and high returns to stockholders. Each mission statement tends to stress excellence in some specified industry.

strategic plan intended to identify a firm's main business focus over a long-term period, perhaps three to five years

Strategic Plan

The **strategic plan** identifies the firm's main business focus over a long-term period. The strategic plan is more detailed than the mission statement and describes in general terms how the firm's mission is to be achieved. For example, if a firm's mission is to produce quality computer products, its strategic plan might specify the particular computer products to be produced and the manner in which they will be sold (retail outlets, Internet, etc.).

The strategic plan typically includes goals and strategies that can be used to satisfy the firm's mission. For example, a recent annual report of Bristol-Myers Squibb listed the following among its main goals and strategies:

Goals:

❝ *Leadership in each product category and in each geographic market in which we compete. We aim to achieve number one or number two position with increasing market shares.* ❞

❝ *Superior customer satisfaction by providing the highest quality products and services to our customers. We will strive to be rated number one or two with continuous improvement as rated by our customers.* ❞

❝ *Superior steady shareholder returns, as measured by a number one or two competitive position in economic performance within our industry.* ❞

❝ *An organization which is committed to winning through teamwork, empowerment, customer focus, and open communications.* ❞

Strategies:

❝ *Our mission and goals will be achieved by adhering to the following core strategies:*

- *Achieve unit growth fueled internally by new products, geographic expansion, and marketing innovation, and externally through acquisition, joint venture and licensing agreements.*
- *Dedicate ourselves to being recognized as the best in research and development across our businesses . . .*
- *Achieve continuous improvement in our cost structure . . .*
- *Attract, develop, motivate, and retain people of the highest caliber. The company's reporting, reward and recognition systems will be built around attainment of the goals identified above.* ❞

Once a firm specifies its mission, it can develop plans to achieve that mission.

tactical planning smaller-scale plans (over one or two years) that are consistent with the firm's strategic (long-term) plan

Tactical Planning   High-level and middle managers also engage in **tactical planning,** or smaller-scale plans (over one or two years) that are consistent with the firm's strategic (long-term) plan. Tactical planning normally focuses on a short-term period, such as the next year or so. To develop their tactical plan, managers of AT&T and other firms assess economic conditions, the general demand for various products, the level of competition among firms producing those products, and changes in technology. They use their vision to capitalize on opportunities in which they have some advantages over other firms in the industry. If a firm's strategic plan is to increase its market share by 20 percent, its tactical plans may focus on increasing sales in specific regions that have less competition. As time passes, additional tactical planning will be conducted in accordance with the strategic plan.

operational planning establishes the methods to be used in the near future (such as the next year) to achieve the tactical plans

Operational Planning   Another form of planning, called **operational planning,** establishes the methods to be used in the near future (such as the next year) to achieve the tactical plans. Continuing our example of a firm whose tactical plan is to increase sales, the operational plan may specify the means by which the firm can increase sales. That is, the operational plan may specify an increase in the amount of funds allocated to advertising and the hiring of additional salespeople.

The goals of operational planning are somewhat dependent on the firm's long-term goals. For example, a firm's top managers may establish a goal of 12 percent annual growth in sales over the next several years. The firm's salespeople may be asked to strive for a 1 percent increase in total sales per month during the upcoming year. Their month-to-month goals are structured from the long-term goals established by top management.

policies guidelines for how tasks should be completed

When firms engage in operational planning, they must abide by their **policies,** or guidelines for how tasks should be completed. For example, a policy on the hiring of employees may require that a specific process be followed. Policies enforced by firms ensure that all employees conduct specific tasks in a similar manner. The policies are intended to prevent employees from conducting tasks in a manner that is inefficient, dangerous, or illegal.

procedures steps necessary to implement a policy

Most policies contain **procedures,** or steps necessary to implement a policy. For example, a policy for hiring may specify that an ad is to be placed in the local newspaper for so many days, and the procedure should be posted in a visible spot at the firm. It may also specify a maximum number of days that an applicant has to accept or reject a job offer. Through such procedures, the firm attempts to ensure that people who apply for a position are treated fairly. Without procedures, managers could make decisions that conflict with the company's goals.

contingency planning alternative plans developed for various possible business conditions

Contingency Planning   Some of a firm's plans may not be finalized until specific business conditions are known. For this reason, firms use **contingency planning,** in which alternative plans are developed for various possible business conditions. That

Exhibit 7.3

Illustration of Contingency
Planning

Situation	Contingency Plan
Overbooked reservations	To reduce the number of customers who need that flight, offer customers who are willing to be bumped (wait for next flight) a free round-trip ticket to the destination of their choice in the future.
Minor airplane repair needed	Have airline engineers available at each major airport in the event that a minor repair is needed.
Major airplane repair needed	If the airplane is not suitable for flying, attempt to reroute the passengers who were supposed to be on that plane by reserving seats for them on other flights.

is, the plan to be implemented is contingent on the business conditions that occur. For example, a firm that produces sports equipment may plan to boost its production of rollerblades in response to recent demand. At the same time, however, it may develop an alternative plan for using its resources to produce other equipment instead of rollerblades if demand declines. It may also develop a plan for increasing its production if the demand for its rollerblades is much higher than expected.

Some contingency planning is conducted to prepare for possible crises that may occur. For example, airlines may establish contingency plans in the event that various problems occur, as illustrated in Exhibit 7.3.

The relationships among planning functions are shown in Exhibit 7.4. Notice how the tactical plan is dependent on the strategic plan. Also, the operational plan is based

Exhibit 7.4

How Planning Functions Are
Related

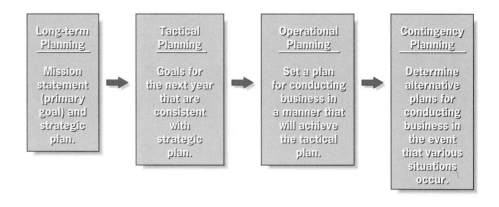

Example

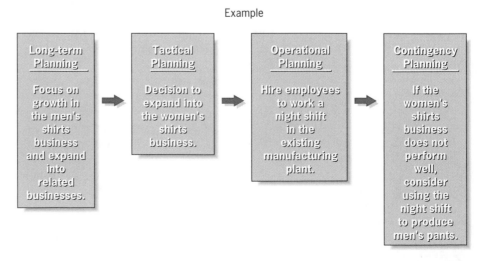

CROSS-FUNCTIONAL TEAMWORK

Interaction of Functions to Achieve the Strategic Plan

 The development of a strategic plan requires interaction among the firm's managers who are responsible for different business functions. Recall that the strategic plan of Bristol-Myers Squibb mentioned earlier includes goals of increased market share, customer satisfaction, and continuous improvement. The firm's strategies to achieve those goals include the creation of new products, continuous improvement in cost structure (high production efficiency), and retaining good employees.

The management function of Bristol-Myers Squibb can help achieve the firm's goals by assessing the needs of consumers in order to create new products. It can also attempt to assess customers' satisfaction with existing products and use marketing strategies to increase the market share of these products. The financing function of Bristol-Myers Squibb can help achieve the firm's goals by determining the level of borrowing that will be sufficient to support the firm's operations.

Since the business functions are related, a strategic plan can be implemented only when the interaction among business functions is recognized. A strategic plan that focuses on increased sales will likely require more production and financing. Exhibit 7.5 shows some common ways that the goals of a strategic plan can be achieved by each function.

Exhibit 7.5

How Various Business Functions Are Used to Achieve the Strategic Plan

Function	Typical Goals or Strategies That Can Be Achieved by This Function
Management	High production efficiency
	High production quality
	Customer satisfaction
	Employee satisfaction
Marketing	Innovation (new products)
	Increase market share of existing products
	Customer satisfaction
Finance	Reduce financing costs
	Efficient use of funds

on the tactical plan. The contingency plan offers alternatives to consider instead of the operational plan in specific situations (such as higher or lower demand for the product than anticipated).

To fully understand how these plans fit together, assume that your firm is created to produce men's shirts. Assume that your strategic plan specifies goals of expanding into related products. In this case, your tactical plan may focus on producing one other product along with men's shirts, such as women's shirts. The operational plan will specify the changes in the firm's operations that are necessary to produce and sell women's shirts. Specifically, the plan will determine how much more fabric must be purchased each month, how the women's shirts will be priced, and where they will be sold. A contingency plan can also be created in the event that excessive competition develops in the market for women's shirts. If this occurs, the contingency plan may be to expand into different products, such as men's pants.

Organizing

organizing the organization of employees and other resources in a manner that is consistent with the firm's goals

The **organizing** function represents the organization of employees and other resources in a manner that is consistent with the firm's goals. Once a firm's goals are established (from the planning function), resources are obtained and organized to achieve those goals. For example, employees of DaimlerChrysler are organized among assembly lines to produce cars or trucks in a manner consistent with the company's goals.

The organizing function occurs continuously throughout the life of the firm. This function is especially important for firms that frequently restructure their operations. Organizational changes such as the creation of a new position or the promotion of an employee occur frequently. These changes may even necessitate revisions in job assignments of employees whose job positions have not changed.

To illustrate the importance of the organizing function, consider a construction company that builds homes. The general contractor assigns tasks to the employees. From the laying of the foundation to painting, most tasks must be completed in a particular order. Since all tasks cannot be completed simultaneously, the contractor has workers working on different homes. In this way, employees can apply their respective specialties (such as painting, electrical, and so on) to whatever homes are at the proper stage of construction. In the next chapter, we will look at organizational structure in more detail.

Leading

leading the process of influencing the habits of others to achieve a common goal

The **leading** function is the process of influencing the habits of others to achieve a common goal. It may include the communication of job assignments to employees and possibly the methods of completing those assignments. It may also include serving as a role model for employees. The leading should be conducted in a manner that is consistent with the firm's strategic plan.

The leading function involves not only instructions on how to complete a task but also incentives to complete it correctly and quickly. Some forms of leading may help motivate employees. One method is to delegate authority by assigning employees more responsibility. Increased responsibility can encourage employees to take more pride in their jobs and raise their self-esteem. If employees are brought closer to the production process and allowed to express their concerns, problems can be resolved more easily. Managers who allow much employee feedback may prevent conflicts between management and employees, or even conflicts among employees. To the extent that the leading function can enhance the performance of employees, it will enhance the performance of the firm.

initiative the willingness to take action

For managers to be effective leaders, they need **initiative,** which is the willingness to take action. Managers who have all other skills but lack initiative may not be very effective. Some managers who recognize the need to enact changes are unwilling to take action because making changes takes more effort than leaving the situation as is, and change may upset some employees. For example, consider a manager who recognizes that the firm's expenses could be reduced, without any adverse effect on the firm, by eliminating a particular department. Nevertheless, this manager may refrain from suggesting any action because it might upset some employees. Managers are more likely to initiate change if they are directly rewarded for suggesting any changes that enhance the firm's value.

Leadership Styles Although all managers have their own leadership styles, styles can be classified generally as autocratic, free rein, or participative. Managers who use an **autocratic** leadership style retain full authority for decision making; employees have little or no input. For example, if managers believe that one of their manufacturing plants will continue to incur losses, they may decide to close the plant without asking for input from the plant's workers. Autocratic managers may believe that employees cannot offer input that would contribute to a given decision. Employees are instructed to carry out tasks ordered by autocratic leaders and are discouraged from being creative. In general, employees who desire responsibility are likely to become dissatisfied with such a management style.

autocratic a leadership style in which the leader retains full authority for decision making

free-rein a leadership style in which the leader delegates much authority to employees

Managers who use a **free-rein** (also called "laissez-faire") management style delegate much authority to employees. This style is the opposite extreme from the auto-

Steve Jobs, chief executive officer of Apple Computer, is shown here introducing new colors of the popular IMacs during his keynote address at the MacWorld Expo in San Francisco. Steve Jobs encourages input from Apple's managers and other employees. His leadership style is one of the reasons for Apple's success.

cratic style. Free-rein managers communicate goals to employees but allow the employees to choose how to complete the objectives. For example, managers may inform workers in a manufacturing plant that the plant's performance must be improved and then allow the workers to implement an improvement strategy. Employees working under a free-rein management style are expected to manage and motivate themselves daily.

participative a leadership style in which the leaders accept some employee input but usually use their authority to make decisions

In the **participative** (also called democratic) leadership style, the leaders accept some employee input but usually use their authority to make decisions. This style requires frequent communication between managers and employees. Participative management can allow employees to express their opinions, but it does not pressure employees to make major decisions. For example, managers of a General Motors plant may consider the ideas of assembly-line workers on how to improve the plant's performance, but the managers will make the final decisions.

A comparison of leadership styles is provided in Exhibit 7.6. The optimal leadership style varies with the situation and with employees' experience and personalities.

Exhibit 7.6

How Leadership Style Affects Employee Influence on Management Decisions

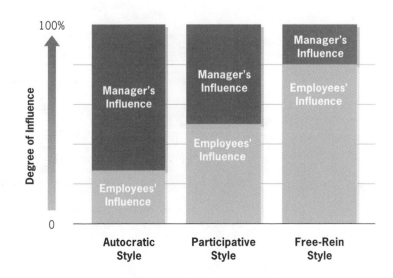

The free-rein style may be appropriate if employees are highly independent, creative, and motivated. An autocratic style may be most effective for managing employees with low skill-levels or high turnover rates. Participative management is effective when employees can offer a different perspective because of their closer attention to daily tasks.

Within a given firm, all three leadership styles may be used. For example, the top management of General Motors may use autocratic leadership to determine the types of automobiles (large versus small cars, luxury versus economy cars, and so on) to design in the future. These plans are made without much employee input because the top managers can rely on recent surveys of consumer preferences along with their own vision of what types of cars will be in demand in the future.

Once top management identifies the types of automobiles to produce, a participative leadership style may be used to design each type of car. That is, top management may establish general design guidelines for a particular type of car to be produced (such as specifying a small economy car) and ask employees for their suggestions on developing this type of car. These employees have experience on specific assembly-line operations and can offer useful input based on various production or quality problems they experienced with other cars. The top managers will make the final decisions after receiving the engineers' proposed designs, which are based on input from numerous employees. This example reflects a participative style because managers use their authority to decide on the particular type of product to be produced but solicit input from many employees.

After the design of a specific car is completed, managers use a free-rein style for some parts of the production process. For example, a group of employees may be assigned to a set of assembly-line tasks. They may be allowed to assign the specific tasks among themselves. They may also be allowed to rotate their specific jobs to avoid boredom. This example reflects the free-rein style because the employees are allowed to choose how to achieve the firm's objectives.

BUSINESS ONLINE

Training in Managerial Functions

http://www.rebrown.com

FIRMS SUCH AS R.E. BROWN PROVIDE MANAGERIAL TRAINING SERVICES AND use the Internet to make companies and potential managers aware of their products and services. For example, this site lists products consistent with the necessary managerial functions, such as planning, organizing, and leading.

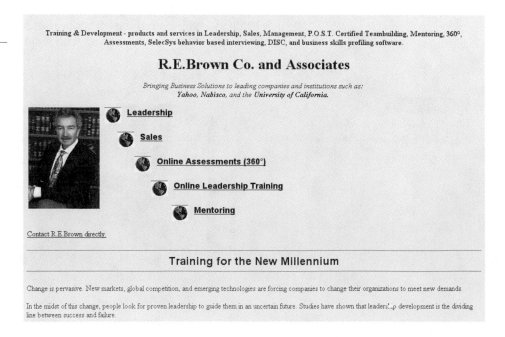

Training & Development - products and services in Leadership, Sales, Management, P.O.S.T. Certified Teambuilding, Mentoring, 360°, Assessments, SelecSys behavior based interviewing, DISC, and business skills profiling software.

R.E.Brown Co. and Associates

Bringing Business Solutions to leading companies and institutions such as:
Yahoo, Nabisco, and the University of California.

- Leadership
- Sales
- Online Assessments (360°)
- Online Leadership Training
- Mentoring

Contact R.E.Brown directly.

Training for the New Millennium

Change is pervasive. New markets, global competition, and emerging technologies are forcing companies to change their organizations to meet new demands.

In the midst of this change, people look for proven leadership to guide them in an uncertain future. Studies have shown that leadership development is the dividing line between success and failure.

Controlling

controlling the monitoring and evaluation of tasks

The **controlling** function represents the monitoring and evaluation of tasks. To evaluate tasks, managers should measure performance in comparison with the standards and expectations they set. That is, the controlling function assesses whether the plans set within the planning function are achieved. Standards can be applied to production volume and cost, sales volume, profits, and several other variables used to measure a firm's performance. The controlling function allows for continual evaluation so that the firm can ensure that it is following the course intended to achieve its strategic plan.

The strategic plan of Bristol-Myers Squibb (presented earlier) states that its reward systems will be based on standards set by the goals identified within that plan. An example of how the controlling function can be used to assess a firm's operations is shown in Exhibit 7.7.

Some standards such as profits are general and apply to all departments of a firm. Thus, no single department is likely to be entirely accountable if the firm's profits are not sufficient. Other standards focus on a particular operation of the firm. For example, production volume, production cost per unit, and inventory level standards can be used to monitor production. A specified volume of sales can be used as a standard to monitor the effectiveness of marketing strategies.

The main reason for setting standards is to detect and correct deficiencies. When deficiencies are detected, managers must take corrective action. For example, if labor and equipment repair expenses are too high, the firm will attempt to identify the reason for these deficiencies so that it can prevent them in the future. If a firm finds that its sales volume is below standards, its managers will determine whether to revise the existing marketing strategies or penalize those employees who are responsible for the deficiency. Deficiencies that are detected early may be more easily corrected. By identifying deficiencies that must be corrected, the controlling function can help to improve a firm's performance.

In some cases, the standards rather than the strategies need to be corrected. For example, a particular advertising strategy to boost automobile sales may fail when interest rates are high, since consumers are unwilling to borrow money to purchase automobiles at those interest rates. The failure to reach a specified sales level may be due to the high interest rates rather than a poor advertising strategy.

Integration of Management Functions

management the utilization of human resources (employees) and other resources (such as machinery) in a manner that best achieves the firm's plans and objectives

To illustrate how the four different functions of **management** are used, consider a firm that makes children's toys and decides to restructure its operations. Because of low sales, the top managers create a new strategic plan to discontinue production of plastic toys and to begin producing computer games. This planning function will require the use of the other management functions, as shown in Exhibit 7.8. The organizing function is needed to reorganize the firm's production process so that it can produce

Exhibit 7.7

Example of the Controlling Function

	Actual Level Last Week	Standards (Expected Level)	Assessment
Sales volume	300 units	280 units	OK
Production volume	350 units	350 units	OK
Labor expenses	$10,000	$9,000	Too high
Administrative expenses	$14,500	$15,000	OK
Equipment repair	$3,000	$1,000	Too high

Exhibit 7.8

Integration of Management
Functions

 Planning

Top Managers:
Change strategic plan to replace
plastic toy production with
computer game production.

 Communicate the plan
to middle management and ask
middle management to
implement the plan.

❷ Organizing

Middle Managers:
Reorganize the plastic toy
production plant so that it can
now be used to produce
computer games. Retrain the
plant's employees for this
production and hire four new
employees to help with the
technical production aspects.

Communicate the
reorganization to supervisors
and ask them to implement
the new production
process.

❸ Leading

Supervisors:
Explain each employee's tasks
required to produce computer
games and how to perform the
tasks.

Communicate
the tasks.

 Employees:
Perform the tasks assigned;
may have some input on job
assignments.

❹ Control

Top Management:
Assess the expenses and sales
from producing computer
games every month. Determine
whether the new strategic plan
is successful.

❹ Control

Middle Management:
Determine whether the
production is efficient (based on
monitoring the plant's output and
expenses each month).

❹ Control

Supervisors:
Monitor employees to ensure
that they are completing their
new assignments properly.

computer games. The leading function is needed to provide employees with instructions on how to produce the computer games. The controlling function is needed to determine whether the production process established to produce computer games is efficient and whether the sales of computer games are as high as forecasted. The controlling function may also provide feedback as to whether employees satisfied the firm's expectations.

In a small business, the owner may frequently perform all the management functions. For example, an owner of a small business may revise the strategic plan (planning function), reorganize the firm's production facility (organizing function), assign new tasks to the employees (leading function), and then assess whether all these revisions lead to acceptable results (controlling function).

GLOBAL BUSINESS

Leadership Styles for Global Business

WHEN U.S. FIRMS ESTABLISH BUSINESSES IN FOREIGN COUNTRIES (CALLED "foreign subsidiaries"), they must determine the type of leadership style to use in those countries. The firms do not automatically apply the style they use in the United States because conditions in foreign countries may be different. In some countries that have only recently encouraged private ownership of businesses (such as Hungary, Ukraine, and China), people are not accustomed to making business decisions that will maximize the value of the business. Many people had experience only in managing government-owned businesses. Consequently, their management decisions sometimes focused on satisfying government goals that conflicted with maximizing the value of the business. Furthermore, the businesses had little or no competition, so managers could make decisions without concern about losing market share. Faced with such conditions, some U.S. firms have used a more autocratic leadership style for their foreign subsidiaries. That is, instructions come from the U.S. headquarters, and the managers of the foreign subsidiaries are responsible for carrying out those instructions. When the managers have problems, they contact U.S. headquarters for advice.

Although many U.S. firms have recently adopted free-rein and participative styles in the United States, they may nevertheless be reluctant to give too much power to managers of some foreign subsidiaries. As the managers of the foreign subsidiaries gain experience working for the firm and in a competitive environment, they may be given more power to make decisions.

When a U.S. firm has foreign subsidiaries in several different countries, its choice of a leadership style may vary with the characteristics of the foreign country. For example, it may allow a participative style in some industrialized countries where managers are experienced in making business decisions aimed at maximizing the firm's value. The same firm may impose an autocratic style in a country where most business managers are not accustomed to making business decisions in this manner. No one particular leadership style is always appropriate for all countries. The firm must consider the country's characteristics before deciding which leadership style to use. Furthermore, the proper leadership style for any particular country may change over time in response to changes in the country's conditions.

Managerial Skills

3 Describe the skills that managers need.

To perform well, managers rely on four types of skills:

▶ Conceptual skills
▶ Interpersonal skills
▶ Technical skills
▶ Decision-making skills

Jeff Bezos used his conceptual skills to organize Amazon .com's business. Bezos, CEO of Amazon.com, recently named Time Magazine's Person of the Year, demonstrates an educational toy, "Gus's Guts," to talk show host Jay Leno during his appearance on the "Tonight Show with Jay Leno," at NBC studios in Burbank. The toy, which allows children to pull out the doll's internal organs, is one of the new items featured on Bezos' Internet superstore.

Conceptual Skills

conceptual skills the ability to understand the relationships between the various tasks of a firm

Managers with **conceptual skills** (also referred to as analytical skills) have the ability to understand the relationships between the various tasks of a firm. They see how all the pieces fit together. For example, top managers of Motorola understand how the production process is related to the marketing and finance functions. Their emphasis is not so much on the precise method of accomplishing any specific task as on having a general understanding of the firm's operations. This enables them to anticipate the potential problems that could arise if, for example, a particular production plant experiences shortages. Managers need conceptual skills to make adjustments when problems like this occur. Managers with good conceptual skills have backup strategies when problems in the production process occur. Such strategies allow the firm to continue using its resources effectively.

Conceptual skills are commonly used by the top-level and middle-level managers who are not directly involved in the production assembly process. These skills are necessary to optimally utilize employees and other resources in a manner that can achieve the firm's goals. Managers with good conceptual skills tend to be creative and are willing to consider various methods of achieving goals.

Consider the conceptual skills of Louis Gerstner, chief executive officer (CEO) of IBM. When he became CEO in 1993, Gerstner recognized that IBM had excessive production costs. To reduce these costs, he reorganized the firm's operations. This was a primary reason why IBM's stock price rose by more than 90 percent within two years after Gerstner became CEO.

Interpersonal Skills

interpersonal skills the skills necessary to communicate with customers and employees

Virtually all managers perform tasks that require good **interpersonal skills** (also referred to as communication skills), which are the skills necessary to communicate with customers and employees, as discussed next.

Communication with Customers Many managers must communicate with customers to ensure satisfaction. They listen to customer complaints and attempt to respond in an acceptable manner. They may also bring other complaints to the attention of top management. Managers lacking good interpersonal skills may ignore customer complaints. Consequently, problems go unnoticed until a sufficient number of dissatisfied customers stop buying the firm's products. By that time, it may be too late for the firm to regain customers' trust.

One of the most important interpersonal skills is the ability to ask good questions. Without this, the real story behind customer or employee dissatisfaction may not be uncovered.

Communication with Employees Managers need good interpersonal skills when communicating with employees. They must be able to clearly communicate assignments to employees and must communicate with employees who have made mistakes on the job so that they can be corrected. In addition, they must listen to complaints from employees and attempt to resolve their problems.

Middle- and top-level managers who use good interpersonal skills in communicating with lower management will be better informed about problems within the firm. Interpersonal skills are often used by top and middle managers when their decisions are influenced by information of other managers. For example, financial managers who develop next year's budget rely on projections of sales volume and prices provided by the marketing department. They also rely on production cost projections provided by the production department. All these managers must communicate with each other, since their projections are interrelated.

Ford Motor Company has initiated an e-mail newsletter from the CEO to all 145,000 employees. The employees are allowed to use e-mail to reply to the CEO. This has encouraged more communication between management and other employees.

Technical Skills

technical skills skills used to perform specific day-to-day tasks

Managers need **technical skills** to understand the types of tasks that they manage. Managers who are closer to the actual production process use their technical skills more frequently than high-level managers. For example, first-line managers of an assembly line of a computer manufacturer must be aware of how computer components are assembled. A technical understanding is important for all managers who evaluate new product ideas or are involved in solving problems.

D∉LL COMPUTER'S FORMULA FOR SUCCESS

In the recent past, Dell Computer launched online sales and service at **www.dell.com**, believing that the Internet is a natural extension of its model for doing business directly with customers without intermediaries. Both individual and institutional customers are increasingly using the Internet to buy desktop and notebook computers, workstations, and servers. To take advantage of the opportunities the Internet offers, managers at Dell Computer clearly need interpersonal and technical skills.

Decision-Making Skills

decision-making skills skills for using existing information to determine how the firm's resources should be allocated

Managers need **decision-making skills** so that they can use existing information to determine how the firm's resources should be allocated. The types of decisions made by managers vary with the position. The following are some typical decisions regarding the utilization of the firm's resources:

▶ Should more employees be hired?
▶ Should more machinery be purchased?
▶ Should a new facility be built?
▶ Should the assembly-line operation be revised?
▶ Should more supplies be ordered?
▶ Should salaries be adjusted?

Exhibit 7.9

Stages Involved in Making a Decision

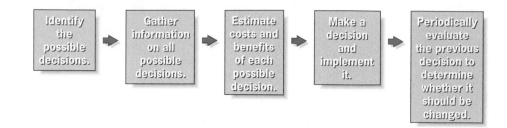

These decisions affect either the revenue or the operating expenses of the firm and therefore affect its earnings. Managers who make proper decisions can improve the firm's earnings and thereby improve its value.

Steps for Decision Making The decision-making process involves several specific stages. First, any possible decisions that are consistent with the firm's strategic plan are identified. Then, information relevant to each possible decision is compiled. Using this information, the costs and benefits of each possible decision are estimated. From these estimates, one or more managers can make and implement the best decision. As time passes, this decision should be evaluated to determine if any changes are necessary. The stages of the decision-making process are summarized in Exhibit 7.9.

As an example, consider the task of accommodating increased demand for products at Compaq Computer. Managers first think of alternative means of achieving this goal, such as hiring more workers or allowing more overtime for existing workers. Compiling the relevant information, including the cost of adding more workers or allowing more overtime, enables the managers to estimate the costs and benefits of each alternative. Once managers have this information, they can conduct a cost-benefit analysis and select the better alternative. As time passes, the cost of each alternative may change and the managers may reconsider their decisions.

BUSINESS ONLINE

Employment Opportunities and Job Descriptions

http://careers.yahoo.com

EMPLOYMENT OPPORTUNITIES, JOB DESCRIPTIONS, AND POSITION OPENINGS are frequently disclosed on the Internet by companies such as Yahoo! Websites such as this assist existing and aspiring managers to determine the skills required for the position they wish to apply for in the future.

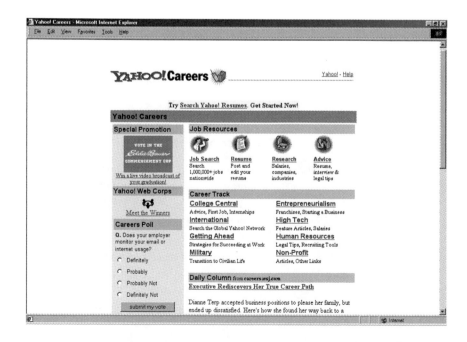

Exhibit 7.10

Summary of Key Managerial Skills

Skill	How the Skill Is Used by a Firm
Conceptual	Used to understand how the production level must be large enough to satisfy demand and how demand is influenced by the firm's marketing decisions.
Interpersonal	Used to inform employees about the goals of the firm and about specific policies that they must follow; also used to hear complaints from employees or customers and to resolve any conflicts among people.
Technical	Used to understand how components must be assembled to produce a product; also used to understand how machines and equipment should be used.
Decision making	Used to determine whether the firm should expand, change its pricing policy, hire more employees, or obtain more financing; proper decision making requires an assessment of the costs and benefits of various possible decisions that could be implemented.

Summary of Management Skills

The various management skills that have been described are summarized in Exhibit 7.10. All of these skills are necessary for managers to be successful.

As an example of how a firm's performance is dependent on the skills of its managers, consider the case of Boston Market. This firm was initially successful, but its managers made several poor decisions about the firm's growth and the pricing of its meals. It then experienced a high degree of management turnover, which resulted in additional poor decisions made by inexperienced managers. In the summer of 1997, its performance declined as a result of the poor management decisions, and so did its value (as measured by its stock price), as shown in Exhibit 7.11.

Exhibit 7.11

Impact of Poor Management on Boston Market's Stock Price

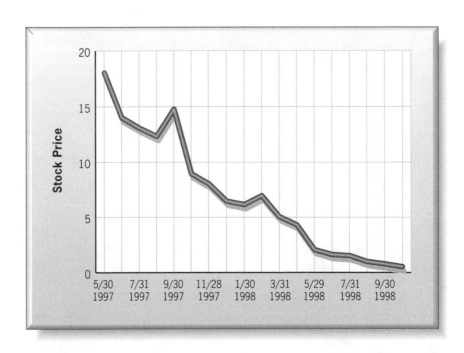

How Managers Manage Time

4 Describe methods that managers can use to utilize their time effectively.

time management the way managers allocate their time when managing tasks

Managers have a limited amount of time to manage their responsibilities. Therefore, they use **time management,** which refers to the way managers allocate their time when managing tasks. Although there is no single perfect formula for using time efficiently, the following guidelines should be followed:

▶ Set proper priorities.
▶ Schedule long time intervals for large tasks.
▶ Minimize interruptions.
▶ Set short-term goals.
▶ Delegate some tasks to employees.

Each of these guidelines is discussed in turn.

SPOTLIGHT ON TECHNOLOGY

Software to Improve Management

Effective management is particularly difficult in a small business where a single manager is responsible for many tasks. Recently, computer software packages have been developed to help managers in other areas. This new category of software, referred to as "MBA-ware" by *PC Magazine,* supports a wide range of activities, including the following:

▶ **Personnel Hiring:** Software for screening job applicants, based upon psychological principles, can be used to assess attitudes and potential fit with the company. Software of this type has long been used at a number of well-known companies, such as Mrs. Field's Cookies.
▶ **Personnel Evaluation:** Reviewing and evaluating personnel has long been a sensitive task, dreaded by many managers. Software is available that helps managers in constructing and writing reviews, as well as recording employee progress toward goals. Such software can help managers get through the review process and can be extremely valuable in documenting poor performance leading to an employee termination. Such documentation can be extremely valuable if the terminated employee sues his or her former employer.
▶ **General Management:** A wide range of software products are available to assist managers in day-to-day management activities. Among these, calendar and scheduling software can be used for appointments and

for time management. Personnel software can form the basis of a personnel system, keeping track of assorted information such as vacation usage, medical benefits, pension contributions, and so forth. In addition, some versions of personnel software provide managers with templates for creating complete personnel manuals. Contact management software can help sales personnel keep track of customer calls. Financial software can aid managers in making reasonable projections of future business. A wide range of software supports specific activities, such as creating presentations and business planning.

▶ **Negotiating:** A number of software packages have been developed that employ psychological models to help managers devise negotiating strategies for various situations. The software design is based on the principle that different negotiating styles should be employed when dealing with different types of individuals.
▶ **Decision Making:** A growing number of software packages are designed to help managers make decisions more rationally. Using tested decision-making techniques, they force managers to identify and prioritize alternatives in such a way that they can be ranked in an internally consistent fashion.
▶ **Creativity:** Some software is designed to stimulate managerial creativity. Such packages employ techniques drawn from brainstorming research and may also employ question-and-answer sessions designed to inspire managers with new ideas.

Although it is unlikely that software will ever substitute for managerial experience, more and more managers will undoubtedly use such tools to supplement their own management techniques.

Set Proper Priorities

One of the main reasons for time management problems is that managers lose sight of their role. Consider a regional sales manager who has two responsibilities: (1) resolving any problems with existing sales orders and (2) entertaining new clients. The sales manager may allocate much more time to entertaining because it is more enjoyable. Consequently, problems with sales orders may accumulate. Time management is a matter of priorities. Managers who set priorities according to what is best for the firm, rather than what they enjoy the most, are more successful.

Schedule Long Time Intervals for Large Tasks

Managers may be able to complete large tasks efficiently by scheduling large intervals (blocks) of time to focus on those tasks. Within each block, managers can focus all of their attention on the large task. In general, more work on a large project can be accomplished within one three-hour interval than in three separate one-hour intervals spread throughout a day or a week. When using short time intervals, managers waste time refreshing their memories on the issue of concern and the potential solutions. They would be more efficient if they could focus on the issue for a longer interval.

The best strategy for a task that requires less than one day of work may be to focus completely on that task until it is done. Short appointments that must be kept during a given day and are unrelated to the large task should be consolidated so that they do not continually break up the time allocated to the large task.

Minimize Interruptions

Virtually all managers are interrupted during the normal working day. Some problems may require immediate attention, but others can be put off until later. Managers should stay focused on the task at hand before allowing interference by unscheduled interruptions (except for emergencies).

Some managers have a natural tendency to create their own interruptions. For example, they may stop in offices of other employees to socialize. Although socializing during work hours may help reduce stress or boredom, managers should attempt to complete a certain amount of work before taking a social break. In this way, the break is a reward for accomplishing some work, not simply a means of putting off work.

Set Short-Term Goals

A common problem for managers is meeting deadlines, especially on large tasks. Managers should set short-term goals so that they can chip away at large tasks. For example, consider a manager who is assigned the task of purchasing a new computer system for the firm. The manager should break down the assignment into smaller tasks, such as (1) obtaining all the relevant information from other employees on the features that the computer system should have, (2) calling firms that sell computer systems to obtain price quotes, and (3) visiting firms where similar computer systems are in place to determine how well they work. Task C cannot be done until Task B is completed, and Task B cannot be done until Task A is completed.

If the assignment must be done in ten weeks, the manager may set a goal of completing Task A during the first three weeks, Task B during the fourth and fifth weeks, and Task C during the sixth and seventh weeks. This schedule allows a few extra weeks before the deadline in case any unexpected problems cause a task to take more time than was planned.

SMALL BUSINESS SURVEY

How Managers Run Meetings Efficiently

A recent survey asked managers of small firms how they run meetings. The following figure identifies some common methods of running a meeting efficiently, along with the percentage of respondents who use those methods.

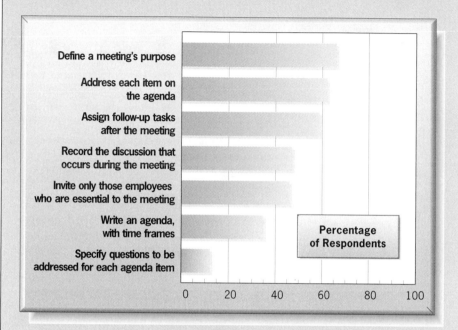

The results suggest that many managers attempt to keep meetings organized by defining the meeting's purpose and providing an agenda. However, most managers do not specify questions to be addressed for each agenda item.

Delegate Some Tasks to Employees

Managers only have so much time to complete the tasks they are assigned. If they can delegate some authority to their employees, they will have more time to be creative. By delegating, managers may even increase the job satisfaction of employees who prefer extra responsibility. However, managers should delegate only those tasks that employees can handle.

BUSINESS DILEMMA | **College Health Club**

Planning at College Health Club

SUE KRAMER, PRESIDENT OF COLLEGE HEALTH CLUB (CHC), IS ATTEMPTING to develop a long-term plan for her business. Her health club has been moderately successful so far, but Sue wants her business to grow over time. She decides to establish the following plans:

1 A strategic plan that will identify the future direction of the business over a period of three to five years.

2 A tactical plan that will include smaller-scale plans that are consistent with her strategic plan and will be implemented over the next year or so.

3 An operational plan that will identify methods to be used to achieve the tactical plans.

Dilemma

Sue believes that her concept of a health club that focuses on college students could be applied to other college campuses, but no other college campuses are nearby. Offer suggestions on how Sue could develop a strategic plan to attract college students to health clubs.

Solution

Sue offered convenience to college students by establishing the health club across the street from the campus and set the membership fee at a level that the students could afford. She plans to further capitalize on this strategy, as explained in her strategic plan.

1 *Strategic Plan* Focus on providing health club services to college students around the state by establishing health clubs near various college campuses. Provide convenient services at a reasonable price.

2 *Tactical Plan* Assess various college campuses throughout the state. Also determine whether competitive health clubs have already attracted those students. Estimate the costs of establishing a health club next to each campus.

3 *Operational Plan* Determine which college campus has the most potential for establishing a new health club. Survey the students on that campus to determine whether there is a demand for health club services. Get quotes on the rent for various places near the campus. Forecast the annual expenses and revenue if a health club were established. If the idea seems feasible, develop an official business plan to be presented to a commercial bank to obtain financing for this new business.

If she establishes a new health club, Sue will monitor its performance and determine whether to expand the service to other campuses. Her ultimate goal is to have a chain of health clubs around the state. Although Sue has a long-term vision, she cannot achieve her long-term plans immediately. She plans to pursue one new health club at a time to ensure that she can adequately manage the business as it expands. She will need to hire employees to help manage any new health clubs. Her strategic plan set the foundation for developing her tactical and operational plans.

Additional Issues for Discussion

1 What situations would discourage Sue Kramer from pursuing her strategic plan?

2 Explain why Sue Kramer needs good interpersonal skills to be successful when running her health club.

3 As Sue hires employees (mostly students who work part-time) for the existing health club over time, which leadership style should she use?

SUMMARY

 The levels of management are:

▶ top (high-level) management, which concentrates on the firm's long-run objectives;

▶ middle management, which is responsible for intermediate and short-term decisions;

▶ supervisory management, which is highly involved with employees who engage in the day-to-day production process.

 The key functions of management are:

▶ planning for the future (objectives);

▶ organizing resources to achieve objectives;

▶ leading employees by providing them with instructions on how they should complete their tasks;

▶ controlling, which involves monitoring and evaluating employee tasks.

 The most important managerial skills needed are:

▶ conceptual skills, used to understand relationships between various tasks;

▶ interpersonal skills, used to communicate with other employees and with customers;

▶ technical skills, used to perform specific day-to-day tasks, such as accounting skills to develop financial statements or electrical skills to understand how the wiring of a product is arranged;

▶ decision-making skills, used to assess alternative choices on the allocation of the firm's resources.

 Some of the key guidelines for effective time management are:

▶ set proper priorities in order to focus on the most important job responsibilities;

▶ schedule long time intervals for large tasks in order to focus on large tasks until the work is done;

▶ minimize interruptions in order to complete assignments;

▶ set short-term goals in order to chip away at long-term projects;

▶ delegate tasks that employees can complete on their own.

KEY TERMS

autocratic *186*
conceptual skills *192*
contingency planning *183*
controlling *189*
decision-making skills *193*
free-rein *186*
initiative *186*
interpersonal skills *192*
leading *186*

management *189*
middle management *180*
mission statement *181*
operational planning *183*
organizing *185*
participative *187*
planning *181*
policies *183*

procedures *183*
strategic plan *182*
supervisory (first-line) management *180*
tactical planning *183*
technical skills *193*
time management *196*
top (high-level) management *180*

REVIEW QUESTIONS

1 Identify and give examples of the functions of managers and how they vary at each level of management within the firm.

2 Describe the various functions a manager will perform on the job.

3 Discuss how a manager would implement the various types of planning functions within a firm. With which type of planning function would a president of a firm most likely be involved?

4 Distinguish management from leadership. Do you think a person could be effective in one area and ineffective in the other?

5 Describe the different leadership styles that you could develop and explain which style would be most appropriate if you wanted to consult with employees before making a decision.

6 Define the concept of management and explain what resources are available in a manager's budget to make decisions.

7 When U.S. firms establish businesses in foreign countries (called "foreign subsidiaries"), management must determine the appropriate leadership style. Discuss the appropriate style for each of the following: an underdeveloped country and an advanced industrialized country.

8 Discuss the different types of skills that a manager should possess. Explain what skills are necessary for a supervisor within a machine shop.

9 Explain the stages of decision making for a manager who has just decided to enter a new market with an existing product line.

10 Explain how you would utilize the guidelines for time management for an important project due today.

DISCUSSION QUESTIONS

1 Assume that you are thinking of becoming a manager. Define management. What are the most important skills you should have to become an effective manager?

2 Discuss how global competition is changing our thinking about managing firms and subsidiaries in foreign countries.

3 How could a firm use the Internet to provide information on its levels of management? How could a firm use the Internet to attract new managers?

4 Have you witnessed examples of effective and ineffective management? Cite some examples of both.

5 Explain the different leadership styles you would use if you were the manager of a project you were doing with other students.

INVESTING IN THE STOCK OF A BUSINESS

Using the annual report of the firm in which you would like to invest, complete the following:

1 What is the firm's mission and strategic plan?

2 How does the firm intend to achieve its strategic plan? Is it restructuring its operations to achieve its objectives?

3 Explain how the business uses technology to enhance its management function. For example, does it use the Internet to provide information regarding its levels of management and the managerial functions stressed most by the company?

4 Go to **http://hoovers.com** and locate the NEWS SEARCH. Type in the name of the firm in the space provided, and review the recent news stories about the firm. Summarize any (at least one) recent news story about the firm that applies to one or more of the key concepts within this chapter.

CASE APPLYING MANAGEMENT SKILLS

Maggie Wiltz manages a high-fashion specialty store in Atlanta, Georgia. Her daily activities start one hour before her store normally opens for business. She starts her day by opening the morning mail. Maggie must read numerous memos before the day starts. These memos are typically related to the coming day's business activities.

Half an hour before the store opens, Maggie meets with her employees. She plans to discuss important issues, most notably the fact that sales were off in the first quarter by 10 percent. She also wants to discuss her concern over returned merchandise.

Maggie's employees are relatively new and inexperienced. She believes she should select an appropriate leadership style to fit the situation and elects to use a participative style. Once Maggie starts the meeting, she wants the employees to participate and provide solutions to the problems discussed. The employees cannot offer any reasons why sales are declining, but they do suggest that a quality issue may be involved in the returns of merchandise.

After the store opens, Maggie is frequently interrupted by her employees. Another item on her agenda for the day is a midday luncheon with the Rotary Club, where she is to be the guest speaker. Later in the day, at the close of business, Maggie is to meet with her regional sales manager to discuss the excessive return of merchandise. She intends to provide him with the solutions that resulted from the meeting with her employees. She does not look forward to this meeting.

QUESTIONS

1 Define time management. What recommendations could you make to help Maggie improve in this area?

2 Discuss the management functions that Maggie utilizes on her job.

3 Should Maggie have developed a plan of action before her meeting with her employees?

4 Discuss the management skills that Maggie is using in this case.

VIDEO CASE EFFECTIVE LEADERSHIP AT VERMONT TEDDY BEAR COMPANY

Vermont Teddy Bear Company produces stuffed teddy bears ordered by customers to be sent as gifts to friends or family members. It competes with other firms that send candy, flowers, or other gifts in the mail. Vermont Teddy Bear Company needs a CEO who can provide effective leadership in order to maintain the firm's success. Liz Robert (pronounced *Robear*), president and chief executive officer of Vermont Teddy Bear Company, has a special leadership style. Her previous job position for the firm was chief financial officer, which forced her to pay attention to detail (estimating costs and revenue for the firm). Yet, she also recognizes that she now needs to use a broad vision when planning the future business for the firm.

The board of directors was initially concerned that Liz was overly focused on details and would not have the broad vision. However, she has adapted by using a broad vision to set goals for the firm in the future. In addition, she still uses her attention to detail by ensuring that employees are assigned tasks intended to achieve the firm's goals. This reflects leadership, because she is influencing the habits of others to achieve a common goal.

QUESTIONS

1 What is the potential advantage for Liz to use a participative leadership style in which other employees are allowed to provide their input?

2 How can Liz use leadership to improve the value of the firm?

3 When Liz was the chief financial officer, Liz was focused on all of the revenue and expenses of the firm. Now that she is CEO, she needs the conceptual skills to understand the relationships between the various tasks of the firm. Do you think that Liz's previous job helped develop her conceptual skills?

INTERNET APPLICATIONS

http://www.ibm.com/ibm/history/story

How many presidents has IBM had in its history? Who is currently the CEO of IBM? What are some of the managerial skills these presidents have used? What functions do you think IBM's CEOs have had to use to develop their key products and innovations?

THE *Coca-Cola* COMPANY ANNUAL REPORT PROJECT

Questions for the current year's annual report are available on the text website at **http://madura_intro_bus.swcollege.com.**

The following questions apply concepts learned in this chapter to The Coca-Cola Company. Go to The Coca-Cola Company website (**http://www.cocacola.com**) and find the index for the 1999 annual report.

QUESTIONS

1 Click on "Message to Share Owners." The Coca-Cola Company has built its credibility by being a dynamic company that is always moving to anticipate and meet customers' desires. Thus, it attempts to consistently hit its long-term targets (goals). Why do you think this builds credibility among its stockholders?

2 Click on "Message to Share Owners." What did The Coca-Cola Company do to empower its employees?

3 Click on "Message to Share Owners." How does the new Chairman feel about his position and to whom is he grateful?

4 Click on "Message to Share Owners." How does the Chairman feel about The Coca-Cola Company's employees?

5 Go to **http://hoovers.com** and locate the NEWS SEARCH. Type in The Coca-Cola Company in the space provided, and review the recent news stories about the firm. Summarize any (at least one) recent news story about The Coca-Cola Company that applies one or more of the key concepts within this chapter of the text.

IN-TEXT STUDY GUIDE

Answers are in an appendix at the back of the book.

TRUE OR FALSE

1 Planning is the managerial function that influences the habits of others to achieve a common goal.

2 The controlling function of management involves organizing employees and other resources in order to achieve the firm's goals.

3 Leading is the management function that provides employees with the instructions they need to complete a task, as well as incentives to encourage the employees to do the job correctly and quickly.

4 Top management is usually highly involved with employees who are engaged in the day-to-day production process.

5 Contingency planning is intended to identify the firm's main business focus over a long-term period.

6 In a small business, the owner may frequently perform all the management functions.

7 A U.S. firm with several foreign subsidiaries should vary its leadership style in the different countries, depending upon the characteristics of the foreign country.

8 A firm's mission statement will identify the goals of the firm.

9 Conceptual skills are commonly required by assembly-line employees who are directly involved in the production assembly process.

10 The free-rein leadership style is more appropriate than the autocratic style if employees are highly independent, creative, and motivated.

MULTIPLE CHOICE

11 The function of management that evaluates employee performance in comparison with established standards is:
a) planning.
b) controlling.
c) organizing.
d) leading.
e) time management.

12 The skills managers use to understand the relationships between the various tasks of the firm are:
a) interpersonal skills.
b) technical skills.
c) decision-making skills.
d) conceptual skills.
e) problem-solving skills.

13 All of the following guidelines should be followed when using time management except:
a) setting proper priorities.
b) centralizing responsibility.
c) scheduling long intervals of time for large tasks.
d) minimizing interruptions.
e) delegating some tasks to employees.

14 Since they are closer to the production process, first-line managers use their _____ skills more frequently than do high-level managers.
a) conceptual
b) interpersonal
c) decision-making
d) management
e) technical

15 The type of planning that identifies the methods used to achieve a firm's tactical plans is called:
a) operational planning.
b) tactical planning.
c) strategic planning
d) contingency planning.
e) procedure planning.

16 All of the following are typical goals that the management function can help to achieve except:
a) high production efficiency.
b) high production quality.
c) limited competition.
d) customer satisfaction.
e) employee satisfaction.

17 Using existing information, managers need _____ to determine how the firm's resources should be allocated.
a) conceptual skills
b) interpersonal skills
c) technical skills
d) decision-making skills
e) autocratic management skills

18 The style of leadership that is the opposite extreme of the autocratic style is:
a) free-rein.
b) authoritative.
c) manipulation.
d) boss-centered.
e) commanding.

19 The management of a firm would benefit from having _____ in order to effectively handle various possible business conditions.
a) interpersonal plans
b) various leadership styles
c) strategic plans
d) tactical management
e) contingency plans

20 The leading function of management should be conducted in a manner that is consistent with the firm's:
a) competition.
b) strategic plan.
c) customers.
d) industry demands.
e) labor union.

21 For managers to understand the relationships between the types of tasks, they must possess:
a) conceptual skills.
b) interpersonal skills.
c) top-management skills.
d) technical skills.
e) tactical plans.

22 Which of the following is the first step involved in making a decision?
a) gathering information
b) estimating costs and benefits of each possible decision
c) identifying the possible decisions
d) making a decision and implementing it
e) evaluating the decision to determine whether any changes are necessary

23 When employees have little or no input in decision making, managers use a(n):
a) free-rein style.
b) interpersonal communication style.
c) autocratic leadership style.
d) participative style.
e) employee-centered style.

24 The type of leadership style that allows employees to express their opinions to their managers is the _____ style.
a) autocratic
b) command-oriented
c) contingency
d) authoritative
e) participative

25 The managers of foreign subsidiaries are responsible for carrying out instructions provided to them from:
a) the corporate headquarters.
b) time management.
c) contingency planning.
d) standing plans.
e) single-use plans.

26 The position of chief financial officer is considered to be a:
a) supervisory position.
b) top-management position.
c) first-line management position.
d) bottom-line position.
e) middle management position.

27 Business firms develop and enforce _____ to prevent employees from conducting tasks in an inefficient, dangerous, or illegal manner.
a) kickbacks.
b) reciprocity.
c) policies.
d) time management.
e) prioritizing tasks.

28 A strategic plan that focuses on increased sales will likely require more:
a) production and financing.
b) policies.
c) rules.
d) authoritarian management.
e) autocratic management.

29 Managers who lack initiative may not be very effective even if they possess the necessary:
a) financial backing.
b) reciprocity.
c) support.
d) skills.
e) patronage.

30 The controlling function requires managers to establish performance standards. All of the following are areas where standards can be applied except:
a) sales volume.
b) profits.
c) production costs.
d) quality.
e) number of competing companies.

31 The skills that managers need to communicate with customers and employees are:
a) organizing skills.
b) control skills.
c) motivating skills.
d) conceptual skills.
e) interpersonal skills.

32 Which of the following describes the primary goal of a firm?
a) tactical plan
b) mission statement
c) operating plan
d) bottom-up plan
e) contingency plan

33 Middle and high-level managers engage in short-term, small-scale plans that are consistent with the firm's strategic plan. These short-term, smaller-scale plans are known as:
a) tactical plans.
b) mission statements.
c) leadership plans.
d) bottom-up plans.
e) contingency plans.

34 The steps necessary to implement a policy are known as:
a) contingency plans.
b) operational goals.
c) initiative statements.
d) production standards.
e) procedures.

35 The function of management that involves the monitoring and evaluation of tasks is:
a) planning.
b) organizing.
c) controlling.
d) leading.
e) motivating.

The Learning Goals of this chapter are to:

1 Explain how an organizational structure may be used by a firm to achieve its strategic plan.

2 Identify methods that can be used to departmentalize tasks.

Organizational Structure

Each firm should have a strategic plan that identifies the future direction of its business. The responsibilities of its managers should be organized to achieve the strategic plan.

Each firm establishes an organizational structure or the structure within the firm that identifies responsibilities for each job position and the relationships among those positions. The organizational structure also indicates how all the job responsibilities fit together. The organizational structure affects the efficiency with which a firm produces its product and therefore affects a firm's value.

Consider the case of Heinz, which manufactures hundreds of different products. Should a different manager be responsible for overseeing the operations of each product? How much responsibility should Heinz assign to the employees who produce its products? What factors should Heinz consider when determining how much authority to assign to its employees? This chapter provides a background on organizational structure that can be used to address these questions.

How a Firm's Organizational Structure Achieves Its Strategic Plan

1 Explain how an organizational structure may be used by a firm to achieve its strategic plan.

organizational structure identifies responsibilities for each job position and the relationships among those positions

organization chart a diagram that shows the interaction among employee responsibilities

An **organizational structure** identifies responsibilities for each job position and the relationships among those positions. The organizational structure typically varies among firms.

A firm's organizational structure can be illustrated with an **organization chart,** which is a diagram that shows the interaction among employee responsibilities. Exhibit 8.1 provides an example of an organization chart.

Chain of Command

The organizational structure indicates the **chain of command,** which identifies the job positions to which all types of employees must report. The chain of command also indicates who is responsible for various activities. Since employees often encounter problems that require communication with other divisions, it helps to know who is responsible for each type of task.

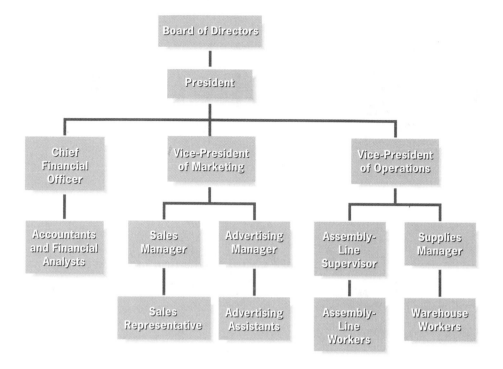

chain of command identifies
the job position to which each
type of employee must report

The president (who also typically holds the position of chief executive officer) has
the ultimate responsibility for the success of a firm. The president normally attempts
to coordinate all divisions and provide direction for the firm's business. In most firms,
many managerial duties are delegated to other managers. Vice-presidents normally oversee specific divisions or broad functions of the firm and report to the president.

BUSINESS ONLINE

Corporate
Organization
Charts

http://www.danka.com

ORGANIZATION CHARTS FOR MANY DIFFERENT COMPANIES CAN OFTEN BE
found on the Internet, as shown here for Danka. This information is useful to company employees, investors, and customers who wish to assess a company's chain of
command or the organizational height.

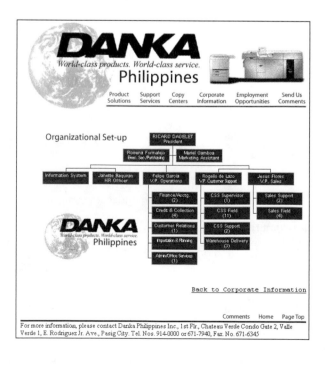

Authority of the Board of Directors

board of directors a set of executives who are responsible for monitoring the activities of the firm's president and other high-level managers

Each firm has a **board of directors,** or a set of executives who are responsible for monitoring the activities of the firm's president and other high-level managers. Directors are selected by shareholders; they serve as representatives for the shareholders, as confirmed by a quotation from Sears' annual report:

❝ The board of directors regularly reviews the corporation's structure to determine whether it supports optimal performance and thus serves the best interests of shareholders by delivering shareholder value. ❞

Directors have the authority to approve or disapprove key business proposals made by a firm's managers, such as acquisitions or layoffs. For example, America Online's decision to merge with Time Warner required board approval. Board members who are also managers of the same firm (such as the chief executive officer) are referred to as **inside board members.** Board members who are not managers of the firm are referred to as **outside board members.** In general, the board focuses only on key decisions and normally is not involved in the day-to-day activities of the firm. Board meetings generally are scheduled every few months or are called when the directors' input is needed regarding a key business decision.

inside board members board members who are also managers of the same firm

outside board members board members who are not managers of the firm

The one thousand largest U.S. firms have twelve directors on their boards on average. Some firms, such as General Electric and PepsiCo, provide directors with stock

SMALL BUSINESS SURVEY

Who Are the Board Members of Small Firms?

A recent survey asked the chief executive officers (CEOs) of small firms (with less than $50 million in annual sales) about the background of their outside board members. The results of the survey follow.

Background	Percentage of Firms Whose Board Members Have That Background
Executives of other firms	69%
Major investors in the firm	36%
Retired business executives	30%
Attorneys	29%
Accountants	22%
Bankers	18%
Business consultants	13%
Customers	2%
Others	3%

The results suggest that these firms rely heavily on executives and major investors to serve as their outside board members. The attorneys, accountants, and business consultants who are hired as outside board members typically also perform other duties (such as legal or banking duties) for the firm.

as partial compensation. This type of compensation may motivate the directors to serve the interests of the firm's shareholders, because the board members will benefit if the firm's stock price rises. Some firms, such as Travelers Group, pay their board members entirely with stock to ensure that they focus on decisions that may boost the stock's price for shareholders.

Directors not only oversee the key decisions of managers but may also initiate changes in a firm. For example, the board may decide that the firm's chief executive officer needs to be replaced or that the firm's businesses should be restructured. The boards of numerous well-known firms such as American Express, W. R. Grace, IBM, and KMart have recently initiated major changes. In many cases, the board becomes more involved after a period of poor performance by the firm. Board members of numerous firms have become more active in recent years as a result of pressure from shareholders.

A board of directors may be more willing to take action if most of its members are outside members (and therefore are not employees of the firm). The outside board members may suggest policies that will benefit shareholders, even if the policies are not supported by the firm's top managers. For example, the directors may recommend that the salaries of some high-level managers be reduced. Such a policy is less likely to be suggested by inside board members who are also high-level managers of the firm.

BUSINESS ONLINE

Board of Director Information

http://product.info.apple.com/ pr/press.releases/1997/q4/ 970806.pr.rel.board.html

CORPORATIONS SUCH AS APPLE COMPUTER OFTEN DISPLAY SIGNIFICANT changes in their company's organizational structure on the Internet. For example, in 1997, Apple changed the composition of its board of directors. The board of directors is elected by the shareholders, who can use websites such as this to confirm the timing and results of their vote. Furthermore, since the board of directors makes the key decisions within a corporation, both managers and investors can use these websites to assess the background and decisions of a company's directors.

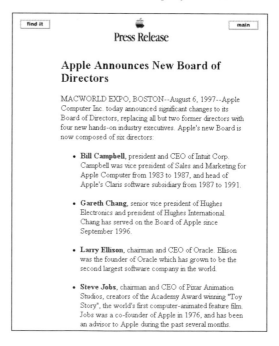

Span of Control

span of control the number of employees managed by each manager

Top management determines the firm's **span of control,** or the number of employees managed by each manager. When an organizational structure is designed so that each manager supervises just a few employees, it has a narrow span of control. Conversely, when it is designed so that each manager supervises numerous employees, it has a wide span of control. When a firm has numerous employees performing similar tasks, a wide span of control is used, since these employees can be easily managed by one or a few managers. A firm with highly diverse tasks may need more managers with various skills to manage the different tasks, resulting in a narrow span of control.

Exhibit 8.2 illustrates how the span of control can vary among firms. The organizational structure at the top reflects a narrow span of control. Each employee oversees only one other employee. The nature of the business may require highly specialized skills in each position so that employees may focus on their own tasks and not have to monitor a large set of employees. The organizational structure at the bottom reflects a wide span of control. The president directly oversees all the other employees. Such a wide span of control is more typical of firms in which many employees have similar positions that can easily be monitored by a single person.

Organizational Height

The organizational structure can also be described by its height. A tall organizational structure implies that there are many layers from the bottom of the structure to the top. Conversely, a short (or flat) organizational structure implies that there is not much distance from the bottom of the structure to the top because there are not many layers of employees between the bottom and top. Many firms that are able to use a wide span of control tend to have a flat organizational structure, as they do not require as many layers. Conversely, firms that need to use a narrow span of control tend to have a tall organizational structure with many layers. Notice that in Exhibit 8.2, the organizational structure with the narrow span of control is tall, while the organizational structure with the wide span of control is flat.

Exhibit 8.2

Distinguishing between a Narrow and a Wide Span of Control

Narrow Span of Control

President

Vice-President of Operations

Sales Manager

Salesperson

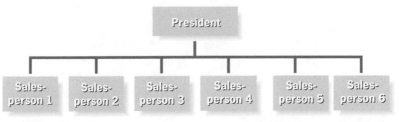

Wide Span of Control

President

Salesperson 1 | Salesperson 2 | Salesperson 3 | Salesperson 4 | Salesperson 5 | Salesperson 6

Centralization

centralization keeping most authority among the high-level managers

Some firms make an effort to keep most authority among the high-level managers, which is referred to as **centralization.** In centralized firms, middle and supervisory managers are responsible for day-to-day tasks and for reporting to the top managers, but they are not allowed to make many decisions.

Decentralization

decentralized authority is spread among several divisions or managers

autonomy divisions can make their own decisions and act independently

In recent years, many firms have **decentralized,** meaning that authority is spread among several divisions or managers. An extreme form of decentralization is **autonomy,** in which divisions are permitted to make their own decisions and act independently. The trend toward decentralization is due to its potential advantages. The delegation of authority can improve the morale of the employees, who may have more enthusiasm if they are assigned more responsibilities. In addition, these managers become more experienced in decision making. Therefore, they will be better

---

SELF-SCORING EXERCISE

How Decentralized Is Your Company?

Decentralization is one of the key design dimensions in an organization. It is closely related to several behavioral dimensions of an organization, such as leadership style, degree of participative decision making, teamwork, and the nature of power and politics within the organization.

The following questionnaire allows you to get an idea of how decentralized your organization is. (If you do not have a job, have a friend who works complete the questionnaire to see how decentralized his or her organization is.) Which level in your organization has the authority to make each of the following decisions? Answer the questionnaire by circling one of the following:

0 = The board of directors makes the decision.
1 = The CEO makes the decision.
2 = The division/functional manager makes the decision.
3 = A sub-department head makes the decision.
4 = The first-level supervisor makes the decision.
5 = Operators on the shop floor make the decision.

Decision Concerning:	Circle Appropriate Level					
a. The number of workers required.	0	1	2	3	4	5
b. Whether to employ a worker.	0	1	2	3	4	5
c. Internal labor disputes.	0	1	2	3	4	5
d. Overtime worked at shop level.	0	1	2	3	4	5
e. Delivery dates and order priority.	0	1	2	3	4	5
f. Production planning.	0	1	2	3	4	5
g. Dismissal of a worker.	0	1	2	3	4	5
h. Methods of personnel selection.	0	1	2	3	4	5
i. Method of work to be used.	0	1	2	3	4	5
j. Machinery or equipment to be used.	0	1	2	3	4	5
k. Allocation of work among workers.	0	1	2	3	4	5

Add up all your circled numbers. Total = _____. The higher your number (for example, 45 or more), the more decentralized your organization. The lower your number (for example, 25 or less), the more centralized your organization.

qualified for high-level management positions in the future. Decentralization has contributed to innovation at many technology firms, as more managers have become more creative.

Decentralization can be useful in accelerating the decision-making process. Decisions are made more quickly if the decision makers do not have to wait for approval from top managers. Many firms, including IBM, have decentralized to accelerate their decision making.

Johnson and Johnson is a prime example of a firm that has benefited from decentralization. It has numerous operating divisions scattered among more than 50 countries, and most of the decision making is done by the managers at those divisions. This has enabled each of Johnson and Johnson's units to make quick decisions in response to local market conditions.

Advantages   A decentralized organizational structure can improve a firm's performance for the following reasons. First, decentralization reduces operating expenses because salaries of some employees who are no longer needed are eliminated. Second, it accelerates the decision-making process, as lower-level employees are assigned more power. Third, it motivates some employees by assigning them more responsibilities. Fourth, it allows those employees who are closely involved in the production of a particular product to offer their input.

Disadvantages   A decentralized organizational structure can also have disadvantages. It could force some managers to make major decisions even though they lack the experience to make such decisions or prefer not to do so. Also, if middle and supervisory managers are assigned an excessive amount of responsibilities, they may be unable to complete all of their tasks.

Proper Degree of Decentralization   The proper degree of decentralization for any firm is dependent on the skills of managers who could be assigned more responsibilities. Decentralization can be beneficial when the managers who are given more power are capable of handling their additional responsibilities. For example, assume that, historically, top managers determined annual raises for all assembly-line workers but decide to delegate this responsibility to supervisors who monitor those workers. The supervisors are closer to the assembly line and are possibly in a better position to assess worker performance. Therefore, this type of decentralization may be appropriate. The top managers may still have final approval of the raises that supervisors propose for their workers.

As a second example, assume that top managers allow supervisors of assembly lines to decide the price to bid for a specific business that is for sale. Assembly-line supervisors normally are not trained for this type of task and should not be assigned to it. Determining the proper price to bid for a business requires a strong financial background and should not be delegated to managers without the proper skills.

The two examples demonstrate that high-level managers should retain authority for tasks that require their specialized skills but should delegate authority when the tasks can be handled by other managers. Routine decisions should be made by the employees who are closely involved with the tasks of concern. Decision making may improve because these employees are closer to the routine tasks and may have greater insight than top managers on these matters.

Some degree of centralization is necessary when determining how funds should be allocated to support various divisions of a firm. If managers of each division were given the authority to make this decision, they might request additional funds even if their division did not need to expand. Centralized management of funds can prevent division managers from making decisions that conflict with the goal of maximizing the firm's value.

DELL COMPUTER'S FORMULA FOR SUCCESS

Dell Computer has been careful not to grow faster than its ability to support customers. The company's core strategy has been segmentation. As a business grows, Dell's management divides it into defined pieces that can focus specifically on the unique requirements of that customer group; therefore, each Dell organization is directly accountable for the needs of Dell customers within that segment. Thus, Dell clearly follows a decentralized structure.

downsizing an attempt by a firm to cut expenses by eliminating job positions

Effect of Downsizing on Decentralization As firms expanded during the 1980s, additional management layers were created, resulting in taller organization charts. In the 1990s, however, many firms attempted to cut expenses by eliminating job positions. This so-called **downsizing** has resulted in flatter organization charts with fewer layers of managers. Continental Airlines, IBM, General Motors, Sears, and many other firms have downsized in recent years.

As some management positions were eliminated, many of those responsibilities were delegated to employees who previously reported to the managers whose positions were eliminated. For example, Amoco (now part of BP Amoco) eliminated a middle layer of its organizational structure. When managers in the middle of the organization chart are removed, other employees must be assigned more power to make decisions. Thus, downsizing has resulted in a greater degree of decentralization.

Downsizing has also affected each manager's span of control. The decentralization caused by eliminating many middle managers resulted in the remaining managers having more diverse responsibilities. Consequently, the organizational structure of many firms now reflects a wider span of control, as illustrated in Exhibit 8.3.

Downsizing not only has removed some management layers and created a wider span of control, but it also has combined various job responsibilities within the organizational structure. Whereas job assignments traditionally focused on production tasks, more attention is now given to customer satisfaction. Many firms recognize that they must rely on their current customers for additional business in the future and

Exhibit 8.3

Effect of Downsizing on Span of Control

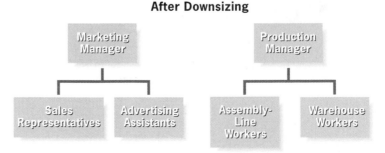

have revised their strategic plan to focus on achieving repeat business from their customers. In many cases, customers would prefer to deal with a single employee rather than several different employees. Consequently, employees are less specialized because they must have diverse skills to accommodate the customers.

Line versus Staff Positions

line positions job positions established to make decisions that achieve specific business goals

staff positions job positions established to support the efforts of line positions

line organization an organizational structure that contains only line positions and no staff positions

line-and-staff organization an organizational structure that includes both line and staff positions and assigns authority from higher-level management to employees

The job positions in an organizational structure can be classified as line positions or staff positions. **Line positions** are established to make decisions that achieve specific business goals. **Staff positions** are established to support the efforts of line positions, rather than to achieve specific goals of the firm. For example, managers at Black and Decker who are involved in the production of power tools are in line positions. Employees in staff positions at Black and Decker offer support to the managers who are in line positions. The staff positions provide assistance to the line positions, while the authority to make decisions is assigned to the line positions.

An organizational structure that contains only line positions and no staff positions is referred to as a **line organization.** This type of organizational structure may be appropriate for a business that cannot afford to hire staff for support, such as a small manufacturing firm.

Most firms need some staff positions to provide support to the line positions. An organizational structure that includes both line and staff positions and assigns authority from higher-level management to employees is referred to as a **line-and-staff organization.**

Exhibit 8.4 depicts a line organization and a line-and-staff organization. The line-and-staff organization in this exhibit includes a director of computer systems, who oversees the computer system, and a director of human resources, who is involved with hiring and training employees. These two positions are staff positions because they can assist the finance, marketing, and production departments but do not have the authority to make decisions that achieve specific business goals.

Creating a Structure That Allows More Employee Input

Firms commonly rely on the input of employees from various divisions for special situations. For this reason, they may need to temporarily adjust their formal organiza-

Firms such as Louisville Slugger (producer of baseball bats, shown here) benefit when employees involved in the production process are allowed to offer input on how to improve production efficiency.

Exhibit 8.4

Comparison of a Line Organization with a Line-and-Staff Organization

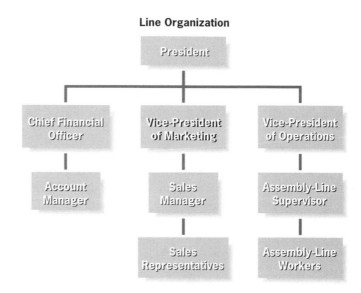

Line Organization

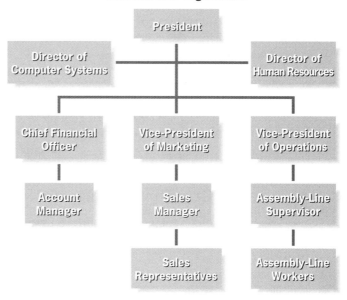

Line-and-Staff Organization

tional structure so that some extra responsibilities may be assigned. The following are two common methods for revising the organizational structure to obtain employee input:

▶ Matrix organization
▶ Intrapreneurship

Each of these methods is discussed in turn.

Matrix Organization Firms are often confronted with special circumstances that require input from their employees. In a **matrix organization,** various parts of the firm interact to focus on specific projects. Because the projects may take up only a portion of the normal workweek, participants can continue to perform their normal tasks and are still accountable to the same boss for those tasks. For example, a firm that plans to install a new computer system may need input from each division on

matrix organization an organizational structure that enables various parts of the firm to interact to focus on specific projects

Exhibit 8.5

A Matrix Organization for a Special Project to Design a New Computer System

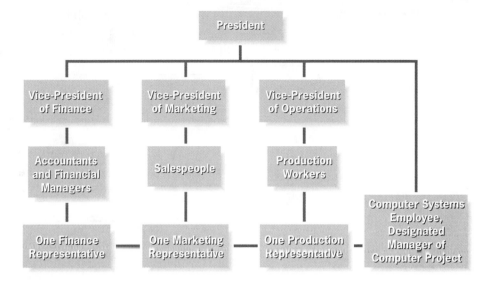

the specific functions of the system that are necessary. This example is illustrated in Exhibit 8.5. The team of employees periodically works on any assigned project until it is completed. Some employees may be assigned to two or more projects during the specific period. As Exhibit 8.5 shows, the finance, marketing, and production divisions each have one representative on the team; each representative can offer insight from the perspective of his or her respective division. The lower horizontal line in Exhibit 8.5 shows the interaction among the representatives from different divisions. The manager of this project is a computer systems employee, who will report the recommendations of the matrix organization to the president or to some other top manager.

An advantage of the matrix approach is that it brings together employees who can offer insight from different perspectives. Each participant who is assigned to a specific group (or team) has particular skills that can contribute to the project. By involving all participants in decision making, this teamwork may provide more employee satisfaction than typical day-to-day assignments. Firms such as Intel, IBM, and Boeing commonly use teams of employees to complete specific projects.

One possible disadvantage of a matrix organization is that no employee may feel responsible because responsibilities are assigned to teams of several employees. Therefore, a firm that uses teams to complete various tasks may designate one job position with the responsibility of organizing the team and ensuring that the team's assignment is completed before the deadline. The person designated as project manager (or team leader) of a specific project does not necessarily have authority over the other participants for any other tasks.

Another disadvantage of the matrix organization is that any time used to participate in projects reduces the time allocated for normal tasks. In some cases, ultimate responsibility is not clear, causing confusion. Many firms eliminated their matrix structure for this reason.

BUSINESS ONLINE

Matrix Organization Chart

SOME ORGANIZATIONS UTILIZE A MATRIX APPROACH TO THEIR ORGANIZAtional structure. The website on the next page shows the matrix organization chart for the Division of Cancer Prevention of the National Cancer Institute. Notice how

http://dcp.nci.nih.gov/matrix
.html

project teams are formed using the subdivisions of organ systems and foundations of prevention research groups. Each project team consists of employees from different areas of the organization.

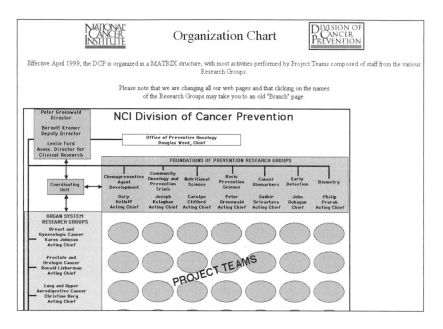

Intrapreneurship   Some firms not only require input from employees on specific issues but also encourage employees to offer ideas for operational changes that will enhance the firm's value. These firms may even create a special subsidiary within their organizational structure in which particular employees are given the responsibility to innovate. In this way, the costs and benefits of innovation can be estimated separately from the rest of the business operations.

Particular employees of a firm can be assigned to create ideas, as if they were entrepreneurs running their own firms. This process is referred to as **intrapreneurship,** as employees are encouraged to think like entrepreneurs within the firm. They differ from entrepreneurs, however, in that they are employees rather than owners of the firm. Some employees may even be assigned the responsibility of developing new products or ideas for improving existing products. Intrapreneurship can pull employees away from normal, day-to-day production tasks. Nevertheless, it can also allow firms to be more innovative because employees are encouraged to search for new ideas. Many firms, including Apple Computer and 3M Company, have used intrapreneurship to encourage new ideas.

Intrapreneurship is likely to be more successful if employees are rewarded with some type of bonus for innovations that are ultimately applied by the firm. The firm should also attempt to ensure that any ideas that employees develop are seriously considered. If managers shoot down ideas for the wrong reasons (jealousy, for instance), employees may consider leaving the firm to implement their ideas (by starting their own business).

Informal Organizational Structure

intrapreneurship the assignment of particular employees of a firm to create ideas, as if they were entrepreneurs running their own firms

informal organizational structure an informal communications network among a firm's employees

All firms have both a formal and an informal organizational structure. The **informal organizational structure** is the informal communications network that exists among a firm's employees. This network (sometimes called a "grapevine") develops as a result of employee interaction over time. Some employees interact because they work on similar tasks. Interaction among employees in unrelated divisions often occurs in a common lunch area, at social events, or even as a result of a decision that requires input from two different divisions.

SPOTLIGHT ON TECHNOLOGY

Impact of Information Technology on Organizational Structure

Advances in technology often bring change to a firm's organizational structure. All parts of a firm use technology, and a wide variety of departments include technology experts among their employees. Technology and the professionals working in the field must support and connect every area of the organization.

The integration of information technology (IT) requires communication among employees. A conscious effort must be made to maintain relationships with the groups each participant represents. IT representatives must communicate the options under consideration and solicit expertise when needed. Other members of the project team or department should inform the ultimate end users about the key issues under consideration and request feedback. These relationships are often overlooked and lost as the immediate challenge of the design overwhelms everything else. Therefore, relationships with other future participants should be maintained through planned communication as the project progresses.

Technology and the knowledge-based economy are not constrained by the physical objects and materials of a firm. Information is flexible and can be structured and organized in a number of different ways. For example, videoconferencing and telecommuting allow project teams and departments to work together regardless of where they are located and what department they work for. Thus, technology enables departments within a firm to communicate more easily.

These same technologies also allow different companies to communicate with each other. Apple Computer is essentially a computer design and marketing company. All of its production is completed by other firms (outsourced). Yet the different firms that are responsible for bringing an Apple computer to market are able to collaborate and communicate easily.

Advantages The informal organizational structure can benefit a firm in several ways. Employees who need help in performing a task may benefit from others. If employees had to seek help through the formal structure, they would have to go to the person to whom they report. If that particular person is not available, the production process could be slowed. An informal structure may also allow employees to substitute for one another, which can ensure that a task will be completed on time. In addition, an informal structure can reduce the amount of manager involvement.

Another advantage of an informal structure is that friendships result from it. Friendships with other employees are a common reason for employee satisfaction with their jobs. It could be the major factor that discourages them from looking for a new job. This is especially true of lower-level jobs that pay low wages. Because friendship can strongly influence employee satisfaction, firms commonly encourage social interaction by organizing social functions.

Informal communication can occur among employees on different levels. This allows information to travel informally from the top down or from the bottom up throughout the organization.

Disadvantages Along with the advantages just described, an informal structure also has some disadvantages. Perhaps the main disadvantage is that employees may obtain incorrect or unfavorable information about the firm through the informal structure. Even if the information is untrue or is a gross exaggeration, it can have a major impact on employee morale. Unfavorable information that has an adverse impact tends to travel faster and further throughout an informal structure than favorable information does.

② Identify methods that can be used to departmentalize tasks.

Methods of Departmentalizing Tasks

When developing or revising an organizational structure, high-level management must first identify all the different tasks and responsibilities that the firm performs. The next

An informal organizational structure allows employees to communicate, even if they have different tasks.

departmentalize assign tasks and responsibilities to different departments

step is to **departmentalize** those tasks and responsibilities, which means to assign the tasks and responsibilities to different departments. The best way of departmentalizing depends on the characteristics of the business. By using an efficient method of departmentalizing tasks and responsibilities, a firm can minimize its expenses and maximize its value. The following are four of the more popular methods of departmentalizing:

▶ By function
▶ By product
▶ By location
▶ By customer

Departmentalize by Function

When firms departmentalize by function, they allocate their tasks and responsibilities according to employee functions. The organization chart shown in Exhibit 8.6 is departmentalized by function. The finance, marketing, and production divisions are separated. This system works well for firms that produce just one or a few products, especially if the managers communicate across the functions.

Exhibit 8.6

Departmentalizing by Function

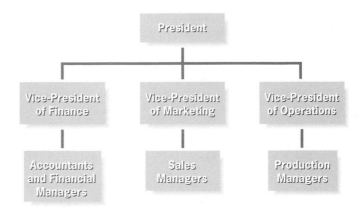

Exhibit 8.7

Departmentalizing by Product

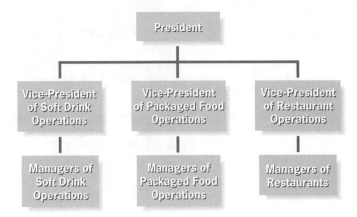

Departmentalize by Product

In larger firms with many products, departmentalizing by product is common. Tasks and responsibilities are separated according to the type of product produced. The organization chart shown in Exhibit 8.7 is departmentalized by product (soft drink, food, and restaurant). This type of organizational structure is used by General Motors, which has created divisions for Buick, Cadillac, Oldsmobile, and Chevrolet.

Many large firms departmentalize by both product and function, as shown in Exhibit 8.8. The specific divisions are separated by product, and each product division is departmentalized by function. Thus, each product division may have its own marketing, finance, and production divisions. This system may appear to be inefficient because it requires several divisions. Yet, if the firm is large enough, a single division would need to hire as many employees as are needed for the several divisions. Separation by product allows employees to become familiar with a single product rather than having to keep track of several different products.

When a firm is departmentalized by product, the expenses involved in the production of each product can be more easily estimated. Therefore, the firm can be viewed as a set of separate business divisions (separated by product), and each division's profits can be determined over time. This allows the firm to determine the contribution of each business division to its total profits, which is useful when the firm is deciding which divisions should be expanded.

Exhibit 8.8

Departmentalizing by Product
and Function

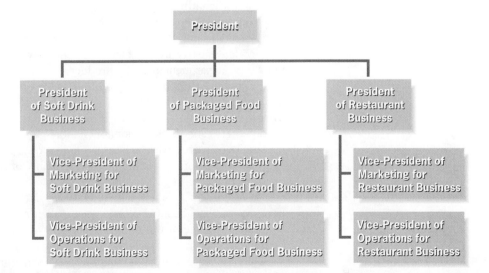

For a small or medium-sized firm with just a few products, departmentalizing by product would cause an inefficient use of employees, resulting in excessive expenses. A single financial manager should be capable of handling all financial responsibilities, and a single marketing manager should be capable of handling all marketing responsibilities. Thus, there is no reason to departmentalize by product.

Departmentalize by Location

Tasks and responsibilities can also be departmentalized by location by establishing regional offices to cover specific geographic regions. This system may be appealing if corporate customers in particular locations frequently purchase a variety of the firm's products. Such customers would be able to contact the same regional office to place all of their orders. Large accounting firms departmentalize by location in order to be close to their customers.

When a firm is departmentalized by location, the expenses incurred at each location can be more easily estimated. Therefore, the firm can be viewed as a set of divisions separated by location, with each location generating its own profits. This allows the firm to identify the locations that have been performing well, which may help it determine which locations should attempt to expand their business.

Departmentalize by Customer

Some firms have separate divisions according to the type of customer. For example, some airlines have a separate reservations division to focus exclusively on group trips. Computer firms such as IBM have designated some salespeople to focus exclusively on selling computers to school systems. They also have some divisions that focus on on-line sales to individuals, while others focus on large corporate customers.

GLOBAL BUSINESS

Organizational Structure of a Multinational Corporation

THE ORGANIZATIONAL STRUCTURE OF A MULTINATIONAL CORPORATION IS complex because responsibilities must be assigned not only to U.S. operations but also to all foreign operations. To illustrate, consider General Motors, which has facilities in Europe, Canada, Asia, Latin America, Africa, and the Middle East. It has departmentalized by location, so either a president or a vice-president is in charge of each foreign region. Specifically, a president is assigned to GM of Mexico, a president to GM of Brazil, a vice-president to Asian and Pacific operations, a president to GM of Canada Limited, and a vice-president to Latin American, African, and Middle East operations. In Europe, one vice-president is assigned to sales and marketing, and a second vice-president is assigned to Europe's manufacturing plants. Thus, the European operations are also departmentalized by function.

Even when firms departmentalize their U.S. operations by product or by function, they commonly departmentalize their foreign operations by location. Since some foreign operations are distant from the firm's headquarters, departmentalizing operations in a foreign country by product or function would be difficult. If the foreign operations were departmentalized by product, an executive at the U.S. headquarters would have to oversee each product produced in the foreign country. If the operations were departmentalized by function, an executive at the U.S. headquarters would have to oversee each function conducted at the foreign facility. Normally, executives at the U.S. headquarters cannot easily monitor the foreign operations because they are not there on a daily or even a weekly basis. Consequently, it is more appropriate to assign an executive at the foreign facility the responsibility of overseeing a wide variety of products and functions at that facility.

In recent years, some multinational corporations have begun to select people who have international business experience for their boards of directors. Such directors are better able to monitor the firm's foreign operations. Furthermore, some multinational corporations are more willing to promote managers within the firm who have substantial experience in international business. Sometimes a corporation will assign employees to its foreign facilities so that they can gain that experience.

CROSS-FUNCTIONAL TEAMWORK

Interaction among Departments

Although the organizational structure formally indicates to whom each employee reports, it still allows interaction among different departments. For example, a firm may departmentalize by function, so that one executive is responsible for the management of operations, a second executive is responsible for the marketing function, and a third executive is responsible for the financing function.

Though each function appears independent of the others on the organization chart, executives in charge of their respective functions must interact with the other departments. Exhibit 8.9 shows how the marketing, production, and finance departments rely on each other for information before making decisions. The marketing department needs to be aware of any changes in the production of a product and the volume of the product that will be available before it finalizes its marketing strategies. The production department needs customer satisfaction information as it considers redesigning products. It also needs to receive forecasts of expected sales from the marketing department, which affect the decision of how much to produce. The marketing and production departments provide the finance department with their forecasts of funds needed to cover their expenses. The finance department uses this information along with other information to determine whether it needs to obtain additional financing for the firm.

Exhibit 8.9

Flow of Information across Departments

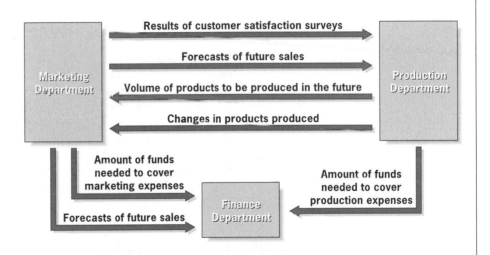

BUSINESS DILEMMA	College Health Club

Organizational Structure of College Health Club

WHEN SUE KRAMER CREATED COLLEGE HEALTH CLUB (CHC), THE ORGANIzational structure consisted of only herself and one part-time employee. Now, however, she is planning to establish a second health club near a college campus about sixty miles away from CHC.

Sue recognizes that an organizational structure can be created by departmentalizing by (1) function, (2) product (service), or (3) location. She must decide which method of departmentalizing to use. To help her decide, she summarizes the characteristics of each method:

Function

1 Marketing: To attract more members.

2 Production: To produce the services for its members.

Product (Service) Offered

1 Ensure that weight machines are working properly.

2 Provide aerobics classes.

Location

1 First health club located next to a local college.

2 Second health club to be located next to a college sixty miles away.

Dilemma

Another way of describing Sue's dilemma is as follows. Should Sue departmentalize responsibilities according to function so that one person conducts the marketing and another manages the production? Or should Sue departmentalize responsibilities by service so that one person focuses on tasks related to the weight machines while another focuses on tasks related to aerobics classes? Or should Sue departmentalize responsibilities by location so that one person manages all functions and services of the health club at the local college campus, while another person manages all functions and services of the health club at the campus sixty miles away?

Solution

Given that the two health clubs are sixty miles apart, Sue may prefer to departmentalize by location. She could focus on the duties at the new health club and allow one or more employees to manage the existing health club. There is no reason to departmentalize by service because that would force one person to manage the weight machines at both clubs (which are sixty miles apart) and another to manage aerobics classes at both clubs. It would be more efficient if the two tasks were performed at each health club by one person. This method avoids travel time between the two clubs. Even if Sue allows someone to perform the key functions at one of the health clubs, she would still have the authority as president to oversee or change any major decisions at that club.

Additional Issues for Discussion

1 As the memberships at CHC increase, Sue Kramer will hire some college students on a part-time basis. Will most of these positions be line positions or staff positions? Why?

2 Sue is considering hiring a college student for an intrapreneurship position for the summer months only. How could this student be beneficial to CHC?

3 If Sue hires employees at CHC, what types of jobs will possibly be needed? To whom will these employees report?

SUMMARY

1 The organizational structure of a firm identifies responsibilities for each job position within a firm and the relationships among those positions. The structure enables employees to recognize which job positions are responsible for the work performed by other positions.

Most firms use a line-and-staff organizational structure. However, they may also use a matrix organization to obtain employee input on various projects. They may also encourage intrapreneurship in which some employees are assigned to create new products or ideas.

2 The main methods of departmentalizing are by:

▶ function, in which tasks are separated according to employee functions;

▶ product, in which tasks are separated according to the product produced;

▶ location, in which tasks are concentrated in a particular division to serve a specific area; and

▶ customer, in which tasks are separated according to the type of customer that purchases the firm's products.

KEY TERMS

autonomy *212*
board of directors *209*
centralization *212*
chain of command *207*
decentralized *212*
departmentalize *220*
downsizing *214*

informal organizational structure *218*
inside board members *209*
intrapreneurship *218*
line organization *215*
line positions *215*
line-and-staff organization *215*

matrix organization *216*
organization chart *207*
organizational structure *207*
outside board members *209*
span of control *210*
staff positions *215*

REVIEW QUESTIONS

1 Define organizational structure and explain how it can affect the value of the firm.

2 Explain why no one specific organizational structure is optimal for all firms.

3 Define inside board members and outside board members. What type of compensation may motivate these directors to serve the interests of the firm's shareholders?

4 Describe the different spans of control you would use for a firm with numerous employees who perform similar tasks and for a firm with highly diverse tasks.

5 Define decentralization of management and explain its advantages and disadvantages.

6 Explain the difference between line positions and staff positions within an organization and cite examples of each.

7 Assume that you are creating a new organizational structure for your firm that allows more employee input. Identify and explain the two common methods you could implement.

8 Explain the advantages and disadvantages of an informal organizational structure.

9 Explain why the organizational structure of a multinational corporation that operates a global business is so complex.

10 Explain how cross-functional teamwork interacts among departments.

DISCUSSION QUESTIONS

1 Assume that you are high-level management and you are revising the organizational structure of your firm. Identify and explain the main methods for departmentalizing the tasks and responsibilities to the different departments.

2 Assume that you have just been named the project manager for a firm. You must bring together line-and-staff personnel in formulating a temporary organizational structure for this project. What type of organizational structure would you recommend and why?

3 Describe how departmentalization is the building block for organizational structure.

4 How could a firm use the Internet to provide information on its organizational structure?

5 Express your opinion of the informal organization. Is it the same as the "grapevine"? Should a manager ever participate in the "grapevine" with employees?

INVESTING IN THE STOCK OF A BUSINESS

Using the annual report of the firm in which you would like to invest, complete the following:

1 Describe the organizational structure of the firm.

2 Does it appear that there are many high-level managers in the firm?

3 Has the firm downsized in recent years by removing middle managers from its organizational structure?

4 Explain how the business uses technology to promote its organizational structure. For example, does it use the Internet to provide information about its organizational structure? Does it provide information regarding the methods of departmentalizing tasks?

5 Go to **http://hoovers.com** and locate the NEWS SEARCH. Type in the name of the firm in the space provided, and review the recent news stories about the firm. Summarize any (at least one) recent news story about the firm that applies to one or more of the key concepts within this chapter.

CASE CREATING AN ORGANIZATIONAL STRUCTURE

Janet Shugarts is president of a barbecue sauce manufacturer in Austin, Texas. A manager in production has come up with a new barbecue recipe that he claims will be the best on the market because it's hot and spicy and has a flavor that the competition cannot match.

Janet has just received new marketing research information. The research indicates that most Europeans prefer a hot and spicy barbecue sauce. The marketing manager is excited about this new product and believes it can be exported to Western Europe.

Janet has just come out of a meeting with her four managers. They have decided to establish a sales office in Paris, France. The plan is to create a project team to set up a production facility within a year in France. The marketing manager will head this project team and has requested that this subsidiary be decentralized to provide him with an opportunity to make timely decisions in this local market.

Because of this expansion, Janet is planning to increase her existing workforce of 120 employees by 20 percent. She has recently hired a human resource manager to take charge of the recruiting and selection function. A rumor circulating around the plant through the "grapevine" hints that employees may attempt to bring in a union. The human resource manager is alarmed because of his position on the organization chart. His position is listed as a support position; thus, he can only advise and make recommendations to a line manager concerning issues relating to recruiting and selection.

QUESTIONS

1 Has Janet created an organizational structure? If so, how?

2 Why would the marketing manager request decentralization of authority in Paris, France?

3 Does this organization reflect a line-and-staff organizational structure? If so, explain.

VIDEO CASE ORGANIZATIONAL STRUCTURE AT JIAN

JIAN creates business software. It wanted to focus on developing additional software and on marketing these products. Because it was a small firm, it wanted to focus on tasks that it did well and to avoid problems that could result if it tried to perform all necessary business functions with a small number of employees. Therefore, it decided to use a unique organizational structure that could achieve its objectives. JIAN relies on other firms for its manufacturing and for its employee payroll, benefits, and recruiting functions. Thus, its own employees can focus completely on software development and marketing.

QUESTIONS

1 Has JIAN departmentalized by product? By function? Explain.

2 Explain how JIAN's unique organizational structure avoids friction between departments.

3 Explain why JIAN's unique organizational structure would be short (flat) rather than tall.

INTERNET APPLICATIONS

Go to the website that provides the annual report of any company that you want to assess. Many companies describe their organizational structure in their annual reports.

Describe the organizational structure based on the information that you find. Does it appear that there are many layers to the structure? Does it appear that tasks are departmentalized? Or is the company departmentalized by product or location?

THE Coca-Cola COMPANY ANNUAL REPORT PROJECT

 Questions for the current year's annual report are available on the text website at **http://madura intro_bus.swcollege.com.**

The following questions apply concepts in this chapter to The Cola-Cola Company. Go to The Coca-Cola Company website (**http://www.cocacola.com**) and find the index for the 1999 annual report.

QUESTIONS

1 Click on "Selected Market Results." Why may The Coca-Cola Company put a new management team into a foreign country?

2 Click on "Note 12: Restricted Stock, Stock Options and Other Stock Plans." Why may monitoring by institutional investors of The Coca-Cola Company's

management be less of a concern than at other companies?

3 Click on "Investments." How does The Coca-Cola Company's marketing approach relate to the company's organizational structure?

4 Click on "Selected Market Results." How could The Coca-Cola Company contribute to people development in Africa? How do you think the company will be able to benefit from these actions in the long run?

5 Go to **http://hoovers.com** and locate the NEWS SEARCH. Type in The Coca-Cola Company in the space provided, and review the recent news stories about the firm. Summarize any (at least one) recent news story about The Coca-Cola Company that applies one or more of the key concepts within this chapter of the text.

IN-TEXT STUDY GUIDE

Answers are in an appendix at the back of the book.

TRUE OR FALSE

1 When a firm is departmentalized by location, its expenses involved in each location can be more easily estimated.

2 An organization chart shows the interaction among employee responsibilities.

3 A company's board of directors normally takes an active role in managing the firm's day-to-day activities.

4 Most firms departmentalize their foreign operations by function.

5 Inside board members are more likely than outside members to support changes that will benefit the firm's stockholders, especially if the firm's top managers do not support the changes.

6 An organizational structure identifies the responsibilities of each job position and the relationships among those positions.

7 Firms will have either a formal organizational structure or an informal organizational structure, but

can never have both types of organizational structures at the same time.

8 An advantage of a firm's informal organizational structure is that it encourages the formation of friendships, which can improve morale and job satisfaction.

9 In recent years, most firms have attempted to centralize authority in the hands of a few key executives.

10 An organizational structure that is designed to have each manager supervise just a few employees has a narrow span of control.

MULTIPLE CHOICE

11 One outcome of the downsizing by many corporations during the 1990s was:
a) an increase in the layers of management.
b) a narrower span of control for most managers.
c) decentralization of authority.
d) increased costs of production.
e) a big reduction in the importance of the informal organizational structure.

12 The _____ for a firm identifies the job position to which each type of employee must report.
a) chain of command   d) flow chart
b) job matrix   e) informal structure
c) staffing chart

13 Employees who serve in _____ positions provide assistance and support to employees who serve in line positions.
a) secondary   d) nonlinear
b) nominal   e) staff
c) reserve

14 The outside members of the board of directors of a company are those directors who:
a) live outside the state in which the corporation received its charter.
b) are not managers of the firm.
c) are not stockholders in the firm.
d) serve on the board without direct compensation.
e) were appointed by the president of the firm rather than selected by the firm's stockholders.

15 A possible disadvantage of decentralization is that it:
a) may require inexperienced managers to make major decisions they are not qualified to make.
b) usually increases the firm's operating expenses.
c) slows down the decision-making process.
d) harms employee motivation by forcing them to take on more responsibilities.
e) prevents employees from making creative decisions.

16 Firms use a(n) _____ organization to allow the various parts of a firm to interact as they focus on a particular project.
a) matrix   d) extracurricular
b) quasi-linear   e) cellular
c) tabular

17 It is common for larger firms with many products to departmentalize by:
a) function.
b) customer.
c) manufacturing process.
d) geographic area.
e) product.

18 A tall organization is characterized by:
a) many stockholders.
b) many layers of employees.
c) a wide span of control.
d) a very decentralized management structure.
e) heavy reliance on inside directors.

19 The responsibilities of a firm's managers should be organized to achieve the:
a) grapevine.
b) formal contingency.
c) strategic plan.
d) chain of command.
e) bureaucratic organization.

20 The board of directors has the responsibility of representing the interests of the firm's:
a) top management.   d) creditors.
b) employees.   e) shareholders.
c) customers.

21 Jobs that are established to make decisions that achieve specific business goals are:
a) staff positions.
b) line positions.
c) line-and-staff functions.
d) temporary jobs.
e) job placement.

22 The strategy of spreading authority among several divisions or managers is called:
a) centralization.
b) decentralization.
c) decision rationing.
d) abdication of authority.
e) adjudication of authority.

23 The ultimate responsibility for the success of a firm lies with the:
a) president.   d) competition.
b) employee.   e) labor union.
c) customer.

24 All of the following are common ways of departmentalizing a firm except by:
a) function.   d) time period.
b) product.   e) location.
c) customer.

25 Members of a firm's board of directors are selected by the firm's:
a) top management.
b) management council.
c) shareholders.
d) creditors.
e) employees.

26 The _____ refers to the number of employees managed by each manager.
a) scope of authority
b) management ratio
c) employee limit
d) span of control
e) manager-employee multiplier

27 Members of the board of directors who are also managers of the same firm are known as:
a) ex-officio board members.
b) primary board members.
c) unelected board members.
d) inside board members.
e) organizational board members.

28 The president of a company:
a) determines which members of the board of directors will be reappointed.
b) coordinates the actions of all divisions and provides direction for the firm.

c) directly supervises the actions of all other employees.

d) seldom delegates managerial duties to other managers.

e) operates independently of the board of directors.

29 An extreme form of decentralization in which divisions can make their own decisions and act independently is called:

a) centralization.

b) autonomy.

c) span of control.

d) span of management.

e) departmentalization.

30 Span of control is determined by

a) consultants.

b) staff.

c) top management.

d) employees.

e) customers.

31 A firm in which managers have narrow spans of control tends to have:

a) a tall organizational structure.

b) very decentralized decision making.

c) a small number of employees.

d) very few layers of management.

e) a very large number of people serving on its board of directors.

32 A(n) _____ is a diagram that shows the formal organizational structure of a firm.

a) chain of command chart

b) PERT diagram

c) organization chart

d) job matrix

e) corporate charter

33 One possible disadvantage of a matrix organization is that it:

a) makes it difficult for different departments to communicate with each other.

b) reduces employee satisfaction by requiring workers to perform monotonous tasks.

c) reduces the time employees have to perform their normal duties.

d) puts too much power in the hands of a small number of top managers.

e) allows top management to make decisions without input from the board.

34 A process whereby particular employees of a firm can be assigned to create ideas as if they were entrepreneurs is referred to as:

a) staff organization.

b) intrapreneurship.

c) co-ownership.

d) leadership.

e) line organization.

35 Employees who serve in _____ positions make decisions that achieve specific business goals.

a) adjunct

d) paraprofessional

b) line

e) interior

c) staff

The Learning **(1)** Identify the key resources used for production.

Goals of this **(2)** Identify the factors that affect the plant site decision.

chapter are to: **(3)** Describe how various factors affect the design and layout decision.

(4) Describe the key tasks that are involved in production control.

CHAPTER 9

Production Management

Firms are created to produce one or more products or services. Production management (also called operations management) is the management of a process in which resources (such as employees and machinery) are used to produce products and services. The process by which a firm's products (or services) are produced can affect the firm's value.

Consider the case of Samsung, a manufacturing firm that produces electronics. Consider these questions for its production. How can Samsung determine the combination of employees and ma-

chinery needed to offer its products? Should it focus its business at one site or use several different sites? How should its facilities be designed to make the

most efficient use of space? This chapter provides a background on production management that can be used to address these questions.

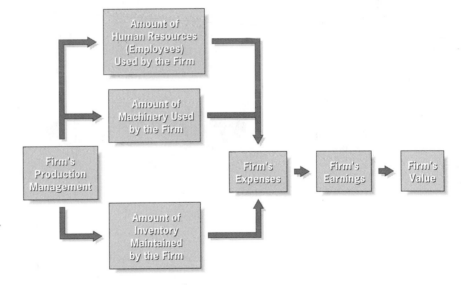

Resources Used for the Production Process

1 Identify the key resources used for production.

production process (conversion process) a series of tasks in which resources are used to produce a product or service

Whether a firm produces products or services, it needs a **production process** (also called **conversion process**), or a series of tasks in which resources are used to produce a product or service. A process identifies the mixture of resources allocated for production, the assignment of tasks, and the sequence of tasks.

Many possible production processes can achieve the production of a specific product. Thus, effective **production management** can develop an efficient (relatively low-cost) and high-quality production process for producing specific products and services. Specifically, production management can achieve efficiency by determining the proper amount of materials to use, the proper mix of resources to use, the proper assignments of the tasks, and the proper sequence of the tasks. The success of some firms, such as Motorola and Compaq Computer, is partially attributed to their production management. The success of service-oriented firms such as Southwest Airlines is attributed to

production management (operations management) the management of a process in which resources (such as employees and machinery) are used to produce products and services

their low-cost production of air transportation for customers. Thus, the profits and value of each firm are influenced by its production management.

The main resources that firms use for the production process are human resources (employees), materials, and other resources (such as buildings, machinery, and equipment). Firms that produce products tend to use more materials and equipment in their production process. Firms that produce services (such as Internet firms) use more employees and information technology.

Human Resources

Firms must identify the type of employees needed for production. Skilled labor is necessary for some forms of production, but unskilled labor can be used for other forms. Some forms of production are labor-intensive in that they require more labor than materials. The operating expenses involved in hiring human resources are dependent both on the number of employees and on their skill levels. Because of the employee skill level required, an Internet firm incurs much larger salary expenses than a grocery store.

BUSINESS ONLINE

Human Resource Information

http://www.generalmotors.com/ careers/job_opp.htm

MANY COMPANIES, SUCH AS GENERAL MOTORS, UTILIZE THE INTERNET TO provide human resource information to current and potential employees. Human resources are vital to the production process. Websites such as the one shown here provide companies with a broader range of potential candidates and provide potential candidates with a broader range of job opportunities.

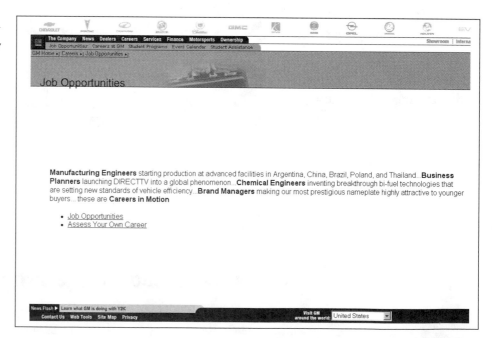

Materials

The materials used in the production process are normally transformed by the firm's human resources into a final product. Tire manufacturers rely on rubber, automobile manufacturers rely on steel, and book publishers rely on paper. Service firms such as travel agencies and investment advisers do not rely as much on materials because they do not engage in manufacturing.

This photo shows how special machinery and human resources are used in the production process for AMD Computer Chip Assembly Plant.

Other Resources

A building is needed for most forms of production. Manufacturers use factories and offices. Service firms use offices. The site may be owned or rented by the firm. Since purchasing a building can be expensive, some firms simply rent the buildings they use. Renting also allows the firm to move at the end of the lease period without having to sell the building. Machinery and equipment are also needed by many manufacturing firms. Technology may also be a necessary resource for manufacturing and service firms.

Combining the Resources for Production

work station an area in which one or more employees are assigned a specific task

assembly line a sequence of work stations in which each work station is designed to cover specific phases of the production process

Managers attempt to utilize the resources just described in a manner that achieves production at a low cost. They combine the various resources with the use of work stations and assembly lines. A **work station** is an area in which one or more employees are assigned a specific task. A work station may require not only employees but also machinery and equipment.

An **assembly line** consists of a sequence of work stations in which each work station is designed to cover specific phases of the production process. The production of a single product may require several work stations, with each station using employees, machinery, and materials. Since the cost of all these resources along with the building can be substantial, efficient management of the production process can reduce expenses, which can convert into higher profits.

A typical example of the production process is shown in Exhibit 9.1. Employees use buildings, machinery, and equipment to convert materials into a product or service. For example, employees of printing firms use machines for typesetting, printing, and binding to produce books. Employees of General Nutrition (GNC) use its manufacturing plant (which is the size of four football fields) to produce more than 150,000 bottles of vitamins per day.

Most production processes are more efficient when different employees are assigned different tasks. In this way, employees can utilize their unique types of expertise to specialize in what they do best.

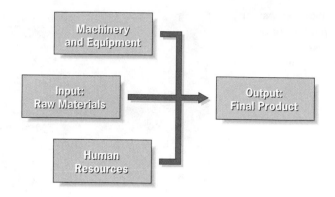

Selecting a Site

2 Identify the factors that affect the plant site decision.

A critical decision in production management is the selection of a site (location) for the factory or office. Location can significantly affect the cost of production and therefore the firm's ability to compete against other firms. This is especially true for industrial firms such as Bethlehem Steel and DaimlerChrysler, which require a large investment in plant and equipment. Site selection can also affect revenue because it may influence the demand for the product produced if the product is to be sold at the site.

Factors Affecting the Site Decision

Several factors must be considered when determining the optimal site. The most relevant factors are identified here.

Cost of Workplace Space The cost of purchasing workplace space (such as buildings or offices) can vary significantly among locations. This is one major reason why companies located in northern cities have relocated to the South during the last ten years. The cost of workplace space is likely to be high near the center of any business district where the land cost is high. W. R. Grace and IBM recently moved some of their facilities to locations where land prices are lower.

The cost of leasing workplace space can also vary substantially among locations. For example, the office rental rates are generally higher in the northeastern states than in other areas. The rental rate is typically higher in cities where the cost of land is high.

Cost of Labor The cost of hiring employees varies significantly among locations. Salaries within a city tend to be higher than outside the city for a given occupation. Salaries are also generally higher in the North than the South for a given occupation. This is another reason why many companies have relocated to the South.

Tax Incentives Some local governments may be willing to offer tax credits to attract companies to their area. This incentive is provided to increase the employment level and improve economic conditions in the area.

Source of Demand If a firm plans to sell its product in a specific location, it may establish its site there. The transporting and servicing costs of the product can be minimized by producing at a site near the source of demand.

Access to Transportation When companies sell products across the nation, they may choose a site near their main source of transportation. They also need to be accessible so that materials can be delivered to them. Some factories and offices are established near interstate highways, rivers, or airports for this reason.

The selection of this automobile manufacturing site of General Motors in Silao, Mexico, is partially influenced by the cost of the workplace space, the cost of labor, and the supply of labor available.

Supply of Labor Firms that plan to hire specialized workers must be able to attract the labor needed. They may choose a location where a large supply of workers with that particular specialization exists. For instance, high-tech companies tend to locate near universities where there is an abundance of educated labor.

DELL® COMPUTER'S FORMULA FOR SUCCESS

Dell Computer has achieved its largest regional market share and sales volume in North and South America. To accommodate growth in these regions, Dell recently opened a new 285,000-square-foot facility in Austin, Texas, where it manufactures corporate desktop computers. The company also recently broke ground on an even larger manufacturing plant for servers and work stations. At the same time, Dell is expanding sales, engineering, and administrative facilities at its headquarters in Round Rock, Texas. The supply of labor was an important consideration for Dell in constructing its new plants.

Evaluating Possible Sites

When a firm considers various sites, it must compare their desirability. First, it may assign a weight to represent the importance of each of the various factors that will influence its decision. Labor-intensive firms would likely place a high weight on the cost of human resources; other firms would be less concerned about this factor.

Once the firm has determined which factors should have the most influence on its decision, it attempts to rate these factors for each possible site. An easy method of comparing alternative sites is to develop a site evaluation matrix, as shown in Exhibit 9.2. Possible sites are listed at the left. Each column identifies a factor that needs to be evaluated. These factors may be rated from 1 (outstanding) to 5 (poor). The overall rating assigned to any potential site can be determined by averaging the ratings for that site. If some factors are more important than others, however, they deserve to have a relatively higher influence on the overall ratings.

The site evaluation matrix in Exhibit 9.2 is simplified in that it focuses on only two factors for each city. The land cost is presumed to be the more important factor and has an 80 percent weight. The supply of labor is allocated the remaining 20

Exhibit 9.2   Example of a Site Evaluation Matrix

Possible Sites	Land Cost		Supply of Labor		Total Rating
	Rating	Weighted Rating (80% of Weight)	Rating	Weighted Rating (20% Weight)	
Austin, TX	3	2.4	1	.2	2.6
Chicago, IL	4	3.2	2	.4	3.6
Los Angeles, CA	5	4.0	3	.6	4.6
Omaha, NE	1	.8	3	.6	1.4

percent weight. The weighted rating shown in Exhibit 9.2 is equal to the rating times the weight of the rating. The weighted ratings for each factor are combined to determine the total rating for each city. For example, the Austin, Texas site received a land cost rating of 3, which converts to a weighted rating of 2.4 (computed as 3 × .8). It also received a supply of labor rating of 1, which converts to a rating of .2 (computed as 1 × .2). Its total rating is 2.6 (computed as 2.4 + .2).

Once the firm determines a rating for each factor, it can derive the total rating for each site considered. Based on the ratings for the four sites in Exhibit 9.2, the Omaha site had the best rating and thus would be selected as the site.

If another firm assessed the same four sites in Exhibit 9.2, it might come to a different conclusion for two reasons. First, it might use different factors in its matrix. Second, it might rate the factors differently. For example, one city may have an abundance of people who have computer development skills, but it may not have many people with skills to manage a bank.

Once a particular area (such as a city or county) has been chosen, the precise location must be decided. Some of the factors already mentioned will influence this decision. In addition, factors such as traffic, crime rate, and worker access to public transportation may influence this decision.

GLOBAL BUSINESS

Selecting a Foreign Production Site

THE SELECTION OF A FOREIGN PRODUCTION SITE BY A U.S. FIRM IS CRITICAL because location affects the firm's operating expenses and therefore its earnings. Consider the case of Warner-Lambert, a U.S. firm that produces pharmaceutical and consumer products, including Listerine, Halls cough drops, Clorets mints, Certs mints, and Trident gum. Warner-Lambert has operations in more than one hundred countries. Its extensive development of foreign operations was motivated by global demand for its products. Warner-Lambert's marketing goal is "every product, everywhere." It is attempting to sell its products in virtually every country. Consequently, it established production sites that were convenient to the foreign markets where it planned to expand. It also considered the land and labor costs in the foreign countries when determining where to establish production facilities. In addition, it considered the locations of its other sites to ensure that each site could accommodate consumer demand within that region. Warner-Lambert has substantial production facilities in Europe, the Middle East, Africa, Latin America, and East Asia, and recently expanded its operations in Australia, New Zealand, and various parts of Europe.

The selection of a production site by any multinational corporation is crucial because costs vary substantially among countries. Annual office rental rates per square foot are more than 5 times higher in Paris than in Mexico City and more than 2 times higher in Tokyo than in Paris. The cost of human resources is generally much lower in less-developed countries, but the supply of labor in those countries may be inadequate. Furthermore, consumer demand for products in those countries may be low, so the products would have to be transported to other countries with much higher demand. Multinational corporations must assess the trade-offs involved. If the products are light in weight (and therefore involve low transportation expenses), a multinational corporation might be willing to use facilities in less-developed countries and transport the products to areas where demand is higher.

Selecting the Design and Layout

Once a site for a manufacturing plant or office is chosen, the design and layout must be determined. The **design** indicates the size and structure of the plant or office. The **layout** is the arrangement of the machinery and equipment within the factory or office.

The design and layout decisions directly affect operating expenses because they determine the costs of rent, machinery, and equipment. They may even affect the firm's interest expenses because they influence the amount of money that must be borrowed to purchase property or machinery.

A study by the management consulting firm Ernst & Young found that firms can improve their profits by using innovative ideas for their plant design and layout. A firm may assign employee teams the responsibility of identifying methods to make its plant design and layout more efficient. Employees may be highly motivated to offer cost-cutting solutions when they realize that the alternative solution may prevent lay-offs.

Factors Affecting Design and Layout

Design and layout decisions are influenced by the following characteristics.

Site Characteristics Design and layout decisions are dependent on some characteristics of the site selected. For example, if the site is in an area with high land costs, a high-rise building may be designed so that less land will be needed. The layout of the plant will then be affected by the design.

Production Process Design and layout are also dependent on the production process to be used. If an assembly-line operation is to be used, all tasks included in this operation should be in the same general area. A **product layout** positions the tasks in the sequence that they are assigned. For example, one person may specialize in creating components, while the next person assembles components, and the next person packages the product. The product layout is commonly used for assembly-line production.

Alternatively, some products (such as airplanes, ships, or homes) are completely produced in one fixed position, which requires a **fixed-position layout.** The employees go to the position of the product, rather than having the product come to them.

The design and layout should allow the sequence of tasks to take place efficiently. For example, the production process is commonly completed near the outside of the plant so that the finished products can be easily loaded onto trucks.

Many firms now use **flexible manufacturing,** a production process that can be easily adjusted to accommodate future revisions. This enables the firm to restructure its layout as needed when the types of products demand change. Merck and Company commonly uses flexible manufacturing, which allows it to produce more than one product within an assembly line. Many auto plants use flexible manufacturing so they can produce whatever cars or trucks are in demand. The production process must be flexible to accommodate customer demand.

A flexible layout normally requires that employees have flexible skills. Although employees may have some specialization, they must have other skills so that when the layout of the plant is rearranged, they can focus on the production of other products.

---

3 Describe how various factors affect the design and layout decision.

design the size and structure of a plant or office

layout the arrangement of machinery and equipment within a factory or office

product layout a layout in which tasks are positioned in the sequence that they are assigned

fixed-position layout a layout in which employees go to the position of the product, rather than waiting for the product to come to them

flexible manufacturing a production process that can be easily adjusted to accommodate future revisions

Product Line   Most firms produce more than one product or service at their site. Firms with a narrow product line focus on the production of one or a few products, which allows them to specialize. Firms with a broad product line offer a wide range of products. Such firms must have a design and layout that can be revised as the product line is revised.

As market preferences change, demand for products changes. The layout must be revised to accompany these changes. For example, the popularity of sports utility vehicles has caused many automobile manufacturers to allocate more of their layout for the production of these vehicles. The allocation of more space for one product normally takes space away from others, unless the initial design and layout allowed extra space for expansion.

Desired Production Capacity   When planning both design and layout, the firm's desired production capacity (maximum production level possible) must be considered. Most firms attempt to plan for growth by allowing flexibility to increase the production capacity over time. The design of the building may allow for additional levels to be added. The proper layout can open up more space to be used for more production. For example, Ford revised its assembly-line operations to produce 25 percent more cars.

If firms do not plan for growth, they will be forced to search for a new site when demand for their product exceeds their production capacity. When a firm maintains its existing site and develops a second site to expand, it must duplicate the machinery and job positions assigned at the original site. Consequently, production efficiency tends to decrease. To avoid this problem, the firm may relocate to a site with a larger capacity. Reassessing all potential plant sites and developing a new design and layout can be costly, however. Firms can avoid these costs by ensuring that the layout at their initial site allows for growth.

Although having a layout that allows for growth is desirable, it is also expensive. A firm must invest additional funds to obtain additional land or floor space. This investment ties up funds that might be better used by the firm for other purposes. Furthermore, if growth does not occur, the firm will not have an efficient layout because some of the space will continue to be unused.

Production facilities such as this one attempt to use all the space efficiently, yet allow some extra room for possible expansion.

Reducing the Layout Space

Recently, many firms have reduced their investment in property and buildings to reduce their expenses. Many large firms, such as IBM, General Motors, and ExxonMobil, have more than one hundred thousand employees. They incur massive expenses in the property or buildings that they own or rent. The potential for reducing costs is great if these firms can use their work space more efficiently and sell any property or buildings they do not need. Alternatively, they can reduce expenses by canceling their rent agreements on buildings they were renting. When firms reduce (downsize) their workforce, they no longer need as many offices and may reduce their work space as well.

Flexible Layout

As firms reduce their work space, they may need to adjust their layout to accommodate their employees. One solution is to allow more employees to work at home. Given the improvement in telecommunications (computer networks, e-mail, and fax machines), some employees may be able to do most of their work at home. AT&T is experimenting with this strategy for some employees. When the employees who work at home need to come in to work, they use work spaces that are not permanently assigned to anyone. For example, a firm may have an office available with a desk, a computer, and a telephone for any employee who normally works at home but needs to use work space at the firm. This concept is referred to as **hotelling** (or **just-in-time office**). Such shared office space may be a little less convenient for employees but can help reduce operating expenses. Salespeople who travel frequently often use a home office rather than a company office.

hotelling (just-in-time office) the firm provides an office with a desk, a computer, and a telephone for any employee who normally works at home but needs to use work space at the firm

Production Control

Once the plant and design have been selected, the firm can engage in **production control**, which involves the following:

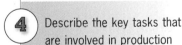

Describe the key tasks that are involved in production control.

▶ Purchasing materials
▶ Inventory control
▶ Routing
▶ Scheduling
▶ Quality control

production control involves purchasing materials, inventory control, routing, scheduling, and quality control

Purchasing Materials

Managers perform the following tasks when purchasing supplies. First, they must select a supplier. Second, they attempt to obtain volume discounts. Third, they determine whether to delegate some production tasks to suppliers. These tasks are discussed next.

Selecting a Supplier of Materials In selecting among various suppliers, firms consider characteristics such as price, speed, quality, servicing, and credit availability. A typical approach to evaluating suppliers is to first obtain prices from each supplier. Next, a sample is obtained from each supplier and inspected for quality. Two or three suppliers may be selected according to these criteria. Then, these suppliers are asked to provide further information on their speed of delivery and their service warranties in case any delivery problems occur. The firm may then try out a single supplier and evaluate its reliability over time.

Alternatively, a firm may initially use a few suppliers and later select the supplier that has provided the best service. Some firms avoid depending on a single supplier, since any problems originating from that supplier could have a major impact on the firm.

Obtaining Volume Discounts Firms that purchase a large volume of materials from suppliers may obtain a discounted price on supplies while maintaining quality. This practice has enabled firms such as AT&T and General Motors to reduce their production expenses in recent years.

outsourcing purchasing parts from a supplier rather than producing the parts

Delegating Production to Suppliers Manufacturers commonly use **outsourcing;** that is, they purchase parts from suppliers rather than producing the parts. Outsourcing can reduce a firm's expenses if suppliers can produce the parts at a lower cost than the manufacturer. Some manufacturers have even begun delegating some parts of the production process to suppliers. Consider a firm located in a city where wages are generally high. Assume that, historically, this firm ordered several components from a supplier and assembled them at its own plant. It may be better to have the supplier partially assemble the components before sending them to the manufacturer. Some of the assembly task is thereby shifted to the supplier. Partial assembly by the supplier may cost less than paying high-wage employees at the manufacturing plant.

deintegration the strategy of delegating some production tasks to suppliers

This strategy of delegating some production tasks to suppliers is referred to as **deintegration** and is illustrated in Exhibit 9.3. The production process within the plant is no longer as integrated, because part of the production is completed by the supplier before the supplies or components are delivered to the manufacturing plant. Automobile manufacturers have deintegrated their production processes by delegating some production tasks to suppliers or other firms. For example, General Motors has delegated the production of its radiator caps, vacuum pumps, and many other parts to suppliers. Ford Motor Company purchases automobile seats that are fully assembled from Lear Seating. This act of deintegration has saved manufacturers hundreds of dollars per automobile, because the supplier's cost of labor is lower than that of the manufacturer.

Deintegration is not restricted to automobile manufacturing. Firms such as General Mills and Hewlett-Packard have also delegated some production to other firms.

Exhibit 9.3

Effects of Deintegration

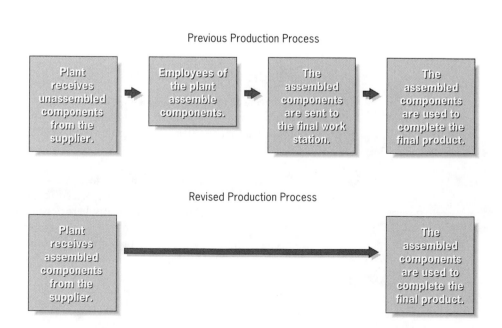

Production
Control
Information

**http://www.johnsontech.com/
products.htm**

BECAUSE PRODUCTION CONTROL IS A MAJOR FACTOR IN PRODUCTION MAN-
agement, websites such as the one shown below for Johnson Technologies are highly
useful. New software, such as "EZ Stock," which aids companies in linking their accounting, inventory, and purchasing functions, is frequently developed and displayed
by companies on the Internet.

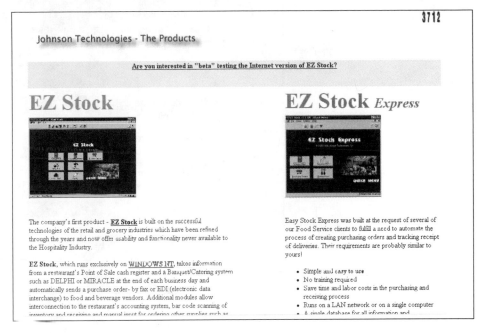

Inventory Control

inventory control the process
of managing inventory at a level
that minimizes costs

Inventory control is the process of managing inventory at a level that minimizes costs.
To appreciate the importance of inventory management, consider the following comments from a recent annual report:

> *Inventory difficulties were a factor in last year's weak financial perfor-
> mance. This year, inventory management was a key to our success. . . .
> Over the past two years, we have implemented new processes and de-
> veloped an inventory management team to work side by side with their
> marketing partners.*

—Best Buy

Inventory control requires the management of materials inventories, work-in-process
inventories, and finished goods inventories, as explained next.

carrying costs costs of
maintaining (carrying)
inventories

order costs costs involved in
placing orders

just-in-time (JIT) a system that
attempts to reduce materials
inventories to a bare minimum
by frequently ordering small
amounts of materials

Control of Materials Inventories When firms carry excessive inventories of materials, they may need to borrow more funds to finance these inventories. This increases
their so-called **carrying costs,** or their costs of maintaining (carrying) inventories. Carrying costs include financing costs as well as costs associated with storing or insuring
inventories. Although firms can attempt to reduce their carrying costs by frequently
ordering small amounts of materials, this strategy increases the costs involved in placing orders (called **order costs**). Any adjustment in the materials purchasing strategy
will normally reduce carrying costs at the expense of increasing order costs, or vice
versa.

A popular method for reducing carrying costs is the **just-in-time (JIT)** system originated by Japanese companies. This system attempts to reduce materials inventories to
a bare minimum by frequently ordering small amounts of materials. It can reduce the
costs of maintaining inventories. However, there is a cost of managerial time required

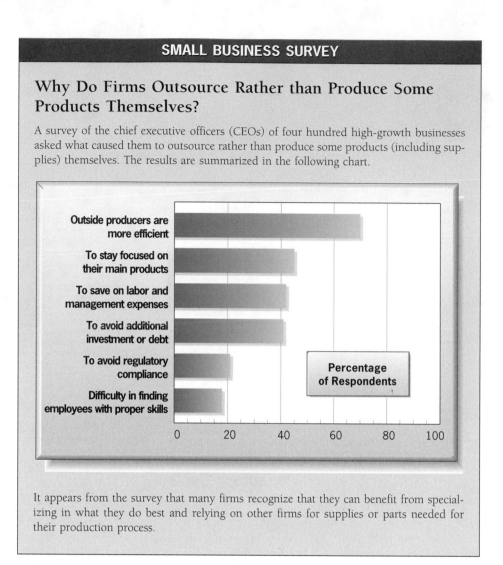

for frequent ordering and a cost of frequent deliveries. In addition, the just-in-time system could result in a shortage if applied improperly. U.S. firms such as Applied Magnetics Corporation and Black and Decker Corporation have improved their productivity by effectively using just-in-time inventory management.

materials requirements planning (MRP) a process for ensuring that materials are available when needed

Materials requirements planning (MRP) is a process for ensuring that the materials are available when needed. Normally requiring the use of a computer, MRP helps managers determine the amount of specific materials that should be purchased at any given time. The first step in MRP is to work backward from the finished product toward the beginning and determine how long in advance materials are needed before products are completely produced. For example, if computers are to be assembled by a specific date, the computer components must arrive by a specific date before then, which means that they must be ordered even earlier. As the firm forecasts the demand for its product in the future, it can determine the time at which the materials need to arrive to achieve a production level that will accommodate the forecasted demand.

work-in-process inventories inventories of partially completed products

Control of Work-in-Process Inventories

Firms must also manage their **work-in-process inventories,** which are inventories of partially completed products. They attempt to avoid shortages of all three types of inventories. The direct consequence of a shortage in raw materials inventory or work-in-process inventory is an interruption in production, while the direct consequence of a shortage in completed goods is forgone sales. A shortage of completed products inventory can be caused by a shortage of raw materials inventory or work-in-process inventory.

Bristol-Myers Squibb Company has attempted to reduce the so-called *cycle time* from when raw materials are purchased until the completion and sale of the final product. This reduces the length of time during which funds must be borrowed to finance purchases, because the firm receives cash from the sale of the product sooner. Therefore, the firm's cost of financing is reduced.

Control of Finished Goods Inventories   As demand for a firm's product changes over time, managers need to monitor the anticipated supply-demand differential. If an excess supply of a product is anticipated, firms can avoid excessive inventories by redirecting their resources toward the production of other products. For example, Ford Motor Company redirects resources away from the production of cars that are not selling as well as expected. Alternatively, firms that experience an excess supply of products can continue their normal production schedule and implement marketing strategies (such as advertising) that will increase demand.

If an increase in demand is anticipated, firms become concerned about possible shortages and must develop a strategy to boost production volume. They may schedule overtime for workers or hire new workers to achieve higher levels of production.

When the forecasted demand is underestimated, the firm may not produce a sufficient volume to accommodate all customers. Compaq Computer, Apple Computer, and many other firms have experienced severe shortages when they underestimated demand. For this reason, some firms maintain more inventories than their expected volume of sales.

Just as firms attempt to avoid shortages, they also attempt to avoid holding excess inventories of products. When firms produce too much of a product, they are sometimes forced to reduce its price to ensure that they can sell all that they have produced. Sometimes they sell the product at a price below cost just to reduce their excess inventories. Kodak recently produced more of its products than it could sell, resulting in excess inventories of some products. When this problem was announced to the public, Kodak's value (as measured by its stock price) declined significantly, as shown in Exhibit 9.4.

Many firms, such as Wal-Mart, Land's End, and Cemex, have improved their efficiency by using computer networks. Changes in inventory level are updated as soon as a customer order is received. IBM refocused its retail sales over the Internet in order to reduce its inventory and reduce its costs, as shown in Exhibit 9.5.

Exhibit 9.4

Impact of Excessive Inventories on Kodak's Stock Price

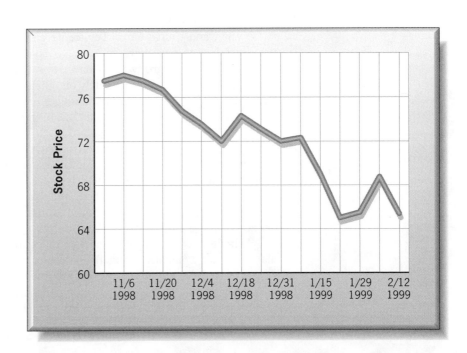

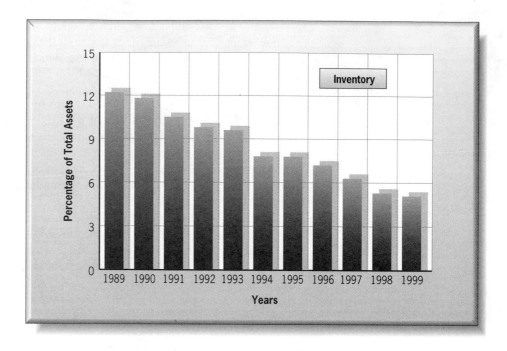

Its inventory as a percentage of its total assets was cut by more than half over a recent ten-year period.

Routing

routing the sequence (or route) of tasks necessary to complete the production of a product

Routing is the sequence (or route) of tasks necessary to complete the production of a product. Raw materials are commonly sent to various work stations so that they can be used as specified in the production process. A specific part of the production process is completed at each work station. For example, the production of a bicycle may require (1) using materials to produce a bike frame at one work station, (2) assembling wheels at a second work station, and (3) packaging the frames and wheels that have been assembled at a third work station.

The routing process is periodically evaluated to determine whether it can be improved to allow a faster or less expensive production process. General Motors, DaimlerChrysler, and United Parcel Service have streamlined their routing process to improve production efficiency.

In recent years, many firms have revised their routing to allow for more outsourcing. Some firms rely completely on other firms to manufacture their product. For example, Hewlett-Packard commonly relies on Solectron Corporation to manufacture its printers according to its specifications. In this way, Hewlett-Packard can focus more on marketing its printers.

Many firms outsource the production of their product whenever they cannot satisfy the demand through their normal production process. For example, some firms experience an increase in demand when they begin to use the Internet (along with their traditional methods) to sell their products. These firms commonly outsource their additional production to manufacturing firms that can quickly manufacture the product according to specifications.

Although outsourcing can be beneficial, it places much responsibility on another manufacturing company. Thus, the ability of a firm that outsources to meet its production schedule depends on the manufacturing companies that it relies on. For this reason, a firm must be very careful when selecting a manufacturing company to which it outsources some of its production tasks.

Impact of Information Technology on Production Processes

The business environment continues to change and place pressure on companies to lower costs, improve quality, and increase customer service. Many companies have been able to use advances in technology to achieve these goals. Inventory control was the main focus of the early computer systems that were popular in the 1970s. The idea was to reduce costs by eliminating the need to carry finished inventory.

The inventory systems expanded to include scheduling of materials needed for production. These early systems were called materials requirements planning (MRP) systems and focused on reducing costs through closer coordination of supply inventories. Prior to MRP, inventory control had been concerned about replacing materials once they had been used. MRP used forecasting to create a master schedule so that the production process could be divided into separate assembly periods. Once the schedule for the different assembly periods was known, appropriate raw materials and other components could be purchased and delivered at the appropriate times. This eliminated the costs of purchasing and warehousing all the raw materials needed for the entire production process.

In the 1980s, these systems expanded to include the major functional manufacturing areas and were renamed manufacturing resources planning (MRP-II) systems. MRP-II systems included planning, customer service (order entry, inventory, forecasting, and sales), and execution systems (production, purchasing, and supply inventory). MRP-II is a software product that allows a firm to organize and control different functions.

As computers continue to evolve, their use has extended to finance, human resources, projects management, service and maintenance, transportation, and nearly every area of the business. These systems became popular in the 1990s and have been renamed enterprise resource planning (ERP) systems. ERP systems are complex software packages that connect the computer systems from different departments. The process can be difficult as the department systems are often incompatible and outdated. The goal is to automate accounting, production, order taking, and the other basic processes of the business. ERP achieves this by recording every transaction, from taking an order to delivering a finished product, and updating the entire system. The practical application allows the customer to place an order (either through traditional sales channels or electronically) that automatically schedules the items in the production line, adjusts raw materials inventories, and schedules the delivery. At the same time, the appropriate accounting entries are made and invoices sent. This high degree of integration allows every user at the company to be better informed of the company's resources and commitments.

Integration is the key difference between ERP systems and the mainframe systems that have been used by many large production companies. Mainframe systems offered little flexibility and resulted in companies becoming departmentalized. For instance, different production facilities would each have their own departments for obtaining supplies. Each production facility would order a material according to its own needs, even though all facilities used the same material. The different systems made it difficult to have consolidated knowledge of how much material was purchased, who it was purchased from, and the costs involved. An ERP system puts all of the production facilities on the same platform so that the overall process can be consolidated and costs reduced.

Companies can extend their ERP system to the Internet where customers can access a website to learn which products are available and which have been committed to other customers. These same companies may also demand that their suppliers offer the same ability so that supplies can be ordered quickly. This coordination allows companies to eliminate inventory, improve connections with suppliers, and decrease overall costs.

Pitney Bowes is one of the companies that allow suppliers to link to their enterprise resource planning system through the Internet. Suppliers have access to Pitney's inventory and anticipated demand and are allowed to send and receive messages. Another company, Boeing, operates a Part Analysis and Requirements Tracking (PART) website designed to allow its customers to purchase and track spare parts orders. The site processes thousands of transactions each day and has reduced order-processing costs by more than 25 percent.

Prior to this technology, companies would have to take inventory manually and order supplies months in advance. Employees who once spent their time counting and ordering supplies are now able to focus their time on more productive tasks. ERP systems can be expensive, however. The systems are priced based on the complexity of the system and the number of users that will access it. Installation requires data to be reformatted and network systems overhauled.

Scheduling

scheduling the act of setting time periods for each task in the production process

production schedule a plan for the timing and volume of production tasks

Scheduling is the act of setting time periods for each task in the production process. A **production schedule** is a plan for the timing and volume of production tasks. For example, the production schedule for a bicycle may set a time of two hours for each frame to be assembled and one hour for each wheel to be assembled. Scheduling is useful because it establishes the expected amount of production that should be achieved at each work station over a given day or week. Therefore, each employee recognizes what is expected. Furthermore, the scheduling allows managers to forecast how much will be produced by the end of the day, week, or month.

If a firm does not meet its production schedule, it will not be able to accommodate customer orders in a timely fashion and will lose some of its customers. Consider the case of Iridium, a cell phone provider, which experienced production problems and delays. Its value (as measured by its stock price) declined shortly thereafter, as shown in Exhibit 9.6. As a related example, Boeing could not fulfill many of its orders in 1998 because it experienced shortages in materials, employee turnover, and other production scheduling problems. Consequently, its value declined, as shown in Exhibit 9.7.

Impact of Technology on Production Scheduling Weyerhaeuser also experienced production scheduling problems, but it has recently used technology to correct those problems. Its customized doors were previously ordered by phone calls, faxes, and mail through various suppliers and distributors. The doors were delivered on schedule less than 50 percent of the time. Weyerhaeuser now allows customers to access its website where they can specify the features of the door they desire and receive instant pricing on a door with those features. Consequently, orders are now placed more quickly. In addition, there is less chance of error because the customers specify the desired features themselves rather than communicating the information to someone who would then have to communicate the information to the manufacturing department. Deliveries are now almost always on schedule. Not only does Weyerhaeuser receive its payments more quickly as a result of the on-time deliveries, but it has also increased the satisfaction level of its customers and therefore generates more repeat business.

Exhibit 9.6

Impact of Production Delays on Iridium's Stock Price

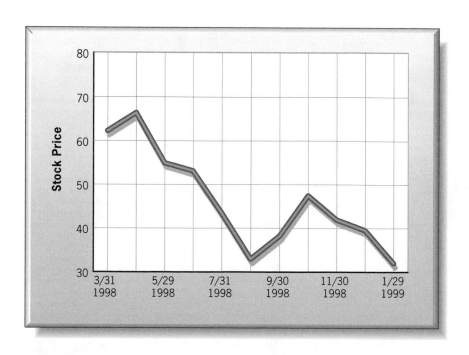

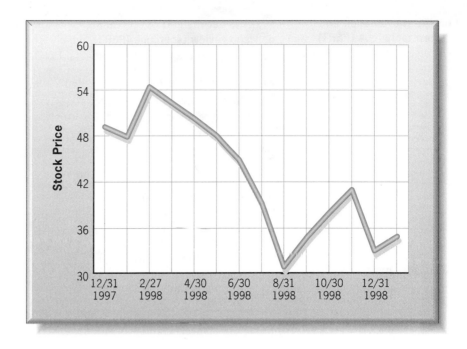

Scheduling for Special Projects

Scheduling is especially important for special long-term projects that must be completed by a specific deadline. If many related tasks must be completed in a specific sequence, scheduling can indicate when each task should be completed. In this way, managers can detect whether the project is likely to be completed on time. If any tasks are not completed on time, managers must search for ways to make up the time on other tasks.

Gantt chart a chart illustrating the expected timing for each task in the production process

One method of scheduling tasks of a special project is to use a **Gantt chart** (named after its creator, Henry Gantt), which illustrates the expected timing for each task within the production process. To show how a Gantt chart can be applied, consider an example in which a chemical firm must produce five hundred one-gallon containers of Chemical Z for a manufacturer. The production process involves creating large amounts of Chemicals X and Y, which are then mixed in a tank to produce Chemical Z. Next, Chemical Z must be poured into gallon containers and then packaged in cases to be delivered. Notice that while the first two tasks can be completed at the same time, each remaining task cannot begin until the previous task is completed.

The bar for each task on the Gantt chart can be marked when that task is completed, as shown in Exhibit 9.8. According to the exhibit, the first four tasks have been completed, so the focus is now on the fifth task.

Exhibit 9.8

Example of a Gantt Chart

Production Tasks	Week 1	Week 2	Week 3	Week 4	Week 5
1. Produce Chemical X.	▰				
2. Produce Chemical Y.	▰	▰			
3. Mix Chemicals X and Y in a tank to produce Chemical Z.			▰		
4. Pour Chemical Z into 500 one-gallon containers.				▰	
5. Package the one-gallon containers into cases.					☐

program evaluation and review technique (PERT)
schedules tasks in a manner that will minimize delays in the production process

critical path the path that takes the longest time to complete

Another method of scheduling tasks for a special project is the **program evaluation and review technique (PERT),** which schedules tasks in a manner that will minimize delays in the production process. PERT involves the following steps:

1 The various tasks involved in the production process are identified.

2 The tasks are arranged in the order in which they must take place; this sequence may be represented on a chart with arrows illustrating the path or sequence of the production process.

3 The time needed for each activity is estimated.

An example of PERT as applied to a firm's production of Chemical Z is shown in Exhibit 9.9. The production of Chemical X (Task 1) and Chemical Y (Task 2) can be conducted simultaneously. The mixing of Chemicals X and Y (Task 3) cannot begin until Tasks 1 and 2 are completed.

Each sequence of tasks is referred to as a path. For example, the sequence of Tasks 1, 3, 4, and 5 represents one path. A second path is the sequence of Tasks 2, 3, 4, and 5. The accumulated time for this path is five weeks. The **critical path** is the path that takes the longest time to complete. In our example, the critical path is the sequence of Tasks 2, 3, 4, and 5; that path takes five weeks. It is important to determine the time necessary to complete the steps within the critical path, since the production process will take that long.

The five-week period has no slack time (extra time) for the workers involved in the critical path. Once the critical path is determined, the slack time on any other paths can be estimated. Since the other path in Exhibit 9.9 has a completion time of four weeks, it has slack time of one week over a five-week period. Knowing the time involved in the critical path allows managers to reduce inefficiencies that can be caused by slack time on other paths. Some of the workers assigned to Task 1 may be assigned to help with the second task of the critical path sequence. This may reduce the time necessary to complete the critical path.

The tasks that are part of the critical path should be reviewed to avoid delays or increase production speed. Tasks estimated to take a long time are closely monitored, since any delays in these tasks are more likely to cause a severe delay in the entire production process. Furthermore, firms attempt to determine whether these tasks can be performed more quickly so that the critical path is completed in less time.

Managers who oversee special projects recognize that the time necessary for each task may be uncertain. For this reason, they may estimate the longest time for each task to be completed. The critical path represents the sum of the longest times for each task and therefore measures the maximum length of time in which the project would

Exhibit 9.9

Determining the Critical Path Based on a Sequence of Production Tasks

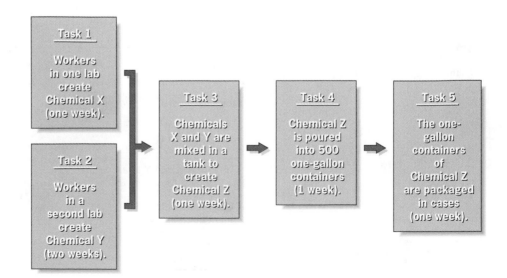

SPOTLIGHT ON TECHNOLOGY

Agile Manufacturing

Many experts believe we are about to enter a new era in manufacturing: the era of mass customization. What distinguishes mass customization from today's mass production is that factory products will no longer consist of multiple copies of the same item. Instead, product specifications will be fed through information pipelines, and factory equipment will reconfigure itself to produce the exact product desired. Further, experts predict that these customized products will cost about the same as today's mass-produced equivalent.

The techniques needed to create such factories of the future are collectively grouped under the heading of agile manufacturing and will depend heavily on information technology. Optical scanning systems combined with telecommunications will be used to get product specifications into the plant. Computer-aided design and computer-aided manufacturing (CAD/CAM) represent the next step. Product specifications, scanned in or drawn by operators, will be translated into instructions for industrial robots and computer-controlled machinery. These pieces of equipment have great flexibility. Rather than accommodating only a single set of repetitive motions, suitable only for doing the same task over and over again, the equipment will be able to do many different activities. This variety of activities will allow a variety of products to be produced.

The U.S. economy is already experiencing some of the benefits of agile manufacturing. A valve maker in Georgia uses CAD/CAM technology to produce customized valves for customers in under three days. In the textile business, agile factories in the United States are able to quickly produce small lots of specialized fabrics to order.

In the near future, agile factories may be the norm in U.S. manufacturing. Experts warn, however, that the appearance of such factories will not necessarily translate into new manufacturing jobs. The key to achieving agility is automation, so the labor required to run such plants will be limited. Substantial growth, however, is expected in the high-tech jobs associated with designing, building, and maintaining the equipment used in these factories.

---

be completed. In our previous example, the expected time of the project was five weeks, but the worst-case time might be seven weeks. That is, the project should be completed in five weeks, but it could take as long as seven weeks if some unfavorable conditions occur (employees call in sick, equipment breaks, and so on). Managers who oversee such a project may guarantee to the customer that the product will be ready within seven weeks. They may be less willing to guarantee five weeks because conditions could delay the production schedule.

Quality Control

quality the degree to which a product or service satisfies a customer's requirements or expectations

Quality can be defined as the degree to which a product or service satisfies a customer's requirements or expectations. Quality relates to customer satisfaction, which can have an effect on future sales and therefore on the future performance of the firm. Thus, firms are increasingly recognizing the impact that the quality of their products or services can have on their overall performance.

quality control a process of determining whether the quality of a product meets the desired quality level

Quality control is a process of determining whether the quality of a product or a service meets the desired quality level and identifying improvements (if any) that need to be made in the production process. Quality can be measured by assessing the various characteristics (such as how long the product lasts) that enhance customer satisfaction. The actual quality of a product can be compared with the desired quality level to determine whether the quality needs to be improved. Given the importance of quality, the following chapter is devoted to this topic.

Integration of the Production Tasks

The production tasks described in this chapter are related, such that each task can be accomplished only after other tasks have been completed. Thus, if any production task breaks down, the entire production schedule is affected. Furthermore, firms are unable to deliver their products to stores or to customers until all production tasks are

Quality control is a critical element when manufacturing any product. Here, IBM technicians are putting new laptop computers through a variety of tests before shipping the finished product to consumers.

supply chain the process from the beginning of the production process until the product reaches the customer

completed. Therefore, firms monitor the so-called **supply chain,** or the process from the very beginning of the production process until the product reaches the consumer. Firms that produce products identify a site for production, hire employees, set up work stations, and determine the design and layout that will ensure efficient production. To recognize the integration required, consider the following example:

▶ After an automobile manufacturer identifies a site for production—a manufacturing plant where automobiles are to be produced—it hires employees and assigns them to assembly lines.

▶ Machinery and tools (such as special wrenches) are placed along the assembly lines to help the employees produce the automobiles.

▶ Materials (including steering wheels, seat cushions, engines, and tires) are delivered to different parts of the assembly line so that they can be installed during the production process. The design and layout are structured so that one task is completed before the automobile frame is moved to the next station on the assembly line, and so on. For example, the dashboard may be inserted at one station and the doors and windshield attached at the next station. The dashboard is installed first because inserting a dashboard is more difficult after the doors have been attached.

▶ A sufficient inventory of materials is ordered to accommodate the scheduled production.

▶ Tasks are scheduled so that each person who is assigned a task on the assembly line has enough time to complete it before the automobile frame is moved to the next station. Too much time should not be allocated for a specific task, however, because that would reduce the production volume.

▶ The quality control process takes place at different stations along the assembly line to ensure that each part of the production process is completed according to standards.

How Breakdowns Disrupt the Production Process To ensure that you understand how the production tasks are integrated, identify the breakdowns that could cause the entire production process to be slowed. This can be accomplished by reviewing the sequence of tasks in order. First, the machinery used by employees in the production process could break down. Does the firm have substitute machinery or tools, or can it quickly purchase new machinery? If it takes a week to replace a machine, a breakdown could disrupt the entire production process for a week. If the dashboard cannot be installed due to a breakdown in machinery, continuing production would be difficult because the dashboard is more easily inserted before some other tasks are completed, as explained earlier.

Second, what if materials needed at different stations along the assembly line do not arrive on time? What if there is no extra inventory of these materials? The production may be stalled. If the manufacturer can easily find an alternative supplier of the materials, the production process is less vulnerable to major problems. If dashboards or other materials are custom-made, however, it may be difficult to find substitutes quickly.

What if some of the employees who were assigned tasks on the assembly line are ill or quit? If the tasks can be done by other employees, the production process may not be disrupted very much. However, the manufacturer can reduce potential problems by having some employees on call in the event that they are needed.

What if the quality control process determines that one specific task needs to be redone? This will disrupt the production process because that task may need to be done properly before the other tasks can be completed. In fact, it is important to catch any production problems when they occur so that the disruption is limited. For example, fixing an incorrectly inserted dashboard is easier before the doors and the windshield are installed.

The integration of tasks is not limited to assembly-line production. Firms such as Motorola, Johnson and Johnson, TRW, and AT&T focus on coordinating all their production tasks in a manner that minimizes production cost while maintaining high quality. In fact, these firms frequently restructure their production process, continually searching for more efficient ways to produce their products. The following statements from recent annual reports illustrate the importance of the production process to such firms:

> ❝ *Motorola is not simply relying on revenue growth to recover its profitability. Our manufacturing consolidation, cost reduction, and restructuring programs are also an important part of our effort to restore our financial performance and increase shareholder value.* ❞
>
> —Motorola

> ❝ *Over the last several years, we have been working hard at improving all aspects of our productivity, including the sharing of common services across the corporation, such as purchasing, information management, administration, and human resources. . . . we have dramatically improved productivity and taken out about $2 billion in annual operating costs.* ❞
>
> —TRW

> ❝ *We announced an aggressive action plan to improve operating profit margins. . . . Activities include closing 10–15 percent of the manufacturing facilities; reducing employment by 7,500; eliminating $75 million a year in administrative costs; consolidating purchasing and reducing the number of suppliers; and stepping up the pace of lean manufacturing efforts.* ❞
>
> —TRW

Integration of Tasks at Service Firms Even service firms use a production process that is integrated and therefore requires that the tasks described in this chapter are completed in a specific order. For example, Amazon.com hires employees to produce the service of fulfilling orders made by customers over a website. The production process for Amazon.com involves forecasting the future demand for books, ordering a sufficient number of each book to satisfy demand in a future period, storing books at warehouses, receiving orders, fulfilling orders, and ensuring that customers receive quality service (such as quick delivery). If Amazon.com does not order a sufficient amount of books relative to the amount customers order, it will not be able to accommodate all of the demand. Alternatively, if it has a sufficient inventory of the books but does not have enough employees and computer facilities to fulfill the orders, the production process will be disrupted.

As an illustration of the importance placed on keeping the production process lean (efficient) as applied to services, consider the following comments from a recent annual report:

> ❝ We will work hard to spend wisely and maintain our lean culture. We understand the importance of continually reinforcing a cost-conscious culture. ❞
>
> —Amazon.com

Service firms, like manufacturing firms, should consider the sequence of production tasks that are required and the order of those tasks. They should then consider whether there is any alternative sequence or alternative design or layout that would allow for more efficient production. Then, they should consider the consequences if any task within the process breaks down. Firms that have ways to quickly substitute materials or employees under such circumstances are less likely to suffer a major slowdown in the production process.

BUSINESS DILEMMA | **College Health Club**

Production at College Health Club

SUE KRAMER, PRESIDENT OF COLLEGE HEALTH CLUB (CHC), IS REVIEWING the production of CHC's health club services.

Site The health club was established at a site next to the college campus where it attracts most of its customers. Thus, its site was established near its source of demand, since most of the demand comes from the college campus.

Design and Layout The design of the health club allows for some expansion so that it can attract more members without being overcrowded. The layout of the club is intended to separate members who use the exercise equipment from those taking aerobics classes.

Production Efficiency Most of the expenses at CHC (such as rent) are fixed. Therefore, the average cost of serving each customer would decline substantially if CHC could increase its memberships.

Dilemma

Sue Kramer is considering whether to relocate the site of her health club. She wants to determine whether a site closer to the business district of the city would be more appropriate than the site next to a college campus outside the city. Using the typical factors that can affect a site decision (which were identified in this chapter), determine which factors favor a site closer to the business district and which factors favor the present site. Should Sue relocate CHC near the business district or leave CHC near the college campus?

Solution

Factors such as cost of human resources and supply of labor are not relevant in this case because Sue's club does not rely on many employees. If Sue moves the site closer to the business district, the club will attract more customers from that area. One advantage of locating near the business district is that professionals can pay higher membership fees. However, Sue initially decided to establish the club next to the college campus because its source of demand was the students. If she moves the site away from the college, she will lose many of the customers who are students at the college.

Recall that Sue's initial plan was to focus on the college students because she thought no other club was focusing on that target market. Since the source of demand was the key factor involved in the site decision, and the students at the college represent the target market, Sue decides to keep the site next to the college campus.

Additional Issues for Discussion

1 The cost of land is much higher near the middle of the city than it is outside the city, where CHC is located. How does this affect CHC's expenses?

2 The design of the health club allows for some expansion. What is a disadvantage of having extra room to allow for expansion?

3 CHC has been open for about six months. How might Sue Kramer forecast membership (demand) over the next six months?

SUMMARY

 The key resources used for production are human resources, materials, and other resources (such as the plant, machinery, and equipment).

2 The plant site decision is influenced by:

▶ cost of workplace space,
▶ cost of labor,
▶ tax incentives,
▶ source of demand for the product produced,
▶ access to transportation, and
▶ supply of labor.

A site evaluation matrix can be used to assign a rating to each relevant factor and derive a total rating for each possible site.

 The design and layout of a plant are influenced by the:

▶ site characteristics,
▶ production process,
▶ product line, and
▶ desired production capacity.

 Production control involves:

▶ purchasing materials, which requires selecting a supplier, nego-

tiating volume discounts, and possibly delegating production to suppliers;

▶ inventory control, which involves managing various inventories at levels that minimize costs;

▶ routing, which determines the sequence of tasks necessary to complete production;

▶ scheduling, which sets time periods for the tasks required within the production process; and

▶ quality control, which can be used to identify improvements (if any) that need to be made in the production process.

KEY TERMS

REVIEW QUESTIONS

1 If you were a plant manager, what primary resources would you use for production?

2 Explain the use of work stations and assembly lines.

3 You are moving your plant from the West Coast to the East Coast. What key location decisions should be considered?

4 What characteristics influence design and layout decisions?

5 In managing a plant, production control is extremely important. Name the five tasks involved.

6 Define deintegration. How would the use of this method of delegating be beneficial to a manufacturer?

7 Compare just-in-time (JIT) inventory with materials requirements planning (MRP).

8 Why is a production schedule so important for a manager?

9 Define PERT. Explain what steps are involved with PERT. Why is it necessary to identify the critical path when working on a project?

10 Define and explain quality control.

DISCUSSION QUESTIONS

1 How would production management apply to a professional basketball team?

2 Assume that you are a project manager for a large construction company. You have been given an assignment to develop a schedule for the construction of a skyscraper. Discuss how you would implement a schedule.

3 How could a firm use the Internet to provide information on its production management function? How could it use the Internet to provide information on its production control?

4 Assume that your company has given you an assignment to relocate the plant to a new region. What factors would you consider in making the decision?

5 What type of layout is appropriate for the following: (a) aircraft manufacturer, such as Boeing, (b) automotive plant, such as General Motors, (c) new housing construction?

INVESTING IN THE STOCK OF A BUSINESS

Using the annual report of the firm in which you would like to invest, complete the following:

1 Describe (in general terms) the firm's production process. What products are produced? Where are the production facilities located? Are the facilities concentrated in one location or scattered?

2 Have the firm's operations been restructured in recent years to improve efficiency? If so, how?

3 Does your firm need to consider labor supply issues when selecting a site?

4 Explain how the business uses technology to promote its production management function. For example, does it use the Internet to provide information about its production management function? Does it provide information regarding the methods used to control production?

5 Go to **http://hoovers.com** and locate the NEWS SEARCH. Type in the name of the firm in the space provided, and review the recent news stories about the firm. Summarize any (at least one) recent news story about the firm that applies to one or more of the key concepts within this chapter.

CASE SELECTING THE BEST PLANT SITE

Richard Capozzi, an entrepreneur in the high-fashion Italian shoes industry, is planning to relocate his manufacturing operation to the western part of the United States. He is currently considering two different locations. One possible location is outside Los Angeles, and the other is in Oklahoma City.

In analyzing the plant site decision, he is considering several factors. In Los Angeles the cost of land is high. However, local government officials are willing to make tax concessions. This plant location is accessible to transportation; a railroad is adjacent to the plant and an eight-lane interstate is in close proximity. Capozzi has identified the West Coast region as his target market for this type of shoe. An artist by trade, he has developed a unique design that should create mass-market appeal in this geographic area.

The Oklahoma City location has several advantages. Land cost is lower than in Los Angeles. Also, a large supply of trained labor is available in this region.

Another key consideration Capozzi must deal with is raw material availability. The raw material is imported from Italy and is received at the port of entry in Los Angeles. Transportation costs would be lower for the Los Angeles plant, a fact that weighs heavily in Capozzi's decision.

QUESTIONS

1 What will influence the plant site decision for Capozzi, and which alternative appears to be optimal?

2 How can each relative factor be rated or evaluated to determine the optimal plant location?

3 How should the decision regarding plant layout and design be determined?

4 What resources will Capozzi need to implement the production plan?

VIDEO CASE PRODUCTION MANAGEMENT AT VERMONT TEDDY BEAR COMPANY

The Vermont Teddy Bear Company produces and delivers hand-crafted teddy bears. Once the demand for teddy bears has been forecasted, the factory purchases enough materials to result in a sufficient production volume to satisfy demand. The firm creates a production schedule for cutting and sewing the materials and then monitors the production on a daily basis to ensure that it is on schedule. When the company wants to produce unusually large amounts of teddy bears, it outsources some of the sewing to people who are temporarily hired to do the work at their own residences. At each stage in the production process, the teddy bears are checked to make sure that they are not flawed.

QUESTIONS

1 How can the firm benefit from outsourcing some of its production during periods of very high demand rather than hiring workers permanently?

2 How does the firm monitor quality control?

3 How is the production volume determined? Would production volume be higher than normal in the months before Christmas? Why?

INTERNET APPLICATIONS

http://www.cannon.net/~gonyeau/nuclear/
euro-ch.htm

Where in Switzerland is the power plant built by General Electric located? What factors do you think influenced the site selection of this power plant? Describe the relative importance of the various resources used in a nuclear power plant. How important do you think inventory control and quality control are for this type of plant?

THE Coca-Cola COMPANY ANNUAL REPORT PROJECT

 Questions for the current year's annual report are available on the text website at **http://madura _intro_bus.swcollege.com.**

The following questions apply concepts learned in this chapter to The Coca-Cola Company. Go to The Coca-Cola Company website (**http://www.cocacola.com**) and find the index for the 1999 annual report.

QUESTIONS

1 Click on "Investments." How does The Coca-Cola Company ensure the availability of its products on a global basis?

2 Click on "Year 2000." What was The Coca-Cola Company's Year 2000 plan? Was the plan successful?

3 Study the "Selected Market Results" section. How might a trucking strike in a particular geographic area affect The Coca-Cola Company's production?

4 Study the "Worldwide Unit Case Volume" section. In which country do you think The Coca-Cola Company should plan to build new plants over the next five years? What do you think the advantages are of opening a plant in that country versus exporting to that country?

5 Go to **http://hoovers.com** and locate the NEWS SEARCH. Type in The Coca-Cola Company in the space provided, and review the recent news stories about the firm. Summarize any (at least one) recent news story about The Coca-Cola Company that applies one or more of the key concepts within this chapter of the text.

IN-TEXT STUDY GUIDE

Answers are in an appendix at the back of the book.

TRUE OR FALSE

1 Downsizing has enabled firms to reduce the amount of work space required.

2 The critical path is the path that takes the shortest time to complete on a PERT diagram.

3 Hotelling represents the sequence of tasks necessary to complete the production of a product.

4 A work station represents an area in which one or more employees is assigned a specific task.

5 Inventories of partially completed products are called work-in-process.

6 A firm uses outsourcing so that it can hire additional employees.

7 Design and layout decisions will have an impact on operating expenses.

8 The term "just-in-time" refers to a schedule that illustrates the expected timing for each task within a project.

9 A fixed-position layout is commonly used for assembly-line production.

10 Quality control can be measured by assessing the various characteristics that enhance customer satisfaction.

MULTIPLE CHOICE

11 The goal of _____ is to develop an efficient, high-quality process for producing products or services.
   a) conversion management
   b) assembly-line control
   c) flexible manufacturing
   d) production management
   e) routing

12 Firms are forced to search for new sites once demand for their product exceeds their:
   a) quality control.
   b) production capacity.
   c) inspection requirements.
   d) routing schedules.
   e) purchase plans.

13 A critical decision in production management is the selection of a:
   a) contingency plan.   d) consultant.
   b) competitor.   e) site.
   c) customer mix.

14 Production management influences each firm's:
   a) industry demand.   d) union.
   b) competition.   e) benefits policy.
   c) profits and value.

15 A system that attempts to reduce material inventories to a bare minimum by frequently ordering small amounts of materials from suppliers is called:
   a) routing.   d) quality control.
   b) just-in-time.   e) deintegration.
   c) scheduling.

16 Which of the following is used to ensure that materials are available when needed in the production process?
   a) just-in-time inventory system
   b) deintegration
   c) outsourcing
   d) materials requirements planning
   e) material routing management

17 All of the following characteristics influence design and layout decisions except:
   a) production process.
   b) desired production capacity.
   c) product line.
   d) purchasing applications.
   e) site.

18 The act of setting time periods for each task in the production process is called:
   a) routing.   d) dispatching.
   b) scheduling.   e) quality control.
   c) inventory control.

19 To avoid delays or increase production speed, the tasks that are part of the _____ are reviewed.
   a) purchasing applications
   b) Gantt chart   d) raw material inventory
   c) critical path   e) hotelling

20 Which of the following production processes is most commonly used for assembly-line production?
   a) flexible manufacturing
   b) fixed-position layout
   c) product layout
   d) capacity layout
   e) cost-benefit layout

21 The process of managing inventory at a level that minimizes costs is called:
   a) scheduling.   d) production planning.
   b) routing.   e) inventory control.
   c) dispatching.

22 A sequence of work stations in which each work station is designed to cover specific phases of the production process is called a(n):
a) assembly line.
d) product location.
b) hotelling.
e) Gantt chart.
c) deintegration.

23 The location of a firm's factory or office can affect all of the following except:
a) cost of production.
b) revenue.
c) level of taxes.
d) board of directors.
e) supply of labor.

24 A strategy of delegating some production tasks to suppliers is referred to as:
a) routing.
d) quality assurance.
b) dispatching.
e) hotelling.
c) deintegration.

25 Which of the following can be used to reduce a firm's investment in property and buildings?
a) hotelling
b) flexible manufacturing
c) production management
d) materials requirements planning
e) program evaluation and review technique (PERT)

26 Which of the following terms describes the process of monitoring the characteristics of a product to ensure that the firm's standards are met?
a) expectation downsizing
b) quality control
c) critical path management
d) program evaluation and review technique
e) work-in-process control

27 The development of temporary, shared office space for those employees who normally work at home is called:
a) flexible manufacturing.
b) deintegration.
c) production control.
d) hotelling.
e) quality control.

28 A method of scheduling tasks that illustrates the expected timing for each task within the production process is a:

a) Venn diagram.
d) just-in-time system.
b) Gantt chart.
e) production plan.
c) MRP system.

29 A production process where employees go to the position of the product, rather than waiting for the product to come to them is a(n):
a) assembly line.
b) batch process.
c) fixed-position layout.
d) unit production process.
e) mass production process.

30 All of the following are key tasks in production control except:
a) layout and design.
d) scheduling.
b) inventory control.
e) quality control.
c) routing.

31 A _____ represents a series of tasks in which resources are used to produce a product or service.
a) layout chart
d) production process
b) Venn diagram
e) chain of command
c) organization chart

32 Firms attempt to minimize the amount of inventory they have in order to reduce their:
a) purchasing costs.
d) quality control.
b) production costs.
e) human resources.
c) carrying costs.

33 The factors that affect a site decision include the following except for:
a) cost of workplace space.
b) tax incentives.
c) source of demand.
d) access to transportation.
e) quality assurance.

34 Once a site for the manufacturing plant is chosen, the next step to be determined is:
a) design and layout.
d) deintegration.
b) production control.
e) inventory control.
c) hotelling.

35 The sequence of tasks necessary to complete the production of a product is:
a) dispatching.
d) routing.
b) quality control.
e) deintegration.
c) purchasing.

The Learning Goals of this chapter are to:	1	Show how total quality management (TQM) can be applied to monitor and enhance the quality of the products and services produced.
	2	Identify the key methods used to improve production efficiency.

Improving Production Quality and Efficiency

n recent years, firms have given more attention to the quality of the products or services they produce. The act of monitoring and improving the quality of products and services produced is commonly referred to as total quality management (TQM). Firms have also given more attention to production efficiency, which refers to the ability to produce products at a low cost. A firm's earnings and therefore its value can be influenced by TQM and production efficiency.

Consider the case of Motorola, which produces cellular telephones, two-way radios, and various other electronic devices. The superior quality of its products made Motorola the winner of the first Malcolm Baldrige National Quality Award. How can Motorola measure the quality of its products? How can it ensure that its production process achieves specific quality standards? How can it improve its production efficiency? This chapter provides a background on TQM and production efficiency that can be used to address these questions.

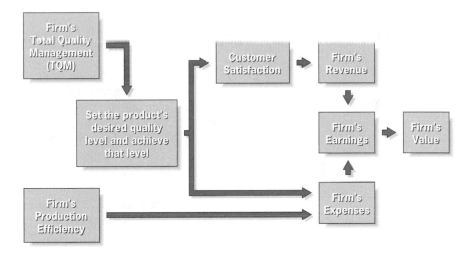

Improving Production Quality with TQM

1 Show how total quality management (TQM) can be applied to monitor and enhance the quality of the products and services produced.

total quality management (TQM) the act of monitoring and improving the quality of products and services produced

The **total quality management (TQM)** concept was developed by W. Edwards Deming and was used extensively by some Japanese firms before being used in the United States. According to W. Edwards Deming, some of the key guidelines for improving quality are (1) provide managers and other employees with the education and training for them to excel in their jobs, (2) encourage employees to take responsibility and to provide leadership, and (3) encourage all employees to search for ways to improve the production process. These guidelines are consistent with giving employees the skills and the freedom to be creative, rather than imposing more restrictions that force employees to focus only on producing a large number of units just to meet some production quota. Deming discouraged the focus on production quotas so that employees could allocate more of their time to leadership and the improvement of the production process.

The chip clean room at Motorola. These Motorola employees are working in a clean room. One speck of dust or dirt can destroy both the product and the equipment in this room. Motorola knows that workers need extensive training to be effective in this environment.

In the last two decades, most U.S. firms have used TQM to some degree. Many firms use teams of employees to assess quality and offer suggestions for continuous improvement.

TQM also stresses the need for firms to measure quality from the customer's perspective. In the past, firms assessed quality solely from their own perspective. For instance, a high-technology computer may satisfy a firm, but it will satisfy a customer only if it is easy to use. Firms are now more aware that their assessment of quality must focus on customer opinions rather than their own. Firms are now paying more attention to quality because they recognize that quality can determine whether customers will purchase the product again. Customers are more likely to purchase the product again from the same producer if they are satisfied with the quality, whether the product is a car, a pair of shoes, or a cellular phone.

Firms now realize that it is easier to retain existing customers than it is to attract new customers who are unfamiliar with their products or services. Historically, firms that focused on quality and customer satisfaction had an advantage over their competitors. Today, most firms recognize the importance of customer satisfaction. Nevertheless, some firms are much better at ensuring customer satisfaction than others.

As an illustration of how a focus on quality and customer satisfaction can affect the value of the firm, consider the case of Bell Atlantic. In September 1997, it initiated a program to focus on complete customer satisfaction and to reward employees based on levels of customer satisfaction. Bell's performance and its value (as measured by its stock price) improved substantially in response to this strategy, as shown in Exhibit 10.1.

Although firms can improve their quality in numerous ways, consider the efforts of Corning Telecommunications Products, which won the Malcolm Baldrige National Quality Award in 1995. First, it developed a technologically advanced product (fiber that transmits phone calls). Second, Corning's purchases of supplies focused less on price and more on quality characteristics (such as durability). The quality of its products is partially dependent on the quality of its supplies. Third, it substantially reduced the number of customer complaints about its products in recent years. Fourth, it created an interactive computer system so that employees can monitor customer feed-

Impact of Increased Focus on Customer Satisfaction on Bell Atlantic's Stock Price

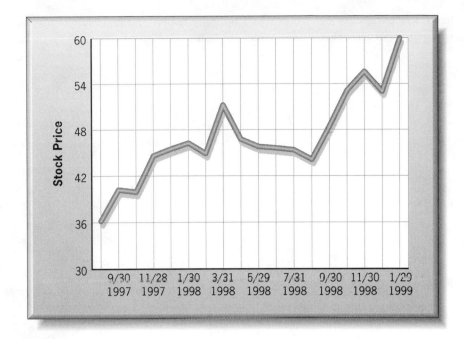

back. This helped employees become aware of what customers liked or disliked about Corning's products and servicing.

Other firms such as Motorola and Saturn, which are noted for their focus on TQM, use their own strategies for improving quality. Although the strategies vary among firms, they all tend to focus on increasing customer satisfaction. Consider these quotations from recent annual reports:

> *We instituted Amoco Progress to unite the best practices of quality management throughout the corporation.*
>
> —Amoco (now part of BP Amoco)

> *The Commitment to Excellence philosophy is Anheuser-Busch's effort to incorporate the key total quality management principles of customer satisfaction, employee involvement, and continuous process improvement into its culture.*
>
> —Anheuser-Busch

> *It's impossible to separate performance for our shareholders from performance for our customers. Our commitment encompasses both. We are committed to rewarding shareholders with above-average returns while constantly exceeding the expectations of our customers.*
>
> —Westinghouse

BUSINESS ONLINE

Total Quality Management Information

BECAUSE OF THE INCREASING IMPORTANCE OF TOTAL QUALITY MANAGEMENT (TQM) in the United States, websites such as the one shown here, which offer differing views on TQM, are very useful to companies attempting to implement TQM.

http://www.goalqpc.com/
research/tqmwheel.html

Notice how the "wheel" contains more areas as another circle is entered. Interested parties can learn more about each area by clicking on the respective area.

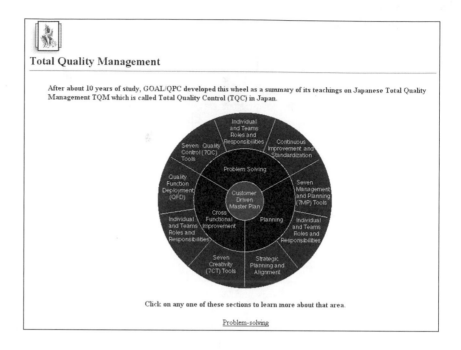

The use of TQM normally involves the following functions:

▶ Specify the desired quality level.
▶ Achieve the desired quality level.
▶ Control the quality level.

Specify the Desired Quality Level

The quality of a product or service typically measures the likelihood that it will perform properly over its expected life. The quality of a computer may be defined by how well it works and how long it lasts. Quality may also be measured by how easy the computer is to use. Alternatively, quality may be defined by the degree of repairs necessary: the more repairs, the lower the quality. Quality may also be defined by how quickly the manufacturer repairs a computer that experiences problems. Each of these characteristics can affect customer satisfaction and therefore should be considered as indicators of quality.

Firms must decide on the amount of resources they will use to enhance a product's quality. At one extreme, they can set a high quality level, which will result in high expenses and a high price. At the other extreme, they can set a low quality level to keep expenses low and charge a lower price. A low quality level does not mean that the product was produced incorrectly. It normally means that the production process was simplified to reduce expenses so that the firm can charge a low price. Low-quality products are appealing to customers who can only afford to pay low prices and who are unwilling to pay higher prices for high-quality products.

When firms set the quality level, they assess the demand for products within different market segments (such as a high-quality segment and a low-quality segment). They also assess the quality levels of products produced by competitors. They attempt to set the quality and price of their products at levels that will satisfy some segment of the market. The Chevrolet Cavalier fits customers who focus more on price and less on quality, while the Cadillac fits customers who focus more on quality.

When setting quality, the focus should be on quality characteristics that customers desire. For example, consider an economy car that could be improved by installing a larger (faster) engine or a higher-quality interior. Assume, however, that a customer survey determines that these improvements would not substantially increase customer satisfaction. Instead, customers are most concerned with possible production defects. In this case, the car manufacturer may decide to focus on ensuring proper production (so that there are fewer defects) rather than upgrading specific parts of the car. With this approach, the firm's desired quality level is focused on increasing customer satisfaction.

Given that customers' future demand for the firm's product may be influenced by the level of customer satisfaction, the firm sets a desired quality level that may result in a higher future demand for its product. Conversely, if the firm sets quality goals that are not relevant to customers, its efforts may not have a favorable effect on future demand.

Achieve the Desired Quality Level

Once the desired quality level is set, employees involved in any stage of the production process can offer suggestions on how the product or service should be produced to achieve that quality level. Employee teams can be organized to provide their suggestions. Having people from different parts of the production process on the same team may enable any potential conflict across the production process to be detected. Higher-quality products will normally require higher-quality materials or more hours of labor to produce the final product. The production process that is developed will specify the types of materials needed to achieve the desired quality level and the amount of time taken by human resources on each part of the process.

DELL COMPUTER'S FORMULA FOR SUCCESS

One of Dell Computer's most distinctive value-added services is its ability to custom-configure hardware and software as it builds computer systems, one order at a time. Such single-step integration is efficient for Dell and its customers and, because it reduces the number of times systems are handled, produces higher-quality products. Thus, Dell is focused on the quality of the products and services it produces.

Control the Quality Level

Quality control is used to ensure that the production process meets specified quality standards. Once the desired quality level has been defined, firms can assess whether that quality level was achieved. To ensure that the quality is maintained, firms periodically evaluate the characteristics used to measure product quality. For example, Microsoft detects some defects in its computer software and General Motors detects some defects in fuel tanks of specific types of cars. By detecting defects, these firms are able to correct the production process and maintain customer satisfaction.

Boeing (manufacturer of aircraft) incurs expenses for implementing a system to remove production defects and raise its quality level. However, Boeing's production process has improved substantially as a result of its ability to identify defects. If firms properly resolve deficiencies detected by quality control, they may be able to increase revenue and cover the expenses associated with quality control.

BUSINESS ONLINE

Corporate
Quality
Information

http://www.gejapan.co.jp/
english/sixsigma.html

MANY FIRMS NOW REALIZE THAT IT IS EASIER TO RETAIN EXISTING CUS-tomers than to attract new ones. Hence, many firms, such as General Electric (GE), use the Internet to provide their customers and investors with information regarding the quality process at their company. For example, GE uses its unique "Six Sigma Quality Coach." Detailed information, such as a description of the approach, can be found on GE's website, as shown here.

quality control circle a group of employees who assess the quality of a product and offer suggestions for improvement

Control by Technology Quality control may be conducted by computers. The firm's computers can determine whether each component of a product produced meets specific quality standards. Computer-controlled machinery has electronic sensors that can screen out defective parts. Firms such as Eastman Kodak and Motorola use computers and software to enhance quality control.

Control by Employees Employees are also used to assess quality. One person may be assigned to assess components at each stage of the assembly line. Alternatively, a team of employees may be responsible for assessing the quality of products at different stages of the production process. Many firms use a **quality control circle,** which is a group of employees who assess the quality of a product and offer suggestions for improvement. Quality control circles usually allow for more interaction among workers and managers and provide workers with a sense of responsibility. Most automobile manufacturers (including DaimlerChrysler and Ford) and computer manufacturers (including IBM) have successfully used quality control circles.

Specific employees of Saturn Corporation (a subsidiary of General Motors) conduct a weekly review of their production process. They search for defects and quickly communicate this information to the employees who are involved with that part of the production process.

sampling randomly selecting some of the products produced and testing them to determine whether they satisfy the quality standards

Control by Sampling Only by testing each unit produced for any possible flaw could quality control ensure that all products satisfied the desired quality level. This is virtually impossible. Firms tend to assess quality control by **sampling,** or randomly selecting some of the products produced and testing them to determine whether they satisfy the quality standards. Firms may check one unit per one hundred units produced and concentrate specifically on possible flaws that have been detected in previous checks.

This photo of a machine sanding a metal auto body before painting at Chrysler's Sterling Heights assembly plant near Detroit shows how technology is used in the production process.

Control by Monitoring Complaints Quality should be assessed not only when the product is produced but also after it is sold. Some products may not show quality deficiencies until after customers use them. One method of assessing the quality of products that have been sold is to monitor the proportion of products returned or to monitor customer complaints. Some firms use a customer complaint staff to identify and resolve quality deficiencies. However, this method does not necessarily indicate the degree of customer satisfaction. It detects only those situations in which customers were extremely dissatisfied.

AT&T has a Consumer Communications Services unit that attempts to ensure customer satisfaction. Firms such as DaimlerChrysler and Saturn attempt to obtain more feedback from their dealers on customer complaints about their production.

Control by Implementing Surveys More customer feedback can be obtained by conducting surveys. Firms can allow customers to offer opinions on product quality control by sending them a survey months after the sale. For example, Saturn and Toyota commonly survey their customers to determine the level of customer satisfaction. The survey can also ask for feedback on the quality of specific parts or functions of the product.

Correcting Deficiencies The quality control process not only detects quality deficiencies but also is used to correct them. If quality is deficient, it is likely caused by one of the following factors. First, the materials provided by suppliers could be inadequate. Second, the quality of work by employees could be inadequate. Third, the machinery and equipment used to produce a product could be malfunctioning.

If the cause of the quality deficiency is materials, the firm either may require the existing supplier to improve the quality or may obtain materials from a different supplier in the future. If the cause is the work of employees, the firm may need to retrain or reprimand those employees. If the cause of quality deficiency is the machinery, the firm may need to use replacements or make repairs.

When a firm detects production deficiencies, it not only must correct the production process but also may need to attend to customer complaints. If the deficiencies were not detected before the product was sold, customers may experience problems with the products. The firm should attempt to respond quickly to customers who

SELF-SCORING EXERCISE

Are You Highly Satisfied as a Customer?

Think of an organization or business with which you have frequent contact and interaction. How satisfied are you with the products or services provided to you by this organization or business? Would the organization or business be competitive in the Customer Satisfaction category for a Malcolm Baldrige National Quality Award?

Complete the following eight questions to rate the quality of the organization's or business's customer satisfaction. Use a scale of 1 (definitely not), 2 (probably not), 3 (unsure), 4 (probably yes), and 5 (definitely yes).

_____ 1. Do you believe the organization knows what you expect as a customer?

_____ 2. Has the organization improved the quality of its customer relationships over a period of time?

_____ 3. Do you receive the same standard of service from different people in this organization?

_____ 4. Do you believe that each and every employee is committed to serving your needs and satisfying you as a customer?

_____ 5. Whenever you have had even the smallest complaint about the organization, has that complaint been resolved satisfactorily?

_____ 6. Have you ever completed any sort of customer satisfaction survey, card, or feedback form for the organization?

_____ 7. Have you heard that people were more satisfied with the organization's products and services in the past than today?

_____ 8. Compared with similar organizations, do you consider this organization to be superior in serving customers?

_____ Total points

Scoring

35–40: This organization provides world-class customer service and deserves quality recognition in this area.

28–34: This organization provides high-quality service to its customers.

20–27: This organization is mediocre in its service to customers.

8–19: This organization needs to improve its service to customers.

purchased the products or services with such quality deficiencies. In this way, it can reduce customer dissatisfaction. For example, when car manufacturers recall cars to repair a deficiency, they may contact customers by phone and offer them loaners until the cars are fixed.

Total quality management is commonly used to correct a firm's perceived deficiencies and therefore improve customer satisfaction. Consider the case of Fairview-AFX, a developer of training facilities, which attempted to assess its customer service record in the early 1990s. Fairview's salespeople called its biggest customers to obtain feedback on its service. About 75 percent of the customers were not satisfied with Fairview's service because of delays in completing work. Recognizing that it might lose much business to competitors, Fairview established a Customer Care program, which obligated employees to complete their work on schedule. Second, it began to contact customers after performing work to ensure that the work was done properly. Third, it set up a communications system among its offices in different cities to monitor inventory so that it could properly estimate delivery times. This resulted in fewer delays in the work it performed and helped to accelerate the production process. Consequently, Fairview was able to substantially improve customer satisfaction.

Broadening the Application of Quality

Traditionally, firms considered quality only in terms of the product that was produced. Today, quality applies not only to the content of the product but to the servicing that surrounds it. Quality involves more than how long the product lasts. It includes the way the product was sold to the customer and the way it was serviced (if necessary) after it was sold. As an illustration of this broadening application of quality, consider the following comments made in a recent annual report:

> **"** *Quality . . . . begins long before the product even exists—in the design and engineering phases. It carries through into manufacturing, marketing and sales, and it doesn't stop when the vehicle goes off the dealer's lot. It continues into the way the product is serviced and the ways the consumer's best interests have been considered every step of the way, through the entire life cycle of the product.* **"**
>
> —Ford Motor Company

Thus, controlling the quality of a product is not limited to testing for defects. Surveys of customer satisfaction are commonly used to determine quality because the firm's perception of quality may not necessarily reflect the customer's perception. Such surveys tend to be more useful if they separate the various aspects that make up quality, including the product itself, its sale, and its servicing.

Assessing Quality of Services

The assessment of quality also applies to services sold to customers. For example, Amazon.com produces a service of fulfilling orders of books, CDs, and other products ordered over the Internet by customers. Its customers assess the quality of the service in terms of the ease with which they can send an order over the Internet, whether they receive the proper order, and how quickly the products are delivered.

Airlines such as American Airlines and Delta Air Lines produce the service of flying customers to their desired destinations. These customers assess the quality of the airline service in terms of safety, the attitude of flight attendants, the comfort of the seats, whether the flight arrived on time, and whether their luggage was lost.

Restaurants produce a service for customers and commonly assess quality by encouraging customers to complete feedback cards left on the tables. Customers are asked to rate not only the product (food) but the service surrounding the product, such as the attitude of the server, how quickly the meal was provided, and the amenities.

GLOBAL BUSINESS

Global Quality Standards

FIRMS THAT CONDUCT INTERNATIONAL BUSINESS MAY ATTEMPT TO SATISFY a set of global quality standards. These standards have been established by the International Standards Organization (ISO), which has representatives from numerous countries. Firms are not required to meet these standards. However, by voluntarily meeting these standards, they can become certified, which may boost their credibility when selling products to foreign customers. The certification process commonly costs at least $20,000 and takes at least one year. The standards focus on the design, manufacturing process, installation, and service of a product. Independent auditors review the firm's operations and decide whether to certify the firm. Foreign customers may be more comfortable if the firm has met the international standards. A publication called *ISO 9000* specifies the standards for production quality. Another set of standards (called *ISO 14000*) applies to the environmental effects of the production process.

Ford Motor Company has certified all of its manufacturing plants around the world under a more recent standard called *ISO 14001*. By meeting this international environment management standard, Ford expects to continue to improve its performance and reduce its costs by hundreds of millions of dollars over a five-year period.

Firms may also have to meet other standards to sell their products in specific foreign countries. For example, the Japanese government assesses any products that are sold in Japan to ensure that they are safe. Japan's safety standards have discouraged firms based in the United States and other countries from attempting to sell products in Japan. The standards established by Japan may serve as a barrier that protects local firms in Japan from foreign competitors.

In addition to meeting standards on global quality, firms must adapt their products to satisfy unique characteristics of countries. U.S. firms that produce automobiles for the United Kingdom must place the steering wheel on the right side. U.S. firms that produce tires to be sold in less-developed countries may use more rubber to withstand rougher road surfaces.

BUSINESS ONLINE

Quality Level Control

http://www.nist.gov/

ORGANIZATIONS SUCH AS NATIONAL INSTITUTE OF STANDARDS AND TECHnology use the Internet to provide information about quality, standards, and quality certifications. This institute offers detailed information for firms that wish to measure their quality standards and improve their quality. Considering the increased importance of TQM, websites such as the one shown here are highly useful to firms attempting to improve the quality of their products.

Methods to Improve Production Efficiency

2 Identify the key methods used to improve production efficiency.

production efficiency the ability to produce products at a low cost

Firms strive to increase their **production efficiency,** which reflects a lower cost for a given amount of output and a given level of quality. Managers continually search for ways to manage human and other resources in a manner that improves production efficiency. Some firms are motivated to reduce their expenses because they are losing market share to their competitors or because their earnings are inadequate. If such a trend continues, these firms will not survive. Even firms that have recently performed well must recognize the need to continually improve, since other competitors may become more efficient.

Production efficiency is important to service firms as well as manufacturing firms. For example, airlines need to be efficient in their service of flying passengers from one location to another so that they can achieve low expenses. This is reinforced by the following comments from a recent annual report:

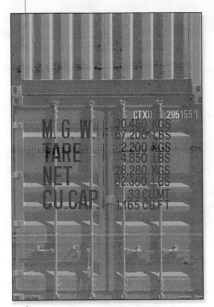

The internationally standardized freight container enables all components of a transport system—air and seaport facilities, railways, highways, and packages—to interface efficiently. This, combined with standardized documents to identify sensitive or dangerous cargoes, makes international trade cheaper, faster, and safer.

benchmarking a method of evaluating performance by comparison to some specified (benchmark) level, typically a level achieved by another company

stretch targets production efficiency targets (or goals) that cannot be achieved under present conditions

automated tasks are completed by machines without the use of employees

" We have a culture that values efficiency, hard work, innovation, and simplicity. . . . That's how the low cost producer keeps finding ways to reduce costs further. . . . Scheduling frequent flights with minimum ground time at efficient airports contributes to the highest productivity in the industry, and, in turn, the lowest operating costs. "

—Southwest Airlines

When Louis Gerstner became chief executive officer of IBM in 1993, he set a goal for IBM to use resources efficiently when producing computers and related products. IBM's restructuring led to an increase in production efficiency, which had several favorable effects. First, the reduction in expenses allowed IBM to lower its prices and therefore become more competitive. Sales of IBM computers increased as demand for its product increased in response to lower prices. IBM's profits increased as a result of its higher sales and more efficient production process (lower operating expenses). IBM's stock price rose substantially as a result of its higher profits. The key to IBM's improvement was more efficient management of its production process. More recently, Motorola has increased its efficiency, which has caused its stock price to increase by more than 100 percent within two years.

Many firms that set production efficiency goals use **benchmarking,** which is a method of evaluating performance by comparison to some specified (benchmark) level. For example, a firm may set a goal of producing baseball caps at a cost of $3 per cap, which is the average cost incurred by the most successful producer of baseball caps.

The top managers of some firms set production efficiency targets (or goals) that cannot be achieved under present conditions. These targets are referred to as **stretch targets** because they are stretched beyond the ordinary. Stretch targets may be established in response to a decline in the firm's market share or performance. For example, 3M Company created a stretch target that 30 percent of its sales be derived from sales of products it created in the last four years. This target was intended to encourage more development of new products so that 3M did not rely on its innovations from several years ago. Boeing also created stretch targets to improve upon its relatively slow process for producing airplanes. It set stretch targets on its time schedule for producing various pieces of the airplane. It also set stretch targets to substantially lower its production expenses so that it could lower its prices. If expenses could be reduced substantially, Boeing could reduce prices and therefore convince airlines to purchase new airplanes rather than repair old ones.

Firms can improve production efficiency through the following methods:

▶ Technology
▶ Economies of scale
▶ Restructuring

Each of these methods is discussed in turn.

Technology

Firms may improve their production efficiency with new technology. New machinery conducts tasks more quickly because of increased technology. Computer systems used by numerous manufacturing firms have improved as a result of technology and have increased the speed at which various tasks can be completed.

Many production processes have become **automated,** whereby tasks are completed by machines without the use of employees. Since expenses incurred from machinery can be less than those incurred from human resources, automation may improve production efficiency. Guidelines for effective automation are summarized in Exhibit 10.2.

Exhibit 10.2

Guidelines for Effective
Automation

To effectively capitalize on the potential benefits from automation, the following guidelines
should be considered:
1. *Plan*—Automation normally does not involve simply speeding up work, but it may require
the elimination of some production steps. Planning is necessary to decide the type of automation that will be most appropriate (computers versus other machinery).
2. *Use Automation Where the Benefits Are Greatest*—It may not be efficient to evenly allocate
automation among all parts of the production process. Some workers will not be able to use
a computer for their type of work.
3. *Train*—To make sure that the automation implemented is effectively utilized; any workers
who use new computers or machinery should be trained.
4. *Evaluate Costs and Benefits over Time*—By assessing the costs and benefits of automation, a firm can decide whether to implement additional automation or revise its existing automation.

Many firms such as Albertson's (a grocery chain) and Home Depot have improved
production efficiency with the use of computer technology. For example, computers
can keep track of the daily or weekly volume of each type of product that is purchased
at the cash register of a retail store. Therefore, the firm does not need an employee to
monitor the inventory of these products. The computer may even be programmed to
automatically reorder some products once the inventory is reduced to a specified level.
Some hospitals use pharmacy robots that stock and retrieve drugs. This technology increases production without additional labor expenses.

Many firms improve technology through ventures with other firms, whereby the
firms pool their specific types of expertise or knowledge. Nucor and U.S. Steel created
an alliance to develop a new method for converting iron ore into steel. Apple, IBM,
and Motorola created an alliance to improve technology for computer hardware. Motorola created an alliance with United Parcel Service (UPS), in which UPS helped Motorola reduce its time on product deliveries by 75 percent. All of these examples reflect the use of technology in ways that can reduce operating expenses and therefore
increase the firm's value.

Economies of Scale

economies of scale as the
quantity produced increases, the
cost per unit decreases

fixed costs operating expenses
that do not change in response to
the number of products
produced

variable costs operating
expenses that vary directly with
the number of products
produced

Firms may also be able to reduce costs by achieving **economies of scale,** which reflect
a lower average cost incurred from producing a larger volume. To recognize how
economies of scale can occur, consider that two types of costs are involved in the production of a product: fixed costs and variable costs. **Fixed costs** are operating expenses
that do not change in response to the number of products produced. For example, the
cost of renting a specific factory is not affected by the number of products produced
there.

Variable costs are operating expenses that vary directly with the number of products produced. As output increases, the variable costs increase, while the fixed costs
remain constant. The average cost per unit typically declines as output increases for
firms that incur large fixed costs.

Automobile manufacturers incur a large fixed cost because they have to pay for
their large facilities (including all the machinery) even if they do not produce many
cars. Therefore, they need to produce a large number of cars to reduce the average cost
per car produced.

Consider the production of a paperback book that requires some materials (ink
and paper) and some manual labor. Assume that a book printing company incurs a
fixed cost (rent plus machinery) of $40,000 per month. These expenses exist regard-
less of the number of books printed. Assume that the variable cost of producing each
book is $2 per book. The total cost of producing books each month is equal to the

fixed cost plus the variable cost. The total cost is estimated for various production levels in Exhibit 10.3. The key measure of production efficiency is the average cost per unit, which is measured as the total cost divided by the number of units produced. Notice how the average cost declines when the production volume increases. This relationship exists because the fixed cost is not affected by the production volume. Therefore, the fixed costs can be spread over a larger production volume. No extra fixed cost is incurred when producing additional products.

Assume that each of the books produced can be sold for $10. Exhibit 10.4 shows the total revenue and total costs for various quantities of books produced. The total

Exhibit 10.3

Relationship between Production Volume and Costs

Quantity of Books Produced	Fixed Cost	Variable Cost ($2 Per Unit)	Total Cost	Average Cost Per Unit
1,000	$40,000	$ 2,000	$42,000	$42.00
3,000	40,000	6,000	46,000	15.33
5,000	40,000	10,000	50,000	10.00
10,000	40,000	20,000	60,000	6.00
15,000	40,000	30,000	70,000	4.67
20,000	40,000	40,000	80,000	4.00
25,000	40,000	50,000	90,000	3.60

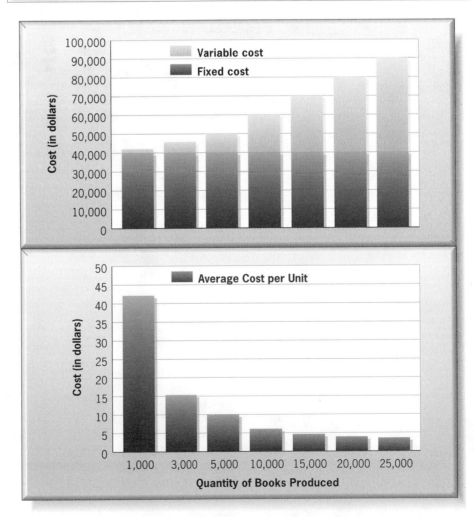

Exhibit 10.4

Relationship between Volume
and Profitability

Quantity of Books Produced	Total Revenue (= Quantity × Price)	Total Cost	Profits
1,000	$ 10,000	$42,000	−$32,000
3,000	30,000	46,000	−$16,000
5,000	50,000	50,000	$0
10,000	100,000	60,000	$40,000
15,000	150,000	70,000	$80,000
20,000	200,000	80,000	$120,000
25,000	250,000	90,000	$160,000

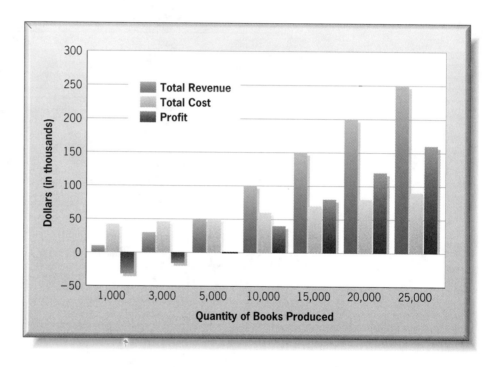

break-even point the quantity of units sold at which total revenue equals total cost

revenue is equal to the quantity produced times the price of $10 per book. The profits represent the difference between the total revenue and the total cost. Notice that the firm experiences losses at small quantities. This is because the fixed costs are incurred even though the production volume is low. At the quantity level of 5,000 books, the total revenue is equal to the total cost. The quantity of units sold at which total revenue equals total cost is referred to as the **break-even point.** At any quantity beyond 5,000 books, the firm experiences profits. The profits are larger for larger quantities produced. This results from the lower average cost incurred from the production of more books.

Some firms strive to achieve a large market share so that they can achieve economies of scale. For example, Compaq Computer typically sets a goal to obtain a substantial market share for each of its products. This results in a large production volume so that Compaq can achieve economies of scale. One of the largest expenses in the production of computers is the research and development to improve computers. That expense is incurred whether Compaq sells only twenty computers or fifty thousand computers. Therefore, the average cost per unit is reduced when Compaq produces a large amount of a specific computer.

Restructuring

restructuring the revision of the production process in an attempt to improve efficiency

Restructuring involves the revision of the production process in an attempt to improve efficiency. When restructuring reduces the expense of producing products or services, it can improve the firm's profits and therefore increase the firm's value. Many firms, including BankAmerica, Federal Express, and IBM, have restructured their operations and have improved their performance as a result.

In October 1998, General Motors began to reorganize its production process to streamline its operations and its management. Its value (as measured by its stock price) increased substantially in response to these efforts, as shown in Exhibit 10.5.

reengineering the redesign of a firm's organizational structure and operations

Many firms periodically assess all aspects of their business to determine whether they should restructure in any way. Many use **reengineering,** which is the redesign of a firm's organizational structure and operations. The reengineering may result in some minor revisions, such as the procedures used to take phone messages or to send packages at the firm. Alternatively, the revisions may be much larger, such as a new facility or a new assembly-line operation for production.

Reengineering requires that the company forget the old way of doing things and attempt to build the best system from scratch. Reengineering has been used by Delta Air Lines, Hallmark, and many other firms. It requires the efforts of many different types of managers within the firm who are willing to think about the optimal method for production without being forced to focus on the method that is currently being used. Reengineering is normally conducted by obtaining input from employees who understand how the production process works. These employees are likely to recognize any inefficient parts of the process that should be eliminated or revised.

A popular method for obtaining employee feedback is to organize employees into cross-functional teams; one employee who is responsible for each specific function of the production process is assigned to the team. For example, a manufacturing firm may have a team that consists of one employee who orders supplies, one who works on the assembly line, one who is responsible for selling the finished product, and one who assesses the quality of the product.

Employees who are asked for input on restructuring do not have to completely understand every function of the production process, because they can rely on their

Exhibit 10.5

Impact of Restructuring on the Stock Price of General Motors

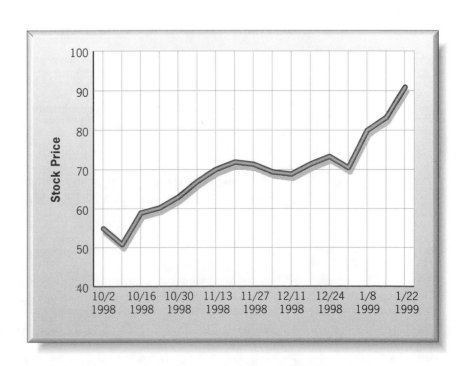

Using Information Technology to Improve Product Quality

Information technology (IT) is increasingly being employed to enhance and monitor product quality. A particularly good example can be found in the elevator industry. The quality of elevators is critical; few people can remember their last trip on an elevator, but everybody can remember the last time they were stuck in one. Otis Elevator, in particular, has been a leader in using IT to improve product quality. A major problem in preventing elevator failures is that small discrepancies that characteristically lead to a failure (such as the elevator not being precisely aligned with the floor when it comes to a stop) are often ignored. Thus, the first indication of a problem that an elevator service company receives may be the emergency call reporting that someone is trapped.

To identify small problems before they become emergencies, Otis developed a Remote Elevator Monitoring (REM) system. The REM system uses a small computer to monitor elevator performance. In addition, some installations employ telecommunications linkages, allowing the elevator itself to call Otis headquarters in the event of any unexpected problems. As a result, the REM system enables service personnel to be sent to a building before small problems escalate to an emergency.

By promoting these capabilities, Otis has been able to charge a premium for its elevators, based upon their perceived quality. Incorporating IT into products to enhance quality can also lead to other economic benefits for a firm. In many industries, ongoing maintenance and servicing of products is, in itself, a huge market. Consequently, the manufacturer can use its expertise in the technology as a competitive advantage in competing for the service business, as Otis has done with its elevators.

team members for specific details. The team of employees can attempt to create a production process that is more efficient. The expenses and other characteristics of this proposed process can be estimated and compared with those of the existing process. When using the team concept, no single employee has excessive influence on the proposed methods for restructuring. Thus, any proposals by the team receive the support of several employees and are not intended to benefit just one particular employee.

Some employees may attempt to focus on changes that will give them more job security or power. This can reduce the potential benefits of reengineering, because the proposed restructuring of the production process may be intended to enhance an employee's position rather than the firm's efficiency. Firms may attempt to prevent such a problem by rewarding those employees who develop cost-cutting ideas that the firm actually uses.

The following statements from recent annual reports confirm how some firms are attempting to restructure their operations:

> ❝ *We believe our restructuring programs will reduce operating costs by approximately $170 million.* ❞
>
> —Westinghouse

> ❝ *Through the reengineering process, we are . . . discarding decades-old processes and starting with a clean sheet of paper.* ❞
>
> —Zenith

downsizing a reduction in the number of employees

Downsizing When firms restructure, they also typically engage in **downsizing;** that is, they reduce the number of employees. Firms identify various job positions that can be eliminated without affecting the volume or the quality of products produced. Some downsizing occurs as a result of technology because automated production processes replace human resources (as explained earlier). However, numerous firms downsize even when they have no plans to further automate their production process.

In recent years, Mobil Corporation (now ExxonMobil), American Airlines, Procter & Gamble, Boeing, IBM, Eastman Kodak, TRW, and numerous other firms have cut thousands of jobs. A reduction in employees results in a reduction of salaries paid by the firm. Firms frequently used downsizing during the recession of the early 1990s. Many firms were experiencing financial problems and restructured their operations to reduce expenses. Job positions were eliminated, resulting in a reassignment of tasks to the remaining employees. Firms noticed that they were able to achieve similar production volume with fewer employees. Even after the recession ended, some firms continued to downsize throughout the 1990s because competition was so intense in many industries. Firms that had an inefficient production process were forced to become more efficient to compete with those firms that had already downsized.

To illustrate the potential savings from downsizing, consider that a firm's cost of employees (labor cost) may be as much as its cost of the materials used to produce the final product. Many large firms, such as IBM and General Motors, spend more than $1 billion in salaries and other compensation each year. If a firm can find a way to cut one hundred employees with an average compensation of $30,000, the savings will be $3 million (computed as $30,000 × 100 employees). For large firms that eliminate thousands of jobs, the cost savings can exceed $100 million per year. If the jobs can

---

CROSS-FUNCTIONAL TEAMWORK

Interaction of Functions Involved in Total Quality Management

Total quality management requires an ongoing product assessment, beginning from the time product materials are ordered and continuing until the customer has purchased and used the product. Consequently, TQM requires an interaction of business functions. The key management functions involved in TQM are ordering the proper types and amounts of supplies, achieving efficient (low-cost) production of the product, and ensuring that the product satisfies the firm's production standards.

The key marketing functions involved in TQM are achieving efficient use of marketing strategies, ensuring customer satisfaction, and obtaining feedback from customers on how to improve the product. When marketing managers receive a similar criticism about a product from many customers, they should contact the production managers, who may redesign the product. This interaction between management and marketing functions is shown in Exhibit 10.6.

The financing function is indirectly affected, as changes in expenses or revenue resulting from TQM may alter the amount of new financing that the firm needs.

Exhibit 10.6

Interaction between Management and Marketing Functions When Implementing Total Quality Management

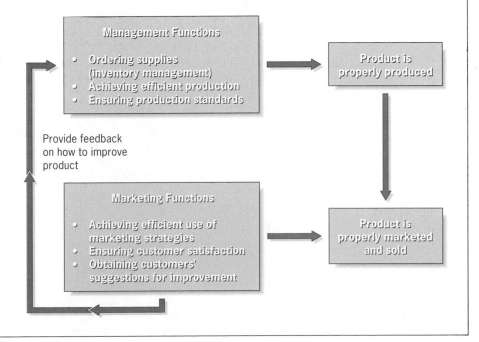

be cut without any other adverse effects, $100 million per year in cost savings should result in an additional $100 million in profit.

Downsizing also has its disadvantages. Some firms become so obsessed with eliminating their inefficient components that they downsize too much. This is referred to as **corporate anorexia.** Downsizing can have the following adverse effects. First, there may be costs associated with the elimination of job positions, such as costs incurred to find other job positions within the firm or outside it for the employees whose jobs were cut. Second, there may be costs associated with training some of the remaining employees whose responsibilities were expanded. Third, if the remaining employees believe their own positions may be cut, their morale may decline, reducing their performance. Fourth, downsizing may result in lower quality, as the remaining employees may be assigned more work and may not detect defects in the production process. For example, when Delta Air Lines reduced its workforce by 10,000 employees, its "on-time" performance declined. Firms must consider such possible adverse effects before they can accurately estimate the cost savings that would result from downsizing.

> **corporate anorexia** the problem that occurs when firms become so obsessed with eliminating their inefficient components that they downsize too much

---

BUSINESS DILEMMA | College Health Club

Total Quality Management at College Health Club

SUE KRAMER, PRESIDENT OF COLLEGE HEALTH CLUB (CHC), HAS HEARD NUmerous business success stories that were attributed to the use of total quality management (TQM). However, most of the TQM examples were manufacturing firms that had elaborate production processes. CHC simply produces a health club service. Nevertheless, Sue believes that the TQM principles could be applied to the production and sale of health club services.

Dilemma

Sue's goal is to apply TQM within her health club business. Offer some suggestions on how Sue could attempt to improve the performance of CHC by applying TQM.

Solution

Recall that the key functions involved in TQM are (1) defining a desired quality level, (2) developing a production process that achieves that level, and (3) controlling the quality level with continuous monitoring and assessment.

No simple formula can measure the quality of a health club service. Sue decides that the best way to measure the quality of the services she provides is to determine whether customers are satisfied with the services. Sue identifies various criteria that may affect customer satisfaction. She asks the customers to rate each of the following criteria, from a 1 ("not satisfied") to a 5 ("very satisfied"):

1 Does CHC have all the desired weight machines and equipment?

2 Does CHC have enough weight machines and equipment so that customers do not have to wait their turn?

3 Is CHC's location convenient?

4 Are CHC's business hours (from 8:00 A.M. to 10:00 P.M. seven days a week) acceptable?

5 Are CHC's aerobics classes effective?

6 Does CHC offer enough aerobics classes?

This survey will help determine the quality level of the health club services as perceived by the customers. Sue can then determine whether the quality level is acceptable to her. If the average score of any criterion is less than 4.0, Sue plans to focus on that item to improve quality and therefore boost customer satisfaction. To determine how customer satisfaction can be improved, she will obtain more detailed feedback on any criterion with an unacceptable score.

To control the quality level over time, Sue plans to place index cards with this survey and a comments box near the club's exit. Thus, whenever customers have concerns about the quality of CHC's services, they can fill out the cards. A high level of customer satisfaction will improve CHC's revenue and could also improve production efficiency due to economies of scale.

Sue recognizes that she not only should search for new members but also should make an effort to keep existing members.

Additional Issues for Discussion

1 How can the quality of a health club be measured?

2 Since so many factors affect quality, how can Sue Kramer decide which factors to focus on for her health club?

3 Explain how the concept of quality control applies to CHC.

SUMMARY

 Total quality management normally involves:

▶ specifying the desired quality level, in which the firm develops a quality standard that can be measured and monitored over time;

▶ achieving the desired quality level, in which the firm establishes a production process that

satisfies the quality standard it established;

▶ controlling the quality level, in which the firm monitors the quality level over time and considers adjustments to achieve continuous improvement.

 The key methods used to improve production efficiency are:

▶ technology, which increases the speed of the production process,

▶ economies of scale, which reduce the average cost per unit as a result of a higher production volume, and

▶ restructuring, which is a revision of the production process to reduce production expenses.

KEY TERMS

automated   *269*
benchmarking   *269*
break-even point   *272*
corporate anorexia   *276*
downsizing   *274*
economies of scale   *270*

fixed costs   *270*
production efficiency   *268*
quality control circle   *264*
reengineering   *273*
restructuring   *273*

sampling   *264*
stretch targets   *269*
total quality management (TQM)   *259*
variable costs   *270*

REVIEW QUESTIONS

1 Discuss how employees can be used to assess the quality level for products produced in a firm.

2 Identify and explain the use of

quality control circles and cite examples where they have enjoyed success.

3 Discuss the global quality standards that a firm can attempt to

achieve in international business.

4 Identify and explain a TQM application for a manufacturing firm that would emphasize efficiency.

5 Define stretch targets for a production manager and discuss why they are established.

6 Identify the methods for improving production efficiency for a firm.

7 Explain why production managers would be interested in the break-even point. Why would a firm be interested in achieving economies of scale?

8 Define downsizing and identify some factors that may force a firm to downsize.

9 Identify some key business functions of management, marketing, and finance that must be performed when implementing a TQM program.

10 Describe corporate anorexia. When can downsizing create adverse effects for a firm?

DISCUSSION QUESTIONS

1 Discuss how the concept of a quality control circle might be used at a local plant in your hometown.

2 How could a firm use the Internet to provide information about its implementation of TQM?

3 Identify a firm in your local area that achieves the highest level of quality and sets a primary objective of customer satisfaction.

4 Assume that you are a plant manager and that your primary objective is to increase production efficiency. Discuss the methods that you could consider to achieve this goal.

5 You have just been assigned to a team in your class and given a research assignment. You are asked to implement a TQM process. Discuss how continuous improvement will take place during this project.

INVESTING IN THE STOCK OF A BUSINESS

Using the annual report of the firm in which you would like to invest, complete the following:

1 Does the firm appear to pay attention to customer satisfaction? Explain.

2 Has the firm improved the quality of its products or services in recent years? If so, how?

3 See if you can find information on reengineering at your firm. Check your annual report and a business magazine or newspaper.

4 Does your firm benefit from economies of scale? Try to identify the fixed and variable costs.

5 Explain how the business uses technology to promote its TQM function. For example, does it use the Internet to provide information about its TQM function? Does it provide information regarding the methods used to improve production efficiency?

6 Go to **http://hoovers.com** and locate the NEWS SEARCH. Type in the name of the firm in the space provided, and review the recent news stories about the firm. Summarize any (at least one) recent news story about the firm that applies to one or more of the key concepts within this chapter.

CASE ASSESSING QUALITY

Genius Books produces manuals that are used by people in making financial and investment decisions. George Egan is the manager overseeing the production of a new manual that is intended to help people fill out their tax forms. He had asked the company's marketing department to determine whether customers would be interested in a manual that would help them calculate their taxes. The marketing department conducted a survey, which found that individuals definitely needed a user-friendly manual to help them determine their income tax.

Although other books and software were available from other companies, George Egan believed that he could produce a tax manual that was just as good but priced lower. George hired some financial experts to help create the manual. He spent much time and money making sure that the income tax tables and instructions were accurate.

He then requested that 50,000 units of the manual be printed, based on his expected demand over the next three years. He thus had all 50,000 manuals ready for delivery when orders came in.

In the first three months, sales reached 5,000 units, but after that they declined. In general, the feedback from customers was that the manual was difficult to use. George defended his strategy, insisting that his manual was definitely accurate. He even hired additional tax experts to assess his manual, and they agreed that it was accurate. Nevertheless, sales remained slow, and he ultimately had to discard about 40,000 manuals that had been printed.

QUESTIONS

1 George believes that he did everything possible to ensure quality control. What mistake did he make in his assessment of quality control?

2 How could George have ensured that customers would be more satisfied with his product?

3 Was it a good idea to produce 50,000 units at once? What might be a better alternative if there is a chance that the manual may have to be revised over time?

VIDEO CASE   PRODUCTION QUALITY CONTROL AT BINDCO CORPORATION

BINDCO Corporation is a leading manufacturer of software for Intel and other firms. Since its clients rely on BINDCO for its products, BINDCO must ensure that its software products are produced properly.

BINDCO has a quality control system that ensures product quality. It requires various employees involved in the production process to confirm that the product meets specified standards at that stage of production. It also uses automated quality control, which involves the use of technology to detect defects. For example, it monitors bar code labeling with scanners. BINDCO also communicates with the client firms for which it produces products to make sure it understands how those firms want their products produced.

1 How can BINDCO's production quality control help it maximize its value?

2 Why is it useful to employees in the production process to monitor production quality at various stages of the production process and to confirm that quality met the specified standards?

3 Why is it important for BINDCO to ensure that it understands how firms want their products produced when producing the software for its clients?

INTERNET APPLICATIONS

http://www.asq.org

What service does the American Society for Quality (ASQ) provide? Briefly describe some of the research and information services provided by ASQ. Describe some of the ASQ products and discuss how they can be used by corporations to develop total quality management at their company. What certifications are available through ASQ? How could corporations use ASQ to improve their production efficiency?

THE Coca-Cola COMPANY ANNUAL REPORT PROJECT

Questions for the current year's annual report are available on the text website at **http://madura_intro_bus.swcollege.com.**

The following questions apply concepts learned in this chapter to The Coca-Cola Company. Go to The Coca-Cola Company website (**http://www.cocacola.com**) and find the index for the 1999 annual report.

QUESTIONS

1 Click on "Message to Share Owners." What do you think enables The Coca-Cola Company to invest where other companies do not? Provide examples in the form of some recent actions.

2 Study the "Management's Discussion and Analysis"

section. Do you think The Coca-Cola Company benefits from economies of scale? Explain.

3 In general, how can The Coca-Cola Company benefit from the process of benchmarking?

4 Click on "Message to Share Owner." How does the Chairman view the company? How does this view apply to the company today and in the future?

5 Go to **http://hoovers.com** and locate the NEWS SEARCH. Type in The Coca-Cola Company in the space provided, and review the recent news stories about the firm. Summarize any (at least one) recent news story about The Coca-Cola Company that applies one or more of the key concepts within this chapter of the text.

IN-TEXT STUDY GUIDE

Answers are in an appendix at the back of the book.

TRUE OR FALSE

1 Economies of scale reflect a lower average cost incurred from producing a larger volume.

2 Production efficiency is important to service firms as well as manufacturing firms.

3 Sampling involves the random selection and testing of some of the products that a firm produces to determine whether they satisfy quality standards.

4 Firms usually find it easier to attract new customers than to retain existing customers.

5 Reengineering involves the redesign of a firm's organizational structure and operations.

6 Restructuring involves the revision of the production process in an attempt to improve efficiency.

7 The aim of production efficiency is to maximize the revenue received for a given volume of sales.

8 Some downsizing occurs as a result of technology because automated production processes replace employees.

9 Total quality management was first used by firms in the United States and was later adopted by firms in Europe, but it has never really caught on with firms in Japan or other Asian countries.

10 The break-even point refers to the quantity of units sold at which the total revenue is equal to the fixed costs of production.

MULTIPLE CHOICE

11 Methods for improving production efficiency would include the following except for:
a) pricing policies.   c) economies of scale.
b) restructuring.   d) technology.

12 The process used to detect and correct quality deficiencies is known as:
a) econometric testing.   d) reengineering.
b) PERT analysis.   e) quality resolution.
c) quality control.

13 A _____ is a group of employees who assess the quality of a product and offer suggestions for improvement.
a) TQM committee
b) quality control circle
c) focus group
d) quality council
e) CORE committee

14 _____ tasks are performed by machines without the use of employees.
a) Automated   d) Retro-engineered
b) Reengineered   e) Labor-intensive
c) Reproducible

15 _____ is a set of international standards dealing with the environmental effects of production processes.
a) TQM 2000
b) The IEPA "Green Book"
c) The United Nations Environmental Resolution of 1996
d) ALERT 2000
e) ISO 14000

16 Managers at TecMax (a medium-sized producer of consumer electronics) want to increase their market share because they believe that the average cost of producing their products will decline as production quantities increase. This suggests that managers at TecMax are trying to take advantage of:
a) diminishing returns.
b) the fact that fixed costs decline as output increases.
c) a monopolistic revenue structure.
d) economies of scale.
e) a decline in marginal costs.

17 A popular method for obtaining employee feedback is by using:
a) cross-functional teams.
b) marketing research.
c) research and development.
d) automation.
e) economies of scale.

18 When firms evaluate performance by comparing their results to some specified level (such as the results achieved by another firm), they are using a procedure known as:
a) comparative analysis.
b) reverse engineering.
c) standardization.
d) relative evaluation.
e) benchmarking.

19 _____ refers to a situation in which a firm becomes so obsessed with eliminating its inefficient components that it downsizes too much.
a) Diminishing returns
b) Marginalization
c) Frictional unemployment
d) Corporate dyslexia
e) Corporate anorexia

20 The purpose of _____ is to redesign a firm's organizational structure and operations to improve production efficiency.
a) benefit analysis
b) reengineering
c) benchmarking
d) role reversal
e) top-down management techniques

21 _____ is the revision of the production process in an attempt to improve production efficiency.
a) Delegation
b) Scientific management
c) Benchmarking
d) Restructuring
e) Production flow realignment

22 Production goals that cannot be achieved under present conditions are called:
a) future targets.
b) objective constraints.
c) opportunity costs.
d) objective functions.
e) stretch targets.

23 TQM stresses the need to measure quality from the perspective of the:
a) competition.
b) customer.
c) government.
d) shareholder.
e) industry.

24 The goal of production efficiency is to:
a) replace labor with machinery.
b) increase revenue by expanding market share.
c) lower the costs of producing a given amount of output at a given level of quality.
d) increase the break-even point.
e) ensure that all products meet the highest possible quality control standards.

25 _____ is commonly used to correct a firm's perceived deficiencies and therefore improve customer satisfaction.
a) TQM
b) Automation
c) Corporate anorexia
d) Downsizing
e) Sampling

26 According to the TQM concept, all of the following are keys to improving quality except:
a) setting up a "quality czar" with ultimate responsibility and authority to initiate any changes that will reduce expenses.
b) providing managers and employees with the education and training needed to excel at their jobs.
c) encouraging all employees to take responsibility and exhibit leadership.
d) encouraging all employees to search for ways to improve the production process.

27 _____ is the process of reducing the number of employees in a firm.
a) Marginalizing
b) Automating
c) Downsizing
d) Realignment
e) Centralization

28 The procedure of randomly selecting and testing products to determine whether they meet quality standards is called:
a) sampling.
b) binary testing.
c) reverse engineering.
d) discrete analysis.
e) surveying.

29 Cross-functional teams consist of:
a) representatives of a firm's employees, suppliers, creditors, customers, and shareholders.
b) members of top and middle management who are experts on quality control.
c) representatives of both the labor union and management.
d) employees responsible for each specific function of the production process.
e) representatives from each firm in a specific industry.

30 The expenses a firm incurs that vary directly with the quantity of output it produces are called:
a) explicit costs.
b) floating costs.
c) variable costs.
d) indirect costs.
e) quantified costs.

31 The total quality management concept was originally developed in Japan by:
a) Frederick Taylor.
b) A. H. Maslow.
c) Malcolm Baldrige.
d) W. Edwards Deming.
e) Frederick Hertzberg.

32 TQM methods were first widely used by firms in:
a) the United States.
b) Japan.
c) China.
d) Western Europe.
e) the former Soviet Union.

33 The two basic types of costs involved in the production of a product are called:
a) observable costs and hidden costs.
b) primary costs and secondary costs.
c) objective costs and subjective costs.
d) fixed costs and variable costs.
e) relative costs and absolute costs.

34 The quantity of output at which a firm's total revenue is exactly equal to its total cost is called the:
a) target quantity.
b) market quantity.
c) equilibrium point.
d) profit point.
e) break-even point.

35 _____ are costs that do not change in response to changes in the quantity produced.
a) Fixed costs
b) Limited costs
c) Marginal costs
d) Objective costs
e) Absolute costs

Summary of Part III

The chapters in Part III describe some of the key components of effective management. These components are (1) recognition of the skills necessary to be effective managers (Chapter 7), (2) proper assignments of job responsibilities (Chapter 8), (3) efficient allocation of resources for production (Chapter 9), and (4) proper monitoring and improvement of product quality (Chapter 10).

The key skills needed for managers to be effective are conceptual skills (to understand relationships among tasks of a firm), interpersonal skills, technical skills, and decision-making skills.

In addition to skills, effective management requires that job responsibilities are properly assigned within the organizational structure. Ideally, the organizational structure allows some control over each job assignment so that all types of tasks can be monitored. The organizational structure may also attempt to ensure employee input on various tasks by assigning extra responsibilities to employees. Job tasks and responsibilities can be departmentalized by function, product, location, or type of customer. The method of departmentalizing job tasks and responsibilities is dependent on the characteristics of the business.

Effective management also requires an efficient production process, which involves the selection of a plant site and the design and layout of the production facilities. The plant site decision is influenced by land cost, access to transportation, and other factors that affect the cost of production. Design and layout decisions are influenced by the characteristics of the plant site,

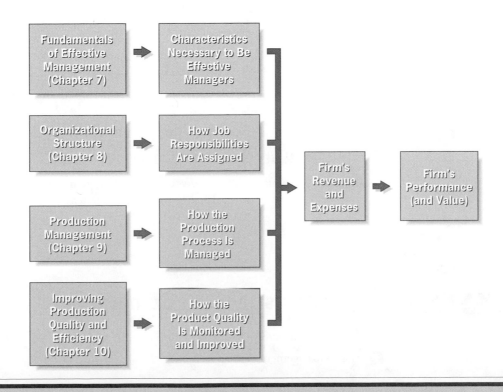

production process, product line, and desired production capacity.

Effective management also requires an effort to continuously improve the quality of each product that is produced. Quality management forces employees to specify the desired quality level, to consider how the production process can be revised to achieve that quality level, and to continuously monitor the quality level by using various quality control methods.

PART III

Developing a Management and Production Plan for Campus.com

Strategic and Tactical Plans (related to Chapter 7)

Develop a strategic plan for Campus.com, and explain what tactical plans would be consistent with the strategic plan. Insert these plans into your business plan for Campus.com.

Organizational Structure (related to Chapter 8)

Given the nature of Campus.com's business, what job positions are needed? Include these positions in your business plan for Campus.com. You (or your team) are responsible for overseeing Campus.com and therefore are the top management of the firm. Do not focus on which members of your team would take each position. Instead focus on identifying the positions needed.

Production Process (related to Chapter 9)

In your business plan for Campus.com, describe the production process used to produce its service. Also, describe how the service will change and how Campus.com might create an efficient system for continued revisions of the service it provides.

Quality Standards (related to Chapter 10)

In your business plan for Campus.com, explain how the firm can maintain the quality of the service it provides.

Communication and Teamwork

You (or your team) may be asked by your instructor to hand in and/or present the part of your business plan that is related to this part of the text.

PART III

Applications for Dell Computer

Refer to Dell Computer's Formula for Success where necessary.

1 Dell's management style

    a. How many levels of management do you think a company such as Dell Computer requires?

    b. What managerial functions do you think are the most important at a company such as Dell? Why?

    c. What managerial skills do you think are the most important at a company such as Dell? Why?

2 Dell's organizational structure

    a. Do you think Dell Computer's organizational structure is centralized or decentralized? Why?

    b. Do you think Dell has a large informal organizational structure? Why or why not?

    c. How do you think Dell's tasks are departmentalized?

3 Dell's quality management

    a. Do you think quality management is important at a company such as Dell Computer?

    b. What methods do you think a company such as Dell could use to improve production efficiency?

    c. Do you think Dell could use the Internet to improve the quality of its products? How?

PART III

The Stock Market Game

Go to **http://www.fantasystockmarket.com**. Enter your name (e-mail address) and password as requested and check your portfolio balance, which is updated continuously by the Fantasy website.

Check Your Stock Portfolio Performance

1 What is the value of your stock portfolio today?

2 What is your return on your investment? (This return is shown on your balance.)

3 How did your return compare to those of other students? (This comparison tells you whether your stock portfolio's performance is relatively high or low.)

Keep in mind that you can change your portfolio at any time during the school term.

Explaining Your Stock Performance

Stock prices are frequently influenced by changes in the firm's management, including changes in the chief executive officer or other high-level managers, the organizational structure, or the production process. A stock's price may rise if such management changes are made and investors expect that the changes will improve the performance of the firm. A stock's price can also decline if the managerial changes are expected to reduce the firm's performance. Review the latest news about some of your stocks on the Fantasy website by clicking on News and typing the ticker symbol of your stock.

1 Identify one of your stocks whose price was affected (since you purchased it) as a result of the firm's management (the main topic in this part of the text).

2 Identify the specific type of managerial changes that caused the stock price to change.

3 Did your stock price increase or decrease in response to the announcement of managerial changes?

<table>
<tr><td>**PART III**</td></tr>
</table>

Running Your Own Business

1 Describe the strategic plan of your business. In this plan, state the business opportunities that exist and the general direction your business will take to capitalize on those opportunities.

2 Explain in detail how your business will operate to achieve your strategic plan.

3 Describe the organizational structure of your business.

4 Provide an organization chart and describe the responsibilities of any employees whom you plan to hire.

5 How might this structure change as the business grows?

6 Describe the production process of your business. That is, describe the tasks that are required to produce your product or service. Indicate the number of employees required and describe other resources (such as machinery) that are needed for production.

7 Describe the facilities needed for production. Will your business require that you rent space in a shopping mall? Describe in general terms the design and layout of the facilities.

8 Estimate the rent expense during the first year for the facilities needed for your business. Also, estimate (if possible) the annual utility expense (such as electricity) for your business facilities.

9 Describe how your business can ensure (a) customer satisfaction, (b) the quality of the product or service you plan to produce, and (c) that customers are treated properly by any employees that you hire.

10 Describe how technology will enable you to improve the quality of the product or service you plan to produce. Explain how your production or customer service may possibly improve over time as a result of technology.

11 Discuss how economies of scale relate to your business.

12 Explain how your business could use the Internet to give customers an opportunity to provide feedback to management.

Managing Employees

Whereas Part III focused on organizational structure and production, Part IV focuses on human resources (employees), another critical component of management. Part IV contains two chapters that explain how managers can improve the performance of their employees. Chapter 11 describes the methods that can be used to motivate employees. Motivation may be necessary for many employees to perform well. To the extent that managers can effectively motivate employees, they can increase the performance of employees and therefore increase the performance of the firm. Chapter 12 explains proper methods used to hire, train, and evaluate the performance of employees. If managers can use these methods effectively, they should be able to improve the firm's performance.

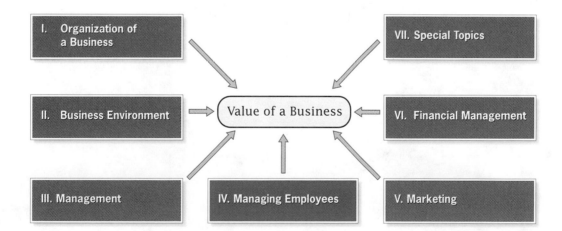

I. Organization of a Business

VII. Special Topics

II. Business Environment → Value of a Business ← VI. Financial Management

III. Management   IV. Managing Employees   V. Marketing

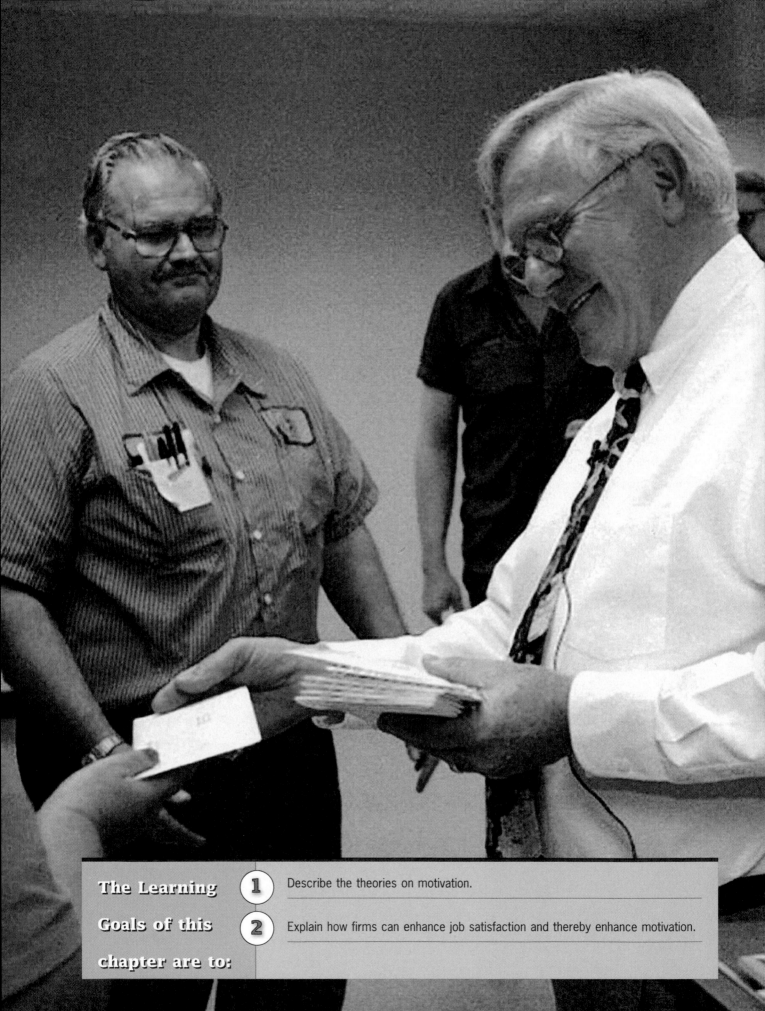

The Learning Goals of this chapter are to:

1 Describe the theories on motivation.

2 Explain how firms can enhance job satisfaction and thereby enhance motivation.

Motivating Employees

A firm has a strategic plan that identifies opportunities and the future direction of the firm's business. When the firm develops strategies to achieve the strategic plan, it relies on its managers to utilize employees and other resources to make the strategies work. The performance of a firm is highly dependent on the performance of its employees. By motivating employees to properly perform the tasks they are assigned, firms can maximize the firm's value.

Consider the case of Wal-Mart Stores, which has a chain of retail stores that sell a wide variety of merchandise. Employees are needed to receive merchandise shipped to them and to periodically stock the shelves. Some employees serve as cashiers, while others are responsible for managing the stores. How can Wal-Mart motivate these employees to perform well at work? Would Wal-Mart employees be more motivated if they were more satisfied with their jobs? How can Wal-Mart ensure a high level of job satisfaction among its employees? This chapter provides a background on motivating employees that can be used to address these questions.

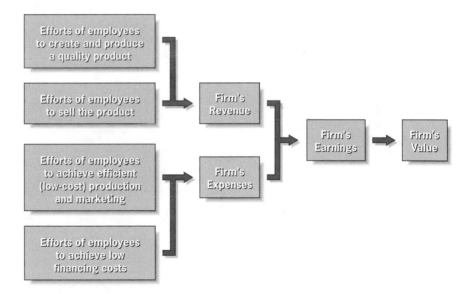

Theories on Motivation

1 Describe the theories on motivation.

job satisfaction the degree to which employees are satisfied with their jobs

The motivation of employees is influenced by **job satisfaction,** or the degree to which employees are satisfied with their jobs. Firms recognize the need to satisfy their employees, as illustrated by the following statements from recent annual reports:

❝ *You will see a greater focus on employee satisfaction . . . which will lead us to higher quality, better growth, and improved profitability.* ❞
—Kodak

> ❝ *The new Quaker State is representative of a new spirit and the promise of a better future for every Quaker State employee. It is the realization that they have it in their power to effect change.* ❞
>
> —Quaker State

> ❝ *Bethlehem's success ultimately depends on the skill, dedication, and support of our employees.* ❞
>
> —Bethlehem Steel

Since employees who are satisfied with their jobs are more motivated, managers can motivate employees by ensuring job satisfaction. Some of the more popular theories on motivation are summarized here, followed by some general guidelines that can be used to motivate workers.

Hawthorne Studies

In the late 1920s, researchers studied workers in a Western Electric Plant near Chicago to identify how a variety of conditions affected their level of production. When the lighting was increased, the production level increased. Yet, the production level also increased when the lighting was reduced. These workers were then subjected to various break periods; again, the production level increased for both shorter breaks and longer breaks. One interpretation of these results is that workers become more motivated when they feel that they are allowed to participate. Supervisors may be able to motivate workers by giving them more attention and by allowing them to participate. These Hawthorne studies, which ignited further research on motivation, are summarized in Exhibit 11.1 and suggest that human relations can affect a firm's performance.

Maslow's Hierarchy of Needs

hierarchy of needs needs are ranked in five general categories. Once a given category of needs is achieved, people become motivated to reach the next category.

physiological needs the basic requirements for survival

In 1943, Abraham Maslow, a psychologist, developed the **hierarchy of needs** theory. This theory suggests that people rank their needs into five general categories. Once they achieve a given category of needs, they become motivated to reach the next category. The categories are identified in Exhibit 11.2, with the most crucial needs on the bottom. **Physiological needs** are for the basic requirements for survival, such as food and shelter. Most jobs can help achieve these needs.

Exhibit 11.1

Summary of the Hawthorne Studies

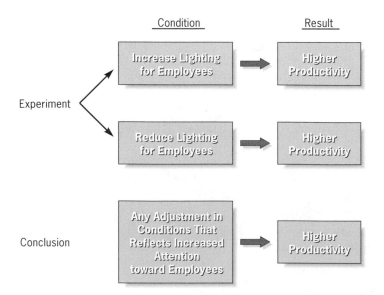

Exhibit 11.2

Maslow's Hierarchy of Needs

safety needs job security and safe working conditions

social needs the need to be part of a group

esteem needs respect, prestige, and recognition

self-actualization the need to fully reach one's potential

Once these needs are fulfilled, **safety needs** (such as job security and safe working conditions) become the most immediate goal. Some jobs satisfy these needs. People also strive to achieve **social needs,** or the need to be part of a group. Some firms attempt to help employees achieve their social needs, either by grouping workers in teams or by organizing social events after work hours. People may also become motivated to achieve **esteem needs,** such as respect, prestige, and recognition. Some workers may achieve these needs by being promoted within their firms or by receiving special recognition for their work. The final category of needs is **self-actualization,** which represents the need to fully reach one's potential. For example, people may achieve self-actualization needs by starting a specific business that fits their main interests and by being successful in running this business.

The hierarchy of needs theory can be useful for motivating employees because it suggests that different employees may be at different places in the hierarchy. Therefore, their most immediate needs may differ. If managers recognize employee needs, they will be better able to offer rewards that motivate employees.

Herzberg's Job Satisfaction Study

In the late 1950s, Frederick Herzberg surveyed two hundred accountants and engineers about job satisfaction. Herzberg attempted to identify the factors that made them feel dissatisfied with their jobs at a given point in time. He also attempted to identify the factors that made them feel satisfied with their jobs. His study found the following:

Common Factors Identified by Dissatisfied Workers	Common Factors Identified by Satisfied Workers
Working conditions	Achievement
Supervision	Responsibility
Salary	Recognition
Job security	Advancement
Status	Growth

hygiene factors work-related factors perceived to be inadequate

motivational factors work-related factors that please employees

Employees become dissatisfied when they perceive work-related factors in the left column (called **hygiene factors**) as inadequate. Employees are commonly satisfied when the work-related factors in the right column (called **motivational factors**) are offered.

Exhibit 11.3

Summary of Herzberg's Job
Satisfaction Study

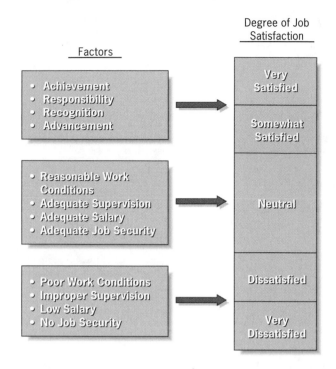

Herzberg's results suggest that factors such as working conditions and salary must be adequate to prevent workers from being dissatisfied. Yet, better-than-adequate working conditions and salary will not necessarily lead to a high degree of satisfaction. Instead, a high degree of worker satisfaction is most easily achieved by offering additional benefits, such as responsibility. If managers can increase worker satisfaction by assigning workers more responsibility, they may motivate workers to be more productive. Exhibit 11.3 summarizes Herzberg's job satisfaction study.

Notice how the results of Herzberg's study correspond with the results of Maslow's hierarchy. Herzberg's hygiene factors generally correspond with Maslow's basic needs (such as job security). This suggests that if hygiene factors are adequate, they fulfill some of workers' more basic needs. Fulfillment of these needs can prevent dissatisfaction as employees become motivated to achieve a higher class of needs. Herzberg's motivational factors (such as recognition) generally correspond with Maslow's more ambitious hierarchy needs.

Several U.S. firms, such as Ford Motor Company, TRW, and Polaroid Corporation, have implemented workshops to stress teamwork and company loyalty. These workshops build self-esteem by focusing on employees' worth to the company. In this way, the workshops may enable employees to achieve a higher class of needs, thereby increasing job satisfaction.

McGregor's Theory X and Theory Y

Another major contribution to motivation was provided by Douglas McGregor, who developed Theory X and Theory Y. Each of these theories represents supervisors' possible perception of workers. The views of Theories X and Y are summarized as follows:

Theory X	Theory Y
Employees dislike work and job responsibilities and will avoid work if possible.	Employees are willing to work and prefer more responsibility.

SELF-SCORING EXERCISE

The Frazzle Factor

Read each of the following statements, and rate yourself on a scale of 0 to 3, giving the answer that best describes how you generally feel (3 points for *always*, 2 points for *often*, 1 point for *sometimes*, and 0 points for *never*). Answer as honestly as you can, and do not spend too much time on any one statement.

AM I ANGRY?

_____ 1. I feel that people around me make too many irritating mistakes.

_____ 2. I feel annoyed because I do good work or perform well in school, but no one appreciates it.

_____ 3. When people make me angry, I tell them off.

_____ 4. When I am angry, I say things I know will hurt people.

_____ 5. I lose my temper easily.

_____ 6. I feel like striking out at someone who angers me.

_____ 7. When a co-worker or fellow student makes a mistake, I tell him or her about it.

_____ 8. I cannot stand being criticized in public.

AM I OVERSTRESSED?

_____ 1. I have to make important snap judgments and decisions.

_____ 2. I am not consulted about what happens on my job or in my classes.

_____ 3. I feel I am underpaid.

_____ 4. I feel that no matter how hard I work, the system will mess it up.

_____ 5. I do not get along with some of my co-workers or fellow students.

_____ 6. I do not trust my superiors at work or my professors at school.

_____ 7. The paperwork burden on my job or at school is getting to me.

_____ 8. I feel people outside the job or the university do not respect what I do.

Scoring

To find your level of anger and potential for aggressive behavior, add your scores from both quiz parts.

40–48: The red flag is waving, and you had better pay attention. You are in the danger zone. You need guidance from a counselor or mental health professional, and you should be getting it now.

30–39: The yellow flag is up. Your stress and anger levels are too high, and you are feeling increasingly hostile. You are still in control, but it would not take much to trigger a violent flare of temper.

10–29: Relax, you are in the broad normal range. Like most people, you get angry occasionally, but usually with some justification. Sometimes you take overt action, but you are not likely to be unreasonably or excessively aggressive.

0–9: Congratulations! You are in great shape. Your stress and anger are well under control, giving you a laid-back personality not prone to violence.

The way supervisors view employees can influence the way they treat the employees. Supervisors who believe in Theory X will likely use tight control over workers, with little or no delegation of authority. In addition, employees will be closely monitored to ensure that they perform their tasks. Conversely, supervisors who believe in Theory Y will delegate more authority because they perceive workers as responsible. These supervisors will also allow employees more opportunities to use their creativity. This management approach would fulfill employee needs to be responsible and to achieve respect and recognition. Consequently, these employees would likely be more motivated because their level of job satisfaction should be higher.

Exhibit 11.4 provides a summary of Theories X and Y. Most employees would prefer that their supervisors follow Theory Y rather than Theory X. Nevertheless, some

Exhibit 11.4

Summary of McGregor's Theories X and Y

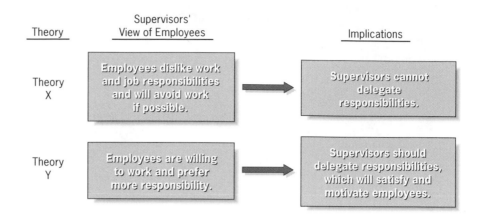

supervisors may be unable to use Theory Y for specific situations. In these cases, they are forced to retain more authority over employees rather than delegate tasks.

Theory Z

In the 1980s, a new theory on job satisfaction was developed. This theory, called Theory Z, was partially based on the Japanese style of allowing all employees to participate in decision making. Participation can increase job satisfaction because it gives employees responsibility. Job descriptions tend to be less specialized so that employees will develop varied skills and have a more flexible career path. To increase job satisfaction, many U.S. firms have begun to allow employees more responsibility.

Expectancy Theory

expectancy theory holds that an employee's efforts are influenced by the expected outcome (reward) for those efforts

Expectancy theory suggests that an employee's efforts are influenced by the expected outcome (reward) for those efforts. Therefore, employees will be more motivated to achieve goals if they are achievable and offer some reward.

As an example, consider a firm that offers the salesperson who achieves the highest volume of annual sales a one-week vacation in Paris. This type of reward will motivate employees only if two requirements are fulfilled. First, the reward must be desirable to employees. Second, employees must believe they have a chance to earn the reward. If the firm employs one thousand salespeople, and only one reward is offered, employees may not be motivated because they may perceive that they have little chance of being the top salesperson. Motivation may be absent even in smaller groups if all employees expect that a particular salesperson will generate the highest sales volume.

Motivational rewards are more difficult to offer for jobs where output cannot easily be measured. For example, employees who repair the firm's machinery or respond to customer complaints do not contribute to the firm in a manner that can be easily measured or compared with other employees. Nevertheless, their performance may still be measured by customer satisfaction surveys or by various other performance indicators.

Equity Theory

equity theory suggests that compensation should be equitable, or in proportion to each employee's contribution

The **equity theory** of motivation suggests that compensation should be equitable, or in proportion to each employee's contribution. As an example, consider a firm with three employees: Employee 1 contributes 50 percent of the total output, Employee 2 contributes 30 percent, and Employee 3 contributes 20 percent. Assume that the firm plans to allocate $100,000 in bonuses based on the relative contributions of each employee. Using the equity theory, the $100,000 would be allocated as shown in Exhibit 11.5.

Exhibit 11.5

Example of Equity Theory

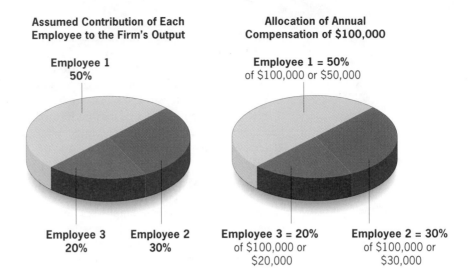

If employees believe that they are undercompensated, they may request greater compensation. If their compensation is not increased, employees may reduce their contribution. Equity theory emphasizes how employees can become dissatisfied with their jobs if they believe that they are not equitably compensated.

Supervisors may prevent job dissatisfaction by attempting to provide equitable compensation. A problem, however, is that their perception of an employee's contribution may differ from that of the employee. If a firm can define how to measure employee contributions and compensate accordingly, its employees will be better satisfied and more motivated.

reinforcement theory suggests that reinforcement can control behavior

positive reinforcement motivates employees by providing rewards for high performance

negative reinforcement motivates employees by encouraging them to behave in a manner that avoids unfavorable consequences

Reinforcement Theory

Reinforcement theory, summarized in Exhibit 11.6, suggests that reinforcement can control behavior. **Positive reinforcement** motivates employees by providing rewards for high performance. The rewards can range from an oral compliment to a promotion or large bonus. Employees may react differently to various forms of positive reinforcement. The more they appreciate the form of reinforcement, the more they will be motivated to continue high performance.

Negative reinforcement motivates employees by encouraging them to behave in a manner that avoids unfavorable consequences. For example, employees may be mo-

Exhibit 11.6

Summary of Reinforcement Theory

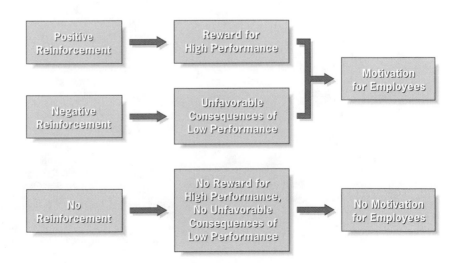

tivated to complete their assignments today to avoid admitting the delay in a group meeting or to avoid negative evaluations by their supervisors.

The various forms of negative reinforcement range from a reprimand to job termination. Some supervisors may prefer to consistently offer positive reinforcement for high performance rather than penalize for poor performance. However, offering positive reinforcement for all tasks that are adequately completed may be difficult. Furthermore, if an employee who has performed poorly is not given negative reinforcement, others may think that employee was given preferential treatment, and their general performance may decline as a result.

Motivational Guidelines Offered by Theories

If supervisors can increase employees' job satisfaction, they may motivate employees to be more productive. All of the theories on motivation are briefly summarized in Exhibit 11.7. Based on these theories, some general conclusions can be offered on motivating employees and providing job satisfaction:

1 Employees commonly compare their perceived compensation and contribution with others. To prevent job dissatisfaction, supervisors should attempt to ensure that employees are appropriately compensated for their contributions.

2 Even if employees are offered high compensation, they will not necessarily be very satisfied. They have other needs as well, such as social needs, responsibility, and self-esteem. Jobs that can fulfill these needs may provide more satisfaction, and therefore may also provide motivation.

3 Employees may be motivated if they believe that it is possible to achieve a level that will result in a desirable reward.

How Firms Can Enhance Job Satisfaction and Motivation

② Explain how firms can enhance job satisfaction and thereby enhance motivation.

Many of the theories on motivation suggest that firms can motivate employees to perform well by ensuring job satisfaction. In general, the key characteristics that affect job

Exhibit 11.7   Comparison of Motivation Theories

Theory	Implications
Theory developed from Hawthorne studies	Workers can be motivated by attention.
Maslow's hierarchy of needs	Needs of workers vary, and managers can motivate workers to achieve these needs.
Herzberg's job satisfaction study	Compensation, reasonable working conditions, and other factors do not ensure job satisfaction but only prevent job dissatisfaction. Thus, other factors (such as responsibility) may be necessary to motivate workers.
McGregor's Theory X and Theory Y	Based on Theory X, workers will avoid work if possible and cannot accept responsibility. Based on Theory Y, workers are willing to work and prefer more responsibility. If Theory Y exists, managers can motivate workers by delegating responsibility.
Expectancy theory	Workers are motivated if potential rewards for high performance are desirable and achievable.
Equity theory	Workers are motivated if they are being compensated in accordance with their perceived contribution to the firm.
Reinforcement theory	Good behavior should be positively reinforced and poor behavior should be negatively reinforced to motivate workers in the future.

job enrichment programs
programs designed to increase the job satisfaction of employees

satisfaction are money, security, work schedule, and involvement at work. To motivate employees, firms provide **job enrichment programs,** or programs designed to increase the job satisfaction of employees. The following are some of the more popular job enrichment programs:

▶ Adequate compensation program
▶ Job security
▶ Flexible work schedule
▶ Employee involvement programs

To the extent that firms can offer these job enrichment programs to employees, they may be able to motivate employees. Each program is discussed in turn.

Adequate Compensation Program

Firms can attempt to satisfy employees by offering adequate compensation for the work involved. However, adequate compensation will not necessarily motivate employees to make their best effort. Therefore, firms may attempt to ensure that those employees with the highest performance each year receive the highest percentage raises.

merit system allocates raises according to performance (merit)

A **merit system** allocates raises according to performance (merit). For example, a firm may decide to give its employees an average raise of 5 percent, but poorly performing employees may receive 0 percent while the highest performing employees receive 10 percent. This system provides positive reinforcement for employees who have performed well and negative reinforcement for those who have performed poorly. The merit system is normally more effective than the alternative **across-the-board system,** in which all employees receive a similar raise. The across-the-board system offers no motivation because the raise is unrelated to employee performance.

across-the-board system all employees are allocated a similar raise

incentive plans provide employees with various forms of compensation if they meet specific performance goals

Firms may attempt to reinforce excellent employee performance with other rewards as well as raises. **Incentive plans** provide employees with various forms of compensation if they meet specific performance goals. For example, a firm may offer a weekly or monthly bonus based on the number of components an employee produced or the dollar value of all products an employee sold to customers.

Some firms such as Long Beach Convention and Entertainment Center (shown here) have implemented an "employee of the month" program in order to motivate employees.

Examples of Compensation Programs The compensation at some firms is composed of base pay and "reward" pay that is tied to specific performance goals. The base pay is set lower than the norm for each job within the industry. However, the additional reward pay (tied to specific goals) can allow the total compensation to exceed the norm. Employees are more motivated to perform well because they benefit directly from high performance.

Some employees of Enterprise Rent-A-Car Company are compensated according to the firm's profits. Steelworkers at Nucor can earn annual bonuses that exceed their annual base salary. Many salespeople earn bonuses based on their own sales volume.

Kodak uses an incentive plan that allows each executive to earn a bonus based on his or her performance. The performance targets are set by the outside board members who are not employees of Kodak. The bonuses are based on performance measures such as revenue and earnings. Procter & Gamble Company provides bonuses to executives based on some nonfinancial measures, such as integrity and leadership.

The bonuses of chief executive officers (CEOs) at General Electric, TRW, and many other firms are tied to the firm's performance. Performance measures may include revenue, earnings, production efficiency, and customer satisfaction.

Firms recognize that tying compensation to performance may increase job satisfaction and motivate employees. The following policies stated in recent annual reports confirm this:

> ❝ *A company lives or dies by results, and at Campbell, executive pay is linked directly to performance . . . and 100 percent of all incentive bonuses are tied to company performance.* ❞
>
> —Campbell's Soup Company

> ❝ *We are working hard to change the culture of the company by emphasizing and rewarding results, not activity.* ❞
>
> —IBM

In addition to linking compensation to performance, some firms also grant stock to their employees as partial compensation for their work. The value of this type of compensation depends on the firm's stock price. To the extent that employees can enhance the firm's stock price with hard work, they can enhance their own compensation.

Initially, firms used stock as compensation only for CEOs. In recent years, however, other top managers of firms have been granted stock as well, to keep them focused on enhancing the value of the stock. Some firms have applied this concept to all or most of their employees. For example, all employees of Avis are given some shares of Avis stock. This may motivate them to perform well because their performance may enhance the value of the stock they own. One limitation of this approach is that some employees who own only a small amount of stock may not believe that their work habits will have much influence on profits (and therefore on the stock price) of the firm. Thus, they will not be motivated because they do not expect that their stock's price will increase as a result of their efforts.

BUSINESS ONLINE

Employee Ownership Strategies

IN LIGHT OF THE TREND TOWARD EMPLOYEE STOCK OWNERSHIP PLANS AND the importance of adequate compensation for job satisfaction, several organizations now use the Internet to advertise products that help companies design compensation programs. The website for the Foundation for Enterprise Development provides equity

http://www.fed.org

compensation and employee ownership strategies to companies. Furthermore, it provides research and information on employee motivation.

As an illustration of how a firm's performance and value can improve when its employee compensation is linked to performance, consider the case of Paychex. In January 1998, Paychex announced its intent to tie employee compensation to its performance. Over the next year, the firm's performance and its value (as measured by its stock price) increased substantially, as shown in Exhibit 11.8.

Developing a Proper Compensation Plan Most compensation plans that tie pay to performance are intended to motivate employees to achieve high performance. The following guidelines can help in designing a compensation plan that motivates employees:

Exhibit 11.8

Impact of New Employee Compensation Policy on the Stock Price of Paychex.

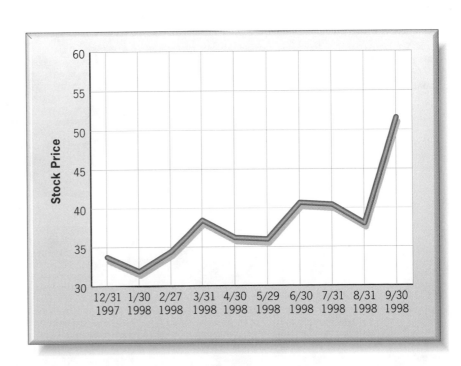

1 *Align Compensation Plan with Business Goals* Compensation formulas for employees should be set only after the goals of the business are established. This ensures that employees are rewarded in line with their ability to satisfy business goals.

2 *Align Compensation with Specific Employee Goals* A compensation plan will motivate employees more if it clearly specifies individual employee goals. Goals for an individual assembly-line employee should focus on specific job responsibilities that the employee can control. Conversely, individual goals that specify high performance for the entire production plant are not under the control of a single employee, and therefore the employee will not be as motivated to perform well.

Employees of some firms are compensated according to the performance of a group to which they belong within the firm. The groups are small enough to allow employees to believe they have some control over the performance measurement.

3 *Establish Achievable Goals for Employees* The compensation plan will work better if the goals specified for each employee are achievable. By offering numerous achievable bonuses, managers can increase each employee's perception of the chance to earn a reward. Firms with limited budgets for bonuses can offer rewards that are less extravagant but still desirable.

Rewards that are desirable and achievable will motivate employees only if they are aware of the bonuses. Offering rewards at the end of the year is too late to motivate employees for that year. Levels of motivation will be higher if employees know about the potential for bonuses at the beginning of the year.

4 *Allow Employee Input on Compensation Plan* The compensation plan should be developed only after receiving input from employees on how they should be rewarded. Although some employee requests may be unreasonable, allowing employee input can improve job satisfaction.

BUSINESS ONLINE

Corporate Employee Information

http://www.saturn.com/ company/index.html

MANY COMPANIES, SUCH AS SATURN, USE THE INTERNET TO PROVIDE POtential employees with information about the company's attitude toward its employees. As the Internet is increasingly becoming a research tool for potential employees, websites such as this are highly useful to them.

UAW Partnership
Saturn in the Community
Saturn in the World
Frequently Asked Questions
Welcome Center
Want a Job?

iShowroom
Pricing
Find a Retailer
Request a Brochure
Buy Saturn Stuff
What's New
Talk to Us
Search
Site Map

A Different Kind *of* Car

A Different Kind *of* Company

Research Center

You've probably noticed folks seem to make a big deal about our company. At the risk of sounding immodest, there's a pretty good reason for that. We think a company that treats employees and customers better will build cars that are better, too. Here's where you can learn about our history, see what we're doing in your community or search for a job here at Saturn.

Home   iShowroom   Pricing   Find a Retailer   Request a Brochure

Job Security

Employees who have job security may be more motivated to perform well. They are less likely to be distracted at work because of concern about finding a more secure job.

Although firms recognize that job security can motivate their employees, they may not be able to guarantee job security. When a weakened U.S. economy lowers the demand for the goods and services provided by U.S. firms, these firms cannot afford to retain all of their employees. Even when the economy is strong, some firms are pressured to lay off employees to reduce expenses.

Firms can provide more job security by training employees to handle various tasks so that they can be assigned other duties if their typical assignments are no longer needed. Nevertheless, the firm may not have any job openings to which employees can be reassigned. Further, the job openings may be so different that reassignments are not possible. Workers on an assembly line normally would not be qualified to perform accounting or financial analysis jobs for an automobile manufacturer.

Flexible Work Schedule

flextime programs programs that allow for a more flexible work schedule

compressed work week compresses the work load into fewer days per week

job sharing two or more persons may share a particular work schedule

Another method of increasing job satisfaction is to implement programs that allow for a more flexible work schedule (called **flextime programs**). Some firms have experimented with a **compressed work week,** which compresses the work load into fewer days per week. Most commonly, a five-day, eight-hour-per-day work week is compressed into four ten-hour days. The main purpose of this schedule is to allow employees to have three-day weekends. When employees are on a schedule that they prefer, they are more motivated to perform well.

Another form of a flexible work schedule is **job sharing,** where two or more persons may share a particular work schedule. For example, a firm that needs a forty-hour work week for deliveries may hire two people to share that position. This allows employees to work part-time and fulfill other obligations such as school or family.

Employee Involvement Programs

As the theories summarized earlier indicate, employees are more motivated when they play a bigger role in the firm, either by being more involved in decisions or by being assigned more responsibility. Firms use various methods to allow more employee involvement and responsibility.

CROSS-FUNCTIONAL TEAMWORK

Spreading Motivation across Business Functions

When a firm uses compensation or other incentives to motivate employees, it must attempt to implement this program across all of its business functions. Since business functions interact, motivating employees who perform one type of function will have limited effects if employees performing other functions are not motivated.

Consider an example in which a firm's production employees are given new incentives to perform well, but marketing employees are not given any new incentives. The quality of the product achieved by the production department is somewhat dependent on the feedback it receives from marketing employees who conduct customer satisfaction surveys. Also, the production department's ability to produce an adequate supply of a product is dependent on the sales forecasts provided by the marketing department. If the sales forecast is too low, the production department may produce an insufficient volume, resulting in shortages.

Production tasks can also affect marketing tasks because effective marketing strategies will result in higher sales only if a sufficient volume of products is produced. Employees assigned to a specific function rely on employees assigned to other functions. Thus, employees who are assigned to a given function and are motivated can achieve high performance only if the other employees they rely on are motivated.

SPOTLIGHT ON TECHNOLOGY

Using Computers to Motivate Employees

In the 1950s and 1960s, using a computer on the job meant sitting at a keyboard, performing mind-numbing data entry tasks. In today's business world, the situation is often radically different. Rather than making jobs more boring, computers are often used to expand the scope of a job and motivate employees. As a result, potential users are often eager to start using such systems.

As an example, consider the application of computers to mortgage loans. For most of this century, mortgage loans for housing were simple financial instruments, offered primarily by savings and loan (S&L) institutions. In the 1980s, however, the number and types of financial institutions able to offer mortgages increased dramatically. These changes in the mortgage industry meant that many banks' branches were unable to offer mortgage products as part of their customer service. Both the branches and the bank headquarters considered the situation undesirable; not only was a potential revenue stream being lost, but the bank was also precluded from becoming a one-stop financial center for its customers.

To alleviate the problem, the Bank of Boston's advanced technology group developed a program called the Mortgage Originator. It applied rules for mortgage origination that were derived from managers at the bank's headquarters. It also maintained a full database of existing mortgage products, contained rules for qualifying customers in accordance with reselling guidelines, and even allowed its users to determine if customers could qualify for larger mortgages. Using the system, branch officers could create complex mortgages for customers. They were motivated to use the system by virtue of its ability to increase the scope of their jobs.

---

job enlargement a program to expand (enlarge) the jobs assigned to employees

Job Enlargement One method of increasing employee responsibility is to use **job enlargement,** which is a program to expand (enlarge) the jobs assigned to employees. Job enlargement has been implemented at numerous firms such as Motorola and Xerox Corporation, which experienced downsizing in the 1990s. The program was implemented not only to motivate employees but also to reduce operating expenses.

job rotation a program that allows a set of employees to periodically rotate their job assignments

Job Rotation **Job rotation** allows a set of employees to periodically rotate their job assignments. For example, an assembly-line operation may involve five different types of assignments. Each worker may focus on one assignment per week and switch assignments at the beginning of the next week. In this way, a worker performs five different assignments over each five-week period.

Job rotation not only may reduce boredom but also can prepare employees for other jobs if their primary job position is eliminated. In this way, employees can remain employed by the firm. For example, if the demand for a specific type of car declines, the manufacturer of that car may attempt to reassign the employees who worked on that car to work on other cars or trucks.

empowerment allowing employees power to make more decisions

Empowerment and Participative Management In recent years, supervisors of many firms have delegated more authority to their employees. This strategy is referred to as **empowerment,** as it allows employees power to make more decisions. Empowerment is more specific than job enlargement because it focuses on increased authority, whereas job enlargement may not necessarily result in more authority. Empowerment may motivate those employees who are more satisfied when they have more authority. Also, they may be in a better position to make decisions on the tasks they perform than supervisors who are not directly involved in those tasks.

participative management employees are allowed to participate in various decisions made by their supervisors or others

Empowerment is related to **participative management,** in which employees are allowed to participate in various decisions. For example, DaimlerChrysler has a program in which individual workers are asked for suggestions on cost cutting or improving quality. Managers are asked to review these suggestions and respond to the workers within a few days.

SELF-SCORING EXERCISE

Are You an Empowered Employee?*

Read each of the following statements carefully. Then, to the right, indicate which answer best expresses your level of agreement (5 = strongly agree, 4 = agree, 3 = sometimes agree/sometimes disagree, 2 = disagree, 1 = strongly disagree, and 0 = undecided/do not know). Mark only one answer for each item, and remember to respond to all items. Remember that *work group* means all persons who report to the same manager as you do, regardless of their job titles.

____ 1. I feel free to tell my manager what I think.	5	4	3	2	1	0
____ 2. My manager is willing to listen to my concerns.	5	4	3	2	1	0
____ 3. My manager asks for my ideas about things affecting our work.	5	4	3	2	1	0
____ 4 My manager treats me with respect and dignity.	5	4	3	2	1	0
____ 5. My manager keeps me informed about things I need to know.	5	4	3	2	1	0
____ 6. My manager lets me do my job without interfering.	5	4	3	2	1	0
____ 7. My manager's boss gives us the support we need.	5	4	3	2	1	0
____ 8. Upper management pays attention to ideas and suggestions from people at my level.	5	4	3	2	1	0

Scoring

To determine if you are an empowered employee, add your scores.

32–40: You are empowered! Managers listen when you speak, respect your ideas, and allow you to do your work.

24–31: You have *some* power! Your ideas are sometimes considered, and you have some freedom of action.

16–23: You must exercise caution. You cannot speak or act too boldly, and your managers appear to exercise close supervision.

8–15: Your wings are clipped! You work in a powerless, restrictive work environment.

*If you are not employed, discuss these questions with a friend who is employed. Is your friend an empowered employee?

Empowerment assigns decision-making responsibilities to employees, whereas participative management simply allows the employees input in decisions. In reality, both terms are used to reflect more responsibilities for employees, whether they have complete or partial influence on decisions. The higher level of involvement by employees is supported by Theory Z, as discussed earlier.

management by objectives (MBO) allows employees to participate in setting their goals and determining the manner by which they achieve their tasks

A popular form of participative management is **management by objectives (MBO),** which often allows employees to work with their managers to set their goals and determine the manner by which they achieve their tasks. The employees' participation can be beneficial because they are closer to the production process. In addition, if their tasks can be completed in various ways, they may use their own creativity to achieve the goals.

MBO is commonly applied to salespeople by assigning a monthly sales *quota* (or goal) that is based on historical sales. The actual sales volume may be dependent on the state of the economy, however. Care must be taken to assign a goal that is achievable.

Do Employees Want More Influence in Business Decisions?

Employees may desire to be involved in business decision making because it increases their influence on the firm's performance. In recent years, the restructuring of firms has resulted in substantially more responsibilities for many employees. A survey of 4,500 workers of various firms was conducted to determine whether workers still wanted to have more influence in business decisions. The results are shown in the following chart:

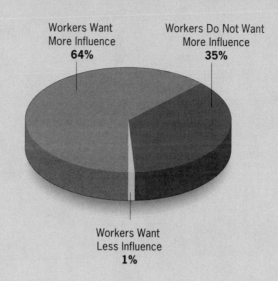

Workers Want
More Influence
64%

Workers Do Not Want
More Influence
35%

Workers Want
Less Influence
1%

The results suggest that even with the recent efforts of firms to give their employees more power and responsibility, employees would generally prefer more responsibility.

For production employees, a production volume goal is specified. Some employees may reduce their quality of work to reach the goal. Thus, objectives must be stated to ensure adequate quality as well as quantity.

teamwork a group of employees with varied job positions is given the responsibility to achieve a specific goal

Teamwork Another form of employee involvement is **teamwork,** in which a group of employees with varied job positions is given the responsibility to achieve a specific goal. Goodyear Tire and Rubber Company uses numerous project teams to achieve its goals. Car manufacturers encourage teamwork to create new ideas. Employees at Yahoo! are encouraged to share their ideas with others to obtain feedback.

DaimlerChrysler, which was created from Chrysler's merger with Daimler-Benz, has continued to design cars with input from assembly-line workers. Executives establish general guidelines on a type of automobile that will satisfy consumers. The workers are then assembled in teams to work out the design details.

When Jaguar (a subsidiary of Ford Motor Company) desired to improve its customer service, its executives initially attempted to instruct employees to provide better service. However, motivating employees was difficult because they were not satisfied with their jobs. The executives decided to create worker involvement teams to develop a plan for improved customer service. The employees were more willing to deal with the problem once they were allowed to search for the best solution.

A classic example of teamwork that all students can relate to is Belmont University's use of teamwork to resolve course registration hassles experienced by students. Students experienced difficulties when attempting to add a class, drop a class, submit a financial aid form, or any other task requiring service from the university. In addition, each task had to be completed at a different location on campus. Consequently, the university formed a team of administrators to find a solution that would make the process easier for students. The team proposed the creation of Belmont Central, a one-stop shop where students could accomplish all administrative tasks from registering for courses to applying for financial aid. For Belmont Central to work, its employees would have to be capable of handling all these tasks. Belmont University implemented the plan and trained the employees so that they were capable of handling a wide variety of tasks. As a result, a student now goes to one place and meets with one employee to perform all administrative tasks. The students are much better satisfied with the service than they were in the past, and the university has received an award from *USA Today* for its excellent use of teamwork to resolve its problems.

open-book management a form of employee involvement that educates employees on their contribution to the firm and enables them to periodically assess their own performance levels

Open-Book Management Another form of employee involvement is **open-book management,** which educates employees on their contribution to the firm and enables them to periodically assess their own performance levels. Open-book management educates employees on how they affect the key performance measures that are relevant for the firm's owners. In this way, it encourages employees to make decisions and conduct tasks as if they were the firm's owners.

Open book management has three distinct characteristics:

1 The firm educates all employees on the key performance measurements that affect the firm's profits and value and ensures that these performance measurements are widely available to employees over time (like an "open book" on the firm's performance). For example, various revenue, expense, and production figures may be displayed daily or weekly in the work area.

2 As employees are given the power to make decisions, they are trained to understand how the results of their decisions will affect the firm's overall performance. Thus, salespeople recognize how their efforts affect the firm's total revenue, while engineers recognize how their efforts reduce the cost of producing a product. Many job positions are not tied directly to revenue or total expenses. Therefore, it is helpful to break performance into pieces that employees can relate to, such as number of customer complaints, proportion of product defects, and percentage of tasks completed on time. Each of these pieces influences the total demand for the firm's product (and therefore the firm's revenue), as well as the expenses incurred.

3 The compensation of employees is typically aligned with their contribution to the firm's overall performance. They may earn some stock so that they are shareholders as well as employees. This reinforces their focus on making decisions that will enhance the firm's value and therefore its stock price. In addition, firms may provide annual pay raises only to employees who helped improve the firm's performance. Although educating employees on how their work affects the firm's value is useful, a firm may still need to compensate employees for their performance in order to motivate them. Firms may set specific annual performance targets for employees and then continually update employees on performance levels throughout the year.

Clad in jeans and a plaid shirt, Southwest Airlines chairman Herb Kelleher attends a luncheon meeting with his employees at Dallas headquarters where every day is dress-down day. Casual attire and employee empowerment and recognition lead to very high job satisfaction.

DELL COMPUTER'S FORMULA FOR SUCCESS

In a recent annual report, Dell Computer's CEO, Michael Dell, stated that it is critical for the company's future success that it recruit, develop, and retain highly skilled people at all levels of the organization. Furthermore, he said that Dell's model of direct customer contact is only as good as the people who apply it to the company's daily business. The CEO also gave credit for the effective implementation of the customer contact model to the 16,000 Dell employees around the world. Thus, Dell used a form of open-book management to motivate the company's employees.

Comparison of Methods Used to Enhance Job Satisfaction

The methods that can enhance job satisfaction and therefore motivate employees are compared in Exhibit 11.9. A combination of methods is especially useful for enhancing an employee's job satisfaction. When firms develop a set of methods that satisfy employees, they will be more effective in motivating employees to achieve high performance. Therefore, methods can improve a firm's profits and value.

Firms That Achieve the Highest Job Satisfaction Level

Many firms use a combination of methods to achieve high job satisfaction. Exhibit 11.10 lists some firms that have been frequently cited as the best firms to work for, along with the methods they use to achieve such high job satisfaction. Notice that each firm has its own way of satisfying employees.

GLOBAL BUSINESS

Motivating Employees across Countries

THE TECHNIQUES USED TO MOTIVATE EMPLOYEES IN THE UNITED STATES may not necessarily be successful for motivating employees in other countries. For example, consider a U.S. firm that has just established a production plant in Eastern Europe. European employees' views on conditions necessary for job satisfaction may differ from those of U.S. production workers. In general, U.S. firms have successfully motivated production workers in the United States by giving them more responsibilities. Assigning additional responsibilities may not motivate production workers in Eastern Europe, however, especially if they have less experience and education. These workers could even be overwhelmed by the extra responsibilities. They might be less capable of striving for efficiency, since their past work experience was in an environment that did not stress efficiency.

In some situations, a U.S. firm may be more capable of motivating foreign workers than U.S. workers. For example, General Motors established a plant in what was then East Germany to produce automobiles. When it trained the workers at this plant, it explained the need for production efficiency to ensure the plant's survival. It asked the workers to provide suggestions on how the plant could increase its production efficiency. These workers offered ten times the number of suggestions that were offered by workers of other General Motors plants in Europe. An entire automobile could be assembled at the East German plant faster than the production time at any other General Motors plant. The efficiency of the workers at the East German plant may be attributed to their background. Although these workers did not have many years of experience on automobile assembly lines, they also had not learned any bad habits that were more prevalent when production assembly systems were less efficient. Thus, these workers were more capable of learning an efficient production system.

Exhibit 11.9 Methods Used to Enhance Job Satisfaction

Method	Description
1. Adequate compensation program	Align raises with performance. Align bonuses with performance. Provide stock as partial compensation.
2. Job security	Encourage employees to have a long-term commitment to the firm.
3. Flexible work schedule	Allow employees flexibility on the timing of their work schedules.
4. Employee involvement programs	Implement job enlargement. Implement job rotation. Implement empowerment and participative management. Implement teamwork. Implement open-book management.

Exhibit 11.10

Examples of Firms That Have Achieved Very High Job Satisfaction

Firm	Methods Used to Achieve High Job Satisfaction
Southwest Airlines	▶ Treats employees with respect. ▶ Empowers employees to solve problems. ▶ Gives awards and recognition to employees.
MBNA	▶ Focuses on hiring employees who get along with other people. ▶ Provides on-site child care.
Microsoft	▶ Casual work environment. ▶ Empowers employees to solve problems.
Eddie Bauer	▶ Two-week paid sick leave for new parents. ▶ Flexible work schedules.
Land's End	▶ No-layoff policy. ▶ Full benefits to part-timers. ▶ 40% discount on catalogue merchandise. ▶ Fitness center and swimming pool on-site.

Overall, a firm's ability to motivate workers in a specific country may depend on characteristics that are not under the firm's control. Workers who will lose their jobs if the firm performs poorly may be more motivated, regardless of the firm's motivation strategies. Workers based in countries with fewer opportunities may be more motivated, since they may appreciate their existing jobs more than workers in other countries. Given these differences, a firm may consider using varying motivation strategies for workers in different countries. In general, a firm should attempt to determine what conditions will increase the job satisfaction of workers in a particular country and provide those conditions for workers who perform well.

| **BUSINESS DILEMMA** | **College Health Club** |

Motivation at College Health Club

SUE KRAMER, PRESIDENT OF COLLEGE HEALTH CLUB (CHC), IS SEARCHING for a way to motivate Lisa Lane, who was hired mainly as an aerobics instructor but also performs other minor tasks. Lisa works part-time and will graduate from college in one year. Sue makes all the decisions, even those related to the scheduling and format of aerobics classes. If CHC's business increases, Sue wants to hire Lisa full-time to help with various tasks and decisions. Lisa's main focus right now is completing her degree. Although Lisa is an adequate aerobics instructor, she has much potential for running a business and will likely become bored if she is used only as an instructor.

Dilemma

Sue wants to enhance Lisa's job satisfaction so that Lisa will be willing to continue her part-time job until Sue can afford to hire her full-time. Currently, however, Sue is not in a position to increase Lisa's hourly wage. Sue needs to develop alternative ways she can satisfy Lisa and encourage her to remain employed at CHC. Offer your own recommendations to Sue on how she may encourage Lisa to remain employed at CHC.

Solution

Although Sue could enhance Lisa's job satisfaction in various ways, she decides on the following:

1 Allow Lisa some flexibility on the hours she will serve as instructor for aerobics classes (although the classes will have to be offered at times desired by CHC members).

2 Allow Lisa to offer input on various decisions, such as ways to increase membership and the types of exercise classes to be offered. If Lisa is more involved in decision making, she may be more willing to take a full-time position at CHC rather than at some other firm once she obtains her degree.

This strategy not only allows Lisa more power but may also improve decision making because Lisa is more involved with the classes and may have ideas about what will satisfy the customers (members).

Sue also considers promising Lisa a future full-time job to discourage her from seeking another job in the future. This would provide Lisa with job security. Sue cannot afford to hire Lisa full-time unless CHC's membership grows. So she promises Lisa a full-time job in one year if membership grows to four hundred.

Overall, Sue is attempting to enhance Lisa's job satisfaction with flextime, empowerment, and job security.

Additional Issues for Discussion

1 Do you think Sue Kramer's esteem and self-actualization needs are fulfilled in her present position at CHC?

2 Do you think Lisa Lane's esteem and self-actualization needs are fulfilled in her present position at CHC?

3 Explain how expectancy theory may be used to explain how Sue is motivated to perform well at CHC.

SUMMARY

1 The main theories on motivation are as follows:

▶ The Hawthorne studies suggest that employees are more motivated when they receive more attention.

▶ Maslow's hierarchy of needs theory suggests that employees are satisfied by different needs, depending on their position within the hierarchy. Firms can satisfy employees at the low end of the hierarchy with job security or safe working conditions. Once basic needs are fulfilled, employees have other needs that must be met. Firms can attempt to satisfy these employees by allowing social interaction or more responsibilities.

▶ Herzberg's job satisfaction study suggests that the factors that prevent job dissatisfaction are different from those that enhance job satisfaction. An adequate salary and working conditions prevent job dissatisfaction, while responsibility and recognition enhance job satisfaction.

▶ McGregor's Theories X and Y suggest that when supervisors believe employees dislike work and responsibilities (Theory X), they do not delegate responsibilities and employees are not motivated; when supervisors believe that employees prefer responsibilities (Theory Y), they delegate more responsibilities, which motivates employees.

▶ Theory Z suggests that employees are more satisfied when they are involved in decision making, and therefore may be more motivated.

▶ Expectancy theory suggests that employees are more motivated if compensation is aligned with goals that are achievable and offer some reward.

▶ Equity theory suggests that employees are more motivated if their compensation is aligned with their relative contribution to the firm's total output.

▶ Reinforcement theory suggests that employees are more motivated to perform well if they are rewarded for high performance (positive reinforcement) and penalized for poor performance (negative reinforcement).

2 Firms can enhance job satisfaction and therefore motivate employees by providing:

▶ an adequate compensation program, which aligns compensation with performance,

▶ job security,

▶ a flexible work schedule, and

▶ employee involvement programs.

KEY TERMS

across-the-board system *297*
compressed work week *301*
empowerment *302*
equity theory *294*
esteem needs *291*
expectancy theory *294*
flextime programs *301*
hierarchy of needs *290*
hygiene factors *291*
incentive plans *297*

job enlargement *302*
job enrichment programs *297*
job rotation *302*
job satisfaction *289*
job sharing *301*
management by objectives (MBO) *303*
merit system *297*
motivational factors *291*
negative reinforcement *295*

open-book management *305*
participative management *302*
physiological needs *290*
positive reinforcement *295*
reinforcement theory *295*
safety needs *291*
self-actualization *291*
social needs *291*
teamwork *304*

REVIEW QUESTIONS

1 Identify the categories of Maslow's hierarchy of needs theory.

2 Describe Herzberg's job satisfaction study on worker motivation.

3 Distinguish Theory X from Theory Y perceptions of management.

4 Describe how expectancy theory can motivate behavior.

5 Discuss the equity theory of motivation.

6 Describe reinforcement theories of motivation and explain how a manager could utilize them.

7 Identify and explain methods that will enhance job satisfaction and motivate employees.

8 Discuss how managers utilize strategic planning to motivate

their employees and to maximize the value of the firm.

9 Describe how empowerment is related to participative management.

10 Discuss the methods used to motivate employees in the United States. Should the same methods be used to motivate employees in other countries?

DISCUSSION QUESTIONS

1 Assume that you are a manager who recognizes that your employees are motivated by money. How could you motivate them at work?

2 Would motivational techniques be more important for the At-

lanta Braves than for an organization such as General Motors? Explain your answer.

3 Assume that you are a manager of a video store. Which theory of motivation would best motivate employee behavior?

4 Would you consider using negative reinforcement to improve the performance of lazy employees? Explain your answer.

5 How could a firm use the Internet and technology to motivate its existing and potential employees?

INVESTING IN THE STOCK OF A BUSINESS

Using the annual report of the firm in which you would like to invest, complete the following:

1 Does the firm appear to recognize that its employees are the key to its success?

2 Does the firm empower its workers? Does it encourage teamwork? Provide details.

3 Explain how the business uses technology to motivate its employees. For example, does it use the Internet to provide information about its compensa-

tion programs? Does it use the Internet or e-mail to provide feedback to its employees?

4 Go to **http://hoovers.com** and locate the NEWS SEARCH. Type in the name of the firm in the space provided, and review the recent news stories about the firm. Summarize any (at least one) recent news story about the firm that applies to one or more of the key concepts within this chapter.

CASE   USING MOTIVATION TO ENHANCE PERFORMANCE

Tom Fry is a plant manager for Ligonier Steel Corporation, located in Ligonier, Pennsylvania. The plant is small, with 250 employees. Its productivity growth rate has stagnated for the past year and a half.

Tom is concerned and decides to meet with employees in various departments. During the meeting, employees disclose that they do not have a chance to interact with one another while on the job. Because they do not receive any recognition for their suggestions, their input of ideas for improvement has stopped.

After a week elapses, Tom calls a meeting to announce a new program. He plans to offer rewards for high performance so that employees will be motivated to surpass their quotas. Bonuses will be awarded to employees who exceed their quotas. Tom believes this program will work because of his perception that "money motivates employees."

A few months later, Tom notices that productivity has increased and that employees are enjoying the bonuses they have earned. Tom decides to provide an additional means of motivation. He wants employees to continue to interact with one another to solve work problems and share information. Supervisors now recognize individual accomplishments. They congratulate employees when suggestions are made and identify an employee of the month in the company newsletter to recognize outstanding performance. Tom strongly supports this feature of the program.

The goal is for employees to grow and develop to their fullest potential. Individuals may be retrained or go back to college to permit job growth within the plant. Employees' ideas and contributions are now perceived as a way to enhance their individual career paths. The results have been overwhelming. Tom Fry, supervisors, and employees have all enjoyed the benefits that have made Ligonier Steel a satisfying place to work for everyone.

QUESTIONS

1 Describe the motivation theory that applies to this case.

2 What needs can employees at Ligonier Steel satisfy in performing their jobs?

3 Describe how bonuses motivated the employees at Ligonier Steel.

4 Describe other rewards besides bonuses that can motivate behavior at work.

VIDEO CASE   MOTIVATING EMPLOYEES AT VALASSIS COMMUNICATIONS, INC.

Valassis Communications, Inc., creates the promotional newspaper inserts for 58 million households. It uses a pay-for-performance system that rewards employees for high performance. The company rewards employees both for individual achievements and for team achievements. The team awards are tied to the performance of the firm overall. In this way, the employees benefit whenever shareholders of the firm benefit.

QUESTIONS

1 How is Valassis's reward system related to "expectancy theory"?

2 How does Valassis use positive reinforcement?

3 Is Valassis's success due entirely to monetary rewards, or are there other reasons for employee satisfaction at the firm?

INTERNET APPLICATIONS

http://www.nceo.org

Click on "Library," and then click on "How ESOPs Work."

Briefly describe an employee stock ownership plan (ESOP). How does it work? How do you think an ESOP motivates employees? How do you think ESOPs benefit the companies using them? Discuss how ESOPs relate to the theories of motivation discussed in the text.

THE Coca-Cola COMPANY ANNUAL REPORT PROJECT

Questions for the current year's annual report are available on the text website at **http://madura_intro_bus.swcollege.com.**

The following questions apply concepts learned in this chapter to The Coca-Cola Company. Go to The Coca-Cola Company website (**http://www.cocacola.com**) and find the index for the 1999 annual report.

QUESTIONS

1 Click on "A Message to Share Owners." Given that The Coca-Cola Company's success depends on recruiting, training, and retaining people who can quickly identify and act on profitable business opportunities, do you think that a Theory X management style would be appropriate at The Coca-Cola Company?

2 Click on "Investments." Do you think rigid salary scales would be appropriate for The Coca-Cola Company?

3 Study the "Selected Market Results" section and the "Investments" section. How might methods of motivating employees differ across countries within The Coca-Cola Company? Do you think you would be motivated to work at The Coca-Cola Company?

4 Click on "A Message to Share Owners." What does the Chairman say in the annual report to motivate The Coca-Cola Company's employees? What does he think about his predecessor and the board of directors?

5 Go to **http://hoovers.com** and locate the NEWS SEARCH. Type in The Coca-Cola Company in the space provided, and review the recent news stories about the firm. Summarize any (at least one) recent news story about The Coca-Cola Company that applies one or more of the key concepts within this chapter of the text.

IN-TEXT STUDY GUIDE

Answers are in an appendix at the back of the book.

TRUE OR FALSE

1 Most compensation plans that tie pay to performance are intended to motivate employees to achieve high performance.

2 Negative reinforcement motivates employees by encouraging them to behave in a manner that avoids unfavorable consequences.

3 A merit system allocates raises for all employees according to sales of the firm.

4 The management strategy of empowerment is favored by Theory X managers.

5 Open-book management encourages employees to make decisions and conduct tasks as if they were the firm's owners.

6 According to Frederick Herzberg, hygiene factors are work-related factors that will motivate and please employees.

7 A supervisor who believes in McGregor's Theory Y will likely monitor employees closely to ensure that their work is completed.

8 Equity theory suggests that an employee's efforts are influenced by the expected outcome of those efforts.

9 An across-the-board system is appropriate when all employees deserve the same reward for their work.

10 Maslow's hierarchy of needs identifies superior compensation as the key to employee motivation.

MULTIPLE CHOICE

11 The compensation of employees is typically aligned with their contribution to the firm's:
a) hierarchy of needs.
b) industry demand.
c) overall performance.
d) reinforcement theory.
e) hygiene theory.

12 By _____ employees to properly perform the tasks they are assigned, management can maximize the firm's value.
a) motivating
b) threatening
c) coercing
d) manipulating
e) harassing

13 Which of the following is an employee involvement program that attempts to encourage employees to make decisions and conduct tasks as if they were the firm's owners?
a) Theory X management
b) open-book management
c) Theory Y management
d) Theory Z management
e) Theory J management

14 In addition to linking compensation with performance, some firms grant employees _____ for good performance.
a) internal satisfaction
b) Theory X involvement
c) Theory Y involvement
d) corporate bonds
e) common stock

15 Which of the following is an employee involvement program where a group of employees with different job positions are given the responsibility of achieving a specific goal?
a) management by objectives (MBO)
b) teamwork
c) job enlargement
d) job rotation
e) job sharing

16 One method of increasing job satisfaction is to implement:
a) Theory X management.
b) Theory Q management.

c) negative reinforcement.
d) flextime programs.
e) across-the-board pay raises.

17 Which of the following theories of management proposes the empowerment of employees?
a) Theory X
b) Theory Y
c) Theory Z
d) expectancy theory
e) equity theory

18 When firms delegate more authority to their employees, this strategy is referred to as:
a) Theory X management.
b) empowerment.
c) the merit system.
d) McGregor's hygiene theory.
e) the equity system.

19 Which of the following allows employees to set their own goals and determine the manner by which they accomplish their tasks?
a) equity theory of motivation
b) expectancy theory of motivation
c) management by objectives
d) Theory X management
e) Theory Y management

20 A program to expand the jobs assigned to employees is called:
a) hygiene theory.
b) downsizing.
c) positive reinforcement.
d) equity theory of motivation.
e) job enlargement.

21 Social interaction and acceptance by others are examples of:
a) physiological needs.
b) esteem needs.
c) safety needs.
d) social needs.
e) self-actualization needs.

22 The reinforcement theory that motivates employees by encouraging them to behave in a manner that avoids unfavorable consequences is _____ reinforcement.
a) positive
b) neutral
c) equity
d) negative
e) expectancy

23 Needs that are satisfied with food, clothing, and shelter are called _____ needs.
a) safety
b) social
c) affiliation
d) self-esteem
e) physiological

24 Herzberg's hygiene factors most closely correspond with Maslow's:
a) physiological needs.
b) psychological needs.
c) social needs.
d) esteem needs.
e) self-actualization needs.

25 Which of the following theories of management suggests that workers will be motivated if they are compensated in accordance with their perceived contributions to the firm?
a) expectancy theory
b) equity theory
c) need theory
d) Theory Y
e) reinforcement theory

26 An employee involvement program that periodically moves individuals from one job assignment to another is:
a) job enlargement.
b) job enrichment.
c) job rotation.
d) job sharing.
e) flextime.

27 All of the following are methods used to enhance job satisfaction except:
a) employee involvement programs.
b) Theory X management.
c) job security.
d) adequate compensation programs.
e) flexible work schedules.

28 According to Herzberg, employees are commonly most satisfied when offered:
a) adequate supervision.
b) adequate salary.
c) recognition.
d) job security.
e) safe working conditions.

29 Theory Z suggests that employees are more satisfied when:
a) they receive above average pay raises.
b) their compensation is consistent with their efforts.
c) managers restrict the delegation of authority.
d) they are involved in decision making.
e) appropriate hygiene factors are available.

30 In an across-the-board system, all employees receive similar:
a) raises.
b) job assignments.
c) offices.
d) work schedules.
e) performance appraisals.

31 _____ can reduce boredom and prepare employees for other jobs if their primary job is eliminated.
a) Job evaluation
b) Job rotation
c) Reengineering
d) Performance appraisal
e) Reinforcement

32 Maslow's hierarchy of needs theory can be useful for motivating employees because it suggests that:
a) people are motivated to achieve their work-related hygiene factors.
b) managers respond to the need for corporate profitability.

c) employee needs are stable.
d) employees are motivated by unsatisfied needs.
e) money is the most important motivating factor.

33 One implication of the Hawthorne studies is that workers can be motivated by receiving:
a) attention.
b) money.
c) stock.
d) bonuses.
e) profit sharing.

34 Which of the following provides employees with various forms of compensation if specific performance goals are met?

a) flextime programs
b) job enlargement
c) participative management
d) open-book management
e) incentive plans

35 Two or more persons sharing a particular work schedule is called:
a) job enlargement.
b) job enrichment.
c) job sharing.
d) flextime.
e) job rotation.

The Learning Goals of this chapter are to:

1 Explain human resource planning by firms.

2 Differentiate among the types of compensation that firms offer to employees.

3 Describe the skills of employees that firms develop.

4 Explain how the performance of employees can be evaluated.

Hiring, Training, and Evaluating Employees

A key to a firm's performance is its human resources (employees). Therefore, a firm's performance is dependent on how human resources are managed. The management of human resources involves recruiting employees, developing their skills, and evaluating their performance.

Consider the case of Southwest Airlines, which has seen great success in recent years and has rapidly expanded its routes throughout most of the United States. What information should Southwest use to determine how many pilots and other types of employees to hire? What type of training can Southwest provide to new pilots beyond what they received when they pursued their pilot's licenses? How can Southwest evaluate the performance of its pilots and other employees? This chapter focuses on managing the hiring, training, and evaluating of employees, which can be used to address these questions.

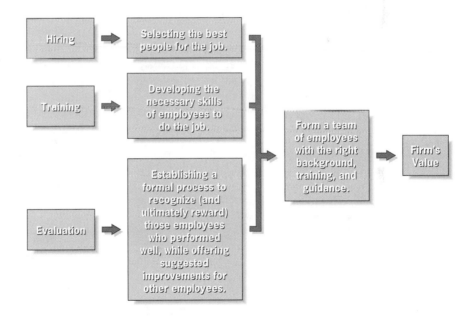

Human Resource Planning

human resource planning
planning to satisfy a firm's needs for employees

Human resource planning involves planning to satisfy a firm's needs for employees. It is composed of three tasks:

▶ Forecasting staffing needs
▶ Job analysis
▶ Recruiting

Forecasting Staffing Needs

If staffing needs can be anticipated in advance, the firm has more time to satisfy those needs. Some needs for human resources occur as workers retire or take jobs with other firms. Retirement can be forecasted with some degree of accuracy, but forecasting when an employee will take a job with another firm is difficult.

Additional needs for employees result from expansion. These needs may be determined by assessing the firm's growth trends. For example, if the firm is expected to increase production by 10 percent (in response to increased sales), it may prepare for the creation of new positions to achieve the projected production level. Positions that handle accounting and marketing-related tasks may not be affected by the increased production level.

If the firm foresees a temporary need for higher production, it may avoid hiring new workers, since it would soon have to lay them off. Layoffs not only affect the laid-off workers but also scare those workers who are still employed. In addition, firms that become notorious for layoffs will be less capable of recruiting people for new positions.

If firms avoid hiring during a temporary increase in production, they must achieve their objective in some other way. A common method is to offer overtime to existing workers. An alternative method is to hire temporarily for part-time or seasonal work.

Once new positions are created, they must be filled. This normally involves job analysis and recruiting, which are discussed in turn.

Job Analysis

job analysis the analysis used to determine the tasks and the necessary credentials for a particular position

job specification states the credentials necessary to qualify for a job position

job description states the tasks and responsibilities of a job position

Before a firm hires a new employee to fill an existing job position, it must decide what tasks and responsibilities will be performed by that position and what credentials (education, experience, and so on) are needed to qualify for that position. The analysis used to determine the tasks and the necessary credentials for a particular position is referred to as **job analysis.** This analysis should include input from the position's supervisor as well as from other employees whose tasks are related. The job analysis allows the supervisor of the job position to develop a job specification and job description. The **job specification** states the credentials necessary to qualify for the job position. The **job description** states the tasks and responsibilities of the job position. An example of a job description is provided in Exhibit 12.1. People who consider applying for

Exhibit 12.1 Example of a Job Description

Title: Sales Representative
Department: Sales
Location: Southern Division, Atlanta, Georgia

Position Summary
The sales representative meets with prospective customers to sell the firm's products and to ensure that existing customers are satisfied with the products they have purchased.

Relationships
▶ Reports to the regional sales manager for the Southern Division.
▶ Works with five other sales representatives, although each representative has responsibility for his or her own region within the Southern Division.

Main Job Responsibilities
1. Serve existing customers; call on main customers at least once a month to obtain feedback on the performance of products previously sold to them; take any new orders for products.
2. Visit other prospective customers and explain the advantages of each product.
3. Check on those customers who are late in paying their bills; provide feedback to the billing department.
4. Meet with the production managers at least once a month to inform them about any product defects cited by customers.
5. Assess the needs of prospective customers; determine whether other related products could be produced to satisfy customers; provide feedback to production managers.
6. Will need to train new sales representatives in the future if growth continues.
7. Overnight travel is necessary for about eight days per month.
8. Sales reports must be completed once a month.

the job position use the job specification to determine whether they could qualify for the position and use the job description to determine what the position involves.

Recruiting

human resource manager

helps each specific department recruit candidates for its open positions

Firms use various forms of recruiting to ensure an adequate supply of qualified candidates. Some firms have a **human resource manager** (sometimes called the "personnel manager") who helps each specific department recruit candidates for its open positions. To identify potential candidates for the position, the human resource manager may check files of recent applicants who applied before the position was even open. These files are usually created as people submit their applications to the firm over time. In addition, the manager may place an ad in local newspapers. This increases the pool of applicants, as some people are unwilling to submit an application unless they are informed of an open position at the firm.

Most well-known companies tend to receive a large number of qualified applications for each position. Many firms retain applications for only a few months so that the number of applications does not become excessive.

BUSINESS ONLINE

Corporate Human Resource Information

http://www.monster.com

INTERNET SITES SUCH AS THE ONE SHOWN HERE ARE INCREASINGLY BEING used by potential employees to research companies and search for job openings. Furthermore, such websites also allow potential employers to post job openings. Prospective employees find these websites highly useful in assessing a particular company's attitude toward its employees and its compensation packages. Also, by allowing employers to post job openings, the websites act as a "clearinghouse" for the labor market.

Internal versus External Recruiting Recruiting can occur internally or externally. **Internal recruiting** seeks to fill open positions with persons already employed by the firm. Numerous firms post job openings so that existing employees can be informed. Some employees within the firm may desire the open positions more than their existing positions.

internal recruiting an effort to fill open positions with persons already employed by the firm

Internal recruiting can be beneficial because existing employees have already been proven. Their personalities are known, and their potential capabilities and limitations

promotion assignment of an employee to a higher-level job with more responsibility and compensation

external recruiting an effort to fill positions with applicants from outside the firm

can be thoroughly assessed. Internal recruiting also allows existing workers to receive a **promotion** (an assignment of a higher-level job with more responsibility and compensation) or to switch to more desirable tasks. This is important to employees because the potential for advancement motivates them to perform well. Such potential also reduces job turnover and therefore reduces the costs of hiring and training new employees. Many of the employees that Walt Disney hires for management positions are recruited internally.

Firms can do more internal recruiting if their employees are assigned responsibilities and tasks that train them for advanced positions. This strategy conflicts with job specialization because it exposes employees to more varied tasks. Nevertheless, it is necessary to prepare them for other jobs and to reduce the possibility of boredom. Even when firms are able to fill a position internally, the previous position that the employee held becomes open, and the firm must recruit for that position.

External recruiting is an effort to fill positions with applicants from outside the firm. Some firms may recruit more qualified candidates when using external recruiting, especially for some specialized job positions. Although external recruiting allows the firm to evaluate applicants' potential capabilities and limitations, human resource managers do not have as much information as they do for internal applicants. The applicant's résumé lists previously performed functions and describes the responsibilities of those positions, but it does not indicate how the applicant responds to orders or interacts with other employees. This type of information is more critical for some jobs than others.

D⌀LL® COMPUTER'S FORMULA FOR SUCCESS

Dell Computer uses the Internet extensively in its human resource planning. For example, the company allows potential employees to search for a specific job at its website. Dell also allows applicants to submit their résumés over the Internet. Furthermore, Dell uses its website to provide potential employees with information about benefits and about the areas where its plants and employment sites are located, such as cost-of-living estimates.

Screening Applicants The recruiting process used to screen job applicants involves several steps. The first step is to assess each application to screen out unqualified applicants. Although the information provided on an application is limited, it is usually sufficient to determine whether the applicant has the minimum background, education, and experience necessary to qualify for the position.

The second step in screening applicants is the interview process. Some firms conduct initial interviews of college students at placement centers on college campuses. Other firms conduct initial interviews at their location. The human resource manager may be able to assess the personalities of remaining applicants from a personal interview, as well as obtain additional information that was not included on the application. Specifically, an interview can indicate an applicant's promptness, communication skills, and attitude. Furthermore, an interview allows the firm to obtain more detailed information about the applicant's past experience.

If the first two screening steps can substantially reduce the number of candidates, the human resource manager can allocate more time during the interview process to assess each remaining applicant. Even when these steps have effectively reduced the number of candidates, however, the first interview with each remaining candidate will not necessarily lead to a selection. A second and even third interview may be necessary. These interviews may involve other employees of the firm who have some interaction with the position of concern. The input of these employees can often influence the hiring decision. A typical questionnaire for obtaining employee opinions about an applicant is shown in Exhibit 12.2.

Exhibit 12.2   Example of Questionnaire to Obtain Employee Opinions about a Job Applicant

	Strongly Agree	Agree	Unsure	Disagree	Strongly Disagree
Applicant's Name _____ Position to be filled _____					
The applicant possesses the necessary skills to perform the tasks required.					
The applicant would work well with others.					
The applicant would be eager to learn new skills.					
The applicant has good communication skills.					
The applicant would accept responsibility.					

Do you detect any deficiencies in the applicant? (If so, describe them.)

Do you recommend that we hire the applicant? Why, or why not?

Signature of employee who is assessing applicant: _____

A third step for screening applicants is to contact the applicant's references. This screening method offers limited benefits, however, because applicants normally list only those references that are likely to provide strong recommendations. A survey by the Society for Human Resource Management found that more than 50 percent of the human resource managers surveyed sometimes receive inadequate information about a job applicant's personality traits. More than 40 percent of these managers said that they sometimes receive inadequate information about the applicant's skills and work habits.

employment test a test of a job candidate's abilities

Another possible step in the screening process is an **employment test,** which is a test of the candidate's abilities. Some tests are designed to assess intuition or willingness to work with others. Other tests are designed to assess specific skills, such as computer skills.

Some firms also request a physical examination for the candidates they plan to hire. This serves as a final screen. The examination can determine whether the candidate is physically able to perform the tasks that would be assigned. In addition, the examination may detect any medical problems. If the firm still decides to hire the candidate, it can at least document any medical problems that existed before the candidate was employed by the firm. This can protect the firm from being blamed for causing a person's medical problems because of unsafe working conditions.

Along with physical examinations, some firms ask candidates to take a drug test. Firms are adversely affected in two ways when their employees take illegal drugs. First, the firm may incur costs of health care and counseling for these employees. Second, the performance of these employees will likely be low and may even reduce the performance of their co-workers.

Some firms outsource the task of screening job applicants. For example, Bristol-Myers Squibb Company relies on the company MRI to identify and screen its job applicants. MRI organizes recruiting conferences, where it identifies candidates who may be suitable for the positions that Bristol-Myers Squibb and other firms need to fill.

Make the Hiring Decision By the time the steps for screening applicants are completed, the application list should have been reduced to a small number of qualified candidates. Some firms take their hiring process very seriously because they recognize that their future performance is highly dependent on the employees that they select, as documented by the following statement:

❝ The past year's success is the product of a talented, smart, hardworking group, and I take great pride in being a part of this team. Setting the bar high [high standards] in our approach to hiring has been, and will continue to be, the single most important element of Amazon.com's success. ❞

—Amazon.com

Careful screening enables firms to recruit people who turn out to be excellent employees. Consequently, careful recruiting can result in low turnover.

Once the screening is completed, the top candidate can be selected from this list and offered the job; the remaining qualified applicants can be considered if the top candidate does not accept the job offer. Exhibit 12.3 summarizes the steps used to screen job applicants. Notice that each step reduces the list of applicants who would possibly qualify for the position.

Once a person is hired, he or she is informed about the firm's health and benefits plans and additional details of the job. A summary of the various tasks necessary to fill a position is provided in Exhibit 12.4.

Providing Equal Opportunity When recruiting candidates for a job position, managers should not discriminate based on factors that are unrelated to potential job performance. Federal laws prohibit such discrimination. The following are some of the laws enacted to prevent discrimination or improper treatment:

▶ The Equal Pay Act of 1963 states that men and women performing similar work must receive the same pay.
▶ The Civil Rights Act of 1964 prohibits discrimination based on race, gender, religion, or national origin.
▶ The Age Discrimination in Employment Act of 1967, amended in 1978, prohibits employers from discriminating against people who are at least forty years old.

Exhibit 12.3

Steps for Screening Job Applicants

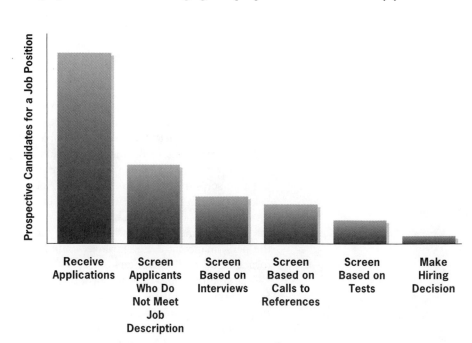

Exhibit 12.4

Summary of Tasks Involved in Human Resource Planning

Forecast Job Needs
- Forecast employee replacement
- Forecast employee expansion

Job Analysis
- Develop job specification
- Develop job description

Recruiting
- Inform potential candidates
- Interveiw qualified candidates
- Make hiring decision

▶ The Americans with Disabilities Act (ADA) of 1990 prohibits discrimination against people who are disabled.

▶ The Civil Rights Act of 1991 enables females, minorities, and disabled people who believe that they have been subject to discrimination to sue firms. This act protects against discrimination in the hiring process or the employee evaluation process. It also protects against sexual harassment in the workplace.

BUSINESS ONLINE

Human Resource Management

http://www.shrm.org

CERTAIN ORGANIZATIONS, SUCH AS THE SOCIETY FOR HUMAN RESOURCE Management (SHRM), provide employers with a variety of services, ranging from publications and an Internet library to international human resource management information. Websites such as these are highly useful to employers attempting to satisfy their firm's employment needs by helping them keep up-to-date on current practices and developments in the field of human resources.

A survey of human resource managers conducted by the Society of Human Resource Management in 1999 found that 85 percent of the managers surveyed expect to see more opportunities for women in the future and 79 percent expect to see more opportunities for minorities.

In 1999, *Fortune* magazine and the Council on Economic Priorities identified several firms that have taken major initiatives to ensure diversity in the workplace. Exhibit 12.5 lists some of these firms and briefly summarizes their efforts. These firms

Exhibit 12.5

Leading Firms in Creating a
Diverse Workplace

Firm	Initiatives in Diversity
Lucent Technologies	9 of its 25 best-paid employees are minorities; 30 percent of its employees are minorities.
Wal-Mart Stores	42 percent of its managers are minorities; 4 of its 15 board members are minorities.
Allstate	35 percent of its new hires are minorities; 21 percent of its managers are minorities.
Chase Manhattan	40 percent of its workforce are minorities; 40 percent of its new hires are minorities.
Marriott International	57 percent of its workforce are minorities; 60 percent of its new hires are minorities.
FedEx	28 percent of its managers are minorities; 42 percent of its workforce are minorities; 52 percent of its new hires are minorities.
AMR (American Airlines)	4 of its 12 board members are minorities; 30 percent of its work force are minorities; 49 percent of its new hires are minorities.
American Express	Provides Diversity Learning Labs for its minority employees; 26 percent of its employees are minorities; 40 percent of its new hires are minorities.
Texas Instruments	6 of the 25 best-paid employees are minorities; 46 percent of new hires are minorities.
Bell Atlantic	Provides a leadership program for promising middle managers, 35 percent of whom are minorities; 4 of its 22 board members are minorities.

demonstrate that diversity in the workplace can be accomplished and that firms with diverse sets of employees can be successful.

Compensation Packages That Firms Offer

2 Differentiate among the types of compensation that firms offer to employees.

Firms attempt to reward their employees by providing adequate compensation. The level of compensation is usually established by determining what employees at other firms with similar job characteristics earn. Information on compensation levels can be obtained by conducting a salary survey or from various publications that report salary levels for different jobs. The wide differences in compensation among job positions are attributed to differences in the supply of people who have a particular skill and the demand for people with that skill. For example, demand for employees who have extensive experience in business financing decisions is high, but the supply of people with such experience is limited. Therefore, firms offer a high level of compensation to attract these people. Conversely, the supply of people who can qualify as a clerk is large, so firms can offer relatively low compensation to hire clerks.

If a firm does not provide adequate compensation and working conditions, it may not be able to retain its employees. Consider the case of Pacific Health Care Systems, which experienced a high level of employee turnover in January 1999. Its value (as measured by its stock price) declined substantially, as shown in Exhibit 12.6.

compensation package the total monetary compensation and benefits offered to employees

A **compensation package** consists of the total monetary compensation and benefits offered to employees. Some employees consider their salary to be their compensation, but the benefits that some firms offer may be more valuable than the salary. The typical elements of a compensation package are salary, stock options, commissions, bonuses, profit sharing, benefits, and perquisites.

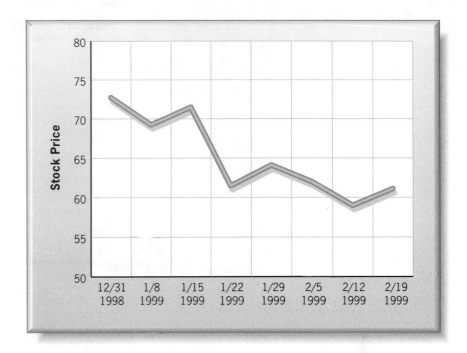

Exhibit 12.6

Impact of High Employee Turnover on Stock Price of Pacific Health Care Systems

Salary

salary (or wages) the dollars paid for a job over a specific period

Salary (or **wages**) is the dollars paid for a job over a specific period. The salary can be expressed per hour, per pay period, or per year and is fixed over a particular time period.

Stock Options

stock options a form of compensation that allows employees to purchase shares of the employing firm's stock at a specific price

Stock options allow employees to purchase the firm's stock at a specific price. Consider employees who have been given stock options to buy 100 shares of stock at a price of $20 per share. This means that they can purchase the stock for this price, regardless of the stock's market price. Thus, even if the stock's market price rises to $30 per share, the employees can still buy the stock for $20 per share. They would need $2,000 (computed as 100 shares × $20 per share) to purchase 100 shares. If the firm performs well over time, the stock price will rise, and their 100 shares will be worth even more. Thus, these employees are motivated to perform well because they benefit directly when the firm performs well. As part-owners of the firm, they share in its profits.

The use of stock or stock options as compensation is becoming more popular, as firms increasingly recognize that their employees work harder when they share in the profits. Consider the following comment from a recent annual report:

> *Chevron's own employees own 11 percent of the company's outstanding shares. . . . In addition, Chevron Success Sharing and employee stock option plans reward employees with incentive pay.*
>
> —Chevron Corporation

Many firms provide stock options to their high-level managers, such as the chief executive officer (CEO), vice-presidents, and other managers. Some firms, however, such as Starbucks and Microsoft, provide stock options to all of their employees. This can motivate all employees to perform well. Starbucks grants stock options to its

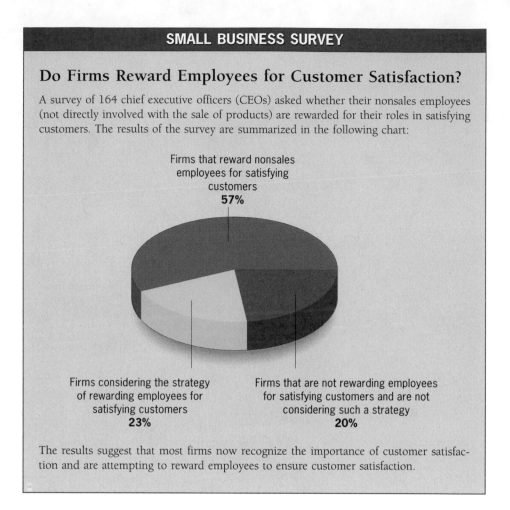

Do Firms Reward Employees for Customer Satisfaction?

A survey of 164 chief executive officers (CEOs) asked whether their nonsales employees (not directly involved with the sale of products) are rewarded for their roles in satisfying customers. The results of the survey are summarized in the following chart:

Firms that reward nonsales
employees for satisfying
customers
57%

Firms considering the strategy
of rewarding employees for
satisfying customers
23%

Firms that are not rewarding employees
for satisfying customers and are not
considering such a strategy
20%

The results suggest that most firms now recognize the importance of customer satisfaction and are attempting to reward employees to ensure customer satisfaction.

employees in proportion to their salaries. An employee who received a salary of $20,000 in 1991 would have earned more than $50,000 by the year 2000 from owning the stock options.

Microsoft attributes much of its success to its use of stock options. Because of its strong performance (and therefore substantial increase in its stock price) since 1992, its managers who were hired in 1992 or before are now millionaires because their shares are worth more than $1 million.

Stock options not only motivate employees but can help to retain employees, as documented by the following comment:

> *We will continue to focus on hiring and retaining versatile and talented employees, and continue to weight their compensation to stock options rather than cash. We know our success will be largely affected by our ability to attract and retain a motivated employee base, each of whom must think like, and therefore must actually be, an owner.*

—Amazon.com

Commissions

commissions compensation for meeting specific sales objectives

Commissions normally represent compensation for meeting specific sales objectives. For example, salespeople at many firms receive a base salary, plus a percentage of their total sales volume as monetary compensation. For jobs in which employee performance cannot be as easily measured, commissions are not used.

Bonuses

bonus an extra one-time payment at the end of a period in which performance was measured

A **bonus** is an extra one-time payment at the end of a period in which performance was measured. Bonuses are usually paid less frequently than commissions (such as once a year). A bonus may be paid for efforts to increase revenue, reduce expenses, or improve customer satisfaction. In most cases, the bonus is not set by a formula; thus, supervisors have some flexibility in determining the bonus for each employee. The total amount of bonus funds that are available for employees may be dependent on the firm's profits for the year of concern.

Profit Sharing

profit sharing a portion of the firm's profits is provided to employees

Some firms, such as Continental Airlines and General Motors, offer employees **profit sharing,** in which a portion of the firm's profits is paid to employees. Boeing, Chase Manhattan, and many other firms offer profit sharing to some of their employees. This motivates employees to perform in a manner that improves profitability.

employee benefits additional privileges beyond compensation payments, such as paid vacation time; health, life, or dental insurance; and pension programs

Employee Benefits

Employees may also receive **employee benefits,** which are additional privileges beyond compensation payments, such as paid vacation time; health, life, or dental insurance; and pension programs. Typically, these employee benefits are not taxed. Many firms provide substantial employee benefits to their employees. The cost of providing health insurance has soared in recent years. Many firms, such as Johnson and Johnson and Tenneco, have responded by offering preventive health-care programs. Some firms now give employees incentives to stay healthy by reducing the insurance premiums charged to employees who receive favorable scores on cholesterol levels, blood pressure, fitness, and body fat.

perquisites additional privileges beyond compensation payments and employee benefits

Ford Motor Co. employees show their profit-sharing checks at the New Jersey assembly plant.

Perquisites

Some firms offer **perquisites** (or "perks") to high-level employees, which are additional privileges beyond compensation payments and employee benefits. Common perquisites include free parking, a company car, club memberships, telephone credit cards, and an expense account.

Comparison across Jobs

The forms of compensation allocated to employees vary with their jobs, as shown in Exhibit 12.7. Employees who are directly involved in the production process (such as assembly-line workers) tend to receive most of their compensation in the form of salary. Low-level managers may also receive most of their compensation as salary but may receive a small bonus and profit sharing.

Many salespeople in the computer and technology sectors earn more compensation in the form of commissions than as salary. High-level managers, such as vice-presidents and CEOs, normally have a high salary and the potential for a large bonus. Their employee benefits are also relatively large, and they normally are awarded various perks as well.

other employees who are attempting to develop new products. Motorola trains its employees to apply new technology to develop new products.

Customer Service Skills

Employees who frequently deal with customers need to have customer service skills. Many employees in tourism industries such as airlines and hotels are trained to satisfy customers. The hotel chain Marriott International provides training on serving customers, with refresher sessions provided after the first and second months. The training is intended not only to ensure customer satisfaction but also to provide employees with an orientation that makes them more comfortable (and increases employee satisfaction). Walt Disney provides extensive training to its newly hired employees. Customer service skills are also necessary for employees hired by firms to sell products or deal with customer complaints.

Safety Skills

Firms educate employees about safety within the work environment. This includes training employees how to use machinery and equipment in factories owned by large manufacturing firms, such as Caterpillar and Goodyear Tire. United Parcel Service (UPS) implements training programs for its employees on handling hazardous materials. Training programs not only reassure employees but also reduce health-care and legal expenses that could be incurred as a result of work-related injuries.

Human Relations Skills

Some training seminars may be necessary for supervisors who lack skills in managing other employees. In general, this type of training helps supervisors recognize that their employees not only deserve to be treated properly but also will perform better if they are treated properly.

Firms commonly provide seminars on diversity to help employees of different races, genders, and religions become more sensitive to other views. Denny's offers employee training on diversity to prevent racial discrimination. Diversity training may allow for an environment in which people work together more effectively, thereby improving the firm's performance. It also may prevent friction between employees and thus can possibly prevent discrimination or harassment lawsuits filed against the firm.

Training seminars are also designed to improve relationships among employees across various divisions so that employees can work within teams. For example, Motorola and Xerox provide seminars for employees on teamwork. Anheuser-Busch organizes regular meetings between employees and executives.

Evaluation of Employee Performance

④ Explain how the performance of employees can be evaluated.

Employees often perceive performance evaluation as only a method for allocating raises. Yet, if supervisors properly conduct the evaluation, it can also provide feedback and direction to employees. An evaluation should indicate an employee's strengths and weaknesses and may influence an employee's chances of being promoted within the firm in the future.

Segmenting the Evaluation into Different Criteria

The overall performance of most employees is normally based on multiple criteria. Therefore, an evaluation can best be conducted by segmenting the evaluation into the

Recruitment Software and Online Recruiting

Recruitment software programs and online recruiting are recent innovations. Recruitment software programs eliminate the need for individuals to read and catalog every résumé received. Online recruiting is a low-cost method of accessing potential employees.

Human resource (HR) departments typically receive numerous résumés on a continual basis. In the past, HR employees had to sift through the résumés to find potential matches for open positions. Résumés that were not an appropriate match were thrown out after a specified amount of time. Recruitment software has reduced costs by creating a more efficient system. Résumés are either received electronically or scanned into the computer and keywords are used to sort them. HR departments or the hiring manager can use the software's searching capabilities to identify specific skill or experience requirements. The system also allows for the creation of a database of applicants. This technology allows HR professionals to spend more time conducting interviews and other important tasks rather than sorting, categorizing, and filing résumés.

Many large firms are using their websites to inform potential applicants about career opportunities and to post open positions. This is particularly useful when the positions are computer related. In the past, positions would be advertised in a newspaper or filled at college recruiting fairs. Online job postings allow more detailed listings at very little cost.

criteria that are relevant for each particular job position. For example, consider employees who have excellent technical skills for their jobs, but are not dependable. Since they rate high on one criterion and low on another, their overall performance might be evaluated as about average. An average rating for overall performance, however, does not specifically pinpoint the employees' favorable or unfavorable work habits.

Segmenting performance evaluation into different criteria can help supervisors pinpoint specific strengths and weaknesses. Evaluating each criterion separately provides more specific information to employees about how they may improve. In our example, the employees who receive a low rating on dependability can focus on improving that behavior. Furthermore, these employees can see from their evaluation that their supervisors recognized their strong technical skills. Without a detailed evaluation, employees may not recognize what tasks they do well (in the opinion of supervisors) and what specific weaknesses need to be improved.

Objective versus Subjective Criteria Some performance criteria are objective, such as parts produced per week, number of days absent, percentage of deadlines missed, and the proportion of defective parts caused by employee errors. Examples of direct measures of performance are provided for specific job positions in Exhibit 12.8 to illustrate how the examples vary by type of job. Other characteristics not shown in Exhibit 12.8 that are commonly assessed for some job positions include organization, communication, and decision-making skills.

Some criteria are less objective but still important. For example, the quality of work cannot always be measured by part defects, because many jobs are not focused on producing a single product. Therefore, quality of work may be subjectively assessed by a supervisor. Also, the willingness of an employee to help other employees is an important criterion that is subjective.

Using a Performance Evaluation Form

Supervisors are typically required to complete a performance evaluation form at the end of each year. An example of such a form is shown in Exhibit 12.9. When supervisors measure the performance of employees, they normally classify the employee in one of several categories such as the following: (1) outstanding, (2) above average, (3)

Exhibit 12.8

Examples of Direct Measures of Performance

Job Position	Direct Measures of Performance
Salesperson	Dollar volume of sales over a specific period Number of new customers Number of delinquent accounts collected Net sales per month in territory
Manager	Number of employee grievances Cost reductions Absenteeism Unit safety record Timeliness in completing appraisals Employee satisfaction with manager Division production Diversity of new hires
Administrative assistant	Number of letters prepared Word processing speed Number of errors in filing Number of tasks returned for reprocessing Number of calls screened

average, (4) below average, and (5) poor. The set of criteria can be more specific for particular jobs within the firm. For example, assembly-line workers may be rated by the total components produced and production quality. A company salesperson may be evaluated by the number of computers sold and the quality of service provided to customers. It is important that employees are informed of the criteria by which they will be rated. Otherwise, they may allocate too much time to tasks that supervisors view as not important.

Assigning Weights to the Criteria

An employee's ratings on all relevant criteria can be combined to determine an overall performance level of the employee. Some firms use weighting systems that weight and rate the criteria used to evaluate the employee. For example, bank tellers may be rated according to their speed in handling customer transactions, their quality (accuracy) in handling money transactions, and their ability to satisfy customers. The speed may be monitored by supervisors over time, while accuracy is measured by balancing the accounts at the end of each day, and customer satisfaction is measured from customer feedback over time.

The different criteria must also be weighted separately because some of the employee's assignments may be perceived as more important than others. Using our example, assume that the weights are determined as follows:

Speed in handling customer transactions	30%
Accuracy in handling customer transactions	50%
Satisfying customers	20% 100%

The sum of the weights of all criteria should be 100 percent. The weighting system should be communicated to employees when they begin a job position so that they understand what characteristics are most important within the evaluation.

To demonstrate how an overall performance measure is derived, assume that in our example the supervisor rated the bank teller as shown in Exhibit 12.10. The overall rating is the weighted average of 4.5; this rating is in between "above average" and "outstanding." Other bank tellers could also be periodically rated in this manner. At

Exhibit 12.9   Example of Performance Appraisal Form

Employee Name _____ Date _____

Position _____

Behavior Ratings: Check the one characteristic that best applies.

Quality of Work (refers to accuracy and margin of error):

_____ **1.** Makes errors frequently and repeatedly
_____ **2.** Often makes errors
_____ **3.** Is accurate; makes occasional errors
_____ **4.** Is accurate; rarely makes errors
_____ **5.** Is exacting and precise

Quantity of Work (refers to amount of production or results):

_____ **1.** Usually does not complete work load as assigned
_____ **2.** Often accomplishes part of a task
_____ **3.** Handles work load as assigned
_____ **4.** Turns out more work than requested
_____ **5.** Handles an unusually large volume of work

Timeliness (refers to completion of task, within time allowed):

_____ **1.** Does not complete duties on time
_____ **2.** Is often late in completing tasks
_____ **3.** Completes tasks on time
_____ **4.** Usually completes tasks in advance of deadlines
_____ **5.** Always completes all tasks in advance of time frames

Attendance and Punctuality (refers to adhering to work schedule assigned):

_____ **1.** Is usually tardy or absent
_____ **2.** Is often tardy or absent
_____ **3.** Normally is not tardy or absent
_____ **4.** Makes a point of being on the job and on time
_____ **5.** Is extremely conscientious about attendance

Responsibility (refers to completing assignments and projects):

_____ **1.** Usually does not assume responsibility for completing assignments
_____ **2.** Is at times reluctant to accept delegated responsibility
_____ **3.** Accepts and discharges delegated duties willingly
_____ **4.** Accepts additional responsibility
_____ **5.** Is a self-starter who seeks out more effective ways to achieve results or seeks additional responsibilities

Cooperation with Others (refers to working and communicating with supervisors and co-workers):

_____ **1.** Has difficulty working with others and often complains when given assignments
_____ **2.** Sometimes has difficulty working with others and often complains when given assignments
_____ **3.** Usually is agreeable and obliging; generally helps out when requested
_____ **4.** Works well with others; welcomes assignments and is quick to offer assistance
_____ **5.** Is an outstanding team worker; always assists others and continually encourages cooperation by setting an excellent example

Performance Summary (include strong areas and areas for future emphasis in improving performance or developing additional job skills):

Employee Comments or Concerns:

Signatures:
Human Resource Manager _____ Date _____
Employee _____ Date _____
Supervisor _____ Date _____

Exhibit 12.10

Developing an Overall Rating

Characteristic	Rating	Weight	Weighted Rating
Speed in handling customer transactions	4 (above average)	30%	4 × 30% = 1.2
Accuracy in handling customer transactions	5 (outstanding)	50%	5 × 50% = 2.5
Satisfying customers	4 (above average)	20%	4 × 20% = .80
			Overall rating = 4.5

the end of each year, the ratings may be used to determine the raise for each teller. The ratings may also be reviewed along with other characteristics (such as experience) when the employees are considered for a promotion.

This system of developing an overall rating is more appropriate when a few key criteria can be used to assess an employee throughout a period. When employees have numerous job assignments, however, accounting for all types of assignments within the performance evaluation is more difficult. Nevertheless, some of the assignments may be combined into a single characteristic, such as "customer service" or "ability to complete tasks on time."

Some supervisors may believe that a weighted system is too structured and does not account for some relevant characteristics, such as ability to get along with other employees. However, characteristics like these could be included within the weighting system.

Steps for Proper Performance Evaluation

Firms can follow specific steps to demonstrate fairness to employees and also satisfy legal guidelines in recognizing employee rights.

1 Supervisors should communicate job responsibilities to employees when they are hired. Supervisors should also communicate any changes in employee job responsibilities over time. This communication can be done orally, but it should be backed up with a letter to the employee. The letters are not as personal as oral communication, but they provide documentation in case a disagreement arises in the future about assignments and responsibilities. The letters may not only provide support to defend against employee lawsuits, but they also force supervisors to pinpoint the specific tasks for employees in a particular job position.

2 When supervisors notice that employees have deficiencies, they should inform the employees of those deficiencies. This communication may occur in the form of a standard periodic review. Supervisors may prefer to inform employees of deficiencies immediately, rather than wait for the review period. Employees should be given a chance to respond to the criticism. Supervisors may also allow a short period of time for employees to correct the deficiencies.

Supervisors should also communicate with employees who were evaluated favorably so that those employees recognize that their efforts are appreciated.

3 Supervisors should use consistency among employees when conducting performance evaluations. That is, two employees who have a similar deficiency should be treated equally in the evaluation process. Many supervisors would prefer communicating deficiencies only to those employees who are more willing to accept criticism. Yet, it is only fair to treat the deficiencies similarly among employees.

Action Due to Performance Evaluations

Some performance evaluations require supervisors to take action. Employees who receive a very favorable evaluation may deserve some type of recognition or even a promotion. If supervisors do not acknowledge such favorable performance, employees may either lose their enthusiasm and reduce their effort or search for a new job at a firm that will reward them for high performance. Supervisors should acknowledge high performance so that such performance continues in the future.

Employees who receive an unfavorable evaluation must also be given attention. Supervisors must determine the reasons for poor performance. Some reasons (such as a family illness) may have a temporary adverse impact on performance and can be corrected. Other reasons, such as a bad attitude, may not be temporary.

When supervisors give employees an unfavorable evaluation, they must decide whether to take any additional actions. If the employees were unaware of their own deficiencies, the unfavorable evaluation can pinpoint the deficiencies that employees must correct. In this case, the supervisor may simply need to monitor the employees closely and ensure that the deficiencies are corrected.

If the employees were already aware of their deficiencies before the evaluation period, however, they may be unable or unwilling to correct them. This situation is more serious, and the supervisor may need to take action. The action should be consistent with the firm's guidelines and may include reassigning the employees to new jobs, suspending them temporarily, or firing them. A supervisor's action toward a poorly performing worker can affect the attitudes of other employees. If no penalty is imposed on an employee for poor performance, other employees may rebel by reducing their productivity as well.

Firms must follow certain procedures to fire an employee. These procedures are intended to prevent firms from firing employees without reason. Specifically, supervisors should identify deficiencies in employees' evaluations and give them a chance to respond

Dealing with Lawsuits by Fired Employees

It is not uncommon for employees to sue the firm after being fired. Some lawsuits argue that the fired employee did not receive due process. Others argue that the firing occurred because of discrimination based on race, gender, age, religion, or national

---

CROSS-FUNCTIONAL TEAMWORK

How Job Responsibilities across Business Functions Can Complicate Performance Evaluations

 Firms have increasingly encouraged employees to perform a variety of business functions to achieve higher levels of job satisfaction and efficiency. Although this form of job enlargement has been successful, it can complicate the evaluation of an employee's performance. Consider an employee of a sporting goods store whose only responsibility is stringing tennis rackets. The performance of this employee is judged by the number of tennis rackets strung and the quality of the stringing (as measured by customer feedback).

The employee's responsibilities are then enlarged to include visiting country clubs and selling tennis rackets to them. Whereas the employee's initial job focused on assembly of tennis rackets, the enlarged responsibilities involve marketing the tennis rackets. Furthermore, other employees are also involved in stringing rackets and making sales calls to country clubs.

The performance evaluation of the employee has become more complicated for two reasons. First, more than one task now must be assessed. Second, other employees are also involved in completing these tasks, which makes it difficult to measure one employee's individual contribution. That is, a firm can easily assess the performance of a team of employees, but it cannot easily assess the performance of each employee within the team.

origin. Complaints of discrimination are first filed with the Equal Employment Opportunity Commission (EEOC), which is responsible for enforcing the discrimination laws. About 20 percent of complaints filed with the EEOC are judged as having a reasonable cause for the fired employee to take action, while 80 percent of the complaints are judged to have no reasonable cause. Even when the EEOC believes the complaint is not valid, however, the fired employee can still sue the firm.

The surge of employee lawsuits in recent years is partially attributed to the following factors. First, as of 1991, plaintiffs were allowed the right to trial by jury. The common perception is that juries are more sympathetic toward plaintiffs than judges are. Also, juries are perceived as more unpredictable, which concerns firms that are sued by employees. A second reason for the surge in lawsuits is the increase in potential damages that can be awarded to plaintiffs. As a result of the Civil Rights Act of 1991, plaintiffs can be awarded not only compensatory damages (such as back pay) but also punitive damages (to penalize the firm) and legal expenses. Therefore, plaintiffs and their attorneys can now receive much larger amounts of money.

Much media attention has been given to employee lawsuits. Firms recognize that such lawsuits can be very costly. However, firms should not ignore an employee's deficiencies out of fear that the employee will sue. Doing so will reduce the motivation of other employees if they recognize that one employee is receiving special treatment. The court system has generally sided with firms in cases in which supervisors followed proper procedures in firing employees.

In recent years, many employees who were dismissed have charged that the dismissal was based on discrimination because of race, religion, gender, or age. Many firms with numerous employees have been sued for this reason, even when their supervisors have followed all proper procedures. Although the laws that prohibit discrimination have good intentions, the court system has not effectively separated the frivolous cases from the valid ones. Consequently, legal expenses for many firms have risen substantially.

Some firms have attempted to settle lawsuits before trial to reduce their legal expenses and negative publicity. However, settling a lawsuit that has no merit may result in other frivolous lawsuits by employees.

Despite the increase in employee lawsuits, firms must still attempt to ensure that their employees are doing the jobs that they are paid to do. While firms cannot necessarily avoid employee lawsuits, they can attempt to establish training and performance evaluation guidelines that will reduce the chances of lawsuits.

Employee Evaluation of Supervisors

upward appraisals used to measure the managerial abilities of supervisors

Some firms allow employees to evaluate their supervisors. The evaluations can then be used to measure the managerial abilities of the supervisors. These so-called **upward appraisals** have been used by many firms, including AT&T and Dow Chemical. An upward evaluation is more effective if it is anonymous. Otherwise, workers may automatically offer a very favorable evaluation either in the hope that their supervisor will return the favor or to avoid retaliation. Evaluations of the supervisor may identify deficiencies, which can then be corrected so that the supervisor can more effectively manage employees in the future. The evaluation form for supervisors should allow each criterion to be evaluated separately so that they can recognize which characteristics need to be improved.

BUSINESS DILEMMA | **College Health Club**

Performance Evaluation at College Health Club

SUE KRAMER, PRESIDENT OF COLLEGE HEALTH CLUB (CHC), IS PLANNING TO establish a second health club about sixty miles away, next to a college campus. If she decides to establish the second club, she will need someone to manage it daily. This manager will need to purchase weight machines, offer aerobics classes, and attract memberships. A second health club could boost Sue's earnings substantially over time.

However, if the club is not managed properly, it could incur losses and could even put Sue out of business.

Sue believes this second club will be successful if it is able to attract local college students as members and ensure that they are sufficiently satisfied to continue their membership. The club's success would also be based on its ability to maintain expenses at a low level. Before hiring a manager, Sue decides to consider the key work characteristics of the manager that would make this second health club successful. These characteristics will serve as the criteria that Sue can use to periodically evaluate the performance of the manager.

Dilemma

Sue's specific goal is to develop a list of three key characteristics that will help determine the manager's performance. Offer your input on the key characteristics that Sue should assess to determine the manager's performance.

Solution

Sue recognizes that the key characteristics are those that will make the second club successful. Since memberships are critical to generate revenue, Sue decides that the manager's ability to sell new memberships is the most relevant characteristic to use in evaluating the manager. The number of new memberships per period will be used to measure this characteristic.

Second, Sue decides that the manager's ability to achieve customer (member) satisfaction is relevant because that will determine future membership renewals. Sue can conduct a survey of existing members to assess customer satisfaction.

Third, she decides that the manager's ability to purchase and repair the equipment at a low cost is relevant. Sue can monitor the expense of the club per period to assess this characteristic. Although other criteria may also be considered, these characteristics are most important for ensuring that the second club's revenue will be high and its costs low.

Additional Issues for Discussion

1 Should Sue ask any job applicants to take drug tests?

2 What type of criteria can Sue use to measure the performance of an aerobics instructor that she hired?

3 Why is it important for Sue to write a detailed job description for managing the new health club (assuming that she decides to open a new health club)?

4 What steps should Sue take if the new manager is not working out?

SUMMARY

 1 The main functions involved in human resource planning are

▶ forecasting human resource needs,
▶ job analysis, and
▶ recruiting.

 2 Compensation packages offered by firms can include salary, stock options, commissions, bonuses, profit sharing, employee benefits, and perquisites.

 3 After firms hire employees, they commonly provide training to enhance technical skills, decision-making skills, customer service skills, safety skills, and human relations skills.

 4 The performance of employees can be evaluated by segmenting the evaluation into different criteria, assigning an evaluation rating to each criterion, and weighting each criterion. The overall performance rating is the weighted average of all criteria that were assigned a rating.

Once supervisors evaluate employees, they should discuss the evaluations with the employees and identify any specific strengths, as well as any specific weaknesses that need to be improved.

KEY TERMS

bonus 325
boycott (chap. appendix) 344
commissions 324
compensation package 322
craft unions (chap. appendix) 341
employee benefits 325
employment test 319
external recruiting 318
human resource manager 317
human resource planning 315
industrial unions (chap. appendix) 341
injunction (chap. appendix) 345
internal recruiting 317

international unions (chap. appendix) 341
job analysis 316
job description 316
job specification 316
labor union (chap. appendix) 341
Landrum-Griffin Act (chap. appendix) 341
local unions (chap. appendix) 341
lockout (chap. appendix) 345
national unions (chap. appendix) 341
Norris-LaGuardia Act (chap. appendix) 341
perquisites 325

picketing (chap. appendix) 344
profit sharing 325
promotion 318
right-to-work (chap. appendix) 341
salary 324
stock options 324
strike (chap. appendix) 344
Taft-Hartley Act (chap. appendix) 341
upward appraisals 334
wages 324
Wagner Act (chap. appendix) 341
yellow-dog contract (chap. appendix) 341

REVIEW QUESTIONS

1 Describe the tasks involved in developing a human resource plan.
2 What is the purpose of a job analysis? What two documents can be developed from a job analysis?
3 Distinguish internal from external recruiting that is undertaken by a firm.
4 Discuss the steps involved in the recruiting process to screen job applicants.
5 Discuss the various types of compensation packages that could be offered to employees.
6 Discuss the types of skills that an employee could receive from a firm's training program.
7 How can segmenting the evaluation into different criteria help the supervisor pinpoint specific strengths and weaknesses of an employee's job performance?
8 Why have recent years seen a surge in employee lawsuits that claim discrimination? How should a firm deal with these lawsuits?
9 What is the purpose of an upward appraisal? How should such an evaluation be conducted?
10 How can management reduce the employee need for union representation? (See the chapter appendix.)

DISCUSSION QUESTIONS

1 Assume that you are a human resource manager and have been assigned to develop a compensation policy with supplemental pay benefits for your employees. Discuss. What do you think is the most desired benefit today for employees?
2 Assume that you are a manager in a company where a group of workers have petitioned for union representation. What factors would cause workers to do this? What can managers do to reduce the possibility that workers will vote in favor of union representation? (See the chapter appendix.)
3 Assume that you are a manager and have an employee with three years' work experience who refuses to be retrained. This employee further refuses to discuss his performance appraisal with you. What is your next step?
4 How could a firm use the Internet to attract new employees? How could it use the Internet to evaluate existing employees?
5 Assume that you have just opened a Jeep Cherokee dealership. Which of your employees would be paid salaries? Which would be paid hourly wages? Which would receive commissions and/or perquisites?

INVESTING IN THE STOCK OF A BUSINESS

Using the annual report of the firm in which you would like to invest, complete the following:

1 Does the firm periodically provide special training to its employees? If so, provide details.

2 Does the firm offer bonuses to its employees as an incentive? If so, are the bonuses tied to employee performance? Provide details.

3 Does the firm offer any other programs that are designed to achieve employee satisfaction, such as a flexible work schedule? If so, provide details.

4 Explain how the business uses technology to hire, train, and evaluate employees. For example, does it use the Internet to provide information about job openings or its compensation programs?

5 Go to **http://hoovers.com** and locate the NEWS SEARCH. Type in the name of the firm in the space provided, and review the recent news stories about the firm. Summarize any (at least one) recent news story about the firm that applies to one or more of the key concepts within this chapter.

CASE   FILLING JOB POSITIONS

George DeCaro, a human resource manager of Bobcat International, has just received a directive from the president of the company. The directive reads: "We have just completed our strategy for the year. The thrust of this strategy is to increase our market share by 22 percent over the next three years." It continues: "We must be ready for this challenge by increasing production, and the human resource department must staff the organization with thirty-seven new jobs."

George's task is to forecast job requirements each year for the next three years. George recognizes that both internal and external recruiting will have to be undertaken. The firm's philosophy is to promote from within whenever possible. This procedure promotes high morale and contributes to the overall success of the organization. Some jobs will have to be filled externally. He ponders the sources for recruiting potential job candidates for semiskilled plant jobs that pay an hourly rate.

George works well with the firm's president and wants to request a meeting to demonstrate how the human resource department will perform a vital role in helping the firm meet its objectives.

QUESTIONS

1 What is the human resource plan? Discuss its major tasks.

2 What is job analysis? How should it be used in this case?

3 Discuss George's sources for recruiting potential employees for the plant jobs.

4 What should be on George's agenda for the meeting with the company's president?

VIDEO CASE   RECRUITING AND TRAINING AT VALASSIS COMMUNICATIONS

Valassis Communications, Inc., creates promotional inserts for newspapers. It attributes much of its success to its employees. Its human resource department spends much time screening and interviewing applicants for jobs. The department also tests applicants in various ways to determine whether they would fit within the firm's environment. Applicants who can be assigned goals and are motivated to meet goals are more likely to be satisfied working at Valassis. Once hired, employees who perform well are rewarded well so that Valassis can retain the best employees.

QUESTIONS

1 Valassis has a close relationship with colleges. How can this relationship help its recruiting?

2 Valassis spends much time and money on its interviews. Why?

3 Valassis mentions employee retention as one of its key tasks. How does this relate to recruiting?

INTERNET APPLICATIONS

http://www.filemaker.com

What are some of the job opportunities available at Filemaker, Inc.? How do you think the company's website helps Filemaker in the human resource planning process?

What benefits does Filemaker offer its employees? What is Filemaker's corporate culture, and how do you think this culture helps the company develop the skills of its employees?

THE Coca-Cola COMPANY ANNUAL REPORT PROJECT

 Questions for the current year's annual report are available on the text website at **http://madura_intro_bus.swcollege.com**.

The following questions apply concepts learned in this chapter to The Coca-Cola Company. Go to The Coca-Cola Company website (**http://www.cocacola.com**) and find the index for the 1999 annual report.

QUESTIONS

1 Click on "Six Beliefs." What are the six beliefs that The Coca-Cola Company's investment strategy focuses on? What kind of corporate culture do these beliefs imply the company is trying to maintain and refine?

2 Click on "Note 13: Pension and Other Postretirement Benefits." Does The Coca-Cola Company restrict its employee pension plans to its U.S. employees? What other benefits do employees receive?

3 Study the "Selected Market Results" and the "Operations Review" sections. What challenges do you think are unique to multinational firms such as The Coca-Cola Company with respect to hiring, training, and evaluating employees?

4 Click on "Operations Review" and study "The Minute Maid Company" section. The Coca-Cola Company also produces Minute Maid. Why would consumers, including children and international customers, drink Minute Maid products?

5 Go to **http://hoovers.com** and locate the NEWS SEARCH. Type in The Coca-Cola Company in the space provided, and review the recent news stories about the firm. Summarize any (at least one) recent news story about The Coca-Cola Company that applies one or more of the key concepts within this chapter of the text.

IN-TEXT STUDY GUIDE

Answers are in an appendix at the back of the book.

TRUE OR FALSE

1 Job analysis represents the forecasting of a firm's employee needs.

2 Federal laws make it illegal to discriminate on the basis of factors not related to potential job performance.

3 Employee benefits such as health insurance and dental insurance are taxed.

4 Firms should offer the same compensation package to their workers in foreign countries that they offer to employees in their home country.

5 The overall performance evaluation of most employees is based on multiple criteria.

6 One task of human resource planning is recruiting.

7 A 1999 survey by the Society of Human Resource Management found that most human resource managers believed that women and minorities would have fewer opportunities in the future than they have now.

8 Employees perceive performance evaluation as a method for allocating wage increases.

9 Firms tend to avoid hiring new full-time workers to meet temporary needs for higher production levels.

10 A job specification states the credentials necessary to qualify for the position.

MULTIPLE CHOICE

11 A performance evaluation:
a) should avoid subjective criteria since they are impossible to measure with any accuracy.
b) is only useful as a means of determining whether employees qualify for pay raises.
c) is typically based on multiple criteria, some of which are objective while others are subjective.
d) is only necessary for workers who are likely candidates for higher-level positions.
e) should be given only to workers who are experiencing job-related problems.

12 The instrument that specifies credentials necessary to qualify for the job position is a:
a) job specification.
b) job description.
c) job analysis.
d) job evaluation.
e) performance evaluation.

13 A major responsibility of a human resource manager is to:
a) help each specific department recruit candidates for its open positions.
b) conduct the performance evaluations for all employees.
c) establish the information system and local area network used by the firm's employees.
d) help select the members of top management who will serve on the firm's board of directors.
e) prevent the formation of labor unions.

14 When firms allow employees to evaluate their supervisors, this process is known as a(n):
a) management audit.   d) peer review.
b) upward appraisal.   e) executive evaluation.
c) forward appraisal.

15 A company gives employees the right to purchase its stock at a specified price when it provides them with:
 a) presumptive rights.
 b) an indenture agreement.
 c) stock options.
 d) a stock preference.
 e) a closed-end agreement.

16 When employees evaluate their supervisors, the results are likely to be more meaningful if the appraisal is done:
 a) verbally, with nothing put in writing.
 b) without the supervisor's knowledge.
 c) no more than once every two years.
 d) anonymously.
 e) only by employees who have known the supervisor for more than two years.

17 A(n) _____ is an assignment to a higher-level job with more responsibility and greater pay.
 a) transfer   d) upward appraisal
 b) lateral assignment e) promotion
 c) perquisite

18 The tasks and responsibilities of a job position are disclosed in a(n):
 a) job specification.   d) organization chart.
 b) indenture agreement. e) staffing report.
 c) job description.

19 _____ are additional privileges, such as paid vacation time and health and dental insurance, given to most or all employees.
 a) Employee benefits
 b) Perquisites
 c) Commissions
 d) Implicit compensations
 e) Kickbacks

20 A firm's human resource manager can obtain detailed information about the applicant's past work experience through a(n):
 a) employment test.   d) orientation program.
 b) physical exam.   e) job analysis.
 c) interview.

21 One of the final steps in the screening process is often the requirement that candidates:
 a) provide a list of references.
 b) fill out an application.
 c) participate in a job analysis.
 d) sign the job description.
 e) take a physical examination.

22 The process used to determine the tasks and the necessary credentials for a particular position is referred to as:
 a) job analysis.
 b) job screening.
 c) human resource planning.

 d) human resource forecasting.
 e) recruiting.

23 Human resource planning includes all of the following tasks except:
 a) designing the appropriate compensation package.
 b) performing job analysis.
 c) forecasting employment needs.
 d) recruiting.

24 When a firm attempts to fill job openings with persons it already employs, it is engaging in:
 a) intrapreneurship.   d) precruiting.
 b) internal recruiting. e) focused recruiting.
 c) entrenchment.

25 Lawsuits against firms by fired employees:
 a) have become much less common in recent years.
 b) allow the fired employees to collect compensatory damages, but not punitive damages.
 c) are decided by a judge rather than a jury.
 d) usually should be settled out of court as soon as possible to avoid negative publicity.
 e) are usually settled in favor of the firm if supervisors followed proper procedures when firing the employees.

26 Efforts to fill open positions with applicants who do not currently work for the firm are referred to as:
 a) up-sizing.   d) job enlargement.
 b) decentralized hiring. e) open staffing.
 c) external recruitment.

27 An extra one-time payment at the end of a period in which performance was measured is a:
 a) salary.   d) piece rate.
 b) wage.   e) bonus.
 c) stock option.

28 Additional privileges given to high-level employees, such as a company car or membership in an exclusive club, are known as:
 a) professional privileges.
 b) commissions.
 c) executive options.
 d) perquisites.
 e) golden parachutes.

29 _____ normally represent compensation for achieving specific sales objectives and often are part of the compensation received by people working in sales positions.
 a) Pensions   d) Stock options
 b) Commissions   e) Dividends
 c) Perquisites

30 A _____ states the credentials necessary to qualify for a job.
 a) job specification
 b) job description
 c) recruiting statement

d) screening form

e) nondiscrimination disclosure form

31 Employees who are directly involved in the production process (such as assembly-line workers) tend to receive most of their compensation in the form of a:

a) bonus.

b) commission.

c) salary.

d) stock option.

e) perquisite.

32 The following are objective criteria in performance evaluation except for:

a) parts produced per week.

b) number of days absent.

c) percentage of deadlines missed.

d) defective parts produced by employee errors.

e) willingness of an employee to help other employees.

33 If firms wish to avoid hiring during a temporary increase in production, they can offer _____ to existing workers.

a) overtime

b) vacations

c) training programs

d) affirmative action

e) orientation programs

34 The use of stock options as a means of compensation:

a) legally can be provided only to top executives and members of the board of directors.

b) is declining in popularity since options reduce the firm's profits.

c) is opposed by labor unions, since options are available only to nonunion employees.

d) has become increasingly popular as firms attempt to motivate employees by allowing them to share in the firm's profits.

e) has allowed workers in many firms to control who serves on the board of directors of their firm.

35 A step in the recruiting process that involves screening applicants is the:

a) training procedure.

b) orientation procedure.

c) upward appraisal.

d) interview.

e) probation period.

APPENDIX

Labor Unions

labor union an association established to represent the views, needs, and concerns of labor

A **labor union** is established to represent the views, needs, and concerns of labor. A union can attempt to recognize the needs of its workers and then negotiate with the firm's management to satisfy those needs. The needs may include job security, safer working conditions, and higher salaries. The union may be able to negotiate for the workers better than they can themselves, because the workers do not have the time or the expertise for negotiating with management. Furthermore, management would not have the time to deal with each worker's needs separately. The union serves as the representative for all workers.

Background on Unions

craft unions unions organized according to a specific craft (or trade), such as plumbing

industrial unions unions organized for a specific industry

local unions unions composed of members in a specified local area

national unions unions composed of members throughout the country

international unions unions that have members in several countries

Unions can be classified as either craft or industrial. **Craft unions** are organized according to a specific craft (or trade), such as plumbing. **Industrial unions** are organized for a specific industry. Unions can also be classified as either local or national. **Local unions** are composed of members in a specified local area. **National unions** are composed of members throughout the country. Some local unions are part of a national union. **International unions** have members in several countries.

History of Union Activities

The popularity of unions has been affected by various laws, summarized next.

Norris-LaGuardia Act restricted the use of injunctions against unions and allowed unions to publicize a labor dispute

yellow-dog contract a contract requiring employees to refrain from joining a union as a condition of employment

The Norris-LaGuardia Act Before 1932, the courts commonly accommodated employer requests to issue injunctions against unions. In 1932, Congress passed the **Norris-LaGuardia Act,** which restricted the use of injunctions against unions and allowed unions to publicize a labor dispute. It also prohibited employers from forcing workers to sign a **yellow-dog contract,** which was a contract requiring employees to refrain from joining a union as a condition of employment.

Wagner Act prohibited firms from interfering with workers' efforts to organize or join unions

The Wagner Act Even with the Norris-LaGuardia Act, firms were able to discourage employees from joining or organizing unions. The **Wagner Act** (also referred to as the National Labor Relations Act) prohibited firms from interfering with workers' efforts to organize or join unions. Employers could not discriminate against employees who participated in union activities. In addition, the act required employers to negotiate with the union representing employees.

Taft-Hartley Act an amendment to the Wagner Act that prohibited unions from pressuring employees to join

right-to-work allows states to prohibit union shops

The Taft-Hartley Act Although the Wagner Act reduced employer discrimination against union participants, it was unable to reduce strikes. The **Taft-Hartley Act,** an amendment to the Wagner Act, prohibited unions from pressuring employees to join. An exception is the union shop, where new employees are required to join the union. The **right-to-work** section of this act allows states to prohibit union shops (several states have used this power).

Landrum-Griffin Act required labor unions to specify in their bylaws the membership eligibility requirements, dues, and collective bargaining procedures

The Landrum-Griffin Act In 1959, Congress passed the **Landrum-Griffin Act** (originally called the Labor-Management Reporting and Disclosure Act of 1959). This act required labor unions to specify in their bylaws the membership eligibility requirements, dues, and collective bargaining procedures.

Trends in Union Popularity

Union membership declined slightly in the early 1930s, as firms discouraged workers from participating in labor activities. After the Wagner Act was passed in 1935, union membership increased rapidly. By 1945, more than one-fourth of all workers were union members. However, union membership consistently declined during the 1980s and 1990s. By 2000, less than 12 percent of all workers were union members. One of the reasons for the decline was the inability of some unionized firms to compete with nonunion firms whose expenses were lower.

BUSINESS ONLINE

Labor Union Homepages

http://www.uaw.org

MOST LABOR UNIONS UTILIZE THE INTERNET TO PROVIDE THEIR MEMBERS with information on recent actions taken by the union, as shown here for the United Auto Workers. The website also provides employees with information about governmental and corporate developments affecting them. Since unions are formed to represent workers, this information is very useful to employees and to employers attempting to assess employee satisfaction.

Negotiations between Unions and Management

Contracts between unions and management commonly last for two to three years. An attempt is made to agree to a new contract before the existing contract expires. The union obtains feedback from its members on what working provisions need to be improved. The union also obtains data on existing wages and employee benefits provided for jobs similar to those of members. Management assesses existing conditions and determines the types of provisions it may be willing to make.

Before the actual negotiations begin, the union may offer a proposed revision of the existing contract. This proposal often includes very high demands, which management will surely refuse. Management may also offer a proposed revision of the existing contract that the union will surely refuse. Normally, the original gap between the two sides is very large. This establishes the foundation for negotiations.

When the union and management meet to negotiate a new contract, the more critical issues to be discussed include the following:

▶ Salaries
▶ Job security
▶ Management rights
▶ Grievance procedures

Salaries

A general concern of unions is to improve or at least maintain their members' standard of living. Unions are credited for negotiating high wages for their members. Unionized grocery store employees commonly receive at least double the salaries of nonunionized employees in the same job positions. Airline pilot captains of unionized airlines, such as American and Delta, earn more than $100,000 per year, while pilot captains of nonunionized airlines commonly earn less than $50,000 per year.

Unions attempt to negotiate for salary increases that will at least match expected increases in the cost of living. They also monitor salaries of workers at other firms to determine the salary increases that they will request. For example, the United Auto Workers (UAW) commonly uses its content contract with one car manufacturer to negotiate its new contract with another car manufacturer.

If the firm has experienced high profits in recent years, a union may use this as reason to negotiate for large wage increases. Conversely, firms that recently experienced losses will argue that they cannot afford to make pay increases. When pilots at Continental Airlines did not receive a salary increase over several years, poor relations developed between the pilots and management at Continental.

Job Security

Job security is a key issue from the perspective of workers. They want to be assured of a job until retirement. Management may not be willing to guarantee job security but may at least specify the conditions under which workers will be laid off. Workers with less seniority are more likely to be laid off.

Although unions are unable to force management to guarantee lifetime jobs, they are somewhat successful at obtaining supplemental unemployment benefits for workers. Firms that offer these benefits contribute an amount for each hour worked into a fund. The fund is used to compensate workers who are laid off. This compensation is a supplement to the normal unemployment compensation workers receive.

Unions may also attempt to prevent management from replacing workers with machines. Management may agree to such demands if the unions reduce some of their other demands. Unions emphasize this issue in industries such as automobile manufacturing, where some tasks are highly repetitive, and therefore workers are more likely to be replaced by machines.

For some workers, job security may be more important than higher wages. Therefore, firms that are willing to provide job security may not have to provide large increases in wages.

Management Rights

Management expects to have various rights as to how it manages its workers. For example, the union-management contract may state a specified number of work hours. Management may also retain the rights to make hiring, promotional, and transferring decisions without influence by unions.

Grievance Procedures

A grievance is a complaint made by an employee or the union. Contracts between a union and management specify procedures for resolving a grievance. The first step normally calls for a meeting between the employee, his or her supervisor, and a union representative. If this meeting does not resolve the grievance, the union normally meets with high-level managers.

Conflicts between Unions and Management

picketing walking around near the employer's building with signs complaining of poor working conditions

boycott refusing to purchase products and services

strike discontinuation of employee services

Unions use various methods to bargain for better working conditions or higher compensation. Employees may attempt to pressure management by **picketing,** or walking around near the employer's building with signs complaining of poor working conditions. Employees can also **boycott** the products and services offered by refusing to purchase them.

Labor Strikes

A more dramatic method of bargaining is a **strike,** which is discontinuation of employee services. Two recent well-publicized strikes were those by employees at UPS and at General Motors. The goal of the UPS strike was to achieve better wages. The objective of the General Motors strike was to ensure that some of GM's plants would not be closed.

The impact of a strike on a firm depends on the firm's ability to carry on operations during the strike. For example, if all machinists of a manufacturing firm strike, the firm's production will be severely reduced unless its other workers can substitute. Most firms carry an inventory of finished products that may be used to accommodate orders during the strike. However, even a large inventory will not be sufficient if the strike lasts long enough.

The publicity of a strike can reduce a firm's perceived credibility. Even though a strike is only temporary, it can create permanent damage. Some firms have long-term arrangements with other companies to provide a specified volume of supplies periodically. If these companies fear that their orders will not be satisfied because of a strike, they will search for a firm that is less likely to experience a strike.

To illustrate how the dissatisfaction of employees can affect a firm's value, consider the case of Caterpillar. About fourteen thousand of Caterpillar's workers went on strike on June 21, 1994. Exhibit 12A.1 shows the stock price of Caterpillar around the time of the strike. Notice how the stock price declined by more than $4 per share in response to the strike. The strike lasted more than seventeen months. Caterpillar replaced many of the strikers with temporary workers and experienced record earnings over the strike period. By the end of the strike, about one-third of the strikers returned to work without any compromise by Caterpillar.

Exhibit 12.A1

Example of How a Strike Can Affect a Firm's Value

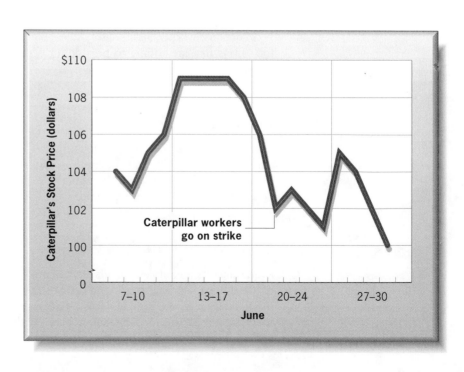

Strikes can damage a firm's reputation if production is halted for a long period of time. A union's bargaining power is greater when a firm cannot easily replace employees who go on strike.

Management Response to Strikes

injunction a court order to prevent a union from a particular activity such as picketing

lockout prevents employees from working until an agreement between management and labor is reached

Management may respond to union pressure by obtaining an **injunction,** which is a court order to prevent the union from a particular activity such as picketing. Alternatively, it could use a **lockout,** which prevents employees from working until an agreement between management and labor is reached.

Another common response by management is to show how large benefits to workers will possibly result in the firm's failure, which would effectively terminate all jobs. The management of Northwest Airlines and US Air (now US Airways) used this approach in the mid-1990s to prevent excessive demands by the union. US Air also offered its pilots partial ownership of the firm in place of salary increases.

The amount of bargaining power a union has is partially dependent on whether the firm can easily replace employees who go on strike. For example, an airline cannot easily replace pilots in a short period of time because of the extensive training needed. Other workers with specialized mechanical skills also have some bargaining power. When thirty-three thousand machinists of Boeing (a producer of aircraft) went on strike in 1995, they forced Boeing to provide a larger salary increase as an incentive to end the strike. However, a strike by workers at Bridgestone/Firestone (a producer of tires) was not as successful, as the firm hired replacement workers.

Management's Criticism of Unions

Unions are criticized by management for several reasons, some of which are discussed here.

Higher Prices or Lower Profits If unions achieve high wages for employees, firms may pass the increase on to consumers in the form of higher prices. If firms do not pass the increase on, their profits may be reduced and the shareholders of the firm will be adversely affected. In essence, the disadvantages to the consumers or shareholders offset the benefits to employees.

A related criticism is that high wages resulting from the union can reduce the firm's ability to compete internationally. This was a major criticism during the 1980s, when many foreign competitors increased their market share in the United States.

Adverse Impact on Economic Conditions A decision to strike by some unions can severely damage a given industry. Unions have the power to close large manufacturing plants, shut down an airline's operations, or even halt garbage collection. Some shutdowns can have a severe impact on the local area.

Production Inefficiency Some unions have negotiated for a minimum number of workers to perform a specific task. In some cases, the number of workers has exceeded the number actually needed. A related criticism is that workers are sometimes perceived to be protected from being fired if they are in a union. Management may be unwilling to fire an unproductive person if it believes the union will file a grievance. If it retains unproductive workers, its efficiency is reduced, and its cost of production increases.

How Firms Reduce Employees' Desire for a Union

The management of some firms has consistently maintained good relations with labor. Consequently, labor has not attempted to organize a union. The following guidelines described are some of the more common methods used to maintain good relations with employees:

1 Management should promote employees from within so that employees are satisfied with their career paths.

2 Management should attempt to avoid layoffs so that employees do not feel threatened whenever business slows down. This may be achieved by reassigning job positions to some employees who are no longer needed in their original positions.

3 Management should allow employees responsibility and input into some decisions. Labor contracts between labor and management may require labor-management committees to be created at each plant to develop methods for improving efficiency. This is a classic example of considering input from employees.

4 Management should maintain reasonable working conditions to demonstrate fairness to employees.

5 Management should offer reasonable and competitive wages so that employees feel properly rewarded and are not continually quitting to take other jobs.

The points just listed represent the key working provisions for which unions negotiate. If the firm adequately maintains these provisions, workers may not need to organize a union.

Summary of Part IV

The performance of a firm is highly dependent on the performance of its employees. Firms commonly attempt to improve employee performance by increasing job satisfaction. The following methods can be used to improve job satisfaction. First, firms can provide compensation that is linked with employee performance. This strategy rewards employees directly for their efforts. Second, firms may provide job security to their employees, which may reduce work-related stress. Third, firms may allow their employees to have a flexible work schedule, which allows employees to have more input on their daily or weekly work schedule. Fourth, firms may implement more employee involvement programs to give employees more input on most business decisions.

Firms can improve their performance by using proper methods of hiring, training, and evaluating their employees. Proper hiring methods ensure that employees have the right background for the types of jobs that may be assigned. Proper training enables employees to apply their skills to perform specific tasks. Proper evaluation methods ensure that employees are rewarded when they perform well and that they are informed of any deficiencies so that they can correct them in the future.

PART IV

Developing the Human Resource Plan for Campus.com

Motivating Employees (related to Chapter 11)

In your business plan for Campus.com, describe how you can offer favorable working conditions (do not include compensation here) that will motivate the employees whom you may need to hire over time. That is, explain how you will ensure that employees help you achieve high performance and are willing to continue working at this business for several years. Identify any disadvantages of these methods that may limit their effectiveness.

Evaluating Employees (related to Chapter 12)

In your business plan for Campus.com, describe how you will assess the performance of your employees. How can you compensate the employees in a manner that will ensure that they will try to maximize the performance of the firm?

Communication and Teamwork

You (or your team) may be asked by your instructor to hand in and/or present the part of your business plan that relates to this part of the text.

PART IV

Applications for Dell Computer

Refer to Dell Computer's Formula for Success where necessary.

1 Employee management at Dell
   a. How do you think the Hawthorne studies apply to Dell Computer?
   b. Explain how a merit system could be implemented at Dell.
   c. How could Dell use the Internet and e-mail to motivate its employees?

2 Dell's human resource management
   a. How do you think Dell Computer could use the Internet to attract new employees?
   b. Which of the employee skills discussed in the text do you think are most important for a service employee at Dell? Why?
   c. Do you think the evaluation of a Dell service representative would be primarily based on objective or subjective criteria?

PART IV

The Stock Market Game

Go to **http://www.fantasystockmarket.com**. Enter your name (e-mail address) and password as requested and check your portfolio balance, which is updated continuously by the Fantasy website.

Check Your Stock Portfolio Performance

1 What is the value of your stock portfolio today?

2 What is your return on your investment? (This return is shown on your balance.)

3 How did your return compare to those of other students? (This comparison tells you whether your stock portfolio's performance is relatively high or low.)

Keep in mind that you can change your portfolio at any time during the school term.

Explaining Your Stock Performance

Stock prices are frequently influenced by changes in the firm's management policies toward its employees, including new policies for awarding bonuses or other compensation. A stock's price may increase if such management policies are changed and investors expect the changes to improve the firm's performance. A stock's price can also decrease if the policy changes are expected to reduce the firm's performance. Review the latest news about some of your stocks on the Fantasy website by clicking on News and typing the ticker symbol of your stock.

1 Identify one of your stocks whose price was affected (since you purchased it) as a result of the firm's motivation and personnel policy changes (the main topic in this part of the text).

2 Identify the specific change in managerial policies related to motivation or personnel decisions that caused the stock price to change.

3 Did the stock price increase or decrease in response to the announcement of new policies related to employee motivation or personnel?

| PART IV |

Running Your Own Business

1 How can you empower your employees so that they have an incentive to perform well?

2 Describe how you might encourage your employees to use teamwork.

3 Describe how each of the theories discussed in this part of the text would apply to your employees or yourself.

4 Develop a job description for the employees that you would need to hire for your business. Include the required education and skills within the job description.

5 Describe the training (if any) that you would have to provide to any employees you hire for your business.

6 Describe how you would compensate your employees. Would you offer bonuses as an incentive? If so, describe how you would determine the bonus.

7 Describe the criteria you would use to evaluate the performance of your employees.

8 Describe how you could use the Internet to attract new employees or to motivate existing employees.

Marketing

Marketing can be broadly defined as the actions of firms to plan and execute the design, pricing, distribution, and promotion of products. A firm's marketing mix is the combination of product, pricing, distribution, and promotion strategies used to sell products. Examples of marketing decisions include the product decision by Kodak to design a miniature video camera, the pricing decision by Ford to price its new model Mustang, the distribution decision by Nike on how to distribute its running shoes across various outlets around the world, and the promotion decision by United Airlines to use television advertising when promoting its airline services.

To recognize how all four strategies are used by a single firm, consider a computer firm that identifies a software package that consumers need. The firm devel-

ops the software (product strategy), sets a price for the software (pricing strategy), decides to sell the software through specific computer stores (distribution strategy), and decides to advertise the software in magazines (promotion strategy). Chapter 13 focuses on product and pricing strategies, Chapter 14 focuses on distribution strategies, and Chapter 15 focuses on promotion strategies.

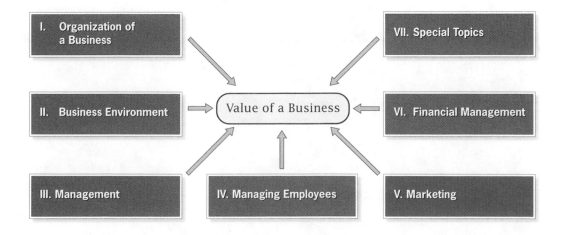

I. Organization of a Business

VII. Special Topics

II. Business Environment

Value of a Business

VI. Financial Management

III. Management

IV. Managing Employees

V. Marketing

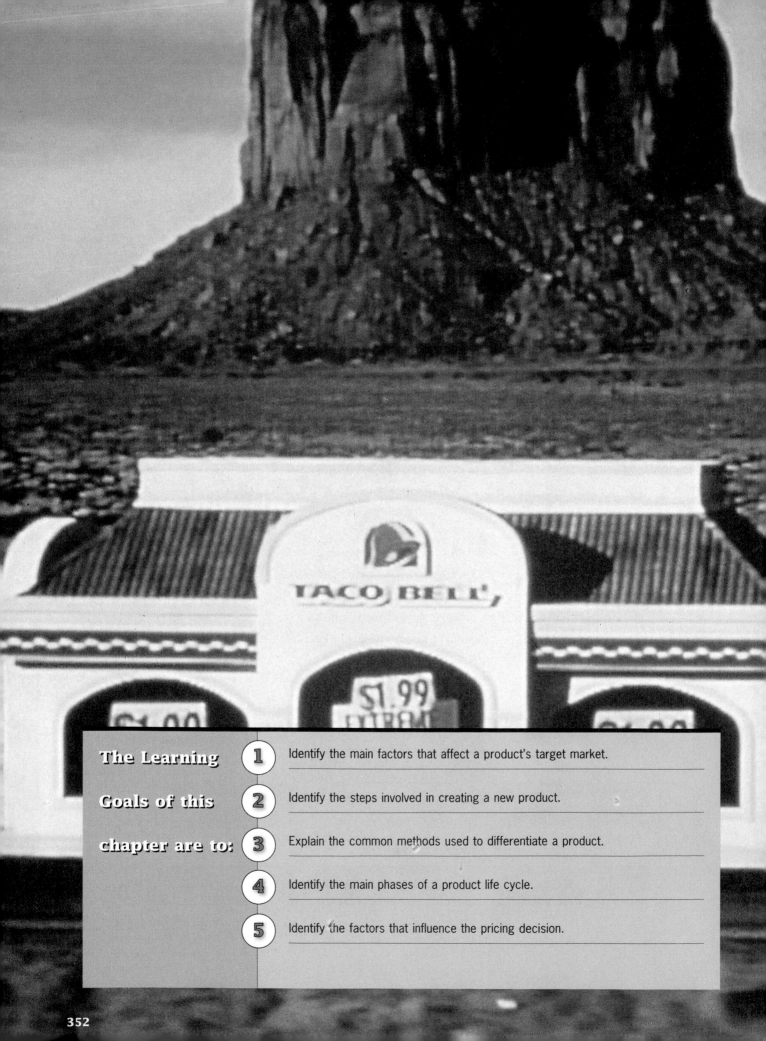

The Learning Goals of this chapter are to:

1. Identify the main factors that affect a product's target market.

2. Identify the steps involved in creating a new product.

3. Explain the common methods used to differentiate a product.

4. Identify the main phases of a product life cycle.

5. Identify the factors that influence the pricing decision.

CHAPTER 13

Product and Pricing Strategies

Product strategies dictate the means by which firms generate revenue, while pricing strategies influence the demand for the products produced. A firm's product and pricing strategies affect its value as follows:

Consider the case of Taco Bell, which sells Mexican fast-food products and beverages. What factors does Taco Bell consider when deciding whether to sell other

types of fast-food items? In what ways can Taco Bell differentiate its food and beverage products from those of its competitors? What factors should Taco Bell

consider when pricing its products? This chapter provides a background on product and pricing strategies that can be used to address these questions.

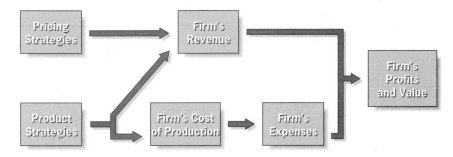

Background on Products

product physical goods as well as services that can satisfy consumer needs

convenience products products that are widely available to consumers, are purchased frequently, and are easily accessible

shopping products products that are not purchased frequently

specialty products products that specific consumers consider to be special and therefore make a special effort to purchase

The term **product** can be broadly defined to include physical goods as well as services that can satisfy consumer needs. Firms must continually improve existing products and develop new products to satisfy customers over time. In this way, firms generate high sales growth, which normally increases their value.

Most products produced to serve consumers can be classified as (1) convenience products, (2) shopping products, or (3) specialty products. **Convenience products** are widely available to consumers, are purchased frequently, and are easily accessible. Milk, newspapers, soda, and chewing gum are typical examples of convenience products.

Shopping products differ from convenience products in that they are not purchased frequently. When consumers are ready to purchase shopping goods, they first shop around and compare quality and prices of competing products. Furniture and appliances are examples of shopping products.

Specialty products are products that specific consumers consider to be special and therefore make a special effort to purchase. A Rolex watch and a Jaguar automobile are examples of specialty products. When evaluating specialty products, consumers base their purchasing decision primarily on personal preference, not on comparative pricing.

Product Line

A **product line** is a set of related products or services offered by a single firm. For example, Coke, Diet Coke, Caffeine-Free Diet Coke, and Sprite are all part of a single product line at The Coca-Cola Company. Pepsi, Diet Pepsi, Mountain Dew, and All-Sport are all part of a single product line at PepsiCo.

A product line tends to expand over time as a firm recognizes other consumer needs. The Coca-Cola Company recognizes that consumers differ with respect to their desire for a specific taste, caffeine versus no caffeine, and diet versus regular. It has expanded its product line of soft drinks to satisfy various needs. Compaq Computer has added portable computers to its product line over time, while Taco Bell has added various low-fat food items to its menus.

Product Mix

The assortment of products offered by a firm is referred to as the **product mix.** Most firms tend to expand their product mix over time as they identify other consumer needs or preferences. Quaker State originally focused on motor oil but has added windshield washer fluid, brake fluid, and many other automobile products to its product mix. Before firms add more products to their product mix, they should determine whether a demand for new products exists and whether they are capable of efficiently producing those products. A firm may even decide to discontinue one of the products in its product mix.

The Coca-Cola Company's product line includes Coke, Diet Coke, and Sprite. PepsiCo's Product line includes Pepsi, Diet Pepsi, and Mountain Dew.

Examples of a Product Mix   The product mix of Liz Claiborne, Inc., includes clothing for women, jewelry, fashion accessories, and clothing for men. IBM's product mix includes software, hardware, and global services, as shown in Exhibit 13.1. The hardware segment generates more sales than either of the other segments, but its proportion of total sales is lower than in previous years. Meanwhile, the proportion of total sales generated by IBM's global services segment (which includes information technology) has increased substantially. This change in the relative proportions reflects IBM's shift away from its hardware product line and into other product lines related to information technology.

Service firms also have a product mix. For example, KPMG is a consulting firm whose services can be segmented into accounting, information systems and technology, and other consulting.

Exhibit 13.1

Product Mix of IBM

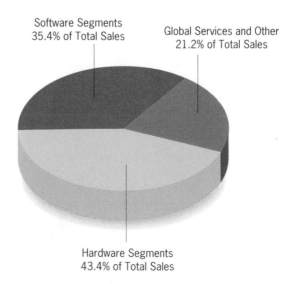

Software Segments
35.4% of Total Sales

Global Services and Other
21.2% of Total Sales

Hardware Segments
43.4% of Total Sales

Actor Tim Allen displays his product mix of "Tim Allen Signature Tools."

Diversifying the Product Mix When their primary product is subject to wide swings in demand, firms tend to diversify their product mix so that they will not be completely dependent on one market. By diversifying, they are not as reliant on a single product whose performance is uncertain. Firms with flexible production facilities that allow for the production of additional goods are more capable of diversifying their product mix.

A common diversification strategy is for a firm to diversify products within its existing production capabilities. For example, hospital supply companies offer a wide variety of supplies that can be sold to each hospital. The Walt Disney Company, which had focused on producing films for children, now offers films for adults. Clothing manufacturers such as Donna Karan offer several types of clothes that can be sold to each retail outlet. A product mix that contains several related products can allow for more efficient use of salespeople.

To understand how firms can benefit from expanding their product mix, consider the case of Amazon.com, which initially focused on filling book orders requested over the Internet. First, it began to offer CDs as well, recognizing that if customers are willing to order books online, they may also order other products. Second, it had already proved that it could provide reliable service, so customers trusted that the additional services would be reliable as well. Third, it could use its existing technology to fill CD orders, which increased efficiency.

In 1999, Amazon.com acquired a stake in Drugstore.com because it believed that it could fill drug orders requested over the Internet. The growth of Amazon.com demonstrates how a firm can expand by using the resources that initially made it successful to offer additional products.

Identifying a Target Market

Identify the main factors that affect a product's target market.

The consumers who purchase a particular product may have specific traits in common, which cause their needs to be similar. Firms attempt to identify these traits so that they can target their marketing toward people with those traits. Marketing efforts

target market a group of individuals or organizations with similar traits who may purchase a particular product

consumer markets markets for various consumer products and services (such as cameras, clothes, and household items)

industrial markets markets for industrial products that are purchased by firms (such as plastic and steel)

are usually targeted toward a particular **target market,** which is a group of individuals or organizations with similar traits who may purchase a particular product.

Target markets can be broadly classified as consumer markets or industrial markets. **Consumer markets** exist for various consumer products and services (such as cameras, clothes, and household items), while **industrial markets** exist for industrial products that are purchased by firms (such as plastic and steel). Some products (such as tires) can serve consumer markets or industrial markets (such as car manufacturers). Classifying markets as consumer or industrial provides only a broad description of the types of customers who purchase products, however. Consequently, firms attempt to describe their target markets more narrowly.

Common traits used to describe a target market are the consumer's gender, age, and income bracket. For example, the target market for dirt bikes may be males under thirty years of age, while the target market for three-month cruises may be wealthy males or females over fifty years of age. Eddie Bauer produces a line of casual clothes for a target market of customers between thirty and fifty years of age, while Carters produces clothes for babies.

D**ELL** COMPUTER'S FORMULA FOR SUCCESS

Dell Computer recently strengthened its focus on Internet sales, which now account for about 40 percent of its total revenue. Dell's management is using its success in Internet sales of computers to widen and redefine its target market. For example, Michael Dell, the company's chief operating officer, recently received 1,700 requests to speak from all around the world. By communicating to its target market that Dell is focused on the Internet, the company will likely further increase its sales in a computer world whose customers are increasingly focused on e-commerce capabilities and high-quality websites.

Factors That Affect the Size of a Target Market

As time passes, the demand for products changes. Firms attempt to be in a position to benefit from a possible increase in demand for particular products. For example, some hotels in Los Angeles and New York have anticipated an increase in Japanese guests and have offered new conveniences to capture that portion of the market. Common conveniences offered are Japanese translators, rooms with bamboo screens, and a Japanese-language newspaper for these guests.

As consumer preferences change, the size of a particular target market can change. Firms monitor consumer preferences over time to anticipate how the size of their target market may be affected. The following are key factors that affect consumer preferences and therefore affect the size of the target market:

▶ Demographics
▶ Geography
▶ Economic factors
▶ Social values

demographics characteristics of the human population or specific segments of the population

Demographics The total demand for particular products or services is dependent on the **demographics,** or characteristics of the human population or specific segments of the population. As demographic conditions change, so does the demand. For example, demographic statistics show an increase in women who work outside the home. Firms have adjusted their product lines to capitalize on this change. Clothing stores have created more lines of business clothing for women. Food manufacturers have created easy-to-fix frozen foods to accommodate the busy schedules of wage-earning women. The tendency for people to have less free time and more income has resulted in increased demand for more convenience services, such as quick oil change and tire replacement services.

One of the most relevant demographic characteristics is age, because target markets are sometimes defined by age levels. Demographic statistics show that the population has grown older. Consequently, sports cars are not as popular. Customers are more interested in cars that are dependable and safe. Automobile manufacturers have adjusted to the demographics by supplying fewer sports cars.

Although the population has generally grown older, the number of children in the United States has recently increased. Many of these recently born children have two parents who work outside the home and spend large sums of money on their children. Firms such as OshKosh B' Gosh and The Gap have capitalized on this trend by producing high-quality (and high-priced) children's clothing.

To illustrate how characteristics of the population can change over time, consider the changes over the twenty-year period 1980–2000, shown in Exhibit 13.2. In general, the population has grown larger, while both the number of people age 65 or older and the number of households earning more than $60,000 annually have increased. Such information is relevant to firms because it suggests that the size of specific target markets may be changing over time.

Geography   The total demand for a product is also influenced by geography. Firms target snow tires to the northern states and surfboards to the east and west coasts of the United States. Tastes are also influenced by geography. The demand for spicy foods is higher in the southwestern states than in other states.

Economic Factors   As economic conditions change, so do consumer preferences. During a recessionary period, the demand for most types of goods declines. Specialty and shopping products are especially sensitive to these conditions. During a recession, firms may promote necessities rather than specialty products. In addition, their pricing may be more competitive. When the economy becomes stronger, firms have more flexibility to raise prices and may also promote specialty products more than necessities.

Interest rates can also have a major impact on consumer demand. When interest rates are low, consumers are more willing to purchase goods with borrowed money. The demand for products such as automobiles, boats, and homes is especially sensitive to interest rate movements because these products are often purchased with borrowed funds.

Social Values   As the social values of consumers change, so do their preferences. For example, the demand for cigarettes and whiskey has declined as consumers have become more aware of the health dangers of using these products. If a firm producing either of these products anticipates a change in preferences, it can begin to shift its marketing mix. Alternatively, it could modify its product to capitalize on the trend. For example, it could reduce the alcohol content of the whiskey or the tar and nicotine content of the cigarettes. It may also revise its promotion strategy to inform the public of these changes.

Exhibit 13.2

Changes in Consumer Characteristics in Last 20 Years (from 1980 to 2000)

1. U.S. population has increased.
2. Higher proportion of people age 65 or older
3. Higher proportion of households with income over $60,000
4. Higher proportion of minority households with income over $60,000
5. Higher proportion of high school students who enter college
6. Higher proportion of minority high school students who enter college

Online Education

http://www.ecollege.com

FREQUENTLY, COLLEGES AND UNIVERSITIES UTILIZE THE INTERNET TO OF-fer online courses. Websites such as eCollege, shown here, allow colleges and universities to reach their target market—potential students—directly. Students can search hundreds of university websites for courses taught online and can compare the courses and their content. Then, the students can register directly over the Internet. Thus, these websites help universities attract new students.

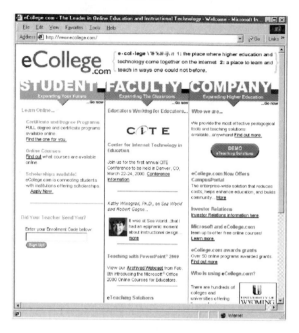

Targeting
Foreign
Countries

WHEN FIRMS SELL THEIR PRODUCT MIX IN FOREIGN COUNTRIES, THEY MUST recognize that consumer characteristics vary across countries. Consider the case of Bestfoods International, a U.S. firm that produces numerous food products, including Skippy peanut butter, Mazola corn oil, and Hellmann's mayonnaise. Its global marketing strategy is to penetrate any foreign markets where there will be sufficient demand. It recognizes that some of its products will be more successful than others in particular foreign markets. Thus, it considers the characteristics of the foreign country before it decides which products to market in that country.

To illustrate how each product is targeted to specific countries, consider the following brief summary of just a few of Bestfoods' products:

1 Bestfoods sells mayonnaise in Argentina, Brazil, and Chile and has recently introduced it in Panama and Venezuela. It has experienced high sales of mayonnaise in the Czech and Slovak Republics and has recently marketed mayonnaise in Spain.

2 Bestfoods sells ready-to-eat desserts and dessert mixes in Europe, including Yabon cakes in France and Ambrosia rice puddings in the United Kingdom. It also sells dessert mixes in Latin America under the Kremel, Maizena, and Maravilla brands.

3 Bestfoods sells pasta in Europe under the Napolina and Knorr brands and in Asia under the Royal and Bestfoods brands.

In general, the product mix marketed by Bestfoods in any given country is dependent on the characteristics of the people in that country. It periodically changes the product mix that is marketed to a particular country in response to changes in that country's characteristics.

Creating New Products

2 Identify the steps involved in creating a new product.

In a given year, firms may offer more than twenty thousand new products. The vast majority of these products will be discontinued within six months. These statistics suggest how difficult it is to create new products that are successful. Nevertheless, the profits from a single successful product may offset losses resulting from several failed products.

A new product does not have to represent a famous invention. Most new products are simply improvements of existing products. Existing products become **obsolete,** or less useful than in the past, for two reasons. They may no longer be in fashion, which is called **fashion obsolescence.** For example, the demand for bell-bottom pants declined once they were no longer in style. Alternatively, products may be inferior to new products that are technologically more advanced, which is called **technological obsolescence.** For example, when Hewlett-Packard creates faster printers, the old models are subject to technological obsolescence.

obsolete less useful than in the past

fashion obsolescence no longer in fashion

technological obsolescence inferior to new products

Use of Marketing Research to Create New Products

When firms develop products, they assess the market to monitor the marketing strategies of their competitors. However, monitoring competitors may cause the firm to be a follower rather than a leader. Many firms prefer to make product decisions that are more innovative than those of their competitors. To obtain more insight on what consumers want, firms use **marketing research,** which is the accumulation and analysis of data in order to make a particular marketing decision.

marketing research accumulation and analysis of data in order to make a particular marketing decision

Marketing research is useful for making product decisions. Computer firms build computers and automobile manufacturers design their new cars to accommodate their perception of what consumers want. Firms' perceptions of consumer preferences are more accurate when backed by marketing research.

A marketing survey may find that many consumers desire a specific product that is not available. It may also identify deficiencies in the firm's existing products; this information can then be used to correct these deficiencies. The design and quality of a product may be revised to accommodate consumer preferences.

New and revised products may be tested with marketing research. The products are given to prospective customers who are asked to assess various features of the products. This type of research allows firms to make further revisions that will satisfy customers.

To enable a firm to have confidence in the implications drawn from marketing research, sample groups of consumers who represent the target market are studied. Many

Ozzie Zehner, president of Imagitrends, an Internet company, tests a tiny camera that could broadcast images (of a car show) directly to the Internet.

marketing research studies lead to a marketing decision that will cost millions of dollars. If the marketing research leads to incorrect conclusions, the decision could result in a large loss to the firm.

One limitation of using marketing research to identify consumer preferences is that tastes change rapidly. Products, such as clothing, that were popular when the marketing research was conducted may be out of style by the time they are designed and distributed to the market.

Use of Research and Development to Create Products

Firms invest funds in research and development (R&D) to design new products or to improve the products they already produce. Manufacturing firms tend to invest more money in R&D than service firms, because technology can improve manufactured products more easily than services.

Firms that spend money on R&D expect the benefits to exceed the expenses. Procter & Gamble's R&D resulted in its two-in-one shampoo and conditioner technology. It attributes the success of its Pantene Pro-V to its product technology. This product is now the leading shampoo in various countries. Procter & Gamble has improved the technology of Tide detergent more than seventy times. Technological development can allow one firm an advantage over its competitors. Many large firms typically spend more than $1 billion on R&D per year.

SMALL BUSINESS SURVEY

What Are the Keys to Creating Successful Products?

A survey asked 550 manufacturers of products to identify the sources of new product ideas. Each possible source listed in the following chart was rated 1 to 5, with 5 meaning that the source was frequently used by a firm for generating new product ideas. The chart shows the average score across the 550 manufacturers for each possible source of new product ideas.

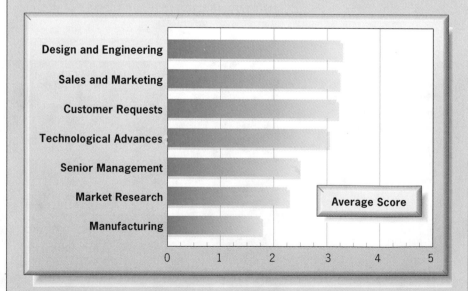

The results indicate that new product ideas most frequently come from the engineering and marketing functions and are less frequently initiated by senior management or the manufacturing process.

Some firms have created alliances to conduct R&D. They share the costs and their technology in attempting to develop products. An alliance not only combines expertise from two or more firms, but it also may reduce the costs to each individual firm.

To expand their product line, many firms have recently increased their investment in R&D. For example, Abbott Laboratories has consistently increased its investment in R&D. Since Abbott Laboratories produces various medical drugs, its future performance is heavily dependent on its ability to create new drugs.

Using Patents to Protect Research and Development One potential limitation of R&D is that it may lead to the production of products that are later copied by other firms. That is, the firms that create the ideas are not always able to prevent competitors from copying the idea. Consequently, the potential to recover all the expenses incurred from R&D may depend on whether the ideas can be protected from competitors. Firms apply for **patents,** which allow exclusive rights to the production and sale of a specific product. The use of patents can allow firms such as IBM, Kodak, and 3M to benefit from their inventions because it prevents competitors from copying the idea. The 3M Company, which created Post-it Notes, commonly obtains at least four hundred patents per year. Patents have even been obtained for specific sunglasses and microwave popcorn. One disadvantage of patents is that they often take several months to obtain approval.

patents allow exclusive rights to the production and sale of a specific product

Steps Necessary to Create a New Product

The following steps are typically necessary to create a new product:

▶ Develop product idea.
▶ Assess the feasibility of a product idea.
▶ Design and test the product.
▶ Distribute and promote the product.
▶ Post-audit the product.

Develop Product Idea The first step in creating a new product is to develop an idea. When the focus is on improving an existing product, the idea already exists, and the firm simply attempts to make it better. When developing an entirely new product, a common method is to identify consumer needs or preferences that are not being satisfied by existing products. The ultimate goal is to develop a product that is superior to existing products in satisfying the consumer.

As firms attempt to improve existing products or create new products, they must determine what will satisfy customers. The commitment of some firms to customer satisfaction is confirmed by the following statements in recent annual reports:

❝ *Kodak's future is in total customer satisfaction.* ❞

—Eastman Kodak

❝ *I [Louis Gerstner, CEO] want everyone in IBM to be obsessed with satisfying our customers.* ❞

—IBM

❝ *We aim to redouble our efforts . . . toward one simple goal: meeting the needs of our customers.* ❞

—Apple Computer

Identifying consumer preferences so as to improve a product or create a new product may involve monitoring consumer behavior. For example, an airline may monitor flights to determine the most disturbing inconveniences, such as cramped seating. This leads to ideas for an improved product, such as wider seats. To satisfy consumer preferences, rental car companies at airports now allow their key customers to go straight from the airplane to their cars (rather than stand in line at the counter).

Technology can be used to monitor consumer behavior. When Amazon.com fills orders, it requests information about the customers. Thus, when Amazon.com considers expanding its product line, it knows the characteristics of the consumers who are buying its existing products. Based on this information about consumer preferences, it can attempt to identify other products that will sell over the Internet.

An alternative to monitoring consumer behavior is surveying people about their behavior. Surveys may be conducted by employees or consulting firms. Again, the goal is to identify consumer preferences that have not been fulfilled. Recognition of heightened consumer concern about health led to many ideas for new products and revisions of existing products. For example, food manufacturers responded by creating cereals and frozen dinners that are more nutritious.

Each consumer preference that deserves attention results from a lack of or a deficiency in an existing product. The firm must determine how this lack or deficiency can be corrected by creating a new product or improving an existing product. In the mid-1990s, IBM decided that it needed to increase the processing speed of its computers. IBM incurred substantial expenses as a result of this decision to improve its products. However, the demand for these improved products increased, resulting in higher revenue.

Assess the Feasibility of a Product Idea Any idea for a new or improved product should be assessed by estimating the costs and benefits. The idea should be undertaken only if the benefits outweigh the costs. For example, American Airlines recently removed some seats to satisfy customers by providing more leg room. The most obvious cost is the work involved in performing this task, but other costs are involved

---

CROSS-FUNCTIONAL TEAMWORK

Interaction among Product Decisions and Other Business Decisions

 When marketing managers create a new product, they must design it in a manner that will attract customers. They must also decide the price at which the product will be sold. These marketing decisions require communication between the marketing managers and the managers who oversee production. Marketing managers explain to the production managers how they would like the product to be designed. The production managers may offer revisions that can improve the design. They also provide estimates on the costs of production. The cost per unit is typically dependent on the volume of products to be produced; therefore, the cost per unit can be estimated only after the marketing managers determine the volume that will need to be produced to satisfy the demand. Since the pricing decision is influenced by the cost of producing the product, the price cannot be determined by the marketing managers until they receive cost estimates from the production managers.

Once the marketing managers have received the necessary input from the production managers and have developed plans for the design and pricing of the product, a financial analysis by the financial managers is necessary to ensure that the proposal is feasible. The financial analysis involves estimating the revenue the firm will generate as a result of creating this product. It also involves estimating production expenses. Using these estimates, the financial managers can determine whether the new product will provide an adequate return to make the firm's investment in the development of this product worthwhile. The marketing managers should attempt to develop the product only if the financial analysis suggests that it will provide an adequate return to the firm. If the marketing managers decide to develop this product, they will inform the production managers, who may need to hire additional production employees. In addition, the financial managers must be informed because they may need to obtain funds to finance production.

Although the marketing managers may be responsible for the creation of new products, they rely on input from the production and financial managers when deciding whether each product is worthwhile and when determining the design and price of the new product.

as well. The strategy causes the airline to reduce its seating capacity. The cost of this reduction is forgone revenue on those flights that were at full capacity. In addition, the work performed may prevent the use of the airplane for a period. Any forgone revenue during that period also represents a cost of improving the product. The benefit of more leg room is greater consumer satisfaction, which may result in a greater demand for the airline's service, resulting in more revenue.

Design and Test the Product If the firm believes the new (or revised) product is feasible, it must determine the design and other characteristics of the product. The new product may be tested before being fully implemented. For example, the airline may first revise its seating structure in a few planes to determine consumer reaction. If the actual costs exceed the benefits, the proposed changes will not be made on other airplanes. If the change has a favorable impact, however, it may be made throughout the entire fleet.

Distribute and Promote the Product When firms introduce new products or improve existing products, they typically attempt to inform consumers. New or improved products are introduced to consumers through various marketing techniques. As an example, an airline that widens its seats may advertise this feature in the media. Additional expenses required to promote the revised design should be accounted for when determining whether it is worthwhile to create a new design.

Post-Audit the Product After the new product has been introduced into the market, the actual costs and benefits should be measured and compared with the costs and benefits that were forecasted earlier. This comparison determines whether the cost-benefit analysis was reasonably accurate. If costs were severely underestimated or benefits were severely overestimated, the firm may need to adjust its method of analysis for evaluating other new products in the future. In addition, the post-audit of costs and benefits can be used for future development of the same product. For example, if the actual costs of improving the airplanes outweigh the benefits, the airline may revert to its original product design when new airplanes are needed.

Summary of Steps Used to Create or Revise a Product A summary of the steps involved in creating or revising a product is shown in Exhibit 13.3. Notice that the whole process is initiated by attempting to satisfy consumer preferences.

③ Explain the common methods used to differentiate a product.

Product Differentiation

Product differentiation is the effort of a firm to distinguish its product from competitive products in a manner that makes it more desirable. Some products are differenti-

Exhibit 13.3

Steps Involved in Creating or Revising a Product

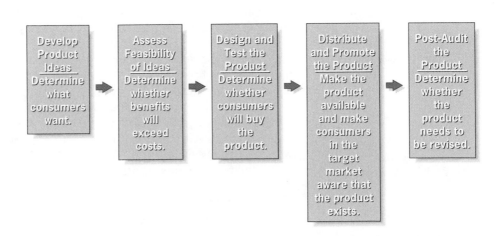

product differentiation a firm's effort to distinguish its product from competitive products in a manner that makes it more desirable

ated from competitive products by their quality. For example, Starbucks has become a popular coffee shop around the country because of its special coffee, even though its prices are high. Kay-Bee Toys used a marketing strategy of specializing in a small selection of high-quality toys, rather than competing with Wal-Mart for the entire line of toys.

All firms look for some type of competitive advantage that will distinguish their product from the rest. The following are some of the more common methods used to differentiate the product:

▶ Unique design
▶ Unique packaging
▶ Unique branding

Unique Design

Some products are differentiated by their design. Consider a homebuilder who builds homes and sells them once they are completed. The builder can attempt to build homes that will satisfy buyers by considering the following questions:

1. Would consumers in this neighborhood prefer one- or two-story homes?
2. Is a basement desirable?
3. Is a fireplace desirable?
4. What is a popular size for homes in this neighborhood?
5. What type of architecture is popular in this neighborhood?

Once these and other issues are resolved, the builder can build homes with specifications that will attract buyers.

Various characteristics can make one product better than others, including safety, reliability, and ease of use. Firms such as AT&T, Kodak, and Audi have a reputation for reliability, which helps create a demand for their products. Producers attempt to improve reliability by using high-quality materials, providing service, and offering warranties. However, attempts to improve reliability usually result in higher costs.

Differentiating the Design of a Service Just as firms that produce products attempt to create unique designs for their products, service firms attempt to develop unique services. For example, Southwest Airlines designed a differentiated service by focusing on many short routes that were previously not available to customers.

Use of Technology to Differentiate Services Amazon.com created a unique design in the service of selling books by taking orders online. The favorable effects on Amazon.com's value (as measured by its stock price) of this unique service are shown in Exhibit 13.4. Amazon.com's stock price increased substantially as a result of the strong demand for its service and the expectations that the demand would grow over time.

Some of the demand for Amazon.com's books online came from customers who previously purchased books at Borders. As customers shifted their business to Amazon.com, Borders experienced a decline in its value, as shown in Exhibit 13.5.

As a related example, Webvan Group provides grocery shopping by e-mail. It has a large warehouse in Oakland, California, and serves an area within forty miles of that warehouse. Customers review a menu of groceries online, check the groceries (such as wine, cheese, vegetables, cereal, and meat) that they wish to purchase, and submit their orders online. The groceries are delivered within a specific thirty-minute interval chosen by the customer. When Webvan receives an order, employees in the warehouse fill boxes with the groceries ordered. Trucks then transport the boxes to various locations, where they are transferred to vans that make the local deliveries.

Exhibit 13.4

How Amazon.com's Differentiated Product Affected Its Stock
Price

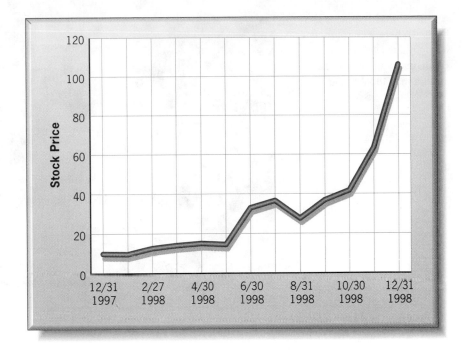

Unique Packaging

A packaging strategy can determine the success or failure of a product, especially for products whose quality levels are quite similar. In an attempt to differentiate themselves from the competition, some firms have repackaged various grocery products in unbreakable or easily disposable containers.

Many packaging strategies are focused on convenience. Motor oil is now packaged in containers with convenient twist-off caps, and many canned foods have pull-tabs. Tide detergent is packaged in both powder and liquid so that consumers can choose their preferred form.

Packaging can also provide advertising. For example, many food products such as microwave dinners are packaged with the preparation instructions on the outside. These

Exhibit 13.5

How Amazon.com's Differentiated Product Affected Borders'
(a Competitor) Stock Price

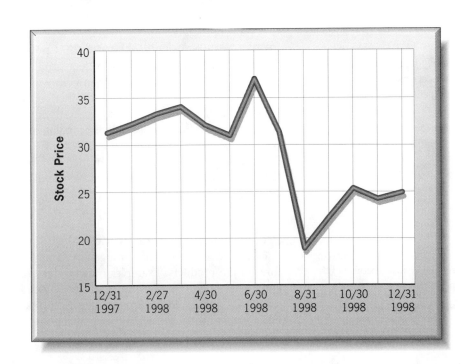

A collection of Pez dispensers is shown here. Pez candy is differentiated from other candy by its unique packaging and its individual brand name.

instructions also demonstrate how simple the preparation is. Packaging also informs consumers about the nutrition of foods or the effectiveness of health-care products. The advertising on the package may be the key factor that encourages consumers to purchase one product instead of others.

Unique Branding

branding a method of identifying products and differentiating them from competitors

Branding is a method of identifying products and differentiating them from competitors. Brands are typically represented by a name and a symbol. A **trademark** is a brand's form of identification that is legally protected from use by other firms. Some trademarks have become so common that they represent the product itself. For example, "Coke" is often used to refer to any cola drink, and "Kleenex" is frequently used to refer to any facial tissue. Some symbols are more recognizable than the brand name. Easily recognized symbols are displayed by Levi's jeans, Nike, Pepsi, and Mercedes.

trademark a brand's form of identification that is legally protected from use by other firms

family branding branding of all or most products produced by a company

Family versus Individual Branding   Companies that produce goods assign either a family or an individual brand to their products. **Family branding** is the branding of all or most products produced by a company. The Coca-Cola Company sells Coca-Cola, Diet Coke, Cherry Coke, and other soft drinks. Ford, RCA, IBM, and Quaker State use family branding to distinguish their products from the competition.

individual branding the assignment of a unique brand name to different products or groups of products

Companies that use **individual branding** assign a unique brand name to different products or groups of products. For example, Procter & Gamble produces Tide, Bold, and Era. General Mills produces numerous brands of cereal. Many clothing manufacturers use different brand names. One product line may be marketed to prestigious clothing shops. A second line may be marketed to retail stores. To preserve the prestige, the top quality brand may not be sold in retail stores.

producer brands brands that reflect the manufacturer of the products

Producer versus Store Brands   Most products can be classified as either a producer brand, a store brand, or a generic brand. **Producer brands** reflect the manufacturer of the products. Examples of producer brands are Black and Decker, Frito-Lay, and Fisher Price. These brands are usually well known because they are sold to retail stores nationwide. **Store brands** reflect the retail store where the products are sold. For example, Sears and J.C. Penney offer some products with their own label. Even if store brands are produced by firms other than the retailer, the names of the produc-

store brands brands that reflect the retail store where the products are sold

ers are not identified. Store brand products do not have as much prestige as popular producer brands; however, they often have a lower price.

Some products are not branded by the producer or the store. These products have a so-called **generic brand.** The label on generic products simply describes the product. Generic brands have become increasingly popular over the last decade because their prices are relatively low. They are most popular for products that are likely to be similar among brands, such as napkins and paper plates. Customers are comfortable purchasing generic brands of these products because there is not much risk in buying a cheaper product.

Benefits of Branding Branding continually exposes a company's name to the public. If the company is respected, new products may be trusted because they carry the company brand name. If they carried a different name, new products introduced by a firm would not likely sell as well.

Many firms with a brand name use their name to enter new markets. The Coca-Cola Company uses its name to promote new soft drinks that it creates. Nabisco can more easily penetrate the market for various specialty foods because of its reputation for quality food products. These firms not only are able to offer new products but also may enter new geographic markets (such as foreign countries) because of their brand name.

The brand is especially useful for differentiating a product when there are only a few major competitors. For example, many consumers select among only two or three brands of some products, such as toothpaste or computers.

The importance of branding is emphasized in a recent annual report of Procter & Gamble:

> 66 *Consumers have to trust that a brand will meet all their needs all the time. That requires superior product technology. And it also requires sufficient breadth of product choices. We should never give consumers a . . . reason to switch away from one of our brands.* 77

Having an established brand name is often crucial to obtaining space in a store. For example, Coca-Cola and Pepsi often receive the majority of a store's soft drink shelf space. The same is true for some cereals, detergents, and even dog food. Retail stores normally allocate more space for products with popular brand names.

Branding also applies to services. When Southwest Airlines begins to serve a new route, it uses its brand (reliability, good service, low prices) to attract customers.

Recently, firms have entered into agreements called **co-branding,** in which two noncompeting products are combined at a discounted price. For example, Blockbuster Entertainment Group issues VISA cards. Blockbuster Video customers can get discounts on video rentals by using their VISA cards.

Summary of Methods to Differentiate Products

Exhibit 13.6 summarizes the methods used to achieve product differentiation. Firms sometimes combine various methods to differentiate their products. For example, if Kodak creates a product that is technologically superior to others, it may also differentiate the product by packaging it in a special manner and by using the Kodak family brand name.

To understand how some firms use all three methods to differentiate their products, consider the following comment from an annual report:

> 66 *Liz Claiborne, Inc., must work more diligently than ever to truly differentiate its brands, . . . applying product innovation [such as a unique design], canny brand marketing, . . . superb customer service and ex-*

generic brands products not branded by the producer or the store

Intel's brand is commonly used to promote computers that contain the Intel chip.

co-branding two noncompeting products are combined at a discounted price

Method	Achieve Superiority by:
Unique design	Higher level of product safety, reliability, or ease of use.
Unique packaging	Packaging to get consumers' attention or to improve convenience.
Unique branding	Using the firm's image to gain credibility, or using a unique brand name to imply prestige.

ceptional in-store presentation [unique packaging] to win over a consumer who has abundant choices. "

—Liz Claiborne, Inc.

BUSINESS ONLINE

Product
Differentiation
Online

http://www.etoys.com/html/
et_home.shtml?sid=a20320597
w59

THE INTERNET HAS ALLOWED NEW AND EXISTING COMPANIES TO DIFFER-entiate their products by making them available directly for purchase from home. One of the largest Internet retailers is eToys, whose website is shown here. The eToys label has become a unique brand, and the company uses its website to sell related products as well as toys. Consumers can also search for a specific toy.

Product Life Cycle

4 Identify the main phases of a product life cycle.

product life cycle the typical set of phases that products experience over their lifetime

Most products experience a **product life cycle,** or a typical set of phases over their lifetime. The marketing decisions made about a particular product may be influenced by the prevailing phase of the cycle. The typical product life cycle has four specific phases:

▶ Introduction
▶ Growth
▶ Maturity
▶ Decline

Introduction

The **introduction phase** is the initial period in which consumers are informed about a new product. The promotion of a product is intended to introduce the product and make consumers aware of it. In some cases, the product is first tested in particular areas to determine consumer reaction. For example, the concept of direct satellite television was tested in various locations. The initial cost of producing and advertising a product may exceed the revenue received during this phase. The price of the product may initially be set high if no other competitive products are in the market yet. This strategy is referred to as **price skimming.**

Growth

The **growth phase** is the period in which sales of the product increase rapidly. The marketing of a product is typically intended to reinforce the product's features. Cellular telephones and direct satellite TVs are in the growth phase. Other firms that are aware of the product's success may attempt to create a similar or superior product. The price of the product may be lowered once competitive products enter the market.

Maturity

The **maturity phase** is the period in which additional competitive products have entered the market, and sales of the product level off because of more competition. At this point, most marketing strategies are used to ensure that customers are still aware that the product exists. Some marketing strategies may offer special discounts to maintain market share. The firm may also revise the design of the existing product (product differentiation) to maintain market share. Standard cable television service is an example of a product at the maturity phase.

Decline

The **decline phase** is the period in which sales of the product decline, either because of reduced consumer demand for that type of product or because competitors are gaining market share. If firms do not prepare for a decline phase on some products, they may experience an abrupt decline in business. Some firms begin to prepare two or more years before the anticipated decline phase by planning revisions in their existing products or services.

The product life cycle is illustrated in Exhibit 13.7. The length of a cycle tends to vary among types of products. It also varies among the firms that sell a particular type of product, because some firms lengthen the cycle by continually differentiating their product to maintain their market share.

Pricing Strategies

5 Identify the factors that influence the pricing decision.

Whether a firm produces industrial steel, textbooks, or haircuts, it needs to determine a price for its product. Managers typically attempt to set a price that will maximize the firm's value. The price charged for a product affects the firm's revenue and therefore its earnings. Recall that the revenue from selling a product is equal to its price times the quantity sold. Although a lower price reduces the revenue received per unit, it typically results in a higher quantity of units sold. A higher price increases the revenue received per unit but results in a lower quantity of units sold. Thus, an obvious trade-off is involved when determining the price for a product.

Exhibit 13.7

Product Life Cycle Phases

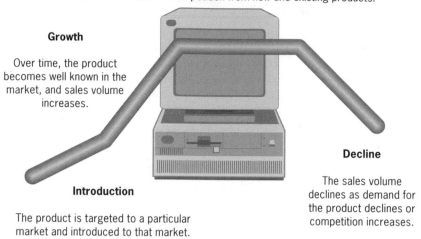

Maturity

Sales volume hits a peak at the end of the growth phase. Then sales begin to level off as a result of competition from new and existing products.

Growth

Over time, the product becomes well known in the market, and sales volume increases.

Decline

The sales volume declines as demand for the product declines or competition increases.

Introduction

The product is targeted to a particular market and introduced to that market.

Firms set the prices of their products by considering the following:

► Cost of production
► Supply of inventory
► Competitors' prices

Pricing According to the Cost of Production

Some firms set a price for a product by estimating the per-unit cost of producing the product and then adding a markup. This method for pricing products is commonly referred to as **cost-based pricing.** If this method is used, the firm must also account for all production costs that are attributable to the production of that product. Pricing according to cost attempts to ensure that production costs are covered. Virtually all firms consider production costs when setting a price. The difference in price between a Cadillac and a Saturn is partially attributed to the difference in production costs. However, other factors may also influence the pricing decision.

cost-based pricing estimating the per-unit cost of producing a product and then adding a markup

Economies of Scale The per-unit cost of production may be dependent on production volume. For products subject to economies of scale, the average per-unit cost of production decreases as production volume increases. This is especially true for products or services that have high fixed costs (costs that remain unchanged regardless of the quantity produced), such as automobiles. A pricing strategy must account for economies of scale. If a high price is charged, not only does sales volume decrease, but also the average cost of producing a small amount increases. For those products or services that are subject to economies of scale, the price should be sufficiently low to achieve a high sales volume (and therefore lower production costs).

Pricing According to the Supply of Inventory

Some pricing decisions are directly related to the supply of inventory. For example, computer firms such as Compaq typically reduce prices on existing personal computers to make room for new models that will soon be marketed. Automobile dealerships frequently use this strategy as well. Most manufacturers and retailers tend to reduce prices if they need to reduce their inventory.

Pricing According to Competitors' Prices

Firms commonly consider the prices of competitors when determining the prices of their products. They can use various pricing strategies to compete against other products, as explained next.

Penetration Pricing If a firm wants to be sure that it can sell its product, it may set a lower price than those of competitive products to penetrate the market. This pricing strategy is called **penetration pricing** and has been used in various ways by numerous firms, including airlines, automobile manufacturers, and food companies.

penetration pricing the strategy of setting a lower price than those of competitive products to penetrate a market

price-elastic the demand for a product is highly responsive to price changes

The success of penetration pricing depends on the responsiveness of consumers to a reduced price. The demand for a product that is **price-elastic** is highly responsive to price changes. Some grocery products such as napkins and paper plates are price-elastic, as price may be the most important criterion that consumers use when deciding which brand to purchase. Many firms, such as Ameritrade, IBM, Taco Bell, and Compaq Computer, were able to increase their revenue as a result of lowering prices.

When Southwest Airlines entered the airline industry, its average fare was substantially lower than the average fare charged by other airlines for the same routes. Southwest not only pulled customers away from other competitors but also created some new customer demand for airline services because of its low prices.

Penetration pricing is not always successful, however. Allstate Insurance increased its market share by lowering its insurance prices (premiums), but its profits declined because it lowered its prices too much.

price-inelastic the demand for a product is not very responsive to price changes

The demand for a product that is **price-inelastic** is not very responsive to price changes. Firms should not use penetration pricing if their products are price-inelastic, because most consumers would not switch to competitive products to take advantage of lower prices. For some products, such as deli products and high-quality automobiles, personalized service and perceived quality may be more important than price. The demand for many services is not responsive to price reductions, because consumers may prefer one firm over others. For example, some consumers may be unwilling to switch dentists, hair stylists, or stockbrokers even if a competitor reduced its price.

Pricing Information-Based Products

As information technology (IT) is increasingly incorporated into products, manufacturers are having to rethink their traditional pricing strategies. Traditionally, most product costs have come from labor and raw materials. This meant that the variable cost of each unit produced (the costs directly associated with a given unit) was a critical factor in the pricing decision. The IT components of products have a markedly different cost structure, however. Although it may cost tens or hundreds of millions of dollars to design and test a single chip, once chips are in production, the variable cost of producing additional chips is very small (such as a few dollars or even pennies). The same is true for producing software. As a result, while incorporating IT into a product may dramatically improve product quality, it can have little impact on the variable cost of that product. Therefore, variable cost is less useful in deciding on price.

How can manufacturers recoup the investment they make in incorporating IT into their products? One way is to raise product prices to reflect the higher value of the redesigned products to consumers. However, other opportunities are available to gain revenue from the technology. Licensing the product to other manufacturers, as Adobe did with its PostScript printer language, is one way of deriving revenue. Another is to market the specialized test equipment needed to service the new technology. Some companies even use technology as a source of ongoing revenue from prior customers, periodically offering upgrades to the on-board information systems in their products.

Whether or not a product contains IT, it is ultimately the market that determines if the "price is right." As such technologies become increasingly important to product performance, however, companies will have to be more creative in their product and pricing strategies.

Defensive Pricing Some pricing decisions are defensive rather than offensive. If a firm recognizes that the price of a competitive product has been reduced, it may use **defensive pricing,** which is the act of reducing product prices to defend (retain) market share. For example, airlines commonly reduce their airfares in response to a competitor that lowers its airfares. This response tends to allow all airlines to retain their market share, but their revenue will decrease (because of the lower price). Computer firms such as IBM and Compaq commonly reduce their prices in response to price reductions by their competitors.

Some firms lower their price to drive out new competitors that have entered the market. This strategy is called **predatory pricing.**

Prestige Pricing Firms may use a higher price if their product is intended to have a top-of-the-line image. This pricing strategy is called **prestige pricing.** For example, GapKids sells baby clothing at relatively high prices to create a high-quality image for customers who are not as concerned about price. Microbreweries use prestige pricing in an attempt to create a high-quality image for their beers.

Firms with a diversified product mix may use a penetration pricing strategy for some products and a prestige pricing strategy for others. For example, Toys "Я" Us has cut prices on some toys to increase market share, but it has a section of the store that uses prestige pricing on educational toys such as computers and computer games.

Example of Setting a Product's Price

To show how a firm may set a product's price, assume that you move to New Orleans and start your own business as a hot dog vendor on the streets of the French Quarter (tourist) district. Assume that you plan to run this business for one year and that a hot dog cooker can be rented for $4,000 annually. This cost is referred to as a **fixed cost** because the cost of production remains unchanged regardless of how many units are produced. Also assume that you purchase your hot dogs, buns, ketchup, and so on, in bulk, and estimate the cost per hot dog to be $.60. These costs are called **variable costs,** since they vary with the quantity of hot dogs produced.

Other vendors in the area charge $2.00 per hot dog. After talking with several other vendors, you forecast that you can sell 20,000 hot dogs in one year as long as your price is competitive.

To determine an appropriate price, begin with the cost information and determine the total cost of production over the first year. The total cost follows:

$$
\begin{aligned}
\text{Total Cost} &= (\text{Fixed Cost}) + [(\text{Quantity}) \times (\text{Variable Cost per Unit})] \\
&= \$4{,}000 + [(20{,}000) \times (\$.60)] \\
&= \$4{,}000 + \$12{,}000 \\
&= \$16{,}000
\end{aligned}
$$

Assume that you price the hot dogs at $1.80 so that your price is slightly lower than those of competitors. Since the total revenue is equal to price times the quantity sold, your total revenue is estimated to be:

$$
\begin{aligned}
\text{Total Revenue} &= (\text{Quantity}) \times (\text{Price per Unit}) \\
&= (20{,}000) \times (\$1.80) \\
&= \$36{,}000
\end{aligned}
$$

Your actual amount of revenue over a future period is subject to uncertainty. For example, if only 10,000 hot dogs are sold, your revenue would be:

$$
\begin{aligned}
\text{Total Revenue} &= (\text{Quantity}) \times (\text{Price}) \\
&= (10{,}000) \times (\$1.80) \\
&= \$18{,}000
\end{aligned}
$$

defensive pricing the act of reducing product prices to defend (retain) market share

predatory pricing the strategy of lowering a product's price to drive out new competitors

prestige pricing the strategy of using a higher price for a product that is intended to have a top-of-the-line image

fixed cost the cost of production that remains unchanged regardless of how many units are produced

variable costs costs that vary with the quantity produced

Your profits would be as follows:

$$\text{Profits} = \text{Total revenue} - \text{Total cost}$$
$$= \$18,000 - \$16,000$$
$$= \$2,000$$

Thus, the profits (revenue minus costs) would only be $2,000. You could attempt to increase your price to make up for the possibility of low sales. However, this may conflict with your goal of using a price that is no higher than the competition. The estimated quantity of hot dogs sold may decline if you sell hot dogs at a higher price.

The total cost and total revenue are depicted in Exhibit 13.8 for various quantities of hot dogs produced. Notice the fixed cost remains unchanged for any quantity

Exhibit 13.8 Estimation of Costs and Revenue at Various Quantities Produced

Quantity (Q)	Fixed Cost	Variable Cost (Q × $.60)	Total Cost	Total Revenue (Q × $1.80)	Profits
1,000	$4,000	$ 600	$ 4,600	$ 1,800	−$ 2,800
3,000	4,000	1,800	5,800	5,400	−400
4,000	4,000	2,400	6,400	7,200	800
7,000	4,000	4,200	8,200	12,600	4,400
10,000	4,000	6,000	10,000	18,000	8,000
15,000	4,000	9,000	13,000	27,000	14,000
20,000	4,000	12,000	16,000	36,000	20,000
25,000	4,000	15,000	19,000	45,000	26,000
30,000	4,000	18,000	22,000	54,000	32,000

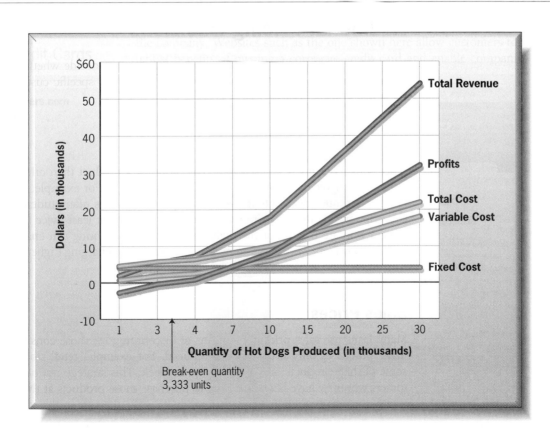

Product Differentiation at College Health Club

SOME OF THE KEY CONCEPTS IN THIS CHAPTER ARE INTEGRATED IN THE following discussion of marketing decisions for College Health Club (CHC). Sue Kramer recently reviewed the firm's product and pricing policies and created the following assessment.

CHC's primary product is health club services. The target market has been men and women between the ages of nineteen and thirty who are or were enrolled in the nearby college.

Since the facilities are not being fully utilized during the mornings and early afternoons, CHC needs to reevaluate its target market. Additional markets should be targeted so that the facilities can be utilized more efficiently. Homemakers should be targeted, since they could utilize the facilities during these off-peak periods. Because they may have children at home, the product (services) that CHC offers may have to be expanded to attract this new market.

The price of an annual membership is $250. This price is lower than most competitors. CHC's sales volume is adequate, but the facilities are rarely crowded. CHC could accommodate a larger group of customers, especially during the morning and early afternoon hours.

Dilemma

Sue considers methods to make CHC more desirable than the competition. CHC's initial success was attributed to its price and convenience for the students at the local college. However, Sue wants to differentiate the services for members to ensure continued interest by students. She also wants to retain the members even after they graduate from college.

Sue follows the steps discussed in this chapter for considering improvements in the service her club offers to members. First, she surveys existing members to determine whether they have specific preferences that she could provide to keep them as long-term customers. The following are the members' main suggestions:

1 Install a small bar in CHC.

2 Install televisions throughout CHC so that customers could watch programs while exercising. Some of the televisions would have a video cassette recorder along with several cassettes on aerobics and exercising.

3 Establish a refreshments area (or at least vending machines) for customers who want to take a break. This would encourage more social interaction between customers and differentiate CHC from competitors. As friendships develop, customers will be less likely to switch to an unfamiliar competitor health club.

4 Install a child care section in CHC so that customers could leave their children there whenever they came to the club.

Sue wants to assess the costs and benefits of each of these ideas so that she can decide which ideas (if any) to implement. Offer your opinion on which of these ideas (if any) Sue should implement.

Solution

Sue decides that the bar is not worth considering because she wants CHC's focus to be on health and does not want to have the responsibility of managing a bar and applying for the necessary ownership licenses. The bar would use up valuable space in the health club, and some college student members are minors. Sue also believes that CHC members would not quit their membership for lack of a bar, since other popular casual bars are nearby.

Sue now focuses on the feasibility of the televisions and the refreshments area. For about $1,500, she could purchase three televisions, which could be installed in three separate areas of CHC for members. Since a CHC membership is currently $250, the televisions would be a feasible purchase if they would bring in six new (or renewal) memberships. That is, six new or renewal memberships would cover the $1,500 expense of three new televisions. Sue believes that the televisions are worth purchasing.

Sue also decides to install some vending machines. They would take up less room than a refreshment stand, and Sue would not need to hire employees to provide refreshments. The vending area would allow for social interaction among members.

Sue also decides to add a child care section that would be available during off-peak periods (mornings). In the afternoon when the club is more crowded, this section would be cleared for more exercise space. Sue recognizes that she might have to buy an insurance policy to cover the potential liability from child care, but she believes that the child care section would result in a substantial increase in members.

Each of Sue's decisions was made based on a comparison of the estimated costs of improving the club's services with the potential extra revenue that would result from increased memberships.

Additional Issues for Discussion

1 How could Sue more closely evaluate the feasibility of targeting homemakers for off-peak periods?

2 When Sue created CHC, she focused on the target market of students at the college nearby. Her promotions and advertising were aimed at the college students. If she now decides to target homemakers as well, how might she revise her promotion and advertising?

3 Would prestige pricing be an effective strategy for CHC based on its target market?

SUMMARY

 The main factors affecting the size of a product's target market are:

▶ demographic trends, such as age and income levels;

▶ geography;

▶ economic factors, such as economic growth;

▶ changes in social values, such as a decline in demand for products perceived to be unhealthy.

2 The main steps involved in creating a new product are:

▶ develop a product idea, which may be in response to changes in consumer needs or preferences;

▶ assess the feasibility of the product idea, which requires comparing the expected benefits with the costs of the product;

▶ design the product and test it with some consumers in the target market;

▶ distribute the product so that it is accessible to the target market, and promote the product to ensure that consumers are aware of it;

▶ post-audit the product to determine whether the product needs to be revised in any way.

 Some common methods used to differentiate a product are:

▶ unique design, in which the product produced is safer, more reliable, easier to use, or has some other advantages;

▶ unique packaging, which can enhance convenience or contain advertising;

▶ unique branding, which may enhance consumers' perception of the product's quality.

 The phases of the product life cycle are:

▶ introduction phase, in which consumers are informed about the product;

▶ growth phase, in which the product becomes more popular and increases its share of the market;

▶ maturity phase, in which the sales volume levels off as a result of competition;

▶ decline phase, in which the sales volume is reduced as a result of competition or reduced consumer demand.

5 The key factors that influence the pricing decision are:

▶ cost of production, so that the price charged can recover costs incurred;

▶ inventory supply, so that the price can be lowered to remove excess inventory;

▶ prices of competitors, so that the price may be set below those of competitors to gain an advantage (penetration pricing) or above those of competitors to create an image of high quality (prestige pricing).

KEY TERMS

branding 366
break-even point 374
co-branding 367
consumer markets 356
contribution margin 374
convenience products 353
cost-based pricing 370
decline phase 369
defensive pricing 372
demographics 356
family branding 366
fashion obsolescence 359
fixed cost 372
generic brands 367

growth phase 369
individual branding 366
industrial markets 356
introduction phase 369
marketing research 359
maturity phase 369
obsolete 359
patents 361
penetration pricing 371
predatory pricing 372
prestige pricing 372
price skimming 369
price-elastic 371
price-inelastic 371

producer brands 366
product 353
product differentiation 363
product life cycle 368
product line 354
product mix 354
shopping products 353
specialty products 353
store brands 366
target market 356
technological obsolescence 359
trademark 366
variable costs 372

REVIEW QUESTIONS

1 Is it in the best interest of management to expand or contract the firm's product mix over time?

2 Identify and explain the factors influencing the size of a product's target market. Identify the target market for the following organizations: (a) Dallas Cowboys, (b) Wal-Mart stores, (c) Midas Muffler, (d) Jeep Cherokee, and (e) Jenny Craig.

3 Discuss the key factors that affect consumer preferences and therefore affect the size of the target market.

4 Discuss the statement: "We are emphatically global in our strategy of building a few core businesses worldwide." Are most large corporations going in this direction today?

5 Describe the use of marketing research by a firm attempting to create new products.

6 Assume that you are an inventor who has just created a new product. Will a patent protect your invention in a domestic market?

7 Assume that you have just come up with a new innovation. Explain the steps that you have gone through in developing this new product.

8 Discuss the product life cycle phases. Identify the current phase for the following products: (a) snowboards, (b) electric typewriters, (c) Harley-Davidson "full-dresser," and (d) 2001 Chrysler PT Cruiser.

9 Discuss different types of pricing strategies. How would the type of strategy used by Calvin Klein jeans differ from that used by community colleges?

10 Assume that you are a manager of a retail outlet that markets T-shirts. You must determine a price. What factors would you consider in setting a pricing strategy?

DISCUSSION QUESTIONS

1 Assume that you are a marketing manager for a nationally known pizza chain. You have just read a marketing research article disclosing the various tastes and preferences of consumers throughout the country. You are planning to introduce this subject to your employees at a meeting. Discuss the topics that you would recommend to this group.

2 How could a firm use the Internet to differentiate its products from the products of competitors? How could it use the Internet to identify its target market?

3 What advice would you give to a retailer when you have purchased a service that you are highly displeased with? What suggestions would you make to improve its operation?

4 Assume that you are a marketing manager for a restaurant chain and you have just become aware of an aging population in this country that has become health conscious. What trends do you see evolving in the early 2000s? Discuss the new products and markets that may be emerging.

5 Although Harley-Davidson "full-dressers" are popular with consumers over thirty-five years of age, younger motorcycle buyers perceive this vehicle as staid and not sporty enough to suit their tastes. These younger motorcycle buyers are more likely to buy foreign-made sport motorcycles like the Kawasaki Ninja. Product managers at Harley-Davidson may want to reposition their top-of-the-line "full-dressers" to appeal to younger consumers as well. Assume that you are the product manager in charge of developing a plan to achieve this goal. What strategy do you think would be most effective for reaching this market segment?

INVESTING IN THE STOCK OF A BUSINESS

Using the annual report of the firm in which you would like to invest, complete the following:

1 Describe the firm's product line or product mix. Does the firm benefit from its brand name?

2 Has the firm developed any new products recently? If so, are these products extensions of the firm's existing product line?

3 Has the firm established any new pricing policies? If so, provide details.

4 Explain how the business uses technology or the Internet to price its products. Explain how the business uses technology or the Internet to identify its target market and to differentiate its product from the products of competitors.

5 Go to **http://hoovers.com** and locate the NEWS SEARCH. Type in the name of the firm in the space provided, and review the recent news stories about the firm. Summarize any (at least one) recent news story about the firm that applies to one or more of the key concepts within this chapter.

CASE   MARKETING T-SHIRTS

Richard Schilo is the owner-operator of Richard's T-Shirts, a manufacturing business. The business has been in operation for two years. Richard has discovered through marketing research that teenagers desire his T-shirts. As a result of this research, Richard introduced a sports line of T-shirts with the endorsements of professional franchises. Richard has had tremendous success with this product line. His business has become highly profitable, having grown 100 percent from the first year's operation of $150,000 in sales to a current level of $300,000 in sales.

Additional marketing research has disclosed that the collegiate market offers growth-oriented potential. In the fall Richard plans to introduce a line of collegiate sweaters at a retail price of $29.95. These sweaters will be sold in college bookstores around the country and will be priced competitively with other comparable sweater lines. The sweaters will be unique in appearance, with embroidered college insignias in school colors and the school mascot on the sweater sleeve. The product will be packaged in a gym bag highlighting the athletic program of the student's choice. An exclusive brand name will be selected for each college and university. The plan is that the brand name will feature that school's athlete of the year.

In the future, Richard plans to introduce his product line to a nationwide network of retail establishments. His pricing strategy will continue during this expansion. His projections show that he will continue to build volume, especially in the retail discount sector, where much growth has taken place in recent years.

QUESTIONS

1 Describe the target market for Richard's T-Shirts.

2 Identify and explain some common methods Richard is planning to use to differentiate his sweaters from other competing products.

3 What is the current phase of the product life cycle for these T-shirts?

4 Discuss the pricing strategy that Richard plans to use with the introduction of sweaters.

VIDEO CASE PRODUCT DEVELOPMENT BY SECOND CHANCE

Second Chance is a company that produces concealable body armor (bullet-proof vests) for police officers. The product was initially relatively heavy and was used only in specific situations. Now, many police officers wish to use concealable body armor every hour that they are on duty. In fact, they may even be required to wear concealable body armor while they are on duty as a means of continual protection. Because police officers now use concealable body armor more than they have in the past, Second Chance recognized the need to make the armor as lightweight and comfortable as possible. However, it was concerned that the lightweight armor would be too expensive, and therefore would not be purchased by police departments. Second Chance then created an expanded product line of body armor, with each product differing in terms of its weight and comfort. It provided the relatively heavy (and low-cost) armor for police departments that could only afford this type of armor. It also provided the relatively lightweight (and more expensive) concealable body armor for police departments that could afford this type of armor.

The incentive to provide a more advanced product comes from the customers (police officers) who want to be comfortable if they are going to wear it all day. When Second Chance uses the latest technology to develop body armor, it first attempts to design the new armor. Then it allows the employees who manufacture the armor to offer their input because they understand the potential manufacturing problems that may result from a particular design. Thus, there is participation by several employees in the development of the new product.

QUESTIONS

1 Why does Second Chance provide a variety of armor types rather than simply selling its most technologically advanced type of armor?

2 How do you think Second Chance determined its target market?

3 The initial body armor that was created more than 20 years ago has become obsolete. Do you think this reflects fashion obsolescence or technological obsolescence?

4 How would Second Chance use marketing research to help it improve its concealable body armor?

INTERNET APPLICATIONS

http://www.autoworld.com

Find the price of a new car of your choice; then find the price of a used car of your choice. How do you think Autoworld makes its pricing decisions? Do you think the company prices cars according to the cost of production, the supply of inventory, or competitors' prices? How do you think Autoworld differentiates its products from other car dealers, if at all?

THE Coca-Cola COMPANY ANNUAL REPORT PROJECT

Questions for the current year's annual report are available on the text website at **http://madura_intro_bus.swcollege.com**.

The following questions apply concepts learned in this chapter to The Coca-Cola Company. Go to The Coca-Cola Company website (**http://www.cocacola.com**) and find the index for the 1999 annual report.

QUESTIONS

1 Study the online annual report. Is Coca-Cola a convenience product, a shopping product, or a specialty product?

2 Click on "Investments." Explain how marketing relates to brand strength at The Coca-Cola Company.

3 Study the "Operations Review" and "Investments" sections.

a. Has The Coca-Cola Company's product line expanded over time? If so, give some examples of recent investments in new products.

b. How do you think the expanded product line benefits The Coca-Cola Company?

4 Click on "A Message to Share Owners." Which stage of the product life cycle do you think Coca-Cola is in?

5 Go to **http://hoovers.com** and locate the NEWS SEARCH. Type in The Coca-Cola Company in the space provided, and review the recent news stories about the firm. Summarize any (at least one) recent news story about The Coca-Cola Company that applies one or more of the key concepts within this chapter of the text.

IN-TEXT STUDY GUIDE

Answers are in an appendix at the back of the book.

TRUE OR FALSE

1 Typical examples of shopping goods include milk, soda, and chewing gum.

2 Firms should use penetration pricing if their products are price-inelastic.

3 Demographics can be used to identify a target market.

4 Consumers purchasing convenience goods will shop around and compare quality and price of similar products.

5 As new consumer needs are identified, firms tend to expand both their product lines and product mix.

6 A change in credit terms can affect a firm's sales.

7 Warranties can be used to achieve product differentiation.

8 Price skimming is a strategy commonly used in highly competitive markets.

9 A change in interest rates can have a major impact on consumer demand.

10 During a recession, the demand for specialty goods tends to increase.

MULTIPLE CHOICE

11 The process of combining two noncompeting products at a discounted price is called:
a) complimentary advertising.
b) multiple discounts.
c) co-branding.
d) sales promotion double.
e) quantity pricing.

12 Sales of the product increase rapidly during the _____ phase of the product life cycle.
a) maturity   d) growth
b) introduction   e) declining
c) saturation

13 Cameras, clothes, and household items are examples of products that exist in:
a) industrial markets.
b) business markets.
c) consumer markets.
d) government markets.
e) foreign industrial markets.

14 When firms develop products, they assess the markets of their competitors to determine their:
a) financial plans.
b) marketing strategies.
c) industrial strategies.
d) geographic segmentation.
e) business segmentation.

15 The first step in creating a new product is to:
a) assess the feasibility of the product.
b) develop a product idea.
c) design the product.
d) test the product.
e) distribute and promote the product.

16 A Rolex watch and a Jaguar automobile are considered:
a) convenience products.
b) shopping goods.
c) industrial products.
d) specialty products.
e) priority products.

17 The size of a particular target market is most likely to change in response to a change in:
a) inflation.
b) consumer preferences.
c) interest rates.
d) the number of competitors.
e) the size of the largest competitor.

18 All of the following are methods commonly used to differentiate products from those of competitors except:
a) quality.   d) packaging.
b) design.   e) branding.
c) tax policies.

19 The Coca-Cola Company sells Coca-Cola, Diet Coke, Cherry Coke, and other soft drinks, which is an example of a(n):
a) family brand.   d) trademark.
b) individual brand.   e) copyright.
c) corporate brand.

20 Products that are not branded by the producer or retail store are called:
a) manufacturer brands. d) obsolete brands.
b) national brands.   e) generic brands.
c) store brands.

21 Personal computers are subject to _____ because of the rapid changes in the development of computer hardware components.
a) product feasibility
b) penetration pricing
c) planned obsolescence
d) the development of generic brands
e) technological obsolescence

22 Which of the following can be used by a firm to protect its investments in research and product development?
a) marketing research   d) target market selection
b) patents   e) product mix
c) demographics

23 All of the following are benefits of product branding except:

a) greater company name recognition.
b) lower prices.
c) easier to introduce new products.
d) easier to enter new geographic markets.
e) easier to obtain retail store shelf space.

24 To develop new ideas for expanding their product line, many firms have recently increased their investment in:
a) research and development.
b) production facilities.
c) distribution facilities.
d) overseas production and assembly operations.
e) inventory control.

25 Many _____ strategies are focused on convenience.
a) packaging
b) economic
c) partnership
d) production
e) finance

26 Which of the following pricing strategies would likely be used in a market where no other competitive products are available?
a) cost-based pricing
b) penetration pricing
c) predatory pricing
d) price skimming
e) defensive pricing

27 When a firm lowers its price and total revenue increases, it tells us that:
a) the demand for the product is price-inelastic.
b) a penetration pricing strategy is being followed.
c) consumers are not very responsive to price changes.
d) the demand for the product is price-elastic.
e) the firm is using a price-skimming strategy.

28 The break-even point occurs when:
a) profits are maximized.
b) sales are at a minimum.
c) total revenue equals total cost.
d) contribution margin is highest.
e) sales discounts are minimized.

29 New and revised products may be tested through:
a) commercialization.   b) geographic sales.

c) product life cycle.   e) marketing research.
d) family brands.

30 When the cost of production remains unchanged regardless of how many units are produced, it is referred to as:
a) variable.
b) semi-finished.
c) fixed.
d) in process.
e) terminal.

31 Which of the following pricing strategies adds a profit markup to the per-unit cost of production?
a) prestige pricing
b) cost-based pricing
c) defensive pricing
d) profit pricing
e) penetration pricing

32 When a hospital supply company offers a wide variety of products to its customers, the firm is:
a) offering quantity price discounts in order to attract price-conscious customers.
b) encouraging customers to pay their outstanding debts in order to take advantage of discounts.
c) practicing product differentiation.
d) diversifying its product mix.
e) responding to the needs of a diverse labor force.

33 Managers typically attempt to set a price that will maximize a firm's:
a) value.
b) cost.
c) production.
d) advertising.
e) promotion.

34 All of the following are key factors that influence consumer preferences and the size of a target market except:
a) social values.
b) anthropology.
c) economic factors.
d) geography.
e) demographics.

35 Some pricing decisions are directly related to the supply of:
a) social values.
b) social norms.
c) maintenance operations.
d) creditors in the marketplace.
e) inventory.

The Learning	1	Explain the advantages and disadvantages of a direct channel of distribution, and identify factors that could determine the optimal channel of distribution.
Goals of this	2	Differentiate between types of market coverage.
chapter are to:	3	Explain how the distribution process can be accelerated.
	4	Explain how retailers can serve manufacturers.
	5	Explain how wholesalers can serve manufacturers and retailers.
	6	Explain the strategy and potential benefits of vertical channel integration.

Distribution Strategies

A distribution channel represents the path of a product from the producer to the customer. The channel often includes marketing intermediaries, or firms that participate in moving the product toward the customer.

A firm's distribution decisions can affect its value by influencing the number of customers that the product reaches (and therefore influencing revenue). Distribution decisions can also affect the firm's value by influencing the costs of delivering a product from the point of production to the consumer.

Consider the case of Wilson Company, which produces a variety of tennis rackets. Should Wilson distribute its tennis rackets directly to consumers, or should it distribute them to retail stores? Should it sell its rackets exclusively to sporting goods stores or to any retail merchandise stores? Should it use a wholesaler or its own employees to distribute the rackets to retail stores? This chapter provides a background on strategies used to distribute products to customers that can address these questions.

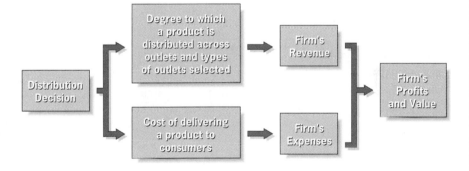

Channels of Distribution

1 Explain the advantages and disadvantages of a direct channel of distribution, and identify factors that could determine the optimal channel of distribution.

A firm's distribution decision determines the manner by which its products are made accessible to its customers. Firms must develop a strategy to ensure that products are distributed to customers at a place convenient to them. Black and Decker distributes its power tools at various retail stores where customers shop for power tools. Liz Claiborne distributes its clothing at upscale clothing stores where customers shop for quality clothing. Ralston Purina distributes its dog food to grocery stores where customers shop for dog food.

Direct Channel

direct channel a producer of a product deals directly with a customer

When a producer of a product deals directly with a customer, marketing intermediaries are not involved; this situation is described as a **direct channel.** An example of a direct channel is a firm such as Land's End that produces clothing and sells the cloth-

A direct channel of distribution is shown here, as the firm's products are advertised in catalogues and ordered directly by consumers.

ing directly to customers. It periodically sends catalogs to consumers, who can mail-order the clothes. It also has a website that allows consumers to place their orders online.

Advantages and Disadvantages of a Direct Channel   The advantage of a direct channel is that the full difference between the manufacturer's cost and the price paid by the consumer goes to the producer. When manufacturers sell directly to customers, they have full control over the price to be charged to the consumer. Conversely, when they sell their products to **marketing intermediaries,** they do not control the prices charged to consumers. Manufacturers also prefer to avoid intermediaries because the prices of their products are increased at each level of the distribution channel, and the manufacturers do not receive any of the markup.

Another advantage of a direct channel is that the producer can easily obtain first-hand feedback on the product. This allows the producer to respond quickly to any customer complaints. Customer feedback also informs the producer about potential problems in the product design and therefore allows for improvement.

A direct channel also has some disadvantages. First, manufacturers that use a direct channel need more employees. If a company that produces lumber wants to avoid intermediaries, it has to hire sales and delivery people to sell the lumber directly to consumers. By using intermediaries, the company can specialize in the production of lumber rather than be concerned with selling the lumber directly to consumers. In addition, producers that use a direct channel may have to incur more expenses to promote the product. Intermediaries can promote products through advertisements or even by placing the product in a visible place for consumers.

Another disadvantage of a direct channel is that the manufacturer may have to sell its products on credit when selling to customers directly. By selling to intermediaries, it may not have to provide credit.

marketing intermediaries firms that participate in moving the product toward the customer

one-level channel one marketing intermediary is between the producer and the customer

merchants marketing intermediaries that become owners of products and then resell them

One-Level Channel

In a **one-level channel,** one marketing intermediary is between the producer and the customer, as illustrated in Exhibit 14.1. Some marketing intermediaries (called **merchants**) become owners of the products and then resell them. For example, wholesalers act as merchants by purchasing products in bulk and reselling them to other firms. In addition, retail stores (or "retailers") such as Wal-Mart and Sears act as merchants by purchasing products in bulk and selling them to consumers. GNC (General Nutrition Centers) uses its chain of more than 4,200 retail stores to distribute its vitamins and related products. Foot Locker has more than 2,700 retail outlets that sell athletic shoes

Exhibit 14.1

Example of a One-Level Channel of Distribution

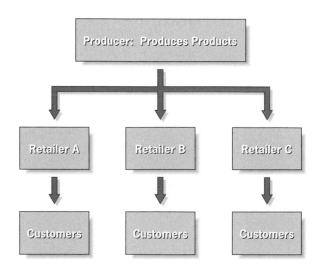

agents marketing intermediaries that match buyers and sellers of products without becoming owners

produced by Nike, Reebok, and other shoe producers. Other marketing intermediaries, called **agents,** match buyers and sellers of products without becoming owners.

Time Warner Corporation (now owned by America Online) commonly uses a one-level channel of distribution for its films and records, tapes, and CDs. Its film company distributes films to movie theaters (the retailer), while its record companies distribute records, tapes, and CDs to retail music shops.

Two-Level Channel

two-level channel two marketing intermediaries are between the producer and the customer

Some products go through a **two-level channel** of distribution, in which two marketing intermediaries are between the producer and the customer. This type of distribution channel is illustrated in Exhibit 14.2. As an example, consider a company that produces lumber and sells it to a wholesaler, who in turn sells it to various retailers. Each piece of lumber goes through two merchants before it reaches the customer.

As an alternative, an agent could take lumber orders from retail stores; then, it would contact the lumber company and arrange to have the lumber delivered to the retailers. In this case, the merchant wholesaler is replaced with an agent, but there are still two intermediaries.

Anheuser-Busch typically uses a two-level channel to distribute Budweiser and its other brands of beer. It relies on nine hundred beer wholesalers to distribute its beer to retail outlets such as grocery and convenience stores.

Benefits for Small Producers Small businesses that produce one or a few products commonly use a two-level channel of distribution. Because these businesses are not well known, they may not receive orders from retail outlets. Therefore, they rely on agents to sell the products to retailers. Consider all the products that a retailer like Home Depot sells. If an entrepreneur creates a new paint product or other home improvement product, it may use an agent to meet with a representative (called a buyer) of Home Depot who will decide whether Home Depot wants to carry this product in its stores. A small business that creates only a few products may have a much better chance of succeeding if it can convince a large retailer to carry its products. Thus, an agent can be critical to the success of such a firm.

Exhibit 14.2

Example of a Two-Level Channel of Distribution

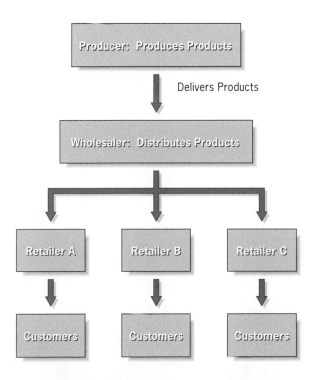

Summary of Distribution Systems

The most common distribution systems are compared in Exhibit 14.3. Firms can use more than one distribution system. Many firms sell products directly to customers through their websites but also sell their products through intermediaries. When firms can avoid a marketing intermediary, they may be able to earn a higher profit per unit on their products, but they will likely sell a smaller quantity unless they use other marketing strategies.

DELL® COMPUTER'S FORMULA FOR SUCCESS

Dell Computer's physical expansion is not limited to the United States. The company will soon open an integrated customer center and production facility in Xiamen, China, which will give Dell its first major presence in the world's most populous country, where it has marketed computers through distributors for several years. Thus, in China Dell will be moving from a two-level distribution channel to a direct distribution channel, which is perfect for a product that may be damaged during transport and is not standardized.

Factors That Determine the Optimal Channel of Distribution

The optimal channel of distribution depends on the product's characteristics, such as its ease of transporting, degree of standardization, and ability to fulfill Internet orders. The effects of these characteristics are described next.

Ease of Transporting If a product can be easily transported, it is more likely to involve intermediaries. If it cannot be transported, the producer may attempt to sell directly to consumers. For example, a manufacturer of built-in swimming pools must deal directly with the consumer, since the product cannot be channeled to the consumer. Conversely, above-ground pools are transportable and are more likely to involve intermediaries.

Degree of Standardization Products that are standardized are more likely to involve intermediaries. When specifications are unique for each consumer, the producer

Exhibit 14.3

Comparison of Common Distribution Systems

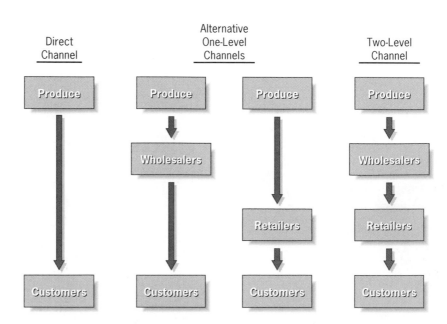

must deal directly with consumers. For example, specialized office furniture for firms may vary with each firm's preferences. Specialized products cannot be standardized and offered at retail shops.

Internet Orders Firms that fill orders over the Internet tend to use a direct channel because their website serves as a substitute for a retail store. For example, Amazon.com provides a menu of books and other products that it can deliver to customers so that customers do not need to go to a retail store to purchase these products. Amazon.com fills orders by having products delivered directly from its warehouses to customers. In fact, Amazon.com has recently built new warehouses in additional locations so that it can ensure quick delivery to customers throughout the United States and in many foreign countries.

Gateway sells its computers directly to customers. It states in its annual report that "the direct channel—delivering goods and services directly from manufacturing to customer—is simply the most efficient channel for business." The Gap uses the Internet to sell clothes directly to customers, but it still maintains its retail stores for customers who wish to shop at the mall rather than online.

BUSINESS ONLINE

Distribution Channel Information

http://www.clubdemo.com/
warehouses/southeast.htm

PRODUCERS, WHOLESALERS, AND RETAILERS FREQUENTLY USE THE INTERnet to provide existing and potential customers with information about the location of their distribution outlets. The website shown here is from *Club Demonstration Services*, a company that provides demonstrations for Costco, a wholesaler selling directly to customers. Customers can obtain a complete list of warehouse demonstrations by region and then decide which warehouse to visit.

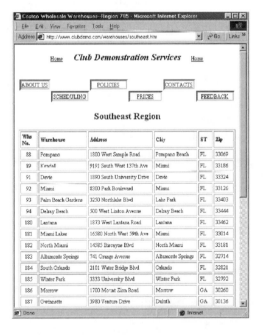

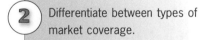

2 Differentiate between types of market coverage.

market coverage the degree of product distribution among outlets

Selecting the Degree of Market Coverage

Any firm that uses a marketing intermediary must determine a plan for **market coverage,** or the degree of product distribution among outlets. Firms attempt to select the degree of market coverage that can provide consumers with an easy access to their products, but they may also need to ensure that the outlets are capable of selling their products. Market coverage can be classified as intensive distribution, selective distribution, or exclusive distribution.

intensive distribution the distribution of a product across most or all possible outlets

selective distribution the distribution of a product through selected outlets

exclusive distribution the distribution of a product through only one or a few outlets

Intensive Distribution

To achieve a high degree of market coverage for all types of consumers, **intensive distribution** is used to distribute a product across most or all possible outlets. Firms that use intensive distribution ensure that consumers will have easy access to the product. Intensive distribution is used for products such as chewing gum and cigarettes, which do not take up much space in outlets and do not require any expertise for employees of outlets to sell.

For example, PepsiCo uses intensive distribution to distribute its soft drinks and snacks. PepsiCo's products are sold through retail outlets that focus on food and drinks. The company distributes its soft drinks and snack foods to virtually every supermarket, convenience store, and warehouse club in the United States and in some foreign countries.

Selective Distribution

Selective distribution is used to distribute a product through selected outlets. Some outlets are intentionally avoided. For example, some specialized computer equipment is sold only at outlets that emphasize computer sales, since some expertise may be necessary. Some college textbooks are sold only at college bookstores and not at retail bookstores. Liz Claiborne distributes its clothing only to upscale clothing stores.

Exclusive Distribution

With **exclusive distribution,** only one or a few outlets are used. This is an extreme form of selective distribution. For example, some luxury items are distributed exclusively to a few outlets that cater to very wealthy consumers. By limiting the distribution, the firm can create or maintain the prestige of the product. Some Nike brands are sold exclusively to Foot Locker's retail stores.

Some products that have exclusive distribution require specialized service. A firm producing high-quality jewelry may prefer to distribute exclusively to one particular jewelry store in an area where the employees receive extensive training.

Selecting the Optimal Type of Market Coverage

Exhibit 14.4 compares the degrees of market coverage achieved by different distribution systems. The optimal degree of coverage depends on the characteristics of the product.

Marketing research can determine the optimal type of coverage by identifying where consumers desire to purchase products or services. For example, a marketing survey could determine whether a firm should distribute its videocassettes for sale through video stores only or through grocery stores as well. If the survey leads to a decision to distribute through grocery stores, the firm can then use additional marketing research to compare the level of sales at its various outlets. This research will help determine whether the firm should continue distributing videocassettes through grocery stores. Marketing research shows that Foot Locker retail stores attract teenagers who are willing to spend $80 or more for athletic shoes. Nike distributes its shoes to Foot Locker because it views these teenagers as its target market.

Selecting the Transportation Used to Distribute Products

Any distribution of products from producers to wholesalers or from wholesalers to retailers requires transportation. The cost of transporting some products can exceed the

Liz Claiborne distributes its clothing to upscale clothing stores, including the retail store shown here that it owns.

Exhibit 14.4   Alternative Degrees of Market Coverage

	Advantage	Disadvantage
Intensive distribution	Gives consumers easy access.	Many outlets will not accept some products if consumers are unlikely to purchase those products there.
Selective distribution	The distribution is focused on outlets where there will be demand for the products and/or where employees have expertise to sell the products.	Since the distribution is selective, the products are not as accessible as they would be if intensive distribution were used.
Exclusive distribution	Since the distribution is focused on a few outlets, the products are perceived as prestigious. Also the producer can ensure that the outlets where the products are distributed are able to service the product properly.	The product's access to customers is limited.

cost of producing them. An inefficient form of transportation can result in higher costs and lower profits for the firm. For each form of transportation, firms should estimate timing, cost, and availability. This assessment allows the firm to choose an optimal method of transportation. The most common forms of transportation used to distribute products are described next.

Truck

Trucks are commonly used for transport because they can reach any destination on land. They can usually transport quickly and can make several stops. For example, The Coca-Cola Company uses trucks to distribute its soft drinks to retailers in a city.

Rail

Railroads are useful for heavy products, especially when the sender and receiver are located close to railroad stations. For example, railroads are commonly used to transport coal to electric plants. If a firm is not adjacent to a station, however, it must reload the product onto a truck. Because the road system allows much more accessibility than railroad tracks, railroads are not useful for short distances. For long distances, however, rail can be a cheaper form of transportation than trucks.

Air

Transportation by airline can be quick and relatively inexpensive for light items such as computer chips and jewelry. For a large amount of heavy products such as steel or wood, truck or rail is a better alternative. Even when air is used, trucks are still needed for door-to-door service (to and from the airport).

Water

For some coastal or port locations, transportation by water deserves to be considered. Shipping is necessary for the international trade of some goods such as automobiles. Water transportation is often used for transporting bulk products.

Pipeline

For products such as oil and gas, pipelines can be an effective method of transportation. However, the use of pipelines is limited to only a few types of products.

The distribution of products is often facilitated by trucks, which transport products from the producer to wholesalers or retailers. Trucks can transport quickly and make several stops.

Additional Transportation Decisions

The selection of the proper form of transportation (such as truck, rail, and so on) is only the first step in developing a proper system for transporting products. To illustrate how complex the transporting of products can be, consider the case of PepsiCo, which may receive orders for its snack foods and soft drinks from one hundred stores in a single city every week. It must determine an efficient way to load the products and then create a route to distribute those products among stores. It must decide the best route and the number of trucks needed to cover the one hundred stores. It must also decide whether to distribute snack foods and soft drinks simultaneously or have some trucks distribute snack foods and others distribute soft drinks.

In reality, no formulas are available to determine the ideal distribution system. Most firms attempt to estimate all the expenses associated with each possible way of delivering products that are ordered. Firms compare the total estimated expenses of each method and select the one that is most efficient.

How to Accelerate the Distribution Process

3 Explain how the distribution process can be accelerated.

The structure of a firm's distribution system affects its performance. A lengthy distribution process has an adverse effect. First, products will take longer to reach customers, which may allow competitors to provide products to the market sooner. This may cause retail stores or customers to order their products from other firms.

A slow distribution process will also result in a long time period from when the firm invests funds to produce the product until it receives revenue from the sale of the product. In most cases, firms will not receive payment until after customers receive the products. Consequently, firms are forced to invest their funds in the production process for a longer period of time.

To illustrate the importance of speed in the distribution process, consider that the actual time required to distribute a typical cereal box from the producer to the retailer (the grocery store) is about one hundred days. Now consider a cereal firm that receives $100 million per year in revenue from the sale of cereal and finds a way to reduce its distribution time from one hundred days to sixty days on average. In a typical year, this firm will receive its $100 million of revenue forty days earlier than before, meaning that it will have forty extra days to reinvest those funds in other projects. Thus, a reduction in distribution time can enhance a firm's value.

Streamline the Channels of Distribution

Many firms are attempting to streamline the channels of distribution so that the final product reaches customers more quickly. For example, by eliminating some of its six regional warehouses, National Semiconductor reduced its typical delivery time by 47 percent and its cost of distribution by 2.5 percent. It now sends its microchips directly to customers around the world from its distribution center. This restructuring has removed one level of the distribution process, as shown in Exhibit 14.5.

Restructuring a distribution process commonly results in the elimination of warehouses. When products are light (such as microchips) and can be easily delivered by mail to customers, warehouses may not be needed. Heavy products (such as beverages), however, cannot be easily delivered by mail, so warehouses are necessary.

Integrate the Production and Distribution Processes

The distribution process can also be accelerated by improving its interaction with the production process. Notice from Exhibit 14.6 how the production process interacts with the distribution process. As an example, if automobiles are produced but not distributed quickly, the production process may be halted until there is room to store the newly produced automobiles. Alternatively, if an insufficient quantity of automobiles is produced, the manufacturer will not be able to distribute the number of automobiles that dealers desire, no matter how efficient its distribution process is.

Saturn ensures that its production and distribution processes interact. Its factories must always have the supplies and parts needed to produce a large volume of automobiles. Then, the automobiles must be distributed to numerous dealerships around the country. Local or economic conditions can cause the amount of new automobiles that dealerships periodically need to change abruptly. Thus, Saturn's production and distribution processes must be able to respond quickly to abrupt changes in the demand by dealerships. Since Saturn allows interaction between its production process and distribution process, it can adjust to satisfy demand.

Compaq Computer has also used interaction between production and distribution to accelerate its process of distributing computers to more than thirty thousand whole-

Exhibit 14.5

Example of a Restructured Distribution Process

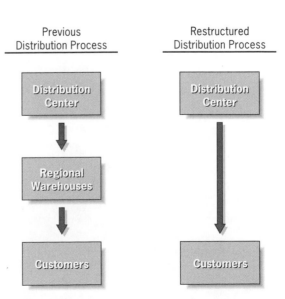

Exhibit 14.6

Exhibit 14.6

Relationship between Production and Distribution

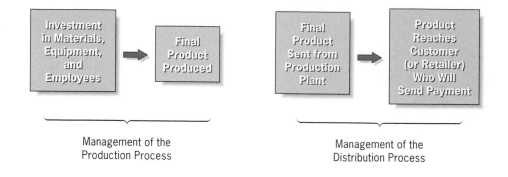

Investment in Materials, Equipment, and Employees → Final Product Produced

Final Product Sent from Production Plant → Product Reaches Customer (or Retailer) Who Will Send Payment

Management of the Production Process

Management of the Distribution Process

salers and retail stores. It has significantly reduced the time from when a final product is produced until it leaves the production plant. Computer technology is now used to indicate which products should be loaded onto specific trucks for delivery purposes.

Exhibit 14.7 provides another perspective on the tasks involved from the time supplies and materials used to produce a product are ordered until the product is delivered to retailers. This exhibit shows how the distribution of products relies on production. If any step in the production process breaks down and lengthens the production period, products will not be distributed on a timely basis.

Assuming that the production process is properly conducted, the firm still needs an efficient distribution system to ensure that products are consistently available for customers. One of the keys to an efficient distribution system is to ensure that any in-

Exhibit 14.7

Steps Involved in the Production and Distribution of Products

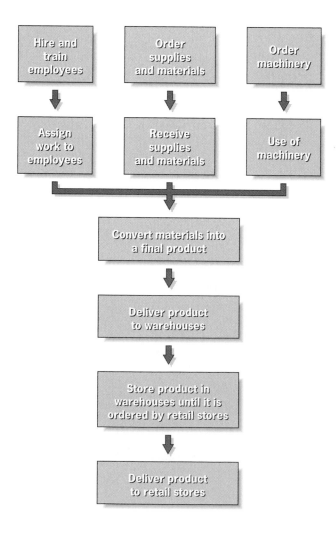

Hire and train employees → Assign work to employees

Order supplies and materials → Receive supplies and materials

Order machinery → Use of machinery

Convert materials into a final product

Deliver product to warehouses

Store product in warehouses until it is ordered by retail stores

Deliver product to retail stores

termediaries used to transfer products from producers to consumers maintain an adequate inventory. The producer must maintain sufficient inventory in anticipation of orders from wholesalers, retailers, or customers. If it does not, it will experience shortages. This task is especially challenging when the firm produces a wide variety of products and sells them to several different intermediaries or customers.

Background on Retailers

Retailers serve as valuable intermediaries by distributing products directly to customers. Most retailers can be described by the following characteristics:

4 Explain how retailers can serve manufacturers.

- ▶ Number of outlets
- ▶ Quality of service
- ▶ Variety of products offered
- ▶ Store versus nonstore

Number of Outlets

independent retail store a retailer that has only one outlet

chain a retailer that has more than one outlet

An **independent retail store** has only one outlet, while a **chain** has more than one outlet. Although there are more independent stores than chain stores, the chain stores are larger on average. Chain stores such as Home Depot, Ace Hardware, and Wal-Mart can usually obtain products at a lower cost because they can buy in bulk from the producer (or its intermediaries). Wal-Mart typically deals with the manufacturer so that it can avoid any markup by marketing intermediaries. Chain stores often have a nationwide reputation, which usually provides credibility. This is a major advantage over independent stores.

WEBSITES SUCH AS MAPQUEST, SHOWN HERE, ALLOW CUSTOMERS TO OBtain maps and driving directions online. Driving directions also include an estimated time for the trip. Thus, these websites enable customers to assess companies' retail outlets and warehouses online and then decide which location is most convenient for them.

BUSINESS ONLINE

Locating Distribution Outlets

http://www.mapquest.com

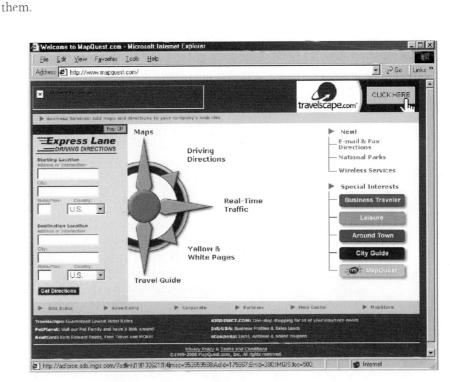

CROSS-FUNCTIONAL TEAMWORK

Interaction between Distribution Decisions and Other Business Decisions

When marketing managers decide how to distribute a product, they must consider the existing production facilities. Firms that have production facilities scattered around the United States can more easily distribute their products directly from those facilities to the retailer or to the customer. Conversely, firms that use a single manufacturing plant may rely on intermediaries to distribute the product. When a large production facility is needed to achieve production efficiency (as in automobile manufacturing), intermediaries are used to distribute the product.

When a firm creates a new product that will be demanded by customers throughout the United States, it must decide where to produce and how to distribute the product. The two decisions are related. Financial managers of the firm use input provided by production managers on estimated production costs and from marketing managers on

estimated distribution costs. If the product is to be produced at a single manufacturing plant, the production cost can be minimized, but the distribution costs are higher. Conversely, if the product is produced at several small manufacturing plants, the production costs are higher, but the distribution costs are relatively low. The financial analysis conducted by financial managers can determine the combination of production and distribution that is most efficient.

Many firms use a single manufacturing plant in the United States and distribute their products throughout the country. If they experience some demand from foreign customers, they may initially attempt to export the products. The cost of distributing products to foreign countries can be very high, however, so U.S. firms often establish a foreign production facility to accommodate the foreign demand. For example, Apple Computer now has three manufacturing plants. Its original plant in California is used to accommodate the demand by U.S. customers. Its plant in Europe produces computer products that are distributed to sales offices throughout Europe. Its plant in Singapore produces computer products that are distributed to sales offices throughout Asia. Apple Computer maintains relatively low distribution expenses by having a manufacturing plant in each region of the world where there is a large demand for its products.

Quality of Service

full-service retail store a retailer that generally offers much sales assistance to customers and provides servicing if needed

self-service retail store a retailer that does not provide sales assistance or service and sells products that do not require much expertise

A **full-service retail store** generally offers much sales assistance to customers and provides servicing if needed. Some products are more appropriate for full service than others. For example, a men's formal wear store offers advice on style and alters the fit for consumers. An electronics store such as Radio Shack provides advice on the use of its products. A **self-service retail store** does not provide sales assistance or service and sells products that do not require much expertise. Examples of self-service stores are Publix Supermarkets and Seven-Eleven.

Variety of Products Offered

specialty retail store a retailer that specializes in a particular type of product

variety retail store a retailer that offers numerous types of goods

A **specialty retail store** specializes in a particular type of product, such as sporting goods, furniture, or automobile parts. Kinney's Shoes is an example of a specialty store because it specializes in shoes. These stores tend to focus on only one or a few types of products but have a wide selection of brands available. A **variety retail store** offers numerous types of goods. For example, KMart, J.C. Penney, and Sears are classified as variety stores because they offer a wide variety of products, including clothes, household appliances, and even furniture.

The advantage of a specialty store is that it may carry a certain degree of prestige. If an upscale clothing store begins to offer other types of products, it may lose its prestige. The disadvantage of a specialty store is that it is not as convenient for consumers who need to purchase a variety of goods. Some consumers may prefer to shop at a store that sells everything they need.

Specialty shops in a shopping mall can retain their specialization and prestige while offering consumers more convenience. Because the mall is composed of various specialty shops, consumers may perceive it as one large outlet with a variety of products.

Kmart is a variety store, but the products it sells vary among its stores. This store in Manhattan focuses more on products for apartments since residents of Manhattan live in apartments or condominiums rather than houses.

To illustrate how these characteristics can be used to describe a retailer, consider Blockbuster Video. It is a chain, a self-service store, and a specialty store. The Athlete's Foot is a chain, a full-service store, and a specialty store.

Store versus Nonstore

Although most retailers use a store to offer their service, others do not. The three most common types of nonstore retailers—mail-order retailers, websites, and vending machines—are described next.

Mail-Order Retailers A mail-order retailer receives orders through the mail or over the phone. It then sends the products through the mail. This type of retailer has become very popular in recent years because many consumers have less leisure time than before and desire shopping convenience. In particular, mail-order clothing retailers have been extremely successful, as consumers find it more convenient to order by phone than to shop in stores. Mail order is more likely to work for products that are light, are somewhat standardized, and do not need to be serviced.

Home shopping networks are a form of mail-order retailing. They have become very popular for specialized items such as jewelry.

Websites Firms have created websites from which their products can be ordered. One of the main advantages of this method over mail order is that catalogues do not have to be sent out. In addition, changes can be made on a frequent basis.

Vending Machines Vending machines have also become popular as a result of consumer preferences for convenience. They are often accessible at all hours. Although they were initially used mainly for cigarettes, candy, and soft drinks, some machines are now being used for products such as aspirin, razors, and travel insurance.

5 Explain how wholesalers can serve manufacturers and retailers.

Background on Wholesalers

Wholesalers serve as intermediaries by purchasing products from manufacturers and selling them to retailers. They are useful to both manufacturers and retailers, as explained next.

How Wholesalers Serve Manufacturers

Wholesalers offer five key services to manufacturers:

- ▶ Warehousing
- ▶ Sales expertise
- ▶ Delivery to retailers
- ▶ Assumption of credit risk
- ▶ Information

Warehousing Wholesalers purchase products from the manufacturer in bulk and maintain these products at their own warehouses. Thus, manufacturers do not need to use their own space to store the products. In addition, manufacturers can maintain a smaller inventory and therefore do not have to invest as much funds in inventory.

To illustrate how manufacturers can benefit from this warehousing, consider Jandy Industries, which produces equipment for swimming pools. Jandy sells its products in bulk to wholesalers that are willing to maintain an inventory of parts. Jandy focuses on maintaining its own inventory of uncommon parts that are not carried by wholesalers.

Sales Expertise Wholesalers use their sales expertise when selling products to retailers. The retailer's decision to purchase particular products may be primarily due to the wholesaler's persuasion. Once wholesalers persuade retailers to purchase a product, they will periodically make contact to determine whether the retailers need to purchase more of that product.

Delivery to Retailers Wholesalers are responsible for delivering products to various retailers. Therefore, manufacturers do not need to be concerned with numerous deliveries. Instead, they can deliver in bulk to wholesalers.

Assumption of Credit Risk When the wholesaler purchases the products from the manufacturer and sells them to retailers on credit, it normally assumes the credit risk (risk that the bill will not be paid). In this case, the manufacturer does not need to worry about the credit risk of the retailers.

Information Wholesalers often receive feedback from retailers and can provide valuable information to manufacturers. For example, they can explain to the manufacturer why sales of the product are lower than expected and can inform the manufacturer about new competitive products that are being sold in retail stores.

How Wholesalers Serve Retailers

Wholesalers offer five key services to retailers:

- ▶ Warehousing
- ▶ Promotion
- ▶ Displays
- ▶ Credit
- ▶ Information

Warehousing Wholesalers may maintain sufficient inventory so that retailers can order small amounts frequently. Thus, the retailers do not have to maintain a large inventory because the wholesalers have enough inventory to accommodate orders quickly.

Promotion Wholesalers sometimes promote their products, which may increase the sales of those products by retail stores. The promotional help comes in various forms, including posters or brochures to be shown in retail stores.

Displays Some wholesalers set up a display of the products for the retailers. The displays are often designed to attract customers' attention but take up little space. This is important to retailers because they have a limited amount of space.

Credit Wholesalers sometimes offer products to retailers on credit. This provides a form of financing for retailers, since they may have to borrow funds if they are required to make payment when receiving the products.

Information Wholesalers can inform retailers about policies implemented by other retailers regarding the pricing of products, special sales, or changes in the hours their stores are open. A retailer can use this type of information when it establishes its own related policies.

Vertical Channel Integration

 Explain the strategy and potential benefits of vertical channel integration.

Some firms use **vertical channel integration,** in which two or more levels of distribution are managed by a single firm. This strategy can be used by manufacturers or retailers, as explained next.

vertical channel integration
two or more levels of distribution are managed by a single firm

Vertical Channel Integration by Manufacturers

Manufacturers may decide to vertically integrate their operations by establishing retail stores. Consider a producer of clothing that has historically sold its clothes to various retailers. It notices that the retailers' prices are typically about 90 percent above what they paid for the clothes. Consequently, the clothing manufacturer may consider opening its own retail shops if it can achieve higher sales by selling its clothes through these shops.

L. L. Bean has created its own outlet stores that sell the clothing it produces. In this way, the firm serves as the producer and as an intermediary. The intermediaries (outlets) allow the product to be widely distributed. Meanwhile, all earnings generated by the producer or the outlets are beneficial to the owners of L. L. Bean.

When a producer or wholesaler considers expanding into retailing operations, it must address the following questions. First, can it absorb the cost of leasing store space and employing workers? These costs can be substantial. Second, can the firm offer enough product lines to make full use of a store? If the firm specializes in producing pullover shirts, it will not have a sufficient variety to attract consumers. Third, will the additional revenue to be earned cover all additional costs incurred? Fourth, will the firm lose the business that it had developed with other retail firms, once it begins to compete with those firms on a retail level? The idea of expansion may become less appealing when the wholesaler addresses these questions.

The trade-off involved in a vertically integrated channel is shown in Exhibit 14.8. The left side of Exhibit 14.8 reflects a strategy in which Zuma Company produces tennis shoes and distributes them to a wholesaler that it owns. Zuma's wholesaler sells the tennis shoes to retailers for $65. The alternative distribution strategy, shown on the right side of Exhibit 14.8, is for Zuma Company to sell its tennis shoes to a marketing intermediary for $50. In this case, it receives $15 less per pair than if it creates

Exhibit 14.8

Trade-off from Using Vertical Integration

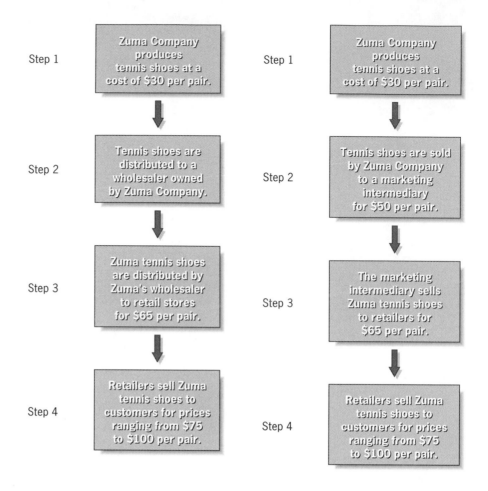

its own wholesaler that sells to retailers. However, it also incurs lower costs if it does not create a wholesale operation.

Vertical Channel Integration by Retailers

Just as a producer may consider establishing retail outlets, a retailer may consider producing its own products. Consider a clothing retailer that has historically purchased its clothes from several different producers. It believes that the producer's cost is about 50 percent less than the price charged to retailers. Consequently, it begins to consider producing the clothes itself. This is the reverse of the previous example. Yet it also involves a firm that is considering vertical integration.

When a retailer considers expanding into production of products, it must address the following questions. First, can it absorb the expenses resulting from production, including the cost of a production plant and new employees? Second, does it have the expertise to adjust the production process as consumer tastes change over time? If a clothing manufacturer cannot adjust, it may be stuck with a large inventory of out-of-date clothing. In general, the firm must decide whether the benefits from producing the clothes itself are greater than the additional costs.

GLOBAL BUSINESS

Global Distribution

IN THE UNITED STATES, THE DISTRIBUTION NETWORK IS WELL ORGANIZED. Manufacturers of most products are able to find distributors that have the knowledge and relationships with retailers to distribute the products. In many foreign countries, however, distribution networks are not well organized. Many products were simply not marketed in some less-developed countries, so a distribution network was never established for these products. Now that U.S. firms have begun to market numerous

SPOTLIGHT ON TECHNOLOGY

Distribution through the Internet

Electronic business has increased the power of the buyer and reduced the importance of sales relationships. Customers have traditionally faced time and distance obstacles when trying to obtain lower prices and quality products. The Internet has eliminated many of those obstacles. Companies and websites now exist that compare prices and quality of products for the consumer.

For example, Autobytel.com provides information about new car purchases, offers suggestions about leasing, gives access to dealer invoices, and enables the consumer to find a low-cost car dealer in the area. Paperexchange.com acts as a broker for paper products and equipment. The way consumers make their purchases is gradually changing. The result is more competition among firms and less brand loyalty.

Companies must adapt to this changing business model. Perhaps the most significant change will be the disruption of traditional distribution channels. As the Internet eliminates the distance between producers and consumers, it also eliminates the need for wholesalers, distributors, and retailers. Amazon.com and Dell Computer are examples of companies that have prospered without traditional retail outlets.

When firms sell their products directly to customers without using retail stores, they can improve their efficiency. They may be able to sell their product at a lower price as a result. Another significant change occurs in firms' relationships with suppliers and freight haulers. A web of communication allows for increased collaboration and the creation of a partnership in the production chain. The ultimate result of electronic business will be increased price competition.

---

products to these countries, they recognize that they cannot necessarily rely on intermediaries to distribute the products. Therefore, they may need to distribute their products directly to retail outlets or to the customers who purchase the products.

To illustrate the potential problems associated with distribution in a foreign country, consider the dilemma of Ben & Jerry's Homemade, which has begun to produce and sell ice cream in Russia. In Russia and in some other countries, the distribution of some products is controlled by organized crime. Consequently, distributing products through the existing distribution network may necessitate extra payoffs to the intermediaries. Also, the intermediaries may decide to focus their efforts on selling other products that offer higher payoffs. Rather than search for an intermediary to distribute its ice cream, Ben and Jerry's decided to distribute the ice cream to outlets itself. It identified a reputable firm in Russia to establish a distribution network.

As Ben and Jerry's was distributing ice cream to outlets, it found that they had limited capacity in their freezers to store ice cream. So it provided the outlets with freezers. This allows Ben and Jerry's to distribute more ice cream to each outlet.

Ben and Jerry's also needed to train the outlets' employees about the different flavors of ice cream, which resulted in another type of expense that is not incurred when selling ice cream in the United States. Ben and Jerry's experience in distributing ice cream to outlets in Russia illustrates how the strategy used for distributing a specific product may vary with the country where the product is being sold.

BUSINESS DILEMMA | College Health Club

Retailing Decision at College Health Club

THE CONCEPTS DISCUSSED IN THIS CHAPTER CAN BE APPLIED TO THE CASE of College Health Club (CHC). Since CHC's main business is the provision of health club services, its potential channels of distribution are somewhat limited. The provision of a service makes it difficult to use intermediaries. However, CHC has an opportunity to be involved in the distribution of a product. CHC was asked by a manufacturer of exercise clothing to serve as a retailer by selling the clothing to its members. The manufacturer would sell the clothing in bulk to CHC, which would be able to mark up the price before selling it to customers.

Dilemma

Sue Kramer, president of CHC, wants to organize a list of key questions that need to be addressed when assessing the idea of selling exercise clothing at the health club. What questions do you believe Sue should address before she decides whether to serve as a retailer?

Solution

Sue identifies the following questions to assess the idea of serving as a retailer for exercise clothing:

1. Would CHC's customers purchase the clothing?

2. What would be the cost of serving as a retailer? The retail shop in the club would take up space that could be used to accommodate future growth in memberships. An employee would have to be hired to serve customers in the retail shop while it was open.

3. Should CHC produce its own "CHC" clothing line to advertise the club instead of purchasing another manufacturer's clothing?

These questions help Sue arrive at a conclusion. Members would like to purchase exercise clothing at the club because it is a convenient place for them to shop. However, Sue does not want to use up valuable space in the club to create a retail shop that would primarily serve customers. The membership is too small to set up a shop.

Sue decides on a compromise solution. She decides to display six different styles of exercise clothing produced by the manufacturer with a poster explaining that members can purchase any of the styles. She will maintain an inventory of the clothing in the back room. Her strategy is to serve as a retailer of only these six styles without using up much space in her health club.

Additional Issues for Discussion

1. If Sue agrees to sell exercise clothing produced by the manufacturer, will the distribution system be a direct channel, a one-level channel, or a two-level channel?

2. Sue has considered producing her own line of CHC exercise clothing and selling it at her health club. Would this type of distribution system be a direct channel, a one-level channel, or a two-level channel?

3. Assume that Sue decides to produce her own line of CHC clothing to sell at her health club. Does this situation reflect intensive distribution, selective distribution, or exclusive distribution?

SUMMARY

The advantages of a direct channel of distribution are:

▶ the full difference between the producer's cost and the price paid by the consumer goes to the producer;

▶ the producer can easily obtain firsthand feedback on the product, allowing for quick response to customer complaints and the opportunity to quickly correct any deficiencies.

The disadvantages of a direct channel of distribution are:

▶ the producer must employ more salespeople;

▶ the producer must provide all product promotions (some intermediaries might be willing to promote the products for producers);

▶ the producer may have to provide credit to customers and incur the risk of bad debt (some intermediaries might be willing to incur this risk).

The optimal channel of distribution is dependent on ease of transportation; the greater the ease, the more likely that intermediaries could be used. It is also dependent on the degree of standardization; the more standardized the product, the more likely that intermediaries could be used.

 The three types of market coverage are:

▶ intensive distribution, which is used to distribute the product across most or all outlets;

▶ selective distribution, which is used to intentionally avoid some outlets;

▶ exclusive distribution, which uses only one or a few outlets.

 A quick distribution process not only satisfies customers but also reduces the amount of funds that must be used to support this process. Firms may accelerate their distribution process by reducing the channels of distribution. Alternatively, they may improve the interaction between the distribution and production processes. The distribution process relies on the production process to have products ready when needed.

 Retailers serve as intermediaries for manufacturers by distributing products directly to customers. Each retailer is distinguished by its characteristics, such as number of outlets (independent versus chain), quality of service (self-service versus full-service), variety of products offered (specialty versus variety), and whether it is a store or a nonstore retailer.

 Wholesalers serve manufacturers by:

▶ maintaining the products purchased at their own warehouse, which allows manufacturers to maintain smaller inventories;

▶ using their sales expertise to sell products to retailers;

▶ delivering the products to retailers;

▶ assuming credit risk in the event that the retailer does not pay its bills;

▶ providing information to manufacturers about competitive products being sold in retail stores.

Wholesalers serve retailers by:

▶ maintaining sufficient inventory so that retailers can order small amounts frequently;

▶ sometimes promoting the products they sell to the retailers;

▶ setting up product displays for retailers;

▶ offering products on credit to retailers;

▶ informing retailers about policies implemented by other retailers regarding the pricing of products, allocation of space, and so on.

 Vertical channel integration is the managing of more than one level of the distribution system by a single firm. For example, a manufacturer of a product may create an intermediary such as a retail store to distribute the product. Alternatively, an intermediary may decide to produce the product instead of ordering it from manufacturers. In either example, a single firm serves as a manufacturer and an intermediary and would no longer rely on another firm to manufacture or distribute its product.

KEY TERMS

REVIEW QUESTIONS

1 Discuss the advantages and disadvantages of direct channel distribution.

2 Compare and contrast one-level and two-level channels of distribution.

3 Discuss the factors that would determine an optimal channel of distribution.

4 What type of distribution system would a manufacturer use for the following products: (a) Calvin Klein jeans, (b) hometown newspapers, (c) Kenmore automatic washers?

5 Explain why Liz Claiborne distributes its clothing at upscale clothing stores as opposed to discount chain stores.

6 How can marketing research determine the optimal type of distribution coverage for a firm?

7 What mode of transportation should be considered by an orchid grower in Hawaii who sends orchids to retail stores in other states? Why?

8 A manufacturer that sells staple products to mini-mart service stations would utilize wholesalers and retailers to reach the final customer. Why?

9 Identify and explain the relationship between production and distribution in reaching the ultimate consumer.

10 In the United States, the distribution network is well organized.

However, in foreign countries, especially developing countries, distribution networks are not well organized. Why has this happened?

DISCUSSION QUESTIONS

1 Discuss the likely events resulting from the elimination of intermediaries for the following products: (a) Rolling Rock beer, (b) Levi's jeans, (c) Jeep Grand Cherokee.

2 How could a firm use the Internet to enhance its degree of market coverage? How could it use the Internet to accelerate the distribution process?

3 Only recently have community colleges started to realize that they, like manufacturers, must give thought to their distribution systems. What distribution decisions might community colleges have to make?

4 Describe an appropriate channel of distribution for (a) a loaf of bread sold in a local grocery store, (b) a Buick Regal, (c) a door-to-door salesperson.

5 Select the appropriate distribution (intensive, selective, or exclusive) for the following products: (a) Ethan Allen furniture, (b) Marlboro cigarettes, (c) Starter jackets, (d) Reebok shoes, (e) *USA Today*.

INVESTING IN THE STOCK OF A BUSINESS

Using the annual report of the firm in which you would like to invest, complete the following:

1 How does the firm distribute its products to consumers? Does it rely on wholesalers? Does it rely on retail stores?

2 Has the firm revised its distribution methods in recent years? If so, provide details.

3 Explain how the business displays its products and

prices over the Internet. Does it distribute products directly to customers who order over the Internet? Does it advertise on the Internet?

4 Go to **http://hoovers.com** and locate the NEWS SEARCH. Type in the name of the firm in the space provided, and review the recent news stories about the firm. Summarize any (at least one) recent news story about the firm that applies to one or more of the key concepts within this chapter.

CASE DISTRIBUTION DECISIONS BY NOVAK INC.

Novak Inc. is a wholesaler in business to sell engine parts for cars. It recently installed a website order system. The system allows a customer (such as a car repair shop) to order inventory parts from anywhere in the United States. Novak can ship directly to the customer.

Larry Novak, president of Novak Inc., decided to sell more than car engine parts. His plan was to sell technical expertise to provide his customers who own repair shops with information pertaining to car engine parts. With recent technological changes and the increased number of imports entering the United States, repair shops must now handle many different car engine parts. Larry placed his company in a position to be more competitive in the industry by emphasizing information rather than price. His website offers numerous product catalogs and handbooks that provide extensive, detailed descriptions and diagrams of every transmission, as well as specific parts needed to complete the repairs.

With the staggering selection of transmissions, shops cannot begin to keep all the essential parts. To help alleviate this problem, Novak has organized a national computer network linking its regional offices around the country. It provides information on the status of in-stock inventory, orders expected to come in, and delivery schedules expected to go out. With this information, salespeople can access data on the availability of a product anywhere in the United States and have it shipped to them directly.

QUESTIONS

1 Is Novak a wholesaler or a retailer?

2 What is the advantage that Novak is now providing to its customers?

3 Is Novak considered an intermediary? How many levels are within Novak's channels of distribution?

4 Does Novak have a quick distribution process? If so, how?

VIDEO CASE DISTRIBUTION STRATEGIES AT BURTON SNOWBOARDS

Burton Snowboards is the leading manufacturer of snowboards and snowboard apparel. Retail stores place orders with manufacturer representatives (reps) before the snowboard season (winter). Burton does not maintain a large inventory, as it attempts to produce its snowboards upon demand. It works closely with retail stores to ensure that the store employees have some knowledge about the snowboards. Burton listens to the feedback that stores receive from customers so that it knows what customers want. Burton also provides advertising signs and promotional brochures to the stores to promote its image. It also offers support over the phone if store employees have specific questions about the products it offers. In addition, Burton has a website that provides much information to customers and answers their specific online questions.

QUESTIONS

1. How is feedback from retail stores within the distribution network related to Burton's production?
2. Why is it important for Burton to screen the potential retail stores that sell its snowboards?
3. How can Burton's website improve the efficiency of its distribution system?

INTERNET APPLICATIONS

http://www.mapquest.com

Obtain driving directions from your home to a location of your choice. How could a business use a website such as MapQuest to direct its customers to appropriate retailers and service locations? How could a company use this website to expand its degree of market coverage?

THE Coca-Cola COMPANY ANNUAL REPORT PROJECT

 Questions for the current year's annual report are available on the text website at **http://madura_intro_bus.swcollege.com**.

The following questions apply concepts learned in this chapter to The Coca-Cola Company. Go to The Coca-Cola Company website (**http://www.cocacola.com**) and find the index for the 1999 annual report.

QUESTIONS

1. Click on "Investments." Who are The Coca-Cola Company's customers? How does the company benefit its customers?
2. Click on "Investments." How does The Coca-Cola Company use "anchor bottlers" to strengthen its distribution system?
3. Click on "Investments." Do you think The Coca-Cola Company utilizes intensive distribution, selective distribution, or exclusive distribution?
4. Click on "Volume." Regarding The Coca-Cola Company's distribution channels, do you think it utilizes one-level or two-level channels?
5. Go to **http://hoovers.com** and locate the NEWS SEARCH. Type in The Coca-Cola Company in the space provided, and review the recent news stories about the firm. Summarize any (at least one) recent news story about The Coca-Cola Company that applies one or more of the key concepts within this chapter of the text.

IN-TEXT STUDY GUIDE

Answers are in an appendix at the back of the book.

TRUE OR FALSE

1. A lengthy distribution process adversely affects a firm's performance.
2. Small business firms that produce only a few products typically use a two-level channel of distribution.
3. Manufacturers can vertically integrate their operations by establishing retail stores.
4. Distribution decisions do not affect the cost of delivering a product.

5 Intensive distribution is used for products such as automobiles and appliances.

6 Wholesalers commonly offer manufacturers sales expertise.

7 Products that are standardized are more likely to involve intermediaries.

8 One reason firms may choose an exclusive distribution strategy is to create or maintain prestige for their product.

9 Retailers sell primarily to wholesalers.

10 Manufacturers that use a direct distribution channel need fewer employees than they would need if they used a one-level or two-level channel.

MULTIPLE CHOICE

11 A firm's distribution process can be accelerated by improving its interaction with its:
- a) social responsibilities.
- b) human resource process.
- c) financing process.
- d) production process.
- e) accounting process.

12 Wholesalers are marketing intermediaries who purchase products from manufacturers and sell them to:
- a) final users.
- b) retailers.
- c) other manufacturers.
- d) primary customers.
- e) secondary customers.

13 Newspaper publishers have their papers available in grocery stores, convenience stores, vending machines, and at many other locations throughout a city. This is an example of a(n) _____ distribution of a product.
- a) nonspecific
- b) specialized
- c) geographically dispersed
- d) intensive
- e) decentralized

14 When a clothing manufacturer sells its own products through a mail-order arrangement, it is using a _____ channel of distribution.
- a) direct
- b) one-level
- c) mixed-mode
- d) nonspecific
- e) wholesale oriented

15 Restructuring a distribution process commonly results in the elimination of:
- a) production.
- b) warehouses.
- c) manufacturers.
- d) product lines.
- e) product mixes.

16 Products that are standardized and easily transported are likely to:
- a) be sold at a high markup.
- b) have limited market areas.

c) use intermediaries in their distribution channels.
- d) be sold at steep discounts.
- e) use a direct channel of distribution.

17 A camera shop that has knowledgeable salespeople who can provide advice to purchasers and also offers to service and repair the cameras it sells is an example of a(n):
- a) mass merchandiser.
- b) agent-seller.
- c) one-stop shopping outlet.
- d) distribution chain.
- e) full-service retailer.

18 Marketing intermediaries that match buyers and sellers of products without becoming the owners of the products themselves are known as:
- a) single-service marketers.
- b) agents.
- c) commission-based wholesalers.
- d) stockers.
- e) mediators.

19 _____ refers to the degree of product distribution among outlets.
- a) The marketing mix
- b) Demographic distribution
- c) Market coverage
- d) Channelization
- e) The retail ratio

20 _____ distribution is used when a producer distributes its products through certain chosen outlets while intentionally avoiding other possible outlets.
- a) Restrictive
- b) Exclusive
- c) Intensive
- d) Narrow
- e) Selective

21 An advantage of exclusive distribution is that it:
- a) makes the product widely available to consumers at a variety of outlets.
- b) eliminates all market intermediaries.
- c) allows the firm to avoid charging a sales tax on the goods.
- d) may allow the firm to create and maintain a level of prestige.
- e) provides the goods to consumers at the lowest possible cost.

22 A wholesaler provides all of the following services to manufacturers except:
- a) production.
- b) warehousing.
- c) delivery to retailers.
- d) sales expertise.
- e) feedback from retailers.

23 _____ are usually the best way to ship goods when the goods must be delivered quickly to several different locations in a local area.
- a) Trucks
- b) Barges

c) The railroads   e) Containerized modules
d) Pipelines

24 Stores that tend to focus on only one or a few types of products are:
a) specialty retailers.
b) variety department stores.
c) retail outlets.
d) discount stores.
e) cash-and-carry retailers.

25 When the wholesaler purchases the products from the manufacturer and sells them to retailers on credit, it normally assumes the:
a) package design.
b) credit risk.
c) promotional expenses of the manufacturer.
d) manufacturer's guarantee.
e) producer's risk.

26 Firms that fill orders over the Internet tend to use a(n) _____ channel of distribution.
a) one-level   d) direct
b) unidirectional   e) intrinsic
c) multimodal

27 The manner by which a firm's products are made accessible to its customers is determined by its:
a) advertising strategies. d) distribution decisions.
b) product decisions.   e) package designs.
c) pricing strategies.

28 One way to accelerate the distribution process is to make sure that it is integrated with the _____ process.
a) marketing   d) advertising
b) financing   e) production
c) credit approval

29 By purchasing products from the manufacturer and selling them to the retailers, wholesalers serve as:
a) producers.
b) intermediaries.
c) end users.
d) cash-and-carry producers.
e) chain stores.

30 A situation in which two or more levels of distribution are managed by a single firm is called:
a) vertical channel integration.
b) horizontal channel integration.
c) multilevel marketing.
d) wheel of retailing.
e) conglomeration.

31 With a direct channel of distribution, the full difference between the manufacturer's cost and the price paid by the consumer goes to the:
a) manufacturer.   d) intermediary.
b) wholesaler.   e) merchant.
c) retailer.

32 For a manufacturer to expose its product to as many consumers as possible, its market coverage should be:
a) selective distribution.
b) intensive distribution.
c) exclusive distribution.
d) zero-level distribution.
e) multilevel distribution.

33 A distribution channel represents the path of a product from producer to:
a) retailer.   d) manufacturer.
b) wholesaler.   e) industrial distributor.
c) consumer.

34 Exclusive distribution can be viewed as an extreme form of:
a) intensive distribution.
b) the one-channel approach.
c) selective distribution.
d) price discrimination.
e) mass merchandising.

35 A(n) _____ is a retailer with only one outlet.
a) exclusive retailer
b) independent retail store
c) wholesaler
d) franchise retailer
e) sole proprietorship

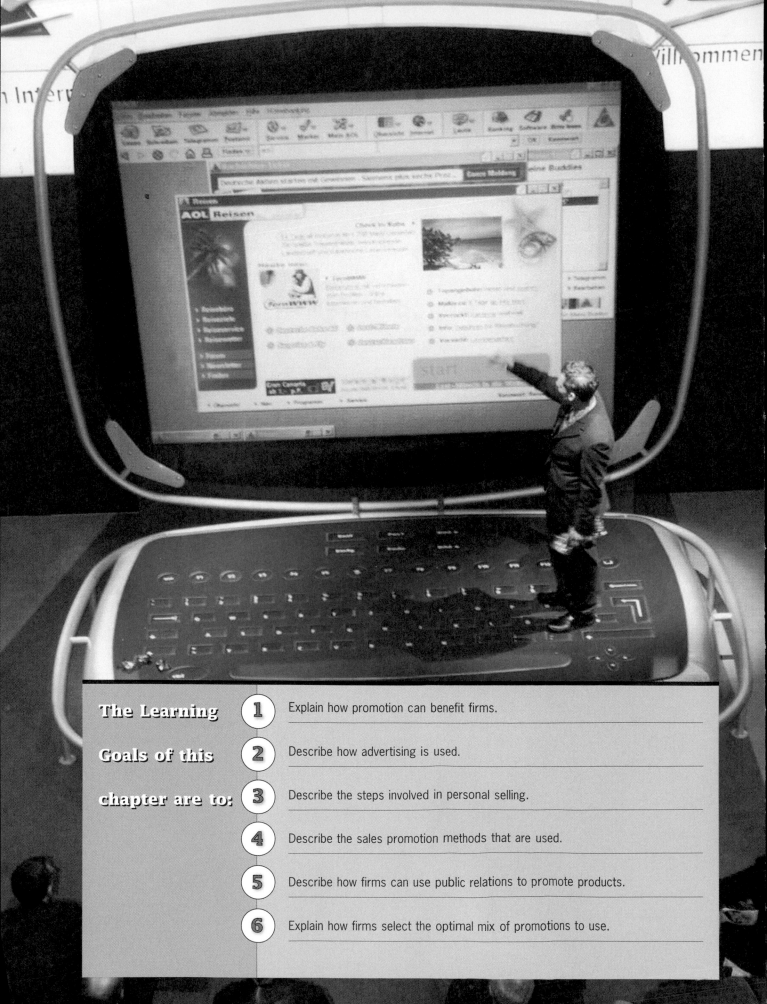

The Learning Goals of this chapter are to:

1. Explain how promotion can benefit firms.

2. Describe how advertising is used.

3. Describe the steps involved in personal selling.

4. Describe the sales promotion methods that are used.

5. Describe how firms can use public relations to promote products.

6. Explain how firms select the optimal mix of promotions to use.

Promotion Strategies

Firms regularly attempt to inform customers about the favorable features of their products. They engage in promotion, which is the act of informing or reminding consumers about a specific product or brand. Firms can use promotion to increase their value.

Consider the case of America Online (AOL), which provides Internet access services. How can AOL benefit from promotion? What promotion strategies and types of

advertising should AOL implement? This chapter provides a background on promotion strategies that can be used to address these questions.

Background on Promotion

promotion the act of informing or reminding consumers about a specific product or brand

Even if a firm's product is properly produced, priced, and distributed, it still needs to be promoted. Firms commonly use **promotion** to supplement the other marketing strategies (product, pricing, and distribution strategies) described in the previous two chapters. For example, the strategy of an automaker to improve product quality is supplemented with promotions that inform consumers about the strategy. An airline's strategy to lower prices is typically supplemented with promotions that inform consumers of the pricing strategy. A quality product that is reasonably priced may not sell unless it is promoted, so that customers are made aware of it.

To make consumers aware of a new product, promotion can be used when the product is introduced. Promotion can also remind consumers that the product exists. Furthermore, it reminds consumers about the product's qualities and the advantages it offers over competing products. Promotion may also include special incentives to induce consumers to purchase a specific product. Promotion may also be used on a long-term basis to protect a product's image and retain its market share.

Effective promotion should increase demand for the product and generate a higher level of sales. To recognize how promotions can enhance product sales, consider the following statement in a recent annual report by Procter & Gamble:

" Our leading brands begin with world-class product technology, but it's advertising that gets consumers' attention and persuades them to use our products again and again. 'Advertising is the lifeblood of our brands,' . . . [A]dvertising is the key driver in all our businesses, but it's especially important for health care products—because consumers want a brand they know and trust. Advertising helps establish the trust. "

As an illustration of how promotion can affect a firm's value, consider the case of Abercrombie & Fitch. It implemented a major promotion to boost awareness of its clothing. Its sales increased substantially just after the promotion, and so did its value (as measured by its stock price), as shown in Exhibit 15.1.

Promotion Mix

promotion mix the combination of promotion methods that a firm uses to increase acceptance of its products

The **promotion mix** is the combination of promotion methods that a firm uses to increase acceptance of its products. The four methods of promotion are:

▶ Advertising
▶ Personal selling
▶ Sales promotion
▶ Public relations

Some firms use one of these promotion methods to promote their products, while other firms use two or more. The optimal promotion mix for promoting the product depends on the characteristics of the target market. Each of the four promotion methods is discussed in detail next.

Advertising

2 Describe how advertising is used.

advertising a nonpersonal sales presentation communicated through media or nonmedia forms to influence a large number of consumers

Advertising is a nonpersonal sales presentation communicated through media or nonmedia forms to influence a large number of consumers. It is a common method for promoting products and services. Although advertising is generally more expensive than other methods, it can reach many consumers. Large firms commonly use advertising agencies to develop their promotion strategies for them. Many firms such as Anheuser-Busch, Compaq, and KMart spend more than $100 million per year on advertising. Procter & Gamble Company spends more than $3 billion a year in advertising.

Although advertising can be expensive, it can increase a product's market share. One reason for Frito-Lay's increase in market share over time is its heavy use of advertising. Frito-Lay typically spends more than $50 million a year on advertising.

Exhibit 15.1

Impact of a Major Promotion on Abercrombie & Fitch's Stock Price

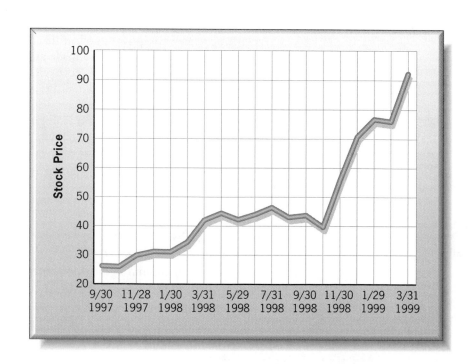

Reasons for Advertising

Advertising is normally intended to enhance the image of a specific brand, institution, or industry. The most common reason is to enhance the image of a specific brand. **Brand advertising** is a nonpersonal sales presentation about a specific brand. Some brands are advertised to inform consumers about changes in the product. GNC (General Nutrition Centers) spends more than $80 million per year on brand advertising. The Gap and The Coca Cola Company also spend heavily on brand advertising. Amazon.com uses extensive brand advertising right on its own website.

Common strategies used to advertise a specific brand are comparative advertising and reminder advertising. **Comparative advertising** is intended to persuade customers to purchase a specific product by demonstrating a brand's superiority by comparison with other competing brands. Some soft drink makers use taste tests to prove the superiority of their respective soft drinks. Volvo advertises its superior safety features, while Saturn advertises that its price is lower than that of its competitors and that its quality is superior.

Reminder advertising is intended to remind consumers of a product's existence. It is commonly used for products that have already proved successful and are at the maturity stage of their life cycle. This type of advertising is frequently used for grocery products such as cereal, peanut butter, and dog food.

A second reason for advertising is to enhance the image of a specific institution. **Institutional advertising** is a nonpersonal sales presentation about a specific institution. For example, firms such as IBM and ExxonMobil sometimes advertise to enhance their overall image, without focusing on a particular product they produce. Utility companies also advertise to enhance their image.

A third reason for advertising is to enhance the image of a specific industry. **Industry advertising** is a nonpersonal sales presentation about a specific industry. Industry associations advertise their respective products (such as orange juice, milk, or beef) to increase industry demand for these products.

Forms of Advertising

Firms can advertise their products through various means. The most effective type of advertising varies with the product and target market of concern. Most types of advertising can be classified as follows:

- ▶ Newspapers
- ▶ Magazines
- ▶ Radio
- ▶ Television
- ▶ Internet
- ▶ Direct mail
- ▶ Telemarketing
- ▶ Outdoor ads
- ▶ Transportation ads
- ▶ Specialty ads

Newspapers Many small and large businesses use newspaper advertising. It is a convenient way to reach a particular geographic market. Because many stores generate most of their sales from consumers within a ten-mile radius, they use a local newspaper for most of their ads. Newspaper ads can be inserted quickly, allowing firms to advertise only a few days after the idea was created. Best Buy, Publix, and other stores frequently use newspapers as a means of advertising.

Magazines Because most magazines are distributed nationwide, the products advertised are distributed nationwide. Some magazines such as *Business Week* have the

---

brand advertising a nonpersonal sales presentation about a specific brand

comparative advertising intended to persuade customers to purchase a specific product by demonstrating a brand's superiority by comparison with other competing brands

reminder advertising intended to remind consumers of a product's existence

institutional advertising a nonpersonal sales presentation about a specific institution

industry advertising a nonpersonal sales presentation about a specific industry

SPOTLIGHT ON TECHNOLOGY

Electronic Shopping Offered by Firms

In the years to come, the process of distributing and promoting products may be revolutionized by information technology. At the leading edge of this revolution is online shopping, such as that provided by Amazon.com (Exhibit 15.2). We will now take a brief tour of that website.

Upon entering Amazon.com, you are provided a list of several "departments" that may be visited.

For this particular trip, we select Electronics & Software. Immediately, we are presented with a main window (see Exhibit 15.3) that not only allows us to begin shopping but also can be used to promote specific products, direct us to featured categories, and provide us with access to other services.

Exhibit 15.2 Main Screen of Amazon.com

Exhibit 15.3 Amazon.com Electronics & Software

Continued

flexibility to offer regional ads that are inserted only in magazines distributed to a certain area.

Radio An advantage of radio advertising is that, unlike magazines and newspapers, it talks to the audience. However, it lacks any visual effect. Because most radio stations serve a local audience, radio ads tend to focus on a particular local area. Furthermore, the particular type of music or other entertainment on each radio station attracts consumers with similar characteristics. Therefore, each station may be perceived to reach a particular target market.

Television Television ads combine the advantages of print media (such as newspapers and magazines) and radio. They can talk to the audience and provide a visual effect. Ads can be televised locally or nationwide. McDonald's, Sears, Duracell, and AT&T commonly show a commercial more than twenty times in a given week. Although television ads are expensive, they reach a large audience and can be highly effective. Some large firms, such as McDonald's and AT&T, run more than 1,000 television ads per year.

Firms attempt to use television advertising during shows that attract their target market. For example, lipstick and fashion firms may focus on the annual Academy Awards because more than 40 million women are watching. Beer and snack food producers focus on football games, which attract mostly men. A one-minute ad during the Super Bowl costs more than $3 million. The rates are much cheaper for ads that are only televised locally or are run on less-popular shows.

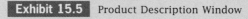

SPOTLIGHT ON TECHNOLOGY

Suppose we are interested in acquiring a pocket organizer. We first choose PDAs from the Electronics & Software page. We are then given a list of different categories of pocket organizers (see Exhibit 15.4). We are then given a list of different models to choose from, along with the prices of each.

After reviewing the list of possible items, we can examine a particular model in a "Product description" window (Exhibit 15.5). If it's what we want, we press a button to order it, which adds it to our "electronic shopping cart." Once we reach the end of our trip to a particular electronic store, we then click a button to "check out," at which point the purchase is billed to a credit card and the items are sent from an Amazon.com distribution facility.

In many ways, these online malls are like an extension of the traditional catalog used to promote products. They offer a number of advantages over paper catalogs, however:

▶ *Firms can update them instantaneously to reflect changing products and competitive conditions.* For example, if a competitor runs a special on a particular product, the online mall can be updated instantly to match the price.
▶ *They have no variable cost.* Catalogs, particularly high-quality catalogs with color photographs, can cost sev-

Exhibit 15.5 Product Description Window

eral dollars apiece to produce and mail, but there is virtually no cost when a consumer accesses an online mall. In addition, there is none of the waste that occurs when a consumer immediately throws away an unwanted catalog.
▶ *They are always accessible to consumers.* Whereas consumers may misplace a traditional catalog, the online mall is always in the same place and is accessible twenty-four hours a day.
▶ *A greater range of effects is available.* Whereas traditional catalogs are limited to print and pictures, online malls can potentially incorporate sound, animation, and special effects as well as permit huge quantities of explanatory material to be attached to the product through the use of online help.

Potential buyers must have the technology necessary to access the catalog and must be willing to purchase by mail. Yet the number of households with PCs is growing dramatically, and mail-order shopping is increasingly being accepted. More than 60 percent of U.S. households order products by mail.

Exhibit 15.4 PDAs & Organizers Window

infomercials commercials that are televised separately rather than within a show

In recent years, many firms (including Procter & Gamble) have created **infomercials,** or commercials that are televised separately rather than within a show. Infomercials typically run for thirty minutes or longer and provide detailed information about a specific product promoted by the firm.

More than 50 percent of total advertising expenditures are used for the four forms of advertising already identified. The allocation is shown in Exhibit 15.6.

Internet

The Internet has become a popular way for firms to advertise their products and services. Some firms use their own website to advertise all of their products. Other firms promote their products on other websites that are commonly viewed by people who may purchase their products.

Exhibit 15.6

Allocation of Advertising
Expenditures

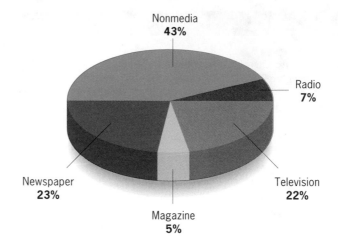

Initially, firms questioned whether people surfing the Internet would pay attention to ads. There is now much evidence that they will and that the Internet can be an effective way to advertise. Consider the case of Bristol-Myers Squibb Company, which experimented with an ad on some financial websites offering a free sample of Excedrin (one of its products) to all viewers who typed in their name and address next to the ad on the websites. Bristol-Myers Squibb expected that it would receive 10,000 responses at the very most over a one-month period. Yet, in one month, 30,000 people responded. Thus, the Internet ad experiment was a success. Furthermore, the ads cost less than traditional methods of advertising. Other firms experienced similar results with ads on the Internet. Firms such as Microsoft and IBM spend more than $10 million per year on technology-based Internet ads. The total amount spent on Internet advertising is now well over $1 billion per year.

One of the most popular types of Internet ads is a "banner ad," which is usually rectangular and placed at the top of a web page. Toyota frequently uses banner ads and found that more than 150,000 Internet users typed in their name and address next to the ad to get more information in a twelve-month period. More than 5 percent of those users purchased a Toyota. An alternative type of Internet ad is the "button ad," which takes the viewer to the website of the firm advertised there if the viewer clicks on the ad. When a firm advertises on a website other than its own, it may pay a set fee to the firm that owns the website. Alternatively, the fee may be based on the number of clicks (by viewers) on the ad itself (to learn more about the advertised product) or on the number of orders of the product by viewers (if the ad results in viewers ordering the product).

DELL COMPUTER'S FORMULA FOR SUCCESS

In June 1994, Dell Computer started using the Internet intensely to promote the idea of selling directly to customers. Specifically, the company launched Dell.com, loading the site first with technical-support information and then with price guides that let customers mix, match, and price components. By late 1996, Dell.com was selling laptops, desktops, and servers, ringing up $1 million in revenue every day. In December 1999, the site had 2 million visitors and sold more than $30 million in products a day. By contrast, Amazon.com's 11 million visitors a month translate into just $3.5 million in sales a day.

Direct Mail   Direct-mail advertising is frequently used by local service firms, such as realtors, home repair firms, and lawn service firms. It is also used by cosmetic firms (including Avon Products), as well as numerous clothing firms that send catalogs directly to homes.

telemarketing the use of the telephone for promoting and selling products

If a firm plans to advertise through the mail, it should first obtain a mailing list that fits its target market. For example, Ford Motor Company sends ads to previous Ford customers. Talbots (a clothing firm) sends ads to a mailing list of its previous customers. Another common approach is for a firm to purchase the subscriber list of a magazine that is read by its targeted consumers. Many mailing lists can be separated by state or even zip code. As the price of paper and postage has increased, advertising by direct mail has become more expensive.

Telemarketing **Telemarketing** uses the telephone for promoting and selling products. Many local newspaper firms use telemarketing to attract new subscribers. Phone companies and cable companies also use telemarketing to sell their services.

Outdoor Ads Outdoor ads are shown on billboards and signs. Such ads are normally quite large because consumers are not likely to stop and look at them closely. Vacation-related products and services use outdoor advertising. For example, Disney World ads and Holiday Inn Hotel ads appear on billboards along many highways.

Seeking to cut through the clutter of billboards, advertisers are turning whole sides of buildings into murals, covering from 5,000 to 20,000 square feet of space.

Transportation Ads Advertisements are often displayed on forms of transportation, such as on buses and on the roofs of taxi cabs. These ads differ from the outdoor ads just described because they are moving rather than stable. The ads generally attempt to provide a strong visual effect that can be recognized by consumers while the vehicle is moving.

Specialty Ads Other forms of nonmedia advertising are also possible, such as T-shirts, hats, and bumper stickers. T-shirts advertise a wide variety of products, from shoes such as Adidas or Nike to soft drinks such as Coca-Cola and Pepsi.

Summary of Forms of Advertising

Exhibit 15.7 summarizes the forms of advertising. It also indicates whether each form targets the national market (nationwide advertising) or a local market.

Exhibit 15.7

Forms of Advertising

Forms of Advertising	Typical Area Targeted
Newspaper	Local
Magazine	National
Radio	Local
Television	National or local
Internet	National
Direct mail	National or local
Telemarketing	Local
Outdoor	Local
Transportation	Local
Specialty	National or local

SEVERAL RETAILERS, SUCH AS WAL-MART, USE THEIR WEBSITES TO PROMOTE the products they sell. By clicking on a product category, customers can view pictures and obtain prices of Wal-Mart's products. Furthermore, customers can order the products directly from the website. Websites such as this allow retailers to simultaneously advertise and sell their products.

Personal Selling

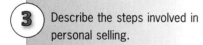

③ Describe the steps involved in personal selling.

personal selling a personal sales presentation used to influence one or more consumers

Personal selling is a personal sales presentation used to influence one or more consumers. It requires a personal effort to influence a consumer's demand for a product. Salespeople conduct personal selling on a retail basis, on an industrial basis, and on an individual basis. The sales effort on a retail basis is usually less challenging because the consumers usually have already entered the store with plans to purchase. In addition, many salespeople in retail stores do not earn a commission. Consequently, they are not as motivated to make a sale.

Selling on an industrial basis involves selling supplies or products to companies. Salespeople in this capacity are normally paid a salary plus commission. The volume of industrial sales achieved by a salesperson is highly influenced by that person's promotional efforts.

Selling on an individual basis involves selling directly to individual consumers. Some insurance salespeople and financial planners fit this description. Their task is especially challenging if they do not represent a well-known firm, since they must prove their credibility.

Salespeople who sell on an industrial or individual basis generally perform the following steps:

▶ Identify the target market
▶ Contact potential customers
▶ Makes sales presentation
▶ Answer questions
▶ Close the sale
▶ Follow up

Identify the Target Market

An efficient salesperson will first determine the type of consumers interested in the product. This reduces time wasted on consumers who will not purchase the product, regardless of the sales effort. If previous sales have been made, the previous customers may be the most obvious starting point.

Industrial salespeople can identify their target market by using library references and the yellow pages of a phone book. If they sell safety equipment, they will call almost any manufacturer in their area. If they sell printing presses, their market will be much more limited.

Individual salespeople have more difficulty identifying their market because they are unable to obtain information on each household. Thus, they may send a brochure to the "resident" at each address, asking the recipient to call if interested. The target market initially includes all households but is then reduced to those consumers who call back. Specific subdivisions of households that fit the income profile of typical consumers may be targeted.

Contact Potential Customers

Once potential customers are identified, they should be contacted by phone, mail, or in person and provided with a brief summary of what the firm can offer them. Interested customers will make an appointment to meet with salespeople. Ideally, the salespeople should schedule appointments so that their time is used efficiently. For example, an industrial salesperson working the state of Florida should not make appointments in Jacksonville (northeast Florida), Miami (southeast), and Pensacola (northwest) within the same week. Half the week would be devoted to travel alone. The most logical approach is to fill the appointment schedule within a specific area. Individual salespeople should also attempt to schedule appointments on a specific day when they are near the same area.

Make Sales Presentation

A sales presentation can range from demonstrating how a printing press is used to explaining the benefits of an insurance policy. Industrial salespeople usually bring equipment with them. They also provide free samples of some products to companies. The sales presentation generally involves the use of each product, the price, and the advantages over competing products. The presentation should focus on how a particular product satisfies customer needs.

Answer Questions

Potential customers normally raise questions during the course of the sales presentation. Salespeople should anticipate common questions and prepare responses to them.

Close the Sale

Most salespeople prefer to make (or "close") a sale right after the sales presentation, while the product's advantages are in the minds of potential customers. For this reason, they may offer some incentive to purchase immediately, such as a discounted price.

Salespeople benefit from the use of technology for staying informed and communicating with their customers, as shown here.

SMALL BUSINESS SURVEY

What Skills Are Needed to Be Successful in Sales?

A survey asked 1,500 sales managers and sales representatives to rank fourteen different types of skills in order of importance for their success. The following table shows the percentage of respondents who ranked each skill as being one of the top four skills in importance:

Type of Skill	Percentage of Respondents
Planning before the sales call	54
Sales approach	48
Assessing potential customer's needs	47
Managing time	45
Overcoming concerns about product	42
Closing the sale	36
Initiating sales calls (cold calling)	30
Making presentations	26
Handling problems with the product	20
Negotiating	19
Following up after the sales calls	16
Using the telephone to make sales calls	15
Managing paperwork	7
Demonstrating the product	4

Notice that the four skills that were perceived to be the most important are conducted before the sales call. This confirms the need for salespeople to plan and organize if they are to be successful in sales.

Follow Up

A key to long-term selling success is the attention given to purchasers after the sale is made. This effort increases the credibility of salespeople and encourages existing customers to call again when they need additional products.

Salespeople should also follow up on potential customers who did not purchase the product after a sales presentation. These potential customers may experience budget changes and become more interested in purchasing the product over time. Exhibit 15.8 summarizes the steps in personal selling.

Sales Promotion

Describe the sales promotion methods that are used.

Sales promotion is the set of activities that is intended to influence consumers. It can be an effective means of encouraging consumers to purchase a specific product. The most common sales promotion strategies are as follows:

▶ Rebates
▶ Coupons
▶ Sampling

sales promotion the set of activities that is intended to influence consumers

Exhibit 15.8

Summary of Tasks Involved in
Personal Selling

Task	Description
Identify target market	Focus on types of customers most likely to purchase the product; contact these potential customers by phone or mail.
Contact potential customers	Schedule appointments with potential customers who are located in the same area on the same days.
Make sales presentation	Demonstrate use and benefits of product.
Answer questions	Prepare for typical questions and allow potential customers to ask questions.
Close the sale	Close the sale after the presentation, perhaps by offering a discount if a purchase is made immediately.
Follow up	Call customers who recently purchased the product to ensure their satisfaction. Call other potential customers who decided not to purchase the product to determine whether they would like to reconsider.

▶ Displays
▶ Premiums

Rebates

rebate a potential refund by the manufacturer to the consumer

A **rebate** is a potential refund by the manufacturer to the consumer. When manufacturers desire to increase product demand, they may offer rebates rather than lowering the price charged at the retail store. Lowering the price to the retail store does not guarantee that the store will pass on the discount. Thus, this strategy could result in lower profit per unit without increasing demand. A rebate ensures that consumers receive the manufacturer's discount. Automobile manufacturers frequently offer rebates of $500 or more.

Coupons

coupons a promotional device used in newspapers, magazines, and ads to encourage the purchase of a product

Coupons are used in newspapers, magazines, and ads to encourage the purchase of a product. They are also commonly packaged with a product so that consumers can use the coupon only if they purchase this same product again. Coupons used in this way can encourage consumers to repeatedly purchase the same brand. Consequently, consumers may become loyal to that brand.

Some coupons are not available until consumers make repeated purchases. For example, airlines offer free flights to frequent fliers, and some hotels offer a free night's stay to frequent customers.

Promoting with coupons may be inefficient for some firms. General Mills had historically used coupons to promote its cereals. However, after learning from marketing research that 98 percent of all cereal coupons are not used, it decided to cut back on this promotion strategy. It reduced annual spending on some promotions by $175 million and focused on improving its product.

Sampling

sampling the act of offering free samples to encourage consumers to try a new brand or product

Sampling is the act of offering free samples to encourage consumers to try a new brand or product. They attempt to lure customers away from competitive products. For example, Clinique samples are provided in cosmetics departments of retail stores. Food samples are offered in grocery stores. Manufacturing firms also provide samples so that consumers can try out equipment. Samples are even sent through direct mail.

Many products on the shelves of this grocery store contain coupons and rebates.

Samples are most commonly used to introduce new products. Firms recognize that once customers get accustomed to a particular brand, they tend to stick with that brand. Thus, the free sample is intended to achieve **brand loyalty,** in which consumers become loyal to a specific brand over time.

brand loyalty consumers become loyal to a specific brand over time

Sampling of Services
Sampling is used for services as well as products. For example, in 1999 America Online (AOL) provided a limited amount of free online time to potential customers. This strategy allowed customers to experience the service that AOL provides and resulted in a large number of subscriptions to AOL's online service. Consequently, AOL's value (as measured by its stock price) increased substantially, as shown in Exhibit 15.9. Subsequently, AOL merged with media giant Time Warner.

Exhibit 15.9

Impact of AOL's Sampling Stretegy on Its Stock Price

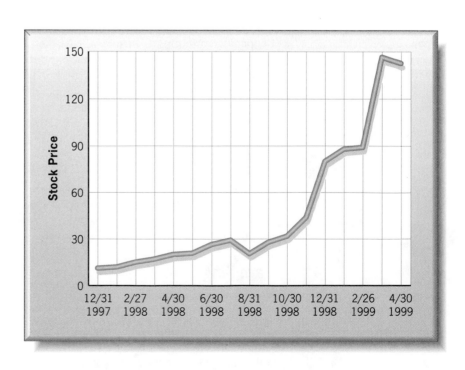

Strategy	Description
Rebates	Firms send refund directly to consumers after product is purchased.
Coupons	Product is sold at a discounted price to consumers with coupons.
Sampling	Free samples of products are distributed to consumers.
Displays	Products are placed in a prominent area in stores.
Premiums	Gifts or prizes are provided free to consumers who purchase a specific product.

Displays

Many stores create special displays to promote particular products. The displays are used to attract consumers who are in the store for other reasons. Products are more likely to get attention if they are located at a point of purchase, such as by the cash registers where consumers are waiting in line. Because there is limited room for displays, companies that want retail stores to display their products are typically willing to set up the display themselves. They may even offer a reduced price to retail stores.

Premiums

premium a gift or prize
provided free to consumers who
purchase a specific product

A **premium** is a gift or prize provided free to consumers who purchase a specific product. For example, *Sports Illustrated* magazine may offer a free sports video to new subscribers. A boat manufacturer may offer a free fishing rod to anyone who purchases its boats. Premiums offer an extra incentive to purchase products.

Summary of Sales Promotion Strategies

Exhibit 15.10 provides a summary of sales promotion methods. The ideal strategy is dependent on the features of the product. Sampling and displays are intended to make the consumer aware of the product's qualities, while other sales promotion strategies are intended to make the price of the product appear more reasonable.

AMAZON.COM, ONE OF THE LARGEST INTERNET RETAILERS, CONDUCTS daily auctions over the Internet. Interested parties can bid on items or put up items for auction. Thus, Amazon.com acts as an intermediary between parties seeking to promote their products and those interested in purchasing them.

BUSINESS ONLINE

Auctions
Online

http://auctions.amazon.com

WHEN FIRMS PROMOTE PRODUCTS, THEY TEND TO EMPHASIZE THE FEA-tures that give those products an advantage over all others. Yet, consumers in different countries may base their purchase decisions on different features. A product may be popular in the United States because it is durable, but it may be popular in another country because of its low price. Therefore, a firm may need to revise its promotion strategy according to the country. In addition, the manner in which a feature is promoted may vary with the country. Television commercials may not reach a large audience in some less-developed countries, where they may be seen by only the relatively wealthy consumers. Some television commercials may still be effective in these countries if the product is being promoted to the type of people who would likely purchase the product. U.S. firms must recognize that the typical profile of the people in foreign countries who watch television or read specific newspapers may vary from the profile in the United States.

Furthermore, firms that hire celebrities to promote products must consider the perceptions of the consumers in each country. Cindy Crawford, Mark McGuire, and Sammy Sosa may be more effective for promotions of products in the United States than in other countries. Arnold Schwarznegger is very popular in Asia because of the distribution of his action films. Another reason promotions of a particular product vary across countries is that each country's government has its own rules and restrictions. A commercial that is acceptable in one country may be restricted in another country. The United Kingdom restricts commercials from directly comparing one product with a competing product. Therefore, commercials that compared Pepsi with Coca-Cola had to be revised to compare Pepsi against Brand X.

Given the different perceptions of products by consumers across countries and different government regulations, a firm may create a different promotion for a particular product in each country where the product is sold. Just as firms create products that are tailored to the unique characteristics of consumers in a specific country, they should also promote products in a manner that appeals to specific consumers.

Public Relations

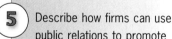

5 Describe how firms can use public relations to promote products.

public relations actions taken with the goal of creating or maintaining a favorable public image

The term **public relations** refers to actions taken with the goal of creating or maintaining a favorable public image. Firms attempt to develop good public relations by communicating to the general public, including prospective customers. Public relations can be used to enhance the image of a product or of the firm itself. It may also be used to clarify information in response to adverse publicity. Many firms have a public relations department, which provides information about the firm and its products to the public. Public relations departments typically use the media to relay their information to the public.

The following are the most common types of public relations strategies:

▶ Special events
▶ News releases
▶ Press conferences

Special Events

Some firms sponsor a special event such as a race. Anheuser-Busch (producer of Budweiser) supports many marathons and festivals where it promotes its name. 7UP promotes local marathons and has even printed the marathon logo and running figures on 7UP cans, which may attract consumers who run or exercise.

Firms commonly attempt to be very accessible to the media, since they may receive media coverage at no charge. When employees of a firm are quoted by the media, the firm's name is mentioned across a large audience. Employees of some banks are assigned to provide economic forecasts, since the bank's name is mentioned in the media.

Tiger Woods, shown here with his father, serves as a spokesperson for American Express. This can enhance the public relations of American Express.

News Releases

news release a brief written announcement about the firm provided by that firm to the media

A **news release** is a brief written announcement about the firm provided by that firm to the media. It enables a firm to update the public about its products or operations. It may also be used to clarify information in response to false rumors that could adversely affect the firm's reputation. The news release may include the name and phone number of an employee who can provide more details if desired by the media. There is no charge for providing a news release, but there is an indirect cost to the firm for hiring employees to promote news releases. Also, there is no guarantee that a news release will be announced by the media.

Press Conferences

press conference an oral announcement about the firm provided by that firm to the media

A **press conference** is an oral announcement about the firm provided by that firm to the media. Like a news release, a press conference may be intended to enhance the firm's image or to eliminate any adverse effects caused by false rumors. A press conference is more personal than a news release, because an employee of the firm makes the announcement directly to the media and may even be willing to answer questions from the media. There is no charge for organizing a press conference, but there is an indirect cost of hiring employees to perform the necessary tasks.

Determining the Optimal Promotion Mix

6 Explain how firms select the optimal mix of promotions to use.

Exhibit 15.11 provides a brief summary of the promotion methods. Each promotion method offers its own advantages and disadvantages, so no single promotion method is ideal for all products. Firms must decide whether to use advertising, personal selling, sales promotion, publicity, or some mix of these promotion methods to promote their products. Firms must consider the characteristics of their target and their promotion budget when determining the optimal promotion mix, as explained next.

| Exhibit 15.11 | Summary of Methods That Make Up the Promotion Mix |

Promotion Method	Advantages	Disadvantages
Advertising	Reaches a large number of customers.	Can be expensive, is not personalized.
Personal selling	Provides personalized attention.	Difficult to reach a large number of customers.
Sales promotion	Offers various incentives for consumers to purchase products.	May not reach as many consumers as advertising.
Public relations	Inexpensive method of enhancing the image of the firm or its products.	Provides only a limited amount of promotion, since news releases and press conferences may not always be covered by the media.

Target Market

If a firm's target market is made up of a wide variety of customers throughout a specific region, it may use advertising to promote its product. If a firm produces a surgical device for a target market of hospital surgeons, it may consider using some advertising to make surgeons aware of the device, along with personal selling to explain how the device is used. If the target market is made up of consumers on tight budgets (such as retired people), the firm may use sales promotion methods such as coupons or rebates.

Any of these promotion methods may be complemented with public relations such as sponsoring a special event when the product appeals to consumers involved in the event. For example, to promote its female athletic shoes, Reebok sponsored a Sports Training Challenge for high school female athletes.

Firms typically attempt to direct their promotion to the target market. Beer commercials by Miller Brewing, Anheuser-Busch, and other beer producers are aired during sports events and directed at a target market of men. Women's clothing ads are placed in fashion magazines and directed at a target market of women. Procter & Gamble promotes its household products on television shows watched by women, since women generally make most of the household purchases.

pull strategy firms direct their promotion directly at the target market, who in turn request the product from wholesalers or producers

When firms direct their promotion directly at the target market, they provide information to the consumers who would most likely purchase the products. Consumers become aware of the product without hearing about it from a retailer. They may request the product from retailers, who in turn request it from wholesalers or producers. This strategy is called a **pull strategy,** because the product was pulled through the distribution channel as a result of consumer demand. As an example, consider a new type of videocassette recorder (VCR) that is advertised to consumers by the producer. As consumers become aware of the product, their demand at retail outlets pulls the product through the distribution channel.

push strategy producers direct their promotion of a product at wholesalers or retailers, who in turn promote it to consumers

Some producers direct their promotion at wholesalers or retailers instead of their target market. When producers promote their products to wholesalers or retailers, their promotion effort is called a **push strategy.** Wholesalers promote the product to retailers, who in turn promote it to consumers. Thus, the product is pushed through the distribution channel. For example, assume that a manufacturer of VCRs has representatives demonstrate their advantages to VCR wholesalers. The wholesalers then promote the VCRs to retailers so they can inform consumers. The difference between a push strategy and a pull strategy is illustrated in Exhibit 15.12. Personal selling is commonly used to apply a push strategy.

Surveying the Target Market Marketing research can enhance the promotion decisions by determining the types of promotions that are favorably received by the target market of concern. For example, a firm that sells clothing to teenagers may survey a sample of teenagers for feedback on various promotions that it may offer. The firm will implement the promotion strategy that is likely to result in the highest level of

Exhibit 15.12

Comparison of Pull and Push Strategies

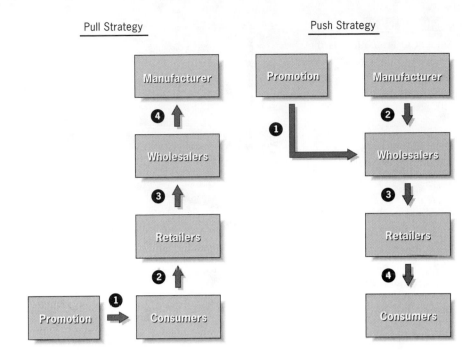

Pull Strategy   Push Strategy

sales (assuming each promotion strategy has the same cost), based on the feedback from the teenagers surveyed.

Promotion Budget

promotion budget the amount of funds that have been set aside to pay for all promotion methods over a specified period

A **promotion budget** is the amount of funds that have been set aside to pay for all promotion methods over a specified period. Firms may create a promotion budget for each product that they produce. The budget may be large if the firm believes that promotion will have a major effect on sales or is necessary to prevent a substantial decline in sales. If the promotion budget for a specific product is small, advertising on television or in widely distributed magazines may not be possible. The firm may have to rely on inexpensive advertising (such as local newspapers) and inexpensive sales promotion methods (such as displays). Perhaps no single type of promotion would be as effective by itself.

The promotion budget varies substantially across firms and may even vary for each firm's product line over time. The promotion budget for a specific product is influenced by the following characteristics:

▶ Phase of the product life cycle
▶ Competition
▶ Economic conditions

Phase of the Product Life Cycle Products that are just being introduced to the market will require more promotions to inform customers about the products. Products that are in the growth phase are promoted to inform and remind customers. Products in the maturity or decline phases of the life cycle may not require as much promotion. However, they may still need some promotion to remind customers and retain their market share. The amount of promotion used for different phases of the life cycle is shown in Exhibit 15.13. Firms that revise their products in an effort to extend the life cycle may use much promotion even in the maturity phase.

Competition A firm may feel compelled to match competitors that frequently advertise with its own promotional campaign. This is a defensive strategy. It implies that

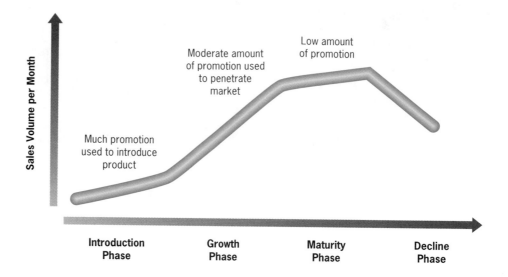

Exhibit 15.13

Amount of Promotion Used throughout the Product's Life Cycle

advertising is used not only as an aggressive strategy to increase market share but also to retain existing market share.

Economic Conditions Firms respond in different ways to favorable economic conditions. Some firms may increase their promotion because they can better afford it. Others will cut back, expecting the strong economy to carry their products. In a stagnant economy, firms may attempt to heavily promote their products in an attempt to maintain demand.

Managing Salespeople

sales manager an individual who manages a group of sales representatives

A common goal of many sales representatives is to become a **sales manager** and manage a group of sales representatives. For example, a company with forty sales representatives around the country may split the geographic markets into four regions. Each region would have ten sales representatives who are monitored by a sales manager.

Sales managers require some of the same skills as sales representatives. They need to have knowledge of the product and the competition. In addition, they must be able to motivate their representatives to sell. They must also be able to resolve customer complaints on the service provided by representatives and reprimand representatives when necessary. Some people are better suited to selling than managing salespeople. There is a distinct difference between motivating consumers to purchase a product and motivating employees to sell a product.

Since sales managers do not perform the daily tasks of selling the product, they can concentrate on special projects, such as servicing a major customer's massive order of products. They should evaluate the long-term prospects of the product and consider possible plans for expanding the geographic market. Information from their sales representatives may help them assess these issues.

Evaluating the Effects of Promotion

Although the costs of a proposed promotion can be accurately estimated, the benefits of the promotion are uncertain. After firms promote products, however, they can determine whether the promotion strategy was successful. If they establish measurable objectives at the time of the promotion, they can assess whether the objectives were achieved. For example, consider a marketing plan that is intended to increase revenue

CROSS-FUNCTIONAL TEAMWORK

Interaction between Promotion Decisions and Other Business Decisions

When marketing managers make promotion decisions, they must interact with other managers of the firm. The amount of promotion that is used for a particular product will influence demand for that product. If marketing managers anticipate a larger demand for the product in response to new promotion strategies, they must inform the production department. The production managers must be aware of the anticipated demand so that they can produce a sufficient volume of products. Promotions that increase demand will increase sales only if the firm produces a larger volume in anticipation of the larger demand. Otherwise, the firm will experience shortages, and customers who are unable to purchase the product may purchase it from a competitor. In some cases, the production may already be at full capacity, which means that the promotion may not be worthwhile until the manufacturing process can be revised to increase capacity.

Marketing managers also interact with financial managers about promotion decisions for the following reasons. First, when marketing managers estimate the costs of a specific promotion and the extra revenue that will be generated over time as a result of that promotion, they may rely on financial managers to assess whether the promotion will provide an adequate return to make it worthwhile to the firm. Second, when marketing managers decide to implement large promotions, they may need a substantial amount of funds; they can inform the financial managers, who may determine the best method to obtain those funds. This discussion illustrates how marketing managers rely on input from the production managers and financial managers when making their promotion decisions.

by 10 percent over the next year. Once the year is over, the actual revenue can be compared with the revenue goal to determine whether the goal was achieved. This type of comparison can be useful for determining whether various promotion strategies are successful over time.

If the objectives of the promotion strategy are not accomplished, the firm may revise its strategy. Sometimes a marketing plan fails because the objectives were overly optimistic. In this situation, the firm may need to revise its objectives rather than its strategies. Firms must also recognize that changes in other conditions may affect revenue. For example, poor economic conditions may cause a firm's revenue to be less than the goal established even if the promotion strategy was effective.

BUSINESS DILEMMA | College Health Club

Promotion Strategy at College Health Club

SUE KRAMER, PRESIDENT OF COLLEGE HEALTH CLUB (CHC), RECOGNIZES that while CHC is moderately successful, it is not being efficiently utilized. Although she has recently succeeded in increasing nonstudent memberships, Sue still believes that she can increase student memberships. Sue's promotions focus on ads in the college newspaper.

Dilemma

Sue's objectives are to attract more students to CHC and persuade existing members to renew their memberships as they expire. Sue needs to assess several promotion decisions that could possibly increase memberships at CHC. Specifically, she wants to identify promotional methods that CHC should implement, given a very limited budget. Also, she wants to decide whether to use local television advertising. Sue must decide which promotional methods to use and whether local television advertising would be worth its high price for CHC.

Solution

Sue considers how each possible promotion method and each form of advertising would possibly enhance CHC's memberships.

Promotion Methods As a form of public relations, Sue decides to provide free seminars on proper exercise at the nearby college. The only cost of this advertising is her time.

She also decides to implement sales promotion methods. First, she will create coupons that will allow a second year of membership at a 20 percent discount for those who sign up for a new annual membership this month. In addition, she considers how to use a sampling method for her club. She allows students and others to "sample" her health club during the mornings (off-peak time) this month for free. She hopes those who "sample" will join the club.

Advertising Sue needs to advertise the sales promotion methods (coupons and sampling) so that college students will be aware of them. She decides that she can obtain the best advertising for the money in the nearby college's student newspaper. She can place the discount coupons described earlier in that newspaper as well. The target market for her club is students at the college. Therefore, she can advertise her promotions to them without using more expensive forms of advertising.

Additional Issues for Discussion

1 Could Sue use direct-mail advertising to focus specifically on the target market?

2 How could Sue use personal selling to promote CHC?

3 How could Sue use premiums to promote CHC?

SUMMARY

1 Promotional efforts can increase sales or at least prevent a decrease in sales because the brand name stays in the consumer's mind, consumers are informed about the product's advantages, and the product's perceived credibility may be enhanced.

2 The key media forms of advertising are newspapers, magazines, radio, television, the Internet, direct mail, telemarketing, outdoor ads, transportation ads, and specialty ads.

3 The main steps involved in personal selling are to:

▶ identify the target market,
▶ contact potential customers,
▶ make sales presentation,
▶ answer questions,

▶ close the sale, and
▶ follow up.

4 The most common sales promotion methods include:

▶ rebates, in which firms give refunds directly to consumers after the product is purchased;
▶ coupons, which allow products to be sold to specific consumers at discounted prices;
▶ sampling, in which consumers receive free samples of products;
▶ displays, in which products are placed in prominent areas of stores; and
▶ premiums, in which gifts or prizes are provided free to consumers who purchase a specific product.

5 Firms can use public relations to enhance a product's or a firm's image. The

most common types of public relations strategies are:

▶ special events, which can be sponsored by a firm to promote a specific product;
▶ news release, which is a brief written announcement about the firm provided by the firm to the media; and
▶ press conference, which is an oral announcement about the firm provided by that firm to the media.

6 When a firm selects the optimal promotion mix to use for promoting a product, it considers the:

▶ target market, so that it can use a promotion method that properly reaches that target market; and
▶ promotion budget, since only those promotion methods that are affordable can be considered.

KEY TERMS

REVIEW QUESTIONS

1 Discuss how promotion can be used when introducing a new product.

2 Identify and explain the four methods of the promotion mix.

3 You are planning to start a florist business in your hometown. Would you use media advertising, nonmedia advertising, or both? Why?

4 Why do newspaper publishers use telemarketing to develop a customer base?

5 You are a salesperson in an office supply business. Why is it important to be persistent and utilize follow-up visits with your customers?

6 Discuss the most common types of sales promotion strategies that a donut shop would utilize.

7 Define public relations and explain the role it would play in the law enforcement department of a major city.

8 Compare the pull strategy with the push strategy.

9 Discuss the different types of promotion that would be utilized throughout the product life cycle for a product or service.

10 How would economic conditions affect your firm's promotional budget?

DISCUSSION QUESTIONS

1 If you are a sales manager in a new automobile dealership, what role would you play in the company and what would your responsibilities be?

2 If you are the owner of a minimart convenience store, what process do you utilize to identify your target market?

3 Identify and explain the different types of promotional methods in the following examples:
  a. Tiger Woods plays golf wearing Nike apparel.

  b. A local supermarket introduces a scratch-and-win ticket.
  c. Ross Perot discusses with the news media his controversial role while on the board of directors at General Motors; his comments will be reported on the evening news.
  d. Assume that you are a college graduate. Your local college telephones, asking you to make a donation for its capital funding program.

4 How could a firm use the Internet to identify its target market? How could it use the Internet to promote its products?

5 Discuss the promotional strategies that would be utilized by a manufacturer in promoting the following brands. Indicate whether the strategy focuses on product position or image building.
  a. Corvette convertible
  b. Dove facial soap
  c. Craftsman tools
  d. Mountain Dew soft drink

INVESTING IN THE STOCK OF A BUSINESS

Using the annual report of the firm in which you would like to invest, complete the following:

1 How does the firm promote its product? Does it use the media to promote its products? Provide details.

2 Does the firm rely heavily on promotion to sell its products? How much money has it allocated toward its promotion budget this year?

3 In reviewing the key terms in this chapter, which do you think could apply to promoting your company's products?

4 Explain how the business uses technology to promote its products over the Internet. Does it provide rebates to customers using the website to purchase products? What do you find most appealing about the firm's website? What do you find least appealing?

5 Go to **http://hoovers.com** and locate the NEWS SEARCH. Type in the name of the firm in the space provided, and review the recent news stories about the firm. Summarize any (at least one) recent news story about the firm that applies to one or more of the key concepts within this chapter.

CASE PROMOTING PRODUCTS ON THE INTERNET

Ken Brabec has created a video, "How to Improve Your Tennis Game," by compiling tips on specific aspects of the game from several tennis pros around the country. He would like to sell the video to video stores, but he realizes that video stores normally deal with large broadcasting and movie companies, and not individuals.

Ken decides that he will try to market the videos to people directly. He can easily mail a video to anyone who orders one, but he needs to decide how to promote the video. Since he can easily mail videos to customers, he wants to promote his video throughout the United States. He first considers advertising in various tennis magazines, but he cannot afford the fee they charge for even a single ad. Ken's funds are limited, and he is not willing to risk all of his money on a few advertisements. Consequently, he decides to advertise his video on various websites, where the advertising fees are relatively low. He still needs to decide the best way to advertise over the Internet, however.

QUESTIONS

1 What types of websites should Ken use to advertise his tennis video?

2 Ken plans to advertise initially on five different websites. He may continue ads on the websites that generate the most sales of his videos. How can Ken determine which of his ads on the Internet are receiving the most attention?

3 Ken is trying to decide whether the promotion on the website should provide an order form for customers to send in. This method would be relatively inexpensive. Alternatively, he could allow customers to order the video over the Internet. This method is more expensive. Is there any benefit to allowing customers to order the video over the Internet using a credit card?

VIDEO CASE PROMOTION STRATEGIES FOR RED ROOF INN

Red Roof Inn provides economy lodging. Its performance declined in 1986, and its slogan "sleep cheap" did not seem to be attracting customers. Consequently, Red Roof Inn hired W. B. Doner & Company to create a new promotional strategy. The strategy focused on the theme that Red Roof Inn was a smart choice for travelers. W. B. Doner & Company had access to bills of American Express credit card holders who used economy hotels and targeted those customers with promotional material. Doner also helped establish a website so that customers can make reservations online and learn where Red Roof Inns are located. The perception of Red Roof Inns has improved over time as a result of this promotional strategy.

QUESTIONS

1 Explain why a new promotional strategy could help Red Roof Inn.

2 One of Red Roof Inn's advertisements suggested that customers can save money by staying at the inn because it does not buy hair nets, shampoo, or mints for its customers as some of its competitors do, but it still offers a comfortable room at a low price. Is this brand advertising, comparative advertising, or reminder advertising?

3 Who is the target market for Red Roof Inn?

INTERNET APPLICATIONS

http://auctions.amazon.com

Click on a category of your choice and view some of the items currently for sale in that category. What types of sales promotion methods does Amazon.com use to auction off other people's products? How do you think Amazon.com generates revenue by selling products for other parties? Do you think Amazon.com advertises its products in other media outlets (other than the Internet)? Why or why not?

THE Coca-Cola COMPANY ANNUAL REPORT PROJECT

 Questions for the current year's annual report are available on the text website at **http://madura_intro_bus.swcollege.com**.

The following questions apply concepts learned in this chapter to The Coca-Cola Company. Go to The Coca-Cola Company website (**http://www.cocacola.com**) and find the index for the 1999 annual report.

QUESTIONS

1 Click on "Operations Review" and study the "North America Group." What happened to retail prices recently? How does this benefit Coca-Cola Company shareholders?

2 Click on "Operations Review" and study "The Minute Maid Company" section. What is the new ad campaign of The Minute Maid Company? How did the campaign affect sales volume of The Minute Maid Company?

3 Study the "Selected Market Results" and the "Operations Review" sections. If The Coca-Cola Company reduced its advertising, do you think sales and profits would fall?

4 Study the "Marketing" section under "Six Beliefs." What does The Coca-Cola Company do to promote its products in India?

5 Go to **http://hoovers.com** and locate the NEWS SEARCH. Type in The Coca-Cola Company in the space provided, and review the recent news stories about the firm. Summarize any (at least one) recent news story about The Coca-Cola Company that applies one or more of the key concepts within this chapter of the text.

IN-TEXT STUDY GUIDE

Answers are in an appendix at the back of the book.

TRUE OR FALSE

1 Comparative advertising is intended to enhance the image of a firm without focusing on a particular product.

2 The promotion mix is the combination of promotion methods that a firm uses to increase the acceptance of its products.

3 Rebates and coupons are used to offer a price discount from retailers to their customers.

4 Television advertising is the most widely used form of personal selling for medium and large businesses.

5 The Internet, magazines, direct mail, and television are all forms of advertising.

6 The most common sales promotion methods are rebates, coupons, sampling, displays, and premiums.

7 One factor that will influence the size of the promotion budget for a product is the phase of the product in the product life cycle.

8 A firm using a push strategy will aim its promotional message directly at the target market customers.

9 Public relations is one of the most expensive forms of sales promotion.

10 A key to successful selling is the follow-up service to customers provided by salespeople.

MULTIPLE CHOICE

11 If a firm's target market is made up of a wide variety of customers throughout a specific region, it would likely use _____ to promote its product.

a) personal selling
b) advertising
c) door-to-door sales
d) one-on-one communication
e) target marketing

12 All of the following are methods of promotion except:
a) target marketing.   d) sales promotion.
b) personal selling.   e) public relations.
c) advertising.

13 Which of the following sales promotion strategies provides a gift or prize to consumers who purchase a specific product?
a) pull   d) rebates
b) push   e) premiums
c) sampling

14 Ads that are televised separately rather than within a show are called:
a) commercials.   d) institutional ads.
b) specialty ads.   e) direct mail ads.
c) infomercials.

15 The use of the telephone for promoting and selling products is known as:
a) telepromotion.
b) telemarketing.
c) online sales promotion.
d) telecommunication mix.
e) annoying phone calls.

16 If marketing managers anticipate a larger demand for a product in response to new promotion strategies, they must inform their:
a) labor union.
b) stockholders.

c) creditors.

d) production department.

e) appropriate government agency.

17 Which of the following promotional strategies is a nonpersonal sales promotion aimed at a large number of consumers?

a) advertising

b) public relations

c) telemarketing

d) retail selling

e) mega-marketing

18 Salespeople generally perform all of the following steps except:

a) identify the target market.

b) follow up.

c) contact potential customers.

d) make sales presentation.

e) advertising.

19 All of the following are methods of sales promotion except:

a) newspaper ads.

b) rebates.

c) coupons.

d) sampling.

e) premiums.

20 The act of informing or reminding consumers about a specific product or brand is referred to as:

a) personal selling.

b) production.

c) finance.

d) promotion.

e) research and development.

21 Which of the following is a strategy where firms focus their promotional messages on the target market customers, who in turn request the product from wholesalers or producers?

a) push

b) co-branding

c) product life cycle

d) sponsorship

e) pull

22 The popular "Louie the lizard" Budweiser commercials are examples of _____ advertising.

a) comparative

b) institutional

c) industry

d) reminder

e) generic

23 When firms promote products, they highlight the advantages over all other products. They emphasize the product's:

a) publicity.

b) features.

c) sales promotion.

d) labeling.

e) life cycle.

24 Even if a firm's product is properly produced, priced, and distributed, it still needs to be:

a) manufactured.

b) inspected.

c) graded.

d) promoted.

e) market tested.

25 A visual method that retail stores use in promoting particular products is a:

a) display.

b) rebate.

c) coupon.

d) premium.

e) market.

26 All of the following are forms of advertising except:

a) direct mail.

b) outdoor ads.

c) personal selling.

d) computer online services.

e) transportation ads.

27 Which of the following is a public relations strategy in which an organization provides the media with a written announcement?

a) special events

b) press conference

c) concert sponsorship

d) direct mail

e) news release

28 Ads that promote the firm, rather than a specific product, are classified as:

a) brand advertising.

b) comparative advertising.

c) reminder advertising.

d) institutional advertising.

e) industry advertising.

29 A salesperson who has just completed an effective sales presentation should attempt to:

a) analyze the market.

b) win at all costs.

c) close the sale.

d) exploit the customer.

e) maximize sales returns and allowances.

30 When producers promote their products to wholesalers or retailers, their promotion effort is called a:

a) push strategy.

b) premium price strategy.

c) sales promotion.

d) market segmentation.

e) pull strategy.

31 The promotion strategy of sampling is most often used to:

a) provide customers with a premium as an incentive to purchase more of the product.

b) introduce new products.

c) give customers a discount if a larger quantity is purchased.

d) serve as a reminder for former customers to buy the product again.

e) unload surplus inventory.

32 A nonpersonal sales presentation about a specific brand is:

a) institutional advertising.

b) personal selling.

c) brand advertising.

d) comparative advertising.

e) reminder advertising.

33 Firms that hire _____ to promote products must consider the perceptions of the consumers in each country.

a) accountants

b) economists

c) suppliers

d) clients

e) celebrities

34 The promotion budget varies substantially across firms and may even vary for each firm's product line over time. Its characteristics are influenced by the following except for:

a) size of human resource department.

b) competition.

c) phase of the product life cycle.

d) economic conditions.

35 The type of advertising that is used for grocery products such as cereal, peanut butter, and dog food is:

a) institutional advertising.

b) reminder advertising.

c) the push strategy.

d) industry advertising.

e) public relations advertising.

Summary of Part V

The key marketing strategies described in Chapters 13 through 15 can be summarized as follows. First, a firm uses market research to define a consumer need. Once a product is developed to satisfy this need, a pricing decision is made. The pricing policy affects the demand for the product and therefore affects the firm's revenue. Then, a method of distributing the product to consumers must be determined. The use of intermediaries tends to make the product more accessible to customers but also results in higher prices. Finally, a promotion strategy must be designed to make consumers aware of the product or to convince them that this product is superior to others.

The marketing strategies just described are continually used even after a product follows the typical life cycle. For example, marketing research may be conducted to determine whether an existing product should be revised or targeted toward a different market. The pricing policy could change if the target market is revised or if the production costs change. The decision regarding the channel of distribution should be periodically reviewed to determine whether some alternative channel is more feasible. The promotional strategy may be revised in response to changes in the target market, pricing, phase of the life cycle, or the channel of distribution.

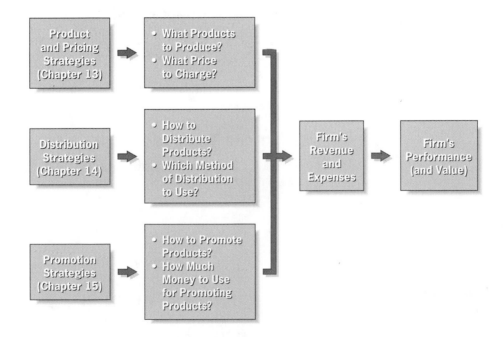

PART V

Developing the Marketing Plan for Campus.com

Product Line and Target Market (related to Chapter 13)

In your business plan for Campus.com, suggest how the firm could expand its product line. That is, what other services could be offered to its customers while it still continues its main type of business? How could it expand its target market?

Pricing (related to Chapter 13)

Campus.com will charge a price per standard service offered (information on one college). What factors should be considered when determining the price to be charged? The initial idea was to charge $1 per request (for information about one college provided to one customer). In your business plan for Campus.com, state your plans for pricing the service. You do not need to use the pricing of $1 per request if you think you have a better pricing policy. If you plan to offer some type of quantity discount, specify that within your business plan.

Distribution (related to Chapter 14)

In your business plan, explain how Campus.com distributes its service. If some customers cannot obtain a hard copy of the information (if their printer is not working), how will Campus.com distribute its services to them?

Promotion (related to Chapter 15)

In your business plan for Campus.com, explain how the firm should advertise its services. Should it focus on high school students, on the parents of the high school students, or on both target markets? Explain. Where should Campus.com advertise its services, assuming it wants to limit its advertising expenditures?

Communication and Teamwork

You (or your team) may be asked by your instructor to hand in and/or present the part of your business plan that relates to this part of the text.

PART V

Applications for Dell Computer

Refer to Dell Computer's Formula for Success where necessary.

1 Dell's product and pricing strategies
   a. Do you think the steps involved in creating a new product are more or less complicated for Dell Computer than for other computer retailers? Why?

b. Do you think Dell's products have a short or a long product life cycle? Why?

c. How does Dell differentiate its products from other computer retailers?

2 Dell's distribution strategies

a. What is Dell's primary channel of distribution? That is, does Dell use a direct channel, a one-level channel, or a two-level channel? Be specific.

b. Does Dell Computer use intensive, selective, or exclusive distribution? Why?

c. Does Dell Computer use vertical channel integration? How?

3 Dell's promotion strategies

a. What is the primary form of media that Dell Computer uses to promote its products? How do you think using this form of media benefits Dell?

b. Do you think personal selling is a big component for Dell in promoting its products? Why?

c. How does Dell combine advertising (an impersonal promotion method) with personal selling (a personalized promotion method)?

PART V

The Stock Market Game

Go to **http://www.fantasystockmarket.com**. Enter your name (e-mail address) and password as requested and check your portfolio balance, which is updated continuously by the Fantasy website.

Check Your Stock Portfolio Performance

1 What is the value of your stock portfolio today?

2 What is your return on your investment? (This return is shown on your balance.)

3 How did your return compare to those of other students? (This comparison tells you whether your stock portfolio's performance is relatively high or low.)

Keep in mind that you can change your portfolio at any time during the school term.

Explaining Your Stock Performance

Stock prices are frequently influenced by changes in the firm's marketing strategies, including new products, pricing, or promotion strategies. A stock's price may increase if such marketing strategies are instituted and investors expect the changes to improve the performance of the firm. A stock's price can also decline if the marketing strategies are expected to reduce the firm's performance. Review the latest news about some of your stocks on the Fantasy website by clicking on News and typing the ticker symbol of your stock.

1 Identify one of your stocks whose price was affected (since you purchased it) as a result of changes in the firm's marketing strategies (the main topic in this part of the text).

2 Identify the specific type of marketing policies that caused the stock price to change.

3 Did your stock price increase or decrease in response to the announcement of new marketing policies?

PART V

Running Your Own Business

1 Describe in detail how the product you plan to produce is different from those offered by competitors. Identify any advantages of your product over those of the competition.

2 Explain how the pricing of your product will be determined. Explain how your product's price will compare with prices of competitive products.

3 Could the unique features of your product be protected from competitors?

4 Describe how your business will distribute the product to customers.

5 Explain whether the cost of distributing your product will be affected substantially if there is a large increase in the price of gasoline or in postal rates.

6 Describe how your business will promote its product. Will it use the Internet? Will it use media to advertise? If so, how?

7 Estimate the amount of money that will be allocated for promotion during the first year.

8 Would coupons or rebates be an effective promotional method for your product? Why or why not?

9 How could your firm use public relations to promote your company or product?

10 How could your firm use the Internet (or other technology) to promote your company or product?

Financial Management

Financial management involves the analysis of financial data, as well as the determination of how to obtain and use funds. Chapter 16 explains how a financial analysis of a firm can be conducted to determine how it is performing, and why. This type of analysis is used to detect a firm's deficiencies so that they can be corrected.

Finance is the means by which firms obtain funds (financing) and invest funds in business projects. Firms may obtain funds to build a new factory, purchase new machinery, purchase more supplies, or even purchase an existing business owned by another company. Chapter 17 describes the common financing methods that firms use and also identifies the types of financial institutions that provide financing. It also explains the factors that influence the ideal type of financing. Chapter 18 describes the tasks that are necessary when a firm determines whether to invest in a particular business project. In addition, it explains why firms sometimes use their funds to acquire other firms. The chapters on financing and business investment are closely related because financing supports the firm's investment in new business projects.

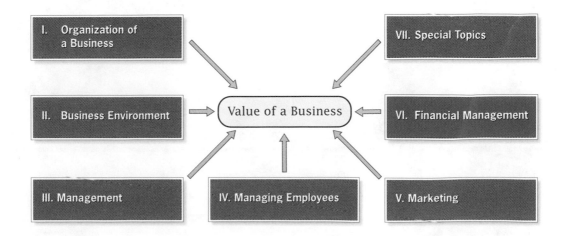

The Learning	1	Explain how firms use accounting.
Goals of this	2	Explain how to interpret financial statements.
chapter are to:	3	Explain how to evaluate a firm's financial condition.

Accounting and Financial Analysis

A ccounting is the summary and analysis of a firm's financial condition. Financial statements are created to disclose detailed information about a firm's recent performance and its financial condition. Managers of all types of businesses use accounting information to make decisions. To the extent that the financial analysis resulting from accounting can detect deficiencies in a firm's operations, it can allow managers to revise those operations and can therefore enhance the firm's value.

To illustrate how accounting and financial analysis can enhance the firm's value, consider the case of Compaq Corporation, which experienced poor performance in 2000. How can a financial analy-

sis be used to identify the cause of Compaq's financial problems? What financial characteristics should Compaq assess when conducting a financial analysis? Why would the financial analysis of

Compaq include an analysis of the entire computer industry? This chapter provides a background on accounting and financial analysis that can be used to address these questions.

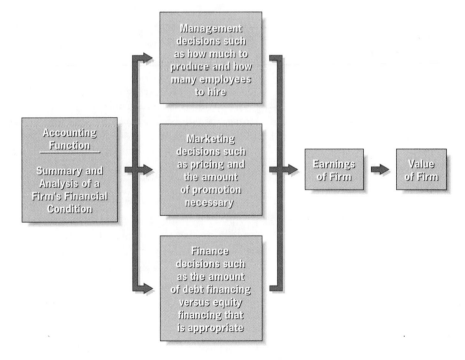

How Firms Use Accounting

1 Explain how firms use accounting.

Firms use **accounting** to report their financial condition, support decisions, and control business operations, as explained in this order next.

Reporting

One accounting task is to report accurate financial data. **Bookkeeping** is the recording of a firm's financial transactions. For example, the recording of daily or weekly revenue and expenses is part of the bookkeeping process.

Firms are required to periodically report their revenue, expenses, and earnings to the Internal Revenue Service (IRS) so that their taxes can be determined. The type of accounting performed for reporting purposes is referred to as **financial accounting.**

Financial accounting must be conducted in accordance with generally accepted accounting principles (GAAP) that explain how financial information should be reported. The Financial Accounting Standards Board (FASB), Securities Exchange Commission (SEC), and IRS establish the accounting guidelines. The use of a common set of guidelines allows for more consistency in reporting practices among firms. Consequently, a comparison of financial statements between two or more different firms may be more meaningful.

Reporting to Shareholders Publicly owned firms are required to periodically report their financial condition for existing or potential shareholders. Shareholders assess financial statements to evaluate the performance of firms in which they invested. If the analysis indicates that the firm has performed poorly, existing shareholders may attempt to replace the board of directors or sell their stock. Some shareholders do not take the time to analyze the firms in which they invest. Instead, they rely on the advice of financial advisers who analyze firms for them.

DELL COMPUTER'S FORMULA FOR SUCCESS

Dell Computer provides its investors and other interested parties with detailed financial information via its website, **www.dell.com**. For example, investors can access Dell's most recent annual report, quarterly "financial fact sheets," and earnings estimates for the coming year. Furthermore, investors can request specific financial information using the website. By making this information available over the Internet, Dell provides investors and other parties with current, up-to-the-minute feedback on its financial performance.

Reporting to Creditors Firms also report their financial condition to existing and prospective creditors. The creditors assess firms' financial statements to determine the probability that the firms will default on loans. Creditors that plan to provide short-term loans assess financial statements to determine the level of the firm's liquidity (ability to sell existing assets). Creditors that plan to provide long-term loans may assess the financial statements to determine whether the firm is capable of generating sufficient income in future years to make interest and principal payments on the loan far into the future.

Certifying Accuracy Private accountants provide accounting services for the firms where they are employed. Although they usually have an accounting degree, they do not have to be certified.

Public accountants provide accounting services for a variety of firms for a fee. A license is required to practice public accounting. Accountants who meet specific educational requirements and pass a national examination are referred to as **certified public accountants (CPAs).**

A common job for a public accountant is auditing to ensure that the firm's financial statements are accurate. All publicly owned firms must have their financial statements audited by an independent accounting firm. When public accountants audit a firm, they examine its financial statements for accuracy. A public accountant's stamp of approval does not imply anything about a firm's performance, only that the information contained within the financial statements is accurate.

---

accounting the summary and analysis of a firm's financial condition

bookkeeping the recording of a firm's financial transactions

financial accounting accounting performed for reporting purposes

public accountants accountants who provide accounting services for a variety of firms for a fee

certified public accountants (CPAs) accountants who meet specific educational requirements and pass a national examination

Decision Support

Firms use financial information developed by accountants to support decisions. For example, a firm's financial managers may use historical revenue and cost information for budgeting decisions. The marketing managers use sales information to evaluate the impact of a particular promotional strategy. The production managers use seasonal sales information to determine the necessary production level in the future. The type of accounting performed to provide information to help managers make decisions is referred to as **managerial accounting.** Financial accounting also reports information, but to shareholders and the IRS (outside the firm). To provide a complete set of information, the information generated by managerial accounting can be included with other information (such as industry characteristics).

managerial accounting the type of accounting performed to provide information to help managers of the firm make decisions

Control

In addition to providing information to support decisions, managerial accounting helps managers maintain control. By reviewing financial information, managers monitor the performance of individuals, divisions, and products. Accounting information on sales is used to monitor the performance of various products and the salespeople who sell them. Information on operating expenses is used to monitor production efficiency.

Managers evaluate their firm's financial statements to monitor operations and to identify the firm's strengths and weaknesses. Financial statements can be generated and analyzed as frequently as necessary to identify problems and resolve them quickly before they become serious.

Another accounting task used for control is **auditing,** which is an assessment of the records that were used to prepare the firm's financial statements. **Internal auditors** specialize in evaluating various divisions within a firm to ensure that they are operating efficiently.

auditing an assessment of the records that were used to prepare a firm's financial statements

internal auditors specialize in evaluating various divisions of a business to ensure that they are operating efficiently

Interpreting Financial Statements

The purpose of financial statements is to inform interested parties about the operations and financial condition of a firm. The most important financial statements are the income statement and the balance sheet. The **income statement** indicates the firm's revenue, costs, and earnings over a period of time (such as a quarter or year), and the **balance sheet** reports the book value of all the firm's assets, liabilities, and owner's equity at a given point in time.

It is possible for a firm to show high earnings on its income statement while being financially weak according to its balance sheet. It is also possible for a firm to show low earnings or even losses on its income statement while being financially strong according to its balance sheet. Because the two statements reveal different financial characteristics, both financial statements must be analyzed along with other information to perform a complete evaluation.

Understanding the information reported on income statements and balance sheets is a necessary part of financial analysis. These financial statements are explained briefly next.

2 Explain how to interpret financial statements.

income statement indicates the revenue, costs, and earnings of a firm over a period of time

balance sheet reports the book value of all assets, liabilities, and owner's equity of a firm at a given point in time

Income Statement

The annual income statement for Taylor, Inc., a manufacturing firm, is presented in Exhibit 16.1. The income statement items shown in Exhibit 16.1 are disclosed in the income statements of most manufacturing firms. **Net sales** reflect the total sales adjusted for any discounts. **Cost of goods sold** is the cost of materials used to produce the goods that were sold. For example, the cost of steel used to produce automobiles

net sales the total sales adjusted for any discounts

cost of goods sold the cost of materials used to produce the goods that were sold

Exhibit 16.1

Example of Income Statement: Taylor, Inc.

Net Sales		$20,000,000
Cost of Goods Sold		16,000,000
Gross Profit		$ 4,000,000
Selling Expense	$1,500,000	
General & Administrative Expenses	1,000,000	
Total Operating Expenses		2,500,000
Earnings before Interest and Taxes (EBIT)		$ 1,500,000
Interest Expense		500,000
Earnings before Taxes		$ 1,000,000
Income Taxes (at 30%)		300,000
Net Income		$ 700,000

gross profit net sales minus the cost of goods sold

operating expenses composed of selling expenses and general and administrative expenses

earnings before interest and taxes (EBIT) gross profit minus operating expenses

earnings before taxes earnings before interest and taxes minus interest expenses

net income (earnings after taxes) earnings before taxes minus taxes

is part of the cost of goods sold for Ford Motor Company. **Gross profit** is equal to net sales minus the cost of goods sold. That is, gross profit measures the degree to which the revenue from selling products exceeded the cost of materials used to produce them.

Operating expenses are composed of selling expenses and general and administrative expenses. For example, the cost of labor and utilities and advertising expenses at Ford Motor Company are part of operating expenses. Gross profit minus a firm's operating expenses equals **earnings before interest and taxes (EBIT).** Earnings before interest and taxes minus interest expenses equals **earnings before taxes**. Finally, earnings before taxes minus taxes equals **net income** (sometimes referred to as **earnings after taxes**).

Firms commonly measure each income statement item as a percentage of total sales, as illustrated in Exhibit 16.2 for Taylor, Inc. The exhibit shows how each dollar of sales is used to cover various expenses that were incurred to generate the sales. Notice that 80 cents of every dollar of sales is used to cover the cost of the goods sold, while 12.5 cents of every dollar of sales is needed to cover operating expenses; 2.5 cents of every dollar of sales is needed to cover interest expense, and 1.5 cents of every dollar of sales is needed to pay taxes. That leaves 3.5 cents of every dollar of sales as net income. This breakdown for a firm can be compared with other firms in the industry. Based on this information, the firm may notice that it is using too much of its revenue to cover the cost of goods sold (relative to other firms in the industry). Therefore, it may search for ways to reduce the cost of producing its goods.

Exhibit 16.2

Income Statement Items as a Percentage of Net Sales for Taylor, Inc.

Net Sales		100.0%
Cost of Goods Sold		80.0%
Gross Profit		20.0%
Selling Expense	7.5%	
General & Administrative Expenses	5.0%	
Total Operating Expenses		12.5%
Earnings before Interest and Taxes (EBIT)		7.5%
Interest Expense		2.5%
Earnings before Taxes		5.0%
Income Taxes (at 30%)		1.5%
Net Income		3.5%

Balance Sheet

asset anything owned by a firm

liability anything owed by a firm

basic accounting equation
Assets = Liabilities + Owner's Equity

Anything owned by a firm is an **asset.** Anything owed by a firm is a **liability.** Firms normally support a portion of their assets with funds of the owners, called "owner's equity" (also called "stockholder's equity"). The remaining portion is supported with borrowed funds, which creates a liability. This relationship is described by the following **basic accounting equation:**

$$Assets = Liabilities + Owner's\ Equity$$

For example, consider a person who purchases a car repair shop for $200,000. Assume that the person uses $40,000 of savings for the purchase and borrows the remaining $160,000 from a local bank. The accounting statement for this business will show assets of $200,000, liabilities of $160,000, and owner's equity of $40,000. As the business acquires equipment and machinery, its total asset value increases. The funds used to purchase more assets are obtained either by additional borrowing or by additional support from the owner. Any increase in assets will therefore be matched by an equal increase in liabilities and owner's equity.

The balance sheet for Taylor, Inc., as of the end of the year, is illustrated in Exhibit 16.3. The assets listed on a balance sheet are separated into current assets and fixed assets. **Current assets** are assets that will be converted into cash within one year. They include cash, marketable securities, accounts receivable, and inventories.

current assets assets that will be converted into cash within one year

Exhibit 16.3

Example of Balance Sheet: Taylor, Inc.

Assets	
Current Assets:	
Cash	$ 200,000
Marketable Securities	300,000
Accounts Receivable	500,000
Inventory	1,000,000
Total Current Assets	$ 2,000,000
Fixed Assets:	
Plant and Equipment	$10,000,000
Less: Accumulated Depreciation	2,000,000
Net Fixed Assets	$ 8,000,000
Total Assets	$10,000,000
Liabilities & Owner's Equity	
Current Liabilities:	
Accounts Payable	$ 600,000
Notes Payable	400,000
Total Current Liabilities	$ 1,000,000
Long-Term Debt	$ 5,000,000
Owner's Equity:	
Common Stock ($5 par value, 200,000 shares)	$ 1,000,000
Additional Paid-In Capital	2,000,000
Retained Earnings	1,000,000
Total Owner's Equity	$ 4,000,000
Total Liabilities and Owner's Equity	$10,000,000

Cash typically represents checking account balances. Marketable securities are short-term securities that can easily be sold and quickly converted to cash if additional funds are needed. Marketable securities earn interest for the firm until they are sold or redeemed at maturity. Accounts receivable reflect sales that have been made for which payment has not yet been received. Inventories are composed of raw materials, partially completed products, and finished products that have not yet been sold.

fixed assets assets that will be used by a firm for more than one year

depreciation a reduction in the value of fixed assets to reflect deterioration in the assets over time

accounts payable money owed by a firm for the purchase of materials

notes payable short-term loans to a firm made by creditors such as banks

owner's equity includes the par (or stated) value of all common stock issued, additional paid-in capital, and retained earnings

Fixed assets are assets that the firm will use for more than one year. They include the firm's plant and equipment. In Exhibit 16.3, depreciation is subtracted from plant and equipment to arrive at net fixed assets. **Depreciation** represents a reduction in the value of fixed assets to reflect deterioration in the assets over time. Specific accounting rules are used to measure the depreciation of fixed assets.

Liabilities and owner's equity are also shown in Exhibit 16.3. Current (short-term) liabilities include accounts payable and notes payable. **Accounts payable** represent money owed by the firm for the purchase of materials. **Notes payable** represent short-term loans to the firm made by creditors such as banks. Long-term liabilities (debt) are liabilities that will not be repaid within one year. These liabilities commonly include long-term loans provided by banks and the issuance of bonds.

Owner's equity includes the par (or stated) value of all common stock issued, additional paid-in capital, and retained earnings. Additional paid-in capital represents the dollar amount received from issuing common stock that exceeds par value. Retained earnings represent the accumulation of the firm's earnings that are reinvested in the firm's assets rather than distributed as dividends to shareholders.

A firm can use its balance sheet to determine the percentage of its investment in each type of asset. An example is provided in Exhibit 16.4. Notice that 80 percent of the firm's assets are allocated to net fixed assets. Most manufacturing firms allocate a large portion of their funds to net fixed assets, since these are the assets used in the production process.

The liabilities and owner's equity can also be broken down to determine where the firm is obtaining most of its financial support. Notice that the firm obtained 50 percent of its funds by issuing long-term debt and another 30 percent from issuing stock. Retained earnings made up 10 percent of the firm's funds.

Exhibit 16.4

Breakdown of Balance Sheet for Taylor, Inc.

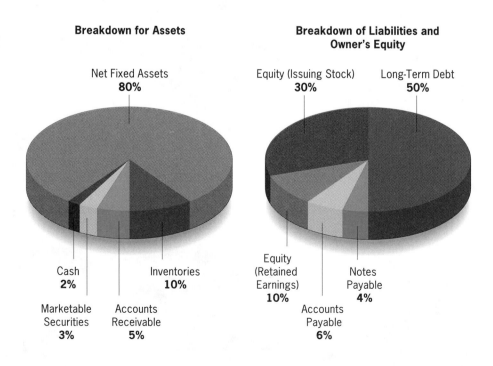

Breakdown for Assets

Net Fixed Assets **80%**

Cash **2%**

Inventories **10%**

Marketable Securities **3%**

Accounts Receivable **5%**

Breakdown of Liabilities and Owner's Equity

Equity (Issuing Stock) **30%**

Long-Term Debt **50%**

Equity (Retained Earnings) **10%**

Notes Payable **4%**

Accounts Payable **6%**

SEVERAL FIRMS USE THE INTERNET TO DISCLOSE RECENT INFORMATION about their financial performance. Marriott, for example, includes virtually its entire annual report on its website. Information such as this is highly useful to current and potential investors seeking to assess Marriott's recent and future performance.

Ratio Analysis

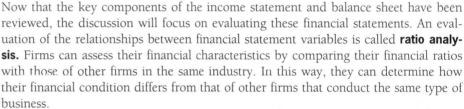

Now that the key components of the income statement and balance sheet have been reviewed, the discussion will focus on evaluating these financial statements. An evaluation of the relationships between financial statement variables is called **ratio analysis.** Firms can assess their financial characteristics by comparing their financial ratios with those of other firms in the same industry. In this way, they can determine how their financial condition differs from that of other firms that conduct the same type of business.

3 Explain how to evaluate a firm's financial condition.

ratio analysis an evaluation of the relationships between financial statement variables

Firms can also assess the ratios over time to determine whether financial characteristics are improving or deteriorating. The industry average serves as a benchmark for what would be considered normal for the firm. Differences from the norm can be favorable or unfavorable, depending upon the size and direction of the difference.

Financial ratios are commonly classified according to the characteristics they measure. These include the following:

▶ Measures of liquidity
▶ Measures of efficiency
▶ Measures of financial leverage
▶ Measures of profitability

The ratios that are used to assess each of these characteristics are defined and discussed next. Each ratio is computed for Taylor, Inc., based on its financial statements in Exhibits 16.1 and 16.3.

Measures of Liquidity

liquidity a firm's ability to meet short-term obligations

Liquidity refers to a firm's ability to meet short-term obligations. Since short-term assets are commonly used to pay short-term obligations (which are current liabilities), most liquidity measures compare current assets with current liabilities. The greater the level of current assets available relative to current liabilities, the greater the firm's liquidity.

A high degree of liquidity can enhance the firm's safety, but an excessive degree of liquidity can reduce the firm's return. For example, an excessive amount of cash is a waste and can reduce a firm's returns. Firms that have excessive cash, marketable securities, accounts receivable, and inventories could have invested more funds in assets such as machinery or buildings (fixed assets) that are used for production. Firms attempt to maintain sufficient liquidity to be safe, but not excessive liquidity. Two common liquidity measures are identified next.

Current Ratio The current ratio compares current assets with current liabilities in ratio form. It is defined as:

$$\text{Current Ratio} = \frac{\text{Current Assets}}{\text{Current Liabilities}}$$

For Taylor:

$$\text{Current Ratio} = \frac{\$2,000,000}{\$1,000,000}$$

$$= 2.00$$

For most manufacturing firms, the current ratio is between 1.0 and 1.5. For Taylor, current assets are twice the amount of its current liabilities. A more detailed comparison of Taylor's liquidity and other financial ratios to the industry norms is conducted later in this chapter after all financial ratios have been discussed.

Quick Ratio The quick ratio requires a slight adjustment in the current ratio. Inventory may not be easily converted into cash and therefore may be excluded when assessing liquidity. To get a more conservative indication of a firm's liquidity, the quick ratio does not include inventory in the numerator:

$$\text{Quick Ratio} = \frac{\text{Cash} + \text{Marketable Securities} + \text{Accounts Receivable}}{\text{Current Liabilities}}$$

For Taylor:

$$\text{Quick Ratio} = \frac{\$1,000,000}{\$1,000,000}$$

$$= 1.00$$

Since the quick ratio does not include inventory in the numerator, it is smaller than the current ratio for any firm that has some inventory. The greater the firm's quick ratio, the greater its liquidity.

Measures of Efficiency

Efficiency ratios measure how efficiently a firm manages its assets. Two of the more popular efficiency ratios are described next.

Inventory Turnover Firms prefer to generate a high level of sales with a low investment in inventory because fewer funds are tied up. However, very low levels of inventory can also be unfavorable because they can result in shortages, which can reduce sales. To assess the relationship between a firm's inventory level and sales, the inventory turnover ratio can be used:

$$\text{Inventory Turnover} = \frac{\text{Cost of Goods Sold}}{\text{Inventory}}$$

For Taylor:

$$\text{Inventory Turnover} = \frac{\$16,000,000}{\$1,000,000}$$

$$= 16.00$$

This ratio suggests that Taylor turns its inventory over sixteen times during the year. The cost of goods sold is used instead of sales in the numerator to exclude the markup that is reflected in sales.

The average inventory over the period of concern should be used in the denominator when it is available, since inventory can change substantially during that period. When it is not available, the year-end inventory is used.

Asset Turnover Firms prefer to support a high level of sales with a relatively small amount of assets so that they efficiently utilize the assets they invest in. Firms that maintain excess assets are not investing their funds wisely. To measure the efficiency with which firms use their assets, the asset turnover ratio can be calculated. It is defined and computed for Taylor as follows:

$$\text{Asset Turnover} = \frac{\text{Net Sales}}{\text{Total Assets}}$$

$$= \frac{\$20,000,000}{\$10,000,000}$$

$$= 2.00$$

Taylor's sales during the year were two times the level of its total assets. Like all other financial ratios, the asset turnover should be evaluated over time and in comparison with the industry norm.

Measures of Financial Leverage

Financial leverage represents the degree to which a firm uses borrowed funds to finance its assets. Firms that borrow a large proportion of their funds have a high degree of financial leverage. This can favorably affect the firm's owners when the firm performs well, because the earnings generated by the firm can be spread among a relatively small group of owners. When the firm experiences poor performance, however, a high degree of financial leverage is dangerous. Firms with a high degree of financial leverage incur higher fixed financial costs (interest expenses) that must be paid regardless of their levels of sales. These firms are more likely to experience debt repayment problems and therefore are perceived as having more risk. Conversely, firms that obtain a larger proportion of funds from equity financing incur smaller debt payments and therefore have less risk.

Although a high proportion of equity financing reduces risk, it may also force earnings to be widely distributed among shareholders. Firms that rely heavily on equity typically have a large number of shareholders who share the firm's earnings. This may dilute the earnings that are distributed to each shareholder as dividends.

debt-to-equity ratio a measure of the amount of long-term financing provided by debt relative to equity

Debt-to-Equity Ratio A measure of the amount of long-term financing provided by debt relative to equity is called the **debt-to-equity ratio.** This ratio is defined and computed for Taylor as follows:

$$\text{Debt-to-Equity Ratio} = \frac{\text{Long-Term Debt}}{\text{Owner's Equity}}$$

$$= \frac{\$5,000,000}{\$4,000,000}$$

$$= 1.25$$

For Taylor, long-term debt is 1.25 times the amount of owner's equity.

times interest earned ratio
measures the ability of a firm to cover its interest payments

Times Interest Earned The **times interest earned ratio** measures a firm's ability to cover its interest payments. If a firm has a low level of earnings before interest and taxes (EBIT) relative to the size of its interest expense, a small decrease in EBIT in the future could force the firm to default on the loan. Conversely, a high level of EBIT relative to the annual interest expense suggests that even if next year's EBIT declines substantially, the firm will still be able to cover the interest expense. The times interest earned ratio is defined and computed for Taylor as follows:

$$\text{Times Interest Earned} = \frac{\text{Earnings before Interest and Taxes (EBIT)}}{\text{Annual Interest Expense}}$$

$$= \frac{\$1,500,000}{\$500,000}$$

$$= 3.0$$

A times interest earned ratio of 3.0 indicates that Taylor's earnings before interest and taxes were three times its interest expense.

Measures of Profitability

Profitability measures indicate the performance of a firm's operations during a given period. The dollar amount of profit generated by the firm can be measured relative to the firm's level of sales, assets, or equity. The ratios that measure these relationships are discussed next.

net profit margin a measure of net income as a percentage of sales

Net Profit Margin The **net profit margin** is a measure of net income as a percentage of sales. This ratio measures the proportion of every dollar of sales that ultimately becomes net income. The net profit margin is computed for Taylor as follows:

$$\text{Net Profit Margin} = \frac{\text{Net Income}}{\text{Net Sales}}$$

$$= \frac{\$700,000}{\$20,000,000}$$

$$= 3.50\%$$

Even with a low profit margin, firms with a high volume of sales can generate a reasonable return for their shareholders. However, firms with a low volume of sales may need a higher profit margin to generate a reasonable return for their shareholders.

return on assets (ROA)
measures a firm's net income as a percentage of the total amount of assets utilized by the firm

Return on Assets A firm's **return on assets (ROA)** measures the return (net income) of the firm as a percentage of the total amount of assets utilized by the firm. It is defined and computed for Taylor as follows:

$$\text{Return on Assets} = \frac{\text{Net Income}}{\text{Total Assets}}$$

$$= \frac{\$700,000}{\$10,000,000}$$

$$= 7.00\%$$

return on equity (ROE)
measures the return to the common stockholders (net income) as a percentage of their investment in the firm

The ROA provides a broad measure of a firm's performance. The higher the ROA, the more efficiently the firm utilized its assets to generate net income.

Return on Equity The **return on equity (ROE)** measures the return to the common stockholders as a percentage of their investment in the firm. This ratio is closely mon-

How Software Has Eased Accounting Functions

Large companies have used complex computer systems to handle their accounting transactions for many years. Now smaller companies have begun to use computer-based accounting as well. These systems ease the process of gathering and summarizing data for financial reporting and tax purposes.

Accounting software designed for small businesses offers online banking, bill paying, time-billing, integration with other popular software packages, and other cost-saving incentives. Another reason to upgrade an accounting system is to accommodate customers who prefer e-bills (bills sent via e-mail). Finally, accounting software ensures that financial practices are kept in line with government regula-

tions. All of the accounting programs follow generally accepted accounting principles (GAAP).

The accounting programs all contain a general ledger, accounts payable, accounts receivable, inventory, and payroll. Repetitive actions are greatly reduced by creating organized databases of business contacts and products. This allows information to be accessed quickly when transactions are entered. For example, once a sale has been completed, an invoice can be created by selecting the customer and product sold from a list. The customer information, payment terms, appropriate sales tax, and product cost are immediately included on the invoice.

These software programs also have the ability to produce business reports. They can sift through large quantities of data to produce customized reports about nearly anything in the business. Cost breakdowns, inventory carrying time and costs, delinquent payments, and outstanding payables are among the reports that can be produced. Such reports would be much more costly to create without software programs.

itored by existing and potential investors because it indicates the recent return on the investment by existing shareholders. The ROE measures the firm's performance from using the equity provided. The return on equity is defined and computed for Taylor as follows:

$$\text{Return on Equity} = \frac{\text{Net Income}}{\text{Owner's Equity}}$$

$$= \frac{\$700,000}{\$4,000,000}$$

$$= 17.50\%$$

Stockholders prefer ROE to be very high because a high ROE indicates a high return relative to the size of their investment. Using high levels of financial leverage can increase ROE (because it restricts the amount of equity used) so that the net income is distributed among fewer shareholders, but high levels of financial leverage increase the firm's exposure to risk.

Comparison of Ratios with Those of Other Firms

Exhibit 16.5 provides the common interpretations for ratios that deviate substantially from what is normal in the industry. Note, however, that there may be a perfectly acceptable reason why a ratio deviates from the norm. For example, consider a firm that has an abnormally large amount of cash according to a comparison with the industry average. Common stockholders may interpret this as evidence of inefficient use of assets. However, further investigation may reveal that the firm has built up its cash because it plans to purchase machinery in the near future. Financial analysis based on an assessment of financial ratios does not necessarily lead to immediate conclusions, but it does lead to questions about a firm that deserve further investigation.

Exhibit 16.6 provides a general summary of the financial ratios commonly used for ratio analysis. Comparing a firm's ratios with an industry average can help identify the firm's strengths and weaknesses. Columns 1 and 2 of Exhibit 16.6 identify and define the financial ratios presented in this chapter. Column 3 lists Taylor's ratios, and

| Exhibit 16.5 | Interpretation of Financial Ratios That Differ from the Industry Norm |

Liquidity Ratios	Common Interpretation if Ratio Is Significantly Lower than Normal	Common Interpretation if Ratio Is Significantly Higher than Normal
Liquidity Ratios		
Current ratio	Insufficient liquidity	Excessive liquidity
Quick ratio	Insufficient liquidity	Excessive liquidity
Efficiency Ratios		
Inventory turnover	Excessive inventory	Insufficient inventory
Asset turnover	Excessive level of assets relative to sales	Insufficient assets based on existing sales
Leverage Ratios		
Debt-to-equity ratio	Insufficient long-term debt	Excessive long-term debt
Times interest earned	Potential cash flow problems, since required interest payments are high relative to the earnings available to pay interest	The firm has far more earnings available to pay interest on debt than it needs.
Profitability Ratios		
Net profit margin	Expenses are high relative to sales.	Expenses are low relative to sales.
Return on assets	Net income is low relative to the amount of assets maintained by the firm.	Net income is high relative to the amount of assets maintained by the firm.
Return on equity	Net income is low relative to the amount of equity invested in the firm.	Net income is high relative to the amount of equity invested in the firm.

the industry averages are provided in column 4. Based on the information in columns 3 and 4, an evaluation of Taylor's ratios relative to those of the industry average is provided in column 5.

In terms of liquidity, Taylor's current and quick ratios are above the industry average. This implies that although Taylor probably has sufficient liquidity, it may have an excessive amount of current assets.

Taylor's inventory turnover ratio is similar to the industry average. This suggests that Taylor maintains the normal amount of inventory.

Taylor's asset turnover ratio is below the industry average. This suggests that Taylor is not using all of its assets efficiently. That is, it has an excessive investment in assets, given the level of sales. It might consider ways of either increasing sales (which would force more production from its assets) or selling some of its assets.

With regard to financial leverage, the debt-to-equity ratio is higher than the industry average. This suggests that Taylor has a relatively high proportion of long-term financing provided by debt relative to equity. The times interest earned ratio for Taylor is lower than the industry norm. Other firms with the same size and in the same industry have lower interest expenses (because they use a lower proportion of debt financing). Since Taylor already uses a relatively high proportion of debt, it may be less able to borrow additional funds.

Regarding profitability, Taylor's net profit margin is lower than the industry norm, which suggests that it is not generating adequate net income based on its level of sales. Also, its return on assets is too low, which is partially attributed to its inefficient use of assets. Since its assets are not efficiently used to generate sufficient sales, they cannot generate a sufficient amount of net income.

Taylor's ROE is too low, which means that it is not generating an adequate net income, given the size of the equity investment in the firm. If it could more efficiently utilize its assets, it could increase net income and therefore increase ROE.

Exhibit 16.7 illustrates how the financial analysis identifies different business functions that may need improvement. Taylor's management, marketing, and finance functions may need to be reassessed to improve its performance. In general, management strategies may be revised to improve production efficiency, marketing strategies may be revised to increase sales, and financing strategies may be revised to establish a more appropriate degree of financial leverage.

Exhibit 16.6   Evaluation of Taylor, Inc., Based on Ratio Analysis

Ratio	Calculation	Ratio for Taylor	Average for Industry	Evaluation of Taylor Based on the Ratio
Liquidity				
Current	$\dfrac{\text{Current Assets}}{\text{Current Liabilities}}$	2.00	1.60	Too high
Quick	$\dfrac{\text{Cash + Marketable Securities + Accts. Receivable}}{\text{Current Liabilities}}$	1.00	0.90	Too high
Efficiency				
Inventory Turnover	$\dfrac{\text{Cost of Goods Sold}}{\text{Inventory}}$	16.00	16.22	OK, unless shortages are occurring
Asset Turnover	$\dfrac{\text{Net Sales}}{\text{Total Assets}}$	2.00	4.11	Too low
Financial Leverage				
Debt-to-Equity Ratio	$\dfrac{\text{Long-Term Debt}}{\text{Owner's Equity}}$	1.25	0.60	Too high
Times Interest Earned	$\dfrac{\text{Earnings before Interest and Taxes}}{\text{Annual Interest Expense}}$	3.0	7.4	Too low
Profitability				
Net Profit Margin	$\dfrac{\text{Net Income}}{\text{Net Sales}}$	3.50%	4.00%	Too low
Return on Assets	$\dfrac{\text{Net Income}}{\text{Total Assets}}$	7.00%	16.44%	Too low
Return on Equity	$\dfrac{\text{Net Income}}{\text{Owner's Equity}}$	17.50%	26.30%	Too low

Limitations of Ratio Analysis

Ratio analysis is useful for detecting a firm's strengths and weaknesses. However, some of its limitations can result in misleading conclusions. The major limitations of ratio analysis are as follows:

1 Comparing some firms with an industry average can be difficult because the firms operate in more than one industry. Consider a firm that produces gas grills, machinery, and aluminum panels. The firm's ratios may deviate from a specific industry norm as a result of the characteristics of the other industries in which the firm operates. Also, the industry used as a benchmark for comparison may include firms that are involved in a variety of other businesses. This distorts the average ratios for the industry.

2 Accounting practices vary among firms. A firm's financial ratios can deviate from the norm because of differences in accounting methods rather than differences in operations.

3 Firms with seasonal swings in sales may show large deviations from the norm at certain times but not at others. Normally, however, the seasonal swings should not distort annual financial statements.

Exhibit 16.7   Example of How Management, Marketing, and Finance Deficiencies Can Be Detected with Ratio Analysis

Management Decisions

One of a firm's relevant management decisions is the production process used to produce products. An efficient production process can result in a relatively higher amount of production and sales with a given level of assets. The asset turnover ratio is an indicator of the efficiency of production because it measures the level of sales generated with a given level of assets. Taylor has a low asset turnover ratio, implying an inefficient use of assets.

Marketing Decisions

Since Taylor's asset turnover ratio is low, it should either eliminate those assets that are not efficiently utilized or maintain its assets but produce and sell a higher volume of products. If it decides to maintain its assets and increase production, it will need effective marketing strategies to sell the extra amount of products produced. Thus, proper marketing strategies may help Taylor to improve its asset turnover ratio.

Finance Decisions

Taylor's debt-to-equity ratio is higher than the norm, which reflects its high degree of financial leverage. Its high proportion of debt financing may make it difficult for Taylor to cover its interest payments. Taylor may use more equity financing in the future, but this will reduce its return on equity. Given its poor utilization of assets, Taylor might consider selling some of its assets and using the proceeds to reduce its debt level. This would allow for a more acceptable degree of financial leverage.

Sources of Information for Ratio Analysis

To help perform ratio analysis, industry data can be obtained from a variety of sources. Some of the more common sources are listed next.

Robert Morris Associates   The booklet *Annual Statement Studies,* published by Robert Morris Associates, provides financial ratios for many different industries. Ratios for firms of various sizes are included so that a firm can compare its ratios with those of similar-sized firms in the same industry.

Dun and Bradstreet   Dun and Bradstreet provides financial ratios for industries and for groups of firms within industries classified by size.

BUSINESS ONLINE

Financial Analysis

http://www.spredgar.com

CORPORATIONS AND GOVERNMENT ORGANIZATIONS CONTINUALLY INTRO-duce new software to facilitate the analysis of financial data. The Securities and Exchange Commission's database, called EDGAR, allows users to download companies' recent earnings filings. As this website shows, an Excel add-in, called SPREDGAR, can be used to facilitate the analysis of information that is downloadable from EDGAR. Considering the amount of information in various filings, new tools such as this are very useful to investors.

GLOBAL BUSINESS

Effect of Exchange Rate Movements on Earnings

A U.S. FIRM THAT HAS SUBSIDIARIES (INCLUDING OFFICES AND FACTORIES) in foreign countries typically generates earnings in the local currencies of the countries where those subsidiaries are located. Any firm with foreign subsidiaries must consolidate the financial data from all subsidiaries when preparing its financial statements. The consolidation process allows changes in exchange rates to have an impact on the firm's reported earnings, as illustrated next.

Consider a U.S. firm that has a subsidiary in the United Kingdom, which generated £10 million in earnings last year. Also assume that the firm's U.S. operations generated $12 million in earnings. The firm must consolidate the £10 million with the $12 million when preparing its income statement. The £10 million cannot simply be added to the $12 million, because the value of the British currency is different from the U.S. currency. Therefore, the British earnings must be "translated" by determining the dollar amount of those earnings. The average exchange rate of the currency of concern over the period in which income was generated is used to translate the foreign earnings. For example, if the average exchange rate of the British pound during the last year was $2.00, the British earnings would be converted into $20 million (computed as £10 million × $2.00 per pound). In this case, the total earnings of the firm would be reported as $32 million (computed as $20 million translated from the British subsidiary plus the $12 million of earnings generated in the United States).

To recognize how the firm's reported earnings are affected by the exchange rate, reconsider the previous example but assume that the average exchange rate during the last year was $1.70 per pound instead of $2.00 per pound. Based on this assumption, the British earnings are translated into $17 million (£10 million × $1.70 per pound). In this example, the British earnings are translated into a smaller amount of dollar earnings. The consolidated earnings of the firm in this example are $29 million (computed as $17 million from the British operations plus $12 million from the U.S. operations), which is $3 million less than in the first example. This illustrates how the reported amount of earnings is affected by the average exchange rate over the period of concern. If the foreign currency has a high value over the period of concern, the foreign earnings will be translated into a higher amount of dollar earnings reported on the income statement. Many U.S. firms with foreign subsidiaries may report unusually high earnings when the values of foreign currencies are high in that period (when the dollar is weak). Under these conditions, the foreign earnings are translated into a large amount of dollar earnings on the income statement. If the values of foreign currencies

General Motors produces cars in various countries, such as China (as shown here). Therefore, its consolidated earnings are partially influenced by the values of foreign currencies in the countries where it produces cars.

decline over a particular year (when the dollar strengthens), the foreign earnings will translate into a smaller amount of dollar earnings, which will reduce the level of consolidated earnings reported on the firm's income statement.

BUSINESS DILEMMA | **College Health Club**

Financial Analysis of College Health Club

SUE KRAMER, PRESIDENT OF COLLEGE HEALTH CLUB (CHC), IS ASSESSING the financial condition of CHC at the end of its first year in operation. She prepares the firm's financial statements and compares them with industry norms for small health clubs. Since she leases all the equipment in the health club, her financial statements are not totally comparable with those health clubs that own their own equipment. Nevertheless, she is able to detect some differences between CHC at the end of its first year and the industry norm for small health clubs:

1 Sue estimates the amount of assets that she rents and determines that if she owned those assets, CHC's asset turnover ratio would have been lower than the industry norm. That is, CHC's sales are relatively low when considering the assets (club's facilities) that are utilized.

2 Sue estimates CHC's degree of financial leverage (based on the debt-to-equity ratio) and determines that it is substantially higher than the industry norm.

3 In its first year, CHC experienced a loss (negative earnings); the profitability ratios for small health clubs showed strong profitability in the last year.

Dilemma

Sue is discouraged by her comparison of CHC with industry norms and considers giving up her business. However, she decides to reexamine and more closely assess the three comparisons just mentioned to determine whether she can improve CHC's performance in the future. Do you expect that these financial characteristics of CHC will improve over time?

Solution

1 CHC's low asset turnover ratio suggests that it is not using its assets as efficiently as other small health clubs. However, Sue must recognize that CHC was only in its first year. As time passes, CHC's membership should grow. She knew that the membership level would be relatively low when she established CHC and developed the business plan (in Chapter 1). Having a small number of memberships caused the relatively low sales level for the first year. If memberships increase over time, so will sales, and the asset turnover ratio will improve.

2 When Sue created CHC one year ago, she invested $10,000 of her own money (equity) and borrowed $40,000 (debt). This resulted in a debt-to-equity ratio of 4.0 (debt is four times the equity). As memberships grow and CHC generates earnings, the earnings will be retained and reinvested in the firm (in the first year, there were no earnings). As earnings are generated and reinvested, the amount of equity financing will increase. Thus, the debt-to-equity ratio will decrease. This will result in a reduction in CHC's degree of financial leverage and therefore reduce CHC's risk.

3 Sue's expenses should not change much from one year to the next because annual expenses are essentially fixed (unless the cost of leasing the space or the equipment rises). The expenses are not related to the number of memberships, so if memberships increase, revenue will increase without any corresponding increase in expenses. Therefore, CHC should be able to improve its profitability if it can increase the number of memberships.

Overall, Sue's detailed assessment helped her realize that CHC's deficiencies (relative to the industry norms) occurred primarily because the club was just one year old and had not yet achieved its potential. If CHC's memberships increase as expected, its efficiency, financial leverage, and profitability ratios will improve.

Although Sue is less concerned after conducting a more detailed assessment of CHC's condition, she recognizes that there is no guarantee that memberships (and therefore sales) will increase as time passes. Sue will have to use much of her time on marketing functions (such as promotion) to increase memberships.

Additional Issues for Discussion

1 Is there any way that Sue can boost the asset turnover ratio immediately?

2 How can Sue immediately reduce her degree of financial leverage?

3 CHC's return on assets was negative at the end of the first year. Does this mean that CHC is failing? Explain.

SUMMARY

1 A firm's financial condition is important to financial managers as well as to the creditors and stockholders of the firm. Financial managers evaluate the firm to detect weaknesses that can be corrected and strengths that can be exploited. Creditors evaluate the firm with a view toward determining creditworthiness, and stockholders evaluate the firm's performance to determine whether they should buy or sell the firm's stock.

2 The key financial statements necessary to perform a thorough evaluation are the income statement and balance sheet. The income statement reports costs, revenue, and earnings over a specified period. The balance sheet reports the book value of assets, liabilities, and owner's equity at a given point in time.

3 Most financial ratios help evaluate one of four characteristics: liquidity, efficiency, financial leverage, and profitability. The liquidity ratios measure a firm's ability to meet its short-term obligations. Efficiency ratios measure how efficiently a firm utilizes its assets. Financial leverage ratios measure the firm's relative use of debt financing versus equity financing and indicate the firm's ability to repay its debt. Profitability ratios measure the firm's net income relative to various size levels. In evaluating a firm's financial ratios, it is useful to compare them with an industry norm. This approach can help detect any deficiencies that exist so that corrective action can be taken. Furthermore, it provides useful input for implementing new policies.

KEY TERMS

accounting *441*

accounts payable *446*

asset *445*

auditing *443*

balance sheet *443*

basic accounting equation *445*

bookkeeping *442*

certified public accountants (CPAs) *442*

cost of goods sold *443*

current assets *445*

debt-to-equity ratio *449*

depreciation *446*

earnings after taxes *444*

earnings before interest and taxes (EBIT) *444*

earnings before taxes *444*

financial accounting *442*

fixed assets *446*

gross profit *444*

income statement *443*

internal auditors *443*

liability *445*

liquidity *447*

managerial accounting *443*

net income *444*

net profit margin *450*

net sales *443*

notes payable *446*

operating expenses *444*

owner's equity *446*

public accountants *442*

ratio analysis *447*

return on assets (ROA) *450*

return on equity (ROE) *450*

times interest earned ratio *450*

The Learning

Goals of this

chapter are to:

1. Identify the common methods of debt financing for firms.

2. Identify the common methods of equity financing for firms.

3. Explain how firms issue securities to obtain funds.

4. Describe how firms determine the composition of their financing.

Financing

irms obtain capital (long-term funds) in the form of debt or equity. Debt financing is the act of borrowing funds. Equity financing is the act of receiving investment from owners (by issuing stock or retaining earnings). The manner in which a firm decides to finance its business can affect its financing costs. By making the proper financing decisions, a firm can minimize the cost of financing its operations, which can enhance its value.

Consider the case of Palm, Inc., producer of the popular Palm Pilot handheld electronic organizer. Palm, Inc.'s stock recently went public. As Palm, Inc. grows, it will need substantial funds to finance its expansion. How can Palm, Inc. finance its expansion? What types of financial institutions would provide financing to Palm, Inc.? What factors would influence Palm, Inc.'s decision to borrow money versus issue new stock? This chapter provides a background on financing that can be used to address these questions.

Methods of Debt Financing

① Identify the common methods of debt financing for firms.

capital long-term funds

debt financing the act of borrowing funds

Firms borrow funds to invest in assets such as buildings, machinery, and equipment. Those firms that invest in more assets typically need to borrow more funds. Service firms spend more money on employees and less on machinery and factories. Thus, they may not need to borrow as much funds because they do not have to purchase machinery for production purposes. In contrast, industrial firms tend to have large investments in assets such as buildings and machinery and therefore need to obtain more **capital.** The common methods of **debt financing** are described next.

Borrowing from Financial Institutions

As a common method of debt financing, firms obtain loans from financial institutions. When a firm applies for a loan, it must present a detailed financial plan that includes specific projections of future revenue and expenses. The plan should demonstrate how the firm will generate sufficient revenue over time to repay the loan.

Many loans are for three years or longer. Lenders assess the creditworthiness of a firm according to several factors, including (1) the firm's planned use of the borrowed funds, (2) the financial condition of the firm's business, (3) the outlook for the industry or environment surrounding the firm's business, and (4) available collateral of the business that can be used to back the loan. Because the lender must assess the financial condition of any business to which it lends, it requires financial statements. The lender will assess the financial statements to determine whether the firm will be able to repay its loan on schedule.

If the lender determines that the firm is creditworthy, it will attempt to establish terms of the loan that are acceptable to the firm. The terms of the loan specify the amount to be borrowed, maturity, collateral, and the rate of interest on the loan.

Pledging Collateral Firms that need to borrow may be asked to pledge a portion of their assets as collateral to back the loan. A common form of collateral is the asset for which the borrowed funds will be used. Lenders are more comfortable providing loans when the loans are backed by collateral. As an example, a firm that borrows funds to purchase a machine may offer that machine as collateral. If lenders expect that they could sell an asset for 70 percent of its existing value, they may finance 70 percent of the purchase and require the asset to be used as collateral. If the firm defaults on the loan, the lender can sell the asset for an amount that covers the loan.

A firm may also pledge its accounts receivable (payments owed to the firm for previous sales of products) as collateral. If the firm defaults on the loan, the lender takes control of the accounts receivable. To ensure that the accounts receivable collateral sufficiently covers the loan balance, the lender would provide a loan amount that is just a fraction of the required collateral. Thus, even if some customers never pay off their accounts receivable, the collateral may still cover the full amount of the loan.

Setting the Loan Rate When setting the loan rate, banks determine the average rate of interest that they pay on their deposits (which represents their cost of funds) and add on a premium. Since deposit rates change over time in response to general interest rate movements, loan rates change as well.

The premium is dependent on the credit risk of the loan or the probability of default. If the firm appears to be in good financial condition and the collateral covers the loan amount, the premium may be about 4 percentage points. For example, if the lender's cost of funds is 6 percent, the loan rate may be 10 percent. However, if the borrowing firm is perceived to have more credit risk, the premium may be more than

Payam Zamani created a firm called Purpletie.com that plans to offer a nationwide chain of Internet-enabled dry cleaning services. This venture will require substantial financing.

prime rate the rate of interest typically charged on loans to the most creditworthy firms that borrow

4 percentage points. The rate of interest typically charged on loans to the most creditworthy firms that borrow is called the **prime rate.**

Fixed-Rate versus Floating-Rate Loans   When firms need funds, they must choose between a fixed-rate loan and a floating-rate loan. Most commercial loans charge floating interest rates that move in tandem with market interest rates. Consider a firm that can obtain a five-year floating-rate loan with an interest rate that is adjusted by the bank once a year according to changes in the prime rate. Assume that the initial loan rate of interest is 8 percent (based on the prevailing prime rate) and will be adjusted once a year. Alternatively, the firm can obtain a fixed-rate loan of 10 percent. Which loan is preferable? The answer depends on future interest rate movements, which are uncertain. Firms that expect interest rates to rise consistently over the five-year period will prefer a fixed-rate loan so that they can avoid the upward adjustments on a floating-rate loan. Firms that expect interest rates to decline or remain stable over the five-year period will prefer a floating-rate loan.

Exhibit 17.1 shows the trend of interest rates that would occur under three different scenarios. If the firm has a fixed-rate loan, the interest rate charged on its loan is I_1, regardless of how market interest rates move over time. If the firm has a floating-rate loan, the interest rate charged on its loan would be I_2 if market interest rates increase over time, or I_3 if market interest rates decrease over time. Firms that obtain floating-rate loans are adversely affected by rising interest rates because the interest rate on their loans will increase.

The interest rate charged on a new loan is based on the general level of interest rates at that time. The top part of Exhibit 17.2 shows how the prime rate has changed over time. The lower part of the exhibit shows the interest expense that a firm would have incurred if it was charged the prime rate on a $1 million loan at that time.

Issuing Bonds

bonds long-term debt securities (IOUs) purchased by investors

Large firms may obtain funds by issuing **bonds,** which are long-term debt securities (IOUs) purchased by investors. Some large firms prefer to issue bonds rather than obtain loans from financial institutions because the interest rate may be lower. Bondholders are creditors, not owners, of the firm that issued the bonds.

Small firms that are not well known are unable to issue bonds. Even if they could issue their own bonds, a bond issuance typically raises more funds than a small firm would need.

par value the amount that bondholders receive at maturity

The **par value** of a bond is the amount that the bondholders receive at maturity. Most bonds have a maturity of between ten and thirty years. The coupon (interest) payments paid per year are determined by applying the so-called coupon rate to the par value. If the coupon rate is 10 percent, the coupon payments paid per year will be $100 for every $1,000 of par value. The coupon payments are normally paid semiannually and are fixed over the life of the bond.

The coupon rate of bonds is influenced by the general level of interest rates at the time the bonds are issued. Firms typically prefer to issue bonds at a time when inter-

Exhibit 17.1

Interest Rate Charged on Loans under Three Different Scenarios

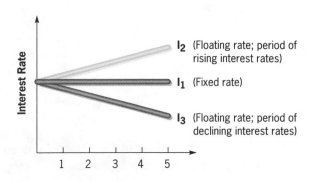

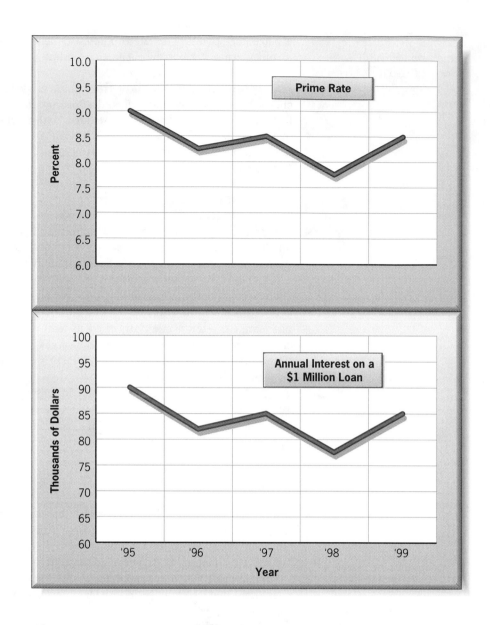

est rates are relatively low. Therefore, they can lock in a relatively low coupon rate over the life of the bond. Forecasting interest rates is difficult, however, so firms cannot easily time the bond issue when interest rates have hit their bottom. Also, firms that need funds immediately cannot wait until interest rates are at a more desirable level.

When a firm plans to issue bonds, it creates an **indenture,** which is a legal document that explains its obligations to bondholders. For example, it states the collateral (if any) that is backing the bonds. **Secured bonds** are backed by collateral, whereas **unsecured bonds** are not backed by collateral. The indenture also states whether the bonds have a **call feature,** which provides the right for the issuing firm to repurchase the bonds before maturity. To recognize the benefits of a call feature, consider a firm that issued bonds when interest rates were very high. If interest rates decline a few years later, the firm could issue new bonds at the lower interest rate and use the proceeds to repay the old bonds. Thus, the call feature gives firms the flexibility to replace old bonds with new bonds that have a lower interest rate. Firms that have a call feature typically need to pay a higher rate of interest.

Default Risk of Bonds The interest rate paid on bonds is influenced not only by prevailing interest rates but also by the issuing firm's risk level. Firms that have more

indenture a legal document that explains the firm's obligations to bondholders

secured bonds bonds backed by collateral

unsecured bonds bonds that are not backed by collateral

call feature provides the right for the issuing firm to repurchase its bonds before maturity

These two owners of "Two Fat Guys" specialty mustard needed financing to develop their new business.

protective covenants restrictions imposed on specific financial policies of a firm

commercial paper a short-term debt security normally issued by firms in good financial condition

risk of default must provide higher interest to bondholders in order to compensate for the risk involved. Rating agencies such as Moody's Investor Service and Standard and Poor's Corporation rate the bonds according to their quality (safety). Investors can use the ratings to assess the risk of the firm issuing the bonds.

Exhibit 17.3 provides a summary of the different ratings that can be assigned. Although each rating agency uses its own method for rating bonds, most bonds are rated within a similar risk level by the agencies. Investors may prefer to rely on the rating agencies rather than develop their own evaluation of the firms that issue bonds. At a given point in time, firms with higher ratings will be able to issue bonds with lower interest rates.

If the financial condition of a firm weakens, the rating on the bonds that it issued can be reduced by a rating agency. As a firm's bond ratings decline, it is less able to issue new bonds because investors are concerned about the lower rating (higher risk). Rating agencies assign ratings after evaluating the financial condition of each firm. They closely assess the amount of debt that a firm has and the firm's ability to cover interest payments on its existing debt. Firms are periodically reevaluated since their ability to repay debt can change in response to economic or industry conditions, or even conditions unique to the firm.

Bondholders may attempt to limit the risk of default by enforcing so-called **protective covenants,** which are restrictions imposed on specific financial policies of the firm. These covenants are enforced to ensure that managers do not make decisions that could increase the firm's risk and therefore increase the probability of default. For example, some protective covenants may restrict the firm from borrowing beyond some specified debt limit until the existing bonds are paid off.

Issuing Commercial Paper

Many firms also issue **commercial paper,** which is a short-term debt security normally issued by firms in good financial condition. Its normal maturity is between three and six months. Thus, the issuance of commercial paper is an alternative to obtaining loans directly from financial institutions. The minimum denomination of commercial paper is usually $100,000. The typical denominations are in multiples of $1 million. Various financial institutions commonly purchase commercial paper. The interest rate on commercial paper is influenced by the general market interest rates at the time of issuance.

Exhibit 17.3

Summary of Risk Ratings Assigned by Bond Rating Agencies

| | Rating Assigned by: | |
	Moody's	Standard & Poor's
Highest quality	Aaa	AAA
High quality	Aa	AA
High-medium quality	A	A
Medium quality	Baa	BBB
Medium-low quality	Ba	BB
Low quality (speculative)	B	B
Poor quality	Caa	CCC
Very poor quality	Ca	CC
Lowest quality (in default)	C	DDD,D

BUSINESS ONLINE

Information on
Commercial
Paper

**http://www.bog.frb.fed.us/
releases/CP**

THE FEDERAL RESERVE, THE CENTRAL BANK OF THE UNITED STATES, PRO-
vides data on various debt instruments on its website. For example, information on
commercial paper rates is available. This information is useful to investors thinking
about investing in commercial paper and to companies thinking about issuing commercial paper in the near future.

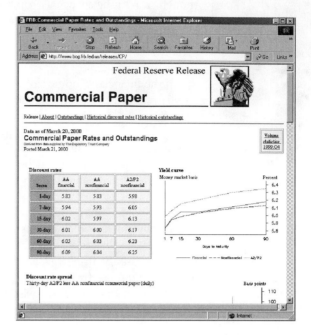

Impact of the Debt Financing Level on Interest Expenses

To illustrate how the level of debt financing (whether by borrowing from financial institutions or by issuing IOUs) affects interest expenses, consider a firm that borrows
$1 million for a five-year period at an interest rate of 9 percent. This firm will pay
$90,000 in interest in each of the next five years (computed as $1,000,000 × 9%).
Thus, the firm will need sufficient revenue to cover not only its operating expenses
(such as salaries) but also its interest expenses. If the firm had borrowed $2 million,
it would have to pay $180,000 in annual interest (computed as $2,000,000 × 9%).
When firms borrow money excessively, they have large annual interest payments that
are difficult to cover. For this reason, the firms have a higher probability of defaulting
on the loans than they would if they had borrowed less funds.

Common Creditors That Provide Debt Financing

Various types of creditors can provide debt financing to firms. **Commercial banks** obtain deposits from individuals and use the funds primarily to provide business loans.
Savings institutions (called "thrift institutions") also obtain deposits from individuals
and use some of the deposited funds to provide business loans. Although savings institutions lend most of their funds to individuals who need mortgage loans, they have
increased their amount of business loans in recent years.

  Finance companies typically obtain funds by issuing debt securities (IOUs) and
lend most of their funds to firms. In general, finance companies tend to focus on loans
to less established firms that have a higher risk of loan default. The finance companies
charge a higher rate of interest on these loans to compensate for the higher degree of
risk.

  Pension funds receive employee and firm contributions toward pensions and invest the proceeds for the employees until the funds are needed. They commonly use
their funds to invest in bonds that are issued by firms.

commercial banks financial
institutions that obtain deposits
from individuals and use the
funds primarily to provide
business loans

savings institutions financial
institutions that obtain deposits
from individuals and use the
deposited funds primarily to
provide mortgage loans

finance companies financial
institutions that typically obtain
funds by issuing debt securities
(IOUs) and lend most of their
funds to firms

pension funds receive employee
and firm contributions toward
pensions and invest the proceeds
for the employees until the funds
are needed

insurance companies receive insurance premiums from selling insurance to customers and invest the proceeds until the funds are needed to pay insurance claims

mutual funds investment companies that receive funds from individual investors, which they pool and invest in securities

bond mutual funds investment companies that invest the funds received from investors in bonds

equity financing the act of receiving investment from owners (by issuing stock or retaining earnings)

Identify the common methods of equity financing for firms.

common stock a security that represents partial ownership of a particular firm

preferred stock a security that represents partial ownership of a particular firm and offers specific priorities over common stock

Insurance companies receive insurance premiums from selling insurance to customers and invest the proceeds until the funds are needed to pay insurance claims. They commonly use their funds to invest in bonds that are issued by firms.

Mutual funds are investment companies that receive funds from individual investors, which they pool and invest in securities. Mutual funds can be classified by the type of investments that they make. Some mutual funds (called **bond mutual funds**) invest the funds received from investors in bonds that are issued by firms.

Methods of Equity Financing

The common methods of **equity financing** are retaining earnings and issuing stock, as explained next.

Retaining Earnings

Firms can obtain equity financing by retaining earnings rather than by distributing the earnings to their owners. Managers retain earnings to provide financial support for the firm's expansion. For example, if a firm needs $10 million for expansion and has just received $6 million in earnings (after paying taxes), it may retain the $6 million as equity financing and borrow the remaining $4 million.

Many small firms retain most of their earnings to support expansion. Larger corporations tend to pay out a portion of their earnings as dividends and retain only part of what was earned. Large firms can more easily obtain debt financing, so they can afford to pay out a portion of their earnings as dividends.

Issuing Stock

Common stock is a security that represents partial ownership of a particular firm. Only the owners of common stock are permitted to vote on certain key matters concerning the firm, such as election of the board of directors, approval to issue new shares of common stock, and approval of merger proposals. Firms can issue common stock to obtain funds. When new shares of stock are issued, the number of shareholders who own the firm increases.

Preferred stock is a security that represents partial ownership of a particular firm and offers specific priorities over common stock. If a firm does not pay dividends over a period, it must pay preferred stockholders all dividends that were omitted before paying common stockholders any dividends. Also, if the firm goes bankrupt, the preferred stockholders have priority claim to the firm's assets over common stockholders. If a firm goes bankrupt, however, there may not be any assets left for preferred stockholders, since creditors (such as lenders or bondholders) have first claim. Preferred stockholders normally do not have voting rights. Firms issue common stock more frequently than preferred stock.

D&LL® COMPUTER'S FORMULA FOR SUCCESS

During a recent fiscal year, Dell Computer used its $1.6 billion cash flows from operations to repurchase 69 million shares of its common stock. By the end of that fiscal year, Dell had repurchased a total of 150 million shares of common stock. Furthermore, Dell carried out two stock splits during that fiscal year. By repurchasing its shares of common stock, Dell demonstrated its ability to generate sufficient cash flow internally without relying on shareholders to provide financing. Moreover, by splitting its stock, Dell signaled to its shareholders that it expects its stock price to increase in the future.

Owners of a new business develop a financial summary that will be presented in order to request additional venture capital.

venture capital firm a firm composed of individuals who invest in small businesses

Issuing Stock to Venture Capital Firms

Firms can issue stock privately to a **venture capital firm,** which is composed of individuals who invest in small businesses. These individuals act as investors in firms rather than as creditors. They expect a share of the businesses in which they invest. Their investments typically support projects that have potential for high returns but also have high risk.

Entrepreneurs who need equity financing can attend venture capital forums, where they are allowed a short time (fifteen minutes or so) to convince the venture capital firms to provide them with equity financing. If an entrepreneur's presentation is convincing, venture capital firms may arrange for a longer meeting with the entrepreneur to learn more about the business that needs financing.

Providers of venture capital recognize that some of the businesses they invest in may generate little or no return. They hope that the successful businesses will more than make up for any unsuccessful ones. Venture capital firms commonly assess businesses that require an equity investment of somewhere between $200,000 and $2,000,000. Small projects are not popular because their potential return is not worth the time required to assess their feasibility.

initial public offering (IPO) the first issue of stock to the public

Going Public

If a small privately held business desires to obtain additional funds, it may consider an **initial public offering (IPO)** of stock (also called "going public"), which is the first issue of stock to the public. Firms such as Yahoo! and Amazon.com went public so that they would have sufficient funds to support their expansion. More recently, firms such as Qualcom and MarketWatch.com have engaged in IPOs.

stock mutual funds investment companies that invest funds received from individual investors in stocks

Insurance companies and pension funds commonly purchase large amounts of stocks issued by firms. In addition, **stock mutual funds** (investment companies that invest pooled funds received from individual investors in stocks) purchase large amounts of stocks issued by firms. An IPO allows a firm to obtain additional funds without boosting its existing debt level and without relying on retained earnings. Firms can obtain a large amount of funds by going public without increasing future interest payments to creditors.

Along with the advantages, IPOs have some disadvantages. First, firms that go public are responsible for informing shareholders of their financial condition. Expenses are associated with developing periodic financial reports that must be filed with the Securities and Exchange Commission (SEC) by all firms that issue stock to the public.

SPOTLIGHT ON TECHNOLOGY

Direct Public Offerings

Smaller firms in need of capital now have a new alternative—the Internet. The Internet is allowing firms to go public without the expenses of a traditional IPO.

The usual process for a small and growing firm would be to seek financing from a venture capitalist or a venture capital fund. After the firm has grown, the venture capitalist assists the firm in a public stock offering. The underwriting, legal, and filing fees are substantial. Now, however, firms can avoid venture capital funding and the fees associated with traditional public offerings by taking their firm public over the Internet.

The communication power of the Internet and a relaxation in the exemption standard by the Securities and Exchange Commission (SEC) have given rise to direct public offerings (DPOs). The SEC allows firms to raise up to $5 million and is supportive of Internet use to distribute offering memoranda and to sell shares.

The issuer usually performs the underwriting, filing, and selling of the offer with an underwriter. Firms such as Wit Capital are available to assist firms interested in DPOs. Their services are available for a much lower fee than investment banks charge for underwriting traditional IPOs.

The DPO also offers an opportunity for investors who are left out of the traditional IPO market. Investment banks underwriting IPOs offer the shares to institutional investors and their other large clients. The individual investor must buy after the firm's shares have begun trading, which is frequently after a large increase in price. The DPO gives individuals the opportunity to invest in a newly public firm at the offer price.

Furthermore, the financial information filed by these firms is accessible to investors. Some firms may prefer not to disclose information that would reveal the success (and perhaps the wealth) of the owners.

A second disadvantage is that when a small business attempts to obtain funding from the public, it may have difficulty convincing the public that its business plans are feasible. This limits the amount of funding that can be obtained from an IPO. It also forces the firm to sell part of the ownership at a relatively low cost. If a firm goes public and cannot obtain funding at a reasonable price, its original owners may feel that they gave away part of the firm for nothing.

A third disadvantage of an IPO is that the ownership structure is diluted. That is, the proportion of the firm owned by the original owners is reduced once shares are

Angus Davis, co-founder of Tellme Networks Inc., received $47 million in funding from high-tech investors in 1999.

sold to the public. Thus, the original owners have less control of the firm, and other investors have more influence on the firm's board of directors and therefore on major decisions. Also, the profits earned by the firm that are distributed among owners as dividends must be allocated among more owners.

A fourth disadvantage of an IPO is that investment banks charge high fees for advising and placing the stock with investors. The firm also incurs legal fees, accounting fees, and printing fees. The fees may be about 10 percent of the total amount of funds received from the IPO. Thus, an IPO of $20 million may result in fees of $2 million.

IPOs are generally more popular when most stock prices are high, as firms may receive a higher price for their newly issued stock under these conditions. For example, stock prices in the late 1990s were very high, and there were numerous IPOs in that period.

BUSINESS ONLINE

Initial Public Offerings

http://www2.ipo.com/ipoinfo/
expected.asp?p=IPO

INFORMATION ABOUT INITIAL PUBLIC OFFERINGS (IPOs) THAT WILL OCCUR in the near future is available on various websites, as shown here for IPO.com. For each company, the date of the IPO, the ticker symbol, the number of shares offered, and the estimated price are shown. Furthermore, more detailed financial data can be obtained by clicking on the company name. Information such as this is useful to investors contemplating a purchase of company stock and to managers of the firm attempting to forecast its financial position.

Listing the Stock   Once a firm has issued stock to the public, it lists its stock on a stock exchange. This allows the investors to sell the stock they purchased from the firm to other investors over time. The stock exchange serves as a **secondary market,** or a market where existing securities can be traded among investors. Thus, investors have the flexibility to sell stocks that they no longer wish to hold.

The most popular stock exchanges in the United States are the New York Stock Exchange (NYSE), the American Stock Exchange (AMEX), and the over-the-counter (OTC) market. Stocks in the over-the-counter market trade via an electronic network known as the National Association of Securities Dealers Automated Quotations (NASDAQ). Each exchange has a set of listing requirements that firms must satisfy to have their stocks listed on that exchange.

secondary market a market where existing securities can be traded among investors

Comparison of Equity Financing with Debt Financing

Equity financing and debt financing are compared in Exhibit 17.4. Notice from the exhibit that the forms of debt financing (loans and bonds) require the firm to make interest and principal payments. Conversely, the forms of equity financing (retained earnings and stock) do not require any payments. Financing with stock may result in dividend payments, but these payments can be omitted if the firm cannot afford them. Also, there are no principal payments to the stockholders, as the stock has no maturity.

Firms use a variety of financing methods to obtain funds. General Motors, Ford Motor Company, Motorola, and many other firms frequently obtain funds by borrowing from banks, issuing bonds, and issuing new stock.

How Firms Issue Securities

A **public offering** of securities (such as bonds or stocks) represents the selling of securities to the public. A firm that plans a public offering of securities can receive help from investment banks, which originate, underwrite, and distribute the securities.

Origination

Investment banks advise firms on the amount of stocks or bonds they can issue. The issuance of an excessive amount of securities can cause a decline in the market price because the supply of securities issued may exceed the demand. Also, the issuance of bonds requires the determination of a maturity date, a coupon rate, and collateral.

Underwriting

When securities offerings are **underwritten,** the investment bank guarantees a price to the issuing firm, no matter what price the securities are sold for. In this way, the investment bank bears the risk that the securities may only be sold at low prices. Alternatively, the investment bank may attempt to sell the securities on a **best-efforts basis,** in which it does not guarantee a price to the issuing firm.

For large issues of securities, the investment bank may create an **underwriting syndicate,** which is a group of investment banks that share the obligations of underwrit-

---

3 Explain how firms issue securities to obtain funds.

public offering the selling of securities to the public

underwritten the investment bank guarantees a price to the issuing firm, no matter what price the securities are sold for

best-efforts basis the investment bank does not guarantee a price to the firm issuing securities

underwriting syndicate a group of investment banks that share the obligations of underwriting securities

Exhibit 17.4

Summary of Firm's Debt and Equity Financing Methods

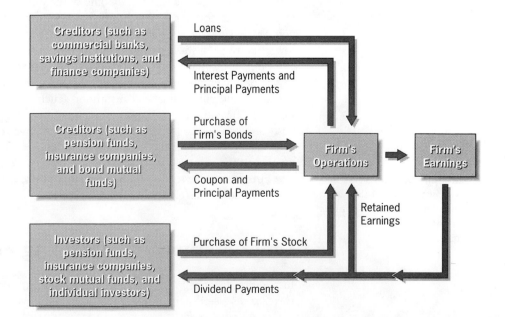

ing the securities. That is, each investment bank in the syndicate is allocated a portion of the securities and is responsible for selling that portion.

INVESTMENT BANKING FIRMS, SUCH AS J.P. MORGAN, FREQUENTLY PROVIDE information about the services they offer on their websites. Furthermore, these websites often allow interested parties to conduct research on specific stocks or bonds. Since investment banking firms frequently underwrite corporate bond or stock issues, this information is highly useful to corporate management.

Distribution

The issuing firm must register the issue with the Securities and Exchange Commission (SEC). It provides the SEC with a **prospectus,** which is a document that discloses relevant financial information about the securities (such as the amount) and financial information about the firm.

Once the SEC approves the registration, the prospectus is distributed to investors who may purchase the securities. Some of the more likely investors are pension funds and insurance companies that have large amounts of funds to invest. Some issues are completely sold within hours. When issues do not sell as well, investment banks may lower the price of the securities to increase demand.

Some firms may prefer to use a **private placement,** in which the securities are sold to one or a few investors. An investment bank may still be used for advisory purposes and for identifying a financial institution (such as an insurance company) that may purchase the entire issue. Firms consider private placements because the actual selling costs are lower since there is only one or a few investors. A disadvantage of a private placement, however, is that many investors cannot afford to purchase an entire issue. Consequently, privately placing the securities may be difficult.

Firms that issue securities incur **flotation costs,** which are costs paid to investment banks for advising, selling the securities, printing expenses, and registration fees.

Other Methods of Obtaining Funds

In addition to debt financing and equity financing, firms may obtain funds in other ways, as discussed next.

prospectus a document that discloses relevant financial information about securities and financial information about the firm issuing them

private placement the selling of securities to one or a few investors

flotation costs costs paid to investment banks for their advice, their efforts to sell the securities, printing expenses, and registration fees

Financing from Suppliers

When a firm obtains supplies, it may be given a specific period to pay its bill. The supplier is essentially financing the firm's investment over that period. If the firm is able to generate adequate revenue over that time to pay the bill, it will not need any more financing. Even if it needs more financing, the supplier's willingness to wait for payment saves the firm some financing costs.

Exhibit 17.5 shows the benefits of supplier financing. In the top diagram, the firm receives supplies on March 1, but does not have to pay its bill until August 1. By August 1, the firm will have sold the product that required the use of the supplies. Thus, it can use a portion of the revenue received from selling the product to pay the supplier.

The lower diagram shows that with no supplier financing, the firm must obtain funds from another source. For example, it may borrow funds from a commercial bank on March 1 to pay the supplier at that time. When it receives its payment for the product on August 1, it can use a portion of the revenue received to pay off the debt. In this case, the firm had to borrow funds for five months and incurs interest expenses over that period. The difference between these two scenarios is that the firm incurs only the expense of the supplies when supplier financing is provided, but it incurs the expense of supplies plus interest expenses if supplier financing is not provided.

Leasing

leasing renting assets for a specified period of time

Some firms prefer to finance the use of assets by **leasing,** or renting the assets for a specified period of time. These firms rent the assets and have full control over them over a particular period. They return the assets at the time specified in the lease contract. Many firms that lease assets cannot afford to purchase them. By leasing, they make periodic lease payments but do not need a large initial outlay.

Some firms prefer to lease rather than purchase when they expect that they may not need the assets for a long period of time. For example, consider a new firm that does not know how much factory space it will need until it can assess the demand for its product. This firm may initially lease factory space so that it can switch factories without having to sell its existing factory if it needs more space.

Exhibit 17.5

How Firms Can Benefit from Supplier Financing

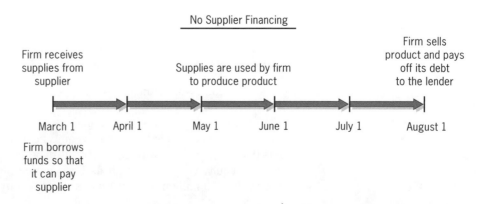

Deciding the Capital Structure

 4 Describe how firms determine the composition of their financing.

capital structure the composition of debt versus equity financing

All firms must decide on a **capital structure,** or the composition of debt versus equity financing. No particular capital structure is perfect for all firms. However, some characteristics should be considered when determining the appropriate capital structure. The use of debt (such as bank loans or bonds) as a source of funds is desirable because the interest payments made by the firm on its debt are tax deductible. Firms can claim their interest payments during the year as an expense, thereby reducing their reported earnings and their taxes. When firms use equity as a source of funds, they do not benefit in this way.

Although debt offers the advantage of tax deductibility, too much debt can increase the firm's risk of default on its debt. A higher level of debt results in a higher level of interest payments each year, which can make it difficult for a firm to cover all its debt payments. When creditors are concerned about the firm's ability to make future interest payments, they are less willing to provide additional credit. A firm's ability to increase its debt level is also constrained by the amount of collateral available.

Firms tend to retain some earnings as an easy and continual form of equity financing. When they need additional funds to support their operations, they typically use debt financing if they have the flexibility to do so. However, when they approach their debt capacity, they may have to retain more earnings or issue stock to obtain additional capital.

Revising the Capital Structure

Many firms revise their capital structure in response to changes in economic conditions, such as economic growth and interest rates. If economic growth declines and their earnings decline, they may reduce debt because it is more difficult to cover interest payments. When interest rates decline, they may increase debt because the interest payments will be relatively low.

To reduce the strain of meeting high interest payments, firms such as Northwest Airlines, American Airlines, and Westinghouse have reduced their debt levels by hundreds of millions of dollars. Conversely, other firms such as IBM have increased debt because they expected that they could easily cover future interest payments that result from the additional debt.

To illustrate how the repurchasing of stock can improve a firm's value (and therefore its stock price), consider the following statements from a recent annual report of Wal-Mart:

> **❝** *In a move to improve shareholder value, the Board of Directors authorized a $2 billion share repurchase program. . . . We started buying [when the stock price was] in the low 20s, and the stock ended up rising 73 percent in the last calendar year.* **❞**

—Wal-Mart

How the Capital Structure Affects the Return on Equity

A firm's earnings performance (as measured by its return on equity) can be significantly influenced by the capital structure decision. Consider a firm that had earnings of $1 million last year and has $10 million in assets. The firm's return on equity (measured as earnings divided by owner's equity) depends on the amount of the firm's assets that were financed with equity versus debt. Exhibit 17.6 shows how the firm's return on equity is dependent on its financial leverage. If the firm used all equity to finance its $10 million in assets, its return on equity (ROE) would be:

How a Firm's Return on Equity Is Dependent on Financial Leverage

Note: Assume that the firm had a net income of $1 million last year and has $10 million in assets.

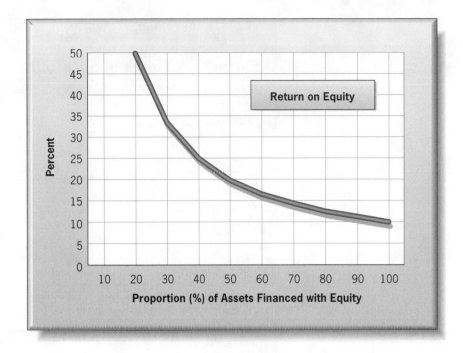

$$\text{ROE} = \frac{\$1,000,000}{\$10,000,000}$$

$$= 10\%$$

At the other extreme, if the firm used only 20% equity ($2 million) to finance its assets, its ROE would be:

$$\text{ROE} = \frac{\$1,000,000}{\$2,000,000}$$

$$= 50\%$$

Although using little equity (mostly debt) can achieve a higher return on equity, it exposes a firm to the risk of being unable to cover its interest payments. To illustrate the risk, Exhibit 17.7 shows how the annual interest expense incurred by a firm

How a Firm's Interest Expense Is Dependent on Financial Leverage

Note: Assume that the firm has $10 million in assets; also assume a 10 percent interest rate on debt.

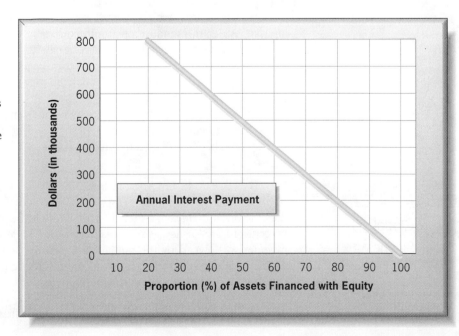

(with $10 million in assets) is dependent on the firm's degree of financial leverage. This exhibit assumes a 10 percent interest rate. For example, if the firm uses all equity, it does not incur any interest expenses. At the other extreme, if it uses only 20 percent ($2 million) of equity financing and relies on 80 percent ($8 million) of debt financing, it will incur an interest expense of $800,000 per year.

The relationship shown in Exhibit 17.7 is simply intended to illustrate how a high degree of financial leverage can force high interest expenses. In reality, the impact of high financial leverage may be even more pronounced than in Exhibit 17.7, because lenders may charge a high interest rate to firms that wish to borrow an excessive amount. An extra premium on the interest rate would compensate those lenders for the risk that the firm may be unable to repay its debt.

Firms weigh the potential higher return on equity that results from using mostly debt financing against the risk resulting from high interest payments. Many firms compromise by balancing their amount of equity and debt financing. For example, a firm could finance its $10 million in assets by using $5 million of equity and the remaining $5 million of debt. Assuming an interest rate of 10 percent on debt, the interest expense would be $500,000 (computed as 10% × $5,000,000), as shown in Exhibit 17.7.

GLOBAL BUSINESS

Global Financing

WHEN U.S. FIRMS ESTABLISH BUSINESSES IN FOREIGN COUNTRIES (CALLED "foreign subsidiaries"), they must obtain sufficient funds to support them. Consider the case of Euro-Disney, a French subsidiary of The Walt Disney Company. About 49 percent of Euro-Disney's stock was owned by The Walt Disney Company, and the remainder was owned by the public. In 1994, Euro-Disney was experiencing financial problems because its theme park was not attracting a sufficient number of customers. It needed to obtain more financial support. However, it was concerned about increasing its debt, since it was already having problems covering its interest payments on debt. It worked out a financial strategy in which it would sell $750 million of stock to The Walt Disney Company. It would also issue new stock to the public to obtain additional funds. Furthermore, the banks that had provided loans to Euro-Disney agreed to forgive interest payments that were owed by Euro-Disney over an eighteen-month period. Many of the European banks who were holding Euro-Disney's debt also purchased some of the firm's stock.

Euro-Disney's financing strategy focused on obtaining French francs because it used that currency to pay most of its expenses. Also, its revenue was in French francs. When it needed to make payments on its debt or dividend payments to its shareholders, it could use the francs received from its theme park's business. Thus, when paying creditors or shareholders, Euro-Disney did not have to convert the francs into any other currency. This was important because it enabled Euro-Disney to avoid potential adverse effects of exchange rate movements.

Consider the potential effects on Euro-Disney if it had obtained U.S. dollars to resolve its financial problems. As it generated French francs from its theme park business, it would have had to convert some of those francs to dollars to make interest or dividend payments. If the value of the French franc had declined over time, Euro-Disney would have needed a larger amount of francs to obtain the amount of dollars necessary to make the payments. This would have placed a greater financial strain on Euro-Disney. This example illustrates that financing foreign projects is complex because it not only involves a decision of debt versus equity financing but also involves selecting the currency to use for financing.

Dividend Policy

dividend policy the decision regarding how much of the firm's quarterly earnings should be retained (reinvested in the firm) versus distributed as dividends to owners

The board of directors of each firm decides how much of the firm's quarterly earnings should be retained (reinvested in the firm) versus distributed as dividends to owners. This decision, referred to as **dividend policy,** is important because it influences the amount of additional financing that firms must obtain. For example, consider a firm that earned $30 million after payment of taxes. Assume that it will need $40 million for various expenses in the near future. If it retains all of the earnings, it will need an additional $10 million. At the other extreme, if it pays out the entire $30 million as dividends, it will need to obtain an additional $40 million.

Some firms target their dividend payment as a percentage of future earnings. For example, General Mills set a dividend target of 50 percent of earnings, while Goodyear Tire set a dividend target of between 20 and 25 percent of earnings.

Factors That Affect a Firm's Dividend Policy

There is no optimal dividend policy to be used by all firms. However, a firm's unique characteristics may influence its dividend policy. Two characteristics that can influence the dividend policy are shareholder expectations and the firm's financing needs.

Shareholder Expectations   A firm's shareholders may expect to receive dividends if they have historically been receiving them. If the firm discontinues or reduces the dividend payment, shareholders could become dissatisfied. Thus, many firms such as ConAgra and Campbell's Soup make an effort to either maintain or increase dividends from year to year.

Firm's Financing Needs   A firm that has no need for additional funds may distribute most of its earnings as dividends. However, it may be concerned that if it pays high dividends, shareholders will continue to expect them. If the firm cannot maintain a continued high dividend payment, it may decide to use a portion of the earnings for another purpose. For example, it may consider replacing old assets or expanding part of its business.

CROSS-FUNCTIONAL TEAMWORK

Interaction between Financing Decisions and Other Business Decisions

When financial managers make financing decisions, they rely on input from other managers. The amount of financing is dependent on the difference between the amount of cash outflows resulting from the payment of expenses and the cash inflows resulting from sales. The larger the difference, the more financing will be needed. Financial managers can ask production managers to estimate the salaries and other production expenses that will be incurred by the firm in the future. They can ask marketing managers to estimate the marketing expenses to be incurred by the firm. They can also ask marketing managers to estimate the future demand for each of the firm's products; this information can be used to estimate the firm's future revenue.

When financial managers decide whether to finance with debt or equity, they rely on input from marketing managers. If the future revenue to be received by the firm is somewhat stable over time, the firm may be willing to finance with debt because cash inflows each month would be sufficient to cover its interest payments on debt. If the monthly revenue is expected to be erratic, however, cash inflows each month may not be sufficient to make interest payments. In this case, the firm may use equity financing instead of debt financing. The marketing managers can offer useful input on this topic because they should know whether the demand for the product will be somewhat stable over time.

A firm's dividend policy will also benefit from the input of its marketing and production managers. If the marketing managers anticipate that the sales will be stable over time, the firm may consistently receive cash each quarter to pay its owners a dividend. However, if it generates erratic sales over time, it may not have a sufficient amount of cash each quarter to make its dividend payment. If the production managers anticipate large expenses in upcoming quarters because of the establishment of new production facilities, they can warn financial managers to retain any earnings rather than distribute them as dividends. Although the financial managers are responsible for decisions such as the amount and type of financing needed, they can make better decisions when considering input from the marketing and production managers.

BUSINESS DILEMMA | **College Health Club**

Financing at College Health Club

SUE KRAMER, PRESIDENT OF COLLEGE HEALTH CLUB (CHC), HAS JUST ESTImated that next year the health club will generate revenue of $100,000, operating expenses of $90,000, and interest expenses of $6,000. There will be a tax of 30 percent on any earnings.

Dilemma

Sue recently inherited $40,000. She realizes that she could invest the $40,000 in CHC, which then could use the funds to repay all of its existing debt.

The capital structure of CHC is currently $10,000 of equity and $40,000 of debt. If Sue pays off the $40,000 in debt, there would be a total equity investment of $50,000 in the health club, and it would have no debt.

Sue wants to determine what the return on her equity investment would be next year under two different situations: (1) she maintains the capital structure as is, with a $10,000 equity investment and $40,000 of debt, or (2) she invests $40,000 of new equity to pay off the debt. She plans to measure the return on equity (ROE) as:

$$ROE = \frac{\text{Earnings after Taxes}}{\text{Owner's Equity}}$$

This comparison will help her decide which capital structure to use. Estimate the return on equity under the two different situations. Sue believes she could earn 18 percent from investing the $40,000 in a new business project. Should she use the $40,000 to pay off CHC's debt or invest the funds in this new project?

Solution

The computation of the earnings after taxes for each situation is shown next, and the ROE is derived from that:

	Situation 1: Use $10,000 of Equity	Situation 2: Use $50,000 of Equity
Revenue	$100,000	$100,000
Operating Expenses	90,000	90,000
Earnings before Interest and Taxes	$ 10,000	$ 10,000
Interest Expenses	6,000	0
Earnings before Taxes	$ 4,000	$ 10,000
Taxes (30%)	1,200	3,000
Earnings after Taxes	$ 2,800	$ 7,000
	ROE = $2,800/$10,000 = 28%	ROE = $7,000/$50,000 = 14%

Notice that there are no interest expenses in Situation 2 because CHC would have no debt. The comparison shows that while Situation 2 results in higher earnings (because it avoids interest expenses), it would result in a lower return on equity. This is because $50,000 of equity is needed in Situation 2, versus only $10,000 in Situation 1.

Sue decides to leave the capital structure as it is, so that she can generate a higher return on her equity investment. She plans to invest her inheritance in some other business project. She recognizes that maintaining the high degree of debt exposes CHC to some risk that it will not have sufficient funds to make its interest payments. This is the trade-off that results from using a high degree of debt.

Additional Issues for Discussion

1 If CHC expands by creating three new health clubs, should it consider issuing stock?

2 Assume that CHC expands and needs more funds but does not wish to borrow additional funds. How can CHC obtain funds if it does not borrow?

3 If interest rates rise over time, how will CHC's cost of funds be affected?

SUMMARY

 The common sources of debt financing are obtaining bank loans, issuing bonds, or issuing commercial paper.

The financial institutions that provide loans to firms are commercial banks, savings institutions, and finance companies. The financial institutions that commonly purchase the corporate bonds issued by firms are insurance companies, pension funds, and bond mutual funds.

2 The common sources of equity financing are retaining earnings and issuing stock. The financial institutions that purchase stocks issued by firms are insurance companies, pension funds, and stock mutual funds.

 When firms issue debt securities or stocks, they normally hire an investment bank. The investment bank may provide advice on the amount of securities the firm should issue, (origination), underwrite the securities, and find buyers of the securities that the firm issues (distribution).

④ Firms may prefer to use debt financing over equity financing because the interest payments are tax deductible. This can allow debt to be a relatively cheap form of financing.

However, a high level of debt financing results in a high level of interest payments, which could make it difficult for the firm to make those payments. Therefore, firms

may prefer to avoid such a risk by using some equity financing as well. With equity financing, the firm does not have to make periodic payments.

KEY TERMS

best-efforts basis   473
bond mutual funds   469
bonds   465
call feature   466
capital   463
capital structure   476
commercial banks   468
commercial paper   467
common stock   469
debt financing   463
dividend policy   479
equity financing   469

finance companies   468
flotation costs   474
indenture   466
initial public offering (IPO)   470
insurance companies   469
leasing   475
mutual funds   469
par value   465
pension funds   468
preferred stock   469
prime rate   465
private placement   474

prospectus   474
protective covenants   467
public offering   473
savings institutions   468
secondary market   472
secured bonds   466
stock mutual funds   470
underwriting syndicate   473
underwritten   473
unsecured bonds   466
venture capital firm   470

REVIEW QUESTIONS

1 Compare the use of funds required by a service firm with the use of funds required by an industrial firm.

2 What factors do lenders use to assess the creditworthiness of firms?

3 When a firm plans to issue bonds, what legal document is created by the firm, and what is included in this document?

4 Identify the various types of creditors that can provide debt financing to firms.

5 Identify and explain common methods of equity financing for a firm.

6 What are the advantages and disadvantages of IPOs (initial public offerings)?

7 Explain the difference between debt financing and equity financing.

8 Identify and explain other methods of obtaining funds that a firm can use in addition to debt financing and equity financing.

9 What factors influence a firm's choice of financing?

10 Discuss the involvement of cross-functional teams in making finance decisions that affect other business decisions.

DISCUSSION QUESTIONS

1 Assume that you are a financial manager. Why would you want to use a very high degree of financial leverage for your firm?

2 Assume that you are a business entrepreneur and you are starting a business that requires a $50,000 investment. You have very little cash; however, you own your own home that is appraised at

$120,000, and you own a car valued at $10,000. Both of these assets are free and clear from any indebtedness. Offer your opinions on how you may negotiate a loan with the bank.

3 How could a firm use the Internet and technology to research financing alternatives?

4 Assume that you are a vice-

president of finance for a large privately held corporation and you must raise $20 million for a project. Discuss why you might consider an IPO.

5 Why do you think stockholders of a firm that is performing very well would prefer that the firm pay only a low percentage of its earnings as dividends?

INVESTING IN THE STOCK OF A BUSINESS

Using the annual report of the firm in which you would like to invest, complete the following:

1. Has the firm obtained new funding over the last year? If so, how?
2. When the firm borrows funds, does it rely mostly on loans from commercial banks, or does it issue bonds?
3. Has the firm's degree of financial leverage changed in the last year because of new financing? If so, has the degree of financial leverage increased or decreased?

4. Explain how the business uses technology to provide information on its financing alternatives and decisions. For example, does it use the Internet to provide information on interest rates on debt instruments that it issues? Does it provide information on the stock price received when issuing stock?
5. Go to **http://hoovers.com** and locate the NEWS SEARCH. Type in the name of the firm in the space provided, and review the recent news stories about the firm. Summarize any (at least one) recent news story about the firm that applies to one or more of the key concepts within this chapter.

CASE THE IPO DECISION

Lauderdale Clothing manufactures shirts and pants with the Lauderdale logo. It is attempting to engage in an initial public offering (IPO). Three years ago, the firm planned an IPO, but because market conditions and earnings for the year came in below expectations, the full value of the firm would not have been realized. Therefore, the plan was scrapped.

Since that time, sales have increased 20 percent (and are currently over $250 million), and profits have increased to more than $60 million, up from last year's profit of $32 million.

The investment banker that will issue the stock for Lauderdale Clothing believes that Lauderdale is in much better financial shape today and better prepared to un-

dertake an IPO of stock. The company has developed stronger management and has aggressively pursued international business.

QUESTIONS

1. Explain why the IPO is expected to be more successful now than it would have been three years ago.
2. What is the role of the investment banker in this IPO?
3. Explain what types of debt and equity financing Lauderdale Clothing could undertake now and in the future.

VIDEO CASE FINANCING DECISIONS BY SCOTSMAN INDUSTRIES

Scotsman Industries sells refrigeration products around the world. It recently acquired several companies and had to decide whether to use equity or debt financing. Scotsman recognizes the benefits from using leverage in which it borrows money rather than issuing stock. Yet, excessive debt could create extreme cash flow pressure to cover interest payment obligations. In addition, the interest rate on some debt varies over time and may rise if market rates rise. Scotsman generally attempts to balance its debt and equity, targeting a 50–50 ratio. In this way, it achieves some benefits from leverage, while minimizing risk by limiting the amount of debt used.

QUESTIONS

1. If Scotsman uses debt rather than equity to finance a profitable project, will the earnings per share be affected more favorably than if it used equity? Explain.
2. How would Scotsman's potential profitability and its risk change if it used a higher proportion of debt in the future?
3. Why might Scotsman's recent willingness to use more debt than its target debt ratio be related to prevailing interest rates?

INTERNET APPLICATIONS

http://www2.ipo.com/ipoinfo/expected.asp?p=IPO

Briefly summarize the information for a future IPO of your choice. How many shares is this firm planning to offer? What will its ticker symbol be? What is the esti-

mated price the firm's stock will sell for? How do you think this price is determined? Also, comment on the firm's recent financial performance, if any. Would you invest in this firm? Why or why not?

THE *Coca-Cola* COMPANY ANNUAL REPORT PROJECT

Questions for the current year's annual report are available on the text website at **http://madura_intro_bus.swcollege.com**.

The following questions apply concepts learned in this chapter to The Coca-Cola Company. Go to The Coca-Cola Company website (**http://www.cocacola.com**) and find the index for the 1999 annual report.

QUESTIONS

1 Click on "Financial Strategies." Why does The Coca-Cola Company say it uses debt financing?

2 Click on "Financial Strategies." The annual report states that The Coca-Cola Company has continued to buy back its own shares of stock. Explain how this affects its financial leverage.

3 Click on "Selected Financial Data." In 1999, The Coca-Cola Company's total return on its shareholders' equity was 27.1 percent. What was the average compound annual growth rate in the company's market price in the last ten years?

4 Click on "Selected Financial Data." Assume that The Coca-Cola Company bought back 20 million shares between 1998 and 1999. Did The Coca-Cola Company issue any stock in 1999? Why?

5 Go to **http://hoovers.com** and locate the NEWS SEARCH. Type in The Coca-Cola Company in the space provided, and review the recent news stories about the firm. Summarize any (at least one) recent news story about The Coca-Cola Company that applies one or more of the key concepts within this chapter of the text.

IN-TEXT STUDY GUIDE

Answers are in an appendix at the back of the book.

TRUE OR FALSE

1 The higher a firm's probability of default, the lower the interest rate charged for a loan.

2 A common form of collateral is the asset purchased with the borrowed funds.

3 A call feature on a bond allows the issuing firm to repurchase the bonds before maturity.

4 Both bonds and commercial paper represent debt financing sources for a firm.

5 Par value represents the rate of interest charged on loans to the most creditworthy firms.

6 When firms obtain all new financing by going public, they do not increase future interest payments to creditors.

7 The issuance of an excessive amount of securities can cause a decline in market prices, because the supply of securities issued may exceed the demand.

8 A firm can increase its financial leverage by increasing the proportion of equity financing in its capital structure.

9 Preferred stock is a security that represents partial ownership of a particular firm and offers specific priorities over common stock.

10 Debt financing is the act of issuing stock or retaining earnings.

MULTIPLE CHOICE

11 Some firms target their dividend payment as a percentage of their:
a) present debt level.   b) past debt level.
c) future earnings.   e) capital structure.
d) revenue.

12 The composition of debt versus equity financing is known as:
a) retained earnings.   d) working capital.
b) revenue.   e) capital structure.
c) asset composition.

13 Investment companies that invest pooled funds from individual investors are:
a) mutual funds.   d) retained earnings.
b) bond indentures.   e) cash dividends.
c) new primary issues.

14 When a firm plans to issue bonds, it explains its obligations to bondholders in a legal document known as a(n):
a) equity ownership.   d) indenture.
b) asset acquisition.   e) note payable.
c) sales revenue.

15 A group of investment banks that share the obligations of underwriting the securities is a(n):
a) bond indenture.
b) corporate charter.
c) savings and loan institution.
d) mutual savings bank.
e) underwriting syndicate.

16 Long-term debt securities purchased by investors are called:
a) corporate bonds.   d) accounts payable.
b) common stock.   e) notes payable.
c) preferred stock.

17 All of the following are creditors that can provide debt financing to firms except:

a) commercial banks.
b) insurance companies.
c) management consultants.
d) pension funds.
e) mutual funds.

18 Firm A and Firm B have identical earnings. Firm A has a higher proportion of debt in its capital structure than does Firm B. Firm A will likely:
a) achieve a lower return on equity than Firm B.
b) achieve a higher return on equity than Firm B.
c) have a lower degree of financial leverage than Firm B.
d) have a lower degree of financial risk than Firm B.
e) have a greater proportion of equity in its capital structure.

19 When comparing manufacturing firms to service businesses, we find that manufacturing firms:
a) borrow more funds.
b) have fewer dollars invested in assets.
c) pay larger dividends than other businesses.
d) use less financial leverage.
e) accumulate less retained earnings.

20 Fees charged by investment banks for their efforts in selling a firm's securities are called:
a) coupon payments.   d) interest fees.
b) best-effort fees.   e) flotation costs.
c) cost of capital.

21 Some firms prefer to finance the use of assets by renting the assets for a specified period of time. This is referred to as:
a) capital structure.   d) sales revenue.
b) leasing.   e) notes payable.
c) retained earnings.

22 Firms that expect interest rates to fall will likely:
a) pay dividends to their stockholders.
b) borrow funds at double the prime rate.
c) borrow funds with a fixed-rate loan.
d) borrow funds with a floating-rate loan.
e) default on their existing bonds.

23 A firm with mostly debt in its capital structure will likely have:
a) low inventory turnover.
b) high accounts receivable.
c) high retained earnings.
d) a large amount of preferred stock.
e) high interest payments.

24 When a business borrows money, the following terms are specified except for:
a) dividend payments.
b) rate of interest.
c) collateral.
d) amount to be borrowed.
e) maturity.

25 When assessing the creditworthiness of a business, a lender will consider all of the following factors except:
a) planned use of the borrowed funds.
b) financial condition of the firm.
c) industry outlook.
d) voting rights of preferred stockholders.
e) availability of collateral.

26 _____ represent earnings of the firm that are reinvested into the business.
a) Dividends   d) Working capital
b) Collateral   e) Capital structure
c) Retained earnings

27 Which of the following describes the best response for a firm anticipating a long-term decline in sales?
a) The firm should increase the proportion of debt in its capital structure.
b) The firm should increase the proportion of bonds in its capital structure.
c) The firm should decrease the proportion of preferred stock in its capital structure.
d) The firm should decrease the proportion of debt in its capital structure.
e) The firm should increase dividends to its stockholders.

28 Corporate stock and bond issues must be registered with the:
a) Federal Trade Commission.
b) Securities and Exchange Commission.
c) Internal Revenue Service.
d) Department of Commerce.
e) Bureau of Labor.

29 When firms apply for loans, they must organize and project their future revenue and expenses in a detailed:
a) marketing mix.   d) financial plan.
b) production plan.   e) production schedule.
c) accounting plan.

30 Firms that conduct international business must consider the potential effects of:
a) exchange rate movements.
b) domestic turnovers.
c) international dividends.
d) international indentures.
e) international proxies.

31 Shareholder expectations and the firm's financing needs are two characteristics that can influence the firm's:
a) exchange rates.
b) governmental relationships.
c) dividend policy.
d) foreign exchange.
e) counter trade.

32 Which of the following forms of financing does not require a fixed payment?

a) bonds   d) leases

b) stocks   e) commercial paper

c) bank loans

33 The interest rate paid on bonds issued by firms is influenced not only by prevailing interest rates but also by the firm's:

a) retained earnings.   d) earnings per share.

b) risk level.   e) return on equity.

c) dividend policy.

34 If a privately held firm desires to obtain additional funds and "go public," it will:

a) borrow funds from a commercial bank.

b) sell bonds in the primary market.

c) merge with a multinational corporation.

d) engage in a public commercial paper offering.

e) engage in an initial public offering.

35 Firms obtain capital (funds) in the form of:

a) inventory and accounts receivable.

b) revenues and expenses.

c) equity and assets.

d) working capital and cost of goods sold.

e) debt and equity.

APPENDIX

How Interest Rates Are Determined

Firms closely monitor interest rates because they affect the cost of borrowing money. The interest rate is the price charged for borrowing money. Managers of firms should understand how interest rates change and should recognize the factors that can cause interest rates to change, as explained by this appendix.

How Interest Rates Change

The interest rate on funds to be borrowed is influenced by the supply of loanable funds (provided by depositors) and the demand for those loanable funds by borrowers. The interaction between demand and supply causes interest rates to change, as explained next.

Demand for Loanable Funds

To illustrate the effects of demand on interest rates, assume that the United States has only one commercial bank. The bank receives all deposits from depositors and uses all the funds to make loans to borrowers. Demand for loans by borrowers will vary with the interest rate the bank charges on loans. The higher the interest rate it charges, the lower the amount of loanable funds demanded (requested for loans). This is because some firms (and other borrowers) are unwilling to pay a high interest rate. If the interest rate is too high, firms may simply not borrow the funds they were hoping to use for expansion.

Consider the demand schedule for loanable funds shown in the second column of Exhibit 17A.1. The demand schedule for loanable funds is also shown on the graph in Exhibit 17A.1 and is labeled D_1. This schedule shows the inverse relationship between the interest rate and the quantity of loanable funds demanded.

Exhibit 17A.1

How the Demand and Supply of Loanable Funds Affect Interest Rates

At an Interest Rate of:	The Quantity of Loanable Funds Demanded by Borrowers Would Be:	The Quantity of Loanable Funds Supplied by Savers Would Be:
12%	$300 billion	$500 billion
10%	350 billion	450 billion
8%	400 billion	400 billion
6%	450 billion	350 billion

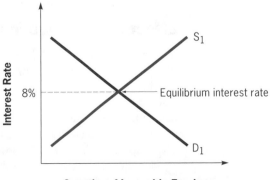

Quantity of Loanable Funds

Supply of Loanable Funds

The quantity of funds supplied (by depositors) to the bank is also related to possible interest rate levels, but in a different manner. The higher the interest rate offered on deposits, the higher the quantity of loanable funds (in the form of deposits) that will be supplied by depositors to banks. The supply schedule for loanable funds to be supplied by depositors is shown in the third column of Exhibit 17A.1. It is also shown on the accompanying graph and is labeled S_1. This schedule shows the positive relationship between the interest rate and the quantity of funds supplied.

Combining Demand and Supply

Interest rates are determined by the interaction of the demand and supply schedules for loanable funds. Notice in Exhibit 17A.1 that at relatively high interest rates (such as 12 percent), the quantity of loanable funds supplied exceeds the quantity of loanable funds demanded, resulting in a surplus of loanable funds. When the interest rate is relatively low (such as 6 percent), the quantity of loanable funds supplied is less than the quantity of loanable funds demanded, resulting in a shortage of funds.

Notice from Exhibit 17A.1 that at the interest rate of 8 percent, the quantity of loanable funds supplied by depositors is $400 billion, which is equal to the quantity of loanable funds demanded by borrowers. At this interest rate, there is no surplus or shortage of loanable funds. The interest rate at which the quantity of loanable funds supplied is equal to the quantity of loanable funds demanded is called the **equilibrium interest rate.**

equilibrium interest rate the interest rate at which the quantity of loanable funds supplied is equal to the quantity of loanable funds demanded

Effect of a Change in the Demand Schedule

As time passes, conditions may change, causing the demand schedule of loanable funds to change. Consequently, a change will occur in the equilibrium interest rate. Reconsider the previous example and assume that most firms suddenly decide to expand their business operations. This decision may result from optimistic news about the economy. Those firms that decide to expand will need to borrow additional funds from the bank. Assume that the demand schedule for loanable funds changes, as shown in Exhibit 17A.2. The graph in the exhibit shows that the demand curve shifts outward from D_1 to D_2.

Now consider the effect of this change in the demand for loanable funds on the equilibrium interest rate, as shown in Exhibit 17A.2. Assuming that the supply schedule of loanable funds remains unchanged, there is now a shortage of loanable funds at the equilibrium interest rate. However, at an interest rate of 10 percent, the quantity of loanable funds supplied by savers will once again equal the quantity of loanable funds demanded by borrowers. Therefore, the new equilibrium interest rate is 10 percent. The graph in Exhibit 17A.2 confirms that the new equilibrium interest rate is 10 percent.

Effect of a Change in the Supply Schedule

Just as the demand schedule for loanable funds may change, so may the supply schedule. To illustrate how a change in the supply schedule can affect the interest rate, reconsider the original example in which the equilibrium interest was 8 percent. Now assume that savers decide to save more funds than they did before, which results in a new supply schedule of loanable funds, as shown in Exhibit 17A.3. At any given interest rate, the quantity of loanable funds supplied is now higher than it was before. The graph in Exhibit 17A.3 shows how the supply curve shifts out from S_1 to S_2.

Now consider the effect of the shift in the supply schedule on the equilibrium interest rate. Assuming that the demand schedule remains unchanged, the supply of loan-

Exhibit 17A.2

Effect of a Change in the Demand for Loanable Funds on Interest Rates

At an Interest Rate of:	The Quantity of Loanable Funds Demanded Was:	But the Quantity of Loanable Funds Demanded Would Now Be:
12%	$300 billion	$400 billion
10%	350 billion	450 billion
8%	400 billion	500 billion
6%	450 billion	550 billion

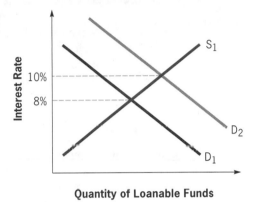

able funds will exceed the demand for loanable funds at the previous equilibrium interest rate of 8 percent. However, at an equilibrium interest rate of 6 percent, the quantity of loanable funds supplied by savers will equal the quantity of loanable funds demanded by borrowers. The graph in Exhibit 17A.3 confirms that the shift in the supply schedule from S_1 to S_2 causes a new equilibrium interest rate of 6 percent.

Exhibit 17A.3

Effect of a Change in the Supply of Loanable Funds on Interest Rates

At an Interest Rate of:	The Quantity of Loanable Funds Supplied by Savers Was:	But the Quantity of Loanable Funds Supplied by Savers Would Now Be:
12%	$500 billion	$600 billion
10%	450 billion	550 billion
8%	400 billion	500 billion
6%	350 billion	450 billion

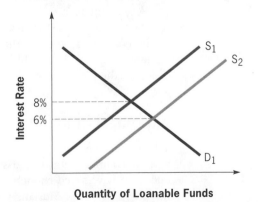

This discussion of interest rates has assumed just one single commercial bank that receives all deposits from savers and provides those funds as loans to borrowers. In reality, many commercial banks and other financial institutions provide this service. Nevertheless, this does not affect the general discussion of interest rates. The equilibrium interest rate in the United States is determined by the interaction of the total demand for loanable funds by all U.S. borrowers and the total supply of loanable funds provided by all U.S. savers.

Factors That Can Affect Interest Rates

Several factors can cause shifts in the demand schedule or supply schedule of loanable funds and therefore can cause shifts in equilibrium interest rates. Firms monitor these factors so that they can anticipate how interest rates may change in the future. In this way, firms can anticipate how their interest owed on borrowed funds may change.

Monetary Policy

Recall that the Federal Reserve System can affect interest rates by implementing monetary policy. As the money supply is adjusted, so is the supply of funds that can be lent out by financial institutions. When the Fed increases the supply of funds, interest rates decrease (assuming no change in demand for funds). Conversely, when the Fed reduces the supply of funds, interest rates increase.

Economic Growth

When economic conditions become more favorable, firms tend to make more plans for expansion. They borrow more money, which reflects an increase in their demand for loanable funds. Assuming that the supply of loanable funds remains unchanged, the increased demand for loanable funds will result in a higher equilibrium interest rate.

To confirm the relationship just described, consider the effects of a strong economy during 1999. In that year, firms increased their demand for loans because of optimism about the future, and interest rates increased substantially.

The Wall Street Journal, Business Week, and other business publications frequently monitor the indicators of economic growth and suggest how interest rates may be affected. A common headline might be something like this: "Economic Growth Increases; Higher Interest Rates Expected." When firms read this headline, they may interpret it as both good news and bad. The good news is higher economic growth, which may increase the demand for the firm's products, thereby increasing the firm's revenue. The bad news is that if the higher economic growth causes higher interest rates, it may also increase the annual interest expenses owed by the firm on its borrowed funds.

As a counterexample, a decline in economic growth can cause firms to reduce their plans for expansion. These firms may see no reason to expand if they expect poor economic conditions, because the demand for their products may decline. If firms demand (borrow) less loanable funds, and the supply of loanable funds remains unchanged, the equilibrium interest rate will decline.

Expected Inflation

When consumers and firms expect a high rate of inflation, they tend to borrow more money. To understand why, assume you plan to purchase a Ford Mustang in two years, once you have saved enough money to pay for it with cash. However, if you believe that the price of the Mustang you wish to purchase will rise substantially by then, you may decide to use borrowed funds to buy it now before the price rises. So when the rate of inflation in the United States is high (or is expected to be high in the near future), many consumers attempt to purchase automobiles, homes, or other products before the prices rise. Firms may also purchase machinery or buildings before the prices rise. These conditions cause an increase in the demand for loanable funds by consumers and firms, which results in higher interest rates. This explains why U.S. interest rates tend to be high when U.S. inflation is high.

Expectations of lower inflation can have the opposite effect. Consumers and firms may be more willing to defer making some purchases if they cannot afford them. They may wait until they are in a better financial situation. When planned purchases are put off until the future, consumers and firms do not need to borrow as much money. Given a lower demand for loanable funds, the interest rate should decline.

Changes in expected inflation could also affect the supply of loanable funds. However, the demand for loanable funds tends to be much more sensitive than the supply of loanable funds to changes in expected inflation.

Savings Behavior

As the savings behavior of people changes, so does the supply schedule of loanable funds, and so does the interest rate. For example, if people become more willing to save money, this increases the amount of money that will be deposited in banks at any possible interest rate. Since the amount of funds that can be loaned out by banks to borrowers has increased, a surplus of funds is available at the previous equilibrium interest rate. Therefore, the new equilibrium interest rate will decline to the level at which the quantity of funds supplied equals the quantity of funds demanded.

Summary of Factors That Affect Interest Rates

Four factors that influence interest rates have been identified and are illustrated in Exhibit 17A.4. The main effects of economic growth and inflation on interest rates occur as a result of influencing the demand for loanable funds. The main effects of savings behavior and monetary policy on interest rates occur as a result of influencing the supply of loanable funds.

The factors that affect interest rates can all change at the same time. One factor may be pushing interest rates up while the others are pushing interest rates down. The final effect on interest rates may depend on which factor has the biggest impact.

Exhibit 17A.4

Summary of Key Factors That Affect Interest Rates

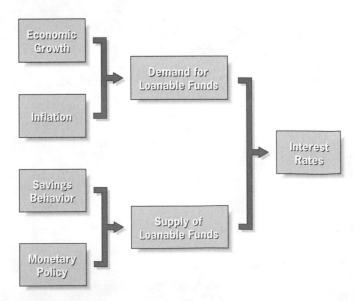

The Learning	①	Describe the tasks necessary to make business investment decisions.
Goals of this	②	Explain how a firm can use capital budgeting to determine whether it should invest in a project.
chapter are to:	③	Describe the factors that motivate investment in other firms (acquisitions).
	④	Explain how firms make decisions for investing in short-term assets.

Business Investment

Whereas the previous chapter focused on how firms obtain funds (financing), this chapter focuses on how firms utilize funds (business investment). A firm can utilize its funds in a wide variety of ways. It makes long-term investment decisions about whether to expand its existing business, develop new businesses, or purchase other companies. It also makes short-term investment decisions regarding the amount it invests in cash, accounts receivable, and inventory. Proper investment decisions will affect the firm's earnings and therefore its value.

To illustrate how business investing can affect the value of a business, consider the case of General Motors (GM), which invests a substantial amount of funds every year in its automobile manufacturing businesses. How can GM determine how much funds to invest in long-term projects? How can GM determine the investment necessary to launch a new product in a foreign market? How can it determine whether it should invest most of its funds to produce new cars or new trucks and vans? This chapter provides a background that can be used to answer these questions.

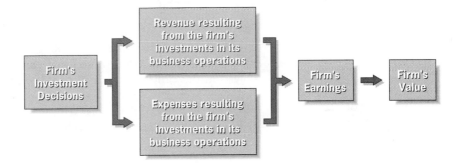

Investment Decisions

 1 Describe the tasks necessary to make business investment decisions.

capital budgeting a comparison of the costs and benefits of a proposed project to determine whether it is feasible

Firms continually evaluate potential projects in which they may invest, such as the construction of a new building or the purchase of a machine. To decide whether any proposed project should be implemented, firms conduct **capital budgeting,** which is a comparison of the costs and benefits of a proposed project to determine whether it is feasible. The costs of a project include the initial outlay (payment) for the project, along with the periodic costs of maintaining the project. The benefits of a project are the revenue it generates.

For example, when McDonald's establishes a new restaurant, the initial outlay includes the construction of the building, the furniture needed, utensils, and cooking facilities. It also includes costs of food as well as labor. The benefits of this project are the revenue that the restaurant will generate over time. In most cases, the precise amounts of a project's costs and benefits are not known in advance and can only be estimated.

Capital budgeting analysis is conducted to justify this firm's investment in trucks.

Exhibit 18.1 shows how Yahoo! has increased its investment in assets over time, so that it can support the growth in its business. Any large investment in assets considered by a firm requires a capital budgeting analysis.

Many decisions that result from capital budgeting are irreversible. That is, if the project does not generate the benefits expected, it is too late to reverse the decision. For example, if a restaurant is unsuccessful, its selling price will likely be much lower than the cost of establishing it.

To illustrate how an inaccurate budgeting analysis can affect the firm, consider the case of Converse, which invested in a company called Apex One. The expenses involved in this project's operations were underestimated, while the revenue from this project was overestimated. Converse terminated the project just three months after it made the initial outlay and incurred a $41.6 million loss on this project. As an illustration of how firms focus on each project's return versus its cost, consider the following statements from recent annual reports:

Exhibit 18.1

How Investment in Assets Has Grown for Yahoo!

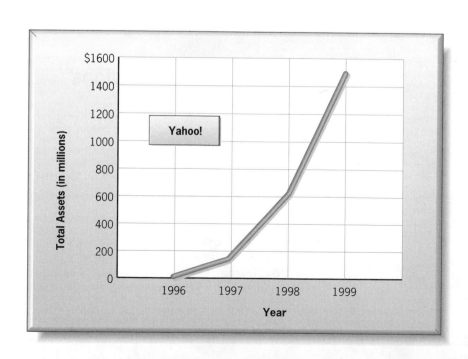

❝ Our goal is to achieve a return on invested capital over the course of each business cycle that exceeds the company's cost of capital. ❞

—Boise Cascade

❝ With a return on capital roughly three times our cost of capital, this strategy [of borrowing more funds to expand] makes even more sense now than before. ❞

—The Coca-Cola Company

❝ All of our divisions use the measurement of return on invested capital relative to the cost of capital as their standard. ❞

—Textron

DELL COMPUTER'S FORMULA FOR SUCCESS

Dell Computer's entire approach to conducting business revolves around the Internet. By investing heavily in supporting its website, **www.dell.com**, the company focuses on its products but uses the Internet to complement that focus. Thus, Dell's servers, which are integral to hosting a website as robust as Dell's, are two of the company's most successful products. This illustrates how investment in a key aspect of Dell's business helps improve the sales of its products.

How Interest Rates Affect Investment Decisions

Interest rates determine the cost of borrowed funds. A change in interest rates can affect the cost of borrowing as well as the project's feasibility. Firms require a return on projects that exceeds their cost of funds. If they use borrowed funds to finance a project and pay 20 percent on those funds, they would require a return of at least 20 percent on that project. If interest rates decrease, the cost of financing decreases, and the firm's required rate of return decreases. Thus, a project once perceived by the firm as unfeasible may be feasible once the firm's required rate of return is lowered.

Capital Budget

capital budget a targeted amount of funds to be used for purchasing assets such as buildings, machinery, and equipment that are needed for long-term projects

Firms plan a **capital budget,** or a targeted amount of funds to be used for purchasing assets such as buildings, machinery, and equipment that are needed for long-term projects. The annual capital budget for firms such as PepsiCo, The Coca Cola Company, IBM, and ExxonMobil commonly exceeds $1 billion. The size of a firm's capital budget is influenced by the amount and size of feasible business projects.

A firm's capital budget can be allocated across its various businesses. PepsiCo distributes its capital budget across snack foods and beverages.

A capital budget can also be segmented by geographic markets. PepsiCo allocates its capital budget for projects in the United States and for projects in foreign countries.

Classification of Capital Expenditures

The types of potential capital expenditures considered by a firm can be broadly classified into the following three categories.

Expansion of Current Business If the demand for a firm's products increases, a firm invests in additional assets (such as machinery or equipment) to produce a large enough volume of products to accommodate the increased demand. For example, many technology firms increased their capital budgets in 2000 because they anticipated an increase in demand for their products.

BUSINESS ONLINE

Information from the SEC

http://www.sec.gov

THE SECURITIES AND EXCHANGE COMMISSION (SEC), WHICH REGULATES A large part of the securities market, provides a variety of information on its website, as shown here. Companies seeking to invest in bonds or stocks can use this information in researching prospective companies. Furthermore, the SEC provides a comprehensive section on small business regulations and investment support for small businesses.

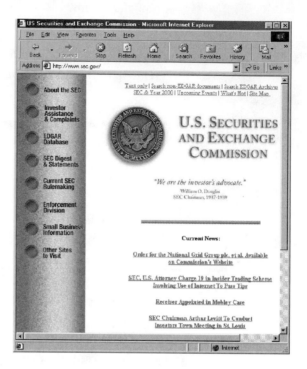

This Burger King, which opened in Reno, Nevada, in 1999, has several innovations. The decision to use these innovations is based on a capital budgeting analysis, which suggests that this investment is feasible.

Development of New Business When firms expand the line of products that they produce and sell, they need new facilities for production. They may also need to hire employees to produce and sell the new products. The car manufacturers frequently invest millions of dollars every year to expand their product line and to improve their exporting capabilities.

Investment in Assets That Will Reduce Expenses Machines and equipment wear out or become technologically obsolete over time. Firms replace old machines and equipment to capitalize on new technology, which may allow for lower expenses over time. For example, a new computer may be able to generate a firm's financial reports more economically than an older computer. The benefits of lower expenses may outweigh the initial outlay needed to purchase the new computer.

Firms also purchase machines that can perform the work of employees. For example, machines rather than employees could be used on an assembly line to package a product. The benefits of these machines are the cost savings that result from employing fewer workers. To determine whether the machines are feasible for this purpose, the cost savings must be compared with the price of the machines.

SEVERAL COMPANIES USE THE INTERNET TO PROVIDE INFORMATION ABOUT their long-term investment strategies, as shown here for Phillips 66. Notice that Phillips uses the website to both explain and comment on the performance of its recent long-term investments. By providing this information, firms such as Phillips give their investors valid financial information to help them in their investment decisions.

BUSINESS ONLINE

Investment Strategies Online

http://www.phillips66.com/ howb3c.html

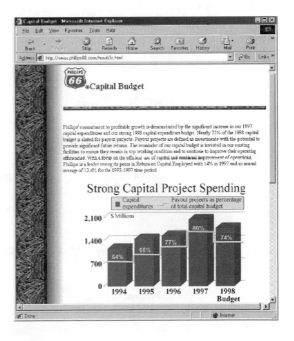

Capital Budgeting Tasks

2 Explain how a firm can use capital budgeting to determine whether it should invest in a project.

The process of capital budgeting involves five tasks:

▶ Proposing new projects
▶ Estimating cash flows of projects
▶ Determining whether projects are feasible
▶ Implementing feasible projects
▶ Monitoring projects that were implemented

John Medica and Michael Dell of Dell Computer introduce a new line of personal computers. Their decision to offer these new products is based on a capital budgeting analysis.

Proposing New Projects

New projects are continually proposed within the firm as various departments or divisions offer input on new projects to consider.

Estimating Cash Flows of Projects

Each potential project affects the cash flows of the firm. Estimating the cash flows that will result from the project is a critical part of the capital budgeting process. Revenue received from the project represents cash inflows, while payments to cover the project's expenses represent cash outflows. The decision whether to make a capital expenditure is based on the size of the periodic cash flows (defined as cash inflows minus cash outflows per period) that are expected to occur as a result of the project.

Determining Whether Projects Are Feasible

Once potential projects are proposed and their cash flows estimated, the projects must be evaluated to determine whether they are feasible. Specific techniques are available to assess the feasibility of projects. One popular method is the net present value (NPV) technique. This technique compares the expected periodic cash flows resulting from the project with the initial outlay needed to finance the project. This process is discussed in more detail later in this chapter. If the present value of the project's expected cash flows is above or equal to the initial outlay, the project is feasible. Conversely, if the present value of the project's expected cash flows is below the initial outlay, the project is not feasible.

mutually exclusive the situation in which only one of two projects designed for the same purpose can be accepted

independent the decision of whether to adopt one project has no bearing on the adoption of other projects

In some cases, the evaluation involves deciding between two projects designed for the same purpose. When only one of the projects can be accepted, such projects are referred to as **mutually exclusive.** For example, a firm may be considering two machines that perform the same task. The two alternative machines are mutually exclusive because the purchase of one machine precludes the purchase of the other.

When the decision of whether to adopt one project has no bearing on the adoption of other projects, the project is said to be **independent.** For example, the purchase of a truck to enhance delivery capabilities and the purchase of a large computer system to handle payroll processing are independent projects. That is, the acceptance (or rejection) of one project does not influence the acceptance (or rejection) of the other project.

The authority to evaluate the feasibility of projects may be dependent on the types of projects evaluated. Larger capital expenditures normally are reviewed by high-level managers. Smaller capital expenditures may be made by other managers.

Implementing Feasible Projects

Once the firm has determined which projects are feasible, it must focus on implementing those projects. All feasible projects should be given a priority status so that those projects that fulfill immediate needs can be implemented first. As part of the implementation process, the firm must obtain the necessary funds to finance the projects.

Monitoring Projects That Were Implemented

Even after a project has been implemented, it should be monitored over time. The project's actual costs and benefits should be compared with the estimates made before the project was implemented. The monitoring process may detect errors in the previous estimation of the project's cash flows. If any errors are detected, the employees who were responsible for project evaluation should be informed of the problem so that future projects can be evaluated more accurately.

A second purpose of monitoring is to detect and correct inefficiencies in the current operation of the project. Furthermore, monitoring can help determine if and when a project should be abandoned (liquidated) by the firm.

Summary of Capital Budgeting Tasks

The five tasks necessary to conduct capital budgeting are summarized in Exhibit 18.2. The most challenging task is the estimation of cash flows, because it is difficult to accurately measure the revenue and expenses that will result from a particular project.

Capital Budgeting Analysis

A firm performs a capital budgeting analysis of each project by comparing the project's initial outlay with the project's expected benefits. The benefits represent the cash flows

Exhibit 18.2

Summary of Capital Budgeting Tasks

Task	Description
Proposing new projects	Propose new projects that require expenditures necessary to support expansion of existing businesses, development of new businesses, or replacement of old assets.
Estimating cash flows of projects	Cash flows in each period can be estimated as the cash inflows (such as revenue) resulting from the project minus cash outflows (expenses) resulting from the project.
Determining whether projects are feasible	A project is feasible if the present value of its future cash flows exceeds the initial outlay needed to purchase the project.
Implementing feasible projects	Feasible projects should be implemented, with priority given to those projects that fulfill immediate needs.
Monitoring projects that were implemented	Projects that have been implemented need to be monitored to determine whether their cash flows were estimated properly. Monitoring may also detect inefficiencies in the project and can help determine when a project should be abandoned.

generated by the project. Before providing an example of a firm's capital budgeting analysis, the procedure for estimating the present value of future cash flows is described.

Background on Present Value

Because money has a time value, a payment received by a firm at a future point in time has less value than the exact payment received today. For this reason, future payments are commonly discounted to determine their present value. For example, if a payment of $50,000 is received in one year, it can be discounted to determine its present value. Assume that the firm could achieve a return of 10 percent over the next year on funds available today. It could use this interest rate to discount the $50,000 payment to be received in one year.

$$\text{Present Value } (PV) \text{ of } \$50,000 \text{ Payment} = \frac{\$50,000}{(1 + .10)}$$

$$\text{to Be Received in One Year} = \$45,455$$

This means that the $50,000 payment to be received in one year has a present value of $45,455. If the firm received $45,455 today (instead of $50,000 in one year) and invested the funds at 10 percent, the funds would accumulate to $50,000 at the end of the year.

Capital budgeting analysis compares future cash flows resulting from the project with the initial outlay needed to purchase the project. The initial outlay is made immediately (if the project is implemented), but the cash flows resulting from the project may be received over several years. Since the timing of the cash flows differs from that of the initial outlay, the cash flows must be converted to a present value so that they can be compared with the initial outlay.

The present value of a project's future cash flows is determined by discounting the cash flows at the rate of return that the firm could have earned on the funds if it had used them for an alternative project with similar risk. That is, the discount rate reflects the return that the firm would require to make the investment. The firm must earn at least that return, or it would simply invest the funds in the alternative project.

For example, assume a firm can invest in a project today that would generate a lump-sum cash flow (CF) of $10,000 from the investment in one year. If the firm has a required return (r) on this investment of 12 percent, the present value (PV) of the cash flow is as follows:

$$PV = \frac{CF \text{ at End of Year 1}}{(1 + r)}$$

$$= \frac{\$10,000}{(1 + .12)^1}$$

$$= \$8,929$$

This suggests that if the cash amount of $8,929 were available today and could be invested at 12 percent, it would be worth $10,000 in one year. If the initial outlay is more than $8,929, the firm should not make the investment, because the initial outlay would exceed the present value of the cash flow generated by the investment.

Now adjust the example to determine the present value of the $10,000 cash flow if it is received at the end of the second year instead of the first year. The present value of this project based on a required return of 12 percent is as follows:

$$PV = \frac{CF \text{ at End of Year 2}}{(1 + r)^2}$$

$$= \frac{\$10,000}{(1 + .12)^2}$$

$$= \$7,972$$

The exponent of the denominator is adjusted to discount the amount based on a period of two years instead of one year. Notice that the present value of cash flows in Year 2 is less than the present value of cash flows in Year 1. The further out the time when a given amount is received, the lower the present value.

The present value of a cash amount in any year can be estimated by adjusting the exponent to reflect the number of years in the future. As one final example, the present value of a $10,000 cash flow to be received three years from now is estimated as follows (assuming the required return is 12 percent):

$$PV = \frac{CF \text{ at End of Year 3}}{(1 + r)^3}$$

$$= \frac{\$10,000}{(1 + .12)^3}$$

$$= \$7,118$$

Now consider a project that generates a cash flow of $10,000 for the firm in Years 1, 2, and 3. Each cash flow can be discounted separately to derive its present value; then, the discounted cash flows are added to determine the present value of the investment. The present value of these cash flows is estimated as follows:

$$PV = \frac{CF \text{ at End of Year 1}}{(1 + r)^1} + \frac{CF \text{ at End of Year 2}}{(1 + r)^2} + \frac{CF \text{ at End of Year 3}}{(1 + r)^3}$$

$$= \frac{\$10,000}{(1 + .12)^1} + \frac{\$10,000}{(1 + .12)^2} + \frac{\$10,000}{(1 + .12)^3}$$

$$= \$8,929 + \$7,972 + \$7,118$$

$$= \$24,019$$

This example is illustrated in Exhibit 18.3. It shows how the present value of cash flows is determined by discounting the cash flows in each year at the firm's required rate of return. Then, those discounted cash flows are added together to determine the present value of the cash flows. If the initial outlay necessary to purchase this project is less than $24,019, the project is feasible and should be implemented. If the initial outlay necessary to purchase the project is more than $24,019, the project is not feasible and should not be implemented.

Estimating the Net Present Value To reinforce the use of capital budgeting analysis, consider a firm that decides to purchase a used delivery truck for $15,000 that will be used to make extra deliveries and will last only two years. By having this truck, the firm estimates that it will generate an extra $8,000 in cash flow at the end of next year and an extra $12,000 at the end of the following year. Assume that the firm requires a return of 15 percent on this project. The present value of these cash flows is estimated as follows:

Exhibit 18.3

Example of Discounting Cash Flows

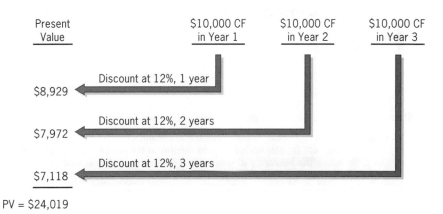

PV = $24,019

GLOBAL BUSINESS

Global Investing

U.S. FIRMS FREQUENTLY CONSIDER INVESTING FUNDS IN FOREIGN PROJECTS. The Coca-Cola Company commonly invests more than $1 billion per year to expand its worldwide business. The Coca-Cola Company typically invests the bulk of its capital budget overseas, because international markets offer more opportunities for the company.

When U.S. firms such as Coca-Cola consider the purchase of a foreign company, they conduct a capital budgeting analysis to determine whether this type of project is feasible. The capital budgeting analysis required to assess a foreign project is more complex than a domestic project because of the need to assess specific characteristics of the foreign country. First, the initial outlay required to purchase the foreign firm will depend on the exchange rate at that time. If Coca-Cola purchased a small Mexican firm for 1,000,000 pesos when the peso is worth $.30, the initial outlay would have been $300,000 (computed as $.30 × P1,000,000). However, if the acquisition is made when the peso is worth $.16, the initial outlay would be $160,000 (computed as P1,000,000 × $.16). The lower the value of the foreign currency needed, the lower the initial outlay needed by the U.S. firm to acquire the foreign company. Firms prefer to invest in foreign companies (or any other foreign projects) under these conditions.

Firms that consider foreign projects must also determine the required rate of return for the foreign project to be feasible. Many foreign projects are considered to be more risky than domestic projects, so U.S. firms require higher rates of return on foreign projects than on domestic projects. Foreign projects in developing countries are especially risky, because the probability is high that these projects could be terminated by the governments of those countries. When a U.S. firm requires a higher return, it uses a higher discount rate to derive the present value of the project's future cash flows. This point is especially important in light of recent trends by U.S. firms to invest in large projects based in developing countries. General Motors typically invests more than $100 million per year in developing countries. The large amount of investment by General Motors in these countries suggests that it expects the projects to generate very high returns, making them worthwhile even though they are riskier than projects in the United States.

Dr. Paul Horn, senior vice president of IBM research, develops new technology that is expected to generate a positive net present value for IBM.

Many other factors also deserve to be considered for foreign projects. The prior discussion is intended to illustrate how a capital budgeting analysis must consider the specific characteristics of the country where the project is to be implemented.

3 Describe the factors that motivate investment in other firms (acquisitions).

Mergers

merger two firms are merged (or combined) to become a single firm owned by the same owners (shareholders)

horizontal merger the combination of firms that engage in the same types of business

vertical merger the combination of a firm with a potential supplier or customer

conglomerate merger the combination of two firms in unrelated businesses

A firm may invest in another company by purchasing all the stock of that company. This results in a **merger,** in which two firms are merged (or combined) to become a single firm owned by the same owners (shareholders). Mergers may be feasible if they can increase the firm's value either by increasing the return to the firm's owners or by reducing the firm's risk without a reduction in return.

Mergers can be classified as one of three general types. A **horizontal merger** is the combination of firms that engage in the same types of business. For example, the merger between Chemical Banking Corporation and Chase Manhattan Corporation represents a horizontal merger, as it combines two of the largest commercial banks. A **vertical merger** is the combination of a firm with a potential supplier or customer, such as General Motors' acquisition of a battery manufacturer that could produce the batteries for many of its automobiles. A **conglomerate merger** is the combination of two firms in unrelated businesses. For example, the merger between a book publisher and a steel manufacturer is a conglomerate merger. The term *conglomerate* is sometimes used to describe a firm that is engaged in a variety of unrelated businesses.

CROSS-FUNCTIONAL TEAMWORK

Cross-Functional Relationships Involved in Business Investment Decisions

When financial managers make capital budgeting decisions, they rely on information from the production and marketing departments, as shown in the diagram below. The expected cash inflows resulting from a project are dependent on the expected sales to be generated by the project, which are normally forecasted by the marketing department. The expected cash outflows resulting from a project are dependent on the expected expenses incurred from the project. Those expenses that are attributed to marketing (such as promotion expenses) can be forecasted by the marketing department. Those expenses that are attributed to production (such as labor expenses) can be forecasted by the production department. The financial manager's ability to estimate a project's net present value is dependent on the input provided by marketing and production managers.

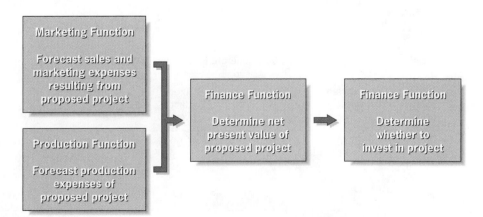

Corporate Motives for Mergers

Mergers are normally initiated as a result of one or more of the following motives.

Immediate Growth A firm that plans for growth may prefer to achieve its objective immediately through a merger. Consider a firm whose production capacity cannot fully satisfy demand for its product. The firm would need two years to build additional production facilities. To achieve an immediate increase in production, the firm may search for a company that owns the appropriate facilities. By acquiring either part or all of such a company, the firm can achieve immediate growth in its production capacity, which allows for growth in its sales. When Walt Disney purchased Capital Cities/ABC, it created more growth potential than if it simply attempted to expand its existing businesses.

Economies of Scale Growth may also be desirable to reduce the production cost per unit. Products that exhibit economies of scale can be produced at a much lower cost per unit if a large amount is produced. A merger may allow for the combination of two production facilities, which achieves a lower production cost per unit.

For example, assume that Firm A and Firm B produce a similar product. Also assume that each firm uses an assembly-line operation for about eight hours per day and sells its product to its own set of customers. Firm A sells five hundred units per month, while Firm B sells four hundred units per month. The variable cost per unit is $10 for each firm. Each firm pays $6,000 per month to rent its own factory. This rent is a fixed cost because it is not affected by the amount of the product produced. If Firm A acquires Firm B, it will be able to serve both sets of customers, which will result in a higher production level. The factory can be used for sixteen hours a day to run a second shift for the assembly line.

Based on the initial assumptions, the average cost per unit for each firm is shown in Exhibit 18.6. Notice that when Firm A acquires Firm B, the average cost per unit is lower than it was for either individual firm. This occurs because only one factory is needed when the firms are merged. Thus, the average cost per unit declines when Firm A makes more efficient use of the factory.

There may be additional ways for the combination of firms to reduce costs, beyond the savings resulting from renting only one factory. For example, assume each firm has its own accountant. Each firm pays a salary for this position, which reflects a fixed cost. However, Firm A's accountant may be able to cover all the accounting duties for the combined firm, which means that it need not incur the cost of Firm B's accountant. Therefore, it can further reduce costs by removing any job positions in Firm B that can be handled by Firm A's existing employees.

Horizontal mergers are more likely to achieve economies of scale than vertical or conglomerate mergers, because they involve firms that produce similar products. Firms with similar operations can allow for the elimination of similar positions once the firms are combined.

Exhibit 18.6 Illustration of How an Acquisition Can Generate Economies of Scale

Firm	Total Output Produced	Variable Cost per Unit	Variable Cost	Fixed Cost (Rent)	Total Cost	Average Cost per Unit
A	500 units	$10	$5,000	$6,000	$11,000	($11,000/500) = $22.00
B	400 units	$10	$4,000	$6,000	$10,000	($10,000/400) = $25.00
A & B Combined	900 units	$10	$9,000	$6,000	$15,000	($15,000/900) = $16.67

Managerial Expertise The performance of a firm is highly dependent on the managers who make the decisions for a firm. Since the firm's value is influenced by its performance, its value is influenced by its managers. To illustrate this point, consider a firm called "Weakfirm" that has had weak performance recently because of its managers. This firm's value should be low if its performance has been weak and is not expected to improve.

However, assume that another firm in the same industry, called "Strongfirm," has more competent managers. If the managers of Strongfirm had been managing the operations of Weakfirm, the performance of Weakfirm might have been much higher. Given this information, Strongfirm may consider purchasing Weakfirm. The price for Weakfirm should be relatively low because of its recent performance. Yet, once Strongfirm purchases Weakfirm, it can improve Weakfirm's performance. The owners (shareholders) of Strongfirm will benefit because their firm is able to acquire another firm at a relatively low price and turn it into something more valuable. In other words, the additional earnings generated by Strongfirm following the acquisition may exceed the cost of the acquisition.

The example just described occurs frequently. Some firms that have had relatively weak performance (compared with other firms in the industry) become targets. Consequently, weak firms are always in danger of being acquired. Kohlberg Kravis Roberts acquired RJR Nabisco because it believed it could improve the firm's performance by using its own managerial expertise.

Some mergers can be beneficial when each firm relies on the other firm for specific managerial expertise. For example, consider Disney's acquisition of the ABC television network. Disney produced movies that were sold to television networks. When television networks began to produce their own movies, Disney could have been prevented from selling its movies to various networks. By acquiring the ABC network, Disney could rely on the network to show some of its movies, while the ABC network was assured that it would be supplied with various popular Disney movies. Disney had expertise as the producer of the product (movies), and ABC had expertise as the distributor of that product. Both firms benefited as a result of the acquisition.

Tax Benefits Firms that incur negative earnings (losses) are sometimes attractive candidates for mergers because of potential tax advantages. The previous losses incurred by the company prior to the merger can be carried forward to offset positive earnings of the acquiring firm. Although the losses of the acquired firm have occurred prior to the acquisition, they reduce the taxable earnings of the newly merged corporation. To illustrate the potential tax benefits, consider an acquisition in which the acquiring firm applies a $1 million loss of the acquired firm to partially offset its earnings. If the acquiring firm is subject to a 30 percent tax rate, it can reduce its taxes by $300,000 (computed as 30 percent times the $1,000,000 in earnings that is no longer subject to tax because of applying the $1,000,000 loss).

Leveraged Buyouts

leveraged buyout (LBO) a purchase of a company (or the subsidiary of the company) by a group of investors with borrowed funds

In a **leveraged buyout**, or **LBO,** a group of investors purchase a company (or the subsidiary of the company) with borrowed funds. In many cases, the investors are the previous managers of the business. For example, consider a diversified firm that plans to sell off its financial services division to obtain cash. The management of this division may attempt to borrow the necessary funds to purchase the division themselves and become the owners. The newly owned business would be supported with mostly borrowed funds.

A well-known LBO was the acquisition of RJR Nabisco by Kohlberg Kravis Roberts for about $25 billion. About 94 percent of the funds used to purchase RJR Nabisco were borrowed.

Any business with characteristics that can adequately operate with a large amount of borrowed funds is a potential candidate for an LBO. Such characteristics include established product lines, stable cash flow, and no need for additional fixed assets. These characteristics increase the probability that a sufficient amount of cash flows will consistently be forthcoming to cover periodic interest payments on the debt. Growth normally is not a primary goal, since the firm does not have excess cash to expand and may have already borrowed up to its capacity.

Although an LBO can place a strain on cash, it does offer an advantage. The ownership of the business is restricted to a small group of people. All earnings can be allocated to this group, which allows the potential for high returns to the owners (although most earnings will likely be reinvested in the business in the early years). However, since businesses that experience LBOs have a debt-intensive capital structure (high degree of financial leverage), they are risky.

Divestitures

divestiture the sale of an existing business by a firm

A **divestiture** is the sale of an existing business by a firm. Firms may have several motives for divestitures. First, a firm may divest (sell) businesses that are not part of its core operations so that it can focus on what it does best. For example, Eastman Kodak, Kmart, W.R. Grace, and Ford Motor Company all sold various businesses that were not closely related to their core businesses.

A second motive for divestitures is to obtain funds. Divestitures generate funds for the firm, because one of the firm's businesses is sold in exchange for cash. For example, Westinghouse made divestitures to focus on its core businesses and also to obtain funds so that it could pay off some of its existing debt. ITT Corporation sold a commercial finance business so that it could use the funds to expand in the entertainment business.

A third motive for divesting is that a firm's "break-up" value is sometimes believed to be worth more than the firm as a whole. In other words, the sum of a firm's individual asset liquidation values exceeds the market value of the firm's combined assets. This encourages firms to sell off what would be worth more when liquidated than when retained.

Short-Term Investment Decisions

 Explain how firms make decisions for investing in short-term assets.

working capital management the management of a firm's short-term assets and liabilities

liquid having access to funds to pay bills when they come due

liquidity management the management of short-term assets and liabilities to ensure adequate liquidity

Treasury bills short-term debt securities issued by the U.S. Treasury

Working capital management represents the management of a firm's short-term assets and liabilities. A firm's short-term assets include cash, short-term securities, accounts receivable, and inventory. Its short-term liabilities include accounts payable and short-term loans. Working capital management is typically focused on the proper amount of investment in a firm's cash, short-term securities, accounts receivable, and inventory. All of these strategies can be classified as a firm's investment strategies. Working capital management can be segmented into liquidity management, accounts receivable management, and inventory management.

Liquidity Management

Firms that are **liquid** have adequate access to funds to pay bills when they come due. **Liquidity management** involves the management of short-term assets and liabilities to ensure adequate liquidity. To remain liquid, firms may maintain cash and short-term securities. For example, they may invest in **Treasury bills,** which are short-term debt securities issued by the U.S. Treasury. Treasury bills have maturities of thirteen weeks, twenty-six weeks, and one year. Treasury bills offer a relatively low return. They provide a firm with easy access to funds because they can easily be sold to other investors.

line of credit an agreement that allows access to borrowed funds upon demand over some specified period

When firms need funds to pay bills, they sell the Treasury bills and use the proceeds to pay the bills. Firms such as DuPont and The Coca-Cola Company hold hundreds of millions of dollars worth of short-term securities to maintain liquidity.

Firms normally attempt to limit their holdings of cash and short-term securities so that they can use their funds for other purposes that generate higher returns. They can be liquid without holding cash and short-term securities if they have easy access to borrowed funds. Most firms have a **line of credit** with one or more banks, which is an agreement that allows access to borrowed funds upon demand over some specified period (usually for one year). If a firm experiences a temporary shortage of funds, it can use its line of credit to obtain a short-term loan immediately. The interest charged by the banks on the loan is normally tied to some specified market-determined interest rate. Thus, the interest rate will be consistent with existing market rates at the time of the loan. Firms with a line of credit do not need to go through the loan application process. They can normally reapply for a new line of credit each year.

Because of its line of credit, its cash, and its short-term securities, The Coca-Cola Company always has access to a sufficient amount of funds to pay its bills.

When firms build up an excessive amount of cash, they search for ways to use the excess. For example, they commonly use excess cash to repurchase some of their existing stock. Alternatively, they may use excess cash to pay off some of their existing debt.

Accounts Receivable Management

Firms have accounts receivable when they grant credit to customers. By granting credit, they may generate more sales than if they required an immediate cash pay-

SMALL BUSINESS SURVEY

Investment Decisions by Small Businesses

About three hundred Entrepreneur of the Year award winners were surveyed by the accounting firm Ernst & Young to determine how they would invest funds if they received the ideal level of financing. The respondents were allowed to select more than one type of investment. Their responses are shown in the following chart:

ment. Allowing credit has two potential disadvantages, however. The first is that the customers may not pay the credit balance for a long time. Thus, the firm does not have use of the cash until several months after the sale was made. Consequently, the firm may have to borrow funds until the cash is received and will have to pay interest on those funds.

The second potential disadvantage of extending credit to customers is that the customers may default on the credit provided. In this case, the firm never receives payment for the products it sold to customers.

Accounts receivable management sets the limits on credit available to customers and the length of the period in which payment is due. The goal is to be flexible enough so that sales increase as a result of credit granted but strict enough to avoid customers who would pay their bills late (beyond the period specified) or not at all.

Given the possibilities of late payments or no payments (default) on the credit, firms need to closely assess the creditworthiness of any customers who wish to pay their bills with credit.

accounts receivable management sets the limits on credit available to customers and the length of the period in which payment is due

Inventory Management

When firms maintain large amounts of inventory, they can avoid stockouts (shortages). However, they invest a large amount of funds by holding so much inventory, and they could have used those funds for other purposes. Consider the case of Wal-Mart, which continuously attempts to order enough of each product to satisfy customers. Yet, it does not want to order an excessive amount of any product so that it can use its funds more efficiently.

Inventory management determines the amount of inventory that is held. Managers attempt to hold just enough inventory to avoid stockouts, without tying up funds in excess inventories. This task is complicated because it requires forecasts of future sales levels, which can be erratic. If sales are more than expected, stockouts could occur unless excess inventory was held.

inventory management determines the amount of inventory that is held

---

BUSINESS DILEMMA	College Health Club

 Capital Budgeting at College Health Club

SUE KRAMER, PRESIDENT OF COLLEGE HEALTH CLUB (CHC), NOTICES THAT the Silver Health Club in a nearby town is for sale for $100,000. It is close to another college campus but has not made much of an effort to attract that college's students. This club's largest expense is the rent. Sue believes that she could improve the performance of the Silver Health Club if she purchased it, but its price seems high.

Sue decides to conduct a capital budgeting analysis of Silver Health Club. She estimates her cash inflows each year and subtracts the estimated cash outflows to derive annual cash flows. Her cash outflows include the hiring of a manager to oversee the club's business, since Sue would still focus most of her time at CHC. She estimates that her cash flows would be $5,000 in each of the first two years and $20,000 over each of the following three years. All cash flows are expected to occur at the end of each year. Sue also estimates that she would be able to sell this health club in five years for $120,000 (after taxes). She decides that she would need to generate a rate of return of at least 20 percent from this health club to make it worth purchasing.

Dilemma

Sue's goal is to determine whether to purchase the health club. Conduct a capital budgeting analysis to determine the net present value of Silver Health Club. Based on your analysis, should Sue purchase the Silver Health Club?

Exhibit 18.7

Capital Budgeting Analysis of a Firm That CHC May Acquire

End of Year	Estimated Cash Flow	Discounted Cash Flow (at 20%)
1	$ 5,000	$ 4,167
2	5,000	3,472
3	20,000	11,574
4	20,000	9,645
5	20,000	8,038
+$120,000 (Salvage Value)		48,225

Present Value = $85,121
− Initial Outlay = $100,000
Net Present Value = −$14,879

Solution

Sue's capital budgeting analysis of the target firm is shown in Exhibit 18.7. The cash flows shown in column 2 of Exhibit 18.7 are discounted at a rate of 20 percent (which represents Sue's required rate of return) to derive their present value in column 3. Notice that the salvage value of $120,000 (the expected sales price of the firm) is also included in the estimated cash flows for Year 5. The discounted annual cash flows are summed at the bottom of Column 3 to derive the present value of future cash flows.

The present value of the Silver Health Club's future cash flows is estimated to be $85,121, which is less than the initial outlay (purchase price) of $100,000. Therefore, the net present value from acquiring the Silver Health Club is negative, causing Sue to reject this project. The present value of future cash flows does not cover the amount she would have to pay for the club. Sue decides to monitor the status of the Silver Health Club over time. If its price is lowered, she will reassess whether to acquire it by conducting a new capital budgeting analysis.

Additional Issues for Discussion

1 If Sue were willing to require a lower rate of return on the Silver Health Club, how would this affect the present value of the club's future cash flows?

2 When Sue estimates the value of Silver Health Club, what is the key information used to estimate its value? Could this information be wrong?

3 A key motive for Sue to consider purchasing Silver Health Club is her belief that she could improve its performance by managing it better. Would economies of scale be a motive for Sue to consider expansion by purchasing another health club?

SUMMARY

1 Capital budgeting analysis is normally applied to determine whether proposed projects are feasible. If the present value of the project's expected cash flows exceeds the project's initial outlay, the project has a positive net present value and should be implemented. If the present value of the project's expected cash flows is less than the project's initial outlay, the project has a negative net present value and should not be implemented.

2 The process of capital budgeting involves five tasks:

▶ proposing new projects that deserve to be assessed;
▶ estimating cash flows of projects, which represent the cash inflows (derived from revenue) minus cash outflows (derived from expenses) per period;
▶ determining which projects are feasible, which can be accom-

plished by comparing the present value of the project's cash flows with the project's initial outlay;

▶ implementing feasible projects based on a priority status; and

▶ monitoring projects that were implemented, so that any errors from estimating project cash flows are recognized and may be avoided when assessing projects in the future.

3 Firms consider investing funds to acquire other companies as a result of one or more of the following motives:

▶ A firm can achieve immediate growth by acquiring another

firm, whereas growth without a merger will be slower.

▶ Mergers can create a higher volume of sales for a firm, which allows it to spread its fixed cost across more units, thereby reducing costs (economies of scale).

▶ Mergers can allow firms to combine resources and contribute those resources in which they have the most managerial expertise.

▶ Mergers can allow the acquiring firm to reduce its taxable earnings when it acquires a company that recently incurred a loss.

4 Firms invest in short-term assets such as cash, short-

term securities, accounts receivable, and inventory. They invest in a sufficient amount of cash and short-term securities to maintain adequate liquidity. However, excessive investment in cash and short-term securities represents an inefficient use of funds.

Firms desire to invest in sufficient accounts receivable so that they can increase revenue over time. They must impose adequate credit standards, however, so that they can avoid excessive defaults on credit they have provided.

Firms desire to invest in a sufficient amount of inventory so that they can avoid stockouts. However, excessive investment in inventory represents an inefficient use of funds.

KEY TERMS

accounts receivable management *510*
capital budget *495*
capital budgeting *493*
conglomerate merger *505*
divestiture *508*
horizontal merger *505*
independent projects *498*

inventory management *510*
leveraged buyout (LBO) *507*
line of credit *509*
liquid *508*
liquidity management *508*
merger *505*
mutually exclusive *498*
net present value *502*

salvage value *502*
tender offer (chapter appendix) *518*
Treasury bills *508*
vertical merger *505*
white knight (chapter appendix) *519*
working capital management *508*

REVIEW QUESTIONS

1 Discuss the investment decisions that financial managers must consider in achieving the firm's objectives.

2 How do interest rates affect the capital budgeting analysis?

3 Identify the classifications of capital expenditures.

4 Discuss the major tasks involved

in the capital budgeting process.

5 Discuss the process of capital budgeting analysis when a firm assesses a foreign project.

6 Identify and explain the different types of mergers that can take place between firms.

7 Explain how cross-functional teamwork is involved in busi-

ness investment decisions.

8 Discuss why a firm's management would consider a divestiture.

9 Identify short-term investment decisions undertaken by a firm.

10 Discuss the pros and cons of carrying a small versus a large inventory for a retailer.

DISCUSSION QUESTIONS

1 How could a firm use the Internet to research investment opportunities?

2 Explain why a horizontal merger

could reduce competition in the automobile industry.

3 Assume that you are a financial manager. How would you work

with production and marketing managers in making capital budgeting decisions to introduce a new product? What must the product generate to make it economically feasible?

4 Jason Boone has just opened a go-cart track. He has timed the opening of the go-cart track with the annual county fair. Because his business has grown rapidly, cash flow remains a problem. Analyze Jason's financial problems. Could this be a good business?

5 Why might a horizontal merger achieve economies of scale?

INVESTING IN THE STOCK OF A BUSINESS

Using the annual report of the firm in which you would like to invest, complete the following:

1 What is the firm's capital budget for this year? Is this budget higher or lower than last year's?

2 What types of new projects has the firm invested in recently?

3 Has the firm divested any of its operations? If so, did it divest to focus more on its core business?

4 Has the firm been involved in any recent merger activity? If so, what is their justification for this action?

5 Explain how the business uses technology to promote its capital budgeting activities. For example, does it use the Internet to provide information about recent investment projects? Does it use the Internet to provide information on planned future capital budgeting activities?

6 Go to **http://hoovers.com** and locate the NEWS SEARCH. Type in the name of the firm in the space provided, and review the recent news stories about the firm. Summarize any (at least one) recent news story about the firm that applies to one or more of the key concepts within this chapter.

CASE DECIDING WHETHER TO ACQUIRE A BUSINESS

Benson, Inc., is a publisher of books that it sells to retail bookstores in the United States. Judith Benson, the owner of Benson, Inc., is concerned because its suppliers continue to increase the price of paper and other materials that Benson purchases from them weekly. One supplier to Benson, Inc., is Hill Company, which provides high-quality supplies but has experienced financial problems recently because of inefficient management.

Judith Benson believes that Benson could benefit from merging with Hill Company. She believes that she could acquire (purchase) Hill at a low price because it has performed poorly in the past. She also believes that she could improve Hill's performance by reorganizing its business. In addition, the merger with Hill would give Benson, Inc.,

more control over the cost of its supplies. It could obtain supplies from Hill, which would now be part of Benson, Inc. Therefore, it would not be subjected to increased prices by other suppliers. Meanwhile, Hill would not only produce supplies for Benson, Inc., but would also sell them to other customers, as it did in the past.

QUESTIONS

1 What type of merger is Judith considering?

2 Explain how Judith Benson would attempt to determine whether the cost of buying Hill Company is worthwhile.

3 How could this investment backfire?

VIDEO CASE INVESTMENT DECISIONS AT MAKSOOD'S, INC.

Maksood's, Inc., is a retailer of leisure products such as swimming pools and lawn furniture. It is a member of the Delta Marketing Group, an organization of fifteen retailers in the Midwest that makes purchases as a group so that they can buy in bulk. Maksood's can maintain a lower inventory because it can turn to the other retailers if it suddenly needs more of a particular item (such as a swimming pool, a pool table, or a gas grill). Thus, Maksood's can obtain the item from another retailer in the group that has excess inventory rather than having to wait for more to be delivered from the manufacturer.

Another advantage of participating in the organization is that the group can buy products in bulk from manufacturers at lower prices. This reduces their costs. In addition, Maksood's and the other retailers in the group are allowed to pay their bills between sixty and ninety days after receiving the products from the manufacturer. Maksood's is allowed a relatively long time to pay its bills because it is a member of the organization, and the manufacturer is more willing to give favorable credit terms to a group of fifteen retailers than to just a single retailer.

Maksood's invests its excess cash in marketable securities. If it needs funding, it can sell some of its marketable securities, or it can draw upon a line of credit that it has with a bank.

QUESTIONS

1 How does Maksood's particiation in the organization of retailers help it minimize its inventory? How can this increase its value?

2 How does Maksood's participation in the organization of retailers help it lengthen its credit terms? How can this increase its value?

3 Identify two sources of funds that Maksood's uses when it needs short-term funds. Which source of funds would it most likely use first? Why?

INTERNET APPLICATIONS

http://biz.yahoo.com/reports/stocks.html

Scroll down and type the word "mergers" next to "Search News." Discuss two articles related to recent merger activity. What types of mergers are they (i.e., horizontal, vertical, or conglomerate)? Do you think these mergers will result in future growth or economies of scale? How do you think these mergers will affect the stock prices of the firms involved in the merger? Why?

THE *Coca-Cola* COMPANY ANNUAL REPORT PROJECT

Questions for the current year's annual report are available on the text website at **http://madura_intro_bus.swcollege.com**.

The following questions apply concepts learned in this chapter to The Coca-Cola Company. Go to The Coca-Cola Company website (**http://www.cocacola.com**) and find the index for the 1999 annual report.

QUESTIONS

1 Click on "Investments." What does The Coca-Cola Company do with the cash flows it receives? What is its criterion for investing in a project?

2 Click on "Selected Financial Data." Describe the trend in capital expenditures of The Coca-Cola Company from 1998 to 1999.

3 Study the "Selected Market Results" section. What type of investments do you think The Coca-Cola Company undertakes in emerging markets? Do you think these investments are different from investments in developed markets? Why?

4 Click on "Investments." Study the table in the "Bottling System" section. What does the difference between fair values and carrying values illustrate?

5 Go to **http://hoovers.com** and locate the NEWS SEARCH. Type in The Coca-Cola Company in the space provided, and review the recent news stories about the firm. Summarize any (at least one) recent news story about The Coca-Cola Company that applies one or more of the key concepts within this chapter of the text.

IN-TEXT STUDY GUIDE

Answers are in an appendix at the back of the book.

TRUE OR FALSE

1 Many decisions that result from capital budgeting decisions are irreversible.

2 Capital budgeting analysis for investment projects in foreign countries tends to be more complex than analysis for domestic projects.

3 Capital budgeting involves the comparison of assets and revenue.

4 One of the most popular methods available to assess the feasibility of projects is the net present value (NPV) technique.

5 A payment received by a firm at a future point in time has more value than the exact payment received today.

6 The amount of money that a firm can receive from selling a project is referred to as the net present value.

7 A payment of $1,000 received two years from today has a higher present value than a payment of $1,000 received one year from today.

8 A firm should invest in a project only if its net present value is less than zero.

9 Firms can merge only if they are producing similar products.

10 Firms can be liquid even if they are not holding large amounts of cash and short-term securities.

MULTIPLE CHOICE

11 A firm's _____ is a targeted amount of funds to be used for purchasing assets such as buildings, machinery, and equipment that are needed for long-term projects.
a) master budget
b) capital budget
c) working capital projection
d) escrow account
e) sinking fund

12 The _____ of an investment is computed by subtracting the initial outlay for the investment from the present value of all future cash flows that result from the investment.
a) net present value
d) investment premium
b) capitalization factor
e) gross cash position
c) discount value

13 If the adoption of investment A has no bearing on whether other investments should be adopted, investment A is said to be:
a) redundant.
d) expedient.
b) irrelevant.
e) unrestricted.
c) independent.

14 The discount rate used to compute the present values of future cash flows from an investment should be equal to the:
a) rate of inflation expected to exist over the life of the investment.
b) tax rate applied to the earnings from the investment.
c) rate of return the firm could have earned on an alternative project of similar risk.
d) rate at which the assets purchased to make the investment will depreciate.
e) rate of interest the government pays on Treasury bills of the same duration as the investment project.

15 All of the following are tasks involved in capital budgeting except:
a) estimating cash flows from the investment.
b) determining which projects are feasible.
c) monitoring projects that are implemented.
d) determining the appropriate size of the line of credit.
e) implementing feasible projects.

16 A merger between a tire manufacturer and a firm that produces clocks and watches is:
a) illegal.

b) a horizontal merger.
c) a diagonal merger.
d) a vertical merger.
e) a conglomerate merger.

17 A firm's short-term assets include all of the following except:
a) cash.
d) inventory.
b) accounts receivable.
e) short-term securities.
c) short-term loans.

18 Firms are said to be _____ if they have adequate access to funds so that they can pay their bills as they come due.
a) leveraged
d) bonded
b) fully endowed
e) liquid
c) vested

19 Firms try to maintain a large enough inventory to avoid:
a) stockouts.
b) the need for trade credit.
c) leveraged financing.
d) default on bonds.
e) undiversified portfolios.

20 The goal of _____ management is to be flexible enough to increase sales to credit customers while being strict enough to limit losses due to customers who pay their bills late or not at all.
a) leverage
d) accounts payable
b) accounts receivable
e) invoice
c) trade credit

21 If the per unit cost of producing a good decreases as a greater quantity is produced, the production process exhibits:
a) economies of scale.
b) diminishing returns.
c) higher fixed costs than variable costs.
d) an exception to the law of supply.
e) a very high break-even point.

22 All of the following are motives for capital budgeting expenditures except:
a) expansion of current business.
b) development of new business.
c) acquisition of assets that will reduce expenses.
d) acquisition of working capital.

23 If the discount rate is 12 percent, the present value of a $20,000 payment received three years from today would be found by:
a) dividing $20,000 by 3 and dividing the result by .12.
b) multiplying $20,000 by .12 and dividing the result by 3.
c) dividing $20,000 by $(1 + .12)^3$.
d) multiplying $20,000 by $(1 + .12)^3$.
e) multiplying $20,000 by 3 and dividing the result by $(1 + .12)$.

24 A capital budgeting project is considered to be feasible if:
a) the sum of future cash flows from the project is greater than the initial outlay.
b) the sum of the present values of all future cash flows from the project is greater than the initial outlay.
c) no other projects have a higher initial outlay.
d) the initial outlay is greater than the sum of all discounted future cash flows that result from the project.
e) the discount rate used to compute present values is less than the rate of inflation.

25 When interest rates rise, a firm will:
a) require a higher discount rate when it evaluates capital budgeting proposals.
b) find that more of its capital budgeting proposals are feasible.
c) find that present values of future cash flows are unaffected.
d) want to borrow more funds.
e) find that cash flows in the early years of a project will be discounted more heavily than cash flows that occur during later years.

26 Economies of scale are more likely to be achieved by:
a) vertical mergers.
b) horizontal mergers.
c) conglomerate mergers.
d) divestitures.
e) accounts receivable management.

27 Firms that incur negative earnings are sometimes attractive candidates for mergers because of potential:
a) tax advantages.   d) retained earnings.
b) cash advantages.   e) divestitures.
c) profit exploitation.

28 A purchase of a company (or the subsidiary of the company) by a group of investors with borrowed funds is a(n):
a) common stock purchase.
b) purchase from retained earnings.
c) equity purchase.
d) preferred stock purchase.
e) leveraged buyout.

29 The three general types of mergers are horizontal, conglomerate, and:
a) cooperative.   d) bureaucratic.
b) vertical.   e) parallel.
c) divestiture.

30 _____ are short-term debt securities offered by the U.S. Treasury that provide firms with easy access to funds since they can be sold to other investors.
a) Federal warrants
b) Treasury trust certificates
c) Treasury stock
d) Treasury bills
e) Federal Reserve notes

31 Which of the flowing is the best example of a vertical merger?
a) A chain of fast-food restaurants merges with a firm that produces electronic components for computers.
b) A small book publisher that specializes in travel and history books merges with another larger book publisher that specializes in biographies and popular fiction.
c) A golf club manufacturer merges with a firm that helps people prepare their income taxes.
d) A firm that publishes a newspaper in the St. Louis area merges with a firm that publishes a newspaper in the Chicago area.
e) A firm that sells flour, sugar, and spices merges with a firm that bakes pies and cakes.

32 When a firm sells off one of its existing businesses, the process is known as a:
a) reverse merger.
b) leveraged buyout.
c) corporate downsizing.
d) conglomeration strategy.
e) divestiture.

33 The result of a firm investing in another company by purchasing all the stock of that company is a(n):
a) divestiture.   d) line of credit.
b) net present value.   e) merger.
c) economies of scale.

34 The management of a firm's short-term assets and liabilities is:
a) accounts receivable management.
b) working capital management.
c) sales management.
d) plant and equipment management.
e) fixed asset management.

35 An agreement that allows a firm access to borrowed funds upon demand over some specified period of time is a:
a) bond indenture.   d) line of credit.
b) stock flotation.   e) note payable.
c) note receivable.

APPENDIX

Merger Analysis

When a firm plans to engage in a merger, it must conduct the following tasks:

▶ Identify potential merger prospects.
▶ Evaluate potential merger prospects.
▶ Make the merger decision.

Identify Potential Merger Prospects

Firms attempt to identify potential merger prospects that may help them achieve their strategic plan. If the firm plans for growth in its current line of products, it will consider purchasing (or "acquiring") companies in the same business. If it needs to restructure its production process, it may attempt to acquire a supplier. If it desires a more diversified product line, it may attempt to acquire companies in unrelated businesses. The firm's long-run objectives influence the selection of merger prospects that are worthy of evaluation.

The size of firms is also a relevant criterion, since some firms may be too small to achieve the desired objectives while others may be too large to acquire. The location is another possible criterion, since a firm's product demand and production costs are dependent on its location.

Evaluate Potential Merger Prospects

Once merger prospects have been identified, they must be analyzed thoroughly, using publicly available financial statements. The financial analysis may detect problems that will eliminate some prospects from further consideration. Prospects with deficiencies that can be corrected should still be considered, however. Along with the firm's financial condition, additional characteristics of each prospect must be assessed, including its reputation and labor-management relations. From this assessment, potential problems that may not be disclosed on financial statements can be detected.

The firm planning the acquisition needs to evaluate the prospect's specific characteristics, such as its facilities, its dependency on suppliers, and pending lawsuits. Unfortunately, a full evaluation of such specific characteristics may not be possible unless the prospect provides the information. The firm planning the acquisition may contact the prospect to request more detailed information. The prospect may comply if it is willing to consider the possibility of a merger.

Make the Merger Decision

Once the firm has identified a specific prospect it wishes to acquire, it can assess the feasibility of acquiring that prospect by using capital budgeting analysis. Thus, the acquisition prospect can be evaluated just like any other project. The cost of this project is the outlay necessary to purchase the firm. The benefits are the extra cash flows that will be generated over time as a result of the acquisition. If the present value of the future cash flows to be received by the acquiring firm exceeds the initial outlay, the acquisition is feasible.

Merger Procedures

If an attempt is made to acquire a prospect, that prospect becomes the "target." It is set apart from all the other prospects that were considered. To enact the acquisition, firms will normally hire an investment bank (such as Morgan Stanley Dean Witter, or Salomon Smith Barney, which is part of Citigroup) for guidance. Some firms that continuously acquire or sell businesses may employ their own investment banking department to handle many of the necessary tasks. Most tasks can be classified into one of the following:

- ▶ Financing the merger
- ▶ Tender offer
- ▶ Integrating the businesses
- ▶ Postmerger evaluation

Financing the Merger

A merger normally requires a substantial amount of long-term funds, as one firm may purchase the existing stock of another firm. One common method for a firm to finance a merger is by issuing more of its own stock to the public. As new stock is sold to the public, the proceeds are used to purchase the target's stock. Alternatively, the acquiring firm may trade its new stock to the shareholders of the target firm in exchange for their stock. Instead of issuing new stock, the acquiring firm may also borrow the necessary funds to purchase the target's stock from its shareholders.

Tender Offer

The acquiring firm first contacts the management of the target firm to negotiate a merger. The acquiring firm normally pays a premium on the target firm's stock to make the deal worthwhile to the target firm's stockholders.

tender offer a direct bid by the acquiring firm for the shares of the target firm

When two firms cannot come to terms, the acquiring firm may attempt a **tender offer.** This is a direct bid by the acquiring firm for the shares of the target firm. It does not require prior approval of the target firm's management. Thus, a tender offer could accomplish a merger even if the management of the target firm disapproves.

The acquiring firm must decide the price at which it is willing to purchase the target firm's shares and then officially extend this tender offer to the shareholders. The tender offer normally represents a premium of 20 percent or more above the prevailing market price, which may be necessary to encourage the shareholders of the target firm to sell their shares. The acquiring firm can achieve control of the target firm only if enough of the target firm's shareholders are willing to sell.

Integrating the Businesses

If a merger is achieved, various departments within the two companies may need to be restructured. The key to successfully integrating the management of two companies is to clearly communicate the strategic plan of the firm. In addition, the organizational structure should be communicated to clarify the roles of each department and position. This includes identifying to whom each position will report and who is accountable for various tasks. If the roles are not clearly defined up front, the newly integrated management will not function properly.

Tensions are especially high in the beginning stages of a newly formed merger, since the employees of the acquired firm are not fully aware of the acquiring firm's plans. Once the merger has occurred, the personnel involved in the initial evaluation of the target firm should guide the integration of the two firms. For example, if the primary reason for a horizontal merger was to reduce the duplication of some managerial functions (to increase production efficiency), management of the newly formed firm should make sure that these reasons for initiating the merger are realized.

A newly formed merger typically requires a period in which the production, financing, inventory management, capital structure, and dividend policies must be reevaluated. Policies are commonly revised to conform to the newly formed firm's characteristics. For example, to deal with the larger volume of sales, inventory of the combined firm may need to be larger than for either original business (although perhaps not as large as the sum of both businesses).

Although identifying ways by which a merger could be beneficial is often easy, it may not be as easy to achieve those benefits without creating any new problems. As a final point, the process of creating the merger can also be much more expensive than originally anticipated and can often place a financial strain on the acquiring company (especially when the target fights the takeover effort). Therefore, firms that are considering acquisitions should attempt to anticipate all types of expenses that may be incurred as a result of the acquisitions.

Postmerger Evaluation

After the merger, the firm should periodically assess the merger's costs and benefits. Were the benefits as high as expected? Did the merger involve unanticipated costs? Was the analysis of the target firm too optimistic? Once the merger takes place, it cannot be easily reversed. Thus, any errors detected from the analysis that led to the merger cannot be washed away. However, lessons can be learned from any errors so that future merger prospects will be more accurately evaluated.

Defense against Takeover Attempts

In some cases, managers of a target firm may not approve of the takeover attempt by the acquiring firm. They may believe that the price offered for their firm is below what it is worth or that their firm has higher potential if it is not acquired. They may view the potential acquiring firm as a shark approaching for the kill (takeover). Under such conditions where the takeover attempt is hostile, management of the target firm can choose from a variety of "shark repellents" to defend itself.

A common defensive tactic against a takeover attempt is an attempt to convince shareholders to retain their shares. Another tactic to avoid a merger is a private placement of stock. By selling shares directly (privately) to specific institutions, the target firm can reduce the acquiring firm's chances of obtaining enough shares to gain controlling interest. The more shares outstanding, the larger the amount of shares that must be purchased by the acquiring firm to gain controlling interest.

A third defensive tactic is for the target firm to find a more suitable company (called a **white knight**) that is willing to acquire the firm and rescue it from the hostile takeover efforts of some other firm. The white knight rescues the target firm by acquiring the target firm itself. Although the target firm no longer retains its independence, it may prefer being acquired by the white knight firm.

white knight a more suitable company that is willing to acquire a firm and rescue it from the hostile takeover efforts of some other firm

Summary of Part VI

The performance of a firm can be assessed by conducting a financial analysis, as discussed in Chapter 16. A financial analysis is also used to identify the reasons for poor performance, such as excessive (or deficient) investment in long-term or short-term assets, or an excessive amount of debt used to finance its investment.

The key financial management decisions made by a firm can be classified as either financing (explained in Chapter 17) or investing funds in business projects (Chapter 18). Firms use either debt financing or equity financing to obtain funds. The common methods of debt financing are obtaining bank loans, issuing bonds, and issuing commercial paper. The common methods of equity financing are retaining earnings or issuing stock. The ideal type of financing is dependent on the firm's characteristics. If the firm does not have a large amount of debt, it may consider debt financing to capitalize on the tax advantage of using debt. If the firm already has a large amount of debt financing, however, it may use equity financing instead.

When firms consider using funds to invest in business projects, they must determine whether the return on the investment is sufficient to make the investment feasible. Capital budgeting analysis is used to determine whether the project is feasible. This analysis determines whether the present value of cash flows exceeds the initial outlay of the project.

In addition to business projects, firms also invest in short-term assets such as accounts receivable and inventory. An investment in accounts receivable is necessary to attract some customers who prefer to purchase products on credit. An investment in inventory is necessary to avoid stockouts. Yet, excessive investment in accounts receivable or in inventory is an inefficient use of funds because the funds could have been used for other purposes.

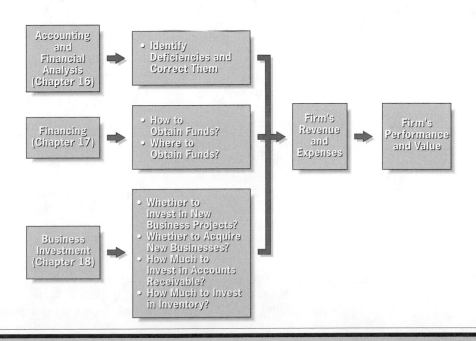

PART VI

Developing the Financial Plan for Campus.com

Monitoring Performance (related to Chapter 16)

In your business plan for Campus.com, explain how the firm will monitor its performance over time. That is, describe the specific financial ratios that it can monitor to measure its performance and its efficiency.

Financing Business Expansion (related to Chapter 17)

In your business plan for Campus.com, identify the alternative choices you have to obtain funds to support additional expansion for Campus.com. Which alternative is the best choice for you? Does the financing method that you selected have any disadvantages?

Business Investment (related to Chapter 18)

In your business plan for Campus.com, briefly explain how Campus.com will determine whether future expansion is feasible. That is, describe how it will decide whether to pursue expansion into a specific project.

Communication and Teamwork

You (or your team) may be asked by your instructor to hand in and/or present the part of your business plan that is related to this part of the text.

PART VI

Applications for Dell Computer

Refer to Dell Computer's Formula for Success where necessary.

1 Financial reporting and financial statement analysis at Dell
   a. Given Dell Computer's focus on the Internet and its customers, what do you think is the most effective way for Dell to provide information to its customers and current and potential investors? Why?
   b. What do you think Dell's primary sales consist of? What do you think its major assets are?
   c. How could Dell be affected by increasing its degree of financial leverage?

2 Dell's financing activities
   a. Assume that Dell Computer needs a loan from a financial institution. Under what circumstances would it prefer a floating-rate loan to a fixed-rate loan?
   b. Based on Dell's recent favorable earnings performance, do you think it needs to issue stock frequently to obtain equity financing? Why or why not?
   c. How could Dell use the Internet to facilitate its financing decisions?

3 Dell's investment activities
   a. Given Dell Computer's high current growth, which classification of capital expenditures listed in your text do you think is most appropriate for Dell?

b. Propose a new project Dell could implement. Describe how this project would benefit Dell and how it would be financed. Be sure to consider Dell's highly competitive industry.

c. How could Dell improve its accounts receivable management? How would your answer differ for a firm operating in retail sales? Take into account that Dell makes a major proportion of its sales over the Internet.

PART VI

The Stock Market Game

Go to **http://www.fantasystockmarket.com**. Enter your name (e-mail address) and password as requested and check your portfolio balance, which is updated continuously by the Fantasy website.

Check Your Stock Portfolio Performance

1 What is the value of your stock portfolio today?

2 What is your return on your investment? (This return is shown on your balance.)

3 How did your return compare to those of other students? (This comparison tells you whether your stock portfolio's performance is relatively high or low.)

Keep in mind that you can change your portfolio at any time during the school term.

Explaining Your Stock Performance

Stock prices are frequently influenced by changes in a firm's financial strategies, including new financing policies and new investment strategies (such as acquisitions). A stock's price may increase if investors expect the new financial strategies to improve the performance of the firm. A stock's price can also decrease if the financial strategies are expected to reduce the firm's performance. Review the latest news about some of your stocks on the Fantasy website by clicking on News and typing the ticker symbol of your stock.

1 Identify one of your stocks whose price was affected (since you purchased it) by changes in the firm's financial strategies (the main topic in this part of the text).

2 Identify the specific type of financial policies that caused the stock price to change.

3 Did the stock price increase or decrease in response to the announcement of new financial policies?

PART VI

Running Your Own Business

1 Forecast the revenue of your business in the first year. (Multiply the amount you expect to sell over the year times the price charged.)

2 Forecast the expenses of your business in the first year. Include the cost of materials and supplies, administrative (management) expenses, marketing expenses, rent expenses, and interest expenses.

3 Forecast the earnings (before taxes) of your business. (This is the difference between the forecasted revenue and the forecasted expenses.)

4 Assuming a tax rate of 20 percent, forecast your taxes. (You can apply a different tax rate if you know what your tax rate would be.)

5 Forecast your earnings after taxes. (This is the difference between your earnings before taxes and the amount of taxes you expect to pay.)

6 State how much of your own money you will invest as a form of equity investment in the business.

7 Indicate whether you will have any co-owners in this business and how much money they will have to invest.

8 State how much money you will need to start your business. (To determine this amount, compare expected expenses with expected revenue. Having a cushion is helpful in case the expenses turn out to be higher than expected or revenue turns out to be less than expected.)

9 State how much money you will need to borrow. (You can estimate this amount by comparing the amount of money you will need to start your business with the amount of equity that will be invested in your business.)

10 Indicate where you plan to obtain borrowed funds. For example, do you plan to obtain a loan from a regular commercial bank or from an Internet bank?

11 State the interest rate that you expect to pay on the borrowed funds.

12 Describe how long you expect to need the borrowed funds before you can pay back the loan.

13 Forecast your return on equity over the first year based on your forecast of earnings after taxes and the amount of equity invested in your business.

14 Describe any big purchases (such as a computer or a machine) that you may need to make for your business someday. What factors would be a part of a cost-benefit analysis of this purchase?

15 Explain how much inventory you would have to maintain to avoid shortages.

16 Would your business generate accounts receivable? If so, how would you manage this asset?

Special Topics

P art VII further explores topics that were introduced in previous chapters and provides a synthesis of the text. Chapter 19 explains how firms use computer information systems to facilitate their operations. Chapter 20 describes the types of risk to which firms are exposed and the methods of managing that exposure. Chapter 21 provides a synthesis of all the key business functions that have been emphasized throughout the text. These functions can be properly conducted only by recognizing how they interact with one another.

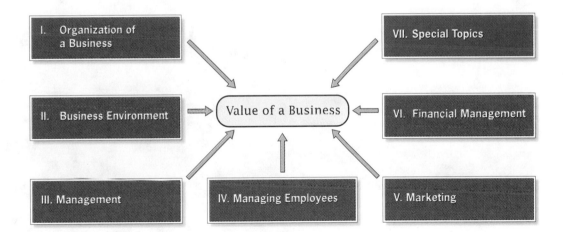

I. Organization of a Business

II. Business Environment

III. Management

IV. Managing Employees

V. Marketing

VI. Financial Management

VII. Special Topics

Value of a Business

The Learning Goals of this chapter are to:

1 Describe the key components of a computer and explain their purpose.

2 Discuss the different ways computers and related technologies contribute to today's businesses.

3 Describe some of the key challenges of managing today's information technologies.

4 Identify emerging technologies and their implications.

IBM

Information Systems and Technology

Management information systems (MIS) are the business function that oversees the adoption, use, and management of information technologies, which include both computers and telecommunications. Over the past fifty years, it has become clear that these technologies can affect the value of a firm in many ways. Decision support systems and end user applications, which enhance managerial decision making, have opened the door to both improved revenue and reduced costs. Traditional data processing systems have streamlined existing business processes, making firms more efficient. Internal information systems, which permit many users to access the same information simultaneously, have improved efficiency and have led to business opportunities that were previously impossible. Interorganizational systems, which allow information to be shared across organizational boundaries, have improved the efficiency of transactions and have promoted better relationships between suppliers and customers. They have also led to the development of entirely new distribution channels. These contributions are only a few of the ways in which information technologies can potentially increase the value of the firm.

Consider the case of United Parcel Service (UPS), which delivers packages to numerous residences and firms around the world. How can UPS use management information systems to keep track of these packages? How can it use management information systems to deliver packages more quickly? This chapter discusses concepts about management information systems that can be used to address these questions.

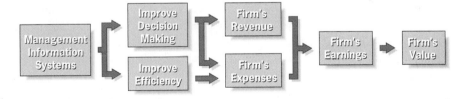

What Is a Computer?

1 Describe the key components of a computer and explain their purpose.

An electronic computer is a device capable of processing and storing vast quantities of information. Such computers, which did not even exist fifty years ago, come in many forms. The early tube-based computers of the 1950s could fill a small warehouse and generated heat equivalent to several hundred hair dryers running full blast. Today's computers more closely resemble the microcomputer in Exhibit 19.1, comfortably fitting on a desktop and using less power than a light bulb. Today's mainframes, large computers used primarily to service entire organizations, have been so miniaturized that their key circuitry often fits into a casing the size of a pizza box. These physical

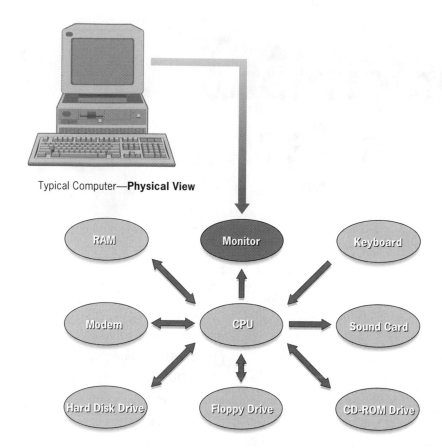

Typical Computer—**Physical View**

Typical Computer—**Logical View**

changes in computers have been accompanied by even more dramatic changes in performance, as illustrated in Exhibit 19.2.

Computer Hardware

hardware the physical components of a computer

system architecture the basic logical organization of a computer

The physical components of a computer are collectively called **hardware.** Although computer hardware is constantly changing, the basic logical organization of computers, often referred to as **system architecture,** has been relatively stable since the mid-1950s. Specifically, nearly all computers are built around four key components:

1 *Central processing unit (CPU)* The heart of the computer, the CPU (commonly referred to as the processor or microprocessor), performs all calculations and moves information between the computer's other components. More than any other single component, the CPU (such as Intel's Pentium processor or Advanced Micro Devices' [AMD] Athlon processor) determines the basic behavior and capabilities of a particular computer. Generally, the faster the processor (as measured in millions of cycles per second, or **megahertz [MHz];** or billions of cycles per second, or **gigahertz [GHz]**), the faster the computer.

megahertz (MHz) one million cycles per second

gigahertz (GHz) one billion cycles per second

The physical changes in computer hardware over the past fifty years have been accompanied by even more dramatic changes in actual performance.

For many key computer components, price-performance ratios have been improving by a factor of ten every five years.

To put such improvements into perspective, had automobiles experienced the same rate of price-performance improvement, the luxury car that cost $10,000 in the mid-1960s would now sell for under a nickel (including a liberal allowance for inflation).

2 *Primary storage* For a computer to function, its processor must have scratch space in which to temporarily store information. In today's computers, such storage typically takes the form of **random access memory (RAM)** chips. RAM is the memory where programs and data in current use are kept and accessed by the CPU. The amount of RAM installed on a particular system is measured in millions of characters (or **megabytes**). Many applications will not run unless a certain amount of RAM is available, and most applications run faster when more RAM is installed.

3 *Secondary storage* Because RAM stores data only as long as the computer is running, computers also have secondary storage available. Today, most secondary storage is in the form of sealed magnetic disks, commonly referred to as a **hard drive.** Hard drives typically contain several billion bytes (**gigabytes**) of storage space.

There are also many forms of removable secondary storage that can be transported from machine to machine. These devices have grown in popularity due to their declining cost, improved performance, and versatility. Some of the more popular secondary storage devices include:

▶ Large capacity disk drives: Different manufacturers offer disk drives with capacity ranging from 100 MB to 1.0 GB per disk. Iomega's ZIP drive is a popular large capacity disk drive with a capacity of 100MB.

▶ CD-Recordable (CD-R): These drives allow users to write data onto a CD once and read many times. Most CDs have a capacity of 650 MB and are an inexpensive method to backup files.

▶ CD-Rewriteable (CD-RW): These drives are similar to CD-Rs except data can be written onto a CD more than once. They can also be used to create CDs that play in audio CD players.

▶ Digital Video Disk (DVD): A bigger and better version of the CD-ROM. The increased capacity allows simultaneous audio and video storage. DVDs are often associated with multimedia presentations.

4 *Peripherals* The devices attached to the CPU that are neither primary nor secondary storage are peripherals. Thousands of different types of general-purpose and special-purpose peripherals exist. Those most often found on desktop computers include a keyboard, mouse, monitor, printer, modem, and sound card. On business machines, peripherals often include scanners and network connectors.

Computer Software

Unlike most pieces of complex machinery, which are designed to accomplish a specific task, computers have no predefined purpose, making them general-purpose machines. The CPU can perform many tasks but needs specific direction. To provide that direction, a collection of step-by-step instructions to the processor, referred to as a **computer program,** is loaded into primary storage (RAM), then run by the CPU. By changing the program that is loaded into RAM, the user can dramatically change how the computer behaves.

Just as the actual machinery of the computer is referred to as hardware, the programs that determine the specific tasks a computer will perform at any given time are called **software.** Software can be divided into a few different categories:

▶ *System software* Programs that manage the other software programs in a system. The system software (or operating system) handles input and output to peripherals, manages the internal memory, and informs the user of the status of application tasks. Windows Millennium and 2000, Linux, and O/S 2 are examples of system software.

▶ *Application software* Programs that perform specific functions for the user. One program is intended to create documents (a word processor), while another program is intended to perform financial analysis (a spreadsheet), and yet another program is intended to generate reports from a firm's client list (a database). Computer programmers can develop applications from scratch. They can also be purchased off the

---

random access memory (RAM) space in which information is temporarily stored in a computer

megabyte millions of characters

hard drive sealed magnetic disks that provide secondary storage in a computer

gigabytes billions of bytes

computer program a collection of step-by-step instructions to the processor

software programs that determine the specific tasks a computer will perform at any given time

shelf and are called software packages. Such packages are typically sold on removable secondary storage media, such as floppy disks or CD-ROMs.

▶ *Middleware* Programs that allow other application programs to cooperate with each other. Frequently, middleware is designed to give applications access to a variety of databases. It is particularly useful in organizations that operate more than one system or network.

▶ *Utility software* Programs that perform specific functions generally for the system. Antivirus and hard drive recovery programs are examples of utility software.

BUSINESS ONLINE

Keeping Up with New Products Online

http://www.techweb.com

SEVERAL WEBSITES, SUCH AS TECHWEB, ALLOW USERS TO EASILY ACCESS RECENT news stories about the introduction of new computer products. Through these websites, a company can keep up with the increasing variety of computer products and determine which new products will be useful for its particular needs.

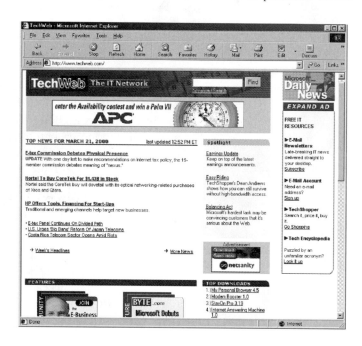

Uses of Computers

2 Discuss the different ways computers and related technologies contribute to today's businesses.

The potential uses for computers are limited only by the imagination of programmers and users. In today's businesses, however, three general types of use have become particularly common:

▶ Computational models
▶ Data processing systems
▶ Interorganizational systems

Each of these is considered in turn.

Computational Models

Ever since their invention, computers have held a tremendous advantage over humans in their ability to perform computations. Today's desktop computers, for example, can perform several million multiplications in a second. A human would take roughly twelve years to perform the same number of computations, assuming the individual was willing to work fifty-five hours a week without vacations and could multiply two fourteen-digit numbers together in an average time of about a minute. Simply stated, when problems require many computations, the use of computers is necessary.

The computational ability of computers is indispensable for creating models that help firms better understand and control business situations. Such computer models are fundamentally different from physical models in that they describe a problem in purely numeric terms. For example, suppose that General Motors wants to predict the wind resistance of a new model of automobile. To use a physical model, GM would have to create a scale model of the car, place it in a wind tunnel, measure the forces at different wind velocities, and then scale the results up to the car's actual size. The computer model of the same problem would use airflow equations and three-dimensional vector images to simulate the wind blowing over the car body. The computer model offers many advantages: there is no need to construct complex equipment (such as the wind tunnel), the same computer can be used to model many different situations, and the computer can often be used to model situations that are impossible to simulate physically.

statistical analysis a computer model that applies statistical principles to understanding relationships between data and certain outcomes

optimization models computer models that are used to represent situations that have many possible combinations of inputs and outputs

"what-if" analysis a computer model that generates different potential business scenarios to answer questions

decision support systems (DSS) computer models that are used to improve managerial decision making

Computer models may take many forms. **Statistical analysis** of data, which is common in finance and operations management, applies statistical principles to understanding relationships between data and certain outcomes. Such analysis often entails billions of computations. **Optimization models,** such as linear programming, are used to represent situations that have many possible combinations of inputs and outputs. Such models are frequently used to help businesses choose their mix of products or design their distribution systems. **"What-if" analysis** involves generating different potential business scenarios to answer questions such as "What if our sales were 10 percent higher?" or "What if interest rates rise by two points?" Managers typically use "what-if" analysis to determine the sensitivity of a business situation to changes in many factors, such as inflation, economic growth, market share, and costs. Computers are necessary for such analysis, as hundreds of scenarios are often considered.

Computer models that are used to improve managerial decision making are called **decision support systems (DSS).** DSS applications come in two forms. Some are complete applications designed to help managers make specific decisions. For example, plant location software can help managers decide where to establish a new facility. DSS applications are also available in tool form, such as the spreadsheet software that managers use to make financial projections. Rather than focusing on a specific problem, such tools are designed to help managers create their own models in a given situation.

Data Processing Systems

As early as the late 1950s, it became clear that computer power could be used for purposes other than fast arithmetic. As more sophisticated forms of secondary storage were developed, such as magnetic tape and hard disks, computers began to replace traditional paper-based record-keeping systems. Among the advantages of these computer-based systems are the following:

▶ *Accuracy* Paper-based systems are subject to arithmetic and transcription errors. Computer-based systems can be designed to greatly reduce these problems.

▶ *Speed* Using computer-based systems, the time required to sort, look up, and format information is a fraction of that required in paper-based systems. Further, the speed of routine tasks, such as closing a company's books at year-end, is similarly improved.

▶ *Space* The physical space required for record keeping can often be significantly reduced by using a computer-based system. For example, a manager at the United Services Automobile Association (USAA) predicted that the online correspondence system the USAA was implementing would ultimately save seventeen acres of storage compared with the company's existing paper-based system.

▶ *Flexibility* Storing information on computers makes it possible to rapidly create new summaries of information that would have taken days or months to prepare manually. Today's information systems often include report-writing tools that enable managers to create their own customized output without the need for programmers.

One area in which data processing systems did not generally produce the initially expected benefits was in labor costs. Some savings were often realized from eliminating the clerical personnel at the heart of the manual system. Such savings, however, were nearly always more than offset by the need to add higher-priced computer programmers and operators. Thus, while early efforts to automate often led to huge increases in capacity and accuracy, they rarely led to reduction in actual labor costs.

Interorganizational Systems

interorganizational systems (IOS) employ computers and telecommunications technology to move information across the boundaries of a firm

remote job entry systems interorganizational systems that allow the user to interact directly with a company's internal systems

electronic data interchange (EDI) an interorganizational system that allows the computers of two or more companies to communicate directly with each other

commercial information service an inter-organizational system that provides a packaged assortment of information services to customers, referred to as subscribers

Interorganizational systems (IOS) employ computers and telecommunications technology to move information across the boundaries of a firm. Such IOS represent the logical extension of a company's internal information systems to its customers, its suppliers, and other interested parties.

IOS come in many forms. Systems such as automatic teller machines (ATMs) and airline reservation systems that allow the user to interact directly with a company's internal systems are referred to as **remote job entry systems.** These systems not only make transactions easier for the customer but also save the company clerical costs.

Another form of IOS, **electronic data interchange (EDI),** allows the computers of two or more companies to communicate directly with each other, without human intervention. EDI systems can produce significant savings in ordering costs, while improving order processing time and accuracy. Even managers skeptical of the benefits of EDI systems may find they have no choice but to install them because a growing number of companies, such as Wal-Mart, refuse to do business with vendors who will not hook up electronically.

A third type of IOS is a **commercial information service,** which provides a packaged assortment of information services to customers, referred to as subscribers. These services, two of the better known of which are CompuServe and America Online, bundle together many different IOS applications, such as Sabre (airline reservations), technical support forums for hardware and software vendors, and electronic shopping malls. They also provide numerous additional services, such as electronic mail, news, and games, to attract subscribers. Most recently, they have provided subscribers with direct connections to the Internet, the global network connecting academic, government, and business institutions. Users subscribe to these services by paying a small monthly fee, usually starting at around $20 per month. They may pay extra for using special services, such as research databases that contain detailed information on public and private companies.

Information systems and technology are necessary to organize functions, including the sequence and timing of plane departures.

Managing Today's Information Technologies

3 Describe some of the key challenges of managing today's information technologies.

The growing importance of information technology to today's businesses means that every manager, not just MIS managers, must become familiar with issues relating to the management of information technology. The following five areas are particularly important:

▶ Managing the firm's information system architecture
▶ Acquiring software
▶ Managing the development of information systems
▶ Managing the implementation of information systems
▶ Managing the security of information systems

Managing the Firm's Information System Architecture

The concept of the system architecture of an individual computer can be generalized to the organization as a whole. With today's technologies, many different system architectures are possible. That choice of architecture can, in turn, play a critical role in determining the capabilities of the firm. For example, the architecture can determine the ability of employees to share information and work together, affect how quickly a company can respond to customer requests, and even alter the ways in which a company offers its goods and services. Several common architectures are considered next.

stand-alone system system architecture consisting of one or more computers that function independently

Stand-Alone System The **stand-alone system** architecture, illustrated in Exhibit 19.3, consists of one or more computers that function independently. Each system has its own software and its own data and typically services the needs of a single user. Stand-alone architecture, sometimes referred to as a "sneaker network" because users must carry disks between computers to transfer data, is most common in small businesses. Its primary advantages are its low cost and technological simplicity. Its weaknesses are the difficulty of moving information between users and the inability to share resources such as printers. For this reason, stand-alone architectures are generally impractical for firms that use shared information extensively.

mainframe (multiuser) system system architecture that uses a single central computer that performs data processing for all users in the organization

Mainframe (Multiuser) System The **mainframe (multiuser) system** architecture, illustrated in Exhibit 19.4, uses a single central computer, usually referred to as a

Exhibit 19.3

Stand-Alone System
Architecture

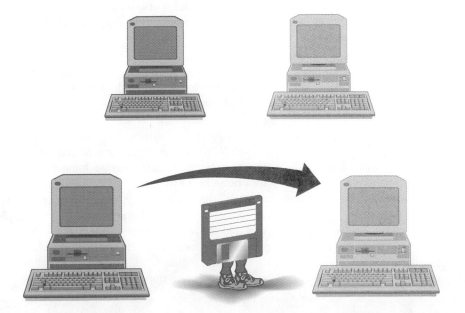

Exhibit 19.4

Mainframe (Multiuser) System
Architecture

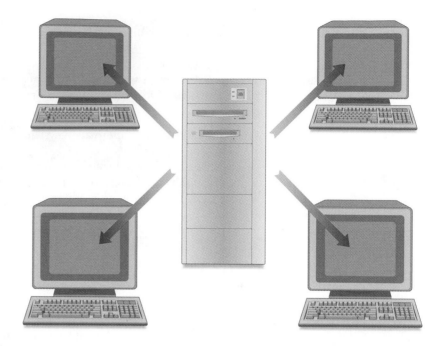

terminals devices that combine
the functions of a monitor and a
keyboard

network system system
architecture that connects
individual microcomputers
together in ways that allow them
to share information

file servers in a network
system, one or more machines
that store and provide access to
centralized data

workstations in a network
system, individual computers that
access the software and data on
the file server

local area network (LAN) a
system in which individual
workstations are directly
connected by network cabling to
the file server

wide area network (WAN) a
system in which
telecommunications technologies
are employed to connect pieces
of the network

modems devices that permit the
digital signals inside computers
to be transmitted over lines
designed primarily for voice
communication

mainframe, that performs data processing for all users in the organization. Users typically interact with the mainframe through **terminals,** devices that combine the functions of a monitor and a keyboard. Under the mainframe architecture, all data storage and computer hardware are centralized, usually under the control of an MIS department within the organization. Although other computers may be present in the organization, such as those used by engineering groups for scientific purposes, such systems are usually kept entirely separate from the company's business systems.

The primary advantage of the multiuser system, which was most popular from the late 1960s to the early 1980s, is that all programs and data are centrally located. The ability to share data led to the development of applications such as online reservation systems. It also made possible sophisticated production management systems capable of sharing data across the entire scope of a business, from raw materials to sales of finished products. The main drawback of the multiuser system is that it tends to prevent users from taking advantage of the sophisticated applications and tools that are now available for PCs but not mainframe computers.

Network System In the past ten years, new system architectures have emerged that provide the benefits of both stand-alone and multiuser architectures. **Network system** architecture connects individual computers together in ways that allow them to share information.

The typical network architecture, illustrated in Exhibit 19.5, consists of one or more machines, known as **file servers,** that store and provide access to centralized data. Connected to these file servers are many individual computers, referred to as **workstations.** Workstations can run their own software but can also access the software and data on the file server, duplicating the benefits of the multiuser system.

Networks are classified according to how the individual workstations are connected. When all are directly connected by network cabling to the file server, as is often the case in a building or headquarters complex, the architecture is called a **local area network (LAN).** When telecommunications technologies are employed to connect pieces of the network, the architecture is called a **wide area network (WAN).** Such telecommunications technologies can be as simple as the use of conventional phone lines and **modems,** devices that permit the digital signals inside computers to be transmitted over lines designed primarily for voice communication. They can also be far more exotic, including the use of leased phone lines, satellites, microwave linkages, and cellular connections.

Exhibit 19.5

Network System Architecture

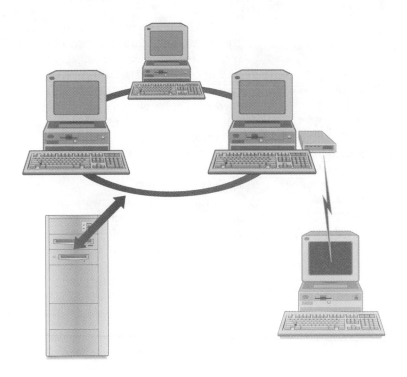

Time Sharing on
Mainframes

**http://www.internet-timeshare
.com**

A RECENT INNOVATION IN COMPUTER TECHNOLOGY MANAGEMENT IS TIME sharing. Internet TimeShare Resources rents IBM mainframe time, allowing users to access IBM mainframe operating systems via the Internet. Alternatives such as this maximize the advantages of mainframe computers (central location) and minimize their disadvantages (lack of PC software).

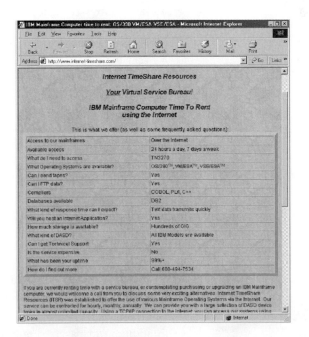

network operating system
software that handles the communications between machines in a network

workgroup software network software that provides a broad array of user-friendly features, such as electronic mail, document management systems, and work-sharing systems

To construct a network, both hardware and software must be acquired. Network hardware costs include the costs of running network cables throughout an office complex, purchasing network adapters for each workstation, and purchasing hubs necessary to connect clusters of workstations. In addition, networks require their own specialized software. At a minimum, that software will include a **network operating system,** such as Novell's Netware or Microsoft's Windows NT, which handles the communications between machines. Recently, many companies have also installed **workgroup software,** such as Lotus Notes, which provides a broad array of user-friendly features, such as electronic mail, document management systems, and work-sharing systems. Together, the hardware and software costs can easily amount to several thousand dollars per workstation.

In many respects, network architectures combine the benefits of the stand-alone and mainframe architectures. The connectivity aspect of a network provides easy access to and sharing of information. Since users access the network with PC-based workstations, the full range of PC software can be run. The main drawbacks of networks over previous architectures are the added costs. In addition, administering and maintaining a network can be far more complex than keeping stand-alone PCs up and running. Thus, the cost of hiring specially trained network engineers and administrators must be considered when establishing a network.

Acquiring Software

Without the proper software, computers are little more than noisy paperweights. The acquisition of software is therefore a critical issue for managers seeking to use information technology effectively. The issue can be further broken down into two parts: how to acquire packaged software and how to acquire customized software, which is written specifically to meet the needs of the organization.

Packaged Software Much, if not all, of the software used in any organization will be packaged software. Such software can be purchased off the shelf and used with no actual programming. The decision as to which software to purchase should not be made lightly. Issues that a manager should consider include the following:

1 *Compatibility* Few firms have the luxury of establishing their information systems from scratch. How the new software will match existing hardware and software must be addressed. Questions the manager should ask include:
  ▶ Will the company's existing hardware handle the new software?
  ▶ Can the new software convert the information created by the old software?
  ▶ Can the new software exchange information with other applications that the firm uses?

2 *Upgradeability* Because computer hardware advances so quickly, businesses should anticipate that they will need to upgrade their software regularly, usually every two to three years. The package's upgrade policy and history are therefore important over the long run. Questions the manager should ask include:
  ▶ How often are upgrades introduced?
  ▶ What do upgrades typically cost?

3 *Support* It is not unusual for the cost of a software package to be far less than the costs of learning to use it. These costs include required training, productivity declines during the period when employees are learning the application, and the use of technical support. Such costs must be factored into the software acquisition decision. Questions the manager should ask include:
  ▶ How hard will it be to learn the new software?
  ▶ What training resources are available?
  ▶ What are the vendor's technical support policies?

In addition, managers should consider the long-term implications of every software decision. Compatibility issues and the need to retrain users mean that all software acquisition decisions ultimately interrelate. Thus, a company should plan a full reevaluation of its entire software policy every four to five years. At such times, software decisions with long-term implications, such as changing PC and network operating systems, should be made and a plan for future acquisitions established.

Customized Software Although packaged software can provide an inexpensive solution for many of a firm's needs, on occasion a firm needs software to accomplish a task that is not directly supported by an existing package. In such a situation, the firm frequently faces three alternatives:

▶ *Modify the company's business processes to fit an existing software package* Although many managers may balk at having to change the way they do business to accommodate the needs of a $100 software tool, sometimes such an approach can make sense. Packaged software, such as accounting applications and project management tools, is usually designed around sound business practices. As a result, adopting a software package can sometimes provide the means for improving the firm's administrative processes.

▶ *Customize an existing application* Particularly in the accounting area, custom development often starts with a basic package that is modified to meet the firm's specific needs. Much less programming must be done than when an entire system is written from scratch. A problem, however, is that modifications to the basic package may make it difficult and expensive to upgrade when new versions of the basic package are introduced. If the required modifications are extensive, this alternative may turn out to be as expensive as programming the entire application from scratch.

▶ *Build an entirely new application* Particularly for complex, specialized applications, creating an application from scratch is often necessary. The chief advantage of this approach is that it allows the firm to design an application specifically to meet its needs. Weighing against this benefit are the high costs of custom development. Custom development also carries two significant risks: the risk of major cost overruns and the risk that the application will not be completed. These risks increase with the size of the application, its complexity, and the firm's lack of experience with the technologies involved.

Even after choosing one of the three alternatives, the manager still faces a classic make-or-buy decision. Should the firm employ a staff of programmers to build and maintain the application? Should it employ third parties, such as consultants or accounting firms, to develop its systems? If so, will it work side-by-side with the third party in developing the system, or will it demand a **turnkey system** that is ready for use upon delivery from the vendor? Such decisions can have a major impact on the long-term success of the application. In today's rapidly changing technology environment, applications must be updated every two to five years, or they become obsolete. In choosing a development strategy, the organization must map out a path that ensures such ongoing maintenance is carried out.

Managing the Development of Information Systems

Whenever a company wants to create an information system for its own purposes, it must address the problem of how to manage the development of that system. The evolution of computer systems, software, and architecture through the years has left many companies with a lack of uniformity in their overall system. To create **connectivity** throughout the entire firm, most large companies and many smaller companies have implemented **enterprise resource planning (ERP) systems** that support the flow of information across all of an organization's departments, including accounting, sales, and manufacturing.

ERP is an elaborate software program that automates all of a firm's business procedures. Customer orders, inventory control, staffing levels, and other functions are

turnkey system a system that is ready for use upon delivery from the vendor

connectivity the ability of a firm's computer systems to work together to permit the flow of information throughout the firm

enterprise resource planning (ERP) systems a software program that automates all of a firm's business procedures and supports the flow of information across departments linked together through ERP software. The system records every transaction and continually updates all of the connected departments.

This software allows all users to be more informed about their company's resources and commitments. A salesperson who records an order into a laptop begins a transaction that will adjust inventory, notify manufacturing, and create an invoice in accounting. Companies that originally used expensive mainframe computing systems have changed to networks of PCs operating with a client-server architecture. These systems work well with ERP software and provide more flexibility.

ERP software has a number of drawbacks, however. The software often costs in excess of $50,000 per user. It is not unusual for large companies to spend more than $100 million and many years to implement ERP systems. A firm must convert data, modify existing systems, overhaul the network infrastructure, and train employees on the new system to create the data warehouse the ERP systems allow. Once completed, ERP allows users to easily generate data on transactions, reports on supplier performance, inventory levels, supply prices, performance reports, and demand forecasts. ERP systems allow simulation to stave off potential problems. Production runs can be simulated to develop schedules and eliminate potential bottlenecks.

Large software development projects have much in common with other large projects, such as building a skyscraper or a ship. They can involve many people, require much coordination, take a long time to complete, and come with hefty price tags: $10 million systems development projects are not uncommon. There are also differences, however. Consider the problem of gauging the progress of software development. Someone who is building a submarine and wants to see how things are going can walk through the dry dock where it's being built and inspect it. With software development projects, walking through the work area will always yield roughly the same view: a group of people sitting in front of workstations typing, talking, or thinking. Simply assessing whether a software development project is on track can represent a significant undertaking, whether it is being done internally or under contract with a third-party developer.

Project Management Techniques

The traditional approach to managing systems development, sometimes referred to as the **systems development life cycle (SDLC),** involves decomposing a system into its functional components. For example, an accounting application would be broken down into modules and submodules, each representing a distinct function in the overall accounting process. Project management techniques, such as PERT charts or critical path analysis, are then employed to organize and monitor the development of the system as a whole. Using such techniques, managers are able to assess how the project is proceeding compared with the original plan.

Unfortunately, the accuracy of project management techniques is not guaranteed. A major source of inaccuracies is the discovery of errors in the code, commonly referred to as **bugs.** For example, a module or submodule may appear to be complete on paper. When that module is connected to other modules, however, previously undiscovered problems may indicate a need for substantial additional work.

Incremental Development Techniques

In recent years, incremental development techniques, which distribute testing more uniformly throughout the development cycle, have gained in popularity. Such techniques usually involve the rapid creation of a working system with limited functionality, know as a **prototype.** Once the initial prototype has been created, additional features are added, with testing being performed at each stage of development. This ongoing testing reduces the number of bugs uncovered at the end of the development process. As the application approaches full functionality, it is often made available to a carefully selected subset of sophisticated users, a process known as **alpha testing.** These users run the software, reporting problems to the developers and making suggestions for additional functionality. Once a fully functional version of the application has been created, a wider group of users is given the software—a process called **beta testing.** These users, who more closely resemble

systems development life cycle (SDLC) an approach to system development that involves decomposing a system into its functional components

bugs errors in software code

prototype a working system with limited functionality

alpha testing during systems development, the process of making the new application available to a carefully selected subset of sophisticated users; done when the application approaches full functionality

beta testing during systems development, the process of testing a fully functional version of the new application with a wider group of users than was used for alpha testing

Sophisticated computer systems such as the one shown here allow businesses to operate more efficiently.

"average" users in their level of experience, generally focus their attention on detecting bugs. The size and scope of alpha and beta testing programs vary widely, but they can be huge. Before introducing Windows 95, for example, Microsoft had literally hundreds of thousands of beta test sites; most of the testers had paid for the privilege in order to acquire the software before its general release.

Managing the Implementation of Information Systems

Managers often assume that the actual development of a system or the acquisition of appropriate software is the major obstacle to creating a successful information system. Experience teaches otherwise, however. Managing system implementation—the process of transferring a system to its intended users—often proves far more difficult than technical development. For some categories of software, when systems are abandoned, it is usually because of unsuccessful implementation, rather than technical or economic issues.

passive resistance occurs when users uncomfortable with a new system overstate difficulties associated with learning the technology

active resistance occurs when users type in bad data or repeatedly crash a new system to make it unusable

The heart of the implementation challenge is overcoming user resistance to a new system or technology. Users uncomfortable with a new system may resort to **passive resistance.** They may overstate the difficulties associated with learning the technology, in effect claiming that they are not using it because they cannot figure out how it works. Users may also indirectly express their displeasure by overstating the impact of any bugs they discover or by dwelling on situations in which the system creates unnecessary work. Users have also been known to engage in **active resistance.** They may, for example, intentionally type in bad data or repeatedly crash the system to make it unusable. Such behaviors can be curtailed with constant management supervision. But as soon as management's attention wanders, resisting users simply return to their old practices. Faced with such active resistance, managers often conclude that the benefits of a system are simply not worth the effort required to keep it in use.

Managers can employ a number of techniques to increase the odds of a successful implementation. Among the most important are the following:

▶ *Ensure that the system has top management support* In study after study, top management support has been reported as a factor that contributed to successful implementation. When such support is lacking, users are less hesitant in resisting the system.

► *Ensure that a need for the system has been established and communicated to users* Users must be aware that a bona fide need for the system exists. The more visible the need, the better. For example, a system that keeps inferior products from getting to the customer has obvious appeal.

► *Allow potential users to participate in the system design and development process* Such participation can lead to an increased sense of involvement for users, giving them a sense of system ownership. That sense of ownership, in turn, can cause users to see themselves as partners in trying to ensure the system's success.

► *Design systems that are intrinsically motivating for users* When a system (1) provides its users with a greater sense of control over their jobs, (2) makes their jobs more interesting, and (3) improves the quality of their job performance in visible ways, potential users are unlikely to resist the system. They may even gravitate toward using it.

Managing the Security of Information Systems

The widespread use of information technology in organizations has significant security implications for management. Information technology increases a firm's vulnerability to both espionage and sabotage.

espionage the process of illegally gathering information

Espionage   A serious security threat that is aggravated by information technology is **espionage,** or the process of illegally gathering information. Prior to the widespread adoption of information systems, the physical nature of paper records such as customer lists made them both hard to steal and hard to analyze. The situation changes when such information is stored in computers, however. Sensitive data, such as a company's entire customer list and sales history, may be secretly copied onto a single data tape. To make matters worse, once such information has been transferred, its electronic form makes it much easier to analyze.

Although achieving fail-safe protection against espionage is impossible, some measure of protection may be achieved by limiting access to information. Most applications, for example, allow passwords to be established so that users can access only data relevant to their assigned duties. Keeping such systems current, however, requires significant management commitment and oversight. Particularly critical in this regard is ensuring that a user's access rights are terminated when the individual quits or is fired.

Another way that managers can reduce the espionage threat is to ensure that users are properly trained in security procedures. Stolen passwords represent a particularly serious threat to security. But that threat can also be significantly reduced through user education (see Exhibit 19.6). Managers can also reduce the threat of compromised passwords by ensuring that users and system administrators periodically change passwords.

Exhibit 19.6

Protecting Passwords

► *Avoid writing a password down.* Never leave a written password anywhere near the system on which it is used, or never write it down next to the user ID for the system.

► *Never type a password when someone is looking.* The easiest way to get someone's password is to watch it being typed.

► *Never use the same password on two systems.* On many systems, the system operator can read users' passwords. An unscrupulous system operator could use that information to access other user accounts with the same password.

► *Never use meaningful personal information for a password.* Using information such as birthdays, children's names, or your brand of car may make it possible for a persistent co-worker to get into your account.

► *Never use an actual word for a password.* The manner in which passwords are stored on many systems makes it possible for hackers, using a dictionary, to determine the password of any user who uses an actual word.

sabotage the malicious destruction of information by a perpetrator

Sabotage Even more chilling to a manager than espionage is **sabotage,** or the destruction of information by a perpetrator. Our reliance on information technology has increased our vulnerability to this threat by making information easier to destroy and by making it possible to destroy records without having physical access to them. For example, the information architecture in many firms makes it possible for a saboteur to destroy data over the phone, without taking the risk of being physically present.

Although sabotage can come from many sources, revenge (by disgruntled employees, for example), commercial gain (by competitors), and vandalism (by hackers who destroy systems for fun) are three of the most common motives. The nature of the sabotage itself can also vary. In some cases, it may consist of the simple erasure of data. In other cases, data may be substituted, as occurred when students in a California school electronically altered their transcripts to get better grades. The best protection against such threats is to employ the same security precautions used against espionage and to back up the system on a regular basis. Such backups, which involve saving all the information on the system's hard disk to tapes or other removable storage media, ensure that lost or damaged data can be restored. In addition, regular backups offer a measure of protection against environmental threats, such as earthquakes, tornadoes, hurricanes, and fires.

computer virus a program that attaches itself to other programs or computer disks

In recent years, a particularly common form of sabotage has been the **computer virus.** A virus is a program that attaches itself to other programs or computer disks, whenever the opportunity presents itself. Because of this replication, users who move programs or disks between machines can inadvertently cause a virus to spread. Viruses can also spread over networks if they are not properly protected.

Viruses differ widely in the damage they cause. Some are relatively benign (for example, drawing peace signs, then disappearing). Others specifically attack the hard disk, erasing data and ultimately rendering the system worthless. Complicating detection,

---

SPOTLIGHT ON TECHNOLOGY

Technology Vocabulary

Learn the vocabulary:

▶ *Bandwidth* The amount of data that can be sent through a connection in a certain amount of time. It is usually measured in bits-per-second (bps) for digital devices. A full page of text may have around 16,000 bits. A modem that operates at 57,600 bps has twice the bandwidth of a modem that operates at 28,800 bps.

▶ *Client/server* A network relationship between two computer programs. Clients are PCs that run applications that request information from other programs, the server. The server is a computer or program that manages disk drives, printers, databases, or network traffic.

▶ *Ethernet* A widely used local area network (LAN).

▶ *Firewall* A set of programs that protect a private network from outside users. The firewall uses a router program to filter all incoming network transmissions to determine whether to forward them toward their destination.

▶ *HTML (HyperText Markup Language)* The language used to create documents on the World Wide Web.

▶ *Intranet* A network that belongs to an organization and is used to share information. It is a secure network accessible by the organization's employees and others with authorization.

▶ *Java* A programming language designed for network environments. It is a simplified version of the C++ language.

▶ *LAN (local area network)* A network of computers sharing the resources of a single server, usually within a single building. It allows users to share data and peripheral devices.

▶ *Router* A device that connects LANs. It maintains a table of available routes to determine the best route for an information packet.

▶ *Standard* A format that has been recognized by a standards organization or accepted by the industry. Standards exist for programming languages, operating systems, data formats, and communication protocols. Standards are particularly important for relationships between businesses.

▶ *Streaming* A method of transferring data that are processed continuously. The user does not have to wait to download the entire file before viewing.

most viruses lie dormant on their host system for a significant period of time so that careless users will give them opportunities to spread to other systems. In other words, a virus may be active on a system for months before actually making its presence known. Some confine their activities to specific days, such as the Michelangelo virus, which destroys hard disks only on the artist's birthday (March 6). Some current viruses include:

▶ *Explore.Zip.Worm,* which uses Microsoft Outlook to disguise itself as a response to an e-mail message sent earlier. Once it is received, it copies itself to the Windows directory and begins to destroy files with certain extensions such as .doc and .xls. It will also search your e-mail inbox for unread messages and respond with a message and the virus attached.
▶ *Melissa,* which spreads itself through Microsoft Outlook. Once opened, it attempts to send e-mail messages to fifty individuals listed in the user's address book. It does little damage to individual hard drives but will quickly overload mail systems by the sheer number of messages that are sent.
▶ *Chernobyl,* which is known as the CIH virus and has been around since 1998. The virus is triggered by the April 26 date of the Chernobyl disaster. It destroys data and completely disables the computer.

Unlike for other forms of sabotage, routing backups do not provide effective virus protection. The problem is that in backing up the system, the virus is saved as well. Thus, restoring the system will also restore the virus. As a result, other forms of protection are usually required. The best is to follow the rules of proper virus hygiene, which include the following:

▶ Avoid all software that has not been acquired from known vendors.
▶ Keep floppy disks from unknown sources out of machines.
▶ Use **antivirus applications,** which are programs that detect and remove viruses. These programs are widely available and can be very effective against *known* viruses. Such programs are often marketed in subscription form, with regular updates that protect against new viruses.

antivirus applications
programs that detect and remove viruses

By establishing and enforcing procedures that clearly state what software can and cannot be installed on company systems and by ensuring that antivirus software is used routinely and kept up-to-date, managers play an important role in protecting their companies against computer viruses.

Emerging Technologies and Their Implications

4 Identify emerging technologies and their implications.

Just as information technologies were transformed over the past few decades, new technologies and new uses for existing technologies will emerge in the next decades. With these new technologies and new uses will come new challenges for managers. Two of the most important developments in technology are the evolution of the worldwide network and the emergence of truly intelligent systems.

The Worldwide Network

Hardly a day goes by when the local newspaper does not carry an article on the Internet. As we discuss at the end of the chapter, however, the Internet has a number of weaknesses when it comes to commercial uses. But what about the global networks of the future? At the present time, new communications infrastructures are being put in place. These infrastructures will ultimately change the ways in which we communicate and work.

E-Commerce The ability to compare and purchase products on the Internet has changed the practices of many businesses. It promises to have a tremendous impact on nearly every industry. Businesses used the Internet to purchase products valued at $43 billion in 1998 and nearly $100 billion in 1999. Consumer purchases rose from about $7 billion in 1998 to about $12 billion in 1999.

The benefits of the Internet to consumers have been obvious and numerous. The ability to research products and compare prices has become dramatically easier. Consumers can simply spend a few minutes at the computer rather than spending time going to assorted retail outlets to get product and price information. Consumers are also able to go to retail outlets to find the product they want to purchase and then go online to find the best price.

Companies also stand to benefit from increased online retailing. Although profit margins are being squeezed, some retailers are able to compensate through increased sales. That is, retailers are able to reach a larger market without a significant investment in traditional outlets. Additionally, online retailers are able to generate revenues through means other than sales of products. Online retailers can profit from advertisement sales, referral fees, and the sale of customer databases.

COMPUTER RETAILERS, SUCH AS SYMANTEC, USE THE INTERNET TO PROVIDE information about their products to individuals and companies. Furthermore, they use the Internet to sell their products. Companies can visit websites such as this to determine whether the products are appropriate for their needs.

Companies that produce homogeneous products and do not require individual service will be greatly influenced by the rising popularity of the Internet. The following are some of the industries that are already changing:

▶ *Books* The popularity of Amazon.com has forced traditional retailers to enter the online arena and to compete based on price. Discounts on best-sellers, historically around 10 percent, have reached 50 percent. Amazon.com's costs are very low because it has low overhead and no retail outlets. Other technological advances allow bookstores to electronically access rare and out-of-print books. This allows traditional booksellers to carry a limited inventory while offering customers a large selection.

▶ *Music* A number of online retailers (including Amazon.com) have focused on selling CDs at deep discounts. Like online book sellers, online music retailers benefit from much lower fixed costs than their traditional retail counterparts. New technology allows consumers to download music almost instantly, giving rise to the possibility that artists may be able to bypass traditional retail outlets and music labels.

▶ *Travel* Airline tickets may be purchased at significant discounts through some online retailers. Additionally, travelers can review resort destinations, reserve hotel rooms, and rent cars, all in a few minutes on the computer.

▶ *Computers and accessories* Consumers are most comfortable with online purchases associated with the technology. Computer packages, peripheral devices, and software can all be purchased online.

▶ *Automobiles* Currently, consumers interested in purchasing automobiles can find referrals online. A consumer can go to a variety of websites to research the autos of interest and their prices. Then the consumer can go to the traditional auto dealer and purchase the car at the agreed-upon price. This essentially forces local dealers to bid for sales. Automakers could offer the public the ability to order cars online and specify the particular features desired.

▶ *Toys and other children's products* Online retailers are beginning to offer all the toys available at the local stores. Additionally, a few websites offer all the products needed to plan a child's party. Instead of spending an evening driving from store to store, a parent can order decorations, games, toys, and everything else needed from the comfort of home or office.

▶ *Pet supplies* A few retailers have been able to achieve significant sales of pet supplies through their websites. They are able to offer better prices and a larger selection than local pet stores.

▶ *Groceries* A number of ventures are entering the online grocery market. The consumer can select the products desired and have them delivered later in the day. The problem of preserving perishable products and the difficulty of satisfying impulse purchases create obstacles to this idea, however.

Many other industries will also be affected by the growth of the Internet. Almost every industry could be changed through an online retail strategy. Firms typically benefit from significantly lower costs achieved by circumventing traditional distribution channels and selling directly to the consumer.

D❤LL COMPUTER'S FORMULA FOR SUCCESS

At a recent conference, Dell Computer's CEO, Michael Dell, promoted Dell's direct-connect philosophy. He said, "We believe that the Internet will be your business. If your business isn't enabled by information, if your business isn't enabled by customers and suppliers having more information and being able to use it, you're probably already in trouble. The Internet is like a weapon sitting on a table to be picked up by either you or your competitors." Thus, Dell's philosophy truly reflects the impact of emerging technologies on corporations. The company's approach of helping firms manage their information technologies reflects a recent trend in customer focus in the computer industry.

---

bandwidth the amount of information a network can carry

Infrastructure The amount of information a network can carry is called its **bandwidth,** which is determined by the physical components that make up the system. Today, a worldwide effort is being made to replace existing wiring with fiber-optic cable. A single optical fiber, the diameter of a human hair, can carry as much information as a cable the diameter of a rolling pin containing thousands of wires. As a result, the potential bandwidth available for telecommunications will increase greatly. In practical terms, that means that information transfers that used to take hours will be possible in under a second.

virtual reality display techniques that combine computerized sights, sounds, and sensations to create a sense of actually "being there"

Implications For businesses, the impact of this change in infrastructure, which will not be fully realized for several decades, will be astounding. As local phone systems are upgraded or replaced, consumers will be able to connect directly into a global network that operates many times faster than today's Internet. The increased bandwidth will make it possible to offer far more goods and services electronically. For example, consumers who wish to purchase clothing online will be able to view three-dimensional photorealistic images of clothing. **Virtual reality** display techniques, which combine computerized sights, sounds, and sensations to create a sense of actually "being there," may make it possible to simulate driving a new car and may also allow the potential home buyer to simulate walking through a new home. Although the services will not be free, they will likely be cheap enough to enable most consumers to be connected. Furthermore, as new services are offered over the network, there will be more opportunities to develop additional sources of revenue.

The high-speed connections between home and office will also have dramatic implications for how we work, manage, and are managed. Global "distances," already reduced by the telephone and air transportation, will shrink further as people from any part of the globe can meet face-to-face through their computers. **Video conferencing,** holding meetings between remote sites using sound and pictures transmitted over telecommunications links, today is limited mainly by the low bandwidth of existing telephone lines, which makes images grainy and jerky. Over the worldwide network, however, image quality will improve dramatically. The distinction between talking to images and talking face-to-face will blur. With such capabilities in place, what will become of the traditional workplace?

video conferencing holding meetings between remote sites using sound and pictures transmitted over telecommunications links

The effects of the worldwide network will be sweeping, and the managers who recognize its potential early enough will be the big winners. To recognize that potential, managers need to be willing to experiment with new technologies as they become available. Today's Internet, for all its weaknesses, affords managers precisely such an opportunity for experimentation, which is perhaps the single best justification for establishing a commercial Internet presence.

Truly Intelligent Systems

Since the 1950s, people have been attracted to—and horrified by—the notion of a truly intelligent computer. Initial efforts to make such a computer a reality led to the

Video conferencing allows audio and video communication between participants based in various locations.

artificial intelligence (AI) a field that focuses on developing computers that can perform tasks traditionally associated with biological intelligence, such as logical reasoning, language, vision, and motor skills

creation of the field of **artificial intelligence (AI).** The goal of AI has been to get computers to perform tasks traditionally associated with biological intelligence, such as logical reasoning, language, vision, and motor skills. Since its founding nearly forty years ago, the field has made some impressive strides (see Exhibit 19.7). The field has also made another important discovery: tasks that are easy for humans are often extremely difficult for computers.

Researchers are now concluding that many of the problems that AI has faced may stem from the fact that human brains and computers are organized very differently. A typical commercial computer has a single processor through which all information passes in a serial fashion, one piece of information at a time. The brain, however, is organized around hundreds of millions of neurons that operate in parallel. Although a single neuron is much slower than a computer CPU, the brain can still process information more than a million times faster than any computer. In pure information processing terms, today's supercomputers are probably less powerful than the brain of a housefly.

massively parallel machines experimental computers with many CPUs that operate simultaneously

That situation will not last forever, however. Experimental computers with many CPUs that operate simultaneously, known as **massively parallel machines,** are already being constructed. If current trends in technology improvement continue (and they are expected to, at least for the next few decades), computers may well reach parity with the human brain around the middle of this century. What will be the implications of these massively parallel machines for the workforce? Even if these machines cannot be trained to think exactly like humans, how many jobs will be left that a computer cannot do? These questions are not purely academic. Today's college freshmen may still be in the workforce when these systems become a reality.

The Future of the Internet

The global euphoria that has recently come to surround the Internet has, in some cases, caused managers to lose perspective on the actual strengths and weaknesses of the system. As we have already noted, the Internet seems to offer unparalleled opportunities for research, public relations, and communications. A number of characteristics of the Internet, however, are far less desirable from a business standpoint. Among the most serious of these are the following:

▶ *Lack of central authority* Unlike other entities a manager deals with, the Internet is more of a community than an organization. Moreover, it is a community with no leader. As a result, managers who find themselves overly dependent on the Internet may find they have nowhere to go when parts of the system go down, as they routinely do.

Exhibit 19.7

Artificial Intelligence Examples

▶ *Robotics* Today, some of the most productive factories in the world make extensive use of adaptive robots that originated from AI research.

▶ *Expert systems* These systems use sophisticated reasoning techniques, developed by AI, to accomplish difficult tasks, such as medical diagnosis. Companies such as American Express save millions of dollars a year by using expert systems.

▶ *Natural language applications* Computers with built-in voice recognition have become commonplace over the past five years, as have voice-driven phone systems. Both owe their existence to speech recognition research done in AI. Grammar checkers and translators depend heavily on natural language interpretation techniques pioneered in AI.

▶ *Object-oriented programming (OOP)* The OOP style, frequently employed in today's advanced systems, owes its existence to years of AI knowledge representation research.

▶ *Lack of underlying organization* Although tremendous amounts of information are present on the Internet, there is no obvious way to find any particular piece of information. Further, even when a piece of information is found, there is no way to ensure its accuracy.

▶ *Network performance* Most managers find it disconcerting to have their business depend on a system whose performance changes from minute to minute, and which could go down at any time. Yet such performance variation is characteristic of the Internet and is largely unavoidable. A substantial fraction of the computers that make up the heart of the Internet, such as the university computers that route communications and messages, are also used for other purposes. Thus, keeping the local Internet connection functioning smoothly is not always the provider's top priority.

▶ *Individual performance* Although universities and corporations generally have networks directly connected to the Internet, individuals usually access "the Net" using dial-up modems. Many of the most expressive features of the Net, including graphics, sound, and full-motion video, can take minutes or more to download. Such delays are a major obstacle to companies wishing to promote their products.

These weaknesses are being addressed as the Internet evolves into the "information superhighway." Two examples of the Internet's progress are:

▶ High-speed connections to private homes, using cable TV wiring.

▶ An increasing amount of Internet network traffic handled by private providers, such as MCI and AT&T.

As these changes continue, the possible uses for the Internet will expand dramatically. The Internet will ultimately become a "necessity" for most firms, much as the phone system is today.

| **BUSINESS DILEMMA** | **College Health Club** |

Information Systems at College Health Club

SUE KRAMER, PRESIDENT OF COLLEGE HEALTH CLUB (CHC), CONSIDERS SOME of the information that she would like to compile and use over time. First, she wants background information on the members so that she can determine their typical profiles. She initially recorded some background information for new members, but the information is on numerous index cards, making it difficult to determine profile characteristics of all members. Second, she wants to provide members with information about their progress (weight loss, endurance tests, and strength tests) from the time that they became members. She initially wrote this information on sheets of paper and then attempted to update the information over time. However, she does not have time to continually ask the members for updates.

Dilemma

Sue's goal is to design a system for more easily compiling information.

Solution

Sue decides to use an information system in which the data are recorded on a computer file. She obtains information from new members when they pay for their memberships and inputs the information into a computer. Each member's name is in the first column, age is in the second column, and other data are recorded as well. The computer can easily determine the average age for all members by computing the average of the numbers in the second column. The average for all other characteristics can be determined in the same manner.

Sue also decides to install a portable computer near the exercise area so that members can record their performance each day. Each member will have access to his or her own file with a code name. The members can input their weight on that day, the number of repetitions when lifting weights, the length of time that they did exercises, and so on. As the file is updated over time, it will indicate the member's progress. This type of information encourages members to continue their workouts (and therefore their memberships), because it shows how they have improved since they first joined CHC.

Additional Issues for Discussion

1 Explain the potential benefits of having a computer determine typical profiles of existing members.

2 Could Sue Kramer use computers for her business in any other ways?

3 Explain how an information system could help Sue send surveys to existing members so that she could obtain their feedback about her health club services.

SUMMARY

1 An electronic computer is a device capable of processing and storing vast quantities of information. The physical components of a computer are called hardware. Most computers are organized around four components: (a) central processing unit (CPU), (b) primary storage, (c) secondary storage, and (d) peripherals.

2 Although firms use computers in many ways, the most common uses are as (a) computational models, (b) data processing systems, and (c) interorganizational systems.

3 Some of the key challenges associated with managing today's information technologies are: (a) managing the firm's information system architecture, (b) acquiring software, (c) managing the development of information systems, (d) managing the implementation of information systems, and (e) managing the security of information systems.

4 Two of the key developments in technology are the evolution of the worldwide network and the emergence of truly intelligent systems. The worldwide network has already allowed for high-speed connections between home and office and between firms and customers. Meanwhile, efforts are being applied to develop truly intelligent computer systems that can think and carry out tasks like humans.

KEY TERMS

REVIEW QUESTIONS

1 Explain how decision support systems can be used to enhance decision making.

2 Define a computer and distinguish between hardware and software.

3 Explain the advantages of computer-based systems.

4 Distinguish the different forms of interorganizational systems (IOS).

5 Identify the issues that managers must become familiar with regarding the management of information technology.

6 Discuss the choice of application software confronting a manager. Why is it such a critical issue?

7 Explain the issues that should concern a manager in making a software applications decision.

8 Identify the techniques for managing the implementation of an information system.

9 Discuss the security threat to a firm with respect to information technology.

10 What is the goal of artificial intelligence? What is the main obstacle in achieving this goal?

DISCUSSION QUESTIONS

1 How do computers influence your everyday life?

2 What is a computer virus? How can you reduce the possibility that the computers you use at home, school, and work will become infected with a virus?

3 How could a firm using the Internet to provide confidential information to certain parties prevent espionage on the Internet? Do you think the Internet has made espionage more or less difficult?

4 How has the introduction of computers changed the way work is done in business offices? Do the benefits of computers outweigh the costs?

5 Discuss the uses of computerized information systems implemented at your college.

INVESTING IN THE STOCK OF A BUSINESS

Using the annual report of the firm in which you would like to invest, complete the following:

1 Does the annual report discuss how the firm uses information systems to monitor its operations?

2 Does the firm use information systems for internal distribution of information or to provide information to external stakeholders (customers, suppliers, stockholders, distributors, and so on)? In what ways could these groups benefit from information systems?

3 Does the firm have its own website on the Internet? Is the address listed in the annual report? If possible, visit this website and describe the information that can be found there.

4 Explain how the business uses technology to promote its information technology management function. For example, does it use the Internet to provide information about its information technology function? Does it provide information about the types of hardware and software it uses to improve production efficiency?

5 Go to **http://hoovers.com** and locate the NEWS SEARCH. Type in the name of the firm in the space provided, and review the recent news stories about the firm. Summarize any (at least one) recent news story about the firm that applies to one or more of the key concepts within this chapter.

b) multiple binary processors.

c) information management systems.

d) massively parallel machines.

e) broadband processors (BBPs).

18 _____ is software that allows other application programs to cooperate with each other.

a) Middleware

b) Shareware

c) Public domain software

d) Background software

e) Mediaware

19 Spreadsheets, database, and word processing software are all types of:

a) operating systems.   d) middleware.

b) utility programs.   e) simulation software.

c) application software.

20 All of the following are advantages that computerized data processing systems have over traditional paper-based record keeping except:

a) they are more accurate.

b) they save space.

c) they are more flexible.

d) they are much faster at performing routine tasks.

e) they prevent espionage.

21 The amount of information a network can carry is called its:

a) information ratings quotient.

b) load factor.

c) megahertz rating.

d) random access capacity.

e) bandwidth.

22 Incremental software development techniques typically involve the rapid creation of a working system with limited functionality known as a(n):

a) alpha version.   d) prototype.

b) mock up.   e) virtual program.

c) simulation program.

23 A system that uses computers and telecommunications technology to share information across organizational boundaries is known as a(n) _____ system.

a) gate-keeping   d) internal information

b) broadband   e) parallel information

c) interorganizational

24 _____ is software that handles input and output to peripherals, manages internal memory, and informs users of the status of application tasks.

a) Middleware   d) Shareware

b) System software   e) Sequencing software

c) Application software

25 In software applications, errors in code are referred to as:

a) bugs.   d) redundancies.

b) quirks.   e) discrepancies.

c) grinches.

26 _____ allows the computers of two or more companies to communicate with each other without human intervention.

a) Remote job entry

b) Decision support system software

c) Electronic data interchange

d) A dual boot system

e) Cryptograhic software

27 The amount of random access memory (RAM) installed on a particular computer is measured in:

a) millibytes.   d) megabytes.

b) megahertz.   e) processing units.

c) kilowatts.

28 Modems, printers, keyboards, monitors, and scanners are all common examples of computer:

a) core components.   d) peripherals

b) CPUs.   e) serial interfaces.

c) externalities.

29 In a mainframe system, individual users typically interact with the computer using a _____ that combines the functions of a keyboard and monitor.

a) file server

b) terminal

c) workstation

d) personal digital assistant (PDA)

e) portable input device (PID)

30 _____, such as America Online and CompuServe, provide a packaged assortment of information services such as e-mail, games, electronic shopping malls, and technical support forums to users who subscribe to their services.

a) Commercial information services

b) Shareware services

c) Management information systems

d) Professional news services

e) Public domain providers

31 _____ software provides a broad array of user-friendly features, such as e-mail, document management systems, and work-sharing systems, to people who are connected to a network.

a) Shareware   d) Database

b) System   e) Workgroup

c) Routing

32 The system architecture where all the networks are directly connected by cabling to the file server is called a:

a) program network.

b) wide area network (WAN).

c) global network.

d) local area network (LAN).

e) computer terminal.

33 When users who are uncomfortable with a new information system overstate difficulties in learning to use the system and exaggerate problems they encounter when trying to use it, they are engaging in:

a) active resistance.
b) passive resistance.
c) sabotage.
d) espionage.
e) organized resistance.

34 In typical network architecture, workstations are connected to a _____, which is a machine that stores and provides access to centralized data.
a) central processing unit
b) mainframe
c) stand-alone computer
d) file server
e) motherboard

35 The goal of _____ is to get computers to perform logical tasks traditionally associated with biological intelligence, such as logical reasoning and language, vision, and motor skills.
a) artificial intelligence
b) optical computing
c) data processing
d) multidimensional computer design
e) evolutionary engineering

discontinuing the use of the machinery. They could avoid the risk of product defects in their toys by eliminating toy production. Although eliminating the operations that caused risk effectively removes particular risks, firms that prefer to continue their existing businesses need an alternative solution.

Shifting Risk   Firms can shift some types of risk to insurance companies by purchasing insurance. **Property insurance** protects a firm against the risk associated with the ownership of property, such as buildings and other assets. Thus, it can provide insurance against property damage by fire or against theft. **Casualty insurance** protects a firm against potential liability for harm to others as a result of product failure or accidents.

Property and casualty insurance companies provide insurance for firms. Firms pay a periodic insurance premium for this type of insurance; the amount of the premium is partially dependent on the types of assets insured. The higher the market value of the insured assets, the higher the insurance premium paid, other things being equal. But not all assets are insured at the same rate. Because a building located in a high-crime area is more vulnerable to theft, the insurance fee will be higher. In addition, the manufacturing operations of some firms are more likely to result in personal injuries than those of other firms. The casualty insurance premium paid is affected by the likelihood of personal injuries.

Insurance companies recognize that the probability of some events occurring can change over time. Consequently, they adjust their premiums to reflect the change in probability. For example, firms experienced an increase in liability lawsuits in recent years. Anticipating a higher level of payouts on liability lawsuits, insurance companies increased their premiums.

Insurance companies employ **actuaries** to forecast the percentage of customers that will experience the particular event that is being insured. This enables insurance companies to set the premium properly on that type of insurance.

The federal and state governments offer business-related insurance. Two popular types are summarized in Exhibit 20.1. Old-age, survivors, disability, and health insurance (OASDHI) is funded by the Social Security taxes paid by employers and employees. Unemployment insurance is funded by unemployment taxes, which are usually paid by employers (although employees also incur an unemployment tax in some states). In general, the two types of insurance summarized in Exhibit 20.1 replace part of the income that is lost because of death, retirement, a layoff, or disability. Although other forms of public insurance are available, they are directed more specifically toward particular types of businesses.

Assuming Risk   Some firms are willing to assume their business risk with **self-insurance,** in which a firm creates a fund to cover any future claims. Rather than pay insurance premiums, firms that self-insure contribute to their own insurance fund. Firms consider self-insurance when they believe the insurance premiums charged by insurance companies are higher than would be needed to cover any claims. However,

property insurance protects a firm against the risk associated with the ownership of property, such as buildings and other assets

casualty insurance protects a firm against potential liability for harm to others as a result of product failure or accidents

actuaries persons employed by insurance companies to forecast the percentage of customers that will experience the particular event that is being insured

self-insurance a firm insures itself by creating a fund to cover any future claims

Exhibit 20.1

Insurance Offered by the Government

| Old-age, survivors, disability, and health insurance (OASDHI) | Workers who are disabled for at least twelve months can receive income payments. People aged sixty-five years or older receive income payments and hospital benefits. Spouses of workers who die receive income payments. |
| Unemployment insurance | Workers who are laid off can receive a portion of their previous earnings until they find a new job. They may also receive assistance in finding a new job. The length of time in which they can receive these benefits varies among states; the maximum period is usually around six months. |

Exhibit 20.2

Illustration of How to Protect
against Risk

Firm's operations	The firm produces ladders and other home repair equipment.
Exposure to risk	Injuries to employees who produce ladders or to customers who purchase ladders.
Protecting against Risk: Possible Solutions	
1. *Eliminating risk*	Discontinue the production and sale of ladders; focus on the production and sale of other home repair equipment that is less risky.
2. *Shifting risk*	Purchase insurance to protect against possible injuries to employees who produce the ladders or customers who use the ladders.
3. *Assuming risk*	Create a fund that can be used to self-insure against possible injuries to employees who produce the ladders or customers who use the ladders.

firms that self-insure may be unable to create a fund large enough to cover some awards granted by the court system. Such firms may be forced into bankruptcy if they are judged to be responsible for damages to an employee or customer, especially when the damages determined by the court system are in millions of dollars.

Comparison of Methods of Protecting against Risk The three methods used to protect against risk are compared for a firm that produces ladders in Exhibit 20.2. Trade-offs are involved when selecting the proper method. A firm is unlikely to eliminate the production of a product if it specializes in that product. Therefore, it would probably purchase insurance or self-insure. If the firm generates only a small amount of its total earnings from a product that creates substantial exposure to risk, it may eliminate the production of that product. The proper method for protecting against risk can be determined by estimating the costs of each method.

LOUISIANA STATE UNIVERSITY PROVIDES A WEBSITE DEVOTED TO RISK MANagement and insurance, as shown here. The website lets professionals and academicians exchange ideas about risk management. Users can be added to Riskmail's e-mail list to receive updates on risk management issues. Considering the high risk exposure of corporations, websites such as this are highly useful to firms' managers.

BUSINESS ONLINE

Risk
Management
Issues

http://riskmail.lsu.edu/

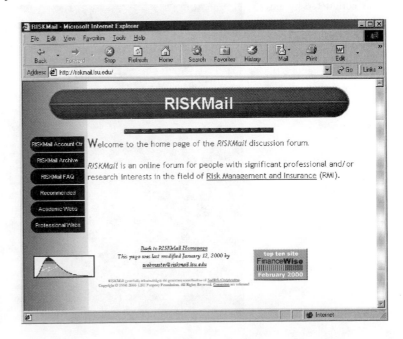

Exposure to the Economic Environment

A firm's **business risk** is dependent on its exposure to the economic environment, including industry conditions, the national economy, and global economies.

2 Identify the ways in which firms are exposed to the economic environment.

business risk the possibility that a firm's performance will be lower than expected because of its exposure to specific conditions

Exposure to Industry Conditions

The performance of a firm is influenced by industry conditions, such as the degree of competition and industry regulations. A firm in a highly competitive industry is subject to a higher degree of business risk because its market share may be reduced. For example, many video stores went bankrupt after the industry became more competitive. A reduction in industry regulations may lead to more competition in the industry. When the banking industry was deregulated in the 1980s, many banks failed because they could not compete effectively.

Exposure to Economic Conditions

The performance of a firm is also influenced by the national economy. The sensitivity of a firm's performance to economic conditions is dependent on the products or services it sells. If the demand for the firm's products or services is very sensitive to the national economy, the firm has a high degree of business risk.

The performance levels of some firms are exposed to interest rate movements. In particular, firms whose products are purchased with borrowed funds may be affected by changes in interest rates. When interest rates rise, the demand for homes and automobiles may decline because the interest payments that would be incurred by consumers purchasing on credit would be higher than they could afford. Therefore, firms such as homebuilders and automobile manufacturers can be affected by interest rate movements. Furthermore, any related firms such as suppliers of homebuilding parts or automobile parts are affected.

Firms that diversify their product mix may reduce their sensitivity to economic conditions (including interest rate movements), because some of the products may still be in demand even when economic conditions are poor.

Some tasks conducted by employees have a relatively high risk of injury. Firms should attempt to provide safe working conditions and can reduce the risk of liability if they offer safe working conditions.

Exposure to Global Conditions

The sensitivity of a firm's performance to global economies is dependent on the firm's target markets and its competition. If the firm exports products to Europe, the demand for its products is influenced by the European economies. A firm that generates a large proportion of its sales in foreign countries can reduce its exposure to its national economy, but it increases its exposure to specific foreign economies.

When firms conduct international business, their performance typically becomes more exposed to exchange rate movements. U.S. firms that rely heavily on exports may be severely affected by the depreciation of foreign currencies because foreign demand for U.S. products declines when the values of foreign currencies decline. U.S. firms that rely heavily on imported materials for their production process may be severely affected by the appreciation of foreign currencies because the cost of the imported materials increases when the values of foreign currencies increase. Firms that conduct international business may reduce their exposure to exchange rate movements by hedging with special exchange rate contracts.

Firms that conduct international business are also exposed to political events that could adversely affect their performance. For example, a foreign government may impose trade barriers or new tax rules that could reduce the earnings of U.S. firms that conduct business in that country. Such forms of so called political risk can increase the firm's business risk. U.S. firms that conduct business in less-developed countries are more exposed to political risk than U.S. firms doing business in industrialized countries.

GLOBAL BUSINESS

Risk of Conducting Business in Less-Developed Countries

ALTHOUGH LESS-DEVELOPED COUNTRIES OFFER NUMEROUS BUSINESS OPportunities, they also present various types of risk for U.S. firms. Consider the following examples:

1 Some U.S. firms made business agreements with Chinese government officials on conducting business in China. They later learned that those officials had no authority to make such business agreements.

2 Some U.S. firms that established businesses in Russia have been exposed to massive corruption by suppliers and government officials.

Although various types of insurance can reduce exposure to risks involved in international business, insurance cannot cover every possible type of risk in a foreign country. Firms can follow some general guidelines to reduce their exposure to risk. First, firms need to fully understand the country's rules regarding the taxes on earnings generated in that country. Second, they must determine whether there are any restrictions on sending funds back to the United States and whether any taxes will be imposed as a result. Third, firms should obtain approval for their business from the proper government officials. These may include city officials as well as central government officials. Fourth, firms should attempt to determine the characteristics of the industry in which they would compete in that foreign country. For example, some industries in foreign countries are controlled by organized crime. These general guidelines can help firms avoid specific countries that may present excessive risk. Alternatively, the guidelines may enable firms to properly prepare for the types of risk that exist in some foreign countries.

Summary of Exposure to the Economic Environment

Exhibit 20.3 summarizes the firm's exposure to the economic environment. The primary reason for the exposure is that the demand for the firm's product is affected by industry, economic, and global conditions. In addition, the firm's expenses may also be affected by these conditions.

Exhibit 20.3

Firm's Exposure to the
Economic Environment

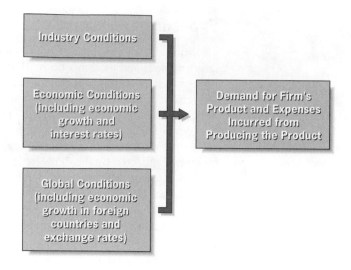

Hedging Risk from Economic Conditions

derivative instruments

instruments whose values are
derived from values of other
securities, indexes, or interest
rates

Derivative instruments are financial instruments whose values are derived from values of other securities, indexes, or interest rates. Firms use many types of derivative instruments to hedge their risk from economic conditions. To illustrate how a firm could use derivative instruments to reduce its risk, consider the following example. Assume that the firm recognizes that it will be adversely affected by rising interest rates. It desires to take a position in a derivative instrument that will generate a gain if interest rates rise, which can offset the adverse effect on the firm. A popular derivative instrument known as an **interest rate swap** allows a firm to swap fixed interest payments for payments that adjust to movements in interest rates. Assume that the firm owes $100 million and that it can negotiate an interest rate swap agreement in which it provides a fixed annual interest payment of $7 million per year over the next five years. In exchange, it will receive a payment based on the existing Treasury bill rate, as applied to $100 million. If interest rates are high at the end of each year, the firm will generate a gain on the interest rate swap. If the Treasury bill rate is 8 percent, the firm will receive 8 percent of $100 million, or $8 million ($1 million more than it pays out per year on the swap). If the Treasury bill rate is 9 percent, the firm will receive 9 percent of $100 million, or $9 million ($2 million more than it pays out per year on the swap). The higher the interest rates, the larger the gain, which can partially offset any adverse effects of the high interest rates on the firm's performance. Many banks and other financial service firms commonly use derivative instruments such as interest rate swaps to reduce potential adverse effects of interest rate movements.

interest rate swap a derivative
instrument that allows a firm to
swap fixed interest payments for
payments that adjust to
movements in interest rates

Some firms, such as Procter & Gamble, experienced losses as a result of improperly using derivative instruments. Consequently, firms began to ensure proper use of derivative instruments. Shortly after Procter & Gamble incurred a loss of about $100 million due to derivative instruments, it made a special effort to monitor its derivative positions more closely, as explained in its annual report:

" *Our policy on derivatives is not to engage in speculative leveraged transactions.* "

" *The Company has taken steps to substantially increase the oversight of the Company's financial activities, including the formation of a Risk Management Council.* "

❝ The Council's role is to insure that the policies and procedures approved by the Board of Directors are being followed within approved limits. ❞

Derivative instruments can reduce risk when used properly. Numerous firms, including PepsiCo and DuPont, use derivative instruments to reduce risk.

Exposure to Firm-Specific Characteristics

3 Identify a firm's exposure to firm-specific characteristics.

A firm's business risk is also influenced by any unique characteristics of the firm that affect its ability to cover its expenses. In general, any characteristics that cause the firm to experience a sudden large loss tend to increase the firm's degree of business risk. Some of the more obvious firm-specific characteristics that influence business risk are identified next.

Limited Funding

Small firms tend to have less access to funding and therefore have less flexibility to cover their expenses. Limited funding results in more business risk. As firms grow, they expand their debt capacity and have more financial flexibility.

Reliance on One Product

Firms that rely on a single product to generate most of their revenue are susceptible to abrupt shifts in their performance and therefore have a high degree of business risk. If the demand for the product declines for any reason, the firm's performance will be adversely affected. Firms that offer a diversified product mix are affected less by a reduction in the demand for a single product.

Reliance on One Customer

Firms that rely on a single customer for most of their business have a high degree of business risk, because their performance would decline substantially if the customer switches to a competitor. There are numerous examples of firms that rely heavily on one customer. For example, firms such as Boeing and Lockheed rely on federal government orders for some of the products they produce. When the federal government reduces its spending, it orders fewer products from these firms. Whirlpool Corporation historically relied on Sears for much of its appliance sales. When Sears experienced a decline in appliance sales, it reduced its orders from Whirlpool. Firms can reduce their reliance on a single customer by spreading the sale of the product across markets.

D∅LL COMPUTER'S FORMULA FOR SUCCESS

In a recent year, less than 15 percent of Dell Computer's $26 billion in sales came from consumers who wanted a PC with easy access to the Internet. The bulk of Dell's business came from corporate and government customers that were not buying web-linked systems. Many companies had frozen information technology spending as they waited out Y2K. With its forward-looking focus on the growing importance of the Internet, Dell Computer was able to reduce its reliance on corporate and government customers, and stay a step ahead of its competition.

Reliance on One Supplier

Firms that rely on a single supplier for most of their supplies may be severely affected if that supplier does not fulfill its obligations. If that supplier suddenly goes out of business, the firm may experience a major shortage of supplies. Firms that use several suppliers are less exposed to the possibility of a single supplier going out of business, because they will still receive their supply orders from the other suppliers.

Reliance on a Key Employee

When a firm relies on a key employee for its business decisions, the death of that employee would have a severe impact on the firm's performance. Consider a computer repair business that has only one employee who can perform the repairs. If the employee dies, this job may not be easily performed by other employees. Until the employee can be replaced, business performance may decline. Since a business cannot be managed as well following the death of a key employee, it may be less capable of covering its expenses.

Hedging against Losses Resulting from a Key Employee's Death Firms can hedge against losses resulting from a key employee's death by purchasing life insurance for their key employees. The policy identifies the firm as the beneficiary in the event that a key employee dies. Thus, when a key employee dies, this type of insurance provides the firm with compensation, which the firm can use to offset the possible losses or reduced performance. The firm is cushioned from the loss of a key employee and may be able to survive while attempting to hire a person to fulfill the key employee's responsibilities.

Consider an individual who runs a small business and applies for a business loan at a local bank. If the individual is killed in an accident, the business may deteriorate and the loan would not be paid off. A life insurance policy could designate creditors (such as a bank) as the beneficiaries to protect them against such a risk. Using this strategy, the business is more likely to be approved for a loan.

To illustrate the use of key employee insurance, consider the case of PRP, a research and development company located in Massachusetts. While PRP was developing a product to be used by cancer patients, the chief executive officer of PRP died. Consequently, investors were unwilling to invest in further development of the product because they were concerned that PRP would not survive without its chief executive officer. However, PRP had a $2.5 million life insurance policy on its chief executive officer, which provided sufficient funding when investors were unwilling to invest more funds in the firm.

From the perspective of the insured policyholder, **whole-life insurance** is life insurance that exists until death or as long as premiums are promptly paid. In addition to providing insurance, whole-life policies provide a form of savings to the policyholder. These policies build a cash value that the policyholder is entitled to even if the policy is canceled.

Term insurance provides insurance for a policyholder only over a specified term and does not build a cash value for the policyholder. The premiums paid by policyholders represent only insurance and not savings. Although term insurance is only temporary and does not build a cash value, it is significantly less expensive than whole-life insurance. Policyholders must compare the cash value of whole-life insurance with its additional costs to determine whether it is preferable to term insurance.

To accommodate firms that need more insurance now than later, **decreasing term insurance** provides insurance benefits to a beneficiary that decrease over time. A firm might use this form of insurance to cover a key employee. As time passes and the firm is more capable of surviving without the employee, less insurance would be needed.

Universal life insurance combines the features of term and whole-life insurance. It specifies a period of time over which the policy will exist but builds a cash value for

whole-life insurance life insurance that exists until death or as long as premiums are promptly paid and has a cash value to which the policyholder is entitled

term insurance provides insurance for a policyholder only over a specified term and does not build a cash value for the policyholder

decreasing term insurance provides insurance benefits to a beneficiary that decrease over time

universal life insurance combines the features of term and whole-life insurance; specifies a period of time over which the policy will exist, but builds a cash value for policyholders over time

the policyholder over time. Interest is accumulated from the cash value until the policyholder uses those funds. Universal life insurance allows flexibility in the size and timing of the premium. The growth in a policy's cash value is dependent on the premium payment, which is divided into two portions. The first portion is used to pay the death benefit identified in the policy and to cover any administrative expenses. The second portion is used for investments and reflects savings for the policyholder. Under Internal Revenue Service rules, the value of these savings cannot exceed the policy's death benefits.

Hedging against the Illness of a Key Employee The illness of one or more key employees may adversely affect the performance of a firm. Many firms offer a program in which their employees obtain health insurance from health insurance companies. The insurance is generally cheaper when purchased through the firm.

Even if a firm has provided some type of health insurance plan for its employees, it may still be affected by the temporary absence of an employee. Firms can reduce the potential adverse effect of an employee's illness by ensuring that more than one employee can perform each task.

Exposure to Property Losses

property losses financial losses resulting from damage to property

Property losses are financial losses resulting from damage to property. The damage may be caused by fire, theft, or weather conditions. The financial losses to the firm can result from payments that must be made to repair the damage or from the interruption of the firm's operations. For example, if a fire forces a firm to close a factory for one month, the financial loss is not just the cost of repairs but also the forgone earnings resulting from closing the factory.

Hedging against Property Losses Property losses may be avoided if the firm enforces policies that can prevent fire or theft. For example, firms that use flammable chemicals may attempt to ensure that all chemicals are kept far away from smoking areas. Firms can also use alarm systems to detect fire or theft. Furthermore, they can design their facilities in a way that protects against burglaries and poor weather conditions.

A small business such as this one is exposed to several types of risk but can use various techniques to eliminate or reduce the risk.

Although firms can take many precautions to prevent property damage, they do not have complete control. Firms cannot completely safeguard against damage caused by fire, theft, or poor weather conditions. Therefore, they normally purchase insurance for protection. Insurance policies vary in what they cover. Some firms may purchase insurance that covers the property in the event of a fire. Other firms may purchase insurance that covers the property under any conditions (including burglary and poor weather).

The annual premium paid for property insurance is dependent on the value of the assets that are to be insured. The annual premium charged to insure the property of a small factory is less than the premium charged for insuring a production plant of General Motors. Insurance companies assess the potential insurance claims that could occur, and set the insurance premiums accordingly.

The annual premium paid for property insurance is also dependent on the probability of damage. The higher the probability, the higher the insurance premium. For example, the insurance premium for a factory that uses flammable chemicals will be higher than one of similar size that does not use flammable chemicals.

BUSINESS ONLINE

Comparing Insurance Quotations

http://www.insurance-online-texas.com/policy_info/transmenu.htm

INSURANCE QUOTATIONS CAN BE EASILY ACCESSED USING THE INTERNET, as shown here. The website of Insurance Online Texas allows users to quickly obtain quotations from various companies for different types of insurance. Furthermore, the website provides a library that can be used to research insurance issues. By pooling insurance quotations, corporations can find the most competitive insurance and choose among various alternatives in hedging against risk.

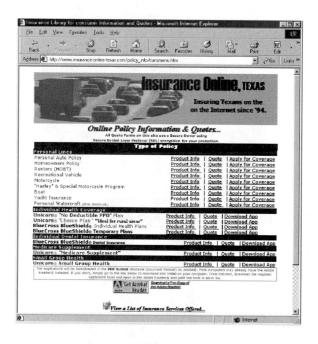

Exposure to Liability Losses

liability losses financial losses due to a firm's actions that cause damages to others or to their property

Liability losses are financial losses due to a firm's actions that cause damages to others or to their property. For example, a firm may be held responsible for an employee who is hurt on the job or for a customer who is hurt because of a defective product produced by the firm.

Hedging against Liability Losses Firms can hedge against liability losses by enforcing policies that ensure safety on the job and quality control of products produced. Nevertheless, they cannot completely safeguard against liability losses with these policies. Consequently, most firms purchase insurance to cover liability damages. Some policies cover damages resulting from injuries to employees, while other policies cover damages resulting from product defects. Because of the large awards granted by the court system for various claims in recent years, liability insurance has become very expensive.

The annual premium paid for liability insurance is dependent on the probability of a liability claim and the size of the claim. Firms in the health-care industry are charged very high liability insurance premiums because their potential liability is so high. Also, firms that produce toys pay high liability insurance premiums because many liability claims result from injuries experienced by children playing with toys.

Exposure to Employee Compensation Claims

Firms must pay compensation (including all medical bills and lost wages) to employees who are injured at work. Proper risk management should assess existing business operations to ensure that all machinery and equipment are safe and that tasks are conducted in ways that will not cause injuries.

The Occupational Safety and Health Administration (OSHA) monitors firms to make sure that they use tools, machinery, and office facilities that are considered safe. In recent years, OSHA has focused on reducing the possibility of cumulative trauma disorder (CTD) that can affect a worker's wrists or hands. The use of computers, word processors, and other equipment that places pressure on the wrists has caused a major increase in compensation claims due to CTDs in recent years.

Hedging against Compensation Claims Firms can use effective risk management techniques to reduce their exposure to employee compensation claims. As an example, consider OshKosh B'gosh, a manufacturer of children's clothing that experienced

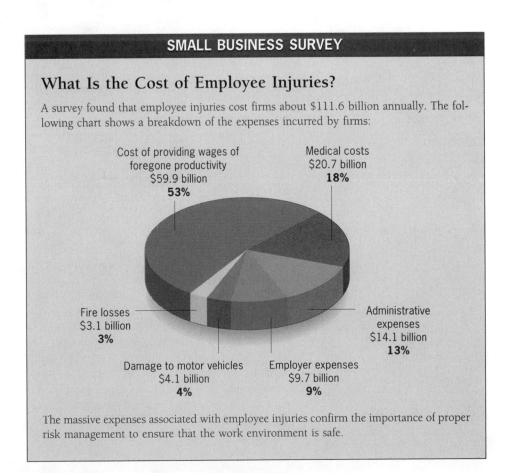

SMALL BUSINESS SURVEY

What Is the Cost of Employee Injuries?

A survey found that employee injuries cost firms about $111.6 billion annually. The following chart shows a breakdown of the expenses incurred by firms:

Cost of providing wages of foregone productivity
$59.9 billion
53%

Medical costs
$20.7 billion
18%

Fire losses
$3.1 billion
3%

Administrative expenses
$14.1 billion
13%

Damage to motor vehicles
$4.1 billion
4%

Employer expenses
$9.7 billion
9%

The massive expenses associated with employee injuries confirm the importance of proper risk management to ensure that the work environment is safe.

a large number of compensation claims because of CTDs. An investigation found that many workers were affected by repetitive tasks that required force with the hands. Consequently, OshKosh B'gosh revised its operations so that employees could avoid motions that could cause CTDs. It also rotated jobs among employees to alleviate stress over time on any particular part of the body. Finally, it provided job safety training to educate employees on how to perform tasks to avoid injuries. When firms use risk management techniques like these, they can improve employee morale and lower the expenses associated with workers' compensation.

Some firms self-insure to establish a fund for covering employee compensation. Other firms purchase employee compensation insurance. The insurance premiums are dependent on the potential employee compensation that a firm may pay for on-the-job injuries.

BUSINESS ONLINE

Insurance Information Online

http://insurance.yahoo.com/

YAHOO! USES ITS WEBSITE TO PROVIDE INDIVIDUALS AND CORPORATIONS with information about several types of insurance. Furthermore, it allows users to access related websites. Websites such as this enable corporations to find ways to hedge their exposure to risk.

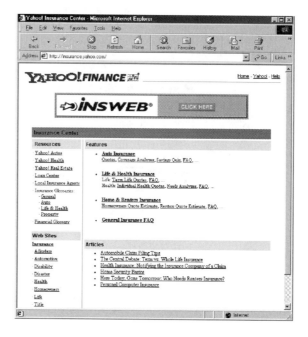

Summary of Exposure to Firm-Specific Characteristics

Exhibit 20.4 summarizes the firm-specific characteristics to which a firm is exposed. The funding can be increased if the firm experiences strong performance. The risk of relying on a single product, customer, or supplier can be reduced by diversifying the firm's product line across many customers and by diversifying among suppliers. The risk of relying on a single employee can be reduced by diversifying job responsibilities or by purchasing insurance. The risk of property, casualty, or employee compensation losses can be covered by purchasing insurance or by self-insuring.

Other firm-specific characteristics may also expose a firm to risk. Insurance may be purchased to cover these types of risk. A brief summary of other types of insurance that can be obtained is provided in Exhibit 20.5.

Exhibit 20.4

Exposure to Firm-Specific
Characteristics

Characteristic	How Firm Is Exposed
Limited funding	Limited ability to cover expenses.
Reliance on one product	Revenue will be reduced substantially if there is a large decline in the demand for a single product.
Reliance on one customer	Revenue will decline substantially if the customer no longer purchases the firm's product.
Reliance on one supplier	Potential shortages of supplies occur if supplier experiences problems.
Reliance on a key employee	Performance will decline if the employee dies, becomes ill, or leaves the firm.
Property losses	Expenses incurred from covering damage to property.
Liability losses	Expenses incurred from covering liability for damages to others or their property.
Employee compensation claims	Expenses incurred from covering compensation claims.

Exposure to Lawsuits

Explain a firm's exposure to
potential lawsuits.

In recent years, firms have been bombarded by lawsuits. To illustrate, consider the following statements from annual reports:

" The company is a defendant in various suits, including environmental ones, and is subject to various claims which arise in the normal course of business. "

—Motorola

Exhibit 20.5

Other Types of Insurance

Type of Insurance	Coverage Provided
Business interruption insurance	Covers against losses due to a temporary closing of the business.
Credit line insurance	Covers debt payments owed to a creditor if a borrower dies.
Fidelity bond	Covers against losses due to dishonesty by employees.
Marine insurance	Covers against losses due to damage during transport.
Malpractice insurance	Covers professionals from losses due to lawsuits by dissatisfied customers.
Surety bond	Covers losses due to a contract not being fulfilled.
Umbrella liability insurance	Provides additional coverage beyond that provided by other existing insurance policies.
Employment liability insurance	Covers claims against wrongful termination and sexual harassment.

> *The Corporation is involved in various lawsuits in the ordinary course of business. These lawsuits primarily involve claims for damages arising out of the use of the Corporation's products and allegations of patent and trademark infringement.*
>
> —Black and Decker

> *PepsiCo is subject to various claims and contingencies related to lawsuits, taxes, environmental and other matters arising out of the normal course of business.*
>
> —PepsiCo

These examples are not the exception but are typical for most large firms. It is not unusual for firms such as retailers or wholesalers to be sued for a product defect, even when they had nothing to do with the design or production of the product.

Assume that you are a firm's risk manager who is responsible for ensuring that the firm's customers and employees are treated properly. Answer the following questions about whether the firm is subject to a possible lawsuit:

1. Your firm's product is tested by a government agency and found to be completely safe. Can your firm be sued by a customer for product defects?

2. Your firm has an employee who is consistently performing poorly at work and has consistently been given clear evaluations citing poor performance. If this employee is fired, can your firm be sued by that employee?

3. Your firm has an employee who not only performs poorly at work but also has begun to take illegal drugs at work. If this employee is fired, can your firm be sued?

4. Your firm recently promoted an employee who was selected as the most qualified for a new position. Can your firm be sued by other employees who are less qualified?

5. An employee recently walked into the firm's offices with a loaded gun. If this employee is fired, can your firm be sued by that fired employee? If this employee is not fired, can your firm be sued by other employees?

The answer to every one of these questions is a definite yes. Furthermore, you may be sued personally along with the firm. That is, the plaintiff may attempt to receive a court judgment on your individual assets as well as the firm's assets. The court system may ultimately prevent a plaintiff from suing other employees personally, but there is nothing to prevent the plaintiff from trying, regardless of the actual circumstances.

The court system may also ultimately rule in favor of a firm that has attempted to treat customers and employees properly. Nevertheless, the firm still incurs the large cost of defending against lawsuits. It may also experience a decline in business when the public is informed by the media about lawsuits. Plaintiffs' attorneys often spread the news of a lawsuit to the media in the hope that public pressure will force the firm to settle the lawsuit before the news does damage to its business. Furthermore, attorneys receive free advertising from the media when their names are mentioned. Many frivolous lawsuits have been settled because firms do not wish to use time or resources to defend against so-called nuisance lawsuits. Even when a firm is willing to defend against a frivolous lawsuit and wins, it may take several years before a court judgment occurs.

In summary, risk managers may have some ability to prevent specific exposure to risk that can result in lawsuits and therefore in major expenses incurred by the firm. However, risk managers cannot prevent frivolous lawsuits that will be filed against the firm. They must simply recognize that such lawsuits may occur and should establish a budget that can be used to defend against them.

Children's toys such as Poké-mon are exposed to the risk of lawsuits because of injuries. Manufacturers of children's toys attempt to ensure safety of the products and use various techniques to manage their risk.

How the Threat of Lawsuits Can Affect Business Strategies

The size of the damages for compensating injured persons can vary among states. Consequently, managers must consider state laws when establishing or expanding a firm in a specific location. In California, large damages imposed by the court system have forced many firms into bankruptcy. Several other firms have moved out of California to reduce their exposure to the risk that a court will impose such damages.

Some products are more likely to result in lawsuits than others. A recent survey found that 47 percent of firms had eliminated at least one of their product lines because of the threat of lawsuits, and 39 percent of firms had withheld new products from the market because of the possible threat of lawsuits.

SPOTLIGHT ON TECHNOLOGY

Risk Management of Information Technology

Information technology has created new risks and increased the complexity of risk management. Risk associated with electronic business is referred to as e-risk, and a number of programs have been developed to minimize it.

Online banking and securities trading have created large exposures to risk. These services are vulnerable to potential losses from security breaches through network hacking, viruses, and electronic thefts. Zurich Financial Services Group offers a risk management program that includes evaluation of current systems by IBM consultants.

The program begins with remote scans of the client's websites, an examination of current security, and a review of previous incidents to determine what is needed to bring the company up to widely accepted security benchmarks. The program also offers insurance coverage against loss of business income, damage to reputation, loss of intellectual property, interruption of service liability, and liabilities incurred as a result of electronically published information. This and similar programs allow firms to aggressively pursue electronic business while protecting against the risk and exposures associated with it.

Concern about Arbitrary Judgments

Since laws cannot be explicitly written to cover every possible aspect of business, there will always be court cases where the judgments are dependent on the specific judges or juries involved. Consequently, attorneys attempt to position the court case so that it will involve judges or jurors who have a favorable bias. Plaintiffs tend to choose a court location where the jury may be biased in favor of the plaintiff. Defendants will likely prefer that the case be conducted in a different court.

To illustrate how positioning can determine the outcome of court cases, consider that in federal court cases, plaintiffs win a larger percentage of their cases heard in the court where the lawsuit was originally filed than those cases that are transferred to other courts.

The preceding discussion suggests that positioning may be more relevant than the law itself. Because some laws are arbitrary, firms may be subject to major damages even if they make every effort to follow the law.

Conclusion for Risk Managers

A firm can use effective risk management to prevent exposure to various types of risk that injure customers or employees. In this way, risk management can also enhance the firm's value by enabling it to avoid the expenses of compensating injured customers or employees or the legal expenses that result from lawsuits.

In reality, risk managers must recognize that their firms may incur major legal expenses even if they conduct risk management properly. Thus, the managers can more accurately estimate their future expenses by anticipating that some lawsuits will be filed against the firms, regardless of their efforts to conduct business properly.

Although a firm cannot prevent arbitrary judgments through risk management, it may be able to avoid unfavorable judgments by attempting to use procedures that are well documented and clearly demonstrate the firm's efforts to treat customers and employees properly.

Remedies for Business Failures

5 Explain the alternative remedies for firms that are failing.

The extreme consequence of business risk is business failure, in which the firm's assets are sold to pay creditors part of what they are owed. In this case, a formal bankruptcy process is necessary. First, however, the firm should consider alternative informal remedies, which could avoid some legal expenses. Common remedies include the following:

- ▶ Extension
- ▶ Composition
- ▶ Private liquidation
- ▶ Formal remedies

Extension

extension provides additional time for a firm to generate the necessary cash to cover its payments

If a firm is having difficulty covering the payments it owes, its creditors may allow for an **extension,** which provides additional time for the firm to generate the necessary cash to cover its payments. An extension is feasible only if the creditors believe that the firm's financial problems are temporary. If formal bankruptcy is inevitable, an extension may only delay the liquidation process and possibly reduce the liquidation value of the firm's assets.

If creditors allow an extension, they may require that the firm abide by various provisions. For example, they may prohibit the firm from making dividend payments until the firm retains enough funds to repay its loans. The firm will likely agree to any reasonable provisions because the extension gives the firm a chance to survive.

No creditor is forced to go along with an extension. Creditors who prefer some alternative action must be paid off in full if an extension is to be allowed. If too many creditors disapprove of an extension, attempting one will not be feasible, as the firm would first have to pay all disapproving creditors what they are owed.

Composition

composition specifies that a firm will provide its creditors with a portion of what they are owed

If the failing firm and its creditors do not agree on an extension, they may attempt to negotiate a **composition** agreement, which specifies that the firm will provide its creditors with a portion of what they are owed. For example, the agreement may call for creditors to receive forty cents on every dollar owed to them. This partial repayment may be as much as or more than creditors would receive from formal bankruptcy proceedings. In addition, the firm may be able to survive, since its future interest payments will be eliminated after paying off the creditors. As with an extension, creditors are not forced to go along with a composition agreement. Any dissenting creditors must be paid in full.

Private Liquidation

private liquidation creditors may informally request that a failing firm liquidate (sell) its assets and distribute the funds received from liquidation to them

If an extension or composition is not possible, the creditors may informally request that the failing firm liquidate (sell) its assets and distribute the funds received from liquidation to them. Although this can be achieved through formal bankruptcy proceedings, it can also be accomplished informally outside the court system. An informal agreement will typically be accomplished more quickly than formal bankruptcy proceedings and is less expensive as it avoids excessive legal fees. All creditors must agree to this so-called **private liquidation,** or an alternative remedy will be necessary.

To carry out a private liquidation, a law firm with expertise in liquidation will normally be hired to liquidate the debtor firm's assets. Once the assets are liquidated, the remaining funds are distributed to the creditors on a pro rata basis.

Formal Remedies

If creditors cannot agree to any of the informal remedies, the solution to the firm's financial problems will be worked out formally in the court system. The formal remedies are either reorganization or liquidation under bankruptcy. Whether a firm should reorganize or liquidate depends on its estimated value under each alternative.

liquidation value the amount of funds that would be received as a result of the liquidation of a firm

Reorganization Reorganization of a firm can include the termination of some of its businesses, an increased focus on its other businesses, revisions of the organizational structure, and downsizing. Consider a firm whose value as a "going concern" (a continuing business) would be $20 million after it reorganizes. Now consider the **liquidation value** of that firm, which is the amount of funds that would be received from liquidating all of the firm's assets. If the firm's liquidation value exceeds $20 million, it should be liquidated. The creditors would receive more funds from liquidation than they would expect to receive if the firm were reorganized. Conversely, if its liquidation value is less than $20 million, the firm should be reorganized.

In the case of reorganization, the firm or the creditors must file a petition. The bankruptcy court then appoints a committee of creditors to work with the firm in restructuring its operations. The firm is protected against any legal action that would interrupt its operations. The firm may revise its capital structure by using less debt, so that it can reduce its periodic interest payments owed to creditors. Once the restructuring plan is completed, it is submitted to the court and must be approved by the creditors.

Liquidation under Bankruptcy If the firm and its creditors cannot agree on some informal agreement, and if reorganization is not feasible, the firm will file for bankruptcy. A petition for bankruptcy must be filed by either the failing firm or the creditors.

The failing firm is obligated to file a list of creditors along with up-to-date financial statements. A law firm is appointed to sell off the existing assets and allocate the funds received to the creditors. Secured creditors are paid with the proceeds from selling off any assets serving as their collateral.

BUSINESS DILEMMA	College Health Club

Managing Risk at College Health Club

SUE KRAMER, PRESIDENT OF COLLEGE HEALTH CLUB (CHC), RECOGNIZES that CHC is exposed to various types of liability risk. Specifically, she knows that customers of the health club could possibly injure themselves when using the exercise or weight machines or when doing aerobics exercises.

Dilemma

Sue wants to determine the alternative methods of dealing with this liability risk so that she can select the most appropriate method. What are the alternative methods for dealing with this risk? Which alternative would you recommend for CHC?

Solution

There are three alternative methods of dealing with the liability risk. One alternative is to eliminate the risk by eliminating the operations that cause the risk. Second, Sue could shift the risk to an insurance company by purchasing liability insurance. Third, Sue could assume the risk by setting up an insurance fund at CHC.

The first method is not feasible because it would require Sue to eliminate most of the services available to CHC members. The second method (purchasing insurance) can be expensive, but it may be necessary even if it means that CHC must borrow funds. Lenders want to make sure that CHC is insured because if it is not, it might be unable to repay its loans if it is liable for a customer's injury. The third method (self-insurance) can be a reasonable solution. However, most new firms like CHC tend to purchase insurance to avoid having to develop their own insurance fund. Firms that have been established for several years may consider self-insurance.

Additional Issues for Discussion

1 How can CHC possibly prevent injuries that result in liability claims?

2 Some firms are viewed as risky because they rely on one product (or service). Does CHC rely too heavily on one service? Is there any logical way that CHC could reduce this risk?

3 CHC currently relies on Sue Kramer (the president) for all of its key business decisions. How could CHC hedge against losses that would occur if Sue became ill?

SUMMARY

1 Business risk is the possibility that the firm's performance will be lower than expected because of its exposure to specific conditions. Risk management involves identifying the risk to which a business is exposed and protecting against that risk. The common ways to protect against risk are to:

▶ eliminate the risk (by eliminating the business operations that caused the risk),

▶ shift the risk (by purchasing insurance), or

▶ assume the risk (by creating self-insurance).

2 Firms are exposed to economic conditions, such as the national and global economies and interest rate movements. Firms can reduce their exposure to the economic environment by producing a variety of products that have different sensitivities to economic conditions.

3 Firms are exposed to risk because of limited funding; reliance on one product, customer, supplier, or key employee; and exposure to property, liability, and employee compensation losses. Firms that are exposed to risk because of reliance on a single supplier, customer, or key employee can reduce their risk by diversifying among suppliers and customers and by diversifying the key managerial responsibilities among employees. Firms can protect against the risk of property or liability losses by purchasing insurance.

4 Firms are exposed to potential lawsuits by customers or employees. They can reduce this risk by ensuring that their products are safe and that working conditions are safe.

5 If a firm is unable to make its payment to creditors, it may consider three informal remedies. First, it can ask creditors to allow an extension, which provides additional time for the firm to cover its payments. Second, it could negotiate a composition agreement, in which it pays creditors a portion of what they are owed. Third, it could liquidate its assets and distribute the proceeds to its creditors.

In addition to these informal remedies, the firm may also consider formal remedies such as liquidation or reorganization through the court system.

KEY TERMS

actuaries *556*
business risk *558*
casualty insurance *556*
composition *571*
decreasing term insurance *562*
derivative instruments *560*

extension *570*
interest rate swap *560*
liability losses *564*
liquidation value *571*
private liquidation *571*
property insurance *556*

property losses *563*
self-insurance *556*
term insurance *562*
universal life insurance *562*
whole-life insurance *562*

REVIEW QUESTIONS

1 Compare the methods a firm could use to protect itself against risk.

2 For insurance purposes, why would a firm eliminate a product from its product line?

3 Discuss a derivative instrument a firm could utilize when it is adversely affected by rising interest rates.

4 Identify specific characteristics of a firm's operations that could expose it to risk.

5 Discuss the different types of life insurance a business can purchase for its key employees.

6 Discuss how a firm can hedge against liability losses.

7 Define product liability for a firm that is attempting to compete in the marketplace. Can the firm hedge against this risk?

8 How can risk managers prevent "nuisance lawsuits" from being filed against their firms?

9 Discuss alternative informal remedies a business should consider before selling its assets to pay creditors and claiming formal bankruptcy.

10 Discuss the advantages of an informal bankruptcy proceeding versus a formal proceeding.

DISCUSSION QUESTIONS

1 Assume that you are a financial manager and your firm is faced with possible bankruptcy. You are in charge of negotiating credit arrangements with your suppliers. Discuss what could be arranged.

2 Why would anyone consider life insurance for a business partner?

After all, it is simply an expense. Defend your answer.

3 How could a firm use the Internet and technology to manage its risk?

4 Assume that you are an entrepreneur and your business has only one customer, the federal government. What are the various types of business risks to which your firm is subjected?

5 Assume that you are a business entrepreneur of a rollerblade manufacturing company. To what extent could you use risk elimination, risk shifting, and risk assumption in your risk management program?

INVESTING IN THE STOCK OF A BUSINESS

Using the annual report of the firm in which you would like to invest, complete the following:

1 Is the firm highly exposed to economic or industry conditions? Has it used any strategies to reduce its exposure to that risk?

2 Is the firm highly exposed to the liability risk that customers or employees may sue the firm? Has it used any strategies to reduce its exposure to that risk? Is it currently being sued by customers, employees, or the government? (Review the notes within the section called "Litigation" or "Contingent Liabilities" near the firm's financial statements.)

3 Explain how the business uses technology to manage risk. For example, does it use the Internet to research the types of risk it is exposed to? Does it use the Internet to obtain insurance quotations?

4 Go to **http://hoovers.com** and locate the NEWS SEARCH. Type in the name of the firm in the space provided, and review the recent news stories about the firm. Summarize any (at least one) recent news story about the firm that applies to one or more of the key concepts within this chapter.

CASE   THE DECISION TO INSURE A BUSINESS

Bruce Leonard and David Mikan own and operate Master Lawncare, located in Cleveland, Ohio. The lawn care business has grown significantly over the years. An insurance agent has called on the partners to recommend an insurance plan. The partners want to protect their investment in case anything happens to either of them. They currently have no insurance on either partner or on the business operations. The partners viewed insurance as a cost of operations with very little benefit to the business. Also, they did not have adequate funds to purchase insurance.

This business concentrates on one major commercial account that keeps the crew busy all summer long landscaping flower gardens, pruning shrubs and trees, and mowing grass. The operation has had few customer-related problems; however, some customers have complained recently about the quality of the mowing and trimming services provided by employees.

Another concern the partners have is with their employees. Several accidents have occurred in the handling of equipment, especially when mowing grass. David states, "We are going to get sued some day by our own employees, and the employees will own this company."

QUESTIONS

1 Is Master Lawncare subject to risk? If so, how can the risk be eliminated?

2 What are the business risks to which this partnership is exposed?

3 Recommend an insurance plan to Bruce and David. Be specific on the types of insurance you would recommend.

4 Should the partnership consider self-insuring its business, even if it needs its funds to support its growth?

VIDEO CASE RISK MANAGEMENT BY JIAN

JIAN created the BizPlan Builder and other software that is used by entrepreneurs to run their businesses. It has focused on creating software that can be used to help manage a business. JIAN attempts to control its risk when creating new products. First, it determines whether there is a niche for the product that it is considering. Second, it tries to focus on creating products that will have no competition. Third, it attempts to determine the potential benefits (cash inflows) and expenses (cash outflows) associated with a new product. JIAN's accounting department plays an important role in providing data that can be used to estimate cash inflows and cash outflows. The company attempts to forecast potential sales of the new product and then determines whether the forecasted sales volume is sufficient to recover the expenses that would be incurred. As with any new product created by any firm, JIAN faces the risk that a new product will not sell enough units to recover the expenses incurred.

QUESTIONS

1 How is JIAN exposed to industry conditions?

2 Some firms are exposed to a high level of risk because they rely solely on one product or on one large customer. Is JIAN highly exposed to this type of risk?

3 Some firms are exposed to a high level of risk because of their exposure to economic conditions. Is JIAN highly exposed to this type of risk?

INTERNET APPLICATIONS

http://www.insurance-online-texas.com/index.htm

Locate insurance quotations for two types of insurance policies. Do you think these quotes are competitive? Why or why not? Discuss some of the other services provided on this website. Do you find these services useful? Overall, how do you think this website could be improved? Be specific.

THE *Coca-Cola* COMPANY ANNUAL REPORT PROJECT

Questions for the current year's annual report are available on the text website at **http://madura_ intro_bus.swcollege.com**.

The following questions apply concepts learned in this chapter to The Coca-Cola Company. Go to The Coca-Cola Company website (**http://www.cocacola.com**) and find the index for the 1999 annual report.

QUESTIONS

1 What type of insurance would protect the manufacturing facilities of The Coca-Cola Company? What other types of insurance might The Coca-Cola Company purchase to reduce its exposure to various types of risk?

2 Click on "Financial Risk Management." Why does The Coca-Cola Company use derivative financial instruments? Does the company ever use derivative financial instruments for trading purposes?

3 Study the "Selected Market Results" section. What type of risk might The Coca-Cola Company expose itself to when it builds plants outside the United States? How might it reduce this risk?

4 In recent years, foreign economies have experienced some turmoil. Do you think The Coca-Cola Company's global presence will help the company reduce the negative impact from these countries' economies? Why?

5 Go to **http://hoovers.com** and locate the NEWS SEARCH. Type in The Coca-Cola Company in the space provided, and review the recent news stories about the firm. Summarize any (at least one) recent news story about The Coca-Cola Company that applies one or more of the key concepts within this chapter of the text.

IN-TEXT STUDY GUIDE

Answers are in an appendix at the back of the book.

TRUE OR FALSE

1 From the perspective of the insured policyholder, term life insurance is in effect until death or as long as premiums are promptly paid.

2 Effective risk management techniques can reduce a firm's exposure to employee compensation claims.

3 Firms in highly competitive industries are subject to a higher degree of risk than firms in less competitive industries.

4 Firms that produce only one type of product are subject to less risk than firms that produce a diversified mix of products.

5 The only effective way to deal with risk is to completely eliminate the factors that contribute to the risk.

6 Creditors are most likely to grant an extension if they believe a firm's financial problems are permanent.

7 Reorganization is a formal remedy for business failure.

8 Under Internal Revenue Service rules, the value of the savings reflected on a universal life insurance policy cannot exceed the policy's death benefits.

9 Firms can usually eliminate their exposure to liability losses by simply following federal and state regulations dealing with product safety and worker safety.

10 Self-insurance represents life insurance for one individual.

MULTIPLE CHOICE

11 A(n) _____ specifies that a firm that is unable to meet all its financial obligations will provide its creditors with a portion of what they are owed.
a) indemnity agreement
b) surety bond
c) composition agreement
d) indenture agreement
e) consolidation bond

12 A firm may be subject to _____ losses if its actions cause damage to others or their property.
a) coincidental   d) second party
b) liability   e) spillover
c) incidental

13 All of the following are examples of firm-specific characteristics that contribute to business risk except:
a) changes in interest rates.
b) reliance on one product.
c) reliance on one supplier.

d) property losses.
e) liability losses.

14 The value of _____ is based on the values of other securities, indexes, or interest rates.
a) derivative instruments
b) spot market assets
c) term insurance
d) flood insurance
e) risk-free funds

15 _____ would be classified as a formal remedy for business failure.
a) An extension agreement
b) Liquidation under bankruptcy
c) A composition agreement
d) Purchase of liability insurance
e) Private liquidation

16 The common ways a firm can protect against risk are to eliminate the risk, assume the risk, or:
a) acquire more risk.
b) redefine the risk.
c) hide the risk from shareholders.
d) ignore the risk.
e) shift the risk by purchasing insurance.

17 Derivative instruments are useful to firms that want to:
a) hedge against risk resulting from economic conditions.
b) liquidate their assets in the event of business failure.
c) reorganize their business to take advantage of new market opportunities.
d) insure against liability losses.
e) sell more shares of stock.

18 When firms believe the casualty insurance premiums charged by insurance companies are higher than the losses they are likely to suffer from casualty claims, they may decide to deal with this type of risk by:
a) using an interest rate swap.
b) creating a fund for self-insurance against future losses.
c) relying more on equity financing.
d) setting up an indenture agreement to avoid responsibility for casualty losses.
e) incurring the legal expenses needed to file a loss exemption form with the local government.

19 _____ insurance is a type of life insurance that remains in effect until death as long as the premiums are promptly paid.
a) Term-life   d) Whole-life
b) Decreasing term-life   e) Mutual-term life
c) Permanent-life

20 _____ insurance protects a firm from lia-

bility for harm to others as a result of product failure or accidents.
a) Term
b) Universal
c) Property
d) Composition
e) Casualty

21 Under a(n) _____ agreement, creditors agree to give a firm more time to generate the necessary cash to cover its debts.
a) no-fault
b) extension
c) composition
d) formal bankruptcy
e) Chapter 11 bankruptcy

22 The two types of insurance offered by the government are:
a) OASDHI and unemployment insurance.
b) life and health insurance.
c) property and casualty insurance.
d) product and performance insurance.
e) term and group insurance.

23 A(n) _____ is a popular form of derivative instrument.
a) term-life policy
b) self-insurance fund
c) extension agreement
d) composition agreement
e) interest rate swap

24 In recent years, the Occupational Safety and Health Administration has focused on:
a) reducing air pollution in the workplace.
b) making sure that firms carry adequate liability insurance.
c) encouraging firms to give their employees better medical care.
d) reducing the possibility of cumulative trauma disorders.
e) revising workers' compensation laws to make sure each state has the same coverage.

25 The amount of funds that would be received if all of a firm's assets were sold off is called its:
a) equity position.
b) net worth.
c) marginal revenue.
d) breakeven value.
e) liquidation value.

26 Universal life insurance is similar to whole-life in that both:
a) are cheaper than term life insurance.
b) cover employees only for periods of ten years or less.
c) build up a cash value.
d) pay the beneficiary only a fraction of the stated coverage if the insured dies less than five years after taking out the policy.
e) invest any premiums received into a "sinking fund."

27 Exposure to lawsuits by customers and employees:

a) has never been a serious problem for most firms, though excessive media attention sometimes makes it seem as though it is.
b) can be eliminated almost completely if a firm simply treats its employees and customers properly.
c) is a problem faced by many large firms.
d) is a serious problem for firms that operate in global markets but not much of a problem for firms operating only in the United States.
e) tends to be very similar regardless of where a firm operates.

28 Which of the following firms is most likely to face the greatest risk from a rise in interest rates?
a) an automobile manufacturer
b) a newspaper publisher
c) the owner of a small shoe repair shop
d) the operator of a barber shop
e) a sole proprietor who operates an income tax preparation service

29 One way for a firm to reduce its sensitivity to economic conditions is to:
a) concentrate authority in the hands of experienced managers.
b) buy liability insurance.
c) avoid the use of any derivative instruments.
d) diversify its product mix.
e) focus most of its efforts on one or two key global markets rather than on the domestic market for its products.

30 _____ are employed by insurance companies to forecast the percentage of customers that will experience a particular outcome that is being insured.
a) Sales agents
b) Actuaries
c) Accountants
d) Brokers
e) Assayers

31 A(n) _____ is a derivative instrument in which firms substitute fixed interest payments for payments that adjust to movements in interest rates.
a) fixed exchange agreement
b) composition agreement
c) bond indenture
d) interest rate swap
e) whole-life policy

32 _____ life insurance has lower premiums than other forms of life insurance, but it does not build up a cash value.
a) Whole-life
b) Universal life
c) Term
d) General purpose
e) Pure coverage

33 A firm's business risk is dependent on its exposure to the economic environment, which includes industry conditions, the national economy, and:

a) actuaries.
b) insurance agents.
c) global economies.
d) casualty insurance agents.
e) universal insurance agents.

34 _____ involves identifying a firm's exposure to risk and protecting against that exposure.
a) Risk management
b) Accounting
c) Marketing
d) Human resource management
e) Capital budgeting

35 When creditors informally request that a firm that is unable to meet its obligations sell off its assets without going through formal bankruptcy proceedings, they are asking the failing firm to:
a) violate the law.
b) enter into a composition agreement.
c) become a limited liability company.
d) become a subsidiary firm.
e) go through a private liquidation.

The Learning
Goals of this
chapter are to:

1 Explain how a firm's value is determined.

2 Summarize the key business decisions and explain how they affect the firm's value.

3 Illustrate how one particular firm (IBM) recently made several key business decisions to increase its value.

CHAPTER 21

Synthesis of Business Functions

anagers of a firm commonly make management, marketing, and finance decisions. These managers must recognize how their decisions may affect a firm's revenue or expenses and therefore its value.

To illustrate how the management, marketing, and finance decisions affect the value of the business, consider the case of the firm Yahoo! as an example. It carefully recruits its employees and communicates each employee's role and contribution in creating a service. Consequently, the firm has been very successful. Yahoo! focuses not only on the development of its employees but also on its marketing and its financing. It uses marketing to promote its services. It also uses financial management to determine

how it should obtain the funds needed to expand its business. The amount of financing needed by Yahoo! is dependent on the cost of providing its services.

Yahoo! must make several business decisions that are related. How many employees are needed to run the organization? What methods should it use to motivate its employees? What type of advertising should it use to promote its services? What other methods should it use beyond advertising to promote its services? How much money will be needed to finance the cost of producing

its services? Will its retained earnings be sufficient to cover its expenses?

The first two questions relate to the management function, the next two questions to the marketing function, and the last two questions to the finance function. This chapter provides a synthesis of business functions, which will illustrate how business decisions are integrated. That is, the proper decision within one business function is dependent on the decisions within the other business functions.

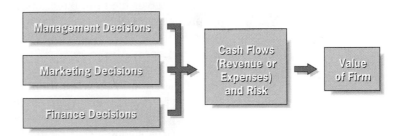

Valuation of a Business

Explain how a firm's value is determined.

Recall that the value of a project is determined by estimating the present value of its expected future cash flows. A firm that assesses a new project is willing to invest in it if the present value of future cash flows exceeds the initial outlay that is needed to invest in the project. When investors consider investing in a firm, they can use the same logic. A firm's value is equal to the present value of its future cash flows. The firm's cash flow in any particular period is equal to its cash inflows minus the cash outflows.

Most of the firm's cash inflows result from its sales. Most of its cash outflows typically result from payment of expenses or taxes. If the payments a firm receives from sales and uses to cover expenses are made with cash, its cash flows normally reflect its earnings (after taxes). Thus, the firm's value is highly influenced by its expected future earnings. The cash flows of a firm may also be affected by some other factors, but earnings are typically the driving force.

How Business Decisions Affect the Firm's Value

2 Summarize the key business decisions and explain how they affect the firm's value.

Managers should manage the firm with the objective of maximizing its value. This objective is in the best interests of the owners who have invested their funds in the firm. Since the value of a firm is the present value of its future cash flows, managers should make decisions that increase these future cash flows.

Most business decisions that are intended to increase the firm's value can be classified as management, marketing, and finance functions. The main types of these decisions have been described throughout the text. When these decisions result in higher cash flows, they enhance the value of the firm. A summary of those decisions is provided next, with an emphasis on how each decision can enhance the firm's value.

Management Decisions

Management is the means by which the firm uses employees and other resources (such as machinery). Some of the key management decisions are focused on strategic planning, determining the organizational structure, determining the production process, and motivating employees.

Strategic Planning Many decisions are based on the firm's strategic plan, which identifies the opportunities and direction of the firm's business. That is, the means by which a firm utilizes its employees and other resources are dependent on the opportunities that exist and the types of business projects that the firm implements. Proper planning can capitalize on opportunities that result in higher revenue or in lower production costs for the firm. Either result can improve earnings, which should increase the present value of the firm's future cash flows.

A firm that develops a more effective strategic plan has more potential to enhance its value. Consider two computer firms that were successful in the United States during the early 1990s but have given up market share to new competitors in recent years. One of these firms may maintain its old strategic plan of simply trying to provide a specific type of computer to U.S. customers. The other firm may revise its strategic plan to change the product it offers and the geographic market that it serves. It may offer a variety of computers to accommodate customers' various needs. It may also develop software packages to complement its computers. Furthermore, it may attempt to serve foreign markets as well. This revised strategic plan gives the firm more ways to maintain or increase its market share.

Organizational Structure An important management decision is the organizational structure, which identifies job descriptions for each job position and the relationships among those positions. The organizational structure determines the manner by which human resources are allocated to various tasks. Organizational structure is not a one-time decision, as the structure must be revised when the firm's strategic plan changes. A properly developed organizational structure can result in a low level of operating expenses.

In recent years, many firms have revised their organizational structures to make more efficient use of human resources. Specifically, firms downsized their workforce and delegated more responsibilities to employees whose job positions were not eliminated. The downsizing was commonly intended to achieve the same level of production at a lower cost. Consequently, firms were able to reduce their salary expenses, which enhanced their values and resulted in higher cash flows.

Production Process A firm develops a production process to produce its products or services. The process defines how human resources are combined with other resources (such as the firm's plant and machinery) to produce the products or services.

Plant Site Decision An important production decision is the selection of the plant site. This decision will determine the land cost. It will also determine the costs of hiring human resources and of transporting products.

Although managers want to select a plant site in an area where costs are low, they must also consider how revenue might be affected. If products can easily be transported, the optimal site may be based in a low-cost location because the products could be sent to other locations where demand is strong. However, some locations that have a low land cost may not have an adequate supply of human resources.

Since the plant site decision can have a major impact on the firm's costs and possibly even its revenue, it can affect the firm's value. A large plant site can achieve a high production volume, but it also results in high expenses. The plant site is not a onetime decision because it is reassessed whenever the firm experiences substantial growth or plans to produce new products.

Design and Layout Decisions The design and layout decisions have a significant impact on production costs. The design represents the size and structure of the plant, while the layout is the manner in which the machinery and equipment are arranged within the plant. In recent years, many firms have begun to use flexible manufacturing in which the layout is easily adjusted to accommodate a revision in the production process. Ideally, the layout can also be easily adjusted to accommodate a revision in the types of products produced. This allows the firm to revise its product line without incurring the costs of moving to a new site.

The plant site decision can affect the cost of labor hired and the cost of transporting materials to the plant. The site should be determined after factoring in the amount of products needed to be produced per week, along with the amount of financing available.

Another recent strategy used by firms is to reduce their layout space in response to the downsizing of their workforce. Consequently, these firms reduced not only their salary expenses but also their expenses resulting from renting or owning work space. This strategy reduced expenses further, resulting in larger cash flows and therefore higher firm values.

Quality Decisions   The quality of the product that the firm produces is dependent on the production process used and the commitment of employees to quality. The higher the quality, the higher the level of customer satisfaction, which affects the product's reputation. Thus, the demand for a product is dependent on its quality and on the production process used. In an effort to increase the amount of referrals and repeat buyers, firms have recently begun to pay more attention to quality and customer satisfaction.

The emphasis on ensuring quality throughout the entire production process is referred to as total quality management (TQM). Although TQM is used in various ways, it typically involves defining a desired quality level, developing a production process that can achieve that quality level, and controlling the quality level over time. TQM has been especially successful when employees have been allowed to help develop the production process intended to achieve the desired quality level. It has also been successful when employee teams have been assigned to monitor and control quality. Since higher quality can lead to higher customer satisfaction, it results in higher sales and therefore in higher cash flows to the firm.

Other Decisions Related to the Production Process   Firms may also improve the production process through the use of technology. They have automated many parts of the production process so that tasks are performed by machines without the help of human resources.

A final method of improving the production process is to produce in large volume so that economies of scale can be realized. Products that have a relatively high level of fixed costs can benefit from economies of scale.

Motivating Employees   Employees tend to be more satisfied with their jobs if they are provided (1) compensation that is aligned with their performance, (2) job security,

The company Excite! recognizes that motivation for its employees may help retain them and increase the company's performance.

(3) a flexible work schedule, and (4) employee involvement programs. Firms have been unable to offer job security, as they continually attempt to reduce their operating expenses by downsizing their workforce. However, they have begun to offer compensation that is tied to employee performance, more flexible work schedules, and more employee involvement programs. To the extent that job satisfaction can motivate employees to improve their performance, firms may be able to achieve a higher production level by providing greater job satisfaction. Therefore, they may be able to increase cash flows (lower production costs per employee) and increase their value as a result of motivating human resources.

Managing Employees Beyond motivation, firms have some control over how well their employees perform. First, they have control at the hiring stage. Proper recruiting and screening can result in the selection of well-qualified employees. Firms can also control how well their employees perform by developing their skills. Specifically, firms focus on developing employees' technical, decision-making, customer service, safety, and human relations skills. Firms can also control employee performance by establishing proper procedures for evaluation. Employees should be informed about the criteria that are used to evaluate their performance and the weight assigned to each criterion. Proper management of human resources can help firms achieve a high level of production, which may enhance their value.

BUSINESS ONLINE

Information on Management Strategies

http://www.ioma.com/

THE INSTITUTE OF MANAGEMENT & ADMINISTRATION (IOMA) ALLOWS USERS of its website to access free samples of its published business management newsletters. The site draws managers and department heads with a full range of free services and information, enticing visitors to subscribe. Websites such as this aid corporations in increasing shareholder wealth.

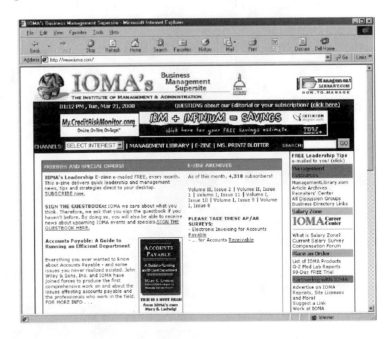

Marketing Decisions

Each firm uses a marketing mix, which is the combination of its product, pricing, distribution, and promotion strategies used to sell products and services.

Product Strategies The success of a firm is highly influenced by the product that it is attempting to sell. Once a firm determines the product (or product line) that it will offer, it must identify its target market so that it can determine the profile of the customers that it must attract. As time passes, firms may attempt to revise their existing products so that they can differentiate their products from those of competitors. To create new products, they may also invest in research and development. In general, strategies to create or improve products can enhance the firm's revenue, which can result in higher cash flows and therefore in a higher firm value.

Pricing Strategies The revenue that a firm generates is directly related to the price charged for its product. The pricing decision can be influenced by the production cost and by competitor prices. Pricing a product too high can limit the quantity that consumers demand, but pricing a product too low may not allow for sufficient profits. Proper pricing decisions can increase future cash flows (higher revenue) and can therefore increase the firm's value.

Distribution Strategies The distribution channel determines the path of a product from the producer to the consumer. It determines the different locations where the product will be available. The firm's distribution strategies will influence the amount of customers that the product reaches. It may also affect the costs of delivering a product from the point of production to the consumer. Therefore, proper distribution strategies can enhance the firm's future cash flows.

SMALL BUSINESS SURVEY

What Are the Major Concerns of Small Businesses?

A survey of small businesses was conducted to determine their major concerns. The businesses were segmented into two groups: those with annual sales of less than $3 million and those with annual sales of more than $3 million. The following table shows the percentage of firms in each group that identified various problems as a serious concern:

Problem	Firms with Less Than $3 Million in Sales	Firms with More Than $3 Million in Sales
Inadequate planning	58%	33%
Inadequate financing	48%	21%
Inadequate managerial skills of some employees in key positions	46%	23%
Not prepared for economic downturns	37%	26%
Inability to respond to market changes	30%	31%
Environmental regulations	29%	38%
Nonenvironmental regulations	18%	22%
Litigation (such as defending against lawsuits)	15%	21%
Employee theft or fraud	13%	11%
Foreign competition	11%	24%

Many of the major concerns detected by this survey have been discussed in this text. Some of the concerns reflect exposure to economic conditions (economic downturns), industry conditions (regulations), and global conditions (foreign competition). Other concerns focus on the firm's management (planning), marketing (response to market changes), and financing.

Promotion Strategies Firms use promotion strategies to increase the acceptance of products through special deals, advertising, and publicity. They commonly use promotions to supplement their product, pricing, and distribution strategies. New products are promoted to introduce them to potential customers. In addition, many popular products are promoted to protect their image and retain their market share. Effective promotion strategies enhance cash flows (by increasing revenue) and can therefore enhance the firm's value.

Finance Decisions

The finance function determines how the firm obtains and invests funds, as summarized next.

Financing Strategies Firms use financing strategies to obtain the amount and type of financing desired. They may borrow from various financial institutions, such as commercial banks, finance companies, or savings institutions. Alternatively, if they have a national reputation and need a large amount of funds, they may issue bonds.

If firms prefer to obtain equity financing instead of debt financing, they may attempt to obtain funds from a venture capital firm. Alternatively, if they need a large amount of funds, they may issue stock. Proper financing strategies can enable the firm to obtain funds at a low cost and can therefore increase the firm's value.

Business Investment Strategies Firms use investing strategies to allocate their funds across their business operations. They use capital budgeting to determine whether potential projects are feasible and should be implemented. For a project to be feasible, the present value of its cash flows must exceed its initial outlay. The discount rate used to discount future cash flows is based on the firm's cost of funds used to support the project. If the firm can obtain funds for the project at a relatively low cost, the project has a better chance of being considered feasible. Since many projects require substantial funding and are irreversible, capital budgeting decisions can have a major impact on the value of the firm.

BUSINESS ONLINE

Stock Market Information Online

http://www.amex.com/

THE WEBSITES OF ORGANIZED STOCK EXCHANGES, SUCH AS THE AMERICAN Stock Exchange (AMEX), provide a variety of information, including recent trends in the stock market and individual stock quotations. Websites such as this help investors make investment decisions and allow corporations to monitor their stock's performance almost continuously.

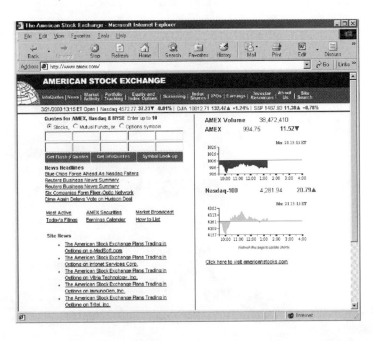

Summary of Business Strategies

The most common types of business strategies are summarized in Exhibit 21.1. Notice from this exhibit that the primary impact of most management strategies is on the firm's cash outflows because these strategies determine the cost of utilizing human resources and other resources. Conversely, the primary impact of most marketing strategies is on the firm's cash inflows because these strategies determine the amount of revenue generated.

D**ELL** COMPUTER'S FORMULA FOR SUCCESS

Dell Computer's strategic decisions (such as global expansion, focus on customers, and focus on the Internet) discussed throughout the text have been very successful in increasing Dell's value. A recent business publication observed that Dell Computer was the best-performing stock (up 68,400 percent since January 2, 1990) during the best bull market of all time. Thus, Dell Computer's forward-looking approach and its various management, marketing, financing, and investment decisions have been very successful in increasing shareholder wealth.

Relationships among Business Strategies

Although the management, marketing, and finance decisions are distinctly different, they are all related. Thus, the management decisions can be determined only after considering marketing information, and marketing decisions can be determined only after considering management information. Finance decisions are dependent on management and marketing information.

Exhibit 21.1

Summary of Key Business Functions

	Primary Impact of Strategy Decision Is on:	
	Cash Inflows	**Cash Outflows**
Type of Management Strategy		
Planning	✓	✓
Organizational structure		✓
Plant site		✓
Production design		✓
Production layout		✓
Production quality	✓	✓
Motivating employees		✓
Managing employees		✓
Type of Marketing Strategy		
Product strategies	✓	
Pricing strategies	✓	
Distribution strategies	✓	
Promotion strategies	✓	
Type of Finance Strategy		
Financing strategies		✓
Investment strategies	✓	

Relationship between Organizational Structure and Production

To illustrate how the management, marketing, and finance decisions are related, consider a firm that produces office desks and distributes them to various retail office furniture outlets. The organizational structure will be partially dependent on the product mix (a marketing decision). If the firm diversifies its product line to include office lamps, file cabinets, and bookcases, its organizational structure will have to specify who is assigned to produce and manage these other products. The plant site selected must be large enough, and the firm's design and layout must be flexible enough, to allow for the production of these other products.

Relationship between Pricing and Production Strategies

The firm's plant site, design, and layout decisions are also influenced by the pricing of the office furniture (another marketing decision). If the pricing strategy is to price the furniture high, the sales volume will be smaller. The firm's plant site, design, and layout should allow for sufficient (but not excessive) work space to achieve the relatively low production level needed to accommodate the expected sales volume.

If the firm prices its office furniture more competitively, it will anticipate a much larger sales volume. In this case, it would use a plant site, design, and layout to achieve a much larger level of production. Most firms determine the type of target market they wish to pursue and then implement a pricing strategy before deciding on the plant's site, design, and layout. That is, the pricing strategy dictates the level of production needed, which influences the plant site, design, and layout.

Relationship between Pricing and Distribution Strategies

The firm's pricing strategy also influences its distribution strategy. If the pricing strategy is intended to focus only on wealthy customers, the office furniture may be distributed exclusively to upscale outlets. If the prices are set lower to attract a wide variety of customers, however, the furniture will be distributed across many outlets to achieve broad coverage.

Just as pricing can influence distribution, distribution can influence pricing. When firms began to offer products directly to consumers over the Internet instead of through retail stores, the firms were able to reduce the prices charged because they avoided any intermediaries.

Relationship between Pricing and Promotion Strategies

The firm's promotion strategies will also be affected by the pricing strategy. If the pricing strategy is intended to focus only on wealthy customers, the promotions will be targeted exclusively toward those customers. If the prices are set lower to attract a wide variety of customers, however, the promotions will be targeted to cover a much broader group of potential customers.

The amount of funds spent on promotion will influence the firm's sales volume and therefore the production level. Consequently, the plant site, design, and layout decisions must consider the amount of promotion planned by the firm.

Relationship between Pricing and Financing Strategies

The firm's finance decisions will be dependent on its pricing decisions. If the firm is using a pricing strategy that will result in a relatively low level of sales (and therefore a low level of production), it will need a small amount of funds to support that production level. If the firm uses a pricing strategy that will result in a high level of sales (and therefore a high level of production), however, it will need a much larger amount of funds to support that production level. If the firm needs a relatively small amount of funds, it may decide to borrow from a commercial bank. If it needs a large amount of funds, it may issue bonds. It may also need to consider using some equity financing if the amount of funds needed would exceed its debt capacity.

GLOBAL BUSINESS

Integrating Business Functions on a Global Basis

U.S. FIRMS THAT CONDUCT INTERNATIONAL BUSINESS MUST APPLY THEIR business strategies in a global environment. As explained in many chapters, when U.S. firms apply a particular business function (such as managing resources, marketing, or financing) to international business, they must consider the unique characteristics of the foreign country. The business functions that are applied to a particular foreign country are integrated. That is, the international management of resources is integrated with the international marketing strategies and financing strategies.

To recognize how these functions are integrated, consider the case of IBM, which generates more than 50 percent of its sales in foreign countries. IBM produces and sells a variety of computer products in numerous foreign countries. Its production decision of how much to produce in a particular country is influenced by input from the marketing function on the expected demand for each product in that area. The number of employees to be hired for production in a specific country is also dependent on the expected demand for IBM's products in that country. The demand for IBM's products within a particular country is partially affected by the degree to which the products are promoted there. The marketing function can consider this information when forecasting the demand for various products in a country. Because of the large demand for its products in Europe, IBM's European production facilities are massive. IBM's Latin American facilities are not as large because the demand for its products in Latin America is much smaller than in Europe.

IBM's decisions regarding the design of various products are influenced by the marketing research that obtains feedback from customers who have purchased IBM's products or from surveys of prospective customers. The design of a product may be revised in a particular country if the marketing research determines that prospective customers in that country would prefer a revised design.

IBM's financing decisions for a particular country are based on the production and marketing decisions, which dictate the amount of funds that are needed to support the planned production volume and the marketing efforts. The larger IBM's anticipated production and marketing expenses in a particular country, the more funds will be needed to cover these expenses. IBM obtains substantial financing for its operations in Europe because it needs a large amount of funds to support its substantial European operations. It requires a smaller amount of funds in Latin America because its operations are not as large there.

Overall, this brief description of IBM illustrates how its management of resources, marketing, and financing decisions for any particular country are integrated, just as they are integrated when managing its operations in the United States.

Summary of Relationships among Business Strategies

Exhibit 21.2 shows the typical sequence of business functions. Many functions can be considered only after deciding on the type of product that will be produced and sold. The management and marketing decisions can be made after identifying the product (or product line). Once all management and marketing decisions are made, the amount of funds needed to support the business can be determined. The financing decision of how to finance the firm is dependent on how much funding is needed. All of these key business decisions will be periodically reassessed as the firm's business grows and its product line expands.

Although accounting and information systems are not illustrated in this exhibit, they are needed to make proper business decisions. The accounting function is used to monitor the firm's financial condition and assess the performance of previous man-

Exhibit 21.2

Common Sequence of
Business Functions

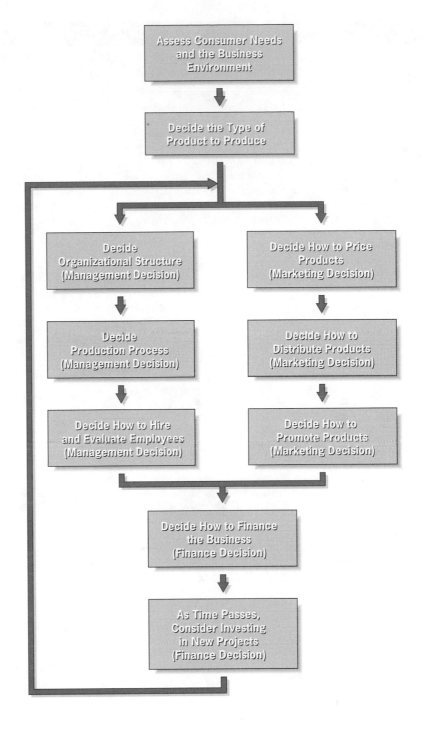

agement, marketing, and finance decisions. It can also be used to detect inefficient business operations so that they can be revised to reduce expenses.

Information systems are continually used to compile and analyze information about the firm's operations. The information can be used to help managers make proper management, marketing, and finance decisions.

3 Illustrate how one particular firm (IBM) recently made several key business decisions to increase its value.

Business Strategies Implemented by IBM

To illustrate how a single firm must consider all the business strategies described throughout the text, recent strategies by IBM are summarized next. The various statements by IBM that follow appeared in IBM's recent annual reports.

SPOTLIGHT ON TECHNOLOGY

Software That Integrates Business Activities

Ten years ago, an important software category for today's businesses didn't even exist. Workgroup software packages are designed to help coordinate the various functions of a business, offering new means of communication and new methods of sharing work and information. In the mid-1990s, their popularity skyrocketed in the business world. Because Lotus Development Corporation held the premier position in this software category with its Lotus Notes package, it was acquired by IBM in 1995.

A workgroup software package typically runs on a computer network. Rather than having a single, well-defined function, workgroup packages offer a collection of features that help users share work. Among these features are the following:

▶ *Electronic mail* Workgroup packages offer sophisticated electronic mail capabilities, allowing users to exchange messages and files across the network. Advanced packages also offer gateways to other mail systems, such as the Internet. As a result, users throughout the world can communicate.

▶ *Time management and scheduling* Packages provide the ability to create centralized company schedules and individual calendars, accessible by all who have the proper security.

▶ *Document sharing systems* Packages allow users to create databases that contain or point to documents they are working on. Using these systems allows remote users to collaborate on the same document.

▶ *External linkages* Most packages provide users with the ability to call into the system and conduct activities remotely (for example, from a hotel room). Some packages also incorporate fax handling capability, allowing faxes to be sent, received, and routed automatically by the package.

▶ *Discussions and conferencing* Packages provide online discussion capability, allowing users to conduct conferences between remote sites and keep a record of the proceedings.

▶ *Work flow processing* Packages can be programmed to allow specific work flows, such as the process of creating and sending a bill, to be completely automated. Once a user initiates a specific job, the software keeps track of each step in the process and, once a given step has been completed, automatically routes it to the next step.

▶ *Security* Packages allow users to designate security for documents, preventing unauthorized reading or editing.

Many managers believe that the real benefit of workgroup software is its use as a platform for further development. It is designed to be customized with add-on products, such as fax servers, video conferencing, project management software, and a host of industry-specific applications.

IBM's Value

Each annual report includes a letter to shareholders from Louis Gerstner, IBM's chief executive officer (CEO). One of the first comments in the letter focuses on the firm's value because the CEO recognizes its importance to shareholders:

" Our market value—probably the most important measure of our progress to investors—grew $69 billion. (It has grown by $146 billion since our major restructuring in 1993.) "

IBM's Mission and Strategic Plan

The primary mission of IBM is as follows:

" We strive to lead in the creation, development, and manufacture of the industry's most advanced information technologies, including computer systems, software, networking systems, storage devices, and microelectronics. "

Most firms do not change their mission very often, but they periodically revise their strategic plan in response to new business opportunities. IBM's strategic plan is as follows:

> *Consistent with the fundamental strategy that it put in place several years ago, the company is well positioned to build integrated e-business solutions. Services software and OEM technology that are required for this business will drive the growth in IBM's revenue and earnings.*

IBM's Social Responsibilities

IBM meets its social responsibilities by focusing on education and the environment, as explained next:

> *Through a $40 million grant program called Reinventing Education, we apply advanced information technologies . . . to improve learning . . . consumers identified IBM as the company that best exemplifies corporate citizenship.*

IBM's expenditures not only demonstrate its social responsibility but may also enable IBM to sell more computers to school systems.

IBM's Assessment of Its Industry

Since IBM is in the information technology industry, it closely monitors this industry and expects that its future performance will be influenced by industry trends:

> *We expect the overall information technology industry to grow at an annual rate of 10 percent, to $1.6 trillion by 2002. Of that, the e-business segment will grow to $600 billion and it will grow twice as fast as the industry overall.*

IBM's Penetration in Foreign Markets

IBM has penetrated numerous foreign markets where competition in the information technology industry is not as intense as in the United States:

> *IBM Global Services has grown in just eight years from a $4 billion to a $24 billion business, with better than 20 percent annual growth.*

IBM's Management Strategies

IBM's key management strategies include its organizational structure, the design and layout of its facilities, its production process, its total quality management, and its training and motivation of employees. Each of these strategies is discussed next.

IBM's Organizational Structure IBM recently revised its organizational structure in two ways. First, it has downsized its workforce. It has also reorganized to focus more on Internet business opportunities.

IBM's Design and Layout Since IBM downsized its workforce, it also revised its work space. It has consolidated work done by data centers and reduced office space worldwide.

IBM's Production Process IBM produces products in large volume to capitalize on economies of scale. Once it develops new technology, it produces and sells its new products and services in bulk. In this way, it spreads the cost over a large volume of units.

A key task in planning the production process is to forecast demand for products so that the volume of products produced is adequate to accommodate the demand. IBM attempts to use flexible production processes so that it can shift production to accommodate the demand.

IBM's Total Quality Management (TQM) Like most successful firms, IBM has increased its efforts to satisfy customers. Specifically, it has developed a variety of methods to enhance customer service. It has created methods over the phone and online by which customers can offer feedback and request assistance.

Training and Motivation of Employees IBM devotes substantial resources to training employees and to rewarding employees who achieve high performance.

IBM's Marketing Strategies

IBM's key marketing strategies include its products, pricing, and distribution. Each of these strategies is discussed next.

IBM's Product Strategies In the information technology industry, IBM and other firms continually assess their product strategies. IBM is commonly granted more than 2,000 patents per year. Improvements in technology have resulted in numerous new products and revisions of existing products.

❝ *IBM's position as the world's premier commercial center of technology is unchallenged. We will continue to invest in that.* **❞**

IBM's product strategies require input about the production cost involved from the marketing employees who recognize the preferences of customers and from the employees who will design the new products. The product strategies will also require input from finance employees regarding whether the design of the new product is financially feasible.

IBM's Pricing Strategies A review of IBM's main product lines suggests that its prices have been lowered in response to intense competition. Given the intense competition throughout the industry, IBM's strategy to reduce prices may have been intended to simply maintain market share. To increase market share, it attempts to capitalize on its technological advantages.

IBM's Distribution Strategies IBM delivers some products directly to the customer. Some of its customers are individuals, while others are businesses that need computer systems.

IBM's Finance Strategies

IBM's key finance strategies include obtaining funds (financing) and investing funds in its businesses, as discussed next.

IBM's Financing Strategies IBM obtains financing in the countries where it conducts its business:

    " The company issued debt to a diverse set of investors, including significant funding in the United States, Japan, and Europe. The funding has a wide range of maturities . . . "

In the mid-1990s, IBM increased its use of equity financing while relying less on debt financing. As a result, Moody's Rating Service upgraded its credit rating on some of IBM's debt. In the late 1990s, IBM increased its use of debt to capitalize on the low interest rates.

IBM's Business Investment Strategies IBM, like most firms, frequently invests in long-term projects as well as in short-term assets. Although IBM reduced its workspace in response to downsizing its workforce, it still uses large amounts of funds on capital expenditures such as new plants and offices. It also uses funds to repurchase some of its stock:

    " The company . . . [made] investments of approximately $20 billion in capital expenditures, research and development, strategic acquisitions, and the repurchase of stock. "

Conclusion about IBM's Strategies

Even with all the management, marketing, and finance decisions made to enhance shareholder wealth, IBM recognized that it must strive for continual improvement. Every year, IBM attempts to capitalize on new opportunities that result from new technology and also continually focuses on improving efficiency.

    " My colleagues are preoccupied not with our achievements of the recent past but with the vast prospects opening before us. "

To assess how IBM's strategies affected its performance, Exhibit 21.3 shows the income statement for 1992 (before many new strategies were implemented) and in 1999 (after these strategies were implemented). In 1999, the revenue was lower than

	Before Strategies Were Implemented (1992)	After Strategies Were Implemented (1999)
Revenue	$64,523	$87,548
Cost of goods sold	35,069	55,619
Gross profit	29,454	31,929
Operating expenses	37,693	20,002
Earnings before interest and taxes	(8,239)	11,927
Interest	787	727
Earnings before taxes	(9,026)	11,757
Taxes	(2,161)	4,045
Earnings after taxes	(6,865)	7,712
Note: Figures are in millions of dollars.		

in 1992 and the operating expenses were about $16 billion less. Consequently, earnings before interest and taxes were much better in 1999.

Exhibit 21.4 compares some of the key income statement items for IBM in 1992 and 1999. The large decline in operating expenses was primarily attributed to downsizing the workforce and the facilities.

Recall that ratio analysis is commonly used to assess a firm's liquidity, efficiency, and financial leverage. Exhibit 21.5 compares IBM's liquidity and efficiency over time to show how the company improved its financial condition as a result of implementing its strategies. The exhibit shows that IBM was able to maintain its liquidity while increasing its efficiency.

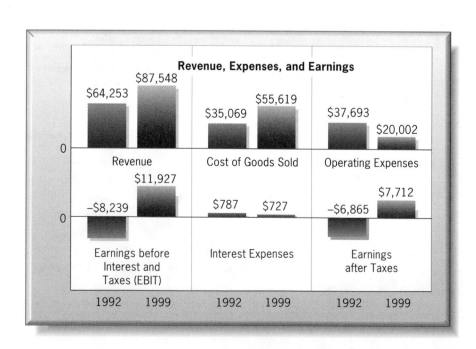

Exhibit 21.5

Change in IBM's Liquidity and
Efficiency

Note: Figures are in millions of
dollars.

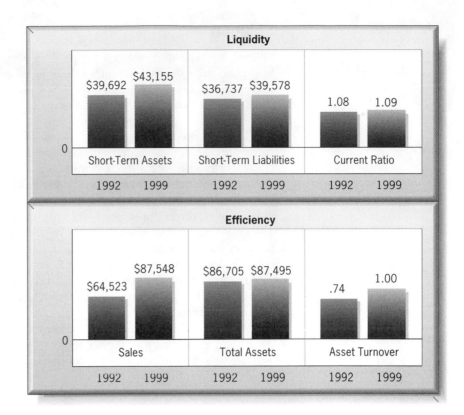

BUSINESS DILEMMA | **College Health Club**

Integrating
Business
Decisions at
College Health
Club

SUE KRAMER, PRESIDENT OF COLLEGE HEALTH CLUB (CHC), IS RECONSID-
ering the business plan she developed about one year ago when she established the
health club. Her key decisions were as follows:

Management Decisions

1 Site of the facilities

2 Design and layout of facilities

Marketing Decisions

1 Customer profile (target market)

2 Product (service) offered

3 Pricing

4 Promotion

Finance Decisions

1 Financing (how much funding?)

Dilemma

Sue is considering the possibility of establishing another health club and needs to assess how these decisions are related. Offer your input on how the health club site,
membership price, design and layout, and promotion strategies are influenced by the
target market.

Solution

The first decision to be made is the product or service to be offered. Sue is planning to expand her existing service (health club) by purchasing another health club in a nearby college town. The health club will be primarily targeted toward the college students in that town. Since the target market is college students, Sue would select a site that is near the local college in that town.

The next decision is pricing or determining the annual membership fee. This decision affects many other decisions because it influences the size of the membership (and therefore the size of the facilities needed). If a low price is charged, the health club will attract more members, and larger facilities will be needed.

The design and layout of the facilities could be determined based on the estimated number of customers (members) who may be using the health club at a given time. The design and layout should also allow for growth in membership over time. Sue does not want too much extra space, however, since she would incur higher expenses (whether leasing or purchasing facilities) for using extra space.

The promotion decisions will be intended to attract enough customers to fill up the facilities. The promotions will be targeted toward college students, who represent the target market.

While the pricing decision will affect the total revenue, the decisions about facilities and promotions will affect the total expenses. Sue can use her decisions to estimate the future cash flows resulting from a new health club and determine whether to establish the new club. If she decides to invest in a new health club, she can assess the cash flows to determine the amount of funds she would need to borrow.

Additional Issues for Discussion

1 Can Sue copy the business plan that she used for CHC when developing a business plan for a new health club near a different college campus?

2 Why might the estimated expenses of the new health club be very different from those of the existing health club?

3 Assume that Sue decides to establish a second health club that focuses on executives instead of college students. What types of business decisions would be affected?

SUMMARY

1 A firm's value is equal to the present value of its expected future cash flows. The cash flows in any period are the difference between cash inflows (revenue) and cash outflows (expenses or taxes).

2 When management, marketing, and finance decisions are implemented in a manner that will increase cash flows, these decisions can enhance the firm's value. Management decisions focus on using human and other resources to produce products or services. Thus, these decisions typically affect cash outflows (expenses). Marketing decisions tend to focus on increasing revenue and therefore affect cash inflows. Finance decisions can affect interest expenses due to financing and future cash flows due to the firm's business investments.

3 IBM applied several key business decisions to increase its value. Specifically, IBM used

▶ management decisions such as downsizing to reduce cash outflows,

▶ product and pricing decisions to increase (or at least maintain) cash inflows, and

▶ finance decisions to fund new investments intended to capitalize on new opportunities.

REVIEW QUESTIONS

1. How can a manager determine the value of a project?
2. Discuss total quality management (TQM) as it relates to production.
3. Explain how a firm can motivate employees and improve job satisfaction.
4. Explain how firms exert some control over employee performance.
5. Discuss how a firm's promotion strategy relates to its pricing strategy.
6. Why is it important for a business to obtain funds at a low cost?
7. Discuss the relationship among business strategies used in management today.
8. Explain why IBM obtains more financing for its European operations than for its Latin American operations.
9. Discuss how IBM has revised its organizational structure.
10. Discuss IBM's marketing strategy.

DISCUSSION QUESTIONS

1. Assume that you are a production manager. Why is TQM important for your firm to be competitive in your industry environment?
2. Assume that you are the promotional manager of a well-known consumer products firm. You have been given the assignment of developing a promotional strategy for a new soap powder that is about to be introduced. Discuss.
3. Discuss why a firm should select a target market before determining a pricing strategy or production capacity (or both).
4. Briefly summarize how a firm could use the Internet to maximize shareholder wealth (i.e., the firm's value).
5. Assume that you are a strategic planner for a computer manufacturer. Your mission is to develop a production strategy for your organization. Discuss.

INVESTING IN THE STOCK OF A BUSINESS

Using the annual report of the firm in which you would like to invest, complete the following:

1. Provide a brief summary of the firm's management strategies.
2. Provide a brief summary of the firm's marketing strategies.
3. Provide a brief summary of the firm's financing strategies.
4. Now that you have briefly summarized the firm's management, marketing, and finance strategies, explain how these strategies are related. For example, suggest how this firm's marketing decisions will af-

fect its production decisions. Also, explain how the amount of financing is dependent on its marketing and production decisions.
5. Explain how the business uses technology to maximize shareholder wealth. For example, does it use the Internet to research or promote any of its business functions?
6. Go to **http://hoovers.com** and locate the NEWS SEARCH. Type in the name of the firm in the space provided, and review the recent news stories about the firm. Summarize any (at least one) recent news story about the firm that applies to one or more of the key concepts within this chapter.

CASE INTEGRATED BUSINESS DECISIONS

Recall from the case in Chapter 1 that Mike Cieplak recently created an idea for a business. He wants to provide lessons on how to use the Internet and e-mail. He believes that this idea will work because many people (especially older people) do not know how to use the Internet. He will provide hands-on experience and show them how to conduct searches for information, buy products online, and use other features that are available. He

will also show people how to create a website. Mike produces a service, and he will try to produce this service by himself. If the demand for the service is more than he can handle, he will hire employees to produce more of the service for his customers.

Mike has decided that instead of renting space, he will initially travel to the customer's home so that he can provide the lessons on the customer's own computer.

Mike has also decided that he will advertise his service under "Services" in the classified ads of the local newspaper.

QUESTIONS

1 Mike initially plans to offer hands-on lessons to each customer individually. If he increases his marketing efforts, how might that decision affect the demand for his services, and how would that affect his decision of whether to hire employees?

2 If Mike increases his marketing efforts, how might that affect his decision about how much financing he needs for his business?

3 Assume that Mike considers renting some space so that he can produce more services at one time, instead of serving one customer at a time. He considers renting a large office where he can provide lessons for groups of forty customers at one time. The rent would be expensive but could be worthwhile if the demand for his service is large. He would incur the rental cost of his office regardless of the demand for his service. How is this production facility decision related to Mike's marketing decision? Do you think he might use a different marketing approach if he decides to rent the office space? Will this affect his financing decision?

VIDEO CASE SYNTHESIS OF BUSINESS STRATEGIES AT VERMONT TEDDY BEAR

Recall that Vermont Teddy Bear Company is a manufacturer of teddy bears. It is one of the fastest growing firms in the United States. It developed a management strategy, a marketing strategy, and a finance strategy that were designed to increase cash flows and therefore increase the value of the firm. It developed a marketing strategy that focused on bear grams, which worked like candy grams that are sent through the mail. Its marketing department decided that this direct selling to the customer was preferable to selling teddy bears through retail stores. It accepts orders directly from customers. It advertises directly to customers using well-known radio personalities. Its marketing department forecasts demand for its teddy bears, and its forecast influences the production decision. When advertising bear grams, it attempts to ensure that there will be sufficient production to satisfy the orders by customers. Thus, its production is tied to the amount of orders expected. If it produces an excessive amount, it is forced to finance the excessive inventory, which increases

financing costs. If it does not produce enough teddy bears, it experiences a shortage, which results in forgone sales. Thus, an accurate forecast can lead to a proper decision on the amount of teddy bears to produce, which increases the firm's value.

QUESTIONS

1 Explain how Vermont Teddy Bear's marketing strategy can affect its decision regarding how much to produce.

2 Explain how Vermont Teddy Bear's marketing and production decisions could affect its financing costs.

3 Explain how Vermont Teddy Bear's marketing and production decisions affect its value.

4 Explain how Vermont Teddy Bear's financing decisions may be affected by its marketing and production decisions.

INTERNET APPLICATIONS

http://www.amex.com

Identify some recent initial public offerings (IPOs) that occurred on the American Stock Exchange and summarize their financial performance since the offering. Also,

summarize the recent market activity. Have firms in the aggregate been performing well recently? Substantiate your answer. What companies recently had earnings surprises? Why do you think the surprises occurred?

THE *Coca-Cola* COMPANY ANNUAL REPORT PROJECT

Questions for the current year's annual report are available on the text website at **http://madura_ intro_bus.swcollege.com**.

The following questions apply concepts learned in this chapter to The Coca-Cola Company. Go to The Coca-

Cola Company website (**http://www.cocacola.com**) and find the index for the 1999 annual report.

QUESTIONS

1 Click on "North America Group." Considering that

Coke is promoted heavily in the United States, how do you think The Coca-Cola Company's marketing and manufacturing functions of Coke soft drink are related?

2 Click on "Financial Strategies." How do you think The Coca-Cola Company's plans for future manufacturing are related to its financing decisions?

3 Click on "Financial Strategies." How do you think The Coca-Cola Company's marketing and financing tasks are related?

4 Based on what you have learned throughout this annual report project, discuss how The Coca-Cola Company integrates marketing, finance, and pro-

duction to achieve the company's ultimate goal—maximizing shareholder value over time.

5 Click on "Financial Review." What is the mission of The Coca-Cola Company? What are the four key objectives of its comprehensive business strategy?

6 Go to **http://hoovers.com** and locate the NEWS SEARCH. Type in The Coca-Cola Company in the space provided, and review the recent news stories about the firm. Summarize any (at least one) recent news story about The Coca-Cola Company that applies one or more of the key concepts within this chapter of the text.

IN-TEXT STUDY GUIDE

Answers are in an appendix at the back of the book.

TRUE OR FALSE

1 The value of a firm is determined by estimating the market value of the firm's assets.

2 The overall objective of a firm's management is to maximize the firm's revenue.

3 The recent downsizing in business organizational structures is intended to achieve lower production costs.

4 The firm's cash flow in any particular period is equal to its cash inflows minus the cash outflows.

5 The selection of the site for a plant or office affects the firm's costs and revenues.

6 Design and layout decisions have a significant impact on both production costs and the value of the firm.

7 Firms with a high level of fixed costs will benefit from large production levels.

8 In an attempt to provide greater job satisfaction, most U.S. firms guarantee the job security of their employees.

9 Because of the size of the U.S. market, firms' business strategies that are successful in the United States will always be successful in other countries.

10 The goal of financing strategies is to lower the cost of funds and increase the value of the firm.

MULTIPLE CHOICE

11 The combination of a firm's product, pricing, distribution, and promotion strategies used to sell products and services is a:
a) production schedule.   d) GANTT chart.
b) PERT diagram.   e) promotional strategy.
c) marketing mix.

12 The process that defines how human resources are combined with other resources to produce products or services is the:

a) financial process.   d) net present value.
b) marketing process.   e) production process.
c) distribution channel.

13 Firms that have a high level of fixed costs can benefit from:
a) economies of scale.
b) higher-priced strategies.
c) curtailing promotional strategies.
d) eliminating distribution channels.
e) more government regulations.

14 The path of a product from the producer to the consumer is determined by the:
a) GANTT chart.   d) distribution channel.
b) PERT diagram.   e) advertising campaign.
c) production schedule.

15 Small firms can attempt to obtain equity financing from:
a) the Small Business Administration.
b) a venture capital firm.
c) a commercial bank.
d) an insurance company.
e) a commercial finance company.

16 Effective marketing strategies are intended to affect the firm's:
a) financial leverage.   d) strategic plan.
b) social responsibilities. e) cash inflows.
c) GANTT chart.

17 Capital budgeting is used to determine:
a) the critical path of a firm's production process.
b) the feasibility of a potential project.
c) the optimum capital structure for the firm.
d) the relationship between the firm's pricing and promotion strategies.
e) the strategic approach to the firm's target market.

18 Which of the following is the most important determinant of a firm's value?
a) earnings   d) liquidity
b) debt   e) asset turnover
c) liabilities

19 A firm's direction and opportunities are identified by the firm's:
a) production schedule.
b) advertising plan.
c) strategic plan.
d) channels of distribution.
e) pricing strategy.

20 Which of the following describes each job position and the relationships between those positions?
a) leadership structure
b) organizational structure
c) control process
d) mission statement
e) job planning process

21 Which of the following is a production process that emphasizes quality?
a) total quality management (TQM)
b) management by objective (MBO)
c) certified production and assembly (CPA)
d) production design and quality (PDQ)
e) just-in-time management (JTM)

22 All of the following provide employees with job satisfaction except:
a) employee involvement programs.
b) job security.
c) maximum corporate profitability.
d) flexible work schedules.
e) compensation aligned with performance.

23 Most business decisions that are intended to increase the firm's value can be classified as management, marketing, and _____ functions.
a) job sharing
b) competitive
c) union
d) finance
e) steering committee

24 Which of the following utilizes employees and other resources of the firm to achieve the organization's goals?
a) value enhancement
b) strategic control
c) government regulation
d) cost control
e) management

25 The selection of a plant site will determine the land cost, the cost of hiring human resources, and:
a) production layout.
b) the cost of transporting products.
c) process layout.
d) production control.
e) dispatching.

26 Downsizing is intended to:
a) increase the firm's commitment to quality.
b) better serve foreign markets.
c) motivate employees.
d) enhance the public image of the firm.
e) decrease the cost of production.

27 Firms use _____ strategies to increase the acceptance of products through special deals, advertising, and publicity.
a) pricing
b) product
c) promotion
d) distribution
e) strategic planning

28 The primary impact of most management strategies is on the firm's:
a) cash outflows.
b) cash budgets.
c) social responsibilities.
d) working capital.
e) debt level.

29 The _____ function is used to evaluate a firm's past business decisions and monitor its current financial condition.
a) marketing
b) accounting
c) finance
d) human resource management
e) production

30 _____ are continually used to compile and analyze information about the firm's operations.
a) Leadership functions
b) Organizing functions
c) Information systems
d) Planning processes
e) Motivating functions

31 Before business strategies are developed, the firm must first decide:
a) the amount of financing required.
b) the type of product to be produced and sold.
c) the elements of the marketing mix to be used.
d) the location of the firm's office and plant facilities.
e) the minimum qualifications of the employees to be hired.

32 How funds are obtained and invested by the firm is determined by the:
a) finance function.
b) marketing function.
c) organizing function.
d) human resource plan.
e) advertising strategy.

33 The pricing decision is influenced mostly by the production cost and by:
a) the size of the firm.
b) competitors' prices.
c) social responsibility.
d) business ethics.
e) public relations.

34 U.S. firms that conduct international business must apply their business strategies in a:
a) global environment.
b) cartel arrangement.
c) noncompetitive spirit.
d) tariff country.
e) quota country.

35 All of the following are job skills that can be developed in employees to improve their performance except:
a) technical skills.
b) decision-making skills.
c) customer service skills.
d) estate planning skills.
e) human relations skills.

PART VII

Completing the Business Plan for Campus.com

Technology (related to Chapter 19)

In your business plan for Campus.com, explain how the firm could use technology to ensure continuous communication with the survey respondents (who provide information about the colleges). Also, explain how Campus.com can use technology to ensure continuous customer feedback from its customers.

Business Risk and Insurance (related to Chapter 20)

In your business plan for Campus.com, explain the potential risk to the business related to its reliance on key managers. That is, if you (or your team) were suddenly unable to oversee its operations due to illness or other reasons, would Campus.com survive? In your business plan, describe the protection you would use (if any) to ensure that Campus.com would still perform well even if you could not oversee the operations. Do you think Campus.com is exposed to any potential lawsuits? If so, describe the conditions under which Campus.com could be sued. Describe how Campus.com could reduce its exposure to lawsuits.

Synthesis (related to Chapter 21)

At this point in the school term, you (or your team) have developed a production plan, a plan for human resources, a marketing plan, and a financial plan. Reassess the plans, and determine whether they fit together. In particular, consider the implications of your plan to run Campus.com's business. Is the production plan consistent with the marketing plan? That is, can more services be accomplished if the marketing plan is very successful?

Are the production and marketing plans consistent with the financial plan? That is, will there be sufficient funds to support any growth that occurs due to the marketing efforts? Does the financial plan allow sufficient funding to support the planned production?

Communication and Teamwork

Your business plan should now be complete. You (or your team) may be asked by your instructor to hand in your business plan and/or to present your plan to the class.

PART VII

Applications for Dell Computer

Refer to Dell Computer's Formula for Success where necessary.

1 Dell Computer's information technology
  a. How do you think Dell Computer uses the Internet to manage its information technology?
  b. How do you think Dell aids companies in managing the challenges of using today's information technologies?

   c. Do you think the security of information systems is a major concern at Dell Computer? Why or why not?

2 Risk management at Dell Computer
   a. What major risk management tasks does Dell Computer face?
   b. How could Dell use the Internet to aid its risk assessment?
   c. What type of insurance against risk do you think is most important at Dell?

3 Dell Computer's value
   a. Do you think there is a single factor that is most important in determining Dell Computer's value? Why?
   b. What business function do you think is most important at Dell?

PART VII

The Stock Market Game

Go to **http://www.fantasystockmarket.com**. Enter your name (e-mail address) and password as requested and check your portfolio balance, which is updated continuously by the Fantasy website.

Check Your Stock Portfolio Performance

It is time to determine the performance of your stock portfolio over the school term.

1 What is the value of your stock portfolio today?

2 What is your return on your investment? (This return is shown on your balance.)

3 How did your return compare to those of other students? (This comparison tells you whether your stock portfolio's performance is relatively high or low.)

Explaining Your Stock Performance

As you learned throughout the school term, stock prices can be influenced by changes in the firm's:

▶ Business environment (economic, industry, and global conditions), covered in Part II
▶ Managerial policies (such as organizational structure and production), covered in Part III
▶ Human resource policies, covered in Part IV
▶ Marketing strategies, covered in Part V
▶ Financial strategies, covered in Part VI

Review the latest news about some of your stocks on the Fantasy website by clicking on News and typing the ticker symbol of your stock.

1 Based on the news about the firms whose stocks you purchased, what business concept covered in this text seems to be most influential on stock prices?

2 Identify a stock in your portfolio that performed relatively well. What caused that stock to perform well (according to related news)?

3 Identify a stock in your portfolio that performed relatively poorly. What caused that stock to perform poorly (according to related news)?

PART VII

Running Your Own Business

1 Explain how you would use information systems to monitor the operations within your business.

2 Explain how you might use the Internet to enhance the performance of your business.

3 What would you do to protect your system from sabotage, espionage, and computer viruses?

4 Describe how your business will reduce the risk of a loss due to a catastrophe such as a flood or fire.

5 Describe how your business will reduce the risk of a loss due to liability.

6 Your business plan to make your business successful contains a set of management strategies (which includes production), marketing strategies, and finance strategies. If you have completed the "Running Your Own Business" exercises in the previous parts, you have already addressed many important decisions on management, marketing, and finance. Provide a brief, general summary of the management (including production) plan for your business idea.

7 Provide a brief, general summary of the marketing plan for your business idea.

8 Provide a brief, general summary of the finance plan for your business idea.

9 Now that you have briefly summarized the management, marketing, and finance plans for your business idea, explain how the different plans are related. That is, explain how your plan for the facilities (in the management plan) is related to the type of product you plan to produce and the price you plan to charge (marketing plan). Also, explain how the financing decisions, such as the amount of financing needed, are dependent on your management and marketing plans.

How to Invest in Stocks

As a firm's business performance changes, so does its stock price. Since performance levels vary among firms, so do stock price movements. Investors who more effectively select the high-performing firms will typically earn higher returns on their investments. From March 20, 1999 to March 20, 2000, the stock price of Qualcomm Inc. increased by 1,500 percent. Thus, an investor who invested $10,000 in Qualcomm stock at the beginning of this period and sold the stock one year later would have received $150,000. Meanwhile, the stock prices of some other firms declined by 100% over that same period. Thus, investors who invested $10,000 in these stocks at the beginning of the period would have lost the entire investment. Investors who understand how stock prices are affected by various factors may be better able to select stocks that will generate high returns.

How the Firm's Stock Price and Value Are Related

A stock's price should represent the value of the firm on a per-share basis. For example, if a firm is valued at $600 million and has 20 million shares, its stock price is:

$$\text{Stock Price} = \frac{\text{Value of Firm}}{\text{Number of Shares}}$$

$$= \frac{\$600,000,000}{20,000,000 \text{ Shares}}$$

$$= \$30 \text{ per Share}$$

As the performance of the firm increases, investors will increase their demand for the stock. Consequently, the stock price will rise.

A stock price by itself does not clearly indicate the firm's value. Consider Firms A and B, each with stock priced at $40 per share. Assume, however, that Firm A has 10 million shares outstanding and Firm B has 20 million shares. Thus, the value of Firm A is $400 million, while the value of Firm B is $800 million.

Understanding Stock Quotations

Financial newspapers such as *The Wall Street Journal, Barrons,* and *Investors Business Daily* publish stock quotations, as do *USA Today* and local newspapers. Although the format of stock quotations varies among newspapers, most quotations provide similar information. Stock prices are always quoted on a per-share basis. Some of the more relevant characteristics that are quoted are summarized next. Use the stock quotations for IBM shown in Exhibit A.1 to supplement the following discussion.

Fifty-Two Week Price Range

The stock's highest price and lowest price over the last fifty-two weeks are commonly quoted just to the left of the stock's name. The high and low prices indicate the range for the stock's price over the last year. Some investors use this range as an indicator of how much the stock fluctuates. Other investors compare this range with the prevailing stock price, as some investors purchase a stock only when its prevailing price is not at its fifty-two week high.

Notice that IBM's fifty-two week high price was $139 and its low price was $81 per share. The low price is about 42 percent below the high price, which suggests

Exhibit A.2

Firms That Make Up the Dow Jones Industrial Average Index

Firm	Recent Stock Price	Weight
Aluminum Co. of America	$ 71.44	3.2
American Express	155.00	6.9
AT&T	58.31	2.6
Boeing	35.87	1.6
Caterpillar	39.56	1.8
Citigroup	60.00	2.7
Coca-Cola	46.37	2.1
Dupont	54.75	2.5
Eastman Kodak	57.18	2.5
ExxonMobil	76.75	3.4
General Electric	158.25	7.1
General Motors	85.62	3.8
Hewlett Packard	142.25	6.4
Home Depot	63.87	2.8
Honeywell	49.43	2.2
IBM	119.81	5.4
Intel	140.75	6.3
International Paper	39.31	1.7
Johnson & Johnson	71.12	3.2
JP Morgan	135.00	6.1
McDonald's	34.81	1.6
Merck	60.62	2.7
Microsoft	100.43	4.9
Minnesota Mining & Mfg	91.12	4.1
Philip Morris	19.75	.8
Procter & Gamble	55.93	2.5
SBC Communications	43.00	1.9
United Technologies	56.50	2.5
Wal-Mart	54.81	2.5
Walt Disney	41.31	1.8

$$\text{Return} = \frac{(\text{Selling Price} - \text{Purchase Price}) + \text{Dividend}}{\text{Purchase Price}}$$

Notice that the numerator reflects a dollar amount composed of the difference between the sales price and purchase price, plus the dividend. This dollar amount is divided by the purchase price to measure the return.

For example, consider a stock that was purchased for $40 per share at the beginning of the year. Assume that a dividend of $2 per share was paid to the investor and that the stock was sold for $44 at the end of the year. The return on this stock over the year is:

$$\text{Return} = \frac{(\text{Selling Price} - \text{Purchase Price}) + \text{Dividend}}{\text{Purchase Price}}$$

$$= \frac{(\$44 - \$40) + \$2}{\$40}$$

$$= .15, \text{ or } 15\%$$

Since the return on the stock is made up of dividends plus the increase in the stock's price, investors cannot just assess a stock's performance by its dividends. Some firms that tend to pay out a higher proportion of their earnings as dividends have less ability to grow in the future, which may limit the potential increase in the stock price. Conversely, firms that retain (reinvest) most of their earnings pay low or no dividends but are more capable of growing. Therefore, investors who are willing to invest in growth firms that do not pay dividends may benefit from larger increases in the stock price.

Return-Risk Trade-Off for Small Stocks

Some investors prefer to invest in stocks of small firms that have potential for a large increase in the stock price. They may attempt to invest before the firms have had much success, because they can purchase the stock at a relatively low price. If these firms become successful, the share price should increase substantially. Many investors realize that if they had purchased shares of successful growing firms such as Microsoft and Compaq Computer when those firms went public, they would be millionaires now. However, for every huge success story, there are many other firms that have failed. Investors who invested in these other unsuccessful firms may have lost 100 percent of their investment.

Stocks of small firms tend to have potential for high return but also tend to have high risk. In addition, many stocks of small firms are not traded frequently, which means that investors who wish to sell their shares of these stocks are less capable of finding a buyer. This can force the investors to sell the stock at a lower price.

To illustrate how stock returns can vary, Exhibit A.3 shows returns for two different airline stocks, UAL (owner of United Airlines) and US Airways. Both airlines were adversely affected by the substantial increase in oil fuel prices in the first quarter of 2000. However, the movements in their stock prices can vary because of differences in firm-specific conditions.

Exhibit A.3

Stock Price Trends of Two
Airline Firms

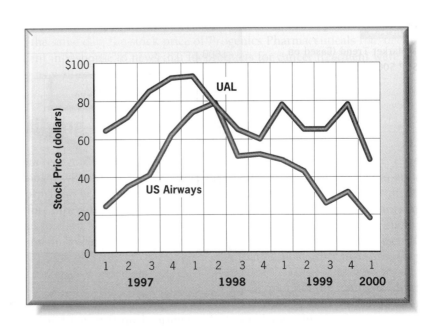

or 5. Assume that most firms in Firm Z's industry have a PE ratio of 9, which means that their stock prices are nine times their recent annual earnings, on average. Since Firm Z's stock price is only five times its recent earnings, some investors may believe that Firm Z's stock is undervalued. They may argue that its price should be nine times its annual earnings, or about $36.

Stock Market Efficiency

The term **stock market efficiency** is used to suggest that stock prices reflect all publicly available information. That is, the prevailing prices have not ignored any publicly available information that could affect the firms' values. Consequently, stocks should not be overvalued or undervalued. The rationale for stock market efficiency is that there are numerous stock analysts who closely monitor stocks. If any stock was undervalued based on existing information, investors would purchase those stocks. The stock's price would be pushed higher in response to the strong demand by all the investors who recognized that the stock was undervalued. Conversely, investors holding overvalued stock would sell that stock once they recognized that it was overvalued. This action would place downward pressure on the stock's price, causing it to move toward its proper level.

Even if the stock market is efficient, investors differ on how to interpret publicly available information. For example, investors may react differently to information that IBM's earnings increased by 20 percent over the last year. Some investors may view that information as old news, while others may believe it is a signal for continued strong performance in the future. Such differences in interpretation are why some investors purchase a stock and others sell that same stock, based on the same information.

Stock Transactions

Investors who wish to purchase stocks use a **stock broker** who facilitates the stock transactions desired. Brokers receive requests of trades from investors and then communicate these trades to people on the trading floor of a stock exchange (called **floor traders**) who execute transactions.

A typical stock transaction order specifies the name of the stock, whether the stock is to be bought or sold, the amount of shares to be traded, and the desired price by the investor. For example, one investor may call a broker and request: "Purchase one hundred shares of IBM; pay no more than $110 per share." A second investor who is holding IBM stock may call a different broker and request: "Sell one hundred shares of IBM at the highest price possible." Both brokers will send this information to the stock exchange. One floor trader will accommodate the buyer, while another floor trader will accommodate the seller. The two traders can agree on a transaction in which one hundred shares of IBM are sold for $110 per share.

Market Orders versus Limit Orders

Investors can place a **market order,** which means they request a transaction for the best possible price. They can also place a **limit order,** which puts a limit on the price at which they would be willing to purchase or sell a stock. Examples of a market order are (1) "Purchase two hundred shares of General Motors stock at the best [lowest] price available" and (2) "Sell three hundred shares of Eastman Kodak stock at the best [highest] price available." Examples of a limit order are (1) "Purchase three hundred shares of Disney; pay no more than $70 per share" and (2) "Sell one hundred shares of PepsiCo; sell for no less than $40 per share."

SELF-SCORING EXERCISE

How Much Risk Can You Take?

Investing in the stock market isn't for those with queasy stomachs or short time horizons. The money you've earmarked for emergencies should be in liquid investments with relatively steady returns, such as money-market funds. But stocks are the backbone of a long-term portfolio for retirement or other goals that are at least ten to fifteen years away.

This simple, self-scoring risk-tolerance test is designed to help you decide what percentage of your long-term money should go into stocks. As you (and your stomach) become more accustomed to the market's ups and downs, you might want to retake the test. Questions come from VALIC (The Variable Annuity Life Insurance Company) and other sources.

_____ 1. Which of the following would worry you the most?
   a) My portfolio may lose value in one of every three years.
   b) My investments won't stay even with inflation.
   c) I won't earn a premium over inflation on my long-term investments.

_____ 2. How would you react if your stock portfolio fell 30 percent in one year?
   a) I would sell some or all of it.
   b) I would stop investing money until it came back.
   c) I would stick with my investment plan and consider adding more to stocks.

_____ 3. You've just heard that the stock market fell by 10 percent today. Your reaction is to:
   a) Consider selling some stocks.
   b) Be concerned, but figure the market is likely to go up again eventually.
   c) Consider buying more stocks, because they are cheaper now.

_____ 4. You read numerous newspaper articles over several months quoting experts who predict stocks will lose money in the coming decade. Many argue that real estate is a better investment. You would:
   a) Consider reducing your stock investments and increasing your investment in real estate.
   b) Be concerned, but stick to your long-term investments in stocks.
   c) Consider the articles as evidence of unwarranted pessimism over the outlook for stocks.

_____ 5. Which of the following best describes your attitude about investing in bonds as compared with stocks?
   a) The high volatility of the stock market concerns me, so I prefer to invest in bonds.
   b) Bonds have less risk but they provide lower returns, so I have a hard time choosing between the two.
   c) The lower return potential of bonds leads me to prefer stocks.

_____ 6. Which of the following best describes how you evaluate the performance of your investments?
   a) My greatest concern is the previous year's performance.
   b) The previous two years are the most important to me.
   c) Performance over five or more years is most significant to me.

_____ 7. Which of the following scenarios would make you feel best about your investments?
   a) Being in a money-market fund saves you from losing half your money in a market downturn.
   b) You double your money in a stock fund in one year.
   c) Over the long term, your overall mix of investments protects you from loss and outpaces the rate of inflation.

_____ 8. Which of the following statements best describes you?
   a) I often change my mind and have trouble sticking to a plan.
   b) I can stay with a strategy only as long as it seems to be going well.
   c) Once I make up my mind to do something, I tend to carry through with it, regardless of the obstacles.

Regulation of Stock Exchanges

insider trading transactions initiated by people (such as employees) who have information about a firm that has not been disclosed to the public

insider information information about a firm that has not been disclosed to the public

The Securities and Exchange Commission (SEC) was created in 1934 to regulate security markets such as the stock exchanges. It enforces specific trading guidelines to prevent unethical trading activities. For example, it attempts to prevent **insider trading,** or transactions initiated by people (such as employees) who have information about a firm that has not been disclosed to the public (called **insider information**). Consider an executive of an engineering firm that has just completed a contract to do work for the government that will generate a large amount of revenue for the firm. If the executive calls a broker to buy shares of the firm, this executive has an unfair advantage over other investors because of the inside information that has not yet been disclosed to the public.

Investing in Foreign Stocks

American depository receipts (ADRs) certificates representing ownership of a stock issued by a non-U.S. firm

U.S. investors can also purchase foreign stocks. When foreign stocks are not listed on a U.S. exchange, the U.S. broker may need to call a broker at a foreign subsidiary, who communicates the desired transaction to the foreign stock exchange where the stock is traded. The commissions paid by U.S. investors for such transactions are higher than those paid for transactions on U.S. exchanges.

Many of the larger foreign stocks are listed on U.S. stock exchanges as **American depository receipts (ADRs).** An ADR is a certificate representing ownership of a stock issued by a non-U.S. firm. Some of the more popular ADRs are British Airways, EuroDisney, and Sony.

Investing in Mutual Funds

net asset value (NAV) the market value of a mutual fund's securities after subtracting any expenses incurred

open-end mutual funds funds that stand ready to repurchase their shares at the prevailing NAV if investors decide to sell the shares

closed-end mutual funds mutual funds that are sold on stock exchanges

growth funds mutual funds that invest in stocks of firms with high potential for growth

income funds mutual funds that invest in stocks that provide large dividends or in bonds that provide coupon payments

international stock funds mutual funds that invest in stocks of foreign firms

Mutual funds sell shares to individual investors and use the proceeds to invest in various securities. They are attractive to investors because they employ portfolio managers with expertise in making investment decisions. Thus, individual investors can place the responsibility of investment decisions with these portfolio managers. Second, individual investors with a small amount of money (such as $500 or $1,000) can invest in mutual funds. In this way, they can be part owners of a widely diversified portfolio with a small amount of money.

The **net asset value (NAV)** of a mutual fund is the market value of the fund's securities after subtracting any expenses incurred (such as portfolio manager salaries) by the fund, on a per-share basis. As the values of the securities contained in a mutual fund rise, so does the mutual fund's NAV.

Types of Mutual Funds

Open-end mutual funds stand ready to repurchase their shares at the prevailing NAV if investors decide to sell the shares. Conversely, shares of **closed-end mutual funds** represent mutual funds that are sold on stock exchanges.

Most mutual funds tend to focus on particular types of securities so that they can attract investors who wish to invest in those securities. For example, **growth funds** invest in stocks of firms with high potential for growth. **Income funds** invest in stocks that provide large dividends or in bonds that provide coupon payments. **International stock funds** invest in stocks of foreign firms. Each mutual fund has a prospectus that describes its investment objectives, its recent performance, the types of securities it purchases, and other relevant financial information.

Load versus No-Load Mutual Funds

load mutual funds open-end mutual funds that can be purchased only by calling a broker

no-load funds open-end mutual funds that can be purchased without the services of a broker

expense ratio for a mutual fund, expenses divided by assets

Open-end mutual funds that can be purchased only by calling a broker are referred to as **load mutual funds.** The term *load* refers to the transaction fees (commissions) charged for the transaction. Other open-end mutual funds that can be purchased without the services of a broker are referred to as **no-load funds.** These mutual funds are purchased by requesting a brief application from the mutual funds and sending it in with the investment.

All mutual funds incur expenses that result from hiring portfolio managers to select stocks and from serving clients (mailing fees and so on). The **expense ratio** (defined as expenses divided by the assets) of each mutual fund can be assessed to determine the expenses incurred by each mutual fund per year. Some mutual funds have an expense ratio of less than .5 percent, while others have an expense ratio above 2 percent. The expense ratio is provided within the mutual funds prospectus. Since high expenses can cause lower returns, investors closely monitor the expense ratio.

KEY TERMS

American depository receipts (ADRs) *618*
bearish *612*
bullish *612*
closed-end mutual funds *618*
commission *616*
discount brokers *616*
expense ratio *619*
floor traders *614*
full-service brokers *616*
growth funds *618*

income funds *618*
insider information *618*
insider trading *618*
international stock funds *618*
limit order *614*
load mutual funds *619*
market order *614*
National Association of Security Dealers Automated Quotation (Nasdaq) *617*

net asset value (NAV) *618*
no-load funds *619*
odd lots *616*
on margin *616*
open-end mutual funds *618*
round lots *616*
stock broker *614*
stock market efficiency *614*

INVESTING IN THE STOCK OF A BUSINESS

Recall from Chapter 1 that you were asked to identify a firm that you would invest in if you had funds to invest. You were asked to record the price of the firm's stock at that time. Now, you should close out your position. That is, determine today's stock price (which is quoted on the Yahoo! website and many other websites). Estimate your return on the stock as follows:

1 If the investment period is about three months, one dividend payment would have been made. Divide the annual dividend per share (which you recorded when you selected your stock) by 4 to determine the quarterly dividend per share (D).

2 Estimate the return (R), based on today's selling price (S), the purchase price (P) you paid at the beginning of the term, and the quarterly dividend (D):

$$R = \frac{S - P + D}{P}$$

3 This return is not annualized. If you wish to annualize your return, multiply R by ($12/n$), where n is the number of months you held your investment. Compare your results with those of other students.

To determine how well your stock performed in comparison with the stock market in general, determine the percentage change in the S&P 500 Index over the term. This index represents a composite of stocks of five hundred large firms.

Offer explanations for the stock performance of your firm. Was the performance driven by the stock market performance in general? Was your firm's performance affected by recent economic conditions, industry conditions, and global conditions? How? Was its performance affected by specific strategies (such as restructuring or acquisitions) that it recently enacted? Discuss.

THE *Coca-Cola* COMPANY ANNUAL REPORT PROJECT

 Questions for the current year's annual report are available on the text website at **http://madura_intro_bus.swcollege.com**.

The following questions apply concepts learned in this appendix to The Coca-Cola Company. Go to the Coca-Cola Company website (**http://www.cocacola.com**) and find the index for the 1999 annual report.

QUESTIONS

1 Using the shareholder information in Coca-Cola's annual report or the business section of a major newspaper, find the stock symbol for The Coca-Cola Company. What is The Coca-Cola Company's stock symbol?

2 On what stock exchanges is The Coca-Cola Company traded?

Careers

This appendix suggests methods that can be used to make career decisions. Some of the more critical career decisions are (1) choosing a career, (2) deciding whether to pursue a career or an additional degree, and (3) determining how to pursue a particular career.

Choosing a Career

Students who prefer to work for a firm rather than start their own businesses must decide what type of job and size of firm would be ideal for them.

Type of Job

A person's salary and level of job satisfaction will depend on the type of job selected. College students should seriously consider this decision before they select their major to ensure that they will have the educational background that is necessary for the type of job they desire.

Salaries Although students should not necessarily choose the major that results in the highest salaries, they should at least be aware of salary differentials before they select a major. This type of information is available at most large libraries and on various websites.

Job Satisfaction Job satisfaction must also be considered when choosing a career. The job satisfaction level for any given career varies among people. Thus, people may not know whether they like a particular type of job until they have worked at it. This is a major dilemma because it is difficult to properly assess job satisfaction without on-the-job experience, which normally occurs after graduation.

Size of Firm

In addition to the type of job, people must determine whether they wish to work for a small or large firm. There are some obvious differences. Some commonly cited advantages of working for a large firm are more prestige, more training, and more opportunities for advancement.

Working for a small firm also offers advantages, including more attention from higher-level management and more diverse responsibilities. Also, fewer promotions are necessary to achieve a higher-level management position.

The advantages listed here do not apply to all large and small firms, as each firm has its own characteristics. Thus, it is strongly recommended that students apply for particular jobs at both small and large firms. The interviewing process may provide more insight on the differences between small and large firms.

Career versus Additional Degree

Students who receive their associates degree are faced with a decision of whether to pursue a bachelor's degree or a full-time career. Students who receive their bachelor's degree are also faced with a decision of whether to pursue a master's degree or a full-time career. Both decisions involve an additional degree versus a career. The following discussion relates to these decisions.

Although the appropriate decision varies among students, some general guidelines deserve consideration. Students should conduct a cost-benefit analysis of the decision to pursue an additional degree. Some of the more obvious costs are tuition, the forgone income that could have been earned by working instead of going to school, and the forgone on-the-job experience that could have been earned by working instead of going to school. Some possible benefits of pursing an additional degree are more marketability in the job market, a higher starting salary, and greater potential for promotion.

The cost and benefits of attaining an additional degree can vary significantly among majors. In addition to the costs and benefits just identified, other factors also deserve to be considered. For example, some people may need a break from school and would prefer to begin their career right away. Others may perform best in school by continuing their education while the previous coursework is still fresh in their minds.

It is often suggested that people get more out of an additional degree if they work full-time for a few years and then return to school. The on-the-job experience may allow for a greater understanding and appreciation of coursework. Such a strategy can have a high cost, however. It is difficult for people to feel motivated on a job knowing they will quit in a few years to pursue an additional degree.

Pursuing a Career and Degree

A popular compromise for those facing the career-versus-degree dilemma is to begin a career and pursue the degree part-time. Many firms will even pay an employee's tuition if the coursework could enhance the employee's performance on the job. This strategy allows people to obtain a degree without giving up the income and on-the-job experience they would forgo if they pursued a degree full-time. However, the disadvantage is that it may take five or more years to achieve the degree part-time. In addition, taking coursework at night after a long day on the job can cause fatigue and stress.

An extra degree does not automatically guarantee immediate success. The number of bachelor's and master's degrees has increased dramatically in recent years. Therefore, competition for existing jobs can be fierce even with additional education. An additional degree can be especially marketable when it complements existing skills. For example, many engineers have pursued master's degrees in business administration so that they can pursue management-level positions at engineering firms.

Internships

Internship programs may enable students to gain on-the-job experience while pursuing a degree. Some internships pay a salary, while others allow students to earn credit for the internship. An internship may also enable students to determine whether they find a particular type of job desirable before they select a major. It may even enhance their understanding of coursework. Perhaps the most important benefit of an internship is the experience, which may increase the student's marketability upon graduation. Numerous firms, including AT&T, Apple Computer, and Boeing, frequently hire interns. Nevertheless, many more students apply for internships than the number of internships available.

Choosing a College

People who decide to pursue a college degree must also select the proper college or university. For those who will be working while pursuing the degree, the choice of a college may be dictated by the location of the job. For others who have the flex-

APPENDIX B • CAREERS **623**

ibility to relocate, several criteria are worth considering. The first step is to identify the colleges that offer a degree in the main field of interest. College catalogs (available at many libraries) should be reviewed to compare the courses offered. Then, each college that offers a degree in the desired field can be more closely assessed to determine the course requirements, possible elective courses, and minor fields available. Other factors such as tuition and location should also be considered. Several colleges offer a degree in any given field.

Some colleges are more prestigious than others, which can be important in attaining a good job. However, colleges' reputations tend to vary. One college may have a strong program in one field but a weak program in others.

For people who plan to find a local job, the college does not need to have a national reputation. Specialized jobs are scarce in many college towns, however. Therefore, even if the college is not nationally recognized, it should be reputable from the perspective of potential employees who may hire its graduates.

Pursuing a Career

The key steps in pursuing a career are as follows:

- ▶ Applying for a position
- ▶ Creating a résumé
- ▶ Interviewing
- ▶ Planning a career path

Each step is discussed in turn.

Applying for a Position

After determining the type of job desired, it is necessary to identify prospective employers that may have job openings in that field. The want ads in the local newspapers may identify firms in the local area that have openings. However, local want ads will not provide a complete listing of companies that wish to fill such a position. Some companies do not advertise openings but simply select from their applicant file to fill positions. For this reason, a worthwhile step is to submit an application to any firms that may potentially hire for the position desired. Very little effort and expense are required to submit an application.

People can improve their chances of being recruited by sending an application in response to an ad, asking friends with jobs to provide referrals, joining associations, conducting a job search on the Internet, and using the college placement service. They might even consider using employment recruiting firms, although these firms normally do not deal with entry-level positions.

Some people who are very interested in a particular job may revise their résumé to fit that job. They could elaborate on any past work experience that is directly applicable to the job.

When students apply for a job, they should send a cover letter along with a résumé. Exhibit B.1 provides an example of a cover letter. Although many formats can be used, the main purpose of the cover letter is to identify the job position desired and explain how one's qualifications fit the job position.

Students pursuing a career should contact the college placement center, which may invite firms to speak about careers. Firms also conduct interviews of students at many placement centers.

Many people are unable to identify the ideal job for which they are qualified. Nevertheless, this does not prevent them from applying for jobs. The human resources department of each firm can determine whether the applicants are qualified for various positions.

Exhibit B.1   Example of a Cover Letter

1022 N. Main Street
Tallahassee, FL 32306

June 9, 2000

Mr. Raymond Jones
President
Jones Manufacturing Co.
550 East 1st Street
Orlando, FL 32816

Dear Mr. Jones:

[State the specific job you are pursuing.]

I noticed that you have a job opening for a tax accountant. I just recently earned my accounting degree from Florida State University. I worked as an intern at Mega Accountants, Inc., in its tax department. Much of the intern work focused on tax accounting for manufacturing firms. I believe that my educational and intern experience has prepared me for your tax accountant position. I have enclosed my résumé, which provides more details about my education and intern background.

[Describe when you are available for work and how you can be reached.]

I am available for work immediately. Please call me at 999-555-1234 if you would like to interview me. I can be reached at that number during the morning on any day of the week. I look forward to hearing from you.

Sincerely,

Robert Smith

Robert Smith

An important factor in managing employees is hiring the right people in the first place. During the past few years, the number of career placement services on the World Wide Web (WWW) has skyrocketed. Several of these services are listed in Exhibit B.2.

Applying for a job is normally the easiest part of pursuing a career. Some people apply at one or two well-known firms and wait to be called. This can be a frustrating experience. People who are willing to consider several firms for employment are more likely to obtain a job. Even if a specific firm is most desirable, it is worthwhile to at least apply for a position at several firms.

Exhibit B.2

Career Placement Services on the World Wide Web

Magellan-Career	http://www.magellan.excite.com/careers
Career Mosaic	http://www.careermosaic.com/
Career.Com	http://www.career.com/
America's Employers	http://www.americasemployers.com/
The Help-Wanted Page	http://www.helpwantedpage.com/
Career Web	http://cweb.com/
Monster.com	http://monster.com/
JobTrak.com	http://www.jobtrak.com
Monster Campus	http://www.studentcenter.com/
College Grad Job Hunter	http://www.collegegrad.com/

Example of a Résumé

Résumé

Robert Smith

1022 N. Main Street

Tallahassee, FL 32306

Job Objective:	Entry-level accountant
Education:	Florida State University, Sept. 1996–May 2000, B.S. in Accounting received May 2000; Grade point average = 3.1 on a 4-point scale.
Work Experience:	Intern at Mega Accountants, Inc., April 1999 to April 2000.

      ☐ Assisted tax accountants in compiling information submitted by clients that would be used to file their tax returns.

      ☐ Researched previous tax court cases to provide information needed to answer clients' specific tax questions.

      ☐ Met with prospective clients to explain the tax services offered by the firm.

Lantern Grocery Store, March 1996 to March 1999.

      ☐ Responsible for ordering stock, monitoring deliveries of stock, and placing stock on shelves.

Professional Organizations:	Treasurer of the Accounting Association at Florida State University, member of Business Club.
Extracurricular Activities:	Volunteer for Salvation Army, Intramural Sports (Baseball and Basketball).
References:	Provided upon request.

Creating a Résumé

The application process normally requires a résumé to be included. Various résumé formats are used, and no format is perfect for all situations. Most résumés for people pursuing entry-level positions are one page long. An example of a typical résumé format is shown in Exhibit B.3. Whatever format is used, it should be designed to describe any characteristics that enhance job skills. The job objective states the desired job position and can be tailored to fit the firm where the application is sent. The education and employment background should be listed in reverse chronological order (most recent experience listed first). Specific details that support job qualifications can be described in this section.

Interviewing

Firms conduct interviews to evaluate applicants more thoroughly. Various characteristics, such as the applicant's personality, cannot be evaluated from résumés alone. Personal interviews allow firms to assess these characteristics. Many firms screen applications and résumés to identify a pool of qualified applicants. Then the qualified applicants are interviewed to determine the optimal applicant for the position. Although strong qualifications on a résumé enable an applicant to be interviewed, they do not guarantee a job. A person who interviews well may be preferable to one with a stronger résumé who interviews poorly.

Firms design most interviews to provide the applicant with additional information about the position and to determine the following:

1 Is the applicant neat and presentable?

2 Would the applicant get along with customers?

3 Does the applicant have good communication skills?

4 Does the applicant have a genuine interest in the position?

5 Would the applicant work well with others?

Applicants cannot prepare for all possible questions that may be asked during an interview, but they should at least prepare for some of the more obvious types of questions that may be asked:

1 Why do you want to work for our company?

2 What do you know about our company?

3 Why do you plan to leave your present employer?

4 Why should our company hire you?

5 What are your strengths?

6 What are your weaknesses?

7 What are your salary requirements?

8 When would you be ready to begin this job?

Although applicants cannot guarantee the outcome of the interview, a few simple but critical rules should be followed:

1 Dress properly.

2 Be on time.

3 Send a follow-up thank-you letter to the persons who interview you.

SELF-SCORING EXERCISE

Evaluating Your Résumé

Once you create a draft of your résumé, ask a friend to evaluate it based on the following criteria.

	Evaluation	Suggestions
Clearly communicates your experience?		
Clearly communicates your skills?		
Clearly communicates your potential?		
Clearly communicates your comparative advantages over other applicants?		
Length of résumé		
Clearly communicates how you could benefit the firm?		
Focus of résumé		
Grammar in résumé		

What to Ask in an Interview A person who is being interviewed is normally allowed time to ask questions about the firm that is conducting the interview. These questions may be just as important as the applicant's answers in determining whether the job is offered. The questions show the applicant's interest in the firm and intelligence about the job. Some possible questions are:

1 How much interaction is there between this position and related divisions?

2 How much responsibility is delegated by the supervisor of this position?

3 What is the typical educational background for this position?

4 Who is involved in the performance evaluation for this position?

5 To what extent does the position involve public relations or contact with customers?

A second set of questions would ask for more details about the position, which could show the interviewee's competency in the area. These questions would vary with the type of position, but a few examples can be provided:

1 What type of computer is used in the department?

2 Which companies are your key suppliers or customers?

3 What are your projections for sales in the division over the next year?

Although asking questions can be valuable, the applicant must recognize the amount of time allocated for the interview and make sure that the interviewer has sufficient time to ask questions.

BUSINESS ONLINE

The Student Center Career Doctor

http://asp.studentcenter.com/
doctor/doctor.asp

AN EXCELLENT SOURCE OF CAREER INFORMATION ON THE WEB IS THE Student Center Career Doctor located at **http://asp.studentcenter.com/doctor/doctor.asp**. This site offers a self-diagnostic test to determine the right career for you.

Planning a Career Path

Even after a job is offered and accepted, career decisions must be made. On-the-job experience may affect the desired career path. Aspiring to a position above the present position is natural. The planned career path to that position may involve either a series of promotions within the firm or switching to a different firm. Although planning a career path is a useful motivator, the plans should be achievable. If everyone planned to be president of a company, most plans would not be achieved. This can cause frustration. A preferable career path would include short-term goals, since some ultimate goals may take twenty years or longer. The use of short-term goals can reinforce confidence as goals are achieved.

Working for a Firm versus Owning a Firm

During the course of a career, many people question whether to continue working for a firm or start their own business. Some people recognize the potential benefits of owning their own firm, such as being their own boss or the potential to earn a high level of income. However, the decision to start a business requires an idea for a product or service that will generate sufficient sales. A successful business also requires proper planning, production, marketing, and financing decisions, as explained throughout the text. Some general guidelines for developing a successful business, which apply to most firms, are listed here:

1 *Create a product (or service) that the market wants.* A new business is typically created when the owner recognizes a product or service desired by customers that is not being offered by a sufficient number (or by any) existing firms.

2 *Prepare for adverse conditions.* An owner of a business should have enough financial backing to prepare for adverse conditions, such as a decline in economic growth or more intense competition. Even if the business is based on a good product (or service) idea, it may experience weak performance in some periods because of factors beyond its control.

3 *Capitalize on new opportunities.* A business should use a flexible strategic plan that adjusts in response to new business opportunities. Businesses that remain more flexible to change are more likely to capitalize on new opportunities.

4 *Ensure customer satisfaction.* The long-run success of many businesses is based on the quality of a product, which leads to customer satisfaction.

5 *Ensure employee satisfaction.* When owners of businesses create conditions that satisfy employees, they motivate employees to perform well and also avoid a high level of employee turnover.

6 *Promote the product.* A good product will not sell unless the market is aware of it. Promotion may be necessary to ensure that the market is informed about the product.

Answers to In-Text Study Guide

Chapter 1

True/False
1. False (pp. 3–4)
2. False (p. 12)
3. True (p. 13)
4. True (p. 14)
5. False (p. 7)
6. False (p. 15)
7. False (p. 13)
8. True (p. 4)
9. True (p. 14)
10. True (p. 6)

Multiple Choice
11. e (p. 3)
12. c (p. 3)
13. c (p. 12)
14. e (p. 3)
15. b (p. 4)
16. b (p. 4)
17. b (p. 12)
18. a (p. 6)
19. a (p. 14)
20. a (p. 14)
21. d (p. 14)
22. e (p. 14)
23. c (p. 4)
24. b (p. 12)
25. c (p. 7)
26. e (pp. 12–13)
27. a (p. 12)
28. d (p. 15)
29. a (pp. 15–16)
30. b (p. 15)
31. c (p. 16)
32. a (p. 12)
33. e (p. 3)
34. e (p. 13)
35. e (p. 12)

Chapter 2

True/False
1. False (p. 30)
2. False (p. 30)
3. False (p. 34)
4. True (p. 33)
5. True (p. 35)
6. True (p. 36)
7. True (p. 33)
8. False (p. 30)
9. True (p. 40)
10. False (p. 31)

Multiple Choice
11. a (p. 34)
12. c (p. 29)
13. c (p. 41)
14. e (p. 30)
15. d (p. 31)
16. b (p. 30)
17. d (p. 41)
18. a (p. 31)
19. a (p. 40)
20. c (p. 43)
21. d (p. 33)
22. c (p. 38)
23. c (p. 40)
24. b (p. 33)
25. a (p. 32)
26. b (p. 33)
27. d (pp. 34–35)
28. a (p. 40)
29. b (p. 43)
30. b (p. 29)
31. c (p. 31)
32. a (p. 35)
33. c (p. 33)
34. a (p. 31)
35. d (p. 29)

Chapter 3

True/False
1. True (p. 58)
2. True (p. 58)
3. True (p. 60)
4. False (p. 67)
5. False (p. 67)
6. False (p. 75)
7. True (p. 64)
8. True (p. 69)
9. False (p. 63)
10. False (p. 60)

Multiple Choice
11. c (p. 60)
12. e (p. 64)
13. a (p. 60)
14. e (p. 58)
15. e (p. 66)
16. c (p. 62)
17. b (p. 61)
18. b (p. 60)
19. a (p. 62)
20. b (p. 56)
21. d (p. 69)
22. c (p. 59)
23. e (p. 59)
24. d (p. 67)
25. c (p. 65)
26. b (p. 58)
27. b (p. 66)
28. d (p. 56)
29. b (p. 67)
30. d (p. 58)
31. d (p. 60)
32. d (p. 60)
33. b (p. 64)
34. b (p. 60)
35. e (p. 60)

Chapter 4

True/False
1. False (p. 94)
2. True (p. 92)
3. False (p. 103)
4. True (p. 104)
5. False (p. 91)
6. False (p. 93)
7. True (p. 98)
8. False (p. 94)
9. False (p. 92)
10. True (p. 92)

Multiple Choice
11. a (p. 92)
12. b (p. 93)
13. c (p. 98)
14. e (p. 95)
15. a (p. 106)
16. c (p. 91)
17. c (p. 94)
18. d (p. 93)
19. a (p. 94)
20. b (pp. 98–99)
21. e (p. 100)
22. a (p. 100)
23. c (p. 105)
24. a (p. 100)
25. c (p. 104)
26. a (p. 103)
27. a (p. 104)
28. c (p. 99)

29. e (p. 104)
30. b (pp. 103–104)
31. b (p. 106)
32. c (pp. 91–93)
33. a (p. 94)
34. d (p. 109)
35. b (p. 109)

Chapter 5

True/False

1. False (p. 121)
2. False (p. 121)
3. True (p. 122)
4. False (p. 127)
5. True (p. 122)
6. False (p. 125)
7. True (p. 127)
8. True (p. 121)
9. True (p. 131)
10. False (p. 120)

Multiple Choice

11. c (p. 122)
12. e (p. 119)
13. b (p. 128)
14. b (p. 128)
15. a (p. 121)
16. d (p. 119)
17. a (p. 122)
18. b (p. 120)
19. d (p. 123)
20. d (p. 121)
21. b (p. 120)
22. c (p. 121)
23. a (p. 125)
24. d (p. 131)
25. c (p. 130)
26. e (p. 128)
27. b (p. 120)
28. a (p. 120)
29. d (p. 128)
30. b (p. 130)
31. b (p. 121)
32. a (p. 127)
33. c (p. 120)
34. c (p. 127)
35. d (p. 126)

Chapter 6

True/False

1. True (p. 142)
2. False (p. 146)
3. False (p. 149)

4. True (p. 156)
5. True (p. 150)
6. False (p. 154)
7. False (p. 155)
8. True (p. 144)
9. False (p. 157)
10. True (p. 156)

Multiple Choice

11. c (p. 141)
12. a (p. 151)
13. d (p. 157)
14. c (p. 146)
15. a (p. 163)
16. d (p. 163)
17. a (p. 151)
18. c (p. 150)
19. a (p. 151)
20. c (p. 150)
21. a (p. 163)
22. b (p. 151)
23. b (p. 163)
24. d (p. 160)
25. a (p. 150)
26. a (p. 155)
27. b (p. 156)
28. c (p. 154)
29. a (p. 150)
30. e (p. 151)
31. c (p. 151)
32. b (p. 153)
33. c (p. 162)
34. a (p. 154)
35. d (p. 163)

Chapter 7

True/False

1. False (p. 182)
2. False (p. 189)
3. True (p. 186)
4. False (p. 180)
5. False (p. 183)
6. True (p. 191)
7. True (p. 191)
8. True (p. 182)
9. False (p. 192)
10. True (p. 186)

Multiple Choice

11. b (p. 189)
12. d (p. 192)
13. b (p. 196)
14. e (p. 193)
15. a (p. 183)
16. c (p. 185)

17. d (p. 193)
18. a (p. 186)
19. e (p. 183)
20. b (p. 182)
21. d (p. 193)
22. c (p. 194)
23. c (p. 186)
24. e (p. 186)
25. a (p. 191)
26. b (p. 180)
27. c (p. 183)
28. a (p. 183)
29. d (p. 186)
30. e (p. 189)
31. e (p. 192)
32. b (p. 182)
33. a (p. 183)
34. e (p. 183)
35. c (p. 189)

Chapter 8

True/False

1. True (p. 221)
2. True (p. 207)
3. False (p. 209)
4. False (p. 222)
5. False (p. 210)
6. True (p. 207)
7. False (p. 218)
8. True (p. 219)
9. False (p. 212)
10. True (p. 210)

Multiple Choice

11. c (p. 214)
12. a (p. 207)
13. e (p. 215)
14. b (p. 209)
15. a (p. 213)
16. a (p. 216)
17. e (p. 221)
18. b (p. 211)
19. c (p. 207)
20. e (p. 209)
21. b (p. 215)
22. b (p. 212)
23. a (p. 208)
24. d (p. 220)
25. c (p. 209)
26. d (p. 210)
27. d (p. 209)
28. b (p. 208)
29. b (p. 212)
30. c (p. 210)
31. a (p. 211)

32. c (p. 207)
33. c (p. 217)
34. b (p. 218)
35. b (p. 215)

Chapter 9

True/False
1. True (p. 239)
2. False (p. 248)
3. False (p. 239)
4. True (p. 233)
5. True (p. 242)
6. False (p. 240)
7. True (p. 237)
8. False (p. 241)
9. False (p. 237)
10. True (p. 250)

Multiple Choice
11. d (p. 231)
12. b (p. 238)
13. e (p. 234)
14. c (p. 231)
15. b (p. 241)
16. d (p. 242)
17. d (p. 237)
18. b (p. 246)
19. c (p. 248)
20. c (p. 237)
21. e (p. 241)
22. a (p. 233)
23. d (p. 234)
24. c (p. 240)
25. a (p. 239)
26. b (p. 250)
27. d (p. 239)
28. b (p. 247)
29. c (p. 237)
30. a (p. 239)
31. d (p. 231)
32. c (p. 241)
33. e (p. 237)
34. a (p. 237)
35. d (p. 244)

Chapter 10

True/False
1. True (p. 270)
2. True (p. 268)
3. True (p. 264)
4. False (p. 260)
5. True (p. 273)
6. True (p. 273)

7. False (p. 268)
8. True (p. 274)
9. False (p. 259)
10. False (p. 272)

Multiple Choice
11. a (p. 269)
12. c (p. 265)
13. b (p. 264)
14. a (p. 269)
15. e (p. 267)
16. d (p. 270)
17. a (p. 273)
18. e (p. 269)
19. e (p. 276)
20. b (p. 273)
21. d (p. 273)
22. e (p. 269)
23. b (p. 260)
24. c (p. 268)
25. a (p. 266)
26. a (p. 259)
27. c (p. 274)
28. a (p. 264)
29. d (p. 273)
30. c (p. 270)
31. d (p. 259)
32. b (p. 259)
33. d (p. 270)
34. e (p. 272)
35. a (p. 270)

Chapter 11

True/False
1. True (p. 297)
2. True (p. 295)
3. False (p. 297)
4. False (p. 302)
5. True (p. 305)
6. False (p. 291)
7. False (p. 293)
8. False (p. 294)
9. True (p. 297)
10. False (p. 290)

Multiple Choice
11. c (p. 297)
12. a (p. 289)
13. b (p. 305)
14. e (p. 298)
15. b (p. 304)
16. d (p. 301)
17. c (p. 294)
18. b (p. 302)
19. c (p. 303)

20. e (p. 302)
21. d (p. 291)
22. d (p. 295)
23. e (p. 290)
24. a (p. 292)
25. b (p. 294)
26. c (p. 302)
27. b (p. 293)
28. c (p. 292)
29. d (p. 294)
30. a (p. 297)
31. b (p. 297)
32. d (p. 290)
33. a (p. 290)
34. e (p. 297)
35. c (p. 301)

Chapter 12

True/False
1. False (p. 315)
2. True (p. 320)
3. False (p. 325)
4. False (p. 326)
5. True (p. 328)
6. True (p. 315)
7. False (p. 321)
8. True (p. 328)
9. True (p. 316)
10. True (p. 316)

Multiple Choice
11. c (p. 329)
12. a (p. 316)
13. a (p. 317)
14. b (p. 334)
15. c (p. 324)
16. d (p. 334)
17. e (p. 318)
18. c (p. 316)
19. a (p. 325)
20. c (p. 318)
21. e (p. 319)
22. a (p. 316)
23. a (p. 315)
24. b (p. 317)
25. e (p. 334)
26. c (p. 318)
27. e (p. 325)
28. d (p. 325)
29. b (p. 324)
30. a (p. 316)
31. c (p. 325)
32. e (p. 329)
33. a (p. 316)

34. d (p. 324)
35. d (p. 318)

Chapter 13

True/False
1. False (p. 353)
2. False (p. 371)
3. True (p. 356)
4. False (p. 353)
5. True (p. 354)
6. True (p. 375)
7. True (p. 364)
8. False (p. 369)
9. True (p. 357)
10. False (p. 357)

Multiple Choice
11. c (p. 367)
12. d (p. 369)
13. c (p. 356)
14. b (p. 359)
15. b (p. 361)
16. d (p. 353)
17. b (p. 356)
18. c (p. 364)
19. a (p. 366)
20. e (p. 367)
21. e (p. 359)
22. b (p. 361)
23. b (p. 367)
24. a (p. 361)
25. a (p. 365)
26. d (p. 369)
27. d (p. 371)
28. c (p. 374)
29. e (p. 363)
30. c (p. 372)
31. b (p. 370)
32. d (p. 355)
33. a (p. 369)
34. b (p. 356)
35. e (p. 370)

Chapter 14

True/False
1. True (p. 392)
2. True (p. 387)
3. True (p. 399)
4. False (p. 385)
5. False (p. 390)
6. True (p. 398)
7. True (p. 388)

8. True (p. 390)
9. False (p. 395)
10. False (p. 386)

Multiple Choice
11. d (p. 393)
12. b (p. 398)
13. d (p. 390)
14. a (p. 385)
15. b (p. 393)
16. c (p. 388)
17. e (p. 396)
18. b (p. 387)
19. c (p. 389)
20. e (p. 390)
21. d (p. 390)
22. a (p. 398)
23. a (p. 391)
24. a (p. 396)
25. b (p. 398)
26. d (p. 389)
27. d (p. 385)
28. e (p. 393)
29. b (p. 398)
30. a (p. 399)
31. a (p. 386)
32. b (p. 390)
33. c (p. 385)
34. c (p. 390)
35. b (p. 395)

Chapter 15

True/False
1. False (p. 411)
2. True (p. 410)
3. False (pp. 419–420)
4. False (p. 412)
5. True (p. 411)
6. True (pp. 418–419)
7. True (p. 425)
8. False (p. 424)
9. False (p. 424)
10. True (p. 418)

Multiple Choice
11. b (p. 410)
12. a (p. 410)
13. e (p. 420)
14. c (p. 413)
15. b (p. 415)
16. d (p. 427)
17. a (p. 410)
18. e (p. 416)
19. a (pp. 418–419)

20. d (p. 409)
21. e (p. 424)
22. d (p. 411)
23. b (p. 409)
24. d (p. 409)
25. a (p. 420)
26. c (p. 411)
27. e (p. 423)
28. d (p. 411)
29. c (p. 417)
30. a (p. 424)
31. b (p. 420)
32. c (p. 411)
33. e (p. 422)
34. a (p. 425)
35. b (p. 411)

Chapter 16

True/False
1. False (p. 442)
2. True (p. 442)
3. False (p. 443)
4. False (p. 442)
5. True (p. 443)
6. True (p. 442)
7. False (p. 445)
8. False (p. 443)
9. False (p. 448)
10. True (p. 449)

Multiple Choice
11. b (p. 443)
12. d (p. 455)
13. a (p. 445)
14. c (p. 443)
15. e (p. 442)
16. c (p. 448)
17. d (p. 442)
18. a (p. 447)
19. b (p. 442)
20. e (p. 443)
21. b (p. 455)
22. e (p. 443)
23. a (p. 450)
24. d (p. 442)
25. e (p. 449)
26. c (p. 442)
27. e (p. 444)
28. b (p. 445)
29. c (p. 445)
30. d (p. 454)
31. b (p. 443)
32. c (p. 450)
33. e (p. 446)

34. a (p. 447)
35. d (p. 446)

Chapter 17

True/False
1. False (p. 464)
2. True (p. 464)
3. True (p. 466)
4. True (p. 467)
5. False (p. 465)
6. True (p. 470)
7. True (p. 473)
8. False (p. 478)
9. True (p. 469)
10. False (p. 469)

Multiple Choice
11. c (p. 479)
12. e (p. 476)
13. a (p. 470)
14. d (p. 466)
15. e (p. 473)
16. a (p. 465)
17. c (p. 468)
18. b (p. 477)
19. a (p. 463)
20. e (p. 474)
21. b (p. 475)
22. d (p. 465)
23. e (p. 478)
24. a (p. 479)
25. d (p. 463)
26. c (p. 469)
27. d (p. 476)
28. b (p. 474)
29. d (p. 463)
30. a (p. 479)
31. c (p. 479)
32. b (p. 479)
33. b (p. 464)
34. e (p. 470)
35. e (p. 463)

Chapter 18

True/False
1. True (p. 494)
2. True (p. 504)
3. False (p. 493)
4. True (p. 502)
5. False (p. 500)
6. False (p. 502)
7. False (p. 501)
8. False (p. 502)
9. False (p. 505)
10. True (p. 509)

Multiple Choice
11. b (p. 495)
12. a (p. 502)
13. c (p. 498)
14. c (p. 500)
15. d (p. 497)
16. e (p. 505)
17. c (p. 508)
18. e (p. 508)
19. a (p. 510)
20. b (p. 510)
21. a (p. 506)
22. d (p. 497)
23. c (p. 501)
24. b (p. 502)
25. a (p. 495)
26. b (p. 506)
27. a (p. 507)
28. e (p. 507)
29. b (p. 505)
30. d (p. 508)
31. e (p. 505)
32. e (p. 508)
33. e (p. 505)
34. b (p. 508)
35. d (p. 509)

Chapter 19

True/False
1. False (p. 546)
2. True (p. 533)
3. True (p. 528)
4. False (p. 541)
5. False (p. 529)
6. True (p. 541)
7. True (p. 532)
8. False (p. 543)
9. True (p. 530)
10. False (p. 546)

Multiple Choice
11. e (p. 540)
12. e (p. 529)
13. b (p. 545)
14. c (p. 528)
15. a (p. 534)
16. e (p. 538)
17. d (p. 546)
18. a (p. 529)
19. c (p. 529)
20. e (p. 531)
21. e (p. 544)
22. d (p. 538)
23. c (p. 532)
24. b (p. 529)
25. a (p. 538)
26. c (p. 532)
27. d (p. 529)
28. d (p. 529)
29. b (p. 534)
30. a (p. 532)
31. e (p. 536)
32. d (p. 534)
33. b (p. 539)
34. d (p. 534)
35. a (p. 546)

Chapter 20

True/False
1. False (p. 562)
2. True (p. 565)
3. True (p. 558)
4. False (p. 561)
5. False (p. 556)
6. False (p. 570)
7. True (p. 571)
8. True (p. 563)
9. False (p. 564)
10. False (p. 556)

Multiple Choice
11. c (p. 571)
12. b (p. 564)
13. a (p. 561)
14. a (p. 560)
15. b (p. 572)
16. e (p. 556)
17. a (p. 560)
18. b (p. 556)
19. d (p. 562)
20. e (p. 556)
21. b (p. 570)
22. a (p. 556)
23. e (p. 560)
24. d (p. 565)
25. e (p. 571)
26. c (p. 562)
27. c (p. 568)
28. a (p. 558)
29. d (p. 558)
30. b (p. 556)
31. d (p. 560)
32. c (p. 562)
33. c (p. 558)
34. a (p. 555)
35. e (p. 571)

Chapter 21

True/False
1. False (p. 582)
2. False (p. 582)
3. True (p. 583)
4. True (p. 582)
5. True (p. 583)
6. False (p. 584)
7. True (p. 584)
8. False (p. 585)
9. False (p. 590)
10. True (p. 587)

Multiple Choice
11. c (p. 585)
12. e (p. 583)
13. a (p. 584)
14. d (p. 586)
15. b (p. 587)
16. e (p. 588)
17. b (p. 587)
18. a (p. 582)
19. c (p. 582)
20. b (p. 582)
21. a (p. 584)
22. c (p. 584–585)

23. d (p. 582)
24. e (p. 582)
25. b (p. 583)
26. e (p. 583)
27. c (p. 587)
28. a (p. 588)
29. b (p. 590)
30. c (p. 591)
31. b (p. 590)
32. a (p. 587)
33. b (p. 586)
34. a (p. 590)
35. d (p. 585)

Glossary

A

accounting the summary and analysis of a firm's financial condition

accounts payable money owed by a firm for the purchase of materials

accounts receivable management sets the limits on credit available to customers and the length of the period in which payment is due

across-the-board system all employees are allocated a similar raise

active resistance occurs when users type in bad data or repeatedly crash a new system to make it unusable

actuaries persons employed by insurance companies to forecast the percentage of customers that will experience the particular event that is being insured

advertising a nonpersonal sales presentation communicated through media or nonmedia forms to influence a large number of consumers

affirmative action a set of activities intended to increase opportunities for minorities and women

agency problem when managers do not act as responsible agents for the shareholders who own the business

agents marketing intermediaries that match buyers and sellers of products without becoming owners

aggregate expenditures the total amount of expenditures in the economy

alpha testing during systems development, the process of making the new application available to a carefully selected subset of sophisticated users; done when the application approaches full functionality

American depository receipts (ADRs) certificates representing ownership of a stock issued by a non-U.S. firm

antivirus applications programs that detect and remove viruses

appreciates strengthens in value

artificial intelligence (AI) a field that focuses on developing computers that can perform tasks traditionally associated with biological intelligence, such as logical reasoning, language, vision, and motor skills

assembly line a sequence of work stations in which each work station is designed to cover specific phases of the production process

asset anything owned by a firm

auditing an assessment of the records that were used to prepare a firm's financial statements

autocratic a leadership style in which the leader retains full authority for decision making

automated tasks are completed by machines without the use of employees

autonomy divisions can make their own decisions and act independently

B

balance of trade the level of exports minus the level of imports

balance sheet reports the book value of all assets, liabilities, and owner's equity of firms at a given point in time

bandwidth the amount of information a network can carry

basic accounting equation Assets = Liabilities + Owner's Equity

bearish periods in which investors are selling their stocks because of unfavorable expectations about the performance of firms

benchmarking a method of evaluating performance by comparison to some specified (benchmark) level, typically a level achieved by another company

best-efforts basis the investment bank does not guarantee a price to the firm issuing securities

beta testing during systems development, the process of testing a fully functional version of the new applications with a wider group of users than was used for alpha testing

board of directors a set of executives who are responsible for monitoring the activities of the firm's president and other high-level managers

bond mutual funds investment companies that invest the funds received from investors in bonds

bonds long-term debt securities (IOUs) purchased by investors

bonus an extra one-time payment at the end of a period in which performance was measured

bookkeeping the recording of a firm's financial transactions

boycott refusing to purchase products and services

brand advertising a nonpersonal sales presentation about a specific brand

brand loyalty consumers become loyal to a specific brand over time

branding a method of identifying products and differentiating them from competitors

break-even point the quantity of units sold at which total revenue equals total cost

bugs errors in software code

bullish periods in which stocks are heavily demanded because of investors' favorable expectations about the performance of firms

business ethics a set of principles that should be followed when conducting business

business plan a detailed description of the proposed business, including a

G-1

description of the business, the types of customers it would attract, the competition, and the facilities needed for production

business risk the possibility that a firm's performance will be lower than expected because of its exposure to specific conditions

bylaws general guidelines for managing a firm

C

call feature provides the right for the issuing firm to repurchase the bonds before maturity

capital long-term funds

capital budget a targeted amount of funds to be used for purchasing assets such as buildings, machinery, and equipment that are needed for long-term projects

capital budgeting a comparison of the costs and benefits of a proposed project to determine whether it is feasible

capital gain the price received from the sale of stock minus the price paid for the stock

capital structure the composition of debt versus equity financing

capitalism an economic system that allows for private ownership of businesses

carrying costs costs of maintaining (carrying) inventories

casualty insurance protects a firm against potential liability for harm to others as a result of product failure or accidents

centralization keeping most authority among the high-level managers

certified public accountants (CPAs) accountants who meet specific educational requirements and pass a national examination

chain a retailer that has more than one outlet

chain of command identifies the job position to which each type of employee must report

chain-style business a type of franchise in which a firm is allowed to use the trade name of a company

and follows guidelines related to the pricing and sales of the product

charter a document used to incorporate a business. The charter describes important aspects of the corporation.

closed-end mutual funds mutual funds that are sold on stock exchanges

co-branding two noncompeting products are combined at a discounted price

commercial banks financial institutions that obtain deposits from individuals and use the funds primarily to provide business loans

commercial paper a short-term debt security normally issued by firms in good financial condition

commissions compensation for meeting specific sales objectives

common stock a security that represents partial ownership of a particular firm

communism an economic system that involves public ownership of businesses

compact disks (CD-ROMS) a form of secondary storage that uses optical techniques

comparative advertising intended to persuade customers to purchase a specific product by demonstrating a brand's superiority by comparison with other competing brands

compensation package the total monetary compensation and benefits offered to employees

competitive advantage unique traits that make a business's products more desirable than those of its competitors

composition specifies that a firm will provide its creditors with a portion of what they are owed

compressed work week compresses the work load into fewer days per week

computer program a collection of step-by-step instructions to the processor

computer virus a program that attaches itself to other programs or computer disks

conceptual skills the ability to understand the relationships between the various tasks of a firm

conglomerate merger the combination of two firms in unrelated businesses

connectivity the ability of a firm's computer systems to work together to permit the flow of information throughout the firm

consumer markets markets for various consumer products and services (such as cameras, clothes, and household items)

consumerism the collective demand by consumers that businesses satisfy their needs

contingency planning alternative plans developed for various possible business conditions

contribution margin the difference between price and variable cost per unit

controlling the monitoring and evaluation of tasks

convenience products products that are widely available to consumers, are purchased frequently, and are easily accessible

corporate anorexia the problem that occurs when firms become so obsessed with eliminating their inefficient components that they downsize too much

corporation a state-chartered entity that pays taxes and is legally distinct from its owners

cost of goods sold the cost of materials used to produce the goods that were sold

cost-based pricing estimating the per-unit cost of producing a product and then adding a markup

cost-push inflation the situation when higher prices charged by firms are caused by higher costs

coupons a promotional device used in newspapers, magazines, and ads to encourage the purchase of a product

craft unions unions organized according to a specific craft (or trade), such as plumbing

creditors financial institutions or individuals who provide loans

critical path the path that takes the longest time to complete

current assets assets that will be converted into cash within one year

customer profile characteristics of the typical customer (based on gender, age, hobbies, and so on)

cyclical unemployment people who are unemployed because of poor economic conditions

D

debt financing the act of borrowing funds

debt-to-equity ratio a measure of the amount of long-term financing provided by debt relative to equity

decentralized authority is spread among several divisions or managers

decision-making skills skills for using existing information to determine how the firm's resources should be allocated

decision support systems (DSS) computer models that are used to improve managerial decision making

decline phase the period in which sales of a product decline, either because of reduced consumer demand for that type of product or because competitors are gaining market share

decreasing term insurance provides insurance benefits to a beneficiary that decrease over time

defensive pricing the act of reducing product prices to defend (retain) market share

deintegration the strategy of delegating some production tasks to suppliers

demand schedule a schedule that indicates the quantity of the product that would be demanded at each possible price

demand-pull inflation the situation when prices of products and services are pulled up because of strong consumer demand

demographics characteristics of the human population or specific segments of the population

departmentalize assign tasks and responsibilities to different departments

depreciates weakens in value

depreciation a reduction in the value of fixed assets to reflect deterioration in the assets over time

derivative instruments instruments whose values are derived from values of other securities, indexes, or interest rates

design the size and structure of a plant or office

direct channel a producer of a product deals directly with a customer

direct foreign investment (DFI) a means of acquiring or building subsidiaries in one or more foreign countries

discount brokers brokers who ensure that a transaction desired by an investor is executed, but do not offer advice

distributorship a type of franchise in which a dealer is allowed to sell a product produced by a manufacturer

divestiture the sale of an existing business by a firm

dividend policy the decision regarding how much of the firm's quarterly earnings should be retained (reinvested in the firm) versus distributed as dividends to owners

dividends income that the firm provides to its owners

downsizing an attempt by a firm to cut expenses by eliminating job positions

E

earnings after taxes earnings before taxes minus taxes

earnings before interest and taxes (EBIT) gross profit minus operating expenses

earnings before taxes earnings before interest and taxes minus interest expenses

economic growth the change in the general level of economic activity

economies of scale as the quantity produced increases, the cost per unit decreases

electronic business use of electronic communications, such as the Internet, to produce or sell products and services

electronic data interchange (EDI) an interorganizational system that allows the computers of two or more companies to communicate directly with each other

employee benefits additional privileges beyond compensation payments, such as a paid vacation; health, life, or dental insurance; and pension programs

employment test a test of a job candidate's abilities

empowerment allowing employees power to make more decisions

enterprise resource planning (ERP) systems a software program that automates all of a firm's business procedures and supports the flow of information across departments

entrepreneurs people who organize, manage, and assume the risk of starting a business

equilibrium interest rate the interest rate at which the quantity of loanable funds supplied is equal to the quantity of loanable funds demanded

equilibrium price the price at which the quantity of the product supplied by firms equals the quantity of the product demanded by customers

equity the total investment by the firm's stockholders

equity financing the act of receiving investment from owners (by issuing stock or retaining earnings)

equity theory suggests that compensation should be equitable, or in proportion to each employee's contribution

espionage the process of illegally gathering information

esteem needs respect, prestige, and recognition

excise taxes taxes imposed by the federal government on particular products

exclusive distribution the distribution of a product through only one or a few outlets

expectancy theory holds that an employee's efforts are influenced by the expected outcome (reward) for those efforts

expense ratio for a mutual fund, expenses divided by assets

exporting the sale of products or services (called exports) to purchasers residing in other countries

extension provides additional time for a firm to generate the necessary cash to cover its payments

external recruiting an effort to fill positions with applicants from outside the firm

F

family branding branding of all or most products produced by a company

fashion obsolescence no longer in fashion

federal budget deficit the situation when the amount of federal government spending exceeds the amount of federal taxes and other revenue received by the federal government

Federal Reserve System the central bank of the United States

file servers in a network system, one or more machines that store and provide access to centralized data

finance means by which firms obtain and use funds for their business operations

finance companies financial institutions that typically obtain funds by issuing debt securities (IOUs) and lend most of their funds to firms

financial accounting accounting performed for reporting purposes

fiscal policy decisions on how the federal government should set tax rates and spend money

fixed assets assets that will be used by a firm for more than one year

fixed costs operating expenses that do not change in response to the number of products produced

fixed-position layout a layout in which employees go to the position of the product, rather than waiting for the product to come to them

flexible manufacturing a production process that can be easily adjusted to accommodate future revisions

flextime programs programs that allow for a more flexible work schedule

floor traders people on the trading floor of a stock exchange who execute transactions

floppy disks removable secondary storage

flotation costs costs paid to investment banks for their advice, their efforts to sell the securities, printing expenses, and registration fees

forward contract states an exchange of currencies that will occur at a specified exchange rate at a future point in time

forward rate the exchange rate that a bank will be willing to offer at a future point in time

franchise arrangement whereby a business owner allows others to use its trademark, trade name, or copyright, under specific conditions

franchisee firm that is allowed to use the trade name or copyright of a franchise

franchisor firm that allows others to use its trade name or copyright, under specified conditions

free-rein a leadership style in which the leader delegates much authority to employees

frictional unemployment people who are between jobs

full-service brokers brokers who provide advice to investors on stocks to purchase or sell, and also ensure that transactions desired by investors are executed

full-service retail store a retailer that generally offers much sales assistance to customers and provides servicing if needed

G

Gantt chart a chart illustrating the expected timing for each task in the production process

general partners partners who manage the business, receive a salary, share the profits or losses of the business, and have unlimited liability

general partnership a partnership in which all partners have unlimited liability

generic brands products not branded by the producer or the store

gigabytes billions of characters

going public the act of initially issuing stock to the public

gross domestic product (GDP) the total market value of all final products and services produced in the United States

gross profit net sales minus the cost of goods sold

growth funds mutual funds that invest in stocks of firms with high potential for growth

growth phase the period in which sales of a product increase rapidly

H

hard drive sealed magnetic disks that provide secondary storage in a computer

hardware the physical components of a computer

hedge action taken to protect a firm against exchange rate movements

hierarchy of needs needs are ranked in five general categories. Once a given category of needs is achieved, people become motivated to reach the next category.

horizontal merger the combination of firms that engage in the same types of business

hotelling (just-in-time office) the firm provides an office with a desk, a computer, and a telephone for any employee who normally works at home but needs to use work space at the firm

human resource manager helps each specific department recruit candidates for its open positions

human resource planning planning to satisfy a firm's needs for employees

hygiene factors work-related factors perceived to be inadequate

I

importing the purchase of foreign products or services

incentive plans provide employees with various forms of compensation if they meet specific performance goals

income funds mutual funds that invest in stocks that provide large dividends or in bonds that provide coupon payments

income statement indicates the revenue, costs, and earnings of firms over a period of time

indenture a legal document that explains the firm's obligations to bondholders

independent the decision of whether to adopt one project has no bearing on the adoption of other projects

independent retail store a retailer that has only one outlet

individual branding the assignment of a unique brand name to different products or groups of products

industrial markets markets for industrial products that are purchased by firms (such as plastic and steel)

industrial unions unions organized for a specific industry

industry advertising a nonpersonal sales presentation about a specific industry

industry demand total demand for the products in an industry

inflation the increase in the general level of prices of products and services over a specified period of time

infomercials commercials that are televised separately rather than within a show

informal organizational structure an informal communications network among a firm's employees

information systems include information technology, people, and procedures that work together to provide appropriate information to the firm's employees so they can make business decisions

information technology technology that enables information to be used to produce products and services

initial public offering (IPO) the first issue of stock to the public

initiative the willingness to take action

injunction a court order to prevent the union from a particular activity such as picketing

inside board members board members who are also managers of the same firm

insider information information about a firm that has not been disclosed to the public

insider trading transactions initiated by people (such as employees) who have information about a firm that has not been disclosed to the public

institutional advertising a nonpersonal sales presentation about a specific institution

institutional investors financial institutions that purchase large amounts of stock

insurance companies receive insurance premiums from selling insurance to customers and invest the proceeds until the funds are needed to pay insurance claims

intensive distribution the distribution of a product across most or all possible outlets

interest rate swap a derivative instrument that allows a firm to swap fixed interest payments for payments that adjust to movements in interest rates

internal auditors specialize in evaluating various divisions of a business to ensure that they are operating efficiently

internal recruiting an effort to fill open positions with persons already employed by the firm

international licensing agreement a type of alliance in which a firm allows a foreign company (called the "licensee") to produce its products according to specific instructions

international stock funds mutual funds that invest in stocks of foreign firms

international unions unions that have members in several countries

interorganizational systems (IOS) employ computers and telecommunications technology to move information across the boundaries of a firm

interpersonal skills the skills necessary to communicate with customers and employees

intrapreneurship the assignment of particular employees of a firm to create ideas, as if they were entrepreneurs running their own firms

introduction phase the initial period in which consumers are informed about a product

inventory control the process of managing inventory at a level that minimizes costs

inventory management determines the amount of inventory that is held

J

job analysis the analysis used to determine the tasks and the necessary credentials for a particular position

job description states the tasks and responsibilities of a job position

job enlargement a program to expand (enlarge) the jobs assigned to employees

job enrichment programs programs designed to increase the job satisfaction of employees

job rotation a program that allows a set of employees to periodically rotate their job assignments

job satisfaction the degree to which employees are satisfied with their jobs

job sharing two or more persons may share a particular work schedule

job specification states the credentials necessary to qualify for a job position

joint venture an agreement between two firms about a specific project

just-in-time (JIT) a system that attempts to reduce materials inventories to a bare minimum by frequently ordering small amounts of materials

L

labor union an association established to represent the views, needs, and concerns of labor

Landrum-Griffin Act required labor unions to specify in their bylaws the membership eligibility requirements, dues, and collective bargaining procedures

layout the arrangement of machinery and equipment within a factory or office

leading the process of influencing the habits of others to achieve a common goal

leasing renting assets for a specified period of time

less-developed countries countries that have relatively low technology

leveraged buyout (LBO) a purchase of a company (or the subsidiary of the company) by a group of investors with borrowed funds

liability anything owed by a firm

liability losses financial losses due to a firm's actions that cause damages to others or to their property

limit order an investor's order that places a limit on the price at which the investor would be willing to purchase or sell a stock

limited liability company (LLC) a firm that has all the favorable features of a typical general partnership but also offers limited liability for the partners

limited partners partners whose liability is limited to the cash or property they contributed to the partnership

limited partnership a firm that has some limited partners

line of credit an agreement that allows access to borrowed funds upon demand over some specified period

line organization an organizational structure that contains only line positions and no staff positions

line positions job positions established to make decisions that achieve specific business goals

line-and-staff organization an organizational structure that includes both line and staff positions and assigns authority from higher-level management to employees

liquid having access to funds to pay bills when they come due

liquidation value the amount of funds that would be received as a result of the liquidation of a firm

liquidity a firm's ability to meet short-term obligations

liquidity management the management of short-term assets and liabilities to ensure adequate liquidity

load mutual funds open-end mutual funds that can be purchased only by calling a broker

local area network (LAN) a system in which individual workstations are directly connected by network cabling to the file server

local unions unions composed of members in a specified local area

lockout prevents employees from working until an agreement between management and labor is reached

M

magnetic tapes removable secondary storage

mainframe (multiuser) system system architecture that uses a single central computer

management the utilization of human resources (employees) and other resources (such as machinery) in a manner that best achieves the firm's plans and objectives

management by objectives (MBO) allows employees to participate in setting their goals and determining the manner by which they achieve their tasks

managerial accounting the type of accounting performed to provide information to help managers of the firm make decisions

managers employees who are responsible for managing job assignments of other employees and making key business decisions

manufacturing arrangement a type of franchise in which a firm is allowed to manufacture a product using the formula provided by another company

market coverage the degree of product distribution among outlets

market order an investor's order requesting a transaction for the best possible price

market share a firm's sales as a proportion of the total market

marketing means by which products (or services) are developed, priced, distributed, and promoted to customers

marketing intermediaries firms that participate in moving the product toward the customer

marketing research accumulation and analysis of data in order to make a particular marketing decision

massively parallel machines experimental computers with many CPUs that operate simultaneously

materials requirements planning (MRP) a process for ensuring that materials are available when needed

matrix organization an organizational structure that enables various parts of the firm to interact to focus on specific projects

maturity phase the period in which additional competitive products have entered the market, and sales of a product level off because of competition

megabyte one million characters

megahertz [MHz] one million cycles per second

merchants marketing intermediaries that become owners of the products and then resell them

merger two firms are merged (or combined) to become a single firm owned by the same owners (shareholders)

merit system allocates raises according to performance (merit)

middle management managers who are often responsible for the firm's short-term decisions

mission statement a description of a firm's primary goal

modems devices that permit the digital signals inside computers to be transmitted over lines designed primarily for voice communication

monetary policy decisions on the money supply level in the United States

money supply demand deposits (checking accounts), currency held by the public, and travelers checks

monopoly a firm that is the sole provider of goods or services

motivational factors work-related factors that please employees

mutual funds investment companies that receive funds from individual investors, which they pool and invest in securities

mutually exclusive the situation in which only one of two projects designed for the same purpose can be accepted

N

National Association of Security Dealers Automated Quotation (Nasdaq) a computerized network within the OTC for firms that meet specific size and capital requirements

national unions unions composed of members throughout the country

negative reinforcement motivates employees by encouraging them to behave in a manner that avoids unfavorable consequences

net asset value (NAV) the market value of a mutual fund's securities after subtracting any expenses incurred

net income earnings before taxes minus taxes

net present value equal to the present value of cash flows minus the initial outlay

net profit margin a measure of net income as a percentage of sales

net sales the total sales adjusted for any discounts

network operating system software that handles the communications between machines in a network

network system system architecture that connects individual microcomputers together in ways that allow them to share information

news release a brief written announcement about the firm provided by that firm to the media

no-load funds open-end mutual funds that can be purchased without the services of a broker

Norris-LaGuardia Act restricted the use of injunctions against unions

and allowed unions to publicize a labor dispute

notes payable short-term loans to a firm made by creditors such as banks

O

obsolete less useful than in the past

odd lots less than one hundred shares

on margin only a portion of the funds needed to purchase a stock is with cash

one-level channel one marketing intermediary is between the producer and the customer

open-book management a form of employee involvment that educates employees on their contribution to the firm and enables them to periodically assess their own performance levels

open-end mutual funds funds that stand ready to repurchase their shares at the prevailing NAV if investors decide to sell the shares

operating expenses composed of selling expenses, and general and administrative expenses

operational planning establishes the methods to be used in the near future (such as the next year) to achieve the tactical plans

optimization models computer models that are used to represent situations that have many possible combinations of inputs and outputs

order costs costs involved in placing orders

organization chart a diagram that shows the interaction among employee responsibilities

organizational structures identifies responsibilities for each job position and the relationships among those positions

organizing the organization of employees and other resources in a manner that is consistent with the firm's goals

outside board members board members who are not managers of the firm

outsourcing purchasing parts from a supplier rather than producing the parts

owner's equity includes the par (or stated) value of all common stock issued, additional paid-in capital, and retained earnings

P

par value the amount that bondholders receive at maturity

participative a leadership style in which the leaders accept some employee input but usually use their authority to make decisions

participative management employees are allowed to participate in various decisions made by their supervisors or others

partners co-owners of a business

partnership a business that is co-owned by two or more people

passive resistance occurs when users uncomfortable with a new system overstate difficulties associated with learning the technology

patents allow exclusive rights to the production and sale of a specific product

penetration pricing the strategy of setting a lower price than those of competitive products to penetrate the market

pension funds receive employee and firm contributions toward pensions and invest the proceeds for the employees until the funds are needed

perquisites additional privileges beyond compensation payments and employee benefits

personal selling a personal sales presentation used to influence one or more consumers

physiological needs the basic requirements for survival

picketing walking around near the employer's building with signs complaining of poor working conditions

planning the preparation of a firm for future business conditions

policies guidelines for how tasks should be completed

political risk the risk that a country's political actions can adversely affect a business

positive reinforcement motivates employees by providing rewards for high performance

predatory pricing the strategy of lowering a product's price to drive out new competitors

preferred stock a security that represents partial ownership of a particular firm and offers specific priorities over common stock

premium a gift or prize provided free to consumers who purchase a specific product

press conference an oral announcement about the firm provided by that firm to the media

prestige pricing the strategy of using a higher price for a product that is intended to have a top-of-the-line image

price skimming the strategy of initially setting a high price for a product if no other competitive products are in the market yet

price-elastic the demand for a product is highly responsive to price changes

price-inelastic the demand for a product is not very responsive to price changes

prime rate the rate of interest typically charged on loans to the most creditworthy firms that borrow

private liquidation creditors may informally request that a failing firm liquidate (sell) its assets and distribute the funds received from liquidation to them

private placement the selling of securities to one or a few investors

privately held ownership is restricted to a small group of investors

privatization the sale of government-owned businesses to private investors

procedures steps necessary to implement a policy

producer brands brands that reflect the manufacturer of the products

product physical goods as well as services that can satisfy consumer needs

product differentiation a firm's efforts to distinguish its product from competitive products in a manner that makes it more desirable

product layout a layout in which tasks are postioned in the sequence that they are assigned

product life cycle the typical set of phases that products experience over their lifetime

product line a set of related products or services offered by a single firm

product mix the assortment of products offered by a firm

production control involves purchasing materials, inventory control, routing, scheduling, and quality control

production efficiency the ability to produce products at a low cost

production management (operations management) the management of a process in which resources (such as employees and machinery) are used to produce products and services

production process (conversion process) a series of tasks in which resources are used to produce a product or service

production schedule a plan for the timing and volume of production tasks

profit sharing a portion of the firm's profits provided to employees

program evaluation and review technique (PERT) schedules tasks in a manner that will minimize delays in the production process

promotion assignment of an employee to a higher-level job with more responsibility and compensation

promotion the act of informing or reminding consumers about a specific product or brand

promotion budget the amount of funds that have been set aside to pay for all promotion methods over a specified period

promotion mix the combination of promotion methods that a firm uses to increase acceptance of its products

property insurance protects a firm against the risk associated with the ownership of property, such as buildings and other assets

property losses financial losses resulting from damage to property

prospectus a document that discloses relevant financial information about securities and financial information about the firm issuing them

protective covenants restrictions imposed on specific financial policies of a firm

prototype a working system with limited functionality

public accountants accountants who provide accounting services for a variety of firms for a fee

public offering the selling of securities to the public

public relations actions taken with the goal of creating or maintaining a favorable public image

publicly held shares can be easily purchased or sold by investors

pull strategy firms direct their promotion directly at the target market, who in turn request the product from wholesalers or producers

push strategy producers direct their promotion of a product at wholesalers or retailers, who in turn promote it to consumers

Q

quality the degree to which a product or service satisfies a customer's requirements or expectations

quality control a process of determining whether the quality of a product meets the desired quality level

quality control circle a group of employees who assess the quality of a product and offer suggestions for improvement

quota a limit on the amounts of specific products that can be imported

R

random access memory (RAM) space in which information is temporarily stored in a computer

ratio analysis an evaluation of the relationships between financial statement variables

rebate a potential refund by the manufacturer to the consumer

recession two consecutive quarters of negative economic growth

reengineering the redesign of a firm's organizational structure and operations

reinforcement theory suggests that reinforcement can control behavior

reminder advertising intended to remind consumers of a product's existence

remote job entry systems interorganizational systems that allow customers and other users to interact directly with a company's internal systems

restructuring the revision of the production process in an attempt to improve efficiency

return on assets (ROA) measures a firm's net income as a percentage of the total amount of assets utilized by the firm

return on equity (ROE) measures the return to the common stockholders (net income) as a percentage of their investment in the firm

right-to-work allows states to prohibit union shops

risk the degree of uncertainty about the firm's future earnings

round lots multiples of one hundred shares

routing the sequence (or route) of tasks necessary to complete the production of a product

S

S-corporation a partnership that has seventy-five or fewer owners and satisfies other criteria. The earnings are distributed to the owners and taxed at the respective personal income tax rate of each owner.

sabotage the malicious destruction of information by a perpetrator

safety needs job security and safe working conditions

salary (or wages) the dollars paid for a job over a specific period

sales manager an individual who manages a group of sales representatives

sales promotion the set of activities that is intended to influence consumers

salvage value the amount of money that a firm can receive from selling a project

sampling randomly selecting some of the products produced and testing them to determine whether they satisfy the quality standards

savings institutions financial institutions that obtain deposits from individuals and use the deposited funds primarily to provide mortgage loans

scheduling the act of setting time periods for each task in the production process

seasonal unemployment people whose services are not needed during some seasons

secondary market a market where existing securities can be traded among investors

secured bonds bonds backed by collateral

segments subsets of a market that reflect a specific type of business and the perceived quality

selective distribution the distribution of a product through selected outlets

self-actualization the need to fully reach one's potential

self-insurance a firm insures itself by creating a fund to cover any future claims, rather than paying insurance premiums

self-service retail store a retailer that does not provide sales assistance or service and sells products that do not require much expertise

sexual harassment unwelcome comments or actions of a sexual nature

shareholder activism the active efforts of stockholders to influence a firm's management policies

shopping products products that are not purchased frequently

shortage the situation when the quantity supplied by firms is less than the quantity demanded by customers

social needs the need to be part of a group

social responsibility a firm's recognition of how its business decisions can affect society

socialism an economic system that contains some features of both capitalism and communism

software programs that determine the specific tasks a computer will perform at any given time

sole proprietor the owner of a sole proprietorship

sole proprietorship a business owned by a single owner

span of control the number of employees managed by each manager

specialty products products that specific consumers consider to be special, and therefore make a special effort to purchase them

specialty retail store a retailer that specializes in a particular type of product

spot exchange rate the exchange rate quoted for immediate transactions

staff positions job positions established to support the efforts of line positions

stakeholders people who have an interest in a business; the business's owners, creditors, employees, suppliers, and customers

stand-alone systems system architecture consisting of one or more computers

statistical analysis a computer model that applies statistical principles to understanding relationships between data elements and predicting future behaviors

stock certificates of ownership of a business

stock broker a person who facilitates desired stock transactions

stock market efficiency a term used to suggest that stock prices reflect all publicly available information

stock mutual funds investment companies that invest funds received from individual investors in stocks

stock options a form of compensation that allows employees to purchase shares of the employing firm's stock at a specific price

stockholders investors who wish to become partial owners of firms

store brands brands that reflect the retail store where the products are sold

strategic alliance a business agreement between firms whereby resources are shared to pursue mutual interests

strategic plan intended to identify a firm's main business focus over a long-term period, perhaps three to five years

stretch targets production efficiency targets (or goals) that cannot be achieved under present conditions

strike discontinuation of employee services

structural unemployment people who are unemployed because they do not have adequate skills

supervisory (first-line) management managers who are usually highly involved with the employees who engage in the day-to-day production process

supply chain the process from the beginning of the production process until the product reaches the customer

supply schedule a schedule that indicates the quantity of a product that would be supplied (produced) by firms at each possible price

surplus the situation when the quantity supplied by firms exceeds the quantity demanded by customers

system architecture the basic logical organization of a computer

systems development life cycle (SDLC) an approach to systems development that involves decomposing a system into its functional components

T

tactical planning smaller-scale plans (over one or two years) that are consistent with the firm's strategic (long-term) plan

Taft-Hartley Act an amendment to the Wagner Act that prohibited unions from pressuring employees to join

target market a group of individuals or organizations with similar traits who may purchase a particular product

tariff tax on imported products

teamwork a group of employees with varied job positions is given the responsibility to achieve a specific goal

technological obsolescence inferior to new products

technology knowledge or tools used to produce products and services

telemarketing the use of the telephone for promoting and selling products

tender offer a direct bid by the acquiring firm for the shares of the target firm

term insurance provides insurance for a policyholder only over a specified term and does not build a cash value for the policyholder

terminals devices that combine the functions of a monitor and a keyboard

time management the way managers allocate their time when managing tasks

times interest earned ratio measures the ability of a firm to cover its interest payments

top (high-level) management managers in positions such as president, chief executive officer, chief financial officer, and vice-president who make decisions regarding the firm's long-run objectives

total quality management (TQM) the act of monitoring and improving the quality of products and services produced

trade deficit amount by which imports exceed exports

trademark a brand's form of identification that is legally protected from use by other firms

Treasury bills short-term debt securities issued by the U.S. Treasury

turnkey system a system that is ready for use upon delivery from the vendor

two-level channel two marketing intermediaries are between the producer and the customer

U

underwriting syndicate a group of investment banks that share the obligations of underwriting securities

underwritten the investment bank guarantees a price to the issuing firm, no matter what price the securities are sold for

universal life insurance combines the features of term and whole-life insurance; specifies a period of time over which the policy will exist, but builds a cash value for policyholders over time

unlimited liability no limit on the debts for which the owner is liable

unsecured bonds bonds that are not backed by collateral

upward appraisals used to measure the managerial abilities of supervisors

V

variable costs operating expenses that vary directly with the number of products produced

variety retail store a retailer that offers numerous types of goods

venture capital firm composed of individuals who invest in small businesses

vertical channel integration two or more levels of distribution are managed by a single firm

vertical merger the combination of a firm with a potential supplier or customer

video conferencing holding meetings between remote sites using sound and pictures transmitted over telecommunications links

virtual reality display techniques that combine computerized sights, sounds, and sensations to create a sense of actually "being there"

W

Wagner Act prohibited firms from interfering with workers' efforts to organize or join unions

"what-if" analysis a computer model that generates different potential business scenarios to answer questions

white knight a more suitable company that is willing to acquire a firm and rescue it from the hostile takeover efforts of some other firm

whole-life insurance life insurance that exists until death or as long as premiums are promptly paid and has a cash value to which the policy-holder is entitled

wide area network (WAN) a system is which telecommunications technologies are employed to connect pieces of the network

work station an area in which one or more employees are assigned a specific task

work-in-process inventories inventories of partially completed products

workgroup software network software that provides a broad array of user-friendly features, such as electronic mail, document management systems, and work-sharing systems

working capital management the management of a firm's short-term assets and liabilities

workstations in a network system, individual computers that access the software and data on the file server

yellow-dog contract a contract requiring employees to refrain from joining a union as a condition of employment

Company Index

Subject Index

Photo and Screen Capture Credits

Chapter 1: *2:* © Corbis; *5:* © Ben Margot/AP/Wide World Photos; *8:* © Will van Overbeek; *14:* Courtesy of the Boston Beer Company; *17:* www.paloaltosoftware.com, 800-229-7526

Chapter 2: *28:* © Tony Stone Images/Andy Sacks; *34:* © AP/Wide World Photos; *34:* © Adobe Systems Inc. Adobe and the Adobe logo are trademarks of Adobe Systems Inc.; *35:* © AP/Wide World Photos; *36:* © Corbis; *39:* © Corbis; *40:* Dairy Queen and related trademarks are owned by American Dairy Queen Corp. and used with permission

Chapter 3: *54:* © AP/Wide World Photos; *62:* © Matthew Mcvay/Tony Stone Images; *64:* Courtesy of The Goodyear Tire and Rubber Company; *65:* Courtesy of Ben & Jerry's; *66:* Info. Resources, Inc./www.WaBio.com; *71:* © AP/Wide World Photos

Chapter 4: *90:* © Tony Stone Images/Peggy Fox; *101:* © David J. Phillip/AP/Wide World Photos; *102:* © Will van Overbeek; *105:* The Gamma Liaison Network

Chapter 5: *118:* © Corbis; *120:* © Buddy Mays/Corbis; *126:* Courtesy of Miller Brewing Company; *130:* © Gail Mooney/Corbis

Chapter 6: *140:* © Arthur Meyerson; *142:* © Sergei Karpukhin/AP/ Wide World Photos; *144:* ©/Corbis; *146:* Blockbuster name, design, and related marks are trademarks of Blockbuster, Inc. © Blockbuster, Inc.; *148:* ©/Corbis; *151:* ©/Corbis

Chapter 7: *178:* © R. W. Jones/Corbis; *182:* © PhotoBank, Inc./Index Stock Imagery; *187:* ©/Corbis; *192:* ©/Corbis

Chapter 8: *206:* ©/Stone; *215:* © Michael Clevenger/AP/ Wide World Photos; *220:* © David Joel/Stone

Chapter 9: *230:* © Mark Segal/Stone; *232:* © 2000 General Motors, used with permission; *233:* © Charles O'Rear/Corbis; *235:* © Danny Lehman/Corbis; *238:* Photodisc/ John A. Rizzo; *250:* © Will van Overbeek

Chapter 10: *258:* © Robert Becker/AP/Wide World Photos; *260:* © Will van Overbeek; *262:* Reprinted with permission of GOAL/QPC, 2 Manor Parkway, Salem NH 03079; *264:* Courtesy General Electric Company, Fairfield, CT; *265:* © Andy Sacks/Stone; *269:* © /International Standards Organization

Chapter 11: *288:* © Chris Sweda/AP/Wide World Photos; *297:* © Michael Newman/ PhotoEdit; *299:* "Foundation FOR Enterprise Development"; *305:* © Tim Sharp/AP/ Wide World Photos

Chapter 12: *314:* © /SuperStock International; *325:* © Richard Harbus/AP/ Wide World Photos; *345:* © Vivianne Moos/Stock Market

Chapter 13: *352:* Courtesy of Taco Bell Corporation; *354:* © Jeff Greenberg/ PhotoEdit; *355:* © Chris Pizzello/AP/Wide World Photos; *359:* © Carlos Osorio/ AP/Wide World Photos; *366:* © Jwe Jay/AP/Wide World Photos; *367:* © Spencer Grant/PhotoEdit

Chapter 14: *384:* © Rachel Epstein/PhotoEdit; *386:* © AP/Wide World Photos; *390:* © David Young-Wolff/PhotoEdit; *392:* © Michael Newman/PhotoEdit; *397:* © Wally Santana/AP/Wide World Photos

Feature and Exhibit Credits

Chapter 2 *Exhibit 2.8, page 44:* IBM 1999 annual report; *Self-Scoring Exercise, page 45:* "Do You Have the Skills Necessary for Achievement" from Nelson and Quick, *Organizational Behavior* © West Publishing Company.

Chapter 3 *Exhibit 3.5, page 61:* Bureau of Labor Statistics and *USA Today,* May 15 1995, 3B; *Exhibit 3.7, page 67: Forbes,* May 17, 1999; *Self-Scoring Exercise, page 72:* J. B. Cullen, B. Victor, and C. Stephens, "An Ethical Weather Report: Assessing the Organization's Ethical Climate." Reprinted with permission of publisher, from *Organizational Dynamics,* Autumn/1989, copyright 1989. American Management Association, New York. All rights reserved; *Self-Scoring Exercise, page 72:* Issues adapted from J. O. Cherrington and D. J. Cherrington, "A Menu of Moral Issues One Week in the Life of the *Wall Street Journal,*" *Journal of Business Ethics* 11(1992): 225–265. Reprinted by permission of Kluwer Academic Publishers.

Chapter 4 *Exhibit 4.1, page 92: Federal Reserve Bulletin; Exhibit 4.2, page 93: Federal Reserve Bulletin; Spotlight on Technology, page 106:* T. Grandon Gill. *American Financial Network, Inc. (A).* Florida Atlantic University, DIS Department case study.

Chapter 5 *Small Business Survey, page 122:* "The State of Small Business," *Inc.,* 1995, 78; *Exhibit 5.5, page 127: Business Week,* 14 August 1995.

Chapter 6 *Exhibit 6.2, page 145:* U.S. Department of Labor, Bureau of Labor Statistics, December 1994; *Exhibit 6.6, page 152:* Federal Reserve Bulletin; *Global Business, page 153:* Adapted from C. Barnum and N. Wolniansky, "Taking Cues from Body Language," *Management Review* 78 (1989): 59. Adapted by permission of publisher, from *Management Review,* June 1989, © 1989. American Management Association, New York. All rights reserved. And from E. Ferrieux, Le Point, *World Press Review,* July 1989. Used with permission; *Spotlight on Technology, page 160:* AUCNET: TV Auction Network System. Harvard Business School Case #9-190-001. 1990.

Chapter 8 *Self-Scoring Exercise, page 212:* Danny Miller and Cornelia Droge, "Psychological and Traditional Determinants of Structure" Figure Only, Vol. 31, No. 4 (December 1986), page 558, © *Administrative Science Quarterly.*

Chapter 10 *Self-Scoring Exercise, page 266:* "Are You A Highly Satisfied Customer?" from Nelson and Quick, *Organizational Behavior,* © West Publishing Company; *Exhibit 10.6, page 275:* Challenger, Gray & Christmas, Inc.

Chapter 11 *Self-Scoring Exercise, page 293:* Questionnaire developed by C. D. Spielberger. Appeared in W. Barnhill, "Early Warning," *The Washington Post,* August 11, 1992, B5. Reprinted from *The Washington Post* (Aug. 11, 1992) with the permission of Dr. Charles D. Spielberger; *Self-Scoring Exercise, page 303:* Survey-Feedback-Action (SFA) Federal Express Company, Memphis, TN; *Small Business Survey, page 304:* Survey by Richard Freeman (London School of Economics) and Joel Rogers (University of Wisconsin), 1995.

Chapter 12 *Exhibit 12.5, page 322: Fortune,* July 19, 1999; *Small Business Survey, page 324: Inc.,* January 1994, 96; *Small Business Survey, page 327:* Survey of Small Business CEOs, Executive Committee, San Diego, March 1993; *Exhibit 12.8, page 330:* Adapted from R. S. Schuler and S. E. Jackson, *Human Resource Management,* 6th ed. (St. Paul: West Publishing, 1996), 370; *Exhibit 12.9, page 331:* Adapted from R. S. Schuler and S. E. Jackson, *Human Resource Management,* 6th ed. (St. Paul: West Publishing, 1996), 412.

Chapter 13 *Exhibit 13.2, page 357: The Wall Street Journal,* 29 March 1995, B1; *Small Business Survey, page 360: Inc.,* June 1995, 88.

Chapter 15 *Exhibit 15.6, page 414:* McCann-Erickson and Standard and Poor's Industry Survey, April 1995, M15; *Small Business Survey, page 418: Inc.,* December 1992, 27.

Chapter 18 *Small Business Survey, page 509: Inc.,* April 1994, 114.

Chapter 20 *Small Business Survey, page 565: Inc.,* April 1995, 112.

Chapter 21 *Small Business Survey, page 586:* "The State of Small Business," *Inc.,* 1995, 79.

Appendix A *Self-Scoring Exercise, page 615:* VALIC (The Variable Annuity Life Insurance Company)®.